MW01226179

SAGE Handbook of

Research on Classroom Assessment

SAGE Handbook of Research on Classroom Assessment

Edited by

James H. McMillan
Virginia Commonwealth University

Los Angeles | London | New Delhi
Singapore | Washington DC

Los Angeles | London | New Delhi
Singapore | Washington DC

FOR INFORMATION:

SAGE Publications, Inc.
2455 Teller Road
Thousand Oaks, California 91320
E-mail: order@sagepub.com

SAGE Publications Ltd.
1 Oliver's Yard
55 City Road
London EC1Y 1SP
United Kingdom

SAGE Publications India Pvt. Ltd.
B 1/I 1 Mohan Cooperative Industrial Area
Mathura Road, New Delhi 110 044
India

SAGE Publications Asia-Pacific Pte. Ltd.
3 Church Street
#10-04 Samsung Hub
Singapore 049483

Acquisitions Editor: Diane McDaniel
Editorial Assistant: Megan Koraly
Production Editor: Brittany Bauhaus
Copy Editor: Megan Markanich
Typesetter: C&M Digitals (P) Ltd.
Proofreader: Jeff Bryant
Indexer: Sylvia Coates
Cover Designer: Candice Harman
Marketing Manager: Terra Schultz
Permissions Editor: Adele Hutchinson

Printed in the United States of America

Library of Congress Cataloging-in-Publication Data

Sage handbook of research on classroom assessment / James H. McMillan, (Ed.).

pages cm
Includes bibliographical references and index.

ISBN 978-1-4129-9587-0 (hardback)

1. Educational tests and measurements.
2. Examinations. 3. Examinations—Validity.
4. Examinations—Interpretation. I. McMillan, James H. editor of compilation.

LB3051.S23 2013
371.26'2—dc23 2012031441

This book is printed on acid-free paper.

SFI label applies to the text stock

12 13 14 15 16 10 9 8 7 6 5 4 3 2 1

BRIEF CONTENTS

DETAILED CONTENTS

FOREWORD

LORRIE A. SHEPARD

University of Colorado Boulder

Why should we care about a topic as mundane as classroom assessment? Assessments used in classrooms are not so elegant as psychometric models, and they are highly local and private to individual teachers' classrooms. Yet, everyday and every-week assessments determine the very character and quality of education; they set the actual, on-the-ground goals for learning and delimit the learning opportunities provided.

In the past decade, a great deal of attention has been paid to the research evidence documenting the potential power of formative assessment to greatly enhance learning – a potential that has yet to be realized. Of even greater potency – often for ill rather than good – is the power of classroom summative assessment to convey what is important to learn. Tests, quizzes, homework assignments, and questions at the end of the chapter implicitly teach students what learning is about. If students come to hold a highly proceduralized view of mathematics or think of science knowledge as vocabulary lists, classroom summative assessments are largely to blame. Classroom assessments can also distort the how and why of learning, if they signal for students that the purpose for learning is to perform well on tests.

To reflect learning that matters, classroom summative measures, whether projects, portfolios – or tests – must be deeply grounded in subject-matter content and processes. And, to support deep learning, formative assessments must elicit student thinking and provide substantive insights rather than quantitative score reports. Research on classroom assessment, therefore, must be the province of subject-matter experts and learning scientists as much as or even more than that of measurement experts.

This handbook is intended for an expanded community of researchers, graduate students in search of dissertation topics, and curriculum reformers. It is a compendium of research, gathering together what we know now and highlighting what we need to learn more about in order to improve practice. The chapters in this volume go deep into studies of specific topics, including feedback, grading, self-assessment, performance assessments, and validity. Unlike recent volumes that consider only the importance of formative assessment, this handbook takes up both formative and summative classroom assessment, which is a critically important step toward conceiving the two in a way that does not put them at cross purposes. But, for the work that follows to be effective, there needs to be a coherent story line that links all of these pieces and the two purposes together. Contemporary learning theory provides the needed conceptual glue and offers a coherent, explanatory framework by which effective practices can be understood and analyzed. Sociocultural learning theory, in particular, subsumes findings from motivational psychology and helps to advance instructional practices that foster both student engagement and higher levels of thinking and reasoning.

A decade ago, when I wrote about "the role of assessment in a learning culture," I chose the concept of culture because of its pervasiveness and integrated nature. I was trying to get at the underlying fabric, linking meanings and classroom interaction patterns that had created a "testing culture" and think instead about the profound shifts that would need to occur to establish a learning culture. Culture is about deeply rooted, but dynamic, shared beliefs and patterns of behavior. It is not a list of cognitive and affective variables elicited one-at-a-time, but a complex set of woven-together assumptions and meanings about what is important to do and be. These shared assumptions may be tacit, invisible, like the air we breathe, yet they are potent. It is this integrated nature of learning environments that must be understood, if we are to design for productive learning. Just as the authors of next-generation science standards are realizing, for example, that big ideas (content) and scientific practices have to be engaged together, classroom assessment researchers and developers must realize how their pieces contribute to the larger picture. There cannot, for example, be one theory of learning and motivation for formative assessment and a different one for summative assessment.

From earlier cognitive research, we know that learning is an act of sense-making whereby learners construct new knowledge and understandings by drawing connections with what they already know. Given the centrality of prior knowledge, formative assessment practices should focus on teacher noticing and instructional routines intended to make student thinking visible. Then, sociocultural theory goes further to explain how social interactions with others and with cultural tools enable co-construction of what is taken into the mind. According to Vygotsky's concept of the zone of proximal development, learning occurs as a student tries out thinking and reasoning with the assistance of more knowledgeable others. This learning-theory idea of supported participation or scaffolding is congruent with Royce Sadler's seminal conception of formative assessment. For assessment to enable new learning, the student must: 1) come to have a shared understanding of quality work similar to that of the teacher, 2) be able to compare the current level of performance using quality criteria, and 3) be able to take action to close the gap. Assessment is the middle step, but it need not be called out as separate from the learning process. For formative assessment practices to be consistent with this view of learning, there should be clear attention to learning goals in terms that are accessible to students, evaluation by means of shared criteria as to where students are in relation to goals, and tailored feedback that offers specific guidance about how to improve.

The foregoing account emphasizing the cognitive aspects of learning, however, tells only half of the story. From a sociocultural perspective, socially supported instructional activity is more than gap closing but rather fully engages the cognitive, meta-cognitive, and motivational aspects of learning. It is not surprising, for example, that self-regulation is a theme that repeats across a dozen of the chapters in this volume. When students are engaged in meaningful activity, they see models of proficient participation and seek to emulate them. They are "motivated" to improve by an increasing identity of mastery and at the same time develop the meta-cognitive skills needed to be able to self-monitor their own performance. Formative assessment practices enhance learning when students are positioned as thoughtful contributors to classroom discourse and have a sense of ownership in criteria used by a community of practice. Author's Chair is an example of an instructional practice that highlights the joint construction of writing skill and identity as an author and also makes "critique" and improvement based on feedback an authentic part of becoming more adept. For these motivational claims to hold true, however, instructional content and activities have to be compelling and worthwhile.

This view of motivation, where students invest effort to get good at something, is often seen in out-of-school contexts – learning so as to *be* a dancer, a musician, a gamer. When in-school experiences lack this sense of purpose, it is most often because of dreary content and grading practices that reward compliance rather than learning. The measurement literature is replete with studies documenting the mixture of considerations that go into teachers' grades. The majority of teachers use points and grades to "motivate" their students. Contrary to their intentions, this leads to the commodification of learning and fosters a performance orientation rather than a mastery or learning orientation. While economists certainly have shown that incentives do work, what we have learned from countless motivational studies is that the use of external rewards diminishes intrinsic motivation. Most poignantly, when young children are rewarded with pizza or stickers for activities like drawing or reading, they like the activities less after the rewards stop than before the reinforcement schedule began. Many teachers also feel strongly about including effort as a factor in determining grades, for motivational reasons. But again this distorts the causal chain. Instead of effort enabling learning that leads to a grade, effort and sometimes the performance of effort produces a grade. In addition to the motivational harm, the achievement goals – toward which student and teacher were working jointly in the formative assessment model – are obscured.

In her chapter on grading, Susan Brookhart reviews the rationale for achievement-based or standards-based grading and the few available studies. Formative assessment and summative assessment are compatible, if they focus on the same rich, challenging, and authentic learning goals and if feedback in the midst of instruction leads to internalized understandings and improved performance on culminating, summative tasks. This is not the same thing as adding up points on multiple interim assignments. Researchers and reformers who want to develop grading practices more in keeping with research on learning and motivation must keep in mind several obstacles. First, they are working against long-standing beliefs on the part of teachers and students, and the older students are, the more explicit negotiations must be to refocus effort on learning. Second, teachers today are under enormous pressure to keep parents informed and to maintain real-time data systems. Often this means that points are given for completing work, not what was learned; and even when quality is assessed, the grade is recorded as if the learning were finished. Third, in an environment of interim and benchmark testing, the nature of feedback is often distorted, emphasizing to students that they need to get three more items correct to pass a standard rather than what substantive aspect of a topic still needs to be understood. The specific ways that these dilemmas can be addressed will vary tremendously according to the age of the students, from the earliest grade levels where letter grades need not be assigned to secondary school contexts where formative processes can serve a coaching purpose to help students attain the verification of skills they need for external audiences.

Of course, all of these claims about processes and meanings of assessment won't amount to much if the contents of assessments are not transformed to direct learning toward more ambitious thinking and reasoning goals. For learning activities to pull students in, they must offer a sense of purpose and meaning. Typically this requires authenticity and a connection to the world (although fantasy worlds with sufficient complexity and coherence can also be compelling). Trying to develop rich curriculum and capture higher-order thinking is an old and familiar problem, going back 100 years if you look hard enough. More immediately, the literature of the past 20 years reminds us that declaring world-class standards and promising to create more authentic assessments – "tests worth teaching to," – are intentions that have been tried before and are frequently undone.

A new round of content standards holds the promise of providing much more coherently developed learning sequences with attention to depth of understanding. And, as previously mentioned, recently-developed standards have also attended to mathematical and scientific practices – arguing from evidence, developing and using models, and so forth – as well as big-idea content strands. The hope, too, is that next-generation assessments will more faithfully represent the new standards than has been the case for large-scale assessments in the past. While the knowledge exists to make it possible to construct much more inventive assessments, this could more easily be done in the context of small-scale curriculum projects than for large-scale, high-stakes accountability tests. In the latter case, the constraints imposed by cost, demands for speedy score reporting, and the need for curriculum neutrality across jurisdictions can quickly drive out innovation and substantive depth. Only time will tell if these new promises for focused and coherent content standards and next-generation assessments will be achieved.

Research on classroom assessment has the potential to make a tremendous contribution to improve teaching and learning, if it were focused on making these grand theoretical claims come true – both regarding learning theory and motivation and more fulsome representations of content and disciplinary practices. We probably do not need more studies documenting limitations of current practice. Instead, a theme repeated across the many studies reported in this handbook is the need to plan for and support teacher learning. Teachers need access to better tools, not disconnected item banks but rather curricular tasks that have been carefully designed to elicit student thinking and for which colleagues and curriculum experts have identified and tested out follow-up strategies. Learning progressions are one way to frame this kind of recursive research and development work. Elsewhere, I've also argued for the design of replacement units, which are carefully designed alternative curriculum units that, because they are modularized, are easier to adopt and try out. Such units would need to include rich instructional activities aimed at a combination of topics and standards (for example, developing and using models and heredity), formative questions and tasks, samples of student work illustrating the range of novice understandings and how to build on them, end-of-unit summative tasks, and possibly longer-term follow up questions and extensions connected to other units. The point is to recognize how much needs to be worked out and to acknowledge the impossibility of every teacher inventing this well for every topic all on her or his own.

What we know about teacher learning, in parallel to student learning, is that teachers need the opportunity to construct their own understandings in the context of their practice and in ways consistent with their identity as a thoughtful professional (rather than a beleaguered bureaucrat). Teachers need social support and a sense of purpose, hence the appeal of communities of practice (although mandated communities of practice may undo the intended meaning). The research literature also warns us that some obstacles are large enough and predictable enough that they should be attended to explicitly in the curriculum, assessment, and professional development design process. Specifically, the articulation between formative assessment (held safe from grading) and summative assessment could be a part of curriculum design, especially for model units used as part of professional development. In my experience, teachers can generalize new curricular and assessment ideas once they get the hang of it, but doing it well when everything is new is much more challenging. Another theme to be addressed explicitly is the relationship of rich, new curricular materials and high-stakes assessments. Groups of teachers jointly analyzing what's on the test, what's not, and how to stay true to more complete learning goals creates both greater awareness and a shared commitment to avoid narrow teaching to the test.

Present-day learning theory has grown to encompass cognition, meta-cognition, and motivation, and has altered what it means to know and participate meaningfully in disciplinary knowledge communities. These perspectives should inform the design of curriculum and of classroom assessments intended to improve student learning and instructional practices. In addition, an understanding of these theories might also be used to examine the heterogeneity in study outcomes, explaining, for example, why two studies with the same-named intervention might produce different learning results.

PREFACE

This book is based on a simple assertion: Classroom assessment (CA) is the most powerful type of measurement in education that influences student learning. This premise lays the foundation for the need for research on CA. Noting the importance of CA is not new, but research in the area is sorely lacking. The measurement community has been and certainly currently is focused on large-scale assessment, mostly for high-stakes accountability testing. Indeed, what is happening with the changing nature of accountability testing, especially its use for teacher evaluation, will only heighten the already high stakes. We know that these large-scale tests influence what happens in the classroom, from what standards are emphasized and how pacing guides are built to cover standards, to the nature of levels of knowledge and understanding that are stressed. But it is in the nature of CAs that student motivation and learning are most affected. Whether summative or formative, classroom tests, quizzes, questioning, papers, projects, and other measures are what students experience on an ongoing basis, and these measures directly impact what and how students study and what they learn. How teachers conceptualize assessments that they use and how they are integrated (or not) with instruction have a direct influence on student engagement and learning.

What we have emphasized in this book is research on and about CA to provide a better understanding of the theoretical, conceptual, and empirical evidence to inform the academic community in a way that will further principles of CA that will lead to best practice. This includes consideration of advances in learning and motivation theory and research that underpin classroom dynamics related to assessment, as well as more direct investigations of specific approaches to assessment.

Our Purpose

The aim of the *SAGE Handbook of Research on Classroom Assessment* is to present a comprehensive source of research on most aspects of K–12 CA and to begin to build an empirical foundation for research that will advance our understanding of CA. In this single text, there is presentation and analysis of all types of research on CA, with an emphasis on important conceptual and theoretical frameworks that are needed for establishing a solid and enduring research foundation. Overall, CA research is summarized and analyzed to convey, in depth, the state of knowledge and understanding that is represented by the research. There is a particular emphasis on how CA practices affect student achievement and teacher behavior. Leading CA researchers served as associate editors and authors, bringing the best thinking and analysis about the nature of research to each area.

The handbook is written primarily for scholars, professors, graduate students, and other researchers and policy makers in universities, organizations, agencies, testing companies, and school districts. Practitioners will find value in specific chapters. The research does have implications for practice, but the main focus of the handbook is on summarizing and critiquing research, theories, and ideas to present a knowledge base about CA and the groundwork for completing research in the future. As such, the handbook will serve as an excellent text for graduate students taking assessment classes. Educational psychology, curriculum, and methods professors can use the handbook as a primary or supplementary text in their classes and as a source of knowledge to inform their research.

Classroom Assessment as a Field of Study?

The identity and research-based field of CA has been developing in earnest over the past two decades, spurred mostly perhaps by the work on formative assessment. Interestingly, while the first three editions of the *Handbook of Research on Teaching* (1963–1986; Gage, 1963; Gage & Travers, 1973; Wittrock, 1986) and *Educational Measurement* (1951–1989; Lindquist & Thorndike, 1951; Linn, 1989; Thorndike, 1971) did not contain a chapter on CA, the fourth editions did (Brennan, 2006; Richardson, 2001), both important chapters by Lorrie Shepard. Shepard's 2006 chapter in the fourth edition of the *Educational Measurement* handbook was one of the first major indications that the larger measurement and research community had interest in how teachers assess students on what is learned in the classroom, apart from the use of large-scale achievement tests (the National Council on Measurement in Education [NCME] has for years, though, promoted some research, training, and activity in CA).

This new emphasis on CA occurred on the heels of work in the nature of cognition that has developed new ways of understanding learning and motivation. Contemporary learning and motivation theory now focus on constructivist paradigms that emphasize the importance of prior learning, social and cultural contexts, and deep understanding. A critically important text in assessment by Pellegrino, Chudowsky, and Glaser, *Knowing What Students Know,* published in 2001, formally integrated newer cognitive and constructivist theories of learning with the need for new and different CAs. The convergence of these factors has resulted in increased attention to CA as a field that has matured considerably since *tests and measurement* courses were used to teach teachers about assessment.

Despite this increased attention, however, it is not entirely clear that CA is a distinct field of study. Perhaps it is an emerging field of study. The hallmarks of a field of study include a recognized, specialized language and terminology; journals, degrees; institutes; conferences; and forums for researchers to exchange and discuss research and ideas, develop new lines of research, and develop new knowledge. The CA community has some of these elements, as evidenced most perhaps by the continuing work on CA in England and the Classroom Assessment Special Interest Group of the American Educational Research Association (AERA). But there are no degrees that I'm aware of, no professional journal, and few conferences. So there is much to be done. The field of CA (if you can call it a field) does not have a strong and recognized research base that builds upon itself and is subject to the level of scrutiny required that transpires in journals, conferences, and degree programs.

Organization

The handbook is organized into six sections. The overall logic of the sequence of chapters is to first present underlying theory and contextual influences, then technical considerations. That is followed by chapters on formative and summative CA. In the last two sections, separate chapters are devoted to different methods of assessments and assessments in different subject areas. This organization was used to show how each of these areas is important in contributing to research that will advance our knowledge and understanding of effective CA.

In the first section, chapters focus on conceptual and theoretical frames of reference and contextual factors that influence CA research. The emphasis is on examining previous CA research, learning and motivation research and theory, and the pervasive impact of large-scale, high-stakes testing. These factors help us to understand how to frame important CA research questions to result in principles that are well aligned with how students are motivated and learn.

The second section, with leadership from Associate Editor Sarah M. Bonner, includes four chapters that examine technical measurement issues and principles that must be considered in conducting CA research. These include the three pillars of high quality CA—(1) validity, (2) reliability, and (3) fairness. Each of these is considered both from traditional measurement and classroom measurement perspectives. There is a long history that documents difficulty in applying principles of validity, reliability, and fairness to CA, and these chapters move our profession toward a more relevant set of principles that apply to what teachers do in the classroom. This section also includes a chapter that looks at techniques for how CA can be measured.

The chapters in the third section, with leadership from Associate Editor Dylan Wiliam, focus on what has become the most recognized topic within measurement: formative assessment. In these chapters, the emphasis is on what occurs in the classroom, the more informal, ongoing process of gathering evidence, providing feedback, and making instructional correctives. In the fourth section, with leadership from Associate Editor Susan M. Brookhart, classroom summative assessment is addressed. This type of assessment should not be ignored or completely consumed by formative dynamics. What teachers do to document student learning is critical, as is the nature and use of reporting grades.

In the fifth section, with leadership from Associate Editor Heidi L. Andrade, research in seven different methods of CAs is presented and analyzed. This includes separate chapters on constructed-response (CR) and selected-response (SR) types of items and tests, performance assessment, and portfolio assessment, as well as chapters that focus on more recently emphasized techniques to examine student self-assessment, peer assessment, and social–emotional traits. The last section, with leadership from Associate Editor Jay Parkes, breaks out assessment by topic, with chapters focused on differentiated instruction (DI), students with disabilities, and different subjects.

References

Brennan, R. L. (Ed.). (2006). *Educational measurement.* Westport, CT: Praeger.

Gage, N. L. (Ed.). (1963). *Handbook of research on teaching.* Chicago: Rand McNally.

Gage, N. L., & Travers, R. M. W. (Eds.) (1973). *Handbook of research on teaching.* Washington, DC: American Educational Research Association.

Lindquist, E. F., & Thorndike, R. L. (1951). *Educational measurement.* Washington, DC: American Council on Education.

Linn, R. L. (Ed.). (1989). *Educational measurement.* Washington, DC: American Council on Education.

Pellegrino, J. W., Chudowsky, N., & Glaser, R. (Eds.). (2001). *Knowing what students know: The science and design of educational assessment.* Washington, DC: National Academy Press.

Richardson, V. (Ed.) (2001). *Handbook of research on teaching.* Washington, DC: American Educational Research Association.

Shepard, L. A. (2006). Classroom assessment. In R. L. Brennan (Ed.), *Educational measurement* (4th ed., pp. 623–646). Westport, CT: Praeger.

Thorndike, R. L. (Ed.). (1971). *Educational measurement.* Washington, DC: American Council on Education.

Wittrock, M. C. (Ed.). (1986). *Handbook of research on teaching.* Washington, DC: American Educational Research Association.

ACKNOWLEDGMENTS

Of course, a project this large can only be completed with much help from many talented people. All the section editors have been great. Their willingness to help select and communicate with chapter authors and edit chapters has been indispensible. I am especially grateful to Susan M. Brookhart, Heidi L. Andrade, and Sarah M. Bonner, who have repeatedly and willingly shared their great ideas and expertise about all aspects of putting this book together, including determining chapter content, organization, and assurance of high quality work. The heart of this book is in the talent and work of chapter authors, and I am grateful to each for their commitment and responsiveness to suggestions. Thanks to Cliff Conrad and Michael Connelly for sharing their experiences with editing previously published handbooks of research and to several anonymous reviewers of the book prospectus. Several graduate students here at Virginia Commonwealth University have been great with editing chores, including Amanda Turner, Divya Varier, and Reggie Brown. Finally, working with SAGE has been wonderful. I appreciate very much the faith showed by Diane McDaniel in approving the book, and Megan Koraly and Megan Markanich have been superb in keeping me on target, providing essential information and suggestions, and ushering the work through to completion.

SECTION 1

Important Contexts for Research on Classroom Assessment

James H. McMillan
Associate Editor

1

Why We Need Research on Classroom Assessment

James H. McMillan

In 1973, I took a measurement class from Bob Ebel at Michigan State University. Bob was a respected measurement authority, educated at an assessment mecca, the University of Iowa, by none other than E. F. Lindquist. We used Ebel's textbook *Essentials of Educational Measurement* (Ebel, 1972), which devoted 400 pages—out of 650 pages for the entire book—to what he said were principles of classroom testing. There were chapters on test reliability and validity, different types of tests, and test score statistics, all directed at what teachers do in the classroom. This suggests that interest in classroom assessment (CA), or perhaps more accurately, how teachers test students in the classroom, has been around for a long time. Looking back, though, the course I took mostly reflected the application of summative psychometric measurement principles to teaching. The classroom, and what teachers did in the classroom, were essentially only the setting in which the principles were applied. There was little regard for CA as integrated with teaching or as a separate field of study.

Fast-forward to today... First, I believe Bob Ebel would be pleased with what has happened to CA, because he was always concerned about student learning. But I think he would be surprised by how CA has matured into a field that is separating itself from traditional notions of psychometrically based measurement, the theories and principles he relied on to write his book. CA is becoming a substantial field of study—one that is increasing a knowledge base so that progress can be made in what Bob was most concerned about: enhancing student achievement. However, the research that is needed to provide a comprehensive foundation for CA is splintered. It has been reported here and there but has not found a home or permanent identity. It is given relatively little attention from the National Council on Measurement in Education (NCME), not withstanding efforts by Rick Stiggins, Jim Popham, Susan M. Brookhart, Lorrie Shepard, and a few others, dwarfed by the psychometrics of large-scale testing.

This handbook is meant to signal the beginning of CA as a separate and distinct field of study with an identifiable research base, a field that integrates three areas: what we know about measurement, student learning and motivation, and instruction. While combining these three areas in a meaningful way is not new (see Cizek, 1997; Guskey, 2003; Pellegrino, Chudowsky, & Glaser, 2001; and Shepard, 2000, 2006), the present volume aims to provide a basis for the research that is needed to establish enduring principles of CA that will enhance as well as document student learning. It is about the need to establish a more formal body of research that can provide a foundation for growing our knowledge about how CA is undertaken and how it can be effective in enhancing student learning and motivation. Our collective assertion is that CA is the most powerful type of measurement in education that influences student learning.

CA is a broad and evolving conceptualization of a process that teachers and students use in collecting, evaluating, and using evidence of student learning for a variety of purposes, including diagnosing student strengths and weaknesses, monitoring student progress toward meeting desired levels of proficiency, assigning grades, and providing feedback to parents. That is, CA is a tool teachers use to gather relevant data and information to make well-supported inferences about what students know, understand, and can do (Shavelson & Towne, 2002), as well as a vehicle through which student learning and motivation are enhanced. CA enhances teachers' judgments about student competence by providing reasoned evidence in a variety of forms gathered at different times. It is distinguished from large-scale or standardized, whether standards-based, personality, aptitude, or benchmark- or interim-type tests. It is locally controlled and consists of a broad range of measures, including both structured techniques such as tests, papers, student self-assessment, reports, and portfolios, as well as informal ways of collecting evidence, including anecdotal observation and spontaneous questioning of students. It is more than mere measurement or quantification of student performance. CA connects learning targets to effective assessment practices teachers use in their classrooms to monitor and improve student learning. When CA is integrated with and related to learning, motivation, and curriculum it both educates students and improves their learning.

A Changing Context for Research on Classroom Assessment

In this section, I want to outline important factors that frame issues and considerations in research on CA. I argue that changes in several areas set the current context, which influences what research questions are appropriate, what methodologies are needed, and what advances can be expected. As depicted in Figure 1.1, there is a dynamic convergence of these contextual factors that influence CA research. The good news is that the emphasis is on how to generate knowledge about effective assessment *for* learning (AFL) and assessment *as* learning. As appropriate, I'll also indicate how subsequent chapters in this handbook address many of these factors.

As illustrated in Figure 1.1, there are six major factors that have a significant influence on the current context in which CA research is conducted. For each of these six, there are important advances in knowledge and practice, and together they impact the nature of the research that needs to be designed, completed, and disseminated. Each is considered in more detail.

Advances in Measurement

Throughout most of the 20th century, the research on assessment in education focused on the role of standardized testing (Shepard, 2006; Stiggins & Conklin, 1992). It was clear that the professional educational measurement community was concerned with the role of standardized testing, both from a large-scale assessment perspective as well as with how teachers used test data for instruction in their own classrooms. Until late in the century, there was simply little emphasis on CA, and the small number of studies that researched CA was made up of largely descriptive studies, depicting what teachers did with testing and grading. For example, an entire issue of the *Journal of Educational Measurement*, purportedly focused on "the state of the art integrating testing and instruction," excluded teacher-made tests (Burstein, 1983). The first three editions of *Educational Measurement* (Lindquist, 1951; Linn, 1989; Thorndike, 1971), which were designed with the goal of presenting important, state-of-the-art measurement topics with chapters written by prominent measurement experts, did not include a chapter on CA (that changed with Lorrie Shepard's chapter in the 2006 edition [Shepard, 2006]. Similarly, the first three editions of the *Handbook of Research on Teaching* (Gage, 1963; Travers, 1973; Wittrock, 1986) had little to say about CA or, for that matter, about testing more broadly (Shepard provided a chapter on classroom assessment in the fourth edition [Shepard, 2001]). The *Standards for Educational and Psychological Testing* (American Educational Research Association [AERA], American Psychological Association [APA], and the National Council on Measurement in Education [NCME], 1999) does not explicitly address

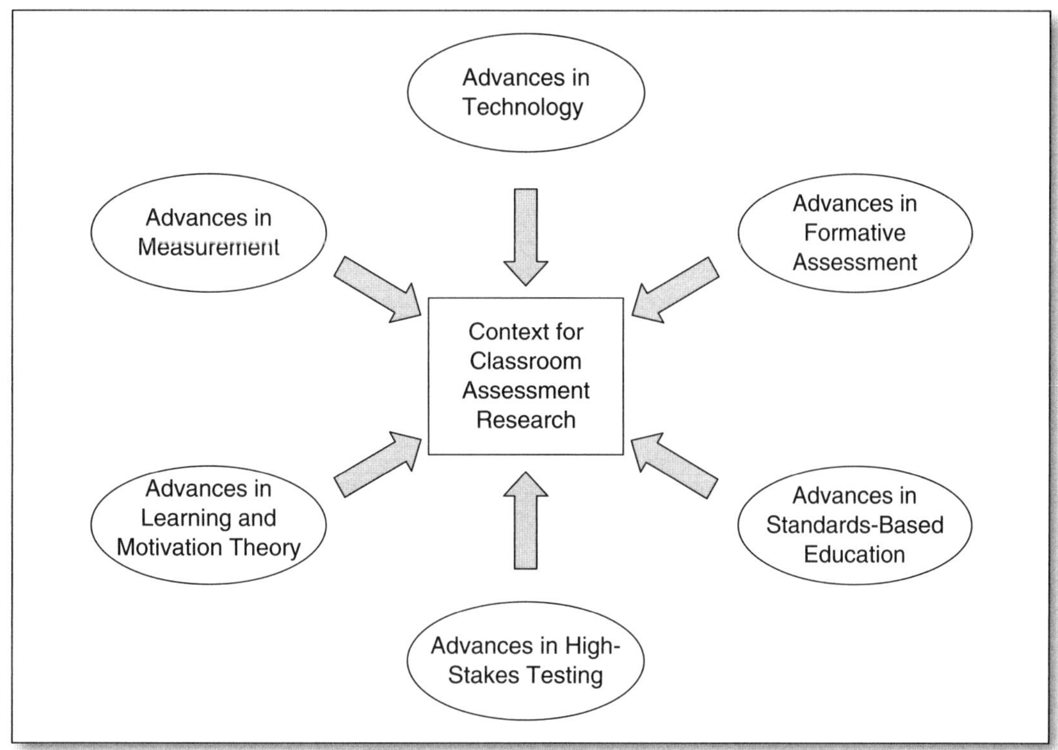

Figure 1.1 Factors Influencing Classroom Assessment Research

CA, nor are the standards written for practitioners. While the *Standards for Educational and Psychological Testing* contains a separate chapter on educational testing and assessment, it focuses on "routine school, district, state, or other system-wide testing programs, testing for selection in higher education, and individualized special needs testing" (p. 137). Clearly, the last century established what could be described as a *psychometric/measurement* paradigm, a powerful context in which attention to assessment focused on the psychometric principles of large-scale testing and corresponding formal, technical, and statistical topics for all educators, including teachers.

The cultural and political backdrop of earlier research examined issues pertaining to "assessment *of* learning" (evidenced by summative test scores; for more information on summative assessments, see Chapter 14 by Connie M. Moss). Inadequacies of assessment training in teacher education were reported many decades ago (Goslin, 1967; Mayo, 1964; Noll, 1955; Roeder, 1972). Subsequent research echoed the shortcomings of teacher education in the assessment area, calling for improved preparation (Brookhart, 2001; Campbell & Evans, 2000; Green & Mantz, 2002; Hills, 1977; Schafer & Lissitz, 1987) and for preparation to be relevant to the assessment realities of the classroom (Stiggins, 1991; Stiggins & Conklin, 1992; Wise, Lukin, & Roos, 1991). Others researched and suggested needed teacher assessment competencies (Plake & Impara, 1997; Schafer, 1993). A generalized finding was that, by and large, teachers lack expertise in the construction and interpretation of assessments they design and use to evaluate student learning (Marso & Pigge, 1993; Plake & Impara, 1997; Plake, Impara, & Fager, 1993), though this referred primarily to constructing, administering, and interpreting summative assessments. When AFL is emphasized, different teacher competencies are needed, including the need for teachers to clearly understand the cognitive elements that are essential to student learning, such as being able to identify errors in cognitive processing that prevent students from advancing along a learning progression (Heritage, 2008).

Similarly, research investigating assessment *as* learning has documented the benefits of student involvement throughout the learning process—in particular, how peer and self-assessment enhances metacognition and ownership of learning as a result of active involvement in evaluating ones own work (Dann, 2002; Shepard, 2000; see also Chapters 21 and 22 of this volume).

A systemic effect on the United States' educational system was fueled by *A Nation at Risk* (National Committee on Excellence in Education, 1983), which suggested the need for substantial improvement in teacher preparation programs. Following this report, many states updated or initiated state-required proficiency exams for beginning teachers. Concurring with the need for teachers to be able to accurately assess student learning, the American Federation of Teachers (AFT), the NCME, and the National Education Association (NEA) developed *Standards for Teacher Competence in Educational Assessment of Students* (American Federation of Teachers (AFT), NCME, and National Education Association [NEA], 1990), which summarized critical assessment knowledge and skills and provided a guide for research, teacher preparation, and professional development. These standards have been *updated* by Brookhart (2011) to incorporate learning and teaching as important components of what teachers need to know to be effective assessors in the classroom.

Though the context of research for CA has shifted away from specific large-scale testing principles, the fundamental ideas of validity, reliability, and fairness are still very much a part of understanding what occurs in the classroom and research on CA. From the perspective of researchers, traditional ideas of validity, reliability, and fairness are used to assure adequate instrumentation and credible data gathering. Our emphasis here is on the validity, reliability, and fairness of CAs. In Chapter 6, Sarah M. Bonner suggests new viewpoints about the validity of CAs. She presents five principles based on new interpretations from traditional conceptualizations of validity. These include (1) alignment with instruction, (2) minimal bias, (3) an emphasis on substantive processes of learning, (4) the effects of assessment-based interpretations, and (5) the importance of validity evidence from multiple stakeholders. These principles extend the idea of validity—evidence of the appropriateness of interpretations, conclusions, and use—to be more relevant to classroom settings. This extends earlier work by Brookhart (2003) and Moss (2003) on the need to reconceptualize validity to be more useful for CA. In addition, Margaret Heritage, in Chapter 11, focuses on validity in gathering evidence for formative assessment.

New thinking is also presented in this volume on reliability and fairness, which also have been conceptualized mainly from technical requirements of large-scale assessment. Jay Parkes, in Chapter 7, posited a reconceptualization of reliability, one that blends measurement and instruction, considers teacher decision making and a subjective inferential process of data gathering, and includes social dynamics in the classroom. He proposes a new conceptual framework for the development of CA reliability. In Chapter 8, Robin D. Tierney argues that fairness for CA, while inconsistently defined in the literature, is best conceptualized as a series of practices, including transparency of assessment learning expectations and criteria for evaluating work, opportunity to learn and demonstrate learning, consistency and equitability for all students, critical reflection, and the creation and maintenance of a constructive learning environment in which assessment is used to improve learning.

This is not to suggest that there were not some attempts during the last part of the 20th century to study CA. Shepard (2006) summarized several of these efforts, which gathered momentum in the 1980s. These studies highlighted the need to understand teachers' everyday decision making concerning both instruction and assessment. Two landmark publications (Crooks, 1988; Stiggins & Conklin, 1992) summarized data to describe the complex landscape of CA and set the stage for a surge of interest in understanding how teachers assess and what the nature of teacher preparation should look like to ensure that teachers have the knowledge and skills to effectively develop, implement, and use assessments they administer in their classrooms. During the 1990s, CA established an independent identity with the publication of textbooks (e.g., Airasian, 1991; McMillan, 1997; Popham, 1995; Stiggins, 1994; Wiggins, 1998), the *Handbook of Classroom Assessment: Learning, Adjustment, and Achievement* (Phye, 1997), and forming of the Classroom Assessment Special Interest Group in AERA. Significantly, in Great Britain, the Assessment Reform Group, which was started in 1989 as a task group of the British Educational

Research Association, initiated study on the relationships between CA, teaching, and student learning. These efforts led to the highly influential and often cited Black and Wiliam (1998) publication that summarized studies showing the dramatic effect of formative assessment on student learning.

Advances in Learning and Motivation

Late in the 20th century, subject-matter experts also began to pay attention to CA as an important component of effective instruction. The work of Grant Wiggins (1993) was instrumental in promoting authentic assessment, and research on learning and motivation was now emphasizing active construction of new knowledge and the importance of student self-assessment as part of self-regulation. Cognitive learning theories led subject-matter experts to change their views of instruction and assessment (Shepard, 2006). As a result, learning is now recognized as a process of connecting new information to existing knowledge. There is an emphasis on the importance of transfer of what is learned, problem solving, and metacognition (as contrasted with knowledge accumulation).

Research in both learning and motivation supports the idea that CA is not solely an end-point (summative). Rather, it is a powerful agent for influencing learning and motivation. This is why research on both learning and motivation, which is extensive and well documented, has a critical role to play in determining the most effective manner in which CAs are planned and implemented. It has also created a conflict with established measurement principles that were based on earlier developed—primarily behavioristic—theories of learning. While this tension still exists, the seminal work *Knowing What Students Know: The Science and Design of Educational Assessment* (Pellegrino et al., 2001) suggests that many technical advancements in assessment can better capture the complexity of student learning to be more consistent with recent cognitive theories of learning and motivation. These newer technical approaches are being used in the design of both summative and formative assessments that will be developed to align with Common Core State Standards (what will essentially be national standards and tests), though the emphasis is on large-scale applications, not on what teachers do day in and day out in their classrooms.

In Chapter 2, Heidi L. Andrade summarizes recent research on self-regulation to show how this knowledge of a process of learning is directly related to assessment. There are four components that are central to self-regulated learning (SRL): (1) goal setting, (2) monitoring progress toward the goal, (3) interpretation of feedback, and (4) adjustment of goal-directed action. Clearly understood, appropriately challenging goals are needed for meaningful learning as well as for intentional engagement that results in intrinsic motivation (as pointed out by Susan M. Brookhart in Chapter 3).

Another model of learning, not necessarily new but with recent interest, is that learning is socially mediated: There is a social nature to learning that is influenced by social norms, expectations, and interpersonal interactions. This sociocultural view of learning has important implications for teaching and assessment (Shepard, 2000). In Chapter 20 of this volume, Susan E. Rivers, Carolin Hagelskamp, and Marc A. Brackett summarize methodological approaches to measuring social–emotional attributes of classrooms and discuss empirical evidence of the relationship of these attributes to student outcomes.

An important result of recent research in learning and motivation is the recognition by those interested in effective instruction that complex and advanced student learning is promoted by active, meaningful learning activities that are accompanied by formative assessment (Shepard, 2006). This realization has also led to the popularity of performance and portfolio assessment as a means of both instruction and assessment. There are now many resources that show how these types of assessments can be effectively implemented. They are generally recognized as essential tools that all teachers may use, as appropriate. In Chapter 18, Suzanne Lane summarizes research on performance assessment, examining technical qualities and concerns of performance assessment as well as the impact of performance assessment on instructional practices and student learning. In the following chapter (Chapter 20), Susan F. Belgrad shows how portfolio assessment is effective in supporting reflection, student self-assessment, and goal setting. These skills are consistent with recent theories of learning of motivation and show how teaching, learning, and assessment can be integrated into a single process. In Chapter 26, Cheryl A. Torrez and Elizabeth Ann Claunch-Lebsack emphasize the growing importance of disciplined inquiry as a critical outcome of social studies education. This includes debating implications, evaluating sources, developing conclusions, and creating interpretive accounts.

As one further illustration of the impact of learning theory on CA, consider recent work by Brookhart (2011), in which she *updated* standards for educational assessment knowledge and skills for teachers. Of 11 *new* standards, note the emphasis on learning in the first three:

1. Teachers should understand learning in the content area they teach.
2. Teachers should be able to articulate clear learning intentions that are congruent with both the content and depth of thinking implied by standards and curriculum goals, in such a way that they are attainable and assessable.
3. Teachers should have a repertoire of strategies for communicating to students what achievement of a learning intention looks like.

High-Stakes, Large-Scale Testing

The now ubiquitous nature of using large-scale testing for accountability has had a dramatic influence on what happens with CA. To understand the nature of this influence, it is helpful to consider the importance of student performance on these tests. State testing for student and school accountability, with the use of common end-of-course testing, is standard. The high-stakes are focused primarily, though not exclusively, on the student, with remediation, grade retention, and high school graduation as possible consequences. These are obviously important for the student, and teachers are pressured to make sure students succeed. Schools are also held accountable, so additional pressure is placed on achieving high scores. This leads naturally to more teaching to the test and test preparation and in turn influences CA to become more like what tests at the end of the year look like. With the Common Core State Standards and new emphasis on using student scores to evaluate teachers and principals, the stakes will become even higher, with more pressure on doing what is needed to obtain high scores (McMillan, 2011). This has led many schools to administer benchmark or interim tests every 9 weeks, to assess progress toward proficiencies needed to do well on the end-of-year test, and to use common assessments in the same grade and/or subject.

There is evidence that the pressure applied by these external tests results in teachers giving more objective tests for their CAs, with less emphasis on constructed-response (CR) formats, performance assessments, or portfolios (Pedulla et al., 2003). Thomas P. Hogan suggests in Chapter 16 that most teachers use both CR and selected-response (SR) (typically multiple-choice) items in their assessments, though the research is far from clear about the differential impact of CR items on student studying and learning. There is no doubt, though, that there is a constant press on teachers to "prepare students for the accountability tests." Often the curriculum is narrowed, along with corresponding CAs. Herman and Baker (2009) summarized the effects numerous studies have documented related to the power of external, high-stakes tests, including signaling of curriculum priorities, teacher modeling of what is assessed, alignment of curriculum with what is tested, and lessening emphasis on what is not tested. Ironically, curriculum narrowing tends to be most severe for students who are at risk.

Furthermore, given the current climate of school accountability and data-driven decision making, teachers are expected to use sound assessment practices as a means for improving student outcomes. They need to integrate large-scale testing approaches and item types with how they assess their students and plan for future instruction.

The important context of external accountability testing is considered in Chapter 4. M. Christina Schneider, Karla L. Egan, and Marc W. Julian describe the nature of high-stakes testing and explain how CAs can be aligned with these tests for a balanced, triangulated understanding of what students know and can do. They point out that the deep understanding and higher thinking skills required by external tests are difficult for teachers to tap with their CAs. The resulting mismatch is problematic. With greater coherence among all major types of assessment (end-of-year, interim, classroom), teachers will have a better understanding of student strengths and weaknesses as well as improved insight into what instructional improvements are needed. Furthermore, as pointed out by Michael C. Rodriguez and Thomas M. Haladyna in Chapter 17, much research is needed to help teachers write SR type items with appropriate formats and attention to the cognitive demands inherent in understanding the item and coming up with an answer.

Formative Assessment

Perhaps the most researched aspect of CA over the past two decades is formative assessment. In contrast to the metaphorical banking model of education, where teachers *deposit* information into their students that can be later *withdrawn* through formal testing, formative assessment is interactive, occurring throughout instruction. Through formative assessment, clues gauging how well learning is coming along are provided. Using assessment to monitor progress and provide feedback reconceptualized the purpose of assessment from a precise, summative, static measure of learning to a means for generating hypotheses about learning progress and the instructional process (Black, Harrison, Lee, Marshall, & Wiliam, 2004; Black & Wiliam, 1998; Shepard, 2000; Stiggins, 2001). As a result, methods that unite instruction and assessment have been studied (e.g., running records, observation, think aloud, and in-the-moment).

Largely as a result of Black and Wiliam (1998), much work by Rick Stiggins, and research by a multitude of individuals and groups (Andrade & Cizek, 2010; McMillan, 2007), formative assessment is at the top of most lists of important measurement topics, as well as many instructional topics, for both CA and large-scale testing. Indeed, it is a concept that is now central to teaching more generally. More recent research on formative assessment has emphasized the extent to which it is embedded in instruction, the extent of student engagement and self-assessment, feedback, and the specific instructional correctives or strategies that are included. These aspects of formative assessment are based on contemporary constructivist learning theories and self-regulation theory (Brookhart, 2011). The emphasis is now on "students as formative decision-makers who need information of a certain type (descriptive at a certain time (in time to act) in order to make productive decisions of their own learning" (Brookhart, 2011, p. 4). Monitoring of progress can be achieved by both teachers and students. The key is for students to know that they are on a path that will lead to success. Ample evidence has accumulated to document the positive impact of formative assessment on student achievement, though there are disputes about the level of impact on student learning (Dunn & Mulvenon, 2009; Kingston & Nash, 2011).

In this volume, we have devoted an entire section to formative assessment, but it is also contained in many other chapters. In Chapter 10, Paul Black discusses contemporary conceptualizations of formative assessment. He points out that while formative assessment is central to instruction it must be supported by summative assessment to be most effective. In Chapter 11, Margaret Heritage focuses on the essential first step in formative assessment: gathering evidence of student understanding. She reviews evidence collection strategies with an emphasis on how the evidence is gathered to have validity and reliability. The critical role of feedback in formative assessment is addressed in Chapters 12 and 13. Dylan Wiliam reviews the history of research on the role of feedback that has now evolved to be essential in the regulation of instruction. Maria Araceli Ruiz-Primo and Min Li summarize a meta-analysis of studies regarding feedback and a theoretical framework to study feedback processes in the classroom. The framework focuses on three components: (1) the assessment activity cycle, (2) formality of the formative assessment episode (FAE), and (3) social participation. The intent is to provide a structure for understanding and researching feedback as it occurs continuously during instruction.

Now that formative assessment is clearly established as a key type of student evaluation, the field is moving toward a greater understanding of student self-assessment as a critical component of formative assessment. In Chapter 21, Gavin T. L. Brown and Lois R. Harris present a synthesis of 84 empirical studies on student self-assessment. They examine several important perspectives about student self-assessment, including the effect of self-assessment on achievement and self-regulation, student perceptions, accuracy, and factors that may mediate effects such as ability and age. They show that there is mixed evidence about the effect of student self-assessment, which points to the need for much more research. Bronwen Cowie, in Chapter 27, summarizes research on the importance of student self-assessment in science, showing how student self-monitoring is helpful in conducting science inquiries. We know student self-assessment can be effective. We now need to parcel out the conditions and factors that need to be present so that the positive impact is significant.

With the increased emphasis on formative assessment, there may be a tendency to mitigate the importance of summative assessment. However, summative assessment is what all teachers do routinely, and the results from these assessments have high stakes. Connie M. Moss, in Chapter 14, reminds us that teachers often use idiosyncratic and flexible criteria in summative judgments of student learning. This allows teachers to *pull* for students and adjust scores to influence final grades (McMillan & Nash, 2000). Moss emphasizes the need for stronger evidence to provide a richer and more comprehensive description about how teachers summarize evidence of learning and how that evidence is reported.

Standards-Based Reform

During the 1990s, standards-based education became ubiquitous, fueling reform for greater accountability for higher and more sophisticated levels of student learning. Popham (2008) describes *standards* effectively:

> *Standards*, of course, is a warmth-inducing word. Although perhaps not in the same league with *motherhood*, *democracy*, and *babies*, I suspect that standards ranks right up there with *oatmeal*, *honor*, and *excellence*. It's really tough not to groove on standards, especially if the standards are *high*. Everyone wants students to reach high standards. (p. 109)

Based on the earlier idea of educational objectives, standards define "what students should know and be able to do." All states now have their standards for student learning, and many are adapting the new Common Core State Standards, which specifies mathematics and English language arts and literacy learning expectations for Grades K–12 (Common Core State Standards Initiative, n.d.). The Common Core State Standards intends to influence what is assessed, as well as the enacted curriculum (Porter, McMaken, Hwang, & Rui, 2011), and with large-scale tests soon aligned with the standards, there is no doubt that these developments will have significant influences on assessments done in the classroom. How will teachers adapt their own formative and summative assessments to the standards and new tests? Will teachers align both content and cognitive skill levels demanded in their CAs to the standards? Add to this the recent Race to the Top federal initiative, which focuses on preparing students for college and/or a career. State and federal efforts in developing and assessing achievement of standards are powerful influences on teaching and assessment and create a context that often conflicts with best practice in CA.

Advances in Technology

Without question, technology will be a key influence on assessment practices in the future and must be considered in research on CA. In Chapter 25, Maggie B. McGatha and William S. Bush summarize studies that use technology in mathematics formative assessment, allowing teachers to obtain immediate knowledge about student understanding and quickly provide feedback. In his chapter on peer assessment (Chapter 22), Keith J. Topping summarizes research on the effectiveness of online systems that allow students to critique each other's work. He also points out that Web-based portfolio assessment is effective for peer assessment. Suzanne Lane, in Chapter 18, discusses computer-based and simulation-based science performance assessments.

Technology now makes it possible to focus on specific details in student knowledge. For example, there are computer programs that quickly evaluate writing and give specific feedback about even the smallest issue or concern. There are now vivid, real-world simulations that can be used in assessments, with engaging and challenging tasks that tap sophisticated and deep understanding.

The Accumulation of Knowledge About Classroom Assessment

Research in education generally has had limited success in producing cumulative knowledge, unlike many scientific fields, including psychology. A recurring theme is that the quality of educational research is low and that in many areas of research there are conflicting findings. There is also a tendency to move quickly to new topics and issues and recently developed techniques and approaches. This has resulted in the lack of a consensus about questions that have enduring importance. At the federal level, reforms to the Education Resources Information Center (ERIC), establishment of the What Works Clearinghouse, and efforts to enhance the scientific rigor of educational research are helping to strengthen the methodology of investigations, but there is still much research reported that does not clearly articulate with established knowledge. What is needed are sustained lines of inquiry that promote deep understanding of important areas of practice, and this need includes CA. Such sustained, focused inquiry eventually leads to generalized principles that move the field forward and increases the certainty of knowledge claims.

The key idea here is in the *accumulation of knowledge*. The need is for research to fit together like building blocks in a sequence that is identifiable. In educational measurement, such accumulation of knowledge is seen with both reliability and validity. The development of reliability progressed over the years from a concept of consistency in how different raters ranked essays (rank-order correlation), to consistency among items on a single test (internal consistency), to providing a formula for measuring consistency on most any type of scale (coefficient alpha), to generalizability theory that enables estimation of consistency by considering multiple sources of error. Jay Parkes, in Chapter 7, discusses the evolution of reliability more completely, identifying the essential building block pieces.

Validity was initially considered a characteristic of a measure based on a correlation between test scores and later performance (e.g., the Army Alpha test). The idea was that a test or survey could be labeled *valid*. By World War II, in an effort to select engineers, it was established that a test could be *intrinsically* valid by the nature of the content. This led to a revised definition of validity to include three types: (1) content-related, (2) criterion-related, and (3) construct-related. At about the same time, it was realized that any single test could be used for different purposes. Later, the definition changed further to emphasize that inferences and uses are valid or invalid, and validity is situation specific and not a characteristic of a test. The language changed to emphasize evidence based on different sources of information. (What's interesting is the notion that there are types of validity that seem to live on despite changes in professional standards in 1985.) In her chapter on validity in this volume (Chapter 6), Sarah M. Bonner extends this development of characteristics of validity by showing how characteristics of CA extend and sharpen how validity is best conceptualized for the purposes of teaching and learning.

In CA more specifically, only the beginnings of cumulative knowledge have been realized. It is difficult to identify a well documented series of studies that focus on a single area. For example, we know much about how teachers grade students and what is used to determine grades, but as Susan M. Brookhart explains in Chapter 15, research on grading shows a wide range of methodological rigor and a mostly singular finding—that teachers combine achievement with other indicators, such as effort and participation, in idiosyncratic ways to give students grades and typically conclude that this is not best practice. With the exception of some grading studies in special education and standards-based approaches, we have not seen a progression of research that moves grading research forward or that shows a cumulative pattern of increasingly sophisticated understandings about the nature and effects of grading.

There are, however, examples of lines of CA research that show promise in establishing cumulative knowledge. Two areas—(1) formative assessment and (2) student self-assessment—illustrate the nature of research that is most likely to result in deep understanding and generalized principles of practice.

Research on Formative Assessment

Formative assessment research has progressed from ideas about formative evaluation to specific studies about different aspects of formative procedures, including investigations of how students interpret learning errors (Leighton, Chu, & Seitz, 2011). It has been bolstered by the use of rich theoretical frameworks and psychological research on the effect of feedback on learning and motivation. As shown by Kingston and Nash (2011), we are now able to conduct meta-analyses on formative assessment studies. For example, while it can be claimed that appropriate formative assessment can have a positive effect on student achievement, the recent meta-analysis conducted by Kingston and Nash (2011) suggests that the effect size of impacts reported in some literature, between 0.40 and 0.70, may be too high. Furthermore, reviews of research have pointed out methodological flaws of many formative assessment studies (Fuchs & Fuchs, 1986). According to Dunn & Mulvenon (2009), previous reviews of research on CA suggest the need for greater methodological soundness in studies—more than conclusions that warrant changes in practice and professional development. What has emerged from these reviews is that there is significant variation in documented effects of formative assessment, depending on differences in how formative assessment is conceptualized and implemented, subject, and age of students. Further understanding of these variations will contribute to useful accumulated knowledge about formative assessment.

Research on Student Self-Assessment

Research on student self-assessment illustrates nicely how a series of studies builds on each other to accumulate knowledge. There has been considerable work on the validity and reliability of scores representing self-assessment that has provided technical adequacy for research in this area. This has been followed by research demonstrating the relationship between self-assessment and learning and then research on implementing interventions to train teachers and students to self-assess. Research in the area is sufficiently mature to consider mediating variables such as task difficulty and academic ability as well as other factors. In addition, as pointed out by Gavin T. L. Brown and Lois R. Harris in this volume (Chapter 21), there is a solid theoretical basis for understanding and researching self-assessment.

Finally, it is important to realize that knowledge generation and accumulation is dynamic, involving continual interactions among empirical findings, methodological advances, and theory building, and it is often nonlinear (Shavelson & Towne, 2002). For instance, as new instruments and ways of understanding and recording student perceptions about CA are developed, these instruments can be used to better understand how students process feedback and think about next steps to improve their understanding. As the theory of formative assessment is further developed, new empirical studies will need to be designed to test proposed theoretical changes. Replication studies will clarify issues of generalization of knowledge across subjects and grade levels. This interplay is most effectively operationalized when researchers continue their empirical investigations in a single area, over and over, to establish depth of understanding.

In addition, it is simply difficult to conduct research on CA. There are considerable obstacles to overcome in doing field-based research, let alone to conducting studies that will elucidate contradictory findings that exist due to variations in field settings. The challenge, it seems to me, is to conduct meaningful field-based studies that will contribute to a generalized knowledge base that will elicit principles and guidelines that will be useful in promoting more effective teaching and more positive student achievement.

New Directions for Classroom Assessment Research

There is much to be done to establish a body of knowledge about CA. The research that is needed is extensive, especially given the differences that exist between subject areas, grade level, and students with different abilities, special needs, and dispositions. The current foundation of knowledge about CA is fragmented. In this section, I'd like to summarize a few key directions for research on CA. Each of the remaining chapters in this volume contains specific recommendations for the area reviewed. While I'm unable to include all of the good suggestions here, the following points are salient in my mind as the field moves ahead.

We are only beginning to map and understand the dynamics of formative assessment. Studies are needed to show how specific aspects of formative assessment are related to student learning and motivation. We need to know more about the conditions that support formative assessment and how formative and summative assessment are related. What student skills are needed for effective formative assessment? How do we educate both teachers and students for formative assessment? In Chapter 27, Bronwen Cowie emphasizes the importance of "on-the-fly" formative assessment and everyday student and student/teacher interaction within science instruction. How are these assessments and interactions different in other subjects? How does immediate and ongoing formative assessment differ from how teachers use results from more formal, planned, and embedded formative assessment?

What prior knowledge, understandings, skills, and interests do students have? It is clear that teachers need to know these incoming understandings and abilities, but how is that best accomplished? We need research on the most efficient, practical approaches to helping teachers know what students bring with them. This is a part of CA—something that has, for the most part, been ignored.

Perhaps the greatest challenge to research on CA is how to account for the effect of student characteristics. It is well known that student abilities, interests, learning preferences, attributional tendencies, and other characteristics related to learning and motivation affect learning, and it is likely that these individual differences also effect the impact of student assessments. As emphasized by Carol Ann Tomlinson and Tonya R. Moon in Chapter 23, there is a need for differentiated assessment that can effectively accommodate differences in student characteristics, method of assessment, and context. Yaoying Xu, in Chapter 24, summarizes important individual differences in children with special needs and implications for CA research and practice.

Another significant challenge is to research present technology used for assessment that will have implications for the future. Hopefully, studies of assessment technology will provide sound conceptual frameworks and underlying principles that can stand the test of time. Specific technologies will surely change. Enduring frameworks and principles will provide a basis for further understanding of what is likely to be most effective. A good example of this need is provided in Chapter 19 by Susan F. Belgrad with her discussion of e-portfolios.

While grading continues to represent a hodgepodge of academic achievement and nonacademic factors, as pointed out by Susan M. Brookhart in Chapter 15, more research is needed on standards-based grading and the place of grading, if at all, in formative assessment. What is the effect of standards-based grading on CA? What is the effect of grading different parts of formative assessment? Can grading be used effectively to encourage student self-assessment and student involvement in selecting new learning goals?

In my view, we will need to continue to be vigilant from a research perspective about the effect of large-scale testing on CA. Given the current proclivity for large-scale testing designs to impinge as interim as well as annual assessments and with increased stakes tied to teacher and principal evaluation, the influence of these tests for what teachers do in their day to day assessments is likely to be very significant. How do teachers translate the cognitive levels emphasized in new large-scale testing in what they design for their students? Research is needed to determine whether teachers' use of CR, authentic assessment based on cognitive theories of motivation and learning will result in sufficiently high levels of student achievement on large-scale tests that are constructed with mostly SR items. There is also a need to examine how teachers will interpret and use computer adaptive and performance-based assessments that are proposed by both the Partnership for Assessment of Readiness for College and Careers (PARCC) and the Smarter Balanced Assessment Consortium (SBAC).

Consistent with the recent call for change by Brookhart (2011) and based on suggestions from Sarah Bonner, Jay Parkes, and Robin Tierney in this volume, research is needed to establish new, more practical ways of applying technical aspects of measurement to CA. Many would agree that the concepts of validity, reliability, and fairness are essential to sound CA, just as they are to large-scale testing, but how can these principles be applied in a practical way to CAs? What materials and instructional practices will effectively educate teachers about these technical concepts? How will we know if CAs demonstrate adequate validity, reliability, and fairness?

Another area that will need development is the construction and validation of measures that can be used to study CA. As pointed out by Bruce Randel and Tedra Clark in Chapter 9 of this volume, there is a scarcity of solid measures and approaches to data collection that can be used to investigate CA. Once more measures with adequate estimates of reliability and validity are established, researchers will find it more convenient, efficient, and significant to study CA.

The research on CA points to the need to focus more on the meaning students give to the assessment tasks and feedback they experience. This is consistent with what we know about what influences learning and motivation—namely that some of the most important factors depend on how students perceive assessments and feedback and how these perceptions affect their motivation and learning.

Conclusion

In this chapter, I have argued for a comprehensive, accumulated research effort that can advance our knowledge and understanding of CA. I summarized the impact of six important influences that drive our research and showed how different chapters in this volume relate to these influences. These chapters show that research in CA is becoming more differentiated and specialized. There is much to be done and no lack of important research questions and directions. The volume as a whole presents CA as a clearly recognized, essential, and critical educational process that needs attention in teaching training and professional development and—for our purposes in this volume—in research to further solidify what we know about how CA influences student learning and motivation.

Research has demonstrated the importance of CA because it clearly influences as well as documents student learning. My hope is that our authors will stimulate engagement in research that taps the process in greater depth by conducting studies to better understand how and why different aspects of CA are important. As part of a larger mission to improve teaching as a profession, student learning, and student motivation, CA is essential. Conducting meaningful, well-designed empirical studies of CA will provide the foundation for enhancing CA as part of our shared quest for educational improvement. Perhaps this will eventually lead to a more formal field called CA, in which there are journal outlets, professional organizations and meetings, self-governance, and other indicators that define a professional field of study and practice.

References

Airasian, P. W. (1991). *Classroom assessment.* New York: McGraw-Hill.

American Educational Research Association, American Psychological Association, and the National Council on Measurement in Education (1999). *Standards for educational and psychological testing.* Washington, DC: American Educational Research Association.

American Federation of Teachers, National Council on Measurement in Education, and National Education Association. (1990). *Standards for teacher competence in educational assessment of students.* Washington, DC: American Federation of Teachers.

Andrade, H. L., & Cizek, G. J. (2010). *Handbook of formative assessment.* New York: Routledge.

Black, P., Harrison, C., Lee, C., Marshall, B., & Wiliam, D. (2004). *Assessment for learning: Putting it into practice.* Buckingham, UK: Open University Press.

Black, P., & Wiliam, D. (1998). Assessment and classroom learning. *Assessment in Education, 5*(1), 7–73.

Brookhart, S. M. (2001). Successful students' formative and summative uses of assessment information. *Assessment in Education, 8*(2), 153–169.

Brookhart, S. M. (2003). Developing measurement theory for classroom assessment purposes and uses. *Educational Measurement: Issues and Practice, 22*(4), 5–12.

Brookhart, S. M. (2011). Educational assessment knowledge and skills for teachers. *Educational Measurement: Issues and Practice, 30*(1), 3–12.

Burstein, L. (1983). A word about this issue [Special issue]. *The Journal of Educational Measurement, 20*(2), 99–101.

Campbell, C., & Evans, J. A. (2000). Investigation of preservice teachers' classroom assessment during student teaching. *Journal of Educational Research, 93,* 350–355.

Cizek, G. J. (1997). Learning, achievement, and assessment: Constructs at a crossroads. In G. D. Phye (Ed.), *Handbook of classroom assessment: Learning, adjustment, and achievement* (pp. 1–32), San Diego, CA: Academic Press.

Common Core State Standards Initiative. (n.d.). Retrieved from www.corestandards.org/the-standards

Crooks, T. J. (1988). The impact of classroom evaluation on students. *Review of Educational Research, 58*(4), 438–481.

Dann, R. (2002). *Promoting assessment as learning: Improving the learning process.* London: RoutledgeFalmer.

Dunn, K. E., & Mulvenon, S. W. (2009). A critical review of research on formative assessment: The limited scientific evidence of the impact of formative assessment in education. *Practical Assessment, Research & Evaluation, 14*(7). Retrieved from http://pareonline.net/pdf/v14n7.pdf

Ebel, R. L. (1972). *Essentials of educational measurement.* Upper Saddle River, NJ: Prentice Hall.

Fuchs, L. S., & Fuchs, D. (1986). Effects of systematic formative evaluation: A meta-analysis. *Exceptional Children, 53,* 199–208.

Gage, N. L. (1963). *Handbook of research on teaching.* Chicago: Rand McNally.

Goslin, D. A. (1967). *Teachers and testing.* New York: Russell Sage.

Green, S. K., & Mantz, M. (2002, April). *Classroom assessment practices: Examining impact on student learning.* Paper presented at the Annual Meeting of the American Educational Research Association, New Orleans, LA.

Guskey, T. R. (2003). How classroom assessments improve learning. *Educational Leadership, 60*(5), 6–11.

Heritage, M. (2008). *Learning progressions: Supporting instruction and formative assessment.* Washington, DC: Council of Chief State School Officers.

Herman, J. L., & Baker, E. L. (2009). Assessment policy: Making sense of the babel. In G. Sykes, B. Schneider, & D. N. Plank (Eds.). *Handbook of Education Policy Research* (pp. 176–190). New York: Routledge.

Hills, J. R. (1977). Coordinators' accountability view of teacher's measurement competence. *Florida Journal of Education Research, 19,* 34–44.

Kingston, N., & Nash, B. (2011). Formative assessment: A meta-analysis and a call for research. *Educational Measurement: Issues and Practice, 30*(4), 28–37.

Leighton, J. P., Chu, M. W., & Seitz, P. (2011, October). *Cognitive diagnostic assessment and the learning errors and formative feedback (LEAFF) model.* Paper presented at the annual MARCES conference, University of Maryland, College Park.

Lindquist, E. F. (Ed.). (1951). *Educational measurement.* Washington, DC: American Council on Education.

Linn, R. L. (Ed.). (1989). *Educational Measurement* (3rd ed.). New York: Macmillan.

Marso, R. N., & Pigge, F. L. (1993). Teachers' testing knowledge, skills, and practices. In S. L. Wise (Ed.), *Teacher training in measurement and assessment skills* (pp. 129–185). Lincoln: Buros Institute of Mental Measurements, University of Nebraska-Lincoln.

Mayo, S. T. (1964). What experts think teachers ought to know about educational measurement. Paper presented at the annual meeting of the National Council on Measurement in Education, Chicago.

McMillan, J. H. (1997). *Classroom assessment: Principles and practice for effective instruction.* Boston: Allyn & Bacon.

McMillan, J. H. (Ed.). (2007). *Formative classroom assessment: Theory to practice.* New York: Teachers College Press.

McMillan, J. H. (2011). The perfect storm: How policy, research, and assessment will transform public education. *Mid-Western Educational Researcher, 24*(1), 39–47.

McMillan, J. H. & Nash, S. (2000). *Teacher classroom assessment and grading practices decision making* (Report). Washington, DC: Education Resources Information Center. (ERIC Document Reproduction Service No. ED447195)

Moss, P. A. (2003). Reconceptualizing validity for classroom assessment. *Educational Measurement: Issues and Practice, 22*(4), 13–25.

National Committee on Excellence in Education. (1983). *A nation at risk: The imperative for educational reform: A report to the nation and the secretary of Education United States Department of Education.* Washington, DC: Government Printing Office.

Noll, V. H. (1955). Requirements in educational measurement for prospective teachers. *School and Society, 80,* 88–90.

Pedulla, J. J., Abrams, L. M., Madaus, G. F., Russell, M. K., Ramos, M. A., & Miao, J. (2003). *Perceived effects of state-mandated testing programs on teaching and learning: Findings form a national survey of teachers.* Boston: Boston College, National Board on Educational Testing and Public Policy.

Pellegrino, J. W., Chudowsky, N., & Glaser, R. (Eds.). (2001). *Knowing what students know: The science and design of educational assessment.* Washington, DC: National Academy Press.

Phye, G. D. (Ed.) (1997). *Handbook of classroom assessment: Learning, adjustment, and achievement.* San Diego, CA: Academic Press.

Plake, B. S., & Impara, J. C. (1997). Teacher assessment literacy: What do teachers know about assessment? In G. D. Phye (Ed.), *Handbook of classroom assessment: Learning, adjustment, and achievement* (pp. 55–70). San Diego, CA: Academic Press.

Plake, B. S., Impara, J. C., & Fager, J. J. (1993). Assessment competencies of teachers: A national survey. *Educational Measurement: Issues and Practice, 12*(1), 10–12.

Popham, W. J. (1995). *Classroom assessment: What teachers need to know.* Boston: Allyn & Bacon.

Popham, W. J. (2008). *Transformative assessment.* Alexandria, VA: Association for Supervision and Curriculum Development.

Porter, A., McMaken, J., Hwang, J., & Rui, Y. (2011). Common core standards: The new U.S. intended curriculum. *Educational Researcher, 40*(3), 103–116.

Roeder, H. H. (1972). Are today's teachers prepared to use tests? *Peabody Journal of Education, 59,* 239–240.

Schafer, W. D. (1993). Assessment literacy for teachers. *Theory Into Practice, 32*(2), 118–126.

Schafer, W. D., & Lissitz, R. W. (1987). Measurement training for school personnel: Recommendations and reality. *Journal of Teacher Education, 38*(3), 57–63.

Shavelson, R. J., & Towne, L. (Eds.). (2002). *Scientific research in education.* Washington, DC: National Academy Press.

Shepard, L. A. (2000). The role of assessment in a learning culture. *Educational Researcher, 29*(7), 4–14.

Shepard, L. A. (2001). The role of classroom assessment in teaching and learning. In V. Richardson (Ed.), *The handbook of research on teaching* (4th ed., pp. 1066–1101). Washington, DC: American Educational Research Association.

Shepard, L. A. (2006). Classroom assessment. In R. L. Brennan (Ed.), *Educational measurement* (4th ed., pp. 623–646). Westport, CT: Praeger.

Stiggins, R. J. (1991). Relevant classroom assessment training for teachers. *Educational Measurement: Issues and Practice, 10*(1), 7–12.

Stiggins, R. J. (1994). *Student-centered classroom assessment.* New York: Macmillan.

Stiggins, R. J. (2001). *Student-involved classroom assessment* (3rd ed.). Upper Saddle River, NJ: Prentice Hall.

Stiggins, R. J., & Conklin, N. F. (1992). *In teachers' hands: Investigating the practices of classroom assessment.* Albany: State University of New York Press.

Thorndike, R. L. (Ed.). (1971). *Educational measurement* (2nd ed.). Washington, DC: American Council on Education.

Travers, R. M. W. (Ed.). (1973). *Second handbook of research on teaching.* Chicago: Rand McNally.

Wiggins, G. P. (1993). *Assessing student performance.* San Francisco: Jossey-Bass.

Wiggins, G. (1998). *Educative assessment: Designing assessments to inform and improve student performance.* San Francisco: Jossey-Bass.

Wise, S. L., Lukin, L. E., & Roos, L. L. (1991). Teacher beliefs about training in testing and measurement. *Journal of Teacher Education, 42*(1), 37–42.

Wittrock, M. C. (Ed.). (1986). *Handbook of research on teaching* (3rd ed.). New York: Macmillan.

2

Classroom Assessment in the Context of Learning Theory and Research

Heidi L. Andrade[1]

Classroom assessment (CA) has long been influenced by program evaluation (Scriven, 1967), psychometrics (Bloom, 1956), and statistics (Shepard, 2000). Only in the past decade or two have we begun to acknowledge that a careful study of the relationship between learning theory and assessment can serve at least two purposes: (1) to inform the design of assessment processes that are grounded in research on how students represent knowledge and develop competence (Bransford, Brown, & Cocking, 2000) and (2) to provide an interpretive lens on the intended and unintended consequences of assessment, including its effects on achievement and motivation.

In 2000, Lorrie Shepard described the ways in which new developments in learning theory had the potential to transform assessment theory and practice. At the time, the consensus among scholars in the field was that the vast majority of what was known about cognition and learning had yet to be applied to CA (Pellegrino, Chudowsky, & Glaser, 2001). Arguing that assessment must reflect cognitive, constructivist, and sociocultural theories in order to enhance learning as well as (or instead of) measuring it, Shepard described the ways in which its form, content, and uses should change to align with and support social-constructivist pedagogy.

This chapter extends Shepard's seminal work via a selective review of current research on learning and assessment. Beginning with an acknowledgment of the need for a model of cognition, the first section discusses recent developments in learning progressions and their implications for assessment in the content areas. The chapter then explores the lessons to be learned by framing assessment in terms of the regulation of learning, a general mega-theory of sorts that comprises everything from goal setting to metacognition, progress monitoring, feedback, and adjustments to learning and teaching. Recommendations for research are integrated into each section of the chapter and summarized at the end.

Classroom Assessment and Learning Progressions

In 2001, the National Research Council (NRC) report *Knowing What Students Know* (Pellegrino et al., 2001) described three necessary components

[1]Thanks go to Fei Chen for her assistance with the search of the literature for this chapter.

of a valid assessment system: "a model of student cognition and learning in the domain, a set of beliefs about the kinds of observations that will provide evidence of students' competencies, and an interpretation process for making sense of the evidence" (p. 44). Brown and Wilson (2011) noted that 10 years later most assessments still lack an explicit model of cognition or a theory about how students represent knowledge and develop competence in a subject domain. They argue that without a model of cognition, assessment designers, presumably including classroom teachers, are handicapped by largely implicit knowledge of how understanding develops and no clear guidance on how to create meaningful assessments.

Enter Learning Progressions

Also known as learning trajectories, Wright maps, construct maps, or construct models, a learning progression is a model of successively more sophisticated ways of thinking about a topic typically demonstrated by children as they learn, from naive to expert (National Research Council [NRC], 2007) (see Chapter 11, this volume). Based on research and conceptual analysis, learning progressions describe development over an extended period of time (Heritage, 2009). For example, if the learning target is to understand that it gets colder at night because part of the earth is facing away from the sun, the students must first understand that the earth both orbits around the sun and rotates on its own axis (see Figure 2.1).

Although learning progressions are often designed with state and federal standards in mind, they are more detailed than most standards, which do not include the significant intermediate steps within and across grade levels that lead to attainment of the standards (Heritage, 2011). Detailed descriptions of typical learning serve as representations of models of cognition that can inform instruction as well as the design and interpretation of the results of assessment. As is shown in Figure 2.1, learning progressions can also indicate common pre- and misconceptions students have about a topic.

Learning progressions can provide teachers with a blueprint for instruction and assessment because they represent a goal for summative assessment, indicate a sequence of activities for instruction, and can inform the design of formative assessment processes that provide indicators of students' understanding (Corcoran, Mosher, & Rogat, 2009; Songer, Kelcey, & Gotwals, 2009). The value of learning progressions for CA lies in the information they provide about what to assess and when to assess it. Teachers and districts can design summative assessments with a learning progression in mind, as well as formative assessments that move learning ahead. Questions that target common misconceptions can be designed in advance and delivered verbally, in writing, to individuals or to groups. For example, at a particular point in a unit on the earth and the solar system, a teacher can ask questions designed to reveal student thinking in relation to a specific learning goal in a progression, such as "How long does it take the earth to go around the sun, and how do you know?" The students' responses to the questions provide insight into their learning and can guide the teacher's next pedagogical steps.

Diagnostic questions can also be implemented in the form of multiple-choice items (Ciofalo & Wylie, 2006; Wylie, Ciofalo, & Mavronikolas, 2010). Briggs, Alonzo, Schwab, and Wilson (2006) have demonstrated that multiple-choice items based on construct maps—that is, learning progressions—can provide diagnostic information to teachers about student understanding. When each of the possible answer choices in an item is linked to developmental levels of student understanding, as in the example in Figure 2.2, an item-level analysis of student responses can reveal what individual students and the class as a whole understand. For example, if one quarter of the students in a class choose option D, which suggests that they believe that darkness is caused by the earth moving around the sun once a day, the teacher might decide to provide opportunities for structured small group discussions between students who understand the day–night cycle and students who are still developing this understanding. Briggs et al. (2006) described the more intensive interventions that may be implemented for the portion of the class who scored at Level 2 or below by selecting options A, C, or E:

> Students who chose option E believe that the Sun and Moon switch places to create night. These students are likely not to believe that the Moon is visible during the day, so daytime observations of the Moon may serve as a catalyst for them to engage in scaffolded reconsideration of this idea.

On the other hand, students who chose option C believe that the Sun moves around the Earth once per day. This is not something which can be easily countered by observation, and a more direct approach may be necessary, for example, having students act out the relative motion of the Earth and Sun. As illustrated here, information from a class summary of a single item can help the teacher see whether there are general patterns in how her students respond to very specific concepts, and might help the teacher plan a subsequent instruction. (pp. 49–51)

4	Student is able to coordinate apparent and actual motion of objects in the sky. Student knows the following: • The earth is both orbiting the sun and rotating on its axis. • The earth orbits the sun once per year. • The earth rotates on its axis once per day, causing the day/night cycle and the appearance that the sun moves across the sky. • The moon orbits the earth once every 28 days, producing the phases of the moon. COMMON ERROR: Seasons are caused by the changing distance between the earth and sun. COMMON ERROR: The phases of the moon are caused by a shadow of the planets, the sun, or the earth falling on the moon.
3	Student knows the following: • The earth orbits the sun. • The moon orbits the earth. • The earth rotates on its axis. However, student has not put this knowledge together with an understanding of apparent motion to form explanations and may not recognize that the earth is both rotating and orbiting simultaneously. COMMON ERROR: It gets dark at night because the earth goes around the sun once a day.
2	Student recognizes the following: • The sun appears to move across the sky every day. • The observable shape of the moon changes every 28 days. Student may believe that the sun moves around the earth. COMMON ERROR: All motion in the sky is due to the earth spinning on its axis. COMMON ERROR: The sun travels around the earth. COMMON ERROR: It gets dark at night because the sun goes around the earth once a day. COMMON ERROR: The earth is the center of the universe.
1	Student does not recognize the systematic nature of the appearance of objects in the sky. Students may not recognize that the Earth is spherical. COMMON ERROR: It gets dark at night because something (e.g., clouds, the atmosphere, or "darkness") covers the sun. COMMON ERROR: The phases of the moon are caused by clouds covering the moon. COMMON ERROR: The sun goes below the earth at night.

Figure 2.1 Excerpt from *Construct Map for Student Understanding of Earth in the Solar System*

SOURCE: Adapted from Briggs, Alonzo, Schwab, & Wilson (2006).

Which is the best explanation for why it gets dark at night?

A. The Moon blocks the Sun at night. [Level 1 response]
B. The Earth rotates on its axis once a day. [Level 4 response]
C. The Sun moves around the Earth once a day. [Level 2 response]
D. The Earth moves around the Sun once a day. [Level 3 response]
E. The Sun and Moon switch places to create night. [Level 2 response]

Figure 2.2 Diagnostic Item Based on *Construct Map for Student Understanding of Earth in the Solar System*

SOURCE: Briggs, Alonzo, Schwab, & Wilson (2006).

Briggs et al. (2006) noted that while diagnostic items based on a model of cognition represent an improvement over tests consisting of traditional multiple-choice items, they complement but do not replace rich, open-ended performance tasks. However, recent evidence suggests that such items are actually better than open-ended items at eliciting responses similar to the understanding that students express in think-alouds and interviews, perhaps because the items probe students' understanding by offering plausible response alternatives (Steedle & Shavelson, 2009).

Future Research on Learning Progressions

A significant amount of research, development, and teacher training is needed in order to take full advantage of recent advances in the use of models of cognition to inform instruction and assessment (Briggs et al., 2006). First, experimental studies are needed of the achievement effects of instruction and assessment based on learning progressions, perhaps with a particular focus on student misconceptions. Research on the effectiveness of learning progression-based pedagogy should also focus on students who do not follow a typical path: Is the usefulness of learning progressions limited by the fact that they describe typical learning pathways? The potential for students' use of learning progressions could also be a fruitful area of inquiry: Would it be useful to have students use learning progressions to set goals, monitor their progress toward them, and make adjustments to the processes and products of their learning? If so, what would that look like and how effective is it in promoting learning, motivation, and self-regulation?

If empirical studies support the popular belief that pedagogy based on learning progressions has the potential to increase student achievement and motivation, further research and development on teacher professional development will be needed. Research indicates that classroom teachers often do not know how to use learning progressions as the basis for their assessments (Heritage, Kim, Vendlinski, & Herman, 2009), nor how to use assessment information to adjust instruction to address student learning needs (Ruiz-Primo & Li, 2011; Schneider & Gowan, 2011). This should come as no surprise, given the documented lack of attention to assessment by most teacher preparation programs (Popham, 2009).

Heritage (2011) has worked with teachers to write learning progressions and map evidence of learning to them. She argued in favor of teacher-developed progressions, while Popham (2011) questioned the usefulness of the practice. Research focused on the role of teachers in the design of learning progressions could be illuminating.

Finally, Steedle and Shavelson (2009) pointed out the difficulties of interpreting results from a collection of items when a student does not reason consistently about the concept being assessed:

> Valid and simple interpretations of learning progression level diagnoses are only possible when students select responses reflecting a single learning progression level with some consistency. When students reason inconsistently, an accurate score report would have to say something like, "The student has scientifically accurate understanding in problem context A, but he or she has a certain problematic belief in contexts B and C and a different problematic belief in context D." Such a characterization of student understanding is more difficult to interpret than

> the small, coherent set of ideas encompassed by a learning progression level, but it may be more accurate. (p. 702)

Careful research on how and how well teachers can apply and interpret formative and summative assessment data based on learning progressions is needed.

Self-Regulated Learning and Classroom Assessment

Another new development in the field of CA is that assessment is frequently framed in terms of the regulation of learning (Clark, 2012). In contrast to learning progressions, which are content specific, self-regulated learning (SRL) is generally considered to be a domain general state or trait. Allal (2010) noted that every theory of learning includes a mechanism of regulation of learners' thinking, affect, and behavior: Behaviorist theory includes reinforcement, Piaget's constructivism has equilibration, cognitive models refer to feedback devices, and sociocultural and social constructivist models include social mediation. Seidel and Shavelson (2007) included a regulative component in their model of teaching and learning components. In one form or another, regulation plays a key role in all major learning theories.

In general, the regulation of learning involves four main processes: (1) goal setting, (2) the monitoring of progress toward the goal, (3) interpretation of feedback derived from monitoring, and (4) adjustment of goal-directed action including, perhaps, redefining the goal itself (Allal, 2010). Research and theory on CA emphasize very similar regulatory goals and processes. Defined as a process of collecting, evaluating, and using evidence of student learning in order to monitor and improve learning (see McMillan, Chapter 1 of this volume), effective CA articulates the learning targets, provides feedback to teachers and students about where they are in relation to those targets, and prompts adjustments to instruction by teachers as well as changes to learning processes and revision of work products by students. Drawing on Sadler (1989), Hattie and Timperley (2007) summarized this regulatory process in terms of three questions to be asked by students: (1) Where am I going? (2) How am I going? and (3) Where to next?

According to Wiliam (2010), this conception of assessment as regulation is common in Francophone countries, where the central concept is regulation, summarized as "feedback + adaptation" (Allal & Lopez, 2005). Defining CA as a regulatory process is also consistent with established notions of SRL, which focus on understanding the processes by which learners set goals and then plan, execute, and reflectively adapt learning (Hadwin, Järvelä, & Miller, 2011) (see also Chapter 21 of this volume). For one example, Hattie and Timperley's first question, "Where am I going?" and the related principle of sharing learning targets with students (Moss, Brookhart, & Long, 2011), resonates with noted SRL scholar Phil Winne's (2011) advice to boost metacognitive monitoring by helping learners set clear standards for themselves.

Nicol and Macfarlane-Dick's (2006) review of the literature on SRL and feedback led them to conclude that good feedback practice is "anything that might strengthen the students' capacity to self-regulate their own performance" (p. 205). Reasoning that if formative assessment is exclusively in the hands of teachers then students are less likely to become empowered and develop the self-regulation skills needed to prepare them for learning outside of school and throughout life, Nicol and Macfarlane-Dick positioned the research on formative assessment and feedback within Butler and Winne's (1995) model of feedback and SRL. Figure 2.3 is an adaptation of Nicol and Macfarlane-Dick's model. The main modifications are the heightened emphasis on other-regulation via feedback from teachers, peers, technologies, and others (H), the inclusion of the processes of interpreting feedback (I), and the closing of the feedback loop for teachers (J).

Following Butler and Winne (1995) and Nicol and Macfarlane-Dick (2006), a key feature of the model in Figure 2.3 is that students occupy a central and active role in all feedback processes, including and especially monitoring and regulating their progress toward desired goals and the evaluating the efficacy of the strategies used to reach those goals. Processes internal to the learner, including activating motivation and knowledge of the domain and relevant strategies; setting goals; selecting learning strategies; and regulating learning, affect, and cognition are depicted inside the shaded area. External feedback from teachers and others must also be

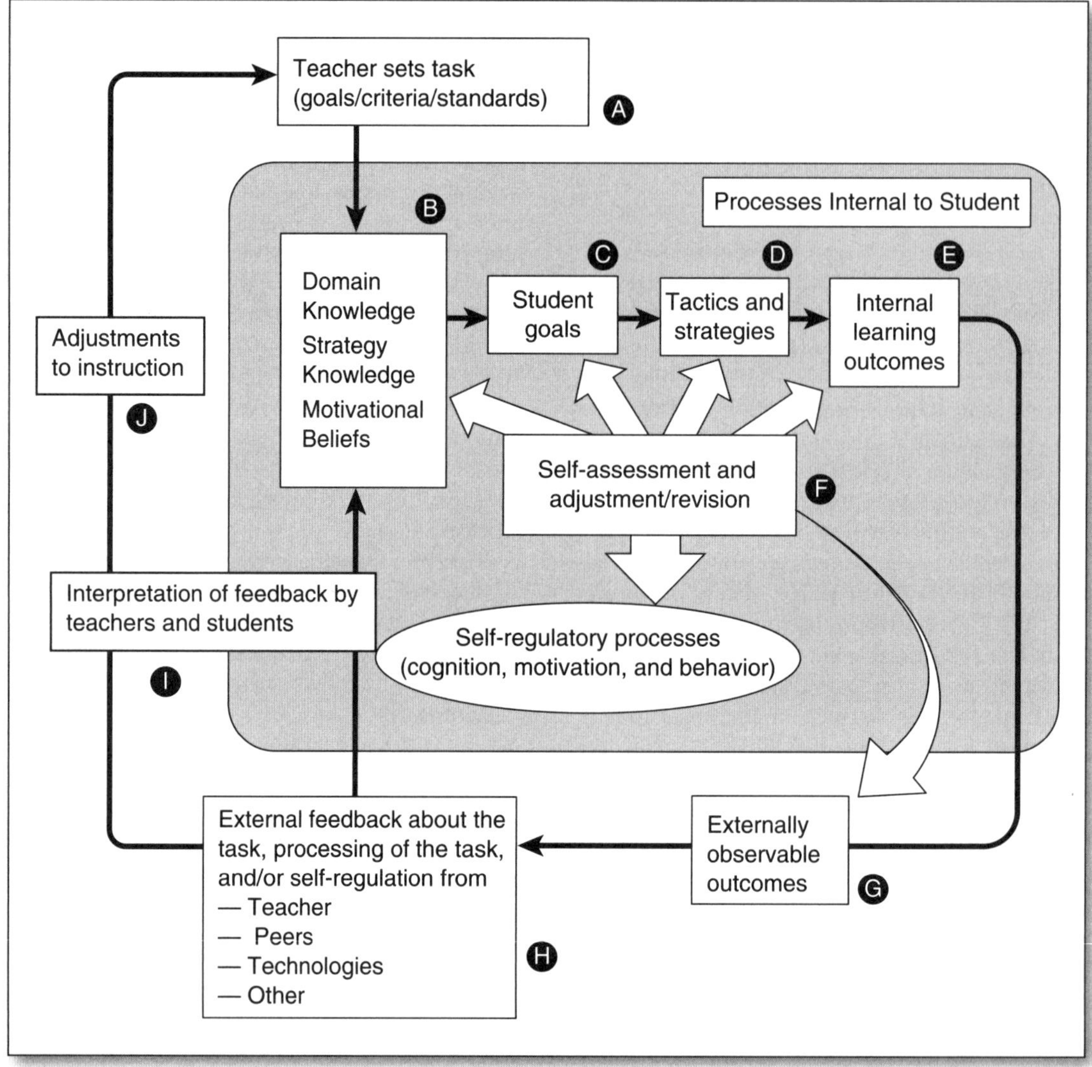

Figure 2.3 Model of Assessment as the Regulation of Learning by Oneself and Others

interpreted by the student if it is to have a significant influence on subsequent learning.

Current views of SRL acknowledge that learning is not just self-regulated by students, but also co-regulated and shared (Hadwin et al., 2011). Regulated learning is as much a social as a solo phenomenon. Black and Wiliam (1998) argued that assessment is also social and that, in fact, "all the assessment processes are, at heart, social processes, taking place in social settings, conducted by, on, and for social actors" (p. 56). In this section of the chapter, I will examine the theoretical and research bases for conceiving of CA as the regulation of learning by students themselves as well as by their peers, their teachers, and assessment technologies. The section is organized in terms of how research on CA is related to the four main regulation processes identified by Allal (2010): (1) goal setting, (2) the monitoring of progress toward the goal, (3) interpretation of feedback derived from monitoring, and (4) adjustment of goal-directed action.

Classroom Assessment and Goal Setting

Variously called learning intentions, learning goals, and learning targets in current scholarship on assessment and SRL, goals describe the skills, concepts, and dispositions that constitute the intended consequences of teaching and learning. Modern theories of regulated learning consider goals to be fundamental to regulatory proficiency and success (Hadwin et al., 2011), and theories of CA consider teachers' learning goals for students to be the basis of good assessment (Green & Johnson, 2010, McMillan, 2011, Nitko & Brookhart, 2011; Stiggins, 2008). The setting of goals by a teacher is step A in Figure 2.3. Goal setting by the student is step C.

Hattie (2009) defined effective goal setting by teachers as setting appropriately challenging goals, developing commitment on the part of teachers and students (especially those with special needs) to attain them, and intending to implement strategies to achieve them. When goals are determined by the teacher, it is necessary to share them with students, who can use them to begin to answer the question, "Where am I going?" For example, Seidel, Rimmele, and Prenzel (2005) found a positive effect of physics teachers' goal clarity and coherence on German students' perceptions of supportive learning conditions, motivation, and competence development as measured by tests on electric circuits and force concepts. The increase in competence corresponded to an increase of more than one standard deviation.

The level of challenge of a goal is quite important (Hill & Rowe, 1998). According to Hattie (2009), there is a direct linear relationship between the degree of goal difficulty and performance, with difficult goals outperforming "do your best" goals. With an average effect size of $d = 0.66$, the support for challenging goals was compelling enough to spur Hattie to recommend that "any school with the motto 'do your best' should immediately change it to 'face your challenges' or 'strive to the highest'" (p. 164). Ideally, of course, the learning goals set for and/or by students must lie within their zone of proximal development (ZPD) (Vygotsky, 1978) in order to ensure that they are appropriately challenging. Learning progressions can play a part in the selection of appropriately challenging goals by teachers and students.

Of course, students also set their own learning goals (step C in the figure), particularly achievement goals. Brookhart (Chapter 3 of this volume) discusses the relationships between students' achievement goals, motivation, and performance. More research is needed, however, on the relationship between unit-, lesson-, and task-specific goal setting by students and achievement, particularly since students' own goals commit them to a particular standard or outcome (Hadwin et al., 2011). Belgrad (Chapter 19 of this volume) reviews the research on portfolios, which tend to highlight goal setting by students. Although quite limited, that research suggests a positive relationship between goal setting and students' performance (Church, Elliot, & Gable, 2001). Additional rigorous research on the effects of student goal setting (with or without portfolios) on self-regulation and achievement is warranted.

Additional research is also needed on the effects on learning outcomes when teachers explicitly share their learning goals with students. Although there have been some recent attempts to encourage teachers to communicate learning goals or targets to students, research indicates that teachers generally do not do so without support (Moss et al., 2011). As with any new development in CA, once the effectiveness of shared learning goals is well defined and understood, research on related professional development for teachers should ensue.

Success Criteria

In contrast with learning goals, which tend to be broad, success criteria describe the qualities of excellent student work on a particular assignment. Success criteria can be communicated to students in a variety of ways. Worked examples, which typically consist of a sample problem and the appropriate steps to its solution, imply success criteria. Hattie's (2009) meta-analysis resulted in an overall effect size of worked examples of $d = 0.52$.

More direct expressions of the success criteria include rubrics and checklists. My colleagues and I (Andrade, Du, & Mycek, 2010; Andrade, Du, & Wang, 2009) engaged elementary and middle school students in reading a model essay, discussing its qualities, and generating a list of criteria that were then included in the rubric they used to self-assess drafts of their essays. This process was more effective than self-assessment according to a rubric that was simply handed out after reviewing and discussing the model essay. Thinking about the qualities of an effective essay and cocreating the success criteria for their own essays appears to make a difference in the potency of self-assessment.

Ross and Starling (2008) also ensured that the Grade 9 geography students in their study understood and could apply the criteria and standards of assessment to their own work. Before asking students to self-assess their projects, they involved them in defining assessment criteria by co-constructing a rubric and taught students how to apply the criteria through teacher modeling. After controlling for the effects of pretest self-efficacy, students in the self-assessment group scored higher than students in the control group on all achievement measures.

It is important to note that the studies discussed in this section involved self-assessment as well as transparent success criteria. My search of the literature revealed only one study that examined the effect of success criteria alone: It was a study I conducted (2001) of the effects of simply providing a rubric to eighth-grade writers before they began to write. Of the three essays students wrote for the study, only one resulted in significant differences between the treatment and comparison groups. Given the results of that study, it seems reasonable to assume that sharing success criteria with students should be part of a more comprehensive process of actively engaging them in assessment by, for example, cocreating success criteria and monitoring their own progress through peer and/or self-assessment. Brown and Harris (Chapter 21 of this volume) draw a similar conclusion.

The quality of the success criteria makes a difference, of course. Citing Moreland and Jones (2000), Brookhart (2007) noted that formative assessment and the instructional decisions based on it can actually thwart the learning process if the success criteria are trivial (e.g., focused on social and managerial issues such as taking turns at the computer) rather than substantive (e.g., focused on procedural and conceptual matters related to learning about computers). Brookhart rightly warned us to "be careful about criteria, which construct the way forward" (p. 51). Informal Google searches of K–12 rubrics strongly suggest that teachers need guidance regarding the identification of high quality success criteria. Research on the effectiveness of professional development would be most welcome.

Classroom Assessment and Monitoring of Progress Toward Goals

A central purpose of both CA and other or self-regulation is to monitor learners' progress toward goals and provide feedback that can be used to deepen their learning and improve their performances (Steps F and H in Figure 2.3). Monitoring progress toward goals can be a process of thinking about one's own thinking, or a related but distinct process of formatively or summatively evaluating the product-based evidence of learning against the standards for it. The former version of progress monitoring is known as metacognition and is largely internal to the learner. The latter version of progress monitoring is feedback and involves the solicitation of critiques from oneself and from others.

Metacognition as Progress Monitoring

Implicit in the nature of formative assessment is the development of the metacognitive awareness needed by students to plan, monitor, and assess their learning and their work (Clark, 2012; Jones, 2007). Metacognition refers to one's knowledge of cognition as well as the processes of monitoring, controlling, and regulating one's own cognition (Pintrich, 2002). Research from a variety of theoretical perspectives has demonstrated that metacognition is associated with better learning and achievement (Azevedo, 2005; Hacker, Dunlosky, & Graesser, 1998).

For example, Mathan and Koedinger (2005) showed that a computer-based program can explicitly model metacognitive skills and use the models to scaffold student performance. Using a less high-tech approach, Allen and Hancock (2008) examined the effects of having students in Grades 4, 5, and 6 metacognitively reflect on their personal profiles of strengths and weaknesses related to reading comprehension. They found that sharing individualized profiles based on the Woodcock–Johnson III and regularly asking students to reflect in writing and make judgments of learning regarding their individual cognitive strengths resulted in greater learning gains as compared to another treatment and a control group. Such programs are excellent examples of using metacognition as a means to an end—better performance—but they typically do not assess metacognition itself.

White and Frederiksen (2005) have developed intelligent software agents that scaffold metacognition and have consistently found that helping students adopt metacognitive roles as they work together on projects can promote learning and foster self-regulation. Unfortunately, metacognition is rarely taught much less assessed in most classrooms. The inclusion of a metacognitive knowledge category in the revised *Taxonomy of Educational Objectives* (Anderson & Krathwohl, 2001) could have spurred the creation and dissemination of ways to assess metacognition but that has not happened. The variety of measures of metacognition used by researchers, including self-report questionnaires, self ratings, think-aloud protocols, written tests, and interviews (Desoete, 2008) have not been adapted for widespread classroom use. There are a variety of explanations for the lack of attention to the assessment of metacognition including the fact that metacognition is not explicitly tested by large-scale examinations, so there is little impetus to teach it, as well as the challenges of assessing a process that is completely internal to the learner.

The good news is that classroom-based assessment of metacognition is a topic flush with opportunities for innovative research. There are at least two categories of inquiry with potential: (1) research on the effects of assessment of metacognition on metacognition itself as well as on learning and (2) research on the effects of CA on metacognition. An obvious starting point for the first category is to study the results of teachers including goals for teaching metacognitive knowledge and strategies in their regular unit planning, sharing those goals with students, and teaching and assessing metacognition along with other content knowledge. Work in this area could build on White and Frederiksen's (2005) research by sharing with students the information about their metacognition gleaned from measures used for research purposes as well as by providing feedback on metacognitive processing from students themselves and, if possible, their teachers and peers.

Research on the effects of assessment of metacognition on metacognition itself as well as on learning can also be done via portfolios. Portfolios provide a rich context for the assessment of metacognition, as they offer students the opportunity to reflect on their work and their approaches to it (see Chapter 19 of this volume). Studies of the development of metacognitive self-knowledge through portfolio assessment seem like a natural extension of existing research.

Inquiry into the effects of CA on metacognition—the second category previously listed—could focus on the relationships between peer or self-assessment and metacognition. Links between self-assessment and metacognition are likely to be found, since the essence of self-assessment is the ability to know what and how one is learning (Jones, 2007). Links between peer assessment and metacognition are also possible, given that students influence each other through co-regulation (Kramarski & Dudai, 2009; White & Frederiksen, 2005).

Feedback as Progress Monitoring

Hattie and Timperley's (2007) review of the research on feedback suggests that it can have very powerful effects on achievement, with an average effect size of 0.79 standard deviations. They put this effect size into perspective by comparing it to other influences on achievement, including direct instruction (0.93), reciprocal teaching (0.86), and students' prior cognitive ability (0.71). They also noted that, compared to over 100 factors known to affect achievement, feedback is in the top 5 to 10 in terms of effect size. They concluded that "feedback is among the most critical influences on student learning" (p. 102). Hattie's more recent (2009) meta-analysis puts the average effect size of feedback at 0.73.

Excellent reviews of research on feedback have recently been published (Brookhart, 2004; Hattie, 2009; Hattie & Timperley, 2007; Lipnevich & Smith, 2008; Shute, 2008; Wiliam, 2010; also see Chapters 12 and 13 of this volume). In general, the research on feedback shows that it tends to be associated with learning and achievement but that not all kinds of feedback are equally effective. Feedback is most effective when it is the right kind (e.g., detailed and narrative, not graded), delivered in the right way (supportive), at the right time (sooner for low-level knowledge but not so soon that it prevents metacognitive processing and later for complex tasks), and to the right person (who is in a receptive mood and has reasonably high self-efficacy). Feedback can come from a variety of sources, including teachers, students, and technology. Each source has a substantive research base that is briefly overviewed next.

Teacher Assessment and Progress Monitoring: Feedback Versus Grades

Assessment information from teachers comes in a variety of forms from informal, formative comments to formal, summative grades. Research suggests that the effects on learning of formative and summative assessments delivered by teachers are quite different. Take, for example, a study by Lipnevich and Smith (2008) of the effects of feedback, grades, and praise on the quality of 464 college students' written essays. The design of the study included three conditions: (1) no feedback, (2) detailed feedback perceived by participants to be provided by the course instructor, and (3) detailed feedback perceived by participants to be computer generated. The conditions were crossed with two factors of grade (receiving a grade or not) and praise (receiving praise or not). Detailed, narrative feedback on individual students' first drafts was found to be strongly related to improvement in essay scores: Students who did not receive detailed feedback obtained substantially lower final exam scores than those who received detailed feedback from either the computer or the instructor. There were no differences in students' performance between computer and instructor conditions. Differences between the no-feedback condition and the instructor- or computer-generated feedback conditions showed effect sizes of between 0.30 to 1.25, depending on the presence of grade and praise.

The influence of grades and praise was more complex. There was a significant difference in the final exam score between students in the grade condition and those in the no-grade condition. Students who were shown the grade they received for their first draft performed less well on the final version than those who were not shown their grade. Lipnevich and Smith (2008) noted that this effect should be viewed in the context of two significant interactions involving grades: Under the grade condition, scores were higher when praise was presented than when it was not. For the no-grade condition, scores were higher when praise was not presented than when praise was presented.

Lipnevich and Smith (2008) concluded that overall, detailed feedback was most effective when given alone, unaccompanied by grades or praise. Their findings echo earlier findings by Butler (1987; Butler & Nisan, 1986), which showed that students who received grades and no comments showed no learning gains, those who received grades and comments also showed no gains, but the students who received comments and no grades showed large gains. Additional research on the relationship between summative grades, achievement, and motivation in K–12 classrooms is needed. If the results indicate that grades do indeed interfere with learning and achievement, the hard work of figuring out how to minimize or even eliminate that negative effect within the context of our grade-addicted society could begin in earnest.

Self-Assessment and Progress Monitoring

I have argued elsewhere (Andrade, 2010) that students are the definitive source of formative feedback because of their access to their own thoughts, feelings, actions, and work. This argument is grounded in research on SRL. Self-assessment is a core element of self-regulation because it involves awareness of the goals of a task and checking one's progress toward them. SRL scholar Dale Schunk (2003) concluded that, as a result of self-assessment, both self-regulation and achievement can increase.

Brown and Harris (Chapter 21 of this volume) survey current research on self-assessment, including investigations of the relationship between it and self-regulation. They conclude that there is evidence of a link between self-assessment and better self-regulation skills, "provided such self-evaluation involves deep engagement with the processes affiliated with self-regulation (i.e., goal setting, self-monitoring, and evaluation against valid, objective standards)" (p. 386). For obvious reasons, simply grading one's own work appears to be less likely to lead to SRL than thoughtful reflection.

Brown and Harris raise an interesting question about whether or not the accuracy of students' self-assessments is a determinant of the effectiveness of the process. They argue that accuracy is a condition of valid student self-assessment, which can be flawed because students, especially younger and less academically proficient students, are often unrealistically optimistic about their own abilities, believe they are above average, neglect crucial information, and have deficits in their knowledge base. On the other hand, insisting on or even simply attending to the accuracy of student's self-assessment could be counterproductive, given the well-known pitfalls of social response bias (Paulhus, 1991); the potential emphasis on a score or grade rather than on forward-looking feedback (Lipnevich & Smith, 2008); and issues of trust, particularly in terms of the quality of the relationship between student and teacher and the student's willingness to be honest in his or her self-assessment (Raider-Roth, 2005). The value of the accuracy of self-assessment by students is an empirical question open to debate and inquiry. Researchers interested in conducting research on this issue are first tasked with creating a method of collecting students' self-assessment that do not also influence them.

Peer Assessment and Progress Monitoring

Topping (Chapter 22 of this volume) summarizes and critiques the research on peer assessment. His review turned up promising findings regarding the potential for criteria-referenced, justified peer assessment to promote achievement for both assessors and assessees. Although his theoretical model of peer assessment includes self-regulation, there were no direct studies available of such a relationship in general nor between peer assessment and progress monitoring in particular. Claims that peer assessment can lead to more effective self- and other-regulation deserve careful empirical study.

Assessment Technologies and Progress Monitoring

The overarching purposes of assessment technologies are to give feedback to students about their progress and to enable teachers to respond to the learning needs of each student with greater speed, frequency, focus, and flexibility. Key features of student-centered assessment technologies include (1) systematic monitoring of student progress to inform instructional decisions; (2) identification of misconceptions that may interfere with student learning; (3) rapid feedback to students, teachers, and others; and (4) information about student learning needs during instruction (Russell, 2010).

Computer-based assessment programs integrate the management of learning (e.g., organizing student assignments, assessments, and performance), curricular resources, embedded assessments, and detailed student-level and aggregate-level reporting of strengths and weaknesses. Perhaps the greatest advantage of these computerized systems is the degree to which they help students and teachers monitor progress. Many programs harness the flexible, adaptive capabilities of artificial intelligence to respond to each student's work with detail and immediacy.

Examples of computer-based programs that feature assessments include ASSISTments, ALEKS, DreamBox Learning, Time To Know, CompassLearning Odyssey, Wowzers, Carnegie Learning, SuccessMaker, and WriteToLearn. Some programs such as DreamBox Learning and Time To Know integrate instruction and assessment into one platform. Others such as WriteToLearn have a more exclusive focus on assessment. WriteToLearn is an example of an assessment technology with research support. WriteToLearn promotes reading comprehension and writing skills by providing students with immediate, individualized feedback (Landauer, Lochbaum, & Dooley, 2009). The program is designed for students in Grades 4 through 12 and is comprised of two components: (1) Summary Street, where students read and summarize articles or book excerpts, and (2) the Intelligent Essay Assessor, where students write topic-prompted essays.

The research on WriteToLearn is promising. One study used a counterbalanced design to find a positive relationship between the use of Summary Street and student summary scores after just 2 weeks of using the program (Wade-Stein & Kintsch, 2004). The researchers also found that students spent significantly more time on generating summaries than students not using the program, which suggests the program may promote motivation and engagement. Another study, using an experimental design, found that eighth-grade students who used Summary Street scored significantly higher on a test of comprehension than students who did not use the program (Franzke, Kintsch, Caccamise, Johnson, & Dooley, 2005). Student writing in the treatment group was also judged as being of higher quality than the writing of students in the control group.

Innovative research on the efficacy of a computerized assessment for learning (AFL) system named Adaptive Content with Evidence-Based Diagnosis (ACED) suggests that even traditional tests can provide feedback that promotes learning (Shute, Hansen, & Almond, 2008). Shute et al. found that the system could enhance student learning by providing test takers with elaborated, task-level feedback without compromising the technical quality of the assessment. The authors concluded that state-mandated tests might be augmented to support student learning with instructional feedback without jeopardizing the primary purpose of the assessment. Since such an augmentation to tests would go a long way toward making them more effective in promoting learning and growth, more research on the potential applications to CA could be quite productive.

Russell (2010) noted that many of the studies of the efficacy of assessment technologies use small samples of students or classrooms and/or were conducted by researchers who were closely linked with the development of the tools. The obvious implications for future research in this area are to expand sample sizes and to involve researchers who do not have vested interest in the outcome of the studies.

Influence of Source of Feedback

The variety of sources of feedback to students, including themselves, their teachers, peers, and technology, raises long-standing questions about how students react and respond to feedback from different agents. For instance, research by Dweck and her colleagues (Dweck & Bush, 1976; Dweck, Davidson, Nelson, & Enna, 1978) and others (Deci & Ryan, 1980; Hollander & Marcia, 1970) has shown that girls are more likely than boys to attribute failure to ability rather than to motivation, effort, or the agent of evaluation. As a result of these attributions, girls' performance following negative adult feedback tends to deteriorate more than boys'. However, a study by Roberts and Nolen-Hoeksema (1989) found no evidence that women's greater responsiveness to evaluative feedback led to performance decrements, suggesting women's tendencies toward maladaptive responses to feedback are not absolute. Earlier studies by Bronfenbrenner (1967, 1970) found that when peers instead of adults delivered failure feedback, the pattern of attribution and response reversed: Boys attributed the failure to a lack of ability and showed impaired problem solving while girls more often viewed the peer feedback as indicative of effort and showed improved performance.

Noting that the more traditional finding of greater helplessness among girls was evident only when the evaluators were adults, Dweck et al. (1978) interpreted these findings to mean that boys and girls have learned to interpret and respond differently to feedback from different sources. Future research on the differential effects of feedback from teachers, peers, technologies, and students themselves would be useful, particularly if it included measures of attributions, self-efficacy, motivation, and performance.

Classroom Assessment and Interpretations of Feedback Derived From Monitoring

We have long known that the action taken by a learner in response to feedback depends, in part, on the way in which it was received (Black & Wiliam, 1998). In terms of SRL, this process involves interpreting feedback, which is Step I in Figure 2.3. Most research on the nature of learners' interpretations of feedback has focused on the powerful effects of feedback on affect, particularly motivation (Brookhart, Chapter 3 of this volume; also see Chapter 13 of this volume). Empirical studies of the effects of students' interpretations of feedback on learning and achievement, however, are scarce.

Draper (2009) has developed a theoretical argument that stresses how students' interpretations of ambiguous feedback determine whether that feedback is useful or not. His perspective can inform future research on the subject. He postulates at least six possible interpretations of feedback:

1. Technical knowledge or method (e.g., concluding that one did not use the best information or method for the task, both of which can be improved)
2. Effort (e.g., deciding that one did not leave enough time to do a task well)
3. Method of learning about a task (e.g., realizing that one did not seek out the right information or did not understand the criteria for the task)
4. Ability (e.g., believing that one does not have the necessary aptitude to succeed at a task)
5. Random (e.g., assuming nothing was done incorrectly so success is possible next time without adjustment or revision)
6. The judgment process was wrong (e.g., determining that the feedback was incorrect)

Students' self-regulatory responses to feedback might be determined by which of the previous six interpretations are brought to bear on any given instance of feedback. Assuming that interpretations 1, 2, and 3 are generally (though not always) more productive than 4, 5 and 6,

Draper contends that teachers should help students construct appropriate interpretations of feedback by offering clear, often very simple, cues. The cues should indicate which interpretation of feedback is correct and constructive—for example, "This is a simple technical issue: You did not use the correct formula to use to solve this problem" (1. Technical method), or "Have you spent enough time and effort on this to do a good job?" (2: Effort), or "It might be helpful to review your method of learning about this task. How did you interpret the third criterion on the rubric?" (3: Method of learning). Research that tests this or related theories and the ways in which CA can influence students' interpretations of feedback is needed.

Classroom Assessment and the Adjustment of Goal-Directed Action

All theories of SRL emphasize learners' adjustments to their goals, strategies, and outcomes in response to feedback from themselves and others about their progress: This is step F in Figure 2.3. But what do we know about the adjustments to goal-directed action that students make in light of CA? Very little. The lack of information about what students actually do in response to feedback reflects the fact that research has tended to employ measures of outcomes and products rather than of the processes of learning and revision. Since this limits our ability as a field to construct a meaningful theory of change, research is needed on the cognitive and behavioral adjustments that students make (if any) in response to both formative and summative assessment.

The literature on CA tends to emphasize teachers' adjustments to instruction, which is represented by step J in Figure 2.3. Wiliam (2010) has championed the view that the most useful assessments are those that yield insights that are instructionally tractable. In other words, assessments are only as good as the insights they provide into the next steps in instruction that are likely to be most effective. Unfortunately, there is plentiful evidence that teachers do not know how to adapt instruction in light of evidence of a lack of student learning (Heritage & Heritage, 2011; Ruiz-Primo & Li, 2011; Schneider & Gowan, 2011). For example, Heritage et al. (2009) and Schneider and Gowan (2011) found empirical evidence that teachers struggle to determine next instructional steps after reviewing student work. Ruiz-Primo, Furtak, Yin, Ayala, and Shavelson (2010) and Fitzpatrick and Schulz (2010) found limited or no evidence that CAs were used directly for formative purposes. Hoover and Abrams (in press) found that 64% of the teachers they studied reported that instructional pacing prohibited reteaching of concepts.

The assessment community should better understand teachers' skills with CA practices so that professional development and instructional materials can better support them and their students in raising student achievement. Schneider and Andrade (2012) propose the following focal research questions:

- How do teachers use formative assessment practices?
- Do teachers have sufficient skill to analyze student work?
- How do teachers use evidence of student learning to adapt instruction on the intended learning target?
- What are the implications of research findings for professional development and instructional materials to support teachers?

Feedback and the Brain

Studies of the brain and learning have produced a new kind of evidence that student achievement is influenced by an interaction between a student's brain and computer-generated feedback (Hinton, Fischer, & Glennon, 2012). For example, Hinton et al. discuss research that shows that the performance of students with a gene that is linked to anxiety can vary significantly based on the availability of feedback (Kegel, Bus, & van Ijzendoorn, 2011). When students with the anxiety-linked gene used a computer literacy instruction program without feedback, they performed poorly compared to students without the gene. When the computer literacy program was adjusted to include positive feedback to students as they work, students with the anxiety-linked gene had better outcomes than students without it. Although brain-based research is generally outside the realm of educational studies, we would do well to keep an eye on new developments in that field.

Recommendations for Future Research

This chapter explored a few select links between learning theory and assessment, with a broad focus on what is known about how students represent knowledge and develop competence, and the intended and unintended consequences of assessment. As Shepard (2000) predicted, new developments in learning have inspired informative research and have at least begun to transform assessment theory and practice. For example, we now have models of cognition that are being used to guide instruction and assessment. We also have an emergent understanding of the ways in which CA can help or hinder the regulation of learning. What we have the most of, however, are questions.

This chapter is peppered with recommendations for future research—particularly research that illuminates the cognitive mechanisms of learning from assessment. The recommendations are summarized in categories of questions that could and perhaps should be addressed:

- Learning progressions: What are the effects of instruction and assessment based on learning progressions? Do they differ for students who do not follow a typical learning path? Is it useful to have students use learning progressions to set goals, monitor their progress toward them, and make adjustments to the processes and products of their learning? If so, what would that look like, and how effective is it in promoting learning, motivation, and self-regulation?
- SRL: What are the effects of student goal setting on self-regulation and achievement? Similarly, what are the effects when teachers explicitly share their learning targets with students? What are the effects of the assessment of metacognition on metacognition itself as well as on learning? What are the effects of peer and self-assessment on metacognition? How do students' interpretations of feedback influence learning and achievement? How does CA affect students' interpretations of feedback? What cognitive and behavioral adjustments do students make in response to formative and summative assessment?
- Peer and self-assessment: What is the relationship among accuracy in self-assessment, self-regulation, and achievement? What is the relationship between peer assessment and SRL?
- Summative assessment: What is the relationship among grades, achievement, and motivation? Can computer-based summative assessments promote learning by providing instant feedback to students without compromising the psychometric qualities of the test?
- Sources of feedback: Are there differential effects of feedback from teachers, peers, technologies, and students themselves? Does the gender of the assessor matter?
- Teacher professional development: What is the best way to involve teachers in the development, use, and interpretation of learning progressions? How do teachers use formative assessment practices, analyze student work, and use evidence of learning to adapt instruction? What are the implications of research findings for professional development and instructional materials to support teachers?

The methods used to investigate questions like those listed here should be varied, rigorous, and appropriate to the questions being asked, of course. Because randomization is generally seen as the gold standard method for making strong inferences about treatment effects (Cook, 2006) but is often difficult to implement with classroom-based studies, researchers might consider using a randomized block design based on matched pairs. Research designs can also be enhanced with the use of sophisticated modern graphics that facilitate highly informative interpretations of results, including causal inferences about treatment effects (Pruzek & Helmreich, 2009). Graphics like those found in *R*, a statistical software package that is freely available on the Internet, can reveal where assessment interventions appear to work especially well or poorly and how and how much results vary across contexts.

References

Allal, L. (2010). Assessment and the regulation of learning. In E. B. P. Peterson (Ed.), *International Encyclopedia of Education* (Vol. 3, pp. 348–352). Oxford: Elsevier.

Allal, L., & Lopez, L. M. (2005). Formative assessment of learning: A review of publications in French. In J. Looney (Ed.), *Formative assessment: Improving learning in secondary classrooms* (pp. 241–264). Paris: Organisation for Economic Cooperation and Development.

Allen, K., & Hancock, T. (2008). Reading comprehension improvement with individualized cognitive profiles and metacognition. *Literacy Research and Instruction, 47,* 124–139.

Anderson, L., & Krathwohl, D. (Eds.). (2001). *A taxonomy for learning, teaching, and assessing: A revision of Bloom's Taxonomy of Educational Objectives (Complete edition).* New York: Longman.

Andrade, H. G. (2001). The effects of instructional rubrics on learning to write. *Current Issues in Education, 4*(4). Retrieved from http://cie.ed.asu.edu/volume4/number4

Andrade, H. L. (2010). Students as the definitive source of formative assessment: Academic self-assessment and the self-regulation of learning. In H. L. Andrade & G. J. Cizek, *Handbook of formative assessment* (pp. 90–105). New York: Routledge.

Andrade, H. L., Du, Y., & Mycek, K. (2010). Rubric-referenced self-assessment and middle school students' writing. *Assessment in Education, 17*(2), 199–214.

Andrade, H. L., Du, Y., & Wang, X. (2009). Putting rubrics to the test: The effect of a model, criteria generation, and rubric-referenced self-assessment on elementary school students' writing. *Educational Measurement: Issues and Practices, 27*(2), 3–13.

Azevedo, R. (2005). Computer environments as metacognitive tools for enhancing learning. *Educational Psychologist, 40*(4), 193–197.

Black, P., & Wiliam, D. (1998). Assessment and classroom learning. *Assessment in Education, 5,* 7–74.

Bloom, B. (Ed.). (1956). *Taxonomy of educational objectives: The classification of educational goals. Handbook 1: Cognitive domain.* New York: David Mckay.

Bransford, J. D., Brown, A. L., & Cocking, R. R. (2000). *How people learn: Brain, mind, experience, and school.* Washington, DC: National Academies Press.

Briggs, D. C., Alonzo, A. C., Schwab, C., & Wilson, M. (2006). Diagnostic assessment with ordered multiple choice items. *Educational Assessment, 11*(1), 33–63.

Bronfenbrenner, U. (1967). Response to pressure from peers versus adults among Soviet and American school children. *International Journal of Psychology, 2*(3), 199–207.

Bronfenbrenner, U. (1970). Reactions to social pressure from adults versus peers among Soviet day school and boarding school pupils in the perspective of an American sample. *Journal of Personality and Social Psychology, 15,* 179–189.

Brookhart, S. (2004). Classroom assessment: Tensions and intersections in theory and practice. *Teachers College Record, 106*(3), 429–458.

Brookhart, S. (2007). Expanding views about formative classroom assessment: A review of the literature. In J. H. McMillan (Ed.), *Formative classroom assessment: Theory into practice.* New York: Teachers College Press.

Brown, N., & Wilson, M. (2011). A model of cognition: The missing cornerstone of assessment. *Educational Psychology Review, 23,* 221–234.

Butler, D., & Winne, P. (1995). Feedback and self-regulated learning: A theoretical synthesis. *Review of Educational Research, 65*(3), 245–281.

Butler, R. (1987). Task-involving and ego-involving properties of evaluation: Effects of different feedback conditions on motivational perceptions, interest, and performance. *Journal of Educational Psychology, 79,* 474–482.

Butler, R., & Nisan, M. (1986). Effects of no feedback, task-related comments, and grades on intrinsic motivation and performance. *Journal of Educational Psychology, 78,* 210–216.

Church, M., Elliot, A., & Gable, S. (2001). Perceptions of classroom environment, achievement goals, and achievement outcomes. *Journal of Educational Psychology, 93,* 43–54.

Ciofalo, J. F., & Wylie, E. C. (2006). Using diagnostic classroom assessment: One question at a time. *Teachers College Record.*

Clark, I. (2012). Formative assessment: Assessment is for self-regulated learning. *Educational Psychology Review.*

Cook, T. D. (2006). Describing what is special about the role of experiments in contemporary educational research: Putting the "gold standard" rhetoric into perspective. *Journal of Multidisciplinary Evaluation, 3*(6), 1–7.

Corcoran, T., Mosher, F. A., & Rogat, A. (2009). *Learning progressions in science: An evidence-based approach to reform* (CPRE Research Report # RR-63). Philadelphia: Consortium for Policy Research in Education.

Deci, E., & Ryan, R. (1980). The empirical exploration of intrinsic motivational processes.

In L. Berkowitz (Ed.), *Advances in experimental social psychology.* New York: Academic Press.

Desoete, A. (2008). Metacognitive prediction and evaluation skills and mathematical learning in third-grade students. *Educational Research & Evaluation, 15*(5), 435–446.

Draper, S. (2009). What are learners actually regulating when given feedback? *British Journal of Educational Technology, 40*(2), 306–315.

Dweck, C., & Bush, E. (1976). Sex differences in learned helplessness: I. Differential debilitation with peer and adult evaluators. *Developmental Psychology, 12*(2), 147–156.

Dweck, C., Davidson, W., Nelson, S., & Enna, B. (1978). Sex differences in learned helplessness: II. Contingencies of evaluative feedback in the classroom and III. An experimental analysis. *Developmental Psychology, 14*(3), 268–276.

Fitzpatrick, B., & Schulz, H. (2010). *Assessing higher order thinking: What teachers think and do.* Paper presented at the annual meeting of the American Educational Research Association, Denver, CO.

Franzke, M., Kintsch, E., Caccamise, D., Johnson, N., & Dooley, S. (2005). Summary Street: Computer support for comprehension and writing. *Journal of Educational Computing Research, 33,* 53–80.

Green, S., & Johnson, R. (2010). *Assessment is essential.* New York: McGraw-Hill.

Hacker, D., Dunlosky, J., & Graesser, A. (1998). *Metacognition in educational theory and practice.* Mahwah, NJ: Lawrence Erlbaum.

Hadwin, A., Järvelä, S., & Miller, M. (2011). Self-regulated, co-regulated, and socially shared regulation of learning. In B. Zimmerman & D. Schunk (Eds.), *Handbook of self-regulation of learning and performance* (pp. 65–86). New York: Routledge.

Hattie, J. (2009). *Visible learning: A synthesis of over 800 meta-analyses relating to achievement.* New York: Routledge.

Hattie, J., & Timperley, H. (2007). The power of feedback. *Review of Educational Research, 77,* 81–112.

Heritage, M. (2009). *The case for learning progressions.* San Francisco: Stupski Foundation.

Heritage, M. (2011). *Developing learning progressions.* Paper presented at the annual conference of the American Educational Research Association, New Orleans, LA.

Heritage, M., & Heritage, J. (2011). *Teacher questioning: The epicenter of instruction and assessment.* Paper presented at the annual meeting of the American Educational Research Association, New Orleans, LA.

Heritage, M., Kim, J., Vendlinski, T., & Herman, J. (2009). From evidence to action: A seamless process in formative assessment? *Educational Measurement Issues and Practice, 28*(3), 24–31.

Hill, P. W., & Rowe, K. J. (1998). Modeling student progress in studies of educational effectiveness. *School Effectiveness and School Improvement, 9* (3), 310–333.

Hinton, C., Fischer, K., & Glennon, C. (2012). *Student centered learning: A mind, brain and education perspective: The Students at the Center series.* Boston: Jobs for the Future. Retrieved from www.studentsatthecenter.org/papers/assessing-learning

Hollander, E., & Marcia, J. (1970). Parental determinants of peer orientation and self-orientation among preadolescents. *Developmental Psychology, 2*(2), 292–302.

Hoover, N., & Abrams, L. (in press). Teachers' instructional use of student assessment data. *Applied Measurement in Education.*

Jones, D. (2007). Speaking, listening, planning and assessing: The teacher's role in developing metacognitive awareness. *Early Child Development and Care, 6/7,* 569–579.

Kegel, C., Bus, A. G., & van Ijzendoorn, M. H. (2011). Differential susceptibility in early literacy instruction through computer games: The role of the dopamine D4 receptor gene (DRD4). *Mind, Brain and Education, 5*(2), 71–78.

Kramarski, B., & Dudai, V. (2009). Group-metacognitive support for online inquiry in mathematics with differential self-questioning. *Journal of Educational Computing Research, 40*(4), 377–404.

Landauer, T., Lochbaum, K., & Dooley, S. (2009). A new formative assesment technology for reading and writing. *Theory Into Practice, 48*(1).

Lipnevich, A., & Smith, J. (2008). *Response to assessment feedback: The effects of grades, praise, and source of information* (Research report RR-08-30). Princeton, NJ: Educational Testing Service.

Mathan, S., & Koedinger, K. (2005). Fostering the intelligent novice: Learning from errors with metacognitive tutoring. *Educational Psychologist, 40*(4), 257–265.

McMillan, J. (2011). *Classroom assessment: Principles and practice for effective standards-based instruction.* New York: Pearson.

Moreland, J., & Jones, A. (2000). Emerging assessment practices in an emergent curriculum: Implications for technology. *International Journal of Technology and Design Education, 10,* 283–305.

Moss, C., Brookhart, S., & Long, B. (2011). *School administrators' formative assessment leadership practices.* Paper presented at the annual meeting of the American Educational Research Association, New Orleans, LA.

National Research Council. (2007). *Taking science to school: Learning and teaching science in grades K–8.* Washington, DC: National Academies Press.

Nicol, D., & Macfarlane-Dick, D. (2006). Formative assessment and self-regulated learning: a model and seven principles of good feedback practice. *Studies in Higher Education, 31*(2), 199–218.

Nitko, A., & Brookhart, S. (2011). *Educational assessment of students* (6th ed.). New York: Pearson.

Paulhus, D. (1991). Measurement and control of response bias. Measures of personality and social psychological attitudes. In J. Robinson, P. Shaver, & L. Wrightsman (Eds.), *Measures of personality and social psychological attitudes, Measures of social psychological attitudes* (Vol. 1, pp. 17–59). San Diego, CA: Academic Press.

Pellegrino, J., Chudowsky, N., & Glaser, R. (Eds.). (2001). *Knowing what students know: The science and design of educational assessment.* Washington, DC: National Academies Press.

Pintrich, P. (2002). The role of metacognitive knowledge in learning, teaching, and assessing. *Theory Into Practice, 41*(4), 219–225.

Popham, J. (2009). Assessment literacy for teachers: Faddish or fundamental? *Theory Into Practice, 48*(1), 4–11.

Popham, J. (2011). *How to build learning progressions: Formative assessment's basic blueprints.* Presentation at the annual meeting of the American Educational Research Association, New Orleans, LA.

Pruzek, R., & Helmreich, J. (2009). Enhancing dependent sample analyses with graphics. *Journal of Statistical Education, 17*(1), 1–21.

Raider-Roth, M. (2005). *Trusting what you know: The high stakes of classroom relationships.* San Francisco: Jossey-Bass.

Roberts, T., & Nolen-Hoeksema, S. (1989). Sex differences in reactions to evaluative feedback. *Sex Roles, 21*(11/12), 725–746.

Ross, J. A., & Starling, M. (2008). Self-assessment in a technology supported environment: The case of grade 9 geography. *Assessment in Education, 15*(2), 183–199.

Ruiz-Primo, M. A., & Li, M. (2011). *Looking into teachers' feedback practices: How teachers interpret students' work.* Paper presented at the annual meeting of the American Educational Research Association, New Orleans, LA.

Ruiz-Primo, M. A., Furtak, E., Yin, Y., Ayala, C. J., & Shavelson, R. (2010). On the impact of formative assessment on student science learning and motivation. In H. L. Andrade & G. J. Cizek (Eds.), *Handbook of formative assessment* (pp. 139–158). New York: Routledge.

Russell, M. (2010). Technology-aided formative assessment of learning. In H. L. Andrade & G. J. Cizek (Eds.), *Handbook of formative assessment* (pp. 125–138). New York: Routledge.

Sadler, D. R. (1989). Formative assessment and the design of instructional systems. *Instructional Science , 18*, 119–144.

Schneider, C., & Andrade, H. (2012). *Teachers' use of evidence of student learning to take action: Conclusions drawn from a special issue on formative assessment.* Manuscript submitted for publication.

Schneider, C., & Gowan, P. (2011). *Deconstructing student work: Investigating teacher's abilities to use evidence of student learning to inform instruction.* Paper presented at the annual meeting of the American Educational Research Association, New Orleans, LA.

Schunk, D. (2003). Self-efficacy for reading and writing: Influence of modeling, goal-setting, and self-evaluation. *Reading & Writing Quarterly, 19*(2), 159–172.

Scriven, M. (1967). The methodology of evaluation. In R. Tyler, R. Gagne, & M. Scriven (Eds.), *Perspectives on curriculum evaluation* (pp. 39–83). Chicago: Rand McNally.

Seidel, T., Rimmele, R., & Prenzel, M. (2005). Clarity and coherence of lesson goals as a scaffold for student learning. *Learning and Instruction, 15*(6), 539–556.

Seidel, T., & Shavelson, R. (2007). Teaching effectiveness research in the past decade: The role of theory and research design in disentangling meta-analysis results. *Review of Educational Research, 77*(4), 454–499.

Shepard, L. (2000). The role of assessment in a learning culture. *Educational Researcher, 29*(7), 4–14.

Shute, V. (2008). Focus on formative feedback. *Review of Educational Research, 78*(1), 153–189.

Shute, V., Hansen, E., & Almond, R. (2008). You can't fatten a hog by weighing it—or can you? Evaluating an assessment for learning system called ACED. *International Journal of Artificial Intelligence in Education, 18*, 289–316.

Songer, N., Kelcey, B., & Gotwals, A. (2009). How and when does complex reasoning occur? Empirically driven development of a learning progression focused on complex reasoning about biodiversity. *Journal of Research in Science Teaching, 46*(6), 610–631.

Steedle, J., & Shavelson, R. (2009). Supporting valid interpretations of learning progression level diagnoses. *Journal of Research in Science Teaching, 46*(6), 699–715.

Stiggins, R. (2008). *An introduction to student-involved assessment FOR learning.* Upper Saddle River, NJ: Pearson.

Vygotsky, L.S. (1978). *Mind and society: The development of higher psychological processes.* Cambridge, MA: Harvard University Press.

Wade-Stein, D., & Kintsch, E. (2004). Summary Street: Interactive computer support for writing. *Cognition and Instruction, 22,* 333–362.

White, B., & Frederiksen, J. (2005). A theoretical framework and approach for fostering metacognitive development. *Educational Psychologist, 40*(4), 211–223.

Wiliam, D. (2010). An integrative summary of the research literature and implications for a new theory of formative assessment. In H. L. Andrade & G. J. Cizek (Eds.), *Handbook of formative assessment* (pp. 18–40). New York: Routledge.

Winne, P. (2011). A cognitive and metacognitive analysis of self-regulated learning. In B. Zimmerman & D. Schunk (Eds.), *Handbook of self-regulation of learning and performance* (pp. 15–32). New York: Routledge.

Wylie, C., Ciofalo, J., & Mavronikolas, E. (2010). *Documenting, diagnosing and treating misconceptions: Impact on student learning.* Paper presented at the annual meeting of the American Educational Research Association, Denver, CO.

3

Classroom Assessment in the Context of Motivation Theory and Research

Susan M. Brookhart

Classroom assessment (CA) and motivation enjoy a chicken-and-egg relationship. On the one hand, performance on assessments serves in a sense as a goal, as the output or desired result of motivated behavior ("I will know I studied hard enough if I do well on this test"). CAs can thus function as the result of a motivational episode, or as "the proof of the pudding is in the eating."

On the other hand, performance on assessments—and to some extent the nature of the assessments—serves as information, or as an input, in various motivational models or theories. There are several ways this can happen—for example, as an expectancy ("It's an essay test, and I always bomb essay tests") or as an external cue ("I better practice explaining my reasoning when I solve a problem, because that's the kind of questions she'll ask"). CAs can thus also function as part of the mechanism driving a motivational episode, more akin to the making of the pudding than the eating.

The purpose of this chapter is not to resolve this chicken-and-egg dilemma but rather to connect motivation theory and research with CA theory and research to see how the connection—and the several roles CA could play in motivation—have been discussed. This article takes two approaches: (1) a review of other literature on the topic of the connection between motivation and CA and (2) an exploration of current trends in motivation theory and CA. Both approaches rely on a selective rather than an exhaustive review of the literature.

Classic Reviews of Motivation Theory and Classroom Assessment

This section reviews previous literature that has explored the connection between motivation and CA. Such literature includes both reviews of the motivation literature where implications for CA have been drawn (Brookhart, 1997; Butler & Winne, 1995; Covington, 1992; Weiner, 1979) and reviews of the impact of assessment on motivation (Crooks, 1988; Harlen & Deakin Crick, 2003; Natriello, 1987). This section thus describes previously explored understandings of CA in the context of motivation theory and research.

Weiner and Attribution Theory

Learning has an obvious, important cognitive component. Motivation for learning is not the same as motivation to eat when one is hungry. Connections between motivation theory and classroom learning became more meaningful as cognitive psychology began to develop. Weiner

(1979) suggested some of these connections in "A Theory of Motivation for Some Classroom Experiences." He characterized this article as a selective review of the motivation literature, applied to the classroom, with a resulting theory (attribution theory) that he felt explained some things conclusively, while other aspects were still open to question. This section begins with Weiner because of the huge impact of attribution theory on future motivation theory, its relevance to classroom learning and assessment, and because Weiner (1979) himself acknowledged that this cognitively based motivational theory represented a new way of thinking about motivation: "A central assumption of attribution theory, which sets it apart from pleasure-pain theories of motivation, is that the search for understanding is the (or a) basic 'spring of action'" (p. 3).

Weiner distilled three dimensions from the literature about attributions of causality—about what people think when they search for the reasons why something happened: (1) locus of causality (internal or external), (2) stability (stable or unstable), and (3) controllability (controllable or uncontrollable). He supported these dimensions with logic as well as theoretical and empirical findings. To illustrate these dimensions concisely here, consider several students who each received the same grade of 96% on a mathematics exam. One student might think, "The teacher wrote an easy test. I lucked out." In attribution theory terms, this explanation says the result was external (the teacher wrote an easy test), unstable (she may or may not write an easy test every time), and uncontrollable (the student himself had nothing to do with it). Another might think, "I really worked hard this time, and finally it paid off" (internal, unstable, controllable). Yet a third might think, "I knew I was good at math" (internal, stable, uncontrollable).

Weiner went on to interpret various experimental results, in an interesting section whose language (e.g., "reinforcement schedule" and "resistance to extinction") recalled the behaviorist tradition even while he was developing what became a very influential theory in cognitive psychology. Nevertheless, he explored the theory and how it predicted reactions to success and failure. Attributions and affect (emotional reactions) are distinct. Emotions about achievement have at least three sources. First, they are related to outcomes (e.g., being pleased with an A on a test no matter what the attribution). Second, some emotions are related to an external locus (e.g., gratitude if a good outcome is attributed to the efforts of another and hostility to the other for a bad outcome). Third, some emotions are related to an internal locus (e.g., pride and shame). As Weiner put it (1979, p. 14), "The affects that are associated with self-esteem . . . are mediated by self-ascriptions."

Landmark Reviews of the Effects of Evaluation on Students

Two studies of the effects of the evaluation process on students (Crooks, 1988; Natriello, 1987) were published at about the same time. These studies took different approaches and reviewed largely nonoverlapping literature to investigate how assessment and evaluation affect students, including effects on achievement as well as motivation. The evaluation these authors investigated was mostly, although not entirely, summative. Today these authors might well have used the term *assessment* for the aspects of evaluation they studied. A decade later, Black and Wiliam (1998) undertook a project to update the Crooks (1988) review; however, they focused on formative assessment. This section focuses on the findings about connections between motivation and assessment in these three reviews.

Crooks (1988, pp. 460–467) described then-modern theories of achievement motivation in his section on motivational aspects of classroom evaluation. Theory regarding attribution (Weiner, 1979), expectancy and value (Eccles, 1983), self-efficacy (Bandura, 1982, 1986; Schunk, 1984), continuing motivation (Maehr, 1976), students' conceptions of ability (Nicholls, 1984), goal orientation (Ames, 1984), self-determination (Ryan, Connell, & Deci, 1985), and research on test anxiety (Hill, 1984) were the primary frameworks by which he described the relationship between classroom evaluation on motivation. Crooks described the curvilinear relationship between text anxiety and achievement, suggesting that tests should provoke enough anxiety for careful work but not so much as to be debilitating. Today that principle is touted as the proverbial "moderate level of challenge."

Some definitions of the main constructs in these motivational theories are required at this point. Table 3.1 summarizes the definitions as Crooks used them. These same definitions still apply today, although the second section of the chapter will describe how relationships among

Construct	*Definition*
Self-efficacy	Students' perceptions of their capability to perform certain tasks or domains of tasks
Intrinsic and extrinsic motivation	Whether the desire to learn comes from factors internal (intrinsic motivation) or external (extrinsic motivation) to the student
Continuing motivation	Persistence, or the tendency to return to and continue working on tasks outside of the instructional context in which they were learned
Attributions for success and failure	The perceived causes or influences on success or failure at a task: ability, effort, luck, or task difficulty
Concept of ability	Whether ability is believed to be the result of learning through effort, and therefore amenable to change, or as a stable trait that is judged normatively
Achievement goals	Task goals—goals of learning or mastering material or skills Ego goals—goals of being smarter or better than someone else

Table 3.1 Motivation Theory Constructs Used in Crooks's Review

SOURCE: Crooks (1988).

these constructs are now the focus of considerable current research. Readers who want more complete definitions than those in Table 3.1 should consult a contemporary handbook of motivation.

These motivation theories allowed Crooks to describe a relationship between assessment and motivation that was complex, mutual, and mediated by student self-perception. In fact, this mediation through student self-perception was the contribution of these "modern" motivational theories and an emphasis they shared. The main basis on which students will build self-efficacy for an assessment is previous successes with similar tasks—a principle that still is one of the primary forces in good assessment design. Evaluations should emphasize the work—the student's performance and level of mastery of the task—rather than engagement. "Thus, for instance, grade credit should be given for the quality of work on an assignment, not merely for handing it in [Schunk, 1984]" (Crooks, 1988, pp. 462–463).

Crooks (1988) also found that intrinsic motivation, as well as intrinsic interest in the content, is important for learning and for continuing learning. Assessment procedures that capitalize on intrinsic interest and—once the student is at work—maintain internal motivation as opposed to switching to external motivators and rewards yield the best results both for achievement and for interest in continuing to learn about the content.

Whether the student perceives the goal of the evaluation to be controlling their behavior or providing them feedback and information to move forward is a key determinant of how they will respond. In addition, whether students view ability in terms of task mastery or in terms of a normative comparison is also a key determinant of how they will respond. All these conclusions (Crooks, 1988) still stand, even as motivation theory has advanced (see next section).

Natriello (1987) framed his review around a model of evaluation from establishing purpose to monitoring outcomes and reported studies of the influence on students of aspects of evaluation at each stage of the model. As did Crooks (1988), Natriello (1987) considered effects on both achievement and motivation. Motivation findings included effects on students' conceptions of ability, self-efficacy, and effort. In classrooms where assessments were less differentiated or undifferentiated, without much opportunity for student choice, and where ability grouping and normative comparisons were made, students were more likely to have a normative conception of ability. In addition to the achievement benefits, students who experience evaluations with clear criteria enjoy higher self-efficacy than those who do not. Higher standards lead to greater student effort on school tasks and to better attendance. When students considered their evaluations of performance on school tasks to be unsound (not accurately reflecting their effort and performance) they were less likely to consider them important and expend effort.

Black and Wiliam (1998) updated Crooks's (1988) review, using a broader title: "Assessment and Classroom Learning." The portion of their review about motivation and classroom learning is in the section on formative assessment and reflects a shift away from the cause–effect language of the previous decade. Black and Wiliam's (1998) emphasis was on "those factors which influence the reception of the message [information from formative assessment] and the personal decisions about how to respond to it" (p. 21).

Goal orientation theory was especially prominent in their review, and they reviewed studies that showed the importance of whether students had a mastery orientation or a performance orientation. The former students were more likely to seek help or to explain lack of help-seeking as trying to work independently, while the latter were likely to avoid seeking help with the rationale of avoiding appearing incapable. Similarly, Black and Wiliam emphasized the importance of self-efficacy and other learners' beliefs about their own learning. Other important beliefs included students' beliefs about the importance of effort, about how much effort should be required for successful learning, and about the nature of learning itself.

The more recent and, in some cases, more sophisticated research and 10 years of development in motivation theory supported for Black and Wiliam (1998) these conclusions about student motivation in formative assessment:

> One is that the "personal features" [student beliefs and perceptions] referred to above can have important effects on a student's learning. The other is that the way in which formative information is conveyed to a student, and the context of the classroom culture and beliefs about the ability and effort within which feedback is interpreted by the individual recipient, can affect these personal features for good or ill. The hopeful message is that innovations which have paid careful attention to these features have produced significant learning gains when compared with the existing norms of classroom practice. (p. 25)

While this seems like the same conclusion as Crooks (1988), there were shifts in the intervening decade. The nuances and complexity of the theories—and hence the research—increased between 1988 and 1998. In part, because of this, the 1998 review emphasized the agency of the student and the primacy of these personal characteristics in defining the student as learner.

A Theory About the Role of Classroom Assessment in Student Motivation and Achievement

Around the same time as the Black and Wiliam (1998) review, I (Brookhart, 1997) proposed a theoretical framework for the role of CA in motivating student effort and achievement. This theory was based on a selective literature review. Its predictions about the role of CA in motivation and achievement were influenced on the motivational side by cognitive evaluation theory (Ryan et al., 1985) and theory about the effects of self-efficacy (Pintrich & Schrauben, 1992), task perceptions (Salomon, 1984), and attribution (Weiner, 1979) on students' amount of invested mental effort (Salomon, 1983, 1984) on classroom tasks in general. These theories were applied to the special case of CA, which was posited to be an "event" that students would experience in similar ways to other classroom activity segments (Stodolsky, 1988).

A series of studies then tested the predictions that arose from the theory. Briefly, students' perceptions of the nature of instructional and assessment tasks, standards and criteria, feedback (including its functional significance), and their self-efficacy beliefs about accomplishing these tasks were predicted to affect the amount of effort students invested in learning, which in turn was predicted to affect achievement. This theory was tested in elementary school (Brookhart & DeVoge, 1999), middle school (Brookhart, Walsh, & Zientarski, 2006), and high school (Brookhart & Durkin, 2003). Interview data to develop a more nuanced understanding of student perceptions were collected in some corollary studies (Brookhart, 2001; Brookhart & Bronowicz, 2003).

The results of this line of research, taken together, seem to indicate that the thinking was on the right track. However, the contribution of self-efficacy perceptions was the only consistent finding across studies (Brookhart & Peretin,

2002). This theory was used in a large-scale study of the Trends in International Mathematics and Science Study (TIMSS) mathematics performance (Rodriguez, 2004), where classroom overall self-efficacy, classroom overall attributions (specifically, fewer uncontrollable attributions), and effort (homework) predicted achievement.

The theory was not complete enough to explain the role of CA in student motivation and achievement completely. Motivation theory has moved on with resulting implications for CA. The second section of this chapter describes recent developments in motivation theory and recent developments in CA and how the two can be described as on course together. Before turning to that portion of the review, one more previous review merits a description.

Harlen and Deakin Crick's Review

Harlen and Deakin Crick's (2003) review of studies of testing and motivation for learning included one from the research agenda described in the previous section (Brookhart & DeVoge, 1999). Harlen and Deakin Crick reviewed research looking for evidence of the impact of testing and other forms of summative assessment on students' motivation for learning. Their final review consisted of 19 studies. The authors described effects on motivation in three categories, which they titled from a student's point of view (Harlen & Deakin Crick, 2003): (1) "what I feel and think about myself as a learner," (2) "the energy I have for the task," and (3) "how I perceive my capacity to undertake the task" (p. 182). They also described some evidence that student characteristics (e.g., age, achievement level, gender, and conditions of assessment) interact with these effects in fairly predictable ways. For example, their review found that high achieving students are less affected by grades than low achieving students.

Harlen and Deakin Crick (2003) stressed that despite the language about the impact of testing on motivation, the relationship was not that of one independent and one dependent variable but rather constellations of each. Still, Harlen and Deakin Crick envisioned the effects as being on motivation while others that were previously noted have also discussed the effects of motivation on learning outcomes. Perhaps it is wisest to talk about mutual effects. This is the approach taken in the next section on current trends in motivation research and CA.

Current Trends in Motivation Research and Classroom Assessment

Advances in motivation theory have brought together motivational constructs that were at one time conceived or studied separately. Self-efficacy, for example, has taken its place as one of the important components of self-regulated learning (SRL) (Zimmerman & Schunk, 2011). Intrinsic and extrinsic sources of motivation and control have become important components of self-determination theory (Ryan & Deci, 2000a, 2000b). Table 3.2 presents definitions for these macro theories of motivation.

Self-regulation of learning is the organizing framework at the more appropriate level of

Construct	*Definition*
Self-regulated learning	"Self-regulated learning and performance refers to the processes whereby learners personally activate and sustain cognitions, affects, and behaviors that are systematically oriented toward the attainment of personal goals" (Zimmerman & Schunk, 2011, p. 1).
Self-determination theory	Self-determination theory posits three basic human needs: (1) feelings of competence, (2) autonomy, and (3) relatedness. Self-determination theory makes "the critical distinction between behaviors that are volitional and accompanied by the experience of freedom and autonomy—those that emanate from one's sense of self—and those that are accompanied by the experience of pressure and control and are not representative of one's self" (Ryan & Deci, 2000a, p. 65).

Table 3.2 More Motivation Theory Constructs

generality for discussing the CA literature for two reasons. The first is evident: Self-regulation of learning is aimed at learning, while self-determination theory seeks to describe overarching motivational needs and patterns throughout life. The second reason for using self-regulation of learning to frame the discussion of CA and motivation is that the constructs represented within this theory extend and refine the constructs the previous literature has addressed. The first section (next) presents a very brief description of current self-regulation theories. The remainder of the sections in this portion of the chapter constitutes a selective exploration of some connections between self-regulation of learning and currently recommended and ongoing reforms in CA, most notably formative assessment and standards-based grading practices.

Self-Regulation of Learning

Self-regulation of learning occurs when learners set goals and then systematically carry out cognitive, affective, and behavioral practices and procedures that move them closer to those goals (Zimmerman & Schunk, 2011). Self-regulation as a topic is usually considered to be part of the field of motivation; however, part of its power is that it organizes cognitive, metacognitive, and motivational aspects into a general view of how learners understand and then pursue learning goals. Different theorists have presented models of how students activate cognition, metacognition, and motivation in order to learn. Three influential models are a nested view (Boekaerts, 1999), an information processing view (Greene & Azevedo, 2007; Winne & Hadwin, 1998), and a phase or cyclical view (Pintrich & Zusho, 2002; Zimmerman, 2011).

Nested View of Self-Regulated Learning

Boekaerts (1999) presented a nested, three-layer model of SRL, based on the kinds of choices students make when they regulate their learning. The inner layer is about students' search for learning or processing styles. Students make choices about how to select, combine, and use cognitive strategies as they learn. The middle layer is about students' direction of their learning processes, or metacognition. Students make choices about how they monitor and evaluate their learning and make decisions about further learning. The outer layer of Boekaerts's model is about students' choices of goals and resources. Even when learning goals are ostensibly set by the teacher and derived from a curriculum, students define these as their own learning goals in light of their own interests, needs, and expectancies and in light of other competing goals they may have for learning or even in other parts of their lives.

Boekaerts (1999) reported that a group of teachers asked her whether SRL was the same thing as successful or optimal learning. Her reply was to separate the notion of "successful learning," which of course is a practical outcome that teachers and students seek, from "self-regulation of learning," which is intended as a theory with explanatory power. Success is a question for evaluation; self-regulation is a question for research. The function of theory is to generate testable hypotheses to help understand and describe components necessary for successful learning. Boekaerts's reply represents a caution for the topic of this chapter: CA in the context of motivation theory and research. CA research has been, up to this point at least, largely practical, seeking to describe successful assessment practices, not theoretical.

Information Processing View of Self-Regulated Learning

Winne and Hadwin (1998, p. 277) pointed out that studying is one aspect of the larger category of learning. It is, however, an aspect of learning where student self-regulation is paramount. Investigating and understanding studying should help with a more general understanding of SRL. In fact, the model they presented in their 1998 chapter as "the COPES model of metacognitive monitoring and control in four stages of studying" (p. 282) has become known as "Winne and Hadwin's model of self-regulation" (Greene & Azevedo, 2007).

The model posits that students have to understand the conditions, operations, products, evaluations, and standards (COPES) for a task at each of four stages of engaging in it: (1) task definition, (2) goals and plans, (3) enactment, and (4) adaptation. The model is an information-processing model that emphasizes students acting on information about the task and standards by making goals and plans and then engaging in both the task and a monitoring-and-control loop to adjusts their understanding and study tactics as they go. Both cognition and metacognition figure largely into this way of looking at studying and self-regulation. Their discussion of the model mentions affect, personality, and self-perceptions as part of the individual differences that contribute to variation in the use of the model, but cognition and motivation are the model's main focus. Greene and Azevedo (2007) reviewed literature through the lens of Winne and Hadwin's (1998) model and found that in general the model served well to organize existing research on SRL and suggest questions for further research.

Phase View of Self-Regulated Learning

Self-regulation of learning, in its present conception in the literature, has subsumed many of the motivation theories that have gone before, for example, theories about self-efficacy, goal orientations, expectancies and values, and interest. The most comprehensive treatments of self-regulation of learning present these aspects in a phase (Pintrich & Zusho, 2002; Wigfield, Klauda, & Cambria, 2011) or cyclical (Zimmerman, 2011) view. A phase or cyclical view allows theorists to place cognitive, metacognitive, and motivational constructs into the sequence of events that occur as students self-regulate. This view of self-regulation of learning affords a way to crosswalk CA literature, which has mostly taken an "event" (Brookhart, 1997) or "episode of learning" (Wolf, 1993) point of view.

Winne (2011) explained SRL as "unfolding over four weakly sequenced and recursive phases" (p. 20). Descriptions of these phases are derived from Winne and Hadwin's (1998) work and include Phase 1, the learner defines the task and its affordances and constraints; Phase 2, the learner sets goals and plans; Phase 3, the learner engages with the task, that is, works on it; and Phase 4, the learner evaluates his or her work (p. 21).

Zimmerman (2011, p. 56) conceived of SRL in three phases, each with several subprocesses. In the forethought phase of self-regulation, the student does task analysis (i.e., sets goals and plans) and makes himself or herself aware of self-motivation beliefs (e.g., self-efficacy, interest, goal orientation, and outcome expectancies). In the performance phase, the student exercises self-control (using various task, interest, and management strategies) and engages in self-observation (metacognitive monitoring and self-recording). In the self-reflection phase, the student engages in self-judgment (self-evaluation and causal attribution) and self-reaction (affect, satisfaction, and potentially adaptive or defensive responses).

Pintrich and Zusho (2002) organized the phases and areas of self-regulation into a "heuristic to organize our thinking and research on self-regulated learning" (p. 251). Table 3.3 presents their framework in four phases and four areas. The four phases are (1) forethought, planning and activation, (2) monitoring, (3) control, and (4) reaction and reflection. Pintrich and Zusho (2002) pointed out that monitoring and control are difficult to separate empirically. The four areas for regulation are (1) cognition, (2) motivation/affect, (3) behavior, and (4) context.

The two-dimensionality of this framework allows for separate consideration of, for example, the cognitive aspects of each phase, the motivational aspects of each phase, and so on, while acknowledging commonalities in occurrence (the phases) and commonalities in constructs (the areas). Aspects of student choice, a centerpiece of Boekaerts's (1999) conception of SRL, are especially salient in the behavior area. Aspects of student cognition and metacognition, a centerpiece of Winne and Hadwin's (1998) conception of SRL, are listed in their own areas. The cyclical nature of self-regulation of learning, a centerpiece of Zimmerman's (2011) conception, is represented in the phases.

Thus Pintrich and Zusho's (2002) framework is simultaneously comprehensive and analytical. For this reason, it is conducive to a crosswalk with the CA literature. The rest of this section discusses aspects of CA research in light of one or more of the phases or areas in Pintrich and Zusho's (2002) framework.

Assessment and the Phases of Self-Regulated Learning

This section unpacks some implications of the first column of the model: the phases of SRL. The first and, to this author, the most obvious area for discussion is the similarities between these phases and the formative assessment cycle. The phases of SRL are a weakly ordered sequence (Pintrich & Zusho, 2002) but a sequence nonetheless. At the forethought and planning stage, the context is student perceptions of the task

	Areas for Regulation			
Phases	*Cognition*	*Motivation/Affect*	*Behavior*	*Context*
Forethought, Planning, and Activation	• Target goal setting • Prior content knowledge activation • Metacognitive knowledge activation	• Goal orientation adoption • Efficacy judgments • Ease of learning judgments (EOLs), perceptions of task difficulty • Task value activation • Interest activation	• Time and effort planning • Planning for self-observations of behavior	• Perceptions of task • Perceptions of context
Monitoring	Metacognitive awareness and monitoring of cognition, judgments of learning (JOLs)	Awareness and monitoring of motivation and affect	• Awareness and monitoring of effort, time use, need for help • Self-observation of behavior	Monitoring, changing task, and context conditions
Control	Selection and adaptation of cognitive strategies for learning, thinking	Selection and adaptation of strategies for managing motivation and affect	• Increase/decrease effort • Persist, give up • Help-seeking behavior	• Change or renegotiate task • Change or leave context
Reaction and Reflection	• Cognitive judgments • Attributions	• Affective reactions • Attributions	Choice behavior	• Evaluation of task • Evaluation of context

Table 3.3 Phases and Areas for Self-Regulated Learning

SOURCE: Reprinted from Pintrich & Zusho (2002), p. 252, with permission from Elsevier.

and of other relevant features of the context. Students set goals; activate prior knowledge; activate beliefs about self-efficacy; the value of the task and the interest it holds for them; and begin to plan how they will spend their time and effort on the task. At the monitoring and control stages, previously noted as difficult to separate, students monitor changing task and context conditions as they learn, using both metacognitive and cognitive strategies to make decisions about changing the task and context and/or their responses to it. In the reaction and reflection phase, students evaluate the task and context as well as their understanding (cognition) and affect (motivations), make attributions about their level of accomplishment, and make choices about what they might learn or do next.

It has become almost a platitude to cite the formative assessment cycle as a series of three questions, but the phases of self-reflection remind us of the importance of the recent shift in thinking in the CA literature from a conception where the goals of learning reside with the teacher to one in which the goals of learning that reside with the student are paramount. It was actually not all that long ago that the idea of assessing goals for learning arose. In the 1930s, Ralph Tyler and his colleagues began planning the "Eight-Year Study" to investigate the effects of using progressive education methods in high school. Part of this effort was the establishment of a set of principles for educational evaluation, based on defining appropriate objectives, establishing and delivering learning experiences, and then evaluating whether the objectives had been achieved (Haertel & Herman, 2005). As common as this objectives-based approach to educational assessment sounds today, it was revolutionary at the time and has been a big influence in educational assessment in the United States to the present day. Note that, as originally conceived, basing assessment and evaluation on goals for learning meant the *educators'* goals.

From the 1950s to the 1970s, interest in curriculum-based assessment (CBA) of learning objectives was taken even further. A widely used taxonomy of educational objectives (Bloom, Englehart, Furst, Hill, & Krathwohl, 1956), behavioral objectives, mastery learning, and measurement-driven instruction (Bloom, Hastings, & Madaus, 1971) all pushed Tyler's principles of evaluating learning to the level of fine-grained, classroom-level lesson objectives. Teachers were the main designers and evaluators of these classroom- and lesson-level objectives.

Current theories of formative assessment have recognized that the agency for learning resides with the student. As this has happened, the theory of assessment now in use has changed from a theory of managing educational programs and classroom lessons to a theory of providing affordances and opportunities for students to manage their own learning. This sea change in thinking about assessment, from what the teacher does to what the student does, happened at approximately the same time that self-regulation theory was developing, although it arose somewhat independently in the field of assessment.

Sadler (1989) noted that "even when teachers provide students with valid and reliable judgments about the quality of their work, improvement does not necessarily follow" (p. 119). He posited that one of the functions of formative assessment is "short-circuiting the randomness and inefficiency of trial-and-error learning" (p. 120). His description of this purposeful-trial concept sounds very much like what could be called self-monitoring of learning: "In other words, students have to be able to judge the quality of what they are producing and be able to regulate what they are doing during the doing of it" (p. 121).

Sadler (1989) described a theory of formative assessment that is dependent on students' understanding of what they are supposed to be learning and on their capacity to monitor the quality of their own work. He wrote (Sadler, 1989) that "the learner has to (a) possess a concept of the *standard* (or goal, or reference level) being aimed for, (b) compare the *actual* (or current) *level of performance* with the standard, and (c) engage in appropriate *action* which leads to some closure of the gap" (p. 121). These three functions have been used as a framework for understanding feedback specifically (Hattie & Timperley, 2007, p. 86: Where am I going? How am I going? Where to next?) and formative assessment, more generally (Wiliam, 2010, p. 31: Where the learner is going, Where the learner is right now, How to get there).

While successful students have at their disposal a repertoire of strategies to participate in this self-regulation of learning (Brookhart, 2001), less successful students do not. In fact, self-regulation strategies and capabilities, or the lack of them, may be the defining feature that separates successful and unsuccessful students. When students are assisted into the self-regulation process with formative assessment methods, such as deliberately teaching what students are to be learning and what constitutes quality in that learning, the provision of feedback and opportunities to use it, even unsuccessful students learn. James, Black, Carmichael, Conner, Dudley, Fox, et al. observed (2006) the following:

> Pupils improve their learning and attainment when they have opportunities to think about what counts as good work. However, much more significantly, the improvements appear to be greater for pupils with weak basic skills. This suggests that, at least in part, low achievement in schools is exacerbated by pupils not understanding what it is they are meant to be learning. (p. 40)

It appears, then, that a major observation about current views of CA in the context of motivation theory and research is that both fields have come, via different paths, to the realization that the *learner* is the major agent of and in CA. The centrality of the learner has begun to take theoretical center stage in understanding the role of assessment information in learning, and studies based in motivational theory have begun to appear in reviews of literature about formative assessment and feedback (Brookhart, 2007; Hattie & Timperley, 2007; Shute, 2008; Wiliam, 2010). In fact, this point has already been made, in greater detail than here, in a chapter titled "Students as the Definitive Source of Formative Assessment" (Andrade, 2010). Andrade's (2010) argument began by pointing out that students have "constant and instant access to their own thoughts, actions, and works" (p. 90). She reviewed research on self-assessment and SRL. In her analysis, she used both the framework of the three formative assessment questions and a model with three phases (forethought, performance and control, and reflection) to describe self-regulation of learning via formative assessment.

Andrade's (2010) chapter is the first time this author is aware of an analyst making the leap from the known effects of feedback and of self-regulation on learning to the assertion that students are the *definitive* source of formative assessment information in the classroom. This section has simply walked through the logic of that position and pointed out that the formative assessment cycle or script (as the three questions have been called) is very consistent with the phases of student self-regulation. The literature cited here has been on the assessment side, in keeping with the purpose of this chapter. Andrade (2010) already has presented a thorough review of studies of student self-regulation of learning from the motivation literature that converges on this point.

Assessment and the Role of Evidence in Self-Regulated Learning: Monitoring and Reaction/Reflection

This section explores some implications of two of the rows of the model of SRL. For two of the phases in the model of self-regulation of learning—(1) the monitoring phase and (2) the reaction and reflection phase—the role of evidence and evidentiary processes are particularly salient across all of the areas. These are, therefore, the phases of SRL that seemingly should be most related to CA, because CAs, both formative and summative, are a main source of evidence of learning. Two questions regarding CA seem especially relevant for both of these phases where students take stock of evidence of their learning: (1) What is the nature of the evidence CAs provide? and (2) How do students interpret that evidence?

Classroom Assessment Evidence of Learning

A lot is known about the types of CA questions, test items, and performance tasks teachers use to elicit evidence of student learning. Other chapters review this literature (see especially Heritage [formative assessment] and Moss [summative assessment] in Chapters 11 and 14 of this volume). Briefly, students get evidence of learning from a range of CA types. Most CA is intended to be criterion-referenced, although the criteria are not always clear (Mavrommatis, 1997). For many teachers, grading is an important reason for assessment (Kusch, 1999; Wilson, 1990), and this limits the kind of assessment teachers do (Schmidt & Brosnan, 1996).

Elementary teachers use more varied assessment methods than secondary (Gullickson, 1985; Wilson, 1990), including a large range of methods (Gipps, McCallum, & Hargreaves, 2000) and assessments of "academic enablers" like effort and improvement (Cizek, Fitzgerald, & Rachor, 1995;

McMillan, Myran, & Workman, 2002). Secondary teachers use fewer commercially prepared tests and more teacher-made tests—often more objective tests (Gullickson, 1985; Stiggins & Bridgeford, 1985; Stiggins & Conklin, 1992; Wilson, 1990; Zhang & Burry-Stock, 2003). They consider "academic enablers" like effort and improvement to be achievement-related constructs; this varies with ability level of class (Cizek et al., 1995; McMillan, 2001). Secondary social studies teachers use constructed response items more than other teachers (McMillan, 2001). While recall questions are dominant, whether teachers write tests (Stiggins, Griswold, & Wikelund, 1989) or whether they are from textbooks (Frisbie, Miranda, & Baker, 1993), teachers do sometimes use questions that tap higher-order thinking (Gullickson, 1985; Kahn, 2000; Stiggins et al., 1989).

For the past 10 years or so, a movement known as standards-based grading (Guskey, 2009) has been gaining momentum in U.S. schools. Teachers using traditional grading practices often combine appraisals of effort and behavior, as well as learning, into a grade (see Brookhart, Chapter 15 of this volume, for a review of the grading literature). In contrast, teachers who employ standards-based or learning-focused grading grade on achievement alone and report measures of effort and behavior separately. One of the main arguments for this grading reform is derived from the logic that if standards of learning are what students are expected to achieve, then their grades should reflect that learning (Brookhart, 2011; Guskey, 2009; O'Connor, 2009). The model of SRL suggests a theoretical, as well as a practical, justification for this. Report card grades should be useful for the reaction/reflection phase of self-regulation of learning. If students are to use their grades in an evidentiary process to regulate even more learning, the grades need to be evidence of learning. An obvious question for future research is whether and how students do use standards-based grades for reaction and reflection and whether that differs from how they use traditional grades.

Student's Strategies for Reflecting on Evidence of Their Learning

The short answer to the question of how students reflect on evidence of their learning gleaned from CAs is "it varies." Successful students are successful, in part, because they actually do monitor and reflect on evidence of their learning and activate comprehension and learning strategies as they do. Successful secondary students can do this in at least four different ways (Brookhart, 2001). They monitor their learning as they are studying for CAs and recognize that studying increases their knowledge. They look for ways to transfer what they are learning to other subjects or to their future (as when a calculus student realizes she is also preparing for her intended engineering career). They activate metacognitive awareness and specifically try to monitor their learning for the immediate CA task. Finally, they use CA evidence to judge the level of their own understanding.

Since the purpose of this chapter is to relate the CA literature to motivation theory and research and not vice versa, it is beyond the scope of this chapter to review all of the motivation literature or even all of the self-regulation literature. However, one recent study (Hulleman, Durik, Schweigert, & Harackiewicz, 2008) of motivation seems to speak clearly to the issue that different students will treat different tasks (including CAs) differently. It is described here because of these implications for CA. How students choose to interpret a task will affect what they take it to be evidence *of* and how seriously they follow up on it in the course of their future learning. In terms of the model of SRL, understanding how students' use of information for monitoring and evaluating their learning varies should contribute to understanding both of those phases of self-regulation and, at the same time, contribute to understanding of the evidentiary reasoning students bring to bear on information from their CAs.

Hulleman and his colleagues (2008) combined three different theoretical perspectives (task value, goal theory, and interest) in order to investigate how a student's interest and view of the task predict what the student gets out of an educational experience in terms of both performance and continuing interest. They did this in two settings: (1) an introductory psychology class at a university (students with a wide range of interest in the subject and little choice about being there) and (2) a high school football camp (students with high interest and ability in football who chose to be there). Task value theory (Eccles, 1983) holds that tasks can have utility value, meaning they are important for some other use—for example success in later coursework—or intrinsic value, meaning they are important to a person because they are enjoyable in themselves. Goal theory (Ames, 1984) suggests that students approach tasks in order to obtain mastery or to perform well (the study did not deal with avoidance goals because the authors were interested in the development of interest and valuing of the tasks). Interest (Hidi & Harackiewicz, 2000) can be task-centered and situational or a more enduring trait focused on a class of tasks.

At the beginning of the course or camp experience, the researchers measured initial interest in the task (learning psychology and playing football, respectively) and achievement goals (mastery and performance). Midway through the course or camp experience, they measured the task value (intrinsic and utility) students placed on their respective tasks. At the end of the course or camp experience, they measured final interest and, ultimately, final performance quality (course grades and coaches' ratings, respectively).

In both settings, initial interest predicted both mastery and performance goals. Students who were more interested were more motivated both to learn and to perform well. Mastery goals were a stronger predictor of how interested students were at the end of their experience for students with high initial interest than for those with low initial interest. Students with higher initial interest and mastery goals were more likely to find both intrinsic and utility value in the task (learning psychology or football). Both kinds of value affected subsequent interest in psychology or football. Performance goals and utility value predicted final performance. Thus perhaps some day, as the fields of self-regulation and CA begin to inform each other more, a body of evidence will build up to allow the conclusion that is tempting here: For monitoring and evaluating their learning, students should find that CAs that are interesting tasks and of obvious utility value (usefulness)—administered in classrooms that foster a learning orientation (mastery goals)—give the best evidence that maximize both learning and future interest in the subject.

Assessment and the Motivation/Affect Area of Self-Regulated Learning

This section explores some implications of one of the columns in the model of SRL: the area of motivation and affect. Motivational and affective variables in this area of the model of SRL include goal orientation, self-efficacy, perceptions of how hard or easy the task will be, task values, interest, awareness and monitoring and control of one's own affective responses, and attributions. Thinking about the CA literature in light of these variables, one finding stands out. The way to develop self-efficacy, expectations of success, and attributions of control is to give students success with similar tasks and materials. That is, students will have more positive self-efficacy and affect and more productive goal orientations for an assessment task if they perceive they have done well at similar tasks (Pajares, 1996; Usher & Pajares, 2008). This finding seems to be robust, having been reported in Crooks's (1988) review a quarter century ago and Harlen and Deakin Crick's (2003) more recent review as well.

Dweck (2000) cautioned that a history of success is a necessary but not sufficient condition for assuring students exhibit mastery-oriented responses and further their learning. She discussed the case of bright girls who often are the highest achievers in school but are also victims of learned helplessness. The problem is that bright girls often hold an entity theory of intelligence, believing their intelligence is fixed and therefore that they will be able to learn so much and no more. When they do hit a failure, they are unable to power through it, and they give up. What students need to conclude from their success, in order to develop self-efficacy for that type of task or assessment, is not that they have a certain level of fixed intelligence but that they can learn when they put their mind to it.

Teachers can change the way children come to understand their abilities related to an activity simply through the choice of feedback they offer in moment-to-moment CA (Johnston & Andrade, in press). For example, Cimpian, Arce, Markman, and Dweck (2007) gave young children the opportunity to role-play drawing pictures using a puppet and had a puppet teacher give them feedback on their pictures. The puppet teacher deemed the first three drawings successful and gave half the children the response of "You're a good drawer." The other half received the feedback of "You did a good job drawing." The difference is subtle, but "You're a good drawer" frames the activity as one in which the child is being judged as an artist (a good drawer). The implicit conclusion is that the person's artistic nature can be deduced from an instance of performance. The "good job drawing" feedback frames the activity as one in which the quality of the process of doing the work is judged, but not the person.

After three instances of one or other of these forms of positive feedback, the children were asked a series of questions about the extent to which they liked a drawing they had done; whether they felt happy or sad and good or not good; and whether they felt like a good or not good boy or girl. There was no difference between the groups. On the next two role-play events, both groups got nonjudgmental feedback suggesting that their drawing had been unsuccessful, such as, "The cat [you just drew] has no ears." Asked the same set of questions again, now about their unsuccessful drawings, the children who had been induced to think that the activity was about deciding who was and was not a good artist became more negative in their responses. Asked which picture they might draw on another day, these students chose one that they had already successfully drawn. Asked whether on another day they would choose to draw or do something else, they were more likely to choose to do something else. The children who had been led to believe the activity was about the process of doing a good job responded more positively in every way and were more likely to choose the more challenging activity on which they had so far been unsuccessful.

The study by Cimpian et al. (2007) shows how formative assessment feedback language mediates the meaning of the children's experience of activity. The two groups of children ostensibly had the same experience but were induced to view it and its significance differently. The different framing affected the students' goals, teacher and student roles, the relationship between teacher and student, and the relationship between the student and the activity. Feedback that frames the outcome of an activity as evidence of a permanent ability trait routinely leads to subsequent avoidance of challenge (Dweck, 2000).

A few studies have looked at whether different types of assessments have different motivational effects. Stefanou and Parkes (2003) investigated "the nature of the effect of particular assessment types on motivation." They noted, for example, that many tout the benefits of using projects for CA, over tests, but such assertions have rarely been tested empirically. They found a significant effect of assessment type on goal orientation in fifth-grade science: Paper–pencil tests and performance assessments both fostered more task-focused orientations than lab tests. Brookhart and Durkin's (2003) study of high school social studies students found that performance assessment may stimulate students' desire for competence in both the absolute sense (mastery goal orientations) *and* the relative sense (performance goal orientations) at the same time. Meece and Miller (1999) did an intervention study in third-grade classrooms. They worked with teachers to encourage them to assign longer (multiday, requiring at least a paragraph response), more collaborative, more thoughtful assignments. The third-grade students became less focused on performance goals, and low achieving students reported less work avoidance.

Turner, Thorpe, and Meyer (1998) investigated the different motivational patterns displayed by different students. They identified four patterns of motivation among students' math achievement goals, negative reactions to making mistakes, and self-regulatory beliefs and behaviors. They named these patterns of student motivation: learning-oriented, success-oriented, uncommitted, and avoidant. By implication, they noted, different kinds of students may perceive the same feedback on classroom tasks and assessments differently. Turner, Thorpe, and Meyer (1998) also found that affect mediated the effects of performance goals on beliefs and self-regulation, which also has implications for classroom formative assessment. For unsuccessful students, that feeling of negative affect after failure is the climate in which much of the formative feedback is given. Feedback for unsuccessful students must first deal with the negative feelings in order to break the cycle of failure. Suggestions for improvement may not be heard or not perceived as constructive otherwise.

Doppelt and Schunn (2008) investigated the effects of many aspects of the learning environment, including teaching methods as well as assessment methods, on various aspects of learning, comparing a group of eighth-grade science classes studying electronics using design-based learning and a group of eighth-grade science classes studying electronics using scripted inquiry. Surprisingly, the two classroom environment features that were most influential (for both groups) in both cognitive and motivational learning outcomes were the perceived importance of homework and instructional worksheets, and the three outcomes most affected were interest in science topics, teamwork skills, and independent learning activities. Their surprise, they reported (Doppelt & Schunn, 2008, p. 208), was because in a previous study of middle school science, the most influential classroom environment features were perceived importance of team projects, class discussions, and performing experiments, and the four outcomes most affected were understanding ideas in class, interest in science topics, independent learning activities, and desire to learn. Perhaps what is best concluded from this line of classroom environment research that includes both teaching and CA methods is that method matters for motivational outcomes but differently for different topics—at least in middle school science.

Assessment and the Context Area of Self-Regulated Learning

This section explores some implications of another of the columns in the model of SRL: the area of context. This area is the last one to be taken up not only because it is the last column of the model but more importantly because it bookends the point with which the chapter began. Assessments are the egg: They are part of the context and the basis of task perceptions that focus cognition, motivation, and behavior. On the other hand, they are the chicken: They are the source of ongoing formative information for monitoring and summative information for reaction and reflection; for successful students, even summative information yields formative suggestions. If CA and SRL do begin to share insights, as Andrade (2010, p. 99) urges that they do, the model of SRL suggests that the nature of assessments (context) and assessment information (evidence) may be the way forward.

Perceptions of the Task

Students' perceptions of the task at hand are the foundation of formative assessment. As noted earlier, "Where am I going?" or "Understanding the learning target and criteria for success" is the compass that guides the formative assessment and feedback process (Sadler, 1989; Wiliam, 2010). Perhaps the kind of studies in which student perceptions of the task are most clearly described—and their effects most clearly studied—are studies of student self-assessment. This is because most self-assessment studies begin with a clear description of the task—the assignment or learning goal—and the criteria for self-assessment, which is often in the form of a rubric or checklist. Sebba, Crick, Yu, Lawson, Harlen, and Durant (2008) located 51 studies of peer and self-assessment and selected the 26 related to secondary education for an in-depth review. Nine of the 15 studies that reported performance outcomes found peer and self-assessment was associated with improved performance. Seven out of nine studies that reported student self-esteem found peer and self-assessment was associated with improved self-esteem. Seventeen out of 20 studies that reported motivational or self-regulation variables found peer and self-assessment was associated with improved engagement, goal clarifying and goal setting, responsibility for learning, and the like.

A closer examination of two additional studies shows how perceptions of the task loom large in student self-evaluation. These studies were selected for description because they were not part of the Sebba (2008) review—they were not at the secondary level—and they provide clear and consistent evidence at different grade levels in two different subjects: (1) mathematics (Ross, Hogaboam-Gray, & Rolheiser, 2002) and (2) writing (Andrade, Du, & Wang, 2008).

Ross et al. (2002) compared treatment and control group students on mathematics problem solving. The self-evaluation treatment group participated in four stages of self-assessment instruction. First, they were involved in defining the evaluation criteria. Second, they were taught how to apply the criteria to their work. Third, students were given feedback on the quality of their self-evaluations. Fourth, students were helped to use the results of their self-evaluations to develop action plans for further learning. For example, in one of the six 30-minute lessons, students solved a problem then cooperated in the development of criteria and described high, medium, and low performance in terms of their criteria. After controlling for pretest performance, students with self-evaluation training outperformed those without on a problem-solving task, with an effect size of 0.40 standard deviations.

Andrade and colleagues (2008) investigated the effects of a model, criteria generation, and rubric-referenced self-assessment on third and fourth graders' writing. The treatment group read a model story or essay and critiqued it in discussion. Then, they generated a list of criteria for writing based on the discussion and were given a rubric.

The treatment group and comparison group in this study both used self-assessment as part of the writing process, but only the treatment group used the rubric to do this. Controlling for previous achievement, the treatment group outperformed the comparison group on final essays, with an effect size of 15% of the variance accounted for (partial eta-squared). Even more interesting, the self-assessment group scored higher on five (ideas, organization, paragraphs, voice, and word choice) of the seven individual criteria in the rubric and not on two (sentences and conventions). That is, the effects of self-assessment showed up on the more thinking-related criteria and not in writing mechanics. The research team had similar findings at the middle school level (Andrade, Du, & Mycek, 2010), except that the group differences were significant for all seven of the criteria for the middle schoolers.

In terms of the model of SRL, both of these studies used treatments where perceptions of the task were activated and made very explicit. These perceptions included both understanding of the nature of the task and of the criteria for performance. Thus while self-assessment was nominally what was studied, what differed most between the groups was the sharpness of perceptions of the task and especially the criteria for quality work on the task.

Perceptions of the Context

Assessment has a long-documented history on students' perceptions of their classroom context. The teacher is responsible for the CA environment (Stiggins & Bridgeford, 1985; Stiggins & Conklin, 1992). Stiggins and Conklin (1992) identified eight dimensions of the CA environment. These are adult-controlled (not student-controlled) aspects of the environment:

1. The purposes for which teachers used CAs
2. The assessment methods teachers used
3. The criteria teachers used for selecting assessments
4. Assessment quality
5. The teacher's use of feedback
6. The teacher's preparation and background in assessment
7. The teacher's perception of students
8. The assessment policy environment

What Stiggins & Conklin (1992) termed the *CA environment* is similar to what sociologists have termed aspects of *classroom structure* (Rosenholtz & Rosenholtz, 1981; Simpson, 1981):

- The level of classroom task differentiation
- The amount of student autonomy granted
- Grouping practices
- Grading practices

Teachers' instructional and assessment choices create different environments in which students "construct identities" (Rosenholtz & Rosenholtz, 1981). Thus while the teacher controls the environment, it is the student who perceives it and is influenced by it, which is consistent with the "perceptions of context" aspect of the forethought phase of SRL.

More unidimensional classroom structures (whole group instruction, little student choice, frequent summative grading) lead to more perceptions that ability is a normally distributed trait and more student perceptions that some students are *smart* and some are *dumb*. In contrast, more multidimensional classrooms (individualized instruction, student choice, less frequent grading) (Rosenholtz & Rosenholtz, 1981; Simpson, 1981) lead to more perceptions that ability is learned and that intelligence can improve.

These constructs from sociology are strikingly similar to Dweck's (2000) descriptions of entity and incremental theories of intelligence, derived from cognitive psychology. Probably the most emphatic description of the effects of the classroom environment in general and the assessment context in particular on students' perceptions of what learning is and their role in it has been Dweck's (2000) career-long investigation into these theories of intelligence. Students who hold an entity theory of intelligence, believing that intelligence is a fixed trait, are more likely to prefer easy tasks on which they can perform well. Students who hold an incremental theory of intelligence, believing that intelligence can change and improve, are more likely to prefer mastery tasks on which they can be challenged and, as a result, learn. Important for the discussion here is that classroom manipulations—such as what students are told and what they are asked to read—can affect students' theories of intelligence and, as a result, their learning goals and ultimately the amount and scope of their learning.

Church, Elliot, and Gable (2001) incorporated theory about the classroom environment with their study of motivation to study the role of CA environment in student motivation and learning. They measured three aspects of student perceptions of the assessment environment in undergraduate chemistry classes: (1) lecture engagement, (2) evaluation focus, and (3) harsh evaluation. They found that the assessment environment had an indirect effect on graded performance, mediated by achievement goals, and both direct and indirect effects on intrinsic motivation.

This section has shown that assessment encompasses two aspects of the context area of self-regulation of learning: (1) when the task at hand is a CA, students' perceptions of the assessment itself are important for self-regulation of learning and (2) the way assessment is handled over time in a classroom creates an assessment context that affects student perceptions, motivation, self-regulation, and performance.

Conclusion

This chapter had two main parts: (1) a review of previous studies that attempted to bring together CA and motivation theory and research and (2) a crosswalk between a current model of self-regulation theory, which has grown to subsume many other motivational theories and variables, and the CA literature. At least one general conclusion seems certain: CA theory and research can be informed by motivation theory and research.

This section highlights three additional—and less global—points that, at least to this reviewer, seem to be important conclusions from the previous sections. One point regards the means-versus-ends, or chicken-and-egg, question with which the chapter began. Point two is about the centrality of the student in both CA and motivation. Point three is about the growing convergence of CA and motivational issues, especially regarding self-regulation.

Conclusion One: Classroom Evidence Can Be at the Same Time the Goal of Motivated Learning, the Summative Purpose, and a Means to It, the Formative Purpose

This is more than the circularity of a chicken-and-egg conundrum. In fact, it is part of the nature of CA itself. The reviews in the first section of the chapter mostly—but not entirely—looked at the effects of assessment on motivation (Crooks, 1988; Harlen & Deakin Crick, 2003; Natriello, 1987), effectively treating motivation as an outcome.

The consideration of CA using Pintrich and Zusho's (2002) framework of the phases and areas of self-regulation paints a more complicated picture. Assessment and motivation have three different relationships simultaneously: (1) coterminal (different ways of conceptualizing the same learning process), (2) as an input and as processing information (perceptions of the assessment task during forethought, formative use of assessment results during monitoring), and (3) as outcome evidence (use of summative assessment results for reaction and reflection). The formative assessment cycle arranges itself nicely across the phases of self-regulation, demonstrating that in one manner of thinking the assessment process is coexistent with the motivational process. Perceptions of the assessment as a task and perceptions of the assessment context are important inputs into the motivational process of SRL. For many classroom learning situations, a formative or summative assessment or assignment *is* the task. Assessment evidence is especially salient in two of the phases of self-regulation of learning, monitoring (where assessment evidence is arguably part of the means to learning) and reacting and reflecting (where assessment evidence arguably certifies the outcome of learning, and perhaps is a catalyst for further learning, as well). In other words, this review has shown that assessment information is both input and outcome for self-regulation of learning and that self-regulation of learning involves both formative and summative assessment. The metaphor breaks down, and the chicken and egg become a casserole.

Conclusion Two: The Student, the Learner, Is at the Center Both of Motivation for Learning and of Assessment for Learning

In the field of motivation, self-regulation as a field is growing and expanding (Zimmerman & Schunk, 2011), subsuming other aspects of motivation (e.g., attribution theory, Weiner, 1979; expectancy value theory, Eccles, 1983; goal theory, Ames, 1984; and so on). This stems from the very important shift from the behaviorism of a previous era to the realization that cognition and metacognition are at the heart of learning and of the regulation of learning (Boekaerts, 1999; Pintrich & Zusho, 2002; Winne & Hadwin, 1998; Zimmerman & Schunk, 2011). Whose cognition and metacognition? The answer is the student's, of course.

In the field of CA, formative assessment is at the growing edge of the field. Much of what is known about teacher use of summative assessment has been established for decades. What is new is the realization that assessment can, and should, be used *for* learning (Sadler, 1989). Theory about formative assessment (Assessment Reform Group, 2002; Wiliam, 2010; Wolf, 1993) has developed in a somewhat parallel track, in a somewhat parallel time frame, to the consolidation of self-regulation theory. The earlier reviews described in the first section of this chapter already recognized that these two fields inform each other (Black & Wiliam, 1998; Brookhart, 1997; Crooks, 1988; Harlen & Deakin Crick, 2003; Natriello, 1987). Andrade (2010) went further, drawing the conclusion that students are the definitive source of formative assessment. The literature reviewed in this chapter converges upon—and underscores—her conclusion.

Conclusion Three: Future Studies of Classroom Assessment Need to Consider Student Motivation, Especially Self-Regulation of Learning, and Future Studies of Self-Regulated Learning Need to Consider the Evidence Students Use for Their Judgments, Much of Which Comes From Classroom Assessment

Research in CA and motivation incline together, more and more. This should continue, and as it does, understanding about both fields should grow. Assessment is already in evidence in most studies of SRL as the measure of learning. A richer description of the requirements of the assessment, students' perceptions of the assessment, and the kind of evidence about student learning that results from it would enhance such studies of motivation. Motivation theory already has a place for task perceptions, students' goals and interests regarding the task, and their choice of strategies (Pintrich & Zusho, 2002; Zimmerman & Schunk, 2011). If the task is a CA, much more information could be available about the task for which students are striving and the nature of the information they must process from its results.

Conversely, motivation is already in evidence in many studies of CA (Brookhart, 1997), especially in studies of formative assessment where student use of information is a focus (Black & Wiliam, 1998). A richer description of individual differences in motivational variables—task perceptions and values, interests, goal orientations, strategy use, decisions about investment of effort—would enhance studies of CA. Motivation theory is the key to the more nuanced understanding of what goes on before, during, and after formative and summative CA that will advance understanding about the meaning and usefulness and hence the validity of the evidence that comes from CA.

Thus the chicken-and-egg conundrum is too simple. And surely *casserole* is the wrong metaphor. Perhaps a busy henhouse, at once bustling with chickens and producing eggs, is a better metaphor to describe the relationship between motivation and assessment.

References

Ames, C. (1984). Competitive, cooperative, and individualistic goal structures: A cognitive-motivational analysis. In R. Ames & C. Ames (Eds.), *Research on motivation in education: Vol. 1. Student motivation.* New York: Academic Press.

Andrade, H. L. (2010). Students as the definitive source of formative assessment: Academic self-assessment and the self-regulation of learning. In H. L. Andrade & G. J. Cizek (Eds.), *Handbook of formative assessment* (pp. 90–105). New York: Routledge.

Andrade, H. L., Du, Y., & Mycek, K. (2010). Rubric-referenced self-assessment and middle school students' writing. *Assessment in Education, 17*(2), 199–214.

Andrade, H. L., Du, Y., & Wang, X. (2008). Putting rubrics to the test: The effect of a model, criteria generation, and rubric-referenced self-assessment on elementary students' writing. *Educational Measurement: Issues and Practice, 27*(2), 3–13.

Assessment Reform Group. (2002). *Assessment for learning: 10 principles.* Retrieved from http://arrts.gtcni.org.uk/gtcni/bitstream/2428/4623/1/Assessment%20for%20Learning%20-%20 10%20principles.pdf

Bandura, A. (1982). Self-efficacy mechanism in human agency. *American Psychologist, 37,* 122–147.

Bandura, A. (1986). *Social foundations of thought and action: A social cognitive theory.* Englewood Cliffs, NJ: Prentice Hall.

Black, P., & Wiliam, D. (1998). Assessment and classroom learning. *Assessment in Education, 5,* 7–74.

Bloom, B. S., Englehart, M. D., Furst, E. J., Hill, W. H., & Krathwohl, D. R. (1956). *Taxonomy of educational objectives: The classification of educational goals, Handbook I: Cognitive domain.* White Plains, NY: Longman

Bloom, B. S., Hastings, J. T., & Madaus, G. F. (1971). *Handbook on formative and summative evaluation of student learning.* New York: McGraw-Hill.

Boekaerts, M. (1999). Self-regulated learning: Where we are today. *International Journal of Educational Research, 31,* 445–457.

Brookhart, S. M. (1997). A theoretical framework for the role of classroom assessment in motivating student effort and achievement. *Applied Measurement in Education, 10*(2), 161–180.

Brookhart, S. M. (2001). Successful students' formative and summative use of assessment information. *Assessment in Education, 8,* 153–169.

Brookhart, S. M. (2007). Expanding views about formative classroom assessment: A review of the literature. In J. H. McMillan (Ed.), *Formative classroom assessment: Theory into practice* (pp. 43–62). New York: Teachers College Press.

Brookhart, S. M. (2011). *Grading and learning: Practices that support student achievement.* Bloomington, IN: Solution Tree.

Brookhart, S. M., & Bronowicz, D. L. (2003). "I don't like writing. It makes my fingers hurt": Students talk about their classroom assessments. *Assessment in Education, 10,* 221–242.

Brookhart, S. M., & DeVoge, J. G. (1999). Testing a theory about the role of classroom assessment in student motivation and achievement. *Applied Measurement in Education, 12,* 409–425.

Brookhart, S. M., & Durkin, D. T. (2003). Classroom assessment, student motivation, and achievement in high school social studies classes. *Applied Measurement in Education, 16,* 27–54.

Brookhart, S. M., & Peretin, J. (2002, April). *Patterns of relationship among motivational and effort variables for different classroom assessments.* Paper presented at the annual meeting of the American Educational Research Association, New Orleans, LA.

Brookhart, S. M., Walsh, J. M., & Zientarski, W. A. (2006). The dynamics of motivation and effort for classroom assessments in middle school science and social studies. *Applied Measurement in Education, 19*(2), 151–184.

Butler, D. L., & Winne, P. H. (1995). Feedback and self-regulated learning: A theoretical synthesis. *Review of Educational Research, 65,* 245–281.

Church, M. A., Elliot, A. J., & Gable, S. L. (2001). Perceptions of classroom environment, achievement goals, and achievement outcomes. *Journal of Educational Psychology, 93,* 43–54.

Cimpian, A., Arce, H. C., Markman, E. M., & Dweck, C. S. (2007). Subtle linguistic cues affect children's motivation. *Psychological Science, 18*(4), 314–316.

Cizek, G. J., Fitzgerald, S. M., & Rachor, R. E. (1995). Teachers' assessment practices: Preparation, isolation, and the kitchen sink. *Educational Assessment, 3,* 159–179.

Covington, M. V. (1992). *Making the grade: A self-worth perspective on motivation and school reform.* Cambridge, UK: Cambridge University Press.

Crooks, T. J. (1988). The impact of classroom evaluation practices on students. *Review of Educational Research, 58,* 438–481.

Doppelt, Y., & Schunn, C. D. (2008). Identifying students' perceptions of the important classroom features affecting learning aspects of a design-based learning environment. *Learning Environments Research, 11*(3), 195–209.

Dweck, C. S. (2000). *Self-theories: Their role in motivation, personality, and development.* New York: Psychology Press.

Eccles, J. (1983). Expectancies, values, and academic behavior. In J. T. Spence (Ed.), *Academic and achievement motives.* San Francisco: Freeman.

Frisbie, D. A., Miranda, D. U., & Baker, K. K. (1993). An evaluation of elementary textbook tests as classroom assessment tools. *Applied Measurement in Education, 6,* 21–36.

Gipps, C., McCallum, B., & Hargreaves, E. (2000). *What makes a good primary school teacher? Expert classroom strategies.* London: Routledge Falmer.

Greene, J. A., & Azevedo, R. (2007). A theoretical review of Winne and Hadwin's model of self-regulated learning: New perspectives and directions. *Review of Educational Research, 77*(3), 334–372.

Gullickson, A. R. (1985). Student evaluation techniques and their relationship to grade and curriculum. *Journal of Educational Research, 79,* 96–100.

Guskey, T. R. (Ed.) (2009). *Practical solutions for serious problems in standards-based grading.* Thousand Oaks, CA: Corwin Press.

Haertel, E., & Herman, J. (2005, June). *A historical perspective on validity arguments for accountability testing.* Los Angeles: National Center for Research on Evaluation, Standards, and Student Testing (CRESST). (ERIC Document Reproduction Service No. ED488709)

Harlen, W., & Deakin Crick, R. (2003). Testing and motivation for learning. *Assessment in Education, 10*(2), 169–207.
Hattie, J., & Timperley, H. (2007). The power of feedback. *Review of Educational Research, 77,* 81–112.
Hidi, S., & Harackiewicz, J. M. (2000). Motivating the academically unmotivated: A critical issue for the 21st century. *Review of Educational Research, 70,* 151–179.
Hill, K. T. (1984). Debilitating motivation and testing: A major educational problem—Possible solutions and policy applications. In R. Ames & C. Ames (Eds.), *Research on motivation in education: Vol. 1. Student motivation.* New York: Academic Press.
Hulleman, C. S., Durik, A. M., Schweigert, S. A., & Harackiewicz, J. M. (2008). Task values, goals, and interest: An integrative analysis. *Journal of Educational Psychology, 100,* 398–416.
James, M., Black, P., Carmichael, P., Conner, C., Dudley, P., Fox, A., et al. (2006). *Learning how to learn: Tools for schools.* London: Routledge.
Johnston, P., & Andrade, H. (in press). *Assessment, teaching and learning in and beyond classrooms.* Graham Nuthall Classroom Research Trust, New Zealand: Sense Publishers.
Kahn, E. A. (2000). A case study of assessment in a grade 10 English course. *Journal of Educational Research, 93,* 276–286.
Kusch, J. W. (1999). The dimensions of classroom assessment: How field study students learn to grade in the middle level classroom. *Journal of Educational Thought (Revue de la Pensee Educative), 33*(1), 61–81.
Maehr, M. L. (1976). Continuing motivation: An analysis of a seldom considered educational outcome. *Review of Educational Research, 46,* 443–362.
Mavrommatis, Y. (1997). Understanding assessment in the classroom: Phases of the assessment process—the assessment episode. *Assessment in Education, 4,* 381–400.
McMillan, J. H. (2001). Secondary teachers' classroom assessment and grading practices. *Educational Measurement: Issues and Practice, 20*(1), 20–32.
McMillan, J. H., Myran, S., & Workman, D. (2002). Elementary teachers' classroom assessment and grading practices. *Journal of Educational Research, 95,* 203–213.
Meece, J. L., & Miller, S. D. (1999). Changes in elementary school children's achievement goals for reading and writing: Results of a longitudinal and an intervention study. *Scientific Studies of Reading, 3,* 207–229.
Natriello, G. (1987). The impact of evaluation processes on students. *Educational Psychologist, 22,* 155–175.
Nicholls, J. G. (1984). Achievement motivation: Conceptions of ability, subjective experience, task choice, and performance. *Psychological Review, 91,* 328–346.
O'Connor, K. (2009). *How to grade for learning* (3rd ed.). Thousand Oaks, CA: Corwin Press.
Pajares, F. (1996). Self-efficacy beliefs in academic settings. *Review of Educational Research, 66*(4), 543–578.
Pintrich, P. R., & Schrauben, B. (1992). Students' motivational beliefs and their cognitive engagement in classroom academic tasks. In D. H. Schunk & J. L. Meece (Eds.), *Student perceptions in the classroom* (pp. 149–183). Hillsdale, NJ: Lawrence Erlbaum.
Pintrich, P. R., & Zusho, A. (2002). The development of academic self-regulation: The role of cognitive and motivational factors. In A. Wigfield & J. S. Eccles (Eds.), *Development of achievement motivation* (pp. 249–284). San Diego, CA: Academic Press.
Rodriguez, M. C. (2004). The role of classroom assessment in student performance on TIMSS. *Applied Measurement in Education, 17,* 1–24.
Rosenholtz, S. J., & Rosenholtz, S. H. (1981). Classroom organization and the perception of ability. *Sociology of Education, 54,* 132–140.
Ross, J. A., Hogaboam-Gray, A., & Rolheiser, C. (2002). Student self-evaluation in grade 5-6 mathematics: Effects on problem-solving achievement. *Educational Assessment, 8,* 43–58.
Ryan, R. M., Connell, J. P., & Deci, E. L. (1985). A motivational analysis of self-determination and self-regulation in the classroom. In C. Ames & R. Ames (Eds.), *Research on motivation in education: Vol. 2. The classroom milieu.* New York: Academic Press.
Ryan, R. M., & Deci, E. L. (2000a). Intrinsic and extrinsic motivations: Classic definitions and new directions. *Contemporary Educational Psychology, 25,* 54–67.
Ryan, R. M., & Deci, E. L. (2000b). Self-determination theory and the facilitation of intrinsic motivation, social development, and well-being. *American Psychologist, 55*(1), 68–78.
Sadler, D. R. (1989). Formative assessment and the design of instructional systems. *Instructional Science, 18,* 119–144.
Salomon, G. (1983). The differential investment of mental effort in learning from different sources. *Educational Psychologist, 18,* 42–50.
Salomon, G. (1984). Television is "easy" and print is "tough": The differential investment of mental effort as a function of perceptions and attributions. *Journal of Educational Psychology, 76,* 647–658.
Schunk, D. (1984). Self-efficacy perspective on achievement behavior. *Educational Psychologist, 19,* 48–58.

Schmidt., M. E., & Brosnan, P. A. (1996). Mathematics assessment: Practices and reporting methods. *School Science and Mathematics, 96,* 17–20.

Sebba, J., Crick, R. D., Yu, G., Lawson, H., Harlen, W., & Durant, K. (2008). Systematic review of research evidence of the impact on students in secondary schools of self and peer assessment. *Research Evidence in Education Library.* London: EPPI-Centre, Social Science Research Unit, Institute of Education, University of London.

Shute, V. J. (2008). Focus on formative feedback. *Review of Educational Research, 78,* 153–189.

Simpson, C. (1981). Classroom structure and the organization of ability. *Sociology of Education, 54,* 120–132.

Stefanou, C., & Parkes, J. (2003). Effects of classroom assessment on student motivation in fifth-grade science. *Journal of Educational Research, 96,* 152–162.

Stiggins, R. J., & Bridgeford, N. J. (1985). The ecology of classroom assessment. *Journal of Educational Measurement, 22,* 271–286.

Stiggins, R. J., & Conklin, N. F. (1992). *In teachers' hands: Investigating the practices of classroom assessment.* Albany, NY: SUNY Press.

Stiggins, R. J., Griswold, M. M., & Wikelund, K. R. (1989). Measuring thinking skills through classroom assessment. *Journal of Educational Measurement, 26,* 233–246.

Stodolsky, S. (1988). *The subject matters: Classroom activity in math and social studies.* Chicago: University of Chicago Press.

Turner, J. C., Thorpe, P. K., & Meyer, D. K. (1998). Students' reports of motivation and negative affect: A theoretical and empirical analysis. *Journal of Educational Psychology, 90,* 758–771.

Usher, E. L., & Pajares, F. (2008). Sources of self-efficacy in school: Critical review of the literature and future directions. *Review of Educational Research, 78*(4), 751–796.

Weiner, B. (1979). A theory of motivation for some classroom experiences. *Journal of Educational Psychology, 71,* 3–25.

Wigfield, A., Klauda, S. L., & Cambria, J. (2011). Influences on the development of academic self-regulatory processes. In B. J. Zimmerman & D. H. Schunk (Eds.), *Handbook of self-regulation of learning and performance* (pp. 33–48). New York: Routledge.

Wiliam, D. (2010). An integrative summary of the research literature and implications for a new theory of formative assessment. In H. L. Andrade & G. J. Cizek (Eds.), *Handbook of formative assessment* (pp. 18–40). New York: Routledge.

Wilson, R. J. (1990). Classroom processes in evaluating student achievement. *Alberta Journal of Educational Research, 36,* 4–17.

Winne, P. H. (2011). A cognitive and metacognitive analysis of self-regulated learning. In B. J. Zimmerman & D. H. Schunk (Eds.), *Handbook of self-regulation of learning and performance* (pp. 15–32). New York: Routledge.

Winne, P. H., & Hadwin, A. F. (1998). Studying as self-regulated learning. In D. J. Hacker, J. Dunlosky, & A. C. Graesser (Eds.), *Metacognition in educational theory and practice* (pp. 277–304). Mahwah, NJ: Lawrence Erlbaum.

Wolf, D. P. (1993). Assessment as an episode of learning. In R. E. Bennet & W. C. Ward (Eds.), *Construction versus choice in cognitive measurement* (pp. 213–240). Hillsdale, NJ: Lawrence Erlbaum.

Zhang, Z., & Burry-Stock, J. A. (2003). Classroom assessment practices and teachers' self-perceived assessment skills. *Applied Measurement in Education, 16,* 323–342.

Zimmerman, B. J. (2011). Motivational sources and outcomes of self-regulated learning. In B. J. Zimmerman & D. H. Schunk (Eds.), *Handbook of self-regulation of learning and performance* (pp. 49–64). New York: Routledge.

Zimmerman, B. J., & Schunk, D. H. (2011). Self-regulated learning and performance: An introduction and overview. In B. J. Zimmerman & D. H. Schunk (Eds.), *Handbook of self-regulation of learning and performance* (pp. 1–12). New York: Routledge.

4

Classroom Assessment in the Context of High-Stakes Testing

M. Christina Schneider

Karla L. Egan

Marc W. Julian

During the school year, students take a variety of assessments. First, students take day-to-day classroom assessments (CAs). Second, they may take interim or common assessments that are meant to gauge their progress in mastering the content knowledge and understanding defined in state standards. Finally, students are given the state's high-stakes end-of-year assessment that measures student achievement of the state standards. Although all three assessments are often believed to be measuring the same construct (the state standards), the observed knowledge, skills, and processes measured by these assessments may differ. When this occurs, teachers, students, and parents may receive mixed messages from each assessment source regarding what the student is actually able to do. Moreover, the ability of the teacher to summarize information either to assist student learning or to understand student progress may be hindered.

The conflicting messages about student achievement that can result from different assessment sources may, in part, be due to substantive differences in how high-stakes assessments are developed as compared to CAs. The interpretation of the state standards plays a central role in how test content is developed on any large-scale K–12 assessment such as those districts use to monitor student progress (interim assessments) or states use for the No Child Left Behind Act of 2001 (NCLB) (U.S. Department of Education, 2002) purposes (year-end assessments). Teachers are often neither aware of nor trained in the research-based and policy-based practices professional test developers use to interpret the state standards for interim or year-end assessments. The research literature cited in this chapter demonstrates that many teachers are also not taught to collect evidence of student learning through best assessment construction practices. To maximize student achievement, teachers and large-scale assessment developers need to (1) have the same interpretations of the standards, (2) identify the same types of student achievement as evidence of mastery of the standards, and (3) collect evidence using the same types of robust practices when building assessments.

The purpose of this chapter is to describe and synthesize research findings from CA, cognitive psychology, and large-scale assessment areas so that these results can support teachers and policy makers as they analyze classroom, interim, and year-end assessment results to determine student knowledge and understanding. In the first section of this chapter, we discuss each source of assessment information, including its purpose, development, and how the results are analyzed and used. In the second section, we propose steps showing how educators can integrate the three assessment sources to result in more valid inferences about student learning and to inform instruction. In the third section, we provide recommended assessment practices based in the research literature that not only allow teachers to elicit student understanding of the content but that also have been shown to help students learn skills that are measured on high-stakes assessments.

Overview of Assessment Sources of Information

In this chapter, we describe classroom, interim, and year-end assessments as sources of assessment information about what students know, rather than a type of assessment. We use the word *type* to describe items—multiple-choice, performance task, constructed-response (CR)—as examples. Before providing a more in-depth analysis of the purposes and uses of each assessment source, we briefly define each source.

CAs are used by teachers to measure student knowledge and understanding of the learning targets the teacher has set throughout the year. Teachers may create the assessment items, they may use published items such as those found in their textbooks or other external sources, or they may use a combination of approaches. Teachers also collect evidence of student learning "on the fly," through formal assessments embedded within an instructional unit, or at the end of an instructional unit. Teachers may use the information gained from the assessments for formative purposes, summative purposes, or both.

Interim assessments are used by districts or states to measure student achievement on state standards and district curricula during the year. The assessments are typically administered two to four times during the year to assess specific aspects of the curricula. They are typically created by district personnel or professional test developers. The results from interim assessments are frequently used to provide diagnostic feedback to aid instruction as well as provide predicative information regarding how a student is likely to perform on year-end assessments.

Year-end assessments are used by the state to measure student achievement on the state standards. These assessments are administered to all students within a state during a specified testing window. They are created by professional test developers—typically in collaboration with personnel at the state department of education. The results from these tests are used primarily for accountability and policymaking purposes.

Classroom Assessment

CAs are the most frequently given assessments during the course of a school year. For this reason, CAs have the greatest potential for providing "diagnostic" information about what students can and cannot do.

Purposes of Classroom Assessment

Teachers use CAs to determine what students know and can do in regard to both district and state standards; but at various times, they may have different purposes for collecting and using evidence of student learning. The terms *formative classroom assessment* (CA) and *summative classroom assessment* (CA) define the teacher's intended use of information, and sometimes, describe the teacher's method of collecting information about student learning.

Formative CA has different connotations depending upon the framework being implemented (see formative assessment chapters [10–13] in this volume). Ruiz-Primo, Furtak, Ayala, Yin, and Shavelson (2010) described a continuum of formative assessment practices that move from informal and perhaps unplanned to those that are formally embedded at specific points during an instructional unit to check whether or not students show evidence of understanding important learning targets. Wiliam, Lee, Harrison, and Black (2004) defined formative CA as teacher questioning, comment-only feedback, sharing grading criteria, and facilitating student self-assessment and peer feedback. These techniques tend to be used by the teacher during his or her instructional sequence. Brookhart (2010) described teacher feedback on summative

CAs. In this model, the teacher provides students feedback on a summative CA to help the student better target the expected outcome on a revision or on a subsequent assignment. Regardless of what practice is used, when teachers collect and analyze evidence regarding individual student learning and use that information to either adjust instruction or provide feedback to students they are using assessment for a formative purpose (Brookhart, Moss, & Long, 2008).

Summative CA answers the question, "How well is the student performing on what the student should know?" With summative CA, teachers often use the proportion of items a student answers correctly to interpret how well a student performed on a set of items or on a diverse set of assessments across a grading period. Proportions are transferred onto a grading scale that historically and implicitly show depth of student achievement on standards covered on a particular test or within a grading period. These grades are then generally interpreted as indicating whether the student is on track toward meeting the year-end proficiency goals of the state.

Designing Classroom Assessment

Ruiz-Primo et al. (2010) maintain that teachers need robust content knowledge and pedagogy skills as a prerequisite to creating effective CAs. Teachers who have limited content knowledge, pedagogy skills, or both are unable to build their assessments to understand gaps in student understanding. To collect accurate evidence regarding what students know and can do, teachers also need to use robust assessment construction principles with content that is accurately aligned to the state standards. That is, teachers and their students need to make instructional and learning decisions based upon valid and reliable information (Airasian & Jones, 1993).

Researchers have found, however, that most teachers lack the necessary knowledge and skills to create high quality CAs. Many teachers lack expertise in using sound assessment construction principles (Aschbacher, 1999; Haydel, Oescher, & Banbury, 1995; Marso & Pigge, 1993; Plake & Impara, 1997). They have difficulty interpreting state standards (Heritage, Kim, Vendlinski, & Herman, 2009; Llosa, 2005; Schneider & Meyer, 2012; Yap et al., 2007). As a result, teachers often focus their learning targets on recall of knowledge (Brookhart, 2005; Oescher & Kirby, 1990; Sobolewski, 2002); whereas, most state standards are written at higher levels of cognitive complexity with the goal that students transfer what they know in the content area to new contexts. It is not surprising that most teachers do not have the knowledge they need to create high quality CAs because most states do not require that teachers demonstrate proficiency in creating assessments.

Tienken and Wilson (2001) found that 35 states do not require that teachers take a course or demonstrate competency in the area of assessment prior to obtaining teacher certification. Stiggins and Herrick (2007) found that, although competence in assessment is oftentimes addressed in teacher standards adopted by a state, states do not typically require that teachers be formally trained in this area. That is, most states do not require a dedicated assessment course in order to become certified.

Without professional development to improve the technical quality of teacher-created (and teacher-used) assessments, the mismatch of the cognitive complexity and content of classroom instruction and the state standards suggests that many students are inadequately prepared to excel on year-end assessments (Corallo & McDonald, 2001). However, such professional development alone is insufficient if student achievement is to be increased. The research studies described next indicate teachers may also need professional development on how to analyze and then use a student's response to determine next instructional steps that are specific to a student's current level of understanding.

Analyzing Student Understanding

Teachers need to analyze and organize student responses to assessments to identify students who may need additional instructional support on a specific learning target (Ruiz-Primo et al., 2010). Although teachers can review student responses to multiple-choice questions to determine students' misconceptions, most research investigating teacher skill in analyzing student responses has focused on *authentic* student work such as science journals or performance tasks (Aschbacher & Alonzo, 2006; Heritage et al., 2009; Ruiz-Primo et al., 2010; Ruiz-Primo & Li, 2011; Schneider & Gowan, 2011).

Ruiz-Primo et al. (2010) found that most teachers did not typically analyze student work to diagnose the level of student understanding in relation to the learning target. In a separate study, Ruiz-Primo and Li (2011) found that when teachers did so, they inaccurately interpreted responses in 4% of the samples reviewed and either ignored or missed inaccurate student responses in 6% of the cases. And the feedback that most teachers did provide to students involved providing grades, symbols, and simple words or phrases. Teachers *rarely* provided thought-provoking feedback that moved students forward in their learning. Similarly, Aschbacher and Alonzo (2006) also found that teachers either ignored or did not address inaccurate information provided by the student. Because of the sparse research investigating how effectively teachers analyze student work, it is difficult to determine how frequently and how well teachers engage in this important practice that sets the direction for reteaching.

Hoover and Abrams (2011) found that 64% of the teachers in their study reported that instructional pacing prohibited reteaching concepts. When teachers did review summative assessments for instructional purposes, they tended to rely on central tendency data to inform their practice rather than reviewing results at the content standard level. In the Fitzpatrick and Schulz (2010) study, teachers reported adjusting their assessments to match what they already knew their students could do. The teachers rationalized this practice by saying they did not have sufficient time to reteach content given the breadth of the standards they were required to cover. Given these pieces of evidence, it seems likely that in current practice teachers rarely analyze and organize samples of student work as a precursor step to moving the student forward in their learning.

Interim Assessments

Interim assessments (sometimes referred to as benchmark assessments) are standardized, periodic assessments of students throughout a school year or subject course. They are focused on providing information about the knowledge, skills, and processes students have developed within a period of time. Interim assessments are more flexibly administered than their year-end assessment counterparts both in content and in administration windows, and they are administered at a school or district level.

Purpose of Interim Assessments

Perie, Marion, and Gong (2009) delineated three purposes for interim assessments: (1) instruction, (2) evaluation, and (3) prediction. Often, interim assessments are designed with the purpose of meeting multiple goals. The instructional purposes for interim assessments are similar to the formative goals associated with CAs, but the information is collected within a more structured framework. For example, an interim assessment may provide diagnostic profiles of student(s) strengths and weaknesses relative to the curriculum, and it can be used to help educators determine which subskills within a content area need additional focus. Such feedback is typically provided for individual students or students grouped by ability level or by classroom.

Interim assessments are also used by districts and schools to evaluate the effectiveness of particular educational policies or instructional programs (Perie et al., 2009). Districts may use different teaching strategies or remediation programs to improve student learning within schools and examine student performance over multiple administrations of the interim assessments to evaluate the success of the different programs. The evaluative purposes of interim assessments are less focused on immediate instructional feedback to the teacher and students. Rather, district and school-level educators use them to guide the implementation of improvements that will support improved learning for future cohorts of students.

Educators also use interim assessments to predict performance on year-end assessments well in advance of the actual administration. Early identification of students for whom consequences may be applied is often important to educators. Because the varying goals of interim assessments are typically interdependent, they can sometimes be confounded. Therefore, Perie et al. (2009) and Christman et al. (2009) recommended interim assessment users articulate and explicitly prioritize the purpose(s) for administering the assessment as an essential step in meeting their various objectives.

Development of Interim Assessments

Interim assessments may undergo different development procedures depending upon the organization charged with their development and the organization's knowledge level of the *Standards for Educational and Psychological Testing* (American Educational Research Association [AERA], American Psychological Association [APA], & National Council on Measurement in Education [NCME], 1999) and professional item-writing practices. Because of the need to use these assessments throughout the year, professional test developers attend to learning progressions and sequences of instruction as well as to the state standards when developing items. Multiple-choice items are typically developed because of their efficiency and because student responses can provide diagnostic insight regarding misconceptions. Given that Goertz, Oláh, and Riggan (2010) found the interim assessments used in their investigation were not frequently developed using student misconceptions, we recommend users of interim assessments verify that student misconceptions are the basis for creating the incorrect responses for each multiple-choice item.

Professional test developers generally use content area experts to develop items. These individuals have received training in how to align items to state standards, how to write items to higher levels of cognitive complexity, how to use content to vary the difficulty of items, how to use student misconceptions as the basis for creating the wrong alternative for each question, and how to evaluate items. For example, the complexity of a text can make items designed to measure a student's ability to make an inference vary in difficulty. If text associated with a reading passage is easier to read, then the associated items will tend to be easier for students to answer correctly. Once items are written, item editors review the items for content accuracy and clarity and then conduct a bias review. Items are then field tested and reviewed from a statistical perspective prior to being used operationally for an interim assessment.

Analyzing Student Understanding

Goertz et al. (2010) wrote that little research exists on how interim assessments are used by teachers or administrators as well as on the effect that interim assessments have on student achievement as measured by year-end assessments. Christman et al. (2009) conducted a multiyear investigation regarding how teachers and principals used interim results in Philadelphia schools. They found that teachers used results to identify students who were predicted to be on the cusp of moving from one performance level to another so that they could receive targeted intervention. Teachers identified skills that needed to be retaught, identified students with similar strengths and weaknesses, modified classroom routines, and determined professional development needs based upon interim assessment findings.

Nearly all the teachers in the Christman et al. (2009) study reviewed items with students and investigated each item. Shepard (2006) noted that item-by-item teacher review is not an effective method of helping teachers determine what to reteach. Christman et al. (2009) found teachers did not explore the intended purpose of items. That is, teachers neither analyzed the conceptual issues that underpinned the items and related them to standards nor did they contrast easy verses difficult items measuring similar content to better determine what students did and did not understand. As a result, teachers made item-specific instructional decisions and missed the opportunity to use the data to inform their pedagogy.

Goertz et al. (2010) found that teachers use interim assessments to determine what content areas that should be retaught and to identify low performing students. However, teachers did not necessarily delve into the content-based reasons for student mistakes. Riggan and Oláh (2011) found that teachers used interim assessment results to target where they needed to collect additional evidence of student understanding within a content area. Based upon the joint pieces of information, teachers could then reteach. It is likely that the teachers in the last study were more sophisticated users of assessment information.

Year-End Assessment

States administer year-end assessments to gauge how well schools and districts are performing with respect to the state standards. These tests are broad in scope because test content is cumulative and sampled across the state-level content standards to support inferences regarding how much a student can do in relation to all of the state standards. Simply stated, these are summative tests. The term *year-end assessment* can be a misnomer because these assessments are sometimes administered toward the end of a school year, usually in March or April and sometimes during the first semester of the school year.

Purposes for Year-End Assessment

Year-end high-stakes assessments tend to be used for two purposes: (1) information and (2) evaluation. Their primary use is to inform the public of how well students, schools, and districts perform relative to the state standards. Students, parents, and teachers can use the results to compare how their school performs relative to another school. And students, parents, and teachers can examine the student-level reports to gauge global student understanding of the state standards in a particular content area.

The controversy surrounding year-end assessments often stems from the use of aggregate test results to evaluate the performance of students, teachers, schools, and districts relative to one another or to evaluate the effectiveness of an instructional program using test performance. At the student level, the results of a year-end assessment are sometimes used to make promotion and retention decisions or as one factor in awarding high school diplomas. Abrams, Pedulla, and Madaus (2003) demonstrated that teachers overwhelmingly disagreed with using year-end assessments to evaluate teachers but found the practice worthwhile for evaluating students for purposes of high school graduation.

Development of Year-End Assessments

Year-end assessments are created through a well-defined development cycle that is based in the state standards and includes psychometric analysis of the tests. For the purposes of this chapter, we limit our discussion to the development cycle after content standards are established and before psychometric analysis begins.

State standards, which are the foundation of year-end assessments, are often broad statements of the knowledge, skills, and processes that students should possess within a content area. Test blueprints outline how a state wishes to emphasize different aspects of a content area. The test blueprints provide guidance on the numbers and types of items that should be developed for each grade and content area.

Professional test developers write the items. These experts include but are not limited to teachers and former teachers in the content area. Item writers are trained in the art of item writing, including how to align items to content standards, write items to assess higher cognitive complexity, vary the content difficulty of items, and analyze the qualities of a good item. Because the implicit intent of many state standards is that students transfer what they know in the content area to new contexts, typically item writers must also develop stimulus materials to be used in conjunction with a question. The use of stimulus materials is one way to have students show that they can transfer what they have learned to a new context.

Once items and stimulus materials are written they are evaluated through formal processes known as content reviews and bias reviews. For the year-end state assessment, this process typically involves having classroom teachers within the state review the items. During the content review, the teachers evaluate the substance of each item, the structure of the item, the accuracy of the content and correct answer, and the appropriateness of the distracters (alternative answers). The teachers also make judgments regarding the suitability of each item for its assigned grade level and the alignment of the item to the state standards. Educators may recommend that an item be realigned to a different standard, removed from the item pool, or revised.

During the bias review, stakeholders representing diverse groups in the community analyze items for potential unfairness in relationship to race and ethnicity, gender, socioeconomic status, regional status (rural/urban), and/or other variables deemed relevant within a particular state. These stakeholders may recommend that an item be removed from the item pool or revised.

Analyzing Student Understanding

A primary question that emerges after the administration of a year-end assessment is how to analyze and use the results. In the aggregate, these results are used to determine how well students within a school and district have performed. Given that the results of the year-end assessments are generally available after the students have moved to the next grade (or graduated), educators may have little interest in the results of particular individuals. Teachers are interested, however, in how much growth their students demonstrated over a year and whether their class of students met state standards (Yen, 2007).

Educators may examine aggregate year-end information to understand how their students performed on the test overall and on specific subskills. Because the subskill information is necessarily based on a small number of items that are likely not parallel in difficulty from year to year, it is inappropriate to make subskill curricular decisions based only on year-end assessments. Only the total test score should be used for such purposes. For this reason, curricular decisions should be made using multiple sources of assessment information.

A Balanced Assessment System

In a balanced assessment system, teachers use CA, interim assessment, and year-end assessments to monitor and enhance student learning in relation to the state standards and to the state's goals for student proficiency. In this section, we will explore the relationship among the three assessment sources, outline steps for investigating why the information about student learning from these assessment sources may differ, and describe the robust practices teachers can use to move student learning forward.

Relationships Among Assessment Sources

Although CAs, interim assessments, and year-end assessments can have different intended uses, all should measure state standards. We assume that in cases where a district has its own set of standards, these standards are also based in the state standards; however, teachers should verify this to be the case. Teachers, administrators, parents, and students should be able to triangulate data from these three assessment sources and find relatively consistent information about student proficiency in regard to the state standards. Figure 4.1 shows the relationship of the three assessment sources to each other and to the state standards. This figure shows that CAs cover both the breadth and depth of the state standards, the interim assessments sample portions of the state content standards at multiple points in time during the school year but less frequently than the CAs, and the year-end assessment samples the state standards covering the breadth but not the depth of the standards at a single point in time.

The figure demonstrates that each assessment source should provide information to the teacher and the student. The knowledge, skills, and processes measured in the CAs will overlap with knowledge, skills, and processes measured by the interim assessments and by the year-end assessment. CAs should cover these knowledge, skills, and process in more depth than either the interim assessment or year-end assessments.

Teachers must understand where students need to be by the end of the year to be proficient. Through teachers' evaluations of the evidence they have collected from students, they must identify whether or not a student is likely to be considered proficient on the year-end assessment given good instruction and multiple opportunities to learn. Interim benchmarks should be used to confirm or disconfirm what the teacher finds to be true in his or her own classroom. When what a teacher predicts is disconfirmed on an interim benchmark assessment, the teacher needs to investigate why a different picture of student performance has emerged.

Steps to Investigate Performance Differences Between Classroom and Large-Scale Assessments

Step 1: Compare What Is Being Measured

Sometimes, teachers consider variables other than student achievement when measuring student achievement in the content area. For example, teachers and principals frequently believe it is ethical to (1) consider student effort or class participation when determining grades, (2) weight homework heavily in the calculation of grades (which a student may not complete independently), or (3) to lower grades for missing or late work (Green, Johnson, Kim, & Pope, 2007; Johnson, Green, Kim, & Pope, 2008). Johnson et al. (2008) wrote that educators who modify grades or test scores because of student effort, late work, or behavior problems do not accurately communicate the student's level of mastery of the learning target. In such instances, different interpretations of student achievement may be expected across the three assessment sources as interim assessments and year-end assessments are designed to measure what a student knows and can do in relation to state standards.

Step 2: Compare How Items Are Aligned to the State Standards

Different pictures of student proficiency can emerge across the three assessment sources due to the complexity of item alignment. Item

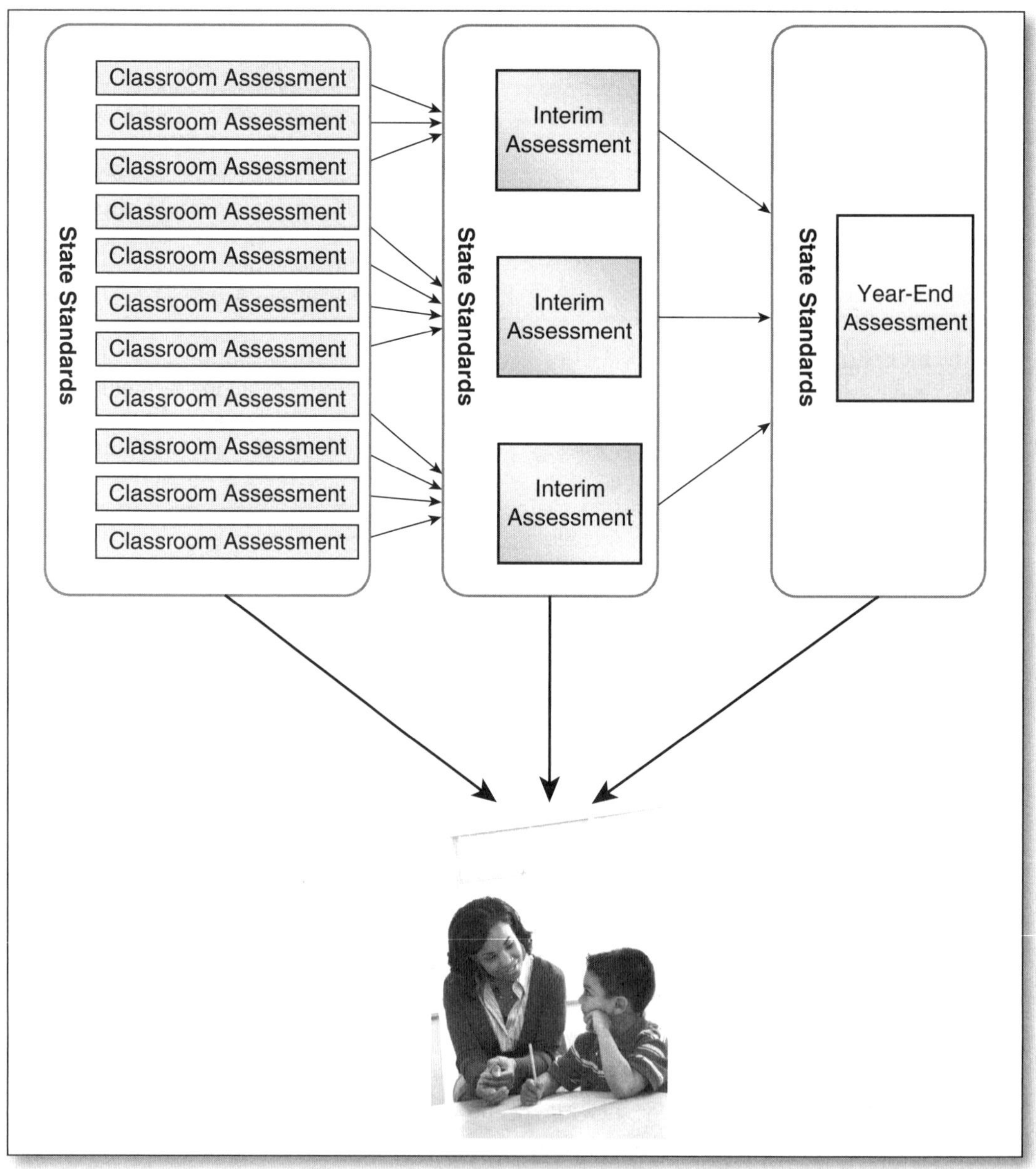

Figure 4.1 Triangulating Information About Student Learning in a Balanced Assessment System

SOURCE: Photo courtesy of iStock.

alignment is central to test score interpretation on any assessment. Because of this, year-end assessment items undergo standards alignment reviews to provide indicators showing the degree to which they exactly match the content and cognitive complexity of the state standards. This is an inferential process, meaning it is a complex cognitive process unto itself.

Within the item alignment process, Webb, Herman, and Webb (2007) noted a certain amount of rater disagreement is caused by differences in how raters interpret state standards. The interpretation of state standards is centered in the expected cognitive complexity in which students are expected to manipulate the content. The confusion is evidenced by the disagreement observed in rater agreement indexes reported in alignment studies (Webb et al., 2007) and the difficulty teachers' have in developing CAs that match rigorous state standards (Carter, 1984; Fleming & Chambers, 1983; Marso & Pigge, 1993). As may be expected, professional test developers appear to be more consistent in their interpretations of standards than are teachers (Nasstrom, 2009).

States use different item alignment policy models within K–12 high-stakes testing, but Webb's (2005) depth of knowledge procedure is the most common process used to conduct item alignment. The item alignment policy model a state uses on the year end assessment it develops and administers is central to how standards should be interpreted and measured by teachers in the classroom.

In the most common policy model, 50% of a test's items have to be aligned at or above the cognitive level of the state standard (Webb et al., 2007) to achieve depth of knowledge consistency. Under this model, the state standards represent the *minimum* a student should know and be able to do at the end of the year. That is, a student is expected to grow beyond what is specified in the standards during the year. Other states use a policy model requiring that items on the year-end assessment match the level specified in the state standard. Under this model, the state standards represent what a student should know and be able to do by the end of the year. This aspect of large-scale assessment is not always transparent to teachers. Without a transparent item alignment process that is shared with teachers, it is not unexpected that what is taught and measured in the classroom may differ than what is measured on interim assessments and summative assessments. For this reason, we recommend that teachers ensure they understand the alignment policy model used in their state and match that policy in their own classroom.

Step 3: Review Student Work From Classroom Assessments

Riggan and Oláh (2011) reported teachers needed to collect additional evidence of student understanding within a content area to use interim assessment results for formative purposes. Although this may be necessary, it is also likely that if teachers keep student work on file, they can review student work on CAs that measured the same standards. This will help teachers develop a path of instruction for the student instead of resorting to teaching students many mini-lessons based upon an item-by-item analysis from the interim assessment.

We recommend that the teacher review the state's performance level descriptor (PLD) for its year-end assessment. These descriptors, which define the likely knowledge, skills, and abilities of students in each performance level, are commonly found on state department of education websites, score reports, and test interpretation guides. PLDs do not describe all things a proficient student is likely able to do in relation to the state standards. However, PLDs should give the teacher a sense of how much of the knowledge, skills, and processes described in the standards a student should possess to be considered, for example, proficient.

Once the teacher identifies the subskill content area weaknesses based upon results from an interim benchmark, those subskill areas should reviewed in the PLD. This will help the teacher conceptualize what the target of expected performance looks like on the year-end assessment. Next, the teacher can analyze samples of student work that are on file from that same standard. Those assessment samples can be reviewed for cognitive complexity in relation to the standard and to the cognitive complexity of tasks described in the PLD to ensure the targets match.

Assuming the teacher finds a match in the cognitive expectations found in the CA, the standard, and the state's PLD describing proficient students, the teacher should analyze the student work on the CAs for the subskill. Table 4.1 shows a Grade 3 mathematics PLD from a large-scale assessment program in South Carolina, and Figure 4.2 shows a Grade 3 mathematics student response to performance task that we will analyze and then compare to the PLD.

On this task, the student correctly shaded in the fraction 3/4; however, we do not have sufficient evidence that the student understands how to model fractions for two reasons. First, in the written explanation the student appears to be targeting the magnitude of numbers in his or her comparison rather than comparing the parts of a whole in the two models. Second, the student is not able to shade the fraction 2/3 onto the first grid. It is likely that the student is simply shading the number of columns on the grid based on the numerator of each fraction without analyzing how to divide the model into the parts denoted by the denominator. Although the student identified that 2/3 is smaller than 3/4, the student did not use adequate mathematical vocabulary to describe why one fraction is smaller than the other and did not show that he conceptualized what a fraction represents.

Below Basic	
What *below basic* students likely can do • estimate whole number computations • perform basic operations with whole numbers • identify simple number sentences and expressions • identify simple patterns • identify common two- and three-dimensional geometric figures and properties • read tables and perform simple computations based upon the data	**What *below basic* students likely cannot do** • solve problems requiring more than one step or operation • alternate between two types of patterns • apply straightforward concepts of probability • use basic mathematics vocabulary
Basic	
What *basic* students likely can do that *below basic* students likely cannot do • solve problems requiring more than one step or operation • alternate between two types of patterns • apply straightforward concepts of probability • use basic mathematics vocabulary	**What *basic* students likely cannot do** • interpret and translate pictorial representations of mathematical concepts • conceptualize fractions and division • apply straightforward measurement concepts • read and interpret scales when the units of the scale are indicated • translate language into numerical concepts
Proficient	
What *proficient* students likely can do that basic students likely cannot do • interpret and translate pictorial representations of mathematical concepts • conceptualize fractions and division • apply straightforward measurement concepts • read and interpret scales when the units of the scales are indicated • translate language into numerical concepts	**What *proficient* students likely cannot do** • make connections among mathematic concepts • communicate their mathematical thinking and reasoning clearly and coherently • use spatial sense • solve long and more complex problems • solve problems requiring approaches that are not commonly used
Advanced	
What *advanced* students likely can do that *proficient* students likely cannot do • make connections among mathematic concepts • communicate mathematical thinking and reasoning clearly and coherently • use spatial sense • solve long and more complex problems • solve problems requiring approaches that are not commonly used	

Table 4.1 Sample South Carolina Performance Level Descriptor for Grade 3 Mathematics

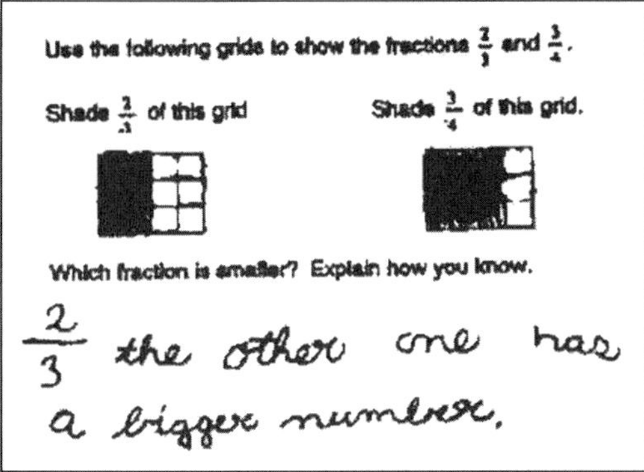

Figure 4.2 Released Item From Grade 3 Mathematics Item and Student Response From South Carolina

SOURCE: South Carolina State Department of Education.

How does the information gained about this student from the performance task align to the performance profiles depicted in the PLD? The proficient Grade 3 student is able to conceptualize fractions and division. The student's performance is inconsistent with a proficient student based upon this single performance task. Similarly, the basic Grade 3 student is able to solve problems that require more than one step and is able to use basic mathematics vocabulary. The student's performance is also inconsistent with a basic student; therefore, we conclude the student's performance is likely similar to that of a below basic student based upon his present level of performance.

This student needs to develop a conceptual understanding of fractions, needs to explain his thinking using the vocabulary of the discipline, and needs to be able to solve straight computation and word problems that use more than one operation. These are multiple skill areas that need to grow, and they go beyond a single item. Based upon this information, the teacher can now determine what additional instruction should occur to support this student's growth. Although we used one performance task to exemplify this process, a classroom teacher should use multiple pieces of CA evidence to analyze the student's content-based current level of performance. The teacher can now compare his or her learning path profile with the predicted performance and determine what knowledge, skills, or processes the student needs to develop to meet the state's conceptualization of proficiency.

Assessment Practices That Facilitate Student Learning

In addition to measuring student learning, a subset of assessment practices can also help students move information into their long-term memory. In this section, we merge research from the CA and cognitive psychology areas to recommend CA practices that teachers can use to help students learn skills that are measured on high-stakes assessments.

Multiple-Choice Items

Teachers are generally not trained to elicit evidence of student learning using a variety of item types. Unfortunately, teachers and administrators sometimes view CA as an opportunity to mimic the item types used on year-end assessments. If all multiple-choice items are used on the year-end assessments then educators will tend to use only multiple-choice items in their classrooms (Abrams et al., 2003). Although this practice is likely caused by the influence of high-stakes assessment on CA, and it may ensure that students are familiar with the multiple-choice item type, this practice surely has unintended consequences for student learning.

Well-constructed multiple-choice items present incorrect answers based upon common misconceptions students have in regard to the content being measured. When a student selects the wrong alternative, his or her misconception may be reinforced. That is, the student may learn the information incorrectly because the misunderstanding is reinforced. This is called a negative suggestion effect. The negative suggestion effect does not mean that multiple-choice items should not be used with students, but it does suggest that teachers need to review the correct answers and cognitive processes needed to answer the question with students after the test has been administered. Butler and Roediger (2006) found that if teachers provided corrective feedback to the students after taking a multiple-choice test, the negative suggestion effect was eliminated.

Performance Tasks

Year-end assessments often use multiple-choice items for standardization, time efficiency, and cost savings purposes. However, the value of high quality performance tasks should not be diminished and should be encouraged as an important tool in CA. Roediger and Karpicke (2006) and McDaniel, Roediger, and McDermott (2007) found when students generate written responses to open-ended items they are better able to retain the information than when they are tested with multiple-choice items. Often the writing of responses helps students retain the information better than simply studying the material.

Newmann, Bryk, and Nagaoka (2001) found that students who routinely received performance tasks that required a generated response connected to content beyond school and went beyond simply reproducing knowledge scored higher on the year-end assessments than peers who had not received such assignments. Performance tasks are ways to engage students in tasks of higher cognitive complexity. They provide evidence regarding the level of student understanding that a teacher can analyze, and they provide the teacher the opportunity to provide the student feedback.

Feedback

Sadler (1989) noted that teacher feedback is effective when it identifies the gap between what is understood and the learning target. Before providing feedback, teachers must first determine whether the student is a good candidate for it. Hattie and Timperley (2007) wrote that when students do not have partial understanding of the learning target, feedback techniques are not effective. These students need to be retaught the material from the beginning. But for students who have partial knowledge, providing feedback can help them recognize and correct their misconception or confusion in regard to the learning target or extend their current level of understanding. This is only likely to happen, however, if students are expected to revise and resubmit their work to the teacher.

To provide effective feedback, the teacher must provide the student information on *how* to move toward mastering the learning target (Hattie & Timperley, 2007). Feedback should not address variables extraneous to the learning target (e.g., correct spelling or neatness when answering a social studies question). Teachers can provide follow-up directions on where to go for information to correct an answer or ask that students provide more details on a particular topic. Such feedback is considered corrective. Attali and Powers (2010) studied the effect providing corrective feedback coupled with a revision requirement for CR items on the scores of college-level students taking a high-stakes exam. Twenty-six percent of the students who revised their responses answered correctly on the second attempt.

Hattie and Timperley (2007) also wrote that feedback can address the processes required to solve a task. When teachers use process-based feedback, they may remind the student of the grading criteria the student may not have addressed or processes previously demonstrated in class. They ask the student to connect the criteria or processes to their own work. Finally, effective feedback can also be used to encourage students to engage in self-regulation. Teachers use self-regulated feedback to help the student evaluate his or her own work and find his or her own errors. Students who are high performing are likely best served by self-regulated feedback or process-based feedback.

Rubrics

Rubrics are another tool to assist students as they engage in the self-regulated learning (SRL) process (see Andrade, 2010; also see Chapter 2 of this volume). Self-assessment is a student driven process in which a student reflects on the attributes of his or her own work, analyzes how well his or her work meets the stipulated criteria, and revises to better meet the criteria (Andrade & Boulay, 2003). When teachers facilitate a culture of critique in their classroom and use high quality student work exemplars, they explicate what good student performance and modes of thinking look like. Research has indicated that such modeling techniques have assisted poor writers improve content, development, and voice in their writing (Andrade, Du, & Wang, 2008; Ross, Rolheiser, & Hogaboam-Gray, 1999) and increase skill in using mathematics vocabulary and in solving word problems (Ross, Hogaboam-Gray, & Rolheiser, 2002; Stallings & Tascione, 1996). These are important components of the constructs measured on year-end assessments.

Future Directions

Substantially more research is needed to determine how often and how accurately teachers analyze and use evidence of student learning to determine next instructional steps based on classroom, interim, and year-end assessment findings. Similarly, more research is needed to determine the quantity and quality of teacher feedback and reteaching based upon classroom, interim, and year-end assessment results. There are currently few experimental designs that have investigated the effects of CA practices and interim assessment practices on student achievement as measured by year-end assessments. Until we better understand strengths and weaknesses in teachers' abilities to use evidence of student learning to support instruction, professional development specialists and researchers will be unable to determine optimal methods of supporting teachers in this endeavor.

It may be necessary for states to carefully document how its standards should be interpreted and assessed. One such example may be found in South Carolina. For each content area, the state provides a support document that explains the content that is relevant to the standard and content that is not, the cognitive expectation for each standard, and appropriate ways to measure student performance of the standard (P. Gowan, personal communication, January 26, 2012). A second tool to assist in this process may be to create sample performance tasks for teachers to use in the classroom that exemplify the intended outcome of a particular standard. Such samples optimally include scoring rubrics and representative student responses for each score point. Along with providing an interpretation of the responses to assist teachers in analyzing and interpreting the work of their own students, the state might also provide a rationale regarding how the task is aligned to the standard and ideas for moving students at each score point forward in their learning. Research should also be undertaken to determine if such a practice improves teacher understanding of the state learning targets.

Developers of interim assessments might also research how to optimally report results from this assessment type. Neither Christman et al. (2009) nor Shepard (2006) supported the notion of item-by-item analysis as an effective method of helping teachers determine what to reteach. Perhaps one solution is to develop student profiles based on test results that not only predict how the student will perform by the end of the year but that also describe what specific skills the student needs to acquire to meet the state proficiency goal. District policy makers should also engage in their own research by investigating the cognitive and content alignment of interim assessment items to ensure they match state standards. CAs should also be investigated from this perspective.

Implications for Classroom Assessment

As a result of the ubiquitous use of interim and year-end assessments teachers now have a new, pervasive large-scale testing context, which they must pay attention to when designing, interpreting, and analyzing results from their CAs. The National Board for Professional Teaching Standards (NBPTS) (2003) in *Adolescence and Young Adulthood: English Language Arts* posited that the accomplished teacher is one who is well versed in the uses and purposes of a variety of assessment tools, shares grading criteria with students prior to assessment, interprets assessment data accurately, and uses data gathered from varied sources of assessments to inform instruction. Central to these attributes is the NBPTS English language arts teacher's ability to interconnect the standards, curriculum, instruction, CAs, and statewide summative assessments. Many of these NBPTS English language arts goals echo those presented in the *Standards for Teacher Competence in Educational Assessment of Students* (American Federation of Teachers [AFT], NCME, & National Education Association [NEA], 1990).

Accurately interpreting state standards is certainly a necessary but not sufficient condition for successfully implementing CA practices. Teachers must also accurately analyze and interpret evidence of student learning and then use that information to help close the gap between the student's present level of performance and the performance required to meet the learning target. Heritage et al. (2009) wrote, "A review of recent literature suggests there is little or no extant research that has investigated teachers' abilities to adapt instruction based on assessment of student knowledge and understanding" (p. 24). The CA and interim assessment research we reviewed in this area shows this is a key area in need of study. It appears that teachers may need much more support in creating, analyzing, and using information from CA and interim assessment than they currently receive. The skills teachers need to acquire to become proficient creators and users of assessment information likely take years to cultivate.

Optimally, teachers select the types of items they give students based upon what it is they want students to learn, what it is they want to measure, and what time constraints they find within the classroom. Just as assessment items built for high-stakes purposes follow a set of written guidelines and undergo multiple content reviews prior to being field tested, teachers should ensure that the items they use in the classroom follow best construction practices and are reviewed by multiple teachers. When teachers ask their colleagues to review their assessments along with corresponding student responses, there is an opportunity to catch unintentional item development errors that can lead to erroneous conclusions about student learning and an opportunity to discuss pedagogy and the intent of state standards.

When teachers rely on CA practices that are best suited to analyzing student learning, they can then link information from performance on a particular assessment to the selection of instructional actions for which implementation leads to gains in student learning (Nichols, Meyers, & Burling, 2009). These are teachers who focus on understanding student learning in relation to the state standards and teach for transfer. They will find their students to be better learners and higher achievers. And these teachers will not place their focus on the *context* of high-stakes assessment. They will place their focus on what a student should know and how to get them there.

References

Abrams, L. M., Pedulla, J. J., & Madaus, G. F. (2003). Views from the classroom: Teachers' opinions of statewide testing programs. *Theory Into Practice, 42*(1), 18–29.

Airasian, P. W. & Jones, A. M. (1993). The teachers as applied measurer: Realities of classroom measurement and assessment. *Applied Measurement in Education, 6*(3), 241–254.

American Educational Research Association, American Psychological Association, & National Council on Measurement in Education. (1999). *Standards for educational and psychological testing.* Washington, DC: American Educational Research Association.

American Federation of Teachers, National Council on Measurement in Education, & National Education Association. (1990). *Standards for teacher competence in educational assessment of students.* Washington, DC: Authors.

Andrade, H. (2010). Students as the definitive source of formative assessment: Academic self-assessment and the self-regulation of learning. In H. L. Andrade & G. J. Cizek (Eds.), *Handbook of formative assessment* (pp. 90–105). New York: Routledge.

Andrade, H., & Boulay, B. (2003). The role of rubric-referenced self-assessment in learning to write. *Journal of Educational Research, 97*(1), 21–34.

Andrade, H. L., Du, Y., & Wang, X. (2008). Putting rubrics to the test: The effect of model, criteria generation, and rubric-referenced self-assessment on elementary school students' writing. *Educational Measurement: Issues and Practice, 27*(2), 3–13.

Aschbacher, P. R. (1999). *Developing indicators of classroom practice to monitor and support school reform* (CRESST Technical Report 513). Los Angeles: University of California, Center for Research on Educational Standards and Student Testing. Retrieved from http://research.cse.ucla.edu/Reports/TECH513.pdf

Aschbacher, P. R., & Alonzo, A. (2006). Examining the utility of elementary science notebooks for formative assessment purposes. *Educational Assessment, 11*(3), 179–203.

Attali, Y., & Powers, D. (2010). Immediate feedback and opportunity to revise answers to open ended questions. *Educational and Psychological Measurement, 70*(1), 22–35.

Brookhart, S. M. (2005, April). *Research on formative classroom assessment.* Paper presented at the annual meeting of the American Educational Research Association, Montreal, Canada.

Brookhart, S. M. (2010). Mixing it up: Combining sources of classroom achievement information for formative and summative purposes. In H. L. Andrade & G. J. Cizek (Eds.), *Handbook of formative assessment* (pp. 279–296). New York: Routledge.

Brookhart, S. M., Moss, C. M., & Long, B. A. (2008, March). *Professional development in formative assessment: Effects on teacher and student learning.* Paper presented at the annual meeting of the National Council on Measurement in Education, New York.

Butler, A. C., & Roediger, H. L., III. (2006). Feedback neutralizes the detrimental effects of multiple choice testing. Unpublished manuscript, Washington University in St. Louis, MO.

Carter, K. (1984). Do teachers understand the principles for writing tests? *Journal of Teacher Education, 35,* 57–60.

Christman, J., Neild, R., Bulkley, K., Blanc, S., Liu, R., Mitchell, C., et al. (2009). *Making the most of interim assessment data. Lessons from Philadelphia.* Philadelphia: Research for Action.

Corallo, C., & McDonald D. (2001). *What works with low-performing schools: A review of research literature on low-performing schools.* Charleston, WV: AEL. (ERIC Document Reproduction Service No. ED462737)

Fitzpatrick, B., & Schulz, H. (2010, May). *Assessing higher order thinking: What teachers think and do.* Paper presented at the meeting of the American Educational Research Association, Denver, CO.

Fleming, M., & Chambers, B. (1983). Teacher-made tests: Windows on the classroom. In W. E. Hathaway (Ed.), *Testing in the schools. New directions for testing and measurement* (pp. 29–38). San Francisco: Jossey-Bass.

Goertz, M. E., Oláh, L. N., & Riggan, M. (2010). *From testing to teaching: The use of interim assessments in classroom instruction.* Philadelphia: Consortium for Policy Research in Education.

Green, S., Johnson, R., Kim, D, & Pope, N. (2007). Ethics in classroom assessment practices: Issues and attitudes. *Teaching and Teacher Education, 23*(7), 999–1011.

Hattie, J., & Timperley, H. (2007). The power of feedback. *Review of Educational Research, 77,* 81–112.

Haydel, J. B., Oescher, J., & Banbury, M. (1995, April). *Assessing classroom teachers' performance assessments.* Paper presented at the annual meeting of the American Educational Research Association, San Francisco.

Heritage, M., Kim, J., Vendlinski, T., & Herman, J. (2009). From evidence to action: A seamless process in formative assessment? *Educational Measurement: Issues and Practice, 28*(3), 24–31.

Hoover, N. R., & Abrams, L. M. (2011, April). *Teachers instructional use of student assessment data.* Paper presented at the meeting of the American Educational Research Association, New Orleans, LA.

Johnson, R., Green, S., Kim, D., & Pope, N. (2008). Educational leaders' perceptions about ethical assessment practices. *The American Journal of Evaluation, 29*(4), 520–530.

Llosa, L. (2005). Assessing English learners' language proficiency: A Qualitative Investigation of Teachers' Interpretations of the California ELD standards. *The CATSOEL Journal, 17*(1), 7–18.

Marso, R. N., & Pigge, F. L. (1993). Teachers' testing knowledge, skills, and practices. In S. L. Wise (Ed.), *Teacher training in measurement and assessment skills* (pp. 129–185). Lincoln: Buros Institute of Mental Measurements, University of Nebraska-Lincoln.

McDaniel, M. A., Roediger, H. L., & McDermott, K. B. (2007). Generalizing test-enhanced learning from the laboratory to the classroom. *Psychonomic Bulletin & Review, 14*(2). 200–206.

Nasstrom, G. (2009). Interpretations of standards with Bloom's revised taxonomy: A comparison of teachers and assessment experts. *International Journal of Research & Method in Education, 32*(1), 39–51.

National Board for Professional Teaching Standards. (2003). *Adolescence and young adulthood: English language arts.* Retrieved from www.nbpts.org/the_standards/standards_by_cert?ID=2&x=49&y=4

Newmann, F., Bryk, A. S., & Nagaoka, J. K. (2001). *Authentic intellectual work and standardized tests: Conflict or coexistence?* Retrieved from http://ccsr.uchicago.edu/publications/p0a02.pdf

Nichols, P. D., Meyers, J. L., & Burling, K. S. (2009). A framework for evaluating and planning assessments intended to improve student achievement. *Educational Measurement: Issuesand Practice, 28*(3), 14–33.

Oescher, J., & Kirby, P. C. (1990). *Assessing teacher-made tests in secondary math and science classrooms.* Paper presented at the annual meeting of the National Council on Measurement in Education, Boston. (ERIC Document Reproduction Service No. ED322169)

Perie, M., Marion, S., & Gong, B. (2009). Moving toward a comprehensive assessment system: A framework for considering interim assessments. *Educational Measurement: Issues and Practice, 28,* 5–13.

Plake, B. S., & Impara, J. C. (1997). Teacher assessment literacy: What do teachers know about assessment? In G. D. Phye (Ed.), *Handbook of classroom assessment, learning, adjustment, and achievement.* San Diego, CA: Academic Press.

Riggan, M., & Oláh, L. A. (2011). Locating interim assessments within teachers' assessment practice, *Educational Assessment, 16*(1), 1–14.

Roediger, H. L. & Karpicke, J. D. (2006). The power of testing memory: Basic research and implications for educational practice. *Perspectives on Psychological Science, 1,* 181–210.

Ross, J. A., Hogaboam-Gray, A., & Rolheiser, C. (2002). Student self-evaluation in grade 5–6 mathematics effects on problem solving achievement. *Educational Assessment, 8*(1), 43–59.

Ross, J. A., Rolheiser, C., & Hogaboam-Gray, A. (1999). Effects of self-evaluation training on narrative writing. *Assessing Writing, 6*(1), 107–132.

Ruiz-Primo, M. A. Furtak, E., Yin, Y., Ayala, C., & Shavelson, R. J. (2010). On the impact of formative assessment on student science learning and motivation. In H. L. Andrade & G. J. Cizek (Eds.), *Handbook of formative assessment* (pp. 139–158). New York: Routledge.

Ruiz-Primo, M. A., & Li, M. (2011, April). *Looking into the teachers' feedback practices: How teachers interpret students' work.* Paper presented at the meeting of the American Educational Research Association, New Orleans, LA.

Sadler, D. (1989). Formative assessment and the design of instructional systems, *Instructional Science, 18,* 119–144.

Schneider, C., & Gowan, P. (2011, April). *Deconstructing student work: Investigating teachers abilities to use evidence of student learning to inform instruction.* Paper presented at the meeting of the American Educational Research Association, New Orleans, LA.

Schneider, M. C. & Meyer, J. P. (2012). Investigating the efficacy of a professional development program in formative classroom assessment in middle school English language arts and mathematics. *Journal of Multidisciplinary Evaluation 8*(17), 1–24.

Shepard, L. A. (2006). Classroom assessment. In R. L. Brennen (Ed.), *Educational measurement* (4th ed.). Westport, CT: Praeger.

Sobolewski, K. B. (2002). *Gender equity in classroom questioning.* Unpublished doctoral dissertation, South Carolina State University, Orangeburg.

Stallings, V., & Tascione, C. (1996). Student self-assessment and self-evaluation. *Mathematics Teacher, 89,* 548–55.

Stiggins, R. J., & Herrick M. (2007). A status report on teacher preparation in classroom assessment. Unpublished research report, Classroom Assessment Foundation, Portland, OR.

Tienken, C., & Wilson, M. (2001). Using state standards and tests to improve instruction. *Practical Assessment, Research & Evaluation, 7*(13). Retrieved from http://pareonline.net/getvn.asp?v=7&n=13

U.S. Department of Education. (2002). *No Child Left Behind Act of 2001* (Title I Paraprofessionals: Draft Non-Regulatory Guidance). Washington, DC: U.S. Department of Education, Office of Elementary and Secondary Education.

Webb, N. L. (2005). *Web alignment tool (WAT): Training manual.* Draft Version 1.1. Wisconsin Center for Education Research, Council of Chief State School Officers. Retrieved from www.wcer.wisc.edu/wat/index.aspx

Webb, N. M., Herman, J. L., & Webb, N. L. (2007). Alignment of mathematics' state-level standards and assessments: The role of reviewer agreement. *Educational Measurement: Issues and Practice, 26,* 17–29.

Wiliam, D., Lee, C., Harrison, C., & Black, P. (2004). Teachers developing assessment for learning: Impact on student achievement. *Assessment in Education, 11*(1), 49–65.

Yap, C. C., Pearsall, T., Morgan, G., Wu, M., Maganda, F., Gilmore, J., et al. (2007). *Evaluation of a professional development program in classroom assessment: 2006–07.* Columbia, SC: University of South Carolina, Office of Program Evaluation.

Yen, W. M. (2007). Vertical scaling and No Child Left Behind. In N. J. Dorans, M. Pommerich, & P. W. Holland (Eds.), *Linking and aligning scores and scales* (pp. 273–282). New York: Springer.

5

Research on Teacher Competency in Classroom Assessment

Cynthia Campbell

As an educational interest in its own right, throughout the years, the purpose and role of classroom assessment (CA) has not been well understood by many educators and consequently has led to its broad definition, implementation, and use. Reflected in this diverseness, phrases such as "tests and measurement" and "student evaluation" have been used interchangeably to describe CA. For many years, CA was viewed predominately as an activity conducted by teachers at the end of instruction as a means for determining the extent of student learning and assigning grades. With advances in understanding about the learning process, CA is now considered a multipurposed activity that can extend over time, occurring before, during, and following instruction. It is an activity that is beneficial to teachers and students alike.

Research investigating evaluation practices of classroom teachers has consistently reported concern about the adequacy of their assessment knowledge and skills. Variations in measurement knowledge and training have been proposed as possible culprits for practicing teachers' assessment difficulties (Stiggins, Frisbie, & Griswold, 1989). For example, inconsistency in teacher scoring of constructed-response (CR) items has been found (Barnes, 1985; Stiggins, 1992; Stiggins & Bridgeford, 1985). Other problematic practices, such as considering nonachievement factors when assigning grades, have been identified through teacher self-report (Barnes, 1985; Brookhart, 1994; Frary, Cross, & Weber, 1993; Griswold, 1993; Hills, 1991; Jongsma, 1991; McMillan, Myran, & Workman, 2002; Stiggins et al., 1989). One implication from these findings is that preservice training in CA has been less than adequate. Another implication is that certain personal characteristics (i.e., attitude and perceived self-efficacy) and cooperating teachers' feedback during supervision of student teachers' assessment practice may have overridden or potentially modified the effects of formal instruction.

The purpose of this chapter is to present a brief overview of the historical context and evolution of research in teacher knowledge and skills in CA as we know it today.

Terms such as *educational measurement* and *tests and measurement* are intentionally preserved to reflect the particular language of the study investigations and conclusions. Such descriptions seem to reflect an era-based understanding of the role and utility of assessment in the classroom (i.e., from an indicator of student learning to an indicator about learning). Also in this chapter, studies examining large-scale school accountability testing, IQ and ability testing, and other assessments of educational interest will not be discussed but rather will be limited to research that has examined various aspects of assessment that pertain directly to the day-to-day activities and decisions of teachers and students within the classroom. Collectively, this chapter aims to describe a chronological and fundamental shift in thinking about the kinds of information that CA should provide along with the manner in which such data are collected and prioritized. In this chapter, teacher skill in CA will be discussed in its major progressions—from assessment *of* learning, to assessment *for* learning (AFL), to assessment *as* learning, although such movements are not necessarily linear. Moreover, it is important to point out that this chapter is not intended to cite all studies investigating teacher assessment competency and practice but rather to present a retrospective sampling of major initiatives and findings.

Research Investigating Teacher Preparation and Competency in Assessment

Teacher competency in CA has been researched for nearly 60 years. Throughout this time, studies have examined what teachers should know and be able to do compared with what they actually know and are skilled in. For example, in 1955, Noll examined mandates for teacher certification and found that very few states required teachers to demonstrate competency in tests and measurement. Additionally, Noll (1955) found that universities by and large did not require prospective teachers to complete coursework in assessment course as a condition of graduation. More than a decade later, Goslin (1967) surveyed 1,450 teachers from 75 public secondary schools sampled across the United States about whether they had a course in tests and measurement. Although less than 25% reported having taken such a course, Goslin's broad definition of tests and measurement, which included topics such as *analysis of the individual*, may have artificially inflated the percentage of teachers reporting having had a course in tests and measurement.

In 1967, Mayo was interested in learning to what extent direct experience in the classroom might affect teachers' assessment knowledge and skills. A random sample of 2,877 senior education majors completed a Measurement Competency Test as a baseline measure. Preservice teachers' scores revealed limited competency in measurement. Two years after graduation, pretest–posttest score comparison ($N = 541$) indicated very small increases in beginning teachers' assessment competency, although such gains were positively related to having had coursework in tests and measurement. Mayo recommended that teacher preparation programs include coursework in assessment as part of the required curriculum. Such findings foreshadowed future decades of research investigating similar concerns.

Relatedly, Hills (1977) reported that Florida accountability coordinators estimated that only 25% of teachers demonstrated evidence of having had effective training in tests and measurement but overwhelmingly believed that requiring assessment coursework during undergraduate training and in-service training would be of value.

When preparing paper-and-pencil exams, Carter (1984) found that teachers spent little time editing or revising tests and reported greater difficulty writing test items that assess higher cognitive processing than developing items that measure lower-level skills. Examining the assessment practices and assessment products created or selected by student teachers, Campbell and Evans (2000) found that, despite having had a specific course in CA, transfer of assessment knowledge and skills was overwhelming absent.

Research continued to document teachers' assessment skills as generally weak (Campbell & Evans, 2000; Cizek, 2000; Cizek, Fitzgerald, & Rachor, 1995; Daniel & King, 1998; Schafer, 1993; Trevison, 2002; Wise, Lukin, & Roos, 1991). Teacher-made tests were often poorly constructed, and the results were frequently interpreted inaccurately (Boothroyd, McMorris, & Pruzek, 1992; Daniel & King, 1998; Hills, 1991; Marso & Pigge, 1993). Moreover, unlike lesson planning or classroom management skills, a deliberate monitoring of teachers' competency in assessment tended to be overlooked in the evaluation process. Hills (1991) wrote, "You would have a hard time finding in the entire U. S. even a single teacher whose career was adversely affected by abysmal ignorance of these skills" (p. 545).

In their literature review of studies investigating teacher assessment practices, Marso and

Pigge (1993) reported that teachers tend to use objectively scored test items (e.g., binary, multiple-choice, and matching) to assess student learning more frequently than nontraditional assessment methods. Yet despite the preference for paper–pencil testing, teachers did not always adhere to item-writing guidelines when constructing their classroom tests.

Investigating the quality of CAs (in particular validity and reliability), Mertler (2000) found teachers' assessment techniques to be less than desired. As a result, Mertler recommended professional development and improved teacher preparation in assessment techniques. Two years later, Green and Mantz (2002) surveyed preservice teachers' CA practices from the perspective of the supervising in-service teacher. Participants ($n = 106$) included in-service supervisors of prekindergarten through Grade 12 preservice teachers. Supervisors were asked to comment on their student teachers' use of a variety of assessment methods. In-service supervisors indicated that the student teachers predominately used informal methods such as oral questioning and guided practice to inform their decisions about instructional effectiveness and student learning. Although these supervising teachers believed that their supervisees had good assessment skills, they indicated that preservice teachers would benefit if their educational preparation had a greater emphasis on assessment and that such training should be a priority.

Brookhart (2001) summarized research from 1990 to 2001 regarding teacher competence in the assessment skills described in the *Standards for Teacher Competence in the Educational Assessment of Students* (American Federation of Teachers [AFT], National Council on Measurement in Education [NCME], & National Education Association [NEA], 1990). She reported that teachers have difficulty (1) selecting (Aschbacher, 1999; Marso & Pigge, 1993) and creating (Aschbacher, 1999; Marso & Pigge, 1993) CAs relative to instructional purpose, (2) using assessment results to make decisions about instructional effectiveness and student learning (McMillan & Nash, 2000; Zhang & Burry-Stock, 1997), (3) devising valid and reliable grading procedures (Brookhart, 1994; McMillan & Nash, 2000), and (4) communicating the results of assessment to students and interested others (Impara, Divine, Bruce, Liverman, & Gay, 1991; Plake, Impara, & Fager, 1993). Brookhart (2001) pointed out that although participant sampling was a limitation of these studies (e.g., convenience), collectively, the findings indicated that "Teachers apparently do better at classroom applications than at interpreting standardized tests," "lack expertise in test construction," and "do not always use valid grading practices" (p. 9). As concluded in the decades before, Brookhart concurred that teachers need additional instruction in assessment.

Teacher Grading Practices

Between 1980 and early 2000, research cited teachers' difficulty developing valid grading procedures (see Chapter 6 of this volume for more on validity). Many teachers admitted to considering nonachievement factors (e.g., attitude, behavior, effort, motivation, improvement, participation, or assignment completion) when grading student work despite the fact that assessment experts disapprove of this practice (Barnes, 1985; Brookhart, 1994; Cox, 1995; Frary et al., 1993; Griswold, 1993; Hills, 1991; Jongsma, 1991; Stiggins et al., 1989). Such research reports that teachers frequently utilize an eclectic mix of achievement and nonachievement considerations when determining and assigning student grades (Brookhart, 1991; Cizek, 2000; Cross & Frary, 1996, 1999). In their investigation of elementary teachers' grading practices, McMillan and colleagues (2002) found that teachers tended to have difficulty separating achievement from nonachievement factors, thereby using a "hodgepodge" system that confounded student achievement with student characteristics such as effort, participation, and improvement.

Teacher Assessment Competency and Standardized Testing

Over the past several decades, educational reform has dominated the thoughts and actions of policy makers and educators. Statewide achievement tests, as a part of educational accountability programs, were mandated for all states. Consequently, standardized achievement tests were (and still are) relied upon heavily to document school performance as a way to verify alignment between local curriculum and state goals and standards. Yet teachers often feel disconnected from this process and unsure of how to make use of such test results within the classroom (see Chapter 4 of this volume).

As public attention shifted to the examination of school achievement through published standardized test results there has been an increase in public and administrative expectations regarding teacher assessment expertise. In an effort to anticipate student achievement on statewide measures, teachers are asked to develop local assessments that align curriculum with state standards as a way to improve test scores. Teachers are also expected to collect and interpret assessment data from a variety of sources, utilizing the information to make instructional decisions that have great impact not only on their classrooms and districts but, perhaps, their careers as well.

Moreover, studies have reported that when interpreting standardized test scores, many teachers have trouble understanding commonly used scores such as percentile bands, grade equivalent scores, and percentile ranks (Hills, 1991; Impara et al., 1991). Additionally, through teacher self-report data, unethical practices such as teaching to the test, giving clues, extending time limits, and changing student answers have been identified (Hall & Kleine, 1992; Nolen, Haladyna, & Haas, 1992). Taken together, these studies suggest that teachers are not skilled in issues related to interpreting and using standardized tests.

Assessment Coursework and Teacher Preparation

Studies investigating how teachers are prepared in assessment have been around for about as long as studies reporting teachers' assessment literacy and competency. In this section, era-based findings about assessment preparation are presented. Sadly, despite decades of research documenting deficiencies, current studies report this is still the case.

In 1972, Roeder initiated a nationwide survey of 916 elementary teacher education programs to determine whether teachers are prepared to use tests and evaluate student performance. Programs were asked to indicate whether completion of coursework in tests and measurement was a prerequisite for graduation. Of the institutions surveyed, approximately 57% did not require assessment coursework. Of the programs in which tests and measurement was a stand-alone and required course, the number of semester hours awarded varied, with approximately 12% reporting a 1- or 2-semester hour course, 17% a 3-hour course, and just over 1% requiring 4 or more semester hours. Approximately 7% indicated that instruction in assessment was embedded within other courses in the required curriculum. Based on his findings, Roeder (1972) concluded, "No! Most of today's elementary teachers are *NOT* prepared to use tests!" (p. 240).

Following *A Nation at Risk* (U.S. Department of Education, 1983), many states updated or initiated state-mandated proficiency exams for beginning teachers requiring that they pass both a basic skills and content area test for certification. In response, many teacher preparation programs considered or modified curricula as a way to improve student pass rate on the certification exams. However, mandating state competency exams did not always prove pivotal for universities to make necessary curricular revisions pertaining to assessment preparation. Subsequent research continued to echo the shortcomings of teacher education in the area of assessment, with calls for improved preparation (Brookhart, 2001; Campbell & Evans, 2000; Green & Mantz, 2002; Schafer & Lissitz, 1987). Likewise, recommendations to make assessment training relevant to the realities of the classroom were emphasized (Stiggins, 1991; Stiggins & Conklin, 1992; Wise et al., 1991).

Ironically, in an era that is apt to be remembered for its increase in emphasis on educational testing, many colleges of education and state certification agencies did not require preservice teachers to take specific coursework in CA (Campbell & Evans, 2000; Cizek, 2000; Hills, 1991; Jett & Schafer, 1992; O'Sullivan & Chalnick, 1991; Schafer, 1993; Schafer & Lissitz, 1987). Stiggins (1999) reported that only 10 states explicitly required assessment courses as part of basic teacher preparation. Moreover, only 15 states had teacher certification standards that included assessment competency. Similar to research pointing to the limitations of teacher assessment preparation, Stiggins (1991) suggested that measurement training has not focused on the day-to-day CA skills teachers routinely need such as diagnosing student strengths and weaknesses, assigning grades, and evaluating instructional effectiveness.

Schafer and Lissitz (1987) surveyed member institutions of the American Association of Colleges for Teacher Education (AACTE) about whether their programs required students to complete a stand-alone course in measurement as a condition of graduation and if such coursework was a state requirement. Respondents could choose from three options: (1) "no," (2) "yes," or (3) "yes and also a state requirement." Examination of the 1,665 responses showed variability in assessment as a curriculum requirement across these programs. Collapsing responses of "yes" and "yes and also a state requirement," school counseling (approximately 98%) and special education (approximately 84%) programs showed the highest percentage. Percentages within the remaining specialty areas ranged from a high of 50.7% in elementary education programs to a low of 42.8% in secondary math education programs, with administration programs reporting only 15.3% to the "yes and also a state requirement." Despite political pressures for states to rethink teacher preparation expectations, many programs curricula requirements did not include a specific course targeting CA. The researchers concluded that without such training, teachers will not be adequately prepared to use assessment effectively in their classrooms. Further, they argued that such findings "can be viewed as but one of a series of reviews documenting the inadequacies of teacher education in the assessment area" (p. 62). Subsequent research by Schafer (1993) would outline several adverse consequences to students as a result of CA practices that are ill conceived. Schafer pointed out that until formal and deliberate preservice preparation in assessment is recognized as a necessary teacher competency and addressed within curriculum, measuring teachers' assessment skill will be of *little worth.* Also investigating the extent that "assessment coursework" is a curriculum requirement, Lambert (1989) reported that although accreditation standards may mandate preservice teachers to have completed some type of coursework in assessment, courses such as statistics, program evaluation, and individual testing could fulfill this requirement.

In March 2012, the National Council on Teacher Quality (NCTQ) released a preliminary report titled *What Teacher Preparation Programs Teach About K–12 Assessment,* which indicated that teachers are not being prepared to effectively use assessment and make data-driven decisions. This conclusion was determined by examining assessment coursework within the preliminary sample institutions, although exactly what that entailed was not made clear. Although such findings may not come as a complete surprise given decades of research documenting the deficiencies of teachers' assessment skills and preparation, it is important to point out that the data represented responses from only 2% of U.S. institutions of higher education. NCTQ cited that many schools did not provide data and that another report is anticipated in May 2012.

Although limits in assessment preparation (e.g., not often required in teacher education, not relevant to practice) have been cited as explanations for teachers' difficulty with assessment, Campbell and Collins (2007) investigated another consideration—whether weakness in teachers' assessment skills could be related to differing views among authors of introductory assessment textbooks regarding content that should be included in such textbooks (i.e., essential assessment topics). Their rationale was that topics included in textbooks are the topics that are likely to guide assessment instruction. Content review of the five top-selling introductory CA textbooks and the five top-selling introductory special education assessment textbooks was conducted to identify assessment topics that were included. Content analysis across the 10 assessment textbooks yielded 73 topics related to 13 categories: (1) decisions, (2) law, (3) technical adequacy, (4) plan assessment, (5) create assessment, (6) score assessment, (7) assessment target, (8) assessment type, (9) assessment method, (10) interpret assessment, (11) communicate assessment results, (12) assessment population, and (13) computer-assisted assessment. Thirty percent of all topics identified were common to both general and special education textbooks. Many of the topics identified were consistent with historically traditional assessment expectations of general and special education environments, while other arguably important topics were not consistently included both within and across texts. Given variability in the inclusion of assessment topics, Campbell and Collins raised concerns that assessment coursework may inconsistently be preparing teachers with core assessment knowledge and skills to inform their educational decision making.

Assuming that the relationship among teaching, assessment, and learning is integral (i.e., proper assessment improves decisions made about teaching and learning), then competency in assessment is one of teachers' most valuable skills. It is important, therefore, that individuals responsible for preparing teachers in assessment concern themselves with the assessment competencies for which teachers will be held accountable. Because institutions of higher education are the primary means for initial teacher preparation, implementers of such programs have a duty to provide curriculum in keeping with modern day expectations. The same responsibility holds true for those providing professional development in assessment to teachers already in the classroom.

Teacher Beliefs About Assessment Knowledge and Skills

Marso and Pigge (1988) found that teachers rated their expertise in CA higher than their expertise in standardized testing, perhaps suggesting that teachers value skills that they view as more practical. Yet despite perceptions of greater knowledge in CA, teachers have consistently indicated not feeling well prepared in assessment and would like professional development opportunities to improve (Stiggins, 1991; Tran, Young, Mathison, & Hahn, 2000; Ward, 1980; Wise et al., 1991). In one state study, less than one-fifth of teachers surveyed reported feeling adequately prepared by their colleges in CA (Mertler, 1999).

Several studies have focused on preservice teacher beliefs regarding the germaneness of assessment coursework and its relationship to teaching self-efficacy. Historically it has been noted that preservice teachers have expressed positive convictions regarding their teaching, including assessment skills (Brookhart & Freeman, 1992; Pigge & Marso, 1987; Weinstein, 1989). A study conducted by Kushner, Carey, Dedrick, and Wallace (1994) with preservice teachers revealed a positive correlation between self-efficacy and their perceived value of coursework pertaining to CA. A follow-up study indicated that participants' self-confidence was perfect and "students who reported increased levels of confidence and less of a decrease in relevance were more successful academically than their classmates" (Kushner et al., 1995, p. 6).

Investigating preservice teachers' beliefs about their assessment training, Wise et al. (1991) found that approximately 47% rated their preparation to be somewhat to very inadequate. Two-thirds reported having taken less than one assessment course during their preservice program. Yet despite perceptions of inadequate or limited preparation in assessment, teachers indicated that being skilled in assessment was essential to their work in the classroom and rated their own skill in measurement to be high. Although teachers reported that much of their assessment knowledge and skills were acquired through trial and error in their own classrooms, most attributed university coursework as having the greatest influence on their understanding of assessment. Consistent with others, Wise et al. recommended that teacher education programs require a course in measurement and that the course content be relevant to the assessment realities of the classroom.

Similarly, Murray (1991) surveyed 148 randomly selected recent teacher graduates about their feelings of preparedness to pass Georgia's state-required Teacher Performance Assessment Instrument (TPAI). Although 92% of the respondents passed the TPAI on the first or second try, they indicated the need for more training in testing and measurement, particularly with regard to interpreting and communicating the results of standardized tests.

Zhang and Burry-Stock (1997) investigated the effects of experience and measurement training on teacher beliefs about their assessment competency. To do this, the researchers developed the *Assessment Practices Inventory* (API), a self-report instrument designed to measure seven major assessment categories identified in literature on classroom testing. A sample of 311 elementary, secondary, and vocational teachers served as respondents. Multivariate analyses of the data revealed that teachers with formal training in educational measurement—and who had four or more years of teaching experience—believed themselves to be more skilled in assessment than teachers with similar experience but without training in interpreting standardized test results, calculating test statistics, using assessment results in decision making, using performance assessment, and conducting informal assessments. Again, recommendations were made for including assessment coursework in teacher preparation programs. Yet like Wise et al. (1991), the findings of this study were based on self-report data, which, although useful for diagnostic information, did not provide a behavioral measure of proficiency.

More recently, the Educational Testing Service (2009–2010) surveyed 7,700 teacher candidates about whether they thought their educational program adequately prepared them for using assessment to identify students' strengths and needs. Participants rated their feelings of preparedness with regard to various assessment methodologies (e.g., tests, rubrics, observation, or performance tasks). Responses ranged between 81% and 95% indicating very well, well, or somewhat well, suggesting that they were satisfied with their preparation in assessment (AACTE, 2012).

Assessment Standards

Following decades of research documenting the limitations of teachers' assessment knowledge and practice, the American Federation of Teachers (AFT), the National Council on Measurement in Education (NCME), and the National Education Association (NEA) (1990) joined together to develop the *Standards for Teacher Competence in Educational Assessment of Students*. The goal of this joint effort was to identify critical assessment knowledge and skills needed by teachers as well as provide a guide for research, teacher preparation, and professional development. The standards outlined seven assessment competencies that teachers should be skilled in:

1. Choosing assessment methods appropriate for instructional decisions
2. Developing assessment methods appropriate for instructional decisions
3. Administering, scoring, and interpreting the results of both externally produced and teacher-produced assessment methods
4. Using assessment results when making decisions about individual students, planning teaching, developing curriculum, and school improvement
5. Developing valid pupil grading procedures that use pupil assessments
6. Communicating assessment results to students, parents, other lay audiences, and other educators
7. Recognizing unethical, illegal, and otherwise inappropriate assessment methods and uses of assessment information

Since their development, the standards have served as a basis for research investigating teacher competency in these areas. Although they continue to be relevant to the assessment expectations of teachers today, some have suggested that the standards omit other important assessment competencies, such as "formative assessment" and "assessment in the context of standards-based reform and accountability" (Brookhart, 2011, p. 4). Consequently, an update of the standards has been recommended (Brookhart, 2011; Stiggins, 1999). Characteristic of the broad wording found in many standards, the seven *Standards for Teacher Competence in Educational Assessment of Students* (AFT et al., 1990) do not spell out the specific knowledge and skills needed by teachers to meaningfully execute the assessment competencies guiding practice. For example, Brookhart (2001) noted that although the term *summative assessment* is not explicitly referred to in the standards, how the competencies relate to summative assessment may be more readily apparent than other assessment practices such as formative assessment. Moreover, she further noted that although formative and summative assessments share certain knowledge, skills, and processes (e.g., well designed and results appropriately interpreted); their purposes and use are fundamentally different; and that such distinctions are not clearly detailed. Limits in specificity could have implications for preservice and in-service assessment preparation.

In 2000, *The Need for Student Evaluation Standards* was developed by the Joint Committee on Standards for Educational Evaluation (Gullickson, 2000). The committee underscored that without a systematic effort, the quality of student evaluation is not likely to change. The committee, chaired by Arlen Gullickson (2000), stated that "critical impediments to sound student evaluation" inhibit the process of implementing "meaningful change in evaluation practices" (p. 5). Specifically, the barriers impeding evaluation practices in schools include the following:

- Inadequate teacher preparation
- Inadequate technical support from administrators
- Changing demands (policies and situations)
- Professional disagreement on evaluation practices
- Lack of shared language between educators and measurement specialists

- Inadequate school policy to guide evaluation of students
- Transitory interventions (lack of time to implement "reforms" or changes)
- Ineffective instruction in educational measurement courses. (Gullickson, 2000, p. 5)

Assessment Literacy Tools

In 1992, Plake et al. (1993) created the Teacher Assessment Literacy Questionnaire (TALQ), a 35-item multiple-choice tool based on the specific assessment competencies outlined in the *Standards for Teacher Competence in Educational Assessment of Students* (AFT et al., 1990). A national survey of in-service teachers from 98 districts in 45 states (N = 555) was conducted to gauge assessment knowledge and skills as evidence by their performance on the TALQ. Approximately 70% of the participants reported having had training in measurement at some time during their preservice preparation or professional development as an in-service teacher. The KR20 (r_{KR20}) reliability for the TALQ was 0.54 (Plake et al., 1993). Examining mean scores by standard revealed the highest performance in items related to Standard 3, Administering, Scoring, and Interpreting the Results of Assessment, and lowest performance in items pertaining to Standard 6, Communicating Assessment Results. Comparing overall scores between those teachers with and without assessment training revealed similar performance on the TALQ (less than a 1 point difference) and an overall score lower than expected or desired (i.e., approximately 23 out of 35 items correct, or 66%). Although this score difference was statistically significant, the general findings indicated that teachers were poorly prepared in assessment and that having had such coursework may not be sufficient for improving assessment practices.

A similar study by Campbell, Murphy, and Holt (2002) tested the TALQ with undergraduate preservice teachers. The renamed Assessment Literacy Inventory (ALI) was administered to 220 undergraduate elementary education majors following completion of a required course in CA. ALI scores demonstrated some similarities in strengths and weaknesses between the preservice teachers and Plake and colleagues' in-service teachers. Comparatively, preservice teachers exhibited somewhat weaker overall scores and greater variability than did in-service teachers, with preservice teachers' answering approximately 21 out of 35 items correct, or roughly 61%, compared to the 1997 in-service teachers' average score of 23, or approximately 66%. This difference raised questions about the value added in having had a course in assessment during teacher preparation compared to learning assessment through trial and error once in the classroom. This finding was in contrast to Mayo (1967), who reported university coursework to be an important contributor to improved practices over experience in the field without having had a course in tests and measurement.

Mertler (2003) studied the assessment literacy of both preservice and in-service teachers. Using a slightly modified version of the TALQ, he obtained similar results to both the Plake et al. (1993) and Campbell et al. (2002) studies. The average score for in-service teachers was equal to 22 items answered correctly—quite similar to the average score of 23 obtained by Plake et al. (1993). Reliability analyses also revealed similar values for internal consistency (r_{KR20} = 0.54 and 0.57 for the original study and the study at hand, respectively). The average score for the preservice teachers was equal to 19—also similar to the average score obtained by Campbell et al. (2002). Reliability analyses revealed identical values (r_{KR20} = 0.74) for internal consistency.

Alternative Assessments and Purpose

In the 1980s and 1990s, growing dissatisfaction with an overreliance on traditional assessment (paper–pencil testing) as an indicator of student achievement, coupled with the notion that students learn best when tasks are meaningful (Glaser, Lesgold, & Lajoie, 1987; Lane, 1989; Shepard, 2000), led to the recommendation that teachers make use of assessments more directly tied to student skills (such as projects, authentic and performance-based assessments, writing samples, and portfolios) (Shavelson, Baxter, & Pine, 1992; Ward & Murray-Ward, 1999; Wiggins, 1989).

Influenced by social constructivist learning theories, later research has investigated teaching, learning, and assessing as an integral meaning-making activity. In contrast to the metaphorical banking model of education (Freire, 1970) where teachers "deposit" information into their students that can be later "withdrawn" through formal testing, AFL is interactive, occurring throughout instruction. Through formative assessment, clues gauging how well learning is coming along are provided. Using assessment to monitor progress and provide feedback reconceptualized the purpose of assessment from a precise, summative, static measure *of* learning to a means *for* generating hypotheses about learning progress and the instructional process (Black, Harrison, Lee, Marshall, & Wiliam, 2004; Black & Wiliam, 1998; Shepard, 2000). This was consistent with the constructivist nature of learning—that students learn best when working with information in personal ways, collaborating with the teacher and student peers (see Chapters 18 and 19 of this volume).

As a result, methods that unite instruction and assessment have been studied (e.g., running records, observation, think aloud, and in-the-moment). See Ward and Murray-Ward (1999) for the historical roots related to the performance assessment movement. Similarly, research investigating assessment *as* learning has documented the benefits of student involvement throughout the learning process. In particular, how self- and peer assessment enhances metacognition and ownership of learning as a result of active involvement in evaluating one's own work has been discussed (Dann, 2002; Shepard, 2000). Yet despite the focus on teacher training and competency in CA, as well as a greater concern for students learning in ways that are constructive and reflective, research during the 2000s continued to document limitations in teachers' assessment skills.

State and Federal Assessment Mandates

The expectation that teachers use sound assessment practices to guide practice and decision making has gained increased focus as a result of statewide testing mandates and the passing of national legislation such as the No Child Left Behind Act of 2001 (NCLB) (U.S. Department of Education, 2002) and the Individuals with Disabilities Education Improvement Act (IDEIA) (2004). By design, the expectation that teachers be skilled in assessment is reflected in both federal laws' statement of purpose, which indicates that high quality education and achievement are more likely when the following occurs:

- ensuring that high-quality academic assessments, accountability systems, teacher preparation and training, curriculum, and instructional materials are aligned with challenging State academic standards so that students, teachers, parents, and administrators can measure progress against common expectations for student academic achievement. [NCLB, Title I, SEC. 1001(1)]
- there are efforts (4) to assess, and ensure the effectiveness of efforts to educate children with disabilities. [IDEIA, Title I, SEC. 601(d)(4)]

Content review of both NCLB and IDEIA legislation was conducted by Campbell and Collins (2009) with the goal of identifying the assessment expectations of classroom and special education teachers. Within each law, hundreds of references to teacher assessment knowledge and skills were found. Some of the assessment expectations of law were consistent with the seven *Standards for Teacher Competence in Educational Assessment of Students* (AFT et al., 1990), while others reflect expectations more in line with what teachers need to know and be able to do in an era of accountability. The expectation that teachers are to be competent in assessment was prominent throughout Titles I, II, and III of NCLB and IDEIA and resulted in the following 10 assessment expectations for teachers:

1. Align goals, curriculum, and assessment to state and local academic standards.
2. Select, create, modify, and implement valid and reliable assessment.
3. Analyze, interpret, and use assessment to inform decisions.
4. Communicate and defend assessment results and procedures.
5. Monitor progress to improve student achievement.
6. Identify students with problems that warrant intervention.
7. Identify student strengths, difficulties, and possible explanations for learning problems.
8. Plan and modify instruction based on student strengths and needs.
9. Use interventions to prevent and remediate learning problems.
10. Use technology to facilitate assessment.

The first 4 expectations are ordered hierarchically and represent a logical sequence of foundational assessment competencies. Expectations 5 through 8 represent sets of decisions that provide a context for applying the foundational assessment sequence. Expectation 9 underscores the importance of using assessment to strengthen general and remedial instruction. Expectation 10 has to do with teachers using technology to facilitate assessment.

Yet as noted earlier, despite educational legislation mandating teacher competency in assessment, research has continued to raise concern about the adequacy of their assessment knowledge and skills, and limits in their assessment preparation. The assertion that teacher assessment skills are underdeveloped in particular areas was supported by President's George W. Bush's Commission on Excellence in Special Education (U.S. Department of Education Office of Special Education and Rehabilitative Services [OSERS], 2002). In order to strengthen educational outcomes for students with special needs, the commission solicited concerns and input from educators, parents, and the public. Problems with the current system of public education were identified in their report, *A New Era: Revitalizing Special Education for Children and Their Families* (U.S. Department of Education OSERS, 2002). Summarized in this report were nine major findings, three of which pertain specifically to the sixth expectation. Of the three findings, two address the prevailing method and model for identifying students with special needs (Findings 2 and 6), while the other relates to teachers feeling unprepared to identify student needs effectively (Finding 7) (Collins & Campbell, 2012).

- Finding 2: The current system uses an antiquated model that waits for a child to fail instead of a model based on prevention and intervention. Too little emphasis is put on prevention, early and accurate identification of learning and behavior problems, and aggressive intervention using research based approaches.
- Finding 6: Many of the current methods of identifying children with disabilities lack validity. As a result, thousands of children are misidentified every year, while many others are not identified early enough or at all.
- Finding 7: Many educators wish they had better preparation before entering the classroom as well as better tools for identifying needs early and accurately.

This is to say that teacher competency in assessment is essential for realizing the ultimate goal of legislation—improved outcomes for all students. An excerpt from IDEIA reflects this charge:

> Reforming special education and regular education teacher certification . . . to ensure that special education and regular education teachers have the training and information necessary to address the full range of needs of children with disabilities. [SEC. 654(b)(1)(A)(i)]

Similarly, one of the three major recommendations for addressing problems with the current system of public education identified by the president's Commission on Excellence in Special Education was to *embrace a model of prevention not a model of failure.*

The current model guiding special education focuses on waiting for a child to fail, not on early intervention to prevent failure. Reforms must move the system toward early identification and swift intervention, using scientifically based instruction and teaching methods. This will require changes in the nation's elementary and secondary schools as well as reforms in teacher preparation, recruitment, and support (Collins & Campbell, 2012).

As discussed earlier, a radical rethinking of the content and method for preparing teachers in assessment is required. Reforming the current system will challenge long-standing traditions concerning pedagogy and the kinds of knowledge and skills that should be developed during assessment instruction—for example, separate and different assessment training for general and special educators. Traditional methods for training general and special educators in assessment, together with topics identified in top selling introductory assessment textbooks (Campbell & Collins, 2007), suggests that current assessment preparation in general and special education will likely omit important competencies expected of teachers. However, reforming teacher assessment preparation must go beyond merely adding more content to an already existing assessment course. Revising coursework using an additive model would not be feasible or effective in preparing teachers and would likely—and understandably—be met with resistance. To address the shared and newly expanded expectations of general and special education teachers identified in law and supported by research driving educational reform, higher education needs to rethink and restructure how *all* teachers are prepared in assessment (Campbell & Collins, 2011).

Summary

Despite the growing demand for highly competent teachers, novice teachers have limited expedients regarding assessment strategies and have relatively few experiences with a variety of alternative assessments (Freiberg, 2002). While it is estimated that a teacher can spend almost one-third (Stiggins & Conklin, 1988) to one-half of his or her time on activities linked to assessment (Stiggins, 1991), this estimate may become conservative as local, state, and federal educational and political bodies require additional forms of accurate assessment of student learning and increases in student achievement (Campbell & Collins, 2011; Crooks, 1988; Stiggins & Conklin, 1992). Accordingly, teachers will be expected to become far more competent in assessment than they are today. Given the current climate of school accountability and data-driven decision making, teachers are expected to use sound assessment practices as a means for improving student outcomes. Research investigating the interplay between CA and high-stakes testing is needed.

Moreover, studies investigating the actual practices and products of teachers in their classrooms as well as how such data are used to enhance student learning and instructional decisions would provide a more authentic gauge of their assessment competency and the effectiveness of assessment training than data collected through self-report. For example, research exploring factors contributing to the disparity between assessment practice and theory (e.g., value congruence between teachers and school administration with regard to assessment emphasis, time constraints, and so forth) could identify informal structures impeding effective assessment. Also needed is research investigating the assessment practices of teachers by grade level and content area. It is possible that contextually unique classroom environments may reveal barriers not previously identified.

Research investigating how and to what magnitude sources of self-efficacy information (e.g., performance, vicarious, or affective) contribute to preservice teachers' enhanced, albeit distorted, perception of their assessment competency may uncover areas to attend to during teacher preparation and assessment coursework. For example, research investigating the criteria used by cooperating teachers to evaluate preservice teachers' assessments and assessment practices during student teaching may shed light on how informational sources contribute to preservice teachers' implicit theories about what constitutes "good assessment," potentially negating the positive effects of assessment training.

Moreover, systematic research examining the quality and reality of teacher assessment preparation in the United States is needed. This is particularly important given the current mandates of educational law and the changing expectations of what teachers need to know and be able to do with assessment and assessment information. Teachers must be prepared, and institutions of higher education must respond. Resolving the ambiguity concerning what assessment knowledge and skills are essential to the work of today's classroom teachers is an important first step to ensure that assessment preparation enhances teaching effectiveness and student learning.

References

American Association of Colleges for Teacher Education. (2012). *AACTE Statement on Teacher Preparation and K–12 Assessment Report.* Retrieved from http://aacte.org/News-Room/Press-Releases-and-Statements/aacte-statement-on-teacher-preparation-and-k-12-assessment-report.html

American Federation of Teachers, National Council on Measurement in Education, & National Education Association. (1990). *Standards for Teacher Competence in Educational Assessment of Students.* Washington, DC: Authors. Retrieved from www.unl.edu/buros/bimm/html/article3.html

Aschbacher, P. R. (1999). *Developing indicators of classroom practice to monitor and support school reform* (CRESST Technical Report 513). Los Angeles: University of California, Center for Research on Educational Standards and Student Testing. Retrieved from www.cse.ucla.edu/products/reports/TECH513.pdf

Barnes, S. (1985). A study of classroom pupil evaluation: The missing link in teacher education. *Journal of Teacher Education, 36*(4), 46–49.

Black, P., Harrison, C., Lee, C., Marshall, B., & Wiliam, D. (2004). Working inside the black box: Assessment for learning in the classroom. *Phi Delta Kappan, 86*(1), 9–21.

Black, P., & Wiliam, D. (1998). Inside the black box: Raising standards through classroom assessment. *Phi Delta Kappan, 80*(2), 139–144.

Boothroyd, R. A., McMorris, R. F., & Pruzek, R. M. (1992, April). *What do teachers know about measurement and how did they find out?* Paper presented at the annual meeting of the National Council on Measurement in Education, San Francisco. (ERIC Document Reproduction Service No. ED351309)

Brookhart, S. M. (1991). Grading practices and validity. *Educational Measurement: Issues and Practice, 10*(1), 35–36.

Brookhart, S. M. (1994). Teachers' grading: Practice and theory. *Applied Measurement in Education, 7*(4), 279–301.

Brookhart, S. M. (2001). *The "standards" and classroom assessment research.* Paper presented at the annual meeting of the American Association of Colleges for Teacher Education, Dallas, TX. (ERIC Document Reproduction Service No. ED451189)

Brookhart, S. M. (2011). Educational assessment knowledge and skills for teachers. *Educational Measurement, Issues and Practice, 30*(1), 3–12.

Brookhart, S. M., & Freeman, D. J. (1992). Characteristics of entering teacher candidates. *Review of Educational Research, 62*(1), 37–60.

Campbell, C., & Collins, V. L. (2007). Identifying essential topics in general and special education introductory assessment textbooks. *Educational Measurement: Issues and Practice, 26*(1), 9–18.

Campbell, C., & Collins, V. L. (2009). *NCLB expectations of teachers.* Unpublished manuscript.

Campbell, C., & Collins, V. L. (2011). *Teacher preparation in assessment: A call to revise and resubmit.* Manuscript submitted for publication.

Campbell, C., & Evans, J. A. (2000). Investigation of preservice teachers' classroom assessment practices during student teaching. *The Journal of Educational Research, 93,* 350–355.

Campbell, C., Murphy, J. A., & Holt, J. K. (2002, October). *Psychometric analysis of an assessment literacy instrument: Applicability to preservice teachers.* Paper presented at the annual meeting of the Mid-Western Educational Research Association, Columbus, OH.

Carter, K. (1984). Do teachers understand principles for writing tests? *Journal of Teacher Education, 35*(6), 57–60.

Cizek, G. J. (2000). Pockets of resistance in the assessment revolution. *Educational Measurement: Issues and Practice, 19*(2), 16–23, 33.

Cizek, G. J., Fitzgerald, S. M., & Rachor, R. E. (1995). *Teachers' assessment practices: Preparation, isolation, and the kitchen sink. Educational Measurement, 3,* 159–180.

Collins, V. L., & Campbell, C. (2012). *IDEIA assessment expectations of teachers.* Manuscript submitted for publication.

Cox, K. B. (1995). *What counts in English class? Selected findings from a statewide study of California high school teachers.* Paper presented at the annual meeting of the American Educational Research Association, San Francisco. (ERIC Document Reproduction Service No. ED384051)

Crooks, T. J. (1988). The impact of classroom evaluation practices on students. *Review of Educational Research, 58,* 438–481.

Cross, L. H., & Frary, R. B. (1996). *Hodgepodge grading: Endorsed by students and teachers alike.* Paper presented at the annual meeting of the National Council on Measurement in Education, New York. (ERIC Document Reproduction Service No. ED398262)

Cross, L. H., & Frary, R. B. (1999). Hodgepodge grading: Endorsed by students and teachers alike. *Applied Measurement in Education, 12*(1), 53–72.

Daniel, L. G., & King, D. A. (1998). Knowledge and use of testing and measurement literacy. *Journal of Educational Research, 91,* 331–344.

Dann, R. (2002). *Promoting assessment as learning: Improving the learning process.* New York: RoutledgeFalmer.

Frary, R. B., Cross, L. H., & Weber, L. J. (1993). Testing and grading practices and opinions of secondary teachers of academic subjects: Implications for instruction in measurement. *Educational Measurement: Issues and Practice, 12*(3), 23–30.

Freiberg, H. J. (2002). Essential skills for new teachers. *Educational Leadership, 59*(6), 56–60.

Freire, P. (1970). *Pedagogy of the oppressed.* New York: Herder and Herder.

Glaser, R., Lesgold, A., & Lajoie, S. (1987). Toward a cognitive theory for the measurement of achievement. In R. R. Ronning, J. A. Glover, J. C. Conoley, & J. C. Witt (Eds.), *The influence of cognitive psychology on testing and measurement* (pp. 41–82). Hillsdale, NJ: Lawrence Erlbaum.

Goslin, D. A. (1967). *Teachers and testing.* New York: Russell Sage Foundation.

Green, S. K., & Mantz, M. (2002, April). *Classroom assessment practices: Examining impact on student learning.* Paper presented at the annual meeting of the American Educational Research Association, New Orleans, LA. (ERIC Document Reproduction Service No. ED464920)

Griswold, P. A. (1993). Beliefs and inferences about grading elicited from students' performance sketches. *Educational Assessment, 1*(4), 311–328.

Gullickson, A. R. (2000, May). *The need for student evaluation standards.* The Joint Committee on Standards for Educational Evaluation. Retrieved from www.wmich.edu/evalctr/jc/pubs/SESNeed.pdf

Hall, J. L., & Kleine, P. F. (1992). Educators' perceptions of NRT misuse. *Educational Measurement: Issues and Practices, 11*(2), 18–22.

Hills, J. R. (1977). Coordinators of accountability view teachers' measurement competence. Florida *Journal of Education Research, 19,* 34–44.

Hills, J. R. (1991). Apathy concerning grading and testing. *Phi Delta Kappa, 72*(7), 540–545.

Impara, J. C., Divine, K. P., Bruce, F. A., Liverman, M. R., & Gay, A. (1991). Does interpretive test score information help teachers? *Educational Measurement: Issues and Practices, 10*(4), 16–18.

Individuals with Disabilities Education Improvement Act. (2004). Retrieved from thomas.loc.gov/cgi-bin/query/z?c108:h.r.1350.enr:%20

Jett, D. I., & Schafer, W. D. (1992). *Classroom teachers move to center stage in the assessment arena—ready or not!* Paper presented at the annual meeting of the American Educational Research Association, San Francisco, CA.

Jongsma, K. S. (1991). Rethinking grading practices. *The Reading Teacher, 45*(4), 319–320.

Kushner, S. N., Carey, L. M., Dedrick, R. F., & Wallace, T. L. (1994, April). *The relationship between preservice teachers' beliefs about the relevance of instruction and their confidence in performing related tasks.* Paper presented at the annual conference of the American Educational Research Association, New Orleans, LA.

Kushner, S. N., Carey, L. M., Dedrick, R. F., & Wallace, T. L. (1995, April). *Preservice teachers' beliefs about the relevance of teacher education coursework and their confidence in performing related skills.* Paper presented at the annual conference of the American Educational Research Association, San Francisco, CA. (ERIC Document Reproduction Service No. ED394 919)

Lambert, N. M. (1989, August). *The crisis in measurement literacy in psychology and education.* Paper presented at the annual meeting of the American Psychological Association, New Orleans, LA. (ERIC Document Reproduction Service No. ED319778)

Lane, S. (1989). Implications of cognitive psychology on measurement and testing. *Educational Measurement: Issues and Practice, 8*(1), 17–19.

Marso, R. N., & Pigge, F. L. (1988). Ohio secondary teachers' testing needs and proficiencies: Assessments by teachers, supervisors, and principals. *American Secondary Education, 17,* 2–9.

Marso, R. N., & Pigge, F. L. (1993). Teachers' testing knowledge, skills, and practices. In S. L. Wise (Ed.), *Teacher training in measurement and assessment skills.* Lincoln: Buros Institute of Mental Measurements, University of Nebraska-Lincoln.

Mayo, S. T. (1967). *Pre-service preparation of teachers in educational measurement. Final report.* Chicago: Loyola University. (ERIC Document Reproduction Service No. ED021784)

McMillan, J. H., Myran, S., & Workman, D. J. (2002). Elementary teachers' classroom assessment and grading practices. *Journal of Educational Research, 95*(4), 203–213.

McMillan, J. H., & Nash, S. (2000, April). *Teacher classroom assessment and grading practice decision making.* Paper presented at the annual meeting of the National Council on Measurement in Education. New Orleans, LA.

Mertler, C. A. (1999). Assessing student performance: A descriptive study of the classroom assessment practices of Ohio teachers. *Education, 120*(2), 285–296.

Mertler, C. A. (2000). Teacher-centered fallacies of classroom assessment validity and reliability. *MidWestern Educational Researcher, 13*(4), 29–35.

Mertler, C. A. (2003, October). Preservice versus inservice teachers' assessment literacy: Does classroom experience make a difference? Paper presented at the annual meeting of the MidWestern Educational Research Association, Columbus, OH.

Murray, D. R. (1991). *An analysis of the perceptions of teacher education graduates on their preparation for service: A five year review.* Rome, GA: Berry College, Department of Education and Psychology. (ERIC Document Reproduction Service No. ED335349)

National Council on Teacher Quality. (2012). *What teacher preparation programs teach about K–12 assessment.* Retrieved from www.nctq.org/p/edschools/docs/assessment_publication.pdf

Nolen, S. B., Haladyna, T. M., & Haas, N. S. (1992). Uses and abuses of achievement test scores. *Educational Measurement: Issues and Practices, 11*(2), 9–15.

Noll, V. H. (1955). Requirements in educational measurement for prospective teachers. *School and Society, 82,* 88–90.

O'Sullivan, R. G., & Chalnick, M. K. (1991). Measurement-related course work requirements for teacher certification and recertification.

Educational Measurement: Issues and Practice, 10(1), 17–19, 23.

Plake, B. S., Impara, J. C., & Fager, J. J. (1993). Assessment competencies of teachers: A national survey. *Educational Measurement: Issues and Practice, 12*(4), 10–12, 39.

Pigge, F. L., & Marso, R. N. (1987). Relationships between student characteristics and changes in attitudes, concerns, anxieties, and confidence about teaching during teacher preparation. *Journal of Educational Research, 81,* 109–115.

Roeder, H. H. (1972). Are today's teachers prepared to use tests? *Peabody Journal of Education, 49*(3), 239–240.

Schafer, W. D. (1993). Assessment literacy for teachers. *Theory into Practice, 32*(2), 118–126.

Schafer, W. D., & Lissitz, R. W. (1987). Measurement training for school personnel: Recommendations and reality. *Journal of Teacher Education, 38*(3), 57–63.

Shavelson, R. J., Baxter, G. P., & Pine, J. (1992). Performance assessments: Political rhetoric and measurement reality. *Educational Researcher, 21*(5), 23–27.

Shepard, L. A. (2000). The role of assessment in a learning culture. *Educational Researcher, 29*(7), 4–14.

Stiggins, R. J. (1991). Relevant classroom assessment training for teachers. *Educational Measurement: Issues and Practice, 10*(1), 7–12.

Stiggins, R. J. (1992). *In teachers' hands: Investigating the practices of classroom assessment.* Albany: State University of New York Press.

Stiggins, R. J. (1999). Evaluating classroom assessment training in teacher education programs. *Educational Measurement: Issues and Practice, 18*(1), 23–27.

Stiggins, R. J., & Bridgeford, N. J. (1985). The ecology of classroom assessment. *Journal of Educational Measurement, 22*(4), 271–286.

Stiggins, R. J., & Conklin, N. F. (1988). *Teacher training in assessment.* Portland, OR: Northwest Regional Educational Laboratory.

Stiggins, R. J., & Conklin, N. F. (1992). *In teachers' hands: Investigating the practices of classroom assessment.* Albany: State University of New York Press.

Stiggins, R. J., Frisbie, D. A., & Griswold, P. A. (1989). Inside high school grading practices: Building a research agenda. *Educational Measurement: Issues and Practices, 8*(2), 5–14.

Tran, M. T., Young, R. L., Mathison, C., & Hahn, B. T. (2000). *New teacher confidence: How does it develop?* Paper presented at the annual meeting of the American Educational Research Association, New Orleans, LA.

Trevison, M. S. (2002). The states' role in ensuring assessment competence. *Phi Delta Kappan, 83*(10), 766–771.

U.S. Department of Education. (1983, April). *A nation at risk.* Washington, DC: National Commission on Excellence in Education. Retrieved from www.ed.gov/pubs/NatAtRisk/risk.html

U.S. Department of Education. (2002). *No Child Left Behind Act of 2001* (Title I Paraprofessionals: Draft Non-Regulatory Guidance). Washington, DC: U.S. Department of Education, Office of Elementary and Secondary Education.

U.S. Department of Education Office of Special Education and Rehabilitative Services. (2002). *A new era: Revitalizing special education for children and their families.* Washington, DC. Retrieved from www.ed.gov/inits/commissionsboards/whspecialeducation/

Ward, A. W., & Murray-Ward, M. (1999). *Assessment in the classroom.* Belmont, CA: Wadsworth Publishing Company.

Ward, J. G. (1980). Teachers and testing: A survey of knowledge and attitudes. In L. M. Rudner (Ed.), *Testing in our schools* (pp. 15–24). Washington, DC: National Institute of Education.

Weinstein, C. S. (1989). Teacher education students' preconceptions of teaching. *Journal of Teacher Education, 40*(2), 53–60.

Wiggins, G. (1989). A true test: Toward more authentic and equitable assessment. *Phi Delta Kappan, 70,* 703–713.

Wise, S. L., Lukin, L. E., & Roos, L. L. (1991). Teacher beliefs about training in testing and measurement. *Journal of Teacher Education, 42*(1), 37–42.

Zhang, Z., & Burry-Stock, J. (1997, March). *Assessment practices inventory: A multivariate analysis of teachers' perceived assessment competency.* Paper presented at the annual meeting of the National Council on Measurement in Education, Chicago. (ERIC Document Reproduction Service No. ED408333)

SECTION 2

Technical Quality of Classroom Assessments

Sarah M. Bonner

Associate Editor

6

Validity in Classroom Assessment: Purposes, Properties, and Principles

Sarah M. Bonner

This chapter presents traditional and contemporary perspectives on the validation of interpretations based on data derived from classroom assessments (CAs). Despite an extensive tradition and literature on validation of standardized educational and psychological tests, appropriate methods for validation of assessments used by teachers in classrooms are not well defined. Further, exemplary cases of CA validation are few to be found. One assumption of this chapter is that the paucity of both prescriptive and descriptive literature on validation of CAs springs from several fundamental ways in which CAs differ from other types of assessment, for which the traditional arsenal of validation approaches has been developed. From some perspectives and for some purposes, CA differs from other educational assessments so radically in its purposes and its qualities that measurement validity may be a secondary concern.

While I support the view that current psychometric approaches to validation have often failed to address issues of validity in CA, I believe that validity or appropriateness of inferences about test scores is a core value. Therefore, I hold it incumbent upon theorists to develop methods that teachers and researchers at the classroom level can use to judge the propriety of inferences. This chapter represents one response to the charge to create a new measurement theory appropriate to the contexts and purposes of CA (Brookhart, 2003); I hope that it will instigate fruitful discourse in the field.

I will limit the scope of this discussion to those CAs administered within the context of the classroom instructional cycle to assist the classroom teacher in planning, guiding, monitoring, or describing the outcomes of instruction. Classroom teachers often are responsible for administering externally produced standardized tests, some of which claim to be formative or valid for instructional purposes. However, the usefulness of those tests for instructional purposes is debatable and is covered in another chapter of this volume (see Schneider, Egan, & Julian in Chapter 4 of this volume). I will discuss CAs in terms of summative and formative uses, although the emphasis will be on formative assessment as the more common classroom activity.

I will begin with a brief review of perspectives on validation of interpretations of test scores or, more generally, of an assessment process and its results. Because validation always involves validation of an *interpretation* or *use* of assessment results (Cronbach, 1971), I will follow with a description of the most typical interpretations and uses of CAs as well as distinctive characteristics of CAs that affect such interpretations and uses. CA often, although not always, purports not only to *measure* learning but to *advance* learning progress. While the learning purpose is an important and desirable one for CA, it poses different validation problems than the measurement purpose. Therefore, I will separately describe approaches to validating CAs for the purpose of *measurement* and for the purpose of supporting claims about *impacts on student learning and other variables* with examples whenever possible. Challenges associated with each purpose will be discussed, and also the issue will be raised as to whether the two purposes are compatible, though it will certainly not be resolved.

I will recommend a set of principles for CA validation that apply equally to both the measurement and learning purposes of assessment. These principles are drawn from traditional frameworks of measurement but avoid the problems of decontextualization, standardization, and pseudo-objectivity associated with traditional validation approaches and do not require large sample sizes. My list of principles for validity in CA is not intended to be exhaustive but is offered as a step in the development of a classroom-based theory of assessment or "classroometric" theory (Brookhart, 2003). I will close the chapter with suggestions of avenues for research on validation of CAs.

Perspectives on Validation of Interpretations of Assessments

Current psychometric approaches present validation as argument for or about the appropriateness of a proposed interpretation or use of test scores or test-based classifications (Bachman, 2005; Kane, 2006; Mislevy, 2003). Some CAs and indeed many other kinds of assessment procedures yield qualitative judgments rather than or in addition to numerical scores or classifications; therefore, the extent to which CAs qualify as measurements—the interpretation of which requires validation at all—should be at least briefly addressed.

As Cizek (2009) pointed out, a test is often other than a paper-and-pencil instrument administered under standardized conditions on a single occasion. Viewed comprehensively, a test is any systematically administered set of procedures that results in some level of measurement of an attribute. Some tests yield more precisely quantified measurements than others, and many CAs, such as end-of-unit tests and comprehensive course exams, do yield scores, although the scoring rules may appear simple. The fact that many other CA procedures do not yield numerical scores does not necessarily mean that they do not qualify as tests. For instance, a classroom essay task that is used to construct mixed ability writing clusters may loosely classify students as demonstrating low, moderate, or high levels of organizational skill, achieving a rough ordinal scale. Further, even informal assessment procedures such as nonrandom questioning that are not administered to all students within a classroom and do not rank students in any way involve many of the assumptions of measurement, such as alignment between an underlying process that stimulates the response and the teacher's inference based on that response. Current psychometric approaches to validation have often failed to meet the needs of teachers using informal methods; however, that does not mean that validity or appropriateness of inferences is not a value for teachers when they use informal methods. Theorists can best support improved validity of inferences drawn from CAs by developing methods that teachers can use to judge the propriety of their inferences, even when they are based on informal procedures.

To summarize the assumptions that allow CA processes to be considered under the umbrella of psychometric theory, CA is a process that sometimes includes measurement but always includes obtaining information about student attributes (in most cases, student achievement), interpreting that information, and using that information for a learning purpose. According to current psychometric theory, the interpretation and use of information for a purpose should be validated by reference to the proposed interpretive argument and the evidence supporting (or refuting) it (Kane, 2006). In other words, interpretations and uses of CAs, whether based on quantitative or qualitative data, have the same theoretical requirement for validation that standardized test interpretations have.

Current Psychometric Theory of Validation

The evolution of traditional approaches to validation of assessment-based interpretations and uses has been well documented elsewhere (Kane, 2001; Moss, 2003); therefore, I will only briefly summarize a few main tenets of current psychometric theory regarding validity. First, validity is not validity of a test per se but of an interpretation and/or use of test scores (Cronbach, 1971). Interpretations of test scores and actions taken on the basis of those interpretations involve a series of inferences first from an observed performance to a score then from score to score meaning, and so on to score use and the consequences of that use (Cizek, 2009; Kane, 2006). Each inference may or may not be correct, and its justification or validity must be established through evidence-based or logical argument.

A corollary of this tenet is that for each distinct proposed interpretation, test purpose, or use, validity must be newly established. According to the *Standards for Educational and Psychological Testing* (American Educational Research Association [AERA], American Psychological Association [APA], & National Council on Measurement in Education [NCME], 1999; hereafter, *Standards*), this holds true when test scores are to be used as a basis for making similar inferences about different populations, or when the scores have been generated in markedly different contexts. The professional expectation to validate a test interpretation within its context poses a challenge for the task of validating CAs, where contextual effects may be large and are not typically controlled through standardization. Nonetheless, according to current theory, an interpretive argument for each test use should be laid out in advance of test administration, although in fluid situations such as classroom and other clinical situations, and during test development, the argument typically develops over time and may be modified in light of emerging evidence (Kane, 2006).

Second, at a theoretical level, the validity of interpretation of test scores is ultimately a question of construct validity; that is, it is based on inquiry into score meaning and the representativeness and relevance of score meaning to the construct that was to be measured (Cronbach, 1971; Messick, 1989). While in some cases, possibly particularly in clinical situations and CA, the inference to be made is practically limited to an inference from observed performance to an observable attribute (Kane, 2006), validation assumptions, issues, and debates generally relate to the need for an inference about an observation to generalize to a broader theoretical construct. Practically speaking, teachers are not always only interested in whether or not a student can demonstrate a specific skill or knowledge component on a given instance and in a specific context but whether skills and knowledge demonstrated (or not) on one occasion generalize to other tasks. For example, knowing whether a student can write an analytic essay on a theme from *Romeo and Juliet* may be used to make relatively direct inferences about the student's current state of knowledge about that theme from *Romeo and Juliet*. A teacher may, however, further wish to use information from such an essay to infer student general knowledge about *Romeo and Juliet*, general ability to interpret Elizabethan drama, and even general analytic essay-writing.

Third, evidence for or against claims about test interpretation or use can be derived from many sources, including both qualitative and quantitative sources, but must be based on the assumptions and plausible rival hypotheses or potential evidence for rebuttals inherent in the interpretive argument for the test use (Kane, 2006; Mislevy, 2003). A case in point relating to the need to probe plausible rival hypotheses can be found in inferences derived from some predictive tests. Historically predictive tests have relied primarily on evidence about their correlation with a criterion to justify their claims to validity. However, a source of construct irrelevant variance contaminating scores on the predictive test may also be present in the criterion, spuriously inflating the correlation between the two measures, beyond the true correlation between the two constructs to be measured. For instance, if advantage afforded by socioeconomic status were found to be systematically associated both with measures of a predictive aptitude test and a criterion measure of job performance, attention only to predictive validity might lead to test use resulting in negative unintended societal consequences. Plausible alternatives to the validity hypothesis should be considered whenever assessment-based claims are made.

New Measurement Theory

In contrast to traditional psychometric perspectives on validation that are rooted in postpositivism, some theorists propose the development of a new measurement theory informed by a social–constructivist epistemology (Black & Wiliam, 2004; Brookhart, 2003; Delandshere, 2001; Gipps, 1999; Moss, 2003; Pellegrino & Chudowsky, 2003; Shepard, 2006; Tittle, 1994).

From these perspectives, test score meaning is co-constructed by test takers and testers within a social context. These perspectives focus on the interpretations, values, and uses given to assessment information within that context rather than a fixed meaning ascribed to scores by external authorities who are artificially given the privileged status of objectivity through standardization processes intended to rob the scores of their contextual origin. Thus the validity of information derived from an assessment depends on perceived qualities of the social context or situation in which the assessment process is embedded, as well as the conceptual frameworks, attitudes, interpretations, and beliefs of all stakeholders in the assessment process. Stakeholders in the assessment process include teachers, students, parents, school administrators, counselors, community leaders, potential employers, and policy makers. An example of this approach to validation is found in Black, Harrison, Hodgen, Marshall, and Serret (2010), who discuss the validation of summative assessments in the light of the teachers' own developing formulations of quality criteria. Validity arguments influenced strongly by social–constructivism would be expected to rely heavily on interpretations of stakeholders in the assessment process for evidence about validity.

The traditional and the sociocultural perspectives on validation in educational measurement differ about what constitutes evidence of validity and about the value placed on psychometric quality of test scores versus values derived from test stakeholders' individual conceptual frameworks. While recognizing these differences in perspectives, I maintain that most theorists accept at least implicitly that the appropriateness of an interpretation or use of an assessment process and the data it generates depends on two things: (1) the justification for the intended interpretation and use (the interpretive argument) and (2) the quality of the evidence that the interpretation and use is appropriate or results in the intended outcomes (the validity argument). Differences among perspectives have more to do with what constitutes a justification or evidence, rather than the need for evidence per se.

Issues that are closely related to validity in assessment are fairness and equity, because lack of fairness can often be attributed to biases that derive from construct irrelevance variance in test scores (Haladyna & Downing, 2004). The many issues relating to fairness and equity are addressed elsewhere in this volume (see Tierney, Chapter 8 of this volume).

Purposes of Classroom Assessment

The purposes served by CAs tend to define arguments about their interpretation and use. The main purposes of cognitive assessments in classrooms are often described as formative and summative, based on terms coined by Scriven (1967). Formative assessments are those whose primary purpose is to guide and improve student learning and/or teacher instructional practice (Shepard, 2006); hence, formative assessment is sometimes referred to as *assessment for learning* (AFL). Contemporary definitions of formative assessment stress the importance of quality feedback and the involvement of students in the assessment process in order to achieve the desired learning gains (Brookhart, 2011). Brookhart (2003) stated that the formative purpose is primary in CA. The term *formative assessment* is sometimes also used to describe externally produced interim or benchmark assessment. (See Chapters 10–13 of this volume.)

Summative purposes of CA are characterized by a reporting function (Harlen, 2005). As with all assessments that include tests, in summative assessment inferences are drawn from evidence gathered systematically. However, the purpose in summative assessment is to use those inferences to report student learning to one or more audiences outside the classroom, such as parents and school administrators, often for highly consequential purposes such as promotion/retention decisions, certification, or selection (see also Chapter 14 of this volume). In the United States, the most common forms that summative assessment in CA take are marking period grades and the tests and performance assessments that are summarized in such grades (unit tests, project grades, etc.). Internationally, responsibility for summative assessment may be held by teachers or external education authorities; in England, for instance, at some key grade levels the summative assessments that are considered authoritative are conducted by external authorities (Black et al., 2010).

Many authors on CA include purposes other than the measurement of learning among purposes for assessment—for example, modeling achievement targets, enhancing student motivation (McMillan, 2011; Nitko & Brookhart, 2011; Stiggins, 2001). Some theorists go further to state that CA *is* learning and that the quality of assessment experiences affects the quality of learning (Torrance, 2007). According to principles of sociocultural theory, meaning-making occurs continuously in the classroom during assessment as well as during explicitly instructional activities so that each assessment is "a head-on encounter with a culture's models of prowess" and an occasion of learning and self-reflection (Wolf, 1993, p. 213). The content of a test communicates the values of instruction—for example, "What is included (or excluded) from a test sends messages to test users about what is considered important, and what is considered to be marginal" (Fulcher, 1999, pp. 233–234). Focus on meaning-making through assessment and assessment's effects on other student variables is related to formative CA in that; to the extent that students actually are motivated by an assessment process or attain instructional support from it, those effects can be considered mediators of the desired goal of learning gain.

The terms *formative* and *summative* suggest a clear distinction between types of interpretations and uses to which teachers put CAs that is often misleading. One expects (and hopes) that most teachers use their mainly summative assessments for purposes of self-reflection and future instructional improvement. In classrooms, learning is perpetual, and a true summation of learning or *payoff* evaluation seldom if ever occurs. Methods used in classrooms for summative purposes appear distinct from formative assessment methods only in terms of whether or not a grade is recorded (Cizek, 2010). Further, teachers assess students for a mixture of purposes, some of which may contradict one another. Scores from a quiz may be used to check student mid-unit progress and adjust instruction accordingly (formative purposes) and entered in the gradebook as part of a marking period grade (summative purpose), based on a teacher's conceptual framework that students will learn more when extrinsically motivated through grades (motivational purpose). The different purposes of CA pose different challenges to validation, and these challenges are heightened when purposes are mixed.

Other Properties of Classroom Assessments

Multiple characteristics distinctive to CA tend to constrain traditional psychometric approaches to gathering evidence to support or refute the validation argument. Some properties of CA that impact validity arguments include the situated nature of CA with essential contextual factors and lack of standardization, perceptions about the level of stakes for inferences in CA, complexity of assessment methods, the nature and number of CA users, the role of theory, and the use of informal assessment methods.

The Situated Nature of Classroom Assessment

A classroom teacher's primary responsibility is to the individual learning needs of her students; therefore, standardizing assessments across multiple classrooms over time or across different sections of a course seems in the informal conceptual framework of many teachers obviously invalid. Instruction varies from section to section, from year to year, and with appropriate differentiation, from student to student. If instruction is differentiated, shouldn't assessment be differentiated accordingly? Moreover, the inferences based on assessments are informed by a host of factors in the classroom, school, and local and regional context in the form of social and economic pressures on teachers, students, and school administrators. The highly situated nature of CAs limits the generalizability of many validation arguments and the number of students and teachers involved in any given argument.

The Level of Stakes

In terms of stakes or consequences associated with CA decision making, philosophic burden of proof or obligation to provide warrant for validity has often been held to be lower for CAs, due to the fact that CAs are usually held to be low stakes. The common wisdom as exemplified in the *Standards* (AERA et al., 1999) is that the higher the stakes, the higher the obligation and vice versa. Kane (2006) used CA as an example of "low-stakes applications involving relatively plausible inferences and assumptions" (p. 26). The assumption that the stakes or consequences associated with CAs are low is seldom questioned, despite evidence that student self-image and motivation are impacted by interpretations and consequences based on CA results (Thomas & Oldfather, 1997). While the consequences of incorrect inferences about a single low-stakes assessment in the classroom may be small, assessment-based decisions accumulate over the school year. One should therefore keep in mind the frequency with which teachers are involved in assessment-related activities, estimated at as much as one-third of their professional time (Stiggins, Conklin, & U.S. Office of Educational Research and Improvement, 1992). McMorris and Boothroyd (1993) described the volume of assessment information this way:

> Every day, the number of tests taken in schools, and the number and type of decisions based on information from those tests, could perhaps best be described as astronomical. Moreover, if we include the other types of assessment information used by teachers and students . . . the amount of information, the number of decisions, and the impact of those decisions become virtually incomprehensible. (p. 336)

It is reasonable to expect that the situation has only intensified since those words were written. Multiple problems with validity of inferences and decisions about multiple assessments can impact students strongly over time, in terms of instructional decisions, course placements, promotion and retention decisions, and lasting effects on student motivation. Also, while individual low-stakes decisions may be open to reconsideration or reversal, in practice prior decisions may influence those in the future so that for instance students pegged as C students may carry that label in a teacher's mind from day to day and in a school from course to course. The stakes of decisions based on CAs should therefore not be discounted, although each individual decision instance may not be highly consequential.

The Complexity of Classroom Assessment Methods

CAs are likely to be multicomponent, evolving records of student processes as well as products, in comparison to most traditional standardized tests which yield single-occasion snapshots of student achievement. An assessment of student essay-writing may include prewriting, drafting, peer and self-editing, responding to feedback, and reviewing the final product components or more. Theoretically, the validation of each of these process components is simultaneously independent and contingent on the others—or at least those preceding it in time. Indeed, the passage of time is an issue in CA that is usually avoided in other educational measurement through standardization. If the same complex essay-writing task that was previously described is administered at the beginning of a term, it should be interpreted in a different light from one administered after instruction, and teacher feedback and instructional responses should be different as well. Validity arguments about CAs must be sensitive to time as a facet of context that is not standardized, as it is in many large-scale assessments.

The Nature and Number of Those Involved

According to the *Standards* (AERA et al., 1999), "validation is the joint responsibility of the test developer and the test user" (p. 11). In classroom contexts, test developers are usually teachers, and test users include teachers, counselors, other school personnel, students, and families. The poor state of training of classroom teachers in assessment has been well documented (Stiggins, 2001; Wise, Lukin, & Roos, 1991). Those responsible for validating assessments in the classroom bring little technical knowledge to the task. Also, the interests and values of teachers and students as they construct assessment-based interpretations may frequently diverge. A critical question to ask regarding CA and validity is "Validity according to whom?" Finally, in many cases, the number of students assessed through a given CA process is small, precluding the use of most quantitative methods traditionally used in validation. The diversity of the CA world should be recalled, however, before precluding all quantitative approaches to validation. It is not unusual in the United States for secondary school teachers to administer the same formal test to 150 students and to use the same secured test over multiple years, and there are many instructors in higher education who routinely administer formal tests to multiple hundreds of students, maintain test banks, and summarize their data quantitatively.

The Role of Theory in Classroom Assessment

Most validity arguments relating to CAs are likely theory-neutral, in that the measurements are intended to describe observable attributes or traits independent of cognitive theory (Kane, 2006). The lack of cognitive theory underlying much educational measurement may be gradually changing, but it is not likely to change within the classroom in the near future. Classroom teachers are not generally testing theory. This reduces the level of inference from the performance to the attribute, without the additional inference from the attribute to its role in theory, in most cases. To refer to a previous example, a teacher may want to use an essay about *Romeo and Juliet* in English language arts to make inferences about analytic essay-writing in general, but he is not likely to wish to make inferences to the validity of a cognitive theory about a specific learning progression from, for instance, conceptual knowledge to deductive reasoning. Thus the interpretation of CA results involves relatively low levels of inference and thus concern about the consequences of a single invalid interpretation are reduced.

The Use of Informal Assessment Methods

In CA, teachers frequently rely on information gleaned from nontest assessment methods. Nontest assessment methods include a wide variety of methods that are rarely documented, such as informal observations of individuals or groups, individualized assignments or common assignments with individualized, nonstandardized grading criteria, and nonrandom questioning. Many classroom instructional decisions such as pacing and temporary grouping are made on the basis of this type of information. In some advanced courses, such as seminars in higher education, even summative decisions may be made on the basis of nonstandardized information (Moss, 2003).

The Measurement Purpose: Traditional and Interpretive Validity Arguments

In this section, I will describe and provide illustrative examples of validation arguments and related studies developed for CAs for the purpose of *measurement of student learning.* I treat the measurement purpose first, based on the assumption that assessments can only begin to help improve student learning when they start by providing accurate and valid information *about* learning. Following a familiar and traditional framework on validation of tests, articulated in the *Standards* (AERA et al., 1999), I will describe approaches that draw on evidence based on test content, internal structure, substantive response processes, relations to other variables, and consequences of assessments. Where relevant exemplars can't be found, examples will be provided that are based on larger-scale assessments but may be considered applicable to the classroom context or that are purely hypothetical.

Content-Based Evidence

Historically, many educational achievement tests have relied heavily on the judgment of subject matter experts about the relationship between test content and the intended curriculum (e.g., state or national standards) to support claims of validity. To demonstrate and improve the content validity of assessments, the *Standards* (AERA et al., 1999) recommend that professional test developers create tables of specifications or test blueprints. Educational experts and authors of textbooks on CA also typically recommend that classroom teachers prepare test blueprints. Guskey (2005) stated that test blueprints "bring added validity and utility to classroom assessments" (p. 37). Among recently reviewed introductory measurement textbooks, authors of textbooks for general educators were found to be in consensus on treating the topic of planning assessments (including creating test blueprints) as essential (Campbell & Collins, 2007). The test blueprint improves and documents validity by mapping the way the test instrument as a whole represents the assessed domain.

Content validation also seeks to demonstrate the relevance of individual test items or tasks to curricular standards. Published guidance to help classroom teachers review the relevance of their assessment tasks to standards dates at least as far back as Mager (1973). Recent technical innovations have allowed test development corporations such as Pearson and the Educational Testing Service to generate item banks with large numbers of assessment tasks linked to state and national standards, to which schools and school districts can purchase access. Teachers can use items from these banks, whose alignment to standards has been attested by subject matter experts, to design standards-relevant CAs.

However, relying solely on content evidence to support claims for validity is problematic according to most theorists. Judgment-based methods tend to suffer from confirmatory bias (Kane, 2006), and evidence about the relationship between test content and curriculum or standards does not address the central question of score interpretation and use (Messick, 1989). Therefore, interpretations based even on highly content-valid tests could be inappropriate, inaccurate, or biased.

Despite its insufficiency as a single source of evidence for validation, educational tests intended to provide information about student progress toward achievement targets are generally considered valid in part according to how well their content relates to and represents the curricular domain, and professional guidelines such as the *Standards* (AERA et al., 1999) still give content-related approaches to test validation primacy of position in the description of sources of validity evidence.

Methods for studying the alignment of an assessment tool to the intended instructional objectives have proliferated in recent years. Many rely on expert judgment of consistencies between test items or tasks and authoritative statements about the expected curriculum (usually operationalized as state or national standards). Some analyze relationships between the test blueprint and the expected curriculum, instead. The focus of recent research has, understandably, been on the relationship between state assessments and published state or national standards rather than on the analysis of classroom tests. In prior decades, however, published studies that reported results of content analyses of classroom tests (Fleming & Chambers, 1983; Marso & Pigge, 1991; McMorris & Boothroyd, 1993) showed that teacher-made tests predominantly favored objectively scored, selected-response (SR) formats and tended to emphasize lower-level aspects of learning.

The finding that teacher-made tests emphasize lower-level aspects of learning does not necessarily mean that teacher-made tests lack validity as measures of instruction and learning goals for students. The question for validity, particularly for content validity, is one of alignment between intended instructional targets and assessment content. Thus, if the expected curricular objectives are at a low level, teacher-made tests at that level may be valid. However, educational policy today promotes critical thinking as a goal of instruction, and state standards and the new Common Core State Standards in the United States reflect this emphasis on critical thinking. Evidence that assessments have traditionally not addressed critical thinking is therefore a concern.

Recent studies about the content validity of CAs were difficult to locate. One recent study about the alignment between teacher-made assessments and intended curricula was unable to determine evidence for or against alignment between instructional goals and teacher-made assessments due to the fact that teachers did not prepare blueprints (Campbell & Evans, 2000). No quality recent studies investigating the relationship between teacher assessments and enacted instruction were found.

Internal Structural Evidence

Many analyses of the internal structure of tests, such as internal consistency and dimensionality analyses, are prohibited in many cases of CAs due to small sample sizes and, in some cases, lack of technical expertise on the part of relevant stakeholders. One of the more basic components of internal structural evidence is evidence based on the reliability of assessments, a topic addressed elsewhere in this volume (Parkes, see Chapter 7 in this volume). Although issues of reliability are beyond the scope of the present chapter, I note here that recent authors who have treated the subject of reliability in CAs have averred that in cases of CA, it is difficult to distinguish issues of reliability from issues of validity (Parkes, 2007; Smith, 2003). The two facets driving quality of assessment-based interpretations become intertwined in the complex process of generating sufficient, trustworthy, and accurate information about student learning within the changing environment of the classroom. Generalizability of assessment interpretations, a related concept, is not likely to be as much a desideratum in CA as it in large-scale assessment, because of the situated, locally embedded nature of most CAs.

A major issue that in traditional psychometrics is typically addressed under the heading of internal structural evidence, or more generally as an aspect of construct validity, is the question of bias. With large-scale assessments, psychometricians attempt to detect differential item functioning, which can be a signal of bias at the test item level. However, differential item functioning analyses require data sets of a size unavailable at the CA level and technical expertise beyond the scope of the classroom teacher who might seek to validate his own assessment-based inferences. Without drawing on differential item functioning analyses, a number of historical experimental studies have found various biases in teacher subjective rating of student work, including effects of extraneous variables such as student race, gender, and handwriting versus word processing (Chase, 1986; Clifton, Perry, Parsonson, & Hryniuk, 1986; Powers, Fowles, Farnum, & Ramsey, 1994). To minimize such sources of bias, training in subjective scoring of essay and performance tasks usually includes advice to use rubrics consistently, refer to anchor papers, score by item or task rather than by student, remove student names prior to scoring, and standardize response formats as much as possible. Little evidence about how well these techniques effectively reduce bias in scoring by classroom teachers was found. One study found considerable variability among trained teachers in rating student essays in English, despite the use of rubrics (Brimi, 2011). Llosa (2008) investigated teachers' decision making about scoring and found that scores on listening/speaking assessments were particularly influenced by teacher perceptions about student personality and behavior, despite the use of rubrics.

Substantive Process Evidence

Another source of evidence for claims for the validity of test score interpretations is gleaned from information about the substantive processes test takers use when they respond to test stimuli. Many cognitive psychologists and contemporary theorists of educational measurement recommend that test design and interpretation be informed by study of cognitive or substantive processes at work in test taking, because such study is important both for understanding the psychological traits that lie behind measures of academic performance and for evaluating the validity of score interpretations (Bonner & D'Agostino, 2012; Embretson & Gorin, 2001; Haladyna, Downing, & Rodriguez, 2002; Leighton, 2004; Pellegrino & Chudowsky, 2003; Pellegrino, Chudowsky, Glaser, & National Research Council Committee on the Foundations of Assessment, 2001). Flaws in assessment tasks can be indicated when tasks elicit thinking or behaviors such as recourse to testwiseness strategies that are different from those the tester wishes to elicit. Inquiry into cognitive processes can enlighten stakeholders as to the causes of bias in test scores, such as vocabulary issues relating to English (or other home) language learning, as opposed to technical vocabulary.

Substantive or cognitive process studies have frequently relied on examinees' reports of their cognitive processes as they complete assessment tasks while thinking aloud (Hamilton, Nussbaum, & Snow, 1997; Morell & Tan, 2009; Nuthall & Alton-Lee, 1995). Procedures used to elicit information about test taker cognitive processes through think-alouds, retrospective debriefing, interaction with test developers, and even techniques such as eye-movement tracking are often components of "cognitive labs," which many professional test developers use during test item tryouts and piloting. Morell and Tan (2009) illustrated the use of think-alouds and analysis of verbal protocols, combined with other methods, to generate a validation argument for a test of environmental science learning. Morell and Tan found that the think-aloud technique provided information about why various test items were more or less difficult for students that was not provided by internal structural analysis. The think-aloud technique also provided information that could be used to improve the partial credit model used to score the test. Although the test in Morell and Tan's study was not a classroom-based assessment, many of the techniques used in cognitive labs and studies of this sort are within the scope of the classroom teacher who seeks to validate her interpretation based on claims about task expectations. Another example of this approach is found in Nuthall and Alton-Lee (1995), who used student questioning to explore the complex cognitive and metacognitive processes students used to respond to nonstandardized achievement tests just after instruction and one year after instruction.

Another way that substantive processes have been studied is in the literature on the decision-making processes that teachers use to arrive at student grades. Using primarily survey methods, researchers have found that teachers endorse and self-report grading practices that result in grades that reflect a range of student attributes other than achievement, such as effort and behavior (Brookhart, 1993; Cizek, Fitzgerald, & Rachor, 1995; McMillan, 2001, 2003). The incorporation of factors outside achievement constitutes a threat to validity if the grade is expected to indicate and is interpreted as representing academic achievement only but actually reflects a "hodgepodge" of factors (Brookhart, 1991).

Evidence Based on Relations to Other Variables

Claims about proposed assessment interpretations that draw on relationships with external variables very frequently involve studies relating test scores to scores on a criterion of success measured in the future, or in some cases, concurrently. These studies are most appropriate when a test is intended to predict future performance and when a high quality measure of that future performance is available. Classroom teacher-made assessments rarely have the psychometric qualities that would make them correlate well with other measures, and scores are usually obtained from small samples, increasing the influence of outlier scores and reducing confidence in the correlation as an estimator. An example of a study that inquired into the relationship between a CA and a criterion measure is found in Mills, Sweeney, & Bonner (2009), which studied the correlation and predictivity of first unit exams in undergraduate general chemistry with semester course outcomes. The study, which originated within a single department where unit exams were not standardized across course sections and incorporated results from several undergraduate institutions, found high correlations between the first exam and course outcomes that were robust over multiple instructors, exam modalities, and undergraduate institutions.

Interestingly, even with evidence leading to doubt about the validity of course grades, as previously described, both individual course grades and combined grade point averages are frequently used as criterion measures in validation studies of other measurement instruments (Cashin & Elmore, 2005; Fewster & Macmillan, 2002). Given that a criterion theoretically should be measured with minimal error, this practice possibly suggests a general consensus about the validity of teacher-generated classroom grades based on their usefulness in association with other variables. In studies on the prediction of postsecondary outcomes, high school grade point average has slightly shown higher validity coefficients than SAT I combined scores (Camara & Echternacht, 2000). Aggregated over multiple courses, the combination of academic achievement with so-called extraneous variables such as effort turns out to relate well to success at the postsecondary level.

Despite evidence just described that demonstrates that CAs can and do predict future student achievement outcomes, the notion of validating CAs based on predictive evidence is conceptually problematic, especially when assessments are at least partly formative. A high correlation between the CA and the criterion measure means that students maintain relative rank in each distribution of scores. If the CA is formative and administered while learning is in progress and the criterion measures learning outcomes, a high correlation means that those who were performing poorly relative to others continued to do so. In other words, instructional efforts to close achievement gaps and help all students reach performance expectations did not succeed. Effective classroom instruction should result in a lower correlation coefficient between assessment of learning-in-progress and learning outcomes compared to the correlation that would be obtained if effective instruction did not occur.

Another kind of evidence from external relationships is obtained through correlational analyses of test scores with other measures of the same construct (convergent evidence), compared to measures of related but distinct constructs (discriminant or divergent evidence). Convergent and discriminant validation studies of CA are practically challenging to conduct with CAs for the same reasons that challenge the use of predictive studies, and no quality recent studies of validation arguments relying heavily on such methods were found, with the exception of Llosa. Llosa (2008), who related the district-wide CA with state English language proficiency scores, found predicted patterns of relationships among the multiple dimensions of English proficiency assessed.

Interpretive Approaches to Validating Measurement Claims

Several studies illustrate investigations into the validity of CA-based interpretations or decisions that focus on the perspectives of key stakeholders and how they generate interpretations. Writing from an interpretivist standpoint, Moss (2003) provided a detailed description of her own practice as a case study, narrating the types of critically inquiring processes she uses as a seminar teacher to make formative and summative assessment inferences and monitor and self-reflect on the validity of actions taken based on those inferences. Several researchers have sought to understand the validity of teachers' summative assessment decisions from the perspective of the teachers' own conceptual frameworks and sense of the classroom and school context (Black et al., 2010; Brookhart, 1993b). Andrade and Du (2005) gathered information through focus groups about undergraduate perspectives on rubric use that provides evidence to support the validity of sharing rubrics with students when the purpose is to foster learning effort.

Interpretive approaches to validation fit CA contexts particularly well when assessment relies heavily on nontest, informal assessments like observations and questioning, such as the graduate seminar described by Moss (2003). Kane (2006) described a classroom teacher's validation argument as a qualitative, iterative process of self-reference to a conceptual framework, gathering informal evidence and making decisions, observing results, and revising the conceptual framework. However, little guidance was found in the literature about techniques that teachers use to improve the credibility and neutrality of their decision-making based on informal assessments. For instance, while values such as minimizing bias and other principles doubtless apply equally to formal and informal assessments, methods for detecting bias in informal assessments are not well defined. Some guidance for supporting teachers in self-reflection about informal observations is found in Bulterman-Bos, Terwel, Verloop, and Wardekker (2002); otherwise, little information was found on methods or technologies to support reflective practice in assessment among K–12 teachers.

Consequential Evidence

Consequential evidence about the validity of assessment-based claims is treated here last among measurement claims because in some ways the role of consequential evidence lies at the boundary between the measurement and the learning purpose.

The more conservative discussion about consequences of measurement focuses on consequences based on decision-accuracy, decision-relevance, and freedom of bias when tests are used for making decisions about individuals or groups that are hard to undo, such as selection and placement decisions. An example of a study that considered the theoretical consequences of classroom test-based advisement for course transfer was Mills et al. (2009), previously described, in which the authors assessed the accuracy of the prediction that students scoring one or more standard deviations below the mean on the first classroom exam were likely to have an unsuccessful course outcome. Evidence from logistic regressions and accuracy rates of predictions about course performance based on the first exam suggested that the first exam could indeed be used as an advisement tool at the undergraduate institution with minimal unintended negative consequences to students in general chemistry.

More progressive concerns about the consequences of test use derive from the assumption—stated or unstated in the test's interpretive argument—that the use of the test will effect some change in test stakeholders: students, teachers, or schools. In short, this research concern reflects the perspective that the primary purpose of assessment is not to *measure* but to *further* learning. This is part of the core theoretical argument for formative assessment, explicitly stated; it is also part of the rationale for test-based accountability programs. The purpose of some tests and assessments in today's schools is explicitly reactive and based on the argument that, because of awareness that they are being assessed, schools will improve programs, teachers will improve instruction, students will try harder, etc. "Increasingly, assessments are viewed as a way not only to measure performance, but also to change it, by encouraging teachers and students to modify their practices" (Pellegrino et al., 2001, p. 39). Arguments about the use of testing to *cause* an *effect* are not wholly similar to arguments about the validity of test score-based interpretations as *measurement* and therefore are discussed separately in the next section.

Reactive Measurement: Validity of Claims About Impacts of Assessments

There are two types of impacts that theorists have ascribed to CA practices. One may occur when the purpose of assessment is *for* learning. Under this paradigm, when assessment tasks are created that are well aligned with learning goals and provide accurate information about student learning through appropriate methods and unbiased interpretations, that information is used formatively to generate feedback to students and instructional responses. If the feedback has certain qualities—for example, if it is prompt, goal-oriented, and directs students to specific actions within their capabilities to improve, and instructional opportunities are offered for such improvement—the entire assessment process can result in improved learning outcomes (Black & Wiliam, 2004). This use of assessment for an instructional effect extends at least one step beyond the measurement purpose of most educational measurement; it extends into the area of intervention, where the validity of inferences from cause to effect is paramount. Even technical tasks such as development of test blueprints have been purported to lead to better instruction and hence better learning (Guskey, 2005). Numerous studies have associated student achievement gains with formative assessment practices (Andrade, Du, & Wang, 2008; Black & Wiliam, 1998, 2004; Rodriguez, 2004). In a mixed methods study comparing effects of portfolio assessment in alternative assessment classrooms to regular assessment classrooms, positive effects of portfolio assessment on student learning orientation and reading were found, supporting the validity claim for use of the portfolio assessments for learning (Underwood, 1998).

Another type of impact is generated almost inadvertently through the assessment process. Humans generate knowledge through all their experiences, including the experience of being assessed (Fulcher, 1999; Wolf, 1993). Impacts of assessment *as* learning may include a range of motivational and attitudinal adjustments that occur among teachers and students daily, as well as learning one another's expectations and boundaries. McMorris and Boothroyd (1993) described the reactive quality in classroom measurement and the often-unintended but unavoidable impacts of teacher assessment practices on student attitudes: "The impacts of a test's characteristics and quality . . . include student attitudes and perceptions that affect what students bring to the next encounter" (p. 324). This constant cognitive and motivational negotiation among stakeholders in the assessment process about the meaning of the assessment is known in research design theory as *measurement reactivity*. In traditional theory, the measurement technique, instrument, or tool should be as unobtrusive as possible, so as not to cause reactivity, which essentially changes the subject being measured through the act of measurement, and potentially changes the perspective of the tester as well. However, in many current contexts test users, developers, and policy makers seek precisely the opposite result.

Because some of these impacts are predictable, they may affect validity of inferences about assessments, especially if one of the claims made for test use is its effect on variables such as motivation. Nitko (1989) pointed out that students were motivated by CAs but went on to note a paucity of evidence about assessment characteristics that promote motivation. The state of research he described still largely pertains today. Understanding the subtle effects of assessment practices on student attitudes and perceptions can help teachers develop and use tests that take educational advantage of such effects and therefore have greater validity as assessments for learning. In the field of language testing, the term *washback* has been used to refer to the effects of testing on instruction (Fulcher, 1999), including both positive effects of washback, such as beneficial changes resulting from use of testing or changes to tests, and negative effects, such as narrowing of curriculum. Washback potentially affects learners, teachers, school administrators, and professional test developers. Washback can also affect institutional processes and products and thus entire systems (Wall, 2000).

Performance assessment is an instance of an assessment method that often claims to capitalize on method effects to improve student motivation and learning or to have positive washback effects. In a descriptive case study of a single high school social studies teacher's classroom environment over multiple occasions of assessment, Brookhart and Durkin (2003) found that performance assessment was associated with higher external and internal motivation and effort compared to paper-and-pencil tests. In a study among high school students in Spanish classes, use of performance assessment predicted student perception of control compared to use of objective testing (Parkes, 2000).

Assessment formats other than performance assessment have also been shown to have predictable relationships to variables other than performance. For instance, O'Neil and Brown (1998) examined the effect of assessment format (constructed-response [CR] versus multiple-choice) on student metacognition (strategy use and self-checking) and affective variables (worry and effort) among a large sample of eighth graders in California using a mixed-model design with format as a within-subjects factor, and found significantly greater strategy use and worry in the CR format, and greater self-checking in the multiple-choice format. Further research is necessary to probe how much the effects of assessment format reported in studies such as those above extend and generalize across multiple content domains, grade levels, and classroom contexts.

Because claims about impacts of assessment practices extend beyond the measurement argument to the validation of inferences about cause and effect, most of the previously cited studies use experimental and quasi-experimental methods. Consistent with such methods, studies address threats to the validity of inferences about the causal link between assessment and outcome through assignment to groups, repeated measures, statistical controls, data triangulation, and so on. Techniques and principles for improving the validity of causal inferences or the credibility of qualitative interpretations are well beyond the scope of this chapter. Attention to validity of causal inferences is crucially important, however, when the purpose of assessment explicitly includes making causal claims, for instance, that a formative assessment practice causes improved writing performance, or the use of performance assessment causes increased motivation. In such cases, at least two validation arguments should be made: (1) for the assessment in its measurement purpose and (2) for the assessment as an intervention.

Five Principles for Valid Teacher Inferences Based on Classroom Assessments

In this section, I propose five principles critical to the process for making claims about the validity of an educational interpretation based on CAs. These principles are reinterpreted from traditional approaches for CA contexts. I select these five because I think they are within the resources available to those working in CA and also reflect the sensitivity to individual learners and learning outcomes that are important for most CA purposes. I specifically refrain from recommending approaches or principles based on technical qualities such as the predictive or convergent properties of test scores, which, for reasons previously described, are prohibited by constraints of classroom contexts or inconsistent with classroom learning purposes. The principles that follow are equally relevant whether the validity claim is made by researchers, teachers, students, or other stakeholders, whether the assessment yields qualitative or quantitative data, and whether the purpose is one of measurement, learning, or both. As such, without providing a new theory of classroom measurement, they distill elements of existing theory into a framework that supports school-based stakeholders in reflecting on and improving the validity of CAs.

1. Assessment Should Be Aligned With Instruction

Approaches based on alignment of test content to curricular standards are not enough; claims for valid inferences about learning within the classroom must be based on tasks that are aligned with instruction in the classroom. Nitko (1989) defined appropriate test usage of tests that are linked with or integrated with instructional materials and procedures. Poor alignment between instruction and CA can have negative impacts on student attitudes, motivation, and classroom climate. If a teacher deems it necessary or educationally valid to use instructional time to provide enrichment or remediation to all or some of her students, she should monitor the results of such enrichment or remediation through her assessments. Her tests and feedback will therefore be better aligned with instruction, though possibly not as well aligned to the expected curriculum. Paradoxically, it appears that when assessments show better warrant for claims about achievement within the classroom, they may correspondingly lack warrant for claims about interpretations of student achievement as defined by state or national standards. In other words, there may be a trade-off between *content* or curricular validity and *instructional* validity, if content has been defined as adherence to state or national grade-level standards. Trade-offs between instructional and content alignment are in themselves appropriate targets for research and inquiry.

Methods for estimating the relatedness and representativeness of CA content include, for a more teacher-centered classroom, analysis of test coverage as represented on a written test, in comparison to instructional time or emphases as represented in lesson plans. For a more student-centered classroom, methods for validating CAs in terms of instructional validity could include eliciting reactions from students following practice tests about the relevance of assessment tasks to instruction.

2. Bias Should Be Minimal at all Phases of the Assessment Process

If task performance requires resources that are not equally available to all types of students, task bias can emerge in the design phase. During test taking, students may be affected by method biases—for instance bias in favor of fluent readers in paper-and-pencil tests, glib writers in essay formats, and gregarious personalities in performance assessments. Teachers can be influenced by biases when scoring assessments as previously described and when providing students with feedback about assessment results. Methods for detecting bias in task design appropriate for CA contexts include analysis of tasks by subject matter experts, which might involve shared task development or review among teacher teams, and/or debriefing assessments with small groups of students. One high school teacher of my acquaintance has 10th-grade students review his 9th-grade tests and rubrics before he administers them, refreshing the 10th graders on prior learning while obtaining the insights of student eyes. Simple techniques of item analysis are appropriate for many classroom contexts; for instance, classroom teachers can easily learn to check the relative difficulty of mathematics test items among English language learners (ELLs) compared to native speakers, which can be informative in settings like secondary schools where the number of students may be relatively large. Methods to reduce bias during scoring and feedback include use of rubrics but also co-scoring and multiple raters for samples of student work. Collaboration around scoring to identify and detect bias can, however, only occur when teachers feel that inquiry into their assessment validity is safe and formative in purpose. (See Chapter 8 of this volume for more discussion of bias and fairness.)

3. Assessment Processes Should Elicit Relevant Substantive Processes

The study of student thinking processes and task-relevant (or irrelevant) behaviors emphasizes the role of process over product, which is consistent with cognitive perspectives on assessment and with the concept that an assessment episode is a learning event for students. In addition to the usefulness of probing student processes to understand possible sources of bias and irrelevant variance, understanding the cognitive processes that are elicited and reinforced through assessments may help teachers create CAs that provide better diagnostic information about flaws in learners' problem solving, develop scoring rubrics that are more sensitive to gradations of student skill and understanding, and develop tests that elicit and reinforce problem-solving approaches that not only measure performance but stimulate motivation, retention, and effective study habits. Teachers should be aware that relevant substantive processes should be elicited not just during task performance but during scoring (whether by teachers or students) and during interpretation of feedback. For instance, if feedback is not promptly provided, students may have difficulty remembering relevant processes that affected their performance and be less able to make use of the feedback. In addition to think-alouds, techniques that yield information about substantive process include observations of students and groups during task-work, peer observations, and retrospective surveys or interviews about assessment tasks.

4. Effects of Assessment-Based Interpretations Should Be Evaluated

Consequences of assessment-based decisions should be justified by strong logical arguments or evidence that the benefits to those affected by the decisions outweigh any negative impacts. Motivational and other types of potential impacts should be considered, as well as effects on learning and achievement. In the case of assessment for formative purposes, where actions are taken based often on informally obtained information about evolving learning, information should be frequently gathered about the effects of such actions on students. Information can be gathered within the fluid context of the classroom both through continued monitoring of student learning with formal and informal assessments and through direct investigation—for example, through questioning students about their perceptions about the usefulness of teacher feedback and ensuing decisions. With formative assessment, teachers should attempt to provide opportunities for students to be reassessed when assessment-based decisions appear to be ineffective or inappropriate and should revise their instructional decisions in light of reassessment as needed.

5. Validation Should Include Evidence From Multiple Stakeholders

Many individuals have stakes in CA processes, interpretations, and decisions, including the classroom teacher and her students, parents, principals, and other teachers. Not all interpretations and decisions require or are expected to be made with input from multiple stakeholders. However, teachers should realize that the validity of their assessment-based interpretations and decisions may be questioned by other stakeholders and be prepared to argue their claims and revise them if needed. Kane (2006) described the validation of an interpretive argument as proceeding in two stages—(1) the development stage and (2) the appraisal stage—and suggests that with some overlap, test developers are highly involved in the development stage of the argument while others who take a more critical stance toward the proposed argument are more involved in the appraisal stage. Without the involvement of stakeholders in validation who are outside the assessment development process, we risk "confirmationist bias" (Kane, 2006) or the assumption that our assessment-based decisions are all valid. On a smaller scale, the same holds true for CAs. Teachers, those closest to the assessment development process, have primary responsibility for evaluating their assessment processes and assessment-based interpretations and decisions but should understand that potentially important validity issues in those processes, interpretations, and decisions can only be detected if the perspectives of others are considered. For some teachers, these others may only include colleagues, mentors, or professional developers, while other teachers may choose to include students in some aspects of assessment validation. As a general principle, responsibility for assessment validation should not depend upon the judgment of a single individual. The involvement of multiple stakeholders in validation helps satisfy the requirement to consider plausible rival hypotheses.

Systemic Validity: A Validation Principle for Teachers?

In addition to the principles that were previously described, teachers should be encouraged through their professional development, professional organizations, and school-based leadership to consider the systemic validity of the assessments they use in their classrooms. The concept of systemic validity was proposed by Frederiksen and Collins (1989) and has not, perhaps, received the attention it deserves. The idea is that educational tests are components of dynamic systems, and thus decisions about assessment methods provide feedback that determines the future of the system. Teachers may adopt classroom-based assessment practices that support the most educationally valid purposes of the system or may adopt practices, such as intensive high-stakes test preparation through drill and practice, that do not support the larger aims intended by the system. The principle that teachers should be responsible for systemically valid assessments is not included under the previously given key principles, due to recognition that to some extent, teachers are not the decision-making authorities in schools about how instruction should be tested. It is likely that teachers are often pressured in their schools to adopt CA practices that focus on test taking strategies, rote memorization, and strategies of testwiseness that are not systemically valid. However, teachers should be at all points encouraged to bear in mind the important educational outcomes of students, rather than a test-as-end-in-itself mentality.

Summary and Recommendations for Research

I have attempted in this chapter to relate the main purposes of CA to both traditional psychometric theory and interpretive and sociocultural discussions of validity. I have borne in mind distinctive purposes and properties of CA that make some traditional validation approaches inappropriate; however, I disagree with some other authors (Brookhart, 2003; Shepard, 2006) that entirely new theory is needed. I argue that different methods and epistemological orientations are not inconsistent with the broader development of theory of measurement validation. Core tenets of contemporary psychometrics recognize the essential contextualization of interpretations, the need to attend to the complex nature of constructs, and the demand for multiple sources of evidence, although psychometric practice often has ignored these principles in favor of standardization. In spite of practical challenges, theory does not value standardization as an end in itself.

I propose a research agenda on CA validity that pays close attention to essential and researchable qualities affecting validity: instructional alignment, minimal bias, substantive processes, effects of assessment-based decisions, and multiple perspectives. I have provided examples of researchers who have practiced critical inquiry into CA validity both from quantitative/traditional and qualitative/interpretive perspectives. I have also argued that validating a CA as a measure of learning alone is inadequate when the purpose is to further student learning and that in such cases, validation approaches based on experimental and quasi-experimental design principles combined with qualitative methods are likely needed.

There are wide gaps in the research literature on validity in CA, and the examples provided in the preceding sections do not constitute a comprehensive literature review nor are they all completely classroom-centered. A more comprehensive review of existing examples of studies relating to the validity of classroom-based assessment practices would clarify strengths and weaknesses in the research literature. Furthermore, it would be desirable to undertake a systematic survey of practices that classroom teachers use to prepare, try out, reflect upon, and revise their assessment methods.

Research might also inquire into the question of potential validation trade-offs between the measurement purpose and the learning purpose of CA. Is measurement validity a necessary but not sufficient condition for validity of an assessment for a learning purpose? How accurate does the validity of the test score interpretation have to be for testing to have a motivational effect, or an effect of directing teacher attention to standards, or to student needs, or to generate effective feedback? Are there conditions that make the validity of the score interpretation secondary or even not an issue, and if so, what are those conditions? For instance, many institutions of higher education require researchers to complete training and be tested on rights of human subjects involved in research. Researchers can retake these tests an unlimited number of times until they achieve the minimum required score for certification. The final scores therefore have little variability among subjects tested and measure essentially nothing except compliance with the regulation. Other purposes (completion of learning modules, compliance) are more important, and the tests are used only to enforce the achievement of these purposes. How frequently do classroom teachers use tests in this way? Should such instruments be considered tests at all? What impact do they have on learning?

Researchers and theorists should also probe practices and make recommendations about the prioritization of assessment uses and its consequent impact on validation. How do teachers prioritize when their assessment use serves multiple purposes, and how should they? The conflicting needs and characteristics of externally developed accountability tests and CAs have been documented (Hickey, Zuiker, Taasoobshirazi, Schafer, & Michael, 2006), and interview-based evidence has suggested that some of the practices teachers use in grading derive from a desire that grades should serve motivational as well as summative purposes (Brookhart, 1993; McMillan, 2003). Such conflicts among purposes are likely more common than not, and here again there may be trade-offs: if the purpose is to model excellence and promote motivation and improvement more than to measure achievement, minor errors in estimating achievement levels may be tolerated if they serve the primary purpose. For instance, I recall an English teacher who asked me about a student of his whose essay, judged solely on the basis of the rubric, earned a perfect score. He was concerned that if the student received the highest possible score, she would not be motivated to improve her writing on the next task. He wished to award a score less than the score representing her level of *true* achievement, for motivational purposes. In general, such problems can be addressed through thoughtful design of rubrics and feedback, but the situation nonetheless illustrates that validity is contingent upon assessment purpose, and the score interpretation that is valid for one purpose might not be valid for another. Recognizing that summative assessments do not always serve formative purposes, weekly teacher-made quizzes without meaningful feedback and instructional responses have been justifiably referred to as mere "frequent summative assessment" (Black & Wiliam, 2004, p. 22). One question that merits study is the extent to which summative reporting of results of formative assessments undermines the learning purpose.

Another issue that deserves both empirical investigation and theoretical development is the question of who bears responsibility for validation of CAs. It is all very well to agree with the *Standards* (AERA et al., 1999) that test developers and users both have stakes in validation, but even in large-scale assessment this shared responsibility can leave ultimate responsibility ambiguous. University-based researchers have conducted many of the studies that were previously described, sometimes enlisting participation of teachers as research subjects or assistants. However, teacher self-inquiry may be more effective than researcher-driven inquiry for improving the validity of teacher practice. Can teachers and students learn to analyze and reflect upon the assessments they use, according to their alignment with their instructional experiences, freedom from bias, the types of thinking and behavior the assessment tasks elicit, and their effects or consequences? How do teachers develop attitudes and skills relating to CA validation, and what supports them in doing so? Teacher assessment knowledge is important but limited by lack of training; learning opportunities for teachers should relate to their specific needs, which develop and change throughout their careers and training, and include needs within their classroom and in relation to external demands for accountability (Brookhart, 2011; Graham, 2005; Popham, 2009; Stiggins, 2001; Zhang & Burry-Stock, 2003). More systematic inquiry should be undertaken into the needs of teachers as assessment developers and validators and what works best to meet those needs. It is interesting to contemplate how our understanding of CA validity might change if there were deep involvement of teachers and students in the validation of the assessments that affect them so much.

References

American Educational Research Association, American Psychological Association, & National Council on Measurement in Education. (1999). *Standards for educational and psychological testing.* Washington, DC: American Educational Research Association.

Andrade, H., & Du, Y. (2005). Student perspectives on rubric-referenced assessment. *Practical Assessment, Research and Evaluation, 10*(3). Retrieved from http://pareonline.net/pdf/v10n3.pdf

Andrade, H. L., Du, Y., & Wang, X. (2008). Putting rubrics to the test: The effect of a model, criteria generation, and rubric-referenced self-assessment on elementary school students' writing. *Educational Measurement: Issues & Practice, 27*(2), 3–13.

Bachman, L. F. (2005). Building and supporting a case for test use. *Language Assessment Quarterly, 2*(1), 1–34.

Black, P., Harrison, C., Hodgen, J., Marshall, B., & Serret, N. (2010). Validity in teachers' summative assessments. *Assessment in Education: Principles, Policy & Practice, 17*(2), 215–232.

Black, P., & Wiliam, D. (1998). Assessment and classroom learning. *Assessment in Education: Principles, Policy & Practice, 5*(1), 7–75.

Black, P., & Wiliam, D. (2004). The formative purpose: Assessment must first promote learning. In M. Wilson (Ed.), *Towards coherence between classroom assessment and accountability: The 103rd yearbook of the national association for the study of education, Part II* (pp. 20–50). Chicago: NSSE: Distributed by the University of Chicago Press.

Bonner, S. M., & D'Agostino, J. V. (2012). A substantive process analysis of responses to items from the multistate bar examination. *Applied Measurement in Education, 25*(1), 1–26.

Brimi, H. M. (2011). Reliability of grading high school work in English. *Practical Assessment, Research & Evaluation, 16*(17), 1–12. Retrieved from www.pareonline.net/pdf/v16n17.pdf

Brookhart, S. M. (1991). Grading practices and validity. *Educational Measurement: Issues and Practice, 10*(1), 35–36.

Brookhart, S. M. (1993a). Teachers' grading practices: Meaning and values. *Journal of Educational Measurement, 30*(2), 123–142.

Brookhart, S. M. (2003). Developing measurement theory for classroom assessment purposes and uses. *Educational Measurement: Issues and Practice, 22*(4), 5–12.

Brookhart, S. M. (2011). Educational assessment knowledge and skills for teachers. *Educational Measurement: Issues and Practice, 30*(1), 3–12.

Brookhart, S. M., & Durkin, D. T. (2003). Classroom assessment, student motivation, and achievement in high school social studies classes. *Applied Measurement in Education, 16*(1), 27–54.

Bulterman-Bos, J., Terwel, J., Verloop, N., & Wardekker, W. (2002). Observation in teaching: Toward a practice of objectivity. *Teachers College Record, 104*(6), 1069–1100.

Camara, W. J., & Echternacht, G. (2000). The SAT I and high school grades: Utility in predicting success in college. The College Board, Research Notes, Office of Research and Development.

Campbell, C., & Collins, V. L. (2007). Identifying essential topics in general and special education introductory assessment textbooks. *Educational Measurement: Issues & Practice, 26*(1), 9–18.

Campbell, C., & Evans, J. A. (2000). Investigation of preservice teachers' classroom assessment practices during student teaching. *Journal of Educational Research, 93*(6), 350–355.

Cashin, S. E., & Elmore, P. B. (2005). The survey of attitudes toward statistics scale: A construct validity study. *Educational and Psychological Measurement, 65*(3), 509–524.

Chase, C. I. (1986). Essay test scoring: Interaction of relevant variables. *Journal of Educational Measurement, 23*(1), 33–41.

Cizek, G. J. (2009). Reliability and validity of information about student achievement: Comparing large-scale and classroom testing contexts. *Theory into Practice, 48*(1), 63–71.

Cizek, G. J. (2010). An introduction to formative assessment: History, characteristics, and challenges. In H. L. Andrade & G. J. Cizek (Eds.), *Handbook of formative assessment* (pp. 3–17). New York: Routledge.

Cizek, G. J., Fitzgerald, S. M., & Rachor, R. A. (1995). Teachers' assessment practices: Preparation, isolation, and the kitchen sink. *Educational Assessment, 3*(2), 159–179.

Clifton, R. A., Perry, R. P., Parsonson, K., & Hryniuk, S. (1986). Effects of ethnicity and sex on teachers' expectations of junior high school students. *Sociology of Education, 59*(1), 58–67.

Cronbach, L. J. (1971). Test validation. In R. D. Thorndike (Ed.), *Educational measurement* (2nd ed., pp. 443–507). Washington, DC: American Council on Education.

Delandshere, G. (2001). Implicit theories, unexamined assumptions and the status quo of educational assessment. *Assessment in Education: Principles, Policy & Practice, 8*(2), 113–133.

Embretson, S., & Gorin, J. (2001). Improving construct validity with cognitive psychology principles. *Journal of Educational Measurement, 38*(4), 343–368.

Fewster, S., & Macmillan, P. D. (2002). School-based evidence for the validity of curriculum-based measurement of reading and writing. *Remedial & Special Education, 23*(3), 149–156.

Fleming, M., & Chambers, B. A. (1983). Teacher-made tests: Windows on the classroom. *New Directions for Testing & Measurement, 19,* 29–38.

Frederiksen, J. R., & Collins, A. (1989). A systems approach to educational testing. *Educational Researcher, 18*(9), 27–32.

Fulcher, G. (1999). Assessment in English for academic purposes: Putting content validity in its place. *Applied Linguistics, 20*(2), 221–236.

Gipps, C. (1999). Chapter 10: Socio-cultural aspects of assessment. *Review of Research in Education, 24*(1), 355–392.

Graham, P. (2005). Classroom-based assessment: Changing knowledge and practice through preservice teacher education. *Teaching and Teacher Education, 21*(6), 607–621.

Guskey, T. R. (2005). Mapping the road to proficiency. *Educational Leadership, 63*(3), 32–38.

Haladyna, T. M., & Downing, S. M. (2004). Construct-irrelevant variance in high-stakes testing. *Educational Measurement: Issues and Practice, 23*(1), 17–27.

Haladyna, T. M., Downing, S. M., & Rodriguez, M. C. (2002). A review of multiple-choice item-writing guidelines for classroom assessment. *Applied Measurement in Education, 15*(3), 309–333.

Hamilton, L. S., Nussbaum, E. M., & Snow, R. E. (1997). Interview procedures for validating science assessments. *Applied Measurement in Education, 10*(2), 181–200.

Harlen, W. (2005). Trusting teachers' judgement: Research evidence of the reliability and validity of teachers' assessment used for summative purposes. *Research Papers in Education, 20*(3), 245–270.

Hickey, D. T., Zuiker, S. J., Taasoobshirazi, G., Schafer, N. J., & Michael, M. A. (2006). Balancing varied assessment functions to attain systemic validity: Three is the magic number. *Studies in Educational Evaluation, 32*(3), 180–201.

Kane, M. T. (2001). Current concerns in validity theory. *Journal of Educational Measurement, 38*(4), 319–342.

Kane, M. T. (2006). Validation. In R. L. Brennan (Ed.), Educational measurement (4th ed., pp. 17–64). Westport, CT: Praeger.

Leighton, J. P. (2004). Avoiding misconception, misuse, and missed opportunities: The collection of verbal reports in educational achievement testing. *Educational Measurement: Issues and Practice, 23*(4), 6–15.

Llosa, L. (2008). Building and supporting a validity argument for a standards-based classroom assessment of English proficiency based on teacher judgments. *Educational Measurement: Issues and Practice, 27*(3), 32–42.

Mager, R. F. (1973). *Measuring instructional intent, or got a match?* Belmont, CA: Fearon.

Marso, R. N., & Pigge, F. L. (1991). An analysis of teacher-made tests: Item types, cognitive demands, and item construction errors. *Contemporary Educational Psychology, 16*(3), 279–286.

McMillan, J. H. (2001). Secondary teachers' classroom assessment and grading practices. *Educational Measurement: Issues and Practice, 20*(1), 20–32.

McMillan, J. H. (2003). Understanding and improving teachers' classroom assessment decision making: Implications for theory and practice. *Educational Measurement: Issues and Practice, 22*(4), 34–43.

McMillan, J. H. (2011). *Classroom assessment: Principles and practice for effective standards-based instruction.* Boston: Pearson.

McMorris, R. F., & Boothroyd, R. A. (1993). Tests that teachers build: An analysis of classroom tests in science and mathematics. *Applied Measurement in Education, 6*(4), 321–342.

Messick, S. (1989). Validity. In R. L. Linn (Ed.), *Educational measurement* (3rd ed., pp. 13–103) New York: Macmillan.

Mills, P., Sweeney, W., & Bonner, S. M. (2009). Using the first exam for student placement in beginning chemistry courses. *Journal of Chemical Education, 86*(6), 738–743.

Mislevy, R. J. (2003). Substance and structure in assessment arguments. *Law, Probability and Risk, 2*(4), 237–258.

Morell, L., & Tan, R. J. B. (2009). Validating for use and interpretation. *Journal of Mixed Methods Research, 3*(3), 242–264.

Moss, P. A. (2003). Reconceptualizing validity for classroom assessment. *Educational Measurement: Issues and Practice, 22*(4), 13–25.

Nitko, A. J. (1989). Designing tests that are integrated with instruction. In R. L. Linn (Ed.), *Educational measurement* (3rd ed., pp. 447–474). New York: Macmillan.

Nitko, A. J., & Brookhart, S. M. (2011). *Educational assessment of students.* Boston: Allyn & Bacon.

Nuthall, G., & Alton-Lee, A. (1995). Assessing classroom learning: How students use their knowledge and experience to answer classroom achievement test questions in science and social studies. *American Educational Research Journal, 32*(1), 185–223.

O'Neil Jr., H. F., & Brown, R. S. (1998). Differential effects of question formats in math assessment on metacognition and affect. *Applied Measurement in Education, 11*(4), 331–351.

Parkes, J. (2000). The interaction of assessment format and examinees' perceptions of control. *Educational Research, 42*(2), 175–182.

Parkes, J. (2007). Reliability as argument. *Educational Measurement: Issues and Practice, 26*(4), 2–10.

Pellegrino, J. W., & Chudowsky, N. (2003). The foundations of assessment. *Measurement, 1*(2), 103–148.

Pellegrino, J. W., Chudowsky, N., Glaser, R., & National Research Council Committee on the Foundations of Assessment. (2001). *Knowing what students know: The science and design of educational assessment.* Washington, DC: National Academy Press.

Popham, W. J. (2009). Assessment literacy for teachers: Faddish or fundamental? *Theory into Practice, 48*(1), 4–11.

Powers, D. E., Fowles, M. E., Farnum, M., & Ramsey, P. (1994). Will they think less of my handwritten essay if others word process theirs? Effects on essay scores of intermingling handwritten and word-processed essays. *Journal of Educational Measurement, 31*(3), 220–233.

Rodriguez, M. C. (2004). The role of classroom assessment in student performance on TIMSS. *Applied Measurement in Education, 17*(1), 1–24.

Scriven, M. (1967). The methodology of evaluation. In R. W. Tyler & R. M. Gagné (Eds.), *Perspectives of curriculum evaluation.* Chicago: Rand McNally.

Shepard, L. A. (2006). Classroom assessment. In R. L. Brennan (Ed.), *Educational measurement* (4th ed., pp. 624–646). Westport, CT: Praeger.

Smith, J. K. (2003). Reconsidering reliability in classroom assessment and grading. *Educational Measurement: Issues and Practice, 22*(4), 26–33.

Stiggins, R. J. (2001). The unfulfilled promise of classroom assessment. *Educational Measurement: Issues and Practice, 20*(3), 5–15.

Stiggins, R. J., Conklin, N. F., & U.S. Office of Educational Research and Improvement. (1992). *In teachers' hands: Investigating the practices of classroom assessment.* Albany: State University of New York Press.

Thomas, S., & Oldfather, P. (1997). Intrinsic motivations, literacy, and assessment practices: "That's my grade. That's me." *Educational Psychologist, 32*(2), 107–123.

Tittle, C. K. (1994). Toward an educational psychology of assessment for teaching and learning: Theories, contexts, and validation arguments. *Educational Psychologist, 29*(3), 149–162.

Torrance, H. (2007). Assessment as learning? How the use of explicit learning objectives, assessment criteria and feedback in post-secondary education and training can come to dominate learning. *Assessment in Education: Principles, Policy & Practice, 14*(3), 281–294.

Underwood, T. (1998). The consequences of portfolio assessment: A case study. *Educational Assessment, 5*(3), 147–194.

Wall, D. (2000). The impact of high-stakes testing on teaching and learning: Can this be predicted or controlled? *System, 28*(4), 499–509.

Wise, S. L., Lukin, L. E., & Roos, L. L. (1991). Teacher beliefs about training in testing and measurement. *Journal of Teacher Education, 42,* 37–42.

Wolf, D. P. (1993). Assessment as an episode of learning. In R. E. Bennett & W. C. Ward (Eds.), *Construction versus choice in cognitive measurement: Issues in constructed response, performance testing, and portfolio assessment* (pp. 213–240). Hillsdale, NJ: Lawrence Erlbaum.

Zhang, Z., & Burry-Stock, J. (2003). Classroom assessment practices and teachers' self-perceived assessment skills. *Applied Measurement in Education, 16*(4), 323–342.

7

Reliability in Classroom Assessment

Jay Parkes

The reliability of scores from classroom assessments (CAs) has long been of interest to researchers in education and psychology though perhaps not so interesting to classroom teachers. This body of research has directly or indirectly provoked huge changes in CA, in educational measurement more broadly, and in what teachers are taught about assessment and what they are expected to know about it. Reliability transcends classroom practice and has philosophical, theoretical, and methodological aspects. In short, it is a critical area for teachers, administrators, policy makers, and researchers, whether they know it or not.

This chapter will outline the traditional measurement approach to reliability theory and methods and summarize the empirical work on the reliability of CAs from that view. It will discuss some of the consequences of those approaches and that research. Then the chapter will detail the philosophical, theoretical, and methodological implications for reliability of a broader conception of CA. Finally, the chapter will provide speculation about where reliability in CA may be headed in the future and some of the implications of those directions.

Traditional Conceptions of Reliability Applied to Classroom Assessment

The most common systems of theory and methodology used to conceptualize and evidence reliability are classical test theory, generalizability theory, and item response theory, the articulation of which is well beyond the scope of this chapter. The relevant chapters of the fourth edition of *Educational Measurement* (Brennan, 2006) would be as good a starting point as any for an in-depth treatment of these systems. Essentially, the measurement principle of reliability expresses the consistency of examinees or raters across measurement occasions.

Both classical test theory and generalizability theory have three fundamental underpinnings that are important to how reliability in CA has been conceived and to how it might evolve into the future (Parkes, 2007). The first is the concept of a replication, the observation of behavior across multiple instantiations. The second is the sampling of observations in a purely statistical sense. The third is unidimensionality—that is, that any single score from a measurement is to represent a single quality. They are important because they define the real limits of where traditional reliability methodology can reasonably be applied (Moss, 2004). They are also important because they inform the debate about whether CA is only measurement or something broader.

Replication is seminal, even definitional, to classical test theory and generalizability theory (Brennan, 2001). Put more plainly, unless a student responds to more than one prompt or question, or more than one rater or judge scores the performance, or the student performs the task on at least two different occasions, there is no replication and thus no way to estimate the consistency of her performance. Multiple items or tasks, multiple raters or judges, or multiple assessment times are required to assess the reliability of the scores.

Consider that old chestnut of a CA technique, the weekly 10-word spelling test, wherein Isabella spells 7 words correctly. Her teacher, Ms. Griegos, might conclude that Isabella's spelling ability is adequate. What is the replication? In this particular instance, it would be the 10 words or items on the spelling quiz. That is, in trying to estimate Isabella's spelling ability on this Friday, the teacher makes 10 different tries, or replications, at that estimation. It would also be possible to have Isabella, a classmate, and/or the teacher each score Isabella's quiz, which would provide multiple judgments across which consistency could be judged. The teacher could give Isabella the same spelling test daily throughout the week and consider each a test–retest occasion.

Standard methodological approaches to collecting reliability evidence for each kind of replication are well established. If the test item is the replication, a measure of internal consistency (usually Cronbach's alpha or KR-20) is a frequent methodology. For raters or judges, some measure of inter-rater consistency or rater agreement can be employed. And for multiple occasions, a test–retest coefficient, for example, is warranted. It is also possible to use multiple approaches together or to use a tool like generalizability theory, which allows the simultaneous consideration of multiple sources of error. The latter is technically considered the better approach.

Classical test theory and, by extension, generalizability theory are built on the true score model wherein each examinee's score is defined as consisting of some *true score* or *universe score*, Isabella's actual spelling ability, and some *error*—the difference between her *observed score* (7 of 10 correct) and that true score. These theories are statistical theories that date back in some ways to Spearman's work of the early 20th century (Suen & French, 2003) and in broader ways back to the foundations of inferential statistics themselves more than 100 years earlier (Stigler, 1986). These theories are statistical sampling theories that assume that the observed information is only a sampling of information available. So the 10 words that Isabella is asked to spell are just 10 of the millions of words that could have been on that spelling test. Statistically speaking, how those 10 words relate to and represent those million is an inferential problem—that is, one of inference from a sample observation to some unknown true score or universe score.

We all remember the probability problems involving three red balls and seven black balls in a bag and determining how likely it would be that we would draw out a red ball. In such problems, the numbers of each color ball were provided to us, and we had to guess what would come out of the bag. The inferential problem is the reverse: Having drawn 10 samples of 4 balls from the bag, noting the number of each color ball among the 4 and replacing the balls in the bag, we want to infer how many balls of each color are actually in the bag.

Ms. Griegos wants to know how good Isabella is at spelling—that is, what her true score on a spelling test is. Ms. Griegos does not ask Isabella to spell every word in existence or even every word that a fifth grader might be expected to know. She asks her to spell 10 words and infers how well she would do at that list of every word that a fifth grader might be expected to know. Classical test theory and generalizability theory also assume that the construct being measured is unidimensional—that is, that the spelling test is tapping into Isabella's spelling ability and only that. Everything that Isabella writes down on that 10-question quiz is taken to be an indication of her spelling ability and not of additional factors.

In addition to the three underpinnings of replication, sampling, and unidimensionality, there are three other considerations that are important here. First is the concept of measurement error. Second is the important context of the purpose of measurement. And third is the idea that reliability is the property of a score not of a test or assessment.

At the heart of classical test theory is the true score model: $o = t + e$, which means that Isabella's 7 of 10, her observed score (o), is considered to be her true score (t) plus some error (e). In classical test theory, the errors are random forces that cause measurement to be imprecise. The term *error* is a strictly and formally inferential statistical concept that describes numerically the distance between the sampled estimate of a true score (i.e., the observed score) and the true score itself. There are two kinds of measurement error: (1) random error and (2) systematic error.

Random here is a strictly and formally inferential statistical term that describes the statistical assumptions used in doing calculations; it may not actually describe the nature of these errors. Random measurement errors in practice are anything that impacts the measurement process that happened in a haphazard or unpredictable way. Isabella might sneeze and mishear a word as Ms. Griegos reads it. She might notice at the eighth word that she should have sharpened her pencil prior to the test and that distracts her. If, while scoring Isabella's spelling test, Ms. Griegos gets interrupted after checking her fourth word and, after the interruption, returns to her sixth word, Isabella will receive credit for spelling the fifth word correctly when perhaps she had not.

Systematic errors impact the measurement process in consistent ways. If Isabella is an English learner, her English proficiency may impact her spelling of each word. If Isabella and her best friend had an argument prior to the test, her distraction and emotions would impact each of her spelling attempts. If Ms. Griegos has the fifth word on the test misspelled on her answer key, she will systematically incorrectly score everyone's test.

While the measurement community, informed by the statistical nature of classical test theory and generalizability theory, tend to think of reliability as consistency of measurement, the more practically helpful way for teachers to think of reliability would be to reduce errors or mistakes while assessing. Fortunately, the layperson's view that error means making a mistake is very useful, because reducing mistakes while measuring will reduce the actual statistical errors too. In a later section, we will discuss practical methods to help teachers avoid measurement errors.

The second consideration in understanding the three underpinnings is the purpose of the assessment in the first place. In traditional measurement practice, there are relative purposes and absolute purposes. Relative purposes involve ranking students, for example, if Ms. Griegos wants to know whom the three best and three worst spellers are in her class. In ranking students like this, Ms. Griegos is making a relative decision—comparing students relative to one another. In relative decisions, systematic errors, such as teacher overall severity or leniency, typically do not make a difference in the outcome since they affect each student equally. Absolute decisions involve comparing students to a standard, for example, if Ms. Griegos wants to identify all her students who missed more than three spelling words. In such a case, a systematic error will make a difference in the outcome. There is the possibility of a systematic error that affects only some of the students, such as language difficulty of the test items, which would be of concern in both relative and absolute decisions. The importance, or stakes, of the decision being made constitutes another sense in which purpose of assessment matters. In other words, how consequential might a measurement error be and how big of a measurement error is consequential. We'll return to these ideas later in the chapter.

The final consideration is that reliability is the property of a score derived from a test or assessment and not a property of the test or assessment itself. Thompson & Vacha-Haase (2000) in a published exchange with Sawilowsky (2000a, 2000b) fully articulated this argument. Since measurement is an inferential process—taking a sample of knowledge from an individual and using it to make a conclusion about his knowledge in its entirety—different measurements, even those made with the same test, can vary in quality. Thus reliability is a way to describe the measurement itself, not the means of making the measurement (Thompson & Vacha-Haase, 2000). In terms of the true score model, a person's true score should remain unchanged (at a single point in time), but that person's observed score could differ contingent on the amount of error present at a particular measurement.

To summarize, the traditional measurement approach is a statistical one, which is to say an inferential one, which is to say is based on drawing samples of human performance of a single quality or construct. In order to make any estimate at all of how well a sample represents the single domain of interest, there must be at least two sampling probes (a replication). Once the samples are drawn—once the test of several items is given, once the portfolio is scored by three peers, or once a poem is recited at least twice—sufficient information exists to estimate how consistently or reliably the (single) domain has been sampled. Considering the nature of measurement errors and the stakes of the assessment are both critical concerns for teachers. Finally, understanding that reliability is the property of a score and not of the measurement process from which it was derived is also important. Using this theoretical and methodological framework, then, how reliable are the scores from CAs?

Reliability of Scores From Classroom Assessments

One of the oldest and most venerable research questions in all of psychology and education arises from this measurement paradigm and has attracted the attention of some of the most luminous names in those fields: How reliable are teacher judgments of student performance? Investigations of this question began at least a century ago (e.g., Kelly, 1914; Rugg, 1918; Starch & Elliott, 1912, 1913a, 1913b); in 1918, Rugg mentioned more than 60 articles in journals about standardizing teachers' marks. This century's worth of research has consistently shown that teachers are not reliable scorers or assessors of student learning without using strategies to reduce the measurement error. The fundamental issue is that human judgment varies (not just among teachers in classrooms) unless it is shaped or channeled or standardized in some way. The century's worth of studies is too much to review systematically here, although a look at some selected examples will illustrate the issues just mentioned.

The Starch and Elliott studies (1912, 1913a, 1913b) and a study by Brimi (2011), which explicitly invoked them 99 years later, highlight the variability of human judgment as well as the improvement that supports provide just as nicely as they bracket the century's research on the topic. Starch and Elliott (1912) took two short- to medium-length essay tests written by Wisconsin high school students, made photocopies (not a trivial thing in the Edwardian age), and distributed those copies to 200 high schools asking that the first-year English teacher score them "according to the practices and standards of the school" (p. 449). The 142 usable responses were provided a score between 0 and 100; some of the schools used 70 and some used 75 as passing grades. One paper received marks ranging from 60 to 97, and the other paper received marks ranging from 50 to 97. Starch and Elliott (1912) concluded, "The first and most startling fact brought out by this investigation is the tremendously wide range of variation" (p. 454).

Other studies in the ensuing years have demonstrated that same variability of unguided teacher scoring. Eells (1930) pointed out that Starch and Elliott were looking at inter-teacher agreement and so explored intra-teacher agreement of 61 teachers rescoring history and geography work 11 weeks after originally scoring them. On a 0 to 20 scale, the number of the 61 teachers who provided the exact same score both times was 10, 55, 14, 21, 17 on each of five questions respectively. None of the teachers exactly replicated their score on all five questions. The intra-rater correlation coefficients across the five questions ranged from 0.25 to 0.51. Eells concluded, "It is unnecessary to state that reliability coefficients as low as these are little better than sheer guesses" (p. 52). The width of the potential scale does not seem to make a difference in rater variability. Starch and Elliott (1912) used a 101-point scale; Eells used a 21-point scale; and Diederich, French, & Carlton (1961), who had 300 essays read by 53 different judges, found that 94% of the essays received seven different scores on a 7-point scale.

One of the most recent such investigations by Brimi (2011) explicitly recalled the Starch and Elliott (1912) study. Brimi asked 90 ninth- and tenth-grade teachers who were specifically trained on the NWREL 6 + 1 Traits of Writing (Culham, 2003) to construct a rubric based on those traits that would produce a score between 0 and 100 and to score a single student essay with it. Seventy-three usable responses were obtained and exhibited a range of scores from 50 to 93, almost precisely the same spread as Starch and Elliott (1912).

Consistently in the last 100 years, human judgment has been shown to be inconsistent. And yet, these studies contain the seeds of understanding how to overcome that variation. Starch and Elliott (1912) wrote about wanting to understand the "personal equation" (p. 442) that teachers use and noted the "utter absence of standards in the assignment of values" (p. 442). Subsequent research has shown that they were essentially correct in both respects: Left to the use of their own personal equation, people will differ in their scores one from another and from themselves as we have just seen, and providing some standards might make judgment more uniform.

Strategies for Reducing Measurement Error in Classroom Assessment

There are several classes of strategies for increasing the reliability of scores from the assessments teachers tend to use in their classrooms. One of the classes of strategies is to reduce or eliminate the need for human judgment. The studies conducted in the early 20th century that were previously mentioned were a key driver in the large-scale standardized objective testing movement in the United States (Shepard, 2006; Suen & French, 2003). The general strategy is to constrain the measurement situation as much as reasonably possible. One strategy is to use objectively scored item formats like multiple choice, where much more acceptable levels of reliability could be obtained. For example, Hammond (1927) reported that a test with several different objective item formats of 301 ninth-grade English students produced an internal consistency estimate of 0.92. Another strategy is to provide very detailed instructions and guidelines to students about how to respond to a more open-ended task (Harlen, 2005). It probably is worth noting that one way to eliminate human judgment is not to use humans at all. Currently, only large-scale testing programs are using computers to score writing (e.g., Attali & Burstein, 2006), but as personal computing applications continue to increase in sophistication, computer scoring for widespread classroom purposes may not be far off (e.g., Jordan & Mitchell, 2009). Another class of strategy is to use established "best practices" (e.g., item-writing rules) for the construction of assessments—whether objective or subjective. Well-constructed multiple-choice questions, for example, produce marginally more reliable scores than poorly constructed items (Haladyna, Downing, & Rodriguez, 2002).

A third class of strategy is to guide the human scoring of more open-ended assessments through the use of scoring guidelines or rubrics (Gamaroff, 2000; Jonsson & Svingby, 2007; Reddy & Andrade, 2010). Jonsson & Svingby's review (2007) concluded that score reliability is higher with a rubric than without one, that providing raters with example performances for each level of the rubric (i.e., anchor papers) aids agreement, and that training boosts reliability.

A fourth class of strategy is to increase teacher understanding of student learning, to inform their consistent interpretation of student responses to assessment tasks. One way to do this is to engage teachers in the construction of assessments and/or rubrics so that they understand the expected nature of student responses (Harlen, 2005) or, if that is not possible, to train them extensively in the tasks and rubrics and forms of student response. A fifth class of strategy is for teachers to form communities of practice in which they can build a common understanding of the expectations of student work (e.g., Pitts, Coles, Thomas, & Smith, 2002), although at least one study has called the effectiveness of this approach specifically to boost reliability into question (Baird, Greatorex, & Bell, 2004).

Questioning the Compatibility of Traditional Reliability and Classroom Assessment

The traditional definitions of reliability and the research literatures based on them discussed in the previous section form a set of boundaries on what reliability is and what it means and how it can be properly shown and how it should be enacted in practice. Such boundaries are important scientifically for setting limits on a discipline, but they also come with costs in terms of what kinds of measurement situations are considered *in bounds* and what teachers are expected to know about assessment. In this next section, we will explore what some of the consequences of these boundaries have been. The overarching consequence has been a rich tapestry of argument woven over the years about the applicability of traditional reliability theories to CA contexts, covering practical, methodological, theoretical, and philosophical considerations.

Stiggins (2001) argued that one of the consequences of the research on the poor reliability of scores from CAs has been the privileging of large-scale testing over CA. He argued that, in the first half of the 20th century, such research brought about a divergence between large-scale testing and CA that left CA unattended by scholarly attention and resources while large-scale testing received all of the monetary, scholarly, curricular, and teacher preparation attention. Thus, in his view, CA skills and abilities were abandoned by 1950 because teachers could not, would not be good at it as understood in purely measurement terms.

Large-scale educational testing pursued largely selected-response (SR) formats from the 1950s through the 1970s when, as cognitive psychology overtook behavioral psychology as the basis for learning theories, those item types began to be called into question (Shepard, 2000). Thus the performance assessment movement ensued with calls for large-scale educational testing to drop SR formats for constructed-response (CR) formats. As large-scale systems tried to incorporate CR assessments, poor reliability moved out of the classroom and into the large-scale assessments. Some have argued that it was the cost and the poor reliability of large-scale performance assessment that doomed the widespread use of them (Black, 2000; Parkes, 2007).

Many of the arguments made and studies conducted during the performance assessment movement, though in large-scale settings and not always with teachers and classrooms, are relevant to understanding where reliability has been and where it is going in CA. In large-scale performance assessment contexts, low reliability estimates of individual-level scores were observed across numerous and diverse subject matters and populations, such as behavioral observation in preschool (McWilliam & Ware, 1994), middle school science (e.g., Shavelson & Baxter, 1992), secondary school writing and mathematics (e.g., Koretz, Stecher, Klein, & McCaffrey, 1994) and college writing (Nystrand, Cohen, & Dowling, 1993) and observed so frequently that they were viewed as a key obstacle to such performance assessments for high-stakes purposes (e.g., Messick, 1994). These disappointing findings from large-scale performance assessment are important for the study of reliability of CAs because both types of assessments make the case that they serve a learning purpose as well as a summative purpose.

The implications for CA of these arguments and studies can be summarized by three main questions: (1) How could traditional psychometric approaches be applied to work better in CA? (2) Should psychometric approaches be abandoned in CA? and (3) How do the demands of traditional reliability mesh with the demands of assessment as/for learning (Earl, 2003)?

It may be useful to consider these questions in light of another example of CA, one that will be useful for the remainder of this chapter. Suppose Ms. Griegos is also trying to teach group work skills to her students. She structures groups and group activities on a daily basis and, at least twice per week, asks the group members to rate two of their peers on the social skills report form (Johnson & Johnson, 2004, p. 140). This form has four main categories of effective group participation, each of which has several specific behaviors relevant to it. Each behavior is rated as (1) needs improvement, (2) making progress, (3) satisfactory, or (4) excellent. At the end of a nine-week marking period, Ms. Griegos now has at least 18 ratings per student of how their peers perceived their social skills in group work. How could traditional psychometric approaches be applied to help Ms. Griegos rate student group work? Should she ignore reliability in this situation? How should she balance demands of traditional perspectives on reliability with her overall assessment and instructional purposes?

More Congruent Applications of Psychometric Approaches to Classroom Assessment

Several different approaches have been proposed to apply classical test theory and generalizability theory methods so that they work better in performance assessment and CA contexts. Parkes (2001) enumerated several of these approaches. One simple way to increase reliability coefficients is to increase the number of replications or observations (in performance assessment contexts, this has been proposed by many, for example, Brennan & Johnson [1995]; it has also been mentioned in CA [e.g., Smith, 2003]). So if Ms. Griegos finds Isabella's 10-question spelling quiz scores unreliable, she could make it a 15- or 20-item spelling quiz. Or if the group work assessment is not sufficiently reliable, Ms. Griegos could ask more peers to rate or increase the number of times per week the rubric is used. But here reliability comes through length, and length comes at additional costs such as more testing time, more raters or rating time, or the need to develop more assessment tasks (Black, 2000; Parkes, 2000). Given the length of instruction blocks in schools, lengthening assessments or assessment time is impractical if not impossible.

Another suggestion for rater agreement issues in performance assessments was careful planning and execution of the scoring (e.g., Gao, Shavelson, & Baxter, 1994). This has also been suggested for CAs (Stuhlmann, Daniel, Dellinger, Denny, & Powers, 1999). Ms. Griegos can provide additional training and practice for her students on completing the social skills rubric and could also support them as they are using the rubric with a brief reminder, or by displaying an expanded rubric with explanations on the wall of the classroom.

Two other suggestions, both technical ones relevant to generalizability theory, have also been proposed. One is to reduce the universe of generalization (Kane, 2011; Reckase, 1995) or to fix some of the facets in the generalizability theory model (Kane, 2011; Suen, Logan, Neisworth, & Bagnato, 1995). As we have seen, when viewing the spelling test as a sampling problem, the 10 words selected for the test represent just 10 of the millions of possible words. Thus the inferential leap from 10 to millions is very large. What if Ms. Griegos changed that universe—the target of the inference? What if she considered that only the 10 words for the week, and no others, are relevant. Those are the only 10 words that she wants to know if Isabella can spell. Suddenly, there is no longer a sampling issue because Ms. Griegos is using the entire universe of words of interest. Suddenly, Isabella's 7 out of 10 words is a completely reliable score. In the social skills example, instead of assuming that each of Isabella's peers is representative of any student in that grade, or even of any student in the class of 25, Ms. Griegos could take Isabella's peers as representative only of the other 3 members of Isabella's group. Alternatively, she could assume that the occasions of group work she has sampled are not samples but the total universe.

There have also been those who argue that CAs and performance assessments have such strong validity that we should tolerate low reliability. Cyril Burt expressed the trade-off well as long ago as 1945:

> We are thus faced with an apparent dilemma: either we can mark the wrong things with much consistency and precision, or we can try to assess the right things at the risk of much inaccuracy and inconsistency. Which course are we to prefer? (p. 80)

Both preferences have received strong support. The arguments in favor of reliability include that reliability is prerequisite to validity (e.g., Brennan, 1998), that consistency in scoring or the minimization of measurement error is always important (e.g., Brennan, 1998), and that reliability is an important social and scientific value that cannot be abandoned (Allchin, 1998; Messick, 1994, 1995; Parkes, 2007). The arguments in favor of validity have also been made. Moss (1994) argued that reliability should be "an option rather than a requirement" (p. 10) because, as it has been understood and enacted, it reduces the number of important learning assessments that are psychometrically permissible. Slomp and Fuite (2004) attempt to unlock the reliability and validity dilemma by combining them to articulate a third characteristic: *quality*. Others have argued that the ability of performance assessments to produce reliable scores is trumped by their authenticity and their ability to capture important learning (e.g., Wiggins, 1989).

In a more nuanced way, however, Kane's (1996, 2011) attempt to introduce tolerance for unreliability is also in this category, and others have mentioned this issue (Mabry, 1995; Shepard, 2006). Tolerance refers to how much reliability matters in a given situation. Traditionally, the higher the stakes—that is, the more important the decision is being made using a score—the more reliable the score needs to be. Low stakes uses can tolerate lower reliability. One permutation here is that several high-tolerance, lower-reliability occasions can add together to form a lower-tolerance, higher-reliability situation. The argument in favor of validity would say that even if one week's spelling test scores are not very reliable, the accumulation of scores over time, and perhaps even Isabella's teacher's multiple other experiences with her, result in very valid information (Burt, 1945) and even an accumulated reliability (Mabry, 1995).

As I've argued elsewhere (Parkes, 2007), while the approaches that were just recounted may work psychometrically to improve the reliability coefficients or to make low coefficients acceptable, their implications for teachers and students in classrooms can be incongruent with current conceptions of what students are to be learning and of student learning itself and especially with the evolving techniques known as formative CA (e.g., McMillan, 2007) or assessment as learning and assessment for learning (AFL) (e.g., Earl, 2003). These approaches also tend to privilege psychometric considerations over other considerations (Mabry, 1995; Moss, 1994, 2004). In CA, that has meant that students, teachers, and learning have been subordinated to measurement quality. Even the arguments to accept lower reliability in classroom contexts do this. Thus while Way, Dolan, & Nichols (2010) "are optimistic that . . . psychometric techniques will evolve . . . that will support formative assessment in new and exciting ways" (p. 298), the incongruities between psychometric and other considerations are sufficiently large that some argue the psychometric considerations should be subordinated to the learning considerations (Munoz, 2009; Wiggins, 1989). As Smith (2003) succinctly summarized, "A de-emphasis on reliability for CA may seem a good idea to some, a bad idea to others, and perhaps just recognition of reality to most" (p. 29). Those making these arguments place the demands of traditional reliability methodology up against the demands for assessment as/for learning (Earl, 2003), grounded in contemporary learning theories, and draw conclusions.

The Incommensurability of Traditional Reliability and Assessment as/for Learning

The three underpinnings of traditional reliability discussed at the beginning of this chapter have implications for what constitutes sound measurement and form boundaries of sound, reliable measurement. In general, traditional reliability demands consistency of performance: Isabella, if she takes a spelling test of those 10 words every day that week should spell the same 7 words right and the same 3 words wrong. Replications imply that each spelling word is interchangeable, that there are not easier words or harder words, more familiar and less familiar words, or words like Isabella uses at home and words that she has never heard at home. Sampling also implies an interchangeability of the words. And unidimensionality implies that her 7 out of 10 words correct measures pure spelling ability and nothing else. What is the replication in Ms. Griego's assessment of social skills in group work? Clearly, different peers form a replication as do each occasion. Thus peers are sampled from a universe of fellow group members and each group assignment is sampled from some universe of assignments. And all of the ratings measure the unidimensional construct of social skills in group work.

How well do the demands of traditional reliability methodology actually fit these two CA situations? A more biased way to ask that question is as follows: If one demanded that these situations be reliable through traditional means, what would you have to do to make it so? Are the 10 words on Isabella's spelling test interchangeable? No, they're really not. Are Isabella's peers really interchangeable judges of her social skills? Given that some classmates really like her and some really do not and given gender and ethnic and language biases inherent in an elementary school classroom, no they absolutely are not interchangeable. Given that the groups' tasks change day by day and week by week such that the demands of the group tasks on strong social skills change, it is not fair to assume that occasions are interchangeable. And are social skills unidimensional? Or each subcategory? It is very doubtful.

The assumptions about the nature of learning under the demands of traditional reliability theory are no longer congruent with current learning theories (Shepard, 2000). To assume that occasions of group work are interchangeable, more specifically, that the observations in the first week and those in the eighth week of the term can be swapped, ignores the fact that Isabella and her classmates are actually supposed to be getting better at social skills so that consistency among observations is the last thing Ms. Griegos wants (Kane, 2011; Smith, 2003). Traditional reliability demands a linear trajectory of Isabella's spelling ability, when, in fact, such trajectories tend to be at best monotonic if not somewhat erratic with plateaus and backslides as new knowledge becomes assimilated with existing knowledge and restructured. This weakness has been noted in the traditional reliability literature (e.g., Brennan, 2001). And Kane (2011) posited that such deviation in and of itself does not constitute measurement error.

But learning theories and the instructional systems built on them are not the only things that have changed in the past 60 years. Stiggins articulated the split of large-scale testing from CA, and this chapter thus far has followed the path more traveled of pure measurement and pure measurement thinking. But what of the path less traveled: What of CA? Throughout this chapter, the term *traditional reliability* has been used for the measurement principle and methodologies. It is critical to understand that reliability is a principle of measurements and that the tools used to gauge reliability are meant to be used in measurement situations. Reliability, routinely considered a prerequisite to validity (on largely statistical grounds), is perhaps the quintessential psychometric property, a property of measurements. Haertel, in his 2006 eponymous chapter on reliability, was very clear on this: "Reliability is concerned *only* [italics added] with the replicability of measurement" (p. 66), is applicable to "measurement problems" (p. 66), and "quantif[ies] the precision of test scores and other measurements" (p. 65). So the history of the reliability of CAs as discussed to this point has always taken the mostly implicit approach that CAs are measurements, only measurements, and purely measurements. If that is one's stance, then it is perfectly right to ask the questions that researchers and theorists have been asking for a century—for example, how reliable are scores from CAs? Why can't teachers make and score classroom tests that produce reliable scores? What knowledge, skills, and abilities should teachers have about measurement? Do they have them? Where should they get them?

If, however, one's stance is that CA may at one time have been pure measurement but has been for some time and is increasingly being seen as a blend of instruction and measurement or even pure instruction and not measurement, then those are no longer key, or perhaps even relevant, questions. Large-scale testing, as Stiggins (2001) suggested, diverged from CA so that large-scale testing could be purely measurement. But CA is not purely measurement. Writing about formative assessment, Way et al. (2010) explained the following:

> Traditional psychometric notions . . . are much narrower in focus. . . . The development and evaluation of tests used for either summative or formative purposes are, for the most part, steeped in the psychometric traditions that have held court for the past 60 years and thus only partially address considerations unique to formative assessment. (p. 297)

Thus at the heart of the mismatch between traditional reliability and CA is that CA is not purely measurement. Brookhart (2007) explained that "Effective formative assessment blends assessment and instruction functions" (p. 49), and in her 2005 review, she labeled this also as an incontrovertible finding of the research literature. As CA expands beyond classroom measurement, different definitions of and approaches to reliability become possible. The final section will provide an overview of some of the possibilities for the future of reliability in CA.

Reconceptualizing and Researching Reliability in Classroom Assessment

If CA is viewed as a blend of measurement and instruction, then aspects of quality measurement must have some place in CA but will no longer be the only considerations. This view of CA now has implications for conceptualizing and capturing the reliability of CAs and what sound CA—not just classroom measurement—should look like. How, then, will the reliability in CA move forward?

Key Concepts Guiding the Development of Reliability

There are six key concepts around which the development of reliability will likely move forward: (1) CA is, to oversimplify, a blend of measurement and instruction; (2) CA will always involve the use of information to make decisions; (3) CA will always be an inferential process; (4) the need for explicit dimensions of quality CA will remain; (5) learning is dynamic, a moving target; and (6) learning and, therefore, CA is social.

CA is, to oversimplify, a blend of measurement and instruction. This is true in a number of ways. First, the sheer array of CA activities—from formal end-of-unit or end-of-year course examinations to informal teacher questioning and observation and from teacher-centered SR quizzes to student-centered peer feedback—will demand and permit varying conceptual and methodological approaches to reliability. For those subsets of CA activities that are, indeed, purely measurement, traditional reliability approaches will continue to work very well. It is the subset that is much more instructional in nature—formative CA, AFL, and assessment as learning—that require the most reconceptualization. Second, the varying purposes of CA activities—from assigning summative grades to determining what to do with the next 5 minutes of class time to keying a learner into their next action—proportion measurement and instruction in different ways. While this blending is superficially easy to see, as McMillan (2003) reminded us, "What is needed is an understanding of how assessment and instruction are interwoven, with new conceptions about what assessment is and how it affects learning" (p. 39).

Regardless of the format or the purpose, all CA activities fundamentally rest on a process of arranging information-gathering opportunities, gathering information, interpreting that information, and making a decision (McMillan, 2003). Bennett (2011) called this a "basic definition of educational measurement" (p. 16), though this chapter has used a much more narrow definition of "measurement" and will employ the above as a definition of CA, a broader range of activity than classroom measurement (e.g., Delandshere & Petrosky, 1998). Thus issues of what information is gathered, how well it is gathered, if the gathering itself influences the information, of what quality is the information, if there is enough information of sufficient quality to make a decision (Smith, 2003), and how consequential the decision is all remain pertinent questions.

And if CA is fundamentally about information-gathering and decision making, an important corollary follows: Not all possible information can be gathered. Thus, CA remains an inferential process (Bennett, 2011), which Chase (1999) referred to as an "axiom of assessment" (p. 6). Mislevy (2004) argued that "the challenge to assessment specialists more broadly, is to first recognize, then harness, the power of probability-based reasoning for more complex assessments" (p. 243). If CA is more than measurement and yet always an inferential process, the pitfalls of inference still obtain but the methods for addressing them should not be confined to purely measurement ones (e.g., Moss, 1994). Heretofore, the predominant approach to the inferential problems has been to address them through inferential statistics, and yet, that is just one branch of the domain of inferential reasoning. CA should draw on that broader domain in seeking ways to address the inferential pitfalls of informed decision making in the classroom (McMillan, 2003), what Shepard (2006) called "an interpretivist approach to analysis and synthesis of data" (p. 642).

The fourth key concept then follows: If CA is inferential, informed decision making, then questions of the quality of the information, the process, and the decision are unavoidable (cf. Smith [2003]: "We do not want to give up on the notion of reliability" [p. 29]). They are moderated by the potential consequences of the decision (Bennett, 2011), but they are unavoidable. So the reliability baby cannot be thrown out with the psychometric bathwater.

Contemporary learning theories conceive of learning as dynamic, redefining the nature of drawing inferences about learning and demanding that CA also be a dynamic, evolving process (Bennett, 2011; McMillan, 2003; Shepard, 2006). This presents a particular challenge to reliability methodologies based on instances rather than processes, occasions rather than durations, and student responses rather than student thinking. Learning is no longer a static target, and even to call it now a moving target may be describing it too discretely. This will likely involve shifting conceptions and methodologies away from the information used to make decisions and on to the decision-making process.

Finally, learning, and therefore CA, is a social process (Shepard, 2000). Therefore, our approaches to the reliability of CA could (and perhaps should) also draw on social processes (Camburn & Barnes, 2004; Moss, 1994, 2004). Generalizability theory provides flexibility to define either Isabella or the group she's in as the object of measurement, which can capture Isabella's learning or the group's learning, but it is not flexible enough to capture the interplay between the two.

Currently Proposed Directions for the Development of Reliability in Classroom Assessment

Those writing about the future of reliability in CA or formative assessment draw upon one or more of these key concepts in developing their suggestions. They have been assembled in several different ways among those writing about the future of reliability (and psychometrics more generally) in CA. Shepard (2006) acknowledged the broad decision-making nature of CA but argued that trying to stretch reliability to that breadth confounds it with validity. Thus, she wrote, "I prefer to use the term validity to refer to the process of warranting interpretations and to limit the term reliability to narrower consistency requirements such as inter-judge agreements for scoring rubrics" (Shepard, 2006, p. 642). Smith (2003), in his own way, narrows reliability to refer to the amount of information contributing to the decision, and it is no longer about the quality or qualities of the information.

> What teachers really need to know, from a reliability perspective, is, "Do I have enough information here to make a reasonable decision about this student with regard to this domain of information?" The essential reliability issue is: Is there enough information here? (Smith, 2003, p. 30)

Ms. Griegos sitting with her 18 ratings of Isabella's social skills during group work then is asking herself, "Is there enough information here for me to be able to make a determination about Isabella's social skills?"

I have made the case elsewhere (Parkes, 2007) that reliability as a scientific value, or as we have been discussing here, as a property of necessarily inferential decision making, must be maintained but that new methods for demonstrating evidence of that value need to be developed. I proposed the conceptual framework of the reliability argument inside of which new techniques might emerge. The six steps to making a reliability argument are (1) determine exactly what social and/or scientific value(s) are most important in an assessment situation (e.g., dependability, consistency, and accuracy); (2) make a clear statement of the purpose and the context of the assessment; (3) define a replication in the particular assessment; (4) decide how little error and/or how much reliability is needed in that situation; (5) collect the evidence—that is, conduct the assessment; and (6) make a final judgment, pulling all of these pieces together. Neither I nor anyone else to my knowledge has as yet made a reliability argument in practice nor derived a new reliability technique using this approach.

Moss (1994, 2004) has proposed a hermeneutical instead of a psychometric approach to reliability. In this approach, interpretations of assessment information are made holistically, playing individual performances off against a larger set of performances, and this is done by someone with knowledge of the student and the larger context in which the assessment was conducted. It is also an iterative and collaborative process. So we imagine Ms. Griegos and Isabella having a conference with the different ratings in front of them, discussing several of them, and Ms. Griegos thus arriving at a final interpretation of Isabella's social skills in group work. Traditional reliability would look at the consistency of the scores from those ratings only, while Moss's approach might consider that but would cast reliability as the firmness of the interpretation Ms. Griegos ultimately draws. Moss's approach has drawn the most discussion in the literature of all of these approaches, though even a concise summary is beyond the scope of this chapter. Li (2003) wrote that Moss's reasoning had "serious flaws" and was writing to "correct the record" (p. 90), and Moss (2004) rebutted those claims. Mislevy (2004) acknowledged to some extent the appropriateness of Moss's approach, but advised that more and deeper knowledge of psychometrics, not less, is necessary to be able to enact her approach.

Implications for Teachers

Teacher knowledge and practice of reliability have been no small part of the developments described in this chapter. Many studies have documented what teachers know about psychometric best practices and what they actually do while assessing students and have mostly concluded that teachers do not know enough and do enough. At issue in such conclusions, though, are whether the expectations against which teachers are being judged are the right expectations and whether the teachers had sufficient opportunity to learn what was expected. With the key concepts underpinning reliability in CA shifting as was just described, the expectations of teachers may also be shifting.

Studies have shown that teachers have limited knowledge of fundamental measurement concepts as revealed in examination of the assessments they create (Campbell & Evans, 2000; Fleming & Chambers, 1983; Haynie, 1992; Marso & Pigge, 1991; McMorris & Boothroyd, 1993; Valentin, 2005), objective tests of their knowledge (Daniel & King, 1998; Impara & Plake, 1995; Mertler, 2003, 2004), and by self-report

(Carter, 1984; Cizek, Fitzgerald, & Rachor, 1995; Gullickson & Ellwein, 1985; McMorris & Boothroyd, 1993) (see also Chapter 5 of this volume). The Marso and Pigge (1991) study is an example of an examination of teacher-created assessments. They gathered 175 assessments used by Ohio teachers from kindergarten through 12th grade in a variety of subjects and coded them for, among other things, format and item construction errors. Among the 455 separate items or exercises identified in the sample, there were 853 errors of construction. Impara & Plake (1995), as an example of a measure of teacher knowledge, administered an objective test of assessment knowledge to 325 Virginia teachers. The test consisted of 21 items, 3 for each of the seven standards from the *Standards for Teacher Competence in Educational Assessment of Students* (American Federation of Teachers [AFT], National Council on Measurement in Education, & National Education Association, 1990). The teachers averaged a score of 14.9 ($SD = 2.61$) out of the 21 possible points, which Impara and Plake (1995) interpreted as "knowledgeable" (p. 7). As an example of a teacher survey of practices, Gullickson and Ellwein (1985) surveyed 323 teachers about their use of posttest analyses and found that 28% of them directly reported calculating an estimate of reliability of the scores from an assessment they gave. But when they *verified* that use by looking at those who reported computing a total score, mean, standard deviation, and reliability estimate, they concluded that probably only 1% reported having actually derived the information needed to do so. With respect to reliability in particular, teachers do not seem to understand it or use it. Impara and Plake (1995) concluded that many teachers do not have a basic understanding of reliability or measurement error, and Gullickson and Ellwein (1985) saw little self-reported evidence of its use.

The expectations of what teachers should know about measurement properties, including reliability, come from different quarters and through different formats. There are statements and sets of standards from professional associations (*The Student Evaluation Standards* [Gullickson & The Joint Committee on Standards for Educational Evaluation, 2002]; *Standards for Teacher Competence in Educational Assessment of Students* [AFT et al., 1990]) and from professionals (e.g., Brookhart, 2011; McMillan, 2000; Rudner & Shafer, 2002). There are also empirical studies of what professors of educational measurement think is important (e.g., Gullickson, 1986) and of what classroom measurement and assessment textbooks include (e.g., Campbell & Collins, 2007). Teachers also have their own expectations about what they should know (Borg, Worthen, & Valcarce, 1986; Onocha & Okpala, 1991). All of the sources that were just given, with one exception, tend to focus either on knowledge of the psychometric properties of large-scale testing information or on generic statements about the quality of information being used to make decisions about students, all largely representing the traditional psychometric approach. The one exception among those cited is Brookhart (2011), who called for the *Standards* (AFT et al., 1990) to be updated to reflect better both formative assessment practices and the current standards-based reform climate. She has also made her own list, based on a review of literature, of what teachers should know. She essentially retained the concepts that, while designing or selecting CAs, teachers need to consider reliability and that they should understand it in large-scale, standardized settings.

Even though such varied constituencies expect teachers to understand reliability and errors in assessment, the research suggests that many teachers have insufficient educational opportunities to learn about measurement concepts. In the early 1990s, only 15 states required assessment coursework to be licensed to teach (O'Sullivan & Chalnick, 1991). As of 1998, Stiggins (1999) reported that 15 states required competence in assessment, 10 explicitly required coursework in assessment, and 25 required neither. A 2005 survey of National Council for Accreditation of Teacher Education (NCATE) accredited teacher preparation institutions in 46 states indicated that 4 of their states required an assessment course though 15 states reported that such a course was institutionally mandated (McKenzie, 2005). The remaining 28 states reported teaching assessment diffused throughout the curriculum. If most preservice teachers are not getting specific measurement coursework, professional development of in-service teachers should be given serious consideration, although "one-shot" programs are not as effective as ongoing, sustained experiences (Koh, 2011; Lukin, Bandalos, Eckhout, & Mickelson, 2004). Interestingly, the latter study included data about reliability specifically: Teachers mentioned specific changes they had made that aided the reliability of their students' scores.

While much of the existing literature documents that teachers do not know or adhere to best psychometric practices—and given what and where and how they receive any education about them, that is little wonder perhaps best psychometric practices are the wrong things for teachers to know. Gullickson and Ellwein (1985), for example, found very few teachers who actually looked at reliability statistics for their exams, and Gullickson and Ellwein interpreted that as poor practice. Another interpretation is that teachers feel sufficiently satisfied with their CA practice that they do not need to know the Cronbach's alpha value for their assessments. Brookhart (2011) has argued that the *Standards* (AFT et al., 1990) need to be updated because they do not capture formative assessment practices very well, a point that would generalize to most of the sources of expectations reviewed here. And while the research shows that teachers do not receive sufficient training in educational measurement, there is also the view that the course in educational measurement they do get contains the wrong things (Linn, 1990; Stiggins, 1991). Another consideration, simply put, is that the traditional psychometric approach to reliability is a technical one such that psychometricians use the word *reliability* differently than the general public does (Ennis, 2000), and teachers in this case are essentially general public.

The shifting methodological, theoretical, and philosophical underpinnings of reliability as described in this chapter will have implications for teachers and for teaching, although it is too soon to be sure what those might be. One of the themes of this chapter is that it is time for teachers and teaching to be having an impact on reliability and best psychometric practice rather than the other way around as it has been for at least 100 years.

Fruitful Directions for Research

One of the main themes of this chapter has been the divergence between the measurement community and its conception of reliability and the teaching/teacher community and its strong need for learning-centered, student-centered, and classroom-based assessment. Any further conceptualization of reliability or research about reliability issues must synthesize these two perspectives. With that in mind, there are some specific needs for continued theoretical, methodological and practical work.

There have been several new starts in the last decade to reconceptualize reliability as we have seen, although they have been long on theory and short on methodological or practical development. These suggestions need some road testing in actual classrooms. The reconceptualization of reliability in CA might benefit from multidisciplinary, or transdiciplinary, teams at work (e.g., Moss, Pullin, Gee, & Haertel, 2005) rather than lone voices.

In terms of immediately researchable agendas, several seem evident here at the end of this chapter. Each of the areas here discussed generate researchable questions in them but need some refocusing in order to move forward. More studies about what teachers know about traditional reliability are not needed, but studies that articulate what teachers *do know* and actually *do* to reduce the errors in their inferences might be useful to reliability theorists and those who help teachers gain proficiency with assessment. As Brookhart (2011) has pointed out, CA in the present standards-based age is very different than what has come before, so what reliability is and what it means in standards-based settings needs some definition. Finally, much of the literature on the expectations for and the training available to teachers about assessment is aging, so replications of studies in those areas would inform practice.

Conclusion

The scientific value of reliability is as old as science, and the measurement principle and attendant methodologies stretches back over a century. In the time since those foundations were laid, what we measure in classrooms, why we measure in classrooms, and whether we are only measuring have all changed. The field of CA has found itself needing new and better theoretical and methodological approaches to the quality of assessments (Brookhart, 2003). Way et al. (2010) have explained, "Extant psychometric procedures largely do not directly support the development and evaluation of formative assessment systems" (p. 305).

In this chapter, we have examined reliability theory and methodology and their rocky relationship with assessments in classrooms. Shepard's (2006) description of the *Educational Measurement: Issues and Practice* special issue remains apt: "[The special issue] is only the beginning of a major reconceptualization effort" (p. 642). The developments described in this chapter are perhaps best summarized by the well-known quote from Winston Churchill: "Now this is not the end. It is not even the beginning of the end. But it is, perhaps, the end of the beginning."

References

Allchin, D. (1998). Values in science and in science education. In B. J. Fraser & K. G. Tobin (Eds.), *International handbook of science education* (pp. 1083–1092). Dordrecht, Netherlands: Kluwer Academic Publishers.

American Federation of Teachers, National Council on Measurement in Education, & National Education Association. (1990). *Standards for teacher competence in educational assessment of students.* Retrieved from www.eric.ed.gov/ERICWebPortal/contentdelivery/servlet/ERICServlet?accno=ED323186

Attali, Y., & Burstein, J. (2006). Automated essay scoring with E-Rater V.2. *The Journal of Technology, Learning, and Assessment.* Retrieved from http://citeseer.ist.psu.edu/viewdoc/summary?doi=10.1.1.173.2655

Baird, J.-A., Greatorex, J., & Bell, J. F. (2004). What makes marking reliable? Experiments with UK examinations. *Assessment in Education: Principles, Policy and Practice, 11*(3), 331–348.

Bennett, R. E. (2011). Formative assessment: A critical review. *Assessment in Education: Principles, Policy & Practices, 18*(1), 5–25.

Black, P. (2000). Research and the development of educational assessment. *Oxford Review of Education, 26*(3/4), 407–419.

Borg, W. R., Worthen, B. R., & Valcarce, R. W. (1986). Teachers' perceptions of the importance of educational measurement. *The Journal of Experimental Education, 55*(1), 9–14.

Brennan, R. L. (1998). Misconceptions at the intersection of measurement theory and practice. *Educational Measurement: Issues and Practice, 17*(1), 5–9.

Brennan, R. L. (2001). An essay on the history and future of reliability from the perspective of replications. *Journal of Educational Measurement, 38*(4), 295–317.

Brennan, R. L. (2006). *Educational measurement.* Westport, CT: American Council on Education/Praeger.

Brennan, R. L., & Johnson, E. G. (1995). Generalizability of performance assessments. *Educational Measurement: Issues and Practice, 14*(4), 9–12, 27.

Brimi, H. M. (2011). Reliability of grading high school work in English. *Practical Assessment, Research & Evaluation, 16*(17). Retrieved from http://pareonline.net/getvn.asp?v=16&n=17

Brookhart, S. M. (2003). Developing measurement theory for classroom assessment purposes and uses. *Educational Measurement: Issues and Practice, 22*(4), 5–12.

Brookhart, S. M. (2007). Expanding views about formative classroom assessment: A review of the literature. In J. H. McMillan (Ed.), *Formative classroom assessment: Theory into practice* (pp. 43–62). New York: Teachers College Press.

Brookhart, S. M. (2011). Educational assessment knowledge and skills for teachers. *Educational Measurement: Issues and Practice, 30*(1), 3–12.

Burt, C. (1945). The reliability of teachers' assessments of their pupils. *British Journal of Educational Psychology, 15*(2), 80–92.

Camburn, E., & Barnes, C. A. (2004). Assessing the validity of a language arts instruction log through triangulation. *Elementary School Journal, 105*(1), 49–74.

Campbell, C., & Collins, V. L. (2007). Identifying essential topics in general and special education introductory assessment textbooks. *Educational Measurement: Issues and Practice, 26*(1), 9–18.

Campbell, C., & Evans, J. A. (2000). Investigation of preservice teachers' classroom assessment practices during student teaching. *The Journal of Educational Research, 93*(6), 350–355.

Carter, K. (1984). Do teachers understand principles for writing tests? *Journal of Teacher Education, 35*(6), 57–60.

Chase, C. I. (1999). *Contemporary assessment for educators.* New York: Longman.

Cizek, G. J., Fitzgerald, S. M., & Rachor, R. E. (1995). Teachers' assessment practices: Preparation, isolation and the kitchen sink. *Educational Assessment, 3*(2), 159–179.

Culham, R. (2003). *6 + 1 traits of writing: The complete guide.* New York: Scholastic.

Daniel, L. G., & King, D. A. (1998). Knowledge and use of testing and measurement literacy of elementary and secondary teachers. *The Journal of Educational Research, 91*(6), 331–344.

Delandshere, G., & Petrosky, A. R. (1998). Assessment of complex performances: Limitations of key measurement assumptions. *Educational Researcher, 27*(2), 14–24.

Diederich, P. B., French, J. W., & Carlton, S. T. (1961). *Factors in judgments of writing ability.* Princeton, NJ: Educational Testing Service.

Earl, L. M. (2003). *Assessment as learning: Using classroom assessment to maximize learning.* Thousand Oaks, CA: Corwin Press.

Eells, W. C. (1930). Reliability of repeated grading of essay type examinations. *Journal of Educational Psychology, 21*(1), 48–52.

Ennis, R. L. (2000). Test reliability: A practical exemplification of ordinary language philosophy. *Philosophy of Education 1999,* 242–248. Champaign, IL: Philosophy of Education Society.

Fleming, M., & Chambers, B. (1983). Teacher-made tests: Windows on the classroom. *New Directions for Testing and Measurement, 19,* 29–38.

Gamaroff, R. (2000). Rater reliability in language assessment: The bug of all bears. *System, 28*(1), 31–53.

Gao, X., Shavelson, R. J., & Baxter, G. P. (1994). Generalizability of large-scale performance assessments in science: Promises and problems. *Applied Measurement in Education, 7*(4), 323–342.

Gullickson, A. R. (1986). Teacher education and teacher-perceived needs in educational measurement and evaluation. *Journal of Educational Measurement, 23*(4), 347–354.

Gullickson, A. R., & Ellwein, M. C. (1985). Post hoc analysis of teacher-made tests: The goodness-of-fit between prescription and practice. *Educational Measurement: Issues and Practice, 4*(1), 15–18.

Gullickson, A. R., & The Joint Committee on Standards for Educational Evaluation. (2002). *The student evaluation standards: How to improve evaluations of students.* Thousand Oaks, CA: Corwin Press.

Haertel, E. (2006). Reliability. In R. L. Brennan (Ed.), *Educational measurement* (Vol. 4, pp. 65–110). Westport, CT: American Council on Education/Praeger.

Haladyna, T. M., Downing, S. M., & Rodriguez, M. C. (2002). A review of multiple-choice item-writing guidelines for classroom assessment. *Applied Measurement in Education, 15*(3), 309–334.

Hammond, E. L. (1927). A study of the reliability of an objective examination in ninth-grade English. *The School Review, 35*(1), 45–51.

Harlen, W. (2005). Trusting teachers' judgment: Research evidence of the reliability and validity of teachers' assessment used for summative purposes. *Research Papers in Education, 20*(3), 245–270.

Haynie, W. J. (1992). Post hoc analysis of test items written by technology education teachers. *Journal of Technology Education, 4*(1), 26–38.

Impara, J. C., & Plake, B. S. (1995). Comparing counselors', school administrators' and teachers' knowledge in student assessment. *Measurement and Evaluation in Counseling and Development, 28*(2), 78–87.

Johnson, D. W., & Johnson, R. T. (2004). *Assessing students in groups: Promoting group responsibility and individual accountability.* Thousand Oaks, CA: Corwin Press.

Jonsson, A., & Svingby, G. (2007). The use of scoring rubrics: Reliability, validity and educational consequences. *Educational Research Review, 2*(2), 130–144.

Jordan, S., & Mitchell, T. (2009). E-assessment for learning? The potential of short-answer free-text questions with tailored feedback. *British Journal of Educational Technology, 40*(2), 371–385.

Kane, M. (1996). The precision of measurements. *Applied Measurement in Education, 9*(4), 355–379.

Kane, M. (2011). The errors of our ways. *Journal of Educational Measurement, 48*(1), 12–30.

Kelly, F. J. (1914). *Teachers' marks: Their variability and standardization.* New York: Teachers College Contributions to Education.

Koh, K. H. (2011). Improving teachers' assessment literacy through professional development. *Teaching Education, 22*(3), 255–276.

Koretz, D., Stecher, B., Klein, S., & McCaffrey, D. (1994). The Vermont portfolio assessment program: Findings and implications. *Educational Measurement: Issues and Practice, 13*(3), 5–16.

Li, H. (2003). The resolution of some paradoxes related to reliability and validity. *Journal of Educational and Behavioral Statistics, 28*(2), 89–95.

Linn, R. L. (1990). Essentials of student assessment: From accountability to instructional aid. *Teachers College Record, 91*(3), 424–436.

Lukin, L. E., Bandalos, D. L., Eckhout, T. J., & Mickelson, K. (2004). Facilitating the development of assessment literacy. *Educational Measurement: Issues and Practice, 23*(2), 26–32.

Mabry, L. (1995). *Naturally occurring reliability.* Paper presented at the annual meeting of the American Educational Research Association, San Francisco.

Marso, R. N., & Pigge, F. L. (1991). An analysis of teacher-made tests: Item types, cognitive demands, and item construction errors. *Contemporary Educational Psychology, 16*(3), 279–286.

McKenzie, J. W. (2005). *Assessment requirements for school personnel in NCATE institutions.* Pullman, WA: Washington State University.

McMillan, J. H. (2000). Fundamental assessment principles for teachers and school administrators. *Practical Assessment, Research & Evaluation, 7*(8). Retrieved from www.eric.ed.gov/ERICWebPortal/detail?accno=EJ638496

McMillan, J. H. (2003). Understanding and improving teachers' classroom assessment decision making: Implications for theory and practice. *Educational Measurement: Issues and Practice, 22*(4), 34–43.

McMillan, J. H. (2007). *Formative classroom assessment.* New York: Teachers College Press.

McMorris, R. F., & Boothroyd, R. A. (1993). Tests that teachers build: An analysis of classroom tests in science and mathematics. *Applied Measurement in Education, 6*(4), 321–342.

McWilliam, R. A., & Ware, W. B. (1994). The reliability of observations of young children's engagement: An application of generalizability theory. *Journal of Early Intervention, 18*(1), 34–47.

Mertler, C. A. (2003, October). *Preservice versus inservice teachers' assessment literacy: Does classroom experience make a difference?* Paper presented at the annual meeting of the Mid-Western Educational Research Association, Columbus, OH.

Mertler, C. A. (2004). Secondary teachers' assessment literacy: Does classroom experience make a difference? *American Secondary Education, 33*(1), 49–64.

Messick, S. J. (1994). The interplay of evidence and consequences in the validation of performance assessments. *Educational Researcher, 23*(2), 13–23.

Messick, S. J. (1995). Validity of psychological assessment: Validation of inferences from persons' responses and performances as scientific inquiry into score meaning. *American Psychologist, 50*(9), 741–749.

Mislevy, R. J. (2004). Can there be reliability without "reliability?" *Journal of Educational and Behavioral Statistics, 29*(2), 241–244.

Moss, P. A. (1994). Can there be validity without reliability? *Educational Researcher, 23*(2), 5–12.

Moss, P. A. (2004). The meaning and consequences of "reliability." *Journal of Educational and Behavioral Statistics, 29*(2), 245–249.

Moss, P. A., Pullin, D., Gee, J. P., & Haertel, E. H. (2005). The idea of testing: Psychometric and sociocultural perspectives. *Measurement: Interdisciplinary Research and Perspectives, 3*(2), 63–83.

Munoz, D. (2009). Reliability as a context-dependent requirement for writing proficiency assessment. *Language Studies Working Papers, 1,* 46–54.

Nystrand, M., Cohen, A. S., & Dowling, N. M. (1993). Addressing reliability problems in the portfolio assessment of college writing. *Educational Assessment, 1*(1), 53–70.

O'Sullivan, R. G., & Chalnick, M. K. (1991). Measurement-related course work requirements for teacher certification and recertification. *Educational Measurement: Issues and Practice, 10*(1), 17–19, 23.

Onocha, C. O., & Okpala, P. N. (1991). Teachers' perceptions of the relevance of topics taught in educational measurement courses. *Educational Research, 33*(3), 228–232.

Parkes, J. (2000). The interaction of assessment format and examinees' perceptions of control. *Educational Research, 42*(2), 175–182.

Parkes, J. (2001). The role of transfer in task variability in performance assessments. *Educational Assessment, 7*(2), 143–164.

Parkes, J. (2007). Reliability as argument. *Educational Measurement: Issues and Practice, 26*(4), 2–10.

Pitts, J., Coles, C., Thomas, P., & Smith, F. (2002). Enhancing reliability in portfolio assessment: Discussions between assessors. *Medical Teacher, 24*(2), 197–201.

Reckase, M. D. (1995). Portfolio assessment: A theoretical estimate of score reliability. *Educational Measurement: Isses and Practice, 14*(1), 12–14, 31.

Reddy, Y. M., & Andrade, H. (2010). A review of rubric use in higher education. *Assessment & Evaluation in Higher Education, 35*(4), 435–448.

Rudner, L. M., & Shafer, W. D. (2002). Reliability. In L. M Rudner & W. D. Shafer (Eds.), *What teachers need to know about assessment* (pp. 17–23). Washington, DC: National Education Association.

Rugg, H. O. (1918). Teachers' marks and the reconstruction of the marking system. *The Elementary School Journal, 18*(9), 701–719.

Sawilowsky, S. S. (2000a). Reliability: Rejoinder to Thompson and Vacha-Haase. *Educational and Psychological Measurement, 60*(2), 196–200.

Sawilowsky, S. S. (2000b). Psychometrics versus datametrics: Comment on Vacha-Haase's "reliability generalization" method and some EPM editorial policies. *Educational and Psychological Measurement, 60*(2), 157–173.

Shavelson, R. J., & Baxter, G. P. (1992). What we've learned about assessing hands-on science. *Educational Leadership, 49*(8), 20–25.

Shepard, L. A. (2000). The role of assessment in a learning culture. *Educational Researcher, 29*(7), 4–14.

Shepard, L. A. (2006). Classroom assessment. In R. L. Brennan (Ed.), *Educational measurement* (4th ed.). Westport, CT: American Council on Education/Praeger.

Slomp, D. H., & Fuite, J. (2004). Following Phaedrus: Alternate choices in surmounting the reliability/validity dilemma. *Assessing Writing, 9*(3), 190–207.

Smith, J. K. (2003). Reconsidering reliability in classroom assessment and grading. *Educational Measurement: Issues and Practice, 22*(4), 26–33.

Starch, D., & Elliott, E. C. (1912). Reliability of grading high-school work in English. *The School Review, 20*(7), 442–457.

Starch, D., & Elliott, E. C. (1913a). Reliability of grading work in history. *The School Review, 21*(10), 676–681.

Starch, D., & Elliott, E. C. (1913b). Reliability of grading work in mathematics. *The School Review, 21*(4), 254–259.

Stiggins, R. J. (1991). Assessment literacy. *Phi Delta Kappan, 72*(7), 534–539.

Stiggins, R. J. (1999). Evaluating classroom assessment training in teacher education programs. *Educational Measurement: Issues and Practice, 18*(1), 23–27.

Stiggins, R. J. (2001). The unfulfilled promise of classroom assessment. *Educational Measurement: Issues and Practice, 20*(3), 5–15.

Stigler, S. M. (1986). *The history of statistics: The measurement of uncertainty before 1900.* Cambridge, MA: Belknap Press of Harvard University Press.

Stuhlmann, J., Daniel, C., Dellinger, A., Denny, R., & Powers, T. (1999). A generalizability study of the effects of training on teachers' abilities to rate children's writing using a rubric. *Journal of Reading Psychology, 20*(2), 107–127.

Suen, H. K., & French, J. L. (2003). A history of the development of psychological and educational testing. In C. R. Reynolds & R. Kamphaus (Eds.), *Handbook of psychological and educational assessment of children: Intelligence, aptitude, and achievement* (Vol. 2, pp. 3–23). New York: Guilford Press.

Suen, H. K., Logan, C., Neisworth, J., & Bagnato, S. (1995). Parent/professional congruence: Is it necessary? *Journal of Early Intervention, 19*(3), 257–266.

Thompson, B., & Vacha-Haase, T. (2000). Psychometrics is datametrics: The test is not reliable. *Educational and Psychological Measurement, 60*(2), 174–195.

Valentin, J. D. (2005, August). *Ascertaining the reliability and content-related validity of mathematics tests constructed by teachers: A snapshot in the primary schools in Seychelles.* Paper presented at the Third East Asia Regional Conference on Mathematics Education, Shanghai.

Way, W. D., Dolan, R. P., & Nichols, P. (2010). Psychometric challenges and opportunities in implementing formative assessment. In H. L. Andrade & G. J. Cizek (Eds.), *Handbook of formative assessment* (pp. 297–315). New York: Routledge.

Wiggins, G. (1989). A true test: Toward more authentic and equitable assessment. *Phi Delta Kappan, 70*(9), 703–13.

8

Fairness in Classroom Assessment

Robin D. Tierney

Fairness is an ideal that has pervaded the history of education in democratic societies, from the establishment of merit-based systems centuries ago to the organization of contemporary classrooms. Common classroom practices, such as raising hands and taking turns, reflect shared beliefs about fairness (Campbell, 2003; Jackson, Boostrom, & Hansen, 1993; Shulman, 2004). Fairness is considered a desirable quality in a wide range of educational assessments, from the diagnosis of individual learning needs to large-scale international surveys of student achievement. As Green, Johnson, Kim, and Pope (2007) noted in their work on the ethics of assessment, fairness is a "general principle that no one contests in the abstract" (p. 1001). In practice, however, the fairness of assessment is less readily assumed and far more contentious.

Concern has long been expressed about the fairness of educational assessment. Early in the 20th century, objective tests were hailed as a means of bypassing the "injustice" caused by teachers' inconsistent grading practices (Finklestein, 1913, p. 6). In subsequent decades, educational measurement experts concentrated on the development and use of standardized tests, but research on classroom assessment (CA) was limited. During the late 1960s and 1970s, political upheaval, shifting social ideals, and new insights in learning theory affected the educational landscape (Bredo, 2006; Giordano, 2005; Gipps, 1999). By the close of the century, reform was underway in many educational systems. As part of this process, there was a growing interest in performance-based or authentic assessment (Clarke, Madaus, Horn, & Ramos, 2000; Horn, 2002; Lam, 1995), emphasis on the pedagogical potential of formative assessment (Black & Wiliam, 1998; Shepard, 2006), increasing recognition of the need to serve diverse students (Kornhaber, 2004; Nettles & Nettles, 1999), and greater awareness of the social, political, and value-laden nature of assessment (Gipps, 1994; Horn, 2002). These changes led to questions about the relevance of measurement theory for the dynamics of CA, and they gave rise to new concerns about fairness for the 21st century.

At present, consensus regarding the meaning of fairness in CA is limited in both practice and theory. While teachers generally aim to be fair in their assessment practices (Brookhart, 1994; Tierney, Simon, & Charland, 2011), their interpretations of fairness vary considerably (Yung, 2001; Zoeckler, 2005). The statistical techniques that help determine fairness in testing are not useful for teachers because of the time constraints and the relatively small number of students typically involved in CA (Camilli, 2006). While measurement theory supports the development and use of standardized and large-scale assessment, its appropriateness for CA was strenuously questioned during the 1990s (e.g., Brookhart, 1993; Delandshere, 2001; Gipps, 1994; Moss, 1994; Shepard, 2000; Stiggins & Bridgeford, 1985; Whittington, 1999; Wiggins, 1993; Wiliam, 1994). The reconceptualization of validity and reliability for CA has since been ongoing (e.g., Black & Wiliam, 2006; Moss, 2003; Parkes, 2007; Smith, 2003; Stobart, 2006; see also Chapters 6 and 7 of this volume), but less attention has been paid to fairness. Although the moral intent underlying the quest for fairness in standardized testing and CA may not be all that different, the concept of fairness needs reworking to take the dynamics and purposes of CA into account.

Greater interest in formative and performance-based assessment in recent years is in keeping with the shift from a testing culture to a learning culture, as described by Gipps (1994) and Shepard (2000). However, caution has been repeatedly voiced regarding the assumption that these forms of assessment are necessarily fairer than traditional written tests (Elwood, 2006; Gipps, 2005; Linn, Baker, & Dunbar, 1991). Some alternative methods, such as discussion circles, reflective journals, and self-assessments, may even have a greater potential for unfairness because they involve personal contact or ask students to reveal weaknesses (Brookfield, 2001; Gynnild, 2011; Schendel & O'Neill, 1999). The conceptual shift from a testing to a learning culture alters the relationships and power dynamics among peers and between students and teachers, resulting in a learning environment that has yet to be fully explored in terms of fair assessment. Furthermore, it is now widely recognized that teachers' assessments, which were once considered low stakes in comparison to standardized tests, can also have significant and long-lasting personal, social, and educational effects for students. For example, the results of summative CAs, such as final examinations or culminating projects, weigh heavily in the selection and placement decisions made for students in many educational systems. Consequently, they can play the same "gatekeeping role" (Nagy, 2000, p. 262) as high-stakes tests. Informal and spontaneous judgments by teachers can also affect students' self-identity, motivation, and approach to learning, which in turn influence teachers' perceptions in ongoing classroom interactions (Brookhart, 1994; Cowie, 2005; Gipps, 1994; Morgan & Watson, 2002; Watson, 1999). Given current ideals regarding the use of assessment for multiple purposes, changing classroom dynamics, and the impact this may have on diverse learners, strong imperative now exists for investigating fairness as a quality of CA.

The purpose of this chapter is to review how fairness has been interpreted from a range of perspectives in order to inform its conceptualization for CA. Specifically, the aim is to answer the following two questions: (1) How has the concept of fairness been interpreted in different types of texts? (2) Which interpretations of fairness are most relevant for the purposes of CA? The goal is not to prescribe how fair assessment should be practiced by all teachers but to provide avenues for further research, discussion, and guidance relating to fairness in CA. An assumption in undertaking this review is that fairness is for the student. What might or might not be fair for teachers, school or system administrators, and test developers involved in educational assessment is beyond the scope of this work.

The next two sections of this chapter provide a background for understanding fairness in CA, first by looking at common usage of the word *fair* and then by tracing the development of the concept in educational measurement. While this may seem peripheral to research on CA, ideas about fairness have not developed in isolation. Examining the link to daily language and measurement terminology illuminates the "a priori reasoning" (Bredo, 2006, p. 4) embedded in thinking about fairness for CA. This is followed by an overview of the different types of literature that contain interpretations of fairness and by a discussion of research relating to key aspects of fairness in CA.

The Multiple Meanings of *Fair*

Like many words in the English language, the word *fair* has multiple definitions. As an adjective or adverb, its meaning changes according to the noun or verb it describes. Fair hair is light, fair weather is temperate, and a fair deal is straight, especially if it's square. Fair play involves following the rules of the game, whereas anything that is fair game is open to attack. When someone gets a fair shake or a fair go it means they have a clear chance. In contrast, rating a service as fair indicates that it is less than perfect but still passable (fair to middling). When a statement is deemed fair enough it is acceptable, or just not sufficiently radical to elicit disagreement. Beneath these disparate uses of the word there often lies a sense of openness, or absence—no clouds, no shady business, no undue impedance in the pursuit of an appropriate target. This is reflected in the dictionary definition of *fair* as that which is "marked by impartiality or honesty, and free from self-interest, prejudice, or favouritism." What is most important about this openness or absence is that opportunity is not constrained.

A second sense that underlies how the word *fair* is used is that of neutral alignment. In carpentry, to square something means to check the accuracy of angles and straighten all sides. In business, fair and square means playing above board and not swaying from the law. In any kind of decision making, the opposite of fair is biased. When fabric is cut on the bias, it is cut on an angle, diagonally to the warp and weft. Thus, a biased line leans one way or another, whereas an unbiased report takes a neutral stance, and an unbiased jury remains objective. To be unbiased or fair in this sense is to adhere to established principles, or a framework, in the same way that a square window fits its casing. Related to the idea of alignment is the sense of being between extremes, or balanced. Fair weather is pleasant, meaning neither too hot nor too cold. Fairly well off is comfortable, meaning neither rich nor poor. Fair trade, evenhandedness, the scales of justice, and a level playing field all involve the idea of balance. As such, despite what appears to be a multiplicity of definitions, common use of the word *fair* generally conveys a sense of openness, neutrality, or balance.

The Evolution of Fairness in Testing

Testing is pervasive in education, and concerns about its fairness are perennial. Questions were raised about the fairness of psychological and educational tests at their inception more than a century ago (Cole & Zieky, 2001; Giordano, 2005; Kornhaber, 2004), and fairness issues continue to figure prominently in discussions about large-scale assessment systems (e.g., National Research Council [NRC], 2010). It is, therefore, an irony in the history of educational assessment that written examinations were initially devised as a method for improving fairness. For example, entry into government positions in ancient China was gained through examinations (Ebel, 1972; Gipps, 1994; Popham, 1981), and European and North American universities began using them to select candidates for admissions during the 19th century (Camilli, 2006; Gipps, 1994). While it may seem naive in retrospect (Stobart, 2005, p. 285), the intent of these examinations was to remove social class as a barrier and equalize opportunity in education and employment. It is now evident that by controlling access they have the reverse effect as gatekeepers in that they bar some students from further learning opportunities.

With the advent of public education during the late 19th and early 20th centuries came an unprecedented number of students, which resulted in a need to distinguish between those capable of higher education and those destined for fields and factories. Psychology was emerging as a branch of science (rather than philosophy) around the same time, and the creation of intelligence tests strongly influenced the development of testing in education (Giordano, 2005; Kornhaber, 2004). High regard for scientific technique during this period supported the general assumption that standardized tests were inherently fairer than the subjective methods (i.e., oral recitation and essays) that had been used previously to assess student achievement (Clarke et al., 2000). However, by the 1960s, questions about the fairness of testing were sufficiently vociferous to command attention from the measurement community. In response to the growing "public hostility" to testing (Messick, 1965, p. 136), the prospect of culture-fair tests garnered interest, and there was a concerted effort to develop an algorithm for fair use of test results in the selection of candidates (Cole & Zieky, 2001). By the end of the 1970s, various statistical models for fair decision making had been put forward but were found wanting within the measurement community. Although educational reforms continued to augment the role of testing in education (Clarke et al., 2000), public faith in the inherent fairness of standardized tests was eroding.

Four revisions of the *Standards for Educational and Psychological Testing* (the first two were named the *Standards for Educational and Psychological Tests*) (American Educational Research Association [AERA], American Psychological Association [APA], & National Council on Measurement in Education [NCME], 1985, 1999; APA, AERA, & NCME, 1966, 1974) reflect how ideas about fairness changed during the latter half of the 20th century. While the 1966 edition does not mention fairness, the 1974 edition acknowledges that "some unfairness may be built into a test" (p. 2). The words *biased* and *unfair* were often used interchangeably at this point; essentially one was tantamount to the other, and both were subsumed by validity. However, as advancements in statistical techniques allowed more vigorous examination of how test items functioned, biased items that favored or disadvantaged different groups of test takers could be identified (Cole & Zieky, 2001). As a result of this development, clearer distinction was made between bias and fairness. The 1985 edition of the *Standards* reflects this in stating that unlike bias, "fairness is not a technical psychometric term" (p. 13). The word *fairness* continued to be used in reference to the utilization of test results, but it was excluded from the technical terminology of measurement. In contrast, bias was increasingly used as a measurement term (e.g., Childs, 1990), but its meaning was restricted to the idea of neutrality rather than the sense of openness that is also seen in common usage of the word *fair*.

With the evolution of validity theory and Messick's (1989) emphasis on consequential evidence, awareness was heightened in the measurement community about the role of values and ethics in testing (Moss, 1998; Shepard, 1997). While fairness had been vaguely positioned under the broader umbrella of validity, by the end of the century it had become comparable to validity, and discussion about the quality of assessment had become as much about ethics as metrics. The revision of the *Standards* in 1999 illustrates this change with four chapters in a section devoted specifically to fairness. Previous editions contained similar content, but the gathering of these chapters under one heading reflects the change in the significance accorded to fairness. The *Standards* (AERA et al., 1999) emphasized the "importance of fairness in all aspects of testing and assessment" (p. 73). Four interpretations are discussed in defining fairness. Two of these—(1) the absence of statistical bias and (2) equitable treatment in the testing process—are described as having generally been accepted in the measurement community. A third interpretation, equality of test outcomes, is rejected. This rejection is hardly radical given that measurement experts have argued for decades that group score differences do not necessarily indicate test bias (e.g., Messick & Anderson, 1970). The fourth interpretation, opportunity to learn, is less straightforward. Several problems with this interpretation are identified for the context of testing, but the *Standards* (AERA et al., 1999) acknowledge that the opportunity to learn test material is necessary for test-based decisions to be fair. As a whole, these interpretations indicate that fairness is larger than and inclusive of bias. Fairness in testing also includes equitable treatment and access to test materials. Equitable treatment involves a balance, and access requires some degree of openness. Thus, the qualities that underlie common usage of the word *fair* are also reflected in the interpretations of fairness for testing.

At present, it is generally accepted in measurement theory that fairness is an important quality that is distinct from but related to validity (Camilli, 2006; Messick, 2000; Stobart, 2005). Like validity, fairness cannot be determined dichotomously because it is a matter of degree (Cole & Zieky, 2001; Lane & Silver, 1999). Research and debate on the relationship between validity and fairness is ongoing (e.g., Xi, 2010; responses by Davies, 2010; Kane, 2010; Kunnan, 2010), but the earlier distinction made between bias and fairness has been maintained. Camilli (2006), for example, explained that bias is a measurement issue whereas fairness relates to "factors beyond the scope of the test" (p. 225). According to Stobart (2005), fairness is a "social process" and a "qualitative judgment" (p. 285) that must take the curriculum and students' learning opportunities into account. Moss, Pullin, Gee, and Haertel (2005) argued further that the influence of measurement and testing on constructs such as opportunity and success in education must be considered in terms of social justice. Through ongoing revisions to the standards, and as thinking about testing evolves, it has become evident that fairness is a complex issue and an enduring concern in education.

Overview of Literature Relating to Fairness in Classroom Assessment

Until recently, most research on fairness in educational assessment has pertained to standardized testing or large-scale assessment. Changes in the educational landscape have provided the imperative for investigating fairness as a quality of CA, but three challenges are apparent in this process. The first is that no single context exists for CA. An enormous diversity of learners and subjects is involved in classroom learning, which makes possible a wide range of circumstances and methods for CA. What might be fair, for example, in determining the literacy of an English language learner (ELL) at the beginning of the term in a primary classroom, might not be fair when medical students take their final pharmacology exam in a university classroom. To discuss the characteristics of the concept as a whole, it is necessary to generalize across classroom contexts, but the particulars of practice should be kept in mind.

The second challenge is that despite being frequently mentioned in CA literature, fairness is not often defined. This may be because fairness is considered an essential virtue in teaching practice (Campbell, 2003) or because fair assessment is commonly accepted as a student's right (Dann, 2002; Robinson, 2002). The definitions and interpretations of fairness that are found in the extant literature vary, and they are sometimes conflicting. This section examines these definitions and interpretations in comparison to those in testing and common usage in order to provide a fuller sketch of the concept than seen to date.

A third complicating factor in this process is the plethora of terminology. Related terms—specifically objectivity, bias, values, ethics, equality, and equity—are often used in conjunction or interchangeably with fairness. This sometimes results in circularity, such as defining fair assessment as "equitable assessment" immediately after stating that equity is "about fairness" (Szpyrka, 2001, p. 5). As precision and consistency are currently lacking in the terminology, literature using related terms that pertains substantively to fair CA is included.

Research literature documents the questions asked and answers given, the discussion of ideas, and the statement of ideals within a community. As such, it is a form of dialogue among stakeholders, and different types of literature capture different aspects of this dialogue. In the following sections, literature is discussed in two main categories: (1) conceptual and (2) empirical. Within these are subcategories that reveal differences in how fairness in CA is interpreted by groups of stakeholders—particularly students, teachers, and researchers.

Conceptual Literature

Three different types of texts are identified as conceptual here because they discuss concepts, usually for the purpose of directing research or practice. The first, committee documents, are developed by members of educational organizations to provide principles or standards for practice. The second contains practical guidance on fair assessment for classroom teachers, and the third aims to further scholarly discussion within the academic community. While some texts are clearly of one type or the other, many contain both practical guidance and theoretical discussion, and others are situated in the movement between practice and theory. As such, the second and third types of texts are discussed together under the rubric of CA theory.

Committee Standards

Two major documents containing principles or standards specifically for CA are the *Principles for Fair Assessment Practices for Education in Canada* (Joint Advisory Committee, 1993) and *The Student Evaluation Standards* (Joint Committee on Standards for Educational Evaluation, 2003). Because these documents were collaboratively constructed with input from many educational organizations, they carry the weight of consensus in reflecting the ideals of the educational community at the time of their publication.

The *Principles* (Joint Advisory Committee, 1993) were developed primarily in response to inappropriate use of large-scale assessment results in Canada (T. Rogers, personal communication, May 10, 2011), but they also include a set of guidelines specifically for CA. Fairness is not explicitly defined, but the principles are said to be "indicative of fair assessment practice" (p. 3) overall. Although they were forward-looking at the time, their sequenced structure is suitable for planned, summative assessment, and there is very little guidance for fairness in informal assessment interactions. The evolution of assessment ideals over the following decade is reflected in *The Student Evaluation Standards* (Joint Committee on Standards for Educational Evaluation, 2003), which presents assessment as "central to student learning" (p. 1). Once again, fairness is not explicitly defined, but 21 of the 28 standards are cross-referenced to fairness in the functional table of contents. As a result, fairness is associated with a wide range of related assessment qualities, including sound, equitable, consistent, balanced, ethical, feasible, accurate, and useful. This breadth supports the idea that ensuring fairness is not a straightforward process, but such a nebulous definition limits the usefulness of the guidance.

Both the *Principles* (Joint Advisory Committee, 1993) and *The Student Evaluation Standards* (Joint Committee on Standards for Educational Evaluation, 2003) emphasized that the purpose, criteria, and results of any assessment should be explicitly and clearly communicated. This is consistent with the sense of openness in the common usage of the word *fair*, and it associates fairness with the concept of transparency in assessment (Frederiksen & Collins, 1989). As the *Principles* (Joint Advisory Committee, 1993) and *The Student Evaluation Standards* (Joint Committee on Standards for Educational Evaluation, 2003) were written a decade apart, it also suggests that the association between fairness and transparency has been accepted in the educational community for some time. In addition, both documents are concerned with administrative issues that extend beyond assessment interactions in classrooms, such as maintaining the confidentiality of assessment results and records at the school and system levels. Fairness is presented in both documents as a general ideal that pervades all assessment phases and concerns all stakeholders. In comparison to the *Standards* (AERA et al., 1999) for testing, the principles and standards for CA delineate fairness less clearly, but the breadth of associated issues far exceeds the few interpretations that are accepted for testing.

Classroom Assessment Theory

The ethics of CA have not been addressed comprehensively in assessment theory. Discussion pertaining to fairness in CA is scattered through journal articles, book chapters, textbooks, monographs, and professional magazines. In this overview, references are generally given as examples as more comprehensive discussion of the key aspect of fairness follows later in this chapter.

CA theory differs considerably in terms of perspective. For example, it includes measurement (e.g., Camilli, 2006), post-modern (e.g., Schendel & O'Neill, 1999), critical theory (e.g., Tierney, 2005), social justice (e.g., Drummond, 2003), and sociocultural (e.g., Poehner, 2011) interpretations of fairness. There is also a difference in the degree of focus; in some texts, fairness issues are mentioned as part of a broader discussion (e.g., Shepard, 2000), whereas others relate specifically to one aspect of fairness (e.g., Gee, 2003). Nonetheless, patterns emerge in terms of the fairness issues that are identified. In two ways, these texts are similar to the *Principles* (Joint Advisory Committee, 1993) and *The Student Evaluation Standards* (Joint Committee on Standards for Educational Evaluation, 2003). First, fairness is most frequently discussed without explicit definition. Only a handful of authors attempt to operationalize the concept with strategies or steps for practice (Camilli, 2006; McMillan, 2011; Russell & Airasian, 2012; Suskie, 2002; Volante, 2006). Second, fairness is often associated with validity and reliability. Given the centrality of these concepts in measurement theory, this in itself is not surprising, especially in texts written by assessment specialists (e.g., Andrade, 2005; Lam, 1995; Whittington, 1999). What is interesting is the evolution of the discussion from its initial concerns about validity and reliability (e.g., Brookhart, 1994; Gipps, 1999; Schendel & O'Neill, 1999) to the reconceptualization of these qualities for CA (Moss, 2003; Smith, 2003), which has led to the realization that different criteria may be needed for fair CA (Camilli, 2006; Cowie, in press).

In CA theory, four needs that are often raised in relation to fairness are for transparent communication (e.g., Guskey & Jung, 2009), for assessments to be appropriate for individual learners (e.g., Poehner, 2011), for thoughtfulness about bias (e.g., Russell & Airasian, 2012), and for students to have opportunities to learn (e.g., Shepard, 2000). Two of these needs—(1) opportunity to learn and (2) bias—appear in the definition of fairness for testing but with significant differences. Opportunity to learn is described in the *Standards* (AERA et al., 1999) as a social issue beyond the confines of testing, and it is accepted as a fairness issue only in the narrow terms of test preparation. In CA theory, opportunity to learn is more widely associated with the alignment of instruction and assessment, the provision of time, access to materials, the quality of student–teacher interactions, and the teacher's ability to understand and support diverse students (e.g., Camilli, 2006; DeLain, 2005; Drummond, 2003; McMillan, 2011). Some CA theorists discuss bias in terms of avoidance (e.g., Volante, 2006), which is similar to how it is addressed in testing (i.e., controlling construct-irrelevance). Rather than avoiding a negative, others suggest that what is needed is increased cultural awareness (e.g., Tierney, 2005) and recognition of the knowledge, skills, and interests that diverse students bring to the classroom (e.g., Badger, 1999; Jiménez, 2005; Cowie, in press; Shepard, 2000; Tomlinson, 2005). Thus being fair in CA requires more than being unbiased; it also involves being receptive to diversity. While a sense of neutrality underlies the meaning of fairness in both testing and CA, a greater degree of openness is reflected in the latter. Overall, CA theory is influenced by a wide range of perspectives, and the interpretation of fairness is broader than in the definition for testing.

In contrast, the overall interpretation of fairness in CA theory is not as comprehensive as in the *Principles* (Joint Advisory Committee, 1993) and *The Student Evaluation Standards* (Joint Committee on Standards for Educational Evaluation, 2003). Some of the recommendations associated with fairness in the committee documents, such as writing clear policies, securely storing results, and analyzing statistical bias, receive scant mention in CA theory. Discussion about fairness in CA theory relates mainly to sharing expectations and criteria, providing abundant opportunity to learn, and ensuring that learners are appropriately assessed. The influence of social values and cultural expectations are frequently acknowledged, and consequently, the importance of teachers' critical reflection during and about assessment is repeatedly underscored.

Empirical Literature

While the conceptual literature represents thinking about how fair assessment should be practiced, empirical literature provides insight into how it is or is not practiced in various classroom contexts. Two groups of studies in this section serve different purposes. Studies in the first group are not about fairness per se, but fairness issues emerge from their results. They are presented here as examples and not as an exhaustive collection. The second group consists of studies that focus intentionally on fairness in CA. These studies were identified through searches in three databases (ERIC, Scopus, and Scholar's Portal) for the purpose of taking stock of what has explicitly been done or learned in this area of research.

Fairness Issues in Classroom Practice

Fairness issues are seen in two areas of classroom research: one focusing on the ethics of teaching and the other on assessment practices. Teachers who participate in classroom-based research voice similar concerns about fairness, but these two areas of research reveal different views of fairness.

Two major works that draw on ethnographic fieldwork to discuss ethics are by Jackson and colleagues (1993) and Campbell (2003). While these texts are primarily concerned with the influence of human morality and ethical knowledge on classroom life, they also shed light on the complexity of assessing learning. A significant issue they observe is that students' learning opportunities are restricted when uniformly low expectations are held for student learning or when a teacher's feedback is either indiscriminant or absent. Teachers are viewed as moral agents who negotiate, whether consciously or not, between conflicting demands that relate to different perceptions or purposes of CA. Fairness from this perspective is an essential quality of both individuals and interactions in the classroom, and it is closely associated with other moral qualities such as honesty and respect. As such, fairness is seen to be in the hands of teachers, with varying degrees of ethical awareness, who strongly influence the quality of students' opportunities to learn.

Research on teachers' assessment practices tends to focus more on methods than morality. A few studies discuss transparency and differentiation in terms of fairness (e.g., Graham, 2005), but concern is most frequently expressed about reflection and consistency. The need for critical reflection, which is emphasized in CA theory, is taken up by several researchers. While the teachers in these studies do reflect about their assessment practices, their thinking is often hampered by misconceptions and traditions that are incompatible with current theory (e.g., Allen & Lambating, 2001; Crossouard, 2011; McMillan, 2003). Nonetheless, they tend to express strong convictions about their practices, particularly the notion that consistency improves the fairness of assessment.

Although consistency is ideal for system-wide assessments that rely on teachers' judgments (e.g., Wyatt-Smith, Klenowski, & Gunn, 2010; Yip & Cheung, 2005), the studies discussed here involve teachers who equate fairness with using the same assessment tasks or criteria for all of the students in their classrooms (e.g., Brighton, 2003; Eggen, 2004; Gummer, 2000; Ryan, 2000). Treating students equally may give the appearance of neutrality, and avoiding favoritism is one definition of fair, but it results in the problem highlighted by the ethical inquiries (Campbell, 2003; Jackson et al., 1993). Essentially, when equal treatment is highly valued, the appropriateness of an assessment is compromised for some students. Whether it is in terms of the method used or the feedback given (e.g., smiley faces on every science poster), students' opportunity to learn and/or demonstrate learning may subsequently be reduced. In summary, classroom-based research provides a glimpse of teachers who struggle with fairness issues in their assessment practices, but a narrower understanding of fairness is evidenced in comparison to the conceptual literature.

Research on Fairness in Classroom Assessment

The studies discussed in this section vary considerably in scope, ranging from a single reflective case (Phillips, 2002) to a nationally sampled survey (Resh, 2009). They are gathered here because they focus on fairness issues, and they provide further evidence regarding the interpretation of the concept in CA.

A growing body of research on students' perceptions about fair CA has gained impetus by the changing needs of universities, for example, to revise programs (e.g., Duffield & Spencer, 2002), understand student evaluations (e.g., Wendorf & Alexander, 2005), reduce student aggression (e.g., Chory-Assad, 2002), and support ELLs (Knoch & Elder, 2010). A few studies are also concerned with the effect of grading practices on the experiences of secondary students (Bursuck, Munk, & Olson, 1999; Dalbert, Schneidewind, & Saalbach, 2007; Resh & Dalbert, 2007). Differences in students' perceptions about fairness sometimes relate to gender and culture (Mauldin, 2009; Resh & Dalbert, 2007; Tata, 2005), but two other patterns are also evident. First, students appreciate transparency, specifically in relation to the provision of study guides, explicit expectations and grading criteria, unambiguous test items, and clear feedback (e.g., Duffield & Spencer, 2002; Gordon & Fay, 2010; Robinson, 2002; Tata, 2005). Students want transparency primarily because it gives them a greater opportunity to learn and/or demonstrate their learning. Second, students tend to prefer equal treatment in grading, with some exceptions for students with learning disabilities (Bursuck et al., 1999). This means that criterion-referenced assessment is considered fairest (Dalbert et al., 2007). Some students' perceptions of fairness are related to their grades (Resh & Dalbert, 2007), but procedural justice is more salient in several contexts, particularly in terms of respectful assessment interactions (Chory-Assad, 2002; Tata, 2005; Wendorf & Alexander, 2005). In keeping with these patterns, long-term memories of fair assessment stem from situations where teachers combine high expectations and clear communication, whereas memories of unfair assessment involve problems in assessment procedures and in teachers' treatment of students (Guskey, 2006).

Teachers' reflections about their assessment practices reveal that they are aware of students' perceptions of fairness (e.g., Phillips, 2002; Tierney, 2010). This may be why consistency is frequently discussed when teachers are involved in research on CA. However, in focusing on fairness, these studies reveal a greater understanding of the idea that equal treatment is not always fair (Szpyrka, 2001; Yung, 2001; Zoeckler, 2005). For example, almost all of the teachers surveyed by Green and colleagues (2007) felt that it would be ethical to accommodate a student with a learning disability during an assessment. Fairness is threatened, however, when differentiation is based on factors other than learning needs. Some teachers' judgments are influenced by student characteristics that should be irrelevant, such as gender (Peterson & Kennedy, 2006), ethnicity (Elhoweris, Mutua, Alsheikh, & Holloway, 2005), socioeconomic status (Minner, 1990), perceptions of ability (Resh, 2009), and behavioral stereotypes (Koch, Steelman, Mulkey, & Catsambis, 2008). Teachers in these studies also continue to weigh student effort in grading (Green et al., 2007; Zoeckler, 2005; Tierney et al., 2011), which is consistent with previous research on grading from Stiggins, Frisbie, and Griswold's (1989) pioneering study to the present.

While teachers consider effort out of a sense of being fair to students, especially lower achieving students, it creates a larger problem that Brookhart (1993) describes as the "double standard of just deserts" (p.140). Some teachers openly state that they consider effort when they believe a student deserves it. However, they don't seem to question the underlying values, the currency of the information, or the quality of the process that they use to determine whether a student is deserving of special consideration. Given that students display effort differently and that teachers' observations of effort are limited by time, class size, and their own beliefs about learning, the fairness of conflating effort and achievement is highly questionable, particularly when assessment decisions have irreversible consequences.

Almost all of this research involves practices within the realm of summative assessment, such as test preparation, grading, and making placement decisions. Very few studies have looked at fairness issues in the assessment interactions that are ongoing in classrooms. Those who do come to a similar conclusion, which in essence is that assessment information is necessarily incomplete (Bulterman-Bos, Terwel, Verloop, & Wardekker, 2002; Morgan & Watson, 2002; Tierney, 2010). Incompleteness suggests missing information, which could threaten fairness, especially given the recommendations for using multiple assessments (e.g., Camilli, 2006) and the reconceptualization of reliability as a "sufficiency of information" (Smith, 2003, p. 30). Students and teachers alike raise concerns about this issue (Duffield & Spencer, 2002; Tierney, 2010). However, while the completeness of information does affect the fairness of final grades or placement decisions, a shift occurs for formative assessment. What is needed is no longer a snapshot but real-time images that are frequently refreshed with new information. Fairness in formative assessment is threatened when the information that teachers use about students' learning is not continuously renewed. This requires receptivity that goes beyond neutrality in classroom interactions, as suggested in the conceptual literature. It tasks teachers with far more than lecturing; it asks for their active and critical engagement as they continuously update and use information about individual learners while directing and facilitating learning in the classroom.

In conclusion, this overview of the literature reveals similarities and differences in how fairness is understood in CA. In the committee documents, fairness is associated with all phases and purposes of assessment, and as a result, it is interpreted more broadly than in any other type of literature examined, including the standards for testing. Interpretations of fairness in CA theory relate primarily to four areas: (1) transparency, (2) appropriateness, (3) students' opportunities, and (4) teachers' critical reflection. Different types of empirical research reveal variations. In the ethical inquiries, fairness is an essential moral quality, and teachers are moral agents who influence classroom interactions for better or worse. In contrast, CA research tends to discuss fairness as a quality of tasks or tools, particularly those for summative assessment. A tension is evidenced between equality and equity. Equality is maintained with the same tasks and criteria for all learners, while equity involves differentiating according to students' needs. Taken together, the students and teachers' voices heard through empirical research give evidence to the complexity of fair CA. Differences in how fairness is interpreted by the various stakeholders represented in the extant literature suggest that it is a matter of perspective, meaning that perceptions of fairness will always depend on who you are and where you stand. However, some interpretations appear so frequently, especially when the flip side is taken into account (e.g., equity–equality and transparency–privacy), that fairness may be more productively considered as a single concept with multiple interrelated facets. This notion is explored further in the following section by looking more closely at specific aspects of fairness in CA.

Aspects of Fairness in Classroom Assessment

There is no single or direct path to guarantee fair CA; the complexity of the concept defies simple solutions. Nonetheless, it is clear from the literature that certain practices relating to transparency, students' opportunities, equitable treatment, critical reflection, and the classroom environment can lead to fairer assessment. Given the diversity of classroom contexts, these should not be taken as a universal checklist but as aspects to consider for the theory and practice of fair CA.

The following elaboration on each of these aspects draws on the extant literature and provides suggestions for further research.

What's Not Clear About Transparency

The merits of transparency are extolled in the theory and practice of educational assessment. Standards for both CA and testing state that clear information should be provided to learners and test takers, and the principles of assessment for learning (AFL) contain a similar statement (Assessment Reform Group, 2002). Assessment specialists have recommended for decades that explicit learning expectations and assessment criteria be shared with students (e.g., Andrade, 2005; Guskey & Jung, 2009; McMillan, 2011; Sadler, 1989; Speck, 1998; Suskie, 2002), and teachers claim wide agreement in principle (Brookhart, 1994; Green et al., 2007; Tierney, 2010; Tierney et al., 2011; Zoeckler, 2005). This would seem to suggest a lack of substantive issues relating to transparency as an aspect of fairness in assessment. Nonetheless, three concerns about transparency arise from the literature.

First, transparency can conflict with the opportunity to learn and demonstrate learning, which are also aspects of fairness. On one hand, explicit criteria support learning because they provide students with a framework for metacognition and encourage learning-oriented dialogue about the desirable qualities of a task (Shepard, 2000). On the other, they restrict or normalize not only the knowledge gained and displayed by students but also that which is recognized and valued by teachers (Crossouard, 2011; Morgan & Watson, 2002). This has made the use of rubrics controversial for teaching and assessing writing (e.g., Badger, 1999; Newkirk, 2004; Wilson, 2006). Several strategies, such as using exemplars and student-generated criteria, have been recommended to ensure that explicit criteria enhance fairness without constraining learning (Tierney, 2010). Empirical evidence regarding the effectiveness of these strategies for learning is emerging (Andrade, Du, & Wang, 2008; see also Chapter 2 of this volume) but has yet to be established in diverse contexts.

A second concern is that despite widespread agreement with the principle of transparency, teachers' assessment practices are still not entirely transparent. CA literature tends to focus narrowly on the explicitness of criteria, which does not necessarily bring the values and biases embedded in an assessment "out into the open" (Gipps, 1999, p. 385). Wyatt-Smith and colleagues (2010) found in their investigation of moderation meetings in Australia that teachers applied their own idiosyncratic values and biases in assessing student work even though task-specific descriptors with exemplars were provided. The addition of unofficial or unacknowledged criteria clouds the meaning of assessment results. Although this issue has long been identified in research on grading (see Chapter 15 of this volume), teachers persist in mediating assessment criteria that should emanate from learning expectations or standards.

A third concern about transparency relates to the communication between students and teachers about assessment. The quality of assessment conversations may vary to a degree that threatens fairness. Some secondary teachers in one study, for example, reported having regular assessment conversations with students, while others seemed to distribute rubrics without explanation (Tierney et al., 2011). The effectiveness of merely handing out rubrics is questionable (Andrade et al., 2008), and different degrees of transparency in communicating about assessment may affect other aspects of fairness, particularly opportunity to learn and demonstrate learning.

Based on these concerns, three questions are recommended for further research on transparency as an aspect of fairness. First, what is the comparative effectiveness of strategies that aim to help diverse students understand and use assessment criteria for learning? Second, how and why are explicit, mandated assessment criteria mediated by tacit values, personal characteristics, and contextual factors? And third, how do the amount, frequency, and clarity of information communicated by teachers affect students' understanding of an assessment task?

Differences in Students' Opportunities

Opportunity to learn and opportunity to demonstrate learning are often discussed in tandem because they are tightly related in practice. However, they are quite distinct phenomena. In the literature, opportunity to learn is discussed temporally, as a phenomenon in the past, present, or future lives of students. When students' backgrounds are considered, opportunity to learn is a social justice issue that involves political, social, and economic forces beyond the classroom. As differences in students' opportunities are central to assessment reform, change has been sought in terms of principles (Gee, 2003; Tierney, 2005) and practical intervention in schools (e.g., Weeden, Winter, & Broadfoot, 2002). Formative assessment is sometimes seen as a means of equalizing disparate opportunities (e.g., Camilli, 2006; Pryor & Crossouard, 2008; Wormeli, 2006). In this light, assessment is more than a technical or moral process; it is a "form of activism" (Poehner, 2011, p. 103). An example of research in this vein is Crossouard's (2011) study on the use of a formative assessment task in schools serving deprived areas in Scotland.

Most frequently, researchers, teachers, and students discuss opportunity to learn in terms of alignment. Sometimes this is specifically as a matter of test preparation (Camilli, 2006; Eggen, 2004; Gordon & Fay, 2010; Green et al., 2007), and other times alignment is described more generally as the fit between what is taught and what is assessed (Drummond, 2003; Duffield & Spencer, 2002; Eggen, 2004; Gummer, 2000; McMillan, 2011; Speck, 1998; Suskie, 2002). For some students and teachers, assessment is fairer when it provides an immediate opportunity to learn, either through completing a task or from subsequent feedback (Duffield & Spencer, 2002; Robinson, 2002; Tierney, 2010). Concerns are also expressed about the long-term consequences of teachers' assessment decisions, particularly when they influence access to scholarships, educational placements, and future employment opportunities (Morgan & Watson, 2002; Tierney, 2010). Differences in the beliefs and expectations that teachers bring to their decision making can result in unevenly distributed opportunities for students within the same school or system (e.g., Nagy, 2000; Watson, 1999; Yung, 2001; Zoeckler, 2005).

The notion that students should have multiple opportunities to demonstrate learning generates little disagreement among teachers (e.g., Green et al., 2007). The rationale for providing students with multiple opportunities is based on the technical need for sufficient information, especially for high-stakes decisions. It is also recommended that opportunities to demonstrate learning be varied (Camilli, 2006; Gipps, 1999; Shepard, 2000; Suskie, 2002). The rationale for varied opportunities is based on the understanding that learning is not a uniform process, especially in the social environment of a classroom. The characteristics of assessment tasks can influence students' perceptions of fairness (Duffield & Spencer, 2002; Knoch & Elder, 2010; Mauldin, 2009) and interact with their demonstration of learning (Shepard, 2000; Tomlinson, 2005; Weeden et al., 2002). Circumstances that can limit opportunity to demonstrate learning include, for example, when expectations are uniformly low (Campbell, 2003; Wiggins, 1993), when student happiness and fun activities are valued over self-efficacy and substantive learning (Brighton, 2003), or when assessment tasks are designed without accurate information about student learning (Moon, 2005). A lack of opportunity to demonstrate learning threatens fairness in both ethical and technical terms; it devalues the learner (Buzzelli & Johnston, 2002), and it limits the opportunities that are subsequently provided (Lam, 1995).

Considering opportunity to learn and opportunity to demonstrate learning as aspects of fairness raises two questions for further investigation. First, how are teachers' assessment practices influenced by their beliefs about students' past opportunities and their expectations for students' future opportunities? Second, to what extent might formative assessment mitigate the effects of social inequity in different educational contexts? Taking multiple perspectives into account, especially those of students and policy makers, could reveal a greater role for CA research in the social justice agenda.

Equal or Equitable for All

Students in varied educational contexts indicate that equal treatment, or consistency in assessment, is highly valued in classrooms (Bursuck et al., 1999; Dalbert et al., 2007; Duffield & Spencer, 2002; Robinson, 2002; Smith & Gorard, 2006). Some teachers agree, and they steadfastly dismiss any accommodation for one student as being unfair to the other students, even if it might be productive for learning (e.g., Allen & Lambating, 2001; Yung, 2001; Zoeckler, 2005). Others are cautious about appearing to differentiate in assigning tasks or giving feedback because they are aware of students' perceptions (e.g., Brighton, 2003; Tierney, 2010; Torrance & Pryor, 2001). A common strategy, reported across contexts, is to go back over a graded set of papers to ensure that assessment criteria is evenly applied without the effect of mood, fatigue, or other rater characteristics (e.g., Eggen, 2004; Gynnild, 2011; Ryan, 2000). In essence, this strategy aims to eliminate construct irrelevant variance, which is central to the definition of fairness in the *Standards* (AERA et al., 1999) for testing, and in keeping with the sense of neutrality and balance underlying common usage in the English language. As Whittington (1999) noted, the imperative for consistency in testing is readily transferred by teachers to their assessment practices because it is congruent with "basic ideas of fairness" (p. 17).

While belief in the need for consistency is strong, teachers' descriptions of their assessment practices reveal that exceptions are frequently made in the name of fairness. Teachers' decisions are often based on their understanding of particular students or situations, and some teachers articulate moral rationale for differentiating assessment tasks or criteria for individual students (e.g., Campbell, 2003; Tierney, 2010; Zoeckler, 2005). The idea that assessment is fairer when it is appropriate for individual learners emerges from three areas. First, special education guidelines (e.g., Guskey & Jung, 2009) have increasingly been adopted in assessment policies aiming to accommodate identified groups, such as students with learning disabilities or ELLs (e.g., Ontario Ministry of Education, 2010). Second, this idea emerges from theories that integrate teaching, learning, and assessing (e.g., Moon, 2005; Poehner, 2011; Tomlinson, 2005). Third, viewing cultural diversity as a wealth has led to a greater awareness not only that students bring varied knowledge and skills to classrooms but also that this must be recognized in assessment practices (Cowie, in press; Jiménez, 2005). Overall, the literature reveals that a shift is underway as convictions about equal treatment yield slowly to the realization that equitable practices result in fairer assessment, particularly in terms of supporting student learning.

The literature also illuminates considerable confusion in this change process. Teachers face a challenge in knowing when and how varying degrees of consistency and differentiation can enhance the fairness of an assessment, especially when it serves multiple purposes. At present, differences in teachers' judgments often seem to be based on students' group membership (e.g., Elhoweris et al., 2005; Minner, 1990; Peterson & Kennedy, 2006), either in officially recognized groups (e.g., gender and special needs) or groups constructed and perceived in varying degrees by teachers (e.g., hardworking and capable). Fairness is threatened when assessment decisions are influenced by stereotypes and personal values, but these are often so entrenched that they are overlooked. This threat is exacerbated when guidance for fair assessment is unclear about the difference between equality and equity and the need for both consistency and differentiation.

Research is needed in this area on both theoretical and practical levels. Tomlinson (2005) highlighted the commonalities in the principles for grading and differentiated instruction (DI) (see Chapter 23 of this volume). Similar discussion is needed to delve further into the relationship between elements of AFL and aspects of fairness. Grounding theoretical discussion with practical examples, such as Mrs. Baca's reliable assessment (Parkes, 2007), would be helpful. Case studies with teachers who are successful in implementing current principles, similar to the one by Ernest, Heckaman, Thompson, Hull, and Carter (2011), would also provide insight for practice. How do successful teachers approach the tension between equality and equity in CA, and what knowledge do they use to assess the learning of diverse students?

Critical Reflection on the Go

All of the aspects of fairness discussed thus far suggest that fairness in CA requires thought. The importance of teachers' reflection is often emphasized in the literature, but discussion about the focus of this reflection is somewhat of a hodgepodge. Exactly what should teachers' reflection be about, and how should they go about it? One topic that clearly stands out for fair assessment is bias. Empirical research has raised concerns for decades about how teachers use or don't use their knowledge or perceptions of students (e.g., from Miner, 1990, to Tierney et al., 2011). The literature that aims to guide teachers' practices is replete with recommendations for thoughtfulness about the biases and stereotypes that constrain fair practice (e.g., Joint Committee on Standards for Educational Evaluation, 2003; McMillan, 2011; Russell & Airasian, 2012). Popham (2008) identified two types of bias: (1) offensiveness in the content of an assessment (i.e., negative stereotypes) and (2) unfair penalization that occurs when the content of an assessment negatively affects students' performance because of their group membership (i.e., gender and ethnicity). Popham's guidance for reflection on this aspect of fairness is particularly helpful because he provides explicit strategies for classroom teachers.

A second topic for teachers' reflection about fair assessment is purpose. A criterion-referenced framework is considered the most appropriate for the purpose of grading (Brookhart, 2004b). While teachers and educational institutions tend to identify their framework as being criterion-referenced, grading often involves informal norm-referencing and student-referencing (e.g., Markus, 2002; McMillan, 2001; Sadler, 2005). As several studies have suggested, confusion about assessment purposes threatens fairness (e.g., Delandshere, 2001; Yip & Cheung, 2005; Yung, 2001). Earl and Katz (2006) highlight three assessment purposes: (1) formative, (2) metacognitive, and (3) summative. This document is also helpful because it provides questions and tips for teachers' reflection about these purposes. In brief, for fairness, teachers need to actively engage in critical reflection about the purposes of their assessments and about the biases that play into their assessment interactions and decisions.

Research on teachers' grading practices over the past few decades shows that while teachers want to be fair, they generally do not think of their practices in terms of principles or theory (Brookhart, 2004a; Dixon & Williams, 2003; McMillan, 2003; Tierney et al., 2011). However, some studies have found that teachers can provide clear descriptions and ethical rationale for their practices (Campbell, 2003; Tierney, 2010). This suggests that teachers' assessment decisions may be guided more strongly by practical knowledge and moral beliefs than theoretical knowledge. Additionally, there is indication that teachers' current vocabularies are insufficient both for the complexity of formative assessment (Crossouard, 2011) and for critical discussion of summative assessment practices (Black, Harrison, Hodgen, Marshall, & Serret, 2010). Sadler (1989) noted that thinking is the source and instrument for professional judgment; it is "not reducible to a formula" (p. 124). However, without opportunities to learn critical assessment literacy, teachers may indeed resort to "formula-based methods" (Shepard, 2000, p. 15) because they provide an illusion of objectivity or they may unquestioningly perpetuate the practices that were practiced upon them.

While the implication for teacher education seems evident, several questions remain for research. First, to what degree do teacher education materials and programs support critical assessment literacy? Is CA presented as a collection of tools and techniques or as a process of equitable decision making? How is the development of professional judgment encouraged, and to what extent are teacher candidates prepared for the inevitable tensions in the use of assessment for multiple purposes? Researchers who have worked with teachers in thinking about assessment quality suggest that assessment literacy needs to begin with the knowledge and values at the heart of teachers' working philosophies (Black et al., 2010; McMillan, 2003; Whittington, 1999). What types of knowledge and values are involved in teachers' thinking as they assess students' learning on the go in a classroom? For research in this area to advance further, it will be important to use methods that probe teachers' responses, such as narrative analysis and think-aloud interviews. The studies by Wyatt-Smith and colleagues (2010) and Crisp (2010) on teachers' judgments in the context moderation and exam marking provide excellent examples. Similar studies that focus on teachers' thinking processes in CA are needed.

Classroom Environment

With growing recognition of the social nature of learning, the importance of the classroom environment has repeatedly been discussed in assessment literature (Brookhart, 2004a; Shepard, 2000; Stiggins, Conklin, & Bridgeford, 1986; Torrance & Pryor, 1998). However, ideas diverge about the nature of a classroom environment that encourages AFL. For example, Pryor and Crossouard (2008) suggested attending to students' personal narratives as a means of nurturing an affective environment, whereas *The Student Evaluation Standards* (Joint Committee on Standards for Educational Evaluation, 2003) recommend the use of balanced feedback (i.e., strengths and weaknesses) to develop a constructive environment. While different ideas may relate to underlying aims or epistemologies, it may also be that the ideal features of a classroom environment depend on the characteristics of the learners and learning involved. As such, the exact nature of the environment needed for assessment to be fair and support learning may depend on the broader context in which it is situated.

Two themes are quite clear, nonetheless, in looking at the relationship between the classroom environment and fair assessment. First is the role of power dynamics. The teachers' authority in classroom relationships has traditionally been recognized, particularly in summative assessment where teachers examine, judge, and grade student achievement (Buzzelli & Johnston, 2002). While students are subjected to this process, they also have some agency in CA. As Bulterman-Bos and colleagues (2002) noted, students "contribute actively to what can be observed," and they sometimes "even compel teachers to take notice" (p. 1085). Involving students in assessment can empower students further (e.g., McDonald & Boud, 2003), but this does not necessarily disrupt traditional power dynamics (Brookfield, 2001; Schendel & O'Neill, 1999), particularly with young children who are not prepared to challenge teachers' decisions (Dann, 2002). Fairness cannot be assumed simply because an assessment aims to support learning.

A second theme is that the virtues of respect and trust are essential for fairness. Tertiary students associate fair assessment with respectful interactions between students and instructors (Gordan & Fay, 2010; Tata, 2005; Wendorf & Alexander, 2005). Trust and respect are also central to secondary students' willingness to disclose their knowledge and engage in AFL (Cowie, 2005). Some experienced teachers emphasize the importance of being proactive in the development of a constructive environment for assessment to be fair and support learning (Tierney, 2010). Many of their recommended strategies center on trust and respect (e.g., monitoring the tone of peer assessment) and take the open nature of classroom interaction into account. This suggests that the relationship between fair assessment and AFL is symbiotic. They are not the same, but they *can* be mutually supportive. The possibility is stressed because student involvement in assessment can also have a negative effect in terms of "poisoning" peer relations (Pryor & Lubisi, 2002, p. 682). The classroom environment is in itself affected by all the other aspects of fairness. Brookhart (2003) noted that the outcomes of CA "fold back into and become part of the classroom environment" (p. 7). Thus, without clear understanding of expectations and criteria, without opportunities to learn and demonstrate learning, without appropriate assessments and some degree of consistency, and without a reflective and responsive approach to interactions and decision making, the classroom environment is unlikely to be one in which desirable learning is achieved through assessment.

Classroom environment research has clearly linked the characteristics of assessment tasks to students' self-efficacy and attitudes about learning (Dorman, Fisher, & Waldrip, 2006). An association between the quality of AFL and the culture in classrooms and schools has also been found (Birenbaum, Kimron, & Shilton, 2011). The relationship between assessment and the culture or environment should be explored further in terms of fairness. How do aspects of fairness interact in different environments, and how does this interaction influence learning? To what extent do contextual factors, such as class size and system requirements, facilitate or constrain teachers' efforts to be fair in assessing student learning, and what are the subsequent effects on the classroom environment? A better understanding of the characteristics of classroom environments that encourage fair assessment and support learning would be valuable for both theory and practice.

Conclusion

There are multiple and conflicting interpretations of the concept of fairness in the literature on educational assessment. To some extent, perspectives on fairness are informed by position, meaning that what is thought to be fair depends on a person's role in a particular context. While test developers focus on eliminating differential item functioning, tertiary students hope for respectful communication about grading. Significant differences are seen between fairness in testing and CA. Opportunity to learn, for example, is clearly more salient in classrooms where the primary purpose of assessment is to support learning. Fairness is particularly complex in AFL because it is a quality of human interaction in perpetually evolving circumstances. A posteriori evidence of fairness determined through investigation or argument is helpful from a theoretical perspective, but it is insufficient for the immediacy of classroom practice, especially for the learners who experience the effects of an assessment. The complexity of fairness is further compounded by the blurring of purposes in CA, which varies from context to context. As a result, fairness cannot be prescribed in universal terms for all students in all classrooms. Ongoing dialogue between stakeholders is absolutely critical to encourage the fairest CA possible. While ideas about what is fair in any given circumstance may often seem at odds, the underlying meaning is often the same. This provides much common ground for the conceptualization and practice of fair assessment in the educational community.

References

Allen, J. D., & Lambating, J. (2001, April). *Validity and reliability in assessment and grading: Perspectives of preservice and inservice teachers and teacher education professors.* Paper presented at the annual meeting of the American Educational Research Association, Seattle, WA.

American Educational Research Association, American Psychological Association, & National Council on Measurement in Education. (1985). *Standards for educational and psychological testing.* Washington, DC: American Educational Research Association.

American Educational Research Association, American Psychological Association, & National Council on Measurement in Education. (1999). *Standards for educational and psychological testing.* Washington, DC: American Educational Research Association.

American Psychological Association, American Educational Research Association, and the National Council on Measurement in Education. (1966). *Standards for educational and psychological tests.* (1966). Washington, DC: Authors.

American Psychological Association, American Educational Research Association, and the National Council on Measurement in Education. (1974). *Standards for educational and psychological tests.* (1966). Washington, DC: Authors.

Andrade, H. G. (2005). Teaching with rubrics: The good, the bad, and the ugly. *College Teaching, 53*(1), 27–30.

Andrade, H. L., Du, Y., & Wang, X. (2008). Putting rubrics to the test: The effect of a model, criteria generation, and rubric-referenced self-assessment on elementary school students' writing. *Educational Measurement: Issues and Practice, 27*(3), 3–13.

Assessment Reform Group. (2002). *Assessment for learning: 10 principles.* Retrieved from www.assessment-reform-group.org/publications.html

Badger, E. (1999). Finding one's voice: A model for more equitable assessment. In A. L. Nettles & M. T. Nettles (Eds.), *Measuring up: Challenges minorities face in educational assessment* (pp. 53–69). Norwell, MA: Kluwer Academic Publishers.

Birenbaum, M., Kimron, H., & Shilton, H. (2011). Nested contexts that shape assessment for learning: School-based professional learning community and classroom culture. *Studies in Educational Evaluation, 37,* 35–48.

Black, P., Harrison, C., Hodgen, J., Marshall, B., & Serret, N. (2010). Validity in teachers' summative assessments. *Assessment in Education: Principles, Policy & Practice, 17*(2), 2215–2232.

Black, P., & Wiliam, D. (1998). Assessment and classroom learning. *Assessment in Education: Principles, Policy & Practice, 5*(1), 7–74.

Black, P., & Wiliam, D. (2006). The reliability of assessments. In J. Gardner (Ed.), *Assessment and learning.* Thousand Oaks, CA: Sage.

Bredo, E. (2006). Philosophies of educational research. In J. L. Green, G. Camilli, & P. B. Elmore (Eds.), *Handbook of complementary methods in education research* (pp. 3–31). Mahwah, NJ: Lawrence Erlbaum.

Brighton, C. M. (2003). The effects of middle school teachers' beliefs on classroom practices. *Journal for the Education of the Gifted, 27*(2/3), 177–206.

Brookfield, S. (2001). Unmasking power: Foucault and adult learning. *Canadian Journal for Studies in Adult Education, 15*(1), 1–23.

Brookhart, S. M. (1993). Teachers' grading practices: Meaning and values. *Journal of Educational Measurement, 30*(2), 123–142.

Brookhart, S. M. (1994). Teachers' grading: Practice and theory. *Applied Measurement in Education, 7*(4), 279–301.

Brookhart, S. M. (2003). Developing measurement theory for classroom assessment purposes and uses. *Educational Measurement: Issues and Practice, 22*(4), 5–12.

Brookhart, S. M. (2004a). Classroom assessment: Tensions and intersections in theory and practice. *Teachers College Record, 106*(3), 429–458.

Brookhart, S. M. (2004b). *Grading.* Upper Saddle River, NJ: Pearson.

Bulterman-Bos, J., Terwel, J., Verloop, N., & Wardekker, W. (2002). Observation in teaching: Toward a practice of objectivity. *Teachers College Record, 104*(6), 1069–1100.

Bursuck, W. D., Munk, D. D., & Olson, M. (1999). The fairness of report card grading adaptations: What do students with and without learning disabilities think? *Remedial and Special Education, 20*(2), 84–92.

Buzzelli, C. A., & Johnston, B. (2002). *The moral dimensions of teaching: Language, power, and culture in classroom interaction.* New York: RoutledgeFalmer.

Camilli, G. (2006). Test fairness. In R. L. Brennan (Ed.), *Educational measurement* (4th ed., pp. 221–256). Westport, CT: Praeger.

Campbell, E. (2003). *The ethical teacher.* Buckingham, UK: Open University Press.

Childs, R. A. (1990). *Gender bias and fairness.* Washington, DC: ERIC Clearinghouse on Tests Measurement and Evaluation, American Institutes for Research. (ERIC Document Reproduction Service No. ED328610)

Chory-Assad, R. M. (2002). Classroom justice: Perceptions of fairness as a predictor of student motivation, learning, and aggression. *Communication Quarterly, 50*(1), 58–77.

Clarke, M. M., Madaus, G. F., Horn, C. L., & Ramos, M. A. (2000). Retrospective on educational testing and assessment in the 20th century. *Journal of Curriculum Studies, 32*(2), 159–181.

Cole, N. S., & Zieky, M. J. (2001). The new faces of fairness. *Journal of Educational Measurement, 38*(4), 369–382.

Cowie, B. (2005). Student commentary on classroom assessment in science: A sociocultural interpretation. *International Journal of Science Education, 27*(2), 199–214.

Cowie, B. (in press). Equity, ethics and engagement: Principles for quality formative assessment in primary science classrooms. In C. Milne, K. G. Tobin, & D. Degenero (Eds.), *Sociocultural studies and implications for science education: The experiential and the virtual.* Dortrecht, The Netherlands: Springer.

Crisp, V. (2010). Towards a model of the judgement processes involved in examination marking. *Oxford Review of Education, 36*(1), 1–21.

Crossouard, B. (2011). Using formative assessment to support complex learning in conditions of social adversity. *Assessment in Education: Principles, Policy & Practice, 18*(1), 59–72.

Dalbert, C., Schneidewind, U., & Saalbach, A. (2007). Justice judgments concerning grading in school. *Contemporary Educational Psychology, 32*(3), 420–433.

Dann, R. (2002). *Promoting assessment as learning: Improving the learning process.* London: RoutledgeFalmer.

Davies, A. (2010). Test fairness: A response. *Language Testing, 27*(2), 171–176.

DeLain, M. T. (2005). Equity and performance-based assessment: An insider's view. In S. J. Barrentine & S. M. Stokes (Ed.), *Reading assessment: Principles and practices for elementary teachers* (2nd ed., pp. 52–55). Newark, DE: International Reading Association.

Delandshere, G. (2001). Implicit theories, unexamined assumptions and the status quo of educational assessment. *Assessment in Education: Principles, Policy & Practice, 8*(2), 113–133.

Dixon, H., & Williams, R. (2003). Teachers' understanding and use of formative assessment in literacy learning. *New Zealand Annual Review of Education.* Retrieved from http://assessment.tki.org.nz/Research/Research

Dorman, J. P., Fisher, D. L., & Waldrip, B. G. (2006). Classroom environment, students' perceptions of assessment, academic efficacy and attitude to science: A LISREL analysis. In D. L. Fisher & M. S. Khine (Eds.), *Contemporary approaches to research on learning environments: Worldviews.* Hackensack, NJ: World Scientific.

Drummond, M. J. (2003). *Assessing children's learning* (2nd ed.). London: David Fulton Publishers, Ltd.

Duffield, K. E., & Spencer, J. A. (2002). A survey of medical students' views about the purposes and fairness of assessment. *Medical Education, 36*(9), 879–886.

Earl, L. M. & Katz, S. (2006). *Rethinking classroom assessments with purpose in mind.* Governments of Alberta, British Columbia, Manitoba, Northwest Territories, Nunavut, Saskatchewan, and Yukon Territory: Western and Northern Canadian Protocol for Collaboration in Education.

Ebel, R. L. (1972). *Essentials of educational measurement* (2nd ed.). Englewood Cliffs, NJ: Prentice Hall.

Eggen, A. B. (2004). *Alfa and omega in student assessment: Exploring identities of secondary school science teachers.* Universitetet i Oslo, Norway. Retrieved from www.ils.uio.no/forskning/pdh-drgrad/.../AstridEggenAvhandling1.pdf

Elhoweris, H., Mutua, K., Alsheikh, N., & Holloway, P. (2005). Effect of children's ethnicity on teachers' referral and recommendation decisions in gifted and talented programs. *Remedial and Special Education, 26*(1), 25–31.

Elwood, J. (2006). Formative assessment: Possibilities, boundaries and limitations. *Assessment in Education: Principles, Policy & Practice, 13*(2), 215–232.

Ernest, J. M., Heckaman, K. A., Thompson, S. E., Hull, K. M., & Carter, S. W. (2011). Increasing the teaching efficacy of a beginning special education teacher using differentiated instruction: A case study. *International Journal of Special Education, 26*(1).

Finklestein, I. E. (1913). *The marking system in theory and practice.* Baltimore: Warwick & York, Inc.

Frederiksen, J. R., & Collins, A. (1989). A system approach to educational testing. *Educational Researcher, 18*(9), 27–32.

Gee, J. P. (2003). Opportunity to learn: A language-based perspective on assessment. *Assessment in Education: Principles, Policy & Practice, 10*(1), 27–46.

Giordano, G. (2005). *How testing came to dominate American schools: The history of educational assessment.* New York: Peter Lang Publishing.

Gipps, C. (1994). *Beyond testing: Towards a theory of educational assessment.* London: RoutledgeFalmer.

Gipps, C. (1999). Socio-cultural aspects of assessment. *Review of Research in Education, 24,* 355–392.

Gipps, C. (2005). Commentary on "the idea of testing: Psychometric and sociocultural perspectives." *Measurement, 3*(2), 98–102.

Gordon, M. E., & Fay, C. H. (2010). The effects of grading and teaching practices on students' perceptions of grading fairness. *College Teaching, 58*(3), 93–98.

Graham, P. (2005). Classroom-based assessment: Changing knowledge and practice through pre-service teacher education. *Teacher and Teacher Education, 21,* 607–621.

Green, S., Johnson, R. L., Kim, D. H., & Pope, N. S. (2007). Ethics in classroom assessment practices: Issues and attitudes. *Teaching and Teacher Education, 23,* 999–1011.

Gummer, E. S. (2000). Rhetoric and reality: Congruence between the knowledge and practice of assessment of the classroom science teacher and the reform initiative of the national science education standards. Unpublished doctoral dissertation, Purdue University, West Lafayette. (UMI No. AAT 3018203)

Guskey, T. R. (2006, April). *"It wasn't fair!" Educators' recollections of their experiences as students with grading.* Paper presented at the American Educational Research Association, San Francisco.

Guskey, T. R., & Jung, L. A. (2009). Grading and reporting in a standards-based environment: Implications for students with special needs. *Theory Into Practice, 48*(1), 53–62.

Gynnild, V. (2011). Student appeals of grades: A comparative study of university policies and practices. *Assessment in Education: Principles, Policy & Practice, 18*(1), 41–57.

Horn, R. A. (2002). Reform in curriculum, instruction, and assessment, *Understanding educational reform: A reference handbook.* Santa Barbara, CA: ABC-CLIO, Inc.

Jackson, P. W., Boostrom, R. E., & Hansen, D. T. (1993). *The moral life of schools.* San Francisco: Jossey-Bass.

Jiménez, R. T. (2005). More equitable literacy assessments for Latino students. In S. J. Barrentine & S. M. Stokes (Eds.), *Reading assessment: Principles and practices for elementary teachers* (2nd ed., pp. 49–51). Newark, DE: International Reading Association.

Joint Advisory Committee. (1993). Principles for fair student assessment practices for education in Canada. Retrieved from www2.education.ualberta.ca/educ/psych/crame/files/eng_prin.pdf

Joint Committee on Standards for Educational Evaluation. (2003). *The student evaluation standards: How to improve evaluations of students.* Thousand Oaks, CA: Corwin Press.

Kane, M. (2010). Validity and fairness. *Language Testing, 27*(2), 177–182.

Knoch, U., & Elder, C. (2010). Validity and fairness implications of varying time conditions on a diagnostic test of academic English writing proficiency. *System, 38*(1), 63–74.

Koch, P. R., Steelman, L. C., Mulkey, L., & Catsambis, S. (2008). Naughty or nice?: Equity, gender and behavior. *Social Psychology of Education: An International Journal, 11*(4), 409–430.

Kornhaber, M. L. (2004). Assessment, standards, and equity. In J. A. Banks (Ed.), *Handbook of research on multicultural education* (2nd ed., pp. 91–109). New York: John Wiley.

Kunnan, A. J. (2010). Test fairness and Toulmin's argument structure. *Language Testing, 27*(2), 183–189.

Lam, T. C. (1995). Fairness in performance assessment. Greensboro, NC: ERIC Clearinghouse on Counseling and Student Services. (ERIC Document Reproduction Service No. ED391982)

Lane, S., & Silver, E. A. (1999). Fairness and equity in measuring student learning using a mathematics performance assessment: Results from the quasar project. In A. L. Nettles & M. T. Nettles (Eds.), *Measuring up: Challenges minorities face in educational assessment* (pp. 97–120). Norwell, MA: Kluwer Academic Publishers.

Linn, R. L., Baker, E. L., & Dunbar, S. B. (1991). *Complex, performance-based assessment: Expectations and validation criteria* (CSE Technical Report 331). Los Angeles: Center for the Study of Evaluation.

Markus, J. (2002). Student assessment and evaluation in studio art. Unpublished doctoral dissertation,

University of Toronto, Canada. (UMI No. AAT NQ69131)

Mauldin, R. K. (2009). Gendered perceptions of learning and fairness when choice between exam types is offered. *Active Learning in Higher Education, 10*(3), 253–264.

McDonald, B., & Boud, D. (2003). The impact of self-assessment on achievement: The effects of self-assessment training on performance in external examinations. *Assessment in Education: Principles, Policy & Practice, 10*(2), 209–220.

McMillan, J. H. (2001). Secondary teachers' classroom assessment and grading practices. *Educational Measurement: Issues and Practice, 20*(1), 20–32.

McMillan, J. H. (2003). Understanding and improving teachers' classroom assessment decision making: Implications for theory and practice. *Educational Measurement: Issues and Practice, 22*(4), 34–43.

McMillan, J. H. (2011). *Classroom assessment: Principles and practice for effective standards-based instruction* (5th ed.). Upper Saddle River, NJ: Pearson.

Messick, S. (1965). Personality measurement and the ethics of assessment. *American Psychologist, 20*(2), 136–142.

Messick, S. (1989). Meaning and values in test validation: The science and ethics of assessment. *Educational Researcher, 18*(2), 5–11.

Messick, S. (2000). Consequences of test interpretation and use: The fusion of validity and values in psychological assessment. In R. D. Goffin & E. Helmes (Eds.), *Problems and solutions in human assessment* (pp. 3–20). Norwell, MA: Kluwer Academic Publishers.

Messick, S., & Anderson, S. (1970). Educational testing, individual development, and social responsibility. *The Counseling Psychologist, 2*(2), 80–88.

Miner. (1990). Teacher evaluations of case descriptions of LD gifted children. *Gifted Child Quarterly, 34*(1), 37–39.

Moon, T. (2005). The role of assessment in differentiation. *Theory Into Practice, 44*(3), 226–233.

Morgan, C., & Watson, A. (2002). The interpretive nature of teachers' assessment of students' mathematics. *Journal for Research in Mathematics Education, 33*(2), 78–110.

Moss, P. (1994). Can there be validity without reliability. *Educational Researcher, 23*(2), 5–12.

Moss, P. (1998). The role of consequences in validity theory. *Educational Measurement: Issues and Practice, 17*(2), 6–12.

Moss, P. (2003). Reconceptualizing validity for classroom assessment. *Educational Measurement: Issues and Practice, 22*(4), 13–25.

Moss, P., Pullin, D., Gee, J. P., & Haertel, E. H. (2005). The idea of testing: Psychometric and sociocultural perspectives. *Measurement, 3*(2), 63–83.

Nagy, P. (2000). Three roles of assessment: Gatekeeping, accountability, and instructional diagnosis. *Canadian Journal of Education, 25*(4), 262–279.

National Research Council. (2010). *State assessment systems: Exploring best practices and innovations: Summary of two workshops.* Washington, DC: The National Academies Press.

Nettles, A. L., & Nettles, M. T. (1999). *Measuring up: Challenges minorities face in educational assessment.* Norwell, MA: Kluwer Academic Publishers.

Newkirk, T. (2004). A mania for rubrics. In A. S. Canestrari & B. A. Marlowe (Eds.), *Educational foundations: An anthology of critical readings.* Thousand Oaks, CA: Sage.

Ontario Ministry of Education. (2010). *Growing success: Assessment, evaluation and reporting in Ontario schools* (1st ed.). Toronto, ON: Queen's Printer for Ontario.

Parkes, J. (2007). Reliability as argument. *Educational Measurement: Issues and Practice, 26*(4), 2–10.

Peterson, S., & Kennedy, K. (2006). Sixth-grade teachers' written comments on student writing. *Written Communication, 23*(1), 36–62.

Phillips, M. (2002). Is "same" treatment "fair" treatment? In J. Shulman, A. K. Whittaker, & M. Lew (Eds.), *Using assessments to teach for understanding.* New York: Teachers College Press.

Poehner, M. E. (2011). Dynamic assessment: Fairness through the prism of mediation. *Assessment in Education: Principles, Policy & Practice, 18*(2), 99–112.

Popham, W. J. (1981). *Modern educational measurement.* Englewood Cliffs, NJ: Prentice Hall.

Popham, W. J. (2008). *Classroom assessment: What teachers need to know* (5th ed.). Upper Saddle River, NJ: Pearson.

Pryor, J., & Crossouard, B. (2008). A socio-cultural theorisation of formative assessment. *Oxford Review of Education, 34*(1), 1–20.

Pryor, J., & Lubisi, C. (2002). Reconceptualising educational assessment in South Africa—testing times for teachers. *International Journal of Educational Development, 22*(6), 673–686.

Resh, N. (2009). Justice in grades allocation: Teachers' perspective. *Social Psychology of Education: An International Journal, 12*(3), 315–325.

Resh, N., & Dalbert, C. (2007). Gender differences in sense of justice about grades: A comparative study of high school students in Israel and Germany. *Teachers College Record, 109*(2), 322–342.

Robinson, J. M. (2002). In search of fairness: An application of multi-reviewer anonymous peer review in a large class. *Journal of Further & Higher Education, 26*(2), 183–192.

Russell, M. K., & Airasian, P. W. (2012). *Classroom assessment: Concepts and applications* (7th ed.). New York: McGraw-Hill.

Ryan, T. G. (2000). An action research study of secondary science praxis. Unpublished doctoral dissertation, University of Toronto, Canada. (UMI No. AAT NQ58601)

Sadler, D. R. (1989). Formative assessment and the design of instructional systems, *Instructional Science, 18*,119–144.

Sadler, D. R. (2005). Interpretations of criteria-based assessment and grading in higher education. *Assessment & Evaluation in Higher Education, 30*(2), 175–194.

Schendel, E., & O'Neill, P. (1999). Exploring the theories and consequences of self-assessment through ethical inquiry. *Assessing Writing, 6*(2), 199–227.

Shepard, L. (1997). The centrality of test use and consequences for test validity. *Educational Measurement: Issues and Practice, 16*(2), 5–8, 13, 24.

Shepard, L. (2000). *The role of classroom assessment in teaching and learning.* CSE Technical Report 517. Washington, DC: Office of Educational Research and Improvement.

Shepard, L. (2006). Classroom assessment. In R. L. Brennan (Ed.), *Educational measurement* (4th ed., pp. 623–646). Westport, CT: American Council on Education/Praeger.

Shulman, L. S. (2004). The wisdom of practice: Managing complexity in medicine and teaching. In S. M. Wilson (Ed.), *The wisdom of practice: Essays on teaching, learning, and learning to teach* (pp. 249–271). San Francisco, CA: Jossey-Bass.

Smith, E., & Gorard, S. (2006). Pupils' views on equity in schools. *Compare, 36*(1), 41–56.

Smith, J. K. (2003). Reconsidering reliability in classroom assessment and grading. *Educational Measurement: Issues and Practice, 22*(4), 26–33.

Speck, B. W. (1998). Unveiling some of the mystery of professional judgment in classroom assessment. In R. S. Anderson & B. W. Speck (Eds.), *Classroom assessment and the new learning paradigm* (pp. 89–96). San Francisco: Jossey-Bass.

Stiggins, R. J., & Bridgeford, N. J. (1985). The ecology of classroom assessment. *Journal of Educational Measurement, 22*(4), 271–286.

Stiggins, R. J., Conklin, N. F., & Bridgeford, N. J. (1986, Summer). Classroom assessment: A key to effective education. *Educational Measurement: Issues and Practice,* 5–17.

Stiggins, R. J., Frisbie, D. A., & Griswold, P. A. (1989). Inside high school grading practices: Building a research agenda. *Educational Measurement: Issues and Practice, 8*(2), 5–14.

Stobart, G. (2005). Fairness in multicultural assessment systems. *Assessment in Education: Principles, Policy & Practice, 12* (3), 275–287.

Stobart, G. (2006). The validity of formative assessment. In J. Gardner (Ed.), *Assessment and learning.* Thousand Oaks, CA: Sage.

Suskie, L. (2002). Fair assessment practices: Giving students equitable opportunities to demonstrate learning. *Adventures in Assessment.* Retrieved from www.sabes.org/resources/publications/adventures/vol14/14suskie.htm

Szpyrka, D. A. (2001). Exploration of instruction, assessment, and equity in the middle school science classroom. Unpublished doctoral dissertation, University of Central Florida, Orlando. (UMI No. AAT 3029061)

Tata, J. (2005). The influence of national culture on the perceived fairness of grading procedures: A comparison of the United States and China. *Journal of Psychology, 139*(5), 401–412.

Tierney, R. D. (2010). Insights into fairness in classroom assessment: Experienced English teachers share their practical wisdom. Unpublished doctoral dissertation, University of Ottawa, Canada. (UMI No. AAT NR69109)

Tierney, R. D., Simon, M., & Charland, J. (2011). Being fair: Teachers' interpretations of principles for standards-based grading. *The Educational Forum, 75*(3), 210–227.

Tierney, R. J. (2005). Literacy assessment reform: Shifting beliefs, principled possibilities, and emerging practices. In S. J. Barrentine & S. M. Stokes (Ed.), *Reading assessment: Principles and practices for elementary teachers* (2nd ed., pp. 29–40). Newark, DE: International Reading Association.

Tomlinson, C. A. (2005). Grading and differentiation: Paradox or good practice? *Theory Into Practice, 44*(3), 262–269.

Torrance, H., & Pryor, J. (1998). *Investigating formative assessment: Teaching, learning and assessment in the classroom.* New York: Open University Press.

Torrance, H., & Pryor, J. (2001). Developing formative assessment in the classroom: Using action research to explore and modify theory. *British Educational Research Journal, 27*(5), 615–631.

Volante, L. (2006). Reducing bias in classroom assessment and evaluation. *Orbit, 36,* 34–36.

Watson, A. (1999). Paradigmatic conflicts in informal mathematics assessment as sources of social inequity. *Educational Review, 51*(2), 105–115.

Weeden, P., Winter, J., & Broadfoot, P. (2002). *Assessment: What's in it for schools?* New York: RoutledgeFalmer.

Wendorf, C. A., & Alexander, S. (2005). The influence of individual- and class-level fairness-related perceptions on student satisfaction. *Contemporary Educational Psychology, 30*(2), 190–206.

Whittington, D. (1999). Making room for values and fairness: Teaching reliability and validity in the classroom context. *Educational Measurement: Issues and Practice, 18*(1), 14–22.

Wiggins, G. (1993). *Assessing student performance: Exploring the purpose and limits of testing.* San Francisco: Jossey-Bass.

Wiliam, D. (1994). *Toward a philosophy for educational assessment.* Paper presented at the British Educational Research Association, Oxford, UK.

Wilson, M. (2006). *Rethinking rubrics in writing assessment.* Portsmouth, NH: Heinemann, Reed Elsevier, Inc.

Wormeli, R. (2006). *Fair isn't always equal: Assessing and grading in the differentiated classroom.* Portland, ME: National Middle School Association.

Wyatt-Smith, C., Klenowski, V., & Gunn, S. (2010). The centrality of teachers' judgement practice in assessment: A study of standards in moderation. *Assessment in Education: Principles, Policy & Practice, 17*(1), 59–75.

Xi, X. (2010). How do we go about investigating test fairness? *Language Testing, 27*(2), 147–170.

Yip, D. Y., & Cheung, D. (2005). Teachers' concerns on school-based assessment of practical work. *Journal of Biological Education, 39* (4), 156–162.

Yung, B. H. W. (2001). Three views of fairness in a school-based assessment scheme of practical work in biology. *International Journal of Science Education, 23*(10), 985–1005.

Zoeckler, L. G. (2005). Moral dimensions of grading in high school English. Unpublished doctoral dissertation, Indiana University, Bloomington. (UMI No. AAT3183500)

9

MEASURING CLASSROOM ASSESSMENT PRACTICES

BRUCE RANDEL AND TEDRA CLARK

This chapter provides an overview of the measurement of classroom assessment (CA) practices. By way of introduction, the chapter begins with a discussion of different ways that measures of CA practice can be used in research. The chapter continues by offering a framework for understanding the many different aspects of CA practice. These different aspects then become the targets of measurement. General issues in measurement as they pertain directly to CA practice are discussed next. Existing measures of CA practice are then reviewed, followed by a discussion of issues to be considered when developing a measure of CA practice. The chapter concludes with final thoughts regarding research and measurement of CA practice.

USING MEASURES OF CLASSROOM ASSESSMENT

Measures of classroom practice have many potential uses in research, and although there are multiple ways to use measures of CA practices in educational research, we propose a specific framework. Measures of CA practice can be used as measures of implementation, as predictors, or as outcomes. Each of these uses will be discussed.

Using measures of CA practice focuses attention on gaining an understanding of the degree to which teachers or other educators are implementing CA practices. This is primarily descriptive, with the aim of capturing and presenting the variations in assessment practice. Questions that this type of descriptive research might address include the following: How much of the important vocabulary of classroom assessment do teachers know? What different assessment methods are teachers using, and how do these methods align with the learning objectives? What type of feedback are teachers providing their students?

Descriptive information of this type typically needs some method to aid data interpretation. Simply knowing a teacher or school had a particular score or rating on a measure of CA practice is often insufficient to gain a full understanding. Some method is needed to help place the score or rating in context. Most instruments discussed next provide a way of interpreting their resulting score or rating.

Measures of CA practice can also be used as predictors. For example, measures of CA practice can be used as independent variables in correlational research to explain variance in dependent variables, such as student achievement. CA measures can also be used as covariates in the analysis for experimental or quasi-experimental studies to reduce unexplained variance in the outcome, thus increasing statistical power. CA measures can also be used to classify or categorize teachers into groups based on their practice. These groups can then be compared on other variables, such as experience or demographic characteristics, to better understand the ways in which teachers differ.

Finally, measures of CA practice can be used as outcomes, or dependent variables. As with the examples with predictors, the research can be correlational, quasi-experimental, or experimental. In correlational research with CA practice as a dependent variable, the goal of the research is typically to understand what variables relate to, predict, or explain variance in CA practice. For example, how does teacher experience relate to CA practice? Does CA practice improve as teachers gain more experience? Is this a linear relationship? Or is there a leveling off where more years of experience do not correspond to better assessment practice? In terms of quasi-experimental or experimental studies, CA practice as an outcome typically would be part of a study that estimates the impact of an intervention on assessment practice. This type of study is useful because it provides researchers and educators with information about the effectiveness of methods and programs for improving CA practice. This information, in turn, informs decisions about the implementation of programs, typically professional development programs.

Measures of CA, therefore, have a variety of uses in research. All these uses help us better understand how assessment is practiced in the classroom, how CA explains variance in other educational outcomes, what explains variance in CA practices, and what programs or methods are effective in improving CA practices. And none of these goals can be accomplished without accurate and reliable measures of CA practice.

But CA is not a single practice. There are many different elements of CA practice, and defining and understanding these elements is required before measuring them. The next section of the chapter provides a framework for understanding and categorizing the diverse practices that make up CA.

Measuring Classroom Assessment Knowledge and Practices

CA is not a product or set of tools. Rather, it is a practice. What matters most is how teachers and learners use the information gleaned from assessments to enhance and/or document student learning. CA is a multifaceted and iterative process that includes several key elements of teacher practice. Quality in CA is based on firm knowledge of the key principles of classroom practice as well as the translation of that knowledge into sound practice including specification of clear and appropriate learning objectives (Ayala et al., 2008; Cowie, 2005; Sadler, 1989; Stiggins & Chappuis, 2008; Valencia, 2008; Wiley, 2008), descriptive feedback to students (Bangert-Drowns, Kulik, Kulik, & Morgan, 1991; Brookhart, 2008; Callingham, 2008; Cowie, 2005; Hattie & Timperley, 2007; Kluger & DeNisi, 1998), student involvement in assessment of learning (Fontana & Fernandes, 1994; Frederiksen & White, 1997; Shepard, 2000; Stiggins & Chappuis, 2006; Valencia, 2008), and informative grading and communication systems (Guskey & Bailey, 2001; Reeves, 2008).

Teacher Pedagogical Content Knowledge

Teacher pedagogical content knowledge (PCK) is a critical component for understanding and implementing high quality classroom practice, including CA (Baxter & Lederman, 2002). According to Shulman's original definition of PCK, the construct "represents the blending of content and pedagogy into an understanding of how particular topics, problems or issues are organized, represented, and adapted to the diverse interests and abilities of learners, and presented for instruction" (Shulman, 1987, p. 4).

Multiple researchers have proposed a contribution of PCK to effective CA practice (Alonzo, 2005; Bell & Cowie, 2000; Black, Harrison, Lee, Marshall, & Wiliam, 2004). Furthermore, certain professional development programs engage teachers in CA as a strategy to support PCK (Van Driel, Verloop, & de Vos, 1998). Specifically, collaborative analysis of student work helps teachers develop new insights into articulating learning goals, tasks for assessing particular goals, the range of student ideas, common patterns in student thinking, and ways in which students represent their thinking (Falk, 2012). In short, CA helps to build teacher knowledge of student understanding and how that knowledge can be used for subsequent interpretation.

Although a complete discussion of the measurement issues related to PCK is beyond the scope of this review (see Baxter & Lederman, 2002, for a large-scale review of assessment and measurement of PCK), accurate measurement of PCK is an important consideration for examining quality in CA. An array of measures and techniques have been developed to examine PCK, including multiple-choice tests, concept maps, pictorial representations, interviews, and mixed-method evaluations (Baxter & Lederman, 2002). However, more research is necessary to identify the best methods for measuring PCK as it relates specifically to CA.

Knowledge of Classroom Assessment

A critical first step to improved practice in CA is enhanced assessment literacy. At this time, many teachers do not use sound CA practice, and there is some evidence that, in fact, many know little about it (Stiggins, 2002). Research and expert opinion suggest that teachers who have high levels of assessment knowledge create more effective assessments and utilize a wider variety of assessments in their classrooms (Bailey & Heritage, 2008; Green & Stager, 1986, 1987; Popham, 2009). Therefore, measurement of CA practice would benefit from evaluation of educators' understanding of the key terminology and underlying principles of CA in order to inform effective use of information gained from various instruments and techniques.

Vocabulary of Classroom Assessment

It is important for educators to develop a precise vocabulary for discussing and thinking about CA. Because CA consists of several diverse aspects, it is often difficult to determine if individuals are referring to the same underlying practices in their vocabulary. Assessment experts recommend collaborative cultures that emphasize continuous learning and improvement in assessment practice (Stiggins, Arter, Chappuis, & Chappuis, 2004). If teachers do not adopt a common vocabulary for the elements of assessment practice, these collaborations may be inefficient if not inhibiting. In addition, if there is confusion about vocabulary, teachers may report that they are using a particular strategy in their classroom when in actuality they are not. This has significant implications for measurement of CA practice, particularly when measurement relies on self-reports.

Principles of Classroom Assessment

In addition to vocabulary, it is important to consider teachers' knowledge of the principles underlying sound CA. For example, measures could attempt to capture teacher's knowledge of the different purposes of CA (e.g., assessment for formative versus summative purposes), examples of assessments (e.g., performance assessments, homework, or portfolios) best suited for certain purposes, and the different ways assessment data can be used to both improve and document student learning. Measurement of CA knowledge may also account for teachers' knowledge of the basic elements of assessment process (e.g., setting learning objectives, delivering feedback, and reporting/grading) and different strategies for engaging in the assessment process in order to maximize its benefits to both teaching and learning.

Classroom Assessment Practices

Teacher knowledge of assessment vocabulary and principles is an important consideration in measuring quality in CA. However, increased knowledge may not actually translate into improved assessment practice. Therefore, separate measures of teacher practice are necessary to accurately capture educators' actual implementation of the important elements of CA as identified in the wide base of assessment literature, to which we now turn.

Learning Objectives

An early step in sound CA practice is the specification of clear and specific learning objectives that are linked to the curriculum and content standards. A learning objective is a statement of what students are expected to learn, understand, or be able to demonstrate as a result of an instructional activity. Learning objectives are usually based on content standards from states, districts, or national subject area organizations. These standards, however, must be translated into more specific academic subskills describing the type and level of student performance that is expected. High quality learning objectives are clearly linked to instruction, and they provide both teachers and learners with an understanding of the information, skills, strategies, and/or processes that demonstrate the attainment of those objectives (Marzano, 2009). High quality learning objectives are often accompanied by rubrics, or scoring tools, that present the criteria for meeting various levels of performance, as well as distinguish various qualities of student thinking, reasoning, and problem solving (Arter & McTighe, 2001).

Assessment Methods

CA can take many forms. Commonly used methods include teacher-made tests, curriculum-embedded evaluations, oral questioning, homework, or performance assessments. In addition, as stated previously, CAs can be used formatively to improve student learning and/or summatively to measure what students have already learned. Assessment methods are not necessarily linked to specific uses. For example, an end-of-chapter test, typically used for evaluative purposes, can also be used to modify instruction. Likewise, an oral questioning strategy, typically used to guide instruction, may be used to form a final evaluation of a student's performance. Measures of quality in assessment practice must capture the diversity in assessment methods in order to reveal the most effective assessment methods and relate them to their most appropriate uses for both enhancing and documenting student learning.

Feedback

Feedback is information that provides learners with an understanding of how they are doing or have done, as well as what they might do in the future to enhance their knowledge and performance (Callingham, 2008; Cowie, 2005; also see Chapters 12 and 13 of this volume). Many assessment scholars agree that feedback is an essential component of the assessment process and a critical support mechanism for student learning (Callingham, 2008; Cauley, Pannozzo, Abrams, McMillan, & Camou-Linkroum, 2006; Center for Comprehensive School Reform and Improvement [CCSRI], 2006; Hattie & Timperley, 2007; Shepard, 2000; Stiggins, 2004; also see Chapter 13 of this volume). However, because not all feedback enhances learning, accurate and reliable measures of feedback are necessary for assessing quality in assessment practice.

The manner in which feedback is delivered is an important consideration for measurement. Research suggests that feedback is most beneficial to student performance when it focuses on features of the task, such as how the student can improve his or her performance in relation to standards and learning objectives (Brookhart, 2008; Crooks, 1988; Hattie & Timperley, 2007; Kluger & DeNisi, 1998; Kulhavy, 1977; Mory, 2004; Shute, 2008). This task-oriented emphasis is advantageous over nonspecific evaluation (e.g., praise or criticism) or normative comparisons because it helps students become aware of misconceptions or gaps between desired goals and current knowledge, understanding, and skills and then helps guide students through the process of obtaining those goals (Brookhart, 2008; Sadler, 1989; Tunstall & Gipps, 1996; for meta-analysis, see Bangert-Drowns et al., 1991).

Measurement of CA practice should also consider the timing of feedback. Research suggests that the most effective feedback is provided during or immediately after a learning experience. If it is provided too early, before students have a chance to fully work through a problem, it may decrease student effort and inhibit learning (Epstein et al., 2002; Kulhavy, 1977; Kulik & Kulik, 1988). If it is provided too late, it is likely that instruction has moved on to address other content, and students may not have an opportunity to demonstrate improved performance (Cauley et al., 2006).

Student Involvement

Another important aspect of assessment is the student's involvement in evaluating his or her own learning (Shepard, 2000; Stiggins, 1998; Valencia, 2008). Self-assessment involves comparison of one's own work with established learning objectives, critiquing one's own work, or simply describing one's own performance by means of self-reflection (see also Chapter 21 of this volume for a review of research on student self-assessment).

Quality in formative assessment is linked to the frequency and manner in which students are involved in assessment of their own learning. Research suggests that children who are given frequent opportunities to reflect on their work relative to established learning objectives show improved academic performance compared to those who do not engage in self-assessment (Fontana & Fernandes, 1994; Frederiksen & White, 1997; see also Stiggins & Chappuis, 2008). Furthermore, students who receive training in self-assessment for monitoring their own understanding show significant learning gains as compared with those who do not receive training (McCurdy & Shapiro, 1992; McDonald & Boud, 2003). Students who self-assess tend to express greater interest in the evaluation criteria and feedback than in the grades they receive (Klenowski, 1995). They also tend to be more honest about the quality of their work, more equitable in their assessment of other students' work, and more prepared to defend their answers and opinions with evidence (Shepard, 2000).

Measurement of student involvement in learning should focus on a number of criteria, including the frequency of student involvement in assessment of their own work or that of their peers, students' understanding of the evaluation criteria, students' use of tools or guidelines for peer and self-assessment (i.e., rubrics, checklists, and examples of high versus low quality work), and the extent to which student peer and self-assessment serves to guide future instruction and classroom activities.

Communication and Grading

Effective communication regarding student work and learning progress is an important, albeit challenging, aspect of CA (Guskey & Bailey, 2001). Typically, students and parents are involved in separate discussions with teachers regarding performance in school, which can often lead to important information being lost in translation. As expressed earlier, descriptive feedback to students that informs them about what they are doing well, what they are struggling with, and what they need to do to improve is a critical component to quality in CA (Brookhart, 2008). Descriptive feedback, however, should not stop at the student level. A key to effective communication is providing students and their families with a common understanding of the student's progress and areas of improvement in order that guidance and learning can be continued outside the classroom (Guskey & Bailey, 2001; Stiggins, Frisbie, & Griswold, 1989). Communication and grading practices go far beyond simply allocating a summary score or grade to represent the learning that has taken place over a certain time period. High quality communication and grading, whether it is directed toward a student or a parent, should provide information that leads to continued growth in learning.

In measuring communication, it is important to consider its many different forms—for example, frequent emails or telephone conversations with parents during the term, student-involved conferences held at key points during the school year, portfolios of student work, report cards, or informal chats about learning progress or difficulties. In fact, it is likely that the more avenues of communication, the more effective it will be for accomplishing the goal of improved student learning, given that the communication is sound (Stiggins et al., 2004).

Sound communication and grading begin with clear performance standards and learning objectives that promote a common understanding of the target levels of performance and where the student stands relative to those targets. Meaningful communication also depends on matching assessment methods to learning targets, as well as gathering sufficient information to ensure that the estimates of student performance are stable and free from bias (Stiggins et al., 2004). When communication involves symbols (i.e., grades), it is important to consider whether all intended recipients have a common understanding of their meaning and the methods used to derive them. More detailed communication methods, such as portfolios of student work and student-led conferences, can provide an important supplement to grading practices by highlighting growth of student performance and communicating more specifically about achievement and areas of improvement.

Measurement Issues and Classroom Assessment Practices

The methods and challenges of measuring educational practice are many and have been documented elsewhere (e.g., Ball & Rowan, 2004; Cohen, Manion, & Morrison, 2007; Gall, Gall, & Borg, 2006). This section of the chapter provides an overview of the methods and challenges of measurement as they pertain to CA practice. The measurement methods are categorized into observations, interviews, self-reports, artifact-based measures, and tests and discussed in turn.

Observations

Observations are a good match with the descriptive purposes of research, such as previously discussed implementation research of a program, practice, or intervention. Naturalistic observations, in which researchers simply observe and record CA activities, are particularly suited to research that is not testing specific hypotheses. Structured observation, where researchers set up a situation to help elicit the assessment activities or use an observation protocol or instrument, are more suited to research that is testing specific hypotheses. For example, researchers might ask specifically to observe teachers as they provide students feedback on a recently administered end-of-chapter quiz in order to examine the relationship between feedback and student performance.

The main advantage of observations is that they measure CA practice directly, typically in the natural setting of the classroom. This is particularly relevant because much of CA practice manifests as interactions between the classroom teacher and students. No other method provides direct measurement of interactions, which is crucial because much CA happens as interactions between the teacher and the student. Observational data often have strong validity because the data are based on direct observation of assessment practices rather than on indirect reports of those practices (Gall et al., 2006). Observations also can be used to measure multiple aspects of assessment practice during a single observation. For example, an observation protocol could include items for observing and recording the clarity of learning objectives provided to the students, the number and type of opportunities for students to be involved in assessment-related activities, and the types and quality of feedback to students.

There are, however, several disadvantages to observations. One disadvantage of observations is that they can be intrusive, possibly changing the learning and assessment dynamics in the classroom (Shaughnessy, Zechmeister, & Zechmeister, 2005). Teachers participating in a research study may be resistant to being observed in their classroom while providing feedback to their students. Observations also require training of those conducting the observations and corresponding evidence that the training results in valid and reliable observational data (Shaughnessy et al., 2005). One common way to show reliability is through inter-observer agreement, where two researchers observe the same teacher, and the researchers' data are compared.

The main disadvantage of observations is their cost (Shaughnessy et al., 2005). The relatively high cost of observations stems primarily from the time required, both for doing the observations but often also for traveling to and from the classroom. The relatively high cost and time-consuming nature of observations means that sampling is typically required because it is too expensive to observe all teachers or classrooms. Sampling can become complicated very quickly if there is a need to sample across teachers (by grade, subject, school, etc.) or to sample across different types of CA, such as quizzes, teacher feedback, and question and answer sessions. The relative high cost also stems from the need to train observers and establish their reliability. Sampling also relates to another disadvantage of observations: The target practice might be missed simply because there was no real opportunity for that practice (Cohen et al., 2007). For example, if class periods were sampled at random for observation and the class period chosen was one where students were doing seat work or even watching a video, the observation would not provide a valid inference regarding the teacher's use of assessment practices. So care has to be taken to sample the appropriate situations where CA has a chance to occur. All this sampling can weaken confidence in the generalizability of the observation data to the individual teacher, the research sample, or target population. This means that the design of the sampling strategy is critical.

Interviews

Interviews, including individual interviews and focus groups, also can be used to study classroom practice and teacher attitudes and perceptions toward different types of classroom practice (Tierney & Dilley, 2002). Interviews are particularly well suited to collecting in-depth information from participants, particularly in the form of qualitative data (Warren, 2002). Interviews allow for follow-up questions and probing of participants' responses to explore issues in greater depth than can typically be done with other data collection methods (Johnson, 2002). For example, teachers could be interviewed about the frequency they used different CA practices, and follow-up questions could explore in-depth the learning objectives addressed by each method and the teachers thoughts about why each method is suited for its respective objective. Interview methods are flexible and adaptable and can range from an open-ended exploratory approach to a close-ended and structured approach. The disadvantages of interview methods include the need for training and expertise of interviewers and relatively large amounts of time and resources needed to conduct the interviews (Warren, 2002). In addition to expertise in the methods for conducting interviews, interviewers must have in-depth knowledge of CA to be able to ask follow-up questions that probe more deeply into underlying issues of CA. Because interviewing is time-consuming and expensive, sample sizes are typically kept small, and subsampling is required within studies with large samples. Interviews and focus groups also can be subject to social desirability. Social desirability occurs when participants respond in a way they think will be seen as more socially desirable (Paulhus, 1991).

Self-Reports

This section includes a number of different measurement methods where the participants are providing information and data on themselves. We have included surveys, questionnaires, and logs in the category of self-reports.

Self-report measures have a number of advantages. First, they are relatively cost effective, particularly those completed by the respondent in an online format. Online measures can be completed at the convenience of the respondent, the data are already in electronic format, and most online survey software has functions that help track response rates and remind respondents to complete surveys. Self-report measures are also good for measuring cognitive constructs, such as perceptions, values, attitudes, and thought processes (Fowler, 2009). Although often not the primary target when measuring assessment practice, teachers' attitudes toward and values for CA may interest some researchers.

Logs have been found to provide a way to measure instructional activities that occur frequently (Camburn & Barnes, 2004). Logs, where teachers simply report activities or other easily defined behaviors, can be particularly relevant and useful for CA. For example, teachers could report the frequency with which they assess their students using different types of assessments. Typically, logs are relatively short and focused and are used more frequently than other self-report instruments such as questionnaires. Logs can provide fine-grained data on assessment practices but increase respondent burden when logs are required very frequently, such as daily or weekly.

Self-reports, like any measurement method, also have disadvantages. One disadvantage is that the data from self-reports may not lend itself to quantitative analysis. Care must be taken when designing and collecting self-reports so that they provide data of the appropriate type for analysis planned. The scale used in surveys and questionnaires also needs to be thought out carefully (Fowler, 2009). Many times, survey data fails to capture variance. For example, an item might ask teachers how important it is to provide students with feedback, and a large portion of the sample responds "important" or "very important" thus failing to capture variance in this trait. Scales used in self-reports also have the problem of multiple interpretations by respondents (Fowler, 2009). If teachers were asked to respond to an item, "How often do you have your students grade themselves using a rubric?" with a scale of "never," "sometimes," "often," or "very often," they can easily interpret these differently, where "very often" means daily to one teacher and weekly to another. A better way to measure frequency is through a log where teachers report the number of times they used an assessment practice during a specific period.

Perhaps the main disadvantage of self-report measures is the difficulty obtaining good evidence to support validity. There are many reasons why the data reported may not accurately reflect what actually happens in the classroom. Teachers may not remember accurately what happened or there may be social desirability issues that influence the teachers to respond in a way they think may please an audience such as researchers or the general public. For example, teachers may overreport the frequency with which they share rubrics with their students because they think that this is desirable.

Artifact-Based Measures

Artifact-based measures are those that use artifacts from the classroom, such as lesson plans and graded tests, as the basis for assessing teacher practice. Several artifact-based measures are available that focus on general classroom instruction (Borko & Stecher, 2005; Matsumura, Patthey-Chavez, Valdés, & Garnier, 2002). The category of artifact-based measures also includes portfolios, where teachers collect examples of their assessments. Portfolios are used in teacher assessment for a number of purposes up to and including high-stakes decision making (Lyons, 2010).

Artifacts have several advantages. First, it is difficult for social desirability to play in, a common criticism of self-reports. Although teachers typically self-select the artifacts that they submit, it is unlikely that teachers could over-represent the quality of their assessment practice in this selection process. Thus artifacts provide a measure of actual practice rather than just a self-report of practice. Another advantage of artifact-based measures is they are much less expensive to collect than observations. Typically all that is needed are clear instructions and self-addressed stamped envelopes. This lower cost means that artifacts can be collected from an entire research sample rather than just a subsample, which is common with observations. Finally, research has shown that artifact-based instruments are well correlated with observations and thus provide an efficient and reliable measure of actual classroom practice (e.g., Aschbacher, 1999; Clare, 2000; Clare, Valdés, Pascal, & Steinberg, 2001; Matsumura, Garnier, Slater, & Boston, 2008; Matsumura et al., 2002). As a measure of CA practice, artifacts and portfolios have an additional advantage over observations. Teachers can be instructed to provide artifacts of a variety of different assessment methods (e.g., homework assignments with grades, rubrics, and definitions of learning objectives) that might not occur or be visible during an observation session. In addition, the artifact or portfolio instructions can require teachers to provide additional information regarding the artifacts provided that could not be obtained during an observation.

Artifact-based measures, and portfolios in particular, have another advantage. Portfolios provide an opportunity for self-reflection (Danielson & Abrutyn, 1997; Wolf, 1989). Most other measurement methods and assessment methods do not provide this same opportunity. Self-reflection can result in improvements in the knowledge and skills being documented in the portfolio.

The primary disadvantage to artifact-based measures is that they do not provide a direct measure of CA practice. Most importantly, artifacts provide only limited information on teacher–student interactions. Artifacts can be collected that show teachers' written feedback to students, but CA often occurs via verbal interactions "in the moment," and artifacts do not provide a window into these interactions. Although the artifacts themselves might represent actual CAs or actual written classroom feedback, these artifacts must be rated to provide a measure of assessment practice and data for analysis.

Rating means that rubrics and training are required. Considerable time, effort, and monetary resources must be devoted to the training and scoring in order to provide reliable scores. Training artifacts may be needed. Multiple rounds of training may be needed. In addition to the training on the procedures used to score the artifacts, the raters will likely need to have considerable expertise in CA in order to apply the scoring procedure and/or scoring rubric. And some type of assessment of raters' accuracy and reliability may be needed before rating actual artifacts used in the research. In addition, some report of inter-rater reliability will likely need to be reported, and this means that at least a sample of artifacts will need to be rated twice.

Tests

The final method of measurement discussed here are tests. Tests, such as selected-response (SR) tests (i.e., multiple-choice, matching, and true/false) and constructed-response (CR) tests (i.e., short answer and essay), are useful primarily for measuring knowledge but also can be used to measure reasoning. For example, a researcher might be interested in measuring the knowledge and reasoning underlying CA practices. As previously argued, knowledge and reasons provide the foundations of assessment literacy and, therefore, are a necessary part of successful implementation of CA practice. CA includes a wide and varied array of practices. If the goal is to measure teachers' knowledge and reasoning across this broad array of practices, a test is the best option because it can provide an efficient way to address many different topics in a single instrument. But tests likely need a large number of items and substantial time on the part of the participants to complete. And test development is time consuming and expensive (see Chapter 14 of this volume).

As can be seen from the previous discussion, each method of measurement has advantages and disadvantages. What's most important is that the method needs to be matched to the construct of interest. If direct measures of classroom practice are needed, then observations likely will provide the best window; although artifact-based measures are also worth considering. If it is teachers' CA literacy that is of interest, than a test will provide the best data. If a research question focuses on teachers' perceptions, attitudes, or values, then a self-report would likely be the most efficient means of measurement.

Existing Measures of Classroom Assessment Practices

This section of the chapter provides brief overviews of existing measures of CA practice. The goal here is to scan the field of CA and inventory existing measures related specifically to CA practice. We hope to provide enough information so that researchers can identify measures of interest and then pursue further information on those measures. These measures pertain directly to CA. There are, of course, numerous measures of general classroom and instructional practices, but a review of those is beyond the scope of this chapter. The existing measures are discussed under the same categories used previously to discuss the advantages and disadvantages of various measurement methods. The end of this section includes a table that compares the instruments on type, purpose, and evidence regarding reliability and validity.

Observational Instruments

At the time of writing this chapter, no formal, validated observational instruments could be found that focused on CA practices, although Lyon, Miller, and Wylie (2011) used a running record of all activities and discourse that occurred during classroom lessons as part of a validation of their self-report measure discussed next.

Self-Reports

This section of the chapter provides an overview of self-report measures of CA practice. This is the most common form of existing measures, likely because of the advantages of this method that was previously described.

Assessment Practices Inventory

The *Assessment Practices Inventory* (API) is a 67-item self-report survey developed by Zhang and Burry-Stock (1994). The API covers a broad range of assessment practices from constructing tests, communicating assessment results, and using assessment results. For each item, teachers use two response scales. One scale is a frequency of use scale designed to measure assessment practices and ranges from 1 = *not at all used* to 5 = *used very often*. The second scale measures teachers' self-perceived assessment skills from 1 = *not at all skilled* to 5 = *very skilled*.

Content validity is supported by the instrument development process that used a table of specifications of major elements of CA based on theoretical framework developed from CA literature and the *Standards for Teacher Competence in Educational Assessment of Students* (American Federation of Teachers [AFT], National Council on Measurement in Education [NCME], & National Education Association [NEA], 1990). Evidence of reliability and validity of the API are provided in several research studies (Zhang, 1996; Zhang & Burry-Stock, 1995, 2003). The API has high reported internal consistency of 0.94 for assessment practices and 0.97 for self-perceived assessment skills (Zhang & Burry-Stock, 2003).

Teacher Report of Student Involvement

The Teacher Report of Student Involvement was developed by researchers for use in a large-scale randomized controlled trial (RCT) (Randel et al., 2011) to study the effectiveness of a widely used professional development program in CA called *Classroom Assessment for Student Learning* (CASL) (Stiggins et al., 2004). This self-report instrument measures the extent to which teachers involve their students in assessment and assessment-related activities over a 2-week period of instruction. The survey includes a list of assessment-related activities, drawn from the larger literature on student involvement (e.g., Sadler, 1989) that could occur in any classroom where students were involved in the learning and assessment process. To complete the survey, teachers respond to 14 items, reporting the number of days they spent on each of the assessment activities within the 2-week time frame.

Psychometric analyses on the scores for the Teacher Report of Student Involvement revealed surprisingly low correlations of scores among four separate waves of data collections (*r*s = 0.15, 0.16, 0.19, 0.56), suggesting that teacher assessment practice, or at least self-reports of teacher practice, may not be stable across time. Internal consistency among the survey items at the final administration wave, however, was very high (alpha = 0.95) (Randel et al., 2011). The Teacher Report of Student Involvement detected an effect size of 0.44 between the treatment and control group in the RCT, although this difference was not statistically significant (Randel et al., 2011).

Assessment Practices Survey

The assessment practices survey (APS) is an online, self-report questionnaire that asks teachers to reflect on their formative assessment practice across five key strategies (Lyon et al., 2011). Teachers are asked to report the frequency of practice (i.e., never, quarterly, monthly, weekly, or daily) across the following eight categories: (1) written feedback, (2) revisions, (3) developing questions, (4) selecting students during questioning, (5) criteria for success, (6) collaborative learning, (7) peer assessment, and (8) self-assessment.

Results from reviews by assessment experts (individuals who had written and presented extensively on assessment) of the definition of formative assessment that provided the basis for the development of the APS and the eight categories of the survey suggested that the definition and categories were adequate for assessing the frequency of teachers' practices of formative assessment. Results from cognitive interviews suggested that teachers were interpreting the items as intended but that the item format needed to be revised, which was subsequently done. Comparison between responses to the APS and daily practices reported in logs showed a weak positive correlation.

Online Formative Assessment Survey

The online formative assessment survey (OFAS) is an instrument that measures teachers' use of the technology-based formative assessment software Diagnostic Online Reading Assessment (DORA) (Karpinski, 2010). The OFAS asked teachers to report the frequency with which they engage in a variety of online formative assessment practices using the following scale: *never* (i.e., zero times a quarter/semester), *rarely* (i.e., one time a quarter/semester), *sometimes* (i.e., two to three times a quarter/semester), and *almost always* (i.e., four or more times a quarter/semester). Items address using DORA, accessing DORA subscale results and using them to inform instruction and provide feedback, communicating results, using grade-level equivalency results, and interpreting DORA results.

Interviews with individuals (teachers and software employees) familiar with DORA were used to create a preliminary survey. A 50-item survey and a 10-item survey were created after item analysis and Rasch scaling of the initial survey. Coefficient alpha for the 50-items was reported at 0.95 and at 0.81 for the 10-item survey. Neither the 50-item nor the 10-item survey, however, was statistically significant, positive predictors of student achievement (Karpinski, 2010).

Classroom Assessment and Grading Practices Survey

The CA and grading practices survey is a 34-item self-report survey of the factors teachers use in determining final semester grades (McMillan, 2001; McMillan, Myran, & Workman, 2002). The survey includes 19 items that cover different factors used to determine grades (e.g., student behavior, improvement, work habits and effort, and extra credit), 11 items that assess the different types of assessments used to determine grades (e.g., exams, oral presentation, and performance assessments), and 4 items that cover the cognitive level of the assessment used (e.g., recall, understanding, or reasoning). Teachers report on a 6-point scale from *not at all* to *completely*.

The survey was based on a previous questionnaire and research literature. Items were reviewed by teachers and pilot tested on a second group of teachers. Item analysis results were used to refine the test and inform item selection. Test–retest reliability after a 4-week interval showed an average of 46% exact agreement of item ratings across 23 teachers and 89% adjacent agreement (McMillan, 2001; McMillan et al., 2002). The survey has been used to describe elementary and secondary teachers' grading practices in math and language arts (McMillan, 2001; McMillan et al., 2002).

Artifact-Based Instruments

Teacher Assessment Work Sample

The Teacher Assessment Work Sample is an artifact-based measure of teachers' assessment practices in the classroom (Randel et al., 2011). The instrument was originally developed at the

National Center for Research on Evaluation, Standards, & Student Testing (CRESST) to measure general classroom practice in elementary and secondary language arts classrooms using language arts assignments (Matsumura et al., 2002). Recently, it was adapted by researchers at Mid-Continent Research for Education and Learning (McREL) to measure CA practice in mathematics using mathematics assessments. In addition, two dimensions that addressed feedback, a critical aspect of formative assessment, were added to the four dimensions of the original CRESST rubric.

To complete the work sample, teachers are asked to copy and submit three mathematics assessments that reflect their lesson objectives, along with four examples of graded student work (including teacher feedback) for each assessment. Of the four examples of student work, two should meet learning objectives set prior to instruction and two should not meet objectives. To measure quality of a variety of assessment options, the artifact should include a typical homework or seat work assessment, a typical in-class project or performance assessment, and a typical quiz or end-of-week assessment. At least one of the homework or in-class assessments should ask students to show their work and explain their answers. Instructions to the assessment work sample ask teachers to attach the activity's directions and indicate via checklist and short-answer responses the following seven criteria: (1) the assignment and its learning goals, (2) how the assignment fits with its unit, (3) how it addressed the range of student skills with the assignment, (4) how much time the students needed to do the assignment, (5) the type of help the students received, (6) how the assignment was assessed including scoring rubric, and (7) how the students performed on the assignment.

The work sample is scored on six rubric dimensions: (1) focus of goals on student learning, (2) clarity of grading criteria, (3) alignment of learning goals and assessment, (4) alignment of learning goals and grading criteria, (5) type of feedback, and (6) student involvement level of feedback. Teachers receive a score from 1 to 4 in each of the six dimensions based on all their submitted materials. Scores from the six areas are then combined, giving each teacher a single score for the work sample.

Researchers utilized the Teacher Assessment Work Sample in their RCT to assess the effectiveness of the CASL professional development program (Randel et al., 2011). For the purpose of the study, two school district personnel with expertise in assessment were trained in work sample scoring and provided independent ratings of the assessment work samples collected from teacher participants. Psychometric analyses showed that inter-rater reliabilities of the work sample by assessment type (i.e., homework, performance, or quiz) and by the six rubric dimensions were moderate to high, with correlations between the two scorers ranging from 0.66 to 0.83 (Randel et al., 2011). In addition, intercorrelations among the six rubric dimensions highlight the existence of three major aspects of formative assessment: (1) learning goals (dimensions 1 and 2), (2) assessment criteria (dimensions 3 and 4), and (3) feedback (dimensions 5 and 6). The results also support the notion that formative assessment is a complex process with key components that are not necessarily related within a single teacher. Lastly, the internal consistency between assessment types was moderate to high (alpha 0.75), indicating that the work sample functions similarly for different assessments.

Tests

Three tests of CA were found. These measures typically used multiple-choice or other SR items to assess teachers knowledge and reasoning in CA. Two tests are based on the *Standards for Teacher Competence in the Educational Assessment of Students* (AFT et al., 1990), whereas the other test was developed to cover common practices and principles in CA.

Teacher Competencies in Assessment

The W. C. Kellogg Foundation provided the National Council on Measurement in Education (NCME) with a grant to improve teacher competencies in educational assessment. Under this grant, an instrument was developed to measure teacher competency levels in assessment as specified in the *Standards for Teacher Competence in the Educational Assessment of Students* (AFT et al., 1990). Items were developed from a table of specifications that identified the knowledge, skills, and abilities represented in each competency area (Plake & Impara, 1997; Plake, Impara, & Fager, 1993). The initial set of items was pilot tested on a sample of 900 educators. In addition, measurement experts reviewed the items and made independent judgment about which standard it measured. These judgments showed a high degree of alignment between the items and the standards. The test was revised based on the pilot and expert review and field tested on 70 teachers. Internal consistency (KR-20) of the final 35-item test was reported at 0.54 (Plake et al., 1993). The overall average score was 66% correct, with teachers scoring highest in the area of administering assessments and lowest in the area of communicating assessment results.

Assessment Literacy Inventory

The Assessment Literacy Inventory (ALI) is a 35-item multiple-choice test with items embedded within five CA scenarios (Mertler & Campbell, 2005). Each scenario presents a brief CA situation followed by seven multiple-choice items. The ALI was developed to directly align to the *Standards for Teacher Competence in the Educational Assessment of Students* (AFT et al., 1990). All of the items within one scenario align with one of the seven American Federation of Teachers (AFT), NCME, and National Education Association (NEA) standards. The ALI was refined through pilot tests, item analyses, and item revision (Mertler & Campbell, 2005). Internal consistency (KR-20) was reported at 0.74. The ALI has been shown to be sensitive to the effectiveness of a 2-week workshop for improving the assessment literacy of inservice teachers (Mertler, 2009).

Test of Assessment Knowledge

The Test of Assessment Knowledge was developed by McREL researchers to sample the knowledge and reasoning skills represented in the key components of formative assessment identified by Stiggins and colleagues (2004) for the CASL professional development program. Specifically, the test samples the content covered in the CASL program, giving more weight to topics that are described in depth and that comprise a large domain of information in that program. Some key components, such as assessment purpose, focus more on conceptual knowledge. Other key components, such as assessments that yield accurate results, emphasize skill in developing CAs, rubrics, and other products to be used in the classroom. The test items cover generally accepted principles and practices of classroom and formative assessment and avoid terminology specific only to the CASL program. Seventy-eight items were initially developed. Item analysis of field test data resulted in the selection of a final 60 multiple-choice, true or false items, and matching items.

In the context of their RCT to study the effectiveness of CASL, McREL researchers found the internal consistency of the Test of Assessment Knowledge to be high (alpha = 0.89). The reliability of the test scores across three waves of administration given over a 2-year time period were relatively low (rs = 0.28, 0.30, 0.37), suggesting that, like teacher practice, teacher knowledge of the key principles and vocabulary of CA may not be stable over time. Furthermore, the correlations between scores on the Test of Assessment Knowledge and two tests of assessment practice (Assessment Work Sample and Teacher Report of Student Involvement) were also low (0.28 and –0.17 respectively), indicating that assessment knowledge may not translate into assessment practice. These results attest to the complexity of formative assessment as a whole and the need to measure various aspects of formative assessment separately. The Test of Assessment Knowledge detected an effect size of 0.42 between the treatment and control group in the RCT of CASL.

Table 9.1 summarizes existing measures of CA knowledge and practices.

Instrument	*Type*	*Purpose*	*Supporting Evidence*
Assessment Practices Inventory (API) (Zhang & Burry-Stock, 1994)	Self-report	Assessment practice and self-perceived assessment skills	Content Internal consistency
Teacher Report of Student Involvement (Randel et al., 2011)	Self-report	Extent of student involvement in assessment related activity	Internal consistency Sensitivity

Instrument	*Type*	*Purpose*	*Supporting Evidence*
Assessment practices survey (APS) (Lyon, Miller, & Wylie, 2011)	Self-report	Frequency of assessment practices	Content
Online formative assessment survey (OFAS) (Karpinski, 2010)	Self-report	Frequency of online formative assessment practices	Internal consistency
Classroom assessment and grading practices survey (McMillan, 2001; McMillan, Myran, & Workman, 2002)	Self-report	Factors used to determine semester grades	Content Test-retest reliability
Teacher Assessment Work Sample (Randel et al., 2011)	Artifact	Classroom assessment practice in mathematics	Test-criterion relationship Inter-rater reliability Internal consistency
Teacher Competencies in Assessment (Plake & Impara, 1997; Plake, Impara, & Fager, 1993)	Test	Knowledge, skills, and abilities in competency area of American Federation of Teachers (AFT), National Council on Measurement in Education (NCME), and National Education Association (NEA) (1990) standards	Alignment with AFT, NCME, and NEA (1990) standards Internal consistency
Assessment Literacy Inventory (ALI) (Mertler & Campbell, 2005)	Test	Knowledge, skills, and abilities in competency area of AFT, NCME, NEA (1990) standards	Alignment with AFT, NCME, NEA (1990) standards Internal consistency Sensitivity
Test of Assessment Knowledge (Randel et al., 2011)	Test	Knowledge and reasoning skills in formative assessment	Internal consistency Sensitivity

Table 9.1 Existing Measures of Classroom Assessment Knowledge and Practice

Developing Measures of Classroom Assessment Practice

The instruments discussed in the previous sections provide a wide variety of measures of CA practices. Measurement in this area, however, is still a relatively new endeavor, and it will be important to continue to develop sound instruments for accurately and reliably measuring teacher practice in CA.

The importance of developing instruments to measure CA practice is highlighted by a large body of research suggesting that there is a critical relationship between teacher assessment practice and student learning (Black & Wiliam, 1998). Sound measurement of classroom practice will contribute to a greater understanding of how the different elements of CA practice are linked to ultimate student outcomes of learning and academic achievement. Sound measurement of classroom practice also can help identify strengths and weaknesses of teacher practices and guide professional development decisions to improve both teaching and learning.

Given the complexity of CA practice, there is no simple way to measure it and no single instrument that will objectively and completely identify quality assessment practice. Measuring assessment practice requires the use of multiple well-constructed measures. No one assessment will be perfect for capturing quality in CA; however, when utilizing multiple measures, the weakness of one measure will be supported by the strength in another. By using multiple measures, we can explore several different characteristics of CA practice—for example, quality of learning objectives, feedback, grading, and reporting systems. When we put the measures together, it will help us determine what matters most for improving student learning. In addition, multiple measures can help us measure a single piece of information in multiple ways—for example, feedback in CA can be measured with artifact-based measures or with self-reports. And data from multiple measures can be used for cross-validation.

Instrument Development

Ideally, instrument development should rely on a team of individuals each with unique expertise relevant to the development process including researchers, technical experts, master teachers, and content experts. The process should be iterative to include several rounds of development, testing, and refinement. The development should be guided by a firm knowledge of the literature on CA, including research-based depictions of high quality CA practice as well as any preexisting measures of the target construct. In addition, the advantages and disadvantages of various instrument formats (i.e., self-reports, observations, tests, and artifact-based measures) should be considered in relation to the specific research and evaluation questions.

Several specifications should inform the development process, including the content and processes to be assessed, the format of the instrument items, and the number and types of items to be included (Johnson, Penny, & Gordon, 2009). The specification of the instrument's content and processes serves to operationalize the construct of interest and helps to ensure congruence between the intended and actual inferences drawn from the measurement data (Millman & Greene, 1993). It is important to precisely define what you want to measure and how scores will be used. In turn, the assessment items should elicit the behavior reflected in your definition. In any assessment situation, the instrument should maximize financial and human investment while minimizing negative consequences for the target population.

Pilot Testing

No matter how many times researchers and their advisors review assessment items, and no matter how familiar they are with the population of teachers whose practice the instrument is designed to measure, instruments are generally not ready to be used in full-scale research or evaluation projects until they have been tested on a small sample of participants. Ideally, the development process will allow enough time to include both pilot testing and field testing phases. Pilot testing is a small-scale tryout of the instrument that generally occurs when the measure is initially being developed. The purpose of the pilot test is to determine the properties of the test in order to direct the revision process, the removal of weak items, and/or the development of additional items.

Pilot testing allows for examination of the psychometric properties of the instrument (Millman & Greene, 1993). Important properties to consider at the item or task level include the difficulty and discrimination, the differential item functioning, and the inter-rater reliability. At the instrument level, it is important to examine score reliability and various types of validity evidence (Johnson et al., 2009).

Field Testing

Field testing is similar to pilot testing, but it generally occurs on a larger scale at the final stage of development to ensure that the instrument is ready to administer in the context of a true intervention or evaluation. The purpose of a field test is to check the adequacy of testing procedures, including test administration, test responding, test scoring, and test reporting. A field test is generally more extensive than a pilot test and occurs on a more diverse population to ensure that it is appropriate for a wide range of participants. Specifically, the field test would reveal if the instrument is valid for measuring CA practice in both high and low performing schools, of varying sizes, in various locales, and serving children of various educational backgrounds and levels of socioeconomic status.

Technical Reporting

The iterative development process should include documentation to support evidence of score validity and reliability, as well as the inclusion/exclusion of particular items. An informative technical report contains sections describing the content or processes the instrument was designed to measure as well as those it was not meant to measure. The technical report should contain a detailed description of the pilot and field test sample and should offer recommendations as to generalizability of the findings to relevant populations. In reporting, both item-level and test-level psychometrics should be included. Item-level analyses provide statistical information about the functioning of a particular item or task and include statistics such as item mean, standard deviation, difficulty, and discrimination. Test-level statistics provide statistical information about the functioning of the test as a whole, including reliability and validity. Whether used in a research study or to evaluate teacher practice or school programming, detailed reporting will guide investigators in selecting instruments matched to their particular questions and help them draw accurate and informative inferences about CA practice from the data provided.

Advantages and Disadvantages of Self-Developed Versus Existing Instruments

Both self-developed and existing measures have advantages and disadvantages. For self-development measures, the primary advantage is that the measure can be developed to focus a specific aspect of CA per the needs of the research, the research questions, or the intervention being study. Self-developed measures have two main disadvantages. The first is the time and cost needed to develop the measure, which can take several months at least. Second, self-developed measures will have little or no validity evidence supporting their use. This evidence will have to be collected as part of the development and use of the measure. The final disadvantage of self-developed measures is that results from these measures cannot be compared directly to results from existing measures. Existing measures are ready for use and often have at least some reliability and validity evidence, but existing measures may not be suited to the research or research questions of every study.

Future Research in the Measurement of Classroom Assessment Practice

The measurement of CA practice has two noticeable areas where more research is needed. First, few direct measures of CA practice are available. There are a number of self-report instruments available that indirectly measure assessment practice, such as teachers' perceived CA competence. The Teacher Assessment Work Sample provides a proxy measure of assessment practice. But no instruments are currently available that directly measure the assessment practice of teachers in the classroom. A direct measure of CA practice would likely be some type of observation. Although there are observational measures of classroom instruction, these measures do not focus on CA practice. An observational measure would add focus on the practices that are critical to CA and formative assessment in particular, such as feedback and teacher–student interactions. Measuring these elements of CA is critical to better understanding how assessment is practiced in the classroom, and an observational measure is likely the best approach.

The second area where research is needed in measurement of CA practice concerns validity (see Chapter 6 of this volume for an extended discussion of validity). While validity has been examined to some extent as previously summarized, and validity evidence has been provided for some of the existing measures of CA practice, many of the measures have little or no validity evidence. Two types of validity evidence could be particularly useful to researchers considering a measure of CA practice. First, predictive validity, particularly in terms of how CA practices correlate with student achievement, would help researchers focus on and better understand the aspects of CA that are related to student achievement.

Second, validity evidence regarding the sensitivity of measures of assessment practice to changes in classroom practice also would be a helpful contribution to the body of knowledge.

Sensitivity to change is important because it allows researchers to determine if professional development programs in CA are impacting teachers' practice. Improvements in teacher practice can, in turn, promote student achievement. Measures that are sensitive to change are critical to studies that examine the effectiveness of professional development programs and especially important to interpreting findings from effectiveness studies, particularly null effects. Without sensitive measures, it can be difficult to make this judgment and understand which programs are truly effective in improving teacher assessment practice.

CONCLUSION

CA practice includes many elements, from defining learning objectives to assigning final grades, and many different methods for measuring CA practice can be used. Each method fits well with some aspects of CA practice and less well with others. Each method has reasons for considering its use and reasons for caution given the data it provides or cannot provide. A number of existing measures are available and have been used in research. The key to using one of these existing measures is ensuring it aligns with the aspects of CA practice under investigation and the hypotheses or goals of the research.

The field of research on CA can use more and better measures of practice. More instruments are needed to measure all the different aspects of CA that was previously described. The measures existing at the time of writing this chapter tend to provide broad indicators of the different aspects, but more measures are needed that provide detailed information about each aspect. For example, enhanced or new measures are needed that provide information about how well students understand the criteria they use to assess themselves or that are used by their teachers. Also, new or better measures of teacher knowledge of CA strategies and principles are needed, with separate, reliable subscales for each of the elements that provide teachers' scores on each element.

CA practice plays a key role in classroom instruction and learning. Building an understanding of CA will help build an understanding of ways to improve it and student achievement. More and better measurement of CA practice is part and parcel to this entire effort.

REFERENCES

Alonzo, A. (2005). *Adopting notebooks as a formative assessment tool: Challenges and contributing factors.* Presentation at the annual meeting of the American Educational Research Association, Montreal, Canada.

American Federation of Teachers, National Council on Measurement in Education, & National Education Association. (1990). *Standards for teacher competence in educational assessment of students.* Washington, DC: National Council on Measurement in Education.

Arter, J., & McTighe, J. (2001). *Scoring rubrics in the classroom: Using performance criteria for assessing and improving student performance.* Thousand Oaks, CA: Corwin Press.

Aschbacher, P. R. (1999). *Developing indicators of classroom practice to monitor and support school reform* (CSE Technical Report 315). Los Angeles: University of California, National Center for Research on Evaluation, Standards, & Student Testing.

Ayala, C. C., Shavelson, R. J., Ruiz-Primo, M. A., Brandon, P., Yin, Y., Furtak, E. M. et al. (2008). From formal embedded assessments to reflective lessons: The development of formative assessment suites. *Applied Measurement in Education, 21*(4), 315–334.

Bailey, A. L., & Heritage, M. (2008). *Formative assessment for literacy grades K–6: Building reading and academic language skills across the curriculum.* Thousand Oaks, CA: Corwin Press.

Ball, D. L., & Rowan, B. (2004). Introduction: Measuring instruction. *Elementary School Journal, 105*(1), 3–10.

Bangert-Drowns, R. L., Kulik, C.-L. C., Kulik, J. A., & Morgan, M. (1991). The instructional effect of feedback in test-like events. *Review of Educational Research, 61*(2), 213–238.

Baxter, J. A., & Lederman, N. G. (2002). Assessment and measurement of pedagogical content knowledge. In J. Gess-Newsome & N. G. Lederman (Eds.), *Examining pedagogical content knowledge: The construct and its implications for science.* London: Kluwer Academic Publishers.

Bell, B., & Cowie, B. (2000). *Formative assessment and science education.* London: Kluwer Academic Publishers.

Black, P., Harrison, C., Lee, C., Marshall, B., & Wiliam, D. (2004). Working inside the black box: Assessment for learning in the classroom. *Phi Delta Kappan, 86*(1), 8–21.

Black, P., & Wiliam, D. (1998). Inside the black box: Raising standards through classroom assessment. *Phi Delta Kappan, 80*(2), 139–144.

Borko, H., & Stecher, B. M. (2005). *Using classroom artifacts to measure instructional practices in middle school mathematics: A two-state field test* (CSE Technical Report 662). Los Angeles: University of California, National Center for Research on Evaluation, Standards, & Student Testing.

Brookhart, S. (2008). *How to give effective feedback to your students.* Alexandria, VA: Association for Supervision and Curriculum Development.

Callingham, R. (2008). Dialogue and feedback: Assessment in the primary mathematics classroom. *Australian Primary Mathematics Classroom, 13*(3), 18–21.

Camburn, E., & Barnes, C. A. (2004). Assessing the validity of a language arts instruction log through triangulation. *Elementary School Journal, 105,* 49–73.

Cauley, K. M., Pannozzo, G., Abrams, L., McMillan, J., & Camou-Linkroum, S. (2006). *The relationship between classroom assessment practices and student motivation and engagement.* Richmond: Virginia Commonwealth University.

Center for Comprehensive School Reform and Improvement. (2006). *Using classroom assessment to improve teaching.* Washington, DC: Author.

Clare, L. (2000). *Using teachers' assignments as an indicator of classroom practice* (CSE Technical Report 532). Los Angeles: University of California, National Center for Research on Evaluation, Standards, & Student Testing.

Clare, L., Valdés, R., Pascal, J., & Steinberg, J. R. (2001). *Teachers' assignments as indicators of instructional quality in elementary schools* (CSE Technical Report 545). Los Angeles: University of California, National Center for Research on Evaluation, Standards, & Student Testing.

Cohen, L., Manion, L., & Morrison, K. (2007). *Research methods in education.* New York: Routledge.

Cowie, B. (2005). Student commentary on classroom assessment in science: A sociocultural interpretation. *International Journal of Science Education, 27*(2), 199–214.

Crooks, T. J. (1988). The impact of classroom evaluation practices on students. *Review of Educational Research, 58*(4), 438–481.

Danielson, C., & Abrutyn, L. (1997). *An introduction to using portfolios in the classroom.* Alexandria, VA: Association for Supervision and Curriculum Development.

Epstein, M. L., Lazarus, A. D., Calvano, T. B., Matthews, K. A., Hendel, R. A., Epstein, B. B., et al. (2002). Immediate feedback assessment technique promotes learning and corrects inaccurate first responses. *The Psychological Record, 52,* 187–201.

Falk, A. (2012). Teachers learning from professional development in elementary science: Reciprocal relations between formative assessment and pedagogical content knowledge. *Science Education, 96*(2), 265–290.

Fontana, D., & Fernandes, M. (1994). Improvements in mathematics performance as a consequence of self-assessment in Portuguese primary school pupils. *British Journal of Educational Psychology, 64*(3), 407–417.

Fowler, F. J. (2009). *Survey research methods.* Thousand Oaks, CA: Sage.

Frederiksen, J. R., & White, B. J. (1997). *Reflective assessment of students' research within an inquiry-based middle school science curriculum.* Paper presented at the annual meeting of the American Educational Research Association, Chicago.

Gall, M. D., Gall, J. P., & Borg, W. R. (2006). *Educational research: An introduction* (8th ed.). Boston: Allyn & Bacon.

Green, K. E., & Stager, S. F. (1986). Measuring attitudes of teachers toward testing. *Measurement and Evaluation in Counseling and Development, 19*(3), 141–150.

Green, K. E., & Stager, S. F. (1987). Differences in teacher test and item use with subject, grade level taught, and measurement coursework. *Teacher Education and Practice, 4,* 55–61.

Guskey, T. R., & Bailey, J. M. (2001). *Developing grading and reporting systems for student learning.* Thousand Oaks, CA: Corwin Press.

Hattie, J., & Timperley, H. (2007). The power of feedback. *Review of Educational Research, 77*(1), 81–112.

Johnson, J. M. (2002). In-depth interviewing. In J. F. Gubrium & J. A. Holstein (Eds.), *Handbook of interview research: Context and methods.* Thousand Oaks, CA: Sage.

Johnson, R. L., Penny, J. A., & Gordon, B. (2009). *Assessing performance: Designing scoring, and validating performance tasks.* New York: Guilford Press.

Karpinski, A. C. (2010). *The relationship between online formative assessment scores and state test scores: Measure development and multilevel growth modeling.* Unpublished doctoral dissertation, The Ohio State University, Columbus.

Klenowski, V. (1995). Student self-evaluation process in student-centered teaching and learning contexts of Australia and England. *Assessment in Education, 2,* 145–163.

Kluger, A. N., & DeNisi, A. (1998). Feedback interventions: Toward the understanding of a double-edged sword. *American Psychological Society, 7*(3), 67–72.

Kulhavy, R. W. (1977). Feedback in written instruction. *Review of Educational Research Association, 47*(2), 211–232.

Kulik, J. A., & Kulik, C.-L. C. (1988). Timing of feedback and verbal learning. *Review of Educational Research, 58*(1), 79–97.

Lyon, C., Miller, S., & Wylie, E. C. (2011, April). *A validity argument for the Assessment Practices Survey: A measure of teachers' enactment of formative assessment.* Paper presented at the 2011 annual meeting of the American Educational Research Association, New Orleans, LA.

Lyons, N. (2010). Approaches to portfolio assessment of complex evidence of reflection and reflective practice. In N. Lyons (Ed.), *Handbook of reflection and reflective inquiry: Mapping a way of knowing for professional reflective inquiry.* New York: Springer.

Marzano, R. J. (2009). *Designing & teaching learning goals & objectives.* Bloomington, IN: Marzano Research Laboratory.

Matsumura, L. C., Garnier, H. E., Slater, S. C., & Boston, M. D. (2008). Toward measuring instructional interactions "at scale." *Educational Assessment, 13,* 267–300.

Matsumura, L. C., Patthey-Chavez, G. G., Valdes, R., & Garnier, H. E. (2002). Teacher feedback, writing assignment quality, and third-grade students' revision in lower- and higher-achieving urban schools. *Elementary School Journal, 103*(1), 3–25.

McCurdy, B. L., & Shapiro, E. S. (1992). A comparison of teacher monitoring, peer monitoring, and self-monitoring with curriculum-based measurement in reading among students with learning disabilities. *Journal of Special Education, 26*(2), 162–180.

McDonald, B., & Boud, D. (2003). The effects of self assessment training on performance in external examinations. *Assessment in Education, 10*(2), 210–220.

McMillan, J. H. (2001). Secondary teachers' classroom assessment and grading practices. *Educational Measurement: Issues and Practice, 20*(1), 20–32.

McMillan, J. H., Myran, S., & Workman, D. (2002). Elementary teachers' classroom assessment and grading practices. *Journal of Education Research, 95*(4), 203–213.

Mertler, C. A. (2009). Teachers' assessment knowledge and their perceptions of the impact of classroom assessment professional development. *Improving Schools, 12,* 101–113.

Mertler, C. A., & Campbell, C. (2005, April). *Measuring teachers' knowledge & application of classroom assessment concepts: Development of the Assessment Literacy Inventory.* Paper presented at the annual meeting of the American Educational Research Association, Montréal, Quebec, Canada.

Millman, J. & Greene, J. (1993). The specification and development of tests of achievement and ability. In R. Lynn (Ed.), *Educational measurement* (3rd ed., pp. 335–366). Washington, DC: American Council on Education.

Mory, E. H. (2004). Feedback research revisited. In D. H. Jonassen (Ed.), *Handbook of research on educational communications and technology* (pp. 745–783). Mahwah, NJ: Lawrence Erlbaum.

Paulhus, D. L. (1991). Measurement and control of response biases: Measures of personality and social psychological attitudes. In J. P. Robinson, P. R. Shaver, & L. S. Wrightsman (Eds.), *Measures of personality and social psychological attitudes, Measures of social psychological attitudes* (Vol. 1, pp. 17–59). San Diego, CA: Academic Press.

Plake, B. S., & Impara, J. C. (1997). Teacher assessment literacy: What do teachers know about assessment? In G. D. Phye (Ed.), *Handbook of classroom assessment: Learning, adjustment, and achievement* (pp. 55–68). San Diego, CA: Academic Press.

Plake, B. S., Impara, J. C., & Fager, J. J. (1993). Assessment competencies of teachers: A national survey. *Educational Measurement: Issues and Practice, 12*(4), 10–12, 39.

Popham, W. J. (2009). Assessment literacy for teachers: Faddish or fundamental? *Theory into Practice, 48*(1), 4–11.

Randel, B., Beesley, A. D., Apthorp, H., Clark, T. F., Wang, X., Cicchinelli, L. F. et al. (2011). *Classroom assessment for student learning: The impact on elementary school mathematics in the central region* (NCEE 2011-4005). Washington, DC: National Center for Education Evaluation and Regional Assistance, Institute of Education Sciences, U.S. Department of Education.

Reeves, D. (2008). Effective grading practices. *Educational Leadership, 65*(5), 85–87.

Sadler, D. R. (1989). Formative assessment and the design of instructional systems. *Instructional Science, 18*(2), 119–144.

Shaughnessy, J., Zechmeister, E., & Zechmeister, J. (2005). *Research methods in psychology.* New York: McGraw-Hill.

Shepard, L. A. (2000). *The role of classroom assessment in teaching and learning* (CSE Technical Report). Los Angeles: National Center for Research and Evaluation, Standards, & Student Testing.

Shulman, L. S. (1987). Knowledge and teaching: Foundations of the new reform. *Harvard Educational Review, 57*(1), 1–23.

Shute, V. J. (2008). Focus on formative feedback. *Review of Educational Research, 78*(1), 153–189.

Stiggins, R. J. (1998). *Classroom assessment for student success. Student assessment series.* Annapolis Junction, MD: NEA Professional Library.

Stiggins, R. J., (2002) Assessment crisis! The absence of assessment FOR learning. *Phi Delta Kappan, 83*(10), 758–765.

Stiggins, R. J. (2004). New assessment beliefs for a new school mission. *Phi Delta Kappan, 86*(1), 22–27.

Stiggins, R. J., Arter, J. A., Chappuis, J., & Chappuis, S. (2004). *Classroom assessment for student learning: Doing it right—using it well.* Portland, OR: Assessment Training Institute.

Stiggins, R. J., & Chappuis, J. (2006). What a difference a word makes: Assessment for learning rather than assessment of learning helps students succeed. *Journal of Staff Development, 27*(1), 10–14.

Stiggins, R. J., & Chappuis, J. (2008). Enhancing student learning. *District Administration, 44*(1), 42–44.

Stiggins, R. J., Frisbie, D. A., & Griswold, P. A. (1989). Inside high school grading practices: Building a research agenda. *Educational Measurement: Issues and Practices, 8*(2), 5–14.

Tierney, W. G., & Dilley, P. (2002). Interviewing in education. In J. F. Gubrium & J. A. Holstein (Eds.), *Handbook of interview research: Context and methods.* Thousand Oaks, CA: Sage.

Tunstall, P., & Gipps, C. (1996). Teacher feedback to young children in formative assessment: A typology. *British Educational Research Journal, 22*(4), 389–404.

Valencia, S. W. (2008). Understanding assessment: Putting together the puzzle. *Beyond the Book.* Retrieved from www.beyond-thebook.com/strategies/strategies_100307.html

Van Driel, J., Verloop, N., & de Vos, W. (1998). Developing science teachers' pedagogical content knowledge. *Journal of Research in Science Teaching, 35*(6), 673–695.

Warren, C. A. B. (2002). Qualitative interviewing. In J. F. Gubrium & J. A. Holstein (Eds.), *Handbook of interview research: Context and methods.* Thousand Oaks, CA: Sage.

Wiley, C. R. H. (2008). Traditional teacher tests. In T. L. Good (Ed.), *21st century education: A reference handbook* (Vol. 1, pp. 431–442). Thousand Oaks, CA: Sage

Wolf, D. (1989). Portfolio assessment: Sampling student work. *Educational Leadership, 46,* 35–39.

Zhang, Z. (1996). *Teacher assessment competency: A Rasch model analysis.* Paper presented at the 1996 annual meeting of the American Educational Research Association, New York.

Zhang, Z., & Burry-Stock, J. A. (1994). *Assessment Practices Inventory.* Tuscaloosa: The University of Alabama.

Zhang, Z., & Burry-Stock, J. A. (1995). *A multivariate analysis of teachers' perceived assessment competency as a function of measurement training and years of teaching.* Paper presented at the 1995 annual meeting of the Mid-South Education Research Association, Biloxi, MS.

Zhang, Z., & Burry-Stock, J. A. (2003). Classroom assessment practices and teachers' self-perceived assessment skills. *Applied Measurement in Education, 16*(4), 323–342.

SECTION 3

FORMATIVE ASSESSMENT

DYLAN WILIAM

Associate Editor

10

Formative and Summative Aspects of Assessment: Theoretical and Research Foundations in the Context of Pedagogy

Paul Black

The past 20 years have seen an accelerating growth in studies of formative assessment (Black, Harrison, Lee, Marshall, & Wiliam, 2003; Black & Wiliam, 1998, 2009). However, this has not been matched by a corresponding development in summative assessment. The net effect has been that the changes have not improved the state of discord between these two functions of assessment; however, they may have highlighted more clearly the awareness of this discord and of its harmful effects on teaching and learning. This chapter analyzes the nature of this discord, the conditions necessary for resolving it, and the importance of doing so by enhancing the quality of teachers' summative assessments.

The first section considers the purposes of assessment within the broader framework of a theory of pedagogy, setting out a simple model of the design and implementation of a program for teaching and learning. The next two sections then discuss in turn formative assessment in the light of that model and the use of the model to examine the relationship, in principle and in practice, between the formative and the summative purposes of assessment. This analysis is then taken up in a section that contrasts the importance of enhancing the quality of teachers' summative assessment with the problems encountered in systemic initiatives that aimed to achieve improved summative assessment. Following, there is a more detailed discussion of the problems of enhancing the quality of teachers' summative assessments. A concluding section presents some reflections on the outcome of the argument.

Assessment in a Model of Pedagogy

Studies of teaching and learning in schools use the terms *pedagogy* and *instruction,* but often these terms are not precisely defined. Pedagogy is often used as an inclusive term to cover all aspects of teaching and learning. Such authors focus on the exercise of power through curriculum and teaching. Examples would be the study by Paolo Freire (1992) and similar works that add such adjectives as *critical, conflict, liberatory,* and *gender,* all of which highlight the political function of pedagogy. This view was expressed very clearly by Alexander (2008b), who stated the following:

> Pedagogy is the act of teaching together with its attendant discourse of educational theories, values, evidence and justifications. It is what one needs to know, and the skills one needs to command, in order to make and justify the many different kinds of decision of which teaching is constituted. Curriculum is just one of its domains, albeit a central one. (p. 47)

In these approaches, the term *instruction* represents one component of the broader realm of pedagogy. Examples are Shulman (1999) and Hallam and Ireson (1999). By contrast, Bruner (1966) used a broad definition of instruction in which it is seen as a guide to pedagogy, the latter being a collection of maxims. These contrasting definitions do not seem to reflect any fundamental difference between those who use these terms in these different ways. What is notable in most of this literature is that assessment receives scant attention. Alexander (2008b), for example, listed the core acts of teaching as "task, activity, interaction, and assessment" (p. 49) but gave the last of these very little attention.

In order to focus on assessment in the context of classroom teaching and learning, I attempt here to consider ways to model pedagogy and instruction in a way that includes assessment and then to show how the literature contributes to this approach, even although the studies quoted pay little attention to assessment as such. The need to consider formative assessment in the broader perspective of pedagogy was argued by Perrenoud (1998). Commenting on the Black and Wiliam (1998) review of formative assessment, he posited as follows:

> This [feedback] no longer seems to me, however, to be the central issue. It would seem more important to concentrate on the theoretical models of learning and its regulation and their implementation. These constitute the real systems of thought and action, in which feedback is only one element. (p. 86)

The following model, from Black (2009) but similar to models set out by Hallam and Ireson (1999) and Wiske (1999), is an attempt to respond to this challenge. It considers any piece of instruction as comprising five components:

1. *Clear aims.* Here choice or compromise between different aims is often involved.
2. *Planning activities.* Any activity should have the potential to elicit responses that help clarify the student's understanding. A *closed* question with a right answer cannot do this. Other relevant features are the task's level of cognitive demand, its relation to previous learning experiences, and its potential to generate interest and engagement.
3. *Interaction.* The way in which a plan is implemented in the classroom is crucial. If pupils are engaged, then the teacher can elicit responses and work with these to help advance students' learning. This may be described as *interactive regulation,* a phrase that stresses the need to build on the students' contributions. Such formative interaction is a necessary condition for successful learning.
4. *Review of the learning.* At the end of any learning episode, there should be review, to check before moving on. It is here that tests, perhaps with both formative and summative use of their outcomes, can play a useful part.
5. *Summing up.* This is a more formal version of the *Review:* Here the results may be used to make decisions about a student's future work or career, to report progress to other teachers, school managements and parents, and to report overall achievements more widely to satisfy the need for accountability.

It is around these last two steps, and particularly Step 5, that tensions arise between the formative and summative functions, both about the instruments and methods used and about the relative roles of teachers, schools, and state agencies in the generation and analysis of assessment evidence. While the five components can represent successive stages in the planning and implementation of any piece of teaching, the model, for which the term *instruction* will be used next, does not deal with the complex interaction of cultural and political factors that bear on pedagogy. In addition, while its simplicity lies in its representation of a time sequence of decisions, it does not follow that links between these steps are implemented in only one direction: There have to be cyclic interactions between the five.

The Formative Purpose in Assessment

The first step specifies the learning aims that subsequent steps must seek to achieve: This can be a practical issue. Feedback in a classroom that is designed to promote, say, the understanding of a particular concept, will not be the same as feedback that is designed to develop particular reasoning skill, using the conceptual problems merely as a vehicle for such development.

Step 2 is more closely involved in formative assessment. Given that the learning purpose calls for dialogic interaction—of teachers with students and of students with one another—a classroom task ought to be designed so that it engages the students' attention and challenges them to reflect on, express, and exchange their ideas about the task. These exchanges will serve the purposes underlying the teaching plan if the planned activity has the potential to explore aspects of the students' learning, which are central to the learning aims.

It is in the third step that the learning plan is implemented. Here, activity is designed to assess, in that it leads to the generation of evidence about learning, and to be formative, in that there are opportunities for using that evidence to develop a learning dialogue. The key idea here is *dialogue*: Alexander (2008a) emphasized the importance of the learners' engagement in dialogue:

> Children, we now know, need to talk, and to experience a rich diet of spoken language, in order to think and to learn. Reading, writing and number may be acknowledged curriculum "basics," but talk is arguably the true foundation of learning. (p. 9)

This point is developed further in Wood's (1998) reference to Vygotsky:

> Vygotsky, as we have already seen, argues that such external and social activities are gradually internalized by the child as he comes to regulate his own internal activity. Such encounters are the source of experiences which eventually create the "inner dialogues" that form the process of mental self-regulation. Viewed in this way, learning is taking place on at least two levels: the child is learning about the task, developing "local expertise"; and he is also learning how to structure his own learning and reasoning. (p. 98)

This link between dialogue and structuring of one's own learning and reasoning draws attention to the fact that self-assessment is not only secured by special self-assessment exercises but is also stimulated insofar as each student is actively involved in the learning dialogue. This is promoted both in whole class teaching and when pupils work together in peer-assessment activities.

The plan of activities (Step 2) may have to be changed as the work in Step 3 reveals unforeseen opportunities or problems. This interaction between these two steps has led some to describe Step 2 as preparatory formative assessment and Step 3 as interactive formative assessment (Cowie & Bell, 1999). Here, I shall use the term *formative* only for the third and fourth steps.

The growth of formative practices has met many difficulties and distortions. Teachers may use open questions but then judge the responses, as correct or not, and move on rather than take up and explore these responses to develop a dialogue. This may happen because the responses of learners are often unpredictable, so facing the teacher with the challenge of finding ways to make use of a contribution that may be at best divergent and at worst unintelligible (Black & Wiliam, 2009): The easy way out is to just give the right answer. Further problems are presented by the need to give students time to think about and discuss between themselves in order to develop their ideas and by the risk that the student contributions may lead the dialogue in unforeseen directions so that teachers are afraid that they are closing control. Thus the teacher has to steer any discussion, encouraging diverse involvements while working toward the aims of the lesson.

Another obstacle is the interpretation of formative assessment as a practice of frequent testing, often linked to emphasis on target setting, aiming to keep students on track, and have a frequently updated measure of their progress. Emphasis on specifying targets may not help if students do not understand what it might be like to achieve them. When the meaning of the target and an understanding of what it would be like to achieve it are clear to the learner, a key stage in the learning has already been accomplished. Here the overlap with the summative purpose is evident, which leads to the need to consider Step 4.

To serve a formative purpose, writing, whether in seat work or homework, should lead to feedback giving the student advice about the strength and weaknesses of the work and about how to improve (see also Chapter 28 in this volume). This is only effective if such feedback is not accompanied with an overall judgment in terms of a mark or grade (Butler, 1988; Dweck, 2000). Where such judgment is avoided, the purpose of the interaction is clearly formative. The considerations in Steps 1, 2 and 3 still apply—that is, the writing task must generate evidence about learning and serve a formative purpose by providing opportunities for using that evidence to develop a learning dialogue. However, teachers might keep a record of the comments offered and of the responses of the student to those comments. Such a record, built up throughout a learning episode, might be used by the teacher to lead to a summative judgment of the progress made—one that can be shared with the student. This is clearly Step 4, and the evidence might contribute to Step 5. The formative purpose should have priority in the formulation of any one writing task, but the assembly of such tasks over the whole learning period could serve the review purpose.

A different example is the test, albeit informal, set at the end of a learning episode to provide an overall review of the learning. The mark or grade awarded for this would serve the summative purpose, and this use might be given first priority in the formulation of the test and its associated marking. However, time could be devoted at the end of a learning episode to provide opportunity for discussion by the students of their results, perhaps to engage them in the marking so that they can be helped to reflect on their work, to see where extra work might be needed and to develop their understanding of the criteria that reflect the purposes of the learning (see pp. 53–57 in Black, Harrison, Osborne, & Duschl, 2004). However, while the summative purpose calls for an overall aggregated judgment, the formative purpose calls for attention to the details of the student's responses. These arguments lay the basis for developing discussion of the formative–summative relationship in the next section.

Formative and Summative: From Discord to Harmony

The scheme of Steps 1 to 5 that were just set out represents summative assessment as an integral part of any teaching and learning system, not as an unwelcome necessity. The aim of this section is to discuss several examples of attempts to enhance teachers' summative work, illustrating the pressures that bear, in contrary directions, on such attempts (see also Connie Moss's chapter in this volume on summative assessment: Chapter 14).

Any assessment is merely a means to gather evidence about learning. It is the use of the evidence that distinguishes the formative from the summative, although of course the methods used and the interpretations of the outcomes may differ according to the uses envisaged. The effect of the intended purposes can be illustrated by the example of assessment in early years education. Young children may be frequently assessed at this stage—not by intrusive assessment tools but rather by systematic observation of their behavior as they take advantage of opportunities to play and talk (see e.g., Fleer & Quinones, 2012). The children's participation may be steered by teachers' interventions, but they will be unaware of the practice of frequent summative assessment that is being implemented. However, this benign relationship is in contrast to that explained in the account by Fitzgerald and Gunstone (2012) of the engagement of primary stage (8-year-old) children in a science investigation. They were encouraged on completion of their work to work in groups to compose posters summing up what they had learned, as in Step 4, but the teacher reported that she did not formally assess these (Step 5), explaining that "Because they're trying to explain their science, I don't want them actually worrying about anything else. I want them to concentrate on telling each other about the science."

This teacher was concerned about the conflict between the pressures of testing and her aim of supporting good learning practices: She saw Step 5 as undermining such practices. This is a common perception where pupils have to take externally set terminal tests in the formulation of which schools play no part and which are the means often adopted to make schools accountable for their students' achievements. Teachers are thereby driven to replicate as closely as possible, in their own summative assessments, the external state tests in order to achieve high scores, thereby losing control of Step 4.

These effects may be even more negative where an external test system is based on a single examination paper, or a set of a few such papers, taken over no more than a few days at the end of a course. The tests are then inexpensive and easy to mark, but they undermine validity as well as making reliability more fragile to short-term health and other variable factors.

One example of this is the narrowing effect of the mandatory national tests at age 14 that operated in England from 1993 until 2008 (Gardner, Harlen, Hayward, & Stobart, 2010). An analysis of the science tests showed that these called mainly for low levels of thinking, with one line or box-ticking items accounting for over 80% of the marks (Fairbrother, 2008).

Similarly, in the United States, external accountability tests, often commercially generated, are dominant in most states, with attempts being made at the federal level to enhance national testing by linking it to the federal funding on which many states depend. Multiple-choice items are predominant in the instruments. Various stakeholders also make use of grades awarded by schools, while higher education institutions supplement these sources with results of tests produced by private agencies. As a consequence, teacher judgment for summative assessment in the United States had often been "found wanting" (Brookhart, 2011). Attempts to broaden the scope of assessments in three states by promoting the use of pupil portfolios assessed by teachers were unsuccessful: Weak guidelines for the inclusion of evidence in portfolios and inadequate training in marking were identified as causes of difficulty (Koretz, 1998; Shapley & Bush, 1999). (Also see Chapter 5 in this volume.)

Such shortcomings were highlighted in the National Research Council (NRC) study (Pellegrino, Chudowsky, & Glaser, 2001), which emphasized the need for multiple measures to "enhance the validity and fairness of the inferences drawn by giving students various ways and opportunities to demonstrate their competence" (p. 255). However, that report also stressed that if classroom assessments (CAs) were to be widely used, careful scrutiny would be needed to ensure that they were adequate in terms of their validity, reliability, and fairness.

This brings the discussion back to the role of teachers in high-stakes assessments. In the systems previously referred to, the teacher has no control over the tests and has to compromise between work that engages students in learning and a short-term emphasis on test preparation. Thus, external test pressures lower teachers' status, deprive them of full ownership of their work, and undermine the development of their own skills in assessment. If teachers had more control over the accountability measures, they would be better able to reconcile, within their own practices, the formative and summative purposes. Thus, one way to redeem the situation is for teachers to have more control over Step 5.

However, the discussion here ought not to be limited to the problems specific to high-stakes testing. For many of the years of schooling, teachers have responsibility for those regular, year-on-year, or more frequent summative assessments on which decisions important for each pupil's future are taken—so the quality of those assessments is a cause for concern.

Developing Teachers' Summative Assessments: The System Problems

This section develops further the arguments for the importance of teachers summative assessments and then presents brief accounts of a variety of innovations at national or state levels, which have tried, and in some cases failed, to achieve what is needed (see also Chapter 14 in this volume, which focuses on summative assessment).

Teachers should play a more active role in high-stakes summative assessments because even the best external tests are bound to be of limited validity. This point was emphasized by Stanley, McCann, Gardner, Reynolds, & Wild (2009):

> The teacher is increasingly being seen as the primary assessor in the most important aspects of assessment. The broadening of assessment is based on a view that there are aspects of learning that are important but cannot be adequately assessed by formal external tests. These aspects require human judgment to integrate the many

> elements of performance behaviors that are required in dealing with authentic assessment tasks. (p. 31)

A similar argument has been expressed in working papers of the inter-country meetings of the European Union (EU) ministers of education (European Commission, 2010). The validity of high-stakes tests—whether external, internal, or both—should be more rigorously challenged in the future, and at least some of the instruments needed to meet these new requirements will have to be implemented and assessed by teachers' themselves. This necessity poses significant challenges, to which we now turn.

Effective Use of Summative Assessments: The Challenges for Teachers

Teachers have to have the understanding and skills to produce valid and reliable assessments, yet the instruments and procedures they use have to be comparable within and between different teachers and schools, although the procedures needed to ensure this comparability must not be so inflexible that they lead to "teaching to the test" practices. Such development has to be supported by a strategy coordinated at national and/or state levels between the various agencies involved. An account by Kuiper and Oettevanger (in press) of the current struggles to establish a new national system in the Netherlands shows how conflict between the perspectives of different institutions responsible—for testing, for the curriculum, or for teacher training intertwined with issues of status and power—creates obstacles to the establishment of a coherent national system.

One cause of difficulty arises when those responsible for the formulation of a mandatory curriculum do not consider the assessment of their stated aims. Where this happens, as is frequently the case, those who design assessments may have to transform those aims into concrete assessment activities so that, in effect, the implemented curriculum is determined by the assessment agency—a power they may not be qualified to exert. Moreover, formal external tests that are inexpensive to compose and administer—and easy to mark reliably—cannot reflect and support in full some of the aims, so Step 1 is distorted. The net effect is that the whole process is controlled by the requirements of Step 5—that is, by the summative assessment agencies so that they control both curriculum and instruction. There are national and state systems for which this would be a fair description.

This fault is one aspect of the broader problem of misalignment between curriculum, instruction, and assessment (a more detailed discussion is set out in the study by the NRC [Pellegrino et al., 2001, pp. 52–53], where it is argued that alignment requires consistent adherence of all involved to a core model of effective learning). Where this is lacking, teachers find guidance about aims in the high-stakes tests, so they "teach to the test." Where teachers have more agency in, and ownership of, the high-stakes test instruments, they can explore and question the meaning of the curriculum formulations, not accept the interpretation of test agencies who work to constraints that are not those of the classroom.

Programs in England and Sweden

There have been attempts, in several national systems, to give teachers' summative assessments a role in the production of high-stakes assessments. Black (1994) described how a plan, recommended in England by a government-appointed committee that gave teachers the responsibility for producing national assessment results by combining scores on external tests with their own assessments, was accepted in principle but undermined in practice. The two undermining steps were to reject a proposition that inter-school moderation groups be developed and to give external tests priority in public reporting of the results.

The combination of national tests with teachers' own assessments is the basis for the national system in Sweden (Black & Wiliam, 2007). Final decisions about the grade of each student is left to the teacher at all stages, the national tests provide an overall calibration, and there are also banks of test items in some subjects for teachers to use for their own assessments. For the school-leaving grades, teacher judgments are one main instrument, but this is complemented by a national aptitude test. As the competition for university places became more intense, this test was becoming relatively more important (Wikström & Wikström, 2005).

Program in Australia

The state of New South Wales allocates 50% of the weight of final assessments to the judgment of each school; the other 50% is based on the state's formal tests. However, the latter is used both to calibrate the school-based results, leading in a few cases to scaling overall, and also to detect and correct anomalies in the results of particular schools. The state of Queensland goes further, with school leaving certificates wholly dependent on school-based assessments, although there is also a benchmarking test. However, both of these states are having to resist pressure from the Australian federal government to impose the same national test in all states.

What is significant is that in each of these two states there is a coherent state system to train teachers as assessors and as participants in inter-school alignment (moderation) procedures, which ensures that the outcomes are comparable across schools. This aim is seen to require inter-school collaborations in local groups, to secure inter-school consistency in judging the final portfolios produced by individual students, but it is also to ensure this comparability through collaborative professional development at earlier stages in the school year. Another significant difference between these systems and that in (say) England is that the state has responsibility for all aspect of the assessment system but also for the curriculum and for the support of all aspects of teacher training, including the funding of in-service training work. In consequence, the assessment systems are planned as one aspect of a system that supports teachers in their summative assessment work. Such a policy provides a way to establish positive and coherent relationships between Steps 4 and 5 of the model that was previously described. Stanley et al. (2009) described how the state systems in Queensland and New South Wales provide this training and support.

Programs in Scotland and Wales

Current developments in Scotland and Wales stand in contrast to these Australian examples. The system in both is in a process of change (Gardner et al., 2010). A study by Hayward, Dow, & Boyd (2008) of the situation in Scotland provides evidence of the problems that arise when national changes do not take account of the help schools might need to implement them. For over 10 years, the implementation of formative assessment had been effectively developed by the Scottish government and is a successful and positive initiative (Hallam, Kirton, Peffers, Robertson, & Stobart, 2004). Over the same period, the only external national test was for the school-leaving years. For summative assessments in earlier years, schools were provided with tests on a national database, the expectation being that they should use these to inform, not replace, their own assessments. However, this had not happened. Teachers were teaching to the national tests and using the results as evidence of their school's success. One reason for this missed opportunity was innovation *overload*. After adopting the innovation in formative assessment with marked success, schools had to implement a new national curriculum and had not been able to work also on a new approach to their summative assessments (Priestley, Miller, Barrett, & Wallace, 2011). To respond to the aims of this curriculum, schools should have been recognizing a wider range of achievements, thereby exploring assessment validity in relation to these aims, but there was no scheme to support such exploration. A related obstacle was the need to provide summative information in a form acceptable to the local education authorities who felt pressure to respond to a national requirement to demonstrate improvement in their schools. So the collection of purely quantitative data on limited areas of activity continued as before. Boyd and Hayward (2010) concluded the following:

> There is an urgent need to tackle issues of assessment literacy in Scotland. Until individuals and groups have a better understanding of the uses and abuses of assessment data, the tensions emerging in this study are likely to persist. (p. 21)

A study of similar transition problems in the changes in Wales exposed similar problems and highlighted the following two weaknesses: "The first related to the lack of comprehensive planning ('under-designing') of many of the initiatives, whilst the second related to perceptions of what constituted quality assessment practice" (Gardner, Harlen, Hayward, & Stobart, 2011, p. 112).

What emerges from these examples is that a coherent system that aims at alignment between curriculum, assessment, and instruction—and built with close attention to the problems of providing national or state support to enhance teachers' professional development in assessment literacy—are all needed if any system is to support the enhanced quality and status of teachers' summative assessments.

Developing Teachers' Summative Assessments—The Fine Grain of Practice

This section discusses several different approaches to the to the development of teachers' summative assessment work. Some have had the direct aim of including some element of teachers' judgments in high-stakes results. An example of this in the UK was a system of assigning a proportion, typically about 15% of the final marks, to teachers' assessment of classroom-based coursework. Calibration of standards was achieved either by inspection of samples submitted to the examining authority or by visits of *moderators* to inspect assessed work. The study by Black and colleagues (2004) showed how a main aim of the system, to encourage implementation with teacher assessment of open-ended investigation tasks in science, was undermined as teachers used repeatedly, from year to year, tasks for which *successful* outcomes could be assured. Similar stereotyping later led to a majority of teachers of mathematics to vote for the abolition of the coursework requirement in their subject.

The strategy of assisting teachers' summative work by providing sets of questions meant that they could use them at their own discretion. This approach in Scotland has been discussed in the previous section. In England, this was tried in the context of improving schools' own internal assessments by the Assessing Pupils' Progress (APP) program, which provided sets of exemplary items but also advised that progress be checked frequently by detailed auditing of performance against sets of atomized criteria, which for any one year group in (say) mathematics could number of the order of 50 to 80. This both limited the range of teachers' own judgments and encouraged them to adopt a rigid program of teaching that mirrored the list of the target criteria.

Such top-down approaches can be counterproductive. A detailed example is described by Hume and Coll (2009). The New Zealand authority had provided a generic example of an open-ended science activity but with a scheme that included the sequence—plan, execute, interpret, report—to be followed in an investigation, together with a format specified for student reports. The description is of a school where students were taken through the example as a template exercise, but although they could carry this out as instructed, many were lost as to how to proceed when given a different phenomenon to investigate. Good tools are only useful in the hands of skilled and reflective practitioners.

Other examples have moved away from the top-down prescriptive approach to teacher development to one in which teachers are more actively involved so that they become agents of their professional development. Gardner et al. (2010) described both the APP initiative and other contrasting approaches. In one such example, a local authority (district) worked with a pilot group of teachers by both providing useful assessment resources and also arranging a series of meetings between the teachers in which they could discuss their use of these resources, adapting these together with exploration and exchange of their own methods for assessing their pupils.

The study of Wyatt-Smith, Klenowski, & Gunn (2010) took this issue further. They observed in detail the ways in which teachers in Queensland, where they were taking full responsibility for their students' summative assessments, arrived at their decisions in group moderation discussions. This work showed that the teachers' judgment process was not driven solely by published standards, for these on their own were insufficient guides to judgment. The teachers also used exemplary examples, complemented by examples of student responses, a variety of types of tacit knowledge, and social processes of dialogue and negotiation. This mix of factors should enhance the legitimacy of the judgment process, for no formal statement of standards can ever have the precision required to support automatic judgment of all eventualities, and no set of examples can do more that give an overall guide to the complex judgment required for all the diverse products that any class of students will produce. Any attempt to produce *teacher-proof* procedures can only work by so narrowing down the nature of the learning work that its potential validity is undermined.

To illustrate this argument from a different perspective, I describe here a project known as the King's-Oxfordshire Summative Assessment Project (KOSAP) (Black, Harrison, Hogden, Marshall, & Serret, 2010, 2011). Its aim was to develop teachers' summative assessment practices so that they could improve the quality of their judgments and begin to make positive links between Steps 4 and 5 of the model presented earlier. The work involved secondary phase teachers of English and of mathematics in a small-scale intervention involving collaboration between teachers across three schools. The work aimed to focus on those summative assessments over which the schools had full control and which were produced mainly or wholly for internal purposes.

The first question explored whether the summative purposes were well served by the data and the practices that were being used. It emerged that these left much to be desired, in part because the accountability pressures exerted by England's national assessment systems constrained practice, even in the school years in which there was no national testing. This exploration led to a discussion of validity in which teachers' developed their own critique of the *off-the-shelf* test questions that they had been using. The uncertain understanding of validity was more marked among the mathematics teachers than English teachers, probably reflecting the differences between the pedagogic cultures of the two (Hodgen & Marshall, 2005). This critical auditing served as a stimulus for teachers to look afresh at their assessment strategy—as one teacher of English put it (Black et al., 2010):

> The project made me think more critically about what exactly I was assessing. The first question I remember being asked ("what does it mean to be good at English?") gave me a different perspective on assessment. I find myself continually returning to this question. (p. 222)

This phase of the work can be seen to correspond to Step 1. To proceed from this level to consider the actual tasks to be used—that is, to move from Step 1 to Step 2—called for a system that uses the range of different types of tasks needed to establish the overall validity of the assessments—that is, a portfolio. There followed the development of discussions and agreements about a set of details that had to be clarified if comparability, at both intra-school and inter-school levels, between the judgments of all teachers were to be assured. Briefly, these issues were as follows:

- The need to agree on the ways in which each domain was to be sampled within a portfolio. New types of tasks had to be sought, adapted, or invented. It was also agreed that all would use some common tasks but that each teacher could use individual choice for some others.
- The conditions for the presentation and guidance under which students would work in producing the various components of a portfolio had to be specified. The agreed rules differed according to the tasks: Some would call for group work in collecting resources and discussing their analysis, followed by production under controlled conditions of individual reports; for others, students learned to use skills in one open-ended task and then tackled a similar task in formal examination conditions.
- Underlying the previously given steps was the need for an agreed specification of the criteria to which all assessors had to work. Teachers found the criteria in the national curriculum for England too vague and had to adapt and refine the criteria in ways that allowed for the diverse realities of classroom instruction.
- In order to produce results that would be comparable in standard within and between schools, procedures were established to inter-calibrate standards by moderation meetings, in intra-school followed by inter-school discussions. For each such meeting, a set of student responses was selected and marked independently by each of the teachers involved, leading to discussion and resolution of discrepancies.

The extra work for teachers that these procedures required was seen by teachers to be valuable in a variety of ways for these English and mathematics teachers, respectively:

> The moderation and standardisation process was incredibly valuable in ensuring rigour, consistency and confidence with our approach to assessment; that teachers in school were highly motivated by being involved in the process that

> would impact on the achievement of students in their classes. (Black et al., 2010, p. 225)

> But I think if all the teachers had more, possibly more ownership of what we are actually doing in terms of summative assessment then you would have more confidence in saying to parents, which I think is one of the biggest things I find with lower school. (Black et al., 2011, p. 460)

A further benefit was that the new types of CA changed the students' involvement and thereby provided new evidence about their different needs. It is illustrated by this mathematics teacher:

> I think it changed the dynamic of the lesson a little bit, in terms of well, in terms of there being much more an element of them getting on trying to find out . . . they were trying to be more independent, I think, I think some of them struggled with that, and others. . . some of them, some still find it quite difficult if they are not hand held all the way through. When others were happier to sort of, go their own way. (Black et al., 2011, p. 460)

The engagement of pupils in the summative assessments helped by developing their ownership of their individual portfolios and leading them to see that the summative assessment activities were an integral part of their learning progress.

This project, albeit only exploratory, was successful in improving the summative assessment practices of the teachers involved in ways that they saw to be supportive of the teaching and learning work that they valued. Thus, it made a contribution within the context of the topic-by-topic, year-on-year internal assessment responsibilities of those involved. From a different perspective, it illustrated how the Steps 1 to 5 apply to the task of planning summative assessment work.

The fundamental importance of developmental work of this kind is underlined by Stanley et al. (2009) in their review of assessment programs in several countries:

> Evidence from education systems where teacher assessment has been implemented with major professional support, is that everyone benefits. Teachers become more confident, students obtain more focused and immediate feedback, and learning gains can be measured. An important aspect of teacher assessment is that it allows for the better integration of professional judgment into the design of more authentic and substantial learning contexts. (p. 82)

What this example highlights is the fine grain of detail with which professional development must deal. One element is the compromise between uniformity and flexibility—too little uniformity can lead to indefensible variations in standards (e.g., Koretz, 1998), too much can undermine the validity and the development of the professional skills of the teacher. Another challenge is the need to develop all aspects of the teachers' assessment literacy (Gardner, 2007). A significant feature was the strategy of the KOSAP research team to guide teachers' initial growth of the project but to steer only lightly so that the project could then grow in ways that responded to and built on those professional insights and classroom craft skills that the team did not and could not deploy.

CONCLUSION

In conclusion, assessment should be seen as an integral part of teaching and learning. A model of instruction that incorporates the purposes of assessment would be helpful in achieving consistency in the debates and initiatives that aim to improve education. Such a model should make clear the central role of formative assessment, seen as the engagement of students in learning dialogues with one another and with their teachers. It must be supported, rather than hindered, by summative assessment practices.

Systems of summative assessment based solely on external testing are unfit for a single purpose, given their inevitably restricted validity, the manner in which they exert pressures that undermine good practices in teaching and defeat their own stated aim of improving learning, and at the same time undermine that professional status of teachers which is essential for the health of any educational system. The formative and summative purposes of assessment can be so intertwined that they are mutually supportive rather than conflicting. Unless this is done, formative assessment cannot achieve its full potential to improve learning. However, this is a complex and context-sensitive task that can only be carried out by classroom teachers who have responsibility for achieving both purposes.

Programs to support teachers' professional development must be designed to help them to develop their skills, strategies, and values in assessment through support for their collaboration in their own professional learning.

National systems must be coherent in the way they align curriculum, instruction, and assessment and should seek to serve the public interest in the accountability of the education system in ways that support, rather than undermine, the quality of that system's work. This calls for achieving an optimum balance between high-stakes assessments and school-based assessments. A realistic appraisal of the quality and comparability of teachers' summative assessments is needed in judging this balance.

It is obvious that there is no single recipe for achieving all the aims implied in these statements. However, it is clear that there is a need for investment in professional development work over several years, for without this all else may fail. The following was expressed in Gardner et al. (2010): "Unless teachers are committed through self-agency to any particular change, the prospects for any successful dissemination and professional learning, leading to its successful practice, are likely to be slim" (p. 134).

References

Alexander, R. (2008a). *Towards dialogic thinking: rethinking classroom talk.* (4th ed.) York, UK: Dialogos.

Alexander, R. (2008b). *Essays in pedagogy.* Abingdon UK: Routledge.

Black, P. (1994). Performance assessment and accountability: The experience in England and Wales. *Educational Evaluation and Policy Analysis, 16*(2), 191–203.

Black, P. (2009). Looking again at formative assessment. *Learning and Teaching Update, 30,* 3–5.

Black, P., Harrison, C., Hodgen, J., Marshall, M., & Serret, N. (2010). Validity in teachers' summative assessments. *Assessment in Education, 17*(2), 215–232.

Black, P., Harrison, C., Hodgen, J., Marshall, M., & Serret, N. (2011). Can teachers' summative assessments produce dependable results and also enhance classroom learning? *Assessment in Education, 18*(4), 451–469.

Black, P., Harrison, C., Lee, C., Marshall, B., & Wiliam, D. (2003). *Assessment for learning–putting it into practice.* Buckingham, UK: Open University Press.

Black, P., Harrison, C., Osborne, J., & Duschl, R. (2004). *Assessment of Science Learning 14–19.* London: Royal Society. Retrieved from www.royalsoc.ac.uk/education

Black, P., & Wiliam, D. (1998). Assessment and classroom learning. *Assessment in Education, 5*(1), 7–74.

Black, P., & Wiliam, D. (2007). Large-scale assessment systems: Design principles drawn from international comparisons. *Measurement, 5*(1) 1–53.

Black, P., & Wiliam, D. (2009). Developing the theory of formative assessment. *Educational Assessment, Evaluation and Accountability, 21*(1), 5–31.

Boyd, B., & Hayward, L. (2010). *Exploring assessment for accountability.* Glasgow: Universities of Strathclyde and Glasgow.

Brookhart, S. M. (2011, June). *The use of teacher judgment for summative assessment in the United States: Weighed in the balance and found wanting.* Paper presented at the Oxford Centre for Educational Assessment seminar, Oxford, UK.

Bruner, J. (1966). *Toward a theory of instruction.* New York: Norton for Harvard University Press.

Butler, R. (1988). Enhancing and undermining intrinsic motivation; the effects of task-involving and ego-involving evaluation on interest and performance. *British Journal of Educational Psychology, 58*(1), 1–14.

Cowie, B., & Bell, B. (1999). A model of formative assessment in science education. *Assessment in Education, 6*(1), 101–116.

Dweck, C. S. (2000). *Self-theories: Their role in motivation, personality and development.* Philadelphia: Psychology Press.

European Commission. (2010). *Assessment of key competences: Draft background paper for the Belgian presidency meeting for directors-general for school education.* Brussels: Author.

Fairbrother, R. (2008). The validity of key stage 2 science tests. *School Science Review,* (329), 107–114.

Fitzgerald, A., & Gunstone, R. (2012). Embedding assessment within primary school science lessons: A case study. In R. Gunstone & A. Jones (Eds.), *Assessment in Science Education.* Melbourne: Springer.

Fleer, M., & Quinones, G. (2012). Building an assessment pedagogy *for, with,* and *of* early childhood science learning: An assessment *Perezhivanie.* In R. Gunstone & A. Jones (Eds.), *Assessment in Science Education.* Melbourne: Springer.

Freire, P. (1992). *Pedagogy of hope.* New York: Continuum

Gardner, J. (2007, Summer). Is teaching a "partial" profession? *Making the Grade: Journal of the Institute of Educational Assessors,* 18–21.

Gardner, J., Harlen, W., Hayward, L., & Stobart, G. (with Montgomery, M.). (2010). *Developing teacher assessment.* Buckingham, UK: Open University Press.

Gardner, J., Harlen, W., Hayward, L., & Stobart, G. (2011). Engaging and empowering teachers in innovative assessment practice. In R. Berry & B. Adamson (Eds.), *Assessment reform in education* (pp. 105–120). New York: Springer.

Hallam, S., & Ireson, J. (1999). Pedagogy in the secondary school. In P. Mortimore (Ed.), *Understanding pedagogy and its impact on learning* (pp. 68–97). London: Paul Chapman.

Hallam, S., Kirton, A., Peffers, J., Robertson, P., & Stobart, G. (2004). *Evaluation of project 1 of the assessment is for learning development program: Support for professional practice in formative assessment. Final report.* Retrieved from www.scotland.gov.uk/library5/education/ep1aldps-00.asp

Hayward, H., Dow, W., & Boyd, B. (2008). *Sharing the standard.* Report for LTScotland. Retrieved from http://wayback.archive-it.org/1961/20100730134209/http://www.ltscotland.org.uk/resources/s/genericresource_tcm4579679.asp?strReferringChannel=assess

Hodgen, J., & Marshall, B. (2005). Assessment for learning in mathematics and English: Contrasts and resemblances. *The Curriculum Journal, 16*(2), 153–176.

Hume, A., & Coll, R. K. (2009). Assessment of learning, for learning, and as learning: New Zealand case studies. *Assessment in Education: Principals, Policy & Practice, 16*(3), 269–290.

Koretz, D. (1998). Large scale portfolio assessments in the US: Evidence pertaining to the quality of measurement. *Assessment in Education, 5*(3), 309–334.

Kuiper, W., & Oettevanger, W. (in press). Aligning science curriculum renewal efforts and assessment practices. In R. Gunstone & A. Jones (Eds.), *Assessment in science education,* Melbourne: Springer.

Pellegrino, J. W, Chudowsky, N., & Glaser, R. (Eds.). (2001). *Knowing what students know: The science and design of educational assessment.* Washington DC: National Academy Press.

Perrenoud, P. (1998). From formative evaluation to a controlled regulation of learning processes. Towards a wider conceptual field. *Assessment in Education: Principles, Policy and Practice, 5*(1), 85–102.

Priestley, M., Miller, K., Barrett, L., & Wallace, C. (2011). Teacher learning communities and educational change in Scotland. *British Educational Research Journal, 37*(2), 265–284.

Shapley, K. S., & Bush, M. J. (1999). Developing a valid and reliable portfolio assessment in the primary grades: Building on practical experience. *Applied Measurement in Education, 12*(2), 111–132.

Shulman, L. S. (1999). Knowledge and teaching: Foundation of the new reform. In J. Leach & B. Moon (Eds.), *Learners and pedagogy* (pp. 61–71). London: Chapman.

Stanley, G., McCann, R., Gardner, J., Reynolds, L., & Wild, I. (2009). *Review of teacher assessment: What works best and issues for development.* Oxford, UK: Oxford University Centre for Educational Development.

Wikström, C., & Wikström, M. (2005). Grade inflation and school competition: an empirical analysis based on the Swedish upper secondary schools. *Economics of Education Review, 24*(3), 309–322.

Wiske, M.S. (1999). What is teaching for understanding? In J. Leach & B. Moon (Eds.), *Learners and pedagogy* (pp. 230–246). London: Chapman.

Wood, D. (1998). *How children think and learn.* Oxford, UK: Blackwell.

Wyatt-Smith, C., Klenowski, V., & Gunn, S. (2010). The centrality of teachers' judgment practice in assessment: A study of standards in moderation. *Assessment in Education: Principals, Policy & Practice, 17*(1), 59–75.

11

Gathering Evidence of Student Understanding[1]

Margaret Heritage

A central practice in formative assessment is teachers' generation and collection of information about how learning is developing while instruction is underway. Teachers engage in continually taking stock of learning by paying close, firsthand attention to specific aspects of students' developing understanding and skills as teaching and learning is taking place in real time (Erickson, 2007).

Consider the following illustration of one teacher's evidence collecting strategies:

> In Ms. Alonzo's fifth-grade class, the students are working in a *writers' workshop* setting. They are writing a persuasive argument to encourage their readers to take more care of the natural environment. In previous workshops, they have learned about the nature and purpose of arguments and counterarguments and evidence to support the argument as well as how to organize their argument effectively.
>
> While the students are involved in the independent writing part of the workshop, Ms. Alonzo sits with Edgar to discuss his writing progress. She has a three-ring binder open to a page with these headings at the top: Child's Name/Date, Research Compliment, Teaching Point, and What's Next for This Child? Further down the page is a self-adhesive note that lists five students' names. These are the other children she wants to meet with during the session.
>
> Ms. Alonzo's initial purpose with Edgar is to follow up from 2 days ago when she provided him with feedback based on the evidence she had elicited from her interaction with him; in that interaction, she determined that Edgar needed to provide stronger sources of evidence to support his argument. On this occasion, she wants to see how he has used her prior feedback.
>
> Ms. Alonzo begins her interaction with Edgar: "You're working on evidence? What was your source? Where did you find it?"
>
> Edgar responds, "In the book of the Environmental Protection Agency and on the Internet."
>
> Ms. Alonzo continues, "And what do you think about what you found so far? Do you think that it supports your argument?"
>
> Edgar is unsure and responds, "I guess . . . "
>
> At this stage, Ms. Alonzo reminds Edgar that the purpose of the evidence is to support his argument and asks him to read his argument aloud. Having established that the focus of his

[1]My thanks to Fritz Mosher for his insightful comments on an earlier draft of this chapter.

> argument is to "stop dumping in the ocean because all the beautiful animals we see are going to start vanishing," Ms. Alonzo then asks, "So what evidence did you find to support that? What evidence did you find that will help you to strengthen that argument?"
>
> In the ensuing interaction, Ms. Alonzo helps Edgar to recognize which of the information he has located is from a reliable source and will be effective in supporting his argument. Satisfied that Edgar can move forward on his own to incorporate his evidence, she then asks him to go over the organization of his persuasive argument and to let her know where he will place the evidence. When Edgar does this, it is apparent to Ms. Alonzo that he has some confusion about the overall structure and that his writing needs to be reorganized. She goes over the organization with him and writes the organizational elements on a self-adhesive note saying, "So make sure that you put them in order, but when you do that, you know, focus on the organization because that's gonna help it to flow so that once we read it to our audience or somebody else reads it, it makes sense."
>
> And she adds, "You might need some transitional sentences. Remember that we talked about those?"
>
> Edgar nods at this point and she leaves him, saying, "So go ahead and work on those."

Throughout this interaction, Ms. Alonzo has made notes in her three-ring binder. Under Research Compliment she writes that he had recognized the reliability of his source, in the section labeled Teaching Point she wrote that she had discussed how evidence supported his argument, and under the heading What's Next for This Child? she wrote "organization and transitional sentences," noting that Edgar was still unsure about how to organize his writing to effectively convey his argument to the reader. What do we see in this example?

Black and Wiliam (1998) referred to formative assessment as "encompassing all those activities undertaken by teachers, and/or by their students, which provide information to be used as feedback to modify the teaching and learning activities in which they are engaged" (pp. 7–8). In a further elaboration, Torrance and Pryor (2001) considered the practice to be routine classroom assessment (CA) "integrated with pedagogy to maximize its formative potential in promoting learning" (p. 616). In the example of Ms. Alonzo and Edgar, we see a teacher who is gathering evidence in the context of a student's developing learning. The evidence is not gathered in the form of a "test" but rather in a carefully executed investigation through which Edgar's teacher is able to determine the next steps to move his learning forward through pedagogical action, including feedback to him.

In short, we see evidence gathering in action: evidence gathering that is integrated with pedagogy and that provides information that the teacher uses as feedback to further learning.

The focus of this chapter is how teachers and their students can engage in the process of generating tractable information to be used as feedback in support of learning. First is a consideration of the purpose of evidence in formative assessment practice. Then follows a discussion of the range of sources of evidence. Next is a section devoted to assessment quality in relation to evidence sources in formative assessment, which is followed by a consideration of gathering evidence in the context of learning progressions. The chapter concludes with a discussion of the role of the student in gathering evidence.

Purpose of Evidence in Formative Assessment Practice

Assessment has two fundamental purposes: (1) to provide information on students' current levels of achievement to the present time and (2) to inform the future steps that teachers need to take in classrooms to ensure that students make progress toward desired outcomes. In broad terms, assessments that provide information on students' current levels of achievement represent a *past-to-present* perspective of learning in the sense that they indicate what has been learned to date. Many goals of assessment require this past-to-present view of learning, for example, accountability, placement, and certification. By contrast, the goals of assessment in support of prospective learning while it is developing require a *present-to-future* perspective, in which the concern is not solely with the actual level of performance but with anticipating future possibilities (Heritage, 2010). The contrast between these two perspectives is nicely captured by Frederick Erickson, when he observed that in addition to looking "upstream at what has been learned, assessment needs to look downstream at what *can be learned*" (F. Erickson, personal communication, October 28, 2009). In a related discussion, Torrance and Pryor (2001) distinguished between two kinds of assessment. The first centers on trying to find out *if* the learner knows, understands, or can do a predetermined thing and is characterized by closed or pseudo-open questioning and tasks. The second is intended to discover *what* the learner knows, understands, and can do. The latter is characterized by open questioning and tasks and oriented more to future development rather than measurement of past or current achievement.

Anticipating future possibilities for learning inherent in a present-to-future assessment perspective accords with Vygotsky's stance on instruction (Heritage, 2010; Heritage & Heritage, 2011; Torrance & Pryor, 2001). He stated that instruction "must be aimed not so much at the ripe as at the ripening functions" (Vygotsky, 1986, p. 188). To aim instruction at the "ripening functions," teachers need an indication about a student's *zone of nearest development* (also termed *the zone of proximal development [ZPD]*), described by Vygotsky as "those processes in the development of the same functions, which, as they are not mature today, still are already on their way, are already growing through, and already tomorrow will bear fruit" (Vygotsky, 1935, p. 120).

Kozulin, Gindis, Ageyev, and Miller (2003) suggested Vygotsky used the concept of the ZPD in three different contexts. First, in the developmental context, the ZPD refers to the child's emerging psychological functions. Second, in the context of assessment and classroom learning, the ZPD refers to the differences between the unaided and the assisted performance of the child. Third, the ZPD is conceived of as a metaphoric space in which the everyday concepts of the child meet *scientific* concepts introduced by teachers or by other mediators of learning. Elaborating further, Chaiklin (2003) observed that new psychological functions develop in conditions where there is a fundamental contradiction between the child's current capabilities—the developed psychological functions—the child's needs and desires, and the challenges and possibilities afforded by the learning context.

In this vein, one can make a distinction between two types of learning: (1) learning that occurs within an extant paradigm of knowledge (cf., Kuhn, 1962) through the deployment of existing competencies in order to develop and extend them within a common paradigm and (2) the discontinuous moments in learning involving the reorganization of knowledge through the application of new competencies that permit a significantly greater depth of understanding in a particular domain. A learner will bump up against the limits of a paradigm or learning framework before being able to move on to a higher, more sophisticated level. For example, returning to the chapter's opening scenario, Edgar is engaged within a new paradigm of writing that takes him beyond his current competence. Now he has to explicitly recognize and address the positions of others (counterarguments), develop the skills to counter them, and organize his writing so that the evidence he has found effectively bolsters his arguments and counterarguments. Ms. Alonzo's interaction reveals that these are *maturing* functions, intermittently grasped and not yet consolidated.

In the course of teaching and learning, then, teachers have to recognize and act on two orders of learning. One is a progressive steplike form of learning in which the accumulation of observations and actions consolidates and deepens a given understanding. In the other, there is learning that occurs in the midst of change, during which the learner shows a fragmentary and inconsistent grip of new concepts: An accumulation of observations or data points yields confusing or incompatible inferences and conclusions, requiring movement to a different order of generalization or abstraction. From a teacher's perspective, the key element in acting upon both orders of learning is feedback. Feedback *from* evidence of student learning helps the teacher establish if the student is moving forward without the need for tailored intervention or to determine which cognitive structures are emerging so that a subsequent pedagogical move can be made to assist these cognitive structures to mature. Feedback *to* the student is the essential means through which appropriate pedagogical moves can be made.

In his seminal article, Sadler (1989) identified feedback to the student as the essential component in formative assessment. Adopting a cybernetic perspective, he began with Ramaprasad's (1983) definition of feedback as "information about the gap between the actual level and the reference level of a system parameter that is used to alter the gap in some way" (p. 4). Thus, Sadler conceptualized formative assessment as a feedback loop designed to close the gap between the learner's current status and desired goals. For Sadler (1989), a critical component in closing the gap is the "judgments teachers make about student responses that can be used to shape and improve the student's competence by short-circuiting the randomness and inefficiency of trial-and-error learning" (p. 120). This echoes the work of Pellegrino and Glaser (1982), who noted that of prime importance in formative assessment is teachers' careful probing and analysis of student learning, which can lead to sensitive adjustments to individual students' learning and to the pathways along which they will progress. Therefore, the overall purpose of evidence gathering in formative assessment is to enable teachers to respond to student learning in order to enhance that learning while the student is in the process of learning (Bell & Cowie, 2000).

Sources of Evidence

As noted earlier, the term *formative assessment* does not apply to a specific tool or measurement instrument. Over 80 years ago, Dewey (1928) pointed the way to evidence collection in support of learning with his comments that what is required is "a much more highly skilled kind of observation than is needed to note the results of mechanically applied tests" (p. 204). In more current literature, "highly skilled observation" can occur in the context of teacher–student interaction, student–student interaction, tasks, and observations of actions. Griffin (2007) argued that humans can only provide evidence of cognitive and affective learning through four observable actions: (1) what they say, (2) write, (3) make, or (4) do. These behaviors act as indicators of an underlying learning construct and are the ways in which learning can be inferred by the observer. Whatever the source of the evidence, the role of the teacher is to construct or devise ways to elicit responses from students that are revealing of their current learning status (Sadler, 1989).

Interactions

Interaction between teacher and students has been characterized as a principal source of evidence in formative assessment (Allal, 2010; Black & Wiliam, 2009; Harlen, 2007; Heritage & Heritage, 2011; Jordan & Putz, 2004; Ruiz-Primo & Furtak, 2006, 2007; Torrance & Pryor, 1998). More specifically, Black and Wiliam (2005) noted that productive strategies in formative assessment include questions designed by the teacher to explore students' learning and generate teachable moments when they can intervene and further learning. Shavelson et al. (2008) suggested that to find the gap between what students know and what they need to know that teachers need to develop a set of central questions that get at the heart of what is to be learned in a specific lesson. Additionally, teachers have to know the right moment to ask these questions so that they can enable students to reveal what they understand and what evidence they can provide to back up their knowledge.

Chin (2007) illustrated the process of questioning and response in a science context: The teacher asks conceptual questions to elicit students' ideas and assists them to engage in productive thinking, invites and encourages multiple responses and questions, and offers ongoing comments to their responses. Finally, in a more in-depth analysis focused on acquiring evidence of children's cognitive processes in mathematics, Ginsburg (2009) advocated a three-pronged approach centered on observations, task performance, and the clinical interview. The latter is the most significant: In it, the teacher follows up task performance "with questions designed to elicit thinking, and in general follows the child's thought process to where it leads" (p. 113).

The essential point about teacher–student interaction as a source of evidence is that it enables teachers to have access to student thinking so that they can advance from the current state. In this context, the type of questioning reflected in the Initiation-Response-Evaluation (I-R-E) or *recitation* paradigm (Cazden, 1988; Mehan, 1979; Sinclair & Coulthard, 1975) does not lead to productive evidence. In this kind of model, the outcome is not to make student thinking visible but rather to let the students know if their responses are right or wrong, which tends to end the exchange and prevents further dialogue (Webb & Jones, 2009).

In a related discussion, Harlen (2007) pointed out that it is not just the framing of the question that matters but also the timing, particularly the time allowed for answering the question. Rowe (1974) found that teachers generally allow very few seconds for students to answer questions, which as Harlen (2007) noted is very short even for questions that ask for recall—let alone for questions that demand students to provide explanations or express their ideas.

In a project designed to improve teachers' use of formative assessment, researchers worked with 24 science and mathematics teachers and brought together the ideas of improved questioning techniques and wait time—the length of the silence between when a teacher asks a question before speaking again if no student has responded (Black, Harrison, Lee, Marshall, & Wiliam, 2003). Teachers altered their questioning practices to include more wait time—for example, asking students to discuss their thinking in pairs before being randomly called on to respond (a no hands-up policy was instituted). Additionally, teachers did not refer to the answers as correct or incorrect but instead asked students to provide reasons for their answers, which gave them an opportunity to explore student thinking. The net result of this practice was that teachers asked fewer questions and spent more time on each (Black et al., 2003).

Ruiz-Primo (2011) expanded on questions as a source of evidence to extended interactional sequences referred to as assessment conversations. Developed from the notion of instructional dialogues as a pedagogical strategy linked to embedded assessment (Duschl & Gitomer, 1997), assessment conversations are conceived of as dialogues that embed assessment into an activity already occurring in the classroom, which enable teachers to gain insights into the nature of student thinking and act pedagogically on those insights (Ruiz-Primo & Furtak, 2004, 2006, 2007). Ruiz-Primo also noted that research suggests that in classrooms where teachers frequently engage in assessment conversations, students achieve at higher levels (Applebee, Langer, Nystrand, & Gamoran, 2003; Nystrand & Gamoran, 1991; Ruiz-Primo & Furtak, 2006, 2007).

Still in the context of student talk, Harlen (2007) contended that teachers can gain insights about student thinking when they set up a situation in which students converse with each other while the teacher "listens in" without participating in the discussion. Of course, it will be essential that the situation is well structured and promotes student exchanges of ideas so that their thinking is revealed.

Other Sources of Evidence

Beyond questions, interactions, discussions, and assessment conversations, there is a range of other sources of evidence. In mathematics, Lesh, Hoover, Hole, Kelly, & Post (2003) proposed model-eliciting activities that are useful for both assessment and instruction. Lesh and colleagues contrasted their model-based eliciting activities with traditional problem-solving activities found in textbooks. The latter requires students to produce an answer to a question that was formulated by someone else, whereas model-based activities require students to recognize the need to develop a model for interpreting the goals and potential solutions of an authentic, relevant problem. While students are working on the activities, they reveal how they are interpreting and mathematizing the problem.

The approach of Cognitively Guided Instruction in mathematics (Carpenter, Fennema, & Franke, 1996; Carpenter, Fennema, Peterson, & Carey, 1988) provides students with learning tasks created from a model of student thinking in arithmetic that permits teachers to interpret and respond to ongoing events in real time as they unfold during instruction. Also in mathematics, Heritage & Niemi (2006) proposed a framework for considering students' mathematical representations as evidence in formative assessment and, more specifically, Kouba and Franklin (1995) proposed that student representations, for instance, of division and multiplication situations and their explanations of the relationship among those representations, can function as evidence.

Harlen (2007) suggested that students' work, for example writing, drawings, and other artifacts resulting from well-designed tasks, can be a rich source of evidence about their ideas and skills. However, she cautioned that the tasks must be constructed so that students are able to express their ideas and that the teacher must have the knowledge and skills to notice the significant features of the work. Harlen (2007) also added that while student products can provide evidence, they rarely provide sufficient details about how certain skills have been used, noting that observation of how students are working can provide insights into their skills and attitudes. She suggested that observation can, for example, provide detail about how pupils make changes in their investigation of variables in science and in mathematics about how they read scales, draw graphs, and use number grids.

Reporting on a program entitled Every Child a Reader and Writer, which was designed to improve writing instruction, Poppers (2011) echoed Harlen's (2007) caution about teacher knowledge and skills with respect to student work products as sources of evidence. Researchers in this program found that initially teachers did not have sufficient background knowledge to notice the significant features of the written work, but with professional development and analysis tools, such as rubrics, they were able to gain skills in interpretation and the use of the evidence to improve student writing.

With respect to other forms of gathering evidence, in the area of reading, Bailey and Heritage (2008) have offered a range of strategies to gain information about students' reading, including student read-alouds, strategic questions focused on the text, and prompted written responses about text as ways to elicit evidence about students' learning. Specifically in the context of science curricula, but equally relevant to other areas, Shavelson et al. (2008) referred to "embedded-in-the-curriculum" formative assessment. These are assessments placed in the ongoing curriculum by teachers or curriculum developers at key junctures in a unit and designed to create goal-directed teachable moments. Finally, Wiliam (2011) provided 50 *techniques* for eliciting evidence ranging from learning logs to ranking exemplars to students generating test items with correct answers.

Technology

Some promising avenues in the ways in which technology can support gathering evidence are emerging. One such example is ASSISTments, which makes use of digital teaching platforms to blend assessment and assistance in a tool that can be adapted and used in a variety of ways with different cognitive models and different content. ASSISTments is designed to augment, replicate, and promote effective assessment practices, including uncovering detailed diagnosis of misconceptions, providing immediate, specific feedback, and monitoring student practice (Heffernan, Militello, Heffernan, & Decoteau, in press). ASSISTments also has a feature that allows teachers to create their questions (on the fly or prepared in advance), ask the students to respond to them, anonymously post the answers using a projector or interactive white board—one source of evidence—and then generate discussions about the questions that can be an additional source of evidence. Similarly, the online program Agile Assessment enables secondary school teachers to construct a range of cognitively demanding assessments to assess higher-order thinking in mathematics (Cook, Seeley, & Chaput, 2011). A Web-based tool, Strategic Reader, designed for use with struggling middle-school readers, provides a flexible assessment and instruction environment so that teachers can gather evidence of student performance during the instructional episodes and employ interventions as needed for individual students (Cohen, Hall, Vue, & Ganley, 2011).

Evidence Quality

Validity and reliability are central to all assessment, yet to date, the application of these concepts to formative assessment is an underdeveloped area of study (Brookhart, 2003; Ploegh, Tillema, & Segers, 2009; Smith, 2003). Erickson (2007) described formative assessment as different from professional psychometrics because it involves the clinical judgment of teachers about students' actions in the classroom. Similarly, Dierick and Dochy (2001) argued that when the notions of validity and reliability are applied to a new assessment context, the predominant view of them needs to be widened and other more appropriate criteria developed. This section addresses some of the ways in which the view of validity and reliability can be considered in the context of formative assessment.

Validity

In line with the idea of an argument-based approach to validity (Kane, 1992), there are a number of arguments that can underpin validity in formative assessment (see also the extended discussion of validity by Sarah M. Bonner in Chapter 6). Let us first consider two fundamental principles concerned with validity: (1) the assessment measures that it is intended to measure and (2) it provides sound evidence for specific decision-making purposes (Herman, Heritage, & Goldschmidt, 2011). The evidence generated by the variety of means discussed earlier is intended to provide information about the students' learning status in relation to the specific learning goals and to be used to inform decisions about next steps in teaching and learning. Ideas of content relevance, construct underrepresentation, and construct-irrelevant variance can be applied here in the sense that the evidence-gathering strategy should be aligned to the learning goal (the construct being addressed), it should be an appropriate representation of the construct, and should include the important dimensions of the construct. In other words, the strategy should not be so broad that it contains dimensions that are irrelevant to the construct nor too narrow that it fails to include the important dimensions of the construct. From the perspective of content relevance, the assessment strategy should be meaningful to students and situated in an authentic context (Frederiksen & Collins, 1989; Newman, 1990). Selecting the appropriate evidence-gathering strategy to meet the conditions that were previously discussed will require teachers to be very clear about what is to be learned and what evidence is needed to determine their students' current learning status.

In the same way that issues of fairness and bias are applicable in traditional psychometric approaches, they are also relevant to formative assessment. Because students' maturing functions do not develop in lockstep, formative assessment is inevitably personalized and teachers will need to employ strategies that tap into the individual knowledge that students manifest. Whatever strategies a teacher selects, they should account for the range of students present in the class so that all students have the opportunity to show where they are in their learning and have the prospect of moving forward from their current status. Similarly, formative assessment strategies should not include any elements that would prevent some students from showing where they are relative to goals, such as the use of language they cannot understand or images that could be offensive to certain subgroups of students.

Erickson (2007) introduced the notion that there can be threats to the "formativity" of formative assessment (p. 189). He argued that for assessment to be formative it must be both timely and produce information that can inform teaching practice during its ongoing course. For this reason, the immediate or proximate timing of evidence is a key component of formative assessment validity. Moreover, and in addition, for formative assessment to be valid it must also yield tractable insights: insights into students' current learning status that are sufficiently tractable to be used in subsequent pedagogical moves (Heritage, 2010).

Messick (1989) viewed validity as an "integrated evaluative judgment of the degree to which empirical evidence and theoretical rationales support the adequacy and appropriateness of the inferences and actions based on test scores and other modes of assessment" (p. 13). The preceding discussion centered on the rationale for the inferences drawn from evidence gathered in formative assessment. In what follows, the focus is on the actions that are taken based on evidence. Cronbach (1988) developed a functional perspective on the validity argument in terms of whether the actions result in appropriate consequences for individuals and institutions. This issue was taken up in Messick's (1994) discussion of the interplay between evidence and social consequences in validity argument: Because action resulting from the use of formative assessment evidence is intended to result in benefits to student learning, consequences represent an important component of the validity argument. Indeed, Stobart (2006) referred to the arguments made by Wiliam and Black (1996) that formative assessment is validated primarily in terms of its consequences; Black and Wiliam (2005) suggested that even if assessments are formative in intention they may not be so in practice if they do not generate further learning. In a later paper, Stobart (2008) went further, suggesting that if learning does not improve as a result of formative assessment, then the issue of validity should be addressed in terms of an investigation of why the assessment and its use were not successful.

Frederiksen and Collins (1989) argued that assessment has systematic validity if it encourages behaviors on the part of teachers and students that promote the learning of valuable skills and knowledge and conclude that encouraging deep approaches to learning is one aspect that can be explored in considering consequences of assessment use. In a related conceptualization of validity that placed particular emphasis on the importance of social consequences, Crooks, Kane, and Cohen (1996) identified "pedagogical decisions" as an important factor in the validity of formative assessment, noting that two students who had performed similarly on a task might benefit from differential pedagogical responses and encouragement based on their personal preferences and needs.

More recently, Crooks (2011), taking a broader conception of validity in formative assessment, identified a number of considerations that arise from the inclusion of student agents in the gathering and use of evidence (which is discussed later in this chapter). These considerations range from committed, motivated participants (teachers and students) on the one hand through the issue of trust so that students feel able to admit the difficulties and uncertainties they are having and includes the notion of teacher insights into the difficulties students are having.

Reliability

Shepard (2001) has argued that reliability is less critical for CA because errors in instructional decisions can be rectified quickly through gathering more evidence of learning (see also Chapter 7 of this volume for more on reliability in CA). Reliability in relation to instructional decisions has been conceived as "sufficiency of information" (Smith, 2003, p. 30). Teachers have to be confident that they have enough information about the student's learning to make a reasonable judgment about the current status of that learning. In the classroom context, a crucial point with regard to reliability has to do with whether the teacher will get the same result again—whether it is characteristic of the student's level of performance or is alternatively a chance outcome or "fluke" and, correlatively, whether the performance seems to change in response to trivial alterations in the classroom situation or only in response to big/important changes? From a teacher's perspective, the sufficiency issue could be reframed as follows: "How do I know this isn't a fluke or artifact of what is going on today—including whether the student may have gotten up on the wrong side of the bed. Do I know enough to rule that out, or do I have to try again another, brighter day?" (Fritz Mosher, personal communication, October 2011). This conception of reliability argues for multiple sources of evidence before a teacher makes an instructional decision. The wider the range of information and the more frequently the information is collected, the more accurately both specific and generalized learning can be inferred (Griffin, Murray, Care, Thomas, & Perri, 2010).

In practical terms, this might mean that before making a judgment about learning a teacher has evidence from a student representation, from observations of the student constructing the representation, and from probing questions about the nature of the representation—why the student constructed it in a particular way and what it means. The more this kind of evidence can be gathered in the context of learning tasks, and so not to take time away from instruction, the more the number of learning events as assessment tasks can be increased to improve the reliability of the information gathered (Linn & Baker, 1996).

Anastasi (1990) contributed a further dimension to the consideration of reliability: the users' responsibilities in interpreting evidence. She suggested that information needs to be considered in relation to a "backward and forward reference" to past and prospective aspects of the students' experience and performance (p. 482). Thus, assessment evidence is not considered as a single instance but rather within the contextualized knowledge a teacher has of all the dimensions of student learning, both antecedent and anticipated.

A final consideration with regard to the judgments that teachers make based on the evidence is the accuracy of their judgment. In other words, how precise is their interpretation of the evidence they have gathered? To this end, Harlen and James (1997) suggested that teachers need to be given opportunities to develop both the expertise and the confidence to make and use reliable judgments about student learning that they can use as the basis for instructional decisions. It may be that, as Erickson (2007) argued, teachers' clinical judgment is undervalued because of the dominance of summative testing as a tool of evaluation and the associated disprivileging of teachers' discretionary authority relative to professional psychometrics. This is clearly a situation that will need to be readdressed if teachers are to be supported in developing the skills needed for reliable judgments related to students' ongoing learning.

If we return to the chapter's opening scenario, we can see the validity and reliability arguments manifest in the interaction between Ms. Alonzo and her student Edgar. Ms. Alonzo's assessment of Edgar takes place in the context of an authentic task—his ongoing writing of a persuasive argument—and attends to deepening his learning about argumentation and extending his writing skills. She is assessing his current status within a developmental trajectory: She wishes to see how he has incorporated her feedback about use of evidence sources, and she has an eye on his future learning, a more developed piece of writing. Her evidence-gathering strategy is aligned to the learning goal, is an appropriate representation of the construct—well-organized persuasive writing that included arguments, counterarguments, and evidence—and permits Edgar to show how he has used evidence sources as well as to reveal some problems in the organization of his writing. The strategy has relevance to Edgar because it centers directly on the development of his persuasive argument, of which he already has ownership because it is on a topic of importance to him: saving the environment. Ms. Alonzo uses several evidence-gathering strategies: Edgar's writing, his documented sources of evidence, and his responses to questions she asks. From this range of evidence, she draws inferences about his learning and determines his next step is to improve his organization and provides feedback accordingly. The value of her interventions is only enhanced by the fact that she has seen what he has done before and will see what he does next—and again and again.

Using the Evidence

Teachers' use of evidence, particularly in terms of feedback and instructional correctives, is dealt with in greater length by Wiliam (see Chapter 12 of this volume) and the chapter by Black (see Chapter 10 of this volume), which discusses some of the issues involved in integrative summative and formative functions of assessment. Nonetheless, some essential points about gathering and using evidence are in order. The first point is that observations and evidence are in fact distinct. Essentially *observations* do not become *evidence* unless there is a structure, such as teachers' understandings of learning progressions, into which the observations can be fitted in order to support interpretation. Second, even before the evidence is generated, teachers will need to have the knowledge and skills to formulate or select evidence-gathering tasks that reveal the nature of student understanding or skills. Third, evidence gathering is a planned process, and assessment tasks "must have a place in the 'rhythm' of the instruction, built-in as part of the constant interaction that is essential to ensure that the teacher and the learner are mutually and closely involved to a common purpose" (Black, Wilson, & Yao 2011, p. 98). This means teachers should determine in advance at what points in the lesson they will need evidence to maintain the forward momentum of learning. Of course, this does not preclude actionable assessment opportunities arising spontaneously in the lesson but rather that evidence gathering should not be left to chance.

In contrast to standardized assessment, formative assessment practice rests mainly with teachers. In addition to determining how and when to gather evidence, they also determine whom to assess. For example, in Ms. Alonzo's lesson, she had decided on the specific students she wanted to assess in individual one-on-one interactions. In other instances, teachers may use an evidence-gathering strategy that engages the whole class or groups simultaneously.

Once the evidence is gathered, teachers will have to interpret the student response against their knowledge of what a fully formed understanding or skill would look like in the context of the task. Finally, teachers will need to translate that interpretation into an appropriate pedagogical move to take the student's understanding to a more advanced state. Sometimes pedagogical decisions need to be made on the fly, so the interpretation of evidence and the subsequent pedagogical move may need to be made in situ rather than at a later point of reflection. These kinds of interventions require flexibility and the nimble use of evidence and insight in real time. Without the attempt to support or influence new learning from the evidence, the label *formative assessment* cannot be applied to the process of evidence gathering. Instead, the term *dangling data* (Sadler 1989, p. 121) is more apt.

Gathering Evidence in the Context of Learning Progressions

The evolution of the standards movement in the United States has led to the development of academic standards that define what students should know and be able to do in the core academic subjects at each grade level. These standards are often complemented by performance standards that describe what level of performance is needed for students to be classified as advanced, proficient, basic, below basic, or by some other performance level (Phelan, 2003). While these standards may provide better descriptions of what students needed to learn than teachers had before such standards existed—and can serve as guideposts for assessment for summative purposes (e.g., annual tests that provide information about student performance in relation to them)—they fall short of what is needed to engage successfully in the practice of formative assessment. Instead, Black and Wiliam (1998) suggested the following:

> [We need to] develop methods to interpret and respond to the results in a formative way. One requirement for such an approach is a sound model of students' progression in the learning of the subject matter, so that the criteria that guide the formative strategy can be matched to students' trajectories of learning. (p. 37)

To gather evidence that can be used to keep learning moving forward, teachers need to understand the pathways leading to increasing expertise in a domain. Learning progressions can provide such a pathway by specifying the steps that students are likely to traverse with adequate instruction along the way to achieving landmark goals in the development of expertise. In the section that follows, we will consider current views of what learning progressions are, how they can be developed and validated, and how they can be used to support evidence gathering (see also Chapters 2 and 6 of this volume).

Defining Learning Progressions

Alonzo and Steedle (2008) noted that the *learning progression* label has operationalized in a variety of ways. These include the following:

- "Learning progressions are tied to big ideas, the central concepts and principles of a discipline. At the core of learning progressions is enactment or use of big ideas in practices, namely, the learning performances." (Duschl, 2006, p. 116)
- "Learning progressions . . . describe successively more sophisticated ways of reasoning within a content domain that follow one another as students learn: They lay out in words and examples what it means to move toward more expert understanding." (Smith, Wiser, Anderson, & Krajcik, 2006, p. 2)
- "Learning progressions are successively more sophisticated ways of thinking about a topic that can be used as templates for the development of curricular and assessment products." (Songer, Kelcey, & Gotwals, 2009, pp. 2–3)
- Vertical maps that provide "a description of skills understanding and knowledge in the sequence in which they typically develop: a picture of what it means to 'improve' in an area of learning." (Masters & Forster, 1996, p. 1)
- Learning progressions "assume a progression of cognitive states that move from simple to complex; while not linear, the progression is not random and can be sequenced and ordered as 'expected tendencies' or 'likely probabilities'" (Confrey & Maloney, 2010).

Although there are variations in these descriptions of progressions, they share two common views: (1) progressions lay out in successive steps, increasingly more sophisticated understandings of core concepts and principles in a domain and (2) progressions describe typical development over an extended period of time. They reflect the idea that early in their schooling students develop concepts and skills at a rudimentary level, and over time, their understanding of the concepts and their acquisition of skills are developed in progressively more sophisticated forms. Progressions provide a connected map of the steps along the way to increasing expertise. These steps, which are components of a connected and coherent landscape of learning in a domain, can serve as guides for instruction and act as a touchstone for gathering evidence for formative purposes.

Developing and Validating Learning Progressions

Elsewhere, I have suggested that approaches to developing progressions can be loosely characterized in two ways: (1) top down and (2) bottom up (Heritage, 2008). In a top-down approach to progressions, experts in a domain (e.g., physicists, mathematicians, or historians) construct a progression based on their domain knowledge and research on how children's learning unfolds in the domain. They conduct empirical research to determine the extent to which their hypothesis holds up in reality and make refinements based on the resulting data (e.g., Black et al., 2011; Confrey & Maloney, 2010; Songer et al., 2009). Ideally, learning progressions should be developed from a strong research base about the structure of knowledge in a discipline and the kind of thinking that is involved and be subject to a rigorous validation process. However, given that a strong research base does not exist in many domains, a bottom-up approach has to fill the gap until it such a research base materializes.

A bottom-up approach involves teachers and curriculum content experts in developing a progression that is based on their experience of teaching children. Their sources for developing the progression are curricula, their views of what is best taught when, and their knowledge of children's learning. In this context, validation involves working together, testing each other's hypotheses against their professional knowledge, making refinements accordingly, trying out the progression to see if their model actually predicts what happens in terms of student learning, and then making further refinements from this experience (e.g., Riley, 2009). A by-product of teacher-developed progressions is an associated deepening of teacher knowledge about learning in a domain, which can have considerable payoff for evidence gathering and use. In the end, top-down and bottom-up approaches to learning progressions are not, and should not be, mutually exclusive. Indeed, creating institutional contexts for self-conscious and systematic integration of the two approaches will be an important development in the next phase of formative assessment practice.

Learning Progressions and Evidence Gathering

Whatever the source of progressions, if they are to be used to support effective evidence gathering they must reflect clear goal steps to index how learning progresses in a domain. Lest these goal level steps be interpreted as a laundry list of objectives, it should be stressed that progressions document connected steps on the way to increasing expertise in relation to core principles, ideas, or concepts and skills in a domain. They are not discrete objectives. However, even the most well-developed and rigorously validated progressions will not be able to support evidence gathering and formative pedagogical responses if the steps are specified at too gross a level. Herein lies the problem with *summative* standards—even those that suggest elements of progression (e.g., the Common Core State Standards show more of a connected pathway than other standards) are still much too gross-grained for formative assessment. In relation to progressions, the Goldilocks maxim applies: Progressions to support evidence gathering should be at the *just right* level of detail so that they enable teachers to map evidence-gathering strategies onto the progression, to interpret the student responses against the background of the progression, and to make appropriate pedagogical moves that will advance learning.

Black et al. (2011) provided a useful description of how progressions work in the ongoing gathering and use of evidence:

> Success overall then depends *first* on the power of the opening questions or activities to provoke rich discussion, but then *secondly* on the capacity of the teacher to listen, to interpret the responses, and to steer the discussion with a light but firm touch, by summarizing, or by highlighting contradictions, or by asking further questions. To do this skillfully and productively, one essential ingredient that the teacher needs is to have in mind an underlying scheme of *progression* in the topic; such a scheme will guide the ways in which students' contributions are summarized and highlighted in the teacher's interventions and the orientation which the teacher may provide by further suggestions, summaries, questions and other activities. (p. 74)

In the absence of clear progressions, despite their best intentions, teachers may not have the necessary resources to guide their evidence-gathering strategies in planned and systematic ways at the level required for formative assessment, nor be able to recognize the import of spontaneous evidence when it arises. In a worst-case scenario, the evidence gathering will be random, ad hoc, and unconnected to a picture of the progressive development of understanding and skills. The best-case scenario of systematic, planned approaches to gathering evidence that can be used to consistently move learning forward is enabled by progressions.

As an endnote to this section on progressions, it is important to recognize that while progressions offer an important resource to teachers to gather evidence and to use it, teachers' experience and knowledge about responses to the evidence that will benefit students' learning are an essential adjunct to the value of progressions. Without due attention to the skills needed by teachers to formulate the next step (Heritage, Kim, Vendlinski, & Herman, 2009), progressions, while necessary, may not be sufficient to facilitate emergent learning.

The Role of the Student in Gathering Evidence

The practice of formative assessment is a joint enterprise in which teachers and students play distinctive, yet complementary, roles in the common purpose of furthering learning. With respect to evidence gathering, students also play an active role in generating internal feedback on their learning through self-assessment (Black & Wiliam, 1998; see also Chapter 21 of this volume). Self-assessment has two aspects: (1) self-appraisal and (2) self-management (Paris & Winograd, 1990). Self-appraisal refers to students' ability to evaluate their learning status and learning strategies through a range of self-monitoring processes (Hattie & Timperley, 2007). Self-management is the students' capacity to take appropriate action to sustain ongoing learning. Engaging in self-assessment contributes to the development of learners' self-regulation processes when they activate and focus their cognitions and behaviors on attaining their specific, personal goals (Zimmerman & Schunk, 2011). The employment of these processes has been associated with achievement differences among students (Schunk, 1981, 1984; Zimmerman & Martinez-Pons, 1986, 1988). Of most relevance to this chapter is that students who are proactive self-regulators monitor and assess their progress toward goals, using the internal feedback they generate to determine when to seek assistance, when to persist with an approach, and when to adjust their learning strategies (Zimmerman & Schunk, 2011).

That students are involved in self-monitoring does not mean that teachers abrogate their responsibilities with regard to evidence gathering. The point here is that both teachers and students generate evidence that they use in reciprocally supportive ways to progress learning. For this to be an effective process, teachers create the conditions in which they and their students develop a shared understanding of their respective roles. For example, students must come to understand that it is the teachers' role to elicit evidence about their learning status and that it is their responsibility to provide responses that help the teacher gain insights they can use to advance learning. In turn, the students understand that it is their role to generate internal evidence during learning and that the teachers' responsibility is to help them reflect on the evidence and build a repertoire of strategies through feedback that supports them to become self-regulated learners. Without this kind of partnership in relation to gathering evidence, students will remain overwhelmingly dependent on the teacher as the primary resource for learning and lack the capacity to become self-sustained lifelong learners (Heritage, 2010).

Sadler (1989) stressed that for students to be able to monitor their own learning they must come to hold a conception of quality similar to the teacher's and that developing this conception depends on the following:

> (i) possessing a concept of the *standard* (or goal, or reference level) being aimed for; (ii) comparing the *actual* (or current) *level of performance* with the standard; and (iii) engaging in appropriate *action* which leads to some closure of the gap. (p. 121)

He also made clear that self-monitoring does not happen automatically but has to be learned. To enable successful self-assessment then, the teacher needs to help students understand the goal being aimed for, understand the criteria for meeting the goal, assist them to develop the skills to make judgments about their learning in relation to the goal, and establish a repertoire of operational strategies to direct their own learning. Teachers must also ensure that there is time for students to systematically engage in reflection. Teacher Sharon Pernisi—when summing up the changes she had made to preserve time for this—noted, "I used to do more but now I do less. Now I work hard to save time for student reflection rather than filling every minute with activity." (Heritage, 2010, p. 4) This should be the goal of all teachers who are concerned with self-assessment.

In terms of supports for student self-assessment, Allal (2010) suggested that self-assessment tools can be either embedded in the curriculum materials or devised by the teacher. Allal (2010) also advised that self-regulation can be enhanced when teachers assist students to analyze the purposes and uses of the tools and to consider the results of their use. Going further, she proposed teachers can also assist students in developing their own self-assessment tools, for example, checklists, and internal questions to ask oneself when engaging in a task. Hattie and Timperley (2007) suggested that teacher feedback can be focused at the self-regulation level to assist students' evaluative skills. Such feedback draws students' attention to the criteria needed to achieve the goal, puts the responsibility squarely on the student to evaluate the evidence in relation to the criteria, and provides a model for how students can assess their learning.

Another approach to supporting students in the development of self-assessment skills is providing opportunities for peer-assessment and feedback (see Chapter 22 of this volume). These kinds of peer processes help students develop the skills to make judgments about evidence in relation to specific goals, which can then be transferred when students engage in and regulate their own work (Boud, Cohen, & Sampson, 1999; Gibbs, 1999). A by-product of student peer assessment for teachers can be the opportunity to gain insights into how well students understand the learning goal and the quality criteria for meeting the goal.

Ultimately, self-assessment by students is neither an optional extra nor a luxury but has to be seen as essential to the practice of formative assessment (Black & Wiliam, 1998). Students have to be active in their own learning, since no one else can learn for them, and unless they are able to evaluate their own strengths and weaknesses and how they might deal with them, they are unlikely to make progress (Harlen & James, 1996).

Conclusion

This chapter has presented some basic dimensions of evidence gathering in the context of formative assessment practice. It has suggested that evidence gathering is a fundamental means to provide information on students' current levels of learning and to guide what teachers and students do to ensure progress. There is no single way to collect evidence for formative purposes. Evidence-gathering strategies can range from planned interactions between teacher and student, to examinations of student work products, and to technology-assisted affordances. However, evidence gathering will only be effective if a number of criteria obtain. First, teachers must have the knowledge to formulate tasks and occasions that provide insights into student thinking. Second, evidence in and of itself is of little use if it is not used to "form" new learning. To this end, the evidence elicited needs to provide a present-to-future perspective so that teachers and students are able to use it for the purpose of extending current learning within and through the students' ZPD. Third, current standards do not provide teachers or students with a clear pathway of learning that can guide both instruction and assessment. While research-based and empirically validated learning progressions that could fulfill this role are emerging, they are presently insufficient to guide evidence gathering. Teachers will have to find ways to develop these progressions using available expertise. Fourth, while concepts of validity and reliability have not been extensively applied to evidence in the context of formative assessment, whatever strategies are employed must be of sufficient quality to provide actionable evidence that will have a strong probability of improving learning. Finally, evidence gathering is not solely within the purview of teachers. In formative assessment practice, students and teachers are collaborators in the common purpose of progressing learning. Without student involvement in the process, students remain passive recipients of teacher judgment and action. Students, too, must be engaged in reflective practices through the process of self-assessment, which in turn, supports the development of self-regulation, a characteristic of effective learning. Only in this way will they come to understand what it means to learn how to learn and be equipped with the skills they need for success beyond school.

References

Allal, L. (2010). Assessment and the regulation of learning. In P. Peterson, E. Baker, & B. McGraw (Eds.), *International encyclopedia of education* (Vol. 3, pp. 348–352). Oxford, UK: Elsevier.

Alonzo, A. C., & Steedle, J. T. (2008). Developing and assessing a force and motion learning progression. *Science Education, 93,* 389–421.

Anastasi, S. (1990). Ability testing in the 1980's and beyond: Some major trends. *Public Personnel Management, 18,* 471–485.

Applebee, A. N., Langer, J. A., Nystrand, M., & Gamoran, A. (2003). Discussion-based approaches to developing understanding: Classroom instruction and student performance in middle and high school English. *American Educational Research Journal, 40,* 685–730.

Bailey, A., & Heritage, M. (2008). *Formative assessment for literacy, grades K–6.* Thousand Oaks, CA: Corwin Press.

Bell, B., & Cowie, B. (2000). The characteristics of formative assessment in science education. *Science Education, 85,* 536–553.

Black, P., Harrison, C., Lee, C., Marshall, B., & Wiliam, D. (2003). *Assessment for learning: Putting it into practice.* Buckingham, UK: Open University Press.

Black, P., & Wiliam, D. (1998). Assessment and classroom learning. *Assessment in Education: Principles Policy and Practice, 5,* 7–73.

Black, P., & Wiliam, D. (2005). Changing teaching through formative assessment: Research and practice. In *Formative assessment: Improving learning in secondary classrooms* (pp. 223–240). Centre for Educational Research and Innovation (CERI). Paris: Organisation for Economic Cooperation and Development.

Black, P., & Wiliam, D. (2009). Developing the theory of formative assessment. *Educational Assessment, Evaluation, and Accountability, 21,* 5–31.

Black, P., Wilson, M., & Yao, S. Y. (2011). Road maps for learning: A guide to the navigation of learning progressions. *Measurement: Interdisciplinary Research and Perspectives, 9*(2–3), 71–122.

Boud, D., Cohen, R., & Sampson, J. (1999). Peer learning and assessment. *Assessment and Evaluation in Higher Education, 24,* 413–425.

Brookhart, S. M. (2003). Developing measurement theory for classroom assessment purposes and uses. *Educational Measurement: Issues and Practice, 22*(4), 5–12.

Carpenter, T. P., Fennema, E. T., & Franke, M. L. (1996). Cognitively Guided Instruction: A knowledge base for reform in primary mathematics instruction. *The Elementary School Journal, 97,* 3–20.

Carpenter, T. P., Fennema, E., Peterson, P. L., & Carey, D. A. (1988). Teachers' pedagogical content knowledge in mathematics. *Journal for Research in Mathematics Education, 19,* 385–401.

Cazden, C. B. (1988). *Classroom discourse: The language of teaching and learning.* Portsmouth, NH: Heinemann.

Chaiklin, S. (2003). The zone of proximal development in Vygotsky's analysis of learning and instruction. In A. Kozulin, B. Gindis, V. S. Ageyev, & S. M. Miller (Eds.), *Vygotsky's educational theory in cultural context* (pp. 39–64). Cambridge, UK: Cambridge University Press.

Chin, C. (2007). Teacher questioning in science classrooms: Approaches that stimulate productive thinking. *Journal of Research in Science Teaching, 44,* 815–843.

Cohen, N., Hall, T. E., Vue, G., & Ganley, P. (2011). Becoming strategic readers: Three cases using formative assessment, UDL, and technology to support struggling middle school readers. In P. Noyce & D. T. Hickey (Eds.), *New frontiers in formative assessment* (pp. 129–140). Cambridge, MA: Harvard Education Press.

Confrey, J., & Maloney, A. (2010, October). *Building formative assessments around learning trajectories as situated in the CCSS.* Paper presented at fall meeting of the State Collaborative on Assessment and Student Standards: Formative Assessment for Students and Teachers, Savannah, GA.

Cook, K., Seeley, C., & Chaput, L. (2011). Customizing and capture:Online assessment tools for secondary mathematics. In P. Noyce & D. T. Hickey (Eds.), *New frontiers in formative assessment* (pp. 69–85). Cambridge, MA: Harvard Education Press.

Cronbach, L. (1988). Internal consistency of tests: Analyses old and new. *Psychometrika, 53,* 63–70.

Crooks, T. (2011). Assessment for learning in the accountability era: New Zealand. *Studies in Educational Evaluation, 37,* 71–77.

Crooks, T., Kane, M., & Cohen, A. (1996). Threats to the valid use of assessments. *Assessment in Education, 3,* 265–285.

Dewey, J. (1928). Progressive education and the science of education. *Progressive Education, V,* 197–201.

Dierick, S., & Dochy, F. (2001). New lines in edumetrics: New forms of assessment lead to new assessment criteria. *Studies in Educational Evaluation, 27,* 307–329.

Duschl, R. A. (2006). Learning progressions as babushkas. *Measurement, 14*(1 & 2), 116–119.

Duschl, R. D., & Gitomer, D. H. (1997). Strategies and challenges to change the focus of assessment and instruction in science classrooms. *Educational Assessment, 4*(1), 37–73.

Erickson, F. (2007). Some thoughts on "proximal" formative assessment of student learning. *Yearbook of the National Society for the Study of Education, 106,* 186–216.

Frederiksen, J., & Collins, A. (1989). A systems approach to educational testing. *Educational Researcher, 18*(9), 27–32.

Gibbs, G. (1999). Using assessment strategically to change the way students learn. In S. Brown & A. Glasner (Eds.), *Assessment matters in higher education: Choosing and using diverse approaches* (pp. 41–53). Buckingham, UK: Open University Press.

Ginsburg, H. P. (2009). The challenge of formative assessment in mathematics education: Children's minds, teachers' minds. *Human Development, 52*(2), 109–128.

Griffin, P. (2007). The comfort of competence and the uncertainty of assessment. *Studies in Educational Evaluation, 33,* 87–99.

Griffin, P., Murray, L., Care, E., Thomas, A., & Perri, P. (2010). Developmental assessment: Lifting literacy through professional learning teams. *Assessment in Education: Principles, Policy & Practice, 17,* 383–397.

Harlen, W. (2007). Formative classroom assessment in science and mathematics. In J. H. McMillan (Ed.), *Formative classroom assessment: Theory into practice* (pp. 116–135). New York: Teachers College Press.

Harlen, W., & James, M. (1996). *Creating a positive impact of assessment on learning.* Paper presented at the annual meeting of the American Educational Research Association, New York.

Harlen, W., & James, M. (1997). Assessment and learning: Differences and relationships between formative and summative assessment. *Assessment in Education: Principles, Policy & Practice,* 4(3), 365–379.

Hattie, J., & Timperley, H. (2007). The power of feedback. *Review of Educational Research, 77,* 81–112.

Heffernan, N., Militello, M., Heffernan, C., & Decoteu, M. (in press). Effective and meaningful use of educational technology: Three cases from the classroom. In C. Dede & J. Richards (Eds.), *Digital teaching platforms.* New York: Teachers College Press.

Heritage, M. (2008). *Learning progressions: Supporting instruction and formative assessment.* Washington, DC: Council of Chief State School Officers. Retrieved from www.ccsso.org/content/PDFs/FAST Learning Progressions.pdf

Heritage, M. (2010). *Formative assessment: Making it happen in the classroom.* Thousand Oaks, CA: Corwin Press.

Heritage, M., & Heritage, J. (2011). *Teacher questioning: the epicenter of instruction and assessment.* Paper presented at the annual meeting of the American Educational Research Association, New Orleans, LA.

Heritage, M., Kim, J., Vendlinski, T., & Herman, J. (2009). From evidence to action: A seamless process in formative assessment? *Educational Measurement: Issues and Practice, 28*(3), 24–31.

Heritage, M. & Niemi, D. (2006). Toward a framework for using student mathematical representations as formative assessments [Special issue]. *Educational Assessment, 11*(3 & 4), 265–284. Mahwah, NJ: Lawrence Erlbaum.

Herman, J. L., Heritage, M., & Goldschmidt, P. (2011). *Developing and selecting assessments of student growth for use in teacher evaluation systems.* Los Angeles: University of California, National Center for Research on Evaluation, Standards, and Student Testing.

Jordan, B., & Putz, P. (2004). Assessment as practice: Notes on measurement, tests, and targets. *Human Organization, 63,* 346–358.

Kane, M. T. (1992). An argument-based approach to validity. *Psychological Bulletin, 112,* 527–535.

Kouba, V., & Franklin, K. (1995). Multiplication and division: Sense making and meaning. *Teaching Children Mathematics, 1,* 574–577.

Kozulin, A., Gindis, B., Ageyev, V. S., & Miller, S. M. (2003). Introduction: Sociocultural theory and education: Students, teachers, and knowledge. In A. Kozulin, B. Gindis, V. S. Ageyev, & S. M. Miller (Eds.), *Vygotsky's educational theory in cultural context* (pp. 1–11). Cambridge, UK: Cambridge University Press.

Kuhn, T. S. (1962). *The structure of scientific revolutions.* Cambridge: University of Chicago Press.

Lesh, R., Hoover, M., Hole, B., Kelly, A. E., & Post, T. (2003). Principles for developing thought revealing activities for students and teachers. In R. Lesh & H. M. Doerr (Eds.), *Beyond constructivism: Models and modeling perspectives on mathematics problem solving, learning, and teaching.* Mahwah, NJ: Lawrence Erlbaum.

Linn, R. L., & Baker, E. L. (1996). Can performance-based student assessment be psychometrically sound? In J. B. Baron & D. P. Wolf (Eds.), *Performance-based assessment—challenges and possibilities: 95th yearbook of the National Society for the Study of Education part 1* (Vol. 95(1), pp. 84–103). Chicago: National Society for the Study of Education.

Masters, G., & Forster, M. (1996). *Progress maps: Assessment resource kit.* Melbourne, Victoria, Australia: The Australian Council for Educational Research.

Mehan, H. (1979). *Learning lessons.* Cambridge, MA: Harvard University Press.

Messick, S. (1989). Validity. In R. L. Linn (Ed.), *Educational measurement* (3rd ed., pp. 13–103). New York: American Council on Education and Macmillan.

Messick, S. (1994). The interplay of evidence and consequences in the validation of performance assessments. *Educational Researcher, 23*(2), 13–23.

Newman, L. S. (1990). International and unintentional memory in young children: Remembering vs. playing. *Journal of Experimental Child Psychology, 50,* 243–258.

Nystrand, M., & Gamoran, A. (1991). Instructional discourse, student engagement, and literature achievement. *Research in the Teaching of English, 25,* 261–290.

Paris, S. G., & Winograd, P. W. (1990). How metacognition can promote academic learning and instruction. In B. J. Jones & L. Idol (Eds.), *Dimensions of thinking and cognitive instruction* (pp. 15–51). Hillsdale, NJ: Lawrence Erlbaum.

Pellegrino, J. W., & Glaser, R. (1982). Analyzing aptitudes for learning: Inductive reasoning. In R. Glaser (Ed.), *Advances in instructional psychology* (Vol. 2, pp. 269–345). Hillsdale, NJ: Lawrence Erlbaum.

Phelan, R. (2003). *Assessment, curriculum, and instruction: Overview of the standards movement.* Retrieved from www.sonoma.edu/users/p/phelan/423/standards.html

Ploegh, K., Tillema, H., & Segers, M. R. S. (2009). In search of quality criteria in peer assessment practices. *Studies in Educational Evaluation, 35,* 102–109.

Poppers, A. E. (2011). Identifying craft moves: Close observation of elementary students writing. In P. Noyce & D. T. Hickey (Eds.), *New frontiers in formative assessment* (pp. 89–107). Cambridge, MA: Harvard Education Press.

Ramaprasad, A. (1983). On the definition of feedback. *Behavioral Science, 28*(1), 4–13.

Riley, J. (2009, June). *Developing learning progressions.* Paper presented at the Council of Chief State School Officers National Conference on Student Assessment, Detroit, MI.

Rowe, M. B. (1974). Wait time and rewards as instructional variables, their influence in language, logic, and fate control: Part II, rewards. *Journal of Research in Science Teaching, 11,* 291–308.

Ruiz-Primo, M. A. (2011). Informal formative assessment: The role of instructional dialogues in assessing students for science learning. Special issue in assessment *for* learning, *Studies of Educational Evaluation, 37*(1), 15–24.

Ruiz-Primo, M. A., & Furtak, E. M. (2004, April). *Informal assessment of students' understanding of scientific inquiry.* Paper presented at the annual meeting of the American Educational Research Association, San Diego, CA.

Ruiz-Primo, M. A., & Furtak, E. M. (2006). Informal formative assessment and scientific inquiry: Exploring teachers' practices and student learning. *Educational Assessment, 11* (3 & 4), 237–263.

Ruiz-Primo, M. A., & Furtak, E. M. (2007). Exploring teachers' informal formative assessment practices and students' understanding in the context of scientific inquiry. *Journal of Educational Research in Science Teaching, 44*(1), 57–84.

Sadler, D. R. (1989). Formative assessment and the design of instructional strategies. *Instructional Science, 18,* 119–144.

Schunk, D. H. (1981). Modeling and attributional effects on children's achievement: A self-efficacy analysis. *Journal of Educational Psychology, 73,* 93–105.

Schunk, D. H. (1984). Self-efficacy perspective on achievement behavior. *Educational Psychologist, 19,* 48–58.

Shavelson, R. J., Young, D. B., Ayala, C. C., Brandon, P. R., Furtak, E. M., Ruiz-Primo, M. A. et al. (2008). On the impact of curriculum-embedded formative assessment on learning: A collaboration between curriculum and assessment developers. *Applied Measurement in Education, 21*(4), 295–314.

Shepard, L. A. (2001). The role of classroom assessment in teaching and learning. In V. Richardson (Ed.), *Handbook of research on teaching* (4th ed., pp. 1066–1101). Washington, DC: American Educational Research Association.

Sinclair, J. M., & Coulthard, R. M. (1975). *Towards an analysis of discourse: The English used by teachers and pupils.* London: Oxford University Press.

Smith, C., Wiser, M., Anderson, C., & Krajcik, J. (2006). Implications of research on children's learning for standards and assessment: A proposed learning progression for matter and atomic-molecular theory. *Measurement, 14,* 1–98.

Smith, J. (2003). Reconsidering reliability in classroom assessment and grading. *Educational Measurement: Issues and Practice, 22*(4), 26–33.

Songer, N. B., Kelcey, B., & Gotwals, A. W. (2009). How and when does complex reasoning occur? Empirically driven development of a learning progression focused on complex reasoning about biodiversity. *Journal for Research in Science Teaching, 46,* 610–631.

Stobart, G. (2006). The validity of formative assessment. In J. Gardner (Ed.), *Assessment and learning* (pp. 133–146). Thousand Oaks, CA: Sage.

Stobart, G. (2008, November). *Validity in formative assessment.* Paper presented at the Ninth Annual AEA-Europe Conference, Hisar, Bulgaria.

Torrance, H., & Pryor, J. (1998). *Investigating formative assessment.* Buckingham, UK: Open University Press.

Torrance, H., & Pryor, J. (2001). Developing formative assessment in the classroom: Using action research to explore and modify theory. *British Educational Research Journal, 27,* 615–631.

Vygotsky, L. S. (1935). *Umstvennoie razvitie detei v protsesse obuchenia.* Moscow, Russia: Gosudarstvennoie Uchebno-pedagogicheskoie Izdatel 'stvo.

Vygotsky, L. S. (1986). *Thought and language* (Rev. ed.) (A. Kozulin, Ed.). Cambridge, MA: MIT Press.

Webb, M. E., & Jones, J. (2009). Exploring tensions in developing assessment for learning. *Assessment in Education: Principles, Policy & Practice, 16,* 165–184.

Wiliam, D. (2011). *Embedded formative assessment.* Bloomington, IN: Solution Tree Press.

Wiliam, D., & Black, P. J. (1996). Meanings and consequences: A basis for distinguishing formative and summative functions of assessment? *British Educational Research Journal, 22*(5), 537–548.

Zimmerman, B., & Schunk, D. (2011). *Handbook of self-regulation of learning and performance.* New York: Routledge.

Zimmerman, B. J., & Martinez-Pons, M. (1986). Development of a structured interview for assessing student use of self-regulated learning strategies. *American Educational Research Journal, 23,* 614–628.

Zimmerman, B. J., & Martinez-Pons, M. (1988). Construct validation of a strategy model of student self-regulated learning. *Journal of Educational Psychology, 80,* 284–290.

12

Feedback and Instructional Correctives

Dylan Wiliam

For much of the 20th century, the dominant philosophy of psychology was associationism. Learning was the result of associating particular stimuli with particular responses, and failure to learn was therefore, presumably, the result of insufficiently strong associations between stimuli and responses, indicating the need for reinforcement of those associations. While such a view of learning may explain reasonably well some aspects of human learning, such as the learning of multiplication facts, many aspects of learning, particularly in science and mathematics, were difficult to explain within such a philosophy.

When children between the ages of 4 and 7 are asked, "What causes the wind?" a common answer is "trees." This seems unlikely to be the result of poor elementary science instruction, nor the result of misremembering what they have been taught about wind as a result of inadequate reinforcement. Rather, as Driver (1983) has suggested, it is more likely the result of attempts by children to literally "make sense" of the world around them.

The idea that what learners learn is the result of an active, constructive process rather than a passive and receptive one is—at least in many aspects of learning—central to understanding the importance of feedback in learning. If learning is a predictable process, which most of the time proceeds as planned, then instructional correctives should be needed rarely; most of the time, students will learn what they have been taught, but occasionally, they will not. In this view, feedback and instructional correctives are pathological aspects of instruction, needed only when things go wrong. However, if learning is an unpredictable process, then feedback and instructional correctives are central to learning; without them, little effective instruction can take place.

This chapter reviews the history of the understanding of the role of feedback in educational settings. It begins with the origins of the idea of feedback in engineering and traces the development through the work on programmed instruction in the 1960s; the work on mastery learning in the 1970s; and how, beginning in the 1980s, feedback came to be regarded as one (admittedly central) element in the regulation of learning processes.

The Origins of Feedback

Feedback in Engineering System Theory

Norbert Wiener and his colleagues were engaged, during the 1940s, in trying to develop automatic rangefinders for anti-aircraft guns. The challenge of course is that to be effective, the gun needs to fire to where the aircraft will be when the shell arrives, rather than where it is when the gun is fired (much like Wayne Gretzky, the ice hockey player, was said to skate not to where the puck was but to where it was going to be). Wiener and his colleagues realized that automating the process required a system that allowed the effects of actions taken within the system to be evaluated and that evaluation should in turn impact future actions (Wiener, 1948). Wiener pointed out that there were two possible kinds of patterns of behavior or "loops"—positive feedback loops, in which the effect of the evaluation was to push the system further in the direction in which it was already going, and negative feedback loops, in which the evaluation resulted in action to oppose the existing tendency. In an engineering system, positive feedback loops are rarely useful, since they reinforce the existing tendency in the system. For example, the term *feedback* is often used in audio engineering to describe a positive feedback loop in which sound from a loudspeaker is fed back into a microphone, which is then further amplified, which in turn increases the sound received by the microphone, increasing the sound coming out of the loudspeaker further still. In general, positive feedback loops lead either to explosive increase (as in the case of the amplification system) or collapse. For example, when a species has a plentiful food supply and no predators, there is exponential growth. On the other hand, in an economic depression, people stop spending money, which then triggers job losses, leading to further loss of confidence and further job losses. The term *positive* to describe such systems is not therefore a value judgment (quite the reverse in fact) but merely describes the relative alignment of the existing tendency of the system and the impetus provided by the feedback.

Negative feedback loops, on the other hand, are extremely useful in systems engineering because they tend to produce stability. Population growth with limited food supply provides one example of a negative feedback loop. As the population of a species increases, competition for food becomes more intense, and so this slows down the rate of increase of the population. Depending on the initial conditions, the population then either approaches, or oscillates with decreasing amplitude around, a steady state, known as the carrying capacity of the environment (Levins, 1966, p. 427). The room thermostat that is used to control a heating system also uses a negative feedback loop. A desired temperature is set on the thermostat, and when the temperature drops below the desired temperature, the thermostat turns on the heating system until the temperature measured by the thermostat exceeds the desired value. Both the examples of population growth with limited food supply and the room thermostat are examples of negative feedback loops because the effect of the feedback is to oppose the existing tendency in the system. In the case of population growth, the existing tendency of the system is for the population to increase, and the effect of the feedback is to slow the rate of increase. In the case of the room thermostat, the tendency of the system is for the temperature in the room to drop, and the effect of the feedback is to heat the room.

In engineering, therefore, the meaning of the terms *positive feedback* and *negative feedback* are quite clear. When these terms are used in education, however, they are rarely used with such precision.

Feedback in Psychology and Education

First, the term *feedback* is often used for any information provided to a learner. For example, Kulhavy (1977) defined feedback as "any of the numerous procedures that are used to tell a learner if an instructional response is right or wrong" (p. 211). This definition was intended to include a range of forms of information provided to learners including informing learners whether their responses were correct or not (often called knowledge of response, knowledge of results, or just KR), providing the correct response (knowledge of correct response, knowledge of correct results, or just KCR) and telling the learners what they needed to improve (correctional review). However, Kulhavy (1977) went on to say the following:

> If we are willing to treat feedback as a unitary variable, we can then speak of its form or composition as ranging along a continuum from the simplest "Yes-No" format to the presentation of substantial corrective or remedial information that may extend the response content, or even add new material to it. Hence, as one advances along the continuum, feedback complexity increases until the process itself takes on the form of new instruction, rather than informing the student solely about correctness. (p. 212)

Kulhavy (1977) noted that much of the early research into the effects of feedback was rooted in the behaviorist paradigm and strongly tied to the programmed learning movement. The idea was that telling students that their answers were correct *reinforced* the cognitive processes through which the student had gone in order to arrive at the correct response and thus would increase the likelihood that the correct response would be given to a similar prompt in the future. B. F. Skinner (1968) summed it up as follows:

> The machine, like any private tutor, reinforces the student for every correct response, using the immediate feedback not only to shape behavior most effectively but to maintain it in strength in a manner which the layman would describe as "holding the student's interest." (p. 39)

Responding to this, Kulhavy (1977) suggested the following:

> With such confident statements available, it is no surprise that scholars have worked overtime to fit the round peg of feedback into the square hole of reinforcement. Unfortunately, this stoic faith in feedback-as-reinforcement has all too often led researchers to overlook or disregard alternate explanations for their data. One does not have to look far for articles that devote themselves to explaining why their data failed to meet operant expectations rather than to trying to make sense out of what they found. (p. 213)

In fact, as Kulhavy pointed out, a number of studies conducted during the 1960s and 1970s provided evidence that was inconsistent with the assumption that feedback functioned best as reinforcement. First, if the primary effect of feedback was as reinforcement, telling students that they were on the right track should have a greater impact on learning (positive reinforcement) than telling them that they were on the wrong track (negative reinforcement). However, a number of studies showed that positive reinforcements were no better—and sometimes were less effective—than negative reinforcements (e.g., Anderson, Kulhavy, & Andre, 1971). Second, and perhaps more decisive in rejecting the idea of feedback as reinforcement, was the delay-retention effect—the finding that delaying feedback for a day or more seemed to have little impact on the effectiveness of the feedback (Kulhavy, 1977). In fact, Kulhavy found that ensuring that feedback is not given until after the learner has attempted the task—what Kulhavy termed *reducing presearch availability*—consistently enhanced the effects of feedback (Kulhavy, 1977).

Reviews of Research on Feedback in Education

Early Meta-Analyses

Rather than the best evidence approach used by Kulhavy, reviews of research on feedback by Schimmel (1983) and by Kulik and Kulik (1988) investigated the impact of feedback on achievement through a meta-analysis, in which quantitative outcomes are combined to provide an overall indication of the size of the effect of the variable under study, most commonly as a measure of the standardized effect size such as Cohen's *d* (Cohen, 1988).

The review by Schimmel (1983) began by identifying 72 studies of the effects of feedback in computerized or programmed learning, and selected 15 studies that satisfied five inclusion criteria:

- The study involved adults learning meaningful verbal material.
- The study involved questioning about the material with immediate feedback following responses.
- The responses to all criterion test items were measured.
- Participants took an immediate posttest.
- The study included a control group given no feedback.

Schimmel (1983) found that immediate feedback was significantly more effective than no feedback, but Schimmel noted that this might have been due to variations in the prose used in the outcome measures, specifically in terms of concreteness, vividness, and vocabulary. He also found that the amount of information given as feedback was unrelated to its effectiveness.

The review by Kulik and Kulik (1988) also looked at verbal learning and began by identifying a total of 288 potential studies that had included *KR* as a key phrase, in either the title, the description, the abstract, or key words provided by the authors. From these, they selected 53 studies where the full text of the study was available, where the outcomes were reported quantitatively, and which included a contrast between a group given feedback immediately and another group in which feedback was delayed. In the 11 studies that Kulik and Kulik termed *applied studies*—studies where the outcome measure was composed of items related to but different from those used for instruction—delaying feedback significantly reduced student learning (d = 0.28). In the eight studies termed *experiments on the acquisition of test content*—where outcome measures were the same as those used in instruction—delaying feedback significantly *increased* student learning (d = 0.36). In the 27 studies focusing on "list learning," the findings were much more mixed. In 10 of the studies, immediate feedback was significantly better, and in four of the studies, delayed feedback was significantly better, while in the remaining 13, the differences were nonsignificant (6 favoring immediate feedback and 7 favoring delayed feedback). However, in summarizing their analysis, Kulik and Kulik (1988) noted that the studies that found superior results for delayed feedback were mostly in well-controlled laboratory settings, while studies of classroom learning tended to support the advantages of immediate feedback, and they concluded that "to delay feedback was to hinder learning" (p. 94).

Three years later, Bangert-Drowns, Kulik, Kulik, and Morgan (1991) published a meta-analysis of the effects of feedback in what they termed "test-like events typical of classroom education and of text-based and technology-based instruction" (p. 216). Their review concentrated on intentional, mediated feedback (i.e., the feedback was intended to increase learning, and it was mediated, for example by language, rather than being provided directly in an interpersonal reaction) and utilized a five-stage model of the feedback process:

1. The learner's initial state is characterized by degree of interest, kind of goal orientation, degree of self-efficacy, and degree of prior relevant knowledge.
2. Search and retrieval strategies are activated by a question.
3. The learner responds to the question (and has some degree of certainty about the response and thus beliefs about what the feedback will indicate).
4. The learner evaluates the response in light of information given in feedback.
5. The learner adjusts relevant knowledge, self-efficacy, interests, or goals as a result of the response evaluation. These adjusted states, with subsequent experiences, determine the next initial state.

Their review generated four main sets of findings:

> *Feedback type*: *Right/wrong* feedback (what Kulhavy termed *KR*) produced no benefit, or providing correct answers (KCR), provided an intermediate effect (d = 0.22), while "repeating until correct," or providing an explanation, provided large effects (d = 0.53 in each case).
>
> *Presearch availability*: Where presearch availability was not controlled, feedback did not improve learning, but where there was control for presearch availability, feedback had a substantial positive impact on learning (d = 0.46).
>
> *Study design*: In studies where students were given a pretest, feedback had no effect whereas in the studies that relied only on posttests there was a significant impact (d = 0.40), presumably because the pretest acted as a form of advance organizer.
>
> *Type of instruction*: Feedback in programmed instruction and in computer-assisted instruction had no statistically significant impact on learning, but in text comprehension exercises and test performance, feedback had a significant positive effect (d = 0.48 and 0.60 respectively).

Bangert-Drowns et al. (1991) concluded that the crucial factor was that feedback was received in a way that they described as *mindful*, drawing on the work of Salomon and Globerson (1987):

> When mindful responses are activated, the individual can be expected to withhold or inhibit the evocation of a first, salient response . . ., to examine and elaborate situational cues and underlying meanings that are relevant to the task to be accomplished . . ., to generate or define alternative strategies . . ., to gather information necessary for the choices to be made, to examine outcomes . . ., to draw new connections and construct new structures and abstractions made by reflective type processes. . . . (p. 625)

In their concluding discussion, Bangert-Drowns et al. (1991) illustrated how their five-stage model can be used to understand the findings of their meta-analysis:

1. *Initial state*: The student's knowledge, interests, goals, and self-efficacy are influenced by their experience of the instruction. Pretests may lead to student overconfidence so they learn less from feedback.
2. *Activation of search and retrieval strategies*: Feedback given before students construct their responses preempts any mindful reflection that might otherwise have been prompted.
3. *Construction of response.*
4. *Evaluation of response in light of feedback*: Learners use feedback to check the correctness of their answers, particularly in situations that lack other instructional supports.
5. *Adjustment of learner's cognitive state*: Ideally, feedback signals errors to students, and the provision of the correct response initiates a mindful process of knowledge development.

In a review aimed at a professional rather than academic audience, Dempster (1991) confirmed many of the findings of the reviews previously discussed and in particular that regular, frequent well-spaced testing and review improved both short-term and long-term retention. However, he also cautioned that these findings might be more applicable to content knowledge and low-level skills than higher-order thinking—a view that was endorsed by Elshout-Mohr (1994) in a review translated from Dutch. Elshout-Mohr's review included many studies not available in English and suggested that KCR was more effective for simple tasks, but learning more complex material requires the development of new capabilities, which Elshout-Mohr suggested would require a more dialogic approach to feedback and would also require the learner to become more active in managing the process.

The Need for Broader Theories

The reviews previously reported focused primarily on the effects of feedback on schools, further education, and universities in more or less formal settings. In a more comprehensive review, Kluger and DeNisi (1996) sought to synthesize the results of feedback in workplaces as well as in schools and higher education. They defined a feedback intervention as "actions taken by (an) external agent(s) to provide information regarding some aspect(s) of one's task performance" (Kluger & DeNisi, 1996, p. 255). They began their review process by searching the Social Science Citation Index, PsycINFO, and National Technical Information Services for all studies that included either *KR* or *feedback*, as one key word and *performance* as another. This process identified more than 2,500 papers and 500 technical reports. They then selected for inclusion only those studies that met the following five criteria:

1. The study had to contain at least one group of participants that received just feedback (as opposed to, for example, feedback plus goal setting).
2. The performance of those receiving feedback had to be compared with a group not receiving feedback (thus excluding those that compared performance of the same group before and after feedback).
3. Each study had to measure performance rather than just describe it.
4. Each study had to include at least 10 participants (due to the large sampling errors involved in studies with small number of participants).
5. The description of the study had to contain sufficient detail to allow a standardized effect size to be computed.

Only 131 (i.e., less than 5%) of the original 3,000 identified studies satisfied all five criteria. From these studies, Kluger and DeNisi (1996) were able to calculate 607 effect sizes on based on 12,652 participants (with a total of 23,663 observations). Weighting the effect sizes in proportion to the size of the sample generated a mean effect of 0.41 standard deviations, which Kluger and DeNisi (1996) concluded indicated that feedback interventions "had a moderate positive impact on performance" (p. 258). However, in 50 out of the 131 studies, feedback had a deleterious impact on performance. They investigated the idea that these negative effects were somehow artifacts of their approach but after several analyses concluded that the negative effects were real.

Kluger and DeNisi (1996) therefore investigated whether there were any systematic differences between the studies that could account for the large variability in the effect sizes found (the variance in the effect sizes was 0.97). Drawing on a range of theoretical resources, they investigated whether any theoretically relevant aspects of the studies might account for the variation in effect sizes. They concluded that feedback interventions could trigger improvements in performance of the order of one standard deviation in situations where the feedback indicates a gap between current and desired performance on a familiar task and does not draw attention to features beyond the task (e.g., by focusing on the self). However, they pointed out that even if feedback had a positive impact on learning, this might be deleterious in the long run. Where feedback increases performance through an increase in motivation to complete a particular task, feedback may need to be continuous to maintain motivation. Even where the feedback cues attention to task learning, this may be of a shallow sort. Their final comment was that feedback research should focus on the kinds of responses that feedback interventions cued in learners, rather than on the general question of whether feedback improves performance.

One review of research on the effects of feedback that did exactly that was conducted by Butler and Winne (1995). Their review started from the assumption that "Self-regulated learning (SRL) is a pivot on which students' achievement turns" and that "feedback is inherent in and a prime determinant of the processes that constitute SRL" (p. 245). Building on the reviews of the effects that were previously discussed and others, Butler and Winne (1995) proposed five functions that feedback can serve in supporting learning:

> First, when students' conceptual understandings or beliefs are consistent with instructional objectives, feedback can confirm that condition. Second, if students lack information . . . , feedback can help students add information, thereby elaborating and enriching prior knowledge. Third, where elements of prior knowledge are incorrect or prior beliefs are inappropriate, feedback can provide information to replace or overwrite those propositions. Fourth, if students' understandings are basically correct, they still may need to tune those for between understandings, example, by discriminating concepts . . . or by specifying conditions for applying learned rules. . . . Fifth, if students hold false theories that are incompatible with new material to be learned, they may need to completely restructure schemata with which information in the domain is represented. (p. 265)

Most of the studies of feedback that were previously discussed involved students of school age (i.e., up to the age of 18). A review undertaken by Jeffrey Nyquist (2003) looked instead at learners in further and higher education. From an initial sample of approximately 300 studies, he identified 86 that satisfied the following criteria:

1. The study had to involve an experimental manipulation of a characteristic relevant to feedback.
2. Participants had to be college-aged learners.
3. The study had to involve measures of academic performance, reported in sufficient detail for a standardized effect size to be calculated.

The details provided in the studies allowed 185 effect sizes (on a total of 12,920 individuals) to be calculated, the average value of which was 0.40 standard deviations—almost exactly the same as that found by Kluger and DeNisi (1996). Making a number of standard adjustments to the effect size (e.g., reducing extreme values to ±2 standard deviations, adjusting for the upward bias of small sample sizes, and weighting each effect size by the inverse of its associated sampling variance) reduced this mean effect to 0.35 (SE = 0.17). However, like Kluger and DeNisi, Nyquist (2003) found that the range of effects was large, and 24 of the 185 computed effect sizes were negative. In order to attempt to account for these differences in the size of effect, Nyquist developed a typology of different kinds of feedback interventions.

In order to do this, he first characterized the studies in terms of eight conceptual factors:

1. *Feedback type*: KR; KCR, KCR plus explanation (KCR+e), KCR plus activity (KCR+a)
2. *Mode of delivery*: Oral, written
3. *Clarity of objective*: No clarity, low clarity, medium clarity, high clarity
4. *Pedagogy*: No instruction, programmed instruction, lecture-based instruction, criterion-based instruction
5. *Task complexity*: Very low, low, medium, high, very high

6. *Metacognition*: None, low, high
7. *Knowledge type*: All declarative, mostly declarative, mostly procedural, all procedural
8. *Domain structure*: More well-structured, less well-structured

He then allocated each of the studies to one of five categories:

1. *Weaker feedback only*: Studies in which students were given only the knowledge of their own score or grade (i.e., KR)
2. *Feedback only*: Studies in which students were given their own score or grade, together with either clear goals to work toward or feedback on the correct answers to the questions they attempted (KCR)
3. *Weak formative assessment*: Studies in which students were given information about the correct results, together with some explanation (KCR+e) or those with KCR where, in addition, at least three of the seven other factors were at the highest possible values
4. *Moderate formative assessment*: Studies in which students were given information about the correct results together with some explanation (where none of the other seven factors were at the highest or second highest values) or information about correct results plus a specific activity (where at least four of the other factors were at their lowest or second lowest values)
5. *Strong formative assessment*: Studies in which students were given information about the correct results together with some explanation (where each of the other seven factors were at the highest or second highest values) or information about correct results plus a specific activity (with no more than four of the other factors at their lowest or second lowest values).

The average standardized effect size for each type of intervention is shown in Table 12.1 (note that the table contains corrected values that differ from those in the original thesis [J. B. Nyquist, personal communication, May 7, 2007]).

These results underscore the key conclusions of Bangert-Drowns et al. (1991) that were previously discussed. Simply informing students of their results produces small benefits, but when the feedback provides explanations or—even better—specific activities for reducing the gap between the current and desired states, substantial increases in learning are possible. These broad conclusions were endorsed by two more recent reviews of feedback in instructional settings by Shute (2008) and Hattie and Timperley (2007).

Shute's (2008) review was undertaken as part of a broader research program on the development of intelligent tutoring systems. Her initial search, which focused on search terms such as feedback, formative feedback, formative assessment, instruction, learning, computer-assisted/based, tutor, learning, and performance, located over 170 publications of potential relevance. Further focusing on topical relevance, experimental design, and meta-analytic procedures, she identified 141 publications relevant to the review (103 journal articles, 24 books and book chapters, 10 conference proceedings, and four research reports). Her broad findings were consistent with earlier research. First, as Kluger and DeNisi (1996) had noted, there was no simple answer to the question, "What feedback works?"—differences in instructional contexts and in the characteristics of tasks and students mediated the effects of feedback to a significant degree. Second, the quantitative estimates for the effects of feedback that Shute reported were typically in the range 0.40 to 0.80, as found in

Category	*Number of Studies*	*Average Effect Size*
Weaker feedback only	31	0.14
Feedback only	48	0.36
Weak formative assessment	49	0.26
Moderate formative assessment	41	0.39
Strong formative assessment	16	0.56

Table 12.1 Effect Sizes for Different Kinds of Formative Assessment

previous studies. Third, to be effective, feedback should not focus on the learner but on the task at hand, providing guidance on how to improve rather than just on whether the responses were correct or not, and feedback should be detailed enough to provide a *scaffold* for the student to improve but not so detailed as to remove the need for students to think for themselves (in other words, feedback should encourage mindfulness). Fourth, she confirmed that the optimal timing of feedback depended on the kinds of learning being undertaken. She suggested that immediate feedback tended to be more helpful for procedural learning, or in the case of tasks well beyond the learner's initial capability, while delayed feedback tended to be more effective for tasks well within the learner's capability, or where transfer to other contexts was a priority.

The review by Hattie and Timperley (2007) was based on an extraordinary research program in which Hattie and his colleagues sought to synthesize a large body of research findings on "what works" in education. Analyzing over 500 meta-analyses of influences on student achievement, which between them synthesized 450,000 effect sizes from 180,000 studies involving over 20 million participants, Hattie (1999) found that 74 of the meta-analyses (involving 7,000 studies and 13,370 effect sizes) specifically mentioned feedback. Synthesizing the results of these studies yielded an average effect size for feedback interventions of 0.95 standard deviations (Hattie & Timperley, 2007), but as earlier reviews such as that by Kluger and DeNisi (1996) had found, there was considerable variability in the effect sizes across the individual studies.

To examine possible moderators of feedback effects, Hattie and Timperley (2007) built on the definition of feedback proposed by Ramaprasad (1983) as being designed to reduce discrepancies between current understandings of performance and a desired goal. Drawing on the work of Deci and Ryan (1994) and Kluger and DeNisi (1996), they proposed a model in which a learner can reduce the discrepancy between current and desired performance either by changing efforts to reach the goal (for example, by employing more effective strategies or by increasing effort) or by abandoning, lowering, or making less specific the goals they have set for themselves. For their part, teachers can "close the gap" by changing the difficulty or the specificity of the goals or by providing more support, by giving help, or providing more structure.

Hattie and Timperley (2007) further suggested that feedback is designed to answer three questions: (1) Where am I going? (2) How am I going? (3) Where next? Moreover, answers to each of the questions can operate at four levels: (1) feedback about the task, (2) feedback about the processing of the task, (3) feedback about self-regulation, and (4) feedback about the self as a person.

On the basis of the studies under review, they found that feedback about the self as a person was the least effective form of feedback (echoing earlier findings on the effects of ego-involving feedback) and that feedback about self-regulation and feedback about the processing of the task "are powerful in terms of deep processing and mastery of tasks" (Hattie & Timperley, 2007, pp. 90–91) while feedback about the task is powerful when the feedback is used either to improve strategy processing, or for enhancing self-regulation.

In reaching their conclusions about the effects of feedback, Hattie and Timperley (2007) also noted that the conditions necessary for feedback to be optimally effective were not commonly found in practice. This suggests that feedback effects cannot be understood without also taking into account the context in which the feedback is provided, which is the focus of the next section.

Feedback and Classroom Assessment

Early Reviews

Toward the end of the 1980s, three major reviews of the effects of classroom assessment (CA) were published (Crooks, 1988; Fuchs & Fuchs, 1986; Natriello, 1987). While these three studies had a broader focus than the meta-analysis carried out by Bangert-Drowns et al. (1991), it is nonetheless rather surprising that none of these three studies were cited by Bangert-Drowns et al. (1991) and indicates some of the challenges of synthesizing research in the field. Indeed, as Black and Wiliam (1998a) pointed out, while the studies by Natriello and Crooks included 91 and 241 references respectively, only 9 were common to both (and neither included the review by Fuchs & Fuchs [1986]).

Fuchs and Fuchs (1986) examined the effects of what they termed *formative evaluation* with short feedback cycles (i.e., between two and five times each week) on the achievement of students with mild or moderate learning difficulties (MLD). They found that feedback had significant impact on student learning (d = 0.70). When they looked at moderators of effects, they found that the effects were slightly smaller for students without learning disabilities (d = 0.63) although this may have been caused by the increased variation in the population under study (with a more variable population, the denominator in the effect size calculation would be increased, leading to a smaller effect size).

Significantly, where teachers decided ahead of data collection how they would analyze the data and what decisions they would take, the effects were more than twice as large when compared with studies in which follow-up actions were left to the judgment of individual teachers (d = 0.92 and 0.42, respectively). Also, where teachers tracked the performance of individual students by producing graphs, effects were almost three times larger (d = 0.70) than in those where this was not done (d = 0.26).

The following year, Natriello (1987) reviewed the impact of evaluation processes on students. To focus the broad scope of the review, he developed a conceptual framework with eight components and considered, within each of the eight components, the effects of those aspects that might be altered or varied. The eight components of the conceptual framework were as follows:

1. Establishing the purpose of the evaluation
2. Assigning tasks to students
3. Setting criteria for student performance
4. Settings standards for student performance
5. Sampling information on student performance
6. Appraising student performance
7. Providing feedback to student performers
8. Monitoring outcomes of the evaluation of students

Natriello's (1987) conclusion was that the studies he reviewed were limited by a lack of theorization that made it impossible to properly compare and contrast studies. In particular, by focusing on current practice, the studies tended merely to confirm the problems of the status quo rather than indicating how assessment practices could be improved. Moreover, many of the studies considered only one or two aspects of an assessment process that was, in reality, multifaceted and served multiple purposes, and this further limited the conclusions that could be drawn. For example, attempts to improve the way an assessment served one function might have a deleterious impact on the ability of the assessment to serve other functions for which it was used. His broad finding was that little could be concluded beyond the idea that assessments are likely to be more effective at doing the things they were designed to do than those they were not.

Around the same time, a third review that was undertaken by Terry Crooks (1988) had a focus in between the broad focus of Natriello's (1987) review and the narrow studies of specific feedback interventions and sought to understand the impact of classroom evaluation practices on students. Crooks' review included traditional teacher-devised tests and quizzes, more informal assessments such as adjunct questions in instructional texts, and oral questioning by teachers in class. Crooks (1988) concluded, "Too much emphasis has been placed on the grading function of evaluation and too little on its role in assisting students to learn" (p. 468). Not only did testing take time away from other more useful instructional activities but it was, in many cases, actually counterproductive, since testing often caused a range of problems such as reducing intrinsic motivation, increasing debilitating evaluation anxiety, encouraging learners to make ability attributions for success and failure that undermined effort, lowering self-efficacy for learning in weaker students, reducing the use and effectiveness of feedback to improve learning, and engendering poorer social relationships among students.

Later Reviews

Ten years later, Black and Wiliam (1998a) published a review of studies on the effects of CA designed to update the earlier reviews by Natriello (1987) and Crooks (1988). Mindful of the limitations of computerized searches—not least because of the lack of agreed keywords to describe the field—they relied on manual searches of each issue of 76 of the most relevant journals, and this process identified 681 publications of potential interest, 250 of which were selected for inclusion in their review. The first section of their review presented a number of "examples in evidence"—brief descriptions of eight studies that illustrated central themes in the relationship between CA and learning. Subsequent sections dealt with assessment by teachers, the student perspective, the teacher's role, the role of assessment in learning systems, a theoretical account of the role of feedback, and a final section on the prospects for the theory and practice of formative assessment.

Because of the variety of relevant studies, Black and Wiliam (1998a) rejected the idea of a meta-analysis (although their study is frequently described as such) and instead concentrated on attempting a narrative synthesis of the field and did not produce an overall quantitative estimate of the effects of CA. However, in a publication designed to draw out for practitioners and policy makers the implication of what they had found, Black and Wiliam (1998b) estimated that attention to CA could produce increases in achievement of the order of 0.4 to 0.7 standard deviations, which they described as "larger than most of those found for educational interventions" (p. 141).

They concluded their review with the following:

> despite the existence of some marginal and even negative, results, the range of conditions and contexts under which studies have shown that gains can be achieved must indicate that the principles that underlie achievement of substantial improvements in learning are robust. Significant gains can be achieved by many different routes, and initiatives here are not likely to fail through neglect of delicate and subtle features. (Black & Wiliam, 1998a, p. 62)

They also emphasized the importance of this final point:

> This last point is very important because there does not emerge, from this present review, any one optimum model on which such a policy might be based. What does emerge is a set of guiding principles, with the general caveat that the changes in classroom practice that are needed are central rather than marginal, and have to be incorporated by each teacher into his or her individual practice in his or her own way. . . . That is to say, reform in this dimension will inevitably take a long time, and need continuing support from both practitioners and researchers. (Black & Wiliam, 1998a, p. 62)

A more recent review of research by Brookhart (2004) examined 41 empirical studies of CA in K–12 education and concluded that the practice of CA occurs at the intersection of three teaching functions: (1) instruction, (2) classroom management, and (3) assessment, but that many of the studies reviewed came from a single disciplinary perspective (often psychology) or had no clear theoretical foundation at all. A few of the studies, however, combined two or more practical or theoretical perspectives, and where this was the case "the resulting picture of classroom assessment was richer and more multidimensional" (p. 454).

Between 2002 and 2004, the Organisation for Economic Cooperation and Development (OECD) undertook a review of CA practices in lower-secondary schools in the following countries: Australia, Canada, Denmark, England, Finland, Italy, New Zealand, and Scotland. As well as case studies of schools in the eight systems included in the review, the report of the project (Looney, 2005) also contained reviews of the research on CA published only in French (Allal & Lopez, 2005) and German (Köller, 2005).

Allal and Lopez (2005) reported that the most important finding of the review of over 100 studies published in French over the past 30 years is the idea that studies of assessment practices in French speaking classrooms have utilized an "enlarged conception of formative assessment" (p. 245). Allal and Lopez (2005) suggested that the notion of feedback within the Anglophone research tradition can be summarized as "feedback + correction," while in Francophone countries, the focus has been on the regulation of learning processes, which Allal and Lopez summarized as "feedback + adaptation" (p. 245).

Allal and Lopez (2005) identified four major developments in the conception of CA in the French language literature. The first, which they termed *focus on instrumentation*, emphasized the development of assessment tools such as banks of diagnostic items and adaptive testing systems. The second (*search for theoretical frameworks*) engaged in a "search for theories that can offer conceptual orientation for conducting assessment" (Allal & Lopez, 2005, p. 249). The third (*studies of existing assessment practices in their contexts*) took further the work on theoretical frameworks by exploring their relevance for understanding assessment processes in classrooms. Most recently, the fourth (*development of active student involvement in assessment*) has examined students assessing themselves and each other and the ways in which assessments can be jointly constructed by students and teachers.

Although it is not straightforward to evaluate the extent to which the French language literature has had a direct impact in the Anglophone community, there is little doubt that approaches to the understanding of CA process in the English-speaking world have certainly broadened in recent years (Brookhart, 2007), and some have explicitly adopted the idea of CA as being concerned with the regulation of learning processes (Wiliam, 2007).

Brookhart (2007) in her review of the literature on what she termed *formative classroom assessment* charted the development of the conception of formative assessment as a series of nested formulations:

- Formative assessment provides information about the learning process.
- Formative assessment provides information about the learning process that teachers can use for instructional decisions.
- Formative assessment provides information about the learning process that teachers can use for instructional decisions and students can use in improving their performance.
- Formative assessment provides information about the learning process that teachers can use for instructional decisions and students can use in improving their performance, which motivates students.

While this very general formulation calls for the kinds of broader conceptual framing that has been common in the French language literature, there appears to have been little cross-fertilization between the French language and English language research. Allal and Lopez (2005) concluded that "studies of practice are episodic and dispersed in different settings, which makes it difficult to identify patterns or trends. In summary, the theoretical promise of French language work on formative assessment is in need of considerably more empirical grounding" (p. 256). In turn, one might add that the English language research on feedback is in need of considerably better theoretical grounding.

In conducting a review of research on CA in the German language, Köller (2005) began with online searches but, like Black and Wiliam (1998a), also scrutinized all issues from 1980 to 2003 of the six German language research journals most relevant to the field. He noted that although academic journals reported many developments related to CA, few of the studies reported the impact of such practices on student outcomes. However, there were a number of studies that confirmed findings in the Anglophone literature. In particular, Köller reported the work of Meyer who established that praise can sometimes impede learning, while criticism or even blame can be helpful at times. Köller also highlighted the importance of the reference norms used by teachers. Rheinberg and others (see, for example, Rheinberg, 1980) have shown that students learn less when taught by teachers who judge their performance against others in the class (a *social* reference norm) than when taught by teachers who compare a student's performance with the previous performance of the same student (an individual reference norm).

Recently, two important critiques of the research on classroom formative assessment have appeared, one by Bennett (2011) and the other by Kingston and Nash (2011). Both draw attention to the fact that the effect sizes indicated by Black and Wiliam (1998b) are speculative rather than being grounded in firm evidence, although neither critique investigates the limitations of using effect sizes in educational research (see Wiliam, 2010, for a brief review). Both conclude with the traditional researcher's lament that "more research is needed." More research would certainly be useful in clarifying exactly how the research on feedback can best be used in real settings. However, there are a number of studies that have indicated that attention to CA processes along the lines indicated by research on feedback reviewed in this chapter can lead to increased student achievement even on externally mandated standardized tests (Clymer & Wiliam, 2006/2007; Wiliam, Lee, Harrison, & Black, 2004).

Summary of Research on Feedback

H. L. Mencken once wrote, "There is always a well-known solution to every human problem—neat, plausible, and wrong" (Mencken, 1920,

p. 158). Perhaps the most surprising thing about the research on feedback is how complex the answer to the simple question "How much does feedback improve learning?" turned out to be. Driven by the assumptions of behaviorist learning theory, for many years it was assumed that the primary goal of feedback would be to provide reinforcement to learners, but experimental confirmation of the power of feedback for reinforcement proved elusive. Indeed, many experimental results indicated that feedback was more effective when it provided instructional correctives rather than when it merely confirmed the learner was on the right track.

To make matters more complicated, studies exploring whether immediate feedback was superior to delayed feedback were also inconclusive, with some finding delayed feedback superior and others finding greater benefits for immediate feedback. Some of the difference appeared to be accounted for by the kind of setting, however, in that studies in classroom settings seemed to find immediate feedback more successful while those in laboratories tended to show greater effects for delayed feedback.

As researchers developed better theories of how feedback operated, it became clear that feedback could have a powerful role in guiding learning. Where feedback allowed students to repeat until correct, or provided an explanation, the impact on learning was greater than when feedback merely indicated the correct answer, which in turn was more effective than simply informing learners whether their responses were correct or not. Perhaps most importantly, there was emerging evidence that the effects of feedback could not be understood without taking into account the reactions of the recipient. Specifically, when the feedback encouraged a *mindful* response by the learner, the impact of feedback was enhanced considerably.

In their review of 90 years of feedback research, Kluger and DeNisi (1996) argued that the entire venture of quantifying the effects of feedback was misguided. They suggested that even where feedback did show positive impact on learning, this might be at the expense of later learning—for example, feedback might be effective in motivating students to reach a particular goal but in such a way as to undermine intrinsic motivation and thus lead to less learning in the longer term. They proposed that research should concentrate on further developing the theory of feedback interventions:

> To establish the circumstance under which positive [feedback intervention] effects on performance are also lasting and efficient and when these effects are transient and have questionable utility. This research must focus on the processes induced by FIs and not on the general question of whether FIs improve performance—look at how little progress 90 years of attempts to answer the latter question have yielded. (Kluger & DeNisi, 1996 p. 278)

Feedback Interventions, Instructional Correctives, and the Role of the Learner

Within the limitations of space of a chapter such as this, it is impossible to do much more than scratch the surface of what a fully developed theory of feedback interventions might cover. In the remainder of this chapter, therefore, I will review briefly three themes that seem to be of particular importance to such a theory: (1) eliciting the right information, (2) providing instructional correctives, and (3) ensuring appropriate responses by learners to feedback.

Knowledge Elicitation

Vinner (1997) discussed the responses of students in Israel to the following item, taken from the Third International Mathematics and Science Study (now called the Trends in International Mathematics and Science Study, or TIMSS):

Which fraction is the largest?

a) $\frac{1}{3}$ b) $\frac{3}{1}$ c) $\frac{3}{8}$ d) $\frac{7}{10}$

This question was answered correctly by 46% of students in the participating sample. For the students who were unsuccessful, clearly some kind of instructional corrective is indicated, but what form should such instructional correction take? One response would be simply to repeat the instruction already provided, although unless the reason for the initial failure is lack of attention, such an approach is unlikely to be successful. An alternative approach is to teach the material again, but in a different way, and this may be more successful for some students. However, Vinner (1997) also revealed that 39% of those responding selected response (b). If 46% answered this item correctly, then 54% responded incorrectly. If these responses were randomly distributed across the three distractors (i.e., incorrect responses) presented in the item, then we would expect each response to be selected by 18% of the respondents. The proportion of respondents selecting (b) is therefore more than twice as great as we would expect if the errors made by students were random, which suggests that the students are not, in fact, responding randomly. In fact, an earlier item, featuring unitary fractions (fractions with a numerator of 1) had a success rate of 88%. One interpretation of this is that the students choosing (b) did so because they were focusing exclusively on the denominator of the fraction (note that the sum of 46% and 39% is close to 88%). Such a response will yield the correct answer for unitary fractions, but will not, in general, do so when fractions have numbers other than one in the numerator.

Bart, Post, Behr, & Lesh (1994) used the term *cognitive rules* to describe "any sequence of cognitive operations that produces an item response from the processing of an item stem. Cognitive rules include problem solving strategies, decision making strategies, and algorithms" (p. 1). In other words, this item is capable of distinguishing between students with a correct cognitive rule and those who are using the incorrect cognitive rule of relying on denominators.

Consider, however, if the original item had been as follows (the only change is that the denominator of (b) is now 7 rather than 4):

Which fraction is the largest?

a) $\frac{1}{3}$ b) $\frac{3}{7}$ c) $\frac{3}{8}$ d) $\frac{7}{10}$

Students taking into account only the magnitude of the denominator would choose the correct answer (and presumably, the success rate would be close to the 88% for the item involving unitary fractions). In other words, this second item is incapable of distinguishing between correct and (at least some of the) incorrect cognitive rules used by students. Note also, however, that there may be other incorrect cognitive rules that lead to the correct answer in the original version of the item, and some students could still be using an incorrect rule to get a correct answer. In general, we can never be certain even when the student answers all questions correctly that they are using a correct cognitive rule. Von Glasersfeld (1987) put it this way, in the context of interviewing:

> In short, the interviewer is constructing a *model* of the child's notions and operations. Inevitably, that model will be constructed, not out of the child's conceptual elements, but out of the conceptual elements that are the interviewer's own. It is in this context that the epistemological principle of *fit*, rather than *match* is of crucial importance. Just as cognitive organisms can never compare their conceptual organisations of experience with the structure of an independent objective reality, so the interviewer, experimenter, or teacher can never compare the model he or she has constructed of a child's conceptualisations with what actually goes on in the child's head. In the one case as in the other, the best that can be achieved is a model that remains viable within the range of available experience. (p. 13)

Heritage (see Chapter 11 of this volume) and Ruiz-Primo and Li (see Chapter 13 of this volume) discuss a range of knowledge elicitation strategies that can be used to determine the extent to which students are likely to be using appropriate cognitive rules. For the purposes of this chapter, the important point to note is that effective feedback requires that the feedback is related to what needs to be done to close the gap between the current and desired state. Feedback that simply provides information about the gap between the current and desired state could be effective if, for example, all that is needed to reach the required state is increased effort. However, such feedback is likely to be much less effective than feedback that indicates the steps needed to be taken to improve (what Nyquist [2003] referred to as "activities for gap reduction"). In other words, *feedback must be designed as part of an instructional system.* This, of course, clearly requires identifying the desired goal state, but it also requires identifying aspects of current performance that are relevant to the range of possible instructional correctives that can be deployed. Why this is so important can be seen by reference to the classic room thermostat. We can set the desired temperature to 70°F and see that the current temperature is 66°F, but if the wire from the thermostat leads to a dehumidifier, then no feedback loop is possible, since the system does not have the capability of reducing the gap between the current and desired state. Alternatively, if the desired temperature is 70°F but the only sensors in the system measure atmospheric pressure, even if the wires lead to a furnace, again no effective feedback loop is possible. While these examples may seem absurd, they provide appropriate analogies for many instructional contexts where information about the level of current achievement is given to students. The information provided to students might accurately describe the current achievement and the gap between current and desired achievement, but there is no mechanism for actually improving the learner's achievement. Alternatively, the feedback might identify some aspects of current performance but not those that are relevant to reaching the desired level of achievement.

To be effective, a feedback system must be designed with an implicit theory of action, where the information about the current state is identified only once the way in which it will increase student achievement is already determined. In other words, the identification of instructional correctives must precede the identification of appropriate feedback. This is why the separation of feedback from the consequent instructional correctives has had such unfortunate consequences. It has suggested that the two processes, the provision of feedback and the consequent instructional correctives, can be treated separately, whereas, in fact, they are not just connected but mutually constitutive. Both feedback and instructional correctives, and the knowledge-eliciting activity, are part of the feedback system. Any attempt to understand how feedback works by looking at one, or even two, of these components in isolation is likely to be unsuccessful. To compound matters even further, even when feedback is well designed it will only have any effect if it is acted upon by the learner. These two ideas—(1) instructional correctives and (2) the learner's role—are the foci of the next two sections of this chapter.

Instructional Correctives

As suggested earlier, a student's failure to learn might simply be the result of failure to hear the instruction (whether through inattention or perhaps due to auditory problems exacerbated by poor acoustics in the instructional setting) in which case repetition of the instruction might be sufficient. However, in general, it is likely that taking a different approach is likely to be more effective.

In the previous section, it was implied that instructional correctives should, ideally, be designed before evidence about student achievement is elicited because without clarity about what kinds of instructional correctives are possible it is impossible to be sure that the right evidence is elicited in the first place, and the feedback may not be able to increase performance.

There appears to be little systematic research on what kinds of instructional correctives are actually implemented in classrooms, although a number of trends are apparent. The most significant trend in this area appears to be that of response to intervention (RTI), defined by the National Center on Response to Intervention (NCRTI) (2010) at the American Institutes of Research as follows:

> Response to intervention integrates assessment and intervention within a multi-level prevention system to maximize student achievement and reduce behavior problems. With RTI, schools identify students at risk for poor learning outcomes, monitor student progress, provide evidence-based interventions and adjust the intensity and nature of those interventions depending on a student's responsiveness, and identify students with learning disabilities.

The central idea of RTI is that the progress made by students (in some cases all students and in other cases just those students identified as being at risk of not making educational progress) is monitored carefully, and where progress is deemed to be insufficient, an intervention is made. This might take the form of more intensive instruction, such as providing support in a smaller group of students, or in the event that small-group instruction is not effective, even one-to-one tutorial instructions—what Bloom (1984) adopted as the gold standard form of educational provision. Other approaches include removing students from some other instructional activities until the required level of achievement is reached. However, there appears to be little systematic evidence about what kinds of interventions are made, how they are chosen, and the extent to which they are successful.

More importantly, given the focus of this chapter, RTI seems to be based on a very limited view of feedback. In the RTI model, the elicitation of evidence is generally just a form of monitoring whether students are making the progress expected. While monitoring of student progress can identify which students are not making the expected progress, there is a disconnect between the evidence elicitation and the consequent action. All the monitoring assessment does is to identify that the original instruction was not effective and something else needs to be tried, but the evidence elicited does not indicate what kinds of alternative interventions should be tried. While this might be regarded as feedback according to some definitions (e.g., that proposed by Kulhavy [1977]), the notion of feedback is very limited. It is as if the anti-aircraft gunners were told that their attempts to hit the incoming aircraft were unsuccessful and they should try firing again but in a different direction. This may lead to more successful action but more by good fortune than by design.

Consider, as an alternative, the following item. It was designed by teachers of Spanish in Chico, California (Wiliam, 2011):

> Which of the following is the correct translation for "I give the book to him"?
>
> A. Yo lo doy el libro.
> B. Yo doy le el libro.
> C. Yo le doy el libro.
> D. Yo doy lo el libro.
> E. Yo doy el libro le.
> F. Yo doy el libro lo.

This item was designed from a thorough knowledge of two difficulties that native English speakers have with pronouns in Spanish: Which pronoun should be used, and where should it be placed? Students choosing A have chosen an incorrect pronoun, although it is placed correctly; responses B and E indicate placement errors; and responses D and F indicate both pronoun and placement errors. By careful design of the item used to elicit evidence, when students choose incorrect answers, the particular choices made by the students indicate what problems the students are having. Such items might be described as diagnostic, since they support the teacher in doing more than monitoring progress. So if a monitoring assessment indicates whether students are making progress or not, a diagnostic assessment indicates what the problem is, rather than just identifying that there is a problem. However, for the teacher, although knowing what precisely is not being learned is better than knowing that there is a problem somewhere, it would be even better if the evidence elicited indicated what kinds of instructional activities would be most likely to lead to the desired progress—in other words, that the feedback should be "instructionally tractable" (Wiliam, 2010). This, of course, merely endorses the empirical findings of Nyquist (2003) that were previously discussed. The greatest effect sizes were found when feedback indicated specific activities for reducing the gap between the current and the desired level of achievement.

The RTI framework emphasizes actions taken by teachers to promote student progress, but it is also important to acknowledge the vast and significant literature on collaborative learning—what Slavin, Hurley, and Chamberlain (2003) described as "one of the greatest success stories in the history of educational research" (p. 177). An adequate theory of feedback interventions as called for by Kluger and DeNisi (1996) would surely have to deal with the power of students to help each other learn. And, of course, such a theory would also have to account for the role of learners in acting on feedback.

The Learner's Role

Over the past 50 years, an extraordinary range of perspectives has been used to examine the issue of how learners react to feedback, including motivation (Deci & Ryan, 1994), attribution theory (Dweck, 2000), self-efficacy (Bandura 1997), self-regulated learning (SRL) (Butler & Winne, 1995), interest (Hidi & Harackiewicz, 2000), and metacognition (Hacker, Dunlosky, & Graesser, 1998). Clearly in a chapter of this length, one can do little more than scratch the surface of such a complex issue, but one theoretical approach that does seem to hold considerable promise for understanding how students make sense of, and react to, feedback is the dual pathway theory proposed by Boekaerts (1993, 2006).

Boekaerts (2006) defined SRL as "a multilevel, multicomponent process that targets affect, cognitions, and actions, as well as features of the environment for modulation in the service of one's goals" (p. 347). One interesting feature of Boekaerts's definition is that it regards SRL as *both* metacognitively governed *and* affectively charged (p. 348), whereas in the past most accounts appear to have prioritized either cognitive or motivational processes (see Wiliam, 2007 for a discussion of this point).

The assumptions of Boekaerts's (2006) dual processing (or dual pathway) theory are deceptively simple:

> It is assumed that students who are invited to participate in a learning activity use three sources of information to form a mental representation of the task-in-context and to appraise it: (1) current perceptions of the task and the physical, social, and instructional context within which it is embedded; (2) activated domain-specific knowledge and (meta)cognitive strategies related to the task; and (3) motivational beliefs, including domain-specific capacity, interest and effort beliefs. (p. 349)

As a result of the appraisal, the student activates energy and attention along one of two pathways: (1) the *growth* pathway or the (2) *well-being* pathway. Attention to the growth pathway leads the student to attempt to increase competence, while attention to the well-being pathway is designed to prevent threat, harm, or loss. Obviously feedback is intended to cue attention to the growth pathway, but it is important to note that even if feedback cues attention to the well-being pathway, this need not necessarily be counterproductive. For example, by attending to the well-being pathway, the learner may lower the cost of failure, thus changing the cost–benefit trade-off in a way that allows attention to be given to the growth pathway.

The generality of this theory allows much previous work to be brought together within a broad theoretical frame. For example, students who see ability as incremental rather than fixed (Dweck, 2000) are more likely to see the value of investing effort and so are more likely to activate attention along the growth pathway, as are those with mastery, rather than performance goals (Dweck, 2000). Students who are personally interested in a task are obviously likely to activate energy along the growth pathway. Where the student is not personally interested in a task, features of the task-in-context may nevertheless trigger situational interest (Hidi & Harackiewicz, 2000) and the circumstances of the work may lead to the students identifying with the goal (Deci & Ryan, 1994).

CONCLUSION

As has been observed several times in this chapter, the ultimate test of feedback and instructional correctives is whether they lead to long-term improvements in the capabilities of learners. While we can now say with some certainty that some kinds of feedback are likely to be more effective than others (e.g., task-involving feedback is likely to be more effective than ego-involving feedback), it is clear that a useful theory of feedback would need to be very broad, including instructional design and a much fuller understanding of learners' affective reactions in instructional settings. For now, perhaps the most that can be said is that good feedback causes thinking.

REFERENCES

Allal, L., & Lopez, L. M. (2005). Formative assessment of learning: A review of publications in French. In J. Looney (Ed.), *Formative assessment: Improving learning in secondary classrooms* (pp. 241–264). Paris: Organisation for Economic Cooperation and Development.

Anderson, R. C., Kulhavy, R. W., & Andre, T. (1971). Feedback procedures in programmed instruction. *Journal of Educational Research, 62,* 148–156.

Bandura, A. (1997). *Self-efficacy: The exercise of control.* New York: W. H. Freeman.

Bangert-Drowns, R. L., Kulik, C.-L. C., Kulik, J. A., & Morgan, M. (1991). The instructional effect of feedback in test-like events. *Review of Educational Research, 61*(2), 213–238.

Bart, W. M., Post, T., Behr, M. J., & Lesh, R. (1994). A diagnostic analysis of a proportional reasoning test item: An introduction to the properties of a semi-dense item. *Focus on Learning Problems in Mathematics, 16*(3), 1–11.

Bennett, R. E. (2011). Formative assessment: A critical review. *Assessment in Education: Principles Policy and Practice, 18*(1), 5–25.

Black, P. J., & Wiliam, D. (1998a). Assessment and classroom learning. *Assessment in Education: Principles, Policy and Practice, 5*(1), 7–74.

Black, P. J., & Wiliam, D. (1998b). Inside the black box: Raising standards through classroom assessment. *Phi Delta Kappan, 80*(2), 139–148.

Bloom, B. S. (1984). The 2-sigma problem: The search for methods of group instruction as effective as one-to-one tutoring. *Educational Researcher, 13*(6), 4–16.

Boekaerts, M. (1993). Being concerned with well being and with learning. *Educational Psychologist, 28*(2), 149–167.

Boekaerts, M. (2006). Self-regulation and effort investment. In K. A. Renninger & I. E. Sigel (Eds.), *Handbook of child psychology: Vol. 4. Child psychology in practice* (6th ed., pp. 345–377). New York: John Wiley.

Brookhart, S. M. (2004). Classroom assessment: Tensions and intersections in theory and practice. *Teachers College Record, 106*(3), 429–458.

Brookhart, S. M. (2007). Expanding views about formative classroom assessment: A review of the literature. In J. H. McMillan (Ed.), *Formative classroom assessment: Theory into practice* (pp. 43–62). New York: Teachers College Press.

Butler, D. L., & Winne, P. H. (1995). Feedback and self-regulated learning: A theoretical synthesis. *Review of Educational Research, 65*(3), 245–281.

Clymer, J. B., & Wiliam, D. (2006/2007). Improving the way we grade science. *Educational Leadership, 64*(4), 36–42.

Cohen, J. (1988). *Statistical power analysis for the behavioral sciences* (2nd ed.). Hillsdale, NJ: Lawrence Erlbaum.

Crooks, T. J. (1988). The impact of classroom evaluation practices on students. *Review of Educational Research, 58*(4), 438–481.

Deci, E. L., & Ryan, R. M. (1994). Promoting self-determined education. *Scandinavian Journal of Educational Research, 38*(1), 3–14.

Dempster, F. N. (1991). Synthesis of research on reviews and tests. *Educational Leadership, 48*(7), 71–76.

Driver, R. (1983). *The pupil as scientist?* Milton Keynes, UK: Open University Press.

Dweck, C. S. (2000). *Self-theories: Their role in motivation, personality and development.* Philadelphia: Psychology Press.

Elshout-Mohr, M. (1994). Feedback in self-instruction. *European Education, 26*(2), 58–73.

Fuchs, L. S., & Fuchs, D. (1986). Effects of systematic formative evaluation—a meta-analysis. *Exceptional Children, 53*(3), 199–208.

Hacker, D. J., Dunlosky, J., & Graesser, A. C. (Eds.). (1998). *Metacognition in educational theory and practice.* Mahwah, NJ: Lawrence Erlbaum.

Hattie, J. (1999, August 2). *Influences on student learning.* Retrieved from www.education.auckland.ac.nz/uoa/education/staff/j.hattie/papers/influences.cfm

Hattie, J., & Timperley, H. (2007). The power of feedback. *Review of Educational Research, 77*(1), 81–112.

Hidi, S., & Harackiewicz, J. M. (2000). Motivating the academically unmotivated. A critical issue for the 21st century. *Review of Educational Research, 70*(2), 151–179.

Kingston, N. M., & Nash, B. (2011). Formative assessment: A meta-analysis and a call for research. *Educational Measurement: Issues and Practice, 30*(4), 28–37.

Kluger, A. N., & DeNisi, A. (1996). The effects of feedback interventions on performance: A historical review, a meta-analysis, and a preliminary feedback intervention theory. *Psychological Bulletin, 119*(2), 254–284.

Köller, O. (2005). Formative assessment in classrooms: A review of the empirical German literature. In J. Looney (Ed.), *Formative assessment: improving learning in secondary classrooms* (pp. 265–279). Paris: Organisation for Economic Cooperation and Development.

Kulhavy, R. W. (1977). Feedback in written instruction. *Review of Educational Research, 47*(2), 211–232.

Kulik, J. A., & Kulik, C.-L. C. (1988). Timing of feedback and verbal learning. *Review of Educational Research, 58*(1), 79–97.

Levins, R. (1966). The strategy of model building in population biology. *American Scientist, 54*(4), 421–431.

Looney, J. (Ed.). (2005). *Formative assessment: Improving learning in secondary classrooms.* Paris: Organisation for Economic Cooperation and Development.

Mencken, H. L. (1920). The divine afflatus. In H. L. Mencken (Ed.), *Prejudices: second series* (Rev. ed., pp. 155–171). New York: Alfred A. Knopf.

National Center on Response to Intervention. (2010). *Glossary of RTI terms.* Retrieved from www.rti4success.org/RTIGlossary#RTI

Natriello, G. (1987). The impact of evaluation processes on students. *Educational Psychologist, 22*(2), 155–175.

Nyquist, J. B. (2003). *The benefits of reconstruing feedback as a larger system of formative assessment: A meta-analysis.* Unpublished master of science thesis, Vanderbilt University, Nashville, TN.

Ramaprasad, A. (1983). On the definition of feedback. *Behavioral Science, 28*(1), 4–13.

Rheinberg, F. (1980). *Achievement evaluation and learning motivation.* Gottingen, Germany: Hogrefe.

Salomon, G., & Globerson, T. (1987). Skill may not be enough: The role of mindfulness in learning and transfer. *International Journal of Educational Research, 11*(6), 623–637.

Schimmel, B. J. (1983, April). *A meta-analysis of feedback to learners in computerized and programmed instruction.* Paper presented at the annual meeting of the American Educational Research Association held at Montreal, Canada. (ERIC Document Reproduction Service No. 233708)

Shute, V. J. (2008). Focus on formative feedback. *Review of Educational Research, 78*(1), 153–189.

Skinner, B. F. (1968). *The technology of teaching.* New York: Appleton-Century-Crofts.

Slavin, R. E., Hurley, E. A., & Chamberlain, A. M. (2003). Cooperative learning and achievement. In W. M. Reynolds & G. J. Miller (Eds.), *Handbook of psychology: Vol. 7. Educational psychology* (pp. 177–198). Hoboken, NJ: Wiley.

Vinner, S. (1997). From intuition to inhibition—mathematics, education and other endangered species. In E. Pehkonen (Ed.), *Proceedings of the 21st Conference of the International Group for the Psychology of Mathematics Education* (Vol. 1, pp. 63–78). Lahti, Finland: University of Helsinki Lahti Research and Training Centre.

von Glasersfeld, E. (1987). Learning as a constructive activity. In C. Janvier (Ed.), *Problems of representation in the teaching and learning of mathematics* (pp. 3–17). Hillsdale, NJ: Lawrence Erlbaum.

Wiener, N. (1948). *Cybernetics, or control and communication in the animal and the machine.* New York: John Wiley.

Wiliam, D. (2007). Keeping learning on track: Classroom assessment and the regulation of learning. In F. K. Lester Jr. (Ed.), *Second handbook of mathematics teaching and learning* (pp. 1053–1098). Greenwich, CT: Information Age Publishing.

Wiliam, D. (2010). An integrative summary of the research literature and implications for a new theory of formative assessment. In H. L. Andrade & G. J. Cizek (Eds.), *Handbook of formative assessment* (pp. 18–40). New York: Routledge.

Wiliam, D. (2011). *Embedded formative assessment.* Bloomington, IN: Solution Tree.

Wiliam, D., Lee, C., Harrison, C., & Black, P. J. (2004). Teachers developing assessment for learning: Impact on student achievement. *Assessment in Education: Principles Policy and Practice, 11*(1), 49–65.

13

Examining Formative Feedback in the Classroom Context: New Research Perspectives

Maria Araceli Ruiz-Primo

Min Li

The result of decades of research on feedback and learning offers near unanimous agreement on the importance of feedback in improving student learning (e.g., Black, Harrison, Lee, Marshall, & Wiliam, 2003; Butler & Neuman, 1995; Cameron & Pierce, 1994; Hattie & Timperley, 2007; Kluger & DeNisi, 1996; Torrance & Pryor, 1998; Yeany & Miller, 1983). After reviewing 180,000 studies with over 100 variables, Hattie (1999) placed feedback among the five most powerful methods that influence student learning and the most critical mediator for many other successful methods of improving student learning. Similarly, many meta-analyses and reviews have produced encouraging effect sizes of feedback on student achievement, mainly above 0.40, and even reaching 1.13, as measured by immediately administered instruments (e.g., Azevedo & Bernard, 1995; Hattie, 1999; Yeany & Miller, 1983). An exception is the meta-analysis reported by Bangert-Drowns, Kulik, Kulik, and Morgan (1991) with an average effect size of 0.26. Despite these impressive findings, we need to recognize how little is actually understood about the characteristics and quality of studies included in earlier reviews and syntheses. For instance, how do researchers define feedback? How were these studies conducted? What are the characteristics of the tasks used in the studies? What are the methodological characteristics of the studies? What evidence of ecological validity do they provide? Further, because we primarily focus on studies with positive effects, we give insufficient attention to those that showed no impact at all or even negative effects (see Kluger & DeNisi, 1996; Shute, 2008).

The landscape of the feedback literature suggests that the knowledge base about feedback is mainly drawn from studies done in laboratories or in artificial classroom environments in which learning tasks tend to be minimally meaningful or irrelevant to learners and seldom take place over extended periods of time. Although feedback has proven to be effective in laboratory type of studies, we may be too confident in trusting any feedback strategies in the classroom. Furthermore, we are aware of many strategies and techniques suggested in books and papers, but we do not know how they have been used or adapted by teachers and students and then how they have influenced students' learning. Some of these strategies are examples of practices that have been observed in classrooms; however, to some degree, it can be said that they have not been empirically tested. An inconvenient truth that needs to be acknowledged is that we generally know much less about feedback practices in the classroom context than we would like to admit. For example, although classroom-based studies on teachers' feedback practices are not common (but see Carnell, 2000; Gipps, Brown, McCallum, & McAlister, 1995; Hargreaves, McCallum, & Gipps, 2000; Torrance & Pryor, 1998; Tunstall & Gipps, 1996), they still appear more frequently than classroom-based studies in which feedback is introduced as a treatment in the regular teaching context (but see Bower, 2005; Brosvic, Dihoff, Epstein, & Cook, 2006; Inagaki, Hatano, & Morita, 1998; Schunk, 1996; Shih & Alexander, 2000; Tudge, Winterhoff, & Hogan, 1996). Even rarer are studies that include comparative groups and studies in which feedback practices are linked to measures of students' academic learning (e.g., grades, assessment tasks, and state assessments) other than the artificial learning tasks created for the study being reported. It is widely recognized, however, that feedback practices are often reported as one of the weakest areas in teachers' classroom assessments (CAs), especially in science and mathematics (Black & Wiliam, 1998; Ruiz-Primo, Li, Ayala, & Shavelson, 2004; Ruiz-Primo & Li, 2004, 2011). Teachers may be surrounded by feedback and involved in it every day, but feedback is poorly analyzed and poorly used (Askew, 2000).

In this chapter, as a follow-up to Chapter 12, we focus on feedback practices in the classroom context, which is based on both theoretical and empirical information. To provide an overview of this area of research, we first briefly present general results from our meta-analysis applying a framework that focuses on conceptual and methodological issues. We then provide an expanded definition of feedback intended to broaden more familiar definitions described in a variety of books and papers. This section is followed by a description of a theoretical framework previously developed by Ruiz-Primo (2010) to study classroom-based feedback practices. The chapter concludes with a proposed research agenda for guiding future studies, helping to frame new questions, and suggesting methodological approaches for examining feedback practice in the classroom.

Understanding What We Know About Feedback

In this section, we try to direct the reader's attention to certain issues on research discourse related to feedback that have been historically neglected. Rather than exploring these issues in depth, we summarize the kinds of problems that we believe should be considered in future studies.

What Exactly Has Positive Effects? Defining Feedback

In contrast to the robust knowledge base about the positive impact and power of feedback, little is known about how feedback has been defined and manipulated in the studies. Moreover, literature is underdeveloped in terms of how teachers should frame feedback comments, the kind of feedback discourse that should be used, the most effective number of comments, and in what context they should be made (Nicol & Macfarlane-Dick, 2006). Some recent work has sought to tease out what generally makes some feedback effective, some ineffective, and some harmful (Brookhart, 2007; Butler & Winne, 1995; Hattie & Timperley, 2007; Kluger & DeNisi, 1996). None of this work, however, has systematically addressed the specific and nuanced characteristics of effective feedback in different disciplines such as science and mathematics education. Notably, findings about critical characteristics of effective feedback have not been consistently supported beyond commonly held beliefs. For example, although immediate and timely feedback is promoted by many researchers, some have found that immediate feedback improves learning only when the goals are related to rote memory tasks but has an opposite effect when learning goals are process driven, such as classroom activities (Kulhavy, 1977; Kulik & Kulik, 1988).

It is important, then, to reflect on how feedback has been characterized in the studies and how the studies have been clustered according to these characteristics. That is, are all the thousands of cited studies conceptually and methodologically comparable? Based on our experience with meta-analyses (e.g., Li, Ruiz-Primo, Yin, & Morozov, 2011; Ruiz-Primo, Briggs, Iverson, Talbot, & Shepard, 2011; Ruiz-Primo, Li, Yin, & Morozov, 2010), conceptually and methodologically coherent clusters of studies yield a very small pool of papers (at most, dozens rather than thousands) that can be analyzed as a group to represent a congruent set of conceptual characteristics about the treatment and outcomes. In our meta-analysis, we focused on feedback practices in science, technology, engineering, and mathematics (STEM) education. After carefully screening more than 9,000 papers that were originally collected, only 238 papers were kept. Of those 238 papers, 24 were coded as background and synthesis papers, 79 as descriptive papers, 24 as qualitative papers, and 111 as quantitative (experimental or quasi-experimental) studies that were relevant to feedback practices in STEM (i.e., 35 primarily focused on science education, 60 on mathematics education, and 16 on engineering and technology education).

For the studies used in our meta-analyses of feedback, we identified 15 dimensions as comprising a working definition of feedback in the studies (Li et al., 2011; Morozov, Yin, Li, & Ruiz-Primo, 2010; Ruiz-Primo, Li, et al., 2010). Some of the dimensions include (1) who provides the feedback (e.g., teacher, peer, self, or technology-based), (2) the setting in which the feedback is delivered (e.g., individual student, small group, or whole class), (3) the role of the student in the feedback event (e.g., provider or receiver), (4) the focus of the feedback (e.g., product, process, self-regulation for cognitive feedback; or goal orientation, self-efficacy for affective feedback), (5) the artifact used as evidence to provide feedback (e.g., student product(s) or process), (6) the type of feedback provided (e.g., evaluative, descriptive, or holistic), (7) how feedback is provided or presented (e.g., written, video, oral, or video), (8) reference of feedback (e.g., self, others, or mastery criteria), and (9) feedback occurrence in the study (e.g., one time or multiple times; or with or without pedagogical use).

Based on these aspects, only a handful of studies could be clustered by using a comparable type of feedback from which a meaningful effect size could be calculated. For example, we found that in papers focusing on science (Ruiz-Primo, Li, et al., 2010), the largest cluster of papers included only four studies. That is, these four studies were roughly similar to each other in how feedback was defined as treatment (i.e., receiving descriptive feedback from peers). Another set of four studies was found to be conceptually similar about feedback used for self-assessment. Many studies were unique in how they manipulated feedback (i.e., cluster size = one). Similar results were found in mathematics (Li et al., 2011) where clusters contained only three studies or less. The findings reported here are about feedback studies only in science and mathematics. It is highly possible that the cluster sizes may be larger in other disciplines such as literacy.

Clearly, the range of feedback definitions is wide. This leads to the question of how it is possible to identify patterns of results from such a small number of studies clustered around each definition. Or how is it possible to argue for feedback effects without considering the nuances and differences among the studies? Admittedly, from these clusters, each with a small number of studies, the effect sizes are always positive but variable (no less than 0.22 in science and 0.62 in mathematics). Still, we ask how much is known about how feedback has been defined and manipulated in different disciplines by grade, by type of population, and the like. The response is *not much*. This is true despite the number of synthesis studies found on this topic and despite that some of these studies analyzed thousands of papers.

One stunning result of our meta-analysis is to discover that a high percentage of the studies focus on evaluating feedback effects in the same experimental session. That is, the feedback treatment is a single event lasting only minutes (72% of studies in science and 85% in mathematics). Few studies focus on multiple feedback episodes that occur at least in a 1-week instructional period (only 5 studies in science and 10 in mathematics). This is surprising since these studies do not at all reflect what should be expected about feedback practices in the classrooms. Nor can these types of studies be used to explain the effects of feedback when teachers implement feedback as a regular or routine practice (Kluger & DeNisi, 1996; Li et al., 2011; Ruiz-Primo, Li, et al., 2010). Needless to say, the studies focusing on the long-term effects of feedback on cognitive outcomes are nonexistent (e.g., Do students with feedback outperform the control group in delayed measures?).

Another completely unexpected finding in our meta-analysis is that in most of the studies analyzed in science and mathematics we found no evidence of pedagogical advance or follow-up before or after the feedback episode. In these studies, the authors did not provide the receivers of the feedback with any background or introductions to orient them to the purpose of feedback, directions about how to interpret it, or descriptions about how the feedback information could be used to improve their performance. Similarly, in most studies, the teachers (or sometimes researchers) who implemented the feedback treatment—either in oral or written form—seldom took any instructional actions, such as allowing class time for students to read or respond to the feedback. The feedback treatment thus appeared as an add-on that did not fit into the flow of teaching and learning. This is completely in contrast to the assumption that a critical characteristic usually associated with feedback in formative assessment literature is the use of information for improvement in learning. Only four studies in science and none in mathematics were found with some type of subsequent instructional activity.

Finally, many of the studies we reviewed provided little or no information about the learning tasks based on which feedback is provided since the tasks used in the outcome measures may or may not be the exact learning tasks used for the feedback treatment. In other studies that mentioned the learning tasks, the instructional tasks were, quite noticeably, different from the type of tasks usually observed in a classroom. Even when studies were conducted in classrooms (in contrast to a laboratory), the tasks, for the most part, tended to be artificial (e.g., putting together a puzzle) and not directly related to the everyday instructional activities implemented in classrooms. In our meta-analysis, when information was available about the task used, a significant percentage of these tasks could be classified as tasks dealing merely with declarative knowledge (36% in science and 12% in mathematics). Across the two samples of studies we found few tasks involving schematic knowledge as knowing why (0% in science and 9% in mathematics). Identifying the characteristics of the tasks is critical to being able to pinpoint the characteristics of feedback that can be linked to the specific type of learning. Unfortunately, there is no information on this issue so this area remains to be studied.

How Much Should the Results Be Trusted? Validity of the Feedback Studies

A high percentage of papers investigating the impact of feedback did so without using a control group. All studies in our meta-analysis used quasi-experimental designs (e.g., posttest only two groups or pretest–posttest), and none of the studies in the clusters created for calculating the effect sizes used randomized experiments. Kluger and DeNisi (1996) found that 37% of the 3,000 papers they reviewed did not include a control group. In fact, only 131 studies, or 4%, were considered appropriate for reaching some type of valid conclusion based on their selection criteria. We, as a research community, have decided to ignore that quality of research design plays a clear role in defining the validity of the studies. Quasi-experiments, with no pretest administered, make it difficult to reject the possibility of preexisting differences in the studied outcomes between groups. Furthermore, the quasi-experimental designs are likely to produce inflated estimates of effectiveness when compared to experimental design studies. We (Ruiz-Primo et al., 2011) have found that effect sizes for comparative studies with random assignment are lower than for those without random assignment.

Confounded effects, rarely mentioned in the synthesis and meta-analyses, pose another threat to validity when interpreting results of feedback studies. Kluger and DeNisi (1996) found that 16% of the studies had confounded treatments (i.e., feedback was not the only treatment implemented). Similarly, among the 60 empirical articles on mathematics feedback, we identified 10 that confounded either the treatments or outcome measures. In our meta-analysis, we decided to exclude these studies, but it is unclear how this type of studies has been treated in other meta-analyses or syntheses. Thus, a pressing research need is to determine the degree and kind of confounded effects present in empirical studies so that we can have clarity about the impact due to feedback treatment rather than other variables.

Another important methodological problem is that most of the studies do not provide information about the reliability and validity of the instruments used to measure the effects of feedback on the selected outcomes. The validity of feedback studies is threatened by failure to attend to the technical characteristics of the instruments used to measure learning outcomes, if any form of measurement of performance is used. Our meta-analysis found that in science only 63% of the studies reported on the reliability of the instruments used, and only one study reported on content validity. In mathematics, just 39% of the studies reported at least one reliability indicator of the outcome measures, and 24% of the studies reported some type of validity information. Given these measures with ambiguity in technical soundness, can we fully trust results reported in synthesis and meta-analyses studies?

Finally, as mentioned previously there is an issue of ecological validity. For a research study to possess ecological validity and its results to be generalizable, the methods, materials, and setting of the study must sufficiently approximate the real-life situation that is under investigation. Most of the studies reported are laboratory-based or are conducted in classrooms but under artificial conditions (e.g., students were asked to identify unfamiliar uses of familiar objects). In our meta-analysis, only four studies on science were conducted in a classroom, all of which focused on peer feedback. In mathematics—more encouraging—at least half of the studies in our meta-analysis were conducted in classrooms. Furthermore, a high percentage of the studies focus on written feedback, and only a few on oral or other types of feedback, although oral feedback is more frequently observed in teachers' daily assessment practices (see Hargreaves et al., 2000).

Clearly, much remains to be learned about what happens in real classrooms and the effects on students' learning. We know little about what teachers actually do in their classrooms (but see Carnell, 2000; Clarke, 2000; Gipps et al., 1995; Hargreaves et al., 2000; Torrance & Pryor, 1998) and about how they vary feedback according to the tasks and learning goals. The field needs to develop more specific knowledge about the strategies that teachers use to provide feedback and the strategies that students use to respond to that feedback. Equally important is discovering how the effects of these strategies vary according to the classroom context, instructional content, and student characteristics.

An Expanded, Reconceptualized Definition of Feedback: Formative Feedback

In this section, we argue that formative feedback, when studied in the classroom context, is far more complex than it tends to appear in most studies, syntheses, or meta-analyses. Feedback practice is more than simply giving students feedback orally or in written form with externally or self-generated information and descriptive comments. We argue that feedback that is not used by students to move their learning forward is not formative feedback. We thus suggest that feedback needs to be examined more closely in the classroom setting, which should ultimately contribute to an expanded and more accurate and precise definition.

Our definition of feedback is based on critical assumptions about *formative assessment* and the role that feedback plays in formative assessment events that are generally accepted by theorists and researchers. In light of this perspective, formative feedback should do the following:

- *Be seen as a process* strongly guided by the learning goal(s) that the teacher and students work toward. This means that an effective feedback process should define, clarify, or articulate the evidence of learning and/or criteria for successfully meeting intended goals. It should also compare the current or actual level of student performance with the success criteria and communicate and use the assessment information to move student learning forward to reduce or close the gap (Nichols, Meyers, & Burling, 2009; Shepard, 2009).

  The formative role of feedback cannot be fully understood without connecting it to the targeted learning goal and comparing the actual achieved level and the expected level as defined by the criteria of success (Ramaprasad, 1983; Sadler, 1989). All these feedback activities directly contribute to quality formative assessment. The impact of feedback information is determined by how well the teacher can fulfill these activities of the feedback process. A teacher who effectively implements this process will constantly make pedagogical decisions around a range of questions about feedback, such as, how to ensure her feedback focuses on the big ideas of the lesson, how best to react to student work, how to organize the feedback episode with the students so that feedback is the most helpful for them, how to make sure the students read the written feedback or pay attention to the oral feedback, and how to make sure students understand her gestures of praising students' effort.

- *Actively involve students in the feedback process* by engaging them in (1) defining the evidence of learning and/or success criteria (or goal, or reference level) being targeted, (2) comparing the current or actual level of performance with the evidence or the criteria for success, and (3) using assessment information to improve their own learning to reduce the gap. A critical aspect of formative assessment is that both students and teachers participate in generating and using the assessment information (Brookhart, 2009; Brookhart, Moss, & Long, 2009). Similarly, students can discuss with their teacher to collaboratively determine what kind of work is helped by feedback and what kind of feedback is the most appropriate. All of these practices entail the use of peer and self-feedback.

- *Be considered as an instructional scaffold* that goes beyond written or oral comments. Formative feedback can involve any verbal exchange (conversation, dialogue, discussion), modeling, demonstrations, cues, or hints that can support learning, such as when a teacher responds to a students' incorrect answer with a new probing question (Askew & Lodge, 2000; Heritage, 2010; Ruiz-Primo & Furtak, 2006, 2007). Examples of feedback that should be more carefully studied include nonverbal strategies such as gestures or body language, instructional actions such as demonstrating, modeling, or conferring as well as whole-class or small-group discussions that other students can listen to and use to improve their understanding (a vicarious feedback).

- *Be specifically intended to improve learning outcomes* (e.g., deepening conceptual understanding) and *processes* (e.g., reflecting on one's learning and learning strategies or making new connections to what has been learned; see Askew & Lodge, 2000).

  In order to improve learning outcomes, the content of feedback ought to focus not only on reducing the difference between a current understanding or performance level and what is expected but also on improving students' learning strategies, helping them to monitor their own learning, and strengthening their belief in their ability to improve and learn.

  Thus, to fully support student learning processes, feedback should also *focus on self-regulation, metacognition, attribution, self-efficacy,* and *goal orientation.* For these affective attributes, feedback should contain only factors that are under the students' control (e.g., effort, ways to monitor or check the work, or strategies to set up the plan rather than being evaluative of an individual's ability or personality). In this manner, feedback can reinforce students' beliefs that they can always improve their work and that they can master new challenging goals and tasks, thus enhancing students' learning-goal orientation.

- *Ensure its usefulness by making feedback accessible and practical.* Appropriate feedback helps students develop sufficient insights into their own learning and become self-critical, self-reflective, and self-directed (Gipps, McCallum, & Hargreaves, 2000; Rubin, 1987; Wiliam, 2011). Feedback is appropriate if it is (1) *helpful,* by letting the students know what to do next and what future actions to expect (Wiliam, 2011); (2) *precise,* by describing what was right or wrong and in what ways something was right or wrong (Gipps et al., 2000; Tunstall & Gipps, 1996; Wiliam, 2011); and (3) *at the right level* for the students (Carnell, 2000).

  When receiving feedback from an external agent (teacher or peer), students should have an opportunity to act on that feedback and plan next steps to further their own learning (e.g., What could make this a better table? Shall I sort the data based on the first column?; Gipps et al., 2000). When students assess themselves, they should construct their own feedback and develop a plan to use the information learned from self-assessment to improve their work.

- *Consider different sources of information* about students' learning and understanding from highly formal (e.g., taking tests or quizzes, filling in a handout, or completing an investigation report) to very informal (e.g., questions, comments, observations, and evaluative and interpretative listening) (Bell & Cowie, 2001; Ruiz-Primo, 2010; Ruiz-Primo & Furtak, 2006, 2007; Ruiz-Primo, Furtak, Yin, Ayala, & Shavelson, 2010; Shavelson, Yin, Furtak, Ruiz-Primo, & Ayala, 2008).

- *Demonstrate, over time, alignment with a learning trajectory at least within a unit or module.* That is, students will take actions based on feedback aligned to the trajectory used to design and map the instructional and assessment activities (Heritage, 2010; Wiliam, 2011). These actions should eventually lead to attainment of the learning goals.

Our definition of formative feedback emphasizes two characteristics. First, the students are essential players in the feedback process. In addition to being recipients of feedback, the students have a role as partners in each of the formative feedback activities (i.e., clarifying learning goals or success criteria, comparing current performance with success criteria, and using the information to formulate an action plan) and as feedback providers and developers of actions to be followed. These roles should be acknowledged and studied as a critical aspect of high quality feedback activities (Black, 2003; Brookhart, 2001, 2003; Coffey, 2003; Cowie, 2005a, 2005b). Second, our notion expands the feedback definition beyond oral or written comments to students' performance. This definition leads to a more blurred distinction between feedback and instruction (Heritage, 2010). Thus, the feedback event is not a discrete activity; rather, it combines looking for evidence of students' learning on ongoing interactions and communicating to students in the on-the-fly situation (Moss, 2008; Ruiz-Primo, 2011; Ruiz-Primo & Furtak, 2006, 2007).

In summary, we need to learn much more about how teachers use formative feedback in real settings, in the classroom, and not with artificial tasks and strategies. We need to learn how teachers develop and apply formative feedback that focuses on effort, self-regulation, metacognition, or procedures all in the same classroom session and with diverse students. The research question then becomes this: How can informal or formal *formative feedback episodes* be genuinely captured in the classroom? In the next section, we offer a framework for conducting such studies. This framework uses the *assessment cycle activity* as the unit of analysis. A complete assessment cycle contains four activities: (1) clarifying learning goals, (2) eliciting information to check students' understanding, (3) interpreting the information collected, and (4) acting on the information collected. One such action is formative feedback, the focus of this chapter.

A Framework for Characterizing Formative Assessment Episodes in the Classroom

Ruiz-Primo (2010) proposed a framework for characterizing formative assessment episodes (FAEs) in the classroom (Figure 13.1). The framework was originally proposed to approach the study of formative assessment practices in classrooms as part of the project Developing and Evaluating Measures of Formative Assessment Practices (DEMFAP) (Ruiz-Primo & Sands, 2009) conducted by the Laboratory for Educational Assessment, Research and InnovatioN (LEARN) at the University of Colorado Denver.

Much of what teachers and students do every day in their classrooms can be viewed as potential assessment opportunities for collecting evidence of students' understanding. Therefore, this evidence should potentially form the basis for feedback to students (Ruiz-Primo, 2011). It is expected that this framework can illustrate how formative assessments function in "ordinary" classrooms and help identify commonalities than can lead to descriptions of their critical dimensions.

Ruiz-Primo's framework reflects an understanding that development and learning are primarily social processes, and learning cannot be separated from its social context (Laboratory for Comparative Human Cognition, 2010). The framework, then, focuses on collecting assessment information and offering feedback on the complex teacher–student interactions. It also recognizes that interactions are mediated by material and symbolic artifacts/tools in the classroom. It intends to understand better how the teachers define what and how to pay attention in the formative assessment process, their roles and the students' roles, and the tools teachers use (language, physical, or symbolic) to help students gain control of their own learning and grow independence; in sum, to know more about how teachers mediate what students will learn through formative assessment and how they support their independence as learners.

The framework is based on the assertion that formative assessment is influenced and circumscribed by a particular learning context (shown in gray in Figure 13.1). It explicitly takes into account social participation—a component neglected in previous frameworks—so that to stress that assessment is not only a teacher-directed activity but also a shared student–teacher activity (Brookhart, 2007; Moss, 2008). Formative assessment is seen as a process that occurs continuously rather than as a discrete activity that only happens periodically and sporadically during instruction. The framework then is conceived as having three components: (1) assessment activity cycle, (2) formality of the FAE, and (3) social participation.

Assessment Activity Cycle

This component expands upon Ramaprasad's (1983) question loop and adopts Sadler (1989) and Bell and Cowie's (2001) assessment activities—clarifying learning expectations (goals), collecting information, interpreting information, and acting on/using the information collected to move students closer to the learning goals and supporting the needed steps. The assessment activity cycle defines a FAE as a chain of the four related formative assessment activities; each activity can be accomplished with a range of strategies (Ruiz-Primo, 2010). For example, eliciting and collecting

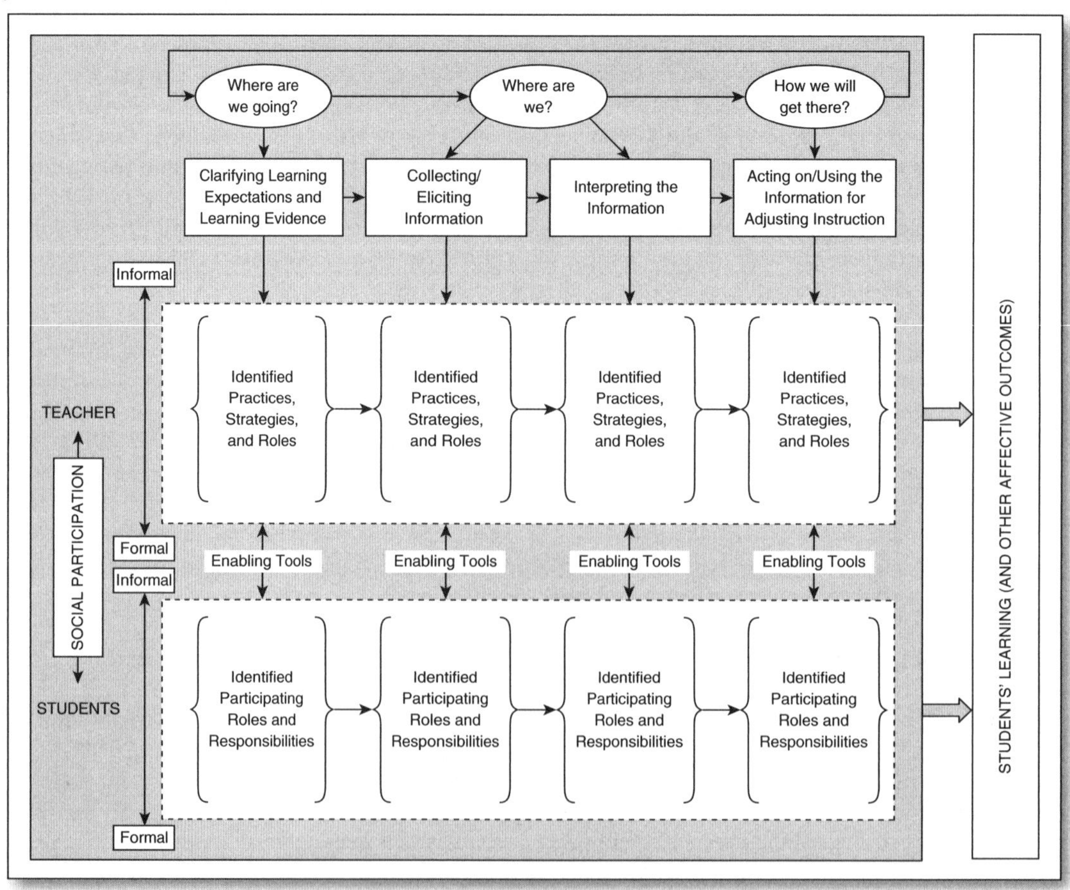

Figure 13.1 Graphic Representation of the Formative Assessment Framework

SOURCE: Ruiz-Primo (2010).

information can be done through questioning, self-assessment, peer-assessment, classroom conversations, or quizzes. All four activities are required in order for an FAE to have occurred. Indeed, poorly implemented practices are characterized by incomplete cycles in which assessment information is not interpreted and/or no subsequent action is taken to address students' learning needs (see Ruiz-Primo & Furtak, 2006, 2007).

Formality of the Formative Assessment Episode

This component is described by an informal-to-formal continuum regarding how FAEs are implemented (see Ruiz-Primo & Furtak, 2006, 2007; Ruiz-Primo, Furtak, et al., 2010; Shavelson et al., 2008). This continuum is related to the assessment characterization proposed by Jordan and Putz (2004): *inherent* assessments as implicit, informal, and nonverbal. For example, students are influenced implicitly by their peers and the teacher in deciding what to do next when working in a group to solve a mathematical problems; *discursive* assessments as explicit when members of a social group talk about what they are doing in an evaluative way; and *documentary* assessments as formal assessments, which are considered more standardized measurements by Jordan and Putz. However, in the context of formative assessment, this formality can refer to quizzes, a gallery of posters, tests, checklists, and the like, which elicit written responses from students.

The formality or informality of a FAE is different for teachers and students. The two components, formality level and teacher–student participation, are closely linked, but one does not necessarily determine the other. For example, an informal formative assessment activity does not necessarily require interaction between the teacher and one or more students. The assessment activity can take place with minimal participation of the teacher, such as a group discussion. In this case, the teacher can serve as an orchestrator of a student–student interaction.

For teachers, level of formality is determined by the interplay of two dimensions, (1) *planning* and (2) *formality of the strategies*. Planning involves teachers' decisions on (1) *type of information to be collected* (e.g., based on the number of hands raised, ideas posted in the parking lot activity, or a written response to a journal prompt); (2) *the precision of the information required* (e.g., having a general sense of how much the whole class of students understands versus knowing the level of understanding for each student or each group); and (3) *timing* (e.g., having a general idea of students' learning for each lesson versus knowing where *all* students are at critical junctures of a unit). A care fully planned assessment episode may require a formal assessment task that is implemented with all students at the same time at critical times during instruction (e.g., formal embedded assessment). This assessment activity will provide information about all students on specific issues that are considered essential to achieving the learning goals. However, a question posed by a student can trigger an informal FAE that is not planned and will involve only the interaction between the teacher and that student. This assessment episode will provide information solely about that particular student. The second dimension of formality, *formality of the strategies*, refers to the formality of the assessment strategies employed (e.g., observing students, listening and commenting to student conversations, and asking questions of students during a classroom conversation versus giving all students a written test). The formality of the strategies largely corresponds to the assessment decisions that are made during planning.

In contrast, for students, formality is determined by two different dimensions: (1) *inclusiveness*, the number of students involved in the activity (e.g., one student versus many or all students), and (2) *formality of participation*, how casually or formally students are expected to participate in the FAEs (e.g., by simply showing thumbs up to indicate they understand versus individually reviewing a peer's science report and providing comments based on a rubric generated by the class).

Social Participation

This component refers to the teacher and students' roles as actors in a FAE. The importance of involving students in FAEs is stressed by Black (2001):

> With better interactions in the classroom teachers will be in closer touch with their pupils' progress in understanding, pupils will become more active and responsible as they become involved in

> expressing their thinking to their teachers and to their peers, and pupils will be drawn into taking responsibility for their learning through self and peer assessment. (p. 76)

If the FAE is exclusively in the hands of the teachers, it can be argued that students cannot be entrusted with managing their own learning, and self-regulation skills thus are less likely to be developed (Andrade, 2010).

The roles that teacher and students fulfill depend on both the specific formative assessment strategy being implemented and the activity that is being conducted (Ruiz-Primo, 2010). This component reflects the participation structure and class norms through which the assessment activity cycle can take place (e.g., one-on-one, peer, teacher with small group, or whole class). This component allows us to identify different roles that students and teachers play and describe how they evolve across assessment activities and diverse episodes.

Formative Feedback Episodes

Figure 13.2 is a representation of the framework with a focus on formative feedback episodes. It provides research questions (in brackets) linked to each assessment activity, which can guide the study of formative feedback episodes in context. Although not every cycle should start with clarification of the learning goals—for example, at the unit level—it should be assumed that any given activity or task should be linked to an articulated learning target or an expectation.

> The learning goals that are the focus of the informal formative assessment practices tend to be discrete and immediate (e.g., what students need to get from a particular activity or from that day's class). However, these discrete, immediate goals are *contextualized* in the larger picture of long-term outcomes; they are part of a *larger learning trajectory* in the context of unit and yearly goals. (Ruiz-Primo, 2011, p. 16)

Since the role of feedback truly lies in reduction of the gap between where students are and where they have to be, feedback should be linked to the attainment of a learning goal, a learning target, or an expected outcome.

Current knowledge about effective feedback practices is insufficient for researchers and practitioners to understand the context in which feedback is provided. It is hard to judge whether feedback is formative or not. It is also difficult to understand the FAE in which a particular feedback occurred and with which characteristics. Analyzing the episode enables researchers to examine the feedback characterization by considering large issues, such as its effectiveness based on certain types of learning goals and expectations, properties of learning tasks, or disciplines.

The Ruiz-Primo framework can help researchers to learn more about the source(s) used to collect information about students' understanding (e.g., Was it formal such as a quiz, or informal, via a question asked by a student or the responses to a teacher's question?). It also helps to identify how teachers make sense of such information and the reference (learning goals, learning targets, success criteria, or task expectations) they use for the interpretation. Specifically for feedback practices, the framework guides a series of research questions about the type of learning task being used to elicit and collect information from students, how tightly the task is linked to the learning goals or targets being pursued, how the task is evaluated and used as the evidence to construct the feedback, and how the feedback is provided and used to shape the next instructional move and inform the learning steps. In our research, we have found that expert teachers frequently clarify learning goals and expectations with students and refer to those goals when providing feedback (Minstrell, Li, & Anderson, 2009).

The framework further emphasizes identifying roles and responsibilities that students and their teacher took in each of the four assessment activities (e.g., Are opportunities provided for them to interpret the information collected?). As it has been mentioned, none of this is new in the literature. What we are missing is a systematic way to approach the study of feedback: how formative feedback episodes evolved in the real classrooms. We do not know a lot about how to implement feedback practices effectively and efficiently so that a formative assessment cycle can be complete and the assessment event actually becomes formative. We know little about the struggles teachers have in collecting and interpreting as well as in

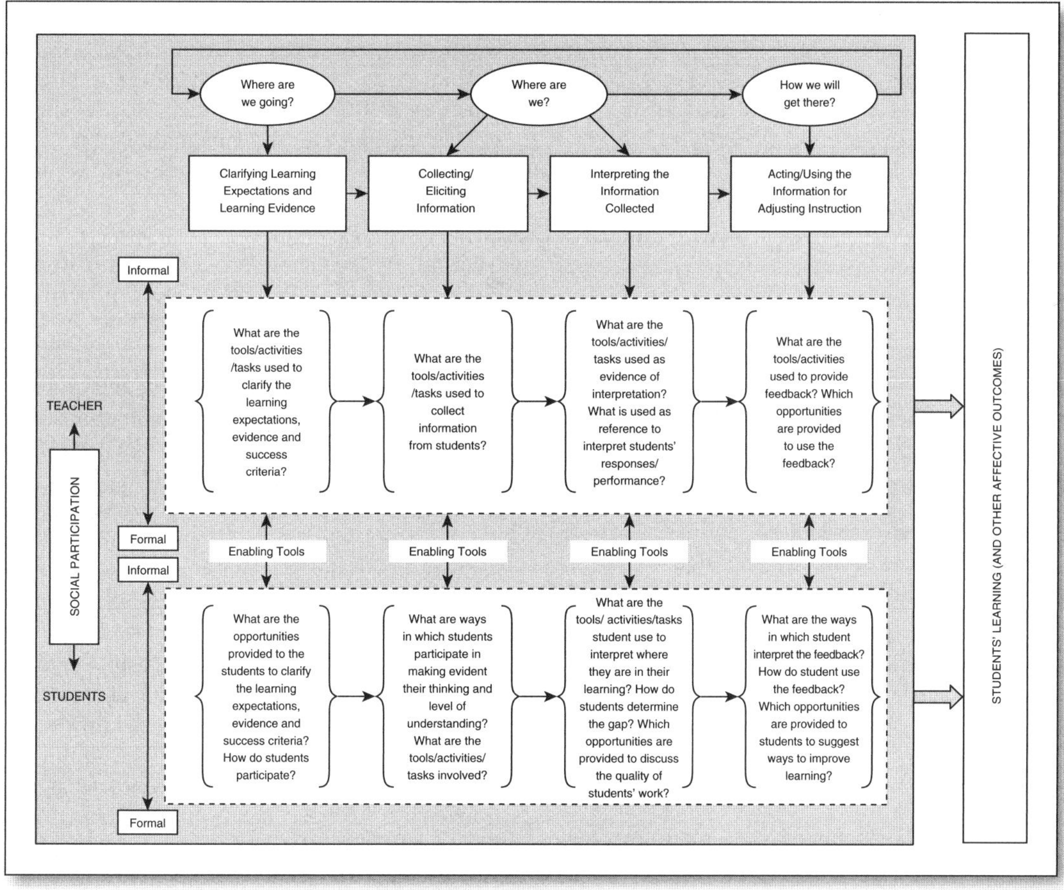

Figure 13.2 Graphic Representation of the Formative Feedback Episodes

SOURCE: Adapted from Ruiz-Primo (2010).

deciding what type of feedback to provide with what content to which students. The framework describes three components, including (1) cycle of activities, (2) formality, and (3) social participation, which at least can be used to systematize the feedback research.

Furthermore, the framework underscores the students' roles in any given formative feedback episode within a classroom context. Research has made clear that students hardly read teachers' written feedback or know how to interpret it (Cowie, 2005a, 2005b). Thus, research needs to be conducted to investigate whether students understand the feedback messages, whether they are aware of the connections between the feedback and the learning goals (and expectations), how they use the feedback information, and how use of the information can affect student learning.

This framework implies four lines of investigation on formative assessment in general and feedback specifically. First, it leads us to consider the social milieu in which formative assessment is contextualized, as well as the social structures that influence the roles that teachers and students play. Second, it focuses on the enabling tools (physical or symbolic) that teachers use to support and mediate students' attention, memory, and thinking. The study of formative assessment should focus on learning more about the mediating tools that teachers use (e.g., exemplary products on boards) and that students initiate to assist themselves in improving their learning. Third, the framework entails addressing the type, frequency, and duration of the assessment activities in the cycle that correspond to the identified roles, along with their occurrence in the instructional sequence in which each actor participates in the FAE. And, fourth, the framework stresses collection of information about students' outcomes, whether cognitive or affective. If there is no evidence of the impact of formative assessment practices on students' performance, then the main reason for conducting research on formative assessment is lost.

Studying Formative Feedback in the Classroom Context

As mentioned previously, most of the publications on formative assessment and feedback include examples of strategies and techniques that teachers can use. Most of them, however, do not provide empirical evidence of the impact of these strategies on student learning; nor do they link them to contextual issues that may affect the effectiveness of the strategies. Here are some key questions researchers should ask: Are the strategies effective independently of the students' characteristics, type of task at hand, the school grade, or the discipline? For whom, when, and under which conditions do these strategies work? How do teachers and students respond to and perceive the different strategies?

It does seem unlikely that we can respond to these questions even if we draw upon information in published papers, meta-analyses, and syntheses. As has been mentioned, there is a lack of studies conducted in real classrooms—the natural setting—where it would be important to see evidence that feedback strategies have substantive impact. Moreover, few studies have focused on feedback over extended periods or on factors that can moderate or mediate the effectiveness of feedback. Therefore, we cannot generalize what we know from the literature to classroom practices.

We have not yet learned enough about how teachers combine different forms of feedback from multiple sources of evidence and across different instructional episodes. Nor do we know enough about the varying strategies teachers use everyday to engage students in the feedback process. "In practice, formative assessment is a complex and challenging process" (Cowie, 2005a, p. 200); we should expect, then, that feedback is complex and challenging too. Rather than persisting with our common belief that feedback is something doable for teachers, we should strive to study formative assessment practices in the classroom, including feedback, to help teachers and students to do better.

Given these unanswered questions, we need different and more trustworthy strategies of inquiry to acquire firsthand knowledge about feedback in the classroom context and to systematically study its effects on student learning. We suggest three major strategies:

1. *Case studies* in which typical and atypical cases, rather than samples of populations, are selected to capture complexities (Stake, 1995) unique to the implementation of appropriate feedback. According to Yin (2003), case studies assume no control over behaviors and events and are especially useful for investigating *how* and *why* research questions. Case studies help us understand the details of interactions with the context in which the cases are being studied (Stake, 1995). Along with student characteristics, the teachers' own background, knowledge, interests, personality, preferences, school, and school district context will influence what the teachers do in their classrooms (Wragg, 1993). Thus, creating case studies allows us to discover and describe the specific elements of interactions in feedback episodes and, further, to explore how the effectiveness of feedback is influenced by all these elements.

A basic source of information for case studies, as well as other research methods, is observations (Angrosino & May de Pérez, 2000). The following is recommended for case studies on formative feedback:

> Careful classroom observation can help illuminate even the most familiar of events. (Wragg, 1993, p. 13)

Although we recognize that classroom observations have been used in multiple studies, unfortunately, many of them have not included data on student learning to support the claims (e.g., Carnell, 2000; Clarke, 2000; Hargreaves et al., 2000).

Classroom observations should be accompanied by interviews with teachers and students, which allow pooling of perceptions about the feedback episodes collected during the classroom observation. The goal is to obtain a more accurate and complete perspective on what happened, how it happened, with what understanding, and with what consequences. Few studies, however, have focused on learning about the students' perspectives, experiences, and expectations with feedback (but see Brookhart, 2001, 2003; Cowie, 2005a, 2005b). This is a fertile source of knowledge on feedback waiting to be tapped.

2. *Observational studies* have variables that are observed rather than manipulated (Rosenbaum, 1995). Observational studies involve a treatment or intervention (e.g., intervention for improving feedback practices) but lack an experimental control. These studies also have been referred to as nonexperimental studies, and they can include correlational studies (Shadish, Cook, & Campbell, 2002). Observational studies can be conducted to explore how feedback strategies are connected to student learning or how a particular professional development method is associated with teacher feedback practice and the learning outcomes of students. We think that this type of study should be considered in cases where, for example, some type of professional development on formative assessment has been implemented. Many school districts are providing professional development on feedback but with almost no information about the impact of the professional development on teacher practices in the classroom or on student learning (but see Brookhart et al., 2009). Different possible designs can be used, including multiple reference groups and multiple control groups.

3. *Experiments* have variables that are manipulated (e.g., an intervention for improving feedback practices), and the effects are measured (Shadish et al., 2002). A common attribute of all genuine experiments is control of treatment(s), although control may take many different forms (Shadish et al., 2002). There are two main experimental subtypes:

a. Randomized experiments, in which units are to be studied, are randomly assigned to the treatment condition or an alternative condition. Educational research commonly uses three types of randomized experiments: (1) completely randomized designs (treatments are randomly assigned to students), (2) block randomized (schools or students are randomized within schools), and (3) cluster randomized (schools are randomly assigned to treatments). These types of experimental designs are most likely to allow the observed effects to be attributed to the treatment(s).

b. Quasi-experiments have units that are not randomly assigned to conditions. To achieve some degree of control, at least two methods can be used: (1) matching based on a source of variations and (2) statistical adjustment. Collecting pretest information, or information about any other variable that can serve as a covariate (e.g., the percent of free and reduced lunch or teacher qualification), is critical for matching and/or statistical adjustment.

We argue that we first should learn more about what expert teachers do (see Minstrell et al., 2009; Gipps et al., 2000; Ruiz-Primo & Sands, 2009) and how they frame their feedback practices. We need to conduct studies in different school contexts to identify patterns by grade, discipline, socioeconomic status, and other such factors. We need populations better described and defined so that the findings can be reasonably generalized. Given how little we know about the characteristics of feedback, it is even more important to compare different versions of feedback treatments than to compare a particular feedback type against no feedback at all. Having clearly defined treatments will greatly improve the construct validity of the studies conducted in this area, in turn facilitating broader accumulation of research knowledge.

A Suggested Agenda for Future Feedback Research

This chapter has purposely raised many questions about formative feedback that we believe establishes a clear agenda for future research on feedback. In this section, we organize these questions by topic/focus and type of study design.

Defining Feedback

Case studies should be applied to develop much needed clarification of the definition of feedback. The studies should address questions such as the following: What are the essential characteristics of effective formative feedback practices in the classroom? Which formative feedback practices are minimally effective in classrooms and why? How do we know the feedback practices provided in informal FAEs are effective?

Variability in Feedback Practices

This line of research includes two groups of questions. The first pertains to describing the feedback variation by carrying out case studies. The questions to be addressed in these studies are as follows: What is the range of formative feedback practices that focus on cognitive goals compared to those focusing on affective goals? What proportion of formative feedback practices used by expert teachers apply to cognitive goals and to affective goals? Do formative feedback practices differ according to the characteristics of the students (e.g., English language learners [ELLs])? Who is exposed to feedback and when? (Heritage, 2010). Do effective formative feedback practices look different in different classrooms depending on classroom characteristics? Do feedback practices differ across different disciplines, and if so, in what ways?

The second set of research questions calls for observational studies aiming to examine the implications for such variation (i.e., variability in feedback practices). For example, do feedback practices produce variations in student learning that can be linked to certain variations in student characteristics? Are all feedback techniques equally effective in all types of activities, with all types of students, in all disciplines and for all grades? In teachers' feedback practices, under what conditions are the variations beneficial and under what conditions do they indicate ineffective practice?

Feedback in Classrooms

Feedback is closely tied to teaching and learning in classrooms. The research, in turn, needs to address teacher and students' everyday realities. This then calls for a related branch of research questions, including how the feedback is linked to the learning goal or target or how the feedback varies in relation to the learning goal or targets that influence student learning. Also, how can this relationship be communicated and made clear to students? What is the impact of vicarious feedback or scaffolding on student learning?

Use of Feedback

Feedback is used by both teachers and students. The key need for the research is related to understanding students' use of feedback and the strategies teachers can apply to facilitate such use. For example, what type of feedback is most easily understood by students? What factors influence students to take up the feedback suggestions to improve their learning? What kinds of instructional and assessment opportunities will most effectively help students to use feedback? What instructional and assessment opportunities can be provided to students to use feedback? What is the impact of these opportunities?

Similarly, more studies are needed to understand the mechanisms and strategies that can be used by teachers in their feedback practices in order to make the new knowledge more relevant, applicable, and influential to the daily work that practitioners deal with. For example, how do teachers use information from their formative assessment practices to plan and formulate feedback? How do teachers use feedback events as part of instructions?

Review of Feedback Research

The synthesis work on feedback should attend to questions that can provide more systematic evidence with accurate effect-size calculations on the type of feedback that works for whom and with which tasks to support which learning goals. For example, how do researchers define feedback? What design was used in the studies conducted? What are the characteristics of the learning tasks used? How much do we know about confounded effects in other syntheses in which studies are reported by the thousands? How reliable and valid are the instruments used?

No doubt, many more questions can be asked about formative feedback practices, but we have raised just a few of the most pressing and which appear to have particular potential for yielding new insights and understandings. We also expect that this discussion will stimulate readers to raise additional critical questions.

Conclusion

The main purpose of this chapter was to offer a different perspective, one that would allow a closer, more critical look at what is known about formative feedback practices. We started by pointing out some basic information about feedback that has been analyzed and reported in reviews, syntheses, and meta-analyses. Based on this information, we concluded that much less is known and understood about formative feedback practices in the classrooms than we had expected.

Motivated by this realization, we first expanded the definition of feedback from written and oral comments to the territory of instruction and interaction with students, ranging from conversation and modeling to asking follow-up questions and using nonverbal strategies. All of these strategies in some way present learners with valuable information about what is right or wrong, what can be done to improve the work, and what to do next. This broadened notion of feedback recognizes the value of situating feedback in the teaching/learning scene by blurring the distinction between instruction and assessment.

In addition, we proposed a theoretical framework to study feedback, which had been developed earlier, specifically to shed light on what it takes to implement effective formative assessment practices in everyday classrooms involving different types of students in different subjects. In this framework, we underscore the necessity of acting on assessment information, enacting complete cycles of assessment activities, and actively engaging students in order to maximize the benefits of formative assessment.

We emphasized that the reported effects of feedback treatment are generally positive, but they are not always easily replicated in the classroom. For example, many teachers provide oral feedback though varying greatly in quality. This is also true about formative assessment strategies since teachers use some forms of simple elicitation as their assessment routines such as the thumbs up/down, entrance and exit tickets, or a mini whiteboard in their classrooms. The troubling issue is that teachers may not be sufficiently aware of the importance of using the information collected from those elicitation strategies to support teaching or learning purposes; rather, they only consider to use those elicitation strategies to just figure out if students got it or not. Therefore, there is more that researchers should inform teachers in professional development rather than just conveying or passing feedback strategies and techniques. Many of the teachers who use such practices are not informed of the nuanced aspects and varying impacts of these techniques due to the subtle yet complex interaction between these techniques, the task features, and learner characteristics. If the implementation of just these routines were effective enough in improving student learning, we should not be concerned about student learning, as these routines are now widely observed in classrooms. This kind of belief and lack of understanding can easily result in ineffective application of formative assessment practices.

We do not know either how teachers implement feedback focused on affective outcomes and how they move back and forth between feedback for cognitive outcomes and feedback for affective outcomes. We also lack sufficient understanding about the long-term effects of effective formative feedback practices, as many studies were conducted in a short time frame.

The issue then is whether we actually have additional knowledge to share with practitioners. Strategies and techniques based on studies conducted in classrooms with ecological validity are not common. Even rarer are studies in which these strategies are empirically supported or where these strategies are presented within a framework that can help teachers to understand when particular strategies are better with what tasks, for which students, and for what subjects. This leads us to question ourselves: Do we know that much about formative feedback?

We end this chapter by encouraging readers to recognize what we actually know and what we still need to learn as a research community about effective formative feedback. It appears that as researchers we know less about formative feedback than would have been predicted. Our degree of not knowing, however, must be appreciated as the accumulation of knowledge resulting from 30 years of research on feedback. To paraphrase Socrates, "The more one knows, the less one knows." This indeed presents abundant opportunities for exciting breakthroughs during the next decade of research, which we would hope will be increasingly classroom-based with methodologies focusing on validity, utility, and rigor.

References

Andrade, H. L. (2010). Students as the definitive source of formative assessment: Academic self-assessment and the self-regulation of learning. In H. L. Andrade & G. J. Cizek (Eds.), *Handbook of formative assessment* (pp. 90–105). New York: Routledge.

Angrosino, M. V., & May de Pérez, K. A. (2000). Rethinking observation: From method to context. In N. K. Denzin & Y. S. Lincoln (Eds.), *Handbook of qualitative research* (2nd ed., pp. 673–702). Thousand Oaks, CA: Sage.

Askew, S. (Ed.). (2000). *Feedback for learning.* New York: Routledge.

Askew, S., & Lodge, S. (2000). Gifts, ping-pong and loops—linking feedback and learning. In S. Askew (Ed.), *Feedback for learning* (pp. 17–32). New York: Routledge.

Azevedo, R., & Bernard, R. M. (1995). A meta-analysis of the effect of feedback in computer-based instruction. *Journal of Educational Computing Research, 13,* 109–125.

Bangert-Drowns, R. L., Kulik, C-L., Kulik, J. A., & Morgan, M. T. (1991). The instructional effect of feedback in test-like events. *Review of Educational Research, 61*(2), 213–238.

Bell, B., & Cowie, B. (2001). *Formative assessment and science education.* Dordrecht, The Netherlands: Kluwer.

Black, P. (2001). Dreams, strategies and systems: Portraits of assessment past, present and future. *Assessment in Education, 8*(1), 65–85.

Black, P. (2003). The importance of everyday assessment. In J. M. Atkin & J. E. Coffey (Eds.), *Everyday assessment in the science classroom* (pp. 1–11). Arlington, VA: National Science Teachers Association Press.

Black, P., Harrison, C., Lee, C., Marshall, B., & Wiliam, D. (2003). *Assessment for learning: Putting it into practice.* Buckingham, UK: Open University Press.

Black, P., & Wiliam, D. (1998). Assessment and classroom learning. *Assessment in Education, 5*(1), 7–74.

Bower, M. (2005). Online assessment feedback: Competitive, individualistic, or . . . preferred form! *Journal of Computers in Mathematics and Science Teaching, 24*(2), 121–147.

Brookhart, S. M. (2001). Successful students' formative and summative uses of assessment information. *Assessment in Education: Principles, Policy & Practice, 8*(2), 153–169.

Brookhart, S. M. (2003). Developing measurement theory for classroom assessment purposes and uses. *Educational Measurement: Issues and Practices, 22*(4), 5–12.

Brookhart, S. M. (2007). Feedback that fits. *Educational Leadership, 65*(4), 54–59.

Brookhart, S. M. (2009). *Exploring formative assessment.* Alexandria, VA: Association for Supervision and Curriculum Development.

Brookhart, S. M., Moss, C. M., & Long, B. A. (2009). Promoting student ownership of learning through high-impact formative assessment practices. *Journal of Multidisciplinary Evaluation, 6*(12), 52–67.

Brosvic, G. M., Dihoff, R. E., Epstein, M. L., & Cook, M. L. (2006). Feedback facilitates the acquisition and retention of numerical fact series by elementary school students with mathematics learning disabilities. *Psychological Record, 56*(1), 35–54.

Butler, R., & Neuman, O. (1995). Effects of task and ego achievement goals on help-seeking behaviors and attitudes. *Journal of Educational Psychology, 87,* 261–271.

Butler, D. L., & Winne, P. H. (1995). Feedback and self-regulated learning: A theoretical synthesis. *Review of Educational Research, 65*(3), 245–281.

Cameron, J., & Pierce, W. D. (1994). Reinforcement, reward, and intrinsic motivation: A meta-analysis. *Review of Educational Research, 64*(3), 363–423.

Carnell, E., (2000). Dialogue, discussion and feedback—views of secondary school students on how others help their learning. In S. Askow (Ed.), *Feedback for learning* (pp. 56–69). New York: Routledge.

Clarke, S. (2000). Getting it right—distance marking as accessible and effective feedback in the primary classroom. In S. Askow (Ed.), *Feedback for learning* (pp. 44–55). New York: Routledge.

Coffey, J. E. (2003). Involving students in assessment. In J. M. Atkin & J. E. Coffey (Eds.), *Everyday assessment in the science classroom* (pp. 75–87). Arlington, VA: National Science Teachers Association Press.

Cowie, B. (2005a). Student commentary on classroom assessment in science: A sociocultural interpretation. *International Journal of Science Education, 27*(2), 199–214.

Cowie, B. (2005b). Pupil commentary on assessment for learning. *The Curriculum Journal, 6*(2), 137–151.

Gipps, C., Brown, M., McCallum, B., & McAlister, S. (1995). *Intuition or evidence? Teachers and national assessment of seven years old.* Buckingham, UK: Open University Press.

Gipps, C., McCallum, B., & Hargreaves, E. (2000). *What makes a good primary school teacher: Expert classroom strategies.* London: RoutledgeFalmer.

Hargreaves, E., McCallum, B., & Gipps, C. (2000). Teacher feedback strategies in primary classrooms—new evidence. In S. Askow (Ed.), *Feedback for learning* (pp. 34–43). New York: Routledge.

Hattie, J. (1999, August). *Influences on student learning.* Inaugural lecture, University of Auckland. Retrieved from www.arts.auckland .ac.nz/staff/index.cfm?P=5049

Hattie, J., & Timperley, H. (2007). The power of feedback. *Review of Educational Research, 77*(1), 81–113.

Heritage, M. (2010). *Formative assessment. Making it happen in the classroom.* Thousand Oaks, CA: Corwin Press.

Inagaki, K., Hatano, G., & Morita, E. (1998). Construction of mathematical knowledge through whole-class discussion. *Learning and Instruction, 8,* 503–526.

Jordan, B., & Putz, P. (2004). Assessment as practice: Notes on measures, tests, and targets. *Human Organization, 63,* 346–358.

Kluger, A. N., & DeNisi, A. (1996). The effects of feedback interventions on performance: A historical review, a meta-analysis, and a preliminary feedback intervention theory. *Psychological Bulletin, 119,* 254–284.

Kulhavy, R. W. (1977). Feedback in written instruction. *Review of Educational Research, 47,* 211–232.

Kulik, J. A., & Kulik, C.-L. C. (1988). Timing of feedback and verbal learning. *Review of Educational Research, 58,* 79–97.

Laboratory for Comparative Human Cognition. (2010). Cultural–historical activity theory. In P. Peterson, E. Baker, & B. McGaw, (Eds.), *International Encyclopedia of Education* (Vol. 6, pp. 360–366). Oxford, UK: Elsevier.

Li, M., Ruiz-Primo, M. A., Yin, Y., & Morozov, A. (2011, April). *Identifying effective feedback practices on student learning of mathematics: A literature synthesis.* Paper presented at the American Educational Research Association. New Orleans, LA.

Minstrell, J., Li, M., & Anderson, R. (2009). *Evaluating science teachers' formative assessment competency.* Technical report, Arlington, VA: National Science Foundation.

Morozov, A., Yin, Y., Li, M., & Ruiz-Primo, M. A. (2010, April). *Effects of classroom feedback practice on motivational outcomes: A synthesis.* Paper presented at the annual meeting of the American Educational Research Association, Denver, CO.

Moss, P. A. (2008). Sociocultural implications for the practice of assessment I: Classroom assessment. In P. A. Moss, D. Pullin, J. P. Gee, E. H. Haertel, & L. J. Young (Eds.), *Assessment, equity, and opportunity to learn* (pp. 222–258). New York: Cambridge University Press.

Nichols, P. D., Meyers, J. L., & Burling, K. S. (2009). A framework for evaluating and planning assessments intended to improve. *Educational Measurement: Issues and Practice, 28*(3), 14–23.

Nicol, D. J., & Macfarlane-Dick, D. (2006). Formative assessment and self-regulated learning: A model and seven principles of good feedback practice. *Studies in Higher Education, 31*(2), 199–218.

Ramaprasad, A. (1983). On the definition of feedback. *Behavioral Science, 28,* 4–13.

Rosenbaum, P. R. (1995). *Observational studies.* New York: Springer.

Rubin, J. (1987). Learner strategies: Theoretical assumptions, research history and typology. In A. Wenden & J. Rubin (Eds.), *Learner strategies in language learning* (pp. 15–30). Englewood Cliffs, NJ: Prentice Hall.

Ruiz-Primo, M. A. (2010). *Developing and evaluating measures of formative assessment practice (DEMFAP) theoretical and methodological approach.* Internal manuscript, Denver, CO: University of Colorado Denver, Laboratory for Educational Assessment, Research, and InnovatioN (LEARN).

Ruiz-Primo, M. A. (2011). Informal formative assessment: The role of instructional dialogues in assessing students' learning [Special issue]. *Assessment for Learning Studies of Educational Evaluation, 37*(1), 15–24.

Ruiz-Primo, M. A., Briggs, D., Iverson, H., Talbot, R., & Shepard, L. (2011). Impact of undergraduate science course innovations on learning. *Science, 331,* 1269–1270.

Ruiz-Primo, M. A., & Furtak, E. M. (2006). Informal formative assessment and scientific inquiry: Exploring teachers' practices and student learning. *Educational Assessment, 11*(3–4), 205–235.

Ruiz-Primo, M. A., & Furtak, E. M. (2007). Exploring teachers' informal formative assessment practices and students' understanding in the context of scientific inquiry. *Journal of Research in Science Teaching, 44*(1), 57–84.

Ruiz-Primo, M. A. Furtak, E., Yin, Y., Ayala, C., & Shavelson, R. J. (2010). On the impact of formative assessment on student science learning and motivation. In H. L. Andrade & G. J. Cizek (Eds.), *Handbook of formative assessment* (pp. 139–158). New York: Routledge.

Ruiz-Primo, M. A., & Li, M. (2004). On the use of students' science notebooks as an assessment tool. *Studies in Educational Evaluation, 30,* 61–85.

Ruiz-Primo, M. A., & Li, M. (2011, April). *Looking into the teachers' feedback practices: How teachers interpret students' work.* Paper presented at the American Educational Research Association. New Orleans, LA.

Ruiz-Primo, M. A., Li, M., Ayala, C. C., & Shavelson, R. J. (2004). Evaluating students' science notebooks as an assessment tool. *International Journal of Science Education, 26*(12), 1477–1506.

Ruiz-Primo, M. A., Li, M., Yin, Y., & Morozov, A. (2010, March). *Identifying effective feedback practices on student learning: A literature synthesis.* Paper presented at the annual meeting for the National Association of Research in Science Teaching, Philadelphia.

Ruiz-Primo, M. A., & Sands, D. (2009). *Developing and evaluating measures of formative assessment practice.* Research proposal proposed and awarded to the Developing and Evaluating Measures of Formative Assessment Practice, Washington, DC.

Sadler, R. D. (1989). Formative assessment and the design of instructional systems. *Instructional Science, 18,* 119–144.

Schunk, D. H. (1996). Goal and self-evaluative influences during children's cognitive skill learning. *American Educational Research Journal, 33,* 359–382.

Shadish, W. R., Cook, T. D., & Campbell, D. T. (2002). *Experimental and quasi-experimental designs for generalized causal inference.* Boston: Houghton Mifflin.

Shavelson, R. J., Yin, Y., Furtak, E. M., Ruiz-Primo, M. A., & Ayala, C. (2008). On the role and impact of formative assessment on science inquiry teaching and learning. In J. Coffey, R. Douglas, & C. Stearns (Eds.), *Assessing science learning. Perspectives from research and practice* (pp. 21–36). Arlington, VA: National Science Teachers Association Press.

Shih, S., & Alexander, J. M. (2000). Interacting effects of goal setting and self- or other-referenced feedback on children's development of self-efficacy and cognitive skill within the Taiwanese classroom. *Journal of Educational Psychology, 92,* 536–543.

Shute, V. (2008). Focus on formative feedback. *Review of Educational Research, 78*(1), 153–189.

Shepard, L. (2009). Commentary: Evaluating the validity of formative and interim assessment. *Educational Measurement: Issues and Practice, 28*(3), 32–37.

Stake, R. E. (1995). *The art of case study research.* Thousand Oaks, CA: Sage.

Torrance, H., & Pryor, J. (1998). *Investigating formative assessment. Teaching, learning and assessment in the classroom.* Buckingham, UK: Open University Press.

Tudge, J., Winterhoff, P., & Hogan, D. (1996). The cognitive consequences of collaborative problem solving with and without feedback. *Child Development, 67,* 2892–2909.

Tunstall, P., & Gipps, C., (1996). Teacher feedback to young children in formative assessment: A typology. *British Educational Research Journal, 22*(4), 389–404.

Wiliam, D. (2011). *Embedded formative assessment.* Bloomington, IN: Solution Tree Press.

Wragg, E. C. (1993). *An introduction to classroom observation.* London: Routledge.

Yeany, R. H., & Miller, P. A. (1983). Effects of diagnostic/remedial instruction on science learning: A meta-analysis. *Journal of Research in Science Education, 20*(1), 19–26.

Yin, R. K. (2003). *Case study research: Design and methods* (3rd ed.). Thousand Oaks, CA: Sage.

SECTION 4

Summative Assessment

Susan M. Brookhart

Associate Editor

14

Research on Classroom Summative Assessment

Connie M. Moss

Assessment is unquestionably one of the teacher's most complex and important tasks. What teachers assess and how and why they assess it sends a clear message to students about what is worth learning, how it should be learned, and how well they are expected to learn it. As a result of increased influences from external high stakes tests, teachers are increasingly working to align their CAs with a continuum of benchmarks and standards, and students are studying for and taking more CAs. Clearly, high-stakes external tests shape much of what is happening in classrooms (Clarke, Madaus, Horn, & Ramos, 2000). Teachers design assessments for a variety of purposes and deliver them with mixed results. Some bring students a sense of success and fairness, while others strengthen student perceptions of failure and injustice. Regardless of their intended purpose, CAs directly or indirectly influence students' future learning, achievement, and motivation to learn.

The primary purpose of this chapter is to review the literature on teachers' summative assessment practices to note their influence on teachers and teaching and on students and learning. It begins with an overview of effective summative assessment practices, paying particular attention to the skills and competencies that teachers need to create their own assessments, interpret the results of outside assessments, and accurately judge student achievement. Then, two recent reviews of summative assessment practices are overviewed. Next, the chapter reviews current studies of summative CAs illustrating common research themes and synthesizing prevailing recommendations. The chapter concludes by drawing conclusions about what we currently know regarding effective CA practices and highlighting areas in need of further research.

Setting the Context: The Research on Summative Classroom Assessments

Assessment is a process of collecting and interpreting evidence of student progress to inform reasoned judgments about what a student or group of students knows relative to the identified learning goals (National Research Council [NRC], 2001). How teachers carry out this process depends on the purpose of the assessment rather than on any particular method of gathering information about student progress. Unlike assessments that are formative or diagnostic, the purpose of summative assessment is to determine the student's overall achievement in a specific area of learning at a particular time—a purpose that distinguishes it from all other forms of assessment (Harlen, 2004).

The accuracy of summative judgments depends on the quality of the assessments and the competence of the assessors. When teachers choose formats (i.e., selected-response [SR], observation, essay, or oral questioning) that more strongly match important achievement targets, their assessments yield stronger information about student progress. Test items that closely align with course objectives and actual classroom instruction increase both content validity and increase reliability so assessors can make good decisions about the kind of consistency that is critical for the specific assessment purpose (Parkes & Giron, 2006). In assessments that deal with performance, reliability and validity are enhanced when teachers specifically define the performance (Baron, 1991); develop detailed scoring schemes, rubrics and procedures that clarify the standards of achievement; and record scoring during the performance being assessed (Stiggins & Bridgeford, 1985).

Teachers' Classroom Assessment Practices, Skills, and Perceptions of Competence

Teacher judgments can directly influence student achievement, study patterns, self-perceptions, attitudes, effort, and motivation to learn (Black & Wiliam, 1998; Brookhart, 1997; Rodriguez, 2004). No serious discussion of effective summative CA practices can occur, therefore, without clarifying the tensions between those practices and the assessment competencies of classroom teachers. Teachers have primary responsibility for designing and using summative assessments to evaluate the impact of their own instruction and gauge the learning progress of their students. Teacher judgments of student achievement are central to classroom and school decisions including but not limited to instructional planning, screening, placement, referrals, and communication with parents (Gittman & Koster, 1999; Hoge, 1984; Sharpley & Edgar, 1986).

Teachers can spend a third or more of their time on assessment-related activities (Plake, 1993; Stiggins, 1991, 1999). In fact, some estimates place the number of teacher-made tests in a typical classroom at 54 per year (Marso & Pigge, 1988), an incidence rate that can yield billions of unique testing activities yearly worldwide (Worthen, Borg, & White, 1993). These activities include everything from designing paper–pencil tests and performance assessments to interpreting and grading test results, communicating assessment information to various stakeholders, and using assessment information for educational decision making. Throughout these assessment activities, teachers tend to have more confidence in their own assessments rather than in those designed by others. And they tend to trust in their own judgments rather than information about student learning that comes from other sources (Boothroyd, McMorris, & Pruzek, 1992; Stiggins & Bridgeford, 1985). But is this confidence warranted?

The CA literature is split on teachers' ability to accurately summarize student achievement. Some claim that teachers can be the best source of student achievement information. Effective teachers can possess overarching and comprehensive experiences with students that can result in rich, multidimensional understandings (Baker, Mednick, & Hocevar, 1991; Hopkins, George, & Williams, 1985; Kenny & Chekaluk, 1993; Meisels, Bickel, Nicholson, Xue, & Atkins-Burnett, 2001). Counterclaims present a more skeptical view of teachers as accurate judges of student achievement. Teacher judgments can be clouded by an inability to distinguish between student achievement and student traits like perceived ability, motivation, and engagement that relate to achievement (Gittman & Koster, 1999; Sharpley & Edgar, 1986). These poor judgments can be further exacerbated when teachers assess students with diverse backgrounds and characteristics (Darling-Hammond, 1995; Martínez & Mastergeorge, 2002; Tiedemann, 2002).

A Gap Between Perception and Competence

For over 50 years, the CA literature has documented the gap between teachers' perceived and actual assessment competence. Teachers regularly use a variety of assessment techniques despite inadequate preservice preparation or in-service professional development about how to effectively design, interpret, and use them (Goslin, 1967; O'Sullivan & Chalnick, 1991; Roeder, 1972). Many teachers habitually include nonachievement factors like behavior and attitude, degree of effort, or perceived motivation for the topic or assignment in their summative assessments. And they calculate grades without weighing the various assessments by importance (Griswold, 1993; Hills, 1991; Stiggins, Frisbie, & Griswold, 1989). When they create and use performance assessments, teachers commonly fail to define success criteria for the various levels of the performance or plan appropriate scoring schemes and procedures prior to instruction. Moreover, their tendency to record their judgments after a student's performance rather than assessing each performance as it takes place consistently weakens accurate conclusions about how each student performed (Goldberg & Roswell, 2000).

In addition to discrepancies in designing and using their own assessments, teachers' actions during standardized testing routinely compromise the effectiveness of test results for accurately gauging student achievement and informing steps to improve it. Teachers often teach test items, provide clues and hints, extend time frames, and even change students' answers (Hall & Kleine, 1992; Nolen, Haladyna, & Haas, 1992). Even when standardized tests are not compromised, many teachers are unable to accurately interpret the test results (Hills, 1991; Impara, Divine, Bruce, Liverman, & Gay, 1991) and lack the skills and knowledge to effectively communicate the meaning behind the scores (Plake, 1993).

Incongruities in teachers' assessment practices have long been attributed to a consistent source of variance: A majority of teachers mistakenly assume that they possess sound knowledge of CA based on their own experiences and university coursework (Gullikson, 1984; Wise, Lukin, & Roos, 1991). Researchers consistently suggest collaborative experiences with assessments as a way to narrow the gap between teacher perceptions of their assessment knowledge and skill and their actual assessment competence. These knowledge-building experiences develop and strengthen common assessment understandings, quality indicators, and skills. What's more, collaboration increases professional assessment language and dispositions toward reflecting during and after assessment practices events to help teachers recognize how assessments can promote or derail student learning and achievement (Aschbacher, 1999; Atkin & Coffey, 2001; Black & Wiliam, 1998; Borko, Mayfield, Marion, Flexer, & Cumbo, 1997; Falk & Ort, 1998; Gearhart & Saxe, 2004; Goldberg & Roswell, 2000; Laguarda & Anderson, 1998; Sato, 2003; Sheingold, Heller, & Paulukonis, 1995; Wilson, 2004; Wilson & Sloane, 2000).

Two Reviews of Summative Assessment by the Evidence for Policy and Practice Information and Co-Ordinating Centre

Impact of Summative Assessments and Tests on Students' Motivation for Learning

The Evidence for Policy and Practice Information and Co-Ordinating Centre (EPPI-Centre), part of the Social Science Research Unit at the Institute of Education, University of London, offers support and expertise to those undertaking systematic reviews. With its support, Harlen and Crick (2002) synthesized 19 studies (13 outcome evaluations, 3 descriptive studies, and 3 process evaluations). The review was prompted by the global standardized testing movement in the 1990s and sought to identify the impact of summative assessment and testing on student motivation to learn. While a more extensive discussion of CA in the context of motivational theory and research is presented in this volume (see Brookhart, Chapter 3 of this volume), several conclusions from this review are worth mentioning here.

The researchers noticed that following the introduction of the national curriculum tests in England, low achieving students tended to have lower self-esteem than higher achieving students. Prior to the tests, there had been no correlation between self-esteem and achievement. These negative perceptions of self-esteem often decrease students' future effort and academic success. What's more, the high-stakes tests impacted teachers, making them more likely to choose teaching practices that transmit information during activities that are highly structured and teacher controlled. These teaching practices and activities favor students who prefer to learn this way and disadvantage and lower the self-esteem of students who prefer more active and learner-centered experiences. Likewise, standardized tests create a performance ethos in the classroom and can become the rationale for all classroom decisions and produce students who have strong extrinsic orientations toward performance rather than learning goals. Not only do students share their dislike for high-stakes tests but they also exhibit high levels of test anxiety and are keenly aware that the narrow test results do not accurately represent what they understand or can do.

Not surprisingly, student engagement, self-efficacy, and effort increase in classrooms where teachers encourage self-regulated learning (SRL) and empower students with challenging choices and opportunities to collaborate with each other. In these classrooms, effective assessment feedback helps increase student motivation to learn. This feedback tends to be task involved rather than ego involved to increase students' orientation toward learning rather than performance goals.

Impact of Summative Assessments on Students, Teachers, and the Curriculum

The second review (Harlen, 2004), which synthesized 23 studies, conducted mostly in England and the United States, involved students between the ages of 4 and 18. Twenty studies involved embedding summative assessment in regular classroom activities (i.e., portfolios and projects), and eight were either set externally or set by the teacher to external criteria. The review was focused on examining research evidence to learn more about a range of benefits often attributed to teachers' CA practices including rich understandings of student achievement spanning various contexts and outcomes, the capacity to prevent the negative impacts of standardized tests on student motivation to learn, and teacher autonomy in pursuit of learning goals via methods tailored to their particular students. The review also focused on the influence of teachers' summative assessments practices on their relationships with students, their workload, and difficulties with reliability and quality. The main findings considered two outcomes for the use of assessment for summative purposes by teachers: (1) impact on students and (2) impact on teachers and the curriculum.

Impact on Students

When teachers use summative assessments for external purposes like certification for vocational qualifications, selection for employment or further education, and monitoring the school's accountability or gauging the school's performance, students benefit from receiving better descriptions and examples that help them understand the assessment criteria and what is expected of them. Older students respond positively to teachers' summative assessment of their coursework, find the work motivating, and are able to learn during the assessment process. The impact of external uses of summative assessment on students depends on the high-stakes use of the results and whether teachers orient toward improving the quality of students' learning or maximizing students' scores.

When teachers use summative assessments for internal purposes like regular grading for record keeping, informing decisions about choices within the school, and reporting to parents and students, nonjudgmental feedback motivates students for further effort. In the same vein, using grades as rewards and punishments both decreases student motivation to learn and harms the learning itself. And the way teachers present their CA activities may affect their students' orientation to learning goals or performance goals.

Impact on Teachers and the Curriculum

Teachers differ in their response to their role as assessors and the approach they take to interpreting external assessment criteria. Teachers who favor firm adherence to external criteria tend to be less concerned with students as individuals. When teacher assessment is subjected to close external control, teachers can be hindered from gaining detailed knowledge of their students.

When teachers create assessments for internal purposes, they need opportunities to share and develop their understanding of assessment procedures within their buildings and across schools. Teachers benefit from being exposed to assessment strategies that require students to think more deeply. Employing these strategies promotes changes in teaching that extend the range of students' learning experiences. These new assessment practices are more likely to have a positive impact on teaching when teachers recognize ways that the strategies help them learn more about their students and develop more sophisticated understandings of curricular goals. Of particular importance is the role that shared assessment criteria play in the classroom. When present, these criteria exert a positive influence on students and teaching. Without shared criteria, however, there is little positive impact on teaching and a potential negative impact on students. Finally, high stakes use of tests can influence teachers' internal uses of CA by reducing those assessments to routine tasks and restricting students' opportunities for learning from the assessments.

Review of Recent Research on Classroom Summative Assessment Practices

What follows is a review of the research on summative assessments practices in classrooms published from 1999 to 2011 and gathered from an Education Resources Information Center (ERIC) search on summative assessments. Studies that were featured in the Harlen and Crick (2002) or the Harlen (2004) reviews were removed. The resulting group of 16 studies investigated summative assessment practices in relation to teachers and teaching and/or students, student learning, and achievement. A comparison of the research aims across the studies resulted in three broad themes: (1) the classroom assessment (CA) environment and student motivation, (2) teachers' assessment practices and skills, and (3) teachers' judgments of student achievement. Table 14.1, organized by theme, presents an overview of the studies.

Theme One: Students' Perceptions of the Classroom Assessment Environment Impact Student Motivation to Learn

Understanding student perceptions of the CA environment and their relationship to student motivational factors was the common aim of four studies (Alkharusi, 2008; Brookhart & Bronowicz, 2003; Brookhart, & Durkin, 2003; Brookhart, Walsh, & Zientarski, 2006). Studies in this group examined teacher assessment practices from the students' point of view using student interviews, questionnaires, and observations. Findings noted both assessment environments and student perceptions of CAs purposes influence students' goals, effort, and feelings of self-efficacy.

As Brookhart and Durkin (2003) noted, even though high profile, large-scale assessments tend to be more carefully studied and better funded, the bulk of what students experience in regard to assessment happens during regular and frequent CAs. Investigations in this theme build on Brookhart's (1997) theoretical model that synthesized CA literature, social cognitive theories of learning, and motivational constructs. The model describes the CA environment as a dynamic context, continuously experienced by students, as their teachers communicate assessment purposes, assign assessment tasks, create success criteria, provide feedback, and monitor student outcomes. These interwoven assessment events communicate what is valued, establish the culture of the classroom, and have a significant influence on students' motivation and achievement goals (Ames, 1992; Brookhart, 1997; Harlen & Crick, 2003).

Teachers' Teaching Experience and Assessment Practices Interact With Students' Characteristics to Influence Students' Achievement Goals

Alkharusi (2008) investigated the influence of CA practices on student motivation. Focusing on a common argument that alternative assessments are more intrinsically motivating than traditional assessments (e.g., Shepard, 2000), the study explored the CA culture of science classes in Muscat public schools in Oman. Participants included 1,636 ninth-grade students (735 male, 901 females) and their 83 science teachers (37 males, 46 females). The teachers averaged 5.2 years of teaching ranging from 1 to 13.5 years of experience. Data came from teacher and student questionnaires. Students indicated their perceptions of the CA environment, their achievement goals, and self-efficacy on a 4-point Likert scale. Teachers rated their frequency of use of various assessment practices on a 5-point Likert scale. Using hierarchical linear models to examine variations present in achievement goals, the study suggests that general principles of CA and achievement goal theory can apply to both U.S. and Oman cultures. Teachers became more aware of the "detrimental effects of classroom assessments that emphasize the importance of grades rather than learning and [focused] on public rather than private evaluation and recognition practices in student achievement motivation" (Alkharusi, 2008, p. 262). Furthermore, the aggregate data suggest that the people and actions around them influence students. Specifically, students are more likely to adopt performance goals such as doing better than others rather than mastery goals of learning more, when assessment environments place value on grades. Students' collective experiences regarding the assessment climate influenced patterns of individual student achievement motivation.

Study	*Research Aim*	*Participants*	*Method*	*Summary of Findings*
Theme One: Classroom Practices and Student Motivation				
Alkharusi (2008)	• Examine the effects of CA practices on students' achievement goals.	• 1,636 ninth-grade students (735 males, 901 females) • 83 science teachers from Muscat public schools in Oman (37 males, 46 females)	Survey	• Both individual student characteristics and perceptions and group characteristics and perceptions influence and explain student mastery goals.
Brookhart & Bronowicz (2003)	• Examine students' perceptions of CAs in relation to assignment interest and importance, student self-efficacy for the task and goal orientation behind their effort.	• Seven teachers (five female, two male) from four schools in Western, Pennsylvania (two elementary, two middle, and two high schools) • 161 students from seven different classrooms in four different schools (63 elementary/middle, 98 high school)	Multiple case analysis	• What matters most to a student affects the student's approach to assessment. • There is a developmental progression in student ability to articulate what it means to succeed in school.
Brookhart & Durkin (2003)	• Describe a variety of CA events in high school social studies classes.	• 1 teacher researcher • 96 students from a large urban high school in the United States	Case study	• The design of the CA, process for completing it, and how much time it takes may affect student motivation and effort. • Performance assessments tap both internal and external sources of motivation.
Brookhart, Walsh, & Zientarski (2006)	• Examine motivation and effort patterns associated with achievement in middle school science and social studies.	• Four teachers (two science, two social studies) from a suburban middle school • 223 eighth-grade students from a suburban Pennsylvania middle school	Field study	• CAs differ on how they are handled and how they engage student motivation and effort, and they have a profound effect on student achievement.
Theme Two: Teacher Assessment Practices and Skills				
Black, Harrison, Hodgen, Marshall, & Serret (2010)	• Explore teachers' understanding and practices in their summative assessments.	• 18 teachers (10 mathematics, 8 English) from three schools in Oxfordshire, England	Partially grounded theory	• Teachers' summative practices were not consistent with their beliefs about validity. • Teacher critiques of their own understandings of validity fostered a critical view of their existing practice.

Study	*Research Aim*	*Participants*	*Method*	*Summary of Findings*
McKinney, Chappell, Berry, & Hickman (2009)	• Investigate pedagogical and instructional mathematical skills of teachers in high-poverty elementary schools.	• 99 teachers from high-poverty schools	Survey	• Teachers rely heavily on teacher-made tests to assess mathematics. • Only a small percentage use alternative assessment strategies.
McMillan (2001)	• Describe assessment and grading practices of secondary teachers.	• 1,483 teachers from 53 middle and high schools in urban/metropolitan Virginia	Survey	• Teachers differentiate cognitive levels of assessments as either higher-order thinking or recall. • Higher ability students receive more assessments that are motivating and engaging while lower ability students receive assessments emphasizing rote learning, extra credit, and less emphasis on academic achievement. • English teachers place more emphasis on constructed-response (CR) items and higher order thinking.
McMillan (2003)	• Determine relationships between teacher self-reported instructional and CA practices and scores on a state high-stakes test.	• 79 fifth-grade teachers from 29 K–5 suburban elementary schools	Survey	• English/language arts teachers used objective tests much more frequently than essay, informal, performance, authentic, or portfolio. • Higher usage of essays in math and English was related to higher objective test scores.
McMillan (2005)	• Investigate relationships between teachers' receipt of high-stakes test results and subsequent changes in instructional and CA practices in the following year.	• 722 teachers from seven Richmond, Virginia, school districts	Survey	• Teachers reported making significant changes to their assessment practices as a result of high-stakes test scores. • Teachers reported placing more emphasis on formative assessments.
McMillan & Lawson (2001)	• Investigate secondary science teachers' grading and assessment practices.	• 213 high school science teachers from urban, suburban and rural schools	Survey	• Secondary science teachers used four assessment types: (1) CR, (2) tests created by or (3) supplied to the teacher, and (4) major examinations. • Teachers tended to use self-made tests, assess as much recall as understanding, use more performance assessments with higher ability students, and assess more recall of knowledge with low ability students.

(Continued)

Table 14.1 (Continued)

Study	*Research Aim*	*Participants*	*Method*	*Summary of Findings*
McMillan & Nash (2000)	• Examine the reasons teachers give for their assessment and grading practices and the factors that influence their reasoning.	• 24 elementary and secondary teachers	Interview	• Tension exists between internal beliefs and values teachers hold regarding effective assessment and realities of their classroom environments and external factors imposed upon them.
Rieg (2007)	• Investigate perceptions of junior high teachers and students at risk of school failure on the effectiveness and use of various CAs.	• 32 teachers from three junior high schools in Pennsylvania • 119 students identified by teachers as being at risk (72 at risk of failing two or more subjects; 20 who also had 10% or greater absenteeism; 27 at risk of dropping out) • 329 students not considered at risk	Survey	• Teachers do not use assessment strategies in their practice that they believe to be effective. • There is a significant difference between what the students at risk felt were effective assessment strategies and the strategies they perceived their teachers actually use. • Students at risk rated 82% of the assessment strategies as more effective than teachers' ratings. • Teachers perceived using certain assessment strategies much more frequently than students perceived that their teachers used them.
Zhang, & Burry-Stock (2003)	• Investigate teachers' assessment practices and perceived skills.	• 297 teachers in two school districts in southeastern United States	Self-reports survey	• As grade level increases, teachers rely more on objective techniques over performance assessments and show an increased concern for assessment quality. • Knowledge in measurement and testing has a significant impact on teachers' self-perceived assessment skills regardless of teaching experience.
Theme Three: Teacher Judgments of Student Achievement				
Kilday, Kinzie, Mashburn, & Whittaker (2011)	• Examine concurrent validity of teachers' judgments of students' math abilities in preschool.	• 33 pre–K teachers in Virginia public school classrooms • 318 students identified as being in at-risk conditions	Hierarchical linear modeling	• Teachers misestimate preschool students' abilities in math both in number sense and in geometry and measurement.

Study	*Research Aim*	*Participants*	*Method*	*Summary of Findings*
Martínez, Stecher, & Borko (2009)	• Investigate teacher judgments of student achievement compared to student standardized test scores to learn if CA practices moderate the relationship between the two.	• 10,700 third-grade students • 8,600 fifth-grade students • Teacher reports of use of standardized test scores and their use of standards for evaluating different students	Unconditional hierarchical linear model	• Teachers judged student achievement in relation to the population in their schools thereby circumventing criterion referencing. • Teachers based evaluations on student needs or abilities. • Gaps in performance of students with disabilities were more pronounced on teacher ratings than standardized test scores. • Teacher judgments incorporate a broader set of dimensions of performance than standardized tests and give more comprehensive picture of student achievement but are susceptible to various sources of measurement error and bias.
Wyatt-Smith, Klenowski, & Gunn (2010)	• Investigate teacher judgment, the utility of stated standards to inform judgment, and the social practice moderation.	• 15 teachers (10 primary and 5 secondary) involved in an assessment communities in Queensland, Australia	Analysis of recordings of talk and conversations	• Common assessment materials do not necessarily lead to common practice or shared understandings. • Teachers tended to view criteria as a guide and perceived it as self-limiting to adhere rigidly to the criteria. • Unstated considerations including perceived value of the benefit of the doubt are included in the judgment making process. • Teachers indicated applying unstated standards they carry around in their head and perceived to have in common to reach an agreement on evaluating ability. • Teachers were challenged practically and conceptually when moving between explicit and tacit knowledge regarding their judgments.

Table 14.1 Overview of 1999 to 2011 Studies on Classroom Summative Assessment

NOTE: CA = classroom assessment.

Student Perceptions of Self-Efficacy May Encourage Students to Consider Classroom Assessment as an Important Part of Learning

Brookhart and colleagues (Brookhart & Bronowicz, 2003; Brookhart & Durkin, 2003; Brookhart et al., 2006) authored the three remaining studies in this theme. The studies reported evidence of CAs and related student perceptions "in their habitats" (Brookhart et al., 2006, p. 163) using classroom observations, artifacts from actual assessment events, and interviews with students and teachers. The three studies yielded the following findings:

- What matters most to a student affects how that student approaches an academic assessment (Brookhart & Bronowicz, 2003).
- There may be a developmental progression in students' ability to articulate what it means to succeed in school (Brookhart & Bronowicz, 2003).
- The CA design, the process for completing it, and the amount of time the assessment takes may influence student motivation and perceptions of effort (Brookhart & Durkin, 2003).
- Teachers can stimulate both mastery and performance goals by designing and using interesting and relevant performance assessments in their classrooms (Brookhart & Durkin, 2003).
- CA environments tend to be more clearly defined by perceptions of the importance and value of assessments coupled with mastery goal orientations (Brookhart et al., 2006).

Summary of Theme One

Taken together, the four studies in this theme present evidence of the profound effects that the CA environment has on student motivation to learn. That motivation is influenced by factors that lie outside the teacher's control—an individual student's interests and needs and students' abilities across grades and developmental levels. What teachers test and how they test over time, however, creates a unique classroom climate that either fuels motivation to learn or derails it. These CA practices are more often than not directly under the teacher's control. Further explorations of student perceptions of self-efficacy in relation to the CA environment may help educators understand the factors that encourage students to study more, try harder, or consider CA as an important part of learning.

Theme Two: Teachers' Summative Assessment Practices and Skills Impact Teacher Effectiveness and Student Achievement

Nine studies investigated summative assessment practices of classroom teachers in relation to seven factors: (1) validity in teachers' summative assessments (Black, Harrison, Hodgen, Marshall, & Serret, 2010), (2) summative assessments in mathematics in urban schools (McKinney, Chappell, Berry, & Hickman, 2009), (3) assessment and grading in secondary classrooms (McMillan, 2001; McMillan, & Lawson, 2001), (4) how teachers' assessment practices relate to and are influenced by scores on high-stakes tests (McMillan, 2003, 2005), (5) the reasons teachers give for their assessment practices (McMillan & Nash, 2000), (6) how teachers' perceptions of assessment practices relate to the perceptions of students at risk of school failure, and (7) relationships between actual assessment practices and teachers' perceived assessment skills (Zhang & Burry-Stock, 2003).

Research Through Professional Development Intervention

Black et al. (2010) implemented the King's-Oxfordshire Summative Assessment Project (KOSAP) to examine and then improve the quality of teachers' summative assessments. Their study examined teachers' understandings of validity and the ways teachers explain and develop that understanding as they learn to audit and improve their existing practices (p. 216). The 35-month project (March 2005 through November 2007) involved 18 teachers from three schools (10 mathematics teachers and 8 English teachers) who taught Grade 8 students (ages 12 to 13). In the first year, teachers were asked to analyze the validity of their assessment practices and create student portfolios that included basic assessment evidence. Working together first in their schools and then across schools, teachers negotiated the portfolio's content, designed common assessment tasks, determined the need for unique assessments for specific purposes, and established procedures for intra- and inter-school moderation. The moderation process occurred as teachers agreed to communal summative assessment standards and grappled with the disparities of their own judgments and those of their colleagues. Data sources included classroom observations of summative assessment events, records of in-school and inter-school moderation meetings, evidence of summative assessments submitted for moderation, and teachers' reflective diaries.

The study revealed the inconsistency between teachers' beliefs about validity and their summative practices; assessment purposes rarely matched assessment practices. Teachers debated assessment validity and their understanding of validity by investigating three issues: (1) the role assessment plays in their judgments of student achievement, (2) the influence these judgments have on learning experiences in their classrooms, and (3) how they deal with the pressure of sharing assessment information with various stakeholders.

While the project impacted teachers' assessment beliefs and practices, the researchers caution that improved assessment competence and skills require sustained commitment over several years. They suggested that interventions should begin with teachers auditing their existing practices, move to engaging communities of teachers in reflection on their individual and shared assessment literacy, and proceed to teachers working together to improve their underlying beliefs and assumptions regarding summative assessment (Black et al., 2010).

Summative Assessments in Mathematics Can Contribute to a "Pedagogy of Poverty"

Historically, traditional and routine instruction and assessment practices dominate mathematics education in urban schools (Hiebert, 2003; Van De Walle, 2006) to produce what Haberman (1991, 2005) framed as the "pedagogy of poverty." McKinney et al. (2009) situated their study in high-poverty schools to investigate current instructional practices in mathematics and compare them to recommendations made by the National Council of Teachers of Mathematics (NCTM) (2000).

They examined practices of 99 elementary teachers from high-poverty schools who attended an NCTM conference and volunteered to complete the *Mathematics Instructional Practices and Assessment Instrument* during the conference. Using a 43-item survey that described effective mathematics instruction (33 indicators) and effective assessment practices (10 indicators), respondents indicated which practices they used and how frequently they used them. Participants were also asked to write in any practices not included in the survey.

The majority of respondents indicated a heavy reliance on traditional teacher-made tests. This finding is in direct opposition to NCTM (2000) principles that encourage its members to match their assessment practices to their CA purpose; be mindful of the ways CA can be used to enhance student learning; and employ alternative strategies like student self-assessments, portfolios, interviews and conferences, analysis of error patterns, and authentic assessments.

As a result of their investigation, McKinney et al. (2009) reported that little had changed in high-poverty mathematics classrooms. Although NCTM encourages its members to employ alternative approaches that allow student inquiry and a concentration on problem solving and reasoning skills, members failed to use them to improve the mathematics success of urban high-poverty students. Only a small number of respondents reported using alternative approaches to mathematics assessment, and even those teachers admitted to using the practices infrequently.

The Influence of High-Stakes Tests on Summative Assessment Practices

Two studies by McMillan (2003, 2005) examined the relationships between high-stakes tests and CA practices. McMillan (2003) warranted the purpose of his first study by citing the lack of empirical evidence about high-stakes testing that relates instructional and CA practices to actual test scores (p. 5). He investigated 70 fifth-grade English and language arts teachers from 29 K–5 suburban elementary schools. The study employed a survey to collect teachers' self-reports of instructional and CA practices. He used average mathematics and reading test scale scores of students in each class as dependent variables and a measure of aptitude as a covariate.

Despite the limitation inherent in self-report data that are not substantiated by classroom observations or artifacts, the findings reveal a positive correlation between the use of essay tests in mathematics and English and higher objective test scores (McMillan, 2003, p. 9). Even given the correlational nature of the findings, the results suggested that essay tests might be a promising CA approach for raising high-stakes test results. This is especially true since the English/language arts teachers in the study reported using objective tests more frequently than essay, performance, authentic, or portfolio assessments.

McMillan's second study (2005), based on previous research (Shepard, 2000) suggesting that tests emphasizing low-level learning influenced more low-level learning practices in classrooms, investigated relationships between teachers' receipt of their students' high-stakes test score results and their revised instructional and CA practices in the following year. McMillan analyzed written survey data from 722 elementary, middle school, and high school teachers from seven Richmond, Virginia, school districts.

Findings showed that teachers believed they had made significant changes to their assessment practices as a direct result of receiving high-stakes test scores (McMillan, 2005, p. 11). Additionally, the teachers reported an increased use of formative assessments, indicating they were more inclined to use assessment data to inform their teaching. Even though changes occurred more often at the elementary level, secondary English teachers were slightly more likely to change their practices than teachers of other subjects. And more secondary social studies teachers seemed to be influenced in their content area practices by the nature of the high-stakes tests since these tests focused on simple knowledge and understanding.

Assessment and Grading Practices in Secondary Classrooms

Most studies examining assessment and grading practices in secondary classrooms use limited sample sizes (ranging from 24 to 150 participants), making it difficult to isolate grade level and subject matter differences and trends (McMillan, 2001, p. 21). In response to this condition, McMillan (2001) and McMillan and Lawson (2001) intentionally used larger participant samples to examine the relationship between assessment and grading in secondary education.

McMillan (2001) examined the practices of 1,438 classroom teachers (Grades 6 through 12) in 53 schools from seven urban/metropolitan school districts in Virginia across a range of content (science, social studies, mathematics, and English). Teachers responded to a questionnaire of closed-form items to indicate the extent to which they emphasized different grading and assessment practices. The questionnaire contained 34 items in three categories (19 items assessed factors teachers used to determine grades, 11 items assessed different types of assessments, and 4 items assessed the cognitive level of the assessments). Three factor analyses reduced the items to fewer components to analyze the relationship among assessment and grading practices and grade level, subject matter, and ability level of the class.

Results indicated an overall tendency for most secondary teachers to differentiate the cognitive level of their assessments into two categories, higher-order thinking, and recall knowledge, with higher-order thinking emphasized more than recall. Analyses of student ability levels and subject matter revealed that class ability level to be a significant variable related to assessment and grading. McMillan (2001) concluded that higher ability students may "experience an assessment environment that is motivating and engaging, because of the types of assessments and cognitive levels of assessments . . . [while] low-ability students [experience] . . . assessment and grading practices that appear to emphasize rote learning" (p. 31).

English teachers differed most from other subject areas when considering types of assessments. These teachers emphasized higher-order thinking more than science and social studies teachers and placed more emphasis on constructed-response (CR) assessments, teacher-developed assessments, and major exams and less reliance on recall items, objective assessments, and quizzes (McMillan, 2001, p. 31). Since teacher reports of their practices were associated to their actions within a specific class and content, McMillan (2001) suggested that future research take subject matter into consideration when examining CA practices since they are "inexorably integrated with instruction and goals for student learning" (p. 32).

McMillan and Lawson (2001) used the survey instrument and data analyses from McMillan's

2001 study to investigate grading and assessment practices of 213 secondary science teachers from urban, suburban, and rural schools. Their findings indicate that though secondary science teachers tended to use teacher-designed, CR assessments, they relied most heavily on objective assessments and emphasized the recall of information nearly as much as they assessed students' understanding. Similar to McMillan's 2001 findings, patterns of differences related to the ability level of the class. Higher-ability students were advantaged by CA environments where teachers used more performance assessments and emphasized higher cognitive levels.

Reasons Teachers Give for Their Assessment and Grading Practices

To better understand the factors that influence teachers' CA and grading, McMillan and Nash (2000) examined those factors in relation to the reasons teachers give for their decisions. They investigated assessment reasoning and decision making of 24 elementary and secondary teachers selected from a pool of 200 volunteers. Teachers were interviewed in their schools during individual sessions that lasted between 45 to 60 minutes. The four-member research team tape-recorded 20 of the interviews and took notes during and after all interviews. Data were coded according to both emerging and preestablished topics identified in the interview guide. The research team organized the coding into five pervasive themes that explained the data and conducted individual case studies for 20 of the 24 teachers adding 10 new categories and one more pervasive theme. The final six themes formed an explanatory model for how and why teachers decided to use specific assessment and grading practices that included the following: (1) teacher beliefs and values, (2) classroom realities, (3) external factors, (4) teacher decision-making rationale, (5) assessment practices, and (6) grading practices. The model illustrated the tension between teachers' internal beliefs and values and the realities of their classrooms along with other mitigating external factors (McMillan & Nash, 2000, p. 9).

The analysis of the reasoning behind teachers' idiosyncratic assessment practices prompted McMillan and Nash (2000) to conclude that the constant tension teachers experience between what they believe about effective CA and the realities of their classrooms, along with pressures from external factors, cause teachers to view assessment as a fluid set of principles that changes each year. Teachers saw assessment and grading as a largely private matter rarely discussed with other teachers, felt most comfortable constructing their own CAs, and often used preassessments to guide their instruction. They reported that learning was best assessed through multiple assessments and that their thinking about how assessments enhance student learning heavily influenced their classroom decisions. Teachers readily admitted that they *pulled for* their students and often used practices that helped them succeed. In fact, their desire to see students succeed was so strong that it prompted the researchers to question whether that desire "promoted assessment practices where students could obtain good grades without really knowing the content or being able to demonstrate the skill" (McMillan & Nash, 2000, p. 36).

Teachers' Perceptions of Their Classroom Assessment Practices and Skills

Teachers routinely use a variety of assessment practices despite being inadequately trained in how to design and use them effectively (Hills, 1991). Two studies in this review investigated this argument by examining teachers' self-perceived assessment skills. In the first study (Rieg, 2007), assessment strategies that teachers perceived to be effective and useful for students who were at risk were compared to the students' view of those same strategies. The second study (Zhang & Barry-Stock, 2003) compared teachers' self-perceived skills with their actual CA practices. A description of each study follows.

Rieg (2007) surveyed 32 teachers from three junior high schools in Pennsylvania. The teachers taught various subjects including language arts, mathematics, social studies, and science. Rieg designed and used two survey instruments (one for teachers and one for students) containing 28 items informed by the literature on students at risk, assessment, grades and motivation, and middle grade students (p. 216). Teachers were asked to rate the effectiveness of the strategies included on the survey and then indicate the frequency with which they used each strategy in their classrooms. She also surveyed 119 students classified as at risk: 72 were at risk of failing two or more subjects, 20 also had 10% or greater absenteeism, and 27 were at risk of dropping out of school. In addition, surveys were given to 329 students who were not considered to be at risk. Surveys were read aloud to all students to eliminate limitations of individual student reading difficulties that might have interfered with the results.

There were significant differences between teacher and student perceptions of the assessment strategies that were effective and in frequent use. Teachers reported not using many of the assessments and assessment-related strategies that they perceived as effective. Students reported that their teachers rarely used the strategies they felt to be helpful. These strategies included providing in-class time to prepare for assessments, giving a detailed review of what would be on a test, supplying rubrics or checklists before a performance assessment, and furnishing a study guide to help prepare for tests (p. 220). There was a positive mean difference on 23 (82%) of the strategies that the students perceived to be more effective than their teacher, and there was a significant difference on seven (25%) items with teachers' perception of use being greater than the students' perception of the teacher's use of those strategies. Overall, Rieg reported statistically significant differences between the perceptions of students at risk on the helpfulness and use of 26 (93%) of the 28 survey items.

Zhang and Burry-Stock (2003) also examined teachers' perceptions of CA practices to learn more about teachers' assessment skills. Their investigation was framed by the *Standards for Teacher Competence in Educational Assessment of Students* (American Federation of Teachers [AFT], National Council on Measurement in Education [NCME], & National Education Association [NEA], 1990). They administered the *Assessment Practices Inventory* (API) (Zhang & Barry-Stock, 1994) to 297 teachers in two southeastern U.S. school districts. Factor analytical technique was applied to study the relationship between the constructs of assessment practices and self-perceived assessment skills on the self-report survey.

Teachers' assessment practices differed by teaching levels with a general difference between elementary and secondary teachers in terms of assessment methods used and teachers' concerns for assessment quality. Secondary teachers relied more heavily on paper–pencil tests and had greater concern for assessment quality. Elementary teachers reported greater reliance on performance assessments. In addition to variance by grade levels, teachers' assessment practices differed across content areas. This finding prompted a call for increased assessment training at the preservice and in-service levels that is specifically linked to effective instructional strategies for particular areas of content and grade levels. Knowledge in measurement and testing had a significant impact on teachers' perceptions of their CA skills regardless of teaching experience. This impact strongly influenced teachers' ability to interpret standardized test scores, revise teacher-made tests, modify instruction based on assessment feedback, use performance assessments, and communicate assessment results (p. 335). In light of this, the researchers called for increased university coursework in tests and measurement as a way to increase teachers' CA expertise.

Summary of Theme Two

The nine studies in this theme reveal tensions and challenges faced by classroom teachers as they compare their summative assessment practices with their own beliefs about effective summative assessments. There were significant discrepancies between teacher perceptions of effective summative assessment practices and their self-reports of their actual classroom practices (Black et al., 2010; McKinney et al., 2009; McMillan & Nash, 2000; Rieg, 2007). Secondary teachers reported a general trend toward objective tests over alternative assessments (McMillan, 2001; McMillan & Lawson, 2001) even though higher usage of essays in mathematics and English was related to higher objective test scores (McMillan & Lawson, 2001). These discrepancies might be explained in part by the influence of high-stakes testing on the choices teachers make based on their changing views of the essential purposes for summarizing student achievement (McMillan, 2003, 2005). Another influence may lie in the level of assessment knowledge that teachers possess and the grade levels that they teach. This tendency may be partially attributed to the teachers' perceived assessment knowledge—a factor found to exert more influence on a teacher's assessment practices than the teacher's actual teaching experience (Zhang & Burry-Stock, 2003).

Theme Three: Many Factors Impact the Accuracy of Teachers' Judgments of Student Achievement.

The final theme includes four studies (Kilday, Kinzie, Mashburn, & Whittaker, 2011; Martínez, Stecher, & Borko, 2009; McMillan, 2001; Wyatt-Smith, Klenowski, & Gunn, 2010) that examine the validity of teachers' judgments of student achievement and the dimensions they consider when making those judgments. Two of the four studies (Kilday et al., 2011; Wyatt-Smith et al., 2010) compared teacher judgments of student achievement to results from standardized test scores to investigate how teachers understand and use assessment criteria. Each study is discussed in turn.

Misestimates of Student Achievement Stem From Characteristics Inherent to the Teacher

Kilday et al. (2011) used hierarchical linear modeling to examine the concurrent validity of teachers' judgments of students' mathematics abilities in preschool. Data from an indirect rating scale assessment and the children's performance on two direct assessments of their number sense, geometry, and measurement skills were used to gauge teachers' judgments of preschool children's mathematics skills. Thirty-three teachers enrolled in a field study of a curriculum designed to enhance students' knowledge of mathematics and science participated in the study. Approximately 10 students in each teacher's class were assessed resulting in a sample of 313 students who exhibited one or more established risk factors. Each teacher rated the mathematics skills of his or her 10 students using a modified version of the Academic *Rating Scale* (ARS) for mathematics, which was developed by the Early Childhood Longitudinal Study—Kindergarten Class of 1998–99 (ECLS-K).

The teachers tended to misestimate preschool students' abilities in number sense, as well as in geometry and measurement. "Approximately 40% of the variation in teachers' ratings of students' mathematics skills stem[med] from characteristics inherent to the teacher and not the skills of the child" (Kilday et al., 2011, p. 7). The researchers attributed these findings to the inherently subjective nature of the rating scales and the amount of domain variance at the preschool level. Both factors can systematically influence teachers to misestimate the mathematics skills of young children. Based on this explanation, the researchers suggest that early childhood teachers must become more familiar with student learning trajectories in subjects like mathematics.

Teachers Base Their Judgments of Student Performance on a Broader Set of Performance Dimensions Than Standardized Test Scores

Martínez et al. (2009) used data from third- and fifth-grade samples of the *Early Childhood Longitudinal Survey* (ECLS) to investigate teacher judgments of student achievement in mathematics. The data came from the follow-up studies (ECLS-K) involving children (15,305 third graders and 11,820 fifth graders) who entered kindergarten in 1998. Data included two independent measures of student achievement in reading, mathematics, and science—one based on a standardized test and the other based entirely on the judgments of the student's teacher. Also included were data on the characteristics and practices of the children's teachers and descriptions of the children's families, classrooms, and school environments. Teacher judgments were compared to students' standardized test scores to see if the measures produced a similar picture of student mathematics achievement and if CA practices moderated the relationship between the two measures.

Teachers who participated in the ECLS-K study reported the various types of assessments they frequently used during the year and which factors they deemed important for assessing student performance. They also described the availability and usefulness of individual standardized test scores for guiding instructional decisions and the time they spent preparing for standardized tests. In addition, teachers described whether they held the same standards for evaluating and grading all students in their classroom of if they applied different standards to different students depending on perceived student need or ability (Martínez et al., 2009, p. 85).

In spite of limitations inherent in a data set that may not contain important features of what teachers do in classrooms to assess their students, Martínez et al. (2009) were able to draw conclusions and report significant findings. First, teachers' achievement ratings of students differed from standardized test scores in important ways.

> [Teachers may] explicitly or instinctively use a school-specific *normative scale* in judging the level of achievement of students in their classrooms . . . [and] may rate students high or low in relation to the achievement levels of other students in the same grade at the school and not necessarily in relation to the descriptors of performance [outlined on test scales in relation to national or state standards]. (Martínez et al., 2009, p. 90)

Second, there were discrepancies between teacher appraisals and standardized test scores in relation to student background characteristics. Teachers' achievement ratings showed a larger disadvantage than standardized test scores for students with disabilities, highlighting the complexity of evaluating students with various challenges. And while standardized tests often disadvantage females, students of minority and low socioeconomic status, and those with low English proficiency, the teachers' judgments appeared less susceptible to bias against traditionally disadvantaged student populations in measuring achievement. The researchers suggested that an alternative explanation might also be the case. Teachers might have deliberately adjusted their ratings upward or their criteria and expectations downward to compensate for disadvantage.

Overall, the findings indicated that teacher judgments incorporated a broader set of performance dimensions than standardized test scores, theoretically providing a more comprehensive picture of student achievement. Some teacher appraisals, however, might be more susceptible to error and bias. Certain teachers may be influenced to appraise student achievement more closely to standardized test scores depending on the specific teacher's background and classroom context. Rating accuracy variance might also be related to the teachers' assessment practices in the classroom that influence their ratings of student achievement. In particular, teachers might not judge student achievement in an absolute manner. They tended to judge achievement in relation to the population of third- and fifth-grade students in their schools thereby "circumventing the criterion referenced . . . scale and adopting a school-specific, norm-referenced scale" (Martínez et al., p. 97).

Teacher Judgment of Student Achievement as a Cognitive and Social Practice

Wyatt-Smith et al. (2010) investigated how stated standards frame teacher judgments and how group moderation (face-to-face and through technology) influences a dynamic process of negotiated meaning. Teacher-based assessment is often characterized as having high validity but questionable reliability (Maxwell, 2001). The study was designed to learn if a strong focus on helping teachers develop a common understanding of standards and recognition of the kinds of performances that demonstrate mastery of those standards might be central to improving reliability.

The study took place in Queensland, Australia, where there is a history of moderated standards-based assessment. "*Moderation* as judgment practices is central . . . [and] involves opportunities for teachers to . . . integrate [their own judgments] with those of other teachers and in so doing share interpretations of criteria and standards" (Wyatt-Smith et al., 2010, p. 61). Both qualitative and quantitative analyses were used to interpret survey data from pre- and post-moderation interviews and recorded conversations from moderation meetings. Fifteen primary and secondary teachers were studied as an assessment community. The teachers first met as a group to raise their awareness of the processes and procedures for moderation. They then met in smaller moderation groups involving three to four teachers.

The teachers received three resources: (1) five marked student work samples representing grades A to F; (2) the *Guide to Making Judgments* that included a matrix of task-specific descriptors and assessable elements that they should consider in their assessments; and (3) annotated student work samples for each question or element of the task and an information sheet of the "reviewing process" (Wyatt-Smith et al., 2010, p. 64). Teachers compared their judgments of each student work sample with each other's ratings to achieve consensus about which grade the work should receive. They cited evidence of the quality of the student work and the application of the assessable elements to justify their individual recommendations. The research team shadowed the teams and recorded their comments and conversations.

Simply providing teachers with assessment materials did not necessarily lead to common practices or shared understandings. Quality standards, no matter how explicitly described, were seen by teachers as inevitably vague or fuzzy. In fact, the teachers' "unstated considerations including the perceived value of 'the benefit of the doubt' were drawn into the judgment-making process" (Wyatt-Smith et al., 2010, p. 69). Teachers needed standards that worked in concert with exemplars to understand how the features of work they were judging satisfied the requirements of a specific level of performance. This might lessen the tendency for teachers to use what Harlen (2005) called "extra-textual considerations" including nonrelevant aspects of student behaviors, work, or performance in their summative assessments (p. 213).

What's more, teachers seemed to have personal standards and criteria that they carry around in their heads. These personal standards come from experience and allow teachers to reach agreement on student ability and what is "average." These *in the head* criteria and standards were not explicitly stated nor elaborated upon. The teachers simply assumed they all held them in common and regarded them as "characteristic of the experienced teacher" (Wyatt-Smith et al., 2010, p. 70). In the head criteria were also assumed to be shared by teachers for summatively judging the characteristics of an average performance.

A tension point emerged as teachers discussed the *fit* of the assessment tasks that yielded the student work samples and the ways the teachers organized their own curriculum and assessed student achievement in their classrooms. Teachers viewed the assessment tasks as distorting and felt that judgments based on them prevented students from getting what they really deserved. This frustration might be attributed to fact that the criteria sheet forced teachers to leave their comfort zone and removed factors they normally employed when judging achievement. Observational data uncovered the ease with which teachers dismissed the assessment criteria preferring to consider student attributes and allowing those attributes to influence their summative judgments. Teachers routinely discussed the merits of linking their assessments to observed student behaviors such as doing a good job, having ability, being deserving, or making an effort.

Although the teachers struggled with biases and flawed judgments, the study ultimately provides insights into the practical and conceptual challenges teachers face. These trials occur daily as teachers try to reconcile their CA practices and beliefs with standardized or common assessments and expectations. These struggles seem to influence teachers to consider both explicit and tacit knowledge about student achievement.

Summary of Theme Three

An accurate and valid description of student achievement is essential to quality teaching and meaningful learning. This knowledge enables teachers to design effective instruction, provide useful feedback, and design effective assessments to collect evidence of student learning. Teachers appear to benefit from talking with each other and experiencing disequilibrium in regard to the validity of their beliefs and practices (Wyatt-Smith et al., 2010). Understanding how teachers view and use assessment criteria provides insights into how their biases and misunderstandings can cause them to misestimate student achievement (Kilday et al., 2011) and prefer their own in the head criteria when it comes to summarizing student achievement (Wyatt-Smith et al., 2010). Teachers may adopt a school-referenced rather than criterion-referenced orientation to summative assessment thereby muddying their decisions and decreasing the reliability and validity of their judgments (Martínez et al., 2009).

Discussion and Recommended Research

The studies reviewed in this chapter reveal areas of need and areas of promise regarding teachers' summative assessment practices. Although teachers are interpreting more test results and testing more frequently, many teachers are underprepared and insufficiently skilled. This leads to summative judgments that are often inaccurate and unreliable. Yet teachers commonly report positive beliefs about and high levels of confidence in their assessments skills and competence despite evidence to the contrary gathered through observations and teacher self-reports (Black et al., 2010; Rieg, 2007). Many teachers misinterpret student achievement or misestimate students' abilities (Kilday et al., 2011). Frequently teachers arrive at their judgments of student achievement through idiosyncratic methods and interpret assessment results using flexible criteria. These tendencies allow teachers to pull for students who *deserve* better grades or adjust scores down for students with poor attitudes or behavior (Wyatt-Smith et al., 2010). Traditional and routine practices are common across the board with low-level recall and objective tests figuring prominently in the assessment arsenals of teachers regardless of grade level or subject area. Low-level testing can be found in many classrooms where it impacts both the quality of the learning that happens there and the motivation of the students who must engage in those assessments (McKinney et al., 2009). Sadly, the impact of this practice cuts even deeper in classrooms with poorer or less able students. Yet even when teachers recognize effective assessment practices, they often see the realities of their classroom environments and other external factors imposed on them as prohibitive (McMillan & Nash, 2000).

Still, teachers' summative assessment practices have the potential to positively influence students and teachers (McMillan, 2003), do so without the negative effects associated with external tests and examinations, and produce more comprehensive pictures of student achievement (Martínez et al., 2009). The influence of high-stakes test scores may even prompt some teachers to make significant changes to their CA practices (McMillan, 2005). The assessment environment that teachers create in their classrooms influences student motivational factors like self-efficacy and self-regulation (Alkharusi, 2008; Brookhart & Durkin, 2003). When teachers collaborate with each other and are coached by those with expertise in summative assessment practices, they are more likely to recognize the realities of their assessment competencies and begin to address their assessment needs. They can mediate for each other a more systematic and intentional inquiry process into the quality of their assessments and become mindful how the quality of those assessments influence student learning and achievement (Black et al., 2010). Moreover, knowledge in summative assessment has a significant impact on teachers' self-perceived assessment skills regardless of their teaching experience (Zhang & Burry-Stock, 2003).

Given the nature of the studies reviewed and those mentioned for historical context, several suggestions appear warranted. First, there is a need for research designs that go beyond teachers' self-reports, surveys, and inventories. Evidence from classroom interactions with students, criteria-based examinations of actual teacher-made summative assessments, observations of professional discussions about what comprises achievement, and other strong evidence from teachers' decisions would provide a richer and more comprehensive picture of how teachers summarize student achievement. Only seven studies reviewed (Black et al., 2010; Brookhart & Bronowicz, 2003; Brookhart & Durkin, 2003; Brookhart et al., 2006; McMillan & Nash, 2000; Wyatt-Smith et al., 2010) took this approach.

Second, there is a critical need for research into the impact that principals and central office administrators have on the summative assessment practices of teachers in their buildings and districts. Investigations of the roles administrators play in perpetuating mediocre assessments of achievement or spearheading quality CA practices would add to our understanding. Teachers do not assess in a vacuum, yet a review of the CA literature might lead us to conclude otherwise. We know little about how building- and district-level administrators might lead a culture of high quality summative assessment to promote accurate decisions about what students know and can do. And studies of college and university certification programs for educational leadership are sorely needed to identify programmatic factors and approaches that produce administrators who understand quality summative assessment, can recognize it when they see it, and are able to effectively intervene when they don't.

Finally, university programs continue to graduate teachers who are overconfident and under competent when it comes to summarizing achievement and using assessment information to promote improved student learning. These studies could inform the design of teacher preparation programs that make quality assessment a focal point of effective pedagogy. This would be especially true if researchers go beyond counting the number of assessment courses in particular curriculum to examining what actually happens in those courses to develop assessment literacy and follow the graduates into the field to see if those courses impact actual assessment practices.

References

Alkharusi, H. (2008). Effects of classroom assessment practices on students' achievement goals. *Educational Assessment, 13*(4), 243–266.

American Federation of Teachers, National Council on Measurement in Education, & National Education Association. (1990). *Standards for teacher competence in educational assessment of students.* Washington, DC: National Council on Measurement in Education. (ERIC Document Reproduction Service No. ED 323 186)

Ames, C. (1992). Classrooms: Goals, structures, and student motivation. *Journal of Educational Psychology, 84,* 261–271

Aschbacher, P. (1999). Helping educators to develop and use alternative assessments: Barriers and facilitators. *Educational Policy, 8,* 202–223.

Atkin, J. M., & Coffey, J. (Eds.) (2001). *Everyday assessment in the science classroom.* Arlington, VA: National Science Teachers Association Press.

Baker, R. L., Mednick, B. R., & Hocevar, D. (1991). Utility of scales derived from teacher judgments of adolescent academic performance and psychosocial behavior. *Educational and Psychological Measurement, 51*(2), 271–286.

Baron, J. B. (1991). Strategies for the development of effective performance exercises. *Applied Measurement in Education, 4*(4), 305–318.

Black, P., Harrison, C., Hodgen, J., Marshall, B., & Serret, N. (2010). Validity in teachers' summative assessments. *Assessment in Education Principles, Policy & Practice, 17*(2), 215–232.

Black, P., & Wiliam, D. (1998). Assessment and classroom learning. *Assessment in Education, 5,* 7–74.

Boothroyd, R. A., McMorris, R. F., & Pruzek, R. M. (1992, April). *What do teachers know about measurement and how did they find out?* Paper presented at the annual meeting of the Council on Measurement in Education, San Francisco. (ERIC Document Reproduction Service No. ED351309)

Borko, H., Mayfield, V., Marion, S., Flexer, R., & Cumbo, K. (1997). Teachers' developing ideas and practices about mathematics performance assessment: Successes, stumbling blocks, and implications for professional development. *Teaching and Teacher Education, 13,* 259–278.

Brookhart, M. S. (1997). A theoretical framework for the role of classroom assessment in motivating student effort and achievement. *Applied Measurement in Education, 10*(2), 161–180.

Brookhart, S. M., & Bronowicz, D. L. (2003). "I don't like writing. It makes my fingers hurt": Students talk about their classroom assessments. *Assessment in Education, 10*(2), 221–241.

Brookhart, S. M., & Durkin, D. T. (2003). Classroom assessment, student motivation and achievement in high school social studies classes. *Applied Measurement in Education 16*(1), 27–54.

Brookhart, S. M., Walsh, J. M., & Zientarski, W. A. (2006). The dynamics of motivation and effort for classroom assessment in middle school science and social studies. *Applied Measurement in Education, 19*(2), 151–184.

Clarke, M. Madaus, G. F., Horn, C. J., & Ramos, M. A. (2000). Retrospective on educational testing and assessment in the 20th century. *Journal of Curriculum Studies, 32*(2), 159–181.

Darling-Hammond, L. (1995). Equity issues in performance-based assessment. In M. T. Nettles & A. L. Nettles (Eds.), *Equity and excellence in educational testing and assessment* (pp. 89–114). Boston: Kluwer

Falk, B., & Ort, S. (1998). Sitting down to score: Teacher learning through assessment. *Phi Delta Kappan, 80,* 59–64.

Gearhart, M., & Saxe, G. B. (2004). When teachers know what students know: Integrating assessment in elementary mathematics. *Theory Into Practice, 43,* 304–313.

Gittman, E., & Koster, E. (1999, October). *Analysis of ability and achievement scores for students recommended by classroom teachers to a gifted and talented program.* Paper presented at the annual meeting of the Northeastern Educational Research Association, Ellenville, NY.

Goldberg, G. L., & Roswell, B. S. (2000). From perception to practice: The impact of teachers' scoring experience on performance-based instruction and classroom assessment. *Educational Assessment, 6,* 257–290.

Goslin, D. A, (1967). *Teachers and testing.* New York: Russell Sage.

Griswold, P. A. (1993). Beliefs and inferences about grading elicited from student performance sketches. *Educational Assessment, 1*(4), 311–328.

Gullikson, A. R. (1984). Teacher perspectives of their instructional use of tests. *Journal of Educational Research, 77*(4), 244–248.

Haberman, M. (1991). The pedagogy of poverty versus good teaching. *Phi Delta Kappan, 73,* 209–294.

Haberman, M. (2005). *Star teachers: The ideology and best practice of effective teachers of diverse children and youth in poverty.* Houston, TX: Haberman Educational Foundation.

Hall, J. L., & Kleine, P. F. (1992). Educators' perceptions of NRT misuse. *Educational Measurement: Issues and Practice, 11*(2), 18–22.

Harlen, W. (2004). A systematic review of the evidence of the impact on students, teachers and the curriculum of the process of using assessment by teachers for summative purposes. In *Research Evidence in Education Library.* London: Evidence for Policy and Practice Information and Co-Ordinating Centre, Social Science Research Unit, Institute of Education.

Harlen, W. (2005). Teachers' summative practices and assessment for learning—tensions and synergies. *The Curriculum Journal, 16*(2), 207–223.

Harlen, W., & Crick, R. D. (2002). A systematic review of the impact of summative assessment and tests on students' motivation for learning (EPPI-Centre Review, version 1.1*). In *Research Evidence in Education Library, Issue 1.* London: Evidence for Policy and Practice Information and Co-Ordinating Centre, Social Science Research Unit, Institute of Education.

Harlen, W., & Crick, R. D. (2003). Testing and motivation for learning. *Assessment in Education: Principles, Policy & Practice, 10,* 169–207.

Hiebert, J. (2003). What research says about the NCTM standards. In J. Kilpatrick, W. G. Martin, & D. Schifter (Eds.), *A research companion to principles and standards for school mathematics* (pp. 5–23). Reston, VA: National Council of Teachers of Mathematics.

Hills, J. R. (1991). Apathy concerning grading and testing. *Phi Delta Kappa, 72*(7), 540–545.

Hoge, R. D. (1984). Psychometric properties of teacher-judgment measures of pupil attitudes, classroom behaviors, and achievement levels. *Journal of Special Education, 17,* 401–429.

Hopkins, K. D., George, C. A., & Williams, D. D. (1985). The concurrent validity of standardized achievement tests by content area using teachers' ratings as criteria. *Journal of Educational Measurement, 22,* 177–182.

Impara, J. C., Divine, K. P., Bruce, F. A., Liverman, M. R., & Gay, A. (1991). Does interpretive test score information help teachers? *Educational Measurement: Issues and Practice, 10*(4), 319–320.

Kenny, D. T., & Chekaluk, E. (1993). Early reading performance: A comparison of teacher-based and test-based assessments. *Journal of Learning Disabilities, 26,* 227–236.

Kilday, C. R., Kinzie, M. B., Mashburn, A. J., & Whittaker, J. V. (2011). Accuracy of teacher judgments of preschoolers' math skills. *Journal of Psychoeducational Assessment, 29*(4) 1–12.

Laguarda, K. G., & Anderson, L. M. (1998). *Partnerships for standards-based professional development: Final report of the evaluation.* Washington, DC: Policy Studies Associates, Inc.

Marso, R. N., & Pigge, F. L. (1988, April). *An analysis of teacher-made tests: Testing practices, cognitive demands, and item construction errors.* Paper presented at the annual meeting of the National Council on Measurement in Education, New Orleans, LA. (ERIC Document Reproduction Service No. ED298174)

Martínez, J. F., & Mastergeorge, A. (2002, April). *Rating performance assessments of students with disabilities: A generalizability study of teacher bias.* Paper presented at the annual meeting of the American Educational Research Association, New Orleans, LA.

Martínez, J. F., Stecher, B., & Borko, H. (2009). Classroom assessment practices, teacher judgments, and student achievement in mathematics: Evidence in the ECLS. *Educational Assessment, 14,* 78–102.

Maxwell, G. (2001). *Moderation of assessments in vocational education and training.* Brisbane, Queensland: Department of Employment and Training.

McKinney, S. E., Chappell, S., Berry, R. Q., & Hickman, B. T. (2009). An examination of the instructional practices of mathematics teachers in urban schools. *Preventing School Failure: Alternative Education for Children and Youth, 53*(4), 278–284.

McMillan, J. H. (2001). Secondary teachers' classroom assessment and grading practices. *Educational Measurement: Issues and Practices, 20*(1), 20–32.

McMillan, J. H. (2003). *The relationship between instructional and classroom assessment practices of elementary teachers and students scores on high-stakes tests* (Report). (ERIC Document Reproduction Service No. ED472164)

McMillan, J. H. (2005). *The impact of high-stakes test results on teachers' instructional and classroom practices* (Report). (ERIC Document Reproduction Service No. ED490648)

McMillan, J. H., & Lawson, S. (2001). *Secondary science teachers' classroom assessment and grading practices* (Report). (ERIC Document Reproduction Service No. ED450158)

McMillan, J. H. & Nash, S. (2000). *Teacher classroom assessment and grading practices decision making* (Report). (ERIC Document Reproduction Service No. ED447195)

Meisels, S. J., Bickel, D. D., Nicholson, J., Xue, Y., & Atkins-Burnett, S. (2001). Trusting teachers' judgments: A validity study of a curriculum-embedded performance assessment in kindergarten–Grade 3. *American Educational Research Journal, 38*(1), 73–95.

National Council of Teachers of Mathematics. (2000). *Principles and standards for school mathematics.* Reston, VA: Author.

National Research Council. (2001). *Inquiry and the National Science Education Standards.* Washington, DC: National Academy Press.

Nolen, S. B., Haladyna, T. M., & Haas, N. S. (1992). Uses and abuses of achievement test scores. *Educational Measurement: Issues and Practice, 11*(2), 9–15.

O'Sullivan, R. G., & Chalnick, M. K. (1991). Measurement-related course work requirements for teacher certification and recertification. *Educational Measurement: Issues and Practice, 10*(1), 17–19.

Parkes, J., & Giron, T. (2006). *Making reliability arguments in classrooms.* Paper presented at the annual meeting of the National Council on Measurement in Education, San Francisco.

Plake, B. S. (1993). Teacher assessment literacy: Teachers' competencies in the educational assessment of students. *Mid-Western Educational Researcher, 6*(1), 21–27.

Rieg, S. A. (2007). Classroom assessment strategies: What do students at-risk and teachers perceive as effective and useful? *Journal of Instructional Psychology, 34*(4), 214–225.

Rodriguez, M. C. (2004). The role of classroom assessment in student performance on TIMSS. *Applied Measurement in Education, 17*(1), 1–24

Roeder, H. H. (1972). Are today's teachers prepared to use tests? *Peabody Journal of Education, 59,* 239–240.

Sato, M. (2003). Working with teachers in assessment-related professional development. In J. M. Atkin & J. E. Coffey (Eds.), *Everyday assessment in the science classroom* (pp. 109–120). Arlington, VA: National Science Teachers Association Press.

Sharpley, C. F., & Edgar, E. (1986). Teachers' ratings vs. standardized tests: an empirical investigation of agreement between two indices of achievement. *Psychology in the Schools, 23,* 106–111.

Sheingold, K., Heller, J. I., & Paulukonis, S. T. (1995). *Actively seeking evidence: Teacher change through assessment development* (Rep. No. MS-94-04). Princeton, NJ: Educational Testing Service.

Shepard, L.A. (2000). The role of assessment in a learning culture. *Educational Researcher, 29,* 4–14.

Stiggins, R. (1991). Relevant classroom assessment training for teachers. *Educational Measurement: Issues and Practice, 10,* 7–12

Stiggins, R. J. (1999). Are you assessment literate? *The High School Journal, 6*(5), 20–23.

Stiggins, R. J., & Bridgeford, N. J. (1985). The ecology of classroom assessment. *Journal of Educational Measurement, 22,* 271–286.

Stiggins, R. J., Frisbie, R. J., & Griswold, P. A. (1989). Inside high school grading practices: Building a research agenda. *Educational Measurement: Issues and Practice, 8*(2), 5–14.

Tiedemann, J. (2002). Teachers' gender stereotypes as determinants of teacher perceptions in elementary school mathematics. *Educational Studies in Mathematics, 50*(1), 49–62.

Van De Walle, J. (2006). *Raising achievement in secondary mathematics.* Buckingham, UK: Open University Press.

Wilson, S. (2004). Student assessment as an opportunity to learn in and from one's teaching practice. In M. Wilson (Ed.), *Towards coherence between classroom assessment and accountability* (National Society for the Study of Education Yearbook, Vol. 103, Part 2, pp. 264–271). Chicago: University of Chicago Press.

Wilson, M., & Sloane, K. (2000). From principles to practice: An embedded assessment system. *Applied Measurement in Education, 13,* 181–208.

Wise, S. L., Lukin, L. E., & Roos, L. L. (1991). Teacher beliefs about training in testing and measurement. *Journal of Teacher Education, 42*(1), 37–42.

Worthen, B. R., Borg, W. R., & White, K. R. (1993). *Measurement and evaluation in schools.* White Plains, NY: Longman.

Wyatt-Smith, C., Klenowski, V., & Gunn, S. (2010). The centrality of teachers' judgment practice in assessment: A study of standards in moderation. *Assessment in Education: Principle, Policy & Practice, 17*(1), 59–75.

Zhang, Z., & Barry-Stock, J. A. (1994). *Assessment Practices Inventory.* Tuscaloosa: The University of Alabama.

Zhang, Z., & Burry-Stock, J. A. (2003). Classroom practices and teachers' self-perceived assessment skills. *Applied Measurement in Education, 16*(4), 323–342.

15

Grading

Susan M. Brookhart

The cartoon shows a boy looking at his report card and then looking up at his teacher. "It may be a report card to you, Ms. Smith, but in my house it's an environmental impact statement." Funny, yes, but it's also too true. Grades and grading have social and motivational impact in addition to their impact as a type of educational assessment. Many students begin school with a desire to learn and change their focus to a desire to get good grades, as early as mid-elementary school (Evans & Engelberg, 1988), because of the way grading is currently done in much of the United States.

Therefore, it is important to understand grades and grading and to use that understanding to inform productive change in grading practices in schools. This chapter summarizes research on teachers' grading practices with the aim of demonstrating some positive changes in grading practice research as well. The chapter will characterize an apparent move from research that finds fault with teacher practices to a more helpful analysis of how teachers' grading practices should fit into a balanced system of instruction and assessment.

The literature reviewed in this chapter is empirical literature—that is, studies that in some way collected and interpreted data to answer research questions. Each of the categories under review—conventional grading practices, grading in special education, and contemporary standards-based grading practices—also has a large professional literature. It is important to distinguish these, because a literature search on "grading" will return some of each. This chapter focuses on grading research, not the professional development literature.

Basic Terms and Concepts

Grading (sometimes called marking) is the process of summing up student achievement with marks or symbols. Teachers grade individual assessments and assignments, and they also combine those grades into one summary mark or symbol for a report period. The focus for this chapter will be on summary grades for report cards in basic (K–12) education. Moss (see Chapter 14 of this volume) discusses research on the kind of individual summative assessments that are combined into report card grades.

The grading scale used on a report card is set by the school district. Letter grading, using a scale of A, B, C, D, F, sometimes with plusses and minuses, is common. Percentage grading, using a scale of 0% to 100%, based on percent of total points earned for various assessments, is also common. Pass/fail grading, using only those two categories, is sometimes used. Narrative grading means writing comments about student achievement, either in addition to or instead of using numbers or letters. Standards-based grading, using proficiency categories (e.g., advanced, proficient, basic, and below basic) has become increasingly common recently, often in conjunction with revised report cards that list reporting standards instead of (or in addition to) subject areas. The standards on these revised report cards are sometimes the same as the state content standards and sometimes are adapted for the report cards.

Grades are assigned based on a referencing framework. The three basic referencing frameworks include (1) norm, (2) criterion, and (3) self. Norm-referenced grading involves comparing students' performances with each other. In a norm-referenced system, the best performers get high grades and the worst performers get low grades. Criterion-referenced grading involves comparing students' performance with established standards. In a criterion-referenced system, students are graded according to where their performance falls on a predefined continuum of quality. This is the method of grading recommended and used for most classroom purposes. Self-referenced grading involves comparing students' performance with their own past performance. In a self-referenced system, students who improve the most get the highest grades.

One more comment about terminology is in order. The term *standards-based* grading (sometimes called grading on absolute standards) for a long time was used to mean grading on established levels of performance (Crooks, 1933). In effect, standards-based meant "criterion-referenced." In recent times, the use of the term *standards-based* has changed. Now it is most often used to mean reporting progress on state or district standards (Guskey & Bailey, 2010). In this contemporary usage, *standards* applies to the content categories (e.g., "numbers and operations" in mathematics) as well as performance levels (e.g., "proficient").

This section has defined basic terms and concepts used in grading. The next three sections review the research literature on grading: (1) research on conventional grading practices, (2) research on grading in special education, and (3) research on contemporary standards-based grading practices. The chapter ends with a brief discussion about the implications for future research.

Research on Conventional Grading Practices

An Inauspicious Beginning

Research on the grading of individual assessments comprised some of the earliest educational research in the United States. Starch and Elliott (1912, 1913a, 1913b) studied what they called the *reliability* of grading. This series of studies became the most famous among similar studies that, taken together, helped influence some schools to change from the percentage grading scale (0–100) to a letter-based system (ABCDF). The motivation behind these studies was perceived unreliability of grades; in effect, Starch and Elliott sought confirmation for this perception (1912):

> The reliability of the school's estimate of the accomplishment and progress of pupils is of large practical importance. For, after all, the marks or grades attached to a pupil's work are the tangible measure of the result of his attainments, and constitute the chief basis for the determination of essential administrative problems of the school, such as transfer, promotion, retardation, elimination, and admission to higher institutions, to say nothing of the problem of the influence of these marks or grades upon the moral attitude of the pupil toward the school, education, and even life. The recent studies of grades have emphatically directed our attention to the wide variation and utter absence of standards in the assignment of values. (p. 442)

Starch and Elliott (1912) sent the same two freshman examination papers in English, from a high school in Wisconsin, to 200 high schools; 142 teachers graded and returned both exams. The exam was comprised of six open-ended questions about grammar, literature, and writing. By more modern standards of essay test question writing (Coffman, 1971), the questions have characteristics known to lead to difficult-to-score variation in student responses. However, they were typical examination questions at the time.

They replicated the same methodology with a geometry exam (Starch & Elliott, 1913a) and with a U.S. history exam (1913b). Starch and Elliott (1913b) concluded that the probable error in grades for English, mathematics, and history was 5.4, 7.5, and 7.7 points (on the 100-point scale), respectively (p. 680). They acknowledged several sources of unreliability, including differences in standards and their relative weights in different schools and among different teachers as well as true teacher inability to distinguish quality levels in student work. Nevertheless, Starch and Elliott's discussion emphasized the teacher's responsibility for grading unreliability. Their studies established a *what's wrong with teachers* tone that has characterized grading research in the United States until recently.

Previous Reviews of Literature

Grading has been a topic of interest in educational research since this inauspicious start. This section describes several reviews that summarize this grading research history.

Crooks (1933) reviewed literature from the 1920s about the various kinds of grading systems (i.e., using ranking, the normal curve, percentages, or absolute standards). Ranking and normal-curve-based grading are both norm-referenced schemes, and Crooks cited scholars' arguments against those. Percentage-based grades, Crooks argued, had already been found to be unreliable. Crooks's review therefore led him to argue for grading on clearly defined, absolute standards, although his review appeared 30 years before the term *criterion-referenced* would be applied to this method of assessment (Glaser, 1963).

Smith and Dobbin (1960) summarized grading research from the 1930s, 1940s, and 1950s. The issue of whether to grade on absolute standards or by comparing students still was an important concern. Smith and Dobbin reported that elementary schools had been somewhat more successful than high schools in moving to what today would be called criterion-referenced grading methods. In high schools, ranking or curving methods persisted because of the perceived sorting function required for using grades for college admissions.

Student unrest in the 1960s was the motivation for perhaps the most unusual review of studies of grading practices (Kirschenbaum, Napier, & Simon, 1971). The authors cite this student unrest as the motivation for their research question—"Is the traditional system of grading the most educationally useful system of evaluation?" (p. 14)—as well as the reason for their presenting their results in the format of a novel. *Wad-ja-get?* (Kirschenbaum et al., 1971) is a novel-length drama about fictional Mapleton High School, followed by an annotated bibliography with 89 sources and an appendix describing alternative grading systems. Because of its readability and accessibility (it was published as an inexpensive paperback book), it became well known. Of interest for this chapter is its conclusion—yet again!—that the best grading system was based on reporting student achievement of established standards. The novel ends with Mapleton High School designing a two-track grading system (letters or credit/no credit), with students and teachers both having choice in the matter. Both tracks were based on clear objectives, shared at the beginning of the course, and included student self-evaluations, teacher comments, and conferences.

I (Susan M. Brookhart) reviewed a set of 19 studies from 1985 to 1994 (Brookhart, 1994). That review considered the theoretical framework and methods of the studies and found that while much of the research was done with a practical, rather than theoretical, framework and with a wide range of methodological rigor, the studies converged on four findings (pp. 288–289):

- Teachers try hard to be fair to students, including informing them up front what the components of a grade will be.
- Achievement measures, especially tests, are the major components in grades, but effort and ability are also commonly considered.
- There is a grade-level effect on grading practices. Elementary teachers use more informal evidence and observation. At the secondary level, paper-and-pencil achievement measures and other written activities comprise a much larger portion of the grade.
- There is individual variation among teachers' grading practices. Different teachers perceive the meaning and purpose of grades differently.

The second and fourth bullets in this summary echo and expand the findings of previous reviews. The variation in grading practices among teachers echoes the "unreliability of grading" issues that have been ongoing in research. Considering effort and ability in addition to achievement and the variation in grading practices among teachers move concerns about grading into the realm of "validity," because the question is about what grades are supposed to measure. These concerns were foreshadowed by previous reviewers' recommendations to grade student achievement of standards.

In some ways, doing the 1994 review was depressing. Some historical concerns about grading have still not been resolved even after

100 years. Reading so many studies at the same time also raised for this author the issue noted at the beginning of the section. Why does an underlying theme under much of this research seem to be "what's wrong with teachers?" Other research about teacher judgment of student achievement does not take this tone. For example, Hoge and Coladarci (1989) interpreted correlations ranging from 0.28 to 0.92 (median = 0.66) between teacher judgment of student achievement and standardized test scores to mean that teacher judgment of student achievement was generally accurate and valid, despite the fact that a correlation of 0.66 means teacher judgment explained less than half the variation in tested student achievement. Yet grading practice studies that show most teachers assign grades based mostly on achievement measures, with some consideration of effort and behavior, have been generally interpreted to mean that grades are unreliable.

Review of Current Literature on Conventional Grading Practices

This section presents a review of 12 studies from 1994 to the present—studies of grading and grading practices published in the years since the previous review. The studies included here were identified via an Education Resources Information Center (ERIC) search on grading, specifying published articles from 1994 to the present, and subsequent review of abstracts. Because grading is part of the larger education system, which differs substantially among countries, only studies of grading in the United States were used for this review.

Table 15.1 presents these studies and their characteristics, in a similar table to the one used in the review of grading studies from 1985 to 1993 (Brookhart, 1994).

Table 15.1 illustrates that the interpretability of grades, a validity issue, continues to be the major finding of research on grading practices. Indeed, the common method of using a survey asking about the use of achievement and nonachievement factors in grades suggests that researchers are looking for that finding.

Grading Practices and Validity: What Is Graded?

Validity is in question when the construct to be measured is not purely achievement but rather some mix of achievement and nonachievement factors. Six of the studies (Cross & Frary, 1999; Feldman, Allibrandi, & Kropf, 1998; McMillan, 2001; McMillan, Myran, & Workman, 2002; Randall & Engelhard, 2009a, 2009b, 2010; Waltman & Frisbie, 1994) reported at least some findings about the mixture of nonachievement factors, most notably effort, with achievement in the assignment of grades. Notably, in this set of studies, five (all but Cross & Frary, 1999) emphasized that achievement was the main factor considered.

Validity is in question when grades mean different things in different schools or subjects, in different teachers' classes, and for different types of student (e.g., lower achieving students). These same six studies found a lot (Cross & Frary, 1999; Feldman et al., 1998; McMillan, 2001; McMillan et al., 2002; Waltman & Frisbie, 1994) or at least some (Randall & Engelhard, 2009b) variation in grading practices by teacher. Grading practice variation was found for different tracks in secondary school (college-preparatory vs. non-college preparatory; Cross & Frary, 1999; McMillan, 2001). Grading practice variation was found for different subjects in secondary school (Feldman et al., 1998; McMillan, 2001) but not in elementary school (McMillan et al., 2002).

Cross and Frary (1999) surveyed 207 middle and high school teachers in one school system and their 8,664 students. Teachers did not always report agreement with recommended practices (for example, only 49% endorsed grading on achievement without regard to ability). Moreover, their reported practices sometimes disagreed with their reported ideals. For example, of the 217 teachers who reported they did consider ability in assigning grades, 49% reported that, ideally, ability should not be considered. Most of their findings demonstrated inconsistencies such as this one, which led Cross and Frary (1999) to conclude that there seems to be resistance to the idea of grading on achievement alone and to speculate that perhaps many teachers have not thought through the negative consequences of mixing constructs when grading (pp. 69–70). Considered this way, the solution to the problem is education and communication and also additional research that demonstrates the benefits of the recommendation to grade on achievement—a theme that will be repeated in the section on standards-based grading.

Study	*Analytical Framework*	*Participants*	n	*Method*	*Summary of Findings*
Cross & Frary, 1999	Practice	Middle and high school teachers Middle and high school students	307 (152 middle, 155 high school) 8,664 (4,174 middle, 4,490 high school)	Survey	• Effort, ability, and behavior included, endorsed by both teachers and students • Difference by track • Practice sometimes inconsistent with reported ideal
Feldman, Allibrandi & Kropf, 1998	Practice	High school science teachers	91 surveyed, of whom 12 were interviewed	Survey, interviews	• Primarily used tests and quizzes, lab, class work, and homework • Subject area difference • Point systems as a "token economy" • Use of grading software
Figlio & Lucas, 2004	Practice	All third-, fourth-, and fifth-grade teachers and students in one Florida district	4 years of data, 1,800 students per year per grade, number of teachers not given	Regressing change in ITBS scores on changes in grading standards, controlling for student and classroom effects	• Teachers vary in grading standards, defined as stringency compared with FCAT scores • Students' year-to-year changes in classroom grading standards are essentially random • High grading standards predict larger ITBS gains
Friedman & Frisbie, 1995	Validity	District report cards	240 elementary, 96 middle, 140 high school sampled for analysis	Content analysis	• Descriptions of K and Grades 1 through 5, 6 through 8, and 9 through 12 report cards • Few included purpose statements • Criterion-referenced meaning intended, but often symbols were ambiguously defined
McElligott & Brookhart, 2009	Legal	State statutes Case law	50	Content and legal analysis	• Most state statutes are silent or vague about grades; legislatures empower school boards to establish grading policies. • Due process and equal protection under the Fourteenth Amendment are the main legal issues in grading litigation.
McMillan, 2001	Practice	Secondary (Grades 6–12) teachers of academic subjects in seven urban Virginia districts	1,483 teachers from 53 schools	Survey	• Teachers vary in factors considered in grading; academic achievement most, much less reliance on academic enablers, external benchmarks, extra credit • Teacher-made assessments used most, measuring reasoning and application more than recall • Subject-area differences, track differences

(Continued)

Table 15.1 (Continued)

Study	*Analytical Framework*	*Participants*	n	*Method*	*Summary of Findings*
McMillan, Myran, & Workman, 2002	Practice	Elementary (Grades 3–5) teachers of academic subjects in seven urban Virginia districts	201 teachers from 105 schools		• Teachers vary in factors considered in grading • A range of teacher-made and publishers' assessments used, measuring reasoning and application more than recall • Few differences by grade level or subject
Randall & Engelhard, 2009a, 2009b, 2010	Practice	Elementary, middle, & high school teachers	516 (of which 234 elementary and middle teachers were used in the 2009 study)	Survey, Guttman mapping sentences to manipulate independent variables	• 2009a study: Level (E, M) effects; achievement and behavior effects • 2009b study: Teachers vary in the way they assign grades, but few were aberrant; achievement main factor used in assigning grades • 2010 study: Achievement, ability, behavior, and effort interactions on assigned grades
Thomas & Oldfather, 1997	Social constructivism Self-determination theory	Students	Selected examples	Theoretical argument/ literature review illustrated by quotations from interviews over a 7-year research agenda	• Grade meanings are socially constructed, situation specific, and subject to multiple interpretations. • Teacher assumptions and beliefs about the nature of learning affect grading practices.
Waltman & Frisbie, 1994	Practice	Fourth-grade math teachers Their students' parents	16 285	Survey	• Parents did not understand the difference between norm- and criterion-referenced and between achievement status and growth. • Teachers gave higher grades (avg. grade B) than parents thought (avg. perceived grade C+)

Table 15.1 Studies of Traditional Grades and Grading Practices

NOTE: FCAT = Florida Comprehensive Assessment Test; ITBS = Iowa Tests of Basic Skills.

Waltman and Frisbie (1994) surveyed 16 fourth-grade mathematics teachers in Iowa and 285 of their students' parents. They compared teachers' reports of the meaning of their grades and parents' perceptions of the meaning of their children's grades. Both parent and teacher responses indicated that most were not able to distinguish between norm-referenced and criterion-referenced grading practices. Most parents thought grades were intended to communicate both achievement and nonachievement factors like effort, and about half the teachers did as well. Overall, parents perceived the average grade to be a C+, when teachers overall reported their average grade was a B–.

Feldman et al. (1998) surveyed 91 high school science teachers in Massachusetts about the types of assessments they included in their grades, the weights of the assessments, and the means of determining the report card grade. They also interviewed 12 of the respondents. Traditional forms of assessment—tests and quizzes, laboratory work, class work, and homework—were the most used. Effort was given a small weight and was the only nonachievement factor teachers indicated was important for grading. Most of the teachers agreed that grades should reflect learning and achievement. One concern the researchers voiced was that in interviews, teachers reported being enthusiastic about *point systems* as a method for determining report card grades, and points could be accumulated by completing assignments, studying, and doing extra credit. Thus, while their reported interest was in learning, the teachers were in fact grading behavior but did not perceive that this was the case.

McMillan (2001) surveyed 1,483 secondary teachers in Virginia about the factors and types of assessment they used in determining grades and about the cognitive level of their assessments. He found that most of the teachers used a combination of factors in determining grades, which could be organized into four types: (1) academic achievement, (2) academic enablers (effort, participation, and the like), (3) external benchmarks (little used), and (4) extra credit (again, little used). Academic achievement was the most important component. In his discussion, McMillan (2001, p. 29) drew on one of his previous studies to suggest that teachers consider effort as a way to judge student motivation and engagement, which are valued under many teachers' philosophies of teaching. Teachers reported using assessments that measured reasoning and understanding as well as recall to measure academic achievement.

McMillan and colleagues (2002) surveyed 921 elementary (Grades 3 and 5) teachers in Virginia about the factors and types of assessment they used in determining grades and about the cognitive level of their assessments, similar to McMillan's (2001) study of secondary teachers. Academic achievement was again the main component used to determine grades, although there was variability in reported use of most of the factors. Elementary teachers used objective tests as well as performance assessments, including both teacher-made and publisher-designed assessments. Again, teachers reported using assessments that measured reasoning and understanding as well as recall.

Randall and Engelhard (2010) surveyed 516 teachers in one district, using a survey built of scenarios using Guttman mapping sentences, so that four factors (ability, achievement, behavior, and effort) could be manipulated. Results indicated a four-way interaction among the factors. With high effort and behavior, low achieving, low-ability students receive an average of a C+, and in general, students with high effort and behavior of any ability get a "boost" (Randall & Engelhard, 2010, p. 1376). And grades increase as behavior improves for students of any ability or effort level. Elementary teachers assigned higher grades than middle school teachers overall—and especially for poor behavior (Randall & Englehard, 2009a).

Despite these differences, teachers did primarily assign grades on the basis of achievement (Randall & Englehard, 2009b). As did McMillan and colleagues, Randall and Englehard suggested the effects of nonachievement factors might stem from teachers' personal beliefs about what supports students (Randall & Englehard, 2010, p. 1378). Thus, the longstanding findings that teachers consider nonachievement factors in grading has not changed in this update to previous literature reviews. What has changed is the nature of reporting that finding, recognizing that achievement is the primary basis for grading and interpreting consideration of nonachievement factors in a positive light as part of teachers' beliefs about what is good for students.

Grading Practices and Validity: How Are Grades Interpreted?

Two studies with very different methodologies emphasized the interpretation of grades by different stakeholders: teachers, parents (Waltman & Frisbie, 1994), and students (Thomas & Oldfather, 1997). Different stakeholders have different views of grades. Parents of fourth graders thought the average grade was a C+, when in fact it was a B (Waltman & Frisbie, 1994). Parents were not able to understand the differences between norm- and criterion-referenced appraisals of achievement or the difference between achievement status (current achievement) and growth (improvement). Students consider grades and the means by which grades are given when they make decisions about who they are as students and what it means to work and learn in the classroom (Thomas & Oldfather, 1997). In sum, grades are subject to multiple interpretations and do not have one universal meaning.

Waltman and Frisbie's (1994) survey study was described in the previous section. Using different methods, Thomas and Oldfather (1997) presented a theoretical literature review illustrated with students' comments about their grades from a 7-year, longitudinal, qualitative study. The described how conventional assessment and grading practices disregard social constructivist understandings about how learning takes place. External, teacher-controlled grades also contravene the support for student autonomy and self-competence called for by self-determination theory (Ryan & Deci, 2000). Therefore, in addition to pointing out that teachers' intentions for grades and students' experiences of them differ, Thomas and Oldfather (1997) suggested that conventional grading practices need to change in order to better support student autonomy and involvement with their learning and, ultimately, support learning itself.

Grading Practices and Achievement

Figlio and Lucas (2004) investigated the effects of teacher-level grading standards on student gains in achievement (as measured by the Iowa Tests of Basic Skills [ITBS]) and on disciplinary problems. They analyzed two sets of year-to-year changes for third, fourth, and fifth graders in a school district in Florida. They constructed a measure of teacher grading standards using students' the Florida Comprehensive Assessment Test (FCAT) scores, such that *higher standards* meant students required a higher FCAT score to achieve a given letter grade in that teacher's class. Figlio and Lucas (2004) found that higher teacher grading standards predicted larger ITBS gains over the year, with modest effect sizes, and that low-ability students in high-ability classes, as well as high-ability students in low-ability classes, benefited the most. Using parent survey data, they found some support for the speculation that home support might be part of the reason. Parents reported giving more help to students with *tougher* teachers.

Thus, two studies (Thomas & Oldfather, 1997; Waltman & Frisbie, 1994) with very different methods converge on the conclusion that students, parents, and teachers interpret grades somewhat differently. One study (Figlio & Lucas, 2004) presented evidence that, however grades are interpreted, external pressure in the form of higher standards can produce learning gains in basic skills (the ITBS is a basic skills test) and better student behavior. Student autonomy and control over learning are not incompatible with high standards; however, taken together these studies suggest looking beyond a simple policy decision (e.g., "enforce high standards") to the classroom perceptions and interactions, and especially the nature of the learning, behind them.

Grading Practices and Validity: Report Cards

Grade meanings are shaped and constrained by the report cards that communicate them. One study in this review (Friedman & Frisbie, 1995) looked at the characteristics of report cards as a way to investigate the validity of the information that could be reported. Friedman and Frisbie (1995) solicited report cards from all school districts in Wisconsin and received report cards from about half of those. They sampled from this pool to arrive at sample sizes for report cards at four levels for detailed coding and analysis: (1) kindergarten, 39; (2) elementary, 59; (3) middle school, 48; and (4) high school, 70.

Friedman and Frisbie (1995) found that few report cards in their sample contained purpose statements explicating what grades were intended to mean, leaving their interpretation open to the reader. Most of the report cards they reviewed were set up to communicate criterion-referenced, achievement-focused information but were limited by symbols whose meanings were vague or muddy—for example when norm-referenced language was used for one or more letters in a grading scale.

This study was the only one in the review that intentionally used validity theory as the theoretical framework for their study. This is interesting, in that the underlying questions for most of the studies of practice—what is graded and how are grades interpreted—are validity issues as well. Grading research has evolved from Starch and Elliott's (1912, 1913a, 1913b) concerns with reliability to broader questions about validity and foreshadow one recommendation for further research—namely, to be more intentional about grounding future studies in validity theory.

Grading Practice and the Law

One study (McElligott & Brookhart, 2009) looked at the legal issues involved in grading. While not purely validity issues, legal issues are certainly centered on intended purposes and meanings for grades. The first author (McElligott) is a lawyer, and it was he who did the legal research on state statues and case law for the study. He reviewed the state statutes and administrative code provisions from the 50 states and also searched case law. McElligott and Brookhart (2009) found that most states' statutes and regulations were silent or vague about grades. As an example of a vague reference to grading, a state statute might specify that grades will be given, and they will be based on multiple assessments. The power to establish the details of grading policies devolves to the local school boards, who usually empower the superintendent and/or principals and teachers to handle the details. McElligott and Brookhart (2009) also found that when grading is challenged in court, most often either the due process or equal protection provisions in the Fourteenth Amendment to the U.S. Constitution are cited.

Conclusion

With a few exceptions, the tone of the grading research does seem to be changing in recent years. Sources of unreliability and invalid grading decisions are often interpreted now in a more nuanced light than previously, with understanding that the causes are more complex than simply lack of teacher competence. Grades are acknowledged to have multiple meanings and multiple contexts, including social and legal contexts.

Because of this changing context for grading in the United States, this chapter includes a review of research on grading in special education and a review of research standards-based grading practices in the next two sections, respectively. The 1994 review did not include either of these kinds of studies. This more complete treatment of research on grading seems warranted because the issues of using standards-based grading with a diverse student population are looming larger and larger. They may become the catalyst that finally, after a century, compels changes in grading practices and a greater focus on communicating achievement.

Research on Grading in Special Education

The review in this section is not the result of an exhaustive literature search, as in the previous section, but rather a selection of articles that highlight the particular issues of grading in special education—in addition, of course, to all the general grading issues from the previous section. The focus of this section is research on special education students working in regular classrooms, not in resource rooms or special classes.

When special education students participate in regular classes and are graded in the same manner as the rest of the class, most pass their classes but end up with grades at about the D level (Donohoe & Zigmond, 1990). This is frustrating to the students and their parents and teachers. McLeskey and Waldron (2002) interviewed teachers in six elementary schools that had implemented an inclusion program. They found that with the inclusion program, teachers had also implemented alterations in grading practices, which before the inclusion program had been the same for all students. McLeskey and Waldron (2002) found that after implementation of the inclusion program, "Grades became reflective of student effort, ability, and improvement. The majority of the teachers, however, placed most emphasis on student improvement" (p. 48). These adaptations may have met the needs of the inclusion program, but they disregard the recommendation to grade students on achievement. The teachers in the study reported continuing to struggle with grading issues, some changing report cards and some changing the curriculum.

Other researchers (Bradley & Calvin, 1998; Jung, 2008) have taken a different approach. Instead of adapting existing grading plans that include nonachievement factors, they focus on specific adaptations that allow grading on achievement for special education students. Here is an example on a writing assignment for which one of the grading criteria for regular students is using complete sentences:

> You may accept partial sentences from a student who is currently working on writing in complete sentences as an IEP goal, without taking off points or lowering that grade. You may want to add a comment on the paper that encourages continued effort on that skill. (Bradley & Calvin, 1998, p. 28)

The literature on grading in special education reveals two research agendas that have taken different approaches to grading adaptations for special education—one by Bursuck, Monk, and their colleagues and one by Jung and her colleagues. Together, these research agendas comprise a large part of the special education grading literature. These plans and their publications are reviewed in the following sections.

Personalized Grading Plans

Classroom teachers use various types of grading adaptations for their special education students—in most cases without a policy mandate from the district (Polloway et al., 1994). Struyk et al. (1995) surveyed a nationally representative sample of secondary teachers and received reasonable response rates. From their survey results (Struyk et al., 1995), the following 10 grading adaptations are ranked in order of perceived helpfulness:

- Give separate grades for process (e.g., effort) and product (e.g., tests).
- Adjust weights of grade components.
- Base grades on meeting academic or behavioral contracts.
- Base grades on improvement.
- Base grades on meeting individualized education program (IEP) objectives.
- Adjust grades based on student ability.
- Modify the grading scale (e.g., A = 90–100 instead of 93–100)
- Base grades on less content than for regular students.
- Pass students if they make an effort to pass.
- Pass students no matter what. (p. 53)

Teacher use of these adaptations varies and differs somewhat between middle and high school teachers (Bursuck et al., 1996). The researchers (Bursuck, Munk, & Olson, 1999) also asked students whether they perceived each of these adaptations as fair. Students with and without disabilities both perceived that adjusting weights, reducing content, passing students for effort, and passing students in any event were "not fair." Students with and without disabilities differed in their perceptions of the fairness of other adaptations.

Informed by their research, Munk & Bursuck (2004) devised a process they call personalized grading plans (PGPs), in which the teacher meets with parents and the student and works through a protocol as a team. The result is either a personalized grading adaptation for the student or, in some cases, the identification of other instructional or assessment adaptations that would eliminate the need for a personalized grading application. The adaptation is added to the student's IEP and subject to ongoing evaluation. The PGP protocol includes eight steps (Munk & Bursuck, 2004):

1. Clarify teacher purposes for grades.
2. Clarify parent and student purposes for grades.
3. Arrive at mutually agreed upon purposes for grades.
4. Examine student learning characteristics and classroom demands; identify potential grading problems.
5. Review current grading system and determine if the grade could be higher and/or more meaningful if a grading adaptation was implemented.
6. Select an adaptation that meets agreed-upon purposes.

7. Document the adaptation in the student's IEP and begin implementation.
8. Monitor the effectiveness of the adaptation. (p. 7)

Munk & Bursuck (2001) reported preliminary findings in a study of implementing PGPs with four middle school students. Each personalized grading plan was different. Most involved a change in the weights assigned to individual assignments and a change in the grading scale, although one of those changes made the percents required for each grade more stringent, not less. Most included participation and homework, although in these classes the regular students' grading plan also included these components. Three of the students received higher grades, and all reported that they were happier with their grades, better understood how they were graded, and tried harder in class. The one student who did not receive a higher grade continued to struggle with the work and ultimately was transferred to a different math class. Teachers and parents reported moderate to high levels of satisfaction with the PGPs. The most commonly cited problem was difficulty learning how to enter modified weights and scales into the district's computerized grading system.

Inclusive Grading Model

Jung (2008) proposed an inclusive grading model that fits with a standards-based grading model now in place in many districts and that focuses on grading achievement. Effort and improvement may be monitored and reported elsewhere, but the academic grade requires inspecting the standards that regular students are expected to achieve during the report period and establishing whether and how these standards should be accommodated, modified, and augmented for the needs of the particular student. Jung's (2008) Inclusive Grading Model has five steps:

1. Determine if accommodations or modifications (to grade-level standards) are needed.
2. Establish standards for modified areas.
3. Determine the need for additional goals.
4. Apply equal grading practices to appropriate standards.
5. Communicate the meaning of grades. (p. 32)

Jung's model has been circulated widely in professional publications (e.g., Jung & Guskey, 2007, 2010). The Inclusive Grading Model was part of a larger study of grading reform in the state of Kentucky (Guskey, Swan, & Jung, 2010). Preliminary results from the 24 general education teachers in the study suggest that although teachers demonstrated the ability to use it in the introductory workshop, the Inclusive Grading Model was not used very frequently in practice. Teacher-written comments indicated a need for more support for daily grading decisions and practices. Study teachers also reported (Guskey et al., 2010, p. 18) that a philosophical shift among their colleagues—toward a better understanding of the differences between three kinds of evidence (grades for academic products, appraisals of process factors like effort, and judgments of progress or improvement)—would be required before modifications of academic product grades could be understood and implemented.

Research on Contemporary Standards-Based Grading Practices

The *standards movement* of the 1990s, which culminated in the mandated, heavy-handed use of large-scale testing in the No Child Left Behind Act of 2001 (NCLB) (U.S. Department of Education, 2002), has led to the realization that "scientific" large-scale testing is not a universal good any more than the reliance on individual teachers' grading practices was expected to be. NCLB led to an increased focus on students' performance against standards, which lends itself to learning-focused grading practices. Paradoxically, then, the standards movement may also be the catalyst needed to finally—after 100 years of advocacy and attempts—move grading practices to more intentionally reflect student achievement of standards.

There is at present much more about standards-based grading in the professional literature (e.g., Brookhart, 2011; Guskey & Bailey, 2010; O'Connor, 2009) than in the research literature. While most evidence about standards-based grading practices is as yet anecdotal, this author located three empirical studies of standards-based grading.

Evaluation of Professional Development in Standards-Based Grading.

Two studies (Guskey et al., 2010; McMunn, Schenck, & McColskey, 2003) of professional development programs were designed to help teachers move toward standards-based grading on achievement outcomes. McMunn et al. (2003) studied professional development in standards-based grading practices in one district in Florida. They reported in detail on changes teachers made, focusing on reporting current student achievement of Florida standards and benchmarks, involving students more in the grading process, using recent high quality evidence, and reducing behavior-related policies (for example, reducing the use of penalties for late work).

In all, however, the level of change did not meet district expectations. One finding in particular stands out for the purposes of this review. McMunn et al. (2003) found that teachers reported that as a result of their professional development in standards-based grading practices, they grew the most in shifting to an achievement-based view of grading by a stunning margin over other categories questioned. A full 75% of teachers reported that they met the goal with full implementation for the category: "I assign grades based on achievement of standards rather than as a means of motivation" (McMunn et al., 2003, p. 20). However, observations in classrooms and examination of classroom artifacts indicated that this was true only for a portion of the teachers. Many still did not understand how to grade based on achievement of standards.

The special education aspects of Guskey and colleagues' (2010) study were reported in the previous section. Their initiative was broader, however, beginning with an attempt to develop a common, statewide, standards-based report card for all levels (K–12). Despite reporting on the same state standards, schools in Kentucky use different report cards, a situation that is similar in all states. Common report cards and an online tool were developed in a summer workshop, and the educators involved returned to their schools and solicited volunteers to use the new report cards. The new report cards derived reporting standards from the Kentucky state standards and reported academic achievement and behavior information separately.

Twenty-four teachers who had used the report cards returned surveys after using the new report cards for one marking period (Guskey et al., 2010). They reported that the standards-based report cards provided more and better quality information than their previous report cards. They reported the new report cards took more time to use but that the additional information was worth the added time. Parents reported similar perceptions. However, some teachers did not understand the full implications of grading on achievement only—for example, confusing formative and summative information about learning.

It seems, then, that a central issue for research on conventional grading practices, mixing achievement and other factors in grades, is also going to be an issue for standards-based grading. A standards-based culture has at least brought lip service to the principle that grades should be based on achievement alone, but more work is needed to bring that to fruition. Guskey and his colleagues reached similar conclusions to those of McMunn and her colleagues, namely that more intensive support, including perhaps alternative strategies for professional development, would be needed to change grading practices as intended and in a timely manner.

The Quality of Information Communicated Via Standards-Based Grades

D'Agostino and Welsh (2007; Welsh & D'Agostino, 2009) investigated the question of whether achievement-only, standards-based grading matches the information about student achievement from their performance on state tests of the same standards. In overall terms, the answer is no. Overall agreement between third and fifth graders' standards-based grades in one district and their proficiency levels on the Arizona Instrument to Measure Standards (AIMS) were 44% for mathematics, 53% for reading, and 51% for writing (D'Agostino & Welsh, 2007). Corrected for chance agreement, those percentages were only 16% to 26%. However, there was wide variation among teachers in how closely their grades matched tested achievement of standards.

To see whether grading practices were related to how well teachers' grading decisions matched tested student proficiency levels, the researchers coded information from interviews of each teacher according to a list of following recommended grading practices, obtained from the same literature reviewed in this chapter. Teacher interviews were coded according to whether each of the following practices was "clearly evident," "somewhat evident," or "not evident" (Welsh & D'Agostino, 2009):

- Assessing most of the performance objectives in state standards
- Grading on achievement, not effort
- Creating or obtaining assessments focused on state standards
- Identifying the objectives assessed by each assessment and tracking students' performance skill by skill
- Focusing on attainment of standards, not objectives listed in textbooks
- Using end-of-unit assessments for grading, not practice work
- Focusing on achievement, not progress (improvement)
- Assessing frequently
- Using multiple assessment approaches to measure different aspects of a skill
- Using a clear method for converting individual assessment results to standards-based grades (p. 85)

The researchers used Rasch modeling to create an *appraisal style* score from these codes. The two heaviest contributors to the scale were (1) basing grades on achievement (performance quality) rather than effort and (2) assessing the full range of objectives (knowledge and skills) within each standard. They found that the higher the appraisal style score—that is, the more a teacher's grading practices followed these recommendations—the more closely that teacher's grades correlated with his or her students' tested proficiency levels.

This study is the only study known to this author that addressed the question of whether grading practices make a difference for the quality of information on standards-based progress reports. It was based on 2 years of data for two grades in one district in Arizona. More studies of this kind would be very helpful to the field.

Conclusion

Research on standards-based grading is in its infancy, so definitive conclusions would be premature. The limited research reviewed here suggests a positive change and a challenge. On the positive side, the culture of "standards-based" learning has succeeded in changing many teachers' attitudes about grading on achievement, something a century of history of conventional grading practices has not succeeded in doing. The challenge is that even teachers who say they are grading on achievement still use practices (e.g., grading homework) that do not completely meet this goal. More research on how teachers can develop knowledge and practice more closely aligned with the new standards-based attitudes and beliefs is needed. Also, more research on the claims that grading on achievement of standards increases students' achievement and development of learning skills is needed. This is the core of the movement.

Conclusion and Recommendations for Future Research

In summary, studies over the last century, with samples from all over the United States, converge on the conclusion that teachers at all levels mix effort and behavior into their academic achievement grades, especially for lower achieving students. However, more recent research finds that achievement is the primary factor considered in grading. Teachers at different grades and in different subjects mix different amounts and kinds of evidence, but often these differences are logical and reasonable (e.g., more lab assessments in science grades and more writing assessments in English grades). It seems fair to conclude that no more inventories of practice are needed to confirm these findings.

Another observation this author believes is justified is that the literature suggests the mixing of effort and behavior into grading practices is robust, not easily changed with professional development. Less evidence is available for this conclusion, but where there is such evidence it always supports this same conclusion. Perhaps, then, it is time for future research to address questions of how best to help teachers focus on grading achievement, as opposed to simply presenting evidence that it is difficult. As Cross and

Frary (1999) put it, "The solution may be in demonstrating the utility of sound measurement advice" (p. 69). Only one study in this review (D'Agostino & Welsh, 2007; Welsh & D'Agostino, 2009) did that.

A third observation about this set of studies is about the lack of theoretical grounding in most of the research. Most of the studies in this review, and those reported in the historical reviews, were based in practice. Questionnaire or interview questions were based on inventories of assessment types and grading practices, perceptions of the usefulness or satisfaction of various methods, and dilemmas of grading (e.g., scenarios regarding effort or improvement). Any studies that centered on questions of the meaning and usefulness of the information communicated in grades could, potentially, be situated in a more theoretically grounded discussion using modern validity theory (Kane, 2006; Messick, 1989).

Considering these three observations, two recommendations for future research seem justified. One, theoretically grounded future grading research should investigate whether, and then demonstrate how, learning-focused grading practices actually do contribute to valid reporting and, ultimately informed by this reporting, meaningful future student learning. Validity arguments seem a promising theoretical mechanism for this purpose. Two, practically relevant future grading research should investigate how state standards, district grading policies, teacher grading practices, student involvement, and computer grading software can be aligned to contribute to valid reporting and meaningful student learning.

References

Bradley, D. F., & Calvin, M. B. (1998). Grading modified assignments: Equity or compromise? *TEACHING Exceptional Children, 31*(2), 24–29.

Brookhart, S. M. (1994). Teachers' grading: Practice and theory. *Applied Measurement in Education, 7*(4), 279–301.

Brookhart, S. M. (2011). *Grading and learning: Practices that support student achievement.* Bloomington, IN: Solution Tree.

Bursuck, W. D., Munk, D. D., & Olson, M. M. (1999). The fairness of report card grading adaptations. *Remedial and Special Education, 20,* 84–92, 105.

Bursuck, W., Polloway, E. A., Plante, L., Epstein, M. H., Jayanthi, M., & McConeghy, J. (1996). Report card grading and adaptations: A national survey of classroom practices. *Exceptional Children, 62,* 301–318,

Coffman, W. E. (1971). Essay examinations. In R. L. Thorndike (Ed.), *Educational measurement* (2nd ed., pp. 271–302). Washington, DC: American Council on Education.

Crooks, A. D. (1933). Marks and marking systems: A digest. *Journal of Educational Research, 27,* 259–272.

Cross, L. H., & Frary, R. B. (1999). Hodgepodge grading: Endorsed by students and teachers alike. *Applied Measurement in Education, 12*(1), 53–72.

D'Agostino, J., & Welsh, M. (2007). *Standards-based progress reports and standards-based assessment score convergence.* Paper presented at the annual meeting of the American Educational Research Association, Chicago.

Donohoe, K., & Zigmond, N. (1990). Academic grades of ninth-grade urban learning-disabled students and low-achieving peers. *Exceptionality, 1,* 17–27.

Evans, E. D., & Engelberg, R. A. (1988). Student perceptions of school grading. *Journal of Research and Development in Education, 21*(2), 45–54.

Feldman, A., Allibrandi, M., & Kropf, A. (1998). Grading with points: The determination of report card grades by high school science teachers. *School Science and Mathematics, 98*(3), 140–148.

Figlio, D. N., & Lucas, M. E. (2004). The gentleman's "A." *Education Next, 4*(2), 60–67.

Friedman, S. J., & Frisbie, D. A. (1995). The influence of report cards on the validity of grades reported to parents. *Educational and Psychological Measurement, 55,* 5–26.

Glaser, R. (1963). Instructional technology and the measurement of learning outcomes: Some questions. *American Psychologist, 18,* 519–521.

Guskey, T. R., & Bailey, J. M. (2010). *Developing standards-based report cards.* Thousand Oaks, CA: Corwin Press.

Guskey, T. R., Swan, G. M., & Jung, L. A. (2010, May). *Developing a statewide, standards-based student report card: A review of the Kentucky initiative.* Paper presented at the annual meeting of the American Educational Research Association, Denver. (ERIC Document Reproduction Service No. ED509404)

Hoge, R. D., & Coladarci, T. (1989). Teacher-based judgments of academic achievement: A review of literature. *Review of Educational Research, 59*(3), 297–313.

Jung, L. A. (2008). The challenges of grading and reporting in special education: An inclusive grading model. In T. R. Guskey (Ed.), *Practical solutions for serious problems in standards-based grading*. Thousand Oaks, CA: Corwin Press.

Jung, L. A., & Guskey, T. R. (2007). Standards-based grading and reporting: A model for special education. *Teaching Exceptional Children, 40*(2), 48–53.

Jung, L. A., & Guskey, T. R. (2010). Grading exceptional learners. *Educational Leadership, 67*(5), 31–35.

Kane, M. T. (2006). Validation. In R. L. Brennan (Ed.), *Educational measurement* (4th ed., pp. 17–64). Westport, CT: Praeger.

Kirschenbaum, H., Napier, R., & Simon, S. B. (1971). *Wad-ja-get? The grading game in American education*. New York: Hart Publishing.

McElligott, J., & Brookhart, S. (2009). Legal issues of grading in the era of high stakes accountability. In T. R. Guskey (Ed.), *Practical solutions for serious problems in standards-based grading* (pp. 57–74). Thousand Oaks, CA: Corwin Press.

McLeskey, J., & Waldron, N. L. (2002). Inclusion and school change: Teacher perceptions regarding curricular and instructional adaptations. *Teacher education and special education, 25*(1), 41–54.

McMillan, J. H. (2001). Secondary teachers' classroom assessment and grading practices. *Educational Measurement: Issues and Practice, 20*(1), 20–32.

McMillan, J. H., Myran, S., & Workman, D. (2002). Elementary teachers' classroom assessment and grading practices. *Journal of Educational Research, 95*, 203–213

McMunn, N., Schenck, P., & McColskey, W. (2003, April). *Standards-based assessment, grading and reporting in classrooms: Can district training and support change teacher practice?* Paper presented at the annual meeting of the American Educational Research Association, Chicago. (ERIC Document Reproduction Service No. ED475763)

Messick, S. (1989). Validity. In R. L. Linn (Ed.), *Educational measurement* (3rd ed., pp. 13–103). Upper Saddle River, NJ: Prentice Hall.

Munk, D. D., & Bursuck, W. D. (2001). Preliminary findings on personalized grading plans for middle school students with learning disabilities. *Exceptional Children, 67*(2), 211–234.

Munk, D. D., & Bursuck, W. D. (2004). Personalized grading plans: A systematic approach to making the grades of included students more accurate and meaningful. *Focus on Exceptional Children, 36*(9), 1–11.

O'Connor, K. (2009). *How to grade for learning K–12* (3rd ed.). Thousand Oaks, CA: Corwin Press.

Polloway, E. A., Epstein, M. H., Bursuck, W. D., Roderique, T. W., McConeghy, J. L, & Jayanthi, M. (1994). Classroom grading: A national survey of policies. *Remedial and Special Education, 15*, 162–170.

Randall, J., & Engelhard, G. (2009a). Differences between teachers' grading practices in elementary and middle schools. *Journal of Educational Research, 102*(3), 175–185.

Randall, J., & Engelhard, G. (2009b). Examining teacher grades using Rasch measurement theory. *Journal of Educational Measurement, 46*(1), 1–18.

Randall, J., & Engelhard, G. (2010). Examining the grading practices of teachers. *Teaching and Teacher Education, 26*(7), 1372–1380.

Ryan, R. M., & Deci, E. L. (2000). Intrinsic and extrinsic motivations: Classic definitions and new directions. *Contemporary Educational Psychology, 25*, 54–67.

Smith, A. Z., & Dobbin, J. E. (1960). Marks and marking systems. In C. W. Harris (Ed.), *Encyclopedia of Educational Research* (3rd ed., pp. 783–791). New York: Macmillan.

Starch, D., & Elliott, E. C. (1912). Reliability of the grading of high-school work in English. *School Review, 20*, 442–457.

Starch, D., & Elliott, E. C. (1913a). Reliability of grading work in mathematics. *School Review, 21*, 254–259.

Starch, D., & Elliott, E. C. (1913b). Reliability of grading work in history. *School Review, 21*, 676–681.

Struyk, L. R., Epstein, M. H., Bursuck, W., Polloway, E. A., McConeghy, J., & Cole, K. B. (1995). Homework, grading, and testing practices used by teachers for students with and without disabilities. *Clearing House, 69*(1), 50–55.

Thomas, S., & Oldfather, P. (1997). Intrinsic motivations, literacy, and assessment practices: "That's my grade. That's me." *Educational Psychologist, 32*, 107–123.

U.S. Department of Education. (2002). *No Child Left Behind Act of 2001* (Title I Paraprofessionals: Draft Non-Regulatory Guidance). Washington, DC: U.S. Department of Education, Office of Elementary and Secondary Education.

Waltman, K. K., & Frisbie, D. A. (1994). Parents' understanding of their children's report card grades. *Applied Measurement in Education, 7*(3), 223–240.

Welsh, M. E., & D'Agostino, J. V. (2009). Fostering consistency between standards-based grades and large-scale assessment results. In T. R. Guskey (Ed.), *Practical solutions for serious problems in standards-based grading* (pp. 75–104). Thousand Oaks, CA: Corwin Press.

SECTION 5

Methods of Classroom Assessment

Heidi L. Andrade

Associate Editor

16

Constructed-Response Approaches for Classroom Assessment

Thomas P. Hogan

This chapter addresses research on the use of constructed-response (CR) approaches for classroom assessment (CA). In accord with the intent of this handbook, the chapter emphasizes research related to the topic, rather than attempting to be an immediate guide to practice. The chapter identifies four major categories of research related to using CR approaches, summarizes research findings, and suggests needed research.

To properly encompass the topic, we need consensual definitions of the two key terms: (1) CR and (2) CA. Providing definitions presents more of a challenge than one might first suppose. However, understanding the research literature in the field, as well as relevant textbooks, requires recognition of variations in definitions. If someone refers to football, and one listener assumes this means soccer while another listener assumes it means American-style football, then confusion in thinking and unpredictable problems in further communication almost certainly ensue.

Definitions of Constructed-Response and Selected-Response Item Formats

Many sources dichotomize item formats into CR and selected-response (SR). The terminology, however, is not universal. Even when these terms are used, what gets classified into each category is not always the same from one source to another. This is an important issue because some of the research findings discussed in this chapter depend on what gets classified as CR versus SR.

Textbook Definitions of Constructed-Response and Selected-Response Item Formats

Textbooks on educational assessment illustrate the lack of clear consensus on the meaning of SR versus CR item formats. I present here a brief summary of the variety of ways textbook authors have classified types of items, including those items variously labeled as short-answer, completion, or fill-in items, which are especially problematic in terms of categorization. This is not intended as an exhaustive list of sources, but those chosen document the assortment of classification schemes.

Many textbooks include short-answer and completion items in chapters devoted to SR items. Examples of such treatment include recent books by Brookhart and Nitko (2008); Kubiszyn and Borich (2003); Miller, Linn, and Gronlund (2009); Nitko and Brookhart (2007); and Stiggins and Chappuis (2012). Grouping short-answer and completion items with other

SR items has a long history in educational measurement books. It occurred, for example, in Ebel's (1965) classic textbook. In contrast, other textbooks clearly place short-answer and completion items in chapters devoted to CR item formats. Examples of this type of treatment include Popham (2011), McMillan (2011), and Hogan (2007). Regardless of how the textbooks treat short-answer items, almost all of them devote separate chapters to essay tests, performance tests, and portfolios, usually without explicitly stating that these three categories are examples of the CR format.

A few sources use the term *performance assessment* as equivalent to CR. For example, following Downing's (2006) chapter on "Selected-Response Item Formats in Test Development," Welch (2006) titled her chapter "Item and Prompt Development in Performance Testing" (p. 303) rather than "in constructed-response testing." The main points of her chapter dealt almost exclusively with the traditional essay test, specifically as implemented in the ACT. Bennett (1993) noted that a widely cited work by the Office of Technology Assessment (U.S. Congress, Office of Technology Assessment, 1992) defined *performance assessment* (rather than CR) as anything other than a multiple-choice item. Thus, according to this usage, a completion item or essay would be a performance assessment, which surely strains the meaning of *performance.*

Definition of Constructed-Response in the *Standards for Educational and Psychological Tests*

Examination of successive editions of the authoritative *Standards for Educational and Psychological Tests* (from this point we will refer to this as *Standards*) (American Educational Research Association [AERA], American Psychological Association [APA], National Council on Measurement in Education [NCME], 1999) proves interesting. Editions of the *Standards* prior to the 1999 edition contain few references to terms such as SR, multiple-choice, CR, or performance types of items. An earlier document, the American Psychological Association's (APA) (1954) *Technical Recommendations*, made no reference to types of items. The *Technical Recommendations for Achievement Tests* (AERA & NCME, 1955) referred to cases where "subjective processes enter into the scoring of the test" (p. 33) and specifically mentioned "completion tests . . . in the scoring of certain products such as handwriting, shorthand, and composition" (p. 33). Thus, the *Standards* identified the human element in scoring as a key characteristic of the CR type of item.

The next three editions of the *Standards* (APA, AERA, & NCME, 1966, 1974, 1985) contained essentially the same treatment of the topic as the 1955 *Technical Recommendations.* Beginning with the 1999 edition, the *Standards* (AERA et al., 1999) referred to "selected-response formats, such as multiple-choice items" (p. 38). These *Standards* then referred to "a short constructed-response format. Short-answer items [requiring] a response of no more than a few words [and] extended-response formats [requiring] the test taker to write a more extensive response of one or more sentences or paragraphs" (AERA et al., 1999, p. 38). The reference to written products in the definition of extended-response formats seems to be a carryover from the days when virtually all items other than SR items were referred to as *essays.*

The 1999 *Standards* clearly place short-answer items in the CR category. The 1999 *Standards* go on to devote entire sections to performance assessments and portfolios, thus constituting a major expansion in treatment of CR measures. The draft of the revision of the 1999 *Standards* (AERA et al., 2011) preserves the coverage of CR, performance assessments, and portfolios virtually unchanged from the 1999 *Standards.*

Terminology in Major Testing Programs

Usage of the terms SR and CR in the *Standards* generally agrees with the usage adopted in such sources as the National Assessment of Educational Progress (NAEP) and Trends in International Mathematics and Science Study (TIMSS). Both sources classified items as either multiple-choice or CR. With the essence of simplicity, the NAEP (2011) glossary defined a CR item as a non-multiple-choice item. Similarly, a TIMSS report (Mullis et al., 2005) noted that "two question formats are used in the TIMSS assessment–multiple-choice and constructed-response" (p. 102). The only distinction among types of CR items in TIMSS is the type of item response theory (IRT) model used to score items as 0/1 or 0/1/2 (Foy, Galia, & Li, 2008). The Programme for International Student Assessment (PISA) (National Center for Education Statistics, n.d.; Organisation for Economic Cooperation and Development [OECD], 2009) also used the distinction between multiple-choice and CR items, although it has a further distinction sometimes labeled closed versus open CR items and sometimes labeled short-answer versus extended-response format. The closed or short-answer items call for simple responses and require little judgment in scoring. The open or extended-response items call for explanations or listing of steps in a process, but even these are relatively brief in terms of total response time.

As will become obvious in later sections, some of the conclusions reached about CR items depend on what gets classified as CR versus SR. In that connection, it is especially important to be alert to varying uses of the terms *new, old, traditional,* and several related descriptors applied to types of items in both the research literature and textbooks about assessment. In the early 20th century, reference to new types of items invariably meant SR items and reference to old or traditional types of items meant CR, especially essay items, although short-answer items also typically fell under this term. Currently, some sources reverse these references. For example, in Stiggins and Chappuis (2012), the first section of the chapter on "Selected-Response Assessments" is labeled "The 'conventional' assessment methods" (p. 92); Frey and Schmitt (2010) lumped together as "traditional" tests any type of SR items as well as completion items and even essays. Thus, sorting through the literature on these matters requires very careful attention to precise use of terms.

The review of research on CR items in this chapter uses the definitions of CR items reflected in the *Standards* and in major testing programs as encompassing the broad array of tasks from simple completions to complex, lengthy responses. As appropriate, comments on the research will try to clarify exactly what the nature of the CR item was in a particular piece of research.

Examples of Constructed-Response Items

It is relatively easy to catalog types of SR items. As indicated by the label, a person must select a response from given alternatives. Thus, even the true–false, other binary-choice (e.g., yes/no), and matching item types all reduce down to some type of SR item, with choices sometimes being among only two alternatives. CR items, in contrast, present a rather wide-open plethora of item formats. A useful way to think about the variety of CR items is along a continuum from simple to more complicated or, perhaps even more operationally, from very short to very long responses. Bennett (1993), Hogan (2007), and Welch (2006) all suggested such a continuum and the terminology is consistent with that found in the *Standards* (AERA et al., 2011). Figure 16.1 depicts this conception of CR items.

At the far left of Figure 16.1 we locate what textbooks usually refer to as fill-in, completion, and short-answer items. Here are examples:

- Who was the first president of the United States? _____
- 46 + 27 = _____
- 4X + 10 = 26, so X = _____
- (Dictated spelling) Spell *executive* as in the following sentence: "The president heads the executive branch of the federal government."
- What is the chemical symbol for water? _____

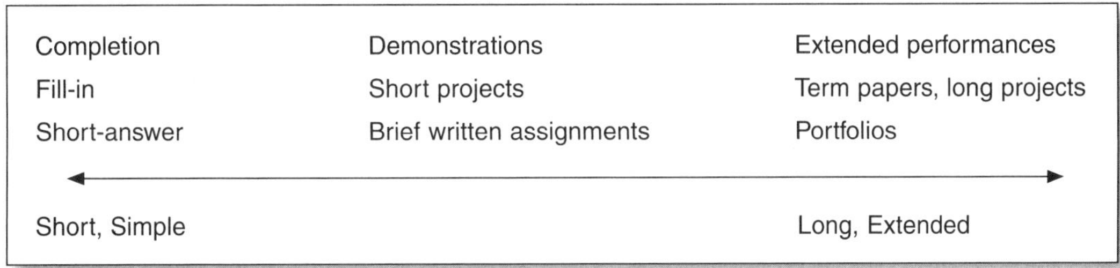

Figure 16.1 Continuum of Constructed-Response Items

At the far right of Figure 16.1 we find such familiar examples as portfolios accumulated over an extended period of time (see Belgrad, Chapter 19 of this volume), assignments such as the conventional term paper, and science or art projects requiring several weeks or more of work. In the middle of the figure, we locate examples such as the following demonstrations and relatively simple performances:

- Using a protractor, bisect this line segment.
- Write an equation to show how to get the perimeter of a rectangle 2 cm wide by 4 cm long.
- Use balloons fully filled and slightly filled to demonstrate that air weighs something.
- Write a letter to the editor of the local newspaper about a community issue.
- Write a brief (20-minute) story about a picture.
- Draw a map of your state and locate your city on the map.
- Do an Internet search to find the world's most used languages. Graph the result.

Assessment of music skill, for example, playing an instrument, and artistic skill, such as drawing a picture or creating a sculpture, are almost necessarily CR in nature and fit in the middle or right side of the figure, depending on the complexity of the task. Assessments of physical fitness commonly used in physical education classes also fit along the continuum. They provide classic examples of performance assessments, including such measures as speed in running 400 meters, distance for throwing a softball, number of basketball free throws made out of 10 shots, and so on. An interesting aspect of these performance assessments in comparison with many other types of performance assessments is that they require virtually no human judgment to score them.

Several of the simple measures of creative or divergent thinking also fall into the middle area of Figure 16.1, for example:

- In 1 minute, list all the words you can think of that begin with the letter L.
- List changes you think might have happened if the South had won the Civil War.

Of course, more extended creative activities, such as writing a short story or a poem, fall further to the right in the figure.

A noteworthy feature of CR items, especially those in the middle and to the right in Figure 16.1, is that they are virtually indistinguishable from instructional activities. Nobody is likely to mistake a multiple-choice or true–false item as being intended for anything other than assessment. But any of the activities listed above for the middle or right side of Figure 16.1 might very well be part of ordinary classroom instruction. They become assessment items only by the intention of the user.

Examples of CR items presented here are limited to the cognitive domain, thus do not include measures of attitudes, dispositions, or the social–emotional attributes of the classroom (see Rivers, Hagelskamp, & Brackett, Chapter 20 of this volume). The examples presented here include reference to performance assessments (see Lane, Chapter 18 of this volume) and portfolios (see Belgrad, Chapter 19 of this volume), both of which are given fuller treatment in other chapters.

Several types of items seem to defy any neat classification into the SR and CR categories. I mention them briefly, for the sake of completeness, without attempting to resolve their proper placement. First, the "grid-in" item, used primarily for mathematics items, contains a problem (e.g., 49×26, or a word problem) requiring a numerical answer. The stem is followed by a numerical grid, say 5 columns by 10 rows where the rows are digits 0 through 9. The student fills in ovals to indicate the answer. The process certainly appears to be a CR. However, scoring requires no human judgment, making it like an SR item. Mathematically, it is an SR item with 10^5 (i.e., 100,000) options.

Curriculum-based assessments or measurements (CBAs or CBMs) present an array of techniques difficult to classify as CR or SR. A CBA in reading, for example, simply counts how many words a student reads in, say, 1 minute. CBA tasks are exceptionally simple. Used primarily by school psychologists, regular classroom teachers can easily use these techniques. In one sense, the techniques are like CR items in that students are not selecting a response. In another sense, they are like SR items in that *scoring* requires no judgment. For general descriptions and examples of CBA techniques, see

Hintze, Christ, and Methe (2006), Kramer (1993), Shapiro (1989), and Shinn (1998). An Internet search of CBA will turn up many other examples.

Several techniques for assessing creative thinking present cases similar to the CBA case, at least for our purposes of classifying items as CR or SR. Some of the simpler forms of creative thinking exercises, like the CBA techniques, require a CR method of responding but require no human judgment. For example, having students list all the words they can think of beginning with the letter L in 1 minute or listing all possible causes of the Civil War in 1 minute—and counting only the number of responses—fall into this category. Of course, it is also possible to score such responses for the quality of answers, which clearly does call for human judgment.

Automated scoring presents a fourth example difficult to classify as SR or CR. In automated scoring, the examinee creates a response, for example, writing an essay—thus clearly placing it in the CR category—but the response is scored by a computer program, thus avoiding any human judgment and giving it one of the key characteristics of the SR category. The primary examples of automated scoring occur in the evaluation of writing ability (see Dikli, 2006, for a summary; see also Drasgow, Luecht, & Bennett, 2004; Shermis & Daniels, 2003).

Teachers' Uses of Constructed-Response Items

To what extent and in exactly what ways do teachers use CR items in CAs? Several investigations have addressed these issues, usually summarizing the variety of assessment techniques employed. Developing generalizations from these studies requires careful attention to the particular definitions used because studies differ in their definitions of CR and SR items.

Studies of Teacher Use of Constructed-Response Items

Fleming and Chambers (1983) classified the types of items used in teacher-made tests in one large-city school district (Cleveland, Ohio). The study covered 342 tests used in Grades 1 through 12 in a variety of school subjects. Short-answer items predominated. In the SR category, matching items were used most frequently, followed by multiple-choice items, then true–false items. Essays received almost no use at any grade level or in any subject, including English. The study included no reference to any type of performance assessment.

Stiggins and Bridgeford (1985) obtained responses from 228 teachers regarding assessment practices. Teachers came from Grades 2, 5, 8, and 11 in eight school districts scattered across the United States. The survey form included short-answer items (thus, CR items in our classification) along with multiple-choice, true–false, and matching items in a category labeled paper-and-pencil objective tests. Another category lumped together standardized objective tests with objective tests supplied with textbooks. Finally, a performance assessment category included structured and spontaneous tests. This study showed that teachers used a great variety of assessment techniques, including both SR and CR items, and that the exact mix of techniques varied by grade. The authors noted concerns about lack of teacher professional development in use of assessment strategies and in following principles of good practice in conducting performance assessments.

Frary, Cross, and Weber (1992) included 536 secondary teachers in a statewide survey. The survey contextualized test usage in terms of grading. Rating categories for types of test items included short-answer, essay, multiple-choice, true–false, math/science problems, and performance. The math/science problems category, which would likely fit under short-answer items in other studies, complicates interpretation of some of the results because the category would be unusually attractive for math and science teachers and virtually unused by teachers of other subjects. For purposes of this review, the main thrust of this study was that teachers used all the item types listed with substantial frequency.

Marso and Pigge (1993) provided a comprehensive review of studies on teachers' testing practices, including several of their own studies. An important distinction incorporated into their summaries was the contrast between self-constructed tests and publisher-constructed tests accompanying textbooks (but not standardized tests). Similar to the results from Fleming and Chambers (1983), Marso and Pigge reported greatest use of short-answer items, followed by matching, multiple-choice, and true–false, with little use of essays.

Cizek, Fitzgerald, and Rachor (1995) queried 143 elementary and secondary teachers in a midwestern state, specifically in a master's-level course in measurement, regarding assessment practices related to grading. The survey classified tests as self-developed versus publishers' tests but did not make distinctions among specific types of items within either of those broad categories. Results showed that teachers use both publisher-prepared and self-developed tests, with the latter category increasing in frequency with increase in grade level.

McMillan, Myran, and Workman (2002) surveyed 901 elementary school teachers from 105 schools in Virginia regarding assessment and grading practices. The survey form listed various types of assessment forms (e.g., essay-type questions or objective assessments). Separate ratings were solicited for mathematics and language arts. The context of the survey form was assessments used specifically for grading, thus not including assessment forms that might be used for other purposes. The authors concluded that "many different types of assessments appear to have been used [and] there was great reliance on assessments prepared by teachers themselves, but also considerable use of assessments provided by publishers" (McMillan et al., 2002, p. 208).

Frey and Schmitt (2010) surveyed 140 teachers from Grades 3 through 12 in 22 school districts in one midwestern state. The principal focus of attention was on the use of traditional tests versus performance tests, with the traditional category including both SR (e.g., MC and TF) items and CR items of the short-answer and essay type. Such traditional items predominated in teachers' assessments. Frey and Schmitt determined that 88% of teachers' assessments were connected to grading, with little devoted to strictly formative assessment.

Burke, Wang, and Bena (2010) surveyed 69 teachers of Grades 3 through 5 in five school districts in Mississippi. Attention focused on specific techniques used for formative assessment. Teachers reported using a great variety of formative assessment techniques but almost no use of portfolios.

Developing generalizations from the studies of teachers' use of various types of assessments presents a challenge because of differences in how authors classified various techniques and in methods for summarizing results of the various surveys. Despite these differences, I venture the following generalizations based on the research on teachers' use of CR items.

1. Nearly all teachers use both SR and CR items. Both categories encompass a variety of specific item types in teachers' practices. For example, SR includes multiple-choice, true–false, and matching items. CR includes short-answer, essays, and performance items.
2. Among CR items, the short-answer type clearly predominates, while the essay receives surprisingly little use. Among SR items, the matching exercise predominates, followed closely by multiple-choice, with true–false trailing far behind.
3. The exact mix of item types varies by grade level. Although, as per the first generalization, teachers at all grade levels use a mixture of item types, CR items occur relatively more often in earlier grades, and SR items tend to increase in higher grades.
4. The relative mix of SR and CR items varies by content area. SR items are more common in science and mathematics and less common in other areas such as language arts and social studies.
5. To date, there appears to be little use of portfolios in ordinary CA.
6. Most assessment, of whatever type, relates to the grading function, with relatively little devoted to strictly formative assessment.
7. The practice of using a mix of SR and CR items has remained relatively stable over at least the past several decades. Of course, SR items were not invented until about 100 years ago, so there certainly has been change over that longer time. While we do not have carefully designed longitudinal studies on the matter of assessment practices, an overview of studies from the past 30 years suggests stability more than change in the mix of assessment techniques used by teachers.

Needed Research

Many of the generalizations just listed must be treated as very tentative. There is much we do not know about teachers' use of CR items. I suggest a need for research on several topics. First, the typical definition of CR items for CA concentrates on items developed by the teacher. The review noted the difficulty of identifying the extent to which teachers use items from tests accompanying textbooks. Certainly most teachers use textbooks and, for all practical purposes, all textbooks supply tests in the form of exercises, end-of-unit tests, and so on. Typically, these tests include both CR and SR items.

The studies by Cizek et al. (1995), Frey and Schmitt (2010), and McMillan et al. (2002) documented that teachers frequently use externally prepared tests. In exactly what way do teachers use these tests? Do teachers combine their own items with the textbook tests? If so, in exactly what ways? A similar question can be raised about the many types of already-prepared tests other than high-stakes tests. These already-prepared tests include both standardized tests (in the sense of having norms, standard instructions, etc.) and nonstandardized tests (e.g., those readily available on the Internet), which many teachers certainly use but are unlikely to think of in the same category as large-scale, standardized tests.

Another topic needing research relates to teachers' use of portfolios. Despite widespread reference to portfolios in textbooks on educational assessment and frequent reference to demonstration projects using portfolios, the research literature on actual uses of various types of assessment techniques in classrooms contains little reference to portfolios. One possible conclusion is that teachers simply do not often use portfolios for routine CA, or perhaps teachers do not consider portfolios an assessment technique. The matter bears additional investigation.

Finally, conspicuously lacking in the research on teachers' use of both CR and SR items is the types of inferences teachers might draw from student response to one or the other type of item. Casual observation suggests there might be differences in these inferences, but research on this matter is lacking.

Recommendations for Use of Constructed-Response Items

Over a considerable period of time and through a variety of publications, Haladyna and colleagues (Haladyna, 1994, 1999, 2004; Haladyna & Downing, 1989a, 1989b; Haladyna, Downing, & Rodriguez, 2002) have identified principles of good practice in the preparation of multiple-choice items. The effort began by identifying recommendations made for writing multiple-choice items in textbooks and articles. Hogan and Murphy (2007) undertook a similar project aimed at CR items by reviewing 25 textbooks and chapters on educational measurement to identify recommendations for preparing CR items. The review expanded to include recommendations on scoring CR items, an issue that is usually irrelevant for SR items except for such matters as differential weighting of options and corrections for guessing.

Hogan and Murphy culled from the 25 sources 15 recommendations for preparation of CR items and 13 recommendations for scoring CR items. I summarize here only the more frequent recommendations. For preparing CR items, the sources recommend covering logistics (e.g., time limits and point values), avoiding the use of optional items, making special effort to clearly define the task, relating the item to instructional objectives or a test blueprint, and using more items with less time per item as opposed to fewer items with more time per item, although on this last point several of the sources actually took exactly the opposite position. For scoring CR items, the sources recommended scoring items anonymously, scoring one item at a time (when there are several items to be scored), developing and using a scoring rubric, separating the evaluation of mechanics from knowledge, and using a second reader.

Treatment of these topics in the sources used by Hogan and Murphy (2007) generally did not distinguish between CA (although that term is used in the title of several of the sources) and large-scale, standardized assessment. The flavor of some of the recommendations certainly seemed to suggest a large-scale context. For example, one of the more frequent recommendations was to use a second reader, a standard practice for large-scale assessment but likely used in a limited way for classroom use. Nevertheless, the recommendations, as a whole, merit attention for classroom use of CR items. Apropos of this point, several of the studies cited earlier on teachers' uses of CR items (Fleming & Chambers, 1983; Marso & Pigge, 1993) noted that teacher-prepared tests often violated professional recommendations for item preparation and scoring. These studies document the need for development of assessment literacy as noted in numerous other reports (Buckendahl, Plake, & Impara, 2004; Daniel & King, 1998; Lukin, Bandalos, Eckhout, & Mickleson, 2004; Mertler, 2005; Plake, Impara, & Fager, 1993; Zhang & Burry-Stock, 2003).

CONSTRUCTED-RESPONSE VERSUS SELECTED-RESPONSE: WHAT DO THEY MEASURE?

A perennial question—perhaps *the* perennial question—about CR items is whether they, in comparison with SR items, measure or *get at* different abilities, traits, or types of achievement. Textbooks and other sources are rife with references to differential measurement by these two item formats. The reasoning often invokes some version of Bloom's (1956) taxonomy or more recently developed but similar taxonomies (Marzano, 2001; Stiggins, Rubel, & Quellmalz, 1988). Bloom's original system ranges from knowledge (at the lower end) through comprehension, application, analysis, and synthesis to evaluation (at the upper end), with the upper categories, usually at some undesignated point of transition, being referred to as higher-order thinking skills (HOTS), a term not used in the original Bloom system. The standard line is that SR items are more appropriate for assessing simpler mental processes, for example, factual knowledge and recognition, whereas measurement of the processes at the upper levels requires CR items. Indeed, the claim is repeated in near mantra-like fashion in many sources and seems firmly entrenched in the educational community's collective consciousness.

The question of whether SR and CR items measure different mental processes, abilities, or traits can be attacked empirically and, indeed, a prodigious research literature has developed to answer this question. The research spans a long period of time, diverse subject matter, and nearly every school grade level, and it originates with authors representing different theoretical dispositions and expectations regarding outcomes of the study.

Methods of Study

Particularly for purposes of suggesting additional research, it will be helpful to describe the various designs used to study the issue. The studies of the relationship between CR and SR measures generally fall into three categories. The first category involves direct correlations between CR and SR measures. For example, suppose we test knowledge of history with an essay test composed of three questions and with a multiple-choice test composed of 50 items. Do the two types of test correlate so highly that they seem to be measuring the same "knowledge of history" trait? Or is the correlation so low as to suggest that the two tests measure somewhat different underlying traits, perhaps even radically different traits? If the correlation is low, we may not know exactly how the measures differ, but rational analysis may suggest that one test is measuring ability to analyze and the other is measuring factual knowledge. I include in this direct correlation category studies using factor analytic methods, which, at root, deal with correlations among tests. The direct correlation method has been the most widely used to study the CR–SR relationship.

A second category includes studies that compare CR and SR measures in terms of their correlations with a third variable that is considered in some sense a superordinate criterion—for example, final grades based on many sources of information accumulated during an entire term. The type of measure (CR or SR) that correlates more highly with the superordinate criterion would be considered the better measure. From a practical viewpoint, if the direct correlation method shows perfect correlation between CR and SR measures, then they should correlate equally with the superordinate criterion.

A third category might be labeled studies of *treatment effect* or *instructional sensitivity*. Given that a group of students has completed a unit of study, which type of measure—CR or SR—does a better job of documenting that learning has occurred? This third method allows for application of a true experimental design. Suppose, for example, that we randomly divide 200 Grade 6 students into two groups, one of which studies Islamic history for one period per day for 2 weeks while the other group does not. We then administer CR and SR tests on Islamic history to the two groups. Which measure, CR or SR, better distinguishes between students who studied the material and students who did not? Note that within each group CR and SR tests might be perfectly correlated, but one may show better differentiation between groups.

For studies employing the direct correlation method or the criterion-correlation method, the correction for attenuation, also known as the correction for unreliability, constitutes a crucial element. The basic idea is that the correlation between two variables is limited by the reliabilities of the two variables. The correction for attenuation provides an estimate of the *true* correlation (often called the disattenuated correlation) after taking into account the reliabilities of the two measures, usually assuming that both reliabilities are perfect. For variations on the basic formula, with applications to a variety of cases, see Gulliksen (1950), Lord and Novick (1968), or Nunnally and Bernstein (1994).

Consider this example as applied to the question of the correlation between a CR and an SR. We test students' knowledge of history with an essay and with a multiple-choice test. The raw, original correlation between the two measures is 0.65. The reliability of the essay test is 0.62 and the reliability of the multiple-choice test is 0.70. Applying the correction for attenuation, the correlation between the two measures is 0.99—virtually perfect. Failure to apply the correction might lead one to believe that the correlation between essay and multiple-choice tests was only moderate (0.65), whereas applying the correction yields quite a different conclusion. In fact, some studies in the research literature did not apply the correction (e.g., Colgan, 1977; Davis & Fifer, 1959; Heim & Watts, 1967) with attendant unfortunate consequences for drawing conclusions.

Two technical points need to be added regarding the correction for attenuation. First, it is important that the reliabilities for the two measures take into account the appropriate sources of error variance. This is not always done. For example, in the illustration just used, if the essay test and multiple-choice tests were given on different days, error variance attributable to time should enter the reliability determination; using an internal consistency reliability for the multiple-choice test and inter-rater reliability for the essay test would underestimate the correction. Second, we need to raise the question about the appropriate standard to apply in determining whether the two measures are virtually equivalent. The purist would maintain that the disattenuated correlation should be 1.00 (or very close to that figure) to merit a declaration of equivalence. For example, Rodriguez (2003) stated, "The primary question is whether or not the average [dissattenuated] correlation based on these studies is at unity" (p. 165). Similarly, Traub (1993) asked "whether or not the coefficient of correlation, after allowance had been made for the attenuating effect of errors of measurement, was different from one" (p. 30). However, one might make the case that a disattenuated correlation of, say, 0.90 is close enough for practical purposes to claim equivalence: That is in the neighborhood of the test–retest reliability of the best-developed tests (see, for example, McCrae & Costa, 2010; Wechsler, 2003, 2008). The work of Sinharay and colleagues (see Sinharay, 2010; Sinharay, Puhan, & Haberman, 2011) on requirements for meaningful differentiation of scores provides another perspective on the question. According to that work, the disattenuated correlation between two measures should fall below 0.85 in order to claim unique information from the two measures.

Research Literature on Constructed-Response Versus Selected-Response Items

In a review prepared for the NAEP, which at the time was struggling with the question of how to allocate items between SR and CR formats, Hogan (1981) summarized 35 reports of the CR–SR relationship, dating from the early 1900s. Many of the reports included multiple individual results—for example, at different grade levels, with different subject matter, and with alternate versions of both SR (e.g., MC and T/F) and CR (e.g., completion and essay). The question raised in the earliest studies differed little from that raised today: Do the two types of items measure the same trait, characteristic, ability, or state of knowledge?

Twenty-six reports relied primarily on the direct correlation method, 7 used the criterion-correlation method, and just 2 used the treatment effect or instructional sensitivity method. The review concentrated on what might be called content knowledge (history, mathematics, science, etc.) and specifically excluded writing, reading, and speaking, as well as noncognitive areas (attitudes, self-concept, etc.). Hogan (1981) concluded, among other points, the following:

> In most instances, free-response and choice-type measures are found to be equivalent or nearly equivalent, as defined by their intercorrelation, within the limits of their respective reliabilities. . . . To the extent that free-response and choice-type tests diverge in what they measure and there is some outside criterion by which to judge which of the two is the better measure, the choice-type measure, more frequently than not, proves to be more valid. . . . (pp. 41–42)

That is, it correlates more highly with the outside criterion.

Traub (1993) reviewed nine studies of CR–multiple-choice equivalence. He selected studies providing more information than the usual CR–multiple-choice correlation. Three studies related to writing skill, two to word knowledge, two to reading comprehension, and three to quantitative ability. Traub concluded in favor of construct equivalence for the reading and quantitative domains, noted contradictory results for word knowledge, and suggested lack of equivalence for the writing domain, although cautioning about methodological problems with two of the three studies he reviewed in that domain. Traub (1993) added, "Regardless of content domain, however, if differences do exist for any domain, they are very likely to be small, at least as measured by the amount of score variance accounted for" (p. 38).

Rodriguez (2002, 2003) identified 67 studies of the construct equivalence of CR and multiple-choice measures and, based on certain inclusion criteria, selected 29 of the studies yielding 56 correlations for meta-analysis. Rodriguez (2002) provided this succinct summary of results: "The primary question is: Do multiple-choice (MC) and CR items measure the same cognitive behavior? The quick answer is: They do if we write them to do so" (p. 214). Near unity corrected correlations between performance on CR and multiple-choice items occurred for stem-equivalent items. Such items equate for content and certain contextual features. They "get at" the raw difference between recall and recognition (not including differences in average scores, which virtually always favor recognition over recall). When stems are not equivalent and/or content is not exactly equivalent, the corrected correlations were not at unity but were still very high. As noted in the discussion of the correction for attenuation earlier, the purist's interpretation of the equivalence question demands corrected correlations at (or very near) unity, but a corrected *r* of, say, 0.90 may be close enough for declaring practical equivalence.

As noted earlier, the majority of studies of the CR–SR relationship have employed the direct correlation method. In fact, the reviews by Rodriguez (2003) and Traub (1993) were limited to studies in this category and approximately two-thirds of the studies in Hogan's (1981) review were in this category. Two early reports used the treatment effect approach. In a series of separate studies, Crawford and Raynaldo (1925) divided college students into three groups. Group A was given enough time to study material carefully, defined as varying from 5 to 30 minutes in different studies; Group B was allowed a few minutes to glance over the material; and Group C was given no opportunity to study the material. Groups were then tested with true–false items and traditional (essay) exams.

Analyses dealt with which type of test showed more separation between groups. The authors relied on a simple count of which type of test showed a greater difference, concluding that the true–false showed a greater difference in five comparisons and the essay exam in eight comparisons; inspection of the summary table shows that many of the differences were quite small. Shulson and Crawford (1928) used two-group contrasts in a series of eight studies (six at the college level, two at the high school level). In each study, one group studied material in a regular class period while a contrasting group did not study the material. Both groups were then tested with a 20-item true–false test and a 20-item completion test.

Again, analyses concentrated on which test gave better separation between groups. The authors concluded that the comparison favored the true–false test in four of the studies while favoring the completion test in the other four studies, leading the authors to state that "the two tests are equally good" (Shulson & Crawford, 1928, p. 583). These two studies are principally of interest for the general approach they took to studying the CR–SR equivalence question. It is difficult to draw definitive conclusions from the two studies due to a lack of crucial information and to shortcomings noted in the original sources. For example, Crawford and Raynaldo (1925) did not say how many items were in their true–false test or how the essays were scored; no reliability information was provided for either test. The authors noted problems with the quality of the true–false items and with the order of administration of the tests that might have influenced results. Shulson and Crawford (1928) also did not report reliability information for any of their tests—"all of the home-made type . . . constructed by the teacher in charge of the regular classes" (p. 581). Kiss and Hogan (2012) used the instructional sensitivity design to contrast differences between SR and CR items in distinguishing students who had studied material for 10 minutes versus 30 minutes. Stem-equivalent SR and CR items proved equally sensitive to the differences in study time for these college students. These studies illustrate methods of studying the CR–SR contrast, which might fruitfully be employed in the future.

Three related studies, not included in any of the reviews just cited, used data from the Advanced Placement (AP) program to examine the relationship between CR and SR (specifically, multiple-choice) items. The studies are noteworthy for the size of their databases and the diversity of CR formats. Depending on the specific exams, the CR formats included extensive (approximately 50-minute), holistically scored essays (e.g., on U.S. history) and a variety of analytically scored problems (e.g., in chemistry). Scores on the CR and multiple-choice items combine into a total score for the AP exam. Lukhele, Thissen, and Wainer (1994) analyzed IRT parameters for 82,842 students on the U.S. history test and for 18,462 students on the chemistry test. They concluded that "there is no evidence to indicate that these two kinds of questions are measuring fundamentally different things" (p. 245). The authors also examined data on the correlations between multiple-choice and CR items, along with their respective reliabilities, for seven AP exams over a 5-year period and concluded that "in all cases, the multiple-choice portion of the test correlates more highly with the constructed response portion than the CR portion does with itself (its reliability)" (p. 246).

Thissen, Wainer, and Wang (1994) examined the factor structure of the AP computer science exam and the chemistry exam, both based on over 5,000 cases. They concluded "that the free-response problems predominantly measure the same thing as the multiple-choice sections" (pp. 120–121) and that "for both tests, the free-response items are intended to measure essentially the same proficiency as the multiple-choice items—and they appear to do so" (p. 122). Wainer and Thissen (1993), in separate analyses of the seven AP tests used in Lukhele et al. (1994), concluded that "for all of the tests, . . . whatever is being measured by the constructed-response section is measured better by the multiple-choice section" (p. 116) than by the CR section itself, due to the lower reliability of the CR section.

An indirect type of analysis of the SR versus CR question arises from the psychometric properties of scaling in major testing projects such as the NAEP and TIMSS. Such programs typically mix SR and CR items when assessing an area such as mathematics or science. The items are scaled with some version of an IRT method that assumes *unidimensionality*. The plain implication is that the two types of items are tapping a single underlying trait (see, e.g., Olson, Martin, & Mullis, 2008). Some of the work with the AP exams by Wainer and colleagues, as previously described, employed this line of reasoning.

On the whole, the conclusions reached by Hogan (1981), Traub (1993), Rodriguez (2002, 2003), and Wainer and colleagues (Lukhele et al., 1994; Thissen et al., 1994; Wainer & Thissen, 1993) are remarkably similar to the conclusions reached in three reviews of research almost 80 years ago by Ruch (1929), Kinney and Eurich (1932), and Lee and Symonds (1933). It is worth noting that studies covered in all these reviews included both short-answer and extended-response (e.g., essays or complex problems) in the CR category.

Some Speculation About the Lack of Differences Between Constructed-Response and Selected-Response Test Items

What might account for the usual finding of a lack of measurement differences between CR and SR tests? Casual observation certainly suggests a difference. I do not know of any consensus explanation for the results, but I will offer the following four points as speculation. First, most of our measures, both CR and SR, provide relatively blunt instruments. We are measuring with yardsticks, not micrometers. Second, in a related vein, we underestimate (or disregard) the considerable measurement error in the measures. Although the correction for attenuation provides a technical solution, that correction probably does not affect our ordinary thinking about the measures. Third, we overestimate the differences in mental processes required by the CR and SR formats. Perhaps this is another example of what Truman Kelley (1927) called the *jangle fallacy*: If you use different words for two things (e.g., abilities), then they really are different. We use multiple distinctions between mental processes, for example, in Bloom-like taxonomies, but research has generally failed to support the distinctions in such systems (see Kreitzer & Madaus, 1994; Seddon, 1978). Fourth, we underestimate the effect of individual differences in general mental ability. Large individual differences tend to swamp any differences attributable to such minor matters as test format.

EFFECTS OF CONSTRUCTED-RESPONSE AND SELECTED-RESPONSE ITEMS ON STUDENTS

Does the use of CR versus SR items have different effects on students? In one sense, this question is a version of the equivalence question addressed in a previous section. However, from a practical perspective, the question of the effect on students has been addressed as a separate issue. Studies have resolved the issue into two questions. First, do students prepare any differently for one type of item? Second, do students learn differentially when tested with one type of item versus the other?

Several studies have addressed these questions. Unfortunately, for our purposes, most of the studies have been conducted with college students or high school students in advanced courses such as physics. I know of no studies in the primary grades and, perhaps, none will ever be done. It is difficult to imagine that, say, a first-grade student could conceptualize the difference between a CR and an SR item. Analysis of the studies requires careful attention to the nature of the learning material and the exact nature of the test items. Nevertheless, we do have some information about these topics.

Meyer (1934, 1935), Hakstian (1971), and Gay (1980) conducted studies to determine the effect of using CR or SR tests on student study habits and degree of learning. The studies reached conflicting conclusions. Meyer indicated type of test did make a difference, Hakstian said it did not make a difference, and Gay concluded the result differed depending on what was used as a criterion. All of these studies were conducted with college students and with small samples within the authors' own classes, thus making generalizations difficult.

Balch (1964) provided an extensive review of nearly 50 studies conducted over a 60-year span on the influence of the evaluating instrument on student learning. The majority of the studies involved college students; a few went as low as the junior high grades. In introducing the topics covered in the review, Balch observed the strong rhetoric surrounding the topic often unsupported by any evidence—a note that might be repeated today. Balch noted that "with the lack of conclusive results and of agreement among the studies reported in the literature, it seems hazardous to draw conclusions" (p. 176) and "the effects of being tested exclusively in one way have not been determined" (p. 177).

In a widely cited study, D'Ydewalle, Swerts, and DeCorte (1983) compared study time and test performance as a function of whether students expected open (CR) or multiple-choice items on a test following a period of studying a text. In introducing the study, the authors noted that "when summarizing the research done so far on the expectation about the type of test [CR versus SR] in text learning, probably the most conspicuous thing is the inconclusiveness of the findings" (p. 55). They found that students who expected open-ended items studied longer than did students who expected multiple-choice items. Curiously, however, study time did not significantly relate to improved performance. This study had an interesting design, but its generalizability seems quite limited for four reasons. First, it was conducted with law school students. Second, the material-to-be-learned was very brief: one page of fact-filled history. Third, total time initially devoted to study was a mere 4 minutes, with increased study time devoted to a second exercise being only about 10 minutes. Fourth, the authors noted that results may have been influenced by lack of ceiling on the multiple-choice test, for which average scores were nearly 90% on the second learning exercise. Scouller (1998) provided another example of a widely cited study on the contrast between multiple-choice and essay tests, in this case with Australian college students. Careful reading of the Scouller article suggests that the "assignment essay" exercise used in that study came closer to what would be called a term paper rather than a traditional essay test.

In two cleverly designed studies, students were led to believe they would receive a particular type of test (CR or SR) but, in fact, may or may not have received that type of test. Sax and Collet (1968) compared the effects of multiple-choice and recall tests on achievement for students in two tests and measurements classes.

Students were given three recall tests or three multiple-choice tests and were told to expect the same format for the final exam. Actually, for the final exam, students were randomly assigned to either the recall or multiple-choice formats. Students who had received multiple-choice exams throughout the semester obtained higher scores on *both* the multiple-choice and recall final exams.

Kumar and Rabinsky (1979) had 60 ninth-grade students read a passage for a test to be taken the next day. One-third of the students were told to expect a recall test, one-third to expect a multiple-choice test, and one-third were left in an ambiguous situation, being told simply that they would be tested for retention of the material. Then, one-half of each group received a multiple-choice test while the other half of each group received a recall test. There was no significant effect due to the set to receive one or the other kind of test. The learning experience in this study was obviously quite limited.

Interaction Effects With Student Characteristics

In a special twist on the question of the effect of CR versus SR items, several studies have examined possible interactions between test format and student characteristics. Longstreth (1978) administered essay, multiple-choice, and true–false tests to college students in a child development course. The correlation between essay and multiple-choice tests reached the usual level (0.99, disattenuated). When results were analyzed separately by race (Asian, Black, White), significant race × test format interactions appeared with Asian and White students scoring higher than Blacks on essay and multiple-choice items but not on true–false items. Snow (1993) suggested possible interactions between test format and student characteristics—specifically that "high need for achievement, as well as high test anxiety, is more likely to be dysfunctional on constructed-response tests than on multiple-choice tests" (p. 55). Snow also suggested an interaction between general ability and test format effects, specifically that the CR format may be particularly advantageous for higher ability students. Martinez (1999) also commented on possible interactions between test format (CR versus SR) and a variety of person characteristics, including test anxiety and self-confidence.

Two large-sample studies examined interactions between gender and test format. Beller and Gafni (2000) compared performance by gender on multiple-choice and open-ended mathematics items in the International Assessment of Educational Progress (IAEP) databases for 1988 and 1991, with approximately 1,000 13-year-olds in 6 countries in 1988 and 1,650 9- and 13-year-olds from 20 countries in 1991. There were larger gender effects for multiple-choice than for open-ended items in 1988 but, inexplicably, the reverse in 1991. Boys did better on more difficult items in both years. Interaction effects also varied by country.

DeMars (2000) examined the performance of several thousand Michigan high school students on multiple-choice and CR items in science and mathematics. One focus of attention was differences in performance for high-stakes tests (which counted for high school diploma) versus low-stakes tests (which did not count for diploma). The results showed an interaction between gender and test format with boys scoring higher than girls on multiple-choice items and girls scoring higher than boys on CR items. There was also an interaction between test format and level of stakes: Scores increased from low to high stakes for both types of items but more so for CR items.

Summary of Effects of Using Constructed-Response and Selected-Response Items

Here is a tentative summary of what the research seems to show about the effects of using CR or SR items. First, students report that they study differently depending on whether they expect a CR or SR test. Specifically, they study more for organization when expecting a CR test and study more for detail when expecting an SR test. Second, despite student reports of differences in study methods, the mode of testing does not usually make any difference in degree of learning. That is, student performance is approximately equal, and this holds regardless of whether performance is defined by a CR or an SR measure. The following was noted by Martinez (1999):

> Of all the issues raised by the use of test response formats, anticipation effects may be the most important in the long run. Although it is commonly believed that expectations

> concerning different response formats lead to different learning outcomes, this connection is still not well-established and described by research. (p. 215)

Third, several studies show that test format (CR or SR) interacts with certain student characteristics, such as gender and level of test anxiety. These interactions provide one of the best reasons for using combinations of CR and SR items when feasible—that is, to counterbalance the interaction effects. For reasons that are not clear, the research on interaction effects is not consistent with the research on the equivalence of what SR and CR tests measure.

To conclude this discussion of the effect of using CR and SR items, note that both types of items seem to share in the benefits of the testing effect. That is, simply testing students, by whatever means (provided that students know they will be tested and that feedback is given), substantially aids learning (Black & Wiliam, 1998; Crooks, 1988; Roediger & Karpicke, 2006).

Conclusion and Recommendations for Research

This chapter identified the following conclusions related to the use of CR approaches in CA:

1. Examining the research literature requires careful attention to what is classified as a CR item or format. Classification of completion or short-answer items varies, particularly in textbook treatments of the topic. Some other types of items—for example, grid-in items and some versions of CBMs—are difficult to classify because they share characteristics of both CR and SR items.
2. Teachers report using a mixture of CR and SR items for CA, with some variations in the exact mix by grade level and subject matter. Although the trends are moderate rather than strong, the use of CR items tends to decline with an increase in grade level. The use of CR items is greater in language and social sciences, less in mathematics and science.
3. Among CR items, the completion or short-answer item clearly predominates. The traditional essay receives little use, and portfolios do not appear in the research on what teachers use. Most assessment, of whatever sort, relates to assigning grades.
4. Experts agree on several key points about using and scoring CR items—for example, giving very clear directions, using a scoring rubric, avoiding optional items, and scoring anonymously. Many teacher-prepared tests violate the experts' recommendations.
5. For measurement of content knowledge, CR and SR approaches are highly correlated. They do not appear to be measuring different traits, abilities, or degrees of knowledge.
6. Students report that they study differently for CR and SR tests. However, students' level of learning does not appear to differ depending on the type of test used or anticipated. Research on this topic yields considerable diversity of results, so conclusions must be quite tentative.
7. Certain student characteristics, such as gender and level of test anxiety, interact with test format (CR versus SR). The CR format tends to favor females, higher-ability students, and lower anxiety students.

This chapter identified the following areas as particularly ripe for further research related to use of CR approaches in CA. It is hoped that the research reviewed in this chapter will help to provide the background for the studies suggested.

1. More research is needed on exact ways in which teachers use externally prepared tests, including those accompanying textbooks and non-high-stakes standardized tests.
2. Research is needed on the inferences teachers might draw from CR versus SR items.
3. Exploration of routine use (i.e., outside of occasional demonstration projects) of portfolios in CA is needed.
4. More studies are needed on possible interactions between student characteristics and test formats (CR versus SR). Student characteristics include more enduring ones such as gender, race, and general ability as well as more transient ones such as anxiety present for a particular test.
5. Additional studies using the treatment effect (instructional sensitivity) design for comparing CR and SR approaches are needed.

References

American Educational Research Association, American Psychological Association, & National Council on Measurement in Education. (1985). *Standards for educational and psychological tests.* Washington, DC: American Psychological Association.

American Educational Research Association, American Psychological Association, & National Council on Measurement in Education. (1999). *Standards for educational and psychological tests.* Washington, DC: American Educational Research Association.

American Educational Research Association, American Psychological Association, & National Council on Measurement in Education. (2011). *Standards for educational and psychological tests* [Draft]. Washington, DC: American Educational Research Association. Retrieved from http://teststandards.net/Revision.htm

American Educational Research Association & National Council on Measurement Used in Education. (1955). *Technical recommendations for achievement tests.* Washington, DC: Authors.

American Psychological Association. (1954). Technical recommendations for psychological tests and diagnostic techniques. *Psychological Bulletin, 51*(2, Pt. 2).

American Psychological Association, American Educational Research Association, & National Council on Measurement in Education. (1966). *Standards for educational and psychological tests and manuals.* Washington, DC: American Psychological Association.

American Psychological Association, American Educational Research Association, & National Council on Measurement in Education. (1974). *Standards for educational and psychological tests.* Washington, DC: American Psychological Association.

Balch, J. (1964). The influence of the evaluating instrument on students' learning. *American Educational Research Journal, 1,* 169–182.

Beller, M., & Gafni, N. (2000). Can item format (multiple choice vs. open-ended) account for gender differences in mathematics achievement? *Sex Roles, 42,* 1–21.

Bennett, R. E. (1993). On the meanings of constructed response. In R. E. Bennett & W. C. Ward (Eds.), *Construction versus choice in cognitive measurement: Issues in constructed response, performance testing, and portfolio assessment* (pp. 1–27). Hillsdale, NJ: Lawrence Erlbaum.

Black, P., & Wiliam, D. (1998). Assessment and classroom learning. *Assessment in Education: Principles, Policy, and Practice, 5*(1), 7–74.

Bloom, B. S. (Ed.). (1956). *Taxonomy of educational objectives, handbook 1: Cognitive domain.* New York: Longman.

Brookhart, S. M., & Nitko, A. J. (2008). *Assessment and grading in classrooms.* Upper Saddle River, NJ: Pearson.

Buckendahl, C. W., Plake, B. S., & Impara, J. C. (2004). A strategy for evaluating district developed assessments for state accountability. *Educational Measurement: Issues and Practice, 23*(2), 17–25.

Burke, G., Wang, Y., & Bena, I. (2010). Methods and uses of classroom assessment employed in teaching grades three through five in five school districts in the Mississippi delta. *Education, 130*(4), 657–665.

Cizek, G. J., Fitzgerald, S. M., & Rachor, R. E. (1995). Teachers' assessment practices: Preparation, isolation, and the kitchen sink. *Educational Assessment, 3*(2), 159–179.

Colgan, L. H. (1977). Reliability of mathematics multi-choice tests. *International Journal of Mathematics Education and Science Technology, 8,* 237–244.

Crawford, C. C., & Raynaldo, D. A. (1925). Some experimental comparisons of true-false tests and traditional examinations. *School Review, 33,* 698–706.

Crooks, T. J. (1988). The impact of classroom evaluation on students. *Review of Educational Research 58*(4), 438–481.

Daniel, L. G., & King, D. A. (1998). Knowledge and use of testing and measurement literacy of elementary and secondary teachers. *Journal of Educational Research, 91,* 331–344.

Davis, F. B., & Fifer, G. (1959). The effect on test reliability and validity of scoring aptitude and achievement tests with weights for every choice. *Educational and Psychological Measurement, 19,* 159–170.

DeMars, C. E. (2000). Test stakes and item format interactions. *Applied Measurement in Education, 13,* 55–77.

Dikli, S. (2006). An overview of automated scoring of essays. *Journal of Technology, Learning, and Assessment, 5*(1). Retrieved from www.jtla.org

Downing, S. M. (2006). Selected-response item formats in test development. In S. M. Downing & T. M. Haladyna (Eds.), *Handbook of test development* (pp. 287–302). Mahwah, NJ: Lawrence Erlbaum.

Drasgow, F., Luecht, R. M., & Bennett, R. (2004). Technology and testing. In R. L. Brennan (Ed.), *Educational measurement* (4th ed., pp. 471–516). Westport, CT: Praeger.

D'Ydewalle, G., Swerts, A., & DeCorte, E. (1983). Study time and test performance as a function of test expectations. *Contemporary Educational Psychology, 8,* 55–67.

Ebel, R. L. (1965). *Measuring educational achievement.* Englewood Cliffs, NJ: Prentice Hall.

Fleming, M., & Chambers, B. (1983). Teacher-made tests: Windows on the classroom. In W. E. Hathaway (Ed.), *Testing in the schools* (pp. 29–38). San Francisco: Jossey-Bass.

Foy, P., Galia, J., & Li, I. (2008). Scaling the data from the TIMSS 2007 Mathematics and Science Assessments. In J. F. Olson, M. O. Martin, & I. V. S. Mullis (Eds.), *TIMSS 2007 technical report* (pp. 233–279). Boston: TIMSS & PIRLS International Study Center, Lynch School of Education, Boston College.

Frary, R. B., Cross, L. H., & Weber, L. J. (1992, April). *Testing and grading practices and opinions in the nineties: 1890s or 1990s.* Paper presented at the annual meeting of National Council on Measurement in Education, San Francisco.

Frey, B. B., & Schmitt, V. L. (2010). Teachers' classroom assessment practices. *Middle Grades Research Journal, 5*(3), 107–117.

Gay, L. R. (1980). The comparative effects of multiple-choice versus short-answer tests on retention. *Journal of Educational Measurement, 17,* 45–50.

Gulliksen, H. (1950). *Theories of mental tests.* New York: John Wiley.

Hakstian, A. R. (1971). The effects of type of examination anticipated on test preparation and performance. *Journal of Educational Research, 64,* 319–324.

Haladyna, T. M. (1994). *Developing and validating multiple-choice test items.* Mahwah, NJ: Lawrence Erlbaum.

Haladyna, T. M. (1999). *Developing and validating multiple-choice test items* (2nd ed.). Mahwah, NJ: Lawrence Erlbaum.

Haladyna, T. M. (2004). *Developing and validating multiple-choice test items* (3rd ed.). Mahwah, NJ: Lawrence Erlbaum.

Haladyna, T. M., & Downing, S. M. (1989a). A taxonomy of multiple-choice item-writing rules. *Applied Measurement in Education, 1,* 37–50.

Haladyna, T. M., & Downing, S. M. (1989b). The validity of a taxonomy of multiple-choice item-writing rules. *Applied Measurement in Education, 1,* 71–78.

Haladyna, T. M., Downing, S. M., & Rodriguez, M. C. (2002). A review of multiple-choice item-writing guidelines for classroom assessment. *Applied Measurement in Education, 15,* 309–334.

Heim, A. W., & Watts, K. P. (1967). An experiment on multiple-choice versus open-ended answering in a vocabulary test. *British Journal of Educational Psychology, 37,* 39–346.

Hintze, J. M., Christ, T. J., & Methe, S. A. (2006). Curriculum-based assessment. *Psychology in the Schools, 43,* 45–56.

Hogan, T. P. (1981). *Relationship between free-response and choice-type tests of achievement: A review of the literature.* Paper prepared under contract for Education Commission of the States. Princeton, NJ: ERIC Clearinghouse on Tests & Measurements.

Hogan, T. P. (2007). *Educational assessment: A practical introduction.* New York: John Wiley.

Hogan, T. P., & Murphy, G. (2007). Recommendations for preparing and scoring constructed-response items: What the experts say. *Applied Measurement in Education, 20,* 427–441.

Kelley, T. L. (1927). *Interpretation of educational measurements.* Yonkers-on-Hudson, NY: World Book.

Kinney, L. S., & Eurich, A. C. (1932). A summary of investigations comparing different types of tests. *School and Society, 36,* 540–544.

Kiss, A. J., & Hogan, T. P. (2012, March). *Instructional sensitivity of constructed-response and selected-response items.* Poster presented at meeting of Eastern Psychological Association, Pittsburgh, PA.

Kramer, J. J. (Ed.). (1993). *Curriculum-based measurement.* Lincoln, NE: Buros Institute of Mental Measurements.

Kreitzer, A. E., & Madaus, G. F. (1994). Empirical investigations of the hierarchical structure of the taxonomy. In L. W. Anderson & L. A. Sosniak (Eds.), *Bloom's taxonomy: A forty-year retrospective* (pp. 64–81). Chicago: University of Chicago Press.

Kubiszyn, T., & Borich, G. (2003). *Educational testing and measurement: Classroom application and practice.* New York: John Wiley.

Kumar, V. K., & Rabinsky, L. (1979). Test mode, test instructions, and retention. *Contemporary Educational Psychology, 4,* 211–218.

Lee, J. M., & Symonds, P. M. (1933). New-type or objective tests: A summary of recent investigations. *Journal of Educational Psychology, 24,* 21–38.

Longstreth, L. (1978). Level I–Level II abilities as they affect performance of 3 races in the college classroom. *Journal of Educational Psychology, 70,* 289–297.

Lord, F. M., & Novick, M. (1968). *Statistical theories of mental test scores.* Reading, MA: Addison-Wesley.

Lukhele, R., Thissen, D., & Wainer, H. (1994). On the relative value of multiple-choice, constructed response, and examinee-selected items on two achievement tests. *Journal of Educational Measurement, 31,* 234–250.

Lukin, L. E., Bandalos, D. L., Eckhout, T. J., & Mickleson, K. (2004). Facilitating the development of assessment literacy. *Educational Measurement: Issues and Practice, 23*(2), 26–32.

Marso, R. N., & Pigge, F. L. (1993). Teachers' testing knowledge, skills, and practices. In S. L. Wise (Ed.), *Teacher training in measurement and assessment skills* (pp. 129–185). Lincoln, NE: Buros Institute of Mental Measurements.

Martinez, M. E. (1999). Cognition and the question of test item format. *Educational Psychologist, 34,* 207–218.

Marzano, R. J. (2001). *Designing a new taxonomy of educational objectives.* Thousand Oaks, CA: Corwin Press.

McCrae, R. R., & Costa, P. T. (2010). *NEO Inventories professional manual.* Lutz, FL: PAR.

McMillan, J. H. (2011). *Classroom assessment: Principles and practice for effective standards-based instruction* (5th ed). Upper Saddle River, NJ: Pearson.

McMillan, J. H., Myran, S., & Workman, D. (2002). Elementary teachers' classroom assessment and grading practices. *Journal of Educational Research, 95*(4), 203–213.

Mertler, C. A. (2005). Secondary teachers' assessment literacy: Does classroom experience make a difference? *American Secondary Education, 33,* 76–92.

Meyer, G. (1934). An experimental study of the old and new types of examination: I. The effect of the examination set on memory. *Journal of Educational Psychology, 25,* 641–661.

Meyer, G. (1935). An experimental study of the old and new types of examination: II. Methods of study. *Journal of Educational Psychology, 26,* 30–40.

Miller, M. D., Linn, R. L., & Gronlund, N. E. (2009). *Measurement and assessment in teaching* (10th ed.). Upper Saddle River, NJ: Pearson.

Mullis, I. V. S., Martin, M. O., Ruddock, G. J., O'Sullivan, C. Y., Arora, A., & Erberber, E. (2005). *TIMSS 2007 Assessment Frameworks.* Chestnut Hill, MA: TIMSS & PIRLS International Study Center.

National Assessment of Educational Progress. (2011). *Glossary.* Retrieved from http://nces.ed.gov/nationsreportcard/glossary.asp

National Center for Education Statistics. (n.d.). *Mathematics concepts and mathematics items.* Retrieved from http://nces.ed.gov/surveys/pisa/pdf/PISA_Math_Concepts_Items.pdf

Nitko, A. J., & Brookhart, S. M. (2007). *Educational assessment of students* (5th ed.). Upper Saddle River, NJ: Pearson.

Nunnally, J. C., & Bernstein, I. H. (1994). *Psychometric theory* (3rd ed.). New York: McGraw-Hill.

Olson, J. F., Martin, M. O., & Mullis, I. V. S. (Eds.). (2008). *TIMSS 2007 technical report.* Boston: TIMSS & PIRLS International Study Center, Lynch School of Education, Boston College.

Organisation for Economic Cooperation and Development. (2009). *PISA 2009 Assessment framework: Key competencies in reading, mathematics and science.* Paris, France: Author.

Plake, B. S., Impara, J. C., & Fager, J. J. (1993). Assessment competencies of teachers: A national survey. *Educational Measurement: Issues and Practice, 12*(4), 10–12, 39.

Popham, W. J. (2011). *Classroom assessment: What teachers need to know* (6th ed.). Upper Saddle River, NJ: Pearson.

Rodriguez, M. C. (2002). Choosing an item format. In G. Tindal & T. M. Haladyna (Eds.), *Large-scale assessment programs for all students: Validity, technical adequacy, and implications* (pp. 213–231). Mahwah, NJ: Lawrence Erlbaum.

Rodriguez, M. C. (2003). Construct equivalence of multiple-choice and constructed-response items: A random effects synthesis of correlations. *Journal of Educational Measurement, 40,* 163–184.

Roediger, H. L. III, & Karpicke, J. D. (2006). The power of testing memory: Basic research and implications for educational practice. *Perspectives on Psychological Science, 1,* 181–210.

Ruch, G. M. (1929). *The objective or new-type examination: An introduction to educational measurement.* Chicago: Scott, Foresman.

Sax, G., & Collet, L. (1968). An empirical comparison of the effects of recall and multiple-choice tests on student achievement. *Journal of Educational Measurement, 5,* 169–173.

Scouller, K. (1998). The influence of assessment method on students' learning approaches: Multiple choice question examination versus assignment essay. *Higher Education, 35,* 453–472.

Seddon, G. M. (1978). The properties of Bloom's Taxonomy of Educational Objectives for the cognitive domain. *Review of Educational Research, 48*(2), 303–323.

Shapiro, E. S. (1989). *Academic skills problems: Direct assessment and intervention.* New York: Guilford Press.

Shermis, M. D., & Daniels, K. E. (2003). Norming and scoring for automated essay scoring. In J. Burstein & M. D. Shermis (Eds.), *Automated essay scoring: A cross-disciplinary perspective* (pp. 169–180). Mahwah, NJ: Lawrence Erlbaum.

Shinn, M. R. (Ed.). (1998). *Advanced applications of curriculum-based measurement.* New York: Guilford Press.

Shulson, V., & Crawford, C. C. (1928). Experimental comparison of true-false and completion tests. *Journal of Educational Psychology, 19,* 580–583.

Sinharay, S. (2010). How often do subscores have added value? Results from operational and simulated data. *Journal of Educational Measurement, 47,* 150–174.

Sinharay, S., Puhan, G., & Haberman, S. J. (2011). An NCME instructional module on subscores. *Educational Measurement: Issues and Practices, 30*(3), 29–40.

Snow, R. E. (1993). Construct validity and constructed-response tests. In R. E. Bennett & W. C. Ward (Eds.), *Construction versus choice in cognitive measurement: Issues in constructed response, performance testing, and portfolio assessment* (pp. 45–60). Hillsdale, NJ: Lawrence Erlbaum.

Stiggins, R. J., & Bridgeford, N. J. (1985). The ecology of classroom assessment. *Journal of Educational Measurement, 22,* 271–286.

Stiggins, R. J., & Chappuis, J. (2012). *Introduction to student-assessment FOR learning* (6th ed.). Upper Saddle River, NJ: Pearson.

Stiggins, R. J., Rubel, E., & Quellmalz, E. (1988). *Measuring thinking skills in the classroom* (Rev. ed.). West Haven, CT: NEA Professional Library.

Thissen, D., Wainer, H., & Wang, X. B. (1994). Are tests comprising both multiple-choice and free-response items necessarily less unidimensional than multiple-choice tests? An analysis of two tests. *Journal of Educational Measurement, 31,* 113–123.

Traub, R. E. (1993). On the equivalence of the traits assessed by multiple-choice and constructed-response tests. In R. E. Bennett & C. W. Ward (Eds.), *Construction versus choice in cognitive measurement: Issues in constructed response, performance testing, and portfolio assessment* (pp. 29–44). Hillsdale, NJ: Lawrence Erlbaum.

U.S. Congress, Office of Technology Assessment. (1992). *Testing in American Schools: Asking the Right Questions, OTA-SET-519.* Washington, DC: Government Printing Office.

Wainer, H., & Thissen, D. (1993). Combining multiple-choice and constructed-response test scores: Towards a Marxist theory of test construction. *Applied Measurement in Education, 6,* 103–118.

Wechsler, D. (2003). *Wechsler Intelligence Scale for Children—Fourth Edition: Technical and interpretive manual.* San Antonio, TX: Psychological Corporation.

Wechsler, D. (2008). *Wechsler Adult Intelligence Scale—Fourth Edition: Technical and interpretive manual.* Upper Saddle River, NJ: Pearson.

Welch, C. (2006). Item and prompt development in performance testing. In S. M. Downing & T. M. Haladyna (Eds.), *Handbook of test development* (pp. 303–328). Mahwah, NJ: Lawrence Erlbaum.

Zhang, Z., & Burry-Stock, J. A. (2003). Classroom assessment practices and teachers' self-perceived assessment skills. *Applied Measurement in Education, 16,* 323–342.

17

Writing Selected-Response Items for Classroom Assessment

Michael C. Rodriguez

Thomas M. Haladyna

Some measurement specialists have referred to selected-response (SR) item writing as an *art*. However, the majority of researchers in this area would argue that item writing is an emerging science with a history of almost 100 years of activity (Haladyna, 2004; Haladyna & Rodriguez, in press; Roid & Haladyna, 1982). Despite this large body of research, there is a need to continue and extend research if item development is to become a useful science for classroom assessment (CA) of student learning. Sources of evidence of this emerging science include automatic item generation methods and theories of item writing to assist item writers (Baker, 1989; Bejar, 1993; Gierl & Haladyna, in press; Irvine & Kyllonen, 2002; Roid & Haladyna, 1982).

The increase in testing for accountability has led to increased pressures for classroom teachers to develop high quality test items to use in their CAs of student learning. Since the early part of the last century to the present, measurement specialists have been writing about the construction of test items and conducting research on item writing (Ebel, 1951; Eurich, 1931; Haladyna, 2004; Monroe, 1918; O'Dell, 1928). However, even with this long and extensive attention to item writing, guidance on item writing and the choice of various SR formats often comes from personal experience.

This chapter reviews research on developing and validating SR test items for assessing learning in kindergarten through secondary classroom settings. Specifically, this chapter focuses on teacher assessment ability, the effectiveness of various SR item formats, the validity of guidelines for SR item writing, and critical issues for researchers. Recommendations for future research are included.

Teachers' Use of Selected-Response Items and Assessment Ability

The quality of teacher-made, SR test items rests on the clarity of the learning objectives, the teachers' subject matter expertise, and their item-writing ability. Strong statements of teacher expectations, or perhaps what teachers should know and be able to do regarding assessment and evaluation of students, have been promoted recently (Brookhart, 2011; Popham,

2009). The *Standards for Teacher Competence in Educational Assessment of Students*, developed by the American Federation of Teachers (AFT), National Council on Measurement in Education (NCME), and the National Education Association (NEA) (1990) has not been revised since its publication. More current is the statement on educational assessment knowledge and skills for teachers (Brookhart, 2011).

Research on teacher assessment ability has shown some interesting results. Salmon-Cox (1980) reviewed the literature on teacher assessment practices and reported a survey of high school teachers that showed 40% used their own tests, 30% used interactions with students, 21% relied on homework performance, 6% used observations of students, and 1% used standardized tests to learn about their students. The use of SR tests was increasing between Grades 2 and 11 and was more frequent with mathematics and science teachers (Stiggins & Bridgeford, 1985). Early efforts focused on descriptions of the assessment environment, also addressing quality of teacher assessments (Stiggins & Conklin, 1992).

Marso and Pigge (1991) reviewed elementary and secondary teacher tests from graduates of Bowling Green State University, including teachers of social studies, science, business education, mathematics, and English. Drawing from 6,529 items across 175 tests, most were in a conventional four- or five-option SR format (20%), matching (19%), short-answer (17%), true–false (15%), problem solving (14%), completion (8%), interpretive (6%), and essay items (1%). Two trained judges classified 72% of the items as knowledge-level items, 11% as comprehension, 15% as application, and less than 2% as measures of higher-order thinking. Nearly half of the higher-order items were on mathematics tests. They also found 853 item-writing errors and 281 test format errors. Finally, Marso and Pigge also found that errors in item writing and form construction were equally common among teachers with 1 to 10 years of experience.

Recent survey-based research has uncovered interesting findings that add to our understanding of teachers' role in assessment, given their attitudes, perceptions, and practices in CAs. Researchers of preservice teachers have found a strong preference for constructed-response (CR) formats for CAs and an inclination toward constructivist approaches to instruction and assessment (Ogan-Bekiroglu, 2009; Volante & Fazio, 2007). Researchers have also suggested that those with some documented measurement and assessment preparation or training and even those with professional development training have higher levels of assessment literacy (Mertler, 2009; Mertler & Campbell, 2005; Plake, Impara, & Fager, 1993). Nearly all researchers evaluating teacher assessment literacy lament the limited knowledge and skills of teachers in the areas of item development, test design, administration, scoring, and reporting.

"Classroom teachers are the ultimate purveyors of applied measurement, and they rely on measurement and assessment-based processes to help them make decision every hour of every school day" (Airasian & Jones, 1993, pp. 241–242). However, researchers have frequently reported the extent and effects of poorly written test items (Downing 2002, 2005; Ellsworth, Dunnell, & Duell, 1990; Jozefowicz et al., 2002; McMorris & Boothroyd, 1993; Tarrant & Ware, 2008). Few teachers make explicit connections between CA performance and student achievement or performance in large-scale assessment programs (Rodriguez, 2004).

Brookhart and her colleagues have investigated the role of assessment in the classroom through her model of the assessment event (Brookhart, 1997, 2003; Brookhart & DeVoge, 1999; Brookhart & Durkin, 2003; Brookhart, Walsh, & Zientarski, 2006). Her model examines the interaction of classroom practices, student perceptions and effort, and achievement within the assessment event. Moreover, these studies have repeatedly found important connections between (1) teacher assessment practices; (2) student perceptions, motivation, and effort; and (3) achievement.

In a large-scale application of the Brookhart model, one that was also consistent with the theoretical framework of the Third International Mathematics and Science Study (TIMSS), Rodriguez (2004) examined the relations among student characteristics, classroom characteristics, assessment practices, and achievement. He found that classes where teachers assigned homework more often tended to perform at a higher level on the TIMSS assessment; classes in which teachers frequently used worksheets from workbooks performed at lower levels; and classes in which teachers frequently used teacher-made objective tests also performed at lower levels. Rodriguez argued that in the absence of quality information about teacher-made tests, it is difficult to understand the role of frequent use of such tests. However, in light of the common finding of low quality teacher-made tests, this is a likely unmeasured mediator; classroom tests of low quality will not provide students with clear information about their performance and can negatively affect academic self-efficacy, motivation, and effort—important elements of the Brookhart model.

The research on teachers' ability in assessment of student learning and, in particular, SR item development has been intermittent with few contemporary studies. As high-stakes testing continues and grows, teachers will need to increase their ability to employ valid CAs.

Research on Selected-Response Item Formats

SR item formats available for CA include conventional multiple-choice, alternate-choice, true–false, multiple true–false, matching, extended matching, and context dependent item sets (also known as testlets) (Haladyna, Downing, & Rodriguez, 2002; Haladyna & Rodriguez, in press). New SR formats are being developed by taking advantage of technology and computer-enabled testing (Sireci & Zenisky, 2006). The research on the quality of these innovative item types is not extensive enough to warrant their widespread use. (For a more thorough review of SR formats, examples of items in each format, and a review of the extensive research on format capabilities and effectiveness, see Haladyna and Rodriguez, in press).

Construct Equivalence

The task of the classroom teacher is to select an SR or CR format for a particular type of content and cognitive demand. What does research inform us about this choice? A review by Rodriguez (2002, 2003) compared SR and CR formats in terms of purpose of assessment, content measured, cognitive demand, and cost with empirical research that experimentally compared scores from SR and CR tasks measuring the same or similar content. He found 56 correlations between SR and CR tasks in the literature spanning 1925 to 1998. These studies covered tests in language arts, mathematics, science, social studies, and computer science. He found that when the stem was identical (i.e., the same question was asked with and without options), the average, disattenuated correlation was 0.95. As the stem and the content became less similar, the correlation between SR and CR scores became smaller; content-equivalent stems were correlated 0.92, not-content-equivalent stems were correlated 0.84, and SR scores and essay scores were correlated 0.81.

Can SR and CR items measure the same construct? They can when we write them to do so. The research on this question points to the intention of the item writer. When items were written to measure the same construct, with identical or comparable stems for example, the items measure the same content. This calls into question the use of CR items given the additional cost in scoring them. For SR and CR items that are not content equivalent, they begin to measure different constructs. This calls into question the practice of combining such items into a common measure. If we value the information obtained from CR items, these items should be written to tap content and cognitive demand not easily measured by SR items. At the same time, if these items really do measure different aspects of the construct—enough to make a difference in the rank ordering of students—it might warrant consideration of separate scores, rather than a combined score, which may hide such differences. The issues here are not easily addressed. However, for CAs, the separation of such items into separate scores may provide useful instructional information.

The Complex Multiple-Choice Format

This format offers the test taker four options that are combined, for example:

What are the ships in Columbus' fleet?

1. Nina
2. Pinta
3. Santa Maria

   A. 1 and 2
   B. 2 and 3
   C. 1 and 3
   D. 1, 2, and 3

Rodriguez (1997) synthesized seven studies of the complex multiple-choice format with 13 independent outcomes. These tests included real estate (six trials), social sciences (three trials), health sciences (two trials), and one each in language arts and mathematics. None of these studies involved elementary and secondary classrooms. Complex multiple-choice items tend to be more difficult and less discriminating than standard SR items (see Table 17.2). This format is not recommended for classroom use.

Research on Other Selected-Response Formats

The true–false, multiple true–false, and alternate-choice formats have received sufficient research study, but most of this research is very dated (Haladyna, 2004). The matching format has received virtually no scholarly attention. The extended-matching format has been used in medical testing, but there is no research or evidence of use in classroom settings.

The testlet is increasing in popularity. It consists of a stimulus (reading passage, picture, chart, graph, or problem) and a set of related test items (Haladyna, 1997, 2004). Considerable attention has been given to testlet scoring, and very little attention has been given to the design and development of testlets.

As noted previously, computer-based item formats are emerging, but there is very little research to report on the efficacy of any of these formats. Research on the capabilities of these various SR item formats has not been extensive. If computerized testing offers a plethora of new formats, each format's capabilities for different types of content and cognitive demand should be determined.

Selected-Response Item-Writing Guidelines

There are dozens of educational measurement textbooks available to students, researchers, and measurement practitioners, all containing one or more chapters on SR item writing (Haladyna et al., 2002). Other resources are designed to be instructive and exhaustive regarding SR item writing, including the *Handbook of Test Development* (see Downing, 2006; Sireci & Zenisky, 2006; Welch, 2006) and more generally *Educational Measurement* (see Ferrara & DeMauro, 2006; Schmeiser & Welch, 2006). There are also entire books devoted to item writing, for example *Writing Test Items to Evaluate Higher Order Thinking* (Haladyna, 1997) and *Developing and Validating Test Items* (Haladyna & Rodriguez, in press). These are strong tools for more in-depth treatment of item writing.

In this section, we present an empirically based taxonomy of item-writing guidelines that we think is researchable; then we review the research on these guidelines.

A Taxonomy of Researchable Item-Writing Guidelines

The taxonomy of SR item-writing guidelines presented in Table 17.1 was developed through a series of reviews and empirical syntheses (Haladyna & Downing, 1989a, 1989b; Haladyna et al., 2002; Haladyna & Rodriguez, in press). The published research available for some of these guidelines is reviewed in the next section. Table 17.1 is instructive to researchers because it shows item-writing guidelines that require research to validate their use.

Item-Writing Guidelines for Other Selected-Response Formats

The guidelines for other SR item formats are largely based on experience from practice. These guidelines include a small number of important considerations for matching items and true–false items. Matching items should employ a set of words, phrases, or statements that are tightly homogenous in content. This is critical in order to focus attention on a single learning objective. It is also important to make sure that the number of options is not the same as the number of items or prompts. This avoids clueing through the process of elimination.

Finally, true–false items require additional attention as well (Frisbie & Becker, 1991). Across a set of true–false items, the number of true or false items should be balanced. Each item should be a simple declarative sentence. A longstanding recommendation has been to write true–false items in pairs, one in the affirmative and one in the negative, only using one on any given test form. Considering the pair together helps the item writer detect ambiguity in the statement itself. A final consideration regarding multiple true–false items is to consider using SR items as a basis but best done when it is possible to write multiple options that are independent but also true. In multiple true–false items, it is probably best to balance the true and false options within each option set.

Feature	*Guideline*
Content Concerns	1. Base each item on one type of content and cognitive demand. 2. Use new material to elicit higher-level thinking. 3. Keep the content of items independent of one another. 4. Avoid overly specific and overly general content. Test important content. 5. Avoid opinions unless qualified. 6. Avoid trick items.
Formatting Concern	7. Format each item vertically instead of horizontally.
Style Concern	8. Edit and proof items. 9. Keep linguistic complexity appropriate for the group being tested. 10. Minimize the amount of reading in each item. Avoid window dressing.
Writing the Stem	11. State the central idea in the stem very clearly and concisely. Avoid repetitious wording. 12. Word the stem positively, and avoid negatives such as *not* or *except.*
Writing the Options	13. Use only options that are plausible and discriminating. Three options are usually sufficient. 14. Make sure that only one of these options is the right answer. 15. Vary the location of the right answer. 16. Place options in logical or numerical order. 17. Keep the content of options independent; options should not be overlapping. 18. Avoid using *none of the above, all of the above,* or *I don't know.* 19. Word the options positively; avoid negatives such as *not.* 20. Avoid giving clues to the right answer: a. Keep the length of options about equal. b. Avoid specific determiners including *always, never, completely,* and *absolutely.* c. Avoid clang associations, options identical to or resembling words in the stem. d. Avoid pairs or triplets of options that clue the test taker to the correct choice. e. Avoid blatantly absurd, ridiculous options. f. Keep options homogeneous in content and grammatical structure. 21. Make all distractors plausible. Use typical errors of students to write your distractors. 22. Avoid humorous options.

Table 17.1 Item-Writing Features and Associated Guidelines

Research on Item-Writing Guidelines

Haladyna and Downing (1989a) reviewed 46 authoritative references dating back to 1935 to develop a taxonomy of SR item-writing guidelines and assessed the level of consensus regarding each guideline. Lack of consensus among references exists for empirically testable guidelines rather than value-laden guidelines (guidelines for which authors did not question the validity). Haladyna and Downing (1989b) assessed the validity of those item-writing guidelines by reviewing research dating back to 1918. Their review of the research uncovered 96 theoretical and empirical studies. Haladyna and Downing concluded that new research was needed on six guidelines in particular, including the use of none of the above (NOTA) and all of the above (AOTA), the complex SR format, negative phrasing in the stem, the number of options, and the use of the question format versus the completion format.

These reviews were updated in 2002 (Haladyna et al.), specifically for the CA context, including reviews of 27 measurement textbooks and an additional 19 empirical item-writing research studies from 1990 to 2001. We based the following section on an overview of these reviews, including the works used in a comprehensive synthesis of the item-writing format effects research literature by Rodriguez (1997) used to update the review of validity evidence for Haladyna et al. (2002).

Across all 57 empirical studies from the Rodriguez review, there were a variety of subject areas and levels of test takers. However, only 18 (32%) were conducted in K–12 classrooms: 31 (54%) included postsecondary contexts, and the remainder were in noneducational or professional settings. Most studies assessed the impact of violating an item-writing guideline on item difficulty (92%), with fewer examining item discrimination (51%), score reliability (69%), or test score validity (17%). The paucity of validity-related research is alarming.

An overall summary of results is provided in Table 17.2. The weighted average effect on each outcome is reported with the standard error of the effect in parentheses under the fixed-effect model. Each effect is in the same metric as the outcome—that is, the difficulty index is in terms of difference in the item difficulty index (item *p*-value), the discrimination index is the effect on item-total point-biserial correlations, the reliability coefficient is based on coefficient alpha or KR-20, and the validity coefficient is in terms of criterion-related correlations. The number of effects (differences) involved is also reported in each cell.

The empirical experimental research on item-writing guidelines is summarized next. Studies conducted in elementary and secondary classrooms are highlighted. It is important to note the small number of classroom-based studies on a small number of item-writing guidelines. These studies are also dated. All 18 studies in elementary and secondary classrooms were published prior to 1995. It is also important to note the limited validity evidence in the elementary and secondary classroom context. The difficulty of conducting rigorous statistical analyses of item format effects on classroom size samples has resulted in analysis limitations.

Guideline Violation	*Difficulty Index*	*Discrimination Index*	*Reliability Coefficient*	*Validity Coefficient*
Using an open, completion-type stem	0.016[b] (0.009) n =17	−0.003[b] (0.076) n = 6	0.031[b] (0.069) n = 10	0.042[b] (0.123) n = 4
Stating the stem negatively	−0.032[a] (0.010) n =18		−0.166 (0.082) n = 4	
Using NOTA	−0.035[a] (0.005) n = 57	−0.027[b] (0.035) n = 47	−0.001[b] (0.039) n = 21	0.073 (0.051) n = 11
Making the correct option longer	0.057[ab] (0.014) n = 17			−0.259* (0.163) n = 4
Using complex SR format	−0.122[ab] (0.011) n = 13	−0.145[ab] (0.063) n = 10	−0.007[b] (0.083) n = 4	

Table 17.2 Summary of Average Effects and Standard Errors for Violating Each Guideline

SOURCE: Rodriguez (1997).

[a]Average effect is significantly different than zero.

[b]Effects are homogenous across studies, based on the meta-analytic *Q*-test statistic.

NOTE: Standard errors are in parentheses. The number of study effects is *n*.

We note the following trends:

- Use of a complete question stem rather than partial stem completed by the options has no systematic effect on item statistics, but some evidence suggests an improvement in test score reliability and validity.
- Use of a negatively worded stem has no consistent effect on item or test score quality.
- Increasing the number of options tended to increase item difficulty and discrimination, as well as test score reliability and validity; however, these effects were not consistent, depending in part on the change in number of options.
- Using NOTA tended to increase item difficulty and reduce test score reliability and validity.
- Using a longer correct option (a clear item-writing flaw) decreased item difficulty as it provides a clue.

State the Stem in Question Form

A first step in item writing is deciding whether to write the stem as a complete question (closed) or in sentence-completion (open) form where the options complete the stem. Forty-one of the 46 sources reviewed by Haladyna and Downing (1989a) addressed this issue, and all supported the use of either format. Haladyna et al. (2002) reviewed the empirical evidence and argued that both formats are appropriate for CA purposes.

Rodriguez (1997) found 10 articles that reported 17 independent outcomes. These tests included social sciences (seven trials), the Army Basic Military Subjects Test (four trials), science (three trials), and language arts (three trials). Three of these studies were conducted in K–12 classrooms, including 5 of the 17 outcomes. In this small set of studies, there was no consistent effect of item format on item difficulty or discrimination, but there was a tendency to improve item score reliability and validity with the closed form of the stem (see Table 17.2).

Eisley (1990) utilized the Utah Core Assessment series in science, creating 20-item forms to test the effect of closed versus open stems. He suggested that the stem be constructed such that it defines a single restricted problem (one which could be solved without options) and that the stem be in open form. Schmeiser and Whitney (1975) created 20 items for reading passages and characterized the open form as an item-writing flaw. Schrock and Mueller (1982) tested this with vocabulary test items and argued that when the stem was truncated severely, it was more difficult to determine the correct meaning of the item. They argued that open and closed stems would result in the same item characteristics when the open stem contains all of the information of the closed question.

Based on the empirical studies of this item format effect, it is difficult to ascertain a consistent set of principals regarding the use of either format. General item-writing guidelines prevail, and this formatting issue may be inconsequential. In sum, items written in either open or closed form should contain a single problem or restricted problem scope, and the item stem, in either format, should contain all necessary information to select the best answer.

Word the Stem Positively

Tamir (1993) recounted an interesting story of a visit he made to Australia. He encountered the biology matriculation exam used in the state of Victoria, comprised completely of negatively worded items. The rationale for this was that it was better for students to be exposed to correct rather than incorrect information—responding to the test is a learning experience and having only one incorrect option per item minimized exposure to incorrect information.

Whether to word the stem positively or negatively was addressed by 35 authors (Haladyna & Downing, 1989a). Of these, 31 suggested avoiding negative stems. This guideline was supported by Haladyna et al. (2002). Rodriguez (1997) reviewed five studies reporting 16 independent outcomes. These tests included science (10 trials), mixed subjects (4 trials), social science (1 trial), and health science (1 trial). Two of these studies were conducted in K–12 classrooms, including 8 of the 16 outcomes. Tamir (1993) identified 35 negatively worded items from a biology exam and made positive variants. Terranova (1969) identified 33 items that could be worded negatively from an intelligence test and administered them in both formats with a set of 36 common items written positively. An interaction with the frequency of switching between negatively and positively worded stems was found: Test forms were much easier when negatively worded items were located together and much more difficult when the negatively worded items were mixed with positively worded items. In these studies, no consistent effect was found on item difficulty or test score reliability.

Several researchers investigated nuances of this guideline, without reporting sufficient statistics to include in the synthesis. Casler (1983) examined the practice of emphasizing the negative term in the stem by underlining it or capitalizing all letters (e.g., not or NOT). By underlining the negative word, the item became less difficult for high-ability students and more difficult for lower-ability students; item discrimination was greater for the emphasized questions. By capitalizing all letters in the negative word, the items were consistently less difficult with no effect on discrimination. Cassels and Johnstone (1984) argued that questions with a negative stem may require at least one additional thinking step than the same question worded positively, since such items were more difficult.

Avoid Using All of the Above

Haladyna and Downing (1989a) found this guideline to be one of the most controversial. Nineteen authors favored the guideline, and 15 suggested that AOTA could be used effectively. Several researchers have empirically examined the AOTA option but confounded it with other format features. Rodriguez (1997) did not include this guideline in the item format synthesis since only Mueller (1975) reported independent outcomes for AOTA.

Mueller (1975) studied a real estate exam including six independent testing periods over 2 years, with 4,642 test takers. One significant limitation of Mueller's design was that items were not stem equivalent across formats: Test takers took one form that contained items in all formats. In order to generalize these findings, we must assume that item difficulties were randomly distributed across each format evaluated (NOTA, AOTA, complex alternatives, and standard specified alternatives). Mueller reported that items with AOTA were the least difficult among the formats examined, and where AOTA was the correct response, the item was very easy. However, AOTA items were the same difficulty on average as the standard SR item. Item discrimination was slightly effected, dropping from 0.30 in standard items to 0.26 in AOTA items.

Haladyna and Downing (1989b) recommended that this guideline be examined more closely, particularly in light of the disagreement among item-writing authors. The recommendation to avoid AOTA could be based on logical reasons more than empirical reasons: If the test taker is certain more than one option is correct, AOTA can be confidently selected without knowing whether other options are also correct. Because of the possible clueing from this option, additional future research on this format is not a priority.

Avoid Using None of the Above

Twenty-six out of 33 authors recommended that NOTA should be avoided (Haladyna & Downing, 1989a). Upon reviewing 10 empirical studies investigating the use of NOTA, Haladyna and Downing (1989b) found that using NOTA generally increased item difficulty and lowered item discrimination and test reliability. They found no advantage to using the NOTA option. Rodriguez (1997) included 17 studies with 56 independent outcomes. Three of these studies were conducted in elementary and secondary classrooms, including 10 of the 56 outcomes. Forsyth and Spratt (1980) wrote 20 SR mathematics items in standard format and alternately with the option "not given." Schmeiser and Whitney (1975) used the 20 items with reading passages also found in the closed-stem versus open-stem study that was previously described to include a form with the NOTA option. Williamson and Hopkins (1967) used items from common K–12 standardized exams and replaced NOTA with a plausible distractor when present or added NOTA to be correct an expected number of times. Overall, NOTA items tended to be more difficult, with lower score reliability and validity.

The reasons for using NOTA vary a great deal and appear to depend, in part, on the subject matter to which it is applied. Boynton (1950), for example, used NOTA as an option in spelling items as a means to increase the number of alternatives and reduce the chance of a correct guess. He found that items that did not contain the correct spelling were much more difficult.

Gross (1994) made an argument for logical rather than empirical guidelines for item writing. He argued against the use of any item feature that might reduce an item's ability to discriminate among test takers with full versus misinformation. He illustrated his argument with the following example. Suppose you are faced with the following conventional MC item.

Which of the following cities is the capital of Texas?

a. Dallas
b. El Paso
c. Houston
d. Lubbock
e. None of the above

Did you answer the question correctly? "The correct answer is NOTA, because, as everyone knows, the capital city of Texas is—*San Antonio. What! The correct answer is not San Antonio, but Austin?*" (Gross, 1994, p. 124). Gross argued that it doesn't matter; neither city is listed. He suggested that the correct answer could be obtained with misinformation.

Several authors offered appropriate uses of NOTA. When NOTA is the correct response, it may prevent simple recognition of the answer for those students who would otherwise not be able to produce it in a CR item. Recognizing NOTA as the correct response may reflect greater understanding of the material (measuring knowledge of what is wrong) than recognizing one answer is correct (Dudycha & Carpenter, 1973; Frary, 1991; Hughes & Trimble, 1965; Mehrens & Lehmann, 1991; Tollefson & Chen, 1986; Wesman & Bennett, 1946).

Second, the NOTA option may motivate test takers to consider each option more carefully (Frary, 1991; Oosterhof & Coats, 1984; Wesman & Bennett, 1946). NOTA can extend the range of possible responses to the entire domain. A third appropriate use applies to math exams, which often use the NOTA option. NOTA may encourage more accurate calculation and discourage repeated attempts to find the correct answer (Forsyth & Spratt, 1980; Frary, 1991; Haladyna, 2004; Oosterhof & Coats, 1984; Rimland, 1960; Tollefson & Tripp, 1983).

Finally, there are at least two cases where NOTA is an *inappropriate* option. The first is when best answer type items are being used. When each option contains some correct content, NOTA should not be used. The correct answer must be exactly correct or NOTA may also be correct. The second case is where the other options exhaust all logical possibilities, then NOTA is not plausible.

Keep the Length of Choices About Equal

All 38 authors reviewed by Haladyna and Downing (1989a) agreed that the length of options should be consistent. This guideline is mentioned because of a tendency of some item writers to be wordier in writing the correct option; item writers tend to be more descriptive for the correct option. Rodriguez (1997) retrieved seven studies including 17 independent outcomes. These studies used tests in the health sciences, social sciences, and the Army Basic Military Subjects Test. Only 1 of these studies was conducted in K–12 classrooms, including 2 of the 17 outcomes. McMorris, Brown, Snyder, and Pruzek (1972) used 42 items based on an 11th-grade social studies state curriculum, alternating half of the items with this item-writing flaw and half without, across two forms. They found a decrease in item difficulty with the flaw but no effect on test score reliability or validity.

Carter (1986) reviewed teacher-made tests from 78 teachers in four states. She found at least one item in 67 of the tests had a longer correct option. The teachers, mostly unaware of this item-writing guideline, said that they needed to make sure the correct answer was worded so that no one would argue about its correctness. Nothing more needs to be said: There is no role for options of different lengths.

Use Three Options

Prior to their review of the empirical research, Haladyna and Downing (1989a) found that the guideline to use as many options as feasible was supported by 16 of the 29 authors addressing this issue. They carefully reviewed theoretical and empirical studies and concluded that the key is not the *number* of options but the *quality* of the options. They also argued that the evidence did not support the standard use of four to five options and that in most testing situations, three options were sufficient (Haladyna & Downing, 1989b). Based on their review, they recommended to use as many functional distractors as possible. Haladyna et al. (2002) also argued that three is probably adequate.

Rodriguez (1997) reviewed 25 studies reporting 51 independent outcomes. Results for this guideline are difficult to summarize, since researchers compared different combinations ranging from two to five options. These studies included tests in language arts (19 trials), math (4 trials), science (6 trials), social science (12 trials), mixed subjects (3 trials), an Air Force instructor exam (4 trials), and a musical acoustics exam (3 trials). Ten of these studies were conducted in K–12 classrooms, including 24 of the 51 outcomes. In terms of these 10 studies, increasing the number of options tended to make items more difficult and test scores more reliable; however, these results depended on the actual change in number of options (Budescu & Nevo, 1985; Denney & Remmers, 1940; Hodson, 1984; Hogben, 1973; Remmers & Adkins, 1942; Remmers & House, 1941; Ruch & Stoddard, 1925; Trevisan, Sax, & Michael, 1991, 1994; Williams & Ebel, 1957).

In a comprehensive meta-analysis of the experimental research on the number of options, Rodriguez (2005) synthesized 56 effects obtained from 27 studies between 1925 and 1999. Of these effects, 25 were conducted in K–12 classrooms, 23 in postsecondary classrooms, and 8 in professional settings. The findings were not dependent on the setting of the research study. The notable effects include the slight increases in item *p*-values when reducing the number of options from five to four (0.02), five to three (0.07), and four to three (0.04), resulting in slightly easier items. The other effects, going from five to two (0.23), four to two (0.19), or three to two options (0.10) resulted in much larger changes in item difficulty.

The notable effects of changing the number of options on item discrimination occur from five to four (–0.04), five to three (–0.004), and four to three options (0.03), all very small. Changing from five, four, or three to two options resulted in larger declines in item discrimination (–0.09 to –0.11). Rodriguez (2005) also found similar results regarding reliability, with negligible changes in reliability when changing the number of options from five to four (–0.035), five to three (–0.016), and four to three (0.020)—effects that mirror those on item discrimination, reflecting the functional association between item discrimination and test score reliability. For the trials deleting ineffective distractors, no change in reliability was observed (0.01), whereas trials randomly deleting distractors yielded an average reduction in reliability of 0.06 (a statistically significant difference). Similarly, there was an average reduction in the reliability of 0.09 when reducing the number of options from four to two; however, this reduction was less than half that for trials deleting ineffective distractors (0.04) as compared to trials deleting distractors randomly. In both cases, random distractor deletion was significantly more damaging than deleting ineffective distractors.

Based on the Rodriguez (2005) synthesis, SR items should consist of three options—one correct option and two plausible distractors. This guideline has support from a variety of sources, including mathematical proof derived by Tversky (1964) that the use of three-option items maximizes the discrimination, power, and information of a test. Other theoretical work has been done to suggest the advantages of three-option items (Ebel, 1969; Grier, 1975; Lord, 1944, 1977). Consider the following implications of employing a model of three-option items: (1) Less time is needed to prepare two distractors rather than three or four distractors, (2) less time is required by test takers to read and consider three options rather than four or five options, and (3) more three-option items can be administered within a given time period than four- or five-option items, potentially improving content coverage.

The threat of guessing resulting in a greater chance of a correct guess with three-option items than with four- or five-option items has also not prevailed. Test takers are unlikely to engage in blind guessing, but rather educated guessing, where they eliminate the least plausible distractors, essentially reducing the four- or five-option item to a three- or two-option item (Costin, 1972, 1976; Kolstad, Briggs, & Kolstad, 1985). The quality of the distractors, not the number of distractors, guards against awarding undeserved credit.

To summarize, the extensive research evidence overwhelmingly favors three-option SR items. From a practical standpoint, item writers will report that writing that fourth or fifth option is very difficult, and research verifies this acknowledged failure (Haladyna & Downing, 1993).

Improving Accessibility for All Test Takers

Accessibility addresses the degree to which students with a wide range of abilities, including students with disabilities or limited English proficiency, can participate in a test without accommodations and perform at their best in a way consistent with the construct. Many resources are available, including recent special issues of journals, for example the *Peabody Journal of Education* (Vol. 84, No. 4, 2009) and *Applied Measurement in Education* (Vol. 23, No. 2, 2010). A common guide for improving access to assessments includes the principles of Universal Design (UD) (see Thompson, Johnstone, & Thurlow, 2002). The main idea behind the use of UD principles is to eliminate barriers to participants so they can display their true abilities by designing tests that provide the greatest access to all possible participants and improve the measurement of important knowledge, skills, and abilities.

Universal Design

The UD framework, originating in architecture, has been extended to a variety of fields, including curriculum and instruction (National Center on Universal Design for Learning, 2011) and psychological and educational testing. Using this framework, tests can be designed for the broadest group of test takers without the need to accommodate specific subpopulations. The National Center for Educational Outcomes (Thompson et al., 2002) adapted the original UD principles into the following assessment features: (1) inclusive assessment population; (2) precisely defined constructs; (3) accessible, nonbiased items; (4) amenable to accommodations; (5) simple, clear, and intuitive instructions and procedures; (6) maximum readability and comprehensibility; and (7) maximum legibility. Thus, in terms of testing, the objectives of UD are to remove all item features that interfere with the measurement of the construct—that is, those contributing construct-irrelevant variance—and extend access to all test takers at all levels of the construct.

The issue of construct relevance and irrelevance is essential to quality item writing. The argument for construct relevance originates from classical measurement theory (Messick, 1989), which indicates that a test score can be separated into components of true score, which relates to the construct, and error score, which relates to everything but the construct. Thus, a well-written test item will reflect the construct (maximize the true score) while minimizing the error. These principles have also been used to modify existing achievement items in large-scale tests and could be applied to CAs as well, thereby maximizing accessibility to classroom tests, which is particularly important for inclusive classrooms.

Research on Item Modifications for Accessibility

Decades of federal requirements for the inclusion of students with disabilities in state accountability-based assessments culminated in the more recent No Child Left Behind Act of 2001 (NCLB) (U.S. Department of Education, 2002) requirements for full participation, substantially increasing attention to alternate assessments (Weigert, 2011; see also Chapter 24 of this volume). States define the eligibility for participation in alternate assessments differently but generally include two primary forms: (1) alternate assessments for alternate academic achievement standards (AA-AAS) for students with the most severe cognitive impairments and (2) alternate assessments for modified academic achievement standards (AA-MAS) for students with moderate to severe cognitive impairments (persistent academic difficulties).

AA-AAS are typically performance-based assessments since students with severe cognitive impairments are generally not able to participate in SR format tests. Studies of the technical quality of AA-AAS are few and limited. Towles-Reeves, Kleinert, and Muhomba (2009) reviewed the empirical research on AA-AAS and recommended more of this work as the first point on their suggested research agenda.

AA-MAS has received much more attention, likely due to the larger population of test takers in this group. A special issue of *Peabody Journal of Education* (Vol. 84, No. 4, 2010) provided a review of current issues related to AA-MAS. Many of the articles also commented on the technical adequacy of AA-MAS, providing useful information regarding test design and administration. Perhaps the most common design approach to AA-MAS is through modification of the general education SR test. Kettler, Elliott, and Beddow (2009) provided a review of the work on the Test Accessibility and Modification Inventory (TAMI), a tool for item modification to enhance test accessibility, guided by the principles of UD, cognitive load theory, test fairness, test accommodations, and item-writing research (also see Beddow, Kurz, & Frey, 2011).

The TAMI provides a rating system to evaluate accessibility, based on elements of (1) the reading passage or other item stimuli, (2) the item stem, (3) visuals, (4) answer choices, (5) page and item layout, and (6) fairness. The rating system is supported by a series of rubrics based on accessibility ratings of each of these elements. The rater then chooses from a set of standard modifications or recommends modifications to improve item and test accessibility. The modifications are largely based on the Haladyna et al. (2002) guidelines to improve the item and remove sources of construct-irrelevant variance (Rodriguez, 2011).

Elliott et al. (2010) and Kettler et al. (2011) reported results from multistate consortium experimental research projects where TAMI was used to modify state tests, focusing on middle school mathematics and reading. These randomized experimental studies provided evidence that modification preserves score reliability and improves performance of students (increases scores) where the performance of students eligible for AA-MAS increased more than for students not eligible for the AA-MAS (the differential boost argument). Rodriguez (2009) analyzed the effect of modification on the functioning of distractors, since a common modification was a reduction of the number of options to three by removing the least functioning or least plausible distractors. The remaining distractors in the mathematics and reading items became more discriminating.

Common item modifications include the following:

- Reducing the number of options to three
- Increasing the white space around the items and between graphics, the stem, and the options
- Simplifying or shortening the stem to essential context words
- Clarifying the question and increasing the size of the visual or graphic associated with the item
- Sometimes eliminating a graphic or figure as many serve as distractions because they are not needed to solve the problem

A significant challenge in this area of research is isolating the effect of any one modification. With the TAMI and other item modification approaches, a package of item modifications is employed, depending on what is needed for each particular item. Because of this, it is impossible to isolate the effect of each individual modification, particularly since modifications are not randomly assigned but chosen because they fit the context of the particular item (see Kettler, 2011, for a review of research on modification packages).

Developing the Science of Item Writing: Future Directions for Research

As previously reviewed, the majority of guidance for SR item writing and test development is not research based. This leaves a wide window of opportunities for researchers to contribute to our knowledge base. In the study of item writing, item format effects, and the influence of item formats on teaching and learning, experimental studies are needed. More than anything, validity-related evidence is in dire need, as very few studies have provided empirical validity evidence.

There is a critical need to evaluate the cognitive behaviors elicited by various SR items and different item features or formatting decisions. New research on SR item writing must be based on a principled and informed approach (Haladyna et al., 2002). A rigorous research endeavor requires that researchers clearly disclose the methods used to write items and design tests used in their research. It would be useful for researchers to consider elements of the "Reporting Standards for Research in Psychology" (American Psychological Association [APA], 2008) and the American Educational Research Association's (AERA) *Standards for Reporting on Empirical Social Science Research in AERA Publications* (American Educational Research Association [AERA], 2006) for guidance on full and complete reporting.

Complete reporting and descriptions of methodology contribute to progress in advancing the science of item writing.

In the context of item-writing research, any number of test design characteristics play a role in the impact of a given item-writing guideline or format manipulation. There are many questions that should be asked. For example, is the effect of using a humorous SR option (see McMorris, Boothroyd, & Pietrangelo, 1997, for a review of the limited research in this area) different when it is used as a distractor versus the correct option? What is the impact of the method used to vary the number of options: Were items originally written with five options with option deletion to create the experimental forms, or were options added to create new forms? These design elements potentially play an important role in item format effects.

In addition, the researcher must attend to, catalogue, and report all other relevant features of items to enable full interpretation of the SR item feature experimentally manipulated. For example, if a researcher is studying the role of a negatively worded stem, is the stem a complete question or a statement completed by the options? In the same study, how many options are provided per item? Are the options ordered alphabetically or logically? Is NOTA an option?

Finally, with respect to experimental studies, researchers rarely evaluate the effects of item formats given individual characteristics, such as age, gender, or ability level. Similarly, researchers rarely examine item characteristics such as the cognitive task or depth of knowledge of each item. Since many of the researchers who have examined these characteristics also have found interesting interactions, researchers should address these when possible.

Item Analysis Considerations

Item analysis methods are key tools for examining the effects of item writing and item formats. Such methods are generally not at the disposal of classroom teachers but clearly are important in the CA researcher toolbox. Item analysis is useful in judging the worth or quality of items and the test. It helps in subsequent revisions of tests and in building item databases for future tests. In the classroom context, with relatively small samples, classical item analysis data should be used carefully (Mehrens & Lehmann, 1991). Item analysis statistics are tentative and sample-specific and highly unstable with small samples. Item difficulty and discrimination can bounce around a great deal with small samples, particularly samples of less than 100. Consider a sample of 50 and the effect of one individual on item difficulty. One person contributes 2% of the sample, so if three individuals incorrectly respond to an item in one format versus another, three individuals make a 0.06 change in item difficulty. Similarly, item discrimination is highly unstable with small samples. Just one or two unexpected responses from individuals with relatively high or low scores can affect the magnitude and the sign of the item-total correlation.

An important tool in this line of research is distractor analysis. As seen in the item-writing guidelines, most of the attention to good item writing concerns distractor characteristics. Consider three good reasons to expand distractor analysis: (1) Each distractor should be useful, (2) useful distractors contribute to more effective scoring with polytomous scoring, improving test sore reliabilities, and (3) information about distractors could potentially provide misconception information to instructors and students (Haladyna, 2004). The information available in the distractor is a direct function of the attention put into writing the distractors, determining the extent to which they become useful to support teaching and learning.

Attention to Score Consistency

Test score reliability has been an important measurement quality index, and many journals require reports of score reliability when the study involves tests or other measurement-based scores (see Chapter 7 of this volume). Of course, we recognize that coefficient alpha is the most commonly reported index of reliability, as it is easily computed with many software packages. However, we also recognize that the assumptions necessary for appropriate use and interpretation of coefficient alpha are rarely met (and rarely tested). Coefficient alpha is appropriate for measures with many items or parts that are at least essentially tau equivalent, and alpha is highly sensitive to both the number of items and observed-score variance (see Rodriguez & Maeda, 2006, for a review). Estimating sample size requirements for alpha is also a function of the degree to which assumptions are met as well as the number of items, desired power, and the desired level of precision (Bonett, 2002). Even Cronbach (2004) lamented the ubiquitous application of alpha as an index of score reliability, noting other more appropriate and flexible approaches including those in the family of generalizability theory indices. For this reason, it may be an important index for CA researchers.

Perhaps more importantly, coefficient alpha is an appropriate index for measures that are intended to spread scores out, as in norm-referenced testing (Feldt & Brennan, 1989). Classroom tests are—virtually by definition—criterion-referenced assessments. They should be built to measure the achievement of learning objectives specific to the classroom or course. As such, it is possible, and desired, to obtain high scores uniformly across students. This leads to score homogeneity and low estimates of coefficient alpha (Feldt & Qualls, 1999) not because the measures produce more measurement error but because the measure is not sensitive to individual differences within a homogenous classroom.

There are more appropriate alternatives. Perhaps the best alternatives are based on a class of indices of classification consistency, particularly for those tests with passing scores or cut-scores (see Haertel, 2006, for a review). Other score-based indices of reliability are those based on more appropriate measurement models, such as the congeneric measurement model, which assumes that each item is a measure of the same latent trait and allows them to be measured on different scales with different levels of precision and different amounts of error (Graham, 2006). Graham suggested that if item variances differ greatly, this may be an indicator that they are being measured on different scales (loading on the common factor differently), which is a likely characteristic of classroom tests. Another feature of classroom tests that likely leads to violations of the tau-equivalence assumptions is the use of items in multiple formats, such as SR items and CR items with partial credit; by default, such items are measured on different scales. Reliability should be estimated using the appropriate measurement model.

Attention to Score Validity

The greatest need in the research on SR item formats is validity evidence, which should be gathered at all stages of research (see Chapter 6 of this volume). Validity evidence should be gathered to ensure the quality of test item development for experimental forms, including the use of item-writing principles. To secure validity evidence in this area, item-writing guidelines could serve as a checklist, such as those previously presented. For each item-writing decision made by the CA researcher in developing experimental forms of items, rationale should be provided. For example, the rationale for the choice of number of options employed should be described. It is not sufficient to follow a set of item-writing guidelines but to have a justification for the many choices in writing and formatting the items. These justifications should be consistent with the validity argument intended through the research.

Perhaps the most common approach to providing validity-related evidence is in the form of criterion-related coefficients, correlations with other measures. In the context of CAs, this form of validity evidence is likely to be less useful. Other criterion measures that might be available include district or state assessments, which are likely based on different learning objectives. Even where state assessments are tied to state subject-matter content standards and classroom curricula are aligned to state standards, state tests do not cover all content standards in the same way a teacher would in the classroom. There may be special cases where a standardized test may be an appropriate criterion reference for CAs, such as the case of Advanced Placement (AP) courses and tests. In this case, the AP exam is directly aligned with the AP approved curriculum and learning objectives. Finally, in the same way that coefficient alpha is not appropriate for criterion-referenced tests because of the limited score variability, homogeneity of scores will also result in lower criterion-related correlations not because the measures are different but because there is too little score variance to observe the full association in scores.

Cognitive psychology offers an important methodology to the study of item writing and item format effects and involves interviewing students as they respond to test items. The think-aloud procedure (or cognitive interview) provides insights into the cognitive processes underlying a student's interaction with a test item (Almond et al., 2009; Willis, 2005). The limitation of this method is that it is labor and time intensive and requires substantial effort to collect data and code and evaluate the findings. However, a review of recent published research based on think-aloud methods (Fox, Ericsson, & Best, 2011) and an experiment in data saturation and variability (Guest, Bunce, & Johnson, 2006) suggests that a relatively small number of participants can yield useful information, perhaps as few as 10 to 15.

Conclusion

In addition to a formal agenda for SR item-writing practices, we can also address a significant limitation in practice: the training and preparation of classroom teachers to develop and use high quality CAs. The evidence in the literature clearly demonstrates the importance of quality assessments, even at the level of item writing. This evidence and existing item-writing guidelines can be used to facilitate teacher preparation for the CA demands they face daily.

Information that increases our understanding of SR items and tests used in K–12 classrooms will improve our ability to support teaching and learning. Empirically grounded evidence to support the item-writing guidelines currently in use will lead to improved item writing, improved test design, stronger tools for teacher preparation and professional development in CA, more appropriate information to support instruction, and better measures of student learning.

References

Almond, P. J., Cameto, R., Johnstone, C. J., Laitusis, C., Lazarus, S., Nagle, K., et al. (2009). *White paper: Cognitive interview methods in reading test design and development for alternate assessments based on modified academic achievement standards (AA-MAS).* Dover, NH: Measured Progress and Menlo Park, CA: SRI International.

American Educational Research Association. (2006). Standards for reporting on empirical social science research in AERA publications. *Educational Researcher, 35*(6), 33–40.

American Federation of Teachers, National Council on Measurement in Education, & National Education Association. (1990). *Standards for teacher competence in educational assessment of students.* Retrieved from www.unl.edu/buros/bimm/html/article3.html

American Psychological Association. (2008). Reporting standards for research in psychology. Why we need them? What might they be? *American Psychologist, 63*(9), 839–851.

Airasian, P. W., & Jones, A. M. (1993). The teacher as applied measurer: Realities of classroom measurement and assessment. *Applied Measurement in Education, 6*(3), 241–254.

Baker, F. B. (1989). Computer technology in test construction and processing. In R. L. Linn (Ed.), *Educational measurement* (3rd ed., pp. 409–428). New York: American Council on Education and Macmillan.

Beddow, P., Kurz, A., & Frey, J. (2011). Accessibility theory: Guiding the science and practice of test item design with the test-taker in mind. In S. N. Elliott, R. J. Kettler, P. A. Beddow, & A. Kurz (Eds.), *Handbook of accessible achievement tests for all students: Bridging the gaps between research, practice, and policy* (pp. 163–182). New York: Springer.

Bejar, I. I. (1993). A generative approach to psychological and educational measurement. In N. Rederiksen, R. Mislevy, & I. Bejar (Eds.), *Test theory for a new generation of tests* (pp. 323–357). Hillsdale, NJ: Lawrence Erlbaum.

Bonett, D. G. (2002). Sample size requirements for testing and estimating coefficient alpha. *Journal of Educational and Behavioral Statistics, 27*(4), 335–340.

Boynton, M. (1950). Inclusion of none of these makes spelling items more difficult. *Educational and Psychological Measurement, 10,* 431–432.

Brookhart, S. M. (1997). A theoretical framework for the role of classroom assessment in motivating student effort and achievement. *Applied Measurement in Education, 10*(2), 161, 180.

Brookhart, S. M. (2003). Developing measurement theory for classroom assessment purposes and uses. *Educational Measurement: Issues and Practice, 22*(4), 5–12.

Brookhart, S. M. (2011). Educational assessment knowledge and skills for teachers. *Educational Measurement: Issues and Practice, 30*(1), 3–12.

Brookhart, S. M., & DeVoge, J. G. (1999). Testing a theory about the role of classroom assessment in student motivation and achievement. *Applied Measurement in Education, 12*(4), 409–425.

Brookhart, S. M., & Durkin, D. T. (2003). Classroom assessment, student motivation, and achievement in high school social studies classes. *Applied Measurement in Education, 16*(1), 27–54.

Brookhart, S. M., Walsh, J. M., & Zientarski, W. A. (2006). The dynamics of motivation and effort for classroom assessments in middle school science and social studies. *Applied Measurement in Education, 19*(2), 151–184.

Budescu, D. V., & Nevo, B. (1985). Optimal number of options: An investigation of the assumption of proportionality. *Journal of Educational Measurement, 22*(3), 183–196.

Carter, K. (1986). Test wiseness for teachers and students. *Educational Measurement: Issues and Practices, 5*(4), 20–23.

Casler, L. (1983). Emphasizing the negative: A note on the not in multiple-choice questions. *Teaching of Psychology, 10*(1), 51.

Cassels, J. R. T., & Johnstone, A. H. (1984). The effect of language on student performance on multiple-choice tests in chemistry. *Journal of Chemical Education, 61,* 613–615.

Costin, F. (1972). Three-choice versus four-choice items: Implications for reliability and validity of objective achievement tests. *Educational and Psychological Measurement, 32,* 1035–1038.

Costin, F. (1976). Difficulty and homogeneity of three-choice versus four-choice objective test items when matched for content of stem. *Teaching of Psychology, 3*(3), 144–145.

Cronbach, L. J. (2004). My current thoughts on coefficient alpha and successor procedures. *Educational and Psychological Measurement, 64*(3), 391–418.

Denney, H. R., & Remmers, H. H. (1940). Reliability of multiple-choice as a function of the Spearman-Brown prophecy formula, II. *Journal of Educational Psychology, 31,* 699–704.

Downing, S. M. (2002). Construct-irrelevant variance and flawed test questions: Do multiple choice item writing principles make any difference? *Academic Medicine, 77,* 103–104.

Downing, S. M. (2005). The effects of violating standard item writing principles on tests and students: The consequences of using flawed test items on achievement examinations in medical education. *Advances in Health Sciences Education, 10,* 133–143.

Downing, S. M. (2006). Selected-response item formats in test development. In S. M. Downing & T. M. Haladyna (Eds.), *Handbook of test development* (pp. 287–301). Mahwah, NJ: Lawrence Erlbaum.

Dudycha, A. L., & Carpenter, J. B. (1973). Effects of item formats on item discrimination and difficulty. *Journal of Applied Psychology, 58,* 116–121.

Ebel, R. L. (1951). Writing the test item. In E. F. Lindquist (Ed.), *Educational measurement* (1st ed., pp. 185–249). Washington, DC: American Council on Education.

Ebel, R. L. (1969). Expected reliability as a function of choices per item. *Educational and Psychological Measurement, 29,* 565–570.

Eisley, M. E. (1990). *The effect of sentence form and problem scope in multiple-choice item stems on indices of test and item quality.* Unpublished doctoral dissertation, Brigham Young University, Provo, UT.

Elliott, S. N., Kettler, R. J., Beddow, P. A., Kurz, A., Compton, E., McGrath, D., et al. (2010). Effects of using modified items to test students with persistent academic difficulties. *Exceptional Children, 76*(4), 475–495.

Ellsworth, R. A., Dunnell, P., & Duell, O. K. (1990). Multiple-choice test items: What are textbook authors telling teachers? *The Journal of Educational Research, 83*(5), 289–293.

Eurich, A. C. (1931). Four types of examination compared and evaluated. *Journal of Educational Psychology, 26,* 268–278.

Feldt, L. S., & Brennan, R. L. (1989). Reliability. In R. L. Linn (Ed.), *Educational measurement* (3rd ed.). New York: American Council on Education and Macmillan.

Feldt, L. S., & Qualls, A. L. (1999). Variability in reliability coefficients and the standard error of measurement from school district to district. *Applied Measurement in Education, 12*(4), 367–381.

Ferrara, S., & DeMauro, G. E. (2006). Standardized assessment of individual achievement in K-12. In R. L. Brennan (Ed.), *Educational Measurement* (4th ed., pp. 579–621). Westport, CT: Praeger Publishers.

Forsyth, R. A., & Spratt, K. F. (1980). Measuring problem solving ability in mathematics with multiple-choice items: The effect of item format on selected item and test characteristics. *Journal of Educational Measurement, 17*(1), 31–43.

Fox, M. C., Ericsson, K. A., & Best, R. (2011). Do procedures for verbal reporting of thinking have to be reactive? A meta-analysis and recommendations for best reporting methods. *Psychological Bulletin, 137*(2), 316–344.

Frary, R. B. (1991). The none-of-the-above option: An empirical study. *Applied Measurement in Education, 4*(2), 115–124.

Frisbie, D. A., & Becker, D. F. (1991). An analysis of textbook advice about true–false tests. *Applied Measurement in Education, 4,* 67–83.

Gierl, M. J., & Haladyna, T. M. (Eds.) (in press). *Automatic item generation.* New York: Routledge.

Graham, J. M. (2006). Congeneric and (essentially) tau-equivalent estimates of score reliability. *Educational and Psychological Measurement, 66*(6), 930–944.

Grier, J. B. (1975). The number of alternatives for optimum test reliability. *Journal of Educational Measurement, 12*(2), 109–112.

Gross, L. J. (1994). Logical versus empirical guidelines for writing test items. *Evaluation and the Health Professions, 17*(1), 123–126.

Guest, G., Bunce, A., & Johnson, L. (2006). How many interviews are enough? An experiment with data saturation and variability. *Field Methods, 18*(1), 59–82.

Haertel, E. H. (2006). Reliability. In R.L. Brennan (Ed.), *Educational Measurement* (4th ed., pp. 111–153). Westport, CT: Praeger Publishers.

Haladyna, T. M. (1997). *Writing test items to evaluate higher order thinking.* Boston: Allyn & Bacon.

Haladyna, T. M. (2004). *Developing and validating multiple-choice test items* (3rd ed.). Mahwah, NJ: Lawrence Erlbaum.

Haladyna, T. M., & Downing, S. M. (1989a). A taxonomy of multiple-choice item-writing rules. *Applied Measurement in Education, 1,* 37–50.

Haladyna, T. M., & Downing, S. M. (1989b). The validity of a taxonomy of multiple-choice item-writing rules. *Applied Measurement in Education, 1,* 51–78.

Haladyna, T. M., & Downing, S. M. (1993). How many options is enough for a multiple-choice test item. *Educational and Psychological Measurement, 53,* 999–1010.

Haladyna, T. M., Downing, S. M., & Rodriguez, M. C. (2002). A review of multiple-choice item-writing guidelines for classroom assessment. *Applied Measurement in Education, 15,* 309–334.

Haladyna, T. M., & Rodriguez, M. C. (in press). *Developing and validating test items.* New York: Routledge.

Hodson, D. (1984). Some effects of changes in question structure and sequence on performance in a multiple choice chemistry test. *Research in Science & Technological Education, 2*(2), 177–185.

Hogben, D. (1973). The reliability, discrimination and difficulty of word-knowledge tests employing multiple choice items containing three, four or five alternatives. *Australian Journal of Education, 17*(1), 63–68.

Hughes, H. H., & Trimble, W. E. (1965). The use of complex alternatives in multiple-choice items. *Educational and Psychological Measurement, 25*(1), 117–126.

Irvine, S. H., & Kyllonen, P. C. (Eds.). (2002). *Item generation for test development.* Mahwah, NJ: Lawrence Erlbaum.

Jozefowicz, R. F., Koeppen, B. M., Case, S., Galbraith, R., Swanson, D. & Glew, H. (2002). The quality of in-house medical school examinations. *Academic Medicine 77,* 156–161.

Kettler, R. (2011). Effects of modification packages to improve test and item accessibility: Less is more. In S. N. Elliott, R. J. Kettler, P. A. Beddow, & A. Kurz (Eds.), *Handbook of accessible achievement tests for all students: Bridging the gaps between research, practice, and policy* (pp. 231–242). New York: Springer.

Kettler, R. J., Elliott, S. N., & Beddow, P. A. (2009). Modifying achievement test items: A theory-guided and data-based approach for better measurement of what students with disabilities know. *Peabody Journal of Education, 84,* 529–551.

Kettler, R. J., Rodriguez, M. C., Bolt, D. M., Elliott, S. N., Beddow, P. A., & Kurz, A. (2011). Modified multiple-choice items for alternate assessments: Reliability, difficulty, and differential boost. *Applied Measurement in Education, 24*(3), 210–234.

Kolstad, R. K., Briggs, L. D., & Kolstad, R. A. (1985). Multiple-choice classroom achievement tests: Performance on items with five vs. three choices. *College Student Journal, 19,* 427–431.

Lord, F. M. (1944). Reliability of multiple-choice tests as a function of number of choices per item. *Journal of Educational Psychology, 35,* 175–180.

Lord, F. M. (1977). Optimal number of choices per item—A comparison of four approaches. *Journal of Educational Measurement, 14*(1), 33–38.

Marso, R. N., & Pigge, F. L. (1991). An analysis of teacher-made tests: Item types, cognitive demands, and item construction errors. *Contemporary Educational Psychology, 16,* 279–286.

McMorris, R. F., & Boothroyd, R. A. (1993). Tests that teachers build: An analysis of classroom tests in science and mathematics. *Applied Measurement in Education, 6,* 321–342.

McMorris, R. F., Boothroyd, R. A., & Pietrangelo, D. J. (1997). Humor in educational testing: A review and discussion. *Applied Measurement in Education, 10,* 269–297.

McMorris, R. F., Brown, J. A., Snyder, G. W., & Pruzek, R. M. (1972). Effects of violating item construction principles. *Journal of Educational Measurement, 9*(4), 287–295.

Mehrens, W. A., & Lehmann, I. J. (1991). *Measurement and evaluation in education and psychology.* Orlando, FL: Harcourt Brace Jovanovich.

Mertler, C. A. (2009). Teachers' assessment knowledge and their perceptions of the impact of classroom assessment professional development. *Improving Schools, 12*(2), 101–113.

Mertler, C. A., & Campbell, C. (2005, April). *Measuring teachers' knowledge and application of classroom assessment concepts: Development of the Assessment Literacy Inventory* (ERIC Document Reproduction Service No. 490355). Paper presented at the annual meeting of the American Educational Research Association, Montreal, Quebec, Canada.

Messick, S. (1989). Validity. In R. L. Linn (Ed.), *Educational measurement* (3rd ed., pp. 13–103).

New York: American Council on Education and Macmillan.

Monroe, W. S. (1918). Existing tests and standards. In G. M. Whipple (Ed.), *The seventeenth yearbook of the National Society for the Study of Education. Part II: The measurement of educational products.* Bloomington, IL: Public School Publishing Company.

Mueller, D. J. (1975). An assessment of the effectiveness of complex alternatives in multiple choice achievement test items. *Educational and Psychological Measurement, 35,* 135–141.

National Center on Universal Design for Learning. (2011). *UDL Guidelines,* Version 2.0. Retrieved from www.udlcenter.org/aboutudl/udlguidelines

O'Dell, C. W. (1928). *Traditional examinations and new type tests.* New York: Century.

Ogan-Bekiroglu, F. (2009). Assessing assessment: Examination of pre-service physics teachers' attitudes toward assessment and factors affecting their attitudes. *International Journal of Science Education, 31*(1), 1–39.

Oosterhof, A. C., & Coats, P. K. (1984). Comparison of difficulties and reliability of quantitative word problems in completion and multiple-choice item formats. *Applied Psychological Measurement, 8*(3), 287–294.

Plake, B. S., Impara, J. C., & Fager, J. J. (1993). Assessment competencies of teachers: A national survey. *Educational Measurement: Issues and Practice, 12*(4), 21–27.

Popham, W. J. (2009). Assessment literacy for teachers: Faddish or fundamental? *Theory Into Practice, 48,* 4–11.

Remmers, H. H., & Adkins, R. M. (1942). Reliability of multiple-choice measuring instruments, as a function of the Spearman-Brown prophecy formula, VI. *Journal of Educational Psychology, 33,* 385–390.

Remmers, H. H., & House, J. M. (1941). Reliability of multiple-choice measuring instruments, as a function of the Spearman-Brown prophecy formula, IV. *Journal of Educational Psychology, 32,* 372–376.

Rimland, B. (1960). The effects of varying time limits and of using "right answer not given" in experimental forms of the U.S. Navy Arithmetic Test. *Educational and Psychological Measurement, 20*(3), 533–539.

Rodriguez, M. C. (1997, March). *The art & science of item writing: A meta-analysis of multiple-choice item format effects.* Paper presented at the annual meeting of the American Educational Research Association, Chicago.

Rodriguez, M. C. (2002). Choosing an item format. In G. Tindal & T.M. Haladyna (Eds.), *Large-scale assessment programs for all students.* Mahwah, NJ: Lawrence Erlbaum.

Rodriguez, M. C. (2003). Construct equivalence of multiple-choice and constructed-response items: A random effects synthesis of correlations. *Journal of Educational Measurement, 40*(2), 163–184.

Rodriguez, M. C. (2004). The role of classroom assessment in student performance on TIMSS. *Applied Measurement in Education, 17*(1), 1–24.

Rodriguez, M. C. (2005). Three options are optimal for multiple-choice items: A meta-analysis of 80 years of research. *Educational Measurement: Issues and Practice, 24*(2), 3–13.

Rodriguez, M. C. (2009). Psychometric considerations for alternate assessments based on modified academic achievement standards. *Peabody Journal of Education, 84,* 595–602.

Rodriguez, M. C. (2011). Item-writing practice and evidence. In S. N. Elliott, R. J. Kettler, P. A. Beddow, & A. Kurz (Eds.), *Handbook of accessible achievement tests for all students: Bridging the gaps between research, practice, and policy* (pp. 201–216). New York: Springer.

Rodriguez, M. C., & Maeda, Y. (2006). Meta-analysis of coefficient alpha. *Psychological Methods, 11*(3), 306–322.

Roid, G. H., & Haladyna, T. M. (1982). *Toward a technology of test-item writing.* New York: Academic Press.

Ruch, G. M., & Stoddard, G. D. (1925). Comparative reliabilities of objective examinations. *Journal of Educational Psychology, 16,* 89–103.

Salmon-Cox, L. (1980, April). *Teachers and tests: What's really happening?* Paper presented at the annual meeting of the American Educational Research Association, Boston.

Schmeiser, C. B., & Welch, C. J. (2006). Test development. In R. L. Brennan (Ed.), *Educational measurement* (4th ed., pp. 307–353). Westport, CT: Praeger Publishers.

Schmeiser, C. B., & Whitney, D. R. (1975, April). *The effect of incomplete stems and "none of the above" foils on test and item characteristics.* Paper presented at the annual meeting of the National Council on Measurement in Education, Washington, DC.

Schrock, T. J., & Mueller, D. J. (1982). Effects of violating three multiple-choice item construction principles. *Journal of Educational Research, 75*(5), 314–318.

Sireci, S. G., & Zenisky, A. L. (2006). Innovative item formats in computer-based testing: In pursuit of improved construct representation. In S. M. Downing & T. M. Haladyna (Eds.), *Handbook of test development* (pp. 329–347). Mahwah, NJ: Lawrence Erlbaum.

Stiggins, R. J., & Bridgeford, N. J. (1985). The ecology of classroom assessment. *Journal of Educational Measurement, 22,* 271–286.

Stiggins, R. J., & Conklin, N. F. (1992). *In teachers' hands: Investigating the practices of classroom assessment.* Albany: State University of New York Press.

Tamir, P. (1993). Positive and negative multiple choice items: How different are they? *Studies in Educational Evaluation, 19*(3), 311–325.

Tarrant, M., & Ware, J. (2008). Impact of item-writing flaws in multiple-choice questions on student achievement in high-stakes nursing assessments. *Medical Education, 42*(2), 198–206.

Terranova, C. (1969). The effects of negative stems in multiple-choice test items. (Doctoral dissertation, State University of New York at Buffalo, 1969). *WorldCatDissertations,* OCLC 52037669.

Thompson, S. J., Johnstone, C. J., & Thurlow, M. L. (2002). *Universal design applied to large scale assessment* (NCEO synthesis report 44). Minneapolis, MN: National Center on Educational Outcomes. Retrieved from http://education.umn.edu/NCEO/OnlinePubs/Synthesis44.html

Tollefson, N., & Chen, J. S. (1986, October). *A comparison of item difficulty and item discrimination of multiple-choice items using none of the above options.* Paper presented at the annual meeting of the Midwest AERA, Chicago.

Tollefson, N., & Tripp, A. (1983, April). *The effect of item format on item difficulty and item discrimination.* Paper presented at the annual meeting of the American Educational Research Association, Montreal, Quebec.

Towles-Reeves, E., Kleinert, H., & Muhomba, M. (2009). Alternate assessment: Have we learned anything new? *Exceptional Children, 75*(2), 233–252.

Trevisan, M. S., Sax, G., & Michael, W. B. (1991). The effects of the number of options per item and student ability on test validity and reliability. *Educational and Psychological Measurement, 51,* 829–837.

Trevisan, M. S., Sax, G., & Michael, W. B. (1994). Estimating the optimum number of options per item using an incremental option paradigm. *Educational and Psychological Measurement, 54*(1), 86–91.

Tversky, A. (1964). On the optimal number of alternatives at a choice point. *Journal of Mathematical Psychology, 1,* 386–91.

U.S. Department of Education. (2002). *No Child Left Behind Act of 2001* (Title I Paraprofessionals: Draft Non-Regulatory Guidance). Washington, DC: U.S. Department of Education, Office of Elementary and Secondary Education.

Volante, L., & Fazio, X. (2007). Exploring teacher candidates' assessment literacy: implications for teacher education reform and professional development. *Canadian Journal of Education, 30*(3), 749–770.

Weigert, S. C. (2011). U.S. policies supporting inclusive assessments for students with disabilities. In S. N. Elliott, R. J. Kettler, P. A. Beddow, & A. Kurz (Eds.), *Handbook of accessible achievement tests for all students: Bridging the gaps between research, practice, and policy* (pp. 19–32). New York: Springer.

Welch, C. (2006). Item and prompt development in performance testing. In S. M. Downing & T. M. Haladyna (Eds.), *Handbook of test development* (pp. 303–327). Mahwah, NJ: Lawrence Erlbaum.

Wesman, A. G., & Bennett, G. K. (1946). The use of "none of these" as an option in test construction. *Journal of Educational Psychology, 37,* 541–549.

Williams, B. J., & Ebel, R. L. (1957). The effect of varying the number of alternatives per item on multiple-choice vocabulary test items. *The Yearbook of the National Council on Measurement in Education, 14,* 63–65.

Williamson, M. L., & Hopkins, K. D. (1967). The use of none-of-these versus homogeneous alternatives on multiple-choice tests: Experimental reliability and validity comparisons. *Journal of Educational Measurement, 4*(2), 53–58.

Willis, G. B. (2005). *Cognitive interviewing: A tool for improving questionnaire design.* Thousand Oaks, CA: Sage.

18

Performance Assessment

Suzanne Lane

Performance assessments are demonstrations of mastery that "emulate the context or conditions in which the intended knowledge or skills are actually applied" (American Educational Research Association [AERA], American Psychological Association [APA], & National Council on Measurement in Education [NCME], 1999, p. 137). Because a defining characteristic of a performance assessment is the close similarity between the performance observed and the performance of interest (Kane, Crooks, & Cohen, 1999), they are often contextualized by linking school activities to real-world experiences (Darling-Hammond, Ancess, & Falk, 1995). They can take the form of demonstrations, oral performances, investigations, or written products and may involve collaboration and reflection.

Performance assessments are considered by policy makers and educators to be key tools in educational reform (Linn, 1993) for three main reasons: (1) They allow for demonstrations of important and meaningful learning targets that cannot be easily assessed with other formats (Resnick & Resnick, 1992). (2) They serve as exemplars of tasks that stimulate and enrich learning rather than just serve as indicators of learning (Bennett, 2010; Bennett & Gitomer, 2009). (3) They help shape sound instructional practices by modeling to teachers what is important to teach and to students what is important to learn (Lane, 2010). These qualities make performance assessments ideal tools for formative, interim, and summative assessments that can be naturally embedded in instruction.

This chapter addresses the importance and use of performance assessments in the classroom, beginning with an overview of their design and scoring. The validity and reliability of classroom-based performance assessments is then discussed. A review of research on the relationship between using classroom-based performance assessment, student learning, and instructional practices is followed by recommendations for research.

Design of Performance Assessments

This section discusses important design decisions, including the type of score inferences, the content and processes to be assessed, the degree of structure of the posed problem and intended response, and models for task design. Design issues related to computer-based performance assessments are also addressed.

In the design or adoption of a performance assessment for classroom use, the type of score inferences that are needed should first be delineated. This includes deciding on whether generalizations to the larger domain are of interest or whether the intent is to provide evidence of a particular accomplishment or performance (Lane, 2010). If the intent is to generalize to the larger domain, sampling tasks from across the domain is required to ensure content representativeness. This is of particular importance for many summative assessments that are designed to assess a range of skills and knowledge, requiring multiple item formats, including performance tasks. To provide evidence of an accomplishment or performance may require the specification of an assessment that allows for the demonstrations of an integrated, complex set of skills, such as a high school project (e.g., using the scientific method to make predictions about phenomenon and conducting an investigation to test the prediction). This performance assessment approach is similar to a merit badge approach. For formative purposes, the performance of interest is much narrower, such as providing a rationale for the solution to a mathematics problem.

It is also important to clearly delineate the content and cognitive processes that need to be assessed. A systematic approach to designing assessment that reflect theories of cognition and learning is evidence-centered design (Mislevy, Steinberg, & Almond, 2003), in which inferences about student learning are based on evidence observed in student performances on complex problem solving tasks that have clearly articulated cognitive demands. The use of evidence-centered design when crafting performance assessments will help ensure that the intended complex thinking skills are being assessed.

The degree of structure for the problem posed and the response expected must also be considered in the design and adoption of performance assessments. Performance assessments can be characterized along two continuums with respect to their task demands (Baxter & Glaser, 1998). One continuum reflects the task demand for cognitive process, ranging from open to constrained, and the other represents the task demand for content knowledge, from rich to lean. An open performance task would provide the opportunity for students to develop their own strategies for solving a problem. A rich task would require substantial content knowledge. Four quadrants are formed by crossing these two continuums so that tasks can be identified to fit one of the quadrants, allowing for clear articulation of the cognitive or content targets in task design (Baxter & Glaser, 1998).

Models for Task Design

Models or templates can be used in the design of performance assessments that assess the same cognitive skills with different tasks. One scoring rubric can then be designed for the model and used in evaluating student responses to the tasks that are model generated. The cognitive demands of tasks, such as generalizing and reasoning, can be systematically represented in a model. The use of task models can enhance the generalizability of score inferences. For example, Baker and her colleagues (Baker, 2007; Niemi, Baker, & Sylvester, 2007) have developed and validated an explanation task model that reflects cognitive demands in key standards for Grades 2 through 9. Tasks derived from the model ask students to read one or more texts that require some prior knowledge in the subject domain, including concepts, principles, and declarative knowledge, in order to understand them and to evaluate and explain important text-based issues.

Computer-Based Performance Assessment Design

Computer-based simulation tasks allow for the assessment of complex reasoning and inferential skills that are not easily measured by most assessment formats. Students' strategies, as well as their products, can be captured in the design of simulation tasks, which is valuable for monitoring the progression of student learning and guiding instruction (Bennett, Persky, Weiss, & Jenkins, 2007). Immediate feedback can be provided to the student in response to the course of actions taken. The use of automated scoring procedures for evaluating student performance can provide an answer to the cost and demands of human scoring.

Important features to consider in the design of computer-based simulations are the nature of the interactions that a student has with the tools in the problem-solving space and the recording of how students use the tools (Vendlinski, Baker, & Niemi, 2008). As in any assessment format, another important issue that needs to be addressed in the design of computer-based simulation tasks is the extent to which the assessment is measuring factors that are irrelevant to the intended content domain. Since performances may be affected by computer skills, the computer interface must be familiar to students, and there should be ample opportunity to practice with it (Bennett, et al., 2007; DeVore, 2002). It is also important to ensure that the range of cognitive skills and knowledge assessed are not narrowed to those skills that are more easily assessed using computer technology (Bennett, 2006).

Computer-based simulation tasks in math, reading, and writing are being designed and evaluated for their potential inclusion in an integrated accountability and formative assessment system (Bennett & Gitomer, 2009; O'Reilly & Sheehan, 2009). In the reading domain, a cognitive model of reading competency has been proposed to serve as the basis for both assessing and advancing learning (O'Reilly & Sheehan, 2009). Three design features ensure that assessments require students to actively construct meaning from text. First, the purpose of reading is clearly articulated because students engage in the reading process in meaningfully different ways, depending on the purpose. Second, students are required to read multiple texts in order to encourage the integration and synthesis of information. Lastly, students read texts of varying quality in order to assess their evaluation skills.

One of the four important components assessed in this reading competency model is the student's ability to extract discourse structure. The assessment provides graphical representations to students so they can map out the structure of the text, including graphic hierarchical organizers and construct maps. As O'Reilly and Sheehan (2009) pointed out, requiring students to construct a lengthy written summary may be more appropriate in the assessment of writing since the quality of students' response to a reading task can be affected by their writing ability. The use of graphical representations helps ensure that a student's writing ability does not affect performance on the reading tasks. Further, the use of graphical representations will more easily allow for automated scoring procedures to be used in scoring students' competency in organizing and summarizing information they have read from texts.

This research program draws on models of cognition and advances in technology to design assessments that capture students' complex thinking skills and provide meaningful information to guide instruction. There are numerous issues that need to be addressed through research on simulation tasks, such as the format of response, content and cognitive skill representativeness, and scoring of performances (Bennett, 2006).

Another assessment project that holds promise in reshaping classroom assessment (CA) involves the design and validation of technology-based virtual performance assessments that measure students' scientific inquiry practices (Clarke-Midura, Code, Zap, & Dede, in press). Evidence-centered design is guiding the development of these virtual performance assessments, and science inquiry practices and problem solving are captured in real-world interactions that require students to make a series of choices. The goal of the project is to provide validity evidence for the use of the virtual performance assessments at the state and classroom level.

Scoring Performance Assessments

Performance assessments are usually scored according to a rubric. Features of scoring rubrics that allow for accurate assignment of scores include (1) consistency with the inferences to be made, (2) clear description of the performance criteria, (3) criteria that reflect the range of intended responses, and (4) alignment with the learning goals (Welch, 2006). The design of scoring rubrics requires specifying the type of rubric, specifying the criteria for judging the quality of performances, and determining whether computers or humans will apply the rubrics (Clauser, 2000). In determining the type of rubric to be used, the purpose of the assessment and the intended score inferences need to be considered. A *holistic rubric* requires a rater to make a single, overall judgment regarding the quality of the response, whereas an *analytic rubric* is used if the assessment provides unique information on more than one feature of the response (Mullis, 1984). Evidence is needed that determines the extent to which analytic scores are able to differentiate aspects of student achievement.

Design of Scoring Rubrics

In scoring performance assessments, student responses are examined using well-articulated criteria. The criteria specified at each score level depends on a number of factors, including the purpose of the assessment, intended score inferences, examinee population, cognitive demands of the tasks, and the degree of structure or openness expected in the response (Lane, 2010; Lane & Stone, 2006). The number of score levels used depends on the extent to which the criteria across the levels can distinguish among various degrees of understanding and skill level. The knowledge and skills reflected at each score level should differ distinctively from those at other levels. When cognitive theories of learning have been delineated within a domain, learning progressions can be reflected in the criteria across the score levels. This allows for criteria specified at each score level to be guided by knowledge of how students acquire understanding within a content domain, and will result in meaningful information that can advance student learning and instruction.

A general rubric may be designed that reflects the skills and knowledge underlying the defined domain. The general rubric can then guide the design of specific rubrics for a particular task. An advantage of this approach is that it helps ensure consistency across the specific rubrics (Messick, 1989). A general rubric can also be used to guide the design of rubrics for task models, with each model measuring a specific set of skills.

Liu, Lee, Hofstetter, and Linn (2008) provided an example of a systematic assessment design procedure that used a general rubric to assess complex science reasoning. First, they identified a key construct within scientific inquiry: *science knowledge integration*. An integrated system of inquiry-based science curriculum modules, assessment tasks, and a scoring rubric was then developed and validated to assess science knowledge integration. The scoring rubric was designed so that the different levels captured qualitatively different types of scientific cognition and reasoning that focused on elaborated links rather than individual concepts. The knowledge integration scoring rubric had four levels: (1) complex (elaborate on two or more scientifically valid links between relevant ideas), (2) full (elaborate on one valid link), (3) partial (state relevant ideas but do not fully elaborate on the link), and (4) none (propose invalid ideas). The rubric is applied to the set of tasks that represent the task model for science knowledge integration, allowing for score comparisons across different items. Using one scoring rubric that can be applied to the set of items that measure knowledge integration makes it more accessible to teachers and provides coherency in the score interpretations. The authors also provided validity evidence for the learning progression reflected in the scoring rubric.

Human and Computer Scoring

Performance assessments used for classroom purposes may be scored by humans or automated scoring procedures. With human scoring, it is important to guard against rater variability or inconsistency. Raters may differ in the extent to which they implement the scoring rubric, the way in which they interpret the scoring criteria, and the extent to which they are severe or lenient in scoring (Eckes, 2008). In addition, they may differ in their understanding and use of scoring levels, and their consistency in rating across examinees, scoring criteria, and tasks. Human raters' interpretation and implementation of the scoring rubric can jeopardize the domain representation of the assessment.

While rater inconsistency is more of an issue in large-scale assessment, it is also important for educators to adhere to scoring procedures to ensure appropriate applications of scoring rubrics to student responses. Well-designed rubrics alone do not ensure accurate and reliable scoring of responses. Teachers need to be well trained in their design, use, and implementation to reap their benefits. In one study that documented increased reliability of scores after training teachers to use a rubric for scoring essays, a teacher reflected on the potential misuse of scoring rubrics in the classroom by saying, "I can't believe I was never trained to use [rubrics]. Without knowing what to look for, I can see how they aren't much better than any other strategy" (Rezaei & Lovorn, 2010, pp. 7–8).

Automated scoring procedures have supported the use of computer-based performance assessments such as computer-delivered writing assessments and simulations. An attractive feature is that they apply the scoring rubric consistently but, more importantly, they allow for the test designer to control the meaning of scores with precise specifications of the skills being assessed and allow for the assessment and reporting of multiple features of student performance (Powers, Burstein, Chodorow, Fowles, & Kukich, 2002). Automated scoring of complex computerized tasks has proven effective for large-scale assessments as well as for CA purposes. A number of Web-based instructional and assessment tools are available to help classroom teachers evaluate student written essays. These tools incorporate automated essay scoring systems, allowing for immediate score reporting and diagnostic information that helps guide instruction for individual students. These systems also include programs to flag essays that are suspicious or unusual and need further evaluation. There is also some evidence of greater gains in state assessment scores for students who have used a Web-based writing instructional and assessment tool as compared to those who have not (White et al., 2010).

Validity and Reliability of Classroom-Based Performance Assessment Score Inferences

It is essential to obtain validity evidence to support the important inferences and decisions made about student learning and the effectiveness of instruction when using performance assessments. As stated in the *Standards for Educational and Psychological Testing* (AERA et al., 1999), validity is the "degree to which evidence and theory support the interpretations of test scores entailed by proposed uses of tests" (p. 9). This requires specifying the purposes and uses of the assessment, designing assessments that match these intentions, and providing evidence to support the proposed uses of the assessment and score inferences. These professional standards mandate the need to collect validity evidence for large-scale assessments; however, it is equally important that inferences made from assessments used for classroom purposes are accurate and fair. The effectiveness of instructional decision making will be compromised if the assessment information is of poor quality. Validity criteria that have been suggested for examining the quality of performance assessments include but are not limited to content representation, cognitive complexity, meaningfulness, transfer and generalizability, fairness, and consequences (Linn, Baker, & Dunbar, 1991). These criteria are closely intertwined with the sources of validity evidence proposed by the *Standards* (AERA et al., 1999): evidence based on test content, response processes, internal structure, relations to other variables, and consequences of testing (see Chapter 6 of this volume).

It is also essential that assessment results are interpreted in light of other relevant information about a student or group of students. Using tests to make important decisions entails "collecting sound collateral information both to assist in understanding the factors that contributed to test results and to provide corroborating evidence that supports inferences based on test results" (AERA et al., 1999, p. 140). As an example, Stone and Lane (2003) demonstrated that a school contextual variable—percent free or reduced lunch, which served as a proxy for socioeconomic status (SES)—was significantly related to school-level performance in five subject areas of the Maryland School Performance Assessment Program (MSPAP), which is no longer used as the state assessment. However, there was no significant relationship between percent free or reduced lunch and growth on the performance assessment at the school-level in four of the five subjects, indicating that school-level growth on these four performance assessments was not related to SES.

Threats to Validity

A potential threat to the validity of score inferences is construct-irrelevant variance (Messick, 1989), which occurs when one or more irrelevant constructs is being assessed in addition to the intended construct. Sources of construct irrelevant variance for performance assessments may include task wording and context, response mode, and raters' attention to irrelevant features of responses or performances (Lane, 2010). For example, Abedi and his colleagues (Abedi & Lord, 2001; Abedi, Lord, Hofstetter, & Baker, 2000) have identified a number of linguistic features that impede the reader, in particular English language learners (ELLs), increasing the likelihood of misinterpreting the task (see Chapter 24 of this volume). Mathematics scores of both ELL students and non-ELL students in low- and average-level mathematics classes improved significantly when their linguistic modification approach was used to reduce the complexity of sentence structure and unfamiliar vocabulary in the task. The linguistic modification approach can be implemented in the design of assessments to help ensure a valid and fair assessment for ELLs and other students who may have difficulty with reading. Construct-irrelevant variance may also occur when student responses to performance tasks are scored according to features that do not reflect the scoring criteria and are irrelevant to the targeted construct (Messick, 1994). This can be addressed by clearly articulated scoring rubrics, a shared understanding of the rubrics by the educators who score student performances, and comprehensive training for the raters.

Another potential threat to the validity of score interpretations for most summative performance assessments is construct underrepresentation (Messick, 1989), which leads to limitations in generalizing from the assessment results to the broader domain (Linn et al., 1991). There are multiple sources of errors that can limit generalizability of the scores, including error due to tasks and raters. Error due to tasks occurs because there are typically only a small number of tasks included in a performance assessment. Students' individual reactions to specific tasks tend to average out on multiple-choice tests because of the relatively large number of items, but such reactions to individual items have a greater effect on scoring performance assessments composed of relatively few items (Haertel & Linn, 1996). It is important to consider the sampling of tasks on a summative assessment: Since summative assessments are intended to measure a broad array of domain skills and content, multiple task formats may be needed.

Research on the Reliability and Validity of Score Inferences

Research provides evidence for the validity and reliability of performance assessments in the classroom. In a demonstration study, Moon, Callahan, Brighton, and Tomlinson (2002) examined the quality of performance assessments for middle school students in four disciplines. Performance assessments were developed using key concepts, processes, and generalizations needed to understand each discipline, and tasks allowed for multiple solution strategies.

Expert reviews provided content validity evidence for the performance tasks. As indicated by the *Standards,* an analysis between the content of the assessment and the domain it is intended to measure provides important validity evidence (AERA et al., 1999) (see Chapter 6 for more discussion of validity evidence based on content). Overall, 46 individuals, including teachers, education officials, curriculum coordinators, and university faculty reviewed the tasks, which were modified based on the reviewers' suggestions. Inter-rater agreement for the analytic scoring rubrics was examined, with Kappa coefficients ranging from 0.55 to 0.95. The study suggests that classroom-based performance assessments can be developed to provide reliable and valid information about student learning.

Conducting scientific investigations is a valued performance assessment, but it may not be practical for teachers to observe all students as they work. As a substitute method, researchers have studied the validity of the score inferences derived from student notebooks. Defined as "a set of student writings and drawings that describe and reflect inquiry experiences as they occur within the science classroom" (Aschbacher & Alonzo, 2006, p. 182), science notebooks emulate practices of scientists in the field. They require students to explain their procedures and reasoning and can serve as valuable performance assessments that inform instruction, promote student learning, and provide a direct measure of student understanding of the implemented curriculum (Aschbacher & Alonzo, 2006). A study of the use of notebooks as a method of assessment found that the correlations between notebook scores and scores from observations of students conducting scientific investigations, which ranged from 0.75 to 0.84, were higher than the correlations between scores from simulations and multiple-choice tests with scores from observations of investigations (0.28–0.53) (Baxter & Shavelson, 1994). These results provide initial evidence of the validity of science notebooks as a form of performance assessment.

A study of the *Early Literacy Profile,* a classroom-based performance assessment designed to support teaching and student literacy, illustrates a comprehensive approach to examining reliability and validity (Falk & Ort, 1999; Falk, Ort, & Moirs, 2007). The research done by Falk and colleagues also provides evidence of the usefulness of performance assessments as accountability tools as well as instructional tools. The *Early Literacy Profile* was developed to monitor K–3 students' progress toward the New York state standards and to provide teachers with instructionally useful information. Features of the assessment include assessing student literacy skills in the context of classroom activities, reporting student performance over time, referencing stages of development and standards, and providing information for reporting. Scales were developed for reading, writing, and oral language that provide information on how literacy skills progress over time.

The reading section has four parts: (1) a reading interview, (2) reading diagnostic tools,

(3) a list of texts read independently by the student, and (4) a written response to a text. The writing section requires students to write an initial and final draft of a narrative and a response to the text from the reading section of the assessment. For the listening/speaking section, teachers complete an assessment form while observing the literacy skills of a student in a group setting.

The *Early Literacy Profile* was reviewed by literacy assessment experts to ensure it was guided by a strong research-based conceptualization of literacy, and it was reviewed to ensure it was sensitive to cultural and language differences (Falk & Ort, 1999), providing content validity and cultural sensitivity evidence. It was field tested with 63 teachers of 1,215 students across 19 school districts. The results suggest that the assessments can differentiate student performance across grades. The percentage of students who scored at each of the four score levels (emergent, beginning, independent, and experienced) at each of the three Grades—1, 2, and 3—indicates that student performance improved from grade to grade and from the fall to the spring administration for the three assessments. For both the reading and writing scales, a person by rater generalizability study was conducted based on data from a summer rating session that involved the participating teachers. The generalizability coefficients for the reading scale were 0.74 for the fall and 0.68 for the spring with one rater, and they increased to 0.85 and 0.81, respectively, with two raters. The writing scale generalizability coefficients were 0.68 for the fall and 0.73 for the spring with one rater, and they increased to 0.81 and 0.85 with two raters. Furthermore, the majority of the rater pairs were in exact agreement (66%–75%), and 100% were in adjacent agreement when assigning the profiles to one of the four levels, providing evidence that the assessments can be scored reliably.

Criterion-related evidence of validity for the reading and writing *Early Literacy Profile* scores of third-grade students was examined using released tasks from the fourth-grade National Assessment of Educational Progress (NAEP) reading and writing assessment and the Degrees of Reading Power (DRP) (Touchstone Applied Science Associates, Inc., 1995). Correlations between the reading and writing *Profile* scores and the NAEP and DRP scores ranged from 0.145 (NAEP multiple-choice scores) to 0.605 (DRP scores). Overall, the correlations are consistent with expectations given that the *Profile* is a performance assessment that measures unique skills that the other measures, consisting of multiple-choice items and short answer items, cannot assess as well.

Predictive validity evidence was provided by examining the third-grade students' scores on the *Profile* with scores on their fourth-grade state English language arts exam. For the *Profile* reading scores and the English language arts scores, the eta coefficient (coefficient of nonlinear association) was 0.63. For the *Profile* writing scores and the English language arts scores, the eta coefficient was 0.53, providing evidence that the classroom-based assessment system predicts achievement on the state assessment system.

Curriculum validity evidence was also obtained by surveying the teachers. Nearly all of the teachers (98%) indicated that "the ways of collecting evidence found in the *Profile* resemble the kinds of activities that they provide for students in their classroom" (Falk et al., 2007, p. 66). Eighty-nine percent indicated that they "felt the evidence provided by the *Profile* is adequate enough for them to look at another teacher's *Profile* evidence and confidently assign his or her students a reading and writing scale score" (p. 66).

Consequential validity evidence was gathered through surveys and interviews across several years. According to Falk and colleagues (2007), the respondents reported that the "*Profile* data provided information about students' literacy progress that was useful to teaching", "*Profile* use expanded teachers' instructional strategies," "*Profile* was useful as a way to help parents understand their child's literacy progress," and "*Profile* led them to reexamine other school structures such as their texts, teaching methods, professional development offerings, assessments and reporting systems" (pp. 67–69). These self-reported examples suggest that the *Profile* helped inform instruction, develop teachers' pedagogical knowledge and strategies, and provide rich information about student learning. Teachers and principals indicated some challenges with the *Profile*, however, including the amount of time that was required, unreliable scoring in some settings, and challenges with implementing it.

Although there were some concerns from the educators, this study provides promising validity evidence for a classroom-based performance assessment of early literacy development. As the authors indicated, money and time needs to be invested in such systems in order for them to provide valuable information that informs instruction and enhances student learning (Falk et al., 2007).

Recent work on simulation-based science assessments for middle school students holds promise for significantly changing the way in which science content knowledge and inquiry skills are assessed and provides a model for coherency of assessment systems. Quellmalz and her colleagues (Quellmalz, Silberglitt, & Timms, 2011; Quellmalz, Timms, & Buckley, 2010) investigated the feasibility and technical quality of simulation-based science assessments for classroom, district, and state assessment purposes. The SimScientists assessments are designed to provide a deep, rich assessment of students' understanding of science systems and inquiry practices by incorporating dynamic animations and interactive simulations of scientific phenomena. The computer-based assessments are developed using evidence-centered design and are based on national frameworks and state standards.

For the classroom embedded assessments, students complete tasks such as making observations, running trials in experiments, recording data, interpreting data, making predictions, and explaining results (Quellmalz, Silberglitt, et al., 2011). The methods for responding to the tasks include selecting a response, changing values of variables in the simulation, drawing, and providing explanations. Formative assessments provide feedback and coaching to scaffold learning; benchmark assessments do not provide coaching. The benchmark assessments, given at the end of curriculum units, are compilations of embedded assessment tasks that have been transferred to a new context.

Initial pilot studies were conducted to provide validity evidence for two simulation-based assessments—(1) ecosystem assessment and (2) force and motion assessment—and included 55 teachers and 5,465 students in three states (Quellmalz, Silberglitt, et al., 2011). The extent to which the simulations elicited the intended thinking and inquiry skills was examined during the development stage using cognitive labs with 26 middle school students and four teachers. As cautioned by Linn (1993), it should not be assumed that a performance assessment measures complex thinking skills; evidence is needed to examine the extent to which tasks and scoring rubrics are capturing the intended cognitive processes. The results, as described in a policy brief, indicated that on average, 84% of the time students were applying the intended content and inquiry practices (Quellmalz, Silberglitt, et al., 2011), providing relatively strong validity evidence that the assessments are measuring complex inquiry skills.

Evidence was also provided for the reliability of the scores: The ecosystem benchmark assessment had a reliability coefficient of 0.76, and for the force and motion benchmark assessment, it was 0.73. Correlations between the benchmark assessment scores and scores on a multiple-choice posttest in the same content area ranged from 0.57 to 0.64. As expected, the correlations for inquiry skills were lower than the correlations for content knowledge.

The authors indicated smaller performance gaps on the simulation assessments than on the traditional posttest for ELL students and students with disabilities. For ELL students, the performance gap for the benchmark assessments averaged 12.1%, whereas the performance gap on the traditional posttest was 25.7%. For students with disabilities, the performance gap averaged 7.7% for the benchmark assessments and 18% for the traditional posttest. Differences in the achievement gaps may suggest that both ELL students and students with disabilities had an easier time accessing the simulations as compared to more traditional tests. This may have been due, in part, to the scaffolding and interactive features used in the design of the simulations.

An independent evaluation of their use revealed that teachers found the embedded assessments useful for understanding student learning and making modifications to their instruction (Herman, Dai, Htut, Martinez, & Rivera, 2010). Teachers also reported that the real-time feedback, interaction capability, and visuals improved upon traditional science assessments.

This section described research that examined the validity and reliability of scores derived from classroom-based performance assessments. The results suggest that complex thinking and reasoning skills can be accurately captured by performance assessments. With the use of computer-based simulation tasks, continued research is needed on the extent to which simulations are more accurate and fair in assessing students as compared to noncomputerized performance assessments.

Research on the Relationship Between Performance Assessments and Student Learning

As part of the validation of classroom-based performance assessments, research has examined the extent to which their use results in both positive and negative consequences, with a focus on the association with the improvement of classroom instruction and student learning. In general, research indicates that the use of performance assessments is related to deeper student understanding of content. Some of the studies discussed next are descriptive, while other studies are quasi-experimental or experimental, using either nonrandomized or randomized groups.

Descriptive Studies

Ruiz-Primo, Li, Tsai, and Schneider (2010) examined the relationship between students' written scientific explanations in their notebooks and learning by analyzing 72 student science notebooks from eight middle school classrooms that used the same scientific inquiry-based curriculum. The study focused on one of the implemented investigations and the resulting student explanations. The curriculum investigations emphasized the importance of students making claims and providing evidence to support their claims, with a focus on six aspects: (1) problem, (2) vocabulary, (3) background, (4) method, (5) reporting results, and (6) conclusions.

Teachers were not instructed on what they should require of students in their notebooks. The researchers scored the following six features: (1) claims, (2) type of evidence provided, (3) nature of evidence provided, (4) sufficiency of evidence, (5) alignment of claim and evidence, and (6) types of link (connection of evidence and claim). A composite score was created and transferred onto a 4-point scale reflecting the student's level of understanding (minimal, partial, complete, and sophisticated). To examine rater reliability, person × rater generalizability studies were conducted using the data from 12 randomly selected notebooks from eight classrooms. The average generalizability coefficient was 0.92, indicating that the notebooks could be reliably scored using detailed scoring rules and trained raters.

The results indicated that the construction of solid explanations by students was not widespread. Although 80% of the students provided some form of an explanation, only 18% provided complete explanations that included claim, evidence, and reasoning. Further, 40% of the explanations were claims only, with no supporting evidence from the investigation. Analyses of the six scores related to claims, evidence, and reasoning also suggested differential performance across the eight classrooms. Complete explanations were observed primarily in two classrooms, most likely due to the teacher's instructional practices and expectations of the students (Ruiz-Primo, Li, et al., 2010).

The relationship between the quality of students' explanations provided in their notebooks and posttests at the end of the scientific investigation instructional unit was examined. The posttests were a multiple-choice test, a short open-ended question assessment, a predict-observe-explain assessment, and a hands-on assessment. They focused on different aspects of student knowledge, including declarative, procedural, and schematic knowledge. In addition, the link between the quality of explanations and a gain score between the multiple-choice pretest score and the posttest score was examined. Overall, the ranking of classrooms based on the mean scores on the posttests was similar to the ranking based on the classroom mean explanation scores. The correlations between the explanation scores and the scores from the hands-on assessment and the predict-observe-explain assessment were higher, at 0.34 and 0.35, respectively, than the correlations between the explanation scores and the multiple-choice test, the short open-ended test, and the gain score for the multiple-choice test, at 0.26, 0.28, and 0.26, respectively, indicating that the science explanations scores were more closely related to assessments that capture similar skills (e.g., hands-on assessment) than assessments that capture other features of understanding (e.g., multiple-choice test).

Teachers indicated that the prompts that were the best for instruction and assessment purposes included scaffolding but also encouraged students to think on their own (Ruiz-Primo, Li, et al., 2010). To enhance the quality of notebooks for both instructional and assessment purposes, future studies are needed that examine the effectiveness of various prompts and degrees of scaffolding on the quality of students' explanations.

Research Using Nonrandomized and Randomized Groups

A number of studies have examined the relationship between the use of classroom-based performance assessments and student learning with either nonrandomized or randomized experimental interventions, providing more direct evidence of the value and effectiveness of performance assessments for monitoring and promoting student understanding. The studies employed various treatment conditions, including providing professional development to teachers on the use of performance-based assessments, on desired learning goals for the students, and on subject matter content, as well as providing students with lessons on assessment.

Science Assessments

The use of notebooks to help fourth- and fifth-grade teachers monitor students' scientific conceptual understanding was examined by Aschbacher and Alonzo (2006). They compared students' conceptual understanding as demonstrated in notebooks to their performance on a performance task and a multiple-choice test for classes of teachers with and without professional development. The professional development provided to teachers emphasized science content knowledge, unit learning goals, assessment, and feedback. The focus was on five types of notebook entries: (1) the research question for the inquiry, (2) record of data collected, (3) data organization to help the analysis, (4) claims that address the research question, and (5) evidence that involves data and reasoning to support the claim. Trained raters scored the notebooks. The percent agreement among raters was 80% or higher.

For the combined 25 classes of students, the notebook scores predicted performance on the other measures but accounted for only a small amount of variance. The scores accounted for a greater amount of variance, however, in the performance assessment scores (0.11) than in the multiple-choice test scores (from 0.04 to 0.06). Notebooks were also more predictive of performance for students in classes taught by teachers who received professional development on their use than for students in classes taught by teachers in the comparison group who did not.

To better understand the predictive validity evidence, the authors analyzed the student notebooks from classes taught by teachers who received professional development. They found four typical patterns in how teachers used the notebooks: (1) minimal guidance to students in what to write, (2) low guidance with some structure but insufficient focus, (3) overly prescriptive guidance that results in students copying from the board, and (4) moderate guidance that focuses students with appropriate directions and questions but allows them to think for themselves. Individual teachers were not consistent in their use of notebooks. The authors attributed this inconsistency to teachers' lack of content knowledge of a particular concept and knowledge of the lesson's learning goals (Aschbacher & Alonzo, 2006). Many teachers reported that they did not use the notebooks as forms of assessments because they were too time consuming. The researchers indicated that the understanding and confidence teachers had with the lesson content and learning goals also contributed to their lack of use for assessment purposes. As the authors suggested, professional development needs to "help teachers to develop a solid conceptual understanding of the big ideas and awareness of key learning goals, as well as how to evaluate student work against those goals, give feedback, and revise practice based on this evidence" (p. 201).

A study by Tilson, Castek, and Goss (2009) provides evidence of the value of teaching students how to demonstrate their scientific knowledge and thinking through writing and of assessing students' scientific reasoning using written assessments. Tilson et al. examined the impact of an integrated science-literacy tool on fourth-grade students' informational writing. A treatment group consisting of 47 classes received the integrated science-literacy unit that included scaffolded instruction on science writing. A control group consisting of 47 classrooms received the science literacy unit but had no instruction on science writing. Students responded to a science writing prompt prior to and after the instructional unit. An analytic rubric with seven dimensions was developed and used for the analysis of student responses. Rater agreement was 90% or greater for each of the scoring rubric dimensions.

Both groups showed some progress in their writing, with the treatment group performing significantly better on the posttest than the control group for five of the dimensions: (1) science content, (2) use of evidence, (3) introduction, (4) writing clarity, and (5) scientific language usage. There were no differences between the groups on two of the dimensions—(1) inclusion of additional information about vocabulary terms and (2) the conclusion. These results suggest the value of instructing students on how to display their scientific knowledge and thinking through writing and assessing students' scientific reasoning using science writing assessments.

In a collaborative project between curriculum specialists and assessment specialists, Shavelson and his colleagues (Shavelson et al., 2008) examined the impact of embedded, performance-based, formative assessments in an inquiry science curriculum on student learning in middle school science classrooms. The curriculum-embedded performance-based/formative assessments included graph prompts that required students to interpret and evaluate a graph based on information from the lesson, as well as predict-observe-explain tasks, constructed-response (CR) tasks that assess procedural and schematic science knowledge, and a concept mapping task to assess the structure of students' declarative knowledge (Ayala et al., 2008).

Twelve middle school classes were randomly assigned to either a group that was provided with the embedded performance/formative assessments or a control group, and the impact of the intervention was examined using four outcome measures: (1) a hands-on performance assessment, (2) a short-answer assessment, (3) a predict-observe-explain assessment, and (4) a multiple-choice test (Yin et al., 2008). Analytic rubrics were developed for the performance assessment, short-answer assessment, and the predict-observe-explain assessment. The agreement among trained raters for the short-answer task was 0.87; for the predict-observe-explain assessment, it was 0.92. The average generalizability coefficient across raters was 0.83 for the performance assessment, indicating that it was scored reliably. Coefficient alphas were 0.86 for the multiple-choice test, 0.83 for the short answer assessment, 0.81 for the performance assessment, and 0.74 for the predict-observe-explain assessment, indicating reasonable internal consistency of each measure.

Using hierarchical linear modeling, the impact of the performance/formative assessment treatment on the outcome measures was examined (Yin et al., 2008). The results indicated that the effects of the intervention on the outcome measures were not significant. However, the authors indicated that the teachers varied greatly in terms of their student outcomes regardless of treatment group. To further investigate the fidelity of the implementation of the embedded performance/formative assessments, Furtak et al. (2008) videotaped and analyzed lessons given by the teachers who received professional development. They obtained a 0.71 Spearman rank order correlation between student gain scores and scores reflecting teachers' enactment of the formative assessments. Although the correlation was not significant (most likely due to the small sample size), it suggests a relationship between the rankings of the enacted treatment and student learning.

The analysis of instruction indicated that students had higher achievement if their teachers' pedagogy had the following characteristics: (1) successful teaching strategies, (2) effective formative assessment implementation, (3) either formal or informal, and (4) classroom management skills (Furtak et al., 2008). Their results indicated that some teachers in the control group provided effective informal assessments and feedback to their students on the fly, whereas some of the teachers in the experimental group did not implement the formative assessments effectively. As stated by Yin et al. (2008), "simply embedding assessments in curriculum will not impact students' learning and motivation, unless teachers use the information from embedded assessment to modify their teaching" (p. 354). In order to use the information, teachers need to have solid knowledge of the science concepts and student learning goals, and professional development to support the instruction-assessment process.

English Language Arts Assessments

As previously noted, the classroom-based English language arts performance assessment, the *Early Literacy Profile,* was related to the performance of students on the state assessment (Falk et al., 2007). The strength of the performance assessments' predictive validity may be a function of the duration and quality of the implementation of the performance assessments for classroom use. Researchers have also examined the impact of the use of other forms of English language arts classroom-based performance assessments, such as the self-assessment of writing, on student learning. There has been a call for the criteria for successful performance on assessments to be transparent to both teachers and students. As indicated by Frederiksen and Collins (1989), students and teachers need to know what is being assessed, by what methods, the criteria used to evaluate performance, and what constitutes successful performance. Students need to be familiar with the task format and scoring criteria. Therefore, engaging students in using a rubric to evaluate their own writing, as well as their peers', can be an effective form of performance assessment for formative purposes.

Self-assessment using a scoring rubric can be considered a form of performance assessment because the activity emulates a meaningful educational practice. Andrade and colleagues (Andrade & Boulay, 2003; Andrade, Du, & Mycek, 2010; Andrade, Du, & Wang, 2008) have examined the relationship between using a rubric for self-assessment and writing performance. In a preliminary study, the relationship between middle school students' use of rubrics to assess their own written essays and their writing performance was examined using comparable groups (Andrade & Boulay, 2003). Students in the treatment group received two lessons on self-assessment and practiced using the rubric to assess their draft essays. A significant relationship was observed between treatment and girls' scores on a historical fiction essay, but there was no significant effect for boys. The scores for a literature essay were not significantly related to the treatment for boys or girls. The authors concluded that the intervention was not sufficient (Andrade & Boulay, 2003), suggesting the need for a more comprehensive approach to instructing students on how to use a rubric to assess their own essays.

In an effort to more fully engage students in learning how to use rubrics to assess their own writing, Andrade, Du, and Wang (2008) examined the relationship between instruction on self-assessment and third- and fourth-grade students' written essay scores. The treatment group read and discussed a model essay, crafted a set of features of an effective essay based on the model essay, and discussed the rubric prior to using it in scoring their draft essays. The comparison group did not discuss a model essay nor use a rubric for their self-assessment, but they did develop a set of features that exemplify an effective essay. In both conditions, the classroom teachers gave each student feedback on their first drafts prior to the students writing their final drafts.

Trained raters scored the students' essays, and those scores were used in the analysis. After controlling for previous achievement in language arts, the results of a two-way analysis of variance indicated that the treatment group's writing scores were significantly higher than the comparison group's writing scores, providing evidence of the effectiveness of engaging students in a discussion of the criteria embedded in a rubric and the use of the rubric to assess their own writing. The effect size was moderate to large ($\eta^2 = 0.15$). Further, there was practical significance in that the treatment group, on average, scored at the low end of a four on the rubric and the comparison group, on average, scored at the upper end of a three on the rubric, thus reflecting meaningful differences in their writing skills.

The procedures used in the Andrade, Du, and Wang (2008) study were replicated in a study that examined middle school students' use of a rubric for self-assessment (Andrade, Du, & Mycek, 2010). After controlling for previous language arts achievement and writing time, the results of a two-way analysis of variance indicated that the treatment group's writing scores were significantly higher than the comparison group's writing scores, with an effect size of $\eta^2 = 0.17$. Future studies would benefit by examining growth in student's writing skills over an extended time period of self-assessment of writing as well as examining the effect of formative assessment strategies during the intervention such as teacher feedback on students' self-assessment.

Mathematics Assessments

A study conducted by Fuchs, Fuchs, Karns, Hamlett, and Katzaroff (1999) examined the relationship between the use of classroom-based mathematics performance assessments and teachers' instructional practices and student learning. Sixteen elementary teachers were randomly assigned to a performance assessment instruction condition or a no performance assessment instruction condition. The teachers in the performance assessment instruction condition participated in a workshop, administered three performance assessments over a few months, and scored and discussed ideas on providing feedback to students with colleagues. The percentage agreement among the raters scoring the assessment was above 0.95.

An analysis of variance indicated a significant interaction between treatment and achievement level for pretest to posttest growth scores on alternate forms of the performance assessment. Growth for above- and at-grade-level students was greater in the performance assessment group than the control group, with an effect size greater than one standard deviation, but there was no treatment effect for below-grade-level students. The authors indicated that the lack of gains for low achieving students on the performance assessment may suggest that teachers need more instructional support to help improve lower achieving students' problem solving skills, with a focus on providing guidance in formulating problem-solving schemas and metacognitive skills.

On a novel problem-solving measure given as a posttest only, scores were significantly higher for the performance assessment group than for the control group for students above-grade-level, whereas there was no significant difference between the treatment groups for students at- and below-grade-level. This indicates that only above-grade-level students benefited from the performance assessment instruction when measured with a novel problem. The authors discussed possible reasons for the lack of a treatment effect for at-grade-level students, including differences in the format and scoring rubric of the novel performance assessment: "metacognitive awareness of the relations across problem-solving situations may have mediated at-grade-level students' problem solving capacity" (Fuchs et al., 1999, p. 637). For struggling learners, it may be necessary to scaffold performance tasks, allowing for the needed support when solving complex tasks.

Teachers were also asked to respond to questions that addressed their level of knowledge about performance assessments. The teachers in the performance assessment group were significantly better at developing math problems that more closely reflected key features of performance assessments (e.g., requiring students to generate information and apply multiple skills) than the teachers in the control group, with an effect size greater than one standard deviation. The teachers in the performance assessment group were significantly better at identifying ways in which performance assessments can facilitate instructional decisions (e.g., track student progress and develop high-level thinking skills) than the teachers in the control group, with an effect size greater than one standard deviation. Teachers in the performance assessment group also reported that they increased their instructional focus on problem solving since participating in the study, whereas teachers in the control group did not, with an effect size of 1.5 standard deviations. When given the opportunity to use performance assessments in their classrooms, teachers reported an increase in their curricular focus on problem solving.

Another study that found differential effects of performance for students of varying achievement levels was conducted by Phelan, Choi, Vendlinski, Baker, and Herman (2011). They examined the effects of including mathematics performance tasks in a formative assessment context on the performance of middle school students. Phelan and colleagues used a transfer measure consisting primarily of multiple-choice and short answer items (with one explanation item). Some of the formative assessment tasks required students to show their solution processes and explain their reasoning. Their formative assessment intervention focused on facilitating student learning of fundamental mathematical principles that support algebra proficiency and helping teachers provide feedback to students and align their instruction to support student understanding. Teachers in the treatment group received professional development to support the implementation and use of the instructional materials and formative assessments. There were approximately eight class periods of intervention and 9 hours of professional development for the teachers. The comparison group received their regular instruction.

Eighty-five teachers from 27 schools and over 4,000 sixth-grade students participated in the study. Students took a pretest and a transfer measure at the end of the school year. Using hierarchical linear modeling, the results indicated that students who received the treatment did not perform better than students in the control group in three of the four areas (rational number equivalence, solving equations, and review and applications) as well as on the overall performance, but the treatment group did outperform the control group on one of the areas—distributive property. A significant interaction effect between treatment and student pretest scores was obtained, indicating that students with higher pretest scores benefited more from the treatment than those students with lower pretest scores, with an effect size of 0.5. This finding is consistent with the results from Fuchs et al. (1999), indicating that the use of performance assessments in the classroom was not related to student learning for low achieving students, whereas it was related to student learning for higher achieving students. Performance assessments require complex thinking that low achieving students have not yet mastered (but they should be provided the opportunity to learn).

Conclusion and Suggestions for Future Research

Performance assessments have been used as key tools in educational reform; however, they are not by themselves an easy cure-all (Shepard et al., 1996). An integrated, coherent approach to curriculum, instruction, assessment, student learning, and professional development is needed to ensure that all students are provided with the opportunity to learn and to show what they know and can do. An excellent example of a program that was designed to ensure coherency among performance-based curriculum, instruction, and assessment was the College Board's English and math Pacesetter program, which was an integrated program of standards, instruction, professional development, and performance assessments. Students in the Pacesetter programs had greater success on performance assessments than did students in control groups (College Board, 2001), providing empirical support for coherency among instruction and assessment.

Studies have provided validity and reliability evidence for the use of classroom-based performance assessment (Falk et al., 2007; Quellmalz, Silberglitt, et al., 2011; Quellmalz et al., 2010; Yin et al., 2008); however, continued research on the design, validation, and use of performance assessments in the classroom is needed, including research on best design principles for computer-based performance tasks. Research should also focus on best practices in using performance assessments and their impact on advancing student learning and informing instruction. Although there is promising evidence that the use of classroom-based performance assessments are related to student learning and instructional practices (Fuchs et al., 1999; Niemi, Wang, Steinberg, Baker, & Wang, 2007), their use in the classroom is limited by the guidance teachers give to students, which may be a function of teachers' content knowledge, knowledge of learning goals, and assessment literacy. In designing studies to examine the effects of performance assessments on student learning, it is essential that teachers are provided with sustained professional development so they become effective users of performance assessments, especially in terms of understanding the skills and knowledge being assessed, how to determine where students are in relation to the learning goals, and how to use the assessment information to improve instruction (College Board, 2001; Ruiz-Primo, Furtak, Ayala, Yin, & Shavelson, 2010; Stiggins, 2010).

It is essential for studies to be implemented over extended time periods to ensure that there is ample opportunity for any intervention to have an impact. Although longitudinal research studies using randomized groups are difficult to implement, they provide the most direct evidence of the impact of the use of performance assessments on student learning and should be implemented in the future.

Some studies revealed that the use of classroom-based performance assessment was significantly related to student learning for middle and/or higher achieving students but not for low achieving students, and the impact on learning was for high achieving students only when a transfer measure was used as the outcome (Fuchs et al., 1999; Phelan et al., 2011). Additional studies are needed to examine the effects of performance assessments on learning for students at different achievement levels. For low achieving students, it may be necessary to scaffold performance tasks, allowing for additional support in solving the tasks.

Abedi and his colleagues (Abedi, 2010; Abedi & Lord, 2001; Abedi et al., 2000) demonstrated that students who have difficulty in reading, including ELL students and low and moderate achieving students, performed significantly better on math assessments when the complexity of the sentence structure and the use of unfamiliar vocabulary in the items was reduced. Their research has direct implications for the design of performance assessments, especially for ELL students and low and moderate achieving students. There is also some emerging evidence that the performance gaps for both ELL students and students with disabilities are smaller on science simulation-based assessments than traditional tests (Quellmalz et al., 2010; Quellmalz, Timms, et al., 2011), which may be a function of the use of scaffolding and the interactive features of the simulation assessments. Additional research is needed to examine the extent to which this finding can be generalized to other simulation assessments and settings, as well as to uncover the features in simulation assessments that may result in narrower performance gaps.

Research is also needed on the impact of performance assessments on teachers' instructional practice. Prior research has provided evidence that the use of performance assessments is related to teacher knowledge of performance assessments and related instructional practices. Teachers in treatment groups (instructed on performance assessment use) were significantly better at designing and identifying uses of performance assessments and were more likely to report changes in their instruction to focus on problem solving and inquiry than those in control groups (Fuchs et al., 1999; Yin et al., 2008). Additional research examining the impact of the use of classroom-based performance assessments on instructional practices needs to go beyond self-report measures of instruction and provide more direct evidence of instruction, such as the observation procedures used by Furtak et al. (2008). Further, more direct measures of how teachers use performance assessments in their classroom will provide a better context for interpretations of the results of studies examining the impact of classroom-based performance assessments on student learning.

References

Abedi, J. (2010). Research and recommendations for formative assessment with English language learners. In H. L. Andrade & G. J. Cizek (Eds.), *Handbook of formative assessment* (pp. 181–195). New York: Routledge.

Abedi, J., & Lord, C. (2001). The language factor in mathematics tests. *Applied Measurement in Education, 14*(3), 219–234.

Abedi, J., Lord, C., Hofstetter, C., & Baker, E. (2000). Impact of accommodation strategies on English language learners' test performance. *Educational Measurement: Issues and Practice, 19*(3), 16–26.

American Educational Research Association, American Psychological Association, & National Council on Measurement in Education. (1999). *Standards for educational and psychological testing*. Washington, DC: American Educational Research Association.

Andrade, H. L., & Boulay, B. A. (2003). Role of rubric-reference self-assessment in learning to write. *The Journal of Educational Research, 97*(1), 23–34.

Andrade, H. L., Du, Y., & Mycek, K. (2010). Rubric-referenced self-assessment and middle school student's writing. *Assessment in Education: Principles, Policy, & Practice, 17*(2), 199–214.

Andrade, H. L., Du, Y., & Wang, X. (2008). Putting rubrics to the test: The effect of a model, criteria generation, and rubric-referenced self-assessment on elementary school students' writing. *Educational Measurement: Issues and Practice, 27*(2), 3–13.

Aschbacher, P., & Alonzo, A. (2006). Examining the utility of elementary science notebooks for formative assessment purposes, *Educational Assessment, 11*(3/4), 179–203.

Ayala, C. C., Shavelson, R. J., Ruiz-Primo, M. A., Brandon, P. R., Young, D. B., Brandon, P.R., et al. (2008). From formal embedded assessments to reflective lessons: The development of formative assessment studies. *Applied Measurement in Education, 21*(4), 315–359.

Baker, E. L. (2007). Model-based assessments to support learning and accountability: The evolution of CRESST's research on multiple-purpose measures. *Educational Assessment, 12*(3&4), 179–194.

Baxter, G. P., & Glaser, R. (1998). Investigating the cognitive complexity of science assessments. *Educational Measurement: Issues and Practice, 17*(3), 37–45.

Baxter, G. P., & Shavelson, R. J. (1994). Performance assessments: Benchmarks and surrogates. *International Journal of Educational Research, 21*, 279–298.

Bennett, R. E. (2006). Moving the field forward: Some thoughts on validity and automated scoring (pp. 403–412). In D. M. Williamson, R. J. Mislevy, & I. I. Behar (Eds.), *Automated scoring of complex tasks in computer-based testing*. Hillside, NJ: Lawrence Erlbaum.

Bennett, R. E. (2010). Cognitively based assessment of, for and as learning: A preliminary theory of action for summative and formative assessment. *Measurement: Interdisciplinary Research and Perspectives, 8,* 70–91.

Bennett, R. E., & Gitomer, D. H. (2009). Transforming K–12 assessment: Integrating accountability testing, formative assessment and professional support (pp. 44–61). In C. Wyatt-Smith & J. Cumming (Eds.), *Educational assessment in the 21st century.* New York: Springer.

Bennett, R. E., Persky, H., Weiss, A. R., & Jenkins, F. (2007). *Problem solving in technology-rich environments: A report from the NAEP Technology-Based Assessment Project* (NCES 2007-466). Washington, DC: National Center for Education Statistics, U.S. Department of Education. Retrieved from http://nces.ed.gov/pubsearch/pubsinfo.asp?pubid=2007466

Clarke-Midura, J., Code, J., Zap, N., & Dede, C. (in press). Assessing science inquiry: A case study of the virtual assessment project. In L. Lennex & K. Nettleton (Eds.), *Cases on inquiry through instructional technology in math and science: Systematic approaches.* New York: IGI Publishing.

Clauser, B. E. (2000). Recurrent issues and recent advances in scoring performance assessments. *Applied Psychological Measurement, 24*(4), 310–324.

College Board. (2001). *Pacesetter research and evaluation findings* (Research Summary-06). New York: College Board.

Darling-Hammond, L., Ancess, J., & Falk, B. (1995). *Authentic assessment in action: Studies of school and students at work.* New York: Teachers' College Press.

DeVore, R. N. (2002). *Considerations in the development of accounting simulations* (Technical Report 13). Ewing, NJ: American Institute of Certified Public Accountants.

Eckes, T. (2008). Rater types in writing performance assessments: A classification approach to rater variability. *Language Testing, 25*(2), 155–185.

Falk, B., & Ort, S. (1999). *Technical report of the New York State Goals 2000 Early Literacy Profile Project.* New York: National Center for Restructuring Education, Schools, and Teaching.

Falk, B., Ort, S. W., & Moirs, K. (2007). Keeping the focus on the child: Supporting and reporting on teaching and learning with a classroom-based performance assessment system. *Educational Assessment, 12*(1), 47–75.

Frederiksen, J. R. & Collins, A. (1989). A systems approach to educational testing. *Educational Researcher, 18*(9), 27–32.

Fuchs, L. S., Fuchs, D., Karns, K., Hamlett, C. L., & Katzaroff, M. (1999). Mathematics performance assessment in the classroom: Effects on teacher planning and student problem solving. *American Educational Research Journal, 36*(3), 609–646.

Furtak, E. M., Ruiz-Primo, M. A., Stemwell, J. T., Ayala, C. C., Brandon, P. R., Shavelson, R. J., et al. (2008). On the fidelity of implementing embedded formative assessments and its relation to student learning. *Applied Measurement in Education, 21*(4), 360–389.

Haertel, E. H., & Linn, R. L. (1996). Comparability. In G. W. Phillips (Ed.), *Technical Issues in Large-Scale Performance Assessment* (NCES 96-802). Washington, DC: U.S. Department of Education.

Herman, J., Dai, Y., Htut, A. M., Martinez, M., & Rivera, N. (2010). CRESST evaluation report: Evaluation of the Enhanced Assessment Grant (EAG). Los Angeles: National Center for Research on Evaluations, Standards, & Student Testing.

Kane, M., Crooks, T., & Cohen, A. (1999). Validating measures of performance. *Educational Measurement: Issues and Practice, 18*(2), 5–17.

Lane, S. (2010). *Performance assessment: The state of the art.* Stanford, CA: Stanford University, Stanford Center for Opportunity Policy in Education.

Lane, S. & Stone, C. A. (2006). Performance assessments. In B. Brennan (Ed.), *Educational measurement* (pp. 387–432). Westport, CT: American Council on Education & Praeger.

Linn, R. L. (1993). Educational assessment: Expanded expectations and challenges. *Educational Evaluation and Policy Analysis, 15,* 1–16.

Linn, R. L., Baker, E. L., & Dunbar, S. B. (1991). Complex performance assessment: Expectations and validation criteria. *Educational Researcher, 20*(8), 15–21.

Liu, O. L., Lee, H. Hofstetter, C., & Linn, M. C. (2008). Assessing knowledge integration in science: Constructs, measures, and evidence. *Educational Assessment, 13*(1), 33–55.

Messick, S. (1989). Validity. In R. L. Linn (Ed.), *Educational Measurement* (3rd ed., pp. 13–104). New York: American Council on Education and Macmillan.

Messick, S. (1994). The interplay of evidence and consequences in the validation of performance assessments. *Educational Researcher, 23*(2), 13–23.

Mislevy, R. J., Steinberg, L. S., & Almond, R. G. (2003). On the structure of educational assessments. *Measurement: Interdisciplinary Research and Perspectives, 1*(1), 3–62.

Moon, T. R., Callahan, C. M., Brighton, C. M., & Tomlinson, C. A. (2002). *Development of differentiated performance assessment tasks for middle school classrooms* (Report No. RM02160). Storrs, CT: National Research Center on the Gifted and Talented.

Mullis, I. V. S. (1984). Scoring direct writing assessments: What are the alternatives? *Educational Measurement: Issues and Practice, 3*(1), 16–18.

Niemi, D., Baker, E. L., & Sylvester, R. M. (2007). Scaling up, scaling down: Seven years of performance assessment development in the nation's second largest school district. *Educational Assessment, 12*(3&4), 195–214.

Niemi, D., Wang, J., Steinberg, D. H., Baker, E. L., & Wang, H. (2007). Instructional sensitivity of a complex language arts performance assessment. *Educational Assessment, 12*(3&4), 215–238.

O'Reilly, T., & Sheehan, K. M. (2009). *Cognitively based assessment of, for and as learning: a framework for assessing reading competency* (RR-09-2006). Princeton, NJ: ETS.

Phelan, J., Choi, K.,Vendlinski, T, Baker, E., & Herman, J. (2011). Differential improvement in student understanding of mathematical principles following formative assessment intervention, *Journal of Educational Research, 104*, 330–339.

Powers, D. E., Burstein, J. C., Chodorow, M. S., Fowles, M. E., & Kukich, K. (2002). Comparing the validity of automated and human scoring of essays. *Journal of Educational Computing Research, 26*(4), 407–425.

Quellmalz, E. S., Silberglitt, M. D., & Timms, M. J. (2011). *How can simulations be components of balanced state science assessment systems?* San Francisco: WestEd.

Quellmalz, E. S., Timms, M. J., & Buckley, B. C. (2010). The promise of simulation-based science assessment: The Calipers project. *International Journal of Learning Technology, 5*(3), 243–263.

Quellmalz, E. S., Timms, M. J., Buckley, B. C., Davenport, J., Loveland, M., & Silberglitt, M. D. (2011). 21st century dynamic assessment. In M. C. Mayrath, J. Clarke-Midura, D. H. Robinson, & G. Schraw (Eds.), *Technology-based assessments for 21st century skills* (pp. 55–89). Charlotte, NC: Information Age Publishing.

Resnick, L. B., & Resnick, D. P. (1992). Assessing the thinking curriculum: New tools for educational reform. In B. G. Gifford & M. C. O'Conner (Eds.), *Changing assessment: Alternative views of aptitude, achievement and instruction* (pp. 37–55). Boston: Kluwer.

Rezaei, A. R., & Lovorn, M. G. (2010). Reliability and validity of rubrics for assessment through writing. *Assessing Writing,* 15(1), 18–39.

Ruiz-Primo, M. A., Furtak, E. M., Ayala, C., Yin, Y., & Shavelson, R. J. (2010). Formative assessment, motivation, and science learning. In H. L. Andrade & G. J. Cizek (Eds.), *Handbook of formative assessment* (pp. 139–158). New York: Routledge.

Ruiz-Primo, M. A., Li, M., Tsai, S., & Schneider, J. (2010). Testing one premise of scientific inquiry in science classrooms: Examining students' scientific explanations and student learning. *Journal of Research in Science Teaching, 47*(5), 583–608.

Shavelson, R. J., Young, D. B., Ayala, C. C., Brandon, P. R., Furtak, E. M., Ruiz-Primo, M.A., et al. (2008). On the impact of curriculum-embedded formative assessment on learning: A collaboration between curriculum and assessment developers. *Applied Measurement in Education, 21*(4), 295–314.

Shepard, L. A., Flexer, R. J., Hiebert, E. H., Marion, S. F., Mayfield, V., & Weston, T. J. (1996). Effects of introducing classroom performance assessments on student learning. *Educational Measurement: Issues and Practice, 15*(3), 7–18.

Stiggins, R. (2010). Essential formative assessment competencies for teachers and school leaders. In H. L. Andrade & G. J. Cizek (Eds.), *Handbook of formative assessment* (pp. 233–250). New York: Routledge.

Stone, C. A., & Lane, S. (2003). Consequences of a state accountability program: Examining relationships between school performance gains and teacher, student, and school variables. *Applied Measurement in Education, 16*(1), 1–26.

Tilson, J. L., Castek, J., & Goss, M. (2009). *Exploring the influence of science writing instruction on fourth graders' writing development.* Retrieved from http://scienceandliteracy.org/sites/scienceandliteracy.org/files/biblio/tilsoncastekgoss_nrc2009_pdf_18057.pdf

Touchstone Applied Science Associates, Inc. (1995). *DRP handbook: G&H test forms.* Brewster, NY: Author.

Vendlinski, T. P., Baker, E. L., & Niemi, D. (2008). *Templates and objects in authoring problem-solving assessments* (CRESST Tech. Rep. No. 735). Los Angeles: University of California, National Center Research on Evaluation, Standards, and Student Testing.

Welch, C. (2006). Item and prompt development in performance testing. In S. M. Downing & T. M. Haladyna (Eds.), *Handbook of test development* (pp. 303–308). Mahwah, NJ: Lawrence Erlbaum.

White, L., Hixson, N., D'Brot, J., Perdue, J., Foster, S., & Rhudy, V. (2010). *Impact of Writing Roadmap 2.0 on WESTEST 2 Online Writing Assessment Scores.* Retrieved from www.ctb.com/ctb.com/control/getAssetListByFilterTypeViewAction?param=459&title=productFamily&p=library.

Yin, Y., Shavelson, R. J., Ayala, C. C., Ruiz-Primo, M. A., Brandon, P. R., Furtak, E. M., et al. (2008). On the impact of formative assessment on student motivation, achievement, and conceptual change. *Applied Measurement in Education, 21*(4), 335–359.

19

Portfolios and E-Portfolios: Student Reflection, Self-Assessment, and Goal Setting in the Learning Process

Susan F. Belgrad

A portfolio is a purposeful collection of student work that illustrates effort, progress, and achievement in one or more areas over time. Portfolio collections typically include evidence of student reflection, as well as student participation in selecting the contents, the criteria for selection, and the criteria for judging merit (Stiggins, 1994). Portfolios grew out of concerns about timed, self-contained assessments of writing, as well as from the recognition that process pedagogy was being undermined by traditional testing and because of a growing awareness of the contextual nature of language use (Belanoff & Dickson, 1991). Portfolios were first implemented during the 1970s in progressive schools and classrooms. They appeared in the National Writing Project as a substitute for a written exit exam in 1983 and became widely used in K–12 classrooms in the 1990s, largely in response to renewed efforts to engage and educate all children through student-centered curriculum and instruction (Belgrad, Burke, & Fogarty, 2008; Stiggins, 1994; Wiggins, 1993).

Portfolios can be important components of a comprehensive evaluation system. Comprehensive systems of evaluation that include portfolios of student performance have been proposed for a number of reasons. One reason is that traditional assessments assume that knowledge has universal meanings, whereas knowledge is complex and can have multiple meanings and perspectives (Bintz & Harste, 1994). Another reason is that standardized assessments treat learning as a passive process, whereas portfolios treat learning as an active process in which students are engaged in the search for meaning. Further, testing emphasizes the mastery of discrete and isolated bits of information or knowledge but advocates of student-centered learning believe the emphasis of assessment should be placed on process as well as products of learning (Herman, Aschbacher, & Winters, 1992).

Perhaps most central to the view of portfolio proponents from the 1990s to today is the way in which high-stakes testing is used to document, sort, and compare students' achievement. Portfolio assessment advocates focus on how the ongoing processes of student inquiry capture the cognitive abilities that underscore successful achievement and engage students themselves as participants in the instructional design and authentic assessment of key learning events in subject areas (Brooks & Brooks, 1993; Johnston, 1989; Wolf, 1990).

This chapter addresses the role that portfolios have played in student assessment. It includes a discussion of portfolio definitions, their contents and processes, and how emerging research may reveal systematic ways to implement e-portfolios for evaluation and accountability purposes at the classroom, school, district, or state level. The chapter also includes a discussion of the purposes and functions of e-portfolios, which have emerged as digital repositories of student performance and achievement, and electronic systems of school and district accountability (High Tech High, 2012). Questions about whether or not e-portfolios can reliably capture evidence of subject area knowledge, skills, and dispositions through both summative and formative measures will be addressed. The goals of this review of research are to clarify definitions and examine the empirical and theoretical bases of K–12 portfolios. A review of the scant research on portfolios and e-portfolios has revealed the need to clarify the terminology used to describe processes used in portfolios to collect, organize, and evaluate student learning and achievement. It is hoped that this review will inform the design of portfolios and portfolio systems and assure that such designs are grounded in a culture of evidence. This review is also intended to provide a holistic perspective on the critically important function of student assessment and on the intended and unintended consequences of dependence on high-stakes assessment that has prevailed during the last decade in American education.

Definitions and Purposes of Portfolios

Although most people think of portfolios as representing an artist's collective works or a financial container of investments, portfolios found in prekindergarten through high school classrooms serve to showcase students' accomplishments and personally selected best works. Portfolios are authentic collections of student work that represent who students are as learners. They are evidence containers that "encourage students to showcase their individuality within the context of the classroom" (Belgrad et al., 2008, p. 1). Carr and Harris (2001) described portfolios as a "purposeful, integrated collection of student work showing effort, progress, or achievement in one or more areas" (p. 181). Portfolios engage students and their teachers in a variety of thinking and reflective processes. Paulson, Paulson, and Meyer (1991) suggested that portfolios provide an intersection of instruction and assessment that encourages students to take charge of their learning. They can promote students' awareness of and attention to standards, as well as progress toward benchmarks and individual learning goals. These processes occur through stages of artifact collection and selection and place students at the center of the learning process through reflective processes that offer them opportunities to become active and creative.

Portfolios offer a high quality learning tool for students within a classroom community of learners where processes of reflection, communication, and collaboration are promoted (Barrett, 2007). They are used to engage K–12 students in the assessment process in order to (1) select and reflect on a variety of documentation or evidence of growth in knowledge, abilities, and dispositions; (2) promote authentic communication about learning with peers, teachers, and parents; (3) promote metacognition through ongoing reflection on their work; and (4) assure student awareness and understanding of external goals and standards so they may set their own goals, self-assess their progress, and pursue new goals to attain achievement.

Portfolios can serve a variety of purposes and take a variety of forms (Belgrad et al., 2008). A number of proponents and researchers state that known purposes are central to success in portfolio assessment (Guskey, 2007; Rolheiser, 1998; Rolheiser & Ross, 2001; Tomlinson & Allan, 2000). There are four main types of portfolios. The *learning* portfolio captures evidence of students' knowledge and skill in order to provide the reader with a holistic picture of how the student has been engaged in learning and achievement over time (Belgrad et al., 2008). The *developmental* portfolio demonstrates the continuing growth and development of students as readers, writers, problem solvers, and so on. The *assessment* or *standards* portfolio demonstrates the achievement of benchmarks or standards and can help students consider how their work meets established criteria, analyze their efforts, and plan for improvement (Belgrad et al., 2008). Finally, the *showcase* portfolio of student work or achievement invites students to focus on, communicate, and celebrate individual achievements or talents. *Multiple intelligences* portfolios and *autobiographical* portfolios often address the purposes of showcase portfolios. Showcase portfolios serve as a counterpoint to traditional forms of assessment because they can illuminate student capabilities not covered by standardized testing (Yancey & Weiser, 1997).

Early Research on Portfolios and Portfolio Processes

In the early 1990s, Vermont led the way in the implementation of statewide performance portfolios in math and writing as an alternative to standardized tests of students' achievement. Authentic student work captured in portfolios was viewed as a viable means to assess student academic progress. But in 1994, a RAND Corporation study responded to the concerns of some teachers, think tanks, and policy groups that portfolios were cumbersome, took up too much teaching time, and were too subjective and unreliable. Instructional inefficiency was seen as another problem with the statewide portfolios. Koretz, McCaffrey, Klein, Bell, and Stecher (1994) found that the inferences being drawn from portfolio assessment were not valid or reliable enough to evaluate schools or students because it was difficult to compare the contents of student work and determine whether the standards were high enough from one school to another.

Given the ways in which portfolio scores were created, their "rater reliability"—the extent of agreement between raters about the quality of student's work—was on average low in both mathematics and writing. Reliability varied, depending on the subject, grade level and the particular scoring criterion, and in a few instances, it could be characterized as moderate. The overall pattern was one of low reliability, however, and in no instance was the scoring highly reliable (Koretz et al., 1994, p. 2).

Recommendations for portfolio reliability from the Vermont study included the following:

- Scoring systems must provide clear and consistent terminology through descriptive rubrics across the system. At the same time, simplicity as contrasted to complexity must characterize the scoring
- Reliability of raters must be insured by providing calibration training with a relatively small number of teachers in order to assure that trainees have reached a high level of proficiency in scoring.
- The system must include a standardization of task and administrative conditions—including standardized benchmarks and sample performance of the precise tasks used in the assessment and administered under standardized conditions (Koretz et al., 1994, pp. 26–27).

The release of the RAND Corporation report on the Vermont Portfolio Project had a strongly negative impact on portfolios as an alternative to statewide tests and as reliable methods of evaluating student performance. Even with Koretz et al.'s (1994) carefully worded assessment that there was no sizable systematic bias in teachers' rating of their own students nor were the scores they assigned systematically too high or too low, the report dampened enthusiasm for portfolio assessment and led to the state and district abandonment of systematic portfolio assessment across the nation.

Kentucky's Education Reform Act of 1990 also implemented a portfolio assessment of students' performance across the state. By 1995, a panel was convened to review its progress in accurately reporting student achievement results. The Pacific Research Institute found many flaws in the system that mirrored some of those reported by the RAND Corporation on Vermont's Portfolio Assessment (Izumi, 1999). When the portfolio assessments were compared to other tests, most notably the National Assessment of Educational Progress (NAEP), the achievement gains reported through the portfolio assessment failed to be matched. Like Vermont, Kentucky's system of portfolios failed to control factors affecting reliability (Izumi, 1999). A second evaluation of Kentucky's portfolio assessment system also indicated it was flawed, with subjectivity arising from its largely unstandardized characteristics (Hambleton et al., 1995). Among the procedures of statewide implementation that were criticized in the report were a lack of specific guidelines about the types of tasks included in each of the subject areas; a lack of specific guidelines on opportunities for student revision of portfolio pieces; a lack of standardization of the contents and processes of portfolios, as well as most aspects of operation and timelines among schools.

The earlier research findings that raised serious questions about the validity of large-scale portfolio assessment systems are important to consider in looking ahead to the assessment of student learning. Educators, researchers, and proponents of comprehensive systems that collect and disseminate evidence of student learning will need to address the role that portfolios in their newest format—e-portfolio—will play in advancing 21st-century national education goals.

The Role of Portfolios in the 21st Century

Portfolios and the student-centered processes they promoted declined in the two decades since the passing of the U.S. Department of Education GOALS 2000: Educate America Act (1994). The No Child Left Behind Act of 2001 (NCLB) (U.S. Department of Education, 2002) provided a comprehensive approach to raising student achievement and closing the achievement gap. It set annual, standardized test-score targets for subgroups of students, based on a goal of 100% proficiency by 2014 and subsequently became the centerpiece of the Title I Elementary and Secondary Education Act (ESEA)—Race to the Top. Yet concerns persist that while testing aligns with key basic skills, it does not measure or address the emerging work force and global education realities that affect national needs for assessments aligned with key student achievement in next-century knowledge and dispositions. Shepard (2000) and Meisels (2003) believe that students in the United States have determined that their performance on standardized tests is more important than the what and the how of their learning experience and achievements. Darling-Hammond (2010) suggested that while higher-order, 21st-century skills are emphasized in other nations' curricula and assessment systems, they have been discouraged by the kind of low-level multiple-choice testing encouraged by the NCLB legislation.

Koretz, McCaffrey, Klein, Bell, and Stecher (2009) and other educational researchers note that in a test-driven curriculum, teachers become constrained from engaging and assessing students in the important 21st-century skills of investigation and collaboration, observation and hypothesis testing, interpreting evidence, applying what they know to new problems, and explaining and defending their answers. The implementation of the Common Core State Standards (National Governors Association, 2010) has addressed these concerns by recommending that the next generation of standardized achievement tests be more reflective of 21st-century learning capabilities and become accessible to educators for informing curricular and instructional decisions that improve student learning (The Smarter Balanced Assessment Consortium [SBAC], 2011). This can be accomplished by not only measuring student performance but also promoting test designs that result in accessibility to the critical information needed to improve achievement (Darling-Hammond, 2010). Balanced systems of student assessments must have a more comprehensive and dimensional capacity to inform teachers and school administrators of how to attain improvement of student performance through curricular, instructional, and formative assessment processes in which students themselves participate. Next-generation assessments must not only measure student knowledge in key subject areas related to student and national needs but also capture higher-order thinking skills (HOTS) that assure success in college and the workplace (Koretz, 2009; The Secretary's Commission on Achieving Necessary Skills [SCANS], 1991; North Central Regional Educational Laboratory [NCREL] & the Metiri Group, 2003).

The emergence of e-portfolios as components of comprehensive systems of student assessment offers some promise. E-portfolios provide qualitative data that can complement and supplement the standardized test scores that provide quantifiable measures of student learning under NCLB. In the recommendations for the reauthorization of the ESEA, the Forum on Educational Accountability (FEA) of FairTest

(2011) asserted that comprehensive assessment systems should do the following:

1. Include classroom-based evidence as part of public reporting and accountability, and for improving teaching and learning
2. Include assessment elements such as performance tasks and projects, which states can make available to educators to use when appropriate and incorporate into large-scale assessments
3. Become part of states' use of multiple sources of evidence in evaluating students, schools, and educators and in constructing any growth/improvement/value-added approaches
4. Address the needs of diverse learners. (para. 2)

Greenberg (2004) and Wall, Higgins, Miller, and Packard (2006) have advanced the need for comprehensive assessment systems that include formative and summative evidence of student performance. In essence, 21st-century learning demands assessments that arise from cultures of evidence that begin within the classroom and become integrated into state and national systems of data collection on K–12 student achievement.

Theoretical Benefits of Portfolio Assessment Processes and Related Research

Educators and their students must know at the outset of instruction *what* is the archival evidence (contents) of portfolios that represents learning in subject areas and *how* it is to be captured and reflected upon. When integrated into a culture of evidence, portfolios bring together the purposes, processes, and tools that represent student learning across the curriculum. Cultures of evidence as currently studied and advanced within the context of e-portfolios in higher education offer criteria that might guide implementation and research into how such a culture would be created in K–12 education:

1. *Claims*: What do I want or need to say about the student?
2. *Evidence*: What does the student have to do to prove that he or she has the knowledge and skills claimed?
3. *Assessment tools and activities*: What assessment tools and/or activities will elicit the evidence that I need about the student's knowledge? (Millett, Payne, Dwyer, Stickler & Aiexiou, 2008, p. 11)

Two key assessment processes—(1) reflection and (2) student self-assessment—have been examined in recent research. However, the research acquired for review was limited to only three classroom-based action research studies. This section of the chapter reviews those studies while at the same time pointing to the clear need for additional, rigorous research.

Reflective Processes

Portfolios integrate summative and formative assessment so that they become "the centerpiece of an integrated standards-based assessment system" (Ainsworth, 2007, p. 79). In this way, portfolios ensure that assessment is an integral and useful part of instruction, as a source of feedback between students and teacher. They provide opportunities for teachers to offer high quality corrective information and give students second chances to demonstrate success (Guskey, 2007) and monitor their progress (Andrade, Chapter 2 of this volume). This is accomplished largely because portfolio selection processes require reflection on the part of both the teacher and the student.

The purposeful design of portfolios supports reflective processes of selection, self-assessment, and goal setting that can lead to increased student voice and motivation and helps students take responsibility for their own learning. Each part of the portfolio process engages students in metacognition as they plan for the inclusion of learning evidence, then monitor and evaluate the evidence shown by individual pieces and the whole portfolio. Metacognition refers to one's knowledge of cognition as well as the processes of monitoring, controlling, and regulating one's own cognition. Andrade (Chapter 2 of this volume) reviews this aspect of classroom assessment (CA) processes.

Research on Reflective Processes

Campos and O'Hern (2007) sought to determine if using portfolios as containers of formative assessment might empower their students to become more motivated and engaged in their own mathematical learning process. They addressed concerns that students viewed mathematics as learning for a test as opposed to acquiring knowledge and skill in mathematics as an important learning capacity. They adopted a reflective stance in which they posed the following questions: What are students supposed to learn? What have they already learned? What do they still need to learn? Which children should be recommended for special services? Are students meeting or progressing toward important achievement standards? The researchers also considered the attitudes of parents toward the grade-level learning and assessment processes used in mathematics and whether they might address these attitudes through portfolio processes that included parent reflection on student work and portfolio conferences. Finally, the researchers' addressed these questions: What are the assessment tools we can apply to create a culture of evidence? and How can evidence become aligned with instruction in such a way that teachers have access to the information needed to lead students to deep learning in mathematics?

An action research inquiry was conducted over a 17-week period in which the use of formative assessments and portfolio conferences were integrated with the ongoing summative assessments of mathematical achievement. Through the use of portfolios, first- and fifth-grade students were engaged in tracking their own progress on benchmarks toward mathematics standards. Students participated in weekly portfolio conferences with teachers about their progress. The teacher–researchers kept class data progression charts for the standards that were used as the basis for the conferences with students.

Campos and O'Hern (2007) surveyed students and parents at the conclusion of the study. Twenty first-grade students and 19 fifth-grade students responded anonymously to a survey designed to learn about new perceptions of their ability to monitor their own learning progress following the use of mathematics portfolios. Seventeen parents of first-grade students and 15 parents of fifth-grade students responded to survey questions designed to assess their awareness of state standards and their understanding of how to use assessment results to enhance their student's learning, for example, "I know the mathematics goals for my child's grade level," "After teachers make students aware of mathematics goals for each unit, my child should be able to talk about these mathematics goals," and "Testing can be used to motivate students' learning" (p. 60).

Analysis of the student survey data as well as scoring of student portfolios showed student self-monitoring toward mathematics goals. Analysis of parent surveys indicated awareness of the grade-level standards, goals, and assessments and their student's progress toward mathematical knowledge. The researchers claimed to have been successful in promoting more student engagement in self-monitoring during mathematics learning, while also increasing parental awareness of students' progress toward achieving grade-level math standards. The reflective practice may have led to a culture of evidence in which teachers, students, and parents became informed of student progress by the information from portfolios and were enabled to make decisions and participate in conversations about learning that could lead to improvement in mathematics teaching and learning.

Student reflection on learning in portfolio processes should become a focus of future research. Empirical studies are needed to test the belief that engagement of students in reflective learning processes has the potential to increase achievement, communication (voice), and motivation. It will also be important to study teacher reflection in portfolio processes. Such research is needed to further inform the preparation and ongoing professional development of teachers who understand the need to create cultures of evidence in their classrooms and schools.

Student Self-Assessment and Communication Processes

Student communication or *voice* can be viewed as the physical representation of individual thinking and perspective within the context of learning and education—in school, at home, and in the community. "Voice spans inflection, tone, accent, style, and the qualities and feelings conveyed by the speaker's words; a commitment to voice attests to the *right* of speaking and *being* represented" (Britzman, 1989, p. 143). It is developed through experience within settings that encourage students to create and communicate opinions, ideas, and beliefs—to give these voice.

Belgrad et al. (2008) have addressed the continuing difficulty of educators to value and promote an intersection where student voice might enhance the evaluative, summative process and promote achievement. The challenge for educators is to create and study portfolio assessment *for* learning (AFL) where the dialogue between learners and teachers becomes thoughtful and reflective and is conducted so that all learners have an opportunity to think and to express their ideas (Stiggins, 2007). This is an area of assessment that is long overdue for careful, empirical study. The role of portfolios in promoting the self-reflective stance that can, in turn, promote achievement and self-efficacy in students requires attention from researchers. Will it be learned that portfolios assure regular opportunities for students to engage in the processes that help them to predict what they can accomplish, self-assess their progress toward attainment (Andrade, Chapter 2 of this volume), and communicate evidence of what they know and what they can do (McMillan et al., 2010; McMillan & Hearn, 2008)?

Rolheiser & Ross (2001) saw the process of self-assessment as one in which students "connect successes and failures to factors they believe have caused the result" (p. 42). Similarly, self-evaluation or regulation is an important part of metacognition (Costa & Kallick, 2008). It occurs when students are regularly encouraged to make judgments about their achievements, reflect on these judgments, and then communicate what they have learned. "This includes conscious control of specific cognitive skills such as checking understanding, predicting outcomes, planning activities, managing time, and switching to different learning activities" (McMillan & Hearn, 2008, p. 42).

Research on Student Self-Assessment and Communication Processes

Another teacher–researcher examined the effects of student reflection, self-assessment, choice, and communication (voice) in a portfolio process. After observing the passive nature of his 86 freshmen students in a ninth-grade English class, Fredrick (2009) became concerned that these first-year secondary students were "losing a very important method of claiming power over themselves and their future" (p. 1918). Recognizing that his high school students felt that their school-based learning was irrelevant, he designed a study in which he hypothesized that the implementation of reflective learning mini-lessons would result in more active, meaningful, and higher quality learning. He believed portfolios and their processes would improve the quality of communication at their culminating performances.

Fredrick (2009) addressed his concerns by (1) identifying and then explicitly teaching the key dispositions students needed to deeply reflect on significant learning experiences; (2) hypothesizing that students would gain a love of learning and improve their overall performance in his English class through achieving more self-reflection in the learning process; and (3) carefully teaching and supporting the portfolio processes of reflection, self-assessment, and goal setting over a period of two semesters. The study was conducted in two parts. In the first semester, students were given a new assignment of a portfolio presentation that replaced what had been only a cover letter to the reader. For the new assignment, they were expected to prepare a 10-minute, one-on-one, student-to-teacher portfolio presentation in which they would be expected to clearly articulate that they had learned a skill and were able to name it; indicate the evidence in their work of that *specific* learning; and communicate their goals for future learning.

Understanding the complexity of the new assignment, Fredrick (2009) analyzed the first semester portfolio presentation statements for the presence of reflective statements and then categorized them as *reflective* or *nonreflective. Reflective* was further classified into three types of statements: (1) *process-related* reflections in which students tell the story of their learning experience on an assignment, (2) *criterion-based assessments* in which students compared their work to criteria discussed in class, and (3) *growth over time* in which the students "compared two different pieces of work and showed how one is better by comparing it with a previous piece of work that was not as good" (p. 1920).

Based on these categories Fredrick (2009) created a rubric that would introduce students to the criteria of student reflection as valued in the portfolio process and would guide his own reflection on his teaching and classroom communication. The rubric was also used to guide students in acquiring information for the reflection on evidence of learning expected to be present in their second semester final portfolio. In reflecting on the creation and use of the rubric and his earlier student communications, Fredrick recognized this about the communications:

> [They were] too one-sided; the students seemed not to have the skills needed to do reflection well, and I had not figured out how to teach those skills. To really use the portfolios in ways that might get students to take a bigger stake in their learning and be more forthcoming about their thinking, I needed to listen to what they had to say and ask probing and follow-up questions when I didn't understand. (p. 1919)

With this awareness, Fredrick (2009) used the criteria on the rubric throughout the second semester to create mini-lessons on reflective communication that provided ongoing instruction and support for students in preparation for their end-of-semester presentations. The subsequent measures of student reflectiveness achieved during the second semester presentations showed improvement when compared to the first semester portfolio presentations. The distribution of scores grew from 4% to 14% rated *outstanding* and 33% to 54% rated *on track*. Conversely, the lower reflectiveness scores from the first semester declined from 36% to 28% *emerging*, and 27% to 8% *off track*.

This action research began with the researcher taking a reflective stance on how to engage students in the collection of evidence, the reflection on evidence, and the communication of evidence through three treatments: (1) a portfolio presentation rather than a cover letter to the reader that deeply engaged students in reflecting on learning evidence, (2) explicit lessons about reflection and the different types of reflective statements on evidence that students could use, and (3) a scoring rubric designed to promote self-assessment and goal setting and guide students in their portfolio presentation design. In reflecting on the outcomes, Fredrick (2009) observed that changes in his expectations for increased student reflectiveness, as well as his enhanced instruction and guidance on reflectiveness and self-assessment in the portfolio process, resulted in more student success in reflecting on and communicating evidence of achievement of the English class objectives. Fredrick concluded that the focus on the nature and criteria of reflective learning practices not only helped students in preparation for self-assessment but also encouraged them to acquire a habit of reflection on evidence year round. The students had "become able to stop and reflect on what they would like to learn and what they've already learned" (Fredrick, 2009, p. 1918).

Steinkruger (2007) investigated self-assessment and goal setting with 126 eighth-grade mathematics students. While this researcher did not utilize a portfolio, the study represents a culture of evidence as it places the teacher and students in a reflective stance by looking at evidence of learning. Steinkruger (2007) hypothesized that "when students look closely at themselves as learners and see the important role they play in the development of themselves and others, ownership of learning is more likely to occur" (p. 3). Her inquiry was led by three questions: (1) What are the effects of self-assessment tools on student group work in math class? (2) What are the effects of self-assessment on student usage of precise mathematical vocabulary? (3) What are the effects of self-assessment on student attitudes in math class? In essence, Steinkruger sought to give her students the opportunity to use self-reflection and self-assessment tools to better engage group learning processes in math. Students' attitudes toward mathematical learning were studied through a pre- and post-intervention survey in order to assess the reflective stance of students at the outset and conclusion of the study. Anecdotal evidence of students' engagement in small-group work using precise mathematical vocabulary was collected through a teacher reflective journal. The students also completed vocabulary monitor sheets that were designed to track their usage of the precise mathematical vocabulary during small-group work. Student self-assessments on their performance, interaction, and attitudes as active group members were completed each week.

In analyzing the data collected from this inquiry, Steinkruger (2007) reported that 84% of her students responded that working in groups helped them understand the math concepts presented weekly. Student comments on surveys revealed that they believed they had achieved new perspectives about the value of working with peers: "If I didn't get something, then someone else might" and "They knew what to do" (p. 10). After taking a closer look at themselves through the study, students' comments on the post-survey indicated that they saw themselves as better group members and more accomplished math thinkers. For example, in response to "The quality of my effort this week in group work has been excellent/pretty good/could have been better," 41 students responded *excellent,* 76 responded *pretty good,* and 9 indicated *could have been better.*

Regarding student perceptions of increased learning as an outcome of their reflective group work, the analysis of post surveys indicated that 84% of students felt working in groups helped them understand the weekly math concepts. Student survey comments suggested that they had become more aware of the role they played in their groups and had made efforts to become "good contributors to the group" (p. 10). In her summary of the classroom inquiry on student self-assessment, Steinkruger (2007) reported that students expressed new perspectives about the value of working with peers and that the overall quality of their effort in group work and math learning outcomes had improved by the conclusion of the study.

This classroom inquiry examined the integration of reflective processes into mathematical learning. In essence, the researcher sought to learn if the metacognitive process of self-assessment would create a stronger sense of responsibility for her students' mathematical learning. The action research conducted in this study led to what the teacher described as a more purposeful effort of students in group learning. As seen in this classroom study, such processes can lead students to acquire a stronger sense of responsibility for the quality of their individual contributions in work with peers as well as achievement of learning objectives.

There is clearly a strong need for K–12 classroom and school-based empirical study of the manner in which portfolio assessment systems might provide for a continuous process of student self-reflection and self-assessment that strengthens individual and group learning performance. Questions that might be asked in such research might be as follows: How does student self-assessment within a culture of evidence affect goal setting related to subject area performance? How do portfolio reflection processes affect individual students' performance in peer groups? Does student participation in portfolio processes lead to increased motivation or achievement?

The Emergence of the E-Portfolio

With the growth of the Internet, Web 2.0 tools, and an array of online social media tools, the paper portfolio of the past is being replaced by the digital or e-portfolio. E-portfolios have emerged as purposeful and efficient collections and records of students' progress in learning. They apply digital technologies that include social media and cloud-based productivity (Barrett, 2007). They support ease of use for students to include multimedia artifacts of products and performances and digital scans and uploads of their work. E-portfolios amplify the reflective nature of paper portfolio formats, where the student describes achievement progress over time, as well as self-assessment of the strengths and weaknesses of selected pieces using scoring rubrics provided by teachers in advance of the work.

Yancey's (2009) study of e-portfolios in higher education has informed the literature regarding K–12 recommendations for implementation. The North Carolina State Board of Education (NCSBE) (2010) utilized her findings that e-portfolios "tend to operate in a larger frame of reference, across courses and often across experiences" (p. 6) in suggesting several advantages that e-portfolios achieved over the print or paper format, including the following:

- Making [student] work or performances easily reviewable and available for reflection and assessment purposes
- Supporting interactive work between student, teacher, and peers
- Making student work in a variety of media types easily accessible, portable, and widely distributable
- Addressing longevity and quantity issues related to storage
- Connecting with other online resources within a cloud-computing framework. (NCSBE, 2010, p. 6)

E-Portfolios and the Demand for Evidence-Based Assessment

Although there is some consensus among U.S. stakeholders that national goals and aligned curricular standards are critically important to assuring the education and preparation of today's students, a divergence of opinion occurs regarding how to assure student achievement and assess achievement of basic and 21st-century skills (Partnership for 21st Century Skills, 2007). The national emphasis on scientifically reliable assessments of student capability and achievement, while achieving some gains in the achievement gap (Darling-Hammond, 2007, 2010), has resulted in what critics charge as a narrowing of curriculum. Science, social studies, the arts, and physical education are less emphasized as schools and educators are increasingly evaluated on the basis of student test scores (Association for Supervision and Curriculum Development Commission on the Whole Child, 2007; Ravitch, 2010).

If the folk wisdom about student assessment is valid—"You get what you assess and you don't get what you don't assess" (Bass, 1993, p. 32)—then emerging research on e-portfolios will be critically important in providing a pathway to more dimensional and reliable systems of evidence of K–12 student achievement. A growing body of research related to e-portfolios (Barrett, 2007; Carney, 2004, 2005; Hartnell-Young, 2007; Yancey & Weiser, 1997) indicates that an important hurdle for e-portfolios to achieve is to address the problems long-associated with inter-rater reliability of student work:

> Even while teachers refined rubrics and received training, it was a challenge to obtain reliability between scorers. The evaluation and classification of results is not simply a matter of right and wrong answers, but of inter-rater reliability, of levels of skill and ability in a myriad of areas as evidenced by text quality and scored by different people, a difficult task at best. (Davies, 2007, p. 6)

The nature of portfolios is that each one is different. The individualization inherent in the portfolio process makes standardization difficult, thus making the evidence requirements of reliability and validity of e-portfolios difficult. Following a review of portfolio efficacy in reliably representing evidence of student achievement, the NCSBE (2010) suggested that "portfolios may be best applied as tools for qualitatively showing individual growth, or as instructional interventions for student learning and goal setting" (p. 834).

In a more recent study of e-portfolios conducted in the United Kingdom, Becta (Hartnell-Young, 2007) found that newly emergent technologies are dimensional enough to meet the recommendation to collect *multiple measures* of students' progress on key learning standards while combining and managing classroom-based evidence and data from test scores in comprehensive systems. "While the capacity is not exploited at present, some e-portfolio systems can be linked with student management systems to store numerical and other attainment data that would assist students and teachers to track their progress" (Hartnell-Young, 2007, p. 21). This is promising research that indicates the critical importance of deepening the research base on large-scale portfolio assessment in the United States. The recommendations issued by Benoit and Yang (1996) following their study of Kentucky's statewide portfolios remain salient today: If e-portfolios are to be used for K–12 student assessment at the district or state level, clear, uniform content selection and judgment guidelines must be explicit to assure high inter-rater reliability and validity.

As evidence containers of assessments and products, e-portfolios have become an effective means of authentically representing student achievement and accomplishments, best work, and goals. In addition, the reflective processes they promote in students are associated with increased motivation and individual responsibility. If students are to become successful, life-long learners who will be prepared to adapt intellectually, socially, and emotionally to the exponential changes in the world and its global economies (Partnership for 21st Century Skills, 2007), they must be engaged in the continuous processes integral to learning. Research on portfolios and e-portfolios as containers of summative and formative evidence of learning is greatly needed to assist educators in assuring that 21st-century knowledge, skills, and dispositions are captured in assessment practices that also enable students to become more autonomous interdependent and successful learners.

The promise of e-portfolios for involving students in every part of the assessment process becomes critical to the "clarion call for a redirection of assessment to its fundamental purpose: The improvement of student achievement, teaching practice, and leadership decision making" (Reeves, 2007, p. 1). Reeves asserted that comprehensive systems of assessment must promote improvement of both instruction and learning: "The most important criterion for educational decision making is evidence and teaching is not merely the act of transmitting knowledge but an inherently collaborative interactive and relationship-based enterprise" (p. 2). In the following review of recent studies of e-portfolios, the focus is on key aspects of portfolio use in classrooms: giving students choices about what to focus on in their learning, opportunities to consider how to provide evidence of their learning (to show what they know), and to reflect and record the learning, the evidence is examined with the culture of evidence lens.

E-Portfolios and Student Reflection

A study of e-portfolios conducted by Chang and Tseng (2009) examined the learning outcomes of junior high school students in a 10-week course on computer animation. The researchers sought to learn if the use of e-portfolios and accompanying reflective processes was associated with their students' achievement and ability to reflect on individual and peer learning related to Web-based presentations. The researchers conducted a review of the literature on portfolio assessment and identified six variables that included the metacognitive processes of reflection, self-assessment, peer assessment, goal setting, and peer interaction. For assessment purposes, they added four variables as course performance outcomes: (1) data gathering, (2) work, (3) continuous improvement, and (4) problem solving.

For this quasi-experimental study, Chang and Tseng (2009) created a self-report questionnaire to query students on the six metacognitive processes that they believed to be inherent in their learning. The questionnaire was used as a pretest–posttest instrument. Thirty students from two classes that met weekly for 2 hours were engaged in this study. After assigning students to an experimental group based on achievement of computer skills acquired in previous semesters, all students were engaged in acquiring the knowledge and skill needed to use PhotoImpact and Dreamweaver to create computer animation projects. Teaching methods remained constant in the comparison and experimental groups, which had the same content, lecture schedule, requirements, submission deadlines, and degree of interaction with teachers and peers. Assessment in the experimental group, however, included portfolio processes that engaged students in reflection, self-assessment, peer assessment, and goal setting. For the ongoing development of the e-portfolio that would include Web pages and PowerPoint presentations, students were engaged in problem solving and data gathering. Only traditional teacher-based assessments of paper-and-pencil testing were used in the comparison group.

Analysis of the pretest and posttest data was conducted at the conclusion of the 10-week course. After excluding the influence of academic achievement and computer achievement, the researchers found that there was a notable difference between the students' performances in the experimental and comparison groups. Chang and Tseng (2009) concluded that the assignment of e-portfolios in the experimental group had a "significant positive influence on students' performances with the most significant indicators related to reflection, followed in order by self-assessment, continuous improvement, goal setting, problem solving, data gathering, work, and peer interaction" (p. 358). An outcome that proved interesting to the researchers was that there was no statistically significant difference between the groups in terms of the peer assessment.

In considering the outcomes of the study, the researchers observed that the e-portfolios showcased students' skills rather than shortcomings, identified their unique learning needs, and encouraged the development of decision-making skills. More research with larger samples of students is needed to substantiate their conclusions. An additional outcome that merits future study regarding peer assessment might be framed around this question: How does teachers' skill and knowledge of promoting a culture of evidence in K–12 classrooms affect student ability to engage in e-portfolio processes that integrate peer review and peer-assessment?

Similar e-portfolio research conducted in Israel (Doppelt, 2007) examined high school students' performance on a culminating project for a course of study called Mechatronics. This high school engineering curriculum encompasses several major subjects related to physics and mathematics, such as civil engineering, computers and electronics, mechanics, and control systems that results in a final graduation project (examination), which is subjected to a calibrated-scoring process conducted by the Israel Ministry of Education.

The purpose of this study was to integrate design-based learning with the authentic assessment processes of e-portfolios to increase success in this high-stakes, project-based examination. It was further expected that students' use of clear criteria and continued documentation of evidence throughout the course would challenge them to think more deeply about the selection of a real-world project that would meet authentic needs, to participate in a showcase of evidence featuring their ongoing consideration of design priorities, to construct a useful product or system using known criteria, and to self-assess their overall project performance before submitting it for external review (Doppelt, 2007).

The researcher conducted a review of the literature on portfolio assessment and creative thinking processes in order to identify elements that would engage the students as designers in their own learning. He believed that the e-portfolio processes of reflection, self-assessment, and goal setting would lead to student choice and voice throughout the course of this high-stakes learning project. Following the literature review, an e-portfolio rubric including the identified elements of the project was developed (creative design process, or CDP). A second instrument, a creative thinking scale (CTS) was designed to measure what the researcher described as four thinking layers that assured success on the Mechatronics project, including student awareness, observation, strategy, and reflection in the design process. A field test of the two instruments was conducted to determine their efficacy in assessing student performance on the projects before they were used in the study.

The intervention had two parts: First, the students were led to document their design projects according to the CTS, and then the projects were assessed using the CDP rubric. A third form of data collection during the intervention was anecdotal record keeping of students' classroom performance and their engagement in the e-portfolio selection, collection, and reflection processes.

The study included 128 high school students from the 10th to 12th grades who were assigned to 57 teams. Students were presented with the descriptive CDP rubric that guided their engagement in the e-portfolio processes and the authentic projects, together with the CTS that guided their thinking to search for, choose, and then design creative and real-world engineering projects. Teachers regularly engaged with the students in online discussions and review of postings in their e-portfolios as a method of assuring continuous engagement and to provide descriptive and evaluative feedback (Davies, 2007). On the examination date, the teams performed a 20-minute presentation in which the instructor directed different questions to each of the individual team members about the project and provided descriptive feedback. Teams were scored on their success in meeting the final project criteria as defined by the Israel Ministry of Education: effective design, construction, and programming of the prototype using the CDP rubric and documenting the entire design process in the e-portfolio. The scoring of the combined e-portfolio (using the CDP rubric) with the design-based thinking scale (CTS) was validated by comparing scores to those that the students achieved in the Israel Ministry of Education external assessment.

The results showed that students in the study had successfully learned how to document the project according to a CDP. It was also learned that e-portfolios supported the teams in achieving high levels of creative thinking while using the CTS. The data revealed that most of the students created portfolios that reflected a high level of achievement in the first domain of the project (purpose, inquiry, solutions, choice, operations, and evaluation) as measured by the CTS. Most importantly, the projects evaluated by the Israel Ministry of Education and the CTS supported the assessment findings of the CTS. All 128 pupils received grades above 80, which exceeded the external examination benchmarks for satisfactory student achievement (matriculation grades in Israel are scaled so that scores above 55 indicate a passing grade; Doppelt, 2007).

This study sought to learn if the use of authentic assessment processes integral to e-portfolios would promote student reflection, engagement, and success in a complex and high-stakes culminating project. The researcher found that student portfolios captured evidence of student reflection that had led to inquiry, problem solving, and self-assessment in the projects. Doppelt (2007) concluded that the use of portfolio assessment assisted students in acquiring the ability to engage in the high-level documentation of the project including how they questioned, analyzed, synthesized, solved problems, created new ideas, designed, and built useful products or systems.

This study offers insight into the potential of student engagement in e-portfolio processes for strengthening complex and creative higher-order thinking while also promoting the self-inspection and documentation of authentic learning. Undoubtedly, this represents a key area in which further study is needed. Questions that arise from the study design and findings might be as follows: How do portfolio tools such as scoring rubrics and checklists presented to students at the outset of high-stakes assessments enable them to set goals, communicate ongoing reflection on progress, and self-assess performances? How do e-portfolios promote communication between students and teachers in a manner that supports and advances key learning or achievement goals? How might e-portfolios in K–12 schools enhance other data collected from standardized tests to provide supplementary evidence of student achievement in critical science, technology, engineering, and mathematics (STEM) learning subject areas? Even more importantly, comparative studies of standardized test results with cumulative K–12 student e-portfolio assessment need to be conducted to learn if together these will have the desired impact of improving student achievement and removing the achievement gap among student populations.

Conclusion and Recommendations for Research

The studies in this review represent classroom-based research on portfolio processes and e-portfolios conducted over the past 10 years. The dearth of empirical research on portfolios—print or digital—presents a challenge to educators and policy makers who wish to consider the inclusion of formative assessment in digital, comprehensive systems of assessment that will capture K–12 student evidence of skills, knowledge, and dispositions. The important purposes, contents, and processes integral to student portfolios and e-portfolios have been presented as still underresearched but important components of CA. In order to ensure that next generation, 21st-century knowledge, dispositions, and abilities are included in K–12 curriculum and instruction, a holistic, systematic approach to collecting and reporting evidence of student achievement is needed.

Due to the inherently subjective nature of showing evidence of complex thinking processes in portfolios, the issues of validity, reliability, and rigor in scoring and calibration of artifacts continue to be critically important to any comprehensive portfolio system of student assessment. An important research goal is to learn how e-portfolios might provide reliable comparative data of student performance at the classroom, district, and state levels. Study of the development of comprehensive systems might promote portfolios as part of a culture of evidence in which classroom-based student performance is captured, scored, calibrated, and integrated with achievement test data.

Metacognitive processes in portfolios are believed to engage students in thinking about learning throughout K–12 curricula. To ensure success in these processes, explicit guidelines for constructing the portfolio that begin with decisions regarding purposes, means of evidence collection, and how students will be placed at the center of the assessment process must be present at each level. The amount of empirical research on these design issues must be increased. The portfolio processes in K–12 student learning, including self-assessment, goal setting, and communication of goal attainment have not been sufficiently researched to provide compelling evidence that such engagements result in students' acceptance of greater responsibility for the acquisition of knowledge, skills, and dispositions aligned with standards of learning.

Districtwide comparative studies are needed to determine the roles of teachers and administrators in the design of portfolio processes that begin with clear purposes and result in student communication through conferences and showcases with parents and key stakeholders in student achievement. Empirical research that measures the effects of e-portfolios in comprehensive systems of assessment on underserved populations who have consistently been left behind is also a moral imperative of researchers.

Research continues to be needed on local and state policies and practices within the formative and summative assessment procedures of e-portfolios to learn how these containers of evidence might ensure that the opportunities for students to revise work following instructional feedback does not result in misleading or inequitable data comparisons. Research on the most efficient systems of establishing the purposes of e-portfolios and means of collection, storage, and showcasing (with assurance of student confidentiality) must be accomplished and results disseminated. Finally, research is needed on the district and school level considerations required for teachers to understand evolving instructional practices that involve new media and technology, including the tools of social media.

It is clear that the emergence of e-portfolios brings with it a new array of researchable questions about how to utilize the media and Internet technology now available in open source (freeware) to assist students in becoming active and motivated learners and creators. Studies are needed that bring attention to the ways in which Internet media tools can provide new formats for clear communication about the progress of student learning to teachers, parents, peers, and others. Studies of successful models of e-portfolios that utilize courseware such as Google Sites, Blackboard, and other emerging Web 2.0 tools will contribute to the knowledge base regarding comprehensive K–12 student assessment. Case study research is also needed to learn about and disseminate universal design standards of these 21st-century learning and assessment tools for schools, districts, and states to implement in a cost- and time-efficient manner. Research on e-portfolios and the portfolio assessment processes they include must expand in order to provide policy makers with clear documentation not only of value-added measures of student achievement but also of the realities of K–12 standards-based curriculum and instruction in order to "place emphasis where it belongs, on teaching and learning, rather than on testing; and do so without sacrificing either the student or the teacher on the altar of accountability" (Meisels, 2003, p. 13).

References

Ainsworth, L. (2007). Common formative assessments: The centerpiece of an integrated standards-based assessment system. In D. Reeves (Ed.), *Ahead of the curve: The power of assessment to transform teaching and learning.* Bloomington, IN: Solution Tree.

Association for Supervision and Curriculum Development Commission on the Whole Child. (2007). *The learning compact redefined: A call to action.* A report of the Commission on the Whole Child. Alexandria, VA: Association for Supervision and Curriculum Development. Retrieved from www.ascd.org/ASCD/pdf/Whole%20Child/WCC%20Learning%20Compact.pdf

Barrett, H. (2007). Researching electronic portfolios and learner engagement: The REFLECT Initiative. *Journal of Adolescent and Adult Literacy, 50*(6), 436–449.

Bass, H. (1993). Let's measure what's worth measuring. *Education Week, 32.* Retrieved from www.edweek.org/ew/articles/1993/10/27/08bass.h13.html

Belanoff, P., & Dickson, M. (1991). *Portfolios: Process and product.* Portsmouth, NH: Boynton/Cook Heinemann.

Belgrad, S. Burke, K., & Fogarty, R. (2008). *The portfolio connection: Student work linked to standards* (3rd ed.). Thousand Oaks, CA: Corwin Press.

Benoit, J., & Yang, H. (1996). A redefinition of portfolio assessment based upon purpose: Findings and implications from a large-scale program. *Journal of Research and Development in Education, 29*(3), 181–191.

Bintz, W. P., & Harste, J. (1994). Where are we going with alternative assessment? And is it really worth our time? *Contemporary Education, 66*(1), 7–12.

Britzman, D. (1989). Who has the floor? Curriculum teaching and the English student teacher's struggle for voice. *Curriculum Inquiry, 19*(2), 143–162.

Brooks, J. G., & Brooks, M. G. (1993). *In search of understanding: The case for constructivist classrooms.* Alexandria, VA: Association of Supervision and Curriculum Development.

Burke, K., Fogarty, R., & Belgrad, S. (1994). *The portfolio connection: The mindful school series.* Palatine, IL: Skylight Publications.

Campos J., & O'Hern, J. (2007). How does using formative assessment empower students in their learning? *Saint Xavier University and Pearson Achievement Solutions,* Chicago.

Carney, J. (2004, April). *Setting an agenda for electronic portfolio research: A framework for evaluating portfolio literature.* Paper presented at the annual meeting of the American Educational Research Association, San Diego, CA. Retrieved from http://it.wce.wwu.edu/carney/Presentations/AERA04/AERAresearchlit.pdf

Carney, J. (2005). *What kind of electronic portfolio research do we need?* Paper presented at the annual meeting of the Society for Information Technology and Teacher Education, Phoenix, AZ.

Carr, J. E, & D. E. Harris. (2001). *Succeeding with standards: Linking curriculum, assessment, and action planning.* Alexandria, VA: Association for Supervision and Curriculum Development.

Chang, C., & Tseng K. (2009). Use and performances of Web-based portfolio assessment. *British Journal of Educational Technology, 40*(2), 358–370.

Costa, A., & Kallick, B. (2008). *Learning and leading with habits of mind: 16 essential characteristics for success.* Alexandria, VA: Association for Supervision and Curriculum Development.

Darling-Hammond, L. (2007, May 7). Evaluating "No Child Left Behind." *The Nation.* Retrieved from www.thenation.com/article/evaluating-no-child-left-behind

Darling-Hammond, L. (2010, May 27). Restoring our schools. *The Nation.* Retrieved from www.thenation.com/article/restoring-our-schools

Davies, A. (2007). Involving students in the classroom assessment process. In D. Reeves (Ed.), *Ahead of the curve: The power of assessment to transform teaching and learning.* Bloomington, IN: Solution Tree.

Doppelt, Y. (2007). Assessing creative thinking in design-based learning. *International Journal of Technology and Design Education, 19,* 55–65.

FairTest. (2011). *2011 Forum on educational accountability recommendations for improving ESEA/NCLB—Summary.* Retrieved from http://fairtest.org/sites/default/files/FEA_2_ Page_ Summary_Recommendations_2011_final.pdf

Fredrick, T. (2009). *Looking in the mirror: Helping adolescents talk more reflectively during portfolio presentations.* Boston: Teachers College Press.

Greenberg, G. (2004). The digital convergence: Extending the portfolio. *Educause Review, 39*(4), 28–36.

Guskey, T. (2007). Using assessments to improve teaching and learning. In D. Reeves (Ed.), *Ahead of the curve: The power of assessment to transform teaching and learning.* Bloomington, IN: Solution Tree.

Hambleton, R., Jaeger, R., Koretz, D., Linn, R., Millman, J., & Phillips, S. (1995, June). Review of the measurement quality of the Kentucky instructional results information system, 1991–1994. Office of Educational Accountability, Kentucky General Assembly.

Hartnell-Young, E. (2007). *Impact study of e-portfolios on learning* (Report). Becta. Retrieved from http://dera.ioe.ac.uk/1469/1/becta_2007_eportfolios_report.pdf

Herman, J., Aschbacher, P., & Winters, L. (1992). *Setting criteria. A practical guide to alternative assessment* (pp. 44–79). Alexandria, VA: Association for Supervision and Curriculum Development.

High Tech High. (2012). *Connectivity at High Tech High.* Retrieved from www.whatkidscando.org/archives/portfoliosmallschools/HTH/portfolios.html

Izumi, L. (1999). *Developing and implementing academic standards.* Pacific Research Institute. Retrieved from www.pacificresearch.org/publications/id.240/pub_detail.asp

Johnston, P. H. (1989). Constructive evaluation and the improvement of teaching and learning. *Instructors College Record, 90*(4), 509–528.

Koretz, D. (2009, December). *Some implications of current policy for educational measurement.* Center for K–12 Assessment and Performance Management. Retrieved from www.k12center.org/rsc/pdf/ExploratorySeminarCompendium.pdf

Koretz, D., McCaffrey, D., Klein, S., Bell, R., & Stecher, B. (1994). *The reliability of scores from the 1992 Vermont Portfolio Assessment Program: Interim report.* Santa Monica, CA: RAND Corporation. Retrieved from www.rand.org/pubs/drafts/DRU159

McMillan, J. H., Cohen, J., Abrams, L. M., Cauley, K., Pannozzo, G., & Hearn, J. (2010). *Understanding secondary teachers' formative assessment practices and their relationship to student motivation.* (ERIC Document Reproduction Service No. ED507712)

McMillan, J. H., & Hearn, J. (2008). Student self-assessment: The key to stronger student motivation and higher achievement. *Educational Horizons, 87,* 40–49.

Meisels, S. (2003). Impact of instructional assessment on elementary children's achievement. *Education Policy Analysis Archives, 11*(9). Retrieved from http://epaa.asu.edu/ojs/article/view/237/363

Millett, C., Payne, D., Dwyer, C., Stickler, L., & Aiexiou, J. (2008). *A culture of evidence: An evidence-centered approach to accountability for student learning outcomes.* Princeton, NJ: Educational Testing Service.

National Governors Association Center for Best Practices and the Council of Chief State School Officers. (2010). *The Common Core State Standards Initiative.* Retrieved from www.corestandards.org/news

North Carolina State Board of Education. (2010). *Electronic portfolio system report and recommendations to the North Carolina State Board of Education.* Retrieved from www.ncpublicschools.org/docs/acre/publications/2010/publications/201003 10-01.pdf

North Central Regional Educational Laboratory & the Metiri Group. (2003). *enGauge 21st century skills: Literacy in the digital age.* Naperville, IL: Author. Retrieved from http://pict.sdsu.edu/engauge21st.pdf

Partnership for 21st Century Skills. (2007). *21st Century Skills Assessment: A partnership for 21st century skills e-paper.* Retrieved from www.vtsbdc.org/assets/files/21st_century_skills_asessment.pdf

Paulson, F. L., Paulson, P. R., & Meyer, C. A. (1991). What makes a portfolio a portfolio? *Educational Leadership, 58*(5), 60–63.

Ravitch, D. (2010). *The death and life of the great American school system: How testing and choice are undermining education.* New York: Basic Books

Reeves, D. (2007). *Ahead of the curve: The power of assessment to transform teaching and learning.* Bloomington, IN: Solution Tree.

Rolheiser, C. (1998). Self-evaluation . . . Helping students get better at it! Ajax, Ontario, Canada: VisuTronx.

Rolheiser, C., & Ross, J. (2001). *Student self-evaluation: What research says and what practice shows.* Retrieved from www.cdl.org/resource-library/articles/self_eval.php

The Secretary's Commission on Achieving Necessary Skills. (1991). *What work requires of schools: A SCANS report for America 2000.* Washington, DC: U.S. Department of Labor. Retrieved from www.gsn.org/web/_shared/SCANS2000.pdf

Shepard, L. A. (2000). The role of assessment in a learning culture. *Educational Researcher, 29*(7), 4–14.

The Smarter Balanced Assessment Consortium. (2011, Spring). An overview of the designs of the PARCC and SMARTER balanced assessment systems. *The Center for K–12 Assessment and Performance Management at ETS,* Version 3. Retrieved from www.k12center.org/publications/all.html

Steinkruger, C. (2007). Do students progress if they self-assess? A study in small-group work Unpublished masters thesis, University of Nebraska, Lincoln.

Stiggins, R. (1994). *Student-centered classroom assessment.* New York: Merrill.

Stiggins, R. (2007). Assessment for learning: An essential foundation for productive instruction. In D. Reeves (Ed.), *Ahead of the curve: The power of assessment to transform teaching and learning.* Bloomington, IN: Solution Tree.

Tomlinson, C. A., & Allan, S. D. (2000). *Leadership for differentiating schools and classrooms.* Alexandria, VA: Association for Supervision and Curriculum Development.

U.S. Department of Education. (2002). *No Child Left Behind Act of 2001* (Title I Paraprofessionals: Draft Non-Regulatory Guidance). Washington, DC: U.S. Department of Education, Office of Elementary and Secondary Education.

U.S. Department of Education GOALS 2000: Educate America Act. (1994). Retrieved from www2.ed.gov/legislation/GOALS2000/TheAct/index.html

Wall, K., Higgins, S., Miller, J., & Packard, N. (2006). Developing digital portfolios: Investigating how digital portfolios can facilitate pupil talk about learning. *Technology, Pedagogy and Education, 15*(3), 261–273.

Wiggins, G. P. (1993). *Assessing student performance.* San Francisco: Jossey-Bass.

Wolf, D. (1990). Assessment as an episode of learning. In R. Bennett & W. Ward (Eds.), *Construction vs. voice in cognitive measurement,* Hillsdale, NJ: Lawrence Erlbaum.

Yancey, K. (2009, Winter). Electronic portfolios a decade into the twenty-first century: What we know; what we need to know. *Association of American Colleges and Universities, 11*(1), 28–32.

Yancey, K., & Weiser, I. (1997). *Situating portfolios: Four perspectives.* Logan: Utah State University Press.

20

Understanding and Assessing the Social–Emotional Attributes of Classrooms[1]

Susan E. Rivers

Carolin Hagelskamp

Marc A. Brackett

The social enterprise of teaching and learning comes to life in the multitude of daily interactions between and among teachers and students, both within and outside of the classroom. Myriad emotions accompany these interactions. For example, questions may be asked with enthusiasm or apathy, responses given with zeal or anxiety, participation encouraged or dismissed, and ideas shared with passion and trust or withheld for fear of ridicule. Every former and current student will recognize the many emotions that comprise the classroom experience—embarrassment, enjoyment, curiosity, boredom, despair, and the list goes on.

Students' social–emotional experiences in the classroom have been linked to a range of outcomes, including grades, study habits, and discipline records (Hamre & Pianta, 2001), as well as students' mental health and achievement motivations (Roeser, Eccles, & Sameroff, 2000) and the quality of teaching (e.g., Juvonen, Wang, & Espinoza, 2011; Ladd, Birch, & Buhs, 1999; Wang, Haertel, & Walberg, 1997). There is increasing recognition at the local, state, and federal level in the United States that schools must meet the social–emotional needs of children and youth for effective teaching and learning to take place (Collaborative for Academic, Social, and Emotional Learning [CASEL], 2012). Under the umbrella term *social and emotional learning* (SEL), schools are increasingly implementing schoolwide policies and curricula that aim to foster caring relationships

[1]Acknowledgment: The writing of this chapter was supported in part by grants awarded to the first and third authors from the William T. Grant Foundation (#s 8364 and 180276) and the NoVo Foundation.

between teachers and students, cooperation, and conflict reduction among students; a greater sense of safety in schools; and specifically, the development of social–emotional skills in students and teachers (Greenberg et al., 2003; Zins, Bloodworth, Weissberg, & Walberg, 2004). SEL programming is an educational strategy designed to foster the acquisition of social–emotional skills, such as social and self-awareness, emotion regulation, responsible decision making and problem solving, and relationship management (Greenberg et al., 2003). To this end, SEL programs aim to enhance the social–emotional climate of a classroom or an entire school. SEL programs also seek to improve academic outcomes for children and youth by creating learning environments that meet their developmental needs, including feelings of belonging, safety, and community and thus provide ideal conditions for academic success (Becker & Luthar, 2002; Catalano, Berglund, Ryan, Lonczek, & Hawkins, 2004).

A number of studies, including large-scale experimental studies, show that targeted SEL interventions can improve the social–emotional attributes of classrooms and facilitate students' social–emotional and academic well-being (e.g., Brown, Jones, LaRusso, & Aber, 2010; Raver et al., 2008; Rivers, Brackett, Reyes, Elbertson, & Salovey, in press-a). Further, a meta-analysis of 213 studies evaluating SEL programming efforts demonstrates benefits to youth across grade levels (elementary through high school) and across urban, suburban, and rural schools in the United States, with primary benefits including increases in students' social–emotional skills (effects sizes ranged from 0.12 to 0.87), improvements in students' prosocial attitudes and behavior (effects sizes ranged from 0.17 to 0.26), mental health (effect sizes ranged from 0.21 to 0.27), and improved academic performance, including an 11-percentile-point gain in achievement as assessed through report card grades and test scores (Durlak, Weissberg, Dymnicki, Taylor, & Schellinger, 2011).

The goal of this chapter is to facilitate the ability of researchers and policy makers to understand, study, and monitor what we call the *social–emotional attributes* of classrooms, given the burgeoning evidence that these attributes matter for student outcomes and are malleable to systematic interventions. The chapter opens with a definition of the measurable components of the social–emotional attributes of classrooms and briefly summarizes empirical evidence of the importance of those attributes for both student outcomes and targeted interventions. The next major section of the chapter discusses methodological approaches to studying social–emotional attributes of classrooms and reviews assessment tools currently available for measuring these classroom attributes. We conclude the chapter with a discussion of directions for future research. Throughout the chapter, we use the term *characteristics* to refer to a classroom's social–emotional attributes and to describe adaptive and maladaptive classroom experiences.

Understanding the Social–Emotional Attributes of Classrooms

Figure 20.1 presents a conceptual model of the social–emotional attributes of classrooms. The model distinguishes between three distinct and measurable attributes: (1) behavioral, (2) affective, and (3) skill-based. The behavioral attributes of classrooms are reflected in the social–emotional characteristics of *interactions* among students and between students and teachers. The affective attributes are the *feelings* students and teachers have for each other. The skill-based attributes are the constellation of social–emotional *skills* in both students and teachers. These skills that students and teachers bring into and develop in the classroom comprise a classroom's basic social–emotional resource.

The model further contextualizes the social–emotional attributes of classrooms by highlighting the potential effects of targeted programs and policies on classrooms' social–emotional characteristics and recognizing the influence of social–emotional attributes of classrooms on students' academic outcomes and social–emotional development. As such, our model is complementary to a number of other recently proposed models of classroom climate (e.g., Jennings & Greenberg, 2009; Jones, Brown, & Aber, 2008; Pianta & Allen, 2008). These other models provide important conceptualizations of classroom quality that also include instructional processes and classroom management, both of which are beyond the scope of this chapter.

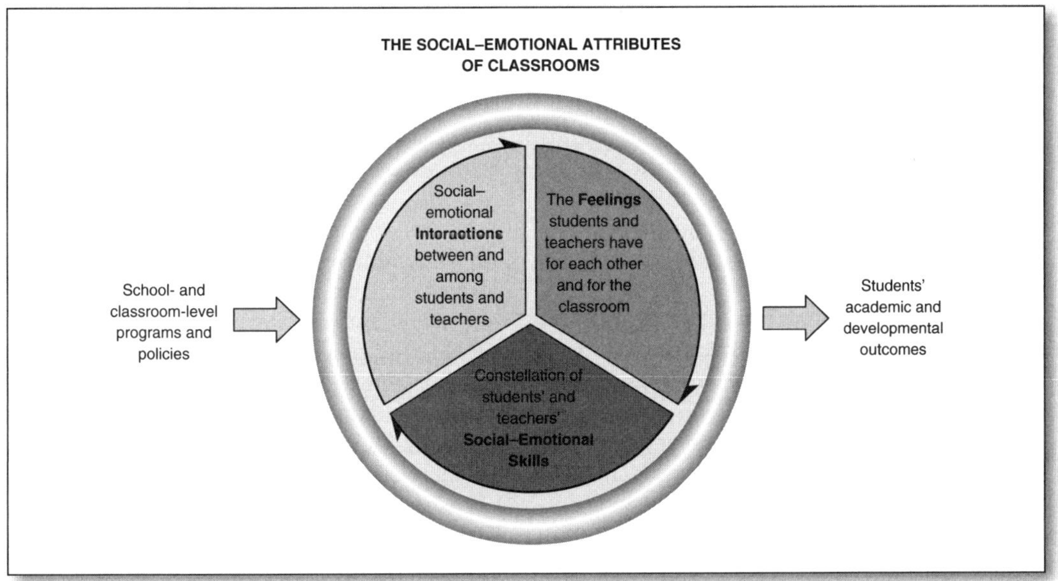

Figure 20.1 Conceptual Model of Classroom Social–Emotional Attributes and Their Relationship to School- and Classroom-Level Programs and Policies and to Students' Outcomes

In this section, we first describe the three social–emotional attributes of classrooms (behavioral, affective, and skill-based) within the context of what might be considered high quality classrooms and then review the literature linking each to student outcomes. As such, we hope to make the case that these classroom-level variables are among the determinants of student performance and well-being and also are indicators by which to measure the effectiveness of intervention programs. Specifically, this necessarily brief review is intended to provide a framework for the detailed methodological part of the chapter.

Interactions Between and Among Teachers and Students

Classroom interactions refer to the social exchanges between and among the persons inhabiting the classroom at any given time. The social–emotional interactions in classrooms may be classified as high quality when they reflect frequent caring, supportive, and cooperative exchanges and a low occurrence or absence of interactions that are hostile, discouraging, and dismissive (Catalano, Hawkins, Berglund, Pollard, & Arthur, 2002; Jones et al., 2008; National Research Council [NRC] & Institute of Medicine, 2002; Pianta & Allen, 2008; Tseng & Seidman, 2007). Studies of these interactions highlight common behaviors that may be evident in high quality social–emotional interactions. Among students, these high quality social–emotional interactions may include sharing of materials; helping each other with lessons; or encouraging each other by listening attentively, clapping, smiling, or asking questions. Positive interactions also are reflected in the absence of interrupting, turning away while someone else is speaking, or mockingly laughing at each other. Positive interactions between teachers and students are observable when teachers include students in decision-making processes (e.g., a teacher asks students to help write a rule for the classroom or decide which book to read); provide students with opportunities to share their work, feelings, and experiences; listen actively; and respond encouragingly when students talk. Additional behaviors that may reflect high quality social–emotional interactions include students and teachers showing mutual respect for each other (e.g., listening when the other is speaking, asking each other for reactions and opinions), responding to each other in constructive ways (e.g., providing suggestions for improvement while being sensitive to others' feelings and needs), and sharing experiences from outside the classroom (e.g., both teachers and students sharing appropriate personal stories relevant to the curriculum).

Although the majority of the research linking the social–emotional characteristics of classroom interactions to students' academic outcomes is correlational, there is consistency in the findings across studies. When supportive and cooperative interactions in classrooms are the behavioral norm and when hostility and disrespect are absent, students report having higher self-esteem and feeling more intellectually competent and self-efficacious. They also show greater academic motivation and report liking school more (Baker, 1999; Barth, Dunlap, Dane, Lochman, & Wells, 2004; Hughes & Kwok, 2006). Moreover, in high quality classrooms, students are observed to participate more, are more likely to complete tasks (Anderson, Hamilton, & Hattie, 2004), have more focused attention (Patrick, Ryan, & Kaplan, 2007), have fewer conduct problems (Brackett, Reyes, Rivers, Elbertson, & Salovey, 2011), and perform better academically (Haertel, Walberg, & Haertel, 1981). In contrast, friction and a lack of cohesion in the classroom are associated with students disconnecting from school and exhibiting greater conduct problems over time (Loukas & Robinson, 2004). In classrooms with more negative social–emotional interactions, students also report a lack of nurturance and encouragement from teachers and are less motivated to participate and follow instructions in class (Wentzel, 2002).

Feelings of Students and Teachers

The feelings of students and teachers capture the subjective and experiential attributes of a classroom. A classroom would be considered to have positive social–emotional qualities when students feel liked, appreciated, and supported by their peers (Baker, Dilly, Aupperlee, & Patil, 2003) and when there are feelings of mutual trust and respect between students and teachers (Ryan & Patrick, 2001). Moreover, in these classrooms, students do not worry about being physically harmed, bullied, or ridiculed. Instead, they experience procedures, rules, and interactions as fair (Ryan & Patrick, 2001). Consequently, students feel that they belong to and enjoy being part of the class. In classrooms with positive social–emotional attributes, teachers, too, feel connected to their students: They feel respected, inspired, and appreciated, and both teachers and students express emotions and humor (Sutton & Wheatley, 2003).

In alignment with the findings on the quality of social–emotional interactions, the way students and teachers feel about their relationships with each other also has been associated with students' academic performance and social–emotional development. This research is largely correlational, preventing causal inferences, but the results are consistent across studies. Compared to students who report feeling rejected and lonely in the classroom, students who feel supported by, connected to, and liked by their peers and their teachers do better in school and are more engaged in learning (Flook, Repetti, & Ullman, 2005; Furrer & Skinner, 2003; Goh, Young, & Fraser, 1995; Haertel et al., 1981; Patrick et al., 2007). Moreover, students who feel a sense of connection to and belonging in the classroom behave more cooperatively and are more likely to abide by classroom norms and values (Solomon, Watson, Battistich, & Schaps, 1996).

Teachers' emotional experiences in the classroom have been associated with their own well-being and performance and their students' performance. Teachers who report feeling generally positive in the classroom also are more motivated, teach more effectively, and are more sensitive toward student needs (Klusmann, Kunter, Trautwein, Lüdtke, & Baumert, 2008). Moreover, their students feel more connected to their school and more engaged in their work (Frenzel, Goetz, Lüdtke, Pekrun, & Sutton, 2009; Solomon et al., 1996). In contrast, when teachers report feeling burned out, stressed, and unhappy about their relationships with students, they also are less effective in keeping classrooms organized, and their students are less motivated in their classes (Klusmann et al., 2008). Teachers report that their feelings of joy and despair in the classroom often originate in the quality of their interactions with students (Sutton & Wheatley, 2003).

Social–Emotional Skills of Teachers and Students

A classroom's unique constellation of social–emotional skills constitutes a third measurable component of its social–emotional attributes. Social–emotional skills refer to the ability to recognize and understand one's own emotional state, to express and regulate one's emotions appropriately, and to show empathy and understanding for the feelings of others (Denham, 1998; Mayer & Salovey, 1997; Saarni, 1999; Salovey & Mayer, 1990). Social–emotional skills include the ability to resolve conflict, recognize social cues, cooperate with others, and solve social problems. These skills also encompass the ability to think about issues from multiple perspectives, including taking into account the point of view of others (Selman, 1981).

Students and teachers come to the classroom with a unique set of social–emotional skills and thus are differentially prepared to cultivate and engage in cooperative and respectful interactions and regulate their emotional responses to their classroom experiences. Social–emotional skills may be considered the building blocks for the types of interactions in which students and teachers engage and for the feelings they experience across the myriad interactions that transpire (Brackett & Katulak, 2006; Brackett, Palomera Martin, Mojsa, Reyes, & Salovey, 2010). The social–emotional skills of teachers are a particularly important asset for the overall social–emotional quality of a classroom. Teachers orchestrate the majority of interactions in the traditional classroom and can do this in ways that promote positive social–emotional interactions and feelings. Teachers with well-developed or sophisticated social–emotional skills should be able to recognize and respond well to students' needs, provide opportunities for students to interact in supportive and cooperative ways, and include students who may be otherwise rejected in less supportive environments (Pianta, 1999). For example, teachers who reported that they were more skilled at recognizing, understanding, and regulating emotions were observed to have classrooms that were more positive and emotionally supportive than did teachers who reported being less skilled in these areas (Brown et al., 2010).

Emotion regulation ability among teachers has been associated positively with their job satisfaction and feelings of personal accomplishment (Brackett et al., 2010). Moreover, teachers with greater skill in regulating their emotions also reported greater support from their principals. Although the causal direction for these relationships remains unknown, these findings suggest that teachers with greater emotion skills create positive interactions and generate positive feelings, which make their principals more supportive.

The social–emotional skills of teachers may be particularly important in difficult environments. For example, teachers who are better able to regulate their emotions may be better at reducing the influence of school-level pressures on their interactions with students in the classroom (Brackett & Katulak, 2006). Moreover, teachers who are attuned to the emotional lives of their students may be more likely to form caring and supportive relationships with them, which may be especially impactful for students from socially disadvantaged backgrounds (O'Connor & McCartney, 2007; Resnick et al., 1997)

Students' social–emotional skills impact the social–emotional quality of the classroom, as well as their own academic and social–emotional developmental outcomes. Across different age groups and over time, students' social–emotional skills, measured through both informant and self-reports as well as skills-based tests, are associated with greater academic motivation, greater engagement, and higher grades (Gil-Olarte Márquez, Palomera Martin, & Brackett, 2006; Rivers et al., in press-b; Valiente, Lemery-Chalfant, & Castro, 2007; Zins et al., 2004). The relationship between social–emotional skills and academic outcomes remains even after controlling for general intelligence, although there is overlap between these constructs (Mayer, Salovey, & Caruso, 2002; Mestre, Lopes, Salovey, & Gil-Olarte Márquez, 2006; see also Rivers, Brackett, & Salovey, 2008, for a review). Students who score higher on skills-based tests of emotional skills report enjoying school and liking their teachers more. Teachers also assess these students as having fewer learning and attention problems than students who score lower on emotional skills (Rivers et al., in press-b). Further, students with better social–emotional skills have an easier time forming friendships and are liked more by adults and peers (Izard et al., 2001; Rubin, Bukowski, & Parker, 2006).

Given these associations, it is expected that classrooms with a higher proportion of students with better social–emotional skills have more caring, supportive, productive, and successful learning environments, resulting in better outcomes for more students. In contrast, classrooms with a higher proportion of students who have less developed social–emotional skills may need extra resources to foster academic success. We did not identify any studies to date that have tested these hypotheses, but findings from research testing SEL interventions provide initial evidence for these ideas (e.g., Brown et al., 2010; Durlak et al., 2011; Raver et al., 2008; Rivers et al., in press-a).

Summary of Social–Emotional Attributes of Classrooms

We defined three measurable characteristics of classrooms that together comprise our model of classroom social–emotional attributes, depicted in Figure 20.1. These attributes are the *social–emotional characteristics of interactions* between and among teachers and students, the *feelings* students and teachers have for each other and the classroom, and the constellation of *social–emotional skills* that students and teachers bring into the classroom. We described empirical evidence linking each attribute to important student outcomes. Having defined the three social–emotional attributes of classrooms, we now turn to their measurement in the next sections, focusing first on methodological approaches to assessments and then to specific measurement tools.

Methodological Approaches to Assessing the Social–Emotional Attributes of Classrooms

The classroom is a setting comprised of its participants—teachers and students—as well as its physical attributes, including its furniture and their spatial arrangement and its resources (books, technology, writing utensils, etc.). Strategies to assess the classroom typically include observations and reports from students, teachers, or both, through surveys, tests, or interviews. To measure the social–emotional attributes of the classroom, a decision must be made as to which level or unit of analysis to examine. Among the levels of analysis from which to choose are the overall classroom itself, one or more students, the teacher, or some combination of these. The level of analysis will drive the selection of instruments and analytical techniques, as well as the conclusions drawn from the data.

When classrooms are the unit of analysis, the assessments typically include observations of the classroom, aggregates of student responses to a survey about the classroom (i.e., the average of responses across the group of students), or teacher reports. Research questions and conclusions would be drawn about how the climate of the classroom is related to, for example, students' grades (Reyes, Brackett, Rivers, White, & Salovey, in press) or their behavior in the classroom (Brackett et al., 2011). When students are the unit of analysis, individual students' perceptions of a classroom attribute are assessed to understand, perhaps, the relationship between each student's feelings in the classroom and that student's academic performance. This may lead to findings such as students who rate their classrooms high in mutual respect also are more motivated and engaged (e.g., Ryan & Patrick, 2001).

Whether the classroom or the student is selected as the level of analysis is dependent upon the research question and, in many cases, the resources available for the assessments and analyses. Below, we briefly discuss methodological and analytic issues that arise when classrooms make up the unit of analysis, followed by a discussion on issues when students are the unit of analysis. More thorough discussions of the statistical issues concerning the assessment and analysis of classroom-level characteristics can be found elsewhere (Raudenbush & Bryk, 2002; Raudenbush & Sadoff, 2008).

Classroom-Level Assessments

By definition, the social–emotional attributes of classrooms are a classroom-level characteristic. As such, they are considered to (1) exist independently of the experience, feelings, and skill set of any one student or teacher (e.g., La Paro, Rimm-Kaufman, & Pianta, 2006); (2) exert a contextual influence on the personal experiences, perceptions, and skills of students (e.g., Bronfenbrenner, 1979); and (3) be relatively stable phenomena, as teachers and students develop a regular rhythm to their interactions over time (e.g., Hamre, Mashburn, Pianta, Locasle-Crouch, & La Paro, 2006; Jones et al., 2008; Kontos & Wilcox-Herzog, 1997; Meehan, Hughes, & Cavell, 2003). This means that, despite some daily variations, classrooms can be distinguished from each other by a general pattern of interactions, feelings, and skills (e.g., Brackett et al., 2011; Hamre, Pianta, Mashburn,

& Downer, 2007) and, presumably, by differences in the constellation of social–emotional skills of teachers (e.g., Brackett et al., 2010) and maybe even the skills of the students. Assessing social–emotional attributes at the classroom level is therefore important when the goal is to (1) compare classrooms to each other; (2) understand the relative impact of classrooms' social emotional attributes on individual or subgroups of students independently of (or interacting with) these students' personal views, skills, or demographic characteristics; or (3) study differences in the impact of interventions on the classroom.

Reliably and validly assessing social–emotional attributes as a classroom-level phenomenon can require considerable resources. For example, to effectively utilize students' perspectives as a measure of classroom social–emotional attributes, data need to be collected from representative samples of students from each classroom. Any single student's opinion or skill set contributes to the overall assessment, but in isolation it would not be considered a valid assessment of the classroom. Collectively, the perspectives and skills of many students from one classroom provide substantively and statistically valuable information that can be used in a number of interesting ways to be discussed later in the chapter. Similarly, if independent observers assess interaction data, they need to collect observational data from each classroom over multiple occasions, and they need to be trained and monitored to ensure the reliability of their ratings (see below for more detail). Moreover, an ample number of classrooms will be required in order to test for differences between them. Bloom (2005) and Raudenbush, Martinez, and Spybrook (2007) explored issues related to power to test effects at the setting level.

Individual-Level Assessments

Even though classroom social–emotional attributes are, by definition, a characteristic of the classroom, there are research questions and practical reasons that may lead one to decide to use responses from individual students or teachers. For example, there may be an interest in comparing the social–emotional experiences of individual students in a classroom, monitoring how changes in an individual student's social–emotional experiences relate to academic outcomes, or examining differential impacts of school-level programs and policies on individual students. Moreover, researchers may decide to use students' perceptions as a proxy for the classroom's social–emotional attributes. This may occur when it is not feasible to create a measure that is reliable at the classroom level, which would require the collection of data from a representative and sufficiently large sample of students and classrooms. What constitutes a sufficiently large sample depends on a number of statistical factors and varies between study designs (Raudenbush & Bryk, 2002; Snijders & Bosker, 1993).

Student Versus Teacher Versus Observer Assessments

Another important question to consider when assessing the social–emotional attributes of classrooms is whether to collect data from students, teachers, independent observers, or, ideally, a combination of these sources. Before reviewing examples from each type of measurement, we outline in this section the value and analytic possibilities of data collected from each source. We also discuss some of the limitations of each data source and suggest ways in which the data can be combined across the three sources.

Student Perspectives

Students can provide a firsthand perspective on what happens in the classroom, including their own personal interactions, feelings, and observations of other students and the teachers in the classroom. However, students may be limited in their ability to reflect or report on some classroom processes; researchers should consider this when selecting measures assessing student perspectives.

To obtain a classroom-level assessment of social–emotional attributes from students' reports, researchers typically aggregate the reports of a representative sample of students from the same classroom. Aggregating responses results in several numerical indicators of classroom social–emotional attributes. By way of example, an aggregated response for classroom interactions may reflect the average frequency with which students, as a class, see themselves helping each other and may reflect the average positivity and negativity of feelings felt by students in the classroom. Averaging the scores from a measure that assesses each student's social–emotional skills can allow for comparisons to other classrooms. The classroom mean also can be used to examine an individual student's deviance from the average experience in the classroom and its influence on outcomes for that student (e.g., Mikami, Lerner, & Lun, 2010). For example, students who act aggressively are less likely to experience social rejection in classrooms where aggressive behaviors are common than in classrooms where aggressive behaviors are not the norm (Sentse, Scholte, Salmivalli, & Voeten, 2007).

Although one purpose of a reliable measure is to capture differences between classrooms and not necessarily differences between students within a classroom, a potentially interesting variance may be explored in student reports within the same classroom (Jones et al., 2008; Shinn, 1990). This is an underutilized technique. For example, the variance between students may reflect the extent to which students vary in their perceptions of helping behaviors in the classroom, the extent to which students feel similarly positive or negative about the classroom, or an estimation of the range of social–emotional skills present in the classroom. Further, when examining variability between classrooms, researchers can examine differences between classrooms in which all students feel interested most of the time and those in which some students feel always interested while others are mostly bored. Classrooms may have the same average interest score but different score distributions. Such variability might bring forth this question: Does variability in student ratings of the classroom predict variability in individual student outcomes, independent of each student's unique experiences? Looking at patterns of variability across classrooms allows for the exploration of questions such as these. Looking at these patterns over time may help to identify when an intervention is needed. For example, discontinuity in students' feelings may indicate the need for teachers to make efforts to target the needs of subgroups of students.

Teacher Perspectives

Teachers are experts of the classroom dynamics they observe, manage, and cocreate on a daily basis. They can offer an intimate and unique perspective on the relationships between students in their classroom, as well as their relationship with each student. Teachers may even be able to make global, evaluative statements about a classroom over time. Many teachers also can contrast their experiences in one classroom with what they have experienced in other classes and over time. Assessing the classroom climate through the eyes of teachers thus adds not only personal experience but also a professional opinion to the data pool.

Nonetheless, because teachers are part of the classroom and often set the social–emotional tone with their behaviors, their reports are subject to response biases. A number of studies have found associations between teachers' evaluation of students' behaviors and their demographic characteristics (i.e., age, gender, and ethnicity) (e.g., Pigott & Cowen, 2000; Saft & Pianta, 2001; Thomas, Coard, Stevenson, Bentley, & Zamel, 2009). For example, there is evidence that teachers rate more positively the behavior and social–emotional competencies of students who are younger, female, and White (Pigott & Cowen, 2000). Students' age and ethnicity, as well as the congruence in teacher and student ethnicity, also have been related to teachers' ratings of their relationship with individual students (Saft & Pianta, 2001). Many other publications discuss biases in teachers' perceptions of prosocial and aggressive behaviors in students (Gregory & Weinstein, 2008; Skiba & Rausch, 2006; Skiba et al., 2008; Thomas et al., 2009). It is beyond the scope of this chapter to discuss the extent to which correlations in teachers' judgments and student demographics reflect biases or are indications of differential developmental trajectories across groups of students. Yet the possibility of systematic bias is important to consider with teacher data, especially when a study does not allow comparisons of two or more teachers' perspectives on the same class or on the same student or group of students.

Keeping the potential for bias in mind, teacher data can be used in at least two ways to create classroom-level scores of social–emotional attributes. First, teachers can report on their relationship with each student or rate the social–emotional skills of each student. When teacher reports are collected for a representative sample of students in the classroom, classroom-level means and variances can be calculated. Second, teachers can rate the quality of interactions in the classroom in general or report on their own feelings in a specific class. Because all students in the classroom are exposed to the teacher, a teacher's report may function as a classroom-level characteristic, despite its being a single indicator (Jones et al., 2008).

Combining teacher and student data may be an optimal approach for understanding the classroom setting. These data, though overlapping to some extent, will usually not be redundant. For example, teachers tend to rate the classroom environment more positively than students, particularly with regard to the quality of student-teacher relationships (Fisher & Fraser, 1983; Fraser, 1998). Teachers and students agree most when rating teachers in terms of their *strictness* and *leadership* but are in least agreement when evaluating teachers on *understanding* and *friendliness* (Wubbels, Brekelmans, & Hermans, 1987). These discrepancies may be useful to attempts to understand and monitor the dynamics of a specific classroom. Researchers examining data from both students and teachers gain a richer and perhaps more valid assessment of a classroom's social–emotional attributes and also can examine which points of view are either more predictive of individual outcomes over time (Fraser, 1982a) or useful indicators of the impact of an intervention (e.g., Rivers et al., in press-a).

Independent Observer Perspectives

Independent observers, who may be researchers or school personnel, can observe and rate the quality of interactions as well as the social–emotional skills of the teacher and of individual students. Four important study design issues should be considered when collecting observational data on a classroom's social–emotional attributes. First, to reduce potential bias, the observations should be conducted by independent or noninvested observers who are not closely affiliated with the school and who have been systematically trained and routinely monitored using a validated assessment tool. Independent observers are better able to judge the quality of specific behaviors, interactions, or other elements of the classroom at a specific moment, independent of the larger social context and of the long-term relationships they represent and in reference to predetermined, research-based criteria.

Second, classrooms need to be observed using time-sampling techniques so that they are systematically sampled to reflect or balance variations in behaviors and interactions that occur over the course of a day (morning versus afternoon), the week (Monday versus Friday), or the year (fall versus spring; e.g., Chomat-Mooney et al., 2008; Hamre, Pianta, & Chomat-Mooney, 2009). Variations related to the timing of lessons sampled for observation should be considered when examining the quality of one specific classroom over time, as well as when the research requires the comparison of multiple classrooms. If it is not feasible to sample lessons to represent all possible time frames then, at a minimum, lessons should be sampled at comparable time points.

Third, the mode by which classrooms are observed—live or filmed observation—should be determined. Live coding involves placing trained observers in the classroom as the lesson takes place and coding the behaviors in real time. Alternatively, trained observers can code filmed observations of classrooms at a later time. The advantages of using live observers are that data is available in real time and no other equipment (cameras, tripods, etc.) is required. The disadvantage is that unless the researchers also film the lesson they attend there are no records available for reliability checks and additional coding, aside from the observers' original notes and ratings. If a study has resources sufficient to place two observers in all classrooms at a time, their agreement can be used as a reliability check. The advantage of filming classrooms is that the data are available for renewed coding and reliability checks. However, film may never capture everything that is going on in a classroom, while a live observer may more flexibly observe different parts of the room during an observation cycle. For further discussions on logistical considerations related to conducting classroom observations for research, see Hamre et al. (2009).

Fourth, several studies have identified coder effects as a significant source of variability in observational ratings (Chomat-Mooney et al., 2008; Mashburn, Downer, Rivers, Brackett, & Martinez, in press). Although little is known about what specifically affects the reliability of coders of classroom observations, a number of biases are imaginable, each linked to personality, experience with a setting, or education level. In our own work, we found that daily variations in emotional states affected trained coders' ratings of behaviors observed in videotapes of classroom sessions as more or less positive (Floman,

Hagelskamp, Brackett, & Rivers, 2012). To eliminate coder biases as much as possible—whether doing live observations or filming—sufficient training and reliability checks need to be included in the timeline and budget of research projects. Moreover, it is important that observers are assigned randomly to the classrooms and lessons they are coding.

Specific Measures to Assess the Social–Emotional Attributes of Classrooms

The previous section discussed methodological approaches for studying the social–emotional attributes of classrooms and addressed many of the basic preliminary questions researchers should consider before data collection. In this section, we present some examples of measurement tools with a focus on student reports, teacher reports, and observational assessments of classroom interactions; the feelings students have about their relationship to each other and to their teacher; and students' social–emotional skills. For each attribute, we describe tools that have been shown to possess both adequate reliability and be predictive of student outcomes. We also focus primarily on the assessment of students' feelings and social–emotional skills and do not include measures that assess these qualities for teachers. We refer readers interested in the latter to other publications (e.g., Brackett et al., 2011; Greene, Abidin, & Kmetz, 1997; Maslach, Jackson, & Leiter, 1996; Sutton & Wheatley, 2003). Fraser (1998) and Gettinger, Schienebeck, Seigel, and Vollmer (2011) are additional resources for measures to assess the social–emotional attributes of classrooms.

Measures to Assess Classroom Interactions: Student Perspectives

Survey Measures

Assessments of students' social–emotional experiences of the classroom date back 50 years. Two broad categories of scales are available: (1) those that assess an individual student's perspective on interactions in the classroom in general (*general classroom judgments*) and (2) those that elicit a student's evaluations of his or her personal relationships and interactions with other students and teachers (*personalized classroom judgments*). The former scales tend to include language about the class, students in the class, or the teacher in the class. The latter scales include first-person language such as "I participate" or "the teacher listens to me."

Among the scales that assess general classroom judgments are two independently developed surveys, both designed to comprehensively capture the experiences of secondary school students in the environments in which they learn and work: the Learning Environment Inventory (LEI) (Fraser, Anderson, & Walberg, 1982; Walberg & Anderson, 1968) and the Classroom Environment Scale (CES) (Moos & Trickett, 1974). Both assessments consist of multiple dimensions representing different aspects of the classroom environment, including social–emotional characteristics of interactions among and between students and the teacher. On the LEI, dimensions are represented by a set of statements on which students rate their agreement. Sample statements include "All students know each other very well," which represents cohesiveness, and "Only the good students are given special projects," which represents favoritism. Statements on the CES reflect dimensions of affiliation (e.g., "Students in this class get to know each other really well") and teacher support (e.g., "The teacher takes a personal interest in students").

These pioneering scales have been modified for use across grade levels, teaching philosophies, and cultures. For example, My Class Inventory (MCI) is a version of the LEI designed for elementary and middle school students and includes simplified statements for these age groups such as, "Children often race to see who can finish first," which represents competitiveness, and "Many children in our class like to fight," which represents friction in the classroom (Fraser et al., 1982). The Questionnaire on Teacher Interactions (QTI), another scale within this category, focuses on students' perceptions of teacher behavior. The QTI includes eight behavioral dimensions, including friendly/helpful behavior ("My teacher is someone we can depend on") and understanding ("If we have something to say, my teacher will listen") (Wubbels & Brekelmans, 1998; Wubbels & Levy, 1993; see also the 2005 special issue of the *Research International Journal of Education* (Vol. 15, no. 1), which provides a comprehensive review of the theoretical model that informed QTI development and research).

With the exception of the LEI, there exist brief versions of these general classroom judgment measures that are easier to administer, less time consuming for students to complete, and require less time to score (Fraser, 1982b; Goh & Fraser, 1996; Goh et al., 1995). Although more practical in these ways, Fraser (1998) stressed that the shorter versions should be reserved for examining classroom-level scores. The longer versions are preferred when measuring individual students' perceptions.

With regards to assessing students' evaluations of their own personal relationships and interactions with other students and teachers (i.e., personalized classroom judgments), there exist several options. On the What Is Happening in This Class? (WIHIC) questionnaire, students respond to questions such as "In this class, I am able to depend on other students for help" (student cohesiveness) and "I do favors for members of my class" (cooperation) (Dorman, 2003). The Network of Relationship Inventory (NRI), designed to assess children and youth's experience of relationship quality with a number of individuals in their social network including their teachers, focuses on instrumental help (i.e., "How much does this person [teacher] help you when you need to get something done?") (Furman & Buhrmester, 1985). The Young Children's Appraisals of Teacher Support (Y-CATS) assesses kindergarteners' perceptions of their relationship with their teachers across three dimensions: (1) warmth (e.g., "My teacher says nice things about my work"), (2) conflict (e.g., "My teacher gets angry with me"), and (3) autonomy support (e.g., "My teacher lets me choose where I sit") (Mantzicopoulos & Neuharth-Pritchett, 2003; Spilt, Koomen, & Mantzicopoulos, 2010).

Assessments that capture student evaluations of the classroom (general classroom judgments) tap into different experiences than assessments that tap into a student's personal relationships in the classroom (personalized classroom judgments) and may lead to different empirical findings (Fraser, 1998). For example, students' general classroom judgments tend to be more favorable than their personalized classroom judgments (Fraser, Giddings, & McRobbie, 1995). Further, more subgroup differences tend to be identified with students' personalized classroom judgments than with their general classroom judgments (Fraser, 1998).

Sociometric and Peer-Nomination Measures

Sociometric and peer-nomination procedures involve providing students with a list of their classmates' names and then asking them to think of the behaviors and interaction styles of each student on the list. This bottom-up approach taps into students' reflections on individual relationships and roles in the classroom. For example, in one study, first-grade students were asked to rate other students' relationships with the teacher, with items such as "Those are the kids that get along with the teacher best" and "Those are the kids who the teacher likes to interact with" (Hughes, Zhang, & Hill, 2006). In this study, each student nominated students from the class list for each descriptor. The total number of nominations each student received constituted that student's individual teacher support score, as perceived by classmates. A classroom-level indicator of normative teacher support also could be created by dividing the median number of nominations students received by the total number of students in the classroom (Stormshak, Bierman, Bruschi, Dodge, & Coie, 1999). Normative classroom teacher–student support predicted an individual student's peer acceptance and classroom engagement above the effect of individual teacher–student support (Hughes et al., 2006) (see also Topping, Chapter 22 of this volume).

Using another peer-nomination protocol, researchers first identified rejected students in first-grade classrooms and then created a classroom-level score that represented the proportion of rejected students in a given classroom (Donohue, Perry, & Weinstein, 2003). A classroom's proportion of rejected students served as a proxy for the frequency of negative interactions and negative feelings in the classroom. In this procedure, rejected students were identified by asking students to name the student in the class who they liked the most and the student they like the least. Dividing the total number of respective nominations by the total number of nominators yields a most-liked and least-liked score for each student. For each student, the least-liked score is then subtracted from the most-liked score to yield a social preference score. A student with a preference score below a certain threshold may be considered rejected (Donohue et al., 2003).

The advantage of sociometric measures is that they provide piecemeal representations of the sum total of relationships that comprise a classroom's social–emotional attributes. As such, they may provide a more precise representation of the overall pattern of relationship quality in a classroom than the more general survey measures (i.e., general classroom judgments). However, sociometric approaches are limited in that they do not capture students' subjective experiences of classroom relationships, which may be better captured with self-report assessments (i.e., general classroom judgments and personalized classroom judgments). Sociometric, peer-nomination, and student self-report measures can be used to complement each other, as each provides a unique perspective on the social–emotional attributes of the classroom.

Measures to Assess Classroom Interactions: Teacher Perspectives

Many prominent student-perspective scales have been adapted for teachers in order to facilitate the comparison of reports from teachers and students, including the CES (Moos & Trickett, 1974) and the QTI (Wubbels & Brekelmans, 1998). The teacher versions typically include a slight rephrasing of items to express the point of view of teachers rather than of students. Another widely used measure is the Student-Teacher Relationship Scale, which assesses teachers' evaluations of their relationship with individual students (Pianta, 2001). Twenty-eight items assess the three dimensions of *closeness* (e.g., "If upset, this child will seek comfort from me"), *conflict* (e.g., "Dealing with this child drains my energy") and *dependency* (e.g., "This child asks for my help when he/she does not need help"). The 26-item Teacher as Social Context questionnaire assesses teachers' relationships with individual students across two dimensions: (1) *autonomy support* (e.g., "I let this student make a lot of his/her decisions regarding schoolwork") and (2) *involvement* (e.g., "I spend time with this student") (Wellborn, Skinner, & Pierson, 1992). It also has a shortened 16-item version (Skinner & Belmont, 1993; Wellborn, Connell, Skinner, & Pierson, 1988).

Measures to Assess Classroom Interactions: Observational

The Classroom Assessment Scoring System (CLASS) is currently the most widely used, validated, and theory-based observational tool to assess the interactions that contribute to the social–emotional classroom climate (Pianta, La Paro, & Hamre, 2006, 2008). The CLASS measures the quality of interactions among teachers and students (La Paro, Pianta, & Stuhlman, 2004) and predicts academic and social adjustment (Brackett et al., 2011; Howes et al., 2008; NICHD Early Child Care Research Network, 2003). It was developed from extensive national, federally funded, observational studies, as well as thorough reviews of the child care and education literature (Hamre et al., 2006).

The CLASS is comprised of three domains, including *emotional support*, *instructional support*, and *classroom organization*. Most relevant to the assessment of the social–emotional attributes of the classroom is the emotional support domain, which is comprised of four dimensions: (1) *positive climate* (degree of warmth and connection observed), (2) *negative climate* (degree of negativity observed; reverse-coded), (3) *teacher sensitivity* (teacher awareness and responsiveness to students' academic and emotional needs), and (4) *regard for student perspectives* (degree to which the classroom is focused on students' interests and motivations). Typically, CLASS coders observe a classroom for 15 to 20 minutes, make note of the presence of behavioral indicators for each dimension, and assign a score or rating for that dimension using a 1 (not at all present) to 7 (present all the time) scale. For example, coders are trained to interpret teacher and student interactions as indicating a concern for students' emotional needs, encouragement and support, and the provision of autonomy and respect. The mean score across the four dimensions constitutes the classroom's level of emotional support. There exist validated versions of the CLASS for preschool through fifth-grade classrooms (Brown et al., 2010; Hamre et al., 2007). A middle school version of the tool is under development.

Two other tools available to assess the social–emotional nature of classroom climate are the Classroom Systems Observational Scale (COS) (Fish & Dane, 2000) and the Early Childhood Environment Rating Scale–Revised (ECERS-R)

(Harms, Clifford, & Cryer, 1998). The 47-item COS assesses three dimensions of the classroom climate, including (1) *cohesion* (i.e., emotional bonding, boundaries, and supportiveness), (2) *flexibility* (i.e., leadership, discipline, and negotiation), and (3) *communication* (i.e., listener's skills, clarity, and self-disclosure). Using the COS, a coder rates statements such as "students speak about friends and families with teachers and with each other" (self-disclosure), "students are helpful to other students" (supportiveness), and "teacher considers circumstances in enforcing consequences" (discipline). The scale was developed for use in kindergarten through sixth-grade classrooms. The ECERS-R is a validated observational tool for kindergarten classrooms. It includes, among others, a dimension assessing warmth and responsiveness in teachers' interaction with students.

By design, most observational tools, particularly the CLASS and the ECERS-R, focus on the behavior of the teacher in the classroom and on the quality of teacher–student relationships. This focus reflects the theoretical framework that informed the development of these scales, namely attachment theory and systems theory (Hamre et al., 2009). It also makes sense given that a teacher typically has greater influence on and responsibility for the classroom climate than individual students. As a result, however, these tools are comparatively insensitive to the influence of peer relationships and peer group dynamics on the experience of students in the classroom. Complementing observational tools with assessments of student perspectives of peer relationships, such as sociometric assessments of peer support and peer rejection, may provide the most useful information about the classroom.

Measures to Assess the Feelings of Students

Several self-report survey tools exist to assess how students feel about their relationships with significant adults and peers in their lives, including teachers and classmates. For example, the Relatedness Scale contains a dimension for students' feelings toward their teacher and a dimension on their feelings toward their classmates (Furrer & Skinner, 2003; Toth & Cicchetti, 1996; Wellborn, & Connell, 1987). For both types of relationships, students respond to 20 items starting with the stem "When I'm with my teacher (classmates) . . . ," followed by responses like "I feel accepted," "I feel like someone special," "I feel ignored," and "I feel happy." Shorter versions of this scale exist, including a 4-item measure (Skinner, Furrer, Marchand, & Kindermann, 2008). The 8-item People in My Life (PIML) scale focuses on emotional qualities of a student's relationship with the teacher with statements such as "My teacher understands me" and "I trust my teacher" (Greenberg, Kusche, Cook, & Quamma, 1995; Murray & Greenberg, 2005). Finally, the 18-item Psychological Sense of School Membership assesses the extent to which middle school students feel accepted, valued, and respected within their classroom (e.g., "I feel like a real part of this class" or "Other students in my class like me the way I am") (Goodenow, 1993).

Other measures assess the perceptions students have of their classmates' feelings while in the classroom. The MCI, reviewed previously in the section on assessing classroom interactions, includes items that assess student perceptions of classroom cohesiveness (e.g., "Students in my class like each other as friends"), satisfaction (e.g., "Some students are not happy in class," reverse scored), and competitiveness (e.g., "Some students feel bad when they do not do as well as others") (Fraser et al., 1982).

Measures to Assess Students' Social–Emotional Skills

Two types of assessments are available to measure students' social–emotional skills: (1) performance-based assessments and (2) informant reports. On performance-based assessments, students engage in problem solving to demonstrate their skills. In contrast, informant reports involve teachers or parents reporting on the skills they observe in a particular student. Self-report measures are problematic because respondents may provide socially desirable responses rather than truthful ones, and they may not know how to evaluate the strength of their social–emotional skills (DeNisi & Shaw, 1977; Paulhus, Lysy, & Yik, 1998). Self-report measures of emotion skills are related weakly to performance assessments and lack discriminant validity (i.e., they are not distinct from existing measures of personality traits; Brackett & Mayer, 2003; Brackett, Rivers, Shiffman, Lerner, & Salovey, 2006).

Among the performance-based assessments is the Mayer-Salovey-Caruso Emotional Intelligence Test–Youth Version (MSCEIT-YV) (Mayer,

Salovey, & Caruso, in press). The 97-item MSCEIT-YV has a criterion of correctness (i.e., there are better and worse answers that are determined using complex scoring algorithms). It can be administered individually or in groups and is appropriate for students aged 10 to 17 years. The MSCEIT-YV is divided into four sections that assess skills related to (1) perceiving emotions expressed in photographs of faces, (2) understanding the meaning of emotion terms (e.g., "When you worry that something awful and dangerous is about to happen, you feel . . . Frustration? Envy? Fear?), (3) the relationship of emotion terms to a variety of physical sensations (e.g., "To what extent is anger like each of the following: hot, red, relaxed, heavy?"), and (4) regulating emotions in hypothetical social situations (i.e., identifying effective responses for managing an emotion; e.g., "Your friend has been sad recently and you want to do something to cheer her up.").

Among the available teacher–informant assessments of students' emotion skills is the 72-item Devereux Student Strengths Assessment (DESSA) (LeBuffe, Shapiro, & Naglieri, 2008). The DESSA is a strength-based, standardized, norm-referenced behavior rating scale that assesses students' social, emotional, and regulatory skills. It is divided into eight subscales: (1) *optimistic thinking* (confidence and hopefulness about various situations), (2) *self-management* (ability to control emotion and behavior), (3) *goal-directed behavior* (initiation of and persistence in completing tasks), (4) *self-awareness* (understanding of personal strengths and limitations), (5) *social awareness* (ability to interact with others), (6) *personal responsibility* (contributions to group efforts), (7) *decision making* (problem solving), and (8) *relationship skills* (behavior that promotes positive interactions with others). Teachers rate the frequency with which students engage in each of the described behaviors. The DESSA has been shown to correlate positively with adaptability, leadership, and study skills and negatively with hyperactivity, aggression, and problems with conduct, attention, and learning (Nickerson & Fishman, 2009).

Directions for Future Research

Decades of research on the social–emotional attributes of classrooms are based on correlational data. Thus, one of the most pressing research tasks in this area is to examine the causal connections between these attributes and student academic and social–emotional outcomes. The research described in this chapter demonstrates associations among the various social–emotional attributes identified in Figure 20.1, as well as between each attribute and student outcomes. In this final section of the chapter, we discuss methodological approaches for future studies that may yield a better understanding of the causal relationships among social–emotional attributes of the classroom and important student-level outcomes.

One promising way to study the causal effects of classrooms' social–emotional attributes is to focus on changing one or more of the attributes through an intervention assigned randomly to classrooms. Evaluating the impact of the intervention through testing its effects in the treatment classrooms versus the control classrooms may yield information about causal relationships. Does the intervention, for example, modify the social–emotional quality of interactions among and between teachers and students in ways that affect student academic performance? Or does the intervention affect individual-level changes in social–emotional skills and academic performance, which then leads to improvements in the feelings students and teachers experience in the classroom? Burgeoning evidence shows that SEL programs can transform social–emotional attributes of the classroom as well as improve the academic outcomes of students; however, these studies have not yet established that improvements at the classroom level indeed precede and cause improvements in student outcomes (e.g., Durlak et al., 2011; Jones, Brown, & Aber, 2011; Rivers et al., in press-a).

A number of scholars have discussed the methodological difficulties in providing conclusive answers regarding the causal relationship between changes in the social–emotional attributes of classrooms and student outcomes. One major methodological hurdle in this area of research is that students and teachers cannot be randomly assigned to high and low quality interactions in the classroom (Bullock, Green, & Ha, 2010). We argue that, in light of these methodological difficulties, it is even more important to develop and properly test theories of change. If an ecological perspective suggests that improvements in the quality of relationships in the classroom will precede and essentially change student outcomes, such a model also needs to predict the time frames of these changes. For instance, how long will it take for a specific SEL program to create a fundamental change in the social–emotional attributes of the classroom level (i.e., create a fundamental change in the classroom)? At what point in the academic year, or the development of a child, are we expecting to see an impact of these classroom-level changes on individual outcomes? Under what circumstances (e.g., school-level policies and community characteristics) do we expect to see these effects? Theories of change should clearly inform research designs and assessment tools in order to increase the likelihood that researchers find program effects, estimate them correctly, and link program effects causally to each other (Cole & Maxwell, 2003).

Studying within-classroom variability in social–emotional processes over time is an exciting and promising way to develop fine-tuned theories of change. For example, hostile interactions and poorer instructional quality may be more common in the latter part of the day than in the morning, which suggests that time-varying factors like fatigue may cause fluctuation in social-emotional attributes within a given classroom (Curby et al., 2011). Sources of variation in teacher–student interactions can be examined by observing segments of the same classrooms across different times of the day (Curby et al., 2011). One approach is the ecological momentary assessment (EMA) method, tracks students' and teachers' experiences in real time, allowing for data collection across multiple time points (Carson, Weiss, & Templin, 2010). Students and teachers respond to prompts to evaluate their momentary interactions on digital devices at different times in the school day. The EMA circumvents hindsight bias and other perceptional errors inherent in surveys that require participants to provide an average rating of their typical feelings or behaviors. For example, with EMA, one could validate the link between social–emotional experiences and academic engagement in the classroom by investigating within-student associations between feeling good and enjoying positive interactions with peers and the teachers on a given day (as reported by the student) and academic engagement on the same day (as reported by the teacher). This method also could shed more light on the dynamics between teachers' emotional states in the classroom, social–emotional characteristics of their interactions with students, and instructional quality. Keeping time of day in mind is critical when comparing intervention effects across classrooms.

Finally, to best understand and assess the social–emotional attributes of classrooms, mixed-methods approaches should be employed (see Maxwell, 2004). This chapter provided an overview of validated survey tools, sociometric assessments, and observational methods that serve to quantify the social–emotional attributes of the classroom, including the interactions between and among students and teachers, the feelings students and teachers have for each other and for the classroom, and the social–emotional skills students and teachers bring into the classroom. These tools can be combined with ethnographic methods and interviews to improve our understanding of rhythms, changes, and temporal associations between the social–emotional attributes across a day, week, semester, or year and within particular school and community contexts.

References

Anderson, A., Hamilton, R. J., & Hattie, J. (2004). Classroom climate and motivated behaviour in secondary schools. *Learning Environments Research, 7,* 211–225.

Baker, J. A. (1999). Teacher-student interaction in urban at-risk classrooms: Differential behavior, relationship quality, and student satisfaction with school. *The Elementary School Journal, 100,* 57–70.

Baker, J. A., Dilly, L. J., Aupperlee, J. L., & Patil, S. A. (2003). The developmental context of school satisfaction: Schools as psychologically healthy environments. *School Psychology Quarterly, 18,* 206.

Barth, J. M., Dunlap, S. T., Dane, H., Lochman, J. E., & Wells, K. C. (2004). Classroom environment influences on aggression, peer relations, and academic focus. *Journal of School Psychology, 42,* 115–133.

Becker, B. E., & Luthar, S. S. (2002). Social-emotional factors affecting achievement outcomes among disadvantaged students: Closing the achievement gap. *Educational Psychologist, 37,* 197–214.

Bloom, H. S. (Ed.). (2005). *Learning more from social experiments: Evolving analytic approaches.* New York: Russell Sage Foundation.

Brackett, M. A., & Katulak, N. A. (2006). Emotional intelligence in the classroom: Skill-based training for teachers and students. In J. Ciarrochi & J. D. Mayer (Eds.), *Applying emotional intelligence: A practitioner's guide* (pp. 1–27). New York: Psychology Press.

Brackett, M. A., & Mayer, J. D. (2003). Convergent, discriminant, and incremental validity of competing measures of emotional intelligence. *Personality and Social Psychology Bulletin, 29,* 1147–1158.

Brackett, M. A., Palomera Martin, R., Mojsa, J., Reyes, M. R., & Salovey, P. (2010). Emotion regulation ability, job satisfaction, and burnout among British secondary school teachers. *Psychology in the Schools, 47,* 406–417.

Brackett, M. A., Reyes, M. R., Rivers, S. E., Elbertson, N. A., & Salovey, P. (2011). Classroom emotional climate, teacher affiliation, and student conduct. *Journal of Classroom Interaction, 46,* 27–36.

Brackett, M. A., Rivers, S. E., Shiffman, S., Lerner, N., & Salovey, P. (2006). Relating emotional abilities to social functioning: A comparison of self-report and performance measures of emotional intelligence. *Journal of Personality and Social Psychology, 91,* 780–795.

Bronfenbrenner, U. (1979). Contexts of child rearing: Problems and prospects. *American Psychologist, 34,* 844–850.

Brown, J. L., Jones, S. M., LaRusso, M. D., & Aber, J. L. (2010). Improving classroom quality: Teacher influences and experimental impacts of the 4Rs program. *Journal of Educational Psychology, 102,* 153–167.

Bullock, J. G., Green, D. P., & Ha, S. E. (2010). Yes, but what's the mechanism? (don't expect an easy answer). *Journal of Personality and Social Psychology, 98,* 550–558.

Carson, R. L., Weiss, H. M., & Templin, T. J. (2010). Ecological momentary assessment: A research method for studying the daily lives of teachers. *International Journal of Research & Method in Education, 33,* 165–182.

Catalano, R. F., Berglund, L., Ryan, J. A. M., Lonczek, H. S., & Hawkins, J. D. (2004). Positive youth development in the United States: Research findings on evaluations of positive youth development programs. *The Annals of the American Academy of Political and Social Science, 591,* 98–124.

Catalano, R. F., Hawkins, J. D., Berglund, L., Pollard, J. A., & Arthur, M. W. (2002). Prevention science and positive youth development: Competitive or cooperative frameworks? *Journal of Adolescent Health, 31,* 230–239.

Chomat-Mooney, L., Pianta, R., Hamre, B., Mashburn, A., Luckner, A., Grimm, K., et al. (2008). *A practical guide for conducting classroom observations: A summary of issues and evidence for researchers.* Unpublished report to the WT Grant Foundation, University of Virginia, Charlottesville.

Cole, D. A., & Maxwell, S. E. (2003). Testing mediational models with longitudinal data: Questions and tips in the use of structural equation modeling. *Journal of Abnormal Psychology, 112,* 558–577.

Collaborative for Academic, Social, and Emotional Learning. (2012). *SEL in your state.* Retrieved from http://casel.org/policy-advocacy/sel-in-your-state/

Curby, T. W., Stuhlman, M., Grimm, K., Mashburn, A. J., Chomat-Mooney, L., Downer, J. T., et al. (2011). Within-day variability in the quality of classroom interactions during third and fifth grade. *The Elementary School Journal, 112,* 16–37.

Denham, S. A. (1998). *Emotional development in young children.* New York: Guilford Press.

DeNisi, A. S., & Shaw, J. B. (1977). Investigation of the uses of self-reports of abilities. *Journal of Applied Psychology, 62,* 641–644.

Donohue, K. M., Perry, K. E., & Weinstein, R. S. (2003). Teachers' classroom practices and children's rejection by their peers. *Journal of Applied Developmental Psychology, 24,* 91–118.

Dorman, J. P. (2003). Cross-national validation of the What Is Happening in this Class? (WIHIC) questionnaire using confirmatory factor analysis. *Learning Environments Research, 6,* 231–245.

Durlak, J. A., Weissberg, R. P., Dymnicki, A. B., Taylor, R. D., & Schellinger, K. B. (2011). The impact of enhancing students' social and emotional learning: A meta-analysis of school-based universal interventions. *Child Development, 82,* 405–432.

Fish, M. C., & Dane, E. (2000). The classroom systems observation scale: Development of an instrument to assess classrooms using a systems perspective. *Learning Environments Research, 3,* 67–92.

Fisher, D. L., & Fraser, B. J. (1983). A comparison of actual and preferred classroom environments as perceived by science teachers and students. *Journal of Research in Science Teaching, 20,* 55–61.

Floman, J., Hagelskamp, C., Brackett, M. A., & Rivers, S. E. (2012). *The association between coder mood and the evaluation of classroom uality using the CLASS.* Manuscript submitted for publication.

Flook, L., Repetti, R. L., & Ullman, J. B. (2005). Classroom social experiences as predictors of academic performance. *Developmental Psychology, 41,* 319–327.

Fraser, B. J. (1982a). Differences between student and teacher perceptions of actual and preferred classroom learning environment. *Educational Evaluation and Policy Analysis, 4,* 511–519.

Fraser, B. J. (1982b). Development of short forms of several classroom environment scales. *Journal of Educational Measurement, 19,* 221–227.

Fraser, B. J. (1998). Classroom environment instruments: Development, validity and applications. *Learning Environments Research, 1,* 7–34.

Fraser, B. J., Anderson, G. J., & Walberg, H. J. (1982). *Assessment of Learning Environments: Manual for Learning Environment Inventory (LEI) and My Class Inventory (MCI).* Perth, Australia: Western Australian Institute of Technology.

Fraser, B. J., Giddings, G. J., & McRobbie, C. J. (1995). Evolution and validation of a personal form of an instrument for assessing science laboratory classroom environments. *Journal of Research in Science Teaching, 32,* 399–422.

Frenzel, A. C., Goetz, T., Lüdtke, O., Pekrun, R., & Sutton, R. E. (2009). Emotional transmission in the classroom: Exploring the relationship between teacher and student enjoyment. *Journal of educational psychology, 101,* 705–716.

Furman, W., & Buhrmester, D. (1985). Children's perceptions of the personal relationships in their social networks. *Developmental Psychology, 21,* 1016–1024.

Furrer, C., & Skinner, E. (2003). Sense of relatedness as a factor in children's academic engagement and performance. *Journal of Educational Psychology, 95,* 148–162.

Gettinger, M., Schienebeck, C., Seigel, S., & Vollmer, L. (2011). Assessment of classroom environments. In M. A. Bray & T. J. Kehle (Eds.), *The Oxford Handbook of School Psychology* (pp. 260–283). New York: Oxford University Press.

Gil-Olarte Márquez, P., Palomera Martin, R., & Brackett, M. A. (2006). Relating emotional intelligence to social competence and academic achievement in high school students. *Psicothema, 18,* 118–123.

Goh, S. C., & Fraser, B. J. (1996). Validation of an elementary school version of the questionnaire on teacher interaction. *Psychological Reports, 79,* 515–522.

Goh, S. C., Young, D. J., & Fraser, B. J. (1995). Psychosocial climate and student outcomes in elementary mathematics classrooms: A multilevel analysis. *The Journal of Experimental Educational, 64,* 29–40.

Goodenow, C. (1993). The psychological sense of school membership among adolescents: Scale development and educational correlates. *Psychology in the Schools, 30,* 79–90.

Greenberg, M. T., Kusche, C. A., Cook, E. T., & Quamma, J. P. (1995). Promoting emotional competence in school-aged children: The effects of the PATHS curriculum. *Development and Psychopathology, 7,* 117–136.

Greenberg, M. T., Weissberg, R. P., O'Brien, M. U., Zins, J. E., Fredericks, L., Resnik, H., et al. (2003). Enhancing school-based prevention and youth development through coordinated social, emotional, and academic learning. *American Psychologist, 58,* 466–474.

Greene, R. W., Abidin, R. R., & Kmetz, C. (1997). The Index of Teaching Stress: A measure of student-teacher compatibility. *Journal of School Psychology, 35,* 239–259.

Gregory, A., & Weinstein, R. S. (2008). The discipline gap and African Americans: Defiance or cooperation in the high school classroom. *Journal of School Psychology, 46,* 455–475.

Haertel, G. D., Walberg, H. J., & Haertel, E. H. (1981). Socio psychological environments and learning: A quantitative synthesis. *British Educational Research Journal, 7,* 27–36.

Hamre, B. K., Mashburn, A. J., Pianta, R. C., Locaslc-Crouch, J., & La Paro, K. M. (2006). *CLASS: Classroom Assessment Scoring System, Technical Appendix.* Charlottesville: University of Virginia. Retrieved from www.classobservation.com

Hamre, B. K., & Pianta, R. C. (2001). Early teacher-child relationships and the trajectory of children's school outcomes through eighth grade. *Child Development, 72,* 625–638.

Hamre, B. K., Pianta, C. R., & Chomat-Mooney, L. (2009). Conducting classroom observations in school-based research. In L. M. Dinella (Ed.), *Conducting science-based psychology research in schools* (pp. 79–105). Washington, DC: American Psychological Association.

Hamre, B. K., Pianta, R. C., Mashburn, A. J., & Downer, J. T. (2007). *Building a science of classrooms: Application of the CLASS framework in over 4,000 U.S. early childhood and elementary classrooms.* Foundation for Child Development. Retrieved from www.icpsr.umich.edu/files/PREK3RD/resources/pdf/BuildingAScienceOfClassroomsPiantaHamre.pdf

Harms, T., Clifford, R. M., & Cryer, D. (1998). *Early Childhood Environment Rating Scale.* New York: Teachers College Press.

Howes, C., Burchinal, M., Pianta, R. C., Bryant, D., Early, D. M., Clifford, R., et al. (2008). Ready to learn? Children's pre-academic achievement in pre-kindergarten programs. *Early Childhood Research Quarterly, 23,* 27–50.

Hughes, J. N., & Kwok, O. M. (2006). Classroom engagement mediates the effect of teacher-student support on elementary students' peer acceptance: A prospective analysis. *Journal of School Psychology, 43,* 465–480.

Hughes, J. N., Zhang, D., & Hill, C. R. (2006). Peer assessments of normative and individual teacher-student support predict social acceptance and engagement among low-achieving children. *Journal of School Psychology, 43,* 447–463.

Izard, C. E., Fine, S., Schultz, D., Mostow, A., Ackerman, B., & Youngstrom, E. (2001). Emotion knowledge as a predictor of social behavior and academic competence in children at risk. *Psychological Science, 12,* 18–23.

Jennings, P. A., & Greenberg, M. T. (2009). The prosocial classroom: Teacher social and emotional competence in relation to student and classroom outcomes. *Review of Educational Research, 79,* 491–525.

Jones, S. M., Brown, J. L., & Aber, J. L. (2008). Classroom settings as targets of intervention and research. In M. Shinn & H. Yoshikawa (Eds.), *Toward positive youth development: Transforming schools and community programs* (pp. 58–77). New York: Oxford University Press.

Jones, S. M., Brown, J. L., & Aber, J. L. (2011). Two-year impacts of a universal school-based social-emotional and literacy intervention: An experiment in translational developmental research. *Child Development, 82,* 533–554.

Juvonen, J., Wang, Y., & Espinoza, G. (2011). Bullying experiences and compromised academic performance across middle school grades. *The Journal of Early Adolescence, 31,* 152–173.

Klusmann, U., Kunter, M., Trautwein, U., Lüdtke, O., & Baumert, J. (2008). Teachers' occupational well-being and quality of instruction: The important role of self-regulatory patterns. *Journal of Educational Psychology, 100,* 702–715.

Kontos, S., & Wilcox-Herzog, A. (1997). Influences on children's competence in early childhood classrooms. *Early Childhood Research Quarterly, 12,* 247–262.

La Paro, K. M., Pianta, R. C., & Stuhlman, M. (2004). The Classroom Assessment Scoring System: Findings from the prekindergarten year. *The Elementary School Journal, 104,* 409–426.

La Paro, K. M., Rimm-Kaufman, S. E., & Pianta, R. C. (2006). Kindergarten to 1st grade: Classroom characteristics and the stability and change of children's classroom experiences. *Journal of Research in Childhood Education, 21,* 189–202.

Ladd, G. W., Birch, S. H., & Buhs, E. S. (1999). Children's social and scholastic lives in kindergarten: Related spheres of influence? *Child Development, 70,* 1373–1400.

LeBuffe, P. A., Shapiro, V. B., & Naglieri, J. A. (2008). *The Devereux Student Strengths Assessment (DESSA).* Lewisville, NC: Kaplan Press.

Loukas, A., & Robinson, S. (2004). Examining the moderating role of perceived school climate in early adolescent adjustment. *Journal of Research on Adolescence, 14,* 209–233.

Mantzicopoulos, P., & Neuharth-Pritchett, S. (2003). Development and validation of a measure to assess head start children's appraisals of teacher support. *Journal of School Psychology, 41,* 431–451.

Mashburn, A. J., Downer, J. T., Rivers, S. E., Brackett, M. A., & Martinez, A. (In press). Improving the power of an experimental study of a social and emotional learning program: Application of generalizability theory to the measurement of classroom-level outcomes. *Prevention Science.*

Maslach, C., Jackson, S., & Leiter, M. P. (1996). *Maslach Burnout Inventory* (3rd ed.). Palo Alto, CA: Consulting Psychologists Press.

Maxwell, J. A. (2004). Causal explanation, qualitative research, and scientific inquiry in education. *Educational Researcher, 33,* 3–11.

Mayer, J. D., & Salovey, P. (1997). What is emotional intelligence? In P. Salovey & D. J. Sluyter (Eds.), *Emotional development and emotional intelligence: Educational implications* (pp. 3–34). New York: Basic Books.

Mayer, J. D., Salovey, P., & Caruso, D. R. (2002). *Mayer-Salovey-Caruso Emotional Intelligence Test, Version 2.0.* Toronto: Multi-Health Systems.

Mayer, J. D., Salovey, P., & Caruso, D. R. (in press). *Mayer-Salovey-Caruso Emotional Intelligence Test–Youth Version: Item booklet.* Toronto: Multi-Health Systems.

Meehan, B. T., Hughes, J. N., & Cavell, T. A. (2003). Teacher-student relationships as compensatory resources for aggressive children. *Child Development, 74,* 1145–1157.

Mestre, J. M., Lopes, P. N., Salovey, P., & Gil-Olarte Márquez, P. (2006). Emotional intelligence and social and academic adaptation to school. *Psicothema, 18,* 112–117.

Mikami, A. Y., Lerner, M. D., & Lun, J. (2010). Social context influences on children's rejection by their peers. *Child Development Perspectives, 4,* 123–130.

Moos, R. H., & Trickett, E. J. (1974). *Classroom Environment Scale Manual.* Palo Alto, CA: Consulting Psychologists Press.

Murray, C., & Greenberg, M. T. (2005). Children's relationship with teachers and bonds with school: An investigation of patterns and correlates in middle childhood. *Journal of School Psychology, 38,* 423–445.

National Research Council & Institute of Medicine. (2002). *Community programs to promote youth development.* Washington, DC: National Academy Press.

NICHD Early Child Care Research Network. (2003). Social functioning in first grade: Associations with earlier home and child care predictors and with current classroom experiences. *Child Development, 74,* 1639–1662.

Nickerson, A. B., & Fishman, C. (2009). Convergent and divergent validity of the Devereux Student Strengths Assessment. *School Psychology Quarterly, 24,* 48–59.

O'Connor, E., & McCartney, K. (2007). Examining teacher-child relationships and achievement as part of an ecological model of development. *American Educational Research Journal, 44,* 340–369.

Patrick, H., Ryan, A. M., & Kaplan, A. (2007). Early adolescents' perceptions of the classroom social environment, motivational beliefs, and engagement. *Journal of Educational Psychology, 99,* 83–98.

Paulhus, D. L., Lysy, D. C., & Yik, M. S. M. (1998). Self-report measures of intelligence: Are they useful as proxy IQ tests? *Journal of Personality, 66,* 525–554.

Pianta, R. C. (1999). *Enhancing relationships between children and teachers.* Washington, DC: American Psychological Association.

Pianta, R. C. (2001). *STRS: Student-Teacher Relationship Scale.* Lutz, FL: Psychological Assessment Resources, Inc.

Pianta, R. C., & Allen, J. P. (2008). Building capacity for positive youth development in secondary school classrooms: Changing teachers' interactions with students. In M. Shinn & H. Yoshikawa (Eds.), *Toward positive youth development: Transforming schools and community programs* (Vol. 1, pp. 21–40). New York: Oxford University Press.

Pianta, R. C., La Paro, K., & Hamre, B. (2006). *Classroom assessment scoring system: Middle/Secondary Version.* Baltimore, MD: Brookes Publishing.

Pianta, R. C., La Paro, K., & Hamre, B. (2008). *Classroom assessment scoring system: K–3.* Baltimore, MD: Brookes Publishing.

Pigott, R. L., & Cowen, E. L. (2000). Teacher race, child race, racial congruence, and teacher ratings of children's school adjustment. *Journal of School Psychology, 38,* 177–195.

Raudenbush, S. W., & Bryk, A. S. (2002). *Hierarchical linear models* (2nd ed.). Thousand Oaks, CA: Sage.

Raudenbush, S. W., Martinez, A., & Spybrook, J. (2007). Strategies for improving precision in group-randomized experiments. *Educational Evaluation and Policy Analysis, 29,* 5–29.

Raudenbush, S. W., & Sadoff, S. (2008). Statistical inference when classroom quality is measured with error. *Journal of Research on Educational Effectiveness, 1,* 138–154.

Raver, C. C., Jones, S. M., Li-Grining, C. P., Metzger, M., Champon, K. M., & Sardin, L. (2008). Improving preschool classroom processes: Preliminary findings from a randomized trial implemented in Head Start settings. *Early Childhood Research Quarterly, 23,* 10–26.

Resnick, M. D., Bearman, P. S., Blum, R. W., Bauman, K. E., Harris, K. M., Jones, J., et al. (1997). Protecting adolescents from harm. *JAMA, 278,* 823.

Reyes, M. R., Brackett, M. A., Rivers, S. E., White, M., & Salovey, P. (in press). The emotional climate of learning: Links to academic achievement. *Journal of Educational Psychology.*

Rivers, S. E., Brackett, M. A., Reyes, M. R., Elbertson, N. A., & Salovey, P. (in press-a). Improving the social and emotional climate of classrooms: A clustered randomized controlled trial testing The RULER Approach. *Prevention Science.*

Rivers, S. E., Brackett, M. A., Reyes, M. R., Mayer, J. D., Caruso, D. R., & Salovey, P. (in press-b). Emotional intelligence in early adolescence: Its relation to academic performance and psychosocial functioning. *Journal of Psychoeducational Assessment.*

Rivers, S. E., Brackett, M. A., & Salovey, P. (2008). Measuring emotional intelligence as a mental ability in adults and children. In G. J. Boyle, G. Matthews, & D. H. Saklofske (Eds.), *Handbook of personality theory and testing* (pp. 440–460). Thousand Oaks, CA: Sage.

Roeser, R. W., Eccles, J. S., & Sameroff, A. J. (2000). School as a context of early adolescents' academic and social-emotional development: A summary of research findings. *The Elementary School Journal, 100*(5), 443–471.

Rubin, K. H., Bukowski, W. M., & Parker, J. G. (2006). Peer interactions, relationships, and groups. In N. Eisenberg, W. Damon, & R. M. Lerner (Eds.), *Handbook of child psychology: Vol. 3. Social, emotional, and personality development* (6th ed., pp. 571–645). New York: John Wiley.

Ryan, A. M., & Patrick, H. (2001). The classroom social environment and changes in adolescents' motivation and engagement during middle school. *American Educational Research Journal, 38,* 437–460.

Saarni, C. (1999). *The development of emotional competence.* New York: Guilford Press.

Saft, E. W., & Pianta, R. C. (2001). Teachers' perceptions of their relationships with students: Effects of child age, gender, and ethnicity of teachers and children. *School Psychology Quarterly, 16,* 125–141.

Salovey, P., & Mayer, J. D. (1990). Emotional intelligence. *Imagination, Cognition and Personality, 9,* 185–211.

Selman, R. L. (1981). The development of interpersonal competence: The role of understanding in conduct. *Developmental Review, 1,* 401–422.

Sentse, M., Scholte, R., Salmivalli, C., & Voeten, M. (2007). Person-group dissimilarity in involvement in bullying and its relation with social status. *Journal of Abnormal Child Psychology, 35,* 1009–1019.

Shinn, M. (1990). Mixing and matching: Levels of conceptualization, measurement, and statistical analysis in community research. In P. Tolan, C. Keys, F. Chertok, & L. A. Jason (Eds.), *Researching community psychology: Issues of theory and methods* (pp. 111–126). Washington, DC: American Psychological Association.

Skiba, R., & Rausch, M. K. (2006). Zero tolerance, suspension, and expulsion: Questions of equity and effectiveness. In C. M. Evertson & C. S. Weinstein (Eds.), *Handbook of classroom management: Research, practice, and contemporary issues* (pp. 1063–1089). Mahwah, NJ: Lawrence Erlbaum.

Skiba, R., Reynolds, C. R., Graham, S., Sheras, P., Conoley, J. C., & Garcia-Vazquez, E. (2008). Are zero tolerance policies effective in the schools? An evidentiary review and recommendations. *American Psychologist, 63,* 852–862.

Skinner, E. A., & Belmont, M. J. (1993). Motivation in the classroom: Reciprocal effects of teacher behavior and student engagement across the school year. *Journal of Educational Psychology, 85,* 571–581.

Skinner, E. A., Furrer, C., Marchand, G., & Kindermann, T. (2008). Engagement and disaffection in the classroom: Part of a larger motivational dynamic? *Journal of Educational Psychology, 100,* 765–781.

Snijders, T. A. B., & Bosker, R. J. (1993). Standard errors and sample sizes for two-level research. *Journal of Educational and Behavioral Statistics, 18,* 237–259.

Solomon, D., Watson, M., Battistich, V., & Schaps, E. (1996). Creating classrooms that students experience as communities. *American Journal of Community Psychology, 24,* 719–748.

Spilt, J. L., Koomen, H. M. Y., & Mantzicopoulos, P. Y. (2010). Young children's perceptions of teacher–child relationships: An evaluation of two instruments and the role of child gender in kindergarten. *Journal of Applied Developmental Psychology, 31,* 428–438.

Stormshak, E. A., Bierman, K. L., Bruschi, C., Dodge, K. A., & Coie, J. D. (1999). The relation between behavior problems and peer preference in different classroom contexts. *Child Development, 70,* 169–182.

Sutton, R. E., & Wheatley, K. F. (2003). Teachers' emotions and teaching: A review of the literature and directions for future research. *Educational Psychology Review, 15,* 327–358.

Thomas, D. E., Coard, S. I., Stevenson, H. C., Bentley, K., & Zamel, P. (2009). Racial and emotional factors predicting teachers' perceptions of classroom behavioral maladjustment for urban African American male youth. *Psychology in the Schools, 46,* 184–196.

Toth, S. L., & Cicchetti, D. (1996). The impact of relatedness with mother on school functioning in maltreated children. *Journal of School Psychology, 34,* 247–266.

Tseng, V., & Seidman, E. (2007). A systems framework for understanding social settings. *American Journal of Community Psychology, 39,* 217–228.

Valiente, C., Lemery-Chalfant, K., & Castro, K. S. (2007). Children's effortful control and academic competence. Mediation through school liking. *Merrill-Palmer Quarterly, 53,* 1–25.

Walberg, H. J., & Anderson, G. J. (1968). Classroom climate and individual learning. *Journal of Educational Psychology, 59,* 414–419.

Wang, M., Haertel, G., & Walberg, H. (1997). Learning influences. In H. Walberg & G. Haertl (Eds.), *Psychology and educational practice* (pp. 199–211). Berkeley, CA: McCutchen.

Wellborn, J. G., & Connell, J. P. (1987). *Manual for the Rochester Assessment Package for Schools.* Rochester, NY: University of Rochester.

Wellborn, J., Connell, J., Skinner, E., & Pierson, L. (1988). *Teacher as social context: A measure of teacher provision of involvement, structure and autonomy support* (Tech. Rep.). Rochester, NY: University of Rochester.

Wellborn J., C., J., Skinner, E., & Pierson, L. (1992). *Teacher as Social Context (TASC), two measures of teacher provision of involvement, structure, and autonomy support.* Rochester, NY: University of Rochester.

Wentzel, K. R. (2002). Are effective teachers like good parents? Teaching styles and student adjustment in early adolescence. *Child Development, 73,* 287–301.

Wubbels, T., & Brekelmans, M. (1998). The teacher factor in the social climate of the classroom. In B. J. Fraser & K. G. Tobin (Eds.), *International Handbook of Science Education* (pp. 565–580). Dordrecht, The Netherlands: Kluwer.

Wubbels, T., Brekelmans, M., & Hermans, J. (1987). Teacher behavior: An important aspect of the learning environment. *The Study of Learning Environments, 3,* 10–25.

Wubbels, T., & Levy, J. (1993). *Do you know what you look like?: Interpersonal relationships in education.* London: Pergamon.

Zins, J. E., Bloodworth, M. R., Weissberg, R. P., & Walberg, H. J. (2004). The scientific base linking social and emotional learning to school success. In J. E. Zins, R. P. Weissberg, M. C. Wang, & H. J. Walberg (Eds.), *Building academic success on social and emotional learning: What does the research say?* (pp. 3–22). New York: Teachers College Press.

21

Student Self-Assessment[1]

Gavin T. L. Brown

Lois R. Harris

The only way any of us can improve—as Coach Graham taught me—is if we develop a real ability to assess ourselves. If we can't accurately do that, how can we tell if we're getting better or worse? (Pausch & Zaslow, 2008, p. 112)

During the past two decades, student self-assessment has been strongly endorsed as an important aspect of formative assessment through the global assessment for learning (AFL) movement. Student self-assessment is not new, with Brookhart (2009) noting that even in the 1930s and 1940s there were numerous authors endorsing the use of student self-evaluation. However, self-assessment is seldom implemented in many classrooms. Hunter, Mayenga, and Gambell (2006) found that 23% of the 4,148 Canadian secondary teachers sampled reported never using self-assessment, with 58% reporting minimal self-assessment use. Only half of 346 surveyed upper secondary students in Finland reported participating in self-assessment (Lasonen, 1995). This limited implementation likely relates to the tensions teachers report between the use of student-led assessment practices and the externally and teacher-controlled summative results generally reported to stakeholders (Harris & Brown, 2010; Volante & Beckett, 2011).

There is general consensus that self-assessment is positive and leads to benefits for students. Perhaps the most powerful promise of self-assessment is that it can raise student academic performance by teaching pupils self-regulatory processes, allowing them to compare their own work with socially defined goals and revise accordingly (Andrade, 2010; Black & Wiliam, 1998; Butler & Winne, 1995; Hattie & Timperley, 2007; Ramdass & Zimmerman, 2008). The logic is that, like self-regulation, self-evaluation of the quality attributes of one's own work draws on metacognitive competencies (e.g., self-observation, self-judgment, self-reaction, task analysis, self-motivation, and self-control) (Zimmerman,

[1]Acknowledgment: We wish to acknowledge the financial support of the Assessment Research Centre grant #C7-R8000-0, Hong Kong Institute of Education that permitted the employment of Ka Ki Kitty Cheng as a research assistant. The first draft of this chapter was written while the first author was employed at the Hong Kong Institute of Education.

2002). Additionally, there is evidence that students can improve their self-regulation skills through self-assessment (i.e., set targets, evaluate progress relative to target criteria, and improve the quality of their learning outcomes) (Andrade, Du, & Mycek, 2010; Andrade, Du, & Wang, 2008; Brookhart, Andolina, Zuza, & Furman, 2004). Furthermore, self-assessment is associated with improved motivation, engagement, and efficacy (Griffiths & Davies, 1993; Klenowski, 1995; Munns & Woodward, 2006; Schunk, 1996), reducing dependence on the teacher (Sadler, 1989). It is also seen as a potential way for teachers to reduce their own assessment workload, making students more responsible for tracking their progress and feedback provision (Sadler & Good, 2006; Towler & Broadfoot, 1992).

This chapter reviews relevant empirical studies concerning the use of student self-assessment in the compulsory school sector (K–12) to help establish which claims about self-assessment are empirically supported. Previous reviews of this topic have focused primarily on higher education students (e.g., Boud & Falchikov, 1989; Dochy, Segers, & Sluijsmans, 1999; Falchikov & Boud, 1989; Mabe & West, 1982). This chapter contributes to our understanding of self-assessment in public schooling.

Defining Self-Assessment

Many terms have been used to describe the process of students assessing and providing feedback on their own work, including self-assessment, self-evaluation, self-reflection, self-monitoring, and more generally, reflection. Since self-assessment requires evaluative consideration of one's own work, the processes of self-grading, self-testing, and self-rating can also potentially be forms of self-assessment. Both the *Thesaurus of ERIC Descriptors* (Educational Research Information Center [U.S.], 2001) and the *Thesaurus of Psychological Index Terms* (Tuleya, 2007) treat self-assessment as a synonym for self-appraisal, and both are classified under the subject heading *self-evaluation (individuals)* or *self-evaluation,* respectively. The *Thesaurus of ERIC Descriptors* defines self-evaluation as "individuals' assessment of themselves" (Educational Research Information Center [U.S.], 2001).

When examining the word *assessment*, the Joint Committee on Standards for Educational Evaluation (2003) defines it as a "process of collecting information about a student to aid in decision making about the student's progress and development" (p. 5). Accepting this definition of assessment, then logically, self-assessment must involve students collecting data to evaluate their own progress, consistent with Klenowski's (1995) statement that self-evaluation requires students "to evaluate and monitor their own performance in relation to identified criteria or standards" (p. 146). Hence, within a compulsory school setting and when serving academic purposes, we take a global and generic approach that self-assessment is a descriptive and evaluative act carried out by the student concerning his or her own work and academic abilities.

Self-assessment can be operationalized in many ways, ranging from a careful consideration of the quality of one's own work guided by a rubric or feedback from the teacher, to scoring one's own work, to practices like predicting one's likely score on an impending task or test. What distinguishes these actions from other assessment practices is that they are carried out by the student (Brooks, 2002), though the degree of autonomy from peers, teachers, or parents will vary in practice. Unlike Boud and Falchikov (1989), who privileged techniques that require an evaluative, criterion-based judgment, we have not excluded self-marking or self-rating techniques. Instead of restricting self-assessment to solely the act of evaluating the quality of work against socially agreed criteria, we include self-assessment acts that involve estimating quantitative aspects of work (e.g., amount, speed, score, or place on a hierarchy/progression). This gives us a broad scope to establish whether there are different effects depending on the type of self-assessment carried out. Thus, self-assessment takes place when students impute or infer that their work or their ability to do that work has some sort of quality characteristics, and this self-assessment may, in its most simple form, be a quantity estimate (i.e., How many task requirements have I satisfied?) or a quality estimate (i.e., How well have I done?).

In taking this broad stance toward self-assessment, we are aware that not all scholars share our perspective. Some classroom assessment

(CA) researchers (e.g., Andrade, 2010) make a robust distinction between assessment and evaluation in which the latter is considered to refer to grading, testing, or marking (hence, summative) rather than the more formative, improvement-oriented emphasis implied by assessment. Other authors (e.g., Clarke, Timperley, & Hattie, 2003) have prioritized a child-centered pedagogical process in which self-assessment focuses the student on processes that lead to improved outcomes without focusing on an evaluative dimension.

Distinguishing between assessment and evaluation has become commonplace in the AFL community, partly as a consequence of Sadler's (1989) assertion that formative and summative evaluations were qualitatively different forms of assessment. This stands in contrast to Scriven's (1967) definition, which focuses on the timing of the interpretations and uses of assessment rather than its form. While agreeing that formative improvement is the fundamental purpose for using any type of assessment (Popham, 2000), it is our position that there is little merit in creating a dichotomy between assessment and evaluation, because all assessments, including formative ones, describe and evaluate the merit, worth, or quality of student work (Hattie & Brown, 2010). Consequently, studies that involve compulsory school students making judgments about their own work or academic ability using a diverse range of assessment methods (e.g., tests, graded assignments, essays, performance tasks, or rubric-guided judgments) have been included in this review.

However, there are limits to what we would consider to be self-assessment. As Kasanen and Räty (2002) pointed out, within an academic context, self-assessment is not about the process of knowing oneself better, as in the notion that an unexamined life is not worth living; rather, it is about judging, evaluating, and considering one's own academic work or abilities. Hence, in this chapter we do not include studies primarily concerned with how children evaluate their self-concept or self-worth (e.g., Burnett, 1996; Byrne & Bazana, 1996; Marsh, 1988; Williams, 1996). The focus in this chapter is on self-assessment of schoolwork, rather than on personal well-being, because a major focus of schools is to help students learn new skills and knowledge and develop their understanding of school curriculum materials.

Self-Assessment Techniques

Methods of Self-Assessment

Research studies tend to emphasize self-assessment methods that focus directly on obtaining from students an estimate or description of how well they believe they will do or have done on a specific test or task. In general, it seems that self-assessment practices can be grouped into three major types: (1) self-ratings, (2) self-estimates of performance, and (3) criteria- or rubric-based assessments. Self-assessment practices may also encourage students to include comments or advice from the student to him or herself about how to improve.

Self-rating requires students to judge quality or quantity aspects of their work using a rating system. In the classroom, checklists that remind students of important task characteristics or task processes are commonplace (e.g., Clarke et al., 2003). Clarke (2005) has also created self-rating prompts that are more evaluative and task-oriented—that is, "a) I am pleased with my work because I . . . ; b) Two improvements I have made are . . . ; c) I would grade myself A B C D E because I . . . ; and d) Next time I need to focus on . . ." (p. 113). In Clarke's (2005) approach to self-rating, students are providing not only a rating of the quality of their work but are also expected to give feedback comments for improvement, mimicking the formative feedback teachers might provide. Another commonplace rating technique is the use of *traffic lights,* where students show the teacher a red, yellow, or green circle to indicate readiness to proceed or quality of understanding, with red signifying difficulty and green meaning comprehension (Black & Harrison, 2001; Clarke, 2005).

Self-marking or grading of one's own work can also be done using either a marking guide for objectively answered questions or a rubric or model answer (Todd, 2002). While some simple self-rating practices like self-marking have sometimes been shown to be trustworthy (Wall, 1982), some teacher educators (e.g., Brooks, 2002) consider that simple mechanical marking (e.g., right versus wrong) is unlikely to be effective in improving learning since high levels of cognitive engagement are absent. Alternatively, self-assessment may involve students estimating their level of performance or ability relative to a test or a task they are about to take, have just taken, or recall having taken some time previously (e.g., How well have I done on this test?). Some of these self-assessments are more global and may also require students to mentally estimate how well they performed on a test in the form of a test mark or score, a rank order position, or a grade.

Lastly, and perhaps most classically associated with AFL, is the practice of using a rubric to ascertain the quality characteristics of the individual's written or performed work. Rubrics may or may not have score indicators (e.g., A, Level 3, or excellence) but always arrange quality indicators in incremental progressions that students use to best fit the various aspects of their work. Rubrics are especially common when students are assessing writing or judging portfolios or collections of work (Andrade & Valtcheva, 2009). These three types of self-assessment show that self-assessments can be global (e.g., How good is my writing?) or anchored to a specific task (e.g., How well did I do on question 3?) as all such tasks require reflection on the quality of the student's work.

Accuracy in Self-Assessment

The role of accuracy of self-assessment is contentious. Brooks (2002) has argued that reliability matters for external assessments, not for formative classroom purposes. Others have argued that grading one's own work (Lipnevich & Smith, 2008) and being required to conform to a teacher's assessment of the student's work (Paulhus, 1991) have negative effects on students' judgments and undermine the constructive processes of self-regulation. Despite evidence students may be motivated to inflate their grades (Harris & Brown, 2010), there is a minority position (e.g., Chang & Tseng, 2011) that advocates using student self-assessments when determining final results so students feel their judgments are valued.

We believe that accuracy is an important facet in determining the validity of any assessment (Messick, 1989) since accurate self-evaluation is a key component within models of self-regulation of learning (Schunk, 1996; Zimmerman, 1998). Thus, from both psychometric and learning theory perspectives, the accuracy of self-assessment is critical, as suggested by the quote at the beginning of the chapter from Pausch, a computer science professor who used self-assessment principles in his teaching. If self-assessment processes lead students to conclude wrongly that they are good or weak in some domain and they base personal decisions on such false interpretations, harm could be done—even in classroom settings (e.g., task avoidance, not enrolling in future subjects) (Ramdass & Zimmerman, 2008).

Consistent with reliability theory (Haertel, 2006), we consider that all self-assessments, no matter how privileged the self is in terms of knowing what the self has done, are imperfect indicators of competence. Indeed, Dunning, Heath, and Suls (2004) identified many reasons self-assessments can be flawed. These include a tendency for humans (1) to be unrealistically optimistic about their own abilities (e.g., "I can finish this in just one week"), (2) to believe that they are above average (e.g., no one admits to being a poor driver, lover, or friend), (3) to neglect crucial information (e.g., ignore key performance indicators that should be used to evaluate their work), and (4) to have deficits in their information (e.g., simply do not know what to look for in determining the quality of their work). Furthermore, lack of competence in a domain (as would be expected in a low progress learner or beginner) has a dual handicapping effect; such people are not very good in the domain and, at the same time, are not aware that they are not good in the domain (Dunning et al., 2004). Additionally, pressure to enhance one's own self-worth may result in overestimation of ability (Saavedra & Kwun, 1993) and inaccurate self-reporting of grades or test scores (Kuncel, Credé, & Thomas, 2005). Students have also been found to take their own effort, which ought to be independent of quality, into account when evaluating their work (Ross, Rolheiser, & Hogaboam-Gray, 1998b). In much simpler terms, as Dr. Gregory House of *House* puts it, "Everybody lies" (Ruff & Barris, 2009, p. 84).

Another pressure on accurate self-assessment is that much of what makes one competent in many domains is relatively ill defined. Consider the great difficulty teachers have in scoring student work against standards or rubrics (Brown, 2009), often providing inaccurate or inconsistent judgments of student work (Topping, 2003). Thus, without putting any responsibility or blame on students, there are many good reasons to expect that their self-assessments of their own work products or performances will be reasonably flawed or inaccurate. Hence, while self-assessment has considerable promise for helping students improve their learning within compulsory school settings, it is not without potential problems and limitations.

Literature Review Method

Selection of Studies

In this chapter, we examined studies of student self-assessment carried out in the compulsory school sector to discern which claims can be empirically supported. Since self-assessment is subsumed by the term *self-evaluation,* that subject heading was initially used to query the Education Resources Information Center (ERIC) and PsycINFO databases. The search initially identified 348 potentially relevant sources. Through a check of abstracts and titles, studies were excluded from this sample when they were the following:

- Not readily available from the authors or the Internet
- In languages other than English
- Conducted outside the K–12 sector (e.g., higher education)
- Related primarily to student self-concept
- Conceptual, not empirical, analyses of self-assessment
- Related specifically to special education (important but outside the scope of this review)

Further searches carried out in these databases, using the key words *self-assessment* and *schools,* resulted in the collection of 11 additional relevant studies. Papers cited in existing reviews (e.g., Andrade & Valtcheva, 2009; Black & Wiliam, 1998; Ross, 2006) were also collected. The current paper provides a synthesis of 84 empirical studies on student self-evaluation in compulsory education.

Research Questions

Drawing on the claims and quality issues raised in the previous section, we reviewed the empirical literature in light of the following questions:

1. What is the relationship between self-assessment and student academic achievement?
2. What is the relationship between self-assessment and self-regulation (including motivation or engagement)?
3. How do students perceive and experience self-assessment?
4. What are the relationships between self-assessment accuracy and student age and ability?
5. What are the relationships between task features, method of self-assessment, and self-assessment accuracy?

Analysis

Studies were read and assigned to thematic categories arising from the research questions of the paper: (1) relationship to academic performance or achievement (achievement); (2) relationship to self-regulating processes (self-regulation); (3) student perspectives (student perspectives); and (4) accuracy concerns relative to student age, student experience, student proficiency, task characteristics, or means of self-assessment (accuracy). Both authors agreed on the classifications of each study.

Where sufficient data were provided, Cohen's (1992) *d* effect sizes (i.e., a standardized measure of difference as a proportion of standard deviation) were computed using an Excel macro developed by Wilson (2001). These standardized effect sizes allow the overall impact of the self-assessment practices described in the studies to be compared within this data set (e.g., average effects on different sample populations) and against effect sizes that have been computed for other educational practices. Within education, the average of all interventions reviewed in a large-scale synthesis of meta-analyses has been estimated to be d = 0.40 and values ≥0.60 are considered large (Hattie, 2009).

Empirical Evaluation of Self-Assessment in Education

The main design, demographic, and thematic content of every reviewed study has been summarized in Table 21.1.

	Source	*Design*	*Country*	*School Level*	*N*	*Description of Study*	*Theme(s)*
1	Alsaker (1989)	Survey	Norway	Middle school (G6–9)	2,309	Examined relationships between self-esteem, perceived academic competence, school importance, and achievement	Accuracy
2	Andrade & Boulay (2003)	Quasi-experiment	United States	Middle school (G7–8)	397	Compared writing results of an experimental group (rubric-guided self-assessment training) with a control group (rubric access only)	Achievement
3	Andrade, Du, & Mycek (2010)	Quasi-experiment	United States	Elementary & middle school	162	Investigated the relationship between writing scores and modeling, generating criteria and self-assessing using a rubric	Achievement
4	Andrade, Du, & Wang (2008)	Quasi-experiment	United States	Elementary school (G3 & 4)	116	Evaluated the effects of modeling, generating criteria, and self-assessing using a rubric on writing performance	Achievement
5	Andrade, Wang, Du, & Akawi (2009)	Quasi-experiment	United States	Elementary & middle school (G3–7)	268	Investigated rubric and self-assessment usage in writing, examining effects on self-efficacy with focus on gender	Self-efficacy
6	Ash (1980)	Survey	United States	High school	156	Examined the usefulness of typing ability self-assessment	Accuracy
7	Barling (1980)	Experiment	South Africa	Elementary school (G3–6)	138	Compared effects of five different treatments (control, control plus feedback, self-monitoring, self-determined performance standards and self-reinforcement, or self-instruction) on academic performance	Achievement
8	Barnett & Hixon (1997)	Quasi-experiment	United States	Elementary school (G2, 4, 6)	62	Investigated how grade level and subject related to students' ability to predict test scores	Accuracy
9	Blatchford (1997a)	Longitudinal survey	United Kingdom	Elementary—high school (ages 7–16)	108	Explored the accuracy and stability over time of students' academic self-assessments	Accuracy
10	Blatchford (1997b)	Longitudinal survey	United Kingdom	Elementary & high school	108	Examined the effects of sex and ethnicity on academic attainment self-assessments	Accuracy

	Source	*Design*	*Country*	*School Level*	*N*	*Description of Study*	*Theme(s)*
11	Bradshaw (2001)	Quasi-experiment	United States	Elementary school (G3–5)	87	Compared student ratings with actual performance	Accuracy
12	Brookhart, Andolina, Zuza, & Furman (2004)	Action research	United States	Elementary school (G3)	41	Investigated self-assessment of strategy use for memorizing and recalling mathematics facts, learning reflection, and using metacognitive skills	Self-regulation; Student perspectives
13	Brown, Irving, Peterson, & Hirschfeld (2009)	Survey	New Zealand	High school (G9–10)	705	Mapped relationships between student definitions and conceptions of assessment	Student perspectives
14	Brown, Peterson, & Irving (2009)	Survey	New Zealand	High school (G9–10)	624	Analyzed relationships between student definition of assessment responses and mathematics achievement	Student perspectives
15	Butler (1990)	Experiment	Israel	Elementary school (GK, 2, & 5)	80	Examined the effects of age and conditions (mastery and competition) on self-assessment accuracy	Accuracy
16	Butler & Lee (2006)	Survey	Korea	Elementary school	151	Investigated the validity of students' self-assessments of oral English performance	Accuracy
17	Chang & Tseng (2011)	Experiment	Taiwan	High school (G8)	60	Examined the effects of students' use of a Web-based portfolio system that incorporated self- and peer assessment tasks	Accuracy
18	Claes & Salame (1975)	Quasi-experiment	Canada	High school (G9, 10)	65	Compared the accuracy of students' self-evaluations of performance on tasks to the students' overall achievement.	Accuracy
19	Connell & Ilardi (1987)	Survey	United States	Elementary school (G4–6)	121	Investigated variables in children's self-ratings of academic competence	Accuracy
20	Cowie (2009)	Multimethod	New Zealand	Elementary, & middle school	22 classes	Investigated student perceptions of experienced formative assessment practices	Student perspectives

(Continued)

Table 21.1 (Continued)

	Source	*Design*	*Country*	*School Level*	*N*	*Description of Study*	*Theme(s)*
21	Daiute & Kruidenier (1985)	Experiment	United States	Middle & high school (G7, 9)	57	Evaluated the effect of using computer self-questioning prompts on writing achievement	Achievement
22	Eccles, Wigfield, Harold, & Blumenfeld (1993)	Survey	United States	Elementary school (G1, 2, 4)	865	Examined students' perceived levels of competence in multiple domains (e.g., sport, music, reading, and math)	Accuracy
23	Elder (2010)	Interview	United States	Elementary school (G1 & G4, 5)	37	Investigated how students self-assess schoolwork	Accuracy
24	Fernandes & Fontana (1996)	Quasi-experiment	Portugal	Elementary school (G3, 4)	354	Examined student self-efficacy beliefs and academic achievement after using self-assessment techniques	Self-regulation
25	Frey & Ruble (1987)	Interview & observation	United States	Elementary school (GK–4)	83	Explored relationships between student self-estimates of ability and their age and sex	Accuracy
26	Gao (2009)	Case study	Hong Kong	High school (G10, 11)	1 class	Examined student perceptions of school-based assessment practices, including self-assessment	Student perspectives
27	Glaser, Kessler, Palm, & Brunstein (2010)	Experiment	Germany	Elementary school (G4)	105	Investigated the effects of self-regulation and evaluation training on writing achievement and efficacy	Self-regulation Achievement
28	Griffiths & Davies (1993)	Action research	UK	Elementary school (G5, 6)	1 class	Explored student self-assessment reflections about the learning process	Self-regulation
29	Harris & Brown (2010)	Interview	New Zealand	Elementary, middle, & high school (G5–7, 10)	40	Studied student and teacher perspectives and experiences of self-assessment practices	Student perspectives

	Source	*Design*	*Country*	*School Level*	*N*	*Description of Study*	*Theme(s)*
30	Harris, Harnett, & Brown (2009)	Focus group interviews	New Zealand	Elementary, middle, & high school (G5/6, 7, 10)	46	Examined student perspectives of experienced classroom assessment (CA) practices	Student perspectives
31	Harward, Allred, & Sudweeks (1994)	Experiment	United States	Elementary (G4)	209	Assessed the effects of four self-corrected test methods on spelling achievement	Achievement
32	Hewitt (2001)	Experiment	United States	Middle, & high school (G7–9)	82	Examined the effects of modeling, self-evaluation, and self-listening on junior high school instrumentalists' music performance	Achievement
33	Hewitt (2005)	Survey	United States	Middle & high school	143	Compared the accuracy of student musical performance self-assessments to expert evaluations	Accuracy
34	Higgins, Harris, & Kuehn (1994)	Survey	United States	Elementary school (G1, 2)	46	Compared student self-ratings of their projects on 5-point scale with teacher ratings	Accuracy
35	Hughes, Sullivan, & Mosley (1985)	Experiment	United States	Elementary school (G5)	250	Examined the effects of self versus teacher assessment and task difficulty on student motivation	Self-regulation
36	Ikeguchi (1996)	Survey	Japan	High school	34	Compared students' self-assessments of language skills with teacher assessments and test scores	Accuracy
37	Johnson & Winterbottom (2011)	Interviews & observation	United Kingdom	High school	28	Examined the motivation and perspectives of students in a girls only biology class implementing self- and peer assessment	Self-regulation Student perspectives
38	Jones, Trap, & Cooper (1977)	Quasi-experiment	United States	Elementary school (G1)	22	Compared student self-rating and recording of handwriting performance with adult ratings	Accuracy

(Continued)

Table 21.1 (Continued)

	Source	*Design*	*Country*	*School Level*	*N*	*Description of Study*	*Theme(s)*
39	Kaderavek, Gillam, Ukrainetz, Justice, & Eisenberg (2004)	Survey	United States	Elementary school (ages 5–12)	401	Examined student self-rating of their narratives relative to actual performance	Accuracy
40	Kasanen & Räty (2002)	Multimethod	Finland	Elementary school (G1)	21	Studied the classroom implementation of self-assessment	Student perspectives
41	Kasanen, Räty, & Eklund (2009)	Interview	Finland	Elementary school (G3, 6)	58	Investigated pupils' evaluations of their academic abilities and potential for improvement in different school subjects	Accuracy
42	Keil, McClintock, Kramer, & Platow, (1990)	Quasi-experiment	United States	Elementary & middle School (G2, 4, 6, 8)	480	Examined the effects of information about children's own outcomes and those of a peer on their self-evaluations	Accuracy
43	Klenowski (1995)	Case Study	Australia & United Kingdom	High school	Not given	Investigated how students self-evaluated work and how teachers implemented these practices	Self-regulation
44	Koivula, Hassmén, & Hunt (2001)	Experiment	Sweden	High school (final year)	550	Compared academic results of students, who completed confidence ratings of answers to standardized test items with normal test takers	Accuracy; Achievement
45	Kwok & Lai (1993)	Survey	Canada & Hong Kong	Elementary school	253	Examined student self-evaluations of academic competence relative to their actual performance in mathematics	Accuracy; Student perspectives
46	Lasonen (1995)	Survey	Finland	High school	346	Explored student experiences of self-assessment and the criteria they use to make judgments	Student perspectives

	Source	*Design*	*Country*	*School Level*	*N*	*Description of Study*	*Theme(s)*
47	Laveault & Miles (2002)	Survey	Canada	Elementary & middle school (G5–8)	770	Investigated the relationship between writing proficiency and accurate self-assessment using a rubric	Accuracy
48	LaVoie & Hodapp (1987)	Survey	United States	Elementary school (G4–6)	311	Compared children's perceptions of standardized test performance with actual performance	Student perspectives; Accuracy
49	Lee & Gavine (2003)	Experiment	Scotland	Middle school (G7)	56	Evaluated the effectiveness of an intervention involving students setting goals and participating in self-evaluation	Accuracy
50	Luyten & Dolkar (2010)	Survey	Bhutan	High school (G10)	365	Compared student and teacher ratings to examination scores	Accuracy
51	McDevitt et al. (2008)	Survey	United States	Middle school (G6–8)	90	Investigated the use of self-assessment and goal setting in reading	Student perspectives; Self-regulation
52	McDonald (2002)	Survey	Barbados	High school	570	Explored student definitions of self-assessment	Student perspectives
53	McDonald (2009)	Mixed methods	Caribbean	High school	515	Compared qualitative data about male student and teacher experiences of self-assessment training with examination results	Self-regulation; Student perspectives
54	McDonald & Boud (2003)	Experiment	Barbados	High school (Final year)	515	Investigated the effects of self-assessment training on student end-of-high-school qualifications results	Achievement
55	Mac Iver (1987)	Survey	United States	Elementary school (G5 & 6)	1,570	Examined the effects of task structure, ability grouping, emphasis on grades, sex, math talent, and math performance on student self-assessments	Accuracy
56	Miller, Duffy, & Zane (1993)	Experiment	United States	Elementary school (G6)	13	Investigated the effects of rewards on accuracy and achievement on mathematics homework self-correction	Accuracy; Achievement

(Continued)

Table 21.1 (Continued)

	Source	*Design*	*Country*	*School Level*	*N*	*Description of Study*	*Theme(s)*
57	Mitman & Lash (1988)	Survey	United States	Elementary school (G3)	131	Compared student perceptions of academic standing with alternative measures	Accuracy
58	Morrison, Montemayor, & Wiltshire (2004)	Quasi-experiment	United States	Middle & high school	141	Compared student self-assessments of musical performance (with and without models) with expert evaluations of performance	Achievement
59	Munns & Woodward (2006)	Action research	Australia	Elementary school (G4)	Not given	Examined relationships between self-assessment, student engagement, behavior, and student–teacher relationship quality	Self-regulation
60	Ng & Earl (2008)	Survey	Australia	High school (Final year)	94	Investigated the role of feedback, goal orientation, and self-efficacy on student self-estimate accuracy	Accuracy
61	Olina & Sullivan (2002)	Experiment	Latvia	High school	189	Explored the effects of teacher evaluation and student self-evaluation on student performance and efficacy attitudes	Achievement; Self-regulation
62	Peterson & Irving (2008)	Focus Group interviews	New Zealand	High school (G9 & 10)	41	Investigated student conceptions of assessment and feedback	Student perspectives
63	Pomerantz & Ruble (1997)	Survey	United States	Elementary school (G2–5)	236	Examined student conceptions of ability and their relationships to self-evaluation	Accuracy
64	Powel & Gray (1995)	Experiment	United States	Elementary school (G1)	124	Investigated if rewards or collaboration with peers improved the accuracy of student predictions of task success.	Accuracy
65	Raider-Roth (2005)	Interview	United States	Elementary school (G6)	9	Examined students' understandings of self-assessment and their experiences with specific self-assessment tasks	Student perspectives
66	Ramdass & Zimmerman (2008)	Experiment	United States	Elementary school (G5–6)	42	Explored relationships between self-correction training, self-efficacy, self-evaluation, and math performance	Self-regulation; Achievement; Accuracy

	Source	*Design*	*Country*	*School Level*	*N*	*Description of Study*	*Theme(s)*
67	Ross, Hogaboam-Gray, & Rolheiser (2002)	Experiment	Canada	Elementary school (G5–6)	516	Studied the effects of self-evaluation training on mathematics achievement	Achievement
68	Ross, Rolheiser, & Hogaboam-Gray (1998a)	Experiment	Canada	Elementary school (G5–6)	300	Explored the effects of self-assessment training on student mathematics achievement	Achievement; Student perspectives
69	Ross, Rolheiser, & Hogaboam-Gray (1998b)	Quasi-experiment	Canada	Elementary & high school (G5–12)	368	Examined student perspectives of self-assessment when classes were in action research and skills training conditions	Student perspectives
70	Ross, Rolheiser, & Hogaboam-Gray (1999)	Experiment	Canada	Elementary school (G5–6)	296	Evaluated the effects of self-evaluation of narrative writing with rubrics on achievement	Achievement
71	Ross, Rolheiser, & Hogaboam-Gray (2002)	Interviews	Canada	Elementary school (G2, 4, 6)	71	Investigated how student cognition mediated evaluation and achievement	Achievement; Student perspectives; Accuracy; Self-regulation
72	Sadler & Good (2006)	Experiment	United States	Middle school (G7)	126	Examined the accuracy and effects on achievement of students grading their own work using rubrics	Achievement; Accuracy
73	Schunk (1996)	Experiment	United States	Elementary school (G4)	44	Investigated how goals and self-evaluation affect motivation and achievement outcomes	Achievement; Self-regulation
74	Spaights (1965)	Survey	United States	Middle school (G7)	80	Examined self-ratings of ability for reading, arithmetic, and language	Accuracy
75	Stipek (1981)	Interview	United States	Elementary school (K–3)	64	Compared students', teachers', and peers' self-ratings of student academic ability	Accuracy
76	Stipek & Tannatt (1984)	Interview	United States	Elementary (pre, K–3) &	96	Investigated how students judge personal and peers' academic ability	Accuracy

(Continued)

Table 21.1 (Continued)

	Source	*Design*	*Country*	*School Level*	*N*	*Description of Study*	*Theme(s)*
77	Sung, Chang, Chang, & Yu (2010)	Survey	Taiwan	Middle school (G7, 8)	226	Investigated self- and peer assessments rating behaviors and examining reliability and validity	Accuracy
78	van Kraayenoord & Paris (1997)	Survey	Australia	Elementary school (G4–6)	93	Tested a classroom interview instrument designed to assess and promote learning self-appraisal	Accuracy; Achievement
79	Wall (1982)	Experiment	United States	Elementary (G4)	85	Investigated the relative effects of systematic self-monitoring and self-reinforcement on children's academic test performances	Achievement
80	Wan-a-rom (2010)	Case Study	Thailand	High school (G11)	5	Evaluated the accuracy of student English vocabulary knowledge self-assessments	Accuracy
81	Watt (2000)	Survey	Australia	Middle school (G7)	400	Investigated change in student self- and task evaluations, and achievement behavior in mathematics and English	Accuracy
82	Wells & Sweeney (1986)	Longitudinal survey	USA	High school (G10 & 11)	1,508	Examined the relationship between self-esteem and self-assessment of ability	Accuracy
83	Wilson & Wright (1993)	Survey	United States	Middle & high school (G8–12)	301	Investigated if student self-evaluations, grades, and teacher assessments predicted standardized test scores	Accuracy
84	Wright & Houck (1995)	Survey	United States	High school (G9–12)	222	Examined gender differences in self-assessments, teacher ratings, and performance on verbal and numerical reasoning tests	Accuracy

Table 21.1 Summary Design, Demographic, and Thematic Characteristics of Reviewed Studies on Student Self-Evaluation

Relationship of Self-Assessment to Academic Achievement

A number of studies have shown that students who engage in self-assessment experience positive gains in their learning (Table 21.2). While most studies report positive effects of having students self-assess, some reported nil to small effects (i.e., $d \leq 0.20$). The median effect lies between 0.40 and 0.45, a moderate effect consistent with values reported in Black and Wiliam (1998).

Training in diverse self-assessment strategies led to learning gains. For example, immediate self-correction of spelling words generated improved test score performances among primary students (Harward, Allred, & Sudweeks, 1994). Mathematics performance was boosted through the classroom implementation of self-assessment strategies (Ross, Hogaboam-Gray, & Rolheiser, 2002), and students taught self-correction strategies for mathematical long division outperformed the control group (Ramdass & Zimmerman, 2008). Students supported in self-questioning their writing with a computerized prompt system had statistically significant advantages in revision quality (Daiute & Kruidenier, 1985). A 12-month training program in the use of self-assessment processes resulted in a statistically significant advantage to students in high school qualifications examinations (McDonald & Boud, 2003). Being taught explicitly to self-regulate their writing processes resulted in both better writing outcomes and more optimistic self-efficacy and ability self-evaluation (Glaser, Kessler, Palm, & Brunstein, 2010). Perhaps the small effects found in Andrade and Boulay (2003) are attributable to the lack of training in self-assessment students received prior to the study.

Using models, answers, or teacher feedback to guide self-assessment judgments also generally improved performance. Self-rating one's own music performance in conjunction with listening to a model performance improved actual performance (Hewitt, 2001). Self-evaluation combined with teacher evaluation produced better quality science project reports than no-evaluation or teacher-only evaluation, though not better test scores (Olina & Sullivan, 2002).

Children who self-evaluated in conjunction with defining criteria and receiving feedback from teachers about their self-evaluations had small gains in narrative writing (Ross, Rolheiser, & Hogaboam-Gray, 1999). However, large gains were reported in writing for a rubric-guided self-evaluation without teacher feedback (Andrade et al., 2008; Andrade et al., 2010). Similarly, science students who self-graded their work with a rubric that they had co-constructed with their teachers gained considerably more on a teacher-marked science test than students who engaged in peer marking (Sadler & Good, 2006), with much larger gains seen among the initially lower performing students. Ross et al. (1999) also found lower achieving students gained considerably ($d = 0.58$) from being taught to self-assess.

Systems where students predicted or monitored their accuracy and achievement and/or rewarded themselves for accuracy or improvement also were correlated with gains. Self-monitoring the number of answers correct and setting stringent performance standards with self-selected rewards for meeting those standards improved learning of vocabulary and mathematics (Barling, 1980). Students taught to give themselves rewards for reaching challenging targets had modest improvements in achievement when they self-corrected their mathematics homework (Miller, Duffy, & Zane, 1993). Likewise, self-determined reinforcement (i.e., giving themselves rewards based on targets relative to previous performances) gave large learning gains relative to just self-marking (Wall, 1982). Schunk (1996) found that when students were asked to self-assess their ability to accurately complete fraction problems, performance goal orientation resulted in greater effects than learning goal orientation, perhaps because students responded positively to the challenge of getting more problems done and solved. Koivula, Hassmén, & Hunt (2001) found that students who were asked to self-assess the accuracy of their responses to particular standardized test items scored better than pupils who did not take part in this additional monitoring and reflection.

Hence, it appears that there is empirical evidence that self-assessment of a task or self-confidence in the quality of the work will generally improve academic performance across a range of grade levels and subject areas, although the extent of these gains varies across studies, with 11 of the 24 effects falling below the 0.40 Hattie (2009) recommends as a cut score for determining if an intervention is academically

Study	*Type of Self-Assessment*	*Effect size (Cohen's d)*
Wall (1982)	Self-marking with self-selected reinforcements	1.62
Ramdass & Zimmerman (2008)	Self-rated confidence in accuracy of own work	1.50
Schunk (1996)	Self-rated confidence in accuracy of own work (performance goal condition)	1.40
Andrade, Du, & Wang (2008)	Rubric guided judgment	0.87
Sadler & Good (2006)	Rubric guided judgment	0.82
van Kraayenoord & Paris (1997)	Student verbal self-assessments evaluated by researchers	0.77
Andrade, Du, & Mycek (2010)	Rubric guided judgment	0.66
Hewitt (2001)	Self-rated performance	0.59
Olina & Sullivan (2002)	Self-rated written work	0.57
Daiute & Kruidenier (1985)	Computer assisted monitoring of work	0.52
McDonald & Boud (2003)	Monitoring of self-regulation processes	0.45
Ross, Hogaboam-Gray, & Rolheiser (2002)	Generic self-assessment of mathematics	0.40
Glaser et al. (2010)	Self-evaluation of written work	0.38
Schunk (1996)	Self-rated confidence in accuracy of own work (learning goal condition)	0.38
Miller, Duffy, & Zane (1993)	Self-correction of homework	0.32
Koivula, Hassmén, & Hunt (2001)	Self-rated confidence in accuracy of quantitative work	0.29
Barling (1980)	Self-monitoring of accuracy with self-selected rewards and standards	0.28
Harward, Allred, & Sudweeks (1994)	Immediate self-correction of test performance	0.27
Ross, Rolheiser, & Hogaboam-Gray (1999)	Rubric guided judgment	0.18
Koivula, Hassmén, & Hunt (2001)	Self-rated confidence in accuracy of verbal work	0.12
Ross, Rolheiser, & Hogaboam-Gray (1998a)	Self-assessment survey rating of performance and strategy usage on a mathematics test	0.08
Andrade & Boulay (2003)	Rubric guided judgment (response to literature essay)	0.04
Andrade & Boulay (2003)	Rubric guided judgment (historical fiction essay)	–0.04

Table 21.2 Effect Sizes for Learning Effects of Self-Evaluation

worthwhile. These findings also reinforce the claim that it is the implementation and complexity of the self-assessment, more so than the type, which generates the positive effects. While studies using rubrics account for some of the higher effect sizes, three of the lowest effect sizes were also of this type, although the two lowest effects occurred in a study where students used rubrics without any training.

Effect of Self-Assessment on Self-Regulation Processes

Studies have demonstrated that engagement in self-assessment also contributes to increased self-regulating skills (Klenowski, 1995; Ramdass & Zimmerman, 2008), a demonstrated precursor of improved achievement (Schunk, 2005). From self-assessment, greater internality of control (Fernandes & Fontana, 1996) and greater self-focused comparison rather than comparing to peer performance (Ross, Rolheiser, & Hogaboam-Gray, 2002) have been reported (see also Chapter 3 of this volume). Greater persistence on a difficult task was found after confidential self-evaluation of performance in word spelling (Hughes, Sullivan, & Mosley, 1985). Through self-assessment, students thought about their use of strategies for memorizing and recalling mathematics facts, instead of just using rote learning (Brookhart et al., 2004).

Improved student motivation, self-efficacy, engagement, student behavior, and quality of student–teacher relationships have all been found as a consequence of self-evaluation (Glaser et al., 2010; Griffiths & Davies, 1993; Munns & Woodward, 2006; Olina & Sullivan, 2002; Schunk, 1996). Student goal setting, a self-regulating skill connected to self-evaluation, was not a statistically significant factor in improved reading performance and motivation—perhaps because students found it difficult to decide on appropriate, challenging goals (McDevitt, et al., 2008). The effects of self-assessment by student sex have not been extensively studied and are varied. Andrade, Wang, Du, and Akawi (2009) found that while mean student self-reported self-efficacy scores generally increased when using rubrics and self-assessment during the writing process, girls appeared to gain more self-efficacy from the self-assessment training than boys. Frey and Ruble (1987) found girls made more negative self-evaluations and attributions than boys—perhaps because of their concern to maintain social relationships. In contrast, McDonald (2009) found that male students especially benefitted from self-assessment training in relation to motivation and achievement. However, Johnson and Winterbottom (2011) found that students in the girls-only class they studied reported lower motivation, lower commitment to a mastery goal orientation, and lower self-efficacy after the implementation of self- and peer assessment, although observed class behaviors suggested some students became more learning oriented.

The research evidence for the connection between self-assessment and self-regulated learning (SRL) is not robust, despite many assertions to that effect. While evidence tentatively appears to suggest that self-assessment can positively contribute to student motivation and self-regulation, some results are mixed. It remains unclear which particular types of students may benefit the most from these practices as it is likely that pupils have highly individualized responses to self-assessment, as discussed in the next section.

Student Perceptions of Self-Assessment

Some studies indicate students seem to enjoy being involved in self-assessment (Brookhart et al., 2004; McDonald, 2009; Ross, Rolheiser, et al., 2002), especially if self-assessment helps them improve their understanding of criteria or work toward their own goals (McDevitt, et al., 2008). Reviews note that rubrics have been found to be particularly helpful for getting students to better understand evaluative criteria (Andrade, 2000; Andrade & Valtcheva, 2009).

Notwithstanding these demonstrated effects, a number of studies have shown that many students raise questions about self-assessment. Students are not always positive about self-assessment or aware of what it is really for. McDonald (2002) found that the students defined self-assessment primarily in terms of autonomous study skills rather than reflections on or evaluations of the merit of their own work, although students in her later study described self-assessment as helpful and motivating (McDonald, 2009). Sometimes students simply fill in the blanks rather than engage in thoughtful self-evaluation (Brookhart et al., 2004). There is evidence that students do not always consider self-assessment to even be assessment (Brown, Irving,

Peterson, & Hirschfeld, 2009; Brown, Peterson, & Irving, 2009; Harris, Harnett, & Brown, 2009; Peterson & Irving, 2008) and question its value (LaVoie & Hodapp, 1987), still wanting thorough, individualized teacher feedback (Lasonen, 1995). Students sometimes see self-assessment as boring, an inappropriate appropriation of the teacher's responsibility, and/or a source of cheating or non-standard scores (Gao, 2009; Harris & Brown, 2010; Johnson & Winterbottom, 2011; Peterson & Irving, 2008; Ross et al., 1998b). Ross et al. (1998b)found that teachers did little to explore student misconceptions and concerns about self-assessment, leading many pupils to become increasingly negative.

Students have also raised concerns about their psychological safety when their self-evaluations are made public to peers, parents, and teachers (Cowie, 2009; Harris & Brown, 2010; Raider-Roth, 2005; Ross, Rolheiser, et al., 1998b, 2002), a common classroom process (Kasanen & Räty, 2002). Consequently, students may provide depressed self-evaluations for fear of being seen as egotistical (Brooks, 2002) or for cultural practices such as self-effacement (Kwok & Lai, 1993). Alternatively, they may give elevated self-assessments to avoid being shamed in front of the class (Harris & Brown, 2010), with studies showing students have differing and highly personal reactions to self-assessment disclosure (Cowie, 2009; Harris et al., 2009). Hence, if self-assessment is to be an effective classroom practice, the valid concerns students have about its legitimacy and practice must be taken into account.

Accuracy in Self-Assessment

Studies reviewed by Ross (2006) indicate that the student as a self can be highly consistent in evaluations, but comparisons between self-evaluations and other measures (e.g., test scores, teacher ratings, and parent ratings) depict a less reliable portrait for self-assessment. The correlation between self-ratings and teacher ratings (Alsaker, 1989; Connell & Ilardi, 1987; Sung, Chang, Chang, & Yu, 2010; van Kraayenoord & Paris, 1997), between self-estimates of performance and actual test scores (Ash, 1980; Barnett & Hixon, 1997; Bradshaw, 2001; Ikeguchi, 1996; Koivula et al., 2001; LaVoie & Hodapp, 1987; Luyten & Dolkar, 2010; Wilson & Wright, 1993; Wright & Houck, 1995), and between student and teacher rubric-based judgments (Higgins, Harris, & Kuehn, 1994; Laveault & Miles, 2002; Sadler & Good, 2006) tended to be positive, ranging from weak to moderate (i.e., values ranging from $r \approx 0.20$ to 0.80), with few studies reporting correlations greater than 0.60. Accuracy was improved when students were taught explicitly to use a self-checking strategy (Ramdass & Zimmerman, 2008), and rewarding accuracy was also found to increase it (Miller et al., 1993). Nonetheless, the accuracy of student self-assessment does not appear to be uniform throughout the student's life course, nor across the full range of learning activities. Some students do not accept that their assessments are inherently less accurate than teachers, believing self-assessments should be used for grading purposes (Chang & Tseng, 2011).

Accuracy, Age, and Schooling Experience

Increasing age is confounded with increasing experience of school so it is not entirely clear whether improved accuracy of self-evaluation is a function of developmental processes or educational experience. Nonetheless, younger children tend to be more optimistic in their self-estimations of performance than older children (Frey & Ruble, 1987; Eccles, Wigfield, Harold, & Blumenfeld, 1993; Ross, Rolheiser, et al., 2002). A review by Stipek and Mac Iver (1989) noted that in elementary school, the criteria children use to judge their intellectual competence starts with emphasis on effort, social reinforcement, and mastery, maturing to a reliance on more objective and normative information.

In studies that used self-ratings, younger students tend to be more optimistic, lenient, or generous than older students (Blatchford, 1997a, 1997b; Kaderavek, Gillam, Ukrainetz, Justice, & Eisenberg, 2004; Kasanen, Räty, & Eklund, 2009; Stipek, 1981; Stipek & Tannatt, 1984; Wilson & Wright, 1993). Elder (2010) found that Grade 1 students reported focusing on superficial features, while Grades 4 and 5 students described making more complex judgments; however, both groups indicated relying heavily on the opinions of others (e.g., parents or teachers) when making decisions about work quality. Older students' self-ratings, while lower than younger students, tend to correlate more strongly with teacher ratings or test scores (Alsaker, 1989; Blatchford, 1997a; Bradshaw,

2001; Butler, 1990; Hewitt, 2005; Kaderavek et al., 2004; Pomerantz & Ruble, 1997; Stipek, 1981; Stipek & Tannatt, 1984) and are generally more sophisticated (Ross, Rolheiser, et al., 2002).

Accuracy and Academic Ability

A large number of studies suggest that accuracy in self-assessment is related to academic ability—that is, higher performing students evaluate their own work more accurately. Only one study was found that contradicted this pattern (Spaights, 1965); although, given the small sample size and its age, the findings may not give an accurate picture of the current situation. Consistent with the notion of double-handicapping related to low ability, high ability students seem to be more severe in assessing their work than their teachers, while low ability students seem to be more lenient on themselves (Barnett & Hixon, 1997; Claes & Salame, 1975; Kwok & Lai, 1993; Laveault & Miles, 2002; Mitman & Lash, 1988; Sung et al., 2010; Watt, 2000). The self-ratings from more able, proficient, or intelligent students tend to correlate more highly with teacher and test measures than the ratings of less proficient students (Claes & Salame, 1975; Keil, McClintock, Kramer, & Platow, 1990; Kwok & Lai, 1993; Laveault & Miles, 2002; Mitman & Lash, 1988; Ng & Earl, 2008; Sung et al., 2010; van Kraayenoord & Paris, 1997). This may suggest that the path to improved performance is not through inflated but inaccurate confidence in one's ability, but through greater humility due to one's appreciation of competence and capability. Hence, empirical data show that age and proficiency are a powerful basis for more accurate self-evaluation.

Accuracy and Task Difficulty

The difficulty of the task being learned interacts with students' ability to self-assess (Barnett & Hixon, 1997; Bradshaw, 2001; Hewitt, 2005). Tasks that are familiar and predictable probably permit more accurate student self-assessment. More technically difficult tasks require greater attention and effort, and this probably interferes with resources needed to monitor and self-rate performance. For example, the simple, concrete task of evaluating the accuracy of letter formation had high levels of agreement between student self-scoring and teacher scoring (Jones, Trap, & Cooper, 1977), and students were 80% to 90% accurate in their self-assessments of whether or not they knew the meaning of a word (Wan-a-rom, 2010). However, Powel and Gray (1995) could not reduce the inaccuracy of young students' self-estimates of success in a beanbag tossing task, despite its obvious concrete nature. Self-assessment in hard tasks can be supported with extra performance-based feedback (Lee & Gavine, 2003). The presence or absence of formal instruction in tested content prior to testing appears to impact student ability to predict accurately their performance (Barnett & Hixon, 1997), and greater accuracy in self-assessment was found when it was explicitly linked to an assessment of the same proficiency (Butler & Lee, 2006).

Basis for Evaluation

Studies have indicated that students value and use criteria based on construct irrelevant factors like effort when evaluating their work (e.g., Ross, Rolheiser, et al., 1998b, 2002). However, self-assessments that use more specific, concrete standards or reference points, rather than subjective criteria (e.g., "I made an effort" or "I'm good at this"), are associated with greater accuracy (Claes & Salame, 1975). Students who received regular teacher feedback in math were found to be more accurate in their self-assessments as they were more likely to use legitimate criteria to judge their abilities (Mac Iver, 1987). More modest and more accurate self-assessments were found among older students who shifted from a general social comparison (i.e., "all children my age") to a more specific social comparison (i.e., "those in my class") as the basis for self-rating (Blatchford, 1997a).

Other Factors Related to Accuracy

It has also been reported that gender, ethnic culture, and personality impact accuracy. For example, Blatchford (1997b) found that as students grew older, White students (especially girls) were less positive and less accurate in their self-assessments of academic achievement than Black students. Wells and Sweeney (1986) identified that students with consistently high self-esteem were more likely to overestimate their abilities, while those with low self-esteem often underestimated their abilities.

Training is also likely to improve accuracy. For example, improved accuracy in rubric-based self-assessment has been demonstrated (1) by teaching students to use explicit, objective criteria (Ramdass & Zimmerman, 2008); (2) by involving students in the co-construction of criteria for the rubric and with practice at using the rubric (Ross, Rolheiser, & Hogaboam-Gray, 1998a); (3) by ensuring students are motivated to pay attention to the rubric (Laveault & Miles, 2002); and (4) by getting students to justify their self-evaluation explicitly to their peers (Dunning et al., 2004).

Summary of Accuracy in Self-Assessment

The general impression formed from the research is that self-assessment is not robustly accurate but also it certainly is not randomly related to external measures of performance. Correlations falling in the range of 0.30 to 0.50 explain some 10% to 25% of variance between the self-assessment and some external measure of performance. Student self-assessments appear to be more accurate among older or more academically able students. Furthermore, students tend to assign lower and less optimistic ratings to their own work with increased experience or ability. Underrating of ability, found in older and more able students, was also correlated with less anxiety and less "emotional investment in achievement outcomes" (Connell & Ilardi, 1987, p. 1303). Hence, as students mature and develop academically, we can expect self-assessments to become less optimistic and more accurate. Educators should not panic when students begin to assign lower ratings for their own work as this may indicate improved competence and a more accurate self-evaluation of performance. While training in self-assessment can improve the accuracy of self-assessment, it seems pedagogically inappropriate to encourage high self-assessment scores independent of increased academic competence; students should not be encouraged to go easy on themselves for ego protection purposes.

Nonetheless, there is a need for instructional input and caution when implementing self-assessment with students likely to be relatively inaccurate (i.e., younger or less proficient students). All self-assessment techniques seem to have similar ranges of agreement with external measures, and rubric-based self-assessment studies appear most promising because of the relatively high learning effects shown when students use them. The studies reviewed also point to the importance of reducing the subjectivity in the criteria students use to evaluate their work. The provision of rubrics and a focus on what others would deem as quality appear to be necessary for high quality self-assessment. Concern must be expressed about the wisdom of using student self-assessments as part of course grades or final summary evaluations because this introduces high-stakes consequences for honest, accurate evaluations.

Conclusion

The reviewed studies suggest that student self-assessment can contribute to improved learning outcomes and better self-regulation skills, provided such self-evaluation involves deep engagement with the processes affiliated with self-regulation (i.e., goal setting, self-monitoring, and evaluation against valid, objective standards). It would appear that it is not the form of self-assessment that matters per se but rather the level of mental engagement students must use to determine how well they have done. Low levels of cognitive engagement can be seen in self-rating satisfaction with a happy or smiley face scale, awarding oneself a grade for a test based on perceived effort, or assigning a rubric characteristic based on a desire to avoid failure. Higher levels of self-assessment cognitive engagement can be seen when students rate themselves relative to challenging goals, evaluate test performance on objective criteria, or use rubrics to which they contributed. Learning and self-regulation gains seem to depend on higher levels of mental involvement in the process of determining the quality of work.

However, as predicted by psychometric and psychological theorization, data suggest that school children are usually not very good at this type of critical, metacognitive reflection unless the accuracy factors identified in this chapter are present, making the use of student self-assessment for grading purposes ill-advised. Improved accuracy appears to be partly a function of cognitive developmental processes (i.e., increasing age) and educational practices (i.e., increasing school experience). Additionally, it appears possible to train students to engage in these deep reflective practices and that such training is associated with better self-regulation of learning, more accurate self-evaluation, and better learning outcomes (Daiute & Kruidenier, 1985; Glaser et al., 2010; McDonald & Boud, 2003; Miller et al., 1993; Morrison, Montemayor, & Wiltshire, 2004; Ramdass & Zimmerman, 2008; Ross et al., 1998a).

Additionally, the teacher clearly has to play an active part in the development and monitoring of self-evaluation, most especially for students who have low academic performance. That low performing students, given they are generally weaker at accurate self-assessment, seem to gain more from this type of self-evaluative reflection is especially good news for educators, as closing the distance between the best and lowest performers is an important goal of schooling. It would appear that, while better students can already self-evaluate effectively, lower performing students need input (i.e., instruction and feedback) to master this key self-regulatory process. Nonetheless, the involvement of teachers in student self-evaluation shifts the ground from a purely personal experience to a shared, public space in which psychological safety, and trust must be present for students to be capable of producing genuine, honest, and accurate self-assessment. Hence, a cautious seal of approval can be given to the use of the best forms of self-assessment in environments that support good teacher–student rapport.

Implications for Current Pedagogical Practices

This review makes it clear that high quality student self-assessment requires active involvement of both students and teachers; self-assessment/evaluation is not an excuse for teacher absence. Ross (2006) provided four essential techniques that need to be incorporated into CA practices: (1) Students need to be involved in the process of establishing criteria for evaluating work outcomes; (2) students need to be taught how to apply those criteria; (3) feedback from others (i.e., teachers and peers) is needed so that students can move from inaccurate, false self-perceptions of their work to more accurate comprehension of the quality of their work; and (4) students need to be taught how to use other assessment data (e.g., test scores or graded work) to improve their work. To extend this list, we would add a fifth condition: There must be psychological safety in the implementation of self-evaluation. Children must know that it is safe to disclose low performance and that they do not need to resort to score-enhancement strategies.

Implications for Future Research

As Barnett and Hixon (1997) pointed out, it is unclear if the association between accurate self-assessment and higher achievement, while consistent with self-regulation models of learning, is a consequence of improved self-regulation or is a by-product of higher achievement. Thus, more studies are needed to determine conditions under which self-evaluation accuracy can be successfully taught to lower performing students, consequently bringing about higher academic performance. Likewise, self-regulation of learning studies (Ramdass & Zimmerman, 2008; Zimmerman, Bonner, & Kovach, 1996) suggests that low performing students can learn to self-regulate, but the generalizability of those studies, given the constraints on accuracy of self-evaluation identified in this chapter, is still in doubt. Hence, studies are needed to explicitly explore the relationships among self-regulation, self-assessment, and academic achievement.

Additionally, questions are raised about the abilities of young students to accurately self-assess. More research is needed to establish if there is a chronological or developmental age beneath which there is little benefit to be reaped through self-assessment. There is clear evidence that low performing students are most inaccurate in their self-assessments, but several studies have shown that the greatest improvement in performance through self-assessment was seen among the low performing students. This suggests that with training in self-assessment accuracy, the gap between low and high performing students might close. Furthermore, it is unknown if there is an interaction between age and academic ability as factors influencing the accuracy of self-assessment judgments.

Psychological safety within classrooms and across cultures is another factor to consider. More research is required to determine if there are some cultures that are more or less able to adopt accurate self-assessment practices due to socially held beliefs about the self, performance, and others. It is also worth investigating classroom environmental factors that make students more or less likely to create and disclose accurate self-assessments. The current studies concerning psychological safety all depend on small-scale narrative techniques; studies are needed that establish in a more generalizable way how student psychological safety can be achieved and whether it improves the quality of self-assessment. How student personality factors mediate self-assessment is also unknown.

A developmental process (e.g., Piagetian development of abstract cognitive reasoning) or an experiential process seems to underlie the general phenomenon of increased accuracy with age. Stipek, Recchia, and McClintic (1992) proposed an empirically derived developmental sequence for reactions to achievement situations in preschool children (ages 1–5) in which children seek positive reactions and avoid potential negative reactions from adults prior to developing a more independent evaluation. However, the inaccuracy of school children's self-estimates suggests that considerable maturation is needed before improvements can be detected (Powel & Gray, 1995). While there may be a developmental trend in accuracy of self-assessment, Alsaker (1989) correctly identified that longitudinal studies are needed before firm conclusions about the underlying processes can be drawn. It is possible that increasing knowledge rather than cognitive or emotional development is sufficient to improve the quality of self-evaluations; the research to date appears insufficient to answer this question. Burnett (1996) rightly pointed out that the decline in self-concept evaluation associated with increasing age may be a function of schooling extinguishing student optimism rather than the development of greater realism; it remains to be seen how this could be tested given ethical and practical constraints about manipulating schooling processes.

Not addressed in this review is a deep analysis of the various techniques of self-assessment. How and when self-evaluations of proficiency, competence, or performance are obtained is still highly variable. Studies have collected self-evaluations before and immediately after assessment events and prior to instruction. Self-estimation of performance has used norm-referencing, absolute referencing, grades and scores, self-centered evaluations, and estimations in terms of the objective criteria of a rubric. The general trend seems to be that the more concrete and immediate the evaluation is and the more the student is cognitively engaged in evaluating quality characteristics, the greater the likelihood that students will make an accurate assessment of their capabilities and improve their learning. Positive effects on learning and self-regulation were seen through self-evaluation techniques that moved most strongly away from simple self-marking or self-rating. Consistent with arguments about the need for metacognitive involvement in self-evaluation (Zimmerman, 2002), these studies show that depth of processing and engagement in self-assessment is required for it to have a learning effect. However, there is no definitive gold standard method for helping students evaluate their own work.

Research into improving the quality of our methods of data collection for research purposes, let alone educational application, is still warranted. It would be useful for large-scale experimental studies to examine which modes of self-assessment allow students to create the most accurate judgments and which, if any, lead to improved motivation, psychological safety, self-regulation, and academic performance over the longer term. Studies that identify the type of learning arising from each method of self-assessment also appear warranted. The trend seems to be that self-assessments that require high levels of cognitive involvement have the greatest learning effects, though it is possible that this is a practice effect from frequent self-assessment rather than a self-regulatory process.

Furthermore, research into the consequential validity of self-evaluations is warranted. When students self-assess and get it wrong or right, what do they do with that information? What are the low- and high-stakes consequences of accurate and inaccurate student self-assessments? While accuracy would appear to be essential, it may be that inaccurate self-assessment in classroom settings—where teachers can structure learning environments and activities—has little negative impact on a student. While this seems improbable to us, the current research literature does not appear to definitively address this problem. Hence, future studies that examine in detail what students do with their self-evaluations—especially when they are palpably wrong—is of great importance to improving our understanding of student self-evaluation.

References

Alsaker, F. D. (1989). School achievement, perceived academic competence and global self-esteem. *School Psychology International, 10*(2), 147–158.

Andrade, H. G. (2000). Using rubrics to promote thinking and learning. *Educational Leadership, 57*(5), 1–7.

Andrade, H. G., & Boulay, B. A. (2003). Role of rubric-referenced self-assessment in learning to write. *The Journal of Educational Research, 97*(1), 21–34.

Andrade, H. L. (2010). Students as the definitive source of formative assessment: Academic self-assessment and the self-regulation of learning. In H. L. Andrade & G. J. Cizek (Eds.), *Handbook of formative assessment* (pp. 90–105). New York: Routledge.

Andrade, H. L., Du, Y., & Mycek, K. (2010). Rubric-referenced self-assessment and middle school students' writing. *Assessment in Education: Principles, Policy & Practice, 17*(2), 199–214.

Andrade, H. L., Du, Y., & Wang, X. (2008). Putting rubrics to the test: The effect of a model, criteria generation, and rubric-referenced self-assessment on elementary school students' writing. *Educational Measurement: Issues and Practice, 17*(2), 3–13.

Andrade, H., & Valtcheva, A. (2009). Promoting learning and achievement through self-assessment. *Theory Into Practice, 28*(1), 12–19.

Andrade, H. L., Wang, X., Du, Y., & Akawi, R. L. (2009). Rubric-referenced self-assessment and self-efficacy for writing. *Journal of Educational Research, 102*(4), 287–302.

Ash, R. A. (1980). Self-assessments of five types of typing ability. *Personnel Psychology, 33*(2), 273–281.

Barling, J. (1980). A multistage, multidependent variable assessment of children's self-regulation of academic performance. *Child Behavior Therapy, 2*(2), 43–54.

Barnett, J. E., & Hixon, J. E. (1997). Effects of grade level and subject on student test score predictions. *Journal of Educational Research, 90*(3), 170–174.

Black, P., & Harrison, C. (2001). Self- and peer-assessment and taking responsibility: The science student's role in formative assessment. *School Science Review, 83*(302), 43–49.

Black, P., & Wiliam, D. (1998). Assessment and classroom learning. *Assessment in Education: Principles, Policy & Practice, 5*(1), 7–74.

Blatchford, P. (1997a). Students' self assessment of academic attainment: Accuracy and stability from 7 to 16 years and influence of domain and social comparison group. *Educational Psychology, 17*(3), 345–359.

Blatchford, P. (1997b). Pupils' self assessments of academic attainment at 7, 11 and 16 years: Effects of sex and ethnic group. *British Journal of Educational Psychology, 67*(2), 169–184.

Boud, D., & Falchikov, N. (1989). Quantitative studies of student self-assessment in higher education: a critical analysis of findings. *Higher Education, 18*, 529–549.

Bradshaw, B. K. (2001). Do students effectively monitor their comprehension? *Reading Horizons, 41*(3), 143–154.

Brookhart, S. M. (2009). *Grading*. Upper Saddle River, NJ: Pearson.

Brookhart, S. M., Andolina, M., Zuza, M., & Furman, R. (2004). Minute math: An action research study of student self-assessment. *Educational Studies in Mathematics, 57*, 213–227.

Brooks, V. (2002). *Assessment in secondary schools: The new teacher's guide to monitoring, assessment, recording, reporting and accountability*. Buckingham, UK: Open University Press.

Brown, G. T. L. (2009). The reliability of essay scores: The necessity of rubrics and moderation. In L. H. Meyer, S. Davidson, H. Anderson, R. Fletcher, P. M. Johnston, & M. Rees (Eds.), *Tertiary assessment and higher education student outcomes: Policy, practice and research* (pp. 40–48). Wellington, New Zealand: Ako Aotearoa.

Brown, G. T. L., Irving, S. E., Peterson, E. R., & Hirschfeld, G. H. F. (2009). Use of interactive-informal assessment practices: New Zealand secondary students' conceptions of assessment. *Learning & Instruction, 19*(2), 97–111.

Brown, G. T. L., Peterson, E. R., & Irving, S. E. (2009). Self-regulatory beliefs about assessment predict mathematics achievement. In D. M. McInerney, G. T. L. Brown, & G. A. D. Liem (Eds.), *Student perspectives on assessment: What students can tell us about assessment for learning* (pp. 159–186). Charlotte, NC: Information Age Publishing.

Burnett, P. C. (1996). Gender and grade differences in elementary school childrens' descriptive and evaluative self-statements and self-esteem. *School Psychology International, 17*(2), 159–170.

Butler, D. L., & Winne, P. H. (1995). Feedback and self-regulated learning: A theoretical synthesis. *Review of Educational Research, 65*(3), 245–281.

Butler, R. (1990). The effects of mastery and competitive conditions on self-assessment at different ages. *Child Development, 61*(1), 201–210.

Butler, Y. G., & Lee, J. (2006). On-task versus off-task self-assessments among Korean elementary school students studying English. *Modern Language Journal, 90*(4), 506–518.

Byrne, B. M., & Bazana, P. (1996). Investigating the measurement of social and academic competencies for early/late preadolescents and adolescents: A multitrait-multimethod analysis. *Applied Measurement in Education, 9*(2), 113–132.

Chang, C. C., & Tseng, K. H. (2011). Using a web-based portfolio assessment system to elevate project-based learning performances. *Interactive Learning Environments, 19*(3), 211–230.

Claes, M., & Salame, R. (1975). Motivation toward accomplishment and the self-evaluation of performances in relation to school achievement. *Canadian Journal of Behavioural Science/Revue Canadienne des Sciences du Comportement, 7*(4), 397–410.

Clarke, S. (2005). *Formative assessment in the secondary classroom.* Abingdon, UK: Hodder Murray.

Clarke, S., Timperley, H. S., & Hattie, J. A. (2003). *Unlocking formative assessment: Practical strategies for enhancing students' learning in the primary and intermediate classroom* (New Zealand ed.). Auckland, New Zealand: Hodder Moa Beckett Publishers Limited.

Cohen, J. (1992). A power primer. *Psychological Bulletin, 112*(1), 155–159.

Connell, J. P., & Ilardi, B. C. (1987). Self-system concomitants of discrepancies between children's and teachers' evaluations of academic competence. *Child Development, 58*(5), 1297–1307.

Cowie, B. (2009). My teacher and my friends helped me learn: Student perceptions and experiences of classroom assessment. In D. M. McInerney, G. T. L. Brown, & G. A. D. Liem (Eds.), *Student perspectives on assessment: What students can tell us about assessment for learning* (pp. 85–105). Charlotte, NC: Information Age Publishing.

Daiute, C., & Kruidenier, J. (1985). A self-questioning strategy to increase young writers' revising processes. *Applied Psycholinguistics, 6*(3), 307–318.

Dochy, F., Segers, M., & Sluijsmans, D. (1999). The use of self-, peer-, and co-assessment in higher education: A review. *Studies in Higher Education, 24*(3), 331–350.

Dunning, D., Heath, C., & Suls, J. M. (2004). Flawed self-assessment: Implications for health, education, and the workplace. *Psychological Science in the Public Interest, 5*(3), 69–106.

Eccles, J., Wigfield, A., Harold, R. D., & Blumenfeld, P. (1993). Age and gender differences in children's self- and task perceptions during elementary school. *Child Development, 64*(3), 830–847.

Educational Research Information Center (U.S.). (2001). *Thesaurus of ERIC descriptors* (14th ed.). Westport, CT: The Oryx Press. Retrieved from www.eric.ed.gov/ERICWebPortal/resources/html/thesaurus/about_thesaurus.html

Elder, A. D. (2010). Children's self-assessment of their school work in elementary school. *Education, 38*(1), 5–11.

Falchikov, N., & Boud, D. (1989). Student self-assessment in higher education: A meta-analysis. *Review of Educational Research, 59*(4), 395–430.

Fernandes, M., & Fontana, D. (1996). Changes in control beliefs in Portuguese primary school pupils as a consequence of the employment of self-assessment strategies. *British Journal of Educational Psychology, 66*(3), 301–313.

Frey, K. S., & Ruble, D. N. (1987). What children say about classroom performance: Sex and grade differences in perceived competence. *Child Development, 58*(4), 1066–1078.

Gao, M. (2009). Students' voices in school-based assessment of Hong Kong: A case study. In D. M. McInerney, G. T. L. Brown, & G. A. D. Liem (Eds.), *Student perspectives on assessment: What students can tell us about assessment for learning* (pp. 107–130). Charlotte, NC: Information Age Publishing.

Glaser, C., Kessler, C., Palm, D., & Brunstein, J. C. (2010). Improving fourth graders' self-regulated writing skills: Specialized and shared effects of process-oriented and outcome- related self-regulation procedures on students' task performance, strategy use, and self-evaluation. *Zeitschrift fur PadagogischePsychologie/ German Journal of Educational Psychology, 24*(3-4), 177–190.

Griffiths, M., & Davies, C. (1993). Learning to learn: Action research from an equal opportunities perspective in a junior school. *British Educational Research Journal, 19*(1), 43–58.

Haertel, E. H. (2006). Reliability. In R. L. Brennan (Ed.), *Educational measurement* (4th ed., pp. 65–110). Westport, CT: Praeger.

Harris, L. R., & Brown, G. T. L. (2010, May). *"My teacher's judgment matters more than mine": Comparing teacher and student perspectives on self-assessment practices in the classroom.* Paper presented to the SIG-Classroom Assessment at the American Educational Research Association Annual Conference, Denver, CO.

Harris, L. R., Harnett, J. A., & Brown, G. T. L. (2009). 'Drawing' out student conceptions: Using pupils' pictures to examine their conceptions of assessment. In D. M. McInerney, G. T. L. Brown, & G. A. D. Liem (Eds.), *Student perspectives on assessment: What students can tell us about assessment for learning* (pp. 321–330). Charlotte, NC: Information Age Publishing.

Harward, S. V., Allred, R. A., & Sudweeks, R. R. (1994). The effectiveness of our self-corrected spelling test methods. *Reading Psychology, 15*(4), 245–271.

Hattie, J. (2009). *Visible learning: A synthesis of meta-analyses in education.* New York: Routledge.

Hattie, J. A., & Brown, G. T. L. (2010). Assessment and evaluation. In C. Rubie-Davies (Ed.), *Educational psychology: Concepts, research and challenges* (pp. 102–117). New York: Routledge.

Hattie, J., & Timperley, H. (2007). The power of feedback. *Review of Educational Research, 77*(1), 81–112.

Hewitt, M. P. (2001). The effects of modeling, self-evaluation, and self-listening on junior high instrumentalists' music performance and practice attitude. *Journal of Research in Music Education, 49*(4), 307–322.

Hewitt, M. P. (2005). Self-evaluation accuracy among high school and middle school instrumentalists. *Journal of Research in Music Education, 53*(2), 148.

Higgins, K. M., Harris, N. A., & Kuehn, L. L. (1994). Placing assessment into the hands of young children: A study of student-generated criteria and self-assessment. *Educational Assessment, 2*(4), 309–324.

Hughes, B., Sullivan, H. J., & Mosley, M. L. (1985). External evaluation, task difficulty, and continuing motivation. *The Journal of Educational Research, 78*(4), 210–215.

Hunter, D., Mayenga, C., & Gambell, T. (2006). Classroom assessment tools and uses: Canadian English teachers' practices for writing. *Assessing Writing, 11*(1), 42–65.

Ikeguchi, C. B. (1996). *Self assessment and ESL competence of Japanese returnees.* Retrieved from http://eric.ed.gov/PDFS/ED399798.pdf

Joint Committee on Standards for Educational Evaluation. (2003). *The student evaluation standards: How to improve evaluations of students.* Thousand Oaks, CA: Corwin Press.

Johnson, N., & Winterbottom, M. (2011). Supporting girls' motivation in science: A study of peer- and self-assessment in a girls-only class. *Educational Studies, 37*(4), 391–403.

Jones, J. C., Trap, J., & Cooper, J. O. (1977). Technical report: Students' self-recording of manuscript letter strokes. *Journal of Applied Behavior Analysis, 10*(3), 509–514.

Kaderavek, J. N., Gillam, R. B., Ukrainetz, T. A., Justice, L. M., & Eisenberg, S. N. (2004). School-age children's self-assessment of oral narrative production. *Communication Disorders Quarterly, 26*(1), 37–48.

Kasanen, K., & Räty, H. (2002). "You be sure now to be honest in your assessment": Teaching and learning self-assessment. *Social Psychology of Education, 5*(4), 313–328.

Kasanen, K., Räty, H., & Eklund, A.-L. (2009). Elementary school pupils' evaluations of the malleability of their academic abilities. *Educational Research, 51*(1), 27–38.

Keil, L. J., McClintock, C. G., Kramer, R., & Platow, M. J. (1990). Children's use of social comparison standards in judging performance and their effects on self-evaluation. *Contemporary Educational Psychology, 15*(1), 75–91.

Klenowski, V. (1995). Student self-evaluation processes in student-centred teaching and learning contexts of Australia and England. *Assessment in Education: Principles, Policy & Practice, 2*(2), 145–163.

Koivula, N., Hassmén, P., & Hunt, D. P. (2001). Performance on the Swedish Scholastic Aptitude Test: Effects of self-assessment and gender. *Sex Roles: A Journal of Research, 44*(11), 629–645.

Kuncel, N. R., Credé, M., & Thomas, L. L. (2005). The validity of self-reported grade point averages, class ranks, and test scores: A meta-analysis and review of the literature. *Review of Educational Research, 75*(1), 63–82.

Kwok, D. C., & Lai, D. W. (1993, May). *The self-perception of competence by Canadian and Chinese children.* Paper presented at the annual convention of the Canadian Psychological Association, Montreal, QC.

Lasonen, J. (1995). A case study of student self-assessment in upper secondary education. In J. Lasonen & M.-L. Stenstrom (Eds.), *Contemporary issues of occupational education in Finland* (pp. 199–215). Jyvaskyla, Finland: University of Jyvaskyla, Institute for Educational Research.

Laveault, D., & Miles, C. (2002, April). *The study of individual differences in the utility and validity of rubrics in the learning of writing ability.* Paper presented at the annual meeting of the American Educational Research Association, New Orleans, LA.

LaVoie, J. C., & Hodapp, A. F. (1987). Children's subjective ratings of their performance on a standardized achievement test. *Journal of School Psychology, 25*(1), 73–80.

Lee, D., & Gavine, D. (2003). Goal-setting and self-assessment in Year 7 students. *Educational Research, 45*(1), 49–59.

Lipnevich, A., & Smith, J. (2008). *Response to assessment feedback: The effects of grades, praise, and source of information* (Research report RR-08-30). Princeton, NJ: Educational Testing Service.

Luyten, H., & Dolkar, D. (2010). School-based assessments in high-stakes examinations in Bhutan: A question of trust? Exploring inconsistencies between external exam scores, school-based assessments, detailed teacher ratings, and student self-ratings. *Educational Research and Evaluation, 16*(5), 421–435.

Mabe, P. A., & West, S. G. (1982). Validity of self-evaluation of ability: A review and meta-analysis. *Journal of Applied Psychology, 67*(3), 280–296.

Mac Iver, D. (1987). Classroom factors and student characteristics predicting students' use of achievement standards during ability self-assessment. *Child Development, 58*(5), 1258–1271.

Marsh, H. W. (1988). *Self Description Questionnaire: A theoretical and empirical basis for the measurement of multiple dimensions of preadolescent self-concept: A test manual and a research monograph.* San Antonio, TX: The Psychological Corporation.

McDevitt, T. M., Sheehan, E. P., Sinco, S. R., Cochran, L. S., Lauer, D., & Starr, N. L. (2008). These are my goals: Academic self-regulation in reading by middle-school students. *Reading Improvement, 45*(3), 115–138.

McDonald, B. (2002). Self assessment skills used by high school students without formal training. *School Psychology International, 23*(4), 416–424.

McDonald, B. (2009). Exploring academic achievement in males trained in self-assessment skills. *Education, 37*(2), 145–157.

McDonald, B., & Boud, D. (2003). The impact of self-assessment on achievement: The effects of self-assessment training on performance in external examinations. *Assessment in Education: Principles, Policy & Practice, 10*(2), 209–220.

Messick, S. (1989). Validity. In R. L. Linn (Ed.), *Educational measurement* (3rd ed., pp. 13–103). New York: Macmillan.

Miller, T. L., Duffy, S. E., & Zane, T. (1993). Improving the accuracy of self-corrected mathematics homework. *Journal of Educational Research, 86*(3), 184–189.

Mitman, A. L., & Lash, A. A. (1988). Student's perceptions of their academic standing and classroom behavior. *Elementary School Journal, 89*(1), 55–68.

Morrison, S. J., Montemayor, M., & Wiltshire, E. S. (2004). The effect of a recorded model on band students' performance self-evaluations, achievement, and attitude. *Journal of Research in Music Education, 52*(2), 116–129.

Munns, G., & Woodward, H. (2006). Student engagement and student self-assessment: The REAL framework. *Assessment in Education: Principles, Policy and Practice, 13*(2), 193–213.

Ng, J. R., & Earl, J. K. (2008). Accuracy in self-assessment: The role of ability, feedback, self-efficacy and goal orientation. *Australian Journal of Career Development, 17*(3), 39–50.

Olina, Z., & Sullivan, H. J. (2002, April). *Effects of teacher and self-assessment on student performance.* Paper presented at the annual meeting of the American Educational Research Association, New Orleans, LA.

Paulhus, D. (1991). Measurement and control of response bias. In J. Robinson, P. Shaver, & L. Wrightsman (Eds.), *Measures of personality and social psychological attitudes, Measures of social psychological attitudes* (Vol. 1, pp. 17–59). San Diego, CA: Academic Press.

Pausch, R., & Zaslow, J. (2008). *The last lecture.* London: Hodder & Stoughton.

Peterson, E. R., & Irving, S. E. (2008). Secondary school students' conceptions of assessment and feedback. *Learning and Instruction, 18*(3), 238–250.

Pomerantz, E. M., & Ruble, D. N. (1997). Distinguishing multiple dimensions of conceptions of ability: Implications for self-evaluation. *Child Development, 68*(6), 1165–1180.

Popham, W. J. (2000). *Modern educational measurement: Practical guidelines for educational leaders* (6th ed.). Boston: Allyn & Bacon.

Powel, W. D., & Gray, R. (1995). Improving performance predictions by collaboration with peers and rewarding accuracy. *Child Study Journal, 25*(2), 141–154.

Raider-Roth, M. B. (2005). Trusting what you know: Negotiating the relational context of classroom life. *Teachers College Record, 107*(4), 587–628.

Ramdass, D., & Zimmerman, B. J. (2008). Effects of self-correction strategy training on middle school students' self-efficacy, self-evaluation, and mathematics division learning. *Journal of Advanced Academics, 20*(1), 18–41.

Ross, J. A. (2006). The reliability, validity, and utility of self-assessment. *Practical Assessment Research & Evaluation, 11*(10). Retrieved from http://pareonline.net/getvn.asp?v=11&n=10

Ross, J. A., Hogaboam-Gray, A., & Rolheiser, C. (2002). Student self-evaluation in Grade 5–6 mathematics: Effects on problem-solving achievement. *Educational Assessment, 8*(1), 43–59.

Ross, J. A., Rolheiser, C., & Hogaboam-Gray, A. (1998a, April). *Impact of self-evaluation training on mathematics achievement in a cooperative learning environment.* Paper presented at the annual meeting of the American Educational Research Association, San Diego, CA.

Ross, J. A., Rolheiser, C., & Hogaboam-Gray, A. (1998b). Skills training versus action research in-service: Impact on student attitudes to self-evaluation. *Teaching and Teacher Education, 14*(5), 463–477.

Ross, J. A., Rolheiser, C., & Hogaboam-Gray, A. (1999). Effects of self-evaluation training on narrative writing. *Assessing Writing, 6*(1), 107–132.

Ross, J. A., Rolheiser, C., & Hogaboam-Gray, A. (2002). Influences on student cognitions about evaluation. *Assessment in Education: Principles, Policy & Practice, 9*(1), 81–95.

Ruff, J. C., & Barris, J. (2009). The sound of one house clapping: The unmannerly doctor as zen rhetorician. In H. Jacoby (Ed.), *House and philosophy: Everybody lies* (pp. 84–97). New York: John Wiley.

Saavedra, R., & Kwun, S. K. (1993). Peer evaluation in self-managing work groups. *Journal of Applied Psychology, 78*(3), 450–462.

Sadler, P. M., & Good, E. (2006). The impact of self- and peer-grading on student learning. *Educational Assessment, 11*(1), 1–31.

Sadler, R. (1989). Formative assessment and the design of instructional systems. *Instructional Science, 18,* 119–144.

Schunk, D. H. (1996). Goal and self-evaluative influences during children's cognitive skill learning. *American Educational Research Journal, 33*(2), 359–382.

Schunk, D. H. (2005). Commentary on self-regulation in school contexts. *Learning & Instruction, 15,* 173–177.

Scriven, M. (1967). The methodology of evaluation. In R. W. Tyler, R. M. Gagne, & M. Scriven (Eds.), *Perspectives of curriculum evaluation* (Vol. 1, pp. 39–83). Chicago: Rand McNally.

Spaights, E. (1965). Accuracy of self-estimation of junior high school students. *Journal of Educational Research, 58*(9), 416–419.

Stipek, D. J. (1981). Children's perceptions of their own and their classmates' ability. *Journal of Educational Psychology, 73*(3), 404–410.

Stipek, D., & Mac Iver, D. (1989). Developmental changes in children's assessment of intellectual competence. *Child Development, 60,* 521–538.

Stipek, D., Recchia, S., & McClintic, S. (1992). Self-evaluation in young children. *Monographs of the Society for Research in Child Development, 57*(1, Serial No. 226).

Stipek, D. J., & Tannatt, L. M. (1984). Children's judgments of their own and their peers' academic competence. *Journal of Educational Psychology, 76*(1), 75–84.

Sung, Y.-T., Chang, K.-E., Chang, T.-H., & Yu, W.-C. (2010). How many heads are better than one? The reliability and validity of teenagers' self- and peer assessments. *Journal of Adolescence, 33*(1), 135–145.

Todd, R. W. (2002). Using self-assessment for evaluation. *English Teaching Forum, 40*(1), 16–19.

Topping, K. (2003). Self and peer assessment in school and university: Reliability, validity and utility. In M. Segers, F. Dochy, & E. Cascallar (Eds.), *Optimising new modes of assessment: In search of qualities and standards* (pp. 55–87). Dordrecht, NL: Kluwer Academic Publishers.

Towler, L., & Broadfoot, P. (1992). Self-assessment in the primary school. *Educational Review, 44*(2), 137–151.

Tuleya, L. G. (2007). *Thesaurus of psychological index terms.* Washington, DC: American Psychological Association.

van Kraayenoord, C. E., & Paris, S. G. (1997). Australian students' self-appraisal of their work samples and academic progress. *The Elementary School Journal, 97*(5), 523–537.

Volante, L., & Beckett, D. (2011). Formative assessment and the contemporary classroom: Synergies and tensions between research and practice. *Canadian Journal of Education, 34*(2), 239–255.

Wall, S. M. (1982). Effects of systematic self-monitoring and self-reinforcement in children's management of test performances. *Journal of Psychology, 111*(1), 129–136.

Wan-a-rom, U. (2010). Self-assessment of word knowledge with graded readers: A preliminary study. *Reading in a Foreign Language, 22*(2), 323–338.

Watt, H. M. (2000). Measuring attitudinal change in mathematics and English over the 1st year of junior high school: A multidimensional analysis. *Journal of Experimental Education, 68*(4), 331–361.

Wells, L., & Sweeney, P. D. (1986). A test of three models of bias in self-assessment. *Social Psychology Quarterly, 49*(1), 1–10.

Williams, J. E. (1996, April). *Academic self-concept to performance congruence among able adolescents.* Paper presented at the annual meeting of the American Educational Research Association, New York.

Wilson, D. B. (2001). *Effect size determination program* (Version 2.0) (Excel Macro Application). College Park: University of Maryland.

Wilson, J., & Wright, C. R. (1993). The predictive validity of student self-evaluations, teachers' assessments, and grades for performance on the Verbal Reasoning and Numerical Ability scales of the Differential Aptitude Test for a sample of secondary school students attending rural Appalachia schools. *Educational and Psychological Measurement, 53*(1), 259–270.

Wright, C. R., & Houck, J. W. (1995). Gender differences among self-assessments, teacher ratings, grades, and aptitude test scores for a sample of students attending rural secondary schools. *Educational and Psychological Measurement, 55*(5), 743–752.

Zimmerman, B. J. (1998). Academic studying and the development of personal skill: A self-regulatory perspective. *Educational Psychologist, 33,* 73–86.

Zimmerman, B. J. (2002). Becoming a self-regulated learner: An overview. *Theory Into Practice, 41*(2), 64–70.

Zimmerman, B. J., Bonner, S., & Kovach, R. (1996). *Developing self-regulated learners: Beyond achievement to self-efficacy.* Washington, DC: American Psychological Association.

22

Peers as a Source of Formative and Summative Assessment

Keith J. Topping

This chapter comprises a review of research on the role of peer assessment in elementary and secondary classrooms (K–12). The function of peer assessment can be formative, summative, or both. A typology of peer assessment is given to help the reader identify the many different kinds. Theoretical perspectives on peer assessment are reviewed and described, and their implications for research are teased out. Studies in elementary schools are then reviewed, describing how both student and teacher behavior changes when peer assessment is deployed, what the consequent effects on student achievement are, and what conditions are necessary for those effects to be maximized. The same is then done for studies in secondary schools. Both kinds of study are then critiqued in relation to future needs for the practical use of peer assessment in classrooms. A summary of the main findings in light of the critique leads to a statement of general directions and specific recommendations for future research.

What Is Peer Assessment?

Peer assessment is generally an arrangement for classmates to consider the level, value, or worth of the products or outcomes of learning of their equal-status peers. However, it can also extend to learning behavior or social behavior and sometimes encompasses both academic products and associated behavior. The intention is that both assessee and assessor benefit from the process.

Typically, students who are themselves learners would look at the work of their colleagues and either grade it by assigning a score reflecting quality, give rich qualitative feedback on the work by considering good and less good aspects and indicating how the work might be improved, or both. Obviously, it is important that participating students are clear about whether grading, rich feedback, or both are to be given. Equally, it is important that the recipient of feedback is ready to respond to it thoughtfully, deciding what points to accept and what not to accept and using this selected information to either improve the existing piece of work (as in formative feedback) or future pieces of work (as in summative feedback). Usually peer assessment is reciprocal—or at least most participants will be both assessee and assessor.

There are immediate benefits of peer assessment for learning (AFL) and achievement but also longer-term benefits with respect to transferable skills in communication and collaboration. There may also be ancillary benefits in terms of the self-regulation of one's own learning. These benefits accrue to both assessors and assessees through the process of peer assessment, not just from the products of the process. Peer assessment of learning and social behavior sharpens and broadens the assessor's capabilities and relates to the processes of learning more than the products. Combining assessment of product and process can enhance student understanding of the consistency or mismatch between these and different ways of learning beyond their own.

Generally, teachers start with peer assessment by pursuing the formative route. Once the students are very familiar with the processes and peer assessment—and reassured about its reliability—then summative aspects can follow. Formative peer assessment is intended to inform or redirect student effort and assist with more appropriate linking of output to objectives. It can also inform future instruction by teachers, although research on this is lacking. Such assessment typically provides much more qualitative detail about what content is good and what content requires further explanation, consolidation, or development. This involves not merely indicating the number of errors but saying exactly where they are, how they are wrong, and possibly suggesting how they might be put right. Of course, a problem with such peer assessment is that it may be less likely to be *correct* than teacher feedback; on the other hand, it is readily available in much larger quantity than teacher feedback. Assessees just need to be somewhat cautious about peer feedback, and assessors cautioned that if they are uncertain they should not claim to be right, since they are not expected to always be right.

With summative peer assessment, on the other hand, feedback is more likely to be numerical or categorical. As the feedback is limited, it is more likely to be reliable. Even though the reasons for the grade might be wrong, the grade itself might still be right. With summative peer assessment, the issues of validity and reliability are important, and teachers will need evidence to address these technical concerns. Once students are somewhat used to peer assessment, however, and have overcome their initial fears and hesitations, reliability is actually likely to be quite high (indeed, not that different from teacher reliability) (Topping, 2003).

Reliability is increased by making model student work available to the assessors—a master version of correctness against which the work to be assessed can be compared. Additionally, assessors can be provided with scoring rubrics, to the design of which they have preferably contributed. Students need to know whether the summative peer assessments will be entered in any kind of high-stakes assessment, such as end-of-year overall grades. Where the answer is yes, they will need to know what proportion of the total grade is determined by the teacher and what proportion by peer assessment.

A Typology of Peer Assessment

Peer assessment can be of many different kinds. As previously indicated, a key difference is whether the peer assessment is formative or summative or both. Similarly, the peer assessment can be quantitative (assigning a number with respect to a grade), qualitative (giving rich verbal feedback on positive and negative aspects and possibilities for improvement), or both. Thus, we see distinctions between formative and summative peer assessment and between qualitative and quantitative peer assessment. Other differences between types of peer assessment are more subtle. For example, are the peer assessments on single pieces of work, or are they of several pieces of work? Peer assessment can operate in different curriculum areas or subjects. The product or output assessed can vary—writing, portfolios, presentations, oral statements, and so on.

Clarification of the assessment criteria is essential, and peers may or may not be involved in establishing these criteria. Rubrics or structured formats for feedback may or may not be provided. Training in peer assessment may be given to assessors and/or assessees to a greater or lesser extent. Is feedback expected to be balanced between positive and negative or only one of these? Is feedback expected to lead to opportunities to rework the product in the light of feedback, or is there no opportunity for this? Is feedback expected to include hints or suggestions for improvement? The nature of subsequent peer assessment activity may be very precisely specified or it may be left loose and open to student creativity. Does the interaction involve guiding prompts, sentence openers, cue cards, or other scaffolding devices?

The participant constellation can vary, with consequent variation in joint responsibility for the assessed product. Assessors and the assessed may be individuals, pairs, or groups. Directionality can vary. Peer assessment can be one-way, reciprocal, or mutual within a group. Matching of students may be deliberate and selective or it may be random or accidental. It may take account only of academic factors or also involve social differences. Assessors and assessees may come from the same year of study or from different years. They may be of the same ability or deliberately of different ability. The amount of background experience students have in peer assessment can be very variable, and it may represent a considerable challenge to and generate considerable resistance in new initiates. If they have previous experience, it may have been positive, negative, or both. Students from different cultural backgrounds may be very different in acceptance of peer assessment. Gender may make a difference, and thought should be given to the implications of same-sex or cross-sex matching. Of course, if there is no face-to-face contact (as in an online environment) gender may not be apparent, but this raises yet another source of variation.

Place can vary: Most peer assessment is structured and occurs in class, but it can also be informal and occur outside of class. Similar variation occurs with respect to the time when the peer assessment takes place: How long are the sessions? How many sessions? The objectives for the exercise may vary: The teacher may target cognitive and/or metacognitive gains, or teacher time saving, or other goals. What degree of justification for opinions is expected of the assessor? Will all peer assessments be confidential to the assessing pair and the teacher, or will they be made publicly available?

The extent to which the process of peer assessment is monitored by supervisory staff (or whether the staff has no idea what actually occurred) is another question. The extent to which the reliability and validity of the peer assessment is moderated by supervising teachers is an issue. Inspecting a sample of the assessments is particularly important where the assessment is summative. Is the task a simple surface task requiring limited cognitive engagement or a highly complex task requiring considerable inference of the part of assesses, or does a simple initial task develop into increasingly complex tasks? In relation to this, what quantity and quality of feedback is expected, and is this elaborated and specific or more concise and general? To what extent is it tending toward the objective and definitive, as it might be in response to a simple task, or to what extent more subjective, as it might be with a more complex task? How are assessees expected to respond to feedback? Are their revisions to be few or many, simple or complex? What extrinsic or intrinsic rewards are made available for participants? Is the peer assessment aligned with the traditional forms of assessment, or do all students have to sit for formal examinations irrespective of their other skills? What transferable skills (e.g., social or communicative) might be measured as by-products of the process? Finally, is the peer assessment being evaluated, as one would hope with any new venture, or is its success or failure just assumed?

Thus, it is clear that peer assessment is not just one method. Labels can be given to some of these variations, distinguishing formative from summative peer assessment, qualitative from quantitative, structured from unstructured, unidirectional from reciprocal or mutual, same-year from cross-year, and same-ability from cross-ability peer assessment, for instance.

Theoretical Perspectives on Peer Assessment

A number of researchers have conducted work that has strong implications for building theories of peer learning (e.g., Chi, Siler, Jeong, Yamauchi, & Hausmann, 2001; King, 1998; Sluijsmans & Prins, 2006). I have developed a model of peer assessment that incorporates several theoretical perspectives (Figure 22.1). The model includes a balance of Piagetian and Vygotskian perspectives and acknowledges the roles of affect and communication. Figure 22.1 includes subprocesses of organization and engagement. These processes are synthesized by the learners to enhance understanding. Actual performance of peer assessment involves practice, leading to consolidation and enhanced performance. An inherently increased quantity of feedback of greater immediacy adds power to this effect. Beyond this, self-monitoring and self-regulation come increasingly into play, developing into fully explicit metacognition. The learners become more able to engage in deep learning.

Level 1

Organization and Engagement	Cognitive Conflict	Scaffolding and Error Management	Communication	Affect
Time on task, time engaged in task		Zone of Proximal Development management	Language← →thought	Motivation
Goals, plans	To liquify primitive cognitions and beliefs	Information modulation	Listen, explain, question	Accountability
Individualization		Modeling and monitoring	Clarify, simplify, prompt	Modeling
Interactivity		Error detection	Rehearse, revise	Ownership,
Immediacy		Diagnosis, correction	Summarize, speculate	self-disclosure
Variety			Hypothesize	

Level 2

Accretion, Retuning, and Restructuring of Knowledge and Skills

Level 3

Intersubjective Cognitive Co-Construction

Level 4

Practice, Fluency, Automaticity, Retention	Generalization
	Supported → independent
Mostly implicit	Implicit → explicit

Level 5

Feedback and Reinforcement

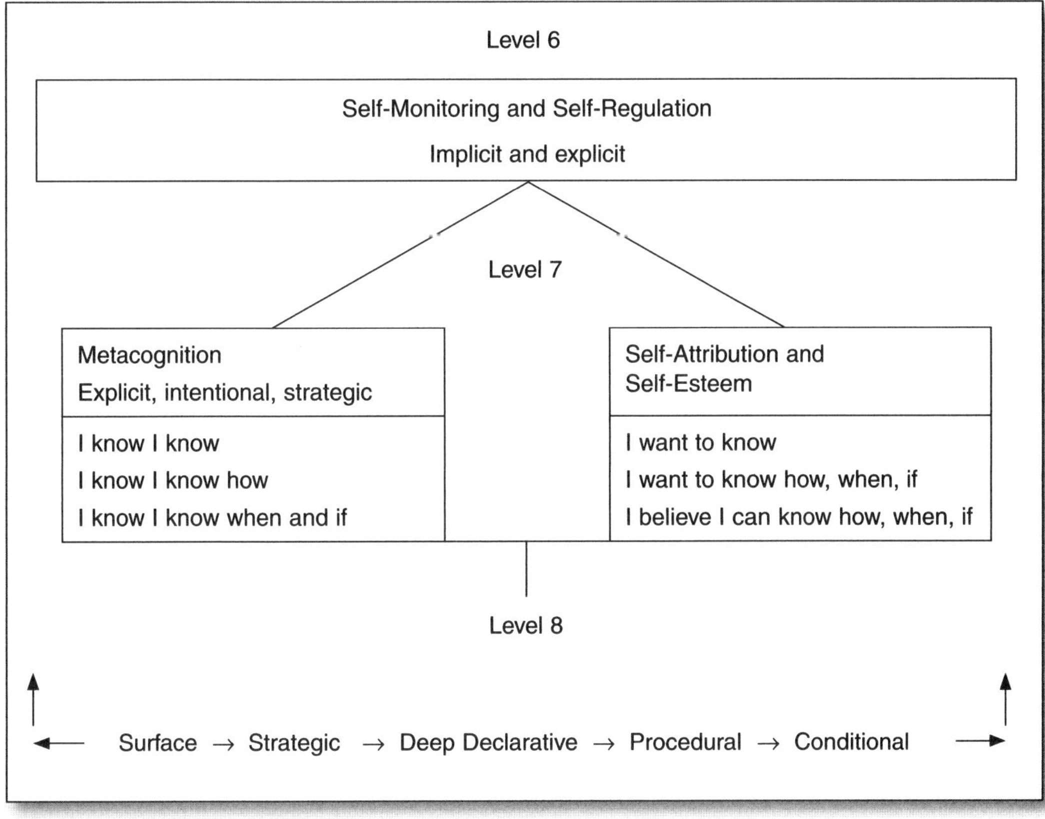

Figure 22.1 Peer Assessment: Groups of Factors Influencing Effectiveness

Organization and Engagement

This model initially assigns some of the main subprocesses of peer assessment into five categories. The first of these includes organizational or structural features of the learning interaction, such as the need and press inherent in peer assessment toward increased time apparently looking at the task and maybe thinking about it (time on task) and time observably involved in doing something active leading to task completion (time engaged with task)—the two being different concepts. The need for both helper and helped to elaborate goals and plans, the individualization of learning and immediacy of feedback possible within the small group or one-on-one situation, and the variety of a novel kind of learning interaction are also included in this category.

Cognitive Conflict

This category encompasses the Piagetian school of thought. It concerns the need to loosen cognitive blockages formed from old myths and false beliefs by presenting conflict and challenge via one or more peers.

Scaffolding and Error Management

By contrast, Vygotskian theory speaks of support and scaffolding from a more competent other, necessitating management of activities to be within the zone of proximal development (ZPD) of both parties in order to avoid any damaging excess of challenge (Vygotsky, 1978). The helper seeks to manage and modulate the information processing demands upon the learner—neither too much nor too little—to maximize the rate of progress. The helper also provides a cognitive model of competent performance. The cognitive demands upon the helper in terms of monitoring learner performance and detecting, diagnosing, correcting, and otherwise managing misconceptions and errors are great; herein lies much of the cognitive exercise and benefit for the helper.

The greater the differential in ability or experience between helper and helped, the less cognitive conflict and the more scaffolding might be expected. Too great a differential might result in minimal cognitive engagement (let alone conflict) for the helper and unthinking but encapsulated acceptance with no retuning or co-construction by the helped. Of course, if the helper is older, more experienced, and therefore more credible but actually has no greater correct knowledge or ability than the helped, then a mismatch and faulty learning might occur in a different way.

Communication

Peer assessment also makes heavy demands upon the communication skills of both helper and helped and in so doing can develop those skills. All participants might never have truly grasped a concept until they had to explain it to another, embodying and crystallizing thought into language—another Vygotskian idea, of course. Listening, explaining, questioning, summarizing, speculating, and hypothesizing are all valuable skills of effective peer assessment that should be transferable to other contexts.

Affect

The affective component of peer assessment is also very powerful. A trusting relationship with a peer who holds no position of authority might facilitate self-disclosure of ignorance and misconception, enabling subsequent diagnosis and correction that could not occur otherwise. Modeling of enthusiasm and competence and belief in the possibility of success by the helper can influence the self-confidence of the helped, while a sense of loyalty and accountability to each other can help to keep the pair motivated and on task.

These five categories, or subprocesses, of Level 1 feed into a larger onward process in Level 2 of extending each other's declarative knowledge, procedural skill, and conditional and selective application of knowledge and skills by adding to and extending current capabilities (accretion), modifying current capabilities (retuning), and, in areas of completely new learning or cases of gross misconception or error, rebuilding new understanding (restructuring). These are somewhat similar to Piagetian concepts of assimilation and accommodation. This leads in Level 3 to the joint construction of a shared understanding between helper and helped, which is adapted to the idiosyncrasies in their perceptions (i.e., is intersubjective), is firmly situated within the current authentic context of application, and forms a foundation for further progress.

As a result of the processes in the first three levels of Figure 22.1, peer assessment enables and facilitates a greater volume of engaged and successful practice, leading to consolidation; fluency and automaticity of thinking; and social, communicative, and other core skills (Level 4). Much of this might occur implicitly—that is, without the helper or helped being fully aware of what is happening with them. Simultaneously or subsequently, peer assessment can lead to generalization from the specific example in which a concept is learned, extending the ability to apply that concept to an ever-widening range of alternative and varied contexts.

As some or all of the processes in the first three levels occur, both helper and helped give feedback to each other implicitly and/or explicitly (Level 5). Indeed, implicit feedback is likely to have already occurred spontaneously in the earlier levels. Peer assessment increases the quantity and immediacy of feedback to the learner very substantially. Explicit reinforcement might stem from within the partnership or beyond it, by way of verbal and/or nonverbal praise, social acknowledgment and status, official accreditation, or an even more tangible reward. However, reinforcement should not be indiscriminate or predominantly focused on effort.

As the learning relationship develops, both helper and helped should become more consciously aware of what is happening in their learning interaction and more able to monitor and regulate the effectiveness of their own learning strategies in different contexts (Level 6). Development into fully conscious explicit and strategic metacognition (Level 7) not only promotes more effective onward learning but it should make helper and helped more confident that they can achieve even more and that their success is the result of their own efforts. In other words, they attribute success to themselves, not external factors, and their self-efficacy is heightened.

As the peer assessment relationship develops, the model continues to apply as the learning moves from the shallow, instrumental surface level to the strategic level and on to the deep level as the students pursue their own goals rather than merely those set for them. Similarly, learning proceeds from the declarative (statements of existing fact) into the procedural (indicating how a situation developed and came to be) and conditional (suggesting what other alternatives might have been possible) (Level 8). These affective and cognitive outcomes feed back into the originating five subprocesses—a continuous, iterative process.

Of course, it is unlikely that peer assessment in practice will neatly follow these levels or stages. Many may be missing. Sometimes one level will occur before another that appears to follow it in the model. Most likely a number of events will occur that seem to be combinations of items in a level or across levels. Even where students work through to Level 8, they may begin again at the outset or later on, usually but not always in relation to a new or varied task.

Research on Peer Assessment

Much of the literature on peer assessment is concerned with students in university or college and rather less with students in K–12 schools. This reflects the ease of access to their own students by university academics for research purposes. I am only concerned with K–12 students in this chapter, although I refer to material from reviews that include older students when it is relevant. Some of the literature is particularly concerned with preservice teachers; I shall ignore this.

Schools can be elementary or secondary, and the organizational differences between these are such that implementation can be very different between the two environments. Consequently, I will take the two kinds of schools separately. Although some studies include both elementary and high school students, they will be treated as a separate group. Middle schools will be treated as elementary.

In what follows, I will first consider peer assessment of academic products and then social behavior. Mostly the literature focuses on typical students, but a few papers focus upon students with special needs or various kinds of disability; these will be noted.

For this review, the literature was newly searched, with a particular focus on 1998 through 2011, although occasionally earlier, classic items have been included. The literature before this has already been searched and the results reported in O'Donnell and Topping (1998). Also see the section on peer assessment in schools in Topping (2003), particularly peer assessment of writing, peer response groups, portfolio peer assessment, and other kinds of peer assessment. For the current chapter, four databases were searched: Education Resources Information Center (ERIC), ScienceDirect, SciVerse Scopus, and ZETOC. Qualitative, quantitative, and mixed methods studies were included, but qualitative studies only where the methodology for data analysis was clearly explicated. Experimental and quasi-experimental studies were included. Action research was excluded as measurement was almost always unstable. ERIC and ScienceDirect were the more productive sources. All yielded largely different items. The search terms were *peer assessment* and *school*. Some retrieved items concerned irrelevant groups, and some lacked any kind of data, but most were relevant. Eleven items were found relating to elementary schools, 10 related to secondary schools, and 5 were reviews.

The next sections discuss the recent studies uncovered by the literature review, divided into elementary school and high school sections. A third section then considers reviews of the literature. At the elementary level, issues included perceptions of the value of peer assessment, modes of presentation in peer assessment, gender effects, social aspects, and implementation with students with special needs. At the secondary level, issues included perceptions of the value of peer assessment, issues of effectiveness of peer assessment, and the exploration of online systems for peer assessment. The reviews variously emphasized the exploration of peer nomination and rating; the balance between a sense of psychological safety, trust, and interdependence coupled with limited diversity in underpinning values; the effect of training and experience on attitudes; classroom climate, the role of peer talk, questioning and discussion, and the richness of feedback; and finally the purpose and quality of peer assessment and the importance of student involvement.

Elementary School

Research reviewed in this section focused on perceptions of the value of peer assessment, modes of presentation in peer assessment, gender effects, social aspects, and students with special needs. There is a relatively high proportion of studies that used a survey methodology, as well as studies of peer assessment of social relations.

Perceptions of the Value of Peer Assessment

While teachers often value the feedback provided by students, students sometimes need to be educated about its benefits. In an early study, Weaver (1995) surveyed over 500 teachers regarding the writing process. Regardless of the stage in the process (early versus late), these teachers generally found peer responses to be more effective than their own. In contrast, students stated they found the teachers' responses to be more helpful in all stages of writing, but they nevertheless improved when they received peer feedback about their writing. There was no doubt that students valued peer assessment, although they may not have liked it at first. There are implications here for how students are introduced to peer assessment. With more resistant students, introduction should be gradual and include much concrete activity before any labeling of the process.

The views of parents are also interesting. Atkinson (2003) conducted two surveys about assessment across the curriculum in Scotland, with the same class of students, and one with their parents, where formative assessment had been used in primary classrooms for many years. Both students and parents wanted assessment integrated with learning. A mix of formal and informal assessment and self- and peer assessment were valued. Parents wanted useful information about their child's progress and not just summative assessment.

From a completely different cultural perspective, Bryant and Carless (2010) conducted extensive interviews and classroom observations in a 2-year case study of Hong Kong classrooms, which tended to be dominated by repetitive learning and many high-stakes tests. Student perceptions of the usefulness of peer assessment varied according to the quality of peer feedback, peer language proficiency, and the novelty or repetitiveness of its processes. Teachers and students viewed peer assessment as having longer-term applications in preparing for secondary school and for examinations. The authors concluded that assessment practices are deeply cultural and, in test-dominated settings, peer assessment may have most potential when explicit links are drawn with preparation for summative assessment.

Overall, these three studies indicate that teachers and parents may value peer assessment more than students, especially inexperienced students. But the cultural context is important, so student concerns about peer assessment quality are exaggerated in a culture of high-stakes testing.

Efficacy of Different Modes of Presentation in Peer Assessment

Two studies examined the efficacy of different methods of applying peer assessment in elementary schools. Chin and Teou (2009) used concept cartoons with two parallel experimental classes of younger (9- to 10-year-olds) and older (10- to 11-year-olds) students in an extended project. The cartoons presented opposing viewpoints about scientific ideas to stimulate talk and argumentation among students in small peer assessment groups. The students were also trained in using scaffolding tools to guide their discussions and to evaluate, challenge, and document each others' ideas. Their dialogic talk and interactive argumentation provided diagnostic feedback about students' misconceptions about scientific principles to the teacher and was helpful in moving students toward better understanding. Students also used drawings to depict their ideas and make their reasoning visible. The conversation from one exemplary small group was audiotaped over the period of the project. This showed that students' assertions and questions encouraged exploratory and reflective discourse that drew on each other's ideas.

In contrast to this face-to-face, verbal dialogic method, Yang, Ko, and Chung (2005) developed a Web-based interactive writing environment that was not subject-specific in a 2-year longitudinal study in the upper years of an elementary school. The environment included three writing themes—(1) *story pass on*, (2) *story chameleon*, and (3) *thousand ideas*—to promote reading comprehension, creativity, and problem-solving skills. Peer assessment was used to provide constructive comments to foster students' ability to review and criticize other writers' essays, to enable students to review their own essay in terms of strengths and weaknesses, and to encourage students to improve their writing skills. The system was integrated with multilayer educational services platforms, which were designed to support the establishment of online social learning communities among K–12 students and teachers.

The online system logs and writing assessment results were analyzed through system usage over 2 years. This showed that students who participated in the writing environment, submitted many essays, interacted with other students online, and reviewed other essays improved their writing skills. Comparing early and late student writing demonstrated a marked improvement in writing. This improvement was greater than the improvement of comparison groups from previous years who had not received the Web-based system.

Gender Effects

An interesting study on the effect of gender in peer assessment was reported by Yurdabakan (2011). This study was conducted in a primary school fourth-grade social sciences course with 46 participants (28 female and 18 male), their ages ranging from 9 to 10. Male and female students scored their fellow and opposite sexes with respect to their contribution to group work and their learning levels. The compatibility between female student and teacher scores was higher than male student and teacher scores (the teacher was male).

Social Aspects

Since students' social status in school can influence their academic achievement, studies have considered social aspects of peer assessment. Studies using standardized measures of academic achievement have found that students who score high on these are more accepted, less rejected and disliked by peers, viewed by teachers as less deviant, and engage in more positive interactions than those who score low on achievement (e.g., Malecki & Elliott, 2002). This may suggest that able students would make the best peer assessors. However, Bryan's (2005) research demonstrated that certain types of social skills interventions (particularly those focused on self-perceptions, self-attributions, and locus of control) had consistent positive effects on academic achievement. The implication of this is that by engaging *all* students in peer assessment, it should be possible to raise the self-esteem and social-connectedness of rejected children and raise their academic achievement.

Several studies of typical students and those with special needs have implications for matching students involved in peer assessment. Frederickson and Furnham (2004) compared behavioral characteristics assessed by 867 typical classmates in mainstream middle schools (8- to 12-year-olds) in one school district for children with moderate learning difficulties (MLD) ($n = 32$) and socially rejected but not MLD children ($n = 38$) and their typical classmates ($n = 287$). Discriminant function analysis was conducted, with peer assessment items as predictors of sociometric status. Systematic differences were identified between MLD and typical students in the peer-assessed behavioral characteristics associated with rejected social status, while there were no differences between typical and socially rejected students. This suggests that the low cognitive ability of MLD students affects their social acceptance.

Four methods of assessing children's friendships were compared by Yugar and Shapiro (2001), addressing peer nominations (naming children you were friendly with), peer ratings (ranking children you were friendly with), and reciprocal peer nominations (naming children you were friendly with when they also named you). There was high agreement between reciprocal peer nominations and peer ratings, but regular peer nominations did not appear reliable. The extent to which social affiliation should be regarded as important when matching for peer assessment is an interesting one. Many practitioners do not match students who are already highly socially affiliated (since they may enjoy their relationship rather than using it to facilitate achievement) but also tend not to match students who are strongly negatively affiliated.

Students With Special Needs

Peer assessment has been used successfully with special needs children (e.g., Scruggs & Mastropieri, 1998). Students as young as Grade 4 (9 years old) have been successfully involved. Importantly, there are gains from functioning as either assessor or assessee. Studies in this category also have implications for matching students involved in peer assessment. O'Keefe (1991) examined the relationship between intellectually challenged children's social status and their social behavior as perceived by their peers in the mainstream classroom. Sociometric surveys and peer assessments of social behavior were conducted in 51 third- through sixth-grade mainstream classrooms in order to identify accepted and rejected intellectually challenged and nonchallenged children. Rejected intellectually challenged children were perceived by their typical peers as engaging in aggressive/disruptive and/or sensitive/isolated behavior. In contrast, accepted intellectually challenged children were perceived as sociable. The same relationships were found for typical children. Factor analyses of the peer assessments revealed that nonchallenged children used similar dimensions in assessing the social behavior of their challenged and nonchallenged peers. This is encouraging, since it suggests that special needs status is no prohibition for involvement in peer assessment focused on achievement, although disruptive or isolated behavior might be.

Similarly, the purpose of a study by Rockhill and Asher (1992) was to examine gender differences in the types of behavior that distinguish between low-accepted children and their better-accepted classmates. Third through fifth graders ($n = 881$) in five elementary schools completed a sociometric scale in which they rated how much they liked to play with each of their classmates and a peer nomination measure on which they nominated classmates who fit each of 19 behavioral descriptions. The same behaviors were important for boys and girls. The most powerful discriminator between children in the low-accepted group and their classmates was the lack of prosocial behavior. Both aggressive and withdrawn low-accepted children received lower peer ratings for prosocial behavior. In both studies, children used similar dimensions in assessing the social behavior of their normal and special peers—they seemed to be blind to the condition or label of the problem individuals and took their behavior at face value. This is encouraging, though the effect may diminish as children grow older.

The implication from these studies for matching students involved in peer assessment is that special care is needed when involving students with aggressive or withdrawn behavior. Such students may need to be matched with peers who are particularly patient and who accept the difficulties that are likely to arise and are prepared to deal with them. However, low intellectual ability is not of itself a disqualification from peer assessment, although matching should probably not be with a high-ability peer. There is no indication that there are any differences for girls and boys, but more boys may be aggressive. Should same-gender matching be practiced with these difficult students? There is no research on this issue.

Summary of Elementary School Studies

In the elementary school sector, there was a relatively high proportion of studies that used a survey methodology and a relatively high proportion of studies of peer assessment of social relations. Relatively few studies showed peer assessment to be successful in promoting achievement, and even in those, the evidence was tenuous. There can be student resistance, and cultural differences may affect the process and outcome. There is some evidence from one small study that females may be more reliable in peer assessment. Other studies consider peer assessment of social factors, sometimes in relation to children with special needs. Aggressive and passive behavior was not peer-assessed positively, but prosocial behavior was, including when generated by children with special needs.

Secondary School

Secondary schools are more complex environments than elementary schools, and what works in the latter may not work in the former. Research reviewed in this section focused on perceptions of the value of peer assessment, issues of effectiveness of peer assessment, and the exploration of online systems for peer assessment.

Perceived Value of Peer Assessment

Black and Harrison (2001) documented case studies of 12 teachers in six schools and reported some concern about whether peer assessment was practicable. Cultural differences were noted by Mok (2011), using interviews and classroom observation to report on moves toward peer assessment in the formerly test-oriented special region of Hong Kong. Average-to-weak ability secondary school students were encouraged to assess their own and peers' oral English. While peer assessment has been recognized as enhancing student learning if sensitively implemented

(Sebba et al., 2008), it is a new concept to many Hong Kong students. Despite the benefits that the participants perceived, they had serious concerns over the new assessment.

Accuracy of Peer Assessment

Tsivitanidou, Zacharia, and Hovardas (2011) investigated secondary school students' peer assessment skills in Greece, in a unit on the topic of a CO_2 friendly house. Students were tasked with adjusting the ecology, architecture, energy, and insulation aspects of the house in order to reduce its CO_2 emissions. Two classes of seventh graders (age 14, $n = 36$, gender balanced), without receiving any kind of support, were anonymously assigned to reciprocally assess their peers' science Web-portfolios. None had any prior experience of peer assessment. Three data sources (i.e., interviews, video observation, and peer assessors' feedback) were used to find that the students had positive attitudes toward unsupported peer assessment and that they intend to implement it again. Students already had some of the skills needed for implementation, irrespective of the degree of mediation. Students in this study were found able to define and use their own assessment criteria. However, the validity and reliability of these criteria were low, suggesting that although students can peer assess without guidance, the quality of their feedback needs attention, perhaps through training in key assessment skills.

In Taiwan, Sung, Chang, Chiou, and Hou (2005) used progressively focused self- and peer assessment procedures with students developing designs for new Web sites. Students assessed random Web sites produced by their colleagues, then best and worst Web sites, and finally the Web site created by their partner. Self-assessment was done before any peer assessment, again after within-group peer evaluation, and once again after between-group peer assessment. Two classes of seventy-six 14- to 15-year-olds of above average ability demonstrated greater objectivity in their self-assessment scores, which were being used as an outcome measure. Teachers rated the quality of student Web site development related to this activity before and after the exercise and found a significant improvement. The quality of the students' performance improved after the peer assessment activities. Similarly, Tseng and Tsai (2007) found that peer assessment scores were highly correlated with teacher scores.

Contrasting results can be found in studies conducted by Chang, Tseng, Chou, and Chen (2011), who examined the reliability and validity of Web-based portfolio peer assessment with seventy-two 15- to 16-year-old students taking a computer course in a senior high school. There was a lack of consistency in ratings of a single portfolio across student assessors (inter-rater reliability), and also two-thirds of the raters demonstrated inconsistency assessing different portfolios. Peer assessment scores were not consistent with teacher assessment scores. Significant differences were found between peer assessment scores and end-of-course examination scores. Web-based portfolio peer assessment was not found to be a reliable and valid method, though the quality of training in peer assessment for these students was questionable. Additionally, a specific assessment rubric was not predefined or negotiated with the students. Further, large and varied portfolios are difficult to assess (see Belgrad, Chapter 19 of this volume). Also, this study used Web-based methods with limited evidence of implementation integrity and was done in a cultural context that is known to militate against effective use of peer assessment.

Effectiveness of Peer Assessment

A Belgian team (Gielen, Peeters, Dochy, Onghena & Struyven, 2010) examined the effectiveness of certain characteristics of peer assessment feedback in a quasi-experimental, repeated measures study of forty-three 13-year-old students. Written assignments showed that receiving justified comments in feedback was related to improvements in writing performance, but this effect diminished for students with higher pretest performance. The effect of accuracy of feedback was less than the effect of justification. Asking assessees to reflect upon feedback after peer assessment was not significantly related to learning gains.

The study by Sung et al. (2005) suggested that not only were students' peer assessments consistent with the assessments of teachers but the quality of the students' work in developing new Web sites improved after the peer assessment activities as well. Similarly, Tseng and Tsai (2007), in Taiwan, found that 184 tenth-grade 16-year-old students significantly improved their projects for a computer course by engaging in successive rounds of peer assessment activities. The study also related the type of peer assessment feedback (i.e., reinforcing, didactic, corrective, or suggestive) to subsequent performance in the student projects. Reinforcing feedback was given when what the student did was proper or correct. Positive feelings about or recognition of the work was expressed. Students could be encouraged without explicitly knowing the reasons. In didactic feedback, a peer provided lengthy explanations with a lecture tone to direct the other student on to the right track. In corrective feedback, if a student's preliminary design or information was incorrect, then a peer could give feedback to point it out or correct it directly. In suggestive feedback, if a student's preliminary design was incomplete rather than incorrect, a peer was likely to give indirect advisory feedback. The peer would have alerted the student that there was a problem without telling him/her exactly what the problem was. Such feedback could be in the form of hints, pauses, or a rising intonation in the voice in order to redirect the student's thinking. This kind of feedback is also considered a kind of scaffolding.

Reinforcing peer feedback was useful in the development of better projects. Suggestive feedback was helpful in the beginning of peer assessment. In the later parts of peer assessment, the effect of this type of feedback on learning was not significant. However, didactic feedback and, to an extent, corrective feedback were negatively correlated with student achievement, suggesting that they might play an unfavorable role for subsequent improvement of students' projects.

Chang and Tseng (2009) conducted a study in Taiwan in which additional questions about the nature of the cultural context of education in that country were raised. They studied the use of peer assessment of Web-based portfolios and its effect on student performance with 13- to 14-year-olds in two computer classes of 30 students each. One class was the intervention group and the other the control class. There was no significant difference between experimental and control groups in terms of academic achievement and computer achievement. Also, a 45-item questionnaire, using a 5-point Likert scale, was designed relating to nine performance dimensions in the portfolio assessment system: (1) goal setting, (2) work, (3) reflection, (4) self-assessment, (5) peer assessment, (6) peer interaction, (7) data gathering, (8) continuous improvement, and (9) problem solving. Among the eight performances that had significant differences, reflection had the highest effect size ($\acute{\eta}$ = 0.261), with self-assessment second ($\acute{\eta}$ = 0.229). Results of an analysis of covariance (ANCOVA) on each factor in relation to academic achievement, computer achievement, and assessment method showed that eight of the nine performance dimensions were significant, except peer assessment. However, peer assessment approached significance ($p = 0.056$), and the experimental group score on peer assessment was the highest for all factors. The overall effect size for assessment method between the two groups was 0.27. (Note that these effect sizes are likely to underestimate the more commonly used Cohen's δ.) The accuracy of peer assessment itself was not enhanced over time.

Similarly, Chang and Chou (2011) examined the effects of reflection quality, defined as the capacity to exercise personal, thoughtful, and explicit introspection, in self-assessment and peer assessment on learning outcomes with forty-five 14-year-old students during a Web-based portfolio assessment process. The immediate influence of reflection quality on learning outcomes was small but positive and statistically significant. Furthermore, follow-up contrasts found reflection quality significantly related to achievement test, work, and attitude outcomes. Thus, low quality reflection in self- and peer assessment was associated with low quality learning, while high quality reflection in self- and peer assessment was associated with higher quality learning.

Positive results were also reported from Hong Kong. Lu and Law (2012) studied 181 high school students engaged in online peer assessment. Peers graded and gave feedback, which was analyzed. Lu and Law found that the provision by student assessors of feedback that identified problems and gave suggestions was a significant predictor of the performance of the assessors themselves and that positive affective feedback was related to the performance of assessees. However, peer grading behaviors were not a significant predictor of project performance.

Summary of High School Studies

In the high school sector, there were several experimental studies of online methods of peer assessment, all authored from Taiwan or Hong

Kong. There were two important studies from Europe. There were no studies of social relations or special needs children. Most studies were positive in terms of indicating a relationship between achievement and peer assessment, but a number (in the online environment and from a particular culture) reported difficulties in implementation, especially with the accuracy of peer assessments. Again, cultural differences were important. Untrained students can still peer assess, although less well. Justification of feedback comments enhances acceptance, except for high-ability students. Some studies were positive in showing the effectiveness of peer feedback for both assessors and assessees.

Literature Reviews

Literature reviews tend to speak about peer assessment as if it were homogeneous, with little differentiation between elementary and secondary levels. Indeed, works referred to here have reviewed relatively little significant literature related to peer assessment in K–12 schools, including more studies of peer assessment in higher education. Nonetheless, the reviews make some interesting and helpful points. An early review by Kane and Lawler (1978) considered research on three methods of peer assessment of their peers' work: (1) peer nomination, (2) peer rating, and (3) peer ranking. They noted that peer assessment could be reliable and valid. Peer nomination appeared to have the highest validity and reliability. Peer rating was the most useful of the three methods for feedback purposes but also produced the least valid and reliable measurements. Peer ranking was the least researched at that time.

A systematic literature review on the effects of peer assessment was reported by Van Gennip, Segers, and Tillema (2009). Peer assessment was seen as fundamentally a social process—interpersonal and interactional. Fifteen studies conducted since 1990 dealt with the effects on achievement of peer assessment. However, only one of these studies included students from a school (in this case, a secondary school), the remainder consisting largely of university students. Interpersonal variables had been measured in only four of these, and even then there were no significant relationships to learning gains. However, the authors developed four underlying constructs based on previous research: psychological safety, value diversity, interdependence, and trust. Psychological safety is defined as a belief that it is safe to take interpersonal risks in a group of people, or the extent of confidence in the rest of the group. Peers who prefer to work with their friends have a narrow view of psychological safety. Those who feel more widely psychologically safe may be less inclined toward friendship marking. Value diversity refers to differences in opinion about what a team's task, goal, or mission should be. It should be low for peer work to be effective. It is likely to be lower where peers have participated in setting the assessment criteria. Interdependence has been long studied, but it needs to be perceived as such by the participants, rather than assumed by the teaching staff. It requires that multiple perspectives are made explicit, and students are individually responsible for an active contribution to group discussions. Peer assessment is commonly used to enhance students' shared responsibility for the assessment processes and learning. However, several studies note that students feel uncomfortable criticizing one another's work, or find it difficult to rate their peers, at least initially. Confidence or trust in both self and the other in relation to learning effects is hardly addressed in empirical studies.

Van Zundert, Sluijsmans, and van Merrienboer (2010) selected 27 papers, all of which studied university students. They found that the psychometric qualities of peer assessment were improved by having trained and experienced peer assessors, which also improved student attitudes toward peer assessment. The development of peer assessment skills benefited from training and experience. Domain-specific skills were positively influenced by enabling students to revise their work on the basis of peer feedback, giving specific peer feedback formats, maintaining small group size, allowing sufficient time for revision, and deploying students having high executive thinking style (i.e., those willing to follow instructional rules rather than be independent and creative). Students with a high level of academic achievement were generally more skillful in peer assessment.

A review of research on the role of peer assessment in the elementary science classroom was undertaken by Hodgson (2010). The themes that emerged consistently were the need for a supportive classroom climate, the role of talk and discussion that was not all teacher-led, the importance of questioning in the process, and the richness of feedback.

Most recently, Tillema, Leenknecht, and Segers (2011) considered what quality criteria were specifically relevant to peer assessment. One hundred and thirty-two studies of measurement quality in peer AFL were selected together with 42 studies for a qualitative analysis of student involvement in peer assessment. Surprisingly, nowhere in the paper is any distinction made between studies based in school, higher education, or other settings. Studies were evaluated with regard to use of two quality criteria: (1) the recognition of educational measurement criteria and (2) the consideration of student involvement in the assessment of learning. These evaluations scrutinized successive parts of the assessment cycle—that is, the process of construction, administration, and follow-up of an assessment. The review regarded the purpose of assessment as important. If the purpose was to enhance future learning rather than assign a category, then formative assessment was important. Where emphasis was placed on authenticity and future learning needs across the life span, peer assessment had much to recommend it in terms of generalizability, particularly utility in contexts beyond the present institution.

In summary, an early review (Kane & Lawler, 1978) considered the relative effectiveness of peer nomination, rating, and ranking and concluded that peer nomination had the highest validity and reliability, while peer rating was the most useful for feedback purposes. A review of peer assessment as a social process (Van Gennip et al., 2009) emphasized the importance of psychological safety, value diversity, interdependence, and trust. Another review (Van Zundert et al., 2010) found that training and experience enhanced the psychometric qualities of peer assessment. Finally, Tillema et al. (2011) found peer assessment met two different kinds of quality criteria, including recognition of educational measurement criteria and consideration of student involvement.

Critique of Studies and Directions for Future Research

It is clear that descriptions of the samples and of the process of implementation of peer assessment were poor in many of the studies. It seems that many authors have spoken about peer assessment with little regard for the way it is operationalized for differences between ages, institutions, countries, subjects, type of output, and other variables. When authors attempt a literature review in this area or conduct a single empirical study, they need to address these variations. In Figure 22.2, a checklist is offered that is designed to facilitate the evaluation of each study with respect to important variations. Of course, many of the items will not be able to be checked at first, since the information will not be in the paper. However, it will at least be clear what is not known. It is hoped that over time authors will learn to report all the features that appear in the checklist.

Check	*Answer*	*Check*	*Answer*	*Check*	*Answer*
Focus		Peers from same or different year of study?		**Feedback**	
Elementary or high school?		Supportive classroom climate?		Quantity of feedback?	
Targeting cognitive and/or metacognitive gains; teacher time saving?		Degree of trust and psychological safety?		Nature of feedback (oral, written, etc.)?	
Formative or summative?		Low-value diversity?		Elaborated and specific or concise and general?	
Formative leading to summative?				Feedback positive, negative, or both?	
Participants clear about this (and reworking)?		**Matching and Contact**		One-way, reciprocal, or mutual within a group?	

Check	*Answer*	*Check*	*Answer*	*Check*	*Answer*
Revisions to be few or many, simple or complex?		Assessors individuals, pairs, or groups?		Feedback quantitative, qualitative, or both?	
Peer nomination, rating, or ranking?		Assessees individuals, pairs, or groups?		Feedback reinforcing suggestive, didactic, or corrective?	
Curriculum areas or subjects?		Matching selective, random, or accidental?		Role of questioning in feedback?	
Single or multiple assessments?		Same-sex or cross-sex matching?		Equal talk and discussion—assessor not "expert"?	
Product—writing, portfolios, presentations, or oral statements?		Matching by same or different ability?		Justification of feedback expected?	
		Matching by social factors?		Confidential or public?	
Nature of Sample		Face-to-face or distant or both?		Monitored by supervisory staff?	
Number of assessors, assessees?		Place: class, informal, home?		Reliability/validity moderated by supervising teachers?	
Cultural background, expectations?		Time: session length, number of sessions?			
Gender?				**Final Issues**	
Student resistance?		**Criteria and Training**		Task surface or complex, or developmental?	
Cultural context favorable or not?		Assessment criteria clear?		Extrinsic or intrinsic rewards?	
Interdependence expected by students?		Students involved in developing criteria?		Evaluation of the peer assessment?	
Experience of students?		Training of assessors, assessees, or both?		Alignment with traditional assessment?	
Previous experience positive or negative?		Activity highly structured or student interpreted?		What social, communicative, or transferable skills measured?	
Preexisting skills?		Interaction with guiding prompts, sentence openers, cue cards, or other scaffolding devices?			

Figure 22.2 Checklist of Important Factors in Peer Assessment Research

Figure 22.2 emphasizes the focus of the peer assessment, the nature of the sample, the matching and contact procedures, criteria and training, variations in feedback, and final issues—in other words, purpose, sample, and implementation. Beyond this, there are, of course, other issues regarding the quality of the studies reviewed here, particularly regarding the nature of the measures used. A tendency to singularity of measures was evident when triangulation of a number of measures would be considerably safer. The general simplicity of modes of analysis, which tended to be either singular inferential statistical procedures or inductive searching for qualitative items, but rarely both, also limits the credibility of some studies.

There are also additional considerations. In the elementary school studies, no study used a control group, although some studies did use comparison groups—in some cases selected post hoc after initial data gathering. No study reported effect sizes. Also in this sector, there was a high proportion of studies that used a survey methodology, a weak approach that harvests the subjective perceptions of participants but does not necessarily couple this with more objective data on what is happening. None of the elementary studies were experimental or quasi-experimental. There was little evidence of the process of peer assessment being studied carefully as assessment proceeded, so implementation quality or integrity was often uncertain. There are perfectly good ways of doing this, involving direct observation, video observation, or analysis of online comments, for example. All of these are time consuming but needed for validity.

The secondary studies fared little better. Again, survey methodologies were quite common (although illuminative). Only one study used a control group, and this study found no positive difference for the peer assessment group, albeit in an unfavorable cultural context and with the difficult area of Web-based portfolio assessment. Only two studies reported effect sizes. In one study, the effect size was negative and in the other rather small, depending on the statistical indicator used. Effect sizes that are at least moderate should be the target of future studies, especially when stemming from larger samples. Only two studies were quasi-experimental. Thus, the secondary studies were only slightly more methodologically respectable than the primary studies. Again, implementation integrity was largely neglected.

The reviews contained little quality research on peer assessment in schools. Although they made interesting points, how those points relate to a K–12 school population has yet to be explored. It is clear that the needs for future research are considerable. We need more studies that relate peer assessment directly to academic achievement, especially in the elementary school sector. More experimental and quasi-experimental studies are needed. Comparison and control groups need to be a ubiquitous feature of such studies. Effect sizes should be quoted as an indicator of impact. Where sample size is relatively small, an indication of the power of the effect size is needed. The tendency for the literature to be dominated by particular types of study, such as online or Web-based studies, should be resisted.

Conclusion

Peer assessment holds considerable promise in both elementary and high schools. The only studies that were not positive related to the online environment in high schools set in an unfavorable cultural context, but even here, as many positive as negative studies were found. Caution is needed in asserting that elementary schools are more promising places to conduct peer assessment, since the quality of the research in elementary schools was not high.

Teachers may wish to involve their students in peer formative assessment until they have reached a level of experience and comfort that enables discussion of moving on to incorporate some peer assessment in a summative manner. However, such peer assessment is unlikely ever to replace teacher or computer assessment as the main form of assessment. Quite apart from any other consideration, time would not permit the engagement of students in peer assessment for too large a proportion of their working week.

It is hoped that peer assessment is capable of engaging students much more effectively in self-regulation and developing other skills relevant to lifelong learning and work. Of course, such long-term developments have yet to be measured and would be difficult to measure. Nonetheless, the logic of short-term measures and theoretical perspectives indicate that such a hope is not forlorn.

References

Atkinson, P. (2003). *Assessment 5–14: What do pupils and parents think?* (ERIC Reproduction Document Service No. ED480897)

Black, P., & Harrison, C. (2001). Self- and peer-assessment and taking responsibility: The science student's role in formative assessment. *School Science Review, 83*(302), 43–49.

Bryan, T. (2005). Science-based advances in the social domain of learning disabilities. *Learning Disability Quarterly, 28,* 119–121.

Bryant, D. A., & Carless, D. R. (2010). Peer assessment in a test-dominated setting: Empowering, boring or facilitating examination preparation? *Educational Research for Policy and Practice, 9*(1), 3–15.

Chang, C. C., & Chou, P. N. (2011). Effects of reflection category and reflection quality on learning outcomes during web-based portfolio assessment process: A case study of high school students in computer application course. *Turkish Online Journal of Educational Technology, 10*(3), 101–114.

Chang, C. C., & Tseng, K. H. (2009). Use and performances of web-based portfolio assessment. *British Journal of Educational Technology, 40*(2), 358–370.

Chang, C. C., Tseng, K. H., Chou, P. N., & Chen, Y. H. (2011). Reliability and validity of web-based portfolio peer assessment: A case study for a senior high school's students taking computer course. *Computers and Education, 57*(1), 1306–1316.

Chi, M. T. H., Siler, S. A, Jeong, H., Yamauchi, T., & Hausmann, R. G. (2001). Learning from human tutoring. *Cognitive Science, 25,* 471–533.

Chin, C., & Teou, L. Y. (2009). Using concept cartoons in formative assessment: Scaffolding students' argumentation. *International Journal of Science Education, 31*(10), 1307–1332.

Frederickson, N. L., & Furnham, A. E. (2004). Peer-assessed behavioural characteristics and sociometric rejection: Differences between pupils who have moderate learning difficulties and their mainstream peers. *British Journal of Educational Psychology, 74*(3), 391–410.

Gielen, S., Peeters, E., Dochy, F., Onghena, P., & Struyven, K. (2010). Improving the effectiveness of peer feedback for learning. *Learning and Instruction, 20*(4), 304–315.

Hodgson, C. (2010). Assessment for learning in science: What works? *Primary Science, 115,* 14–16.

Kane, J. S., & Lawler, E. E. (1978). Methods of peer assessment. *Psychological Bulletin, 85*(3), 555–586.

King, A. (1998). Transactive peer tutoring: Distributing cognition and metacognition. *Educational Psychology Review, 10*(1), 57–74.

Lu, J., & Law, N. (2012). Online peer assessment: Effects of cognitive and affective feedback. *Instructional Science, 40*(2), 257–275.

Malecki, C. K., & Elliott, C. N. (2002). Children's social behaviors as predictors of academic achievement: A longitudinal analysis. *School Psychology Quarterly, 17,* 1–23.

Mok, J. (2011). A case study of students' perceptions of peer assessment in Hong Kong. *ELT Journal, 65*(3), 230–239.

O'Donnell, A. M. & Topping, K. (1998). Peers assessing peers: Possibilities and problems. In K. Topping & S. Ehly (Eds.), *Peer-assisted learning.* Mahwah, NJ: Lawrence Erlbaum.

O'Keefe, P. F. (1991). Relationship between social status and *peer assessment* of social behavior among mentally retarded and nonretarded children. (ERIC Document Reproduction Service No. ED340500)

Rockhill, C. M., & Asher, S. R. (1992). *Peer assessment of the behavioral characteristics of poorly accepted boys and girls.* Educational Resources Information Center document reproduction service ED346372.

Scruggs, T. E., & Mastropieri, M. A. (1998). Tutoring and students with special needs. In K. J. Topping & S. Ehly (Eds.), *Peer-assisted learning.* Mahwah, NJ: Lawrence Erlbaum.

Sebba, J., Crick, R. D., Yu, G., Lawson, H., Harlen, W., & Durant, K. (2008). *Systematic review of research evidence of the impact on students in secondary schools of self and peer assessment* (Technical report). In *Research Evidence in Education Library.* London: EPPI-Centre, Social Science Research Unit, Institute of Education, University of London.

Sluijsmans, D., & Prins, F. (2006). A conceptual framework for integrating peer assessment in teacher education. *Studies in Educational Evaluation, 32,* 6–22.

Sung, Y. T., Chang, K. E., Chiou, S. K., & Hou, H. T. (2005). The design and application of a web-based self- and peer-assessment system. *Computers and Education, 45(2),* 187–202.

Tillema, H., Leenknecht, M., & Segers, M. (2011). Assessing assessment quality: Criteria for quality assurance in design of (peer) assessment for learning—A review of research studies. *Studies in Educational Evaluation, 37*(1), 25–34.

Topping, K. J. (2003). Self and peer assessment in school and university: Reliability, validity and utility. In M. S. R. Segers, F. J. R. C. Dochy, & E. C. Cascallar (Eds.), *Optimizing new modes of assessment: In search of qualities and standards.* Dordrecht: Kluwer Academic Publishers.

Tseng, S. C., & Tsai, C. C. (2007). On-line peer assessment and the role of the peer feedback: A study of high school computer course. *Computers and Education, 49*(4), 1161–1174.

Tsivitanidou, O. E., Zacharia, Z. C., & Hovardas, T. (2011). Investigating secondary school students' unmediated peer assessment skills. *Learning and Instruction, 21*(4), 506–519.

Van Gennip, N. A. E., Segers, M., & Tillema, H. M. (2009). Peer assessment for learning from a social perspective: The influence of interpersonal variables and structural features. *Educational Research Review, 4*(1), 41–54.

Van Zundert, M., Sluijsmans, D., & van Merrienboer, J. (2010). Effective peer assessment processes: Research findings and future directions. *Learning and Instruction, 20*(4), 270–279.

Vygotsky, L. S. (1978). *Mind in society: The development of higher psychological processes.* M. Cole, V. John-Steiner, S. Scribner, & E. Souberman (Eds.). Cambridge, MA: MIT Press.

Weaver, M. E. (1995). Using peer response in the classroom: Students' perspectives. *Research and Teaching in Developmental Education, 12,* 31–37.

Yang, J. C., Ko, H. W., & Chung, I. L. (2005). Web-based interactive writing environment: Development and evaluation. *Educational Technology and Society, 8*(2), 214–229.

Yugar, J. M., & Shapiro, E. S. (2001). Elementary children's school friendship: A comparison of peer assessment methodologies. *School Psychology Review, 30*(4), 68–85.

Yurdabakan, I. (2011). The investigation of peer assessment in primary school cooperative learning groups with respect to gender. *Education 3-13, 39*(2), 153–169.

SECTION 6

Differentiated Classroom Assessment

Jay Parkes

Associate Editor

23

Differentiation and Classroom Assessment

Carol Ann Tomlinson

Tonya R. Moon

In this chapter, we will review research related to assessment in the differentiated classroom, what could be called differentiated assessment. We will first set the stage for the need for differentiation, then review briefly the essential elements of differentiated instruction (DI). We will then explore pre-assessment, formative assessment, and summative assessment as implemented in a differentiated classroom and conclude with practical implications and suggestions for research.

Demographics and Differentiation

It has never been the case that all students of a certain age learn at the same rate, at the same depth, or in the same way. Nonetheless, since the inception of consolidated schools in the early part of the 20th century, educators in the United States have generally sorted students by age and have typically taught largely as though students in a certain grade level could, should, and would respond to one-size-fits-all instruction.

While there has always been evidence that such an approach was less than optimal for a variable number of students, the practice has remained dominant. When students appear to be academic outliers to the degree that single-size instruction clearly misses the mark for them (or more accurately perhaps that the students miss the mark in such settings), the solution of choice has been to place those students in alternate settings such as classrooms designed for English language learners (ELLs), students with special education identification, students identified as gifted, or into low or high track classes. In each instance, one motivation for such arrangements has been to allow teachers to maintain norm-based approaches to planning and delivering instruction.

In contemporary schools, there are at least three noteworthy challenges to this approach to teaching. First, a critical mass of students comes to school with profiles that are ill suited to one-size-fits-all teaching. Indications are that this will continue to be the case for the foreseeable future:

- Approximately 21% of U.S. students, ages 5 to 17, speak a language other than English at home (National Center for Education Statistics, n.d.).
- Approximately 450 languages are currently spoken in U.S. schools (Gray & Fleischman, 2004).

- Estimates are that at least 45% of children younger than 5 are minorities (Center for Public Education, 2007).
- Trends in immigration and birth rate suggest that soon there will be no majority group of students—in other words, that no one group will make up more than 50% of the population (Center for Public Education, 2007).
- The number of students diagnosed with learning disabilities has nearly tripled in the past three decades (National Center for Education Statistics, n.d.).
- Autism spectrum disorder has risen from 4 or 5 children in 10,000 to 1 in 150 (Centers for Disease Control and Prevention, 2007, n.d.).
- One in five children experiences some behavioral or emotional difficulty (Kluger, 2010).
- Approximately 20% of children in the United States live in poverty—a rate as high as 30% is found in some states (Center for Public Education, 2007).

Also, in most schools and classrooms are students who are academically advanced well beyond grade-level expectations. The National Association for Gifted Children (NAGC) (n.d.) estimates that there are over 3 million academically gifted children in American schools or approximately 6% of the U.S. K–12 student population. In addition, some students will belong in more than one category—for example, an ELL with an emotional problem or an advanced learner with a learning disability. The U.S. Department of Education estimates that there are approximately 360,000 of these "twice-exceptional" students in Grades K–12 (National Education Association, 2006).

In this context, addressing learner variance by separating students who function *normally* from those who do not becomes increasingly difficult. These trends suggest that fewer and fewer students will appear to be normal, leading, among other concerns, to a configuration of *splinter* classrooms.

A second challenge to maintenance of a one-size-fits-all approach to instruction augmented by removal of students who do not fit the norm is that ability grouping and tracking in schools tend to result in lower groups dominated by low income students and students of color and higher groups dominated by more affluent students and students from Caucasian and some Asian groups. Further, these demarcations tend to result in less challenging and robust learning opportunities for students in low and middle level classes, with richer and more dynamic learning opportunities often reserved for students in higher groups or tracks (Boykin & Noguera, 2011; Callahan, 2005; Gamoran, Nystrand, Berends, & LePore 1995; Hochschild & Scovronik, 2003). This outcome of restricting high quality curriculum and instruction to a limited segment of the school population—and should be unacceptable under any circumstances—will likely have stunningly negative impacts for a society in which minority students will become the majority in the relatively near term (Marx, 2000).

A third challenge to *standardized* teaching and attempts to deal with student variance via ability grouping derives from admonitions of demographers and futurists who conclude that virtually all students will need to be competent critical and creative thinkers and problems solvers if they are to be successful, contributing adults in the 21st century. In other words, virtually all young people need to develop proficiency with the kinds of knowledge, skills, and attitudes that have previously been thought of as appropriate solely or largely for students in higher level classes (Hochschild & Scovronik, 2003; Marx, 2000). To the degree that such an argument is tenable, it becomes simultaneously less tenable to group students in ways that limit access to rich, relevant, and motivating learning opportunities.

DI offers an alternative to one-size-fits-all classrooms and ability grouping as the mechanism of choice to address students' inevitable learning differences. The model does not advocate elimination of all classes and/or programs for students with specialized learning needs. What it does suggest, however, is that a far greater number of students could access high quality curriculum and instruction in effectively differentiated general classrooms. In addition, differentiation is important even in settings that are designed to be more homogeneous in nature, since the concept of homogeneity is rarely evidenced in any classroom. Thus, students in specialized settings would fare better as well to the degree that teachers were competent and confident in addressing their specific learning needs. In order to differentiate instruction so that all students have access to high quality curriculum and to be able to document student attainment of the curricular goals and objectives, assessment should also be differentiated to ensure alignment among the curriculum, instruction, and assessment. In differentiating assessment, the learning outcomes assessed remain the same (except in the case of students with individual learning plans that prescribe curriculum for the student different from the grade-level curriculum), while the format of the assessment, time allowance, and scaffolding may vary.

Brief Overview of a Model of Differentiation

The model of differentiation referenced in this chapter works from the premise that a classroom is a system of five interdependent elements and that, as with all systems, the whole works more effectively when all of the elements are sound and working in concert—in this case, with an eye to ensuring instructional fit for individuals in the class as well as for the class as a whole. The five elements are (1) classroom environment, (2) curriculum, (3) assessment, (4) instruction, and (5) classroom management. A primary goal of differentiation is maximizing the capacity of each learner to succeed and, whenever possible, exceed essential learning goals established for the class or grade level. Following is a summary of key attributes of the five elements that reflect a current understanding of best educational practices in general and those necessary to ensure appropriate attention to learner variance.

Classroom Environment

Environment refers to the affective tone of the classroom as students perceive it. The nature of that environment predicts much about student attitude toward school learning, student engagement, and student outcomes. Indicators of an environment that supports learning in a differentiated classroom include the following (Dweck, 2000, 2006; Hattie, 2009, 2012; Sousa & Tomlinson, 2011; Tomlinson, Brimijoin, & Narvaez, 2008; Tomlinson & Imbeau, 2010):

- The teacher believes in the capacity of each student to succeed. That is, the teacher operates from a growth mind-set perspective that an individual's effort is the defining factor in his or her achievement rather than primarily the student's genetics or background.
- The teacher's interactions with students and instructional arrangements support a growth mind-set in students.
- The teacher finds each student interesting and worthwhile and makes consistent efforts to connect with each student in order to build the trust and affiliation necessary for students to commit to the risk of learning.
- The teacher's respect for the possibilities in each student leads students to be respectful of one another's abilities.
- The environment enables students to be affirmed and feel safe as they are.
- The environment offers many opportunities for students to affiliate with a wide range of peers so that students feel a sense of belonging to and identification with the class.
- The classroom reflects sense of community or teamwork. It *belongs* to everyone in the class, not just to the teacher, and everyone is responsible for contributing to the smooth operation of the classroom and supporting the success of peers in the classroom.
- The atmosphere is one of high expectations and high support to meet those expectations.

Curriculum

This refers to an articulated and planned set of experiences designed to guide learners to competence with essential knowledge, understanding, and skills. It can be thought of both as what students need to learn and how they gain access to that content. Indicators of high quality curriculum in a differentiated classroom include the following (Darling-Hammond, 2008; Darling-Hammond & Bransford, 2005; Hattie, 2009, 2012; National Research Council [NRC], 2000; Tomlinson, 1999, 2000, 2003; Tomlinson et al., 2008; Tomlinson & McTighe, 2006; Wiggins & McTighe, 1998):

- There are clearly articulated learning goals known to the teacher and students. The goals include essential knowledge, essential understandings, and essential skills. Emphasis is on student understanding of and the ability to apply and transfer those understandings so that students regularly make meaning of what they are asked to learn. Essential knowledge and essential skills may be differentiated in cases where students demonstrate early mastery and in instances where students need to move backward along a continuum of knowledge and skills in order to correct learning deficits that impede their ability to move ahead in a content area, even as they work to master expected knowledge and skills. Essential understandings are central for all learners and provide a basis for discussion and sharing across the class.

- There is a clear plan to engage learners with content. High relevance and focus on student interests support student motivation to learn. Engagement helps students make meaning of or relate to what they are asked to learn.
- Tasks are respectful. That is, when tasks are differentiated, each student's work looks equally interesting to students. In addition, all student work is focused on essential understandings and requires a high level of thought and application.
- Teachers "teach up." Teachers plan learning experiences with advanced learners in mind and plan differentiation as a means of supporting all students in reaching and, when possible, exceeding those advanced expectations. Teaching up is central to ensuring maximum academic growth for all members in a class, including those who perform well beyond grade-level expectations.

Classroom Assessment

Classroom assessment (CA) refers to both formal and informal means by which teachers and students can follow the progress of a learner toward meeting or exceeding the level of knowledge, understanding, and skills designated as essential in the curriculum. This classroom element is the subject of the majority of this chapter and will be explored more fully as the chapter progresses. We do not use the term to apply to assessments that are externally mandated and used for school or teacher accountability purposes.

Indicators of effective use of CA in a differentiated classroom include the following (Darling-Hammond, 2008; Darling-Hammond & Bransford, 2005; Hattie, 2009, 2012; NRC, 2000; Tomlinson, 1999, 2000, 2003; Tomlinson et al., 2008; Tomlinson & Imbeau, 2010; Tomlinson & McTighe, 2006; Wiliam, 2011):

- The teacher is a persistent student of his or her students, consistently seeking to grow in understanding of the student's readiness levels, interests, approaches to learning, and background in order to teach more effectively.
- At various times and in various ways, a teacher assesses student readiness, interest, and approaches to learning.
- Assessments of readiness are tightly aligned with the knowledge, understanding, and skills designated as essential in the curriculum.
- Assessments occur before a unit of study begins so that a teacher is aware of students' starting points relative to both prerequisite knowledge and to knowledge, understanding, and skills designated as essential to a topic or unit of study. They also occur regularly throughout a unit of study to maintain awareness of student progress toward or beyond learning outcomes designated as essential. They occur at summative points in a unit of study to determine the degree to which a student achieved mastery of essential knowledge, understanding, and skills.
- Both pre-assessments and formative assessments are largely used to help teachers plan instruction that is likely to address the varied learning needs of students and to help students understand their own progress so they can contribute to it with greater urgency.
- Assessments themselves may be differentiated to increase the opportunity for students to demonstrate what they know, understand, and can do. However, the knowledge, understanding, and skill targeted in an assessment do not change.

Instruction

This refers to the processes, sequences, and activities in which a teacher and students participate to ensure that students master content designated as essential in the curriculum. While curriculum specifies *what* teachers will teach and what students should learn, instruction specifies *how* teachers will teach and how students will learn. Indicators of effective instruction in a differentiated classroom include the following (Darling-Hammond, 2005; Darling-Hammond & Bransford, 2005; Hattie, 2009, 2012; NRC, 2000; Tomlinson, 1999, 2000, 2003; Tomlinson et al., 2008; Tomlinson & McTighe, 2006):

- Instruction is predicated on the belief that learning must happen in students rather than to them. In other words, instruction is student-centered.
- Instruction is tightly aligned with knowledge, understanding, and skills designated as essential in the curriculum.
- Instruction is guided by formal and informal teacher assessment of student growth, preferences, and needs.
- The teacher attends to student readiness, interest, and learning profile. Attention to readiness is critical for academic growth. Attention to interest supports motivation to learn. Attention to learning profile encourages efficiency of learning.
- A key goal of instruction is to help students understand the learning process and themselves as learners so they can increasingly contribute to their own success.
- The teacher uses a variety of instructional strategies (small group instruction, varied materials and technologies, learning contracts, tiering, etc.) to support student learning. Selection of instructional strategies is guided by the nature of the content and the needs of students.
- Purposeful planning for flexible student grouping enables students to work with a wide variety of peers as well as alone and with the teacher. Both heterogeneous and homogeneous learning groups with regard to readiness, interest, and learning profile are part of flexible grouping plans, as are teacher-choice, student-choice, and random groupings. Grouping patterns attend to both learning goals and student needs.

Classroom Management

Classroom management refers to the organization of the classroom in terms of materials and routines. Effective management in a differentiated classroom is imperative for the teacher and students to feel confidence with flexible instruction or DI. To this end, the teacher balances structure and flexibility, modifying the balance in favor of increased flexibility as students are ready to work with increasing independence. Indicators of effective classroom leadership and management in a differentiated classroom include the following (Darling-Hammond, 2005; Darling-Hammond & Bransford, 2005; Hattie, 2009, 2012; NRC, 2000; Tomlinson, 1999, 2000, 2003; Tomlinson et al., 2008; Tomlinson & Imbeau, 2010):

- Classroom management appears to be designed not to ensure teacher dominance but rather for enhanced student learning.
- Early in the year and consistently throughout the year, the teacher helps students think about and contribute to a conception of a classroom that is designed to help each learner succeed as fully as possible. Students become the teacher's partner in both design and implementation of such a classroom.
- Students understand how to access materials, how to move around the room, where to put work when it is finished, how to get help when the teacher is busy, how to help one another appropriately, what to do when they finish an assignment, and how to do other processes that encourage student growth toward independence as learners.
- The teacher and students practice routines to ensure that students know how to use the routines successfully.
- The teacher and students regularly discuss what is working well in the classroom and what needs additional attention to work as it should.

Interaction of the Elements

Strictly speaking, differentiation is an instructional model and therefore need not be concerned with curriculum and assessment. However, envisioning the classroom as a system of intertwined elements prompts the realization that each of the five key elements that were previously noted impacts and is impacted by the others. For example, when a student or group of students feels diminished by the learning environment for any number of reasons, that student's engagement with curriculum and participation in instruction will likely be inhibited. If a student perceives that the curriculum is flat and uninspired, that sends a message of disrespect for that student's capacity as a learner and makes the learning environment feel less secure.

The role of assessment in differentiation certainly reflects the interdependence of the five classroom elements. Its effectiveness is greatly dependent on alignment with clear curricular goals. Ensuring that students come to see formative assessment as a vehicle to support their academic growth is pivotal in student development of a growth mind-set—a key environmental goal. Only when a teacher understands how to plan for students' differences from formative assessment information is it possible for instruction to robustly address students' readiness needs. And only when a teacher gains comfort in flexibly managing a classroom is the teacher freed up to study students individually—an important means of gaining insights about students' particular strengths, needs, interests, and approaches to learning.

In the remainder of the chapter, we will explore in detail both the nature of formative assessment in an effectively differentiated classroom and its potential impact on the learning environment, curriculum, instruction, and classroom management. We will also examine summative assessment as it relates to differentiation. The discussion that follows is rooted in research where it is available but also provides practical implications for assessment and differentiation since the model is intended for classroom use.

Assessment and Differentiation

As one of the fundamental principles of *defensible differentiation,* or differentiation that is likely to make a meaningful difference in the learning of students, the process of ongoing assessment is pivotal. It involves understanding and taking into account students' varying interests and approaches to learning, as well as their readiness levels related to content so instruction can be adjusted to be a better fit for learners' needs.

The following sections outline research on the influence of assessment prior to, during, and after instruction on student learning as well as the alignment of effective assessment practices with the philosophy and practices of differentiation as a whole.

Assessment of Prior Knowledge

The Context for Pre-Assessment

Assessment of prior knowledge—or pre-assessment—is most often associated with student readiness to learn. The philosophy of differentiation with which we work takes care to distinguish the term *readiness* from alternative terms sometimes used as though they were synonyms. Readiness, as we use the term, is not a synonym for *ability, aptitude,* or *capacity.* It refers simply to what a student knows, understands, and can do at a given point and related to a topic at hand. It includes essential prerequisite knowledge, understanding, and skills that could impact a student's success with the topic as well as the student's status with knowledge, understanding, and skills that a teacher is about to teach in a unit of study. Readiness is fluid. At least some of the time, nearly all students will already know some things about a topic that a teacher assumes they do not yet know. (For example, Nutall, 2005, found that students often already knew about 40% of what teachers planned to teach them.) At least some of the time, nearly all students will lack some segment of knowledge that a teacher assumes they have. Differentiation assumes that most students have far more capacity than is visible to teachers and likely to the students themselves. Working from that perspective, it is not a goal that a teacher knows how *smart* a student is but rather where that student is in a learning sequence or trajectory so that the teacher can help the student move along that route as efficiently and effectively as possible. Assessment of prerequisite and current knowledge enables a teacher to avoid assuming students have mastered what they were taught at earlier points in school, to develop awareness of student misunderstandings, and to keep from wasting a student's time by teaching him or her content the student has already mastered.

Further, persistent, informed pre-assessment (and formative assessment) are important in three central themes of effectively differentiated classrooms. The first is the teacher's early and continuing invitation to students: "I want to make this a classroom that works for every student in it, and I need you to help me create that kind of classroom." Pre- and formative assessment should quickly become a visible way a teacher comes to understand what a student needs next in order to grow as a learner. The second theme is the message to students, through both words and actions, that the teacher believes every student in the class is capable of learning at a high level if the teacher and student are willing to work hard. Pre- and formative assessment in this context communicates a "growth mind-set" message (Dweck, 2006), signals to students that a part of academic success stems from knowing what is expected of them as learners and where the learners currently are relative to those expectations. With that knowledge in place, the student and teacher understand what comes next, and both are better positioned to contribute to the student's success.

The third theme in a differentiated classroom to which pre-assessment (and formative assessment) contributes is that every student has a next step in learning to take each day and that those next steps will not always be the same ones for every student. While all students are working toward—and hopefully beyond—delineated goals, they will sometimes progress and arrive there on different timetables and by different routes. Pre-assessment (and formative assessment) provides a visible logic for that assertion. Teachers, then, should help students early on to see that these two types of assessments are vehicles for planning and support, not instruments of judgment. They are simply designed to help the teacher plan more effectively and to help the student know how to learn in a targeted manner.

Differentiation suggests that pre-assessments themselves can be differentiated with the goal of ensuring that each student has the maximum opportunity to demonstrate knowledge, understanding, and skill. *What* the pre-assessment is designed to measure would not be modified or differentiated except in cases where students have individual education plans indicating learning goals that differ from those specified for a course or grade level. However, the mode in which a student may indicate knowledge or working conditions such as time for response can vary based on student need (Tomlinson & McTighe, 2006).

Research on Pre-Assessment

While no research has specifically focused on the role of pre-assessment in a differentiated classroom or on ways in which teachers' use pre-assessment data to differentiate instruction, there has been extensive research in the area of prior knowledge in general and its influence on student achievement specifically (Bransford & Johnson, 1972; NRC, 2000; Resnick, 1983). As highlighted in the research literature related to prior knowledge, there are several implications regarding the role of assessing prior knowledge in a differentiated classroom.

Extensive research has documented that students connect what they learn to what they already know, or to prior knowledge, beliefs, and assumptions (e.g., Cobb, 1994; Piaget, 1952, 1978; Vygotsky, 1962, 1978). Thus, prior knowledge has long been considered the most important factor in student learning and consequently in student achievement (Tobias, 1994). Not only is knowing the prior knowledge that students bring into a given teaching context important, but the amount and quality of that prior knowledge is also important for a teacher to know because those factors influence the acquisition of new knowledge and the capacity to apply skills (e.g., higher-order problem solving) (Dochy, Segers, & Buehl, 1999).

In some instances, students bring inaccurate prior knowledge into a new learning situation—for example, transferring everyday meanings of language into more technical contexts. Several studies or reviews of research in the area of mathematics (e.g., Raiker, 2010) and statistics (e.g., Kaplan, Fisher, & Rogness, 2009; Makar & Confrey, 2005; Tomlinson, Dyson, & Garratt, 2001) indicate that carrying over everyday meanings of certain technical terms (e.g., spread, variation, and random) can distort learning and ultimately negatively impact performance. Other types of inappropriate prior knowledge that are important to uncover and that have implications in a differentiated classroom are students' misapplication of analogies from one situation to another (e.g., Iding, 1997), transferring linguistic knowledge in a native language to the study of a new language (e.g., Bartlett, 1932; Ellis, 1994) or misapplication of cultural knowledge (Ogbu, 1992) from a familiar context to another that differs in significant ways. Again, in each case, having a clear understanding of students' prior knowledge can aid a teacher in planning instruction to fit the varying range of readiness levels, interests, approaches to learning, and cultural differences that students in a classroom are likely to have.

Students can also bring accurate but incomplete prior knowledge into a new learning context. For example, students may know significant events regarding the Civil War but not have developed inquiry skills to analyze primary source documents. Research in this area indicates that there are a number of typologies or categories of knowledge. For instance, Anderson and colleagues (2001) and Gagné, Yekovich, & Yekovich (1993) emphasized the importance of distinguishing between declarative and procedural knowledge that appear across most subjects. Declarative knowledge is considered static and has to do with facts, theories, events, and objects. Procedural knowledge is considered dynamic and has to do with knowing how to do something—for example, motor skills, cognitive skills, and cognitive strategies (Gagné et al., 1993). Clearly defining the learning goals and the type(s) of knowledge that are required for mastery allows a teacher to assess students' prior knowledge in more a more purposeful way (Jiamu, 2001). In the context of teaching a middle school science course that involves the use of the microscope, for example, a teacher may want to assess students' prior knowledge regarding the use of that tool. Specifically, the teacher may want to gather data regarding students' familiarity with the parts of a typical microscope (eye piece, arm, objective lens, stage, diaphragm, etc.), which is declarative knowledge. She may also want to gather students' prior knowledge regarding the procedures that one uses in creating a wet mount, which is procedural knowledge. In this case, understanding where students are relative to both types of knowledge—declarative and procedural—can facilitate the planning of differentiation to account for the varying levels of readiness in the two areas, thus making instructional planning more effective and efficient.

It is useful to remember that students are not blank slates when they enter classrooms. They bring with them the impact of an array of prior experiences in other classrooms and in their own particular lives. In order for students to grow in those classrooms, teachers must have an understanding not only of the amount of prior knowledge a student brings but also the quality of that prior knowledge. To have prior knowledge that is inaccurate or incomplete will impede new learning. Conversely, it is pointless and likely harmful to persist in *teaching* students things they have long since mastered. Effective pre-assessment in a differentiated classroom enables a teacher to gather information that can lead to opening pathways to achievement responsive to an array of student points of entry into any topic of study.

Differentiation, Pre-Assessment, and Students' Interests

It is commonly accepted that individuals know more about a topic that is of particular interest to them than they do about topics that are of less interest. It is also often the case in many classrooms that students are sometimes disengaged from the learning process because they find the content uninteresting and irrelevant to their lives and experiences. In a differentiated classroom, collecting assessment data on student interests enables a teacher to plan instruction designed to intersect with and build on students' interests, thus engaging students more fully in the learning process. This approach is built upon a foundation of empirical evidence indicating that interests influence students' cognitive engagement and consequently has a positive effect on learning and long-term retention (e.g., Hidi, 2000; Hidi & Harackiewicz, 2000). In order to capitalize on students' engagement, a teacher must find ways to determine students' interests so that she can create learning experiences that tap into those areas. Practical ways that a teacher can gather pre-assessment data regarding students' interests include, among others, interest inventories, online surveys, individual conferences or interviews with students about their interests, and studying students' choices when offered to note patterns in their selections. For example, a high school science teacher began the year by asking students to list four activities they participated in and enjoyed outside of school and to briefly describe duration and level of their participation. In addition, she asked the students to note any connection they saw between the activity and science. She understood that many students would see no connection. She knew, however, that using the information they provided, she could relate science to their interests as the year progressed and help them to do the same.

Questions and tasks that are interesting to students are more likely to lead to increased student engagement with the work and to a student's sense that the work required for a task is rewarding. Tasks that tap student interests also result in greater evidence of student creativity, increased student productivity, a higher level of student autonomy, and greater intrinsic motivation (Amabile, 1983; Collins & Amabile, 1999; Sharan & Sharan, 1992). In general, it appears that interest contributes to a sense of competence and self-determination in learners and to positive learning behaviors, such as willingness to accept challenge and persist in it (Csikszentmihalyi, Rathunde, & Whalen, 1993; Fulk & Montgomery-Grymes, 1994; Zimmerman & Martinez-Pons, 1990). Therefore, a student's experience with content is enhanced, and his or her achievement should benefit when teachers help the student attach key ideas and skills from the content area to the student's own interest areas or enables students to apply relevant knowledge, understanding, and skills from a content area to an area of interest to the student.

Differentiation and Student Learning Profile

Learning profile is a term coined by the author of the model of differentiation that is the focus of this chapter. It is an umbrella term that subsumes literature in four somewhat distinct but interrelated areas that have to do with ways in which learners approach learning—or how individuals learn most efficiently and effectively (Tomlinson, 1999, 2000; Tomlinson & Imbeau, 2012). The four bodies of theory and research address differences in approach to learning that may be shaped by gender, culture, intelligence preference, and/or *learning style*.

Few, if any, sources question the premise that individuals may approach learning in different ways. There are also few, if any, sources that question the existence of gender- or culture-influenced learning differences. In recent years, however, some experts in psychology, neuroscience, and sociology have been critical of both the concept and use of the specific area of learning styles in classrooms (Coffield, Moseley, Hall, & Ecclestone, 2004; Pashler, McDaniel, Rohrer, & Bjork, 2008). Some of these sources incorrectly use the terms *learning style* and *intelligence preference* as synonyms.

Among criticisms relevant to a discussion of assessment and learning profile are that (1) instruments used to determine students' learning styles tend to lack evidence of reliability and validity; (2) to suggest that a student only learns in a specific way is unwarranted; and (3) labeling students by learning style is potentially limiting to individual students and may result in stereotyping of groups of students (Coffield et al., 2004; Pashler et al., 2008).

Based on current knowledge, it would appear that defensible application of learning styles in the classroom would exclude use of surveys to determine a student's learning style, categorizing students by learning style, and assignment of students to tasks based on their perceived learning style. By contrast, examples of appropriate application of learning style might include teachers presenting information in a variety of ways; offering students options for taking in, exploring, and demonstrating key content; planning for multimodal student learning; and helping students become more self-aware in determining which approaches to learning work for them in specific contexts and understanding how to adjust their approach to learning when the approach they are using does not seem to be supporting successful outcomes. For example, if a student is having difficulty following the logic of a text while reading it silently, the student might fare better to diagram or outline the ideas, represent them with icons, talk through the ideas orally, or listen to a recording of the text (Willis, 2006).

Assessment During the Process of Instruction

Collecting assessment information regarding student learning during the process of instruction is also known as formative assessment, ongoing assessment, or assessment for learning (AFL), and its purpose is to facilitate student growth toward identified learning goals. Ongoing assessment can be divided into two categories (Bell & Cowie, 2001), each with sound but limited empirical evidence to support its use during the instructional cycle. The two categories are (1) formal ongoing assessment and (2) informal ongoing assessment. Both categories relate to status checking during times in an instructional cycle when students are learning and practicing rather than at times in the learning cycle that are designated for judging outcomes. Thus, unlike summative assessment, formative assessment is appropriately seen primarily as a source of feedback for a teacher and students rather than as a source of data for a gradebook. In this way, formative or ongoing assessment contributes uniquely to student motivation to learn, a growth mind-set in teachers and students, and a learning environment that feels both safe and challenging (Earl, 2003). All of these elements are central to the philosophy of differentiation, thus indicating the importance of formative assessment in the model.

As is the case with pre-assessment, the model of differentiation discussed here suggests the appropriateness of differentiating a formative assessment in instances where doing so allows students greater opportunity to reveal what they know, understand, and can do. Examples of differentiated formative assessments include a student taking an assessment on a computer or—digitally recording answers when writing by hand is difficult—providing additional time for a student with learning challenges that may be aggravated by time pressure, presenting simplified directions for a student learning English, or allowing a student to draw and annotate a response rather than relying on prose when written language is an impediment to expression and not the sole purpose of the assessment. In each of these cases, the process of collecting data is differentiated in that it is responsive to variations in a student's mode of learning. Differentiating the process to more aptly fit students' learning strengths results in a more accurate picture of a students' prior and current knowledge, thus providing information to more appropriately target instruction.

Formal Ongoing Assessment

Formal ongoing assessments can be defined as assessment procedures conducted during an instructional cycle when specific time is set aside within the instructional sequence to allow students to respond to pre-identified questions that are designed to capture students' learning up to a specific point and that are typically used because of the importance of particular learning objectives for upcoming learning experiences within the same instructional cycle. Examples of formal ongoing assessments include specific prompts to which students respond (e.g., journaling), worksheets, quizzes, and exit cards. They typically occur multiple times throughout a given unit of study in order to assess student progress in mastering or moving beyond essential knowledge, understanding, and skills. Because formal ongoing assessment is preplanned, it can be tightly aligned with knowledge, understanding, and skills specified as essential for the segment of study the teacher is assessing.

Probably the most well-known and cited research investigating the impact of formal ongoing assessment on student achievement was conducted by Black and Wiliam (1998). The findings from this study combined with more recent research in the area (e.g., Wiliam, Lee, Harrison, & Black, 2004; Wininger, 2005) provide some support for the positive impact that formal ongoing assessment can have on student achievement, although several methodological issues have been noted in this research (see Dunn & Mulvenon, 2009).

Informal Ongoing Assessment

Informal formative assessments are more spontaneous instances in which data are gathered about students during any student–teacher interaction (Ruiz-Primo & Furtak, 2006). These types of assessments occur daily throughout the instructional cycle and are sometimes referred to as assessment conversations (Ruiz-Primo & Furtak, 2006) because they tend to occur in exchanges between teacher and student(s). The conversations are based upon three teacher actions (Ruiz-Primo & Furtak, 2007): (1) a question posed by the teacher, (2) teacher recognition and acknowledgment of students' responses, and (3) teacher use of the collected information to make appropriate instructional modifications to support student learning. These types of conversations can range from whole group conversations to small group conversations to one-on-one conversations with individual students and can take a variety of forms (e.g., windshield checks, five-finger checks, student responses during whole class or small group instruction, and student responses during individual conversations between student and teacher). For example, a teacher teaching a lesson on subtracting mixed numbers pauses mid-lesson to gauge students' processing of the content using a five-finger check. She notes that the students who are responding orally to questions do so with accuracy and self-rate their confidence with the information as a "five" and that six students have not volunteered answers and rate their confidence much lower (e.g., one or two). She quickly notes these students' names and structures the second half of the lesson differently to ensure that these six students are tasked with problems to share with the class. In this instance, the teacher uses the students' responses to the five-finger check along with careful attention to patterns of accurate responses to form ad hoc instructional groups.

While this is a recent area of research, empirical evidence that exists suggests that effective informal ongoing assessment practices may be associated with high levels of student learning (e.g., Ruiz-Primo & Furtak, 2007). It is likely that informal ongoing assessment, because of its more fluid and impromptu nature, may sometimes be less tightly aligned with essential content goals than is the case with formal ongoing assessment. It is also less likely to provide the teacher with a clear picture of the status of all students in the class than to yield a snapshot of individuals or small groups of students within the class at a given time. Nonetheless, its immediacy enables a teacher to use assessment information to make rapid and targeted adjustments in the flow of instruction.

The research regarding ongoing assessment, both formal and informal, suggests at best only a modest impact on student achievement. Beyond methodological issues, several plausible explanations can be offered for the findings suggesting limited impact. One explanation is the primacy accorded to grades by students. That is, students may need assistance in understanding both the value of formative feedback and how to use it to benefit their achievement rather than simply focusing on a grade. Earl (2003) referred to this process as AFL, or assessment that involves students in thinking about learning goals and ways in which feedback can help them develop agency as learners. Another explanation for the modest impact of formative assessment on student performance centers on the type of feedback provided by the teacher. In a meta-analysis on the effects of various types of feedback, Kluger and DeNisi (1996) suggest that giving students specific comments directed at what the student did correctly, what needs to be done to improve, and how to go about using the feedback for improvement is necessary to benefit student learning.

In many instances, by contrast, general praise is provided instead of specific feedback. Mueller and Dweck's (1998) research on praise suggests that when praise is given in the absence of specific feedback, students begin to avoid the risk of making mistakes and instead only want to *look smart.* Thus it may be that teachers need the opportunity to learn how to (1) focus students on growth in a learning cycle rather than on grades, (2) provide feedback that is specific and targeted at helping students take next steps in their learning, and (3) help students see themselves as agents in their own success by ensuring their understanding of how to use formative assessment data effectively.

Use of both formal and informal assessment processes requires that the teacher have a clear understanding of essential content goals, elicit information from students that closely aligns with those goals, correctly interpret assessment data to identify students' learning needs, and adjust instruction appropriately based on those needs. These are skills that appear fundamental to effective instruction—differentiated or otherwise—and yet each one is complex and needs to evolve individually and in concert over an extended time during a teacher's career in order to benefit students. It is likely that few teachers receive the sort of persistent, intelligent support necessary to help them develop and hone these skills in ways that would benefit students as a group and individually (Tomlinson et al., 2008).

The practice of eliciting information from students, identifying their needs based on the elicited data, and then adjusting instruction to better scaffold for learning would seem to be fundamental to effective teaching. While ongoing assessment is certainly at the core of the philosophy of differentiation, there is no published empirical research that focuses specifically on the use of ongoing assessment to inform instruction in the context of a differentiated classroom. Thus, it is clear that there is a need for research in the area of ongoing assessment and its role in student learning in a differentiated classroom.

Assessment After Instruction

Whereas the focus of formative assessment is feedback rather than grades, there are points in an instructional cycle when the teacher seeks evidence of student learning that will be graded. Such assessments are summative (i.e., assessment of learning; see also Chapter 14 of this volume) and occur at transitional points in a unit of study, such as at the end of a series of instrumental lessons, at the end of the unit, or the conclusion of a marking period. By their intent, summative assessments are considered key components in a grading system (see Chapter 15 of this volume). The purpose of these assessments is to evaluate the degree to which students have acquired the knowledge, understanding, and skills designated as essential for that particular instructional segment. Summative assessments can be designed to elicit information from students, to determine their proficiency with skills, and/or to reveal their ability to apply and transfer what they have learned. Summative assessments that focus on this latter component of learning are often referred to as performance assessments or authentic assessments and are particularly useful in determining student understanding of content (Wiggins & McTighe, 1998).

It is important to note that summative assessments also have a formative aspect that can occur when detailed feedback is provided to students on those assessments regarding their specific strengths, weaknesses, and next steps in the learning process. Used in this way, summative assessments can be steps in a learning sequence for students. Another way that summative assessment can be used formatively occurs when a teacher uses the results of an assessment to look for patterns in students' learning in order to modify instruction the next time the content is taught. Therefore, what we tend to think of as "end-of-the-line" assessment can become assessment FOR instruction, benefiting teacher planning, and assessment AS instruction, benefiting learner development of autonomy.

Research on the role that differentiation plays in a summative assessment context is limited. Differentiation can be applied to summative assessment in a variety of ways to facilitate optimal conditions for students to demonstrate what they know, understand, and are able to do related to the topic being assessed. This is the case regardless of the type of summative assessment. For example, on more traditional assessments, allowing students who are new to learning English to demonstrate their level of mastery of learning goals in a format other than writing extended English prose—and is therefore more accessible—is a form of differentiation.

Other examples of differentiation of summative assessments are extending the time allowed for a student who has physical difficulty with writing, including items that relate content to student interests or modifying the complexity of language used in writing the assessment based on student readiness (Tomlinson & Moon, 2011). As is the case with formative assessments, it is important that the learning goals and the criteria for evaluating student work remain the same regardless of the type of differentiation used to gather the data regarding student understanding. This is the case regardless of the degree of authenticity of the task. The type of differentiation employed in terms of the ways in which data are gathered regarding students' understandings has to be appropriate for the assessment context, thus differentiated assessment takes into account both the student's needs and the requirements of the assessment situation. However, in most instances, it should be possible to accommodate student needs by viewing the context as flexible as feasible.

The limited empirical work on differentiation and summative assessment focuses on the use of differentiated performance assessment (Moon, Brighton, Callahan, & Robinson, 2005; Moon, Callahan, Brighton, & Tomlinson, 2002). In their work investigating the psychometric properties of differentiated performance assessments for middle school classrooms, Moon et al. (2002) found that differentiated classroom performance assessments could be developed and implemented to provide reliable and valid information about student learning. Examples of differentiation useful with performance assessments include providing resources at the reading levels of various students, varying the level and kinds of structures associated with the tasks, supplying students with competent models of related assessments at varied levels of complexity, and enabling students to apply key knowledge, understanding, and skills to interest areas (Tomlinson & Moon, 2011).

FUTURE DIRECTIONS

As has been noted in previous research (Herman, Osmundson, Ayala, Schneider, & Timms, 2006), "learning must be orchestrated in complex ways that bring together a variety of teacher expertise—strong content knowledge, sophisticated pedagogical knowledge and strategies, effective assessment, and strong routines and norms for student engagement" (p. 35). Given the complexity and interdependence between teaching and student learning, three specific areas emerge as needing systematic investigation.

The first area for future research includes an exploration of the ways in which teachers incorporate or do not incorporate assessment information into their daily practices, particularly as related to differentiation efforts. While the use of assessment in guiding instruction is not a new concept and many teachers collect assessment data, too often teachers lack the knowledge, understanding, and skills to differentiate instruction for subgroups within the class based upon that assessment information. In order for teachers to collect student data, to analyze that data, to provide meaningful feedback to students from that data, and to adjust their instructional plans in order to better fit diverse students' needs in a timely manner, research efforts need to be devoted to understanding the types of professional learning experiences necessary for teachers to be successful in understanding content, content goals, and sequences in which students most effectively learn content and how to use content goals to design assessments, how to interpret student work in light of content goals, and how to understand the implications of that work for instruction. Other areas warranting future study include the exploration of students' responsibility in the assessment process and ways in which students can be more active and informed participants, thus creating a partnership between teacher and students to benefit student academic growth.

While related to the first area, the second area of research that warrants future efforts includes exploration of the ways in which both internal and external structures (e.g., teacher attitudes about teaching and learning, class time, collaboration among colleagues, professional development, and classroom management systems) support or inhibit teachers' use of assessment data to guide their instructional planning and practices. Given the current accountability climate where multiple external assessments (e.g., state assessments, benchmark assessments, and interim assessments) are administered throughout the school year, there is a need to know what structures are needed to assist teachers in incorporating classroom-focused assessments, both informal and formal, as well as the external assessments into their practices. While both types of assessment can be useful in terms of supporting student learning, the varying purposes of each type create a tension in classrooms, since external assessments are associated with accountability while teacher-generated formative assessments have more of a guidance or supportive function.

The third area of study that warrants consideration are the types of research methodologies that can be used to help develop a knowledge base in the area of CA and differentiation. Within the educational community, much criticism has been garnered at the uselessness of educational research (see special issue of *Educational Researcher*, 2002, *31*[8]). In response to these criticisms, the educational field has seen an increase in the emphasis of randomized experimental group designs, with many agencies (e.g., What Works Clearinghouse and Institute for Education Sciences) primarily using these types of designs as the gold standard in terms of effectiveness questions. While some of the criticism may be warranted, the process of teaching and student learning is a complex and dynamic one, and it is because of this complexity that a variety of research methodologies is essential to developing a knowledge base of effective classroom practices. Shavelson and Towne (2002) group educational research questions into three types: (1) description ("What is happening?"), (2) cause ("Is there a systematic effect?"), and (3) process or mechanism ("Why or how is it happening?").

While establishing evidence-based practices is an important and necessary endeavor, guiding principles for researchers and funding organizations are needed for specifying the types and levels of evidence needed to identify a practice as evidence-based and effective. This serves as a cautionary tale. As this needed research is conducted, it is essential that researchers employ a wide range of research methodologies instead of focusing exclusively on one type of methodology (e.g., randomized controlled trial), which often comes at the expense of compartmentalizing the complexities of classrooms into separate and unrelated components, thus overlooking and often ignoring the interrelatedness of the components.

References

Amabile, T. (1983). *The social psychology of creativity.* New York: Springer-Verlag.

Anderson, L. W., Krathwohl, D. R., Airasian, P. W., Cruikshank, K. A., Mayer, R. E., Pintrich, P. R., et al. (Eds.). (2001). *A taxonomy for learning, teaching, and assessing: A revision of Bloom's taxonomy of educational objectives.* Boston: Allyn & Bacon.

Bartlett, F. C. (1932). *Remembering: A study in experimental and social psychology.* New York: Cambridge University Press.

Bell, B., & Cowie, B. (2001). *Formative assessment and science education.* Dordrecht, The Netherlands: Kluwers.

Black, P., & Wiliam, D. (1998). Assessment and classroom learning. *Assessment in Education, 5*(1), 7–73.

Boykin, A., & Noguera, P. (2011). *Creating opportunity to learn: Moving from research to practice to close the achievement gap.* Alexandria, VA: Association for Supervision and Curriculum Development.

Bransford, J. D., & Johnson, M. K. (1972). Contextual prerequisites for understanding: Some investigators of comprehension and recall. *Journal of Verbal Learning and Verbal Behavior, 11,* 717–726.

Callahan, R. (2005). Tracking and high school English learners: Limiting opportunity to learn. *American Educational Research Journal, 42,* 305–328.

Center for Public Education. (2007). *You may also be interested in.* Retrieved from www.centerforpubliceducation.org/You-May-Also-Be-Interested-In-landing-page-level/Organizing-a-School-YMABI/the-United-States-and-their-schools.html

Centers for Disease Control and Prevention. (2007) Autism awareness month. *Morbidity and Mortality Weekly Report, 60*(12), 379. Retrieved from www.cdc.gov/mmwr/preview/mmwrhtml/mm6012a4.htm?s_cid=mm6012a4_w

Centers for Disease Control and Prevention. (n.d). *Prevalence of the autism spectrum disorders in multiple areas of the United States, 2000–2002.* Retrieved from www.cdc.gov/ncbddd/autism/documents/autismcommunityreport.pdf

Cobb, P. (1994). *Theories of mathematical learning and constructivism, A personal view.* Paper presented at the Symposium on Trends and Perspectives in Mathematics Education, Institute for Mathematics, University of Kalgenfurt, Austria.

Coffield, F., Moseley, D., Hall, E., & Ecclestone, K. (2004). *Should we be using learning styles; What research has to say to practice.* London: The Learning and Skills Research Centre, London.

Collins, M., & Amabile, T. (1999). Motivation and creativity. In R. J. Sternberg (Ed.), *Handbook of creativity* (pp. 297–312). New York: Cambridge University Press.

Csikszentmihalyi, M., Rathunde, K., & Whalen, S. (1993). *Talented teenagers: The roots of success and failure.* New York: Cambridge University Press.

Darling-Hammond, L. (2008). *Powerful learning: What we know about teaching for understanding.* San Francisco: Jossey-Bass.

Darling-Hammond, L., & Bransford, J. (2005). *Preparing teachers for a changing world: What teachers should learn and be able to do.* San Francisco: Jossey-Bass.

Dochy, F., Segers, M., & Buehl, M. (1999). The relation between assessment practices and outcomes of students: The case of research on prior knowledge. *Review of Educational Research, 69,* 145–186.

Dunn, K. E., & Mulvenon, S. W. (2009). A critical review of research on formative assessment: The limited scientific evidence of the impact of formative assessment in education. *Practical Assessment, Research, & Evaluation, 14*(7). Retrieved from http://pareonline.net/getvn.asp?v=14&n=7

Dweck, C. (2000). *Self-theories: Their role in motivation, personality, and development.* Philadelphia: Psychology Press.

Dweck, C. (2006). *Mindset: The new psychology of success.* New York: Random House.

Earl, L. (2003). *Assessment as learning: Using classroom assessment to maximize student learning.* Thousand Oaks, CA: Corwin Press.

Ellis, R. (1994). *The study of second language acquisition.* New York: Oxford University Press.

Fulk, B., & Montgomery-Grymes, D. (1994). Strategies to improve student motivation. *Intervention in School and Clinic, 30,* 28–33.

Gagné, E. D., Yekovich, C. W., & Yekovich, F. R. (1993). *The cognitive psychology of school learning* (2nd ed.). New York: HarperCollins.

Gamoran, A., Nystrand, M., Berends, M., & LePore, P. (1995). *American Educational Research Journal, 32,* 687–715.

Gray, T., & Fleischman, S. (2004). Successful strategies for English language learners. *Educational Leadership, 62*(4), 84–88.

Hattie, J. (2009). *Visible learning: A synthesis of over 800 meta-analyses relating to student achievement.* New York: Routledge.

Hattie, J. (2012). *Visible learning for teachers: Maximizing impact on learning.* New York: Routledge.

Herman, J .L., Osmundson, E., Ayala, C., Schneider, S., & Timms, M. (2006). *The nature and impact of teachers' formative assessment practices* (CSE

Report 703). Los Angeles: Center for Assessment and Evaluation of Student Learning, University of California at Los Angeles.

Hidi, S. (2000). An interest researcher's perspective: The effect of intrinsic and extrinsic factors on motivation. In C. Sansome & J. M. Harackiewicz (Eds.), *Intrinsic and extrinsic motivation: The search for optimal motivation and performance* (pp. 309–339). San Diego, CA: Academic Press.

Hidi, S., & Harackiewicz, J. M. (2000). Motivating the academically unmotivated: A critical issue for the 21st century. *Review of Educational Research, 70,* 151–179.

Hochschild, J., & Scovronik, N. (2003). *The American dream and the public schools.* New York: Oxford University Press.

Iding, M. K. (1997). How analogies foster learning from science texts. *Instructional Science, 25,* 233–253.

Jiamu, C. (2001). The great importance of the distinction between declarative and procedural knowledge. *Análise Psicólogica, 4*(XIX), 559–566.

Kaplan, J. J., Fisher, D. G., & Rogness, N. T. (2009). Lexical ambiguity in statistics: What do students know about the words association, average, confidence, random, and spread? *Journal of Statistics Education, 17*(3). Retrieved from www.amstat.org/publications/jse/v17n3/kaplan.html

Kluger, A. N., & DeNisi, A. (1996). The effects of feedback interventions on performance: A historical review, a meta-analysis, and a preliminary feedback intervention theory. *Psychological Bulletin, 119*(2), 254–284.

Kluger, J. (2010, October 21). Keeping young minds healthy. *Time,* 41.

Makar, K., & Confrey, J. (2005). "Variation-talk": Articulating meaning in statistics. *Statistics Education Research Journal, 4*(1), 27–54.

Marx, G. (2000). *Ten trends: Preparing children for a profoundly different future.* Arlington, VA: Educational Research Service.

Moon, T. R., Brighton, C. M., Callahan, C. M., & Robinson, A. E. (2005). Development of authentic assessments for the middle school classroom. *Journal for Secondary Gifted Education, 16*(2/3), 119–133.

Moon, T. R., Callahan, C. M., Brighton, C. M., & Tomlinson, C. A. (2002). *Development of differentiated performance assessment tasks for middle school classrooms* (RM02160). Storrs: The National Research Center on the Gifted and Talented, University of Connecticut.

Mueller, C. M., & Dweck, C. S. (1998). Intelligence praise can undermine motivation and performance. *Journal of Personality and Social Psychology, 75,* 33–52.

National Association for Gifted Children. (n.d.). *Frequently asked questions.* Retrieved from www.nagc.org/index2.aspx?id=548

National Center for Education Statistics. (n.d.) *Fast facts.* Retrieved from http://nces.ed.gov./fastfacts/display.asp?id=96

National Education Association. (2006). *The twice-exceptional dilemma.* Washington, DC: Author.

National Research Council. (2000). *How people learn: Brain, mind, experience, and school.* Washington, DC: National Academy Press.

Nutall, G. (2005). The cultural myths of classroom teaching and learning: A personal journey. *Teachers College Record, 107,* 895–934.

Ogbu, J. U. (1992). Understanding cultural diversity and learning. *Educational Researcher, 21,* 5–14.

Pashler, H., McDaniel, M., Rohrer, D., & Bjork R. (2008). Learning styles: Concepts and evidence. *Psychological Science in the Public Interest, 9*(3), 106–119.

Piaget, J. (1952). *The origins of intelligence in children* (M. Cook, Trans.). New York: International University Press.

Piaget, J. (1978). *Success and understanding.* Cambridge, MA: Harvard University Press.

Raiker, A. (2010). Spoken language and mathematics. *Cambridge Journal of Education, 32*(1), 45–60. Retrieved from http://dx.doi.org/10.1080/03057640220116427.

Resnick, L. B. (1983). A developmental theory of number understanding. In H. P. Ginsburg (Ed.), *The development of mathematical thinking* (pp. 109–151). New York: Academic Press.

Ruiz-Primo, M. A., & Furtak, E. R. (2006). Informal formative assessment and scientific inquiry: Exploring teachers' practices and student learning. *Educational Assessment, 11* (3 & 4), 205–235.

Ruiz-Primo, M. A., & Furtak, E. R. (2007). Exploring teachers' informal formative assessment practices and students' understanding in the context of scientific inquiry. *Journal of Research in Science Teaching, 44*(1), 57–84.

Sharan, Y., & Sharan, S. (1992). *Expanding cooperative learning through group investigation.* New York: Teachers College Press.

Shavelson, R. J., & Towne, L. (Eds.). (2002). *Scientific research in education.* Washington, DC: National Academy Press.

Sousa, D., & Tomlinson, C., (2011). *Differentiation and the brain: How neuroscience supports the learner-friendly classroom.* Indianapolis, IN: Solution Tree.

Tobias, S. (1994). Interest, prior knowledge, and learning. *Review of Educational Research, 64,* 37–54.

Tomlinson, C. (1999). *The differentiated classroom: Responding to the needs of all learners.*

Alexandria, VA: Association for Supervision and Curriculum Development.

Tomlinson, C. (2000). *How to differentiate instruction in mixed ability classrooms* (2nd ed.). Alexandria, VA: Association for Supervision and Curriculum Development.

Tomlinson, C. (2003). *Fulfilling the promise of the differentiated classroom*. Alexandria, VA: Association for Supervision and Curriculum Development.

Tomlinson, C., Brimijoin, K., & Narvaez, L. (2008). *The differentiated school: Making revolutionary changes in teaching and learning*. Alexandria, VA: Association for Supervision and Curriculum Development.

Tomlinson, C., & Imbeau, M. (2010). *Leading and managing a differentiated classroom*. Alexandria, VA: Association for Supervision and Curriculum Development.

Tomlinson, C., & Imbeau, M. (2012). Differentiated instruction: An integration of theory and Practice. In G. Brown, R. Lara-Alicio, & S. Jackson (Eds.), *Handbook of educational theories*. Charlotte, NC: Information Age Publishing.

Tomlinson, C., & McTighe, J. (2006). *Integrating differentiated instruction and understanding by design: Connecting content and kids*. Alexandria, VA: Association for Supervision and Curriculum Development.

Tomlinson, C. A., & Moon, T. R. (2011). The relationship between assessment and differentiation. *Better: Evidence-based education, 3*(3), 3–4.

Tomlinson, J., Dyson, P., & Garratt, J. (2001). Student misconceptions of the language of error. *University Chemistry Education, 5*, 1–8.

Vygotsky, L. (1962). *Thought and language*. Cambridge, MA: MIT Press.

Vygotsky, L. (1978). *Mind in society: The development of the higher psychological processes*. Cambridge, MA: Harvard University Press.

Wiggins, G., & McTighe, J. (1998). *Understanding by design*. Alexandria, VA: Association for Supervision and Curriculum Development.

Wiliam, D. (2011). *Embedded formative assessment*. Indianapolis, IN: Solution Tree.

Wiliam,. D., Lee, C., Harrison, C., & Black, P. (2004). Teachers developing assessment for learning: Impact on student achievement. *Assessment in Education, 11*, 49–65.

Willis, J. (2006). *Research-based strategies to ignite student learning: Insights from a neurologist and classroom teacher*. Alexandria, VA: Association for Supervision and Curriculum Development.

Wininger, R. S. (2005). Using your tests to teach: Formative summative assessment. *Teaching Psychology, 32*(2), 164–166.

Zimmerman, B., & Martinez-Pons, M. (1990). Student differences in self-regulated learning: Relating grade, sex, and giftedness to self-efficacy and strategy use. *Journal of Educational Psychology, 82*, 51–59.

24

CLASSROOM ASSESSMENT IN SPECIAL EDUCATION

YAOYING XU

Classroom assessment (CA) is a broad concept, addressing any form of assessment occurring in the classroom context. CA can be defined as a process of collecting, evaluating, and using information gathered before, during, or after instruction to help the classroom teacher make decisions on improving students' learning (McMillan, 2011). It differs from large-scale or standardized tests in that CA links learning targets directly to assessment practices that lead to the improvement of students' learning through progress monitoring based on the information collected by the classroom teacher. The concept of CA applies to the assessment, planning, and implementation of intervention for students with special needs. While students with special needs have an individualized education program (IEP) that may differ from the general education curriculum in learning targets, the goal of data collection similarly is to improve students' learning by informing teachers to make appropriate decisions in the progress monitoring process. The focus of this chapter is to discuss CA for students with special needs in inclusive settings. Specifically, the purposes of assessing students with special needs are introduced within the theoretical framework of CA. In addition, the approaches of CA for students with special needs are explored, followed by recommendations for teachers to assess students with special needs with evidence-based assessment strategies.

STUDENTS WITH DISABILITIES AND SPECIAL EDUCATION SERVICES

The first special education law, P.L. 94-142, the Education of All Handicapped Children Act, was renamed the Individuals with Disabilities Education Act (IDEA) in 1990. This law states that all children with disabilities will receive free and appropriate public education in the least restrictive environment (LRE). In 1997, the act was amended with several important new provisions to strengthen the implementation of the essential principles included in the initial act. One of the most important new provisions added to IDEA 1997 was that the law required "whenever appropriate" that general education classrooms should be used for children with special needs, recognizing that most students with disabilities spend all or most of their school time in general education settings. As a result, the law included a provision requiring that a general education teacher become a member of the team for a student's IEP. Therefore, it is essential that the general education teacher, collaboratively with the special education teacher and other team members, makes reflective decisions that improve the learning of both students with or without disabilities, based on "the evidence gathered through assessment, reasoning, and experience" (McMillan, 2011, p. 4).

Students With Disabilities

Students served under the IDEA requirement are categorized among 13 disabilities (for the specific definition of each category, see Individuals with Disabilities Education Improvement Act [IDEIA], 2004, pp. 46756–46757). The IDEA provides special education and related services to students who are eligible under these disability areas. Based on prevalence, the categories of disabilities under the IDEA may be described as higher-incidence disabilities and lower-incidence disabilities. Higher-incidence disabilities refer to the disabilities that are more commonly seen in schools. Individuals who have higher-incidence disabilities are a diverse group with a wide range of abilities and disabilities, from mild to severe in intensity. Higher-incidence disabilities make up over 80% of the total population of students ages 6 to 21 with disabilities under the IDEA including the following disability areas: speech or language impairments, specific learning disabilities (SLD), mild or moderate intellectual disabilities, and emotional disturbance (U.S. Department of Education, 2007). In addition to these identified categories under the IDEA, students with attention deficit/hyperactivity disorder (ADHD) make up approximately 3% to 5% of the total student population (Kauffman & Landrum, 2009). Most of these students are served in general education classrooms with appropriate accommodations. These students may or may not qualify for special education and related services under the IDEA. Lower-incidence disabilities refer to disabilities that are far less commonly represented in schools compared with higher-incidence disabilities.

Lower-incidence disabilities can be present at birth or acquired later in life and can be temporary or permanent or life threatening (Mastropieri & Scruggs, 2010). Lower-incidence disabilities involve a wide range of disability areas, including physical and other health impairments, autism, severe and multiple disabilities, visual impairments, and hearing impairments. Traditionally, most students with lower-incidence disabilities were served in separate schools or programs. With the advances in assistive technology and creative adaptations, individuals with lower-incidence disabilities can succeed in inclusive classrooms.

In addition to those commonly defined categories, curriculum adaptations or material accommodations may be necessary to ensure the success of students who may not have a diagnosed disability but do have other special learning needs. Individuals with other special learning needs also represent a wide range of abilities, including students who are gifted and talented, students from culturally and linguistically diverse backgrounds, and students who are at risk for school failure due to environmental and/or biological risk factors. All these students are served in general education classrooms; however, their unique needs may or may not be identified because their disabilities are not one of the 13 IDEA-defined categories. As a result, it often falls to the general education teacher's responsibility to collect, evaluate, and use the assessment data in making plans for the students' learning and improvement. An effective teacher would integrate instruction and assessment before, during, and after instruction on a daily basis (McMillan, 2011).

Special Education and Inclusive Education

Special education is defined as "a specially designed and coordinated set of comprehensive, research-based instructional and assessment practices and related services to students with learning, behavioral, emotional, physical health, or sensory disabilities" (Salend, 2011, p. 7). Specifically, special education involves the following key features: individualized assessment and planning; specialized, intensive, and goal-directed instruction; research-based instructional practices; collaborative partnerships; and student performance evaluation (Heward, 2009). Although individualized instruction or intervention is an essential component to special education, the assessment, planning, and implementation of intervention for students with special needs are relevant to general education and aligns with the concept of CA. Once a student with special needs is determined to be eligible for special education services, the student's IEP is established with individualized educational goals and objectives, including academic and nonacademic areas. The student's IEP team collects data to inform planning, monitor progress, and if necessary, to modify learning goals and objectives based on the progress monitoring. Today, most students with special needs receive their education in general education or inclusive classrooms. In 2007 and 2008, about 95% of students aged 6 to 21 served under the IDEA requirement were enrolled in regular schools (U.S. Department of Education, National Center for Education Statistics, 2010).

The concept of inclusion came along with individual students' rights and was further emphasized through the LRE provision under the IDEA. Both the IDEA 1997 and IDEIA 2004 emphasize the access to the general education curriculum in the provision of educational services for children and students with disabilities. The cornerstone of these two amendments is that the student's IEP must include a statement of the student's present levels of academic achievement and functional performance, including how the student's disability affects his or her involvement and progress in the general education curriculum (IDEIA, 2004; Title I, B, 614 [d]1AiI ([a]). In addition, the law requires that every child with a disability be educated in the LRE. The LRE requires the following:

> To the maximum extent appropriate, children with disabilities, including children in public or private institutions or other care facilities, are educated with children who are not disabled and special classes, separate schooling or other *removal* of children with disabilities *from the regular educational environment occurs only when the nature or severity of the disability of a child is such that education in regular classes with the use of supplemental aids and services cannot be achieved satisfactorily*. (IDEIA, 2004, italics added)

Inclusion as a philosophy is how we interpret the legal requirement of LRE. Inclusion values all students' rights to receive appropriate education within the general education classroom, regardless of their disability status or developmental level. It recognizes that all students are able to learn and benefit from a "meaningful, challenging, and appropriate curriculum delivered within the general education classroom" (Salend, 2011, p. 7). The emphasis on educating all children, with or without disabilities, in the general educational settings or natural environments, was explicit and strong in the legal language. The assumption of the universal relevance of the general education curriculum to all age appropriate students is apparent in the IDEIA (2004). The numerous provisions of this law require that we reference the curriculum for students with disabilities to that of their typically developing peers, which is the right for all students. Therefore, the learning objectives for students with disabilities start with the general education curriculum that targets for the improvement of all students' learning with or without disabilities.

The Conceptual Framework of Classroom Assessment and Response to Intervention

Conceptual Framework of Classroom Assessment for Special Education

Sadler (1989) proposed a conceptual framework of CA within the context of curriculum and instruction that includes three elements: (1) learning goals, (2) information about the present status of learner, and (3) action to close the gap. In special education, these three elements relate directly to CA for students with special needs within the contexts of assessment, curriculum, and instruction. For students with special needs, their learning goals are documented as the IEP goal and objectives that were developed by the IEP team and implemented within the inclusive classrooms and other general education settings whenever applicable. The general education teacher and special education teacher collect formative assessment data to evaluate and monitor progress of the student and, if necessary, to modify the learning goals. The present status of the learner aligns with the present level of academic and functional performance of the student with special needs, as required in the student's IEP statements. Finally, the action or the implementation of the intervention planning takes place based on the assessment data with a purpose of reducing the discrepancy or the gap between the student's present level of performance and the student projected IEP goals, through evidence-based intervention. Response to intervention (RTI) is a proposed approach through the IDEIA 2004 that involves formative assessment within the general education settings. RTI requires CA because consistent progress monitoring is needed to evaluate students' improvement in learning or students' response to intervention.

Response to Intervention

The most recent reauthorization of the special education law (P.L. 108-446) emphasized the need to provide more educational opportunities for students with disabilities. The reauthorization of the special education law seeks multiple innovative ways to improve educational results for students with disabilities. For example, IDEIA or IDEIA 2004 no longer requires the use of discrepancy models for determining SLD (Harris-Murri, King, & Rostenberg, 2006). Instead, the RTI model was proposed as an alternative approach to determining the eligibility for special education and related services.

RTI is referred to as tiered instruction (intervention) because of its different levels of intervention. Most school districts that are using RTI have implemented a three-tier intervention process. Tier 1 refers to high-quality instructional and behavioral supports for all students in general education settings by measuring the rate of academic growth of all students in comparison to other classes in the school or district or nation. Curriculum-based measurement (CBM) would be used to determine the overall achievement level and growth in achievement for the classroom of the struggling student. This tier attempts to rectify the previous difficulty in assessing the quality of past educational experiences to rule out inadequate instruction as a possible reason for underachievement (Drame & Xu, 2008). Interventions at Tier 2 are still provided within general education settings. If students are not making satisfactory performance with the more intensive, specialized intervention at Tier 2, they will be moved to the Tier 3 level, which is further individualized intervention but not yet special education and related services. This intervention level could occur within the general education curriculum but could also be in a setting outside the classroom that is more appropriate for individualized instruction. Some programs proposed an additional level, Tier 4 intervention, before the student is referred for special education.

The continuous progress monitoring that measures how adequately students respond to an intervention is particularly important in an RTI model. Instead of a fixed period of time for a student staying in a specific tier level, most programs use the rate of progress as a means of determining whether a student should move from one tier to the next. For example, in moving a student from Tier 2 to Tier 3, instead of a 15-week fixed schedule, the student may be moved to a Tier 3 intervention after the ongoing documentation shows consistent nonresponsiveness of the student to a scientific, research-based intervention. After Tier 3, the nonresponsiveness could be the cause to suspect that a student has a disability and should be referred for a comprehensive special education evaluation.

Research has demonstrated that the use of IQ-achievement discrepancy models for determining SLD contributes to the disproportionate minority representation in special education programs (Donovan & Cross, 2002). One of the fundamental differences between the RTI and the discrepancy model is in early intervention. Unlike the discrepancy model, which is primarily an assessment system for eligibility requirement, RTI is an intervention delivery system based on formative assessment that is provided for *all* children, regardless of their ability level. Additionally, instead of looking for within-child deficits as evidence of a disability, RTI targets a broader and more contextual analysis by considering day-to-day interpersonal and institutional factors that may affect student achievement and behavior (Harris-Murri et al., 2006). Therefore, RTI is a system that links assessment to intervention within the context of curriculum and instruction. Information collected through CA can help teachers and other RTI members make accurate and timely decisions on how to improve all students' learning, including students with special needs.

Students with learning disabilities are a heterogeneous group with a wide range of abilities (Vaughn, Bos, & Schumm, 2011). Some high ability students with learning disabilities may be excluded from being identified and receiving special education and related services. These students may achieve well enough within the normal range by using their intellectual strengths and coping strategies as well as support services. For example, if they respond well to an intervention by achieving average or above average at Tier 1 within the large group, they are less likely to be moved to Tier 2 or 3 for more individualized intervention and thus may miss the opportunity to reach the level that is consistent with their abilities. On the other hand, some students who do not respond to the intervention due to cultural or linguistic causes than a disability may be identified inappropriately as having a learning disability at the end of the intervention process in the IDEA category. The RTI team members need to be cautious about all these variables that could potentially affect the outcome of intervention.

Purposes of Classroom Assessment for Students With Disabilities

Purposes

As stated earlier, the overall goal of CA is to improve students' learning with well-defined learning objectives through effective assessment practices that teachers use in daily classroom activities to inform their instruction. The assessment and intervention for students with special needs serve the same goal through their IEPs. The IDEA requires that all students with disabilities have the rights to receive an unbiased and nondiscriminatory evaluation conducted by a multidisciplinary team to determine these students' educational needs (Noonan & McCormick, 2006). In the field of special education, the term *evaluation* often refers to procedures that are used to determine the eligibility for special education and related services. Once the student's eligibility for special education services is determined, the term *assessment* is used, which refers to the procedures to identify the needs in each curriculum domain or for young children, in each developmental area, that leads to program planning for effective instruction or intervention. Therefore, before and after the student's IEP is established, the evaluation and assessment may serve very different purposes such as screening, diagnosis, intervention planning, progress monitoring, and program evaluation (Noonan & McCormick, 2006).

After the child is determined to be eligible for special education services, the IEP team is formed, including members such as the special education teacher, general education teacher(s), parents, the student whenever possible, and any other related individuals. This is when CA can be very effective in identifying the student's strengths and weakness, the student's needs and concerns, and the family resources and priorities. All this information can be used by the classroom teacher and the special education teacher to evaluate the student's learning target in this case and the IEP goals and objectives through formative CA techniques. Although CA was not explicitly stated in the IDEA, the support for using CA was evident in the IDEA through the student's IEP content that requires "a statement of the child's present levels of academic achievement and functional performance including how the child's disability affects the child's involvement and progress in the general education curriculum" (34 CFR Part 300, §300.320).

The requirement of the general education curriculum for students with special needs makes CA an important tool to document these students' progress. The assessment types and purposes for students with special needs are relevant to the three elements of CA. For example, the assessment for intervention planning directly relates to the learning goals of CA, including screening and diagnosis to identify the students' current status or level of development and progress monitoring. See Table 24.1 for specific assessment purposes and relevant questions teachers may ask during CA practices.

Assessment Types and Purposes

Screening

Screening is defined as the process of quickly testing students to identify those who *appear* to qualify for special education and related services. Those identified at screening must go on for diagnosis. Screening is a quick and effective assessment process that is administered to all children at a grade- or age-appropriate level. Because of these features, a screening test must be simple, accurate, comprehensive, and cost effective (Filler & Xu, 2006/2007). Simplicity means short, easy to administer, and simple to score. Accuracy requires that the test is both valid and reliable, gives few false positives and no false negatives, and is appropriate for cultural and ethnic groups in the community.

Diagnosis

When a student is referred for comprehensive evaluation, diagnosis is the primary purpose to determine whether the student is eligible for special education and related services. The procedure of diagnosis involves multiple assessment measures such as classroom observations, parent interviews, teacher surveys, and formal and informal tests. It is important to point out that a diagnosis of a disability does not automatically make the student eligible for special education and related services. To be eligible for special

Classroom Assessment Elements				
Learning Goal	*Current Status*	*Action*	*Purpose*	*Questions to Ask*
	Screening		To identify students who appear to have a disability	Is the test comprehensive? Can the classroom teacher administer it? Are parents/families informed?
	Diagnosis		To determine eligibility through comprehensive evaluation only to students who were referred	Are multidisciplinary team members involved? Are multiple measures included? Are the student and his or her family concerns identified?
Intervention planning			To directly benefit the child through effective instructional planning	Are the student's individualized education program (IEP) goals and objectives developed based on the student's current status? Does assessment information link to the intervention? Are accommodations and modifications made to meet the students' individual needs?
		Progress monitoring	To document student's progress through ongoing data collection	Are data collected on a regular basis? Who collects the data? When and where? Are adjustments made based on the student's progress or lack of progress?

Table 24.1 Types and Purposes of Classroom Assessment for Students With Special Needs

education and related services, the student needs to meet two criteria: (1) the student has a disability, based on the diagnosis results and (2) the student has a *need* for special education and related services because of the disability. The need is based on the child's educational performance, including academic and nonacademic needs (IDEIA, 2004).

Intervention Planning

Intervention planning is closely linked to the general education curriculum, specifically the curriculum domain in which the student is identified to have a need for special education—or for young children, the planning targets children's developmental areas in natural environments. Assessment for intervention planning directly leads to the development of the student's IEP goals and objectives and to determine the effectiveness of the intervention. Assessment for intervention planning provides information to guide teachers or interventionists as to what to teach, how to teach, and in what sequence to teach.

Progress Monitoring

Progress monitoring is conducted on a regular basis, such as daily or weekly, following the implementation of intervention based on the planning. Specifically, progress monitoring is to evaluate the effectiveness of intervention strategies or approach relevant to the IEP goals and objectives and what modifications are needed if the intervention is not effective. Systematic data collection in a classroom is essential for teachers to monitor a student's progress.

Any of the assessment types that were previously mentioned can be applied within the CA contexts in general education classrooms. As a member of the IEP team for a student with special needs, the general education teacher plays a critical role in developing and implementing the student's intervention plan with appropriate learning goals. The following section introduces evidence-based approaches to assessing students with special needs within the context of general education curriculum and instruction in inclusive settings.

Approaches to Classroom Assessment for Students With Special Needs

The conceptual framework of CA emphasizes the general education curriculum and instruction as the context of assessment. Effective CA involves student motivation, teacher expectation, quality of the environment, and most important, the purpose of the assessment. According to Stiggins and Chappuis (2005), effective CA is related to clear purpose of assessment, explicit learning expectations, relevant learning objectives, and timely and effective communications with students about the assessment results. In special education, effective CA also means *individualized.* However, individualization does not mean isolation or separation. Whenever possible, the individualized intervention should occur within the general education classroom or inclusive settings.

Developing Learning Objectives for Classroom Assessment

When a student with special needs is included in the general education classroom, the classroom teacher may need to collect additional information to identify the student's learning needs and develop learning targets. The instruction or intervention is expected to be more effective when the student's needs are addressed through prioritized learning objectives. Student-centered planning is an evidence-based approach to collecting accurate and meaningful information for developing learning objectives. Student-centered planning does not necessarily mean that the student is the sole focus; it does mean that the student's needs are assessed and planned in a learning context that is meaningful for the student. In other words, the assessment is authentic, functional, and individualized.

It is well known that successful attempts to meet the educational needs of students with a wide spectrum of needs in a single setting require careful planning. Key to that planning is the identification of activities that allow for the meaningful participation of each student and are, at the same time, valid for the unique cultural identity of the student's family. An example of student-centered planning is the McGill Action Planning System (MAPS). MAPS is a strategy that was originally developed by Marsha Forest, Jack Pearpoint, Judith Snow, Evelyn Lusthaus, and the staff at the Center for Integrated Education in Canada. One particular characteristic of the MAPS is its focus on what the student can do, instead of the student's weaknesses or deficits (Ryan, Kay, Fitzgerald, Paquette, & Smith, 2001). MAPS is a person-centered planning process, bringing together the student with disabilities and his or her family, friends, teachers, and other related service professionals within the curriculum and instruction context (Callicott, 2003; Mount & Zwernick, 1988). MAPS can be used with individuals with mild or moderate disabilities (Vandercook, York, & Forest, 1989). The effectiveness of using the MAPS in identifying the student's strengths, needs, and priorities was illustrated by Sheehy, Ornelles, and Noonan (2009). The process of the MAPS provides a reflective opportunity for each member of the planning team to validate the student's unique social and cultural backgrounds that have influenced the student, which makes the learning objectives relevant and meaningful (O'Brien, O'Brien, & Mount, 1997). This reflective process helps produce a complete picture of the student with disabilities. Based on this information, the MAPS team is able to develop an action plan with specific learning objectives within the general education curriculum that can be prioritized through the IEP goals and objectives.

A critical feature of the MAPS process is the involvement of peers and friends of the student with disabilities in assessment for intervention planning, as well as other aspects of the educational program. Typically, these students provide necessary and fresh perspectives on the needs of their peers related to involvement in general education classes and extracurricular activities. They also serve a key role in supporting their peer with disabilities in regular activities and settings. Additionally, these students can help other team members understand and appreciate the dreams and fears of a student with special needs relative to being accepted and valued as a member of the school community. Because the involvement of peers is an essential feature of the MAPS process, the planning should not occur until the student with disabilities has been a member of the general education classroom or natural community, so that his or her friends without disabilities can be identified and recruited. Ideally, more than one friend should be included. The planning typically occurs in one or two sessions, but for younger children the session can be broken down into shorter periods. The seven key questions to be addressed by MAPS include the following:

1. What is the individual's history?
2. What is your dream for the individual?
3. What is your nightmare?
4. Who is the individual?
5. What are the individual's strengths, gifts, and abilities?
6. What are the individual's needs?
7. What would the individual's ideal day at school look like, and what must be done to make it happen?

Addressing the questions that compose the MAPS process, however, should be an ongoing activity for the planning team. The facilitator may choose to address the questions in different sequences, based on different situations. Peer participation in the planning for inclusion helps the planning team to brainstorm the needs of the student with disabilities, describe the dreams for the student from their typically developing peers, share their concerns or fears for the student in inclusive settings, and develop goals that capitalize on the student's strengths.

When considering the use of the MAPS process, professionals and parents may ask how the MAPS process relates to the IEP development. While the MAPS planning is not a legal process, as is the IEP document and procedure, it complements IEPs in several ways. First, the collaborative process inherent in the MAPS can lead to a clearer sense of mission and greater sense of teamwork, both of which are keys to special education assessment and intervention effectiveness. Second, because the MAPS planning involves the student's siblings and typically developing peers, it provides a source of additional input and perspective that is age and developmentally relevant. Specific IEP goals and objectives should reference skills and concepts taught in general education classes and other typical school and community environments that are chronologically relevant and appropriate (Vandercook et al., 1989). Third, the MAPS planning should provide families with an experience that leads to an appreciation for the value of their active participation in educational planning. Finally, the MAPS provides general education teachers meaningful information on incorporating the student's IEP objectives into the instructional goals within the general education curriculum that targets for all students in the setting.

Developing Learning Objectives Through School–Family Partnerships

CA for students with special needs is not for simply communicating to the parents. Rather, it is to involve parents and other family members as decision makers throughout the assessment process. The student's learning objectives are relevant to his or her IEP objectives and most likely will require that parents implement the plan in settings other than the school. If the learning objectives involve behavior targets or other functional skills, observations across settings between school and home are essential for collecting consistent and valid information based on which the classroom teacher can plan and implement instruction. Therefore, assessing family concerns or needs is an integrated component for CA because the learning target for the student with disabilities needs to be generalized across settings. Pérez Carreón, Drake, and Calabrese Barton (2005) suggested that one way to assess family concerns in a meaningful manner for all involved is to allow parents' life experiences and cultural background to inform and shape the school's climate. Schools need to implement parental participation programs by listening to parents' and other family members' voices. This supports their unique needs and hopes, reflected in their voices. In this way, the home and school may be more integrated, and a truly collaborative team could be formed.

Cooper and Christie (2005) evaluated a District Parent Training Program (DPTP) that was designed to "educate and empower urban school parents" (p. 2249). Although the DPTP was a curriculum-based parent education program with the intent to empower parents in helping their children in content areas such as English and math, findings from the evaluation by Cooper and Christie suggested a mutual benefit between parents and school. While parents felt more empowered through the program, educators and administrators gained a better understanding of family needs by giving those parents the opportunity to articulate their own needs and pinpoint the ways in which they wanted to gain from parent-oriented programs. They also found that establishing true partnerships with parents requires that educators acknowledge and validate parents' views and ultimately share power. Partnership also requires educators to show sensitivity to the culturally relevant values that influence parents' educational priorities and demands and recognize that cultural, socioeconomic, and gender factors affect how parents participate in their children's education. As Dunst, Trivette, Davis, and Cornwell (1988) have noted, it is important to recognize that implicit in such an approach is the assumption on the part of educators that every parent has the capacity to identify his or her own educational concerns and can acquire the skills necessary to play a central role in the education of the child.

Assessing Learning Contexts for Effective Student Learning

Different from the traditional assessment approaches that primarily focus on the student's development and achievement, the alternative assessment models in the past two decades have considered the influence of contexts in students' learning—especially the role of interrelated social and cultural contexts (e.g., Gutiérrez-Clellen, 1996; Keogh & Weisner, 1993; Losardo & Notari-Syverson, 2011; Thorp, 1997). In addition, ongoing research has acknowledged the effect of context on student learning. For example, Keogh and Weisner (1993) argued that the high numbers of students experiencing underachievement and the increasing numbers of students requiring special education services justified a closer look at procedures for identifying and aiding children at a high risk for exhibiting a mild handicapping condition. They cautioned against viewing individual risk factors outside the ecocultural context in which they occur. The social environment contains a complex array of cultural–environmental conditions that influence the participants in the environment. "The ecocultural context also shapes perceptions and responses to child characteristics. For example, individual differences in children's temperaments or behavioral styles may become risky or protective as children interact with adults and peers" (Keogh & Weisner, 1993, p. 6).

Cousin, Diaz, Flores, and Hernandez (1996) proposed a model that emphasizes the relationships among five sociocultural contexts in the educational process. The first level is the social/cultural/community context, which is responsible for fostering development through daily interactions in the community and family. "The social and political contexts that exist in communities affect the interactions that take place and establish relationships that influence school attitudes, policies and practices" (Cousin et al., 1996, p. 441). Second, differences in the district/school context level, such as in school socioeconomic status, institutional referral practices, teacher quality, and financial resources, have the potential to impede or capitalize upon child development begun in the family and community context. Third, the classroom/teacher context level is very influential in the student's transformation into a *student* whose behavior complements the cultural values of the classroom set by the teacher and interactions with other students in the classroom. The last two levels—(4) the group context and (5) the social construction of the mind, are concerned with the impact of peer relationships on cognitive development and the internalization of social interactions. When an individual student's behavior is observed, we need to examine in which learning context that behavior tends to occur to determine the function of that particular behavior.

Recommendations for Teachers to Assess Students With Disabilities

Using Classroom Assessment to Document Students' Individualized Education Program Progress

The IEP team is required by law to complete an IEP document, implement IEP objectives, document the student's progress, and make adjustment for the objectives based on the progress documented. Beyond the legal requirement, effective and devoted classroom teachers are concerned about the student's actual learning in the classroom, which may or may not be included in the student's IEP document. IEP goals and objectives are written in very specific terms to meet the measurability requirement. Often, the instructional objectives related to CA are broad, although still measurable, to guide instruction more effectively and at the same time to help teachers decide what to assess (Popham, 2002). For students with special needs, their IEP goals often include behavior or functional objectives as part of the educational performance in addition to academic goals. One effective approach is to embed the student's specific IEP goals and objectives within the broader instructional objectives of CA the teacher has planned. For example, the specific IEP behavior objective "Mark will raise his hand to ask questions during instructional time" can be embedded within the broader instructional objective "Students will participate in the class discussion and summarize the topics." When the student's IEP objectives are embedded within broader instructional objectives, it makes the learning and teaching consistent and relevant, and more meaningful.

As shown in Figure 24.1, the student's IEP goals and objectives are built upon the student's

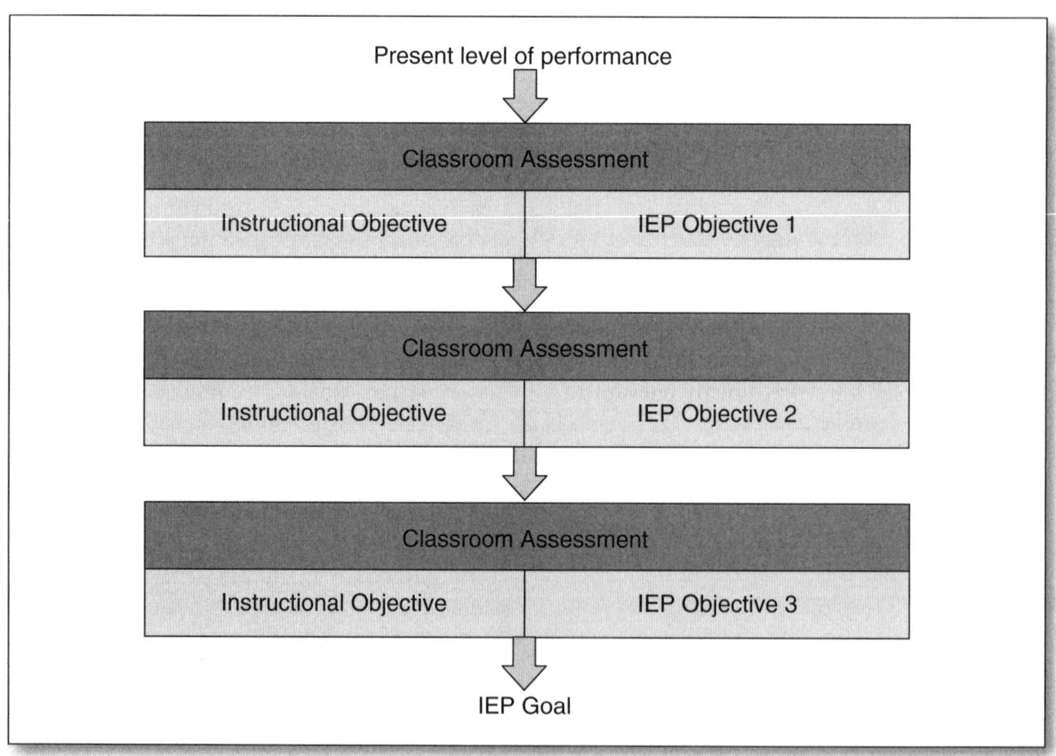

Figure 24.1 Embedding Individualized Education Program Objectives Within Instructional Objectives Using Classroom Assessment

NOTE: IEP = individualized education program.

present level of performance to provide the starting point of step-by-step objectives leading to annual goals. The present level of performance is based on previous test results and CA outcomes, such as direct observation by the classroom teacher, anecdotal notes by the interventionist during a specified instructional time, or a portfolio evaluation provided by the special education teacher. Between the present level of performance and the annual goal are the short-term IEP objectives, which are intermediate steps, one being built upon the other. Each specific IEP objective for an individual child can be embedded within the broader instructional objectives for all students in the general education classroom or inclusive settings. In each step of the objectives, CA plays a critical role in evaluating the effectiveness of the instruction/intervention and documenting the student's progress.

Curriculum-based assessment (CBA) is a type of CA that teachers often use to assess not only the content they are teaching but also the knowledge and skills the students are learning on a regular basis. CBA is a direct application of criterion-referenced assessment strategies to educational content. CBA is a direct means for identifying a student's entry point within an educational program and for refining and readjusting instruction. CBAs focus on skills that are part of the daily curriculum. Item selection in CBAs is determined by how important they are to the student's school performance or daily living. The test results from a CBA indicate how much the student has mastered on a specific subject area or domain. CBAs are often used for intervention planning or programming because items from a CBA test are directly relevant to a student's IEP goals and objectives.

Collecting Functional Assessment Data Within the Classroom Assessment Context

Functional behavioral assessment (FBA) is defined as "a method for identifying the variables that consistently predict and maintain challenging behavior" (Horner & Carr, 1997, as cited in McLean, Wolery, & Bailey, 2004, p. 238). The core of FBA is the analysis of behavior functions, or functional analysis. The goal of FBA is to develop an intervention plan to either decrease the undesirable behavior or to increase an appropriate behavior (McLean et al., 2004).

FBA has been well documented in research in identifying the function(s) of a behavior that will be planned as the target for intervention (Lalli, Browder, Mace, & Brown, 1993; Sprague & Horner, 1992). FBA is an approach to examining the relationship among environmental events, conditions, and interventions that may trigger a problem behavior (Crone & Horner, 2003). Research on FBA suggested the effectiveness and efficiency of behavior support that targets the function of children's behavior (DuPaul & Ervin, 1996; Kamps et al., 1995; Neilsen & McEvoy, 2004). Gettinger and Stoiber (2006) found that FBA and positive behavior support were effective in increasing children's positive behavior and decreasing their challenging behavior in classroom settings. Functional assessment can be conducted within the CA context because the classroom teachers can collect information during routine activities within a typical school day and use the information to plan and implement instruction or intervention.

Assumptions

Functional assessment is based on the following three assumptions: (1) purposefulness of behavior—behavior occurs for a reason and serves as a specific function for the individual student; (2) the change of behavior—behavior can change as a result of a certain presentation of a task and response to the challenging behavior; and (3) the context of behavior—the environmental or contextual meaning of behavior and the relationship between environment and behavior affect the effectiveness of intervention (Foster-Johnson & Dunlap, 1993; McLean et al., 2004; Neel & Cessna, 1993). Previous research suggested that FBA leads to more effective behavioral interventions than traditional intervention approaches, especially in improving students' on-task behaviors and decreasing disruptive behaviors (Ervin et al., 2001; Kamps, Wendland, & Culpepper, 2006; Newcomer & Lewis, 2004).

Functional Assessment Methods

Both indirect and direct methods of functional assessment have been applied in identifying the function of the behavior and the contextual variables that either elicit the behavior (antecedent) or reinforce the behavior (consequence) (McLean et al., 2004; Repp & Karsh, 1994). Indirect methods typically include existing written documents such as the student's previous assessment report, structured or semi-structured interviews, checklists, rating scales, and questionnaires (Arndorfer, Miltenberger, Woster, Rortvedt, & Gaffaney, 1994; McLean et al., 2004). Direct methods usually involve observation assessment, including the combination of scatterplot and antecedent-behavior-consequence (ABC) analysis.

Some studies have suggested that the ABC analysis may lead to hypotheses on the function of the problem behavior (Repp & Karsh, 1994; Sprague & Horner, 1992). For example, a student's problem behavior of talking to a peer during a classroom project may function as obtaining the teacher's attention and escaping undesirable academic tasks, or a peer attention could increase the student's off-task behavior (Kern, Childs, Dunlap, Clarke, & Falk, 1994; Lewis & Sugai, 1996; Meyer, 1999).

One important feature of FBA is that observations are conducted within a relevant context through which the student behavior occurs. Functional analysis is completed through antecedent or consequence environmental manipulation by manipulating and replicating the experimental condition versus control condition. Once the function of the problem behavior is identified through the ABC analysis, the environmental context can be altered so that the student's problem behavior will no longer serve the function (e.g., obtaining teacher's attention). Instead, the student may be arranged to sit next to a peer who serves as a peer mentor to obtain the same function but in the appropriate way (e.g., raising his hand). Therefore, a consistent observation of the general education classroom environment is essential to the validity of functional assessment and the success of intervention.

Assessment Accommodations

Assessment accommodations are defined by changes to the setting, scheduling, materials, or procedures to allow meaningful participation in assessments (U.S. Department of Education, 2002). Cohen and Spenciner (2007) further defined accommodations for students with special needs as "changes to the educational program and assessment procedures and materials that do not substantially alter the instructional level, the content of the curriculum, or the assessment criteria" (p. 4). Disability can pose a serious challenge to learning and to fully demonstrating knowledge and abilities. It is important for teachers to remember that the purpose of any forms of CA is to assess the student's ability level instead of the effects of the disability condition (Salvia, Ysseldyke, & Bolt, 2007). For example, for a student with sensory motor difficulties, if the CA purpose is to assess students' writing skills, then the accommodation for this writing assessment can be a change of the assessment format such as a laptop computer instead of the pencil–paper format. Furthermore, this change of format as an accommodation can be applied to all students in the classroom. Accommodations for assessment can help students overcome or minimize the barriers presented by their disabilities and focus on their ability (Elliott, Kratochwill, & Schulte, 1999; McDonnell, McLaughlin, & Morrison, 1997; Pitoniak & Royer, 2001). The use of testing accommodations is viewed as a central factor in increasing the participation of students with disabilities in assessments (Thurlow, Ysseldyke, & Silverstein, 1993).

As mentioned earlier, general education teachers or teachers of content subjects are most likely to teach students with special needs in the general education or inclusive classrooms. Accommodations will allow teachers to provide appropriate instruction to all students with or without disabilities in the classroom, including students who are gifted or talented. In addition to students with disabilities, gifted students also need support when individualized instruction is provided to accommodate their unique needs. They may not be able to differentiate instruction on their own, and they may need guidance in recognizing their unique learning needs to reach their potential capabilities (Manning, Stanford, & Reeves, 2010). To reach this goal, it is essential to provide effective differentiated instruction (DI) to meet the diverse educational needs, learning styles, and interests of all learners in the inclusive classroom. DI is an alternative approach to teaching and learning that allows teachers options of varying learning contents, contexts, and modes of assessment to meet the individual needs of each student (Stanford & Reeves, 2009; Thousand, Villa, & Nevin, 2007; see also Chapter 23 of this volume).

Universal design for learning (UDL) is one way to implement DI. UDL is a theoretical framework designed to guide the development of curricula that are flexible and supportive of all students (Dolan & Hall, 2001; Meyer & Rose, 1998; Pisha & Coyne, 2001; Rose, 2001). Within the framework of UDL, the individual needs of all students in the setting will be addressed, including students who have disabilities, students who are gifted or talented, and students who are from culturally and linguistically diverse backgrounds. The methods, materials, and assessment are usable by all. UDL helps meet the challenges of diversity by suggesting flexible instructional materials, techniques, and strategies that empower educators to meet the various individual needs within the general education curriculum. The UDL framework guides the development of adaptable curricula by means of three principles: (1) multiple means of representation, (2) multiple means of expression, and (3) multiple means of engagement (Center for Applied Special Technology, 2008). Instead of adapting the existing curriculum to meet the individual needs of students, UDL is promoting flexible *accessibility* for diverse learners through multiple options of materials in representation, expression, and engagement.

The Americans with Disabilities Act of 1990 requires equal access to goods and services for people with disabilities. The concept of UDL came about through the field of architecture as a way to address these legal requirements by providing equal access to physical environments for people with special needs (Story, Mueller, & Mace, 1998). UDL proposes that accessibility features should be considered during the conceptualization, design, and development stages of any environmental interface to provide an environment with the least amount of restrictions or specialized provisions for people with special needs (Pisha & Coyne, 2001). This concept was then applied to the field of education and became known as UDL (Rose & Meyer, 2002). The three principles of UDL are as follows:

- Principle 1: To support recognition learning and provide multiple, flexible methods of presentation
- Principle 2: To support strategic learning and provide multiple, flexible methods of expression and apprenticeship
- Principle 3: To support affective learning and provide multiple, flexible options for engagement

Within the framework of UDL, technology or assistant technology has played an important role in accommodating students' learning in inclusive classrooms. For example, a means of representation can be conducted through video, audio, or text-to-speech methods. Online blogs and searches can be an effective means of engaging the student in a subject relevant project. Similarly, a means of students to express themselves can include PowerPoint presentations, augmentative communication, concept maps, or music and arts.

Through the principles of UDL, accommodations can provide access to assessment and intervention. The term *accommodation* can refer to any tools used during assessment and/or intervention in assisting students with disabilities to access to the learning content without lowering the expectations of outcomes. Assessment accommodations can be grouped into four categories: (1) setting accommodations, (2) scheduling accommodations, (3) testing materials accommodations, and (4) test procedures accommodations (Christensen, Lazarus, Crone, & Thurlow, 2008). A common accommodation may involve a change of the presentation of the test material or a change of the student's mode of response. For example, for a student who needs more time to process the information, additional time can be provided to ensure that the student is able to complete the test, as long as the speed or the testing time is not the purpose of the CA test. A student who is easily distracted may be allowed to take the test in a separate location or a quieter corner of the room. A student with ADHD may take the test with shorter periods of time and take more breaks. If the purpose of the CA is to assess students' reading comprehension, then allowing the students with writing problems to dictate instead of writing their responses is an appropriate accommodation. See Table 24.2 for examples of accommodations of each category that teachers can apply during CA practices. Assessment accommodations for students with disabilities can be provided during CA procedures and ongoing instruction or intervention procedures. For students with IEPs, the accommodations need to be consistent with the IEP statements (Thurlow, House, Boys, Scott, & Ysseldyke, 2000).

Accommodation	*Examples for Classroom Assessment Practices*
Setting	Separate room, quiet location, small group or one-on-one administration, provisions of special furniture
Scheduling	Additional time to complete the test, provision of frequent breaks, completion of a section per day, reduced number of items per section
Testing materials	Laptop, iPad, large-print version, Braille version (if applicable and available), space items so as not to interfere with one another
Test procedures	Directions read aloud, repetition or clarification of directions, answers marked in test booklet, present items in a predictable sequence

Table 24.2 Categories of Assessment Accommodations for Classroom Assessment Practices

Conclusion

As mentioned earlier, CA involves gathering, interpreting, and using the information to support teachers' decision making for instructional practices and to enhance students' learning (McMillan, 2011; Popham, 2002). One primary principle of CA is the direct connection between learning targets and assessment practices that teachers use in the classroom to monitor students' progress, and this principle applies to the assessment for students with special needs. A fundamental principle for assessing students with disabilities is to link assessment to curriculum and instruction. Because the population of students with disabilities is a heterogeneous group, CA learning targets often need to be individualized with accommodations being provided if necessary. Still, individualized learning targets are linked to the general education curriculum and the teaching situation in the classroom. Shepard (2000) also proposed collecting and using the assessment information as part of the ongoing learning process. However, in reality, teachers have not used CA consistently to assess students with special needs. One reason is that the assessment and evaluation for students with special needs are policy driven. Sometimes the classroom teacher may feel legally obligated to conduct an assessment for the IEP requirement instead of gathering meaningful data to benefit the student's learning. Another important reason that teachers use less of CA is the lack of empirical research on CA for students with disabilities. For example, although authentic assessment such as portfolios is well accepted by teachers as a CA technique, it has not been widely used to document the progress of students with disabilities because of the lack of operational definitions of measuring students' progress. The existing literature provides very limited or insufficient data on the effectiveness of using CA for students with special needs (Salvia et al., 2007). There is an urgent need for empirical research on the use of CA for assessing students with special needs in inclusive settings. The issue is not whether students with special needs should be assessed with CA; the key is how students with special needs should be assessed with CA for the purpose of improving their learning.

CA for students with disabilities can be very effective when the purpose of the assessment is clearly described and communicated among the student's team members, including the student himself or herself. Despite the variety of formats and approaches to CA, the main purpose is to directly benefit the students' learning through effective assessment and instructional practices. Although CA occurs mostly in a classroom, the information from beyond the classroom should be obtained for planning instruction or interventions. This is especially the case if the learning target is related to a student's behavior (because a student's problem behavior usually occurs across settings). It is critical to target a behavior for intervention that is consistent across settings and persistent over time. Therefore, for CA to be effective and meaningful, the assessment team needs to include individuals who interact with the student with a disability on a regular basis, including the student's family members and friends. Students' strengths and concerns need to be identified within the culturally relevant contexts, the assessment purpose should be directly related to the instructional objectives, and the focus of the assessment should be on students' learning through effective teaching. Students with special needs are able to succeed in general education classrooms or inclusive settings, but it takes an interdisciplinary team's effort to develop and implement a comprehensive assessment and intervention system to ensure that the student's IEP truly reflects the effectiveness of intervention that enhances the student's learning. Appropriate accommodations must be used when needed.

References

Arndorfer, R. E., Miltenberger, R. G., Woster, S. H., Rortvedt, A. K., & Gaffaney, T. (1994). Home-based descriptive and experimental analysis of problem behaviors in children. *Topics in Early Childhood Special Education, 14,* 64–87.

Callicott, K. J. (2003). Culturally sensitive collaboration within person-centered planning. *Focus on Autism and Other Developmental Disabilities, 18,* 61–68.

Center for Applied Special Technology. (2008). *Universal design for learning (UDL) guidelines 1.0.* Retrieved from www.udlcenter.org/aboutudl/udlguidelines

Christensen, L., Lazarus, S., Crone, M., & Thurlow, M. L. (2008). *2007 state policies on assessment participation and accommodations for students with disabilities* (Synthesis Report 69). Minneapolis: University of Minnesota, National Center on Educational Outcomes.

Cohen, L. G., & Spenciner, L. J. (2007). *Assessment of children & youth with special needs* (3rd ed.). Boston: Pearson.

Cooper, C. W., & Christie, C.A. (2005). Evaluating parent empowerment: A look at the potential of social justice evaluation in education. *Teacher College Record, 107*(10), 2248–2274.

Cousin, P. T., Diaz, E., Flores, B., & Hernandez, J. (1996). Looking forward: Using a sociocultural perspective to reframe the study of learning disabilities. In M. Poplin & P. Cousin (Eds.), *Alternative views of learning disabilities.* Austin, TX: Pro-Ed.

Crone, D. A., & Horner, R. H. (2003). *Building positive behavior support systems in schools: Functional behavioral assessment.* New York: Guilford Press.

Dolan, R. P., & Hall, T. E. (2001). Universal design for learning: Implications for large-scale assessment. *IDA Perspectives, 27*(4), 22–25.

Donovan, S., & Cross, C. (Eds.). (2002). *Minority students in special and gifted education.* Washington, DC: National Academic Press.

Drame, E., & Xu, Y. (2008). Examining sociocultural factors in response to intervention models. *Childhood Education, 85*(1), 26–32.

Dunst, C. J., Trivette, C. M., Davis, M., & Cornwell, J. (1988). Enabling and empowering families of children with health impairments. *Children's Health Care, 17*(2), 71–81.

DuPaul, G. J., & Ervin, R. A. (1996). Functional assessment of behavior related to attention deficit/hyperactivity disorder: Linking assessment to intervention design. *Behavior Therapy, 27,* 601–622.

Elliott, S. N., Kratochwill, T. R., & Schulte, A. G. (1999). *Assessment accommodations guide.* Monterey, CA: CTB/McGraw-Hill.

Ervin, R. A., Radford, P., Bertsch, K., Piper, A., Ehrhardt, K., & Poling, A. (2001). A descriptive analysis and critique of the empirical literature on school-based functional assessment. *School Psychology Review, 30,* 193–210.

Filler, J., & Xu, Y. (2006/2007). Including children with disabilities in early childhood education programs: Individualizing developmentally appropriate practices. *Childhood Education, 83*(2), 92–98.

Foster-Johnson, L., & Dunlap, G. (1993). Using functional assessment to develop effective, individualized interventions for challenging behavior. *Teaching Exceptional Children, 25*(3), 44–50.

Gettinger, M., & Stoiber, K. C. (2006). Functional assessment, collaboration, and evidence-based treatment: Analysis of a team approach for addressing challenging behaviors in young children. *Journal of School Psychology, 44,* 231–252.

Gutiérrez-Clellen, V. F. (1996). Language diversity: Implications for assessment. In K. N. Cole, P. S. Dale, & D. J. Thal (Eds.), *Assessment of communication and language* (pp. 29–56). Baltimore: Brookes Publishing.

Harris-Murri, N., King, K., & Rostenberg, D. (2006). Reducing disproportionate minority representation in special education programs for students with emotional disturbances: Toward a culturally responsive response to intervention model. *Education and Treatment of Children, 29*(4), 779–799.

Heward, W. L. (2009). *Exceptional children: An introduction to special education* (9th ed.). Upper Saddle River, NJ: Merrill/Pearson.

Horner, R. H., & Carr, E. G. (1997). Behavioral support for students with severe disabilities: Functional assessment and comprehensive intervention. *Journal of Special Education, 31,* 84–104.

Individuals with Disabilities Education Improvement Act of 2004. Pub. L. No. 108-446, 20 U.S.C. § 1400 *et seq*. (2004).

Kamps, D. M., Ellis, C., Mancina, C., Wyble, J., Greene, L., & Harvey, D. (1995). Case studies using functional analysis for young children with behavior risks. *Education & Treatment of Children, 18,* 243–260.

Kamps, D., Wendland, M., & Culpepper, M. (2006). Active teacher participation in functional behavior assessment for students with emotional and behavioral disorders risks in general education classrooms. *Behavioral Disorders, 31,* 128–146.

Kauffman, J. M., & Landrum, T. (2009). *Characteristics of emotional and behavioral disorders of children and youth* (9th ed.). Upper Saddle River, NJ: Merrill/Pearson.

Keogh, B. K., & Weisner, T. (1993). An ecocultural perspective on risk and protective factors in children's development: Implications for learning disabilities. *Learning Disabilities & Research, 8*(1), 3–10.

Kern, L., Childs, K. E., Dunlap, G., Clarke, S., & Falk, G. D. (1994). Using assessment based curricular intervention to improve the classroom behavior of a student with emotional and behavioral challenges. *Journal of Applied Behavior Analysis, 27,* 7–9.

Lalli, J. S., Browder, D. M., Mace, F. C., & Brown, D. K. (1993). Teacher use of descriptive analysis data to implement interventions to decrease students' problem behaviors. *Journal of Applied Behavior Analysis, 26,* 227–238.

Lewis, T. J., & Sugai, G. (1996). Descriptive and experimental analysis of teacher and peer attention and the use of assessment-based intervention to improve pro-social behavior. *Journal of Behavioral Education, 6*(1), 7–24.

Losardo, A., & Notari-Syverson, A. N. (2011). *Alternative approaches to assessing young children* (2nd ed.). Baltimore: Brookes Publishing.

Manning, S., Stanford, B., & Reeves, S. (2010). Valuing the advanced learner: Differentiating up. *The Clearing House, 83,* 145–149.

Mastropieri, M. A., & Scruggs, T. E. (2010). *The inclusive classroom: Strategies for effective differentiated instruction* (4th ed.). Upper Saddle River, NJ: Merrill/Pearson.

McDonnell, L. M., McLaughlin, M. J., & Morrison, P. (Eds.). (1997). *Educating one and all: Students with disabilities and standards-based reform.* Washington, DC: National Academy Press.

McLean, M., Wolery, M., & Bailey, D. B. (2004). *Assessing infants and preschoolers with special needs* (3rd ed.). Upper Saddle River, NJ: Pearson.

McMillan, J. H. (2011). *Classroom assessment: Principles and practice for effective standards based instruction* (5th ed). Boston: Allyn & Bacon.

Meyer, K. A. (1999). Functional analysis and treatment of problem behavior exhibited by elementary school children. *Journal of Applied Behavior Analysis, 32*(2), 229–232.

Meyer, A., & Rose, D. H. (1998). *Learning to read in the computer age.* Cambridge, MA: Brookline Books.

Mount, B., & Zwernick, K. (1988). *It's never too early, it's never too late: A booklet about personal futures planning* (Pub. No. 421-88-109). St. Paul, MN: Metropolitan Council.

Neel, R. S., & Cessna, K. K. (1993). Behavioral intent: Instructional content for students with behavior disorders. In K. K. Cessna (Ed.), *Instructionally differentiated programming: A needs-based approach for students with behavior disorders* (pp. 31–39). Denver: Colorado Department of Education.

Neilsen, S., & McEvoy, M. (2004). Functional behavior assessment in early education settings. *Journal of Early Intervention, 26,* 115–131.

Newcomer, L. L., & Lewis, T. J. (2004). Functional behavioral assessment: An investigation of assessment reliability and effectiveness of function-based interventions. *Journal of Emotional and Behavioral Disorders, 12,* 168–181.

Noonan, M. J., & McCormick, L. (2006). *Young children with disabilities in national environments: Methods and procedures.* Baltimore: Brookes Publishing.

O'Brien, L., O'Brien, J., & Mount, B. (1997). Person-centered planning has arrived...or has it? *Mental Retardation, 35,* 470–488.

Pérez Carreón, G., Drake, C., & Calabrese Barton, A. (2005). The importance of presence: Immigrant parent's school engagement experiences. *American Educational Research Journal, 42*(3), 465–498.

Pisha, B., & Coyne, P. (2001). Smart from the start: The promise of universal design for learning. *Remedial and Special Education, 22*(4), 197–203.

Pitoniak, M. J., & Royer, J. M. (2001). Testing accommodations for examinees with disabilities: A review of psychometric, legal, and social policy issues. *Review of Educational Research, 71*(1), 53–104.

Popham, W. J. (2002). *Classroom assessment: What teachers need to know* (3rd ed.). Boston: Allyn & Bacon.

Repp, A. C., & Karsh, K. G. (1994). Hypothesis-based interventions for tantrum behaviors of persons with developmental disabilities in school settings. *Journal of Applied Behavior Analysis, 27,* 21–31.

Rose, D. (2001). Universal design for learning: Deriving guiding principles from networks that learn. *Journal of Special Education Technology, 16*(2), 66–67.

Rose, D., & Meyer, A., (2002). *Teaching every student in the digital age: Universal design for learning.* Alexandria, VA: Association for Supervision and Curriculum Development.

Ryan, A. K., Kay. P. J., Fitzgerald, M., Paquette, S., & Smith, S. (2001). A case study in parent-teacher action research. *Teaching Exceptional Education, 33*(3), 56–61.

Sadler, R. (1989). Formative assessment and the design of instructional systems. *Instructional Science, 18,* 119–144.

Salend, S. J. (2011). *Creating inclusive classrooms: Effective and reflective practices.* Boston: Pearson.

Salvia, J., Ysseldyke, J. E., & Bolt, S. (2007). *Assessment in special and inclusive education* (10th ed.). Boston: Houghton Mifflin.

Sheehy, P., Ornelles, C., & Noonan, M. J. (2009). Biculturalization: Developing culturally responsive approaches to family participation. *Intervention in School and Clinic, 45*(2), 132–139.

Shepard, L. A. (2000). *The role of assessment in a learning culture.* Presidential address presented at the annual meeting of the American Educational Research Association, New Orleans, LA.

Sprague, J. R., & Horner, R. H. (1992). Covariation within functional response classes: Implications for treatment of severe problem behavior. *Journal of Applied Behavior Analysis, 25,* 735–745.

Stanford, B., & Reeves, S. (2009). Making it happen: Using differentiated instruction, retrofit framework, and universal design for learning. *TEACHING Exceptional Children Plus, 5*(6) Article 4. Retrieved from http://escholarship.bc.edu/education/tecplus/vol5/iss6/art4

Stiggins, R., & Chappuis, J, (2005), Using student-involved classroom assessment to close achievement gaps. *Theory Into Practice, 44*(1), 11–18.

Story, M. F., Mueller, J. L., & Mace, R. L. (1998). *The universal design file: Designing for people of all ages and abilities.* Raleigh: North Carolina State University, The Center for Universal Design.

Thorp, E. K. (1997). Increasing opportunities for partnership with culturally and linguistically diverse families. *Intervention in School and Clinic, 32*(5), 261–270.

Thousand, J. S., Villa, R. A., & Nevin, A. I. (2007). *Differentiating instruction: Collaborating planning and teaching for universally designed learning.* Thousand Oaks, CA: Corwin Press.

Thurlow, M. L., House, A. L., Boys, C., Scott, D. L., & Ysseldyke, J. E. (2000). Students with disabilities in large-scale assessments: State participation and accommodation policies. *Journal of Special Education, 34*(3), 154–163.

Thurlow, M. L., Ysseldyke, J. E., & Silverstein, B. (1993). *Testing accommodations for students with disabilities: A review of the literature* (Synthesis Report No. 4). Minneapolis: University of Minnesota, National Center for Educational Outcomes.

U.S. Department of Education. (2002). *No Child Left Behind Act of 2001* (Title I Paraprofessionals: Draft Non-Regulatory Guidance). Washington, DC: U.S. Department of Education, Office of Elementary and Secondary Education.

U.S. Department of Education. (2007). *To assure the free appropriate public education of all children with disabilities: Twenty-seventh annual report to Congress on the implementation of the Individuals with Disabilities Education Act.* Washington, DC: Author.

U.S. Department of Education, National Center for Education Statistics. (2010). *Digest of Education Statistics, 2009* (NCES 2010-013).

Vandercook, T., York, J., & Forest, M. (1989). The McGill Action Planning System (MAPS): A strategy for building the vision. *JASH, 14*(3), 205–215.

Vaughn, S., Bos, C. S., & Schumm, J. S. (2011). *Teaching students who are exceptional, diverse, and at risk in the general education classroom* (5th ed.). Boston: Allyn & Bacon.

25

Classroom Assessment in Mathematics

Maggie B. McGatha

William S. Bush

Classroom assessment (CA) in mathematics has evolved considerably over the past 20 years, from summative assessments like daily quizzes, chapter tests, unit tests, and end-of-course assessments primarily used to assign student grades to formative assessments (or assessments *for* learning), which include teacher questioning and feedback during lessons, student writing assignments, and individual or group projects. Changes in mathematics CAs have been stimulated by changes in national mathematics standards—the National Council of Teachers of Mathematics (NCTM) *Curriculum and Evaluation Standards for School Mathematics* (1989), *Professional Standards for Teaching Mathematics* (1991), the *Assessment Standards for School Mathematics* (1995), the *Principles and Standards for School Mathematics* (2000), and more recently, the Council of Chief State School Officers (CCSSO) *Common Core State Standards in Mathematics* (2010). These documents not only describe important mathematics content for Grades K–12, but they also identify important mathematical processes like problem solving, reasoning, and inquiry that all students should develop.

As a result of widespread acceptance of these national documents, the goals of mathematics teaching have become broader and deeper with regard to student learning. Therefore, CAs must be varied and flexible in order to capture students' levels of learning and thinking and provide teachers with important feedback about different levels of learning. Therefore, teachers now must incorporate a wider range of assessments, like portfolios, projects, and extended-response items, to assess students' higher-level learning.

In this chapter, we examine the research on CA in mathematics by analyzing research findings with regard to teachers' implementation of effective CA practices in mathematics and their effects on student learning and attitudes. We have organized our review of the research on CA in mathematics into three categories: (1) formative assessment practices in mathematics, (2) summative assessment practices in mathematics, and (3) the impact of external mathematics assessments on CA and instruction. We end the chapter with a discussion of topics for further research.

Formative Assessment Practices in Mathematics

As noted in the formative assessment section of this handbook, research has shown that formative assessment can lead to improved student achievement. Formative assessment is multifaceted and complex. Leahy, Lyon, Thompson, and Wiliam (2005) characterized this complexity as teachers paying attention to "everything students do—such as conversing in groups, completing seatwork, answering and asking questions, working on projects, handing in homework assignments, even sitting silently and looking confused..." (p. 19). In order to effectively use formative assessment to improve student achievement, teachers must pay attention to all of this information from students and use it to inform their practices. Hence, classroom practice is where we begin our review of the research on formative assessment in mathematics. We then share insights from the literature about challenges involved in implementing formative assessment in the mathematics classroom and professional development.

Classroom Practice

Several researchers have described formative assessment practices in mathematics classrooms. Generally speaking, even though the task is daunting, teachers are attempting to implement formative assessment into their practice in various ways. Specifically, the research on formative assessment classroom practices falls into four categories: (1) integrated practices, (2) isolated practices, (3) student work analysis, and (4) technology.

Integrated Practices

Three studies, in particular, focused on integrating several aspects of the formative assessment process. Suurtamm, Koch, and Arden (2010) reported that mathematics teachers in their study (Grades 7 through 10) used a variety of assessment strategies in their classrooms. These strategies included math journals, flexible grouping, pre-assessment quizzes, performance tasks, and questioning. Observations of teachers revealed that a variety of assessment strategies were used in formative ways, and teachers integrated assessment with instruction to make assessment a continuous process. They reported that teachers also supported student learning by (1) providing descriptive feedback to students, (2) supporting students in self-assessment, and (3) using assessment data to inform their teaching.

In a 3-year study of National Certified Board Teacher candidates (middle and high school science and mathematics), Sato, Wei, and Darling-Hammond (2008) found an increase in formative assessment practices. In particular, researchers tracked types of assessments, learning goals and criteria, student self-assessment, modification of teaching based on formative assessment data, and quality of feedback. The most significant changes noted in teachers' practice were greater variety of types of assessments and greater use of assessment data for formative purposes. Additionally, teachers moved from teaching discrete facts to focusing more on conceptual understanding and aligning their assessments with learning goals.

Panizzon and Pegg (2007) described a 2-year study with secondary mathematics and science teachers focused on implementing formative assessment practices. Teachers were supported through professional learning communities and were engaged in creating action plans to describe what aspects of formative assessment they wanted to implement. The researchers reported that using a variety of questioning strategies was the most common change for teachers in the project. In particular, mathematics teachers realized that using more open-ended questioning strategies allowed students to demonstrate conceptual understandings. Panizzon and Pegg also reported that teachers experienced shifts in their views of assessment over the 2 years—from collecting scores for grading purposes to gathering information about students that could inform their practice to enhance student learning.

Isolated Practices

A second group of research studies on formative assessment practices in mathematics classrooms focused on single aspects of formative assessment, such as feedback, student self-assessment, and daily quizzes. In contrast to the integrated practices studies that were previously mentioned, formative assessment practices were not a part of a comprehensive formative assessment process. For example, Li, Yin, Ruiz-Primo, and Morozov (2011) provided a synthesis of the literature on teachers' use of feedback in mathematics classrooms. The authors conveyed that there is agreement among scholars that the most effective use of feedback is providing formative comments that support a student in closing the gap between where they are and where they need to be. The synthesis included 18 papers that described 33 experimental or quasi-experimental studies ranging from kindergarten to college in seven countries. In contrast to the recommendations on effective feedback that was previously mentioned, the authors found that in over half of the studies, feedback was evaluative in nature and focused solely on correctness. Only five studies included accounts of descriptive feedback in which students were provided information to improve their work. An alarming finding from the synthesis was that none of the studies incorporated "pedagogical follow-up" after feedback was provided to students. Students often had to interpret the feedback and figure out how to use it to move their learning forward. The authors explained that without the pedagogical follow-up to inform teaching and learning, the impact of the feedback was basically lost.

A few studies in the mid-1990s focused on self-assessment in mathematics and revealed some positive effects, but many studies had limitations that narrowed the generalizability of the findings (Fontana & Fernandes, 1994; Ross, 1995; Schunk, 1996; see Chapter 21 of this volume for more discussion of student self-assessment). In an attempt to overcome some of the limitations of previous studies, Ross, Hogaboam-Gray, and Rolheiser (2002) designed a study with fifth- and sixth-grade students that included a "four stage process: (1) involve students in defining evaluation criteria; (2) teach students how to apply the criteria; (3) give students feedback on their self-evaluations; and (4) help students use evaluation data to create action plans" (p. 48). Researchers in this study found that supporting students in learning how to self-assess in mathematics using the four-stage process that was just described had a positive effect on mathematics achievement. Interestingly, the researchers compared this study (N = 259, treatment; N = 257, control) with a pilot study they conducted the year before (N= 176, treatment; N= 174, control) in which no significant differences between the treatment and control students were found (Ross, Hogaboam-Gray, & Rolheiser, 2001). The researchers addressed two problems from the pilot study in the second study: (1) increasing the length of the study by one-third (8 weeks to 12 weeks) and (2) increasing the in-service time and materials for teachers. They attributed the combination of student self-assessment with appropriate in-service training for teachers to the positive results.

A final area of study focused on isolated formative assessment practices using daily quizzes. Peterson and Siadat (2009) explored the impact of formative assessments (in this case, quizzes) on achievement of college students in an elementary algebra class (N = 1,574). The study included two experimental classes, one with weekly quizzes and one with biweekly quizzes, and two control classes using no quizzes. The quizzes were used as formative assessments in which students were provided with immediate, constructive feedback upon completing the quizzes. This study contrasts other studies with regard to the frequency of assessments, as described in the next section, involving quizzes used as summative measures. The textbook, content covered, and homework assignments were the same in every class. To measure student achievement, teachers gave all students the same internal summative assessments (department midterm and final exams) as well as an external summative assessment (COMPASS test developed by ACT, Inc.). The results revealed that students across all four classes were relatively equal on pretests, and scores on the posttest increased for all student groups. However, scores for students in the experimental group were significantly higher on all internal summative exams and on the COMPASS test. This study supported the use of regular feedback, regardless of frequency, to improve learning in a postsecondary mathematics course.

Student Work Analysis

A third area of CA practice that has been studied in mathematics classrooms is the use of assessment tasks to support teachers in understanding students' thinking is. Lin (2006) conducted a study with four third-grade teachers who were involved in a larger research study, the Assessment Practices in Mathematics Classroom project. The school-based assessment team, consisting of Lin and the four teachers, met weekly over the course of a school year to discuss mathematics assessment tasks and students' responses. Teachers also observed each other teach and reflected in writing about what they were learning. After lesson observations, teachers discussed the mathematics from the lesson, analyzed student work, and then created assessment tasks that could be used in the class. Lin concluded that teachers benefited from the collaboration by becoming more aware of a variety of solution strategies, students' misconceptions and how to address them, and the importance of students' critical thinking.

Technology

Using technology as formative assessment tools in mathematics classrooms is a fourth area of interest to researchers. This is a relatively new area of formative assessment research and, presently, only one study exists. Shirley, Irving, Sanalan, Pape, and Owens (2011) studied secondary mathematics and science teachers' use of connected classroom technology (CCT) in its first year of implementation. The six teachers in the study used the TI-Navigator system, which included handheld graphing calculators for each student, a teacher's computer, projection device, and other software. The system was connected wirelessly to allow the teacher to present problems or tasks for students and then to see the results immediately. Teachers in the study used the CCT to track student learning and provide immediate feedback to students. Researchers found that the technology allowed teachers to more efficiently monitor individual and whole class achievement. In addition, the technology created a rapid feedback cycle that allowed teachers to offer more immediate and appropriate remediation.

Summary

The research on formative assessment classroom practices fell into four categories: (1) integrated practices, (2) isolated practices, (3) student work analysis, and (4) technology. Across three studies that looked broadly at formative assessment practices in mathematics classrooms (Panizzon & Pegg, 2007; Sato et al., 2008; Suurtamm et al., 2010), several findings were consistent. Teachers used a variety of approaches to formative assessment, and they used assessment data in more formative ways. In studies that focused on isolated formative assessment practices, researchers found that the way teachers used feedback was not aligned with recommendations about effective feedback (Li et al., 2011). However, teaching students how to self-assess had positive impacts on student achievement (Ross et al., 2002). Using formative assessments increased student achievement in college algebra courses (Peterson & Siadat, 2009). A third area of formative assessment research focused on using assessment tasks to support teachers in understanding student thinking. Lin (2006) found that analyzing students' work on assessment tasks improved teachers' awareness of student misconceptions and how to address them. The fourth area of formative assessment classroom practices focused on technology. Shirley and colleagues (2011) reported that teachers in their study effectively used technology to monitor students' learning in efficient ways that allowed for a quick feedback cycle.

Challenges

The previous set of studies indicated that mathematics teachers are attempting to implement formative assessment practices. A second set of studies focused on the challenges involved in effectively implementing formative assessment practices in mathematics classrooms. The studies focused on two challenges: (1) teacher content knowledge and (2) fairness and equity.

Heritage, Kim, Vendlinski, and Herman (2009) studied sixth-grade teachers' (N = 118) mathematics knowledge for teaching as it related to formative assessment. The teachers completed tasks that required them to use their mathematical content knowledge and pedagogical content knowledge (PCK) as they would in the classroom. In particular, the researchers studied the teachers' ability to analyze and interpret student work in order to make effective formative assessment decisions. Teachers reviewed student responses to assessment tasks and then discussed (1) the key mathematical principle of the task, (2) inferences they could draw from the students' work, (3) feedback that would be appropriate, and (4) suggested next steps for the student. Researchers found that the most challenging task for teachers was using assessment information to plan next steps and adapt instruction as needed. They concluded that the teachers' ability to adjust instruction based on student evidence was dependent upon strong content knowledge including understanding developmental mathematics content trajectories within a mathematics domain.

Hodgen and Marshall (2005) also concluded that teacher content knowledge was critical to effective formative assessment. They conducted a comparison study of English and mathematics lessons that focused on understanding the differences in subject-specific formative assessment practices. While the scope and content of the mathematics and English lessons were very different, the researchers concluded that there were similarities in what made each lesson formative. For example, both teachers engaged students in high quality tasks; students were encouraged to justify their thinking; and students engaged with one another, which allowed for peer feedback. Hodgen and Marshall found that both teachers had a strong content knowledge that allowed them to create rich tasks and engage students in powerful content-specific lessons. The researchers concluded that even though the pedagogy involved in formative assessment seemed generic, the teachers' content knowledge was the crucial element for creating effective assessment tasks and providing useful feedback.

A second challenge identified in the literature is fairness and equity. Morgan and Watson (2002) reported two studies—one using formative assessment and the other summative assessment. We will discuss the formative assessment study here and the summative study in the next section. The formative assessment study reported case studies of two teachers working with students in Year 7, the first year of secondary school in England. In each classroom, the researcher and teacher identified target students in the study. Researchers took extensive field notes about each target student including all verbal interactions, written work, and behavior and actions during each class session. The researcher and teacher met after each class observation and discussed the events of the class. The purpose of the study was to explore differences in the researcher's and the teacher's interpretations of students' understandings based on formative assessment data collected. Results from the study showed that teachers interpreted similar work quite differently. In particular, researchers found that early impressions of students and exceptionally strong positive or negative behavior were both strong influences on teacher's interpretations of students' work. Morgan and Watson pointed out that teacher's interpretations of formative assessment data were influenced by many factors that might have very little to do with mathematical performance.

In order for teachers to effectively use formative assessment practices, they must have strong mathematics content knowledge that allows them to make informed decisions about next instructional steps based on students' needs (Heritage et al., 2009; Hodgen and Marshall, 2005). Morgan and Watson (2002) found that factors unrelated to student achievement could influence teachers' analysis of formative assessment data.

Professional Development

Several studies on formative assessment practices in mathematics classrooms have focused on professional development to support teachers in changing their assessment practices. Lee and Wiliam (2005) and Wiliam, Lee, Harrison, and Black (2004) reported different aspects of an 18-month professional development intended to support teachers in developing their use of formative assessment. Twenty-four secondary teachers (12 mathematics and 12 science) spent 6 months learning about four strategies of formative assessment: (1) questioning, (2) descriptive feedback, (3) sharing learning criteria with students, and (4) self- and peer assessment. Teachers then created action plans that outlined what aspects of formative assessment they wanted to implement in their classrooms. During the school year, teachers were observed and had opportunities to discuss with other professionals how they were implementing the formative assessment practices described in their action plans. Wiliam and colleagues (2004) reported that teachers participating in the professional development significantly changed their perceptions of themselves as professionals.

Lee and William (2005) identified six issues that seemed to be particularly important characteristics of the professional development that resulted in significant changes in mathematics and science teachers' formative assessment practice:

1. Providing teachers with credible research evidence that formative assessment can positively impact student achievement was a huge motivating factor for teachers.
2. Providing teachers with some practical strategies to get started with formative assessment was important to ease teachers into the process.
3. Providing teachers the support of a professional learning community was critical in firmly establishing formative assessment ideas.
4. Providing teachers time to reflect on their practice through the professional development sessions and the observation cycle was necessary in supporting sustained reflection.
5. Providing teachers the time needed to change their personal practice was essential in order to see significant change.
6. Providing teachers with the flexibility to implement the formative assessment strategies they deemed appropriate was crucial to their success.

Similar to the 18-month study that was previously described, two other studies highlighted the importance of an extended professional learning experience. The study by Panizzon and Pegg (2007), described previously, was organized around a 2-year professional development experience with secondary mathematics and science teachers. Teachers were supported through professional learning communities and were involved in creating action plans to describe what aspects of formative assessment they wanted to implement. The researchers concluded that engaging teachers in extended professional development experiences was a necessary component to support change in classroom practice.

Sato et al. (2008) concluded that professional development activities like the National Board Certification process that is extended over time (3 years in this study) are conducive to supporting teacher change. The researchers reported that engaging teachers in examining their actual classroom practice as well as the artifacts of classroom practice serves as another crucial aspect of professional development.

Two themes that span across all of the professional development studies focused on CA: (1) the importance of extended professional development as opposed to a one-day workshop and (2) providing support to teachers though professional learning communities. Researchers from these studies agreed that removing the barrier of isolation and providing collegial support is critical as teachers grapple with implementing formative assessment practices that are new to them.

Summative Assessments in Mathematics

The use of summative assessments in mathematics classrooms is a long-standing tradition (see Chapter 14 for more discussion of summative assessment). As noted in the previous section, formative assessment practices are emerging as a way to compliment summative assessment in mathematics classrooms. Prior to the past decade, however, researchers found that teachers relied heavily on summative assessments almost exclusively in their mathematics classrooms (Airasian, 1991; Henke, Chen, & Goldman, 1999; Kirtman, 2002; Parsad, Lewis, & Farris, 2001; Stiggins, 2001). The studies focused on summative assessment practices in mathematics cluster into two areas: (1) classroom practice and (2) teacher judgments.

Classroom Practice

In the past 20 years, fewer studies on summative assessment practices in mathematics classrooms have been conducted than on formative assessment practices. This result is due, in large part, to the standards movement in mathematics (CCSSO, 2010; NCTM, 1989, 1991, 1995, 2000) and Black and Wiliam's (1998) seminal work acknowledging the benefits of formative assessment. The research on summative assessment in mathematics classrooms falls into two categories: (1) assessment and grading practices and (2) frequency of summative assessments.

McMillan (2001) investigated the assessment and grading practices of middle and high school teachers of mathematics, science, social studies, and English in seven Virginia school districts. This study attempted to address some of the limitations of previous studies by asking questions about particular classes of students rather than more global assessment practices and by including a large sample (N = 1,483). However, only the findings specific to mathematics teachers, which made up 25% of the sample (N = 381), are reported here. McMillan asked teachers to comment on the extent to which they used assessment and grading practices in three broad categories: (1) factors used in determining grades, (2) types of assessments, and (3) cognitive level of assessments. He found that, in determining grades, mathematics teachers relied more on academic achievement and completed homework and less on academic enablers (i.e., effort, participation, and ability), extra credit, and graded homework/use of zeroes than other subject area teachers. Regarding types of assessments, McMillan reported that mathematics teachers used constructed-response (CR) assessments less than other subject area teachers, and they used quizzes more than English and science teachers. In addition, McMillan found that mathematics teachers used assessment tasks that measured higher-order thinking more than social studies teachers. Regarding the overall findings (all content area teachers), McMillan reported that this study basically replicated what other studies had found and demonstrated that most teachers use a variety of factors in determining grades (Brookhart 1994; Cizek, Fitzgerald, Shawn, & Rachor, 1996; Cross & Frary, 1996).

Ohlsen (2007) conducted a study based on McMillan's work, except she focused only on mathematics teachers and only asked about types of assessments teachers used. In particular, participants in this study were secondary mathematics teachers in nine states who were all members of the NCTM. Ohlsen found that participants used teacher-developed assessments, major exams, and quizzes most often in assigning students' semester grades. The least commonly used assessments were oral presentations, team projects, and essay questions. Similar to McMillan's study, Ohlsen noted that some teachers included multiple assessment strategies across the semester leading to a blending of traditional assessments with some performance-based assessments.

In both of these studies, participants reported the type of assessments they used to determine students' semester grades. Clearly, teachers could use some assessment methods, such as quizzes, for formative or summative purposes. These studies are included under summative assessment practices because, from our perspective, using assessments to assign grades falls into the summative assessment category.

A second area of research on summative assessment practices in mathematics classrooms focused on the frequency in which summative assessments were used. Kika, McLaughlin, and Dixon (1992) studied the effect of frequent testing on the performance of high school algebra students. Fifty-one students were randomly assigned to either a weekly tests group or a biweekly tests group for a 2-month period. At the end of 2 months, the groups received the other treatment schedule for 2 months. This 2-month rotation continued for a period of 8 months. The students were taught by the same teacher and used the same instructional materials. Researchers found that students in the weekly tests group had statistically significant higher scores on their tests than did the biweekly tests group. The outcome was replicated with each 2-month rotation. Also of note in this study, low and middle achieving students had higher gains in the weekly tests group.

Shirvani (2009) studied the effects of more frequent uses of summative assessments by focusing on daily versus weekly quizzes. He based his study on previous work, which showed improvements by students in the daily quizzes group, but it was not statistically significant (Dineen, Taylor, & Stephens, 1989). Participants in Shirvani's study were 69 high school geometry students who were taught by the same teacher using the same instructional materials. Two classes were randomly assigned to each group. The treatment group received a 10-minute quiz at the end of each class period, and the control group received a quiz every Friday. The treatment lasted for 6 weeks, and both groups took the same final exam. Results indicated that the treatment group (daily quizzes) significantly outperformed the control group on the final exam. Shirvani also investigated the effects of homework assignments for each group, and the treatment group also had significantly higher homework scores.

Studies on summative assessment classroom practices focused on assessment and grading practices and frequency of assessments. McMillan (2001) and Ohlsen (2007) found that teachers still rely mainly on more traditional types of summative assessments such as tests and quizzes. However, a small trend toward using more performance-based assessments, such as projects and presentations, in summative ways, was noted in both studies. Using summative assessments more frequently (weekly versus biweekly and daily versus weekly) reflected better student performance in secondary mathematics classrooms (Kika et al., 1992; Shirvani, 2009).

Teacher Judgments

Three studies focused broadly on teachers' judgments relative to summative assessment in mathematics classrooms. Each study looked at teacher judgments in different contexts. Morgan and Watson (2002), as noted in the previous section, reported the results of two studies: one using formative assessment and the other summative. In the summative study, teachers were asked to review student work that was part of the national examination given to students at age 16. This examination had two components: (1) a traditional timed exam scored by external reviewers and (2) one or more extended problem-solving tasks scored by classroom teachers. Eleven experienced teachers from five schools participated in the study. Teachers first solved the task themselves and then assessed the students' work on the task. Next, teachers discussed with interviewers the judgments they made in ranking students' work. Morgan and Watson found great diversity in the judgments that different teachers made about the same work. For example, some teachers ranked one piece of student work highest and other teachers ranked it as lowest. Morgan and Watson explained that many factors such as prior experiences, knowledge, and beliefs influence teacher judgments about student performance in mathematics.

A second study focused on teachers' judgments about students' overall mathematics achievement. Martinez, Stecher, and Borko (2009) analyzed data from the Early Childhood Longitudinal Survey (ECLS) of third- and fifth-grade students ($N = 15{,}305$ and $N = 11{,}820$, respectively) in order to compare teacher judgments of student achievement with students' standardized test scores. They found that teacher judgments correlated strongly with the standardized test scores. While this relationship was maintained across schools, it varied considerably across teachers. The researchers suggested that this variance could be related to teacher background and classroom context. Furthermore, the variation seemed associated with certain CA practices. For example, teachers whose judgments of students' achievement were strongly correlated with standardized tests also exhibited the following characteristics: (1) rated student effort (third grade) and completed homework (fifth grade) as important in student assessment, (2) used formative assessments more than summative assessments to evaluate their students, and (3) held the same standards in evaluating all students.

Black, Harrison, Hodgen, Marshall, and Serret (2010) explored teacher judgments of their own summative assessments, in particular on their judgments of the validity of the assessments. Twelve teachers, 6 in English and 6 in mathematics from three secondary schools in England participated in the study. The 20-month study began with teachers examining their own summative assessments and judging their validity. Initially, teachers thought their assessments were valid until researchers challenged their ideas about validity. Over the course of the study and professional development, teachers engaged in activities that allowed them to better understand validity, create more valid assessments, and make more accurate judgments about the validity of their assessments.

Studies focusing on teacher judgments relative to summative assessments found that many factors impact teacher judgment. Morgan and Watson (2002) found variation in teacher judgments of open-ended student work on a national examination. They reported that prior experiences, knowledge, and beliefs accounted for the variation in teacher judgments. Comparing teacher judgments of students' achievement to standardized tests, Martinez and colleagues (2009) reported strong alignment between the two until data were examined at the teacher level where much variation was detected. The variation was attributed to teacher background and classroom context. Black and colleagues (2010) focused on teachers' judgments of the validity of their summative assessments. As a result of participating in the professional development provided through the study, teachers' judgments about the validity of their assessments improved.

Impact of External Assessments

As a result of the school accountability movement in the 1990s, state education agencies enhanced their student accountability systems and placed more emphasis on student performance results with regard to district, school, and teacher accountability (see Chapter 4 of this volume). Many studies have been conducted to explore the impact of these state assessments. In this section, we provide an overview of the studies conducted specific to mathematics. Three of the studies focus on the impact of state assessments on classroom instructional practices and one study on the impact on CAs.

Firestone, Mayrowetz, and Fairman (1998) examined how implementation of a new state assessment changed middle mathematics teachers' instructional practices. A group of 82 middle school teachers and administrators in five districts in Maryland and Maine were interviewed regarding changes in their mathematics instruction as a result of the state mathematics assessments. The researchers also conducted classroom observations to validate the responses to interviews. The results indicated that the effects of state testing on classroom teaching were not particularly strong. The researchers concluded that while state assessments promoted some changes, like aligning the content of lessons taught with test content, they were less influential in actually changing instructional practices.

Two other studies also investigated the impact of state assessments in Maryland. Lane, Parke, and Stone (2002) investigated the impact of the Maryland School Performance Assessment Program (MSPAP) and the Maryland Learning Outcomes (MLO) on mathematics classroom instructional practices. Ninety elementary and middle schools in Maryland participated in the study. The results were quite different from the previous study and indicated that principals and teachers reported using MSPAP as a source for making changes in instruction, especially with regard to problem solving, reasoning, and communication. They also found that the schools for which teachers reported that MSPAP had an impact on their mathematics instruction also had greater MSPAP performance gains in mathematics over the 5 years. It is important to note that this study did not include any observation data so all results were based on teacher and administrator self-reports and student achievement data.

The third study focused on Maryland's state assessment (Parke & Lane, 2008) explored the extent to which mathematics classroom activities in Maryland were aligned with Maryland learning outcomes and the MSPAP. Data were collected from 3,948 instructional, assessment, and test preparation activities from a statewide stratified random sample of 250 teachers in the tested grades (3, 5, and 8) and nontested grades (2, 4, and 7). Teachers also completed questionnaires about their classroom practice. Parke and Lane found that most classroom activities aligned with aspects of state assessment and standards. They reported minimal differences in classroom activities across grades, but the degree of alignment was higher for instructional activities than for assessment activities. Data from questionnaires indicated that teachers perceived a greater alignment between their instructional practices and MSPAP than the collected activities actually indicated. This finding aligns with the Firestone et al. (1998) study.

A fourth study on the impact of state assessments was conducted in New Jersey. Schorr, Bulgar, Razze, Monfils, and Firestone (2003) conducted a 3-year study on the changes in mathematics teaching in the state as a result of new state assessments. The study focused on the instructional practices of fourth-grade teachers ($N = 63$) who were interviewed and observed during mathematics lessons. Like the previous studies, researchers from this study found that teachers reported making changes in their practice, but observations in classrooms did not provide evidence of the described changes.

The final study on the impact of state assessment on classroom practice focused specifically on CAs. Boyd (2008) found that a pending state assessment had little impact on middle school mathematics teachers' CAs. He collected and analyzed CAs from nine eighth-grade mathematics teachers from 1 year prior to the introduction of the new eighth-grade Ohio Achievement Test (OAT) in mathematics and 1 year after the test had been implemented. The teachers' CAs given across the 2 school years were compared to determine the impact of the state test on the teacher assessments. Findings indicated that about 87% of teachers' CA items were at the lowest depth-of-knowledge level during both years, while state assessments included items with higher levels. Teachers also relied heavily on curriculum materials for their test items, and these materials tended to assess lower-level skills such as students' ability to recall basic facts or perform routine procedures. Boyd concluded that the presence of the state assessment did not entice teachers to assess students at higher depth-of-knowledge levels.

Studies on the impact of state assessments on classroom practices in mathematics revealed mixed results. The four reviewed studies found that state assessments did not radically change teacher practice. Although three of these studies included teacher reports of perceived changes in instructional practice, classroom observations did not confirm these perceptions. The one study that reported significant changes in instructional practice (Lane et al., 2002) was based solely on teacher and administrator self-reports.

Areas of Further Research

In general, more research on the effects and effectiveness of formative assessment practices on student learning is needed. Black and Wiliam's (1998) seminal review of the research on formative assessment has resulted in an increase in the number of research studies focused on formative assessment. However, not many studies have been conducted specific to mathematics. In particular, the use of technology as a formative assessment tool has not been tested or explored sufficiently to determine its effectiveness in this capacity.

The Standards for Mathematical Practice from the *Common Core State Standards in Mathematics* (CCSSO, 2010) present an important area for future research involving CA. As mathematics teachers across the country are encouraged to find ways to engage students in the mathematical practices (make sense of problems, reason abstractly and quantitatively, construct viable arguments and critique the reasoning of others, model with mathematics, use tools strategically, attend to precision, look for and make use of structure, and look for and express regularity in repeated reasoning) research on using formative assessment practices to track this learning will be extremely important. Another challenge will be finding summative ways to validly assess students' understanding of the mathematical practices.

Wiliam (2006) indicated that formative assessment tools or strategies will only be effective if teachers can implement them as part of their regular classroom practice. He suggested, "The task of improving formative assessment is substantially, if not mainly, about teacher professional development" (p. 287). While a few studies have focused on the impact of professional development on mathematics teachers' implementation of formative assessment strategies, much more research is needed. Lee and Wiliam (2005) provided a valuable starting place by identifying six crucial aspects of such professional development. The need for research on professional development is not limited to formative assessment. Black and colleagues (2010) described a professional development model used to assist teachers in developing valid summative assessments. While this study presented some helpful suggestions about professional development, the findings are limited. Research is needed with regard to creating quality experiences for teachers and determining the extent to which the professional development has been effective. Furthermore, additional research focused on teachers' knowledge of assessment methods and practices would provide useful information in developing professional development to assist teachers in developing valid summative CAs.

Student performance on high-stakes accountability assessments has become increasingly more important. Now, more than ever, teachers must develop and organize CAs to ensure that they align both in content and cognitive demand with these assessments. This skill requires that teachers not only know the mathematics content and cognitive demand of the state assessments but how to design classroom assessments that prepare students for the state assessments. And teachers must know how to prepare students for these CAs. Research on professional development strategies that are effective in preparing teachers for these important tasks is needed.

Conclusion

As this research summary reveals, mathematics classrooms are changing. Standards change, curricula change, teaching practices change, students change, and with them, assessments and assessment practices must change. It is critical that high quality research not only documents these changes but identifies strategies and support to help teachers adjust to them. Assessment permeates every level of education, from standardized international and national assessments, to state accountability assessments, to classroom assessments. As high-stakes assessments change and as the mathematical competencies for success change, so classroom assessments should change in mathematics content but more importantly in mathematics processes and practices. Hopefully, this chapter has provided useful information to help researchers and others address issues of change in their work.

References

Airasian, P. (1991). *Classroom assessment.* New York: McGraw-Hill.

Black, P., Harrison, C., Hodgen, J., Marshall, B., & Serret, N. (2010). Validity in teacher's summative assessments. *Assessment in Education: Principles, Policy & Practice, 17*(2), 215–232.

Black, P. & Wiliam, D. (1998). Inside the black box: Raising standards through classroom assessment. *Phi Delta Kappan, 80*(2), 139–147.

Brookhart, S. M. (1994). Teachers' grading: Practice and theory. *Applied Measurement in Education, 7,* 279–301.

Boyd, B. T. (2008). Effects of state tests on classroom test items in mathematics. *School Science and Mathematics, 108*(6), 251–262.

Cizek, G. J., Fitzgerald, S. M., & Rachor, R. E. (1996). Teachers' assessment practices: Preparation, isolation and the kitchen sink. *Educational Assessment, 3*(2), 159–179.

Council of Chief State School Officers. (2010). *Common core state standards in mathematics.* Washington, DC: Author.

Cross, L. H., & Frary, R. B. (1996). *Hodgepodge grading: Endorsed by students and teachers alike.* Paper presented at the annual meeting of the National Council on Measurement in Education, New York.

Dineen, P., Taylor, J., & Stephens, L. (1989). The effect of testing frequency upon the achievement of students in high school mathematics courses. *School Science and Mathematics, 89*(3), 197–200.

Firestone, W., Mayrowetz, D., & Fairman, J. (1998). Performance-based assessment and instructional change: The effects of testing in Maine and Maryland. *Educational Evaluation and Policy Analysis, 20*(2), 95–113.

Fontana, D., & Fernandes, M. (1994). Improvements in mathematics performance as a consequence of self-assessment in Portuguese primary school pupils. *British Journal of Educational Psychology, 64*(4), 407–417.

Henke, R. R., Chen, X., & Goldman, G. (1999). *What happens in classrooms? Instructional practices in elementary and secondary schools, 1994–95.* Washington, DC: National Center for Education.

Heritage, M., Kim, J., Vendlinski, T., & Herman, J. (2009). From evidence to action: A seamless process in formative assessment. *Educational Measurement: Issues and Practice, 28*(3), 24–31.

Hodgen, J., & Marshall, B. (2005). Assessment for learning English and mathematics: A comparison. *Curriculum Journal, 16*(2), 153–176.

Kika, F. M., McLaughlin, T. F. & Dixon, J. (1992). Effects of frequent testing on secondary algebra students. *Journal of Educational Research, 85*(3), 159–162.

Kirtman, L. (2002, May 8). *Policy and practice: Restructuring teachers' work.* Retrieved from http://epaa.asu.edu/epaa/v10n25/

Lane, S., Parke, C. S., & Stone, C. A. (2002). The impact of a state performance-based assessment and accountability program on mathematics instruction and student learning: Evidence from survey data and school performance. *Educational Assessment, 8*(4), 279–315.

Leahy, S., Lyon, C., Thompson, M., & Wiliam, D. (2005). Classroom assessment: Minute-by-minute and day-by-day. *Educational Leadership, 63*(3), 18–24.

Lee, C., & Wiliam, D. (2005). Studying changes in the practices of two teachers developing assessment for learning. *Teacher Development, 9*(2), 265–283.

Li, M., Yin, Y., Ruiz-Primo, M. A., & Morozov, A. (2011). *Identifying effective feedback practices on student mathematics learning: A literature synthesis.* Paper presented at the annual meeting of the American Educational Research Association, New Orleans, LA.

Lin, P. J. (2006). Conceptualization of teachers' understanding of students' mathematical learning by using assessment tasks. *International Journal of Science and Mathematics Education, 4*(3), 545–580

Martinez, F. M., Stecher, B. & Borko, H. (2009). Classroom assessment practices, teacher judgments, and student achievement in Mathematics: Evidence from the ECLS. *Educational Assessment, 14*, 78–102.

McMillan, J. H. (2001). Secondary teachers' classroom assessment and grading practices. *Educational Measurement: Issues and Practice, 20*(1), 20–32.

Morgan, C. & Watson, A. (2002). The interpretative nature of teachers' assessment of students' mathematics: Issues for equity. *Journal for Research in Mathematics Education, 33*(2), 78–110.

National Council of Teachers of Mathematics. (1989). *Curriculum and evaluation standards for school mathematics.* Reston, VA: Author.

National Council of Teachers of Mathematics. (1991). *Professional standards for teaching mathematics.* Reston, VA: Author.

National Council of Teachers of Mathematics. (1995). *Assessment standards for school mathematics.* Reston, VA: Author.

National Council of Teachers of Mathematics. (2000). *Principles and standards for school mathematics.* Reston, VA: Author.

Ohlsen, M. T. (2007). Classroom assessment practices of secondary school members of NCTM. *American Secondary Education, 36*(1), 4–14.

Panizzon, D., & Pegg, J. (2007). Assessment practices: Empowering mathematics and science teachers in rural secondary schools to enhance student learning. *International Journal of Science and Mathematics Education, 6*(2), 417–436.

Parke, C. S. & Lane, S. (2008). Examining alignment between state performance assessment and mathematics classroom activities. *Journal of Educational Research, 101*(3), 132–147.

Parsad, B., Lewis, L., & Farris, E. (2001). *Teacher preparation and professional development: 2000* (NCES 2001-088). Washington, DC: National Center for Education Statistics.

Peterson, E., & Siadat, M. V. (2009). Combination of formative and summative assessment instruments in elementary algebra classes: A prescription for success. *Journal of Applied Research in the Community College, 16*(2), 92–102.

Ross, J. A. (1995). Effects of feedback on student behaviour in cooperative learning groups in a grade 7 math class. *Elementary School Journal, 96*, 125–143.

Ross, J. A., Hogaboam-Gray, A., & Rolheiser, C. (2001). *Effects of self-evaluation training in mathematical achievement.* Paper presented at the annual meeting of the American Educational Research Association, Seattle, WA.

Ross, J. A., Hogaboam-Gray, A., & Rolheiser, C. (2002). Student self-evaluation in grade 5-6 mathematics effects on problem-solving achievement. *Educational Assessment, 8*(1), 43–59.

Sato, M., Wei, R. C., & Darling-Hammond, L. (2008). Improving teachers' assessment practices through professional development: The case of National Board Certification. *American Educational Research Journal, 45*(3), 669–700.

Schorr, R. Y., Bulgar, S., Razze, J. S., Monfils, L. F., & Firestone, W. A. (2003). Teaching mathematics and science. In R. Y. Schorr, W. A. Firestone, & L. Monfils (Eds.), *The ambiguity of teaching to the test: Standards, assessment, and educational reform.* Mahwah, NJ: Lawrence Erlbaum.

Schunk, D. (1996). Goal and self-evaluative influences during children's cognitive skill learning. *American Educational Research Journal, 33*, 359–382.

Shirley, M. L., Irving, K. E., Sanalan, V. A., Pape, S. J., & Owens, D. T. (2011). The practicality of implementation connecting classroom technology in secondary mathematics and science classrooms. *International Journal of Science and Mathematics Education, 9*(2), 459–481.

Shirvani, H. (2009). Examining an assessment strategy on high school mathematics achievement: Daily quizzes vs. weekly tests. *American Secondary Education, 38*(1), 34–45.

Stiggins, R. J. (2001). The unfulfilled promise of classroom assessment. *Educational Measurement: Issues and Practice, 20*(3), 5–15.

Suurtamm, C., Koch, M., & Arden, A. (2010). Teachers' assessment in mathematics: Classrooms in the context of reform. *Assessment in Education: Principles, Policy & Practice, 17*(4), 399–417.

Wiliam, D. (2006). Formative assessment: Getting the focus right. *Educational Assessment, 11*(3 & 4), 283–289.

Wiliam, D. Lee, C. Harrison, C., & Black, P. J. (2004). Teachers developing assessment for learning: Impact on student achievement. *Assessment in Education: Principles Policy and Practice, 11*(1), 49–65.

26

Research on Assessment in the Social Studies Classroom

Cheryl A. Torrez

Elizabeth Ann Claunch-Lebsack

We take a focused approach in addressing research on assessment in the social studies classroom with an emphasis on teaching and learning. The chapter begins with the purpose of social studies education and a definition of assessment in the social studies classroom. Secondly, an overview of social studies assessment in historical contexts is provided, followed by recent trends in social studies curriculum and assessment. Following this, the chapter addresses promising research developments on assessment in social studies classrooms. In conclusion, a discussion and call for further research is offered. A thorough examination and analysis of the extant literature regarding assessment, social studies education, and social studies classrooms was conducted. The following criteria were used to select the works that were reviewed: direct relevance to the topic, dates published, studies addressing K–12 schools in the United States, empirical studies, and literature reviews.

Purpose of Social Studies Education

Academicians have debated, as early as the 19th century with the Committee of Ten (Hertzberg, 1988), and continue to debate the nature and purposes of social studies (e.g., Butts, 1989; Evans, 2004; Saxe, 1991; Thornton, 2005). The National Council for the Social Studies (NCSS) (1994) has defined social studies in the following way:

> Social Studies is the integrated study of the social sciences and humanities to promote civic competence. Within the school program, social studies provides coordinated, systematic study drawing upon such disciplines as anthropology, archaeology, economics, geography, history, law, philosophy, political science, psychology, religion, and sociology, as well as appropriate content from the humanities, mathematics, and natural sciences. The primary purpose of social studies is to help young people make informed and reasoned decisions for the public good as citizens of a culturally diverse, democratic society in an interdependent world. (p. vii)

It is within this citizenship construct that social studies curriculum and instruction in K–12 classrooms generally occurs (Marker & Mehlinger, 1992). Drawing upon the NCSS definition, Parker (2012) indicated two goals for social studies education: (1) social understanding and (2) civic efficacy. Social studies scholars and teacher educators encourage curriculum in which K–12 students engage in inquiry and not in rote memorization of dates and facts (e.g., Bower & Lobdell, 2005; Hoge, Field, Foster, & Nickell, 2004; Thornton, 2005). Levstik & Barton (2011) called for *disciplined inquiry*, which has its roots in the belief that "meaningful learning involves not just mastering the content of a subject but understanding the nature and purpose of that subject" (p. 16). In a social studies classroom, we expect to see students asking questions, finding information to answer their questions, evaluating the sources of information, developing conclusions based upon evidence, and creating interpretive accounts. At a K–12 level, students should engage in authentic work, and classroom assessment (CA) should correspond to authentic activities (NCSS, 2010).

Definition of Assessment in the Social Studies Classroom

The extant literature is replete with studies on assessment, testing, and evaluation, yet there is a paucity of empirical research focusing specifically on assessment in the social studies classroom. The last four editions of the *Handbook of Research on Teaching* included chapters on research on social studies (Armento, 1986; Metcalf, 1963; Seixas, 2001; Shaver & Larkins, 1973), but none of these included a substantive mention of assessment in the social studies classroom. Neither the *Handbook of Research on Social Studies Teaching and Learning* (Shaver, 1991) nor the *Handbook of Research in Social Studies Education* (Levstik & Tyson, 2008) included chapters on research on assessment in the social studies classroom. A search of *Theory and Research in Social Education (TRSE)* also resulted in similar findings. Therefore, in providing an overview of research on assessment focused specifically in the social studies classroom, a larger framework of assessment is essential.

Within the context of any K–12 classroom, curriculum, instruction, and assessment, by design, should be intertwined. Madaus and Kellaghan (1996) defined assessment "as an activity to show what a person knows or can do" (p. 120). They further stated that a teacher uses information derived from assessment to make curricular decisions. Shepard (2001) suggested a framework for understanding a reformed view of assessment "where assessment plays an integral role in teaching and learning" (p. 1066). This is with a view toward transforming CA practices to illuminate and enhance the learning process. Wolf, Bixby, Glenn, and Gardner (1991) suggested a construct for alternative assessment that "might permit the assessment of thinking rather than the possession of information" (p. 33). These definitions and purposes of CA provide a framework for the social studies classroom.

In their 2008 *Handbook of Research in Social Studies Education* chapter on assessment and accountability in the social studies, Grant and Salinas wrote, "the term *assessment* means little because it can mean so much" (p. 119). They clearly differentiated CA from standardized assessment. CA may be formative or summative and can also indicate the "form in which the judgment is instantiated as, for example, multiple-choice tests, oral presentations, worksheets, and the like" (p. 120). Standardized assessment is "any measure of students' aptitude and/or ability that is determined by an agency or organization outside the school" (p. 120).

Within the social studies classroom then, assessment must be linked to the overarching goals of the social studies curriculum; a tangible connection between curriculum and assessment should be visible (NCSS, 1999). The primary characteristic of social studies CA is that it serves a constructive purpose; it benefits teaching and learning (Darling-Hammond, Einbender, Frelow, & Ley-King, 1993; Levstik & Barton, 2011; NCSS, 2004). For students, assessment tasks allow them to show what they know and are able to do rather than what they don't know. Constructive assessment gives students as many ways of showing what they know as possible. This can occur through formal and informal measures; through tasks selected by the teacher and the student; and through writing, speaking, and doing other presentation methods (Levstik & Barton, 2011). The social studies practitioner literature is replete with prescriptive ways for social studies teachers to implement constructive assessment (e.g., social studies methods textbooks, Web sites for teachers, and NCSS journals). For example, Gallavan (2009a, 2009b) described the purpose of assessment and numerous ways to develop and use social studies CAs, and Alleman and Brophy (1999a) set forth a list of principles for teachers when developing alternative assessment tools.

Within the research literature, a clear distinction is made between classroom uses of assessment and external accountability systems (Grant, 2006; Kornhaber, 2004; Shepard, 2001). Grant and Salinas (2008), one of the few reviews of assessment and social studies, addressed standardized assessment (external accountability measures) not CA. However, we limit much of this chapter to research on assessment that informs teacher and student—CA rather than *standardized* assessment.

Since assessment is part and parcel of curriculum and instruction, assessment activities should reflect authentic social studies activities and be performance based (Hart, 1999; NCSS, 2011). This has not always been the case, as the following section illustrates. For decades, testing and measurement served external purposes and did little to provide usable and useful information to social studies teachers (Seixas, 2001).

Social Studies Assessment in a Historical Context

The evolution of assessment in the social studies classroom mirrors the changes to assessment in all content areas, and each of these reflect changes in psychology, curriculum, politics, business, and the purposes of schooling. Educational changes in curriculum, instruction, and assessment do not occur in isolation but as a reflection of external changes in society (Flinders & Thornton, 1998; Marshall, Sears, Anderson Allen, Roberts, & Schubert, 2007).

Historically, the majority of social studies tests, both standardized and objective-classroom based tests, emphasized rote recall (Perkins, 1992). Traditionally, social studies content was taught and assessed in a mimetic manner rather than in transformative manner (Thornton, 1994). Scriven (1967) noted the connection between this type of curriculum and assessment, indicating that a history curriculum that consisted solely of memorizing names and dates could not be thought of as *good*, even if the students memorized the information. There was no thoughtful consideration of content, just repetition of information from the textbook (Hertzberg, 1985).

There is minimal literature on the history of assessment in social studies. Alleman and Brophy (1999b) provided a snapshot of historical trends in social studies assessment highlighting ways in which the field moved beyond testing for the sole purpose of grading students. Superka, Vigliani, and Hedstrom (1978) described instruments used to evaluate aspects of K–12 social studies programs. These included general social studies achievement tests, discipline specific knowledge tests, and tests focused on assessing critical thinking skills. However, Alleman and Brophy (1997) indicated that such instruments were "rarely used at the classroom level because they are costly in time, money and effort" (p. 335). Kurfman's (1982) synthesis of evaluation in social studies indicated that teacher-made tests were implemented more frequently than standardized, norm-referenced tests and tests that were provided with basal curriculum materials. Teachers historically have preferred assessments that inform their next-steps curricular decision making.

By the end of the 20th century, standardized, norm-referenced testing of social studies had become well established. The National Assessment of Educational Progress (NAEP) tests were first administered in 1969 for testing history and geography knowledge (National Center for Educational Statistics, 2011). The New York Regents exam began during the Civil War (Watson, 2010). General knowledge tests such as the Iowa Tests of Basic Skills (ITBS), tests of the College Entrance Exam, and Advanced Placement (AP) tests were widespread by the end of the 20th century. None of these are considered CAs although they may influence the teaching of social studies and the activities in which students engage (Grant & Salinas, 2008; National Assessment of Educational Progress [NAEP], 2011; Nuthall & Alton-Lee, 1995).

Increased high-stakes testing became dominant in the 1980s along with the *back-to-basics movement* (Kurfman, 1991; Marker & Mehlinger, 1992). Popham (1987) defined high-stakes tests as "examinations that are associated with important consequences for examinees" and "examinations whose scores are seen as reflections of instructional quality" (p. 680). Furthermore, in his chapter *Testing as Context for Social Education*, Kurfman (1991) noted that by 1990, "a common criticism of social studies tests is the failure to measure student attainment of more complex, higher-order thinking skills" (pp. 313–314). He further noted that one of the effects of testing on curriculum and instruction is "what gets tested is what gets taught," and Bracey (1987) cautioned against the fragmentation and narrowing of curriculum. Concomitantly, toward the end of the 20th century, increased emphasis on meaningful and alternative assessment in the social studies classroom surfaced in tandem to the evolution of social studies from doing and knowing to experiencing and making meaning (Alleman & Brophy, 1999b; Newmann, 1990). In 1999, the NCSS journal, *Social Education*, published a special issue focused solely on *Authentic Assessment in Social Studies* that included topics such as student self-assessment, observation as an assessment tool, rubrics, and misuse of evaluation tools. Clearly, social studies classroom teachers were being encouraged to move toward assessment that informed their instructional decision making. There is, however, a noticeable absence in the social studies scholarly works investigating the ways in which and the extent to which teachers and students used authentic assessment to illuminate and enhance the learning of social studies.

Recent Trends: Social Studies Curriculum and Assessment

By the beginning of the 21st century, social studies educators' focus on assessment in the social studies classroom had moved squarely into authentic methods of assessment that reflected the disciplined inquiry of the social studies. In 2004, the NCSS issued a position statement regarding assessment indicating that "fair and equitable assessment of all students must be an integral part of any social studies program" (p. 290). It further called for connections between curriculum, instruction, and assessment. Its suggestions for alternative assessments included portfolios, performance assessments, written reports, research projects, and other demonstrations of student knowledge and skills. The NCSS also stated that assessments should be used only for the purpose for which they were designed: to provide information to students, parents, and teachers. Finally, "Assessments of students in social studies should be designed and used to further the goal of educating students to be active citizens in our democratic society" (NCSS, 2004, p. 290).

This position statement was, in part, a response to broader educational changes. In 2001, the No Child Left Behind Act of 2001 (NCLB) (U.S. Department of Education, 2002) was enacted. One consequence of this legislation was that external standardized assessment began to drive curriculum and instruction. "Indeed, assessments not only drive instruction, they often determine whether any instruction occurs at all" (Levstik & Tyson, 2008, p. 8). The national trend to measure all students' learning by standardized testing resulted in an increased use of externally developed social studies curricula (Segall, 2003). Utilizing textbooks *as* curriculum and assessment tools limits the depth of understanding and engagement in social studies by students (Brophy, 1990; Brophy, McMahon, & Prawatt, 1991; Brozo & Tomlinson, 1986; Guzzetti, Kowalinski, & McGowan, 1992; Sewall, 1988).

Predictably, new state standards and attending to the content of standardized tests affected social studies teachers' decisions regarding content and instruction (Grant, 2006; Grant et al., 2002). Social studies assessments, rather than informing teacher and student, were increasingly utilized for test practice (Abrams, Pedulla, & Madaus, 2003; Pedulla et al., 2003; Volger, 2006).

Another consequence was the narrowing of social studies curriculum and instructional time (Boyle-Baise, Hsu, Johnson, Serriere, & Stewart, 2008; Snow-Gerono & Franklin, 2007; von Zastrow & Janc, 2004). A 3-year study conducted in North Carolina found that only 23% of elementary teachers taught social studies on a daily basis all year (Rock et al., 2004). Instead, social studies was integrated into reading and other curricular areas that resulted in a marginalization of social studies content. VanFossen's (2005) study of elementary schools in Indiana indicated that, on average, less than 18 minutes per day was dedicated to social studies. VanFossen and McGrew (2008) concluded that the status of elementary social studies education in Indiana was worsening, when compared to VanFossen's (2005) earlier study, and social studies in the elementary curriculum was a "discipline at risk." The marginalization of social studies instruction is not a new phenomenon (Fitchett & Heafner, 2010; Svengalis, 1992). In the 1960s, the age of Sputnik, social studies as a discipline was deemphasized as greater attention was given to mathematics and science (Marshall et al., 2007). However, the *extent* of social studies marginalization in the early 21st century was a new phenomenon.

Entering the second decade of the 21st century, Levstik (2008), in describing what happens in social studies classrooms, stated the following:

> Patterns of instruction persist, with textbooks still predominating, but with some teachers drawing on other resources, and engaging

> students in the kind of inquiry social studies scholars and NCSS standards tend to call for. Upon closer inspection, though, fault lines begin to appear. Restructuring and high-stakes testing take a toll on social studies. . . . At the elementary level, social studies appears to be in even more trouble. Few elementary teachers perceive themselves as experts in regard to social studies. Moreover, as high-stakes assessment focuses on reading and mathematics, social studies too often disappears entirely, almost disappears as it is integrated into reading programs, or survives at such a low level students are as likely to misunderstand as to understand it. (p. 59)

American social studies classrooms, for the early part of the 21st century, have been in a near state of atrophy as the disconnect between classroom realities and best social studies practices widens. Diminished social studies instruction has resulted in the silencing of constructive assessments of student learning, which may have constrained new classroom research assessment projects. Practitioner research has also been impacted by standardized assessments. VanSledright (2002), in one of the few published studies addressing assessment, albeit implicitly in the social studies classroom, noted that the high-stakes tests his fifth-grade students were required to take seldom assessed the "sorts of ideas and issues that a confrontation with history's interpretive paradox is likely to provoke" (p. 1108).

In many ways, it appears as though social studies curriculum, instruction, and assessment came full circle in one century—as though the field ended up right where it started. As the next section indicates, there are some promising, emerging research developments on assessment in the social studies classroom.

Promising Developments

There is a small, emergent body of research that indicates some social studies teachers are resisting the trend to teach to tests and to test preparation activities. Rather, they believe that assessing and teaching of the social studies must be varied and multidimensional (Gradwell, 2006; Grant & Gradwell, 2005; Segall, 2003; Smith, 2006; van Hover, 2006; van Hover, Hicks, & Washington, 2011). These case studies do not indicate widespread sweeping changes within K–12 classrooms, and more research would benefit the field, but these studies do provide a foundation for further exploration by scholars.

Action Research Studies

Additionally, within the scholarly literature, a small number of action research studies on assessment in social studies classrooms have been published. Brookhart and Durkin's (2003) single-case descriptive study investigated the perceptions of high school students regarding varying CAs. The findings of this teacher research study indicated that common student perceptions for assessments was that their task was to internalize the teacher's or the text's material, and students perceived "hard work" in terms of time rather than conceptually difficult work. The instructional context in terms of the curriculum and instructional strategies used before each of the assessments were not well addressed in the study.

Kelley's (2006) action research study investigated the development of inquiry skills—specifically questioning—in her kindergarten classroom. Her findings were consistent with literature indicating that questioning strategies can be taught to and developed by young learners and that these kindergartners were able to ask social studies specific inquiry questions. VanSledright (2002), in a practitioner–researcher study, investigated his fifth-grade social studies students' disciplined inquiry. Informal formative assessment resulted in additional instructional decision making and shed light on the inherent pedagogical tensions between disciplined inquiry and standardized assessment. These three studies may provide evidence to social studies scholars that a researcher presence in K–12 classrooms is necessary in order to conduct empirical research on assessment in social studies classrooms.

In the following sections on promising developments, qualities of strong assessment practices are provided with a call for disciplined inquiry, along with an example of a program using disciplined inquiry in a systematic fashion and a suggestion for rethinking and expanding CA. These are included, purposefully, not to be prescriptive but rather to suggest that social studies scholars may need to seek alternative means and venues for research on assessment in the social studies classroom.

Research on Social Studies Assessment

Distilling the sparse research on social studies CA reveals the shared qualities of good CA practices: (1) assessments inform both student and teachers (Darling-Hammond et al., 1993; Levstik & Barton, 2011; NCSS, 2004), (2) assessments should illuminate and enhance the learning process (Shepard, 2001), (3) assessments must be varied and ongoing (Stiggins, 1991; Wiggins, 1998), and (4) assessments should reflect authentic social studies activities and be linked to overarching social studies goals (Hart, 1999; NCSS, 2011). Discipline-based inquiry projects, with thoughtful consideration in the implementation, provide opportunities for ongoing formative assessment as the interaction between content and student illuminate the thinking process and a summative assessment in the completed project. Classrooms in which such projects occur are rich sites for social studies scholars to engage in much needed research.

Disciplined Inquiry

The importance of inquiry skills in the social studies is essential as student-generated questions are at the core of the discipline. Since 1963 when Project Social Studies was launched by the Cooperative Research Branch of the United States Office of Education in order to teach inquiry skills systematically, inquiry has been encouraged as part of the social studies curriculum. In defining disciplined inquiry, Levstik & Barton (2011) stated that the term refers "to purposeful investigations that take place within a community that establishes goals, standards, and procedures of study" (p. 19). Here, again, the practitioner literature focuses much attention on how to implement disciplined inquiry and assessment in social studies classrooms, but the absence of empirical research on assessment of disciplined inquiry in classrooms is glaring. Promising systematized programs, such as the one provided next, may provide a stepping ground for research on assessment in social studies classrooms.

National History Day

The National History Day (NHD) program is a research-based example of disciplined inquiry and using the historical research project as both a formative assessment and summative evaluation of student learning (see www.nhd.org). The goals of the program are to improve history teaching and learning by illuminating the research process professional historians follow and engage students in an original research. The structure of the program is for students in Grades 6 to 12 to select a historical topic around an annual theme and engage in original historical research. The program is meant to be integrated into social studies classrooms.

NHD recently published the results of a longitudinal study of the effects of learning history through historical research. The multistate studies, conducted from 2008 to 2010, gathered empirical evidence on the impact of student-driven historical research on student achievement in social studies, and in other core academic areas. The studies also assessed curriculum and instructional strategies that improve the teaching and learning of history. Although not a study of assessment in the social studies classroom, this programmatic evaluation does provide evidence of the connection between curriculum, instruction, and assessment in the social studies classroom.

These studies relied to a large extent on standardized assessment measures such as annual statewide tests, AP tests, end-of-course exams as well as students' grades, GPAs, feedback from teachers and students about engagement, motivation, and attitudes toward history and related subjects. The results were positive and included findings suggesting that NHD students outperform their peers on standardized tests in all subject areas and achieved commended performance on social studies assessments (National History Day [NHD], 2011). The focus on disciplined inquiry, with NHD, has multiple benefits for students. What remains unclear is how teachers and students use formative and summative assessments within these classrooms to improve teaching and learning—a research topic that would immensely benefit the social studies field.

Research on New Ways of Assessing Learning

Additional perspectives on assessment are emerging and show promise. There is evidence that students attend to visual stimulation and engage with images before text (Burmark, 2002; Caviglioli & Harris, 2003; Hyerle, 2000; Moline, 1996; Walling, 2005). Overreliance on language-based assessments creates a blind spot into student understanding. Language is not an indicator of understanding (Claunch, 2002). For instance, in the drawing (see Figure 26.1), students were asked to explain Paul Revere's role in the American Revolution.

This student-created image was used as an unintended yet constructive assessment after a unit on the American Revolution. The setting was a sixth-grade classroom after 9 weeks of studying the American Revolution. The student had participated fully in the reading of the textbook, taking chapter tests (scoring 80% and above), writing a script for the Lexington battle, and reading several fictional novels. The teacher's assessment of this sixth grader was that the student understood the Revolutionary War. When the teacher asked the student to illustrate Henry Wadsworth Longfellow's famous poem, it was a window into understanding (see Figure 26.1). Through the drawing, not the language, the teacher was able to assess the misconceptions and how little the student knew about the American Revolution. This has significant implications for teaching and assessment in the social studies and supports assessments to be varied and less language-based. Bruner (1962) contended that students go through an ionic stage of development (images) before reaching the representational stage (language based). These stages are not tied to chronological stages of development but are experienced based. Because of the complex nature of the social studies, nonlanguage-based assessments are an unexplored research possibility.

Although recent and promising developments in research on assessment in the social studies classroom are inchoate, there are multiple ways to assess student learning in the social studies classroom and to conduct scholarly, empirical research within K–12 social studies classrooms. Furthermore, the relationship among curriculum, instruction, and assessment continues to influence teaching and learning in the social studies classroom. It is therefore vital for educa-

Figure 26.1 Use of Image to Assess Social Studies

SOURCE: From Claunch, A. (2002). *How Nine and Ten year olds Construct Historical Time from Literature.* Unpublished dissertation: University of New Mexico.

tors and researchers to reconsider social studies classrooms as fruitful environments in which to collaboratively teach, learn, and inquire.

Discussion

In this chapter, the purpose of social studies and a definition of assessment in the social studies classroom have been provided, with an emphasis on constructive assessment that reflects disciplined inquiry and informs both students and teachers. The ongoing debates over the nature, meaning, and purposes of social studies (Shaver, 1987) continue into the 21st century (Levstik, 2008; Seixas, 2001) and may continue to impact social studies curriculum, instruction, and assessment. Social studies scholars have focused attention on high-stakes testing and its implications (Grant & Salinas, 2008; Rock et al., 2004; VanFossen, 2005; von Zastrow & Janc, 2004) but not on what actually happens in classrooms with assessment. Grant and Salinas (2008) provided the field with a review of large-scale assessment and accountability in the social studies, and they noted, "It seems cliché to conclude that more inquiry is needed, but in this important area the case for such a conclusion seems especially strong" (p. 219). Their words echo more loudly in relationship to research on assessment in the social studies classroom.

Conversely, there is a plethora of practitioner literature focusing on classroom teaching strategies. Cuban (1991) noted the numerous articles on what students should be doing in social studies and very few on what actually happens in classrooms. Perhaps this is even more true for CA practices. The NCSS journals, *Social Education, Social Studies and the Young Learner,* and *Middle Level Learning,* provide curricular, instructional, and assessment support for classroom educators. In 1999, E. W. Ross, the editor of *TRSE,* issued a call to "reclaim schools as places for learning, rather than places for testing" (p. 128). The subsequent empirical studies published in *TRSE* have not adequately addressed assessment in the social studies classroom. The preponderance of scholarship regarding social studies CA has been prescriptive rather than empirical, even though this prescriptive scholarship has its roots in social studies research (for example, Gallavan & Kottler, 2009; NCSS, 2011). Use of constructive assessment in classrooms is not being adequately investigated by social studies scholars and educators.

Call for Research on Assessment in the Social Studies Classroom

Research on assessment in social studies classrooms is noticeably underdeveloped. Numerous literature searches failed to provide substantive evidence that scholars are engaging in empirical research on assessment in social studies classrooms. Investigations could include the following:

- In what ways do teachers use constructive assessment to make curricular and instructional decisions?
- In what ways do students use constructive assessment?
- Does it make a difference in any measureable or observable way?
- What types of assessment decisions do teachers make?
- Is constructive assessment being used to inform teaching and learning, as the prescriptive literature calls for, or simply being used as another means of grading?
- In what ways are assessments linked to the overarching goals of social studies, specifically in relationship to a citizenship construct?
- In what ways is the prescriptive literature enacted in K–12 social studies classrooms?

There are action research studies that nibble at the edges of a much needed body of research, addressed earlier in this chapter (see Brookhart & Durkin, 2003; Kelley, 2006; VanSledright, 2002). Again, these three case studies, from disparate teacher–researchers, suggest to social studies scholars the importance and necessity of engaging in research within K–12 classroom settings. An extensive case literature would strengthen the knowledge of CA practices and their implications immensely.

We acknowledge challenges to developing empirical and theoretical studies on social studies CA. These may include the marginalization of social studies at the elementary level, the decreased importance of social studies as a discipline at the secondary level, an overreliance on standardized assessment, and researcher access to social studies classrooms in which constructive assessment regularly occurs; however, these obstacles can and should be addressed.

References

Abrams, L., Pedulla, J., & Madaus, G. (2003). Views from the classroom: Teachers' opinions of statewide testing programs. *Theory Into Practice, 42*(1), 18–29.

Alleman, J., & Brophy. (1997). Elementary social studies: Instruments, activities, and standards. In G. Phye (Ed.), *Handbook of classroom assessment* (pp. 321–357). San Diego: Academic Press.

Alleman, J., & Brophy, J. (1999a). Current trends and practices in social studies assessment for the early grades. *Social Studies and the Young Learner, 11*(4), 15–17.

Alleman, J., & Brophy, J. (1999b). The changing nature and purpose of assessment in the social studies classroom. *Social Education, 63*(6), 334–337.

Armento, B. (1986). Research on teaching social studies. In M. C. Wittrock (Ed.), *Handbook of research on teaching* (3rd ed., pp. 942–951). New York: Macmillan.

Bower, B., & Lobdell, J. (2005). *Social studies alive! Engaging diverse learners in the elementary classroom.* Palo Alto, CA: Teachers' Curriculum Institute.

Boyle-Baise, M., Hsu, M., Johnson, S., Serriere, S.C., & Stewart, D. (2008). Putting reading first: Teaching social studies in elementary classrooms. *Theory and Research in SocialEducation, 36*(3), 233–255.

Bracey, G. W. (1987). Measurement-driven instruction: Catchy phrase, dangerous practice. *Phi Delta Kappan, 68*(9), 683–686.

Brookhart, S. M., & Durkin, D. T. (2003). Classroom assessment, student motivation, and achievement in high school social studies classes. *Applied Measurement in Education, 16*(1), 27–54.

Brophy, J. (1990). Teaching social studies for understanding and higher-order application. *The Elementary School Journal, 90*(4), 351–417.

Brophy J., McMahon, S., & Prawatt, R. (1991). Elementary social studies series: Critique of a representative example of six experts. *Social Education, 55*(3), 155–160.

Brozo, W. G., & Tomlinson, C. M. (1986). Literature: The key to lively content courses. *The Reading Teacher, 40*(3), 288–293.

Bruner, J. (1962). *On knowing: Essays for the left hand.* Cambridge, MA: Harvard University Press.

Burmark, L. (2002). *Visual literacy.* Alexandria, VA: Association for Supervision and Curriculum Development.

Butts, R. F. (1989). *The civic mission in educational reform: Perspectives for the public and for the profession.* Stanford, CA: Hoover Institution Press.

Caviglioli, O., & Harris, I. (2003). *Thinking visually.* Portland, ME: Stenhouse Publishers.

Claunch, A. (2002). *How nine and ten year olds construct historical time by reading children's literature.* Unpublished doctoral dissertation, University of New Mexico, Albuquerque.

Cuban, L. (1991). History of teaching in social studies. In J. P. Shaver (Ed.), *Handbook of research on social studies teaching and learning* (pp. 197–209). New York: Macmillan.

Darling-Hammond, L., Einbender, L., Frelow, F., & Ley-King, J. (1993). *Authentic assessment in practice: A collection of performance tasks, exhibitions, and documentation.* New York: National Center for Restructuring Education, Schools and Teaching.

Evans, R. W. (2004). *The social studies wars: What should we teach the children?* New York: Teachers College Press.

Fitchett, P. G., & Heafner, T. L. (2010). A national perspective on the effects of high-stakes testing and standardization on elementary social studies marginalization. *Theory and Research in Social Education, 38*(1), 114–130.

Flinders, D. J., & Thornton, S. J. (Eds.). (1998). *The curriculum studies reader.* New York: Routledge.

Gallavan, N. P. (2009a). *Developing performance-based assessments, grades K–5.* Thousand Oaks, CA: Corwin Press.

Gallavan, N. P. (2009b). *Developing performance-based assessments, grades 6–12.* Thousand Oaks, CA: Corwin Press.

Gallavan, N. P., & Kottler, E. (2009). Constructing rubrics and assessing progress collaboratively with social studies students. *Social Studies, 100*(4), 154–159.

Gradwell, J. M. (2006). Teaching in spite of, rather than because of, the test: A case of ambitious history teaching in New York state. In S. G. Grant (Ed.), *Measuring history: Cases of state-level testing across the United States* (pp. 157–176). Greenwich, CT: Information Age Publishing.

Grant, S. G. (Ed.). (2006). *Measuring history: Cases of state-level testing across the United States.* Greenwich, CT: Information Age Publishing.

Grant, S. G., & Gradwell, J. M. (2005). The sources are many: Exploring history teachers' selection of classroom texts. *Theory and Research in Social Education, 33*(2), 244–265.

Grant, S. G., Gradwell, J. M., Lauricella, A. M., Derme-Insinna, A., Pullano, L., & Tzetzo, K. (2002). When increasing stakes need not mean increasing standards: The case of New York state global history and geography exam. *Theory and Research in Social Education, 30*(4), 488–515.

Grant, S. G., & Salinas, C. (2008). Assessment and accountability in the social studies. In L. S. Levstik & C. A. Tyson (Eds.), *Handbook of research in social studies education* (pp. 219–238). New York: Routledge.

Guzzetti, B. J., Kowalinski, B. J., & McGowan, T. (1992). Using a literature based approach to teaching social studies. *Journal of Reading, 36*(2), 114–122.

Hart, D. (1999). Opening assessment to our students. *Social Education, 63*(6), 343–345.

Hertzberg, H. W. (1985). Students, methods, and materials of instruction. In M. T. Downey (Ed.), *History in the schools* (pp. 25–40). Washington, DC: National Council for the Social Studies.

Hertzberg, H. W. (1988). Foundations, the 1892 committee of ten. *Social Education, 52*(2), 144–145.

Hoge, J. D., Field, S. F., Foster, S. J., & Nickell, P. (2004). *Real-world investigations for social studies: Inquiries for middle and high school students.* Upper Saddle River, NJ: Pearson.

Hyerle, D. (2000). *A field guide to using visual tools.* Alexandria, VA: Association for Supervision and Curriculum Development.

Kelley, L. A. (2006). Learning to question in kindergarten. *Social Studies Research and Practice, 1*(1), 45–54.

Kornhaber, M. L. (2004). Appropriate and inappropriate forms of testing, assessment, and accountability. *Educational Policy, 18*(1), 45–70.

Kurfman, D. (1982). *Evaluation in social studies* (Working projects from Project Span). Boulder, CO: Social Science Education Consortium, 3–27.

Kurfman, D. (1991). Testing as context for social education. In J. Shaver (Ed.), *Handbook of research on social studies teaching and learning* (pp. 310–320). New York: Macmillan.

Levstik, L. S. (2008). What happens in social studies classrooms? In L. S. Levstik & C. A. Tyson (Eds.), *Handbook of research in social studies education* (pp. 50–62). New York: Routledge.

Levstik, L. S., & Barton, K. C. (2011). *Doing history: Investigating with children in elementary and middle schools.* New York: Routledge.

Levstik, L. S., & Tyson, C. A. (Eds.). (2008). *Handbook of research in social studies education.* New York: Routledge.

Madaus, G. F., & Kellaghan, T. (1996). Curriculum evaluation and assessment. In P. W. Jackson (Ed.), *Handbook of research on curriculum* (pp. 119–149). New York: Macmillan.

Marker, G. W., & Mehlinger, H. (1992). Social studies. In P. W. Jackson (Ed.), *Handbook of research on curriculum* (pp. 830–851). New York: Macmillan.

Marshall, J. D., Sears, J. T., Anderson Allen, L., Roberts, P. A., & Schubert, W. H. (2007). *Turning points in curriculum: A contemporary American memoir.* Upper Saddle River, NJ: Pearson.

Metcalf, L. E. (1963). Research on teaching the social studies. In N. L. Gage (Ed.), *Handbook of research on teaching* (pp. 929–965). Chicago: Rand McNally.

Moline, S. (1996). *I see what you mean.* York, MA: Stenhouse Publishers.

National Assessment of Educational Progress. (2011). *2010 geography assessment.* Retrieved from http://nces.ed.gov/nationsreportcard/geography/

National Center for Educational Statistics. (2011). *National assessment of educational progress.* Retrieved from http://nces.ed.gov/nationsreportcard/

National Council for the Social Studies. (1994). *Expectations of excellence: Curriculum standards for social studies.* Washington DC: Author.

National Council for the Social Studies. (1999). Authentic assessment in social studies [Special issue]. *Social Education, 63*(6).

National Council for the Social Studies. (2004). Promoting fair and equitable assessments: A position statement of national council for the social studies. *Social Education, 68*(4), 290.

National Council for the Social Studies. (2010). *National curriculum standards for social studies: A framework for teaching, learning, and assessment.* Washington DC: Author.

National Council for the Social Studies. (2011). Authentic instruction and assessment [Special issue]. *Social Studies and the Young Learner, 23*(3).

National History Day. (2011). *National history day works: National program evaluation.* Retrieved from www.nhd.org/NHDworks.htm

Newmann, F. (1990). Higher order thinking in teaching social studies: A rationale for the assessment of classroom thoughtfulness. *Journal of Curriculum Studies, 22,* 44–56.

Nuthall, G., & Alton-Lee, A. (1995). Assessing classroom learning: How students use their knowledge and experience to answer achievement test questions in science and social studies. *American Educational Research Journal, 32*(1), 185–223.

Parker, W. (2012). *Social studies in elementary education.* Boston: Allyn & Bacon.

Pedulla, J., Abrams, L., Madaus, G., Russell, M., Ramos, M, & Miao, J. (2003) *Perceived effects of state mandated testing programs on teaching and learning: Findings from a national survey of teachers.* Chestnut Hill, MA: National Board on Educational Testing and Public Policy.

Perkins, D. (1992). *Smart schools: From training memories to educating minds.* New York: The Free Press.

Popham, W. J. (1987). The merits of measurement driven instruction. *Phi Delta Kappan, 68*(9), 679–682.

Rock, T. C., Heafner, T., O'Connor, K., Passe, J., Oldendorf, S., Good, A., et al. (2004). One state closer to a national crisis: A report on elementary social studies education in North Carolina schools. *Theory and Research in Social Education, 34*(4), 455–483.

Ross, E. W. (1999). Resisting test mania. *Theory and Research in Social Education, 27*(2), 126–128.

Saxe, D. W. (1991). *Social studies in schools: A history of the early years.* Albany, NY: SUNY Press.

Scriven, M. S. (1967). The methodology of evaluation. In R. Tyler, R. Gagné, & M. Scriven (Eds.), *Perspectives of curriculum evaluation* (pp. 39–83). Chicago: Rand McNally.

Segall, A. (2003). Teachers' perceptions on state mandated standardized testing: The Michigan educational assessment program (MEAP) as a case study of consequences. *Theory and Research in Social Education, 31*(3), 287–325.

Seixas, P. (2001). Review of research on social studies. In V. Richardson (Ed.), *Handbook of research on teaching* (4th ed., pp. 545–565). Washington DC: American Educational Research Association.

Sewall, G. (1988). American history textbooks: Where do we go from here? *Phi Delta Kappan, 69,* 552–558.

Shaver, J. P. (1987). Implications from research: What should be taught in social studies? In V. Richardson-Koehler (Ed.), *Educators' handbook: A research perspective* (pp. 112–138). New York: Longman.

Shaver, J. P. (Ed.). (1991). *Handbook of research on social studies teaching and learning.* New York: Macmillan.

Shaver, J. P., & Larkins, A. G. (1973). Research on teaching social studies. In R. M. W. Travers (Ed.), *Second handbook of research on teaching* (pp. 1243–1262). Chicago: Rand McNally.

Shepard, L. A. (2001). The role of classroom assessment in teaching and learning. In V. Richardson (Ed.), *Handbook of research on teaching* (4th ed., pp. 1066–1101). Washington DC: American Educational Research Association.

Smith, A. M. (2006). Negotiating control and protecting the private. History teachers and the Virginia standards of learning. In S. G. Grant (Ed.), *Measuring history: Cases of state-level testing across the United States* (pp. 221–248). Greenwich, CT: Information Age Publishing.

Snow-Gerono, J. L. & Franklin, C. A. (2007). Accountability systems' narrowing effect on curriculum in the United States: A report within an elementary education teacher certification program. In L. Deretchin & C. Craig (Eds.), *ATE Teacher Education Yearbook XV: International perspective on accountability systems and their impact on students, society and teacher preparation* (pp. 97–112). Lanham, MD: Scarecrow Education Publications.

Stiggins, R. J. (1991). Facing the challenges of a new era of educational assessment. *Applied Measurement in Education, 4*(4), 263–273.

Superka, D. P., Vigliani, A., & Hedstrom, J. E. (1978). *Social studies evaluation sourcebook.* Boulder, CO: Social Science Education Consortium.

Svengalis, C. M. (1992). *National survey of course offerings in social studies, kindergarten–grade 12, 1991–1992.* Washington, DC: Council of State Social Studies Specialists.

Thornton, S. J. (1994). The social studies near century's end: Reconsidering patterns of curriculum and instruction. *Review of Research in Education, 20,* 223-254.

Thornton, S. J. (2005). *Teaching social studies that matters: Curriculum for active learning.* New York: Teachers College.

U.S. Department of Education. (2002). *No Child Left Behind Act of 2001* (Title I Paraprofessionals: Draft Non-Regulatory Guidance). Washington, DC: U.S. Department of Education, Office of Elementary and Secondary Education.

VanFossen, P. J. (2005). "Reading and math take so much time…": An overview of social studies instruction in elementary classrooms in Indiana. *Theory and Research in Social Education, 33*(3), 376-403.

VanFossen, P. J. & McGrew, C. (2008). Is the sky really falling?: An update on the status of social studies in the K–5 curriculum in Indiana. *International Journal of Social Education, 23*(1), 139–182.

van Hover, S. (2006). Teaching history in the Old Dominion: The impact of Virginia's accountability reform on seven secondary beginning history teachers. In S. G. Grant (Ed.), *Measuring history: Cases of state-level testing across the United States* (pp. 195–220). Greenwich, CT: Information Age Publishing.

van Hover, S., Hicks, D., & Washington, E. (2011). Multiple paths to testable content? Differentiation in a high-stakes testing context. *Social Studies Research and Practice, 6*(3), 34–51.

VanSledright, B. (2002). Confronting history's interpretive paradox while teaching fifth graders to investigate the past. *American Educational Research Journal, 39*(4), 1089–1115.

Volger, K. (2006). The impact of high school graduation examination on Mississippi social studies teachers' instructional practices In S. G. Grant (Ed.), *Measuring history: Cases of state-level testing across the United States* (pp. 273–302). Greenwich, CT: Information Age Publishing.

von Zastrow, C., & Janc, H. (2004). Academic atrophy: *The condition of the liberal arts in America's schools.* Washington, DC: Council for Basic Education.

Walling, D. R. (2005). *Visual knowing.* Thousand Oaks, CA: Corwin Press.

Watson, R. S. (2010). *Stability and change in New York state regents mathematics examinations, 1866–2009: A socio-historical analysis* (Doctoral dissertation). Retrieved from http://search.proquest.com/docview/846060249?accountid=14613

Wiggins, G. (1998). *Educative assessment: Designing assessments to inform and improve student performance.* San Francisco: Jossey-Bass.

Wolf, D., Bixby, J., Glenn III, J., & Gardner, H. (1991). To use their minds well: Investigating new forms of student assessment. *Review of Research in Education, 17,* 31–74.

27

Assessment in the Science Classroom: Priorities, Practices, and Prospects

Bronwen Cowie

What counts as assessment in science classrooms—and more importantly, what constitutes quality assessment in science classrooms—is inextricably entwined with what counts as science and how learning takes place. The chapter begins with an overview of the goals of science education and important perspectives on science learning. Wider political influences on science classroom assessment (CA) are then discussed, followed by some illustrative examples of how assessment is accomplished in science classrooms. In all of this, the need for assessment to contribute to learning (formative assessment)—and the affordances and constraints offered by science, science classrooms, and the goals of science education—are emphasized. This leads naturally to the consideration of how the quality of assessment in science classrooms might be conceptualized and whose voice and needs should count most in any decisions about assessment quality, especially as related to consequences. At this time, innovation in assessment in science tends to be mixed with concerns for equity and the matter of differential access and achievement and with local, national, and international accountability and status. The chapter touches on these aspects as part of considering challenges and opportunities for active student involvement in CA and for enhancing teacher CA practice.

The Science Classroom as a Site for Assessment

Science teachers undertake assessment in the classroom for formative, summative, and accountability purposes, and these interact with curriculum and instruction to shape and frame student classroom experiences. A quick scan of the vision statements for the science curricula in countries as diverse as the United States, England, New Zealand, Singapore, and Thailand shows that the primary goal of science education is the development of a scientifically literate citizenry. It is no longer sufficient that only those intending to pursue science as a career engage with science. The expectation is that all students will develop as knowledgeable and confident knowers, commentators on, and users of science as part of their everyday lives now and into the future (Fensham, 2008; National Research Council [NRC], 1996; Roberts, 2007; Tytler, 2007). This requires that, in addition to understanding science concepts, students need to develop an understanding of the social and epistemic basis of science—that is, of how scientific knowledge is warranted and communicated (Duschl, 2008). Students need an appreciation of the disciplinary practices that form the basis of science authority for them to be able to employ these as generative resources for ongoing learning and action (Ford & Forman, 2006).

Inquiry and argumentation-based teaching approaches are prominent among those approaches recommended as effective in moving student learning beyond conceptual goals (European Commission, 2007; NRC, 2000). The emphasis on scientific inquiry in contemporary science education has seen a shift from perceiving science as an activity focusing on exploration and experiment to one which construes argumentation, model building, and explanation as central to learning and knowing science (NRC, 2007). With inquiry, the idea is that if students learn science in the context of inquiry they will know what they know, how they know it, and why they believe it (Duschl, 2003a). As a teaching approach, argumentation focuses attention on the generation, critique, and use of evidence to develop and substantiate knowledge claims (Simon, Erduran, & Osborne, 2006). Both of these approaches come with substantial challenges and, as is illustrated later, potentially productive implications for the conduct of CA.

The focus on scientific literacy for *all* brings students, with their different strengths, interests, and needs, to the forefront of an analysis of science CA. Since 2000, evidence has been mounting of a general decline in student interest in science, with this lack of interest increasing as students move to higher grade levels (Porter & Parvin, 2009; Tytler, 2007). There is even evidence that some students who perform well in standard tests do not see a role for science in their everyday lives or future (Aikenhead, 2006; Calabrese Barton, Tan, & Rivet, 2008). This lack of interest has been attributed to factors such as students not realizing the extent to which science is involved in careers, the negative images of science in the media, and most commonly, the tendency for science to be taught and assessed as a fixed, value-free body of decontextualized knowledge (Harlen, 2010; Southerland, Smith, Sowell, & Kittleson, 2007).

Researchers working with an agenda of *science for all* argue that the persistent achievement gaps in science between mainstream and indigenous, English second language, and students from low socioeconomic backgrounds can be attributed to the way science is taught and not to deficits in students and their communities (Lee & Buxton, 2010). They are emphatic that success in science for these students should not have to come at the expense of their broader cultural values and worldviews (Calabrese Barton, Basu, Johnson, & Tan, 2011). They have provided strong evidence of the value of recognizing and bringing into play the varied linguistic and cultural resources students bring with them into the classroom (Lee, 2001; Warren, Ballenger, Ogonowski, Rosebery, & Hudicourt-Barnes, 2001). Lee (2001) sums up the implications for CA in science of this position: "Equitable instruction and assessment practices for diverse students involve consideration of their cultural and linguistic experiences in preparing them to function competently in the institutions of power as well as in their homes and communities" (pp. 499–500).

These aspirations pose a challenge in the practice of CA. Not only does assessment need to foster student scientific literacy but it needs to do this in a way that empowers students within their own cultures and communities (Bang & Medin, 2010; Lee & Buxton, 2010; Mutegi, 2011; Tan, 2011). All this indicates teachers need to be aware of whom they are teaching and to pay close attention to the critical intersections between canonical science, school science, and the cultural backgrounds of their students (Southerland et al., 2007).

The wider societal political context for curriculum and assessment is an influence on the conduct of assessment in science classrooms. Teacher assessment in science classrooms is influenced by international and national assessment programs as tools to drive school improvement through a focus on standards and accountability. Science features in the Programme for International Student Assessment (PISA) and Trends in International Mathematics and Science Study (TIMSS) international testing programs and in national testing regimes such as the No Child Left Behind Act of 2001 (NCLB) (U.S. Department of Education, 2002) in the United States and the SATs in England. While these assessments are intended to drive positive reform, there is considerable evidence that *teaching-to-the-test* is narrowing the science curriculum and contributing to teaching practices that run counter to those advocated in science reform documents (Carlone, Haun-Frank,

& Webb, 2011; Sadler & Zeidler, 2009; Southerland et al., 2007). At the same time, governments worldwide are endorsing formative assessment because of its potential to support the learning of all students and to raise achievement overall (Black & Wiliam, 1998; NRC, 2000; Organisation for Economic Cooperation and Development [OECD], 2005; Tytler, 2007; see also Chapters 10 through 13 of this volume). In practice, teacher decision making needs to reconcile and find a balance between the simultaneous policy demands for accountability and improvement (McMillan, 2003).

Assessment and the Nature of Learning

How learning is theorized influences what counts as evidence of learning and also how it might be supported. Over the past 30 years, constructivist and, more recently, sociocultural views of learning have predominated in science education (Anderson, 2007). In each case, the role of student prior knowledge is acknowledged, and students are accorded an active role in the learning process. From a constructivist perspective, however, the assessment focus is on making student thinking visible. Then, if student conceptions differ from those of scientists, engaging students in tasks that create cognitive conflict so as to challenge and develop student views toward those of scientists. The extent to which student ideas can be resistant to change and science can appear counterintuitive is a key contribution of the constructivist work—one that has led to an appreciation that CA practices need to access and build on the sense students are making during and not just at the end of a teaching and learning sequence.

From a sociocultural perspective, learning is a process of identity transformation that involves learners gaining proficiency in the valued activities of a particular community (Wenger, 1998). The implication is that assessment needs to focus on what students do with social support, rather than working alone, and on how over time they take up and use various resources in the setting (e.g., ideas, people, tasks, and tools). Evidence of learning, like opportunities for action to enhance learning, is embedded in the ongoing interactions that take place among the ideas, people, tasks, and tools in a setting. A sociocultural approach confronts the problem of conflicts between the identities that are available to students in science classrooms and the identities students find meaningful out of school and also with those to which they aspire (Aikenhead, 1996; Basu, Barton, & Tan, 2011). Consequently, analysis of CA practice needs to consider how it affords students with different opportunities to learn and positions them in different relationships with science, its construction, use, and communication (Moss, 2008).

Moving Into the Science Classroom

In the paragraphs that follow, I begin by elaborating on the overall dynamic of assessment in science classrooms. Next, I consider in more detail aspects of the assessment process, including (1) ways of making student ideas public and available for reflection and discussion, (2) tools and technologies to support teacher assessment, (3) the affordances for active student involvement in assessment, and (4) innovation in summative assessment. For this analysis, I draw on research on assessment in science classrooms and, mirroring Moss's (2008) analysis of Lampert's mathematics teaching to illustrate CA, I interrogate research focused on student inquiry, argumentation, and science for all.

The Dynamic of Classroom Assessment

Classroom studies that focus directly on teacher assessment practices have shown that science teacher formative assessment practices vary along dimensions related to the formality of the assessment, the degree of planning, the type of data collected, the nature and time frame of teacher feedback, and formative actions (Ruiz-Primo, 2011). Teacher assessment focus can be on the whole class, small groups, or the individual student and on any or all of the various aspects of teachers' goals for student science learning.

Informal interactive formative assessment (Cowie & Bell, 1999), or *on-the-fly-formative assessment* (Shavelson et al., 2008), lies at one end of the continuum of formality, teacher planning, and time frame for responding. It relies on teachers noticing, recognizing, and responding to student learning while they are engaged in learning tasks, which places considerable demands on teacher pedagogical and pedagogical content knowledge (PCK) (Bell & Cowie, 2001). It also relies on a classroom culture in which students are willing to disclose and discuss their tentative ideas and to act on teacher feedback (Cowie, 2005). The learning goals that are the focus of informal interactive formative assessment tend to be those associated with the task at hand, albeit contextualized by a teacher's longer-term goals for student learning (Ruiz-Primo, 2011). Feedback typically draws on the relationships and resources in the immediate context and is usually provided during an interaction although teachers can respond the next day and or on multiple occasions.

Planned-for interactions as formative assessment involve a more deliberate creation of and capitalization on "moments of contingency" during instruction (Black & Wiliam, 2009, p. 10). Questions and activities designed to optimize teacher access to student thinking are central to planned-for assessment interactions, as is teachers planning time to interact with students (Black, Harrison, Lee, Marshall, & Wiliam, 2003). For instance, a teacher might plan to use a predict-observe-explain task (White & Gunstone, 1992) as a stimulus and focus for discussion on whether and why a half bar of soap will sink if the full bar does. They might use a *think-pair-share* to provide an opportunity for students to test out and formulate their ideas with a partner before orchestrating a whole class discussion on whether or not a person is an animal—a question known to provoke debate.

With more formal planned and embedded formative assessment, the prompts to elicit student learning are prepared in advance. Teacher-prepared tasks of this sort generally focus on specific aspects of the teacher's intended learning and target the whole class as a process that is discernible as an occasion in which the teacher is gathering data. In a number of countries, teachers also have access to banks of assessment items and curriculum resources that embed formative and summative tasks. As part of their work on formative assessment, Black and Harrison (2004) have demonstrated how science teachers can use test results in formative ways. A more recent study has demonstrated that summative data and results can be generated and presented in a variety of ways and still meet the standards and needs of parents, schools, and public/government authorities (Black, Harrison, Hodgen, Marshall, & Serret, 2011). On the other hand, there is evidence of the value of performance assessment and teachers collecting evidence of student inquiry over time for summative purposes (see Chapters 18 and 19 of this volume). Examples include the development of portfolios (Duschl & Gitomer, 1997), the compilation of evidence from formative interactions (Cowie, Moreland, Jones, & Otrel-Cass, 2008), and/or the use of Web-based performance assessments (e.g., Hickey, Ingram-Goble, & Jameson, 2009; Ketelhut, Nelson, Clarke, & Dede, 2010).

Making Student Learning Public and Available for Reflection and Refinement

A substantial body of research has explored the development and efficacy of different assessment approaches and programs to support and encourage students to make their learning *visible* (or audible)and open for discussion and development. In the case of formative assessment, researchers have emphasized that the tasks that are used to help develop and make particular aspects of student learning visible also need to embed within them features that will help teachers and students make sense of where students are at in terms of understanding a concept/practice, as well as to include possibilities for student and teacher actions to move student learning forward. Science education research about student alternative conceptions and conceptual change/development offers a breadth of insights and strategies, both general and specific, that science teachers can use to help them elicit, interpret, and respond to student ideas (Osborne & Freyberg, 1985; White & Gunstone, 1992). These include, for example, knowing that it is worthwhile to ask students to wire up a bulb to make it glow and once they have worked out how to do this to ask them to explain what they think is happening in the wires. The teacher can then use research that indicates student explanations will include that the second wire is essentially redundant or that the current clashes in the bulb or circulates around the circuit as a basis for making sense of and providing feedback on student ideas.

Dialogue and discussion is central to learning science (Lemke, 1990; Roth, 2005) and formative assessment (Anderson, Zuiker, Taasoobshirazi, & Hickey, 2007; Black & Wiliam, 2009). Black et al. (2003) have highlighted that in order to stimulate productive talk teachers need to engage students with thought-provoking (rich) questions and that these are best prepared in advance. To sustain discussion, teachers need to withhold judgment and encourage students to clarify, compare, challenge, and defend their various views using evidence that can also be subject to critique. Black et al. (2003) documented a significant increase in the depth and extent of student contributions when a teacher shifted to ask more open questions and to allow time for students to think before prompting students to answer.

Teaching based around inquiry, argumentation, and socioscientific issues provides a forum and focus for talk and for teacher assessment and facilitation of student learning (Driver, Newton, & Osborne, 2000; Duschl, 2003b). As Harlen (2003) pointed out, inquiry relies on teachers and students monitoring student developing ideas and interests so that they are able to provide appropriately targeted resources and feedback (see also Minstrell, Anderson, & Li, 2011). Duschl and Gitomer's (1997) use of planned assessment conversations to help teachers scaffold and support student construction of meaning is an often referenced example of effective assessment in science inquiry. Students are presented with authentic problems and proceed through an established sequence of investigations to develop conceptual understanding, reasoning strategies related to ways of knowing in science, and communication skills. Assessment conversations involve teachers eliciting student ideas through a variety of means and recognizing these through a public discussion in which they use student ideas to reach a reasoned consensus based on evidence. Students develop a portfolio as they complete the unit to represent their learning. Studies by Ruiz-Primo and Furtak (2006) and Minstrell, Li, and Anderson (2009a) have endorsed the value of assessment conversations, highlighting that students whose teachers engage more frequently in the full assessment conversation cycle perform better on formal assessment tasks, reinforcing the crucial nature of action on information.

Research by Minstrell and van Zee (2003) has demonstrated positive gains in learning when the authority for science classroom conversation shifts from the teacher to the students. Employing a technique they called the *reflective toss*, Minstrell and van Zee found that students become more active in classroom discourse, with the positive consequence of making student thinking more visible to both the teacher and the students themselves. Herrenkohl and Guerra (1998) provided students with guidelines to support them in asking constructive questions to check and critique peers' work. They found that a focus on listening skills and audience roles helped to foster productive discussion about students' "thinking in science."

The focus within scientific literacy on students coming to understand and be able to use science epistemic criteria as part of inquiry offers a fertile and meaningful context for the development and use of student peer assessment and self-monitoring (see Chapters 21 and 22 of this volume). Science epistemic criteria provide authentic success criteria in the formative assessment sense, making them a legitimate focus for student science learning and learning to learn science.

Current developments in research on students' practical epistemologies indicate that students have developed ideas about how they know what they know and what makes a good reason for believing a claim based on their everyday experiences, and that these can either resource or hinder their science learning (Sandoval, 2003). Sandoval and Cam (2010) found that when students aged 8 to 10 were asked to help two story characters choose the "best reason" for believing a claim, most students appeared to have a loose ordering of the epistemic status of justifications with data being preferred, plausible mechanisms appealing and preferred over ambiguous data, and appeals to authority least preferable. The primary reason for preferring any justification was its credibility, with this related to its firsthand nature. They propose that this preference for data is productive and that instructional attention can usefully be focused on the attributes of measurement and experimentation that make data credible. On the basis of their study of the epistemic criteria for good models generated by middle school students before and after instruction, Pluta, Chinn, and Duncan (2011) proposed that inquiries built from students' own epistemic criteria may engender a greater sense of ownership over and understanding of science epistemic criteria and support the development of classrooms as powerful science learning communities.

A number of researchers have provided evidence that the use of an ensemble of modes and media can support the development and expression of learning (e.g., Givry & Roth, 2006; Kress, Jewitt, Ogborn, & Tsatsarelius, 2001; Varelas et al.,

2010). In providing or negotiating feedback, science teachers are able to capitialize on the material as well as the social aspects of science knowledge generation and validation processes. They can suggest that students revisit earlier, undertake new experiments and observations, or consult other knowledge sources such as textbooks and the Internet, as well as discuss ideas. This means that teachers do not have to rely on their own authority to persuade students toward a more scientific understanding. They also make students aware of the range of sources of information available and the need for critical judgment of the quality and trustworthiness of evidence/information.

Danish and Phelps (2010) have provided rich detail of the assessment conversations of kindergarten and first-grade students as they prepared a storyboard about honeybees. The students' assessed and critiqued each other's work, and they acted on each other's feedback. Kelly and Brown (2003), on the basis of their analysis of an inquiry unit on solar energy, argued that the use of multiple formats, audiences, and media enhances students' abilities to explain their ideas and reasoning, gain feedback on these and thus refine each. They proposed that teachers gain an expanded view of their students' science learning when they gather assessment data while students are working through tasks that have meaning for them, something that can be particularly important for students from linguistically and culturally diverse backgrounds. A study by Crawford, Chen, and Kelly (1997) illustrated the role the audience plays in student demonstrations of learning. The students in Crawford and colleagues' study provided more elaborated explanations when talking with younger children than when they talked with their teacher—thereby presenting quite a different picture of what they knew. O'Byrne (2009) demonstrated the merit of more formally planning to use a combination of written tests, drawings, and picture puzzles. This combination of tasks served to illuminate how young students constructed scientific concepts about wolves out of background knowledge by showing different paths of meaning making.

Science studies have highlighted that being proficient in the discipline involves the ability to "fluently juggle with its verbal, mathematical, and visual-graphical aspects, applying whichever is most appropriate in the moment and freely translating back and forth among them" (Lemke, 2000, p. 248). Studies with a focus on promoting student understanding and use of science-specific representations (Ainsworth, 2006; Waldrip, Prain, & Carolan, 2010), rather than assessment per se, have demonstrated the value of instructing students in why and how particular representations are used and of providing them with opportunities to do this. Hubber, Tytler, and Haslam (2010) documented the value of providing students opportunities for talking through a variety of practical experiences along with opportunities to develop their own representations prior to introducing the science usage of *force* and the conventional arrow representations for it. Hubber et al. (2010) noted that while this approach posed a number of conceptual, epistemological, and pedagogical challenges for teachers it also provided them ongoing access to rich information on student thinking. At the end of the unit, students were able to talk meaningfully about the role of representations in understanding, the function of different representations, and the need to coordinate these—something that is an important aspect of scientific literacy.

Writing to learn and writing to express that learning, often in conjunction with spoken language, has been a sustained focus in science education (Prain & Hand, 2012). Student science notebooks, which are a natural part of most science classrooms, can be used to gauge the quality of student communication and reasoning and the nature of their understanding. However, research has consistently indicated that teachers only sometimes make use of notebooks to improve teaching and learning (Aschbacher & Alonzo, 2006). Research on more formal written assessment tasks has tended to demonstrate that more open response tasks provide a deeper insight into what students actually know. Buck and Trauth-Nare (2009) found that select-response tasks contributed to a teacher overestimating student understanding when compared with interview data. Student written responses to an open response task generated more representative evidence of student understanding. When the teacher responded to student-written comments with suggestions, the teacher–student written exchange acted as a form of assessment conversation that both the teacher and students found valuable, albeit students needed convincing that the aim was formative rather than summative.

Furtak and Ruiz-Primo (2008) have illustrated that open-format formative assessment prompts (e.g., constructed-response [CR] and predict–observe) appear to function better when used as a basis for teachers to elicit a range of middle school students' ideas about sinking and floating in writing, whereas constrained outcome space prompts (predict–observe–explain) may be more appropriate for whole-class conversations that focus students upon scientifically appropriate responses. McNeill, Lizotte, Krajcik, and Marx (2006) demonstrated the value of fading written instructional support (scaffolds) to better prepare students to construct scientific explanations when they were no longer provided with support. Subsequently, this team has developed a rubric to help teachers assess their students' written explanations. The rubric takes into consideration the content knowledge needed to respond to the task and what counts as appropriate evidence and reasoning (McNeill & Krajcik, 2008).

Tools and Technologies to Support Teachers' Assessments

Researchers, largely based in the United States, have developed a range of multiple-choice item formats designed to provide information on *how* as well as *what* students know (e.g., the facet-based items developed for DIAGNOSER, Sadler's [1998] distractor multiple-choice items, and the explanation multiple-choice items being developed by Liu, Lee, & Linn [2011]; see also Chapter 16 on CR items). The DIAGNOSER Web-based assessment system was designed by Minstrell and his colleagues (Minstrell, Anderson, Kraus, & Minstrell, 2008) to assist teachers to elicit and respond to student alternative conceptions. DIAGNOSER is constructed so that each possible student response is associated with a different conception of a science concept. Student responses provide teachers and students with information on student alternative conceptions. DIAGNOSER incorporates sample lessons to help teachers address learning goals and student conceptions. Large numbers of science teachers have used DIAGNOSER with research indicating the tools work best when a teacher already has a perspective of and genuine interest in listening to students and addressing and building on their thinking (Minstrell & Kraus, 2007).

Sadler (1998) has developed a series of multiple-choice questions focused on astronomy and space science and aligned with the K–12 U.S. National Science Standards, which include *distractors* based on student alternative conceptions. Significantly, the trials Sadler has conducted have shown that students' ideas do not change quickly and that in some cases the proportion of students choosing a correct answer first declined and then increased across the grade levels. This indicates that students can sometimes produce correct answers based on invalid reasoning and that as student ideas mature they may start giving wrong answers to questions they previously answered correctly before developing a more stable and comprehensive revised view. Osborne and Freyberg (1985) also found this to be the case when teaching focused on challenging student alternative conceptions. These findings highlight the challenge for science teachers in shifting student conceptions and in deciding when a new idea is securely established.

The inquiry unit on buoyancy developed by Shavelson and colleagues (2008) is an example of collaboration between an assessment and a curriculum research and development group. The assessment tasks embedded in the unit are in the form of focus, multiple-choice, and short-answer questions; concept-mapping tasks; and performance assessments. They focus on different aspects of mass, volume, density and buoyancy. In a series of papers (*Applied Measurement in Education*, Vol. 21, 2008), the researchers documented the variation in teacher use of the embedded tasks, linking this to teacher preconceptions about assessment and its role in student inquiry and inquiry teaching practices. In reflecting on the outcomes of the study the researchers noted that some but not all of the teachers acted on the information they accessed about student learning. They speculated that their teachers would have benefited from a deeper understanding of the nature and purposes of formative assessment, particularly the centrality of action on evidence of student learning.

The work of Gerard, Spitulnik, and Linn (2010) is another example of curriculum-embedded assessment. In their case, the assessments were embedded in inquiry Web-based curriculum materials designed to guide student learning about plate tectonics. The learning activities and assessment tasks include diagrams, maps, written text, developing models, brainstorm, and so on. Teacher customizations to address identified student learning needs included revisions of the embedded questions, the addition of hands-on investigations, and modification to teaching strategies. Student achievement improved in each of the 3 years of instructional customization. Overall, however, studies of this kind have indicated that while embedded assessment curriculum materials can be effective, they are far from a quick fix to the challenge of supporting science teacher formative assessment (Shepard, 2007).

Support for Students as Active Participants in the Assessment Process

Inquiry, argumentation, and socioscientific-based instruction all require active student engagement and self-assessment (Harlen, 2003). Frederiksen and White (1997) have demonstrated that self- and peer assessment can help to build students' understanding of scientific inquiry. Students who had regular opportunities in class to monitor their own progress and the progress of their peers through verbal and written feedback—and were provided with opportunities to improve their performance later in the unit—performed better on both project work and the unit test, with lower performing students showing the greatest improvement. ¶Students posing questions is pivotal to science inquiry and an important component of critical scientific literacy. Several authors have demonstrated the value of student questions in providing feedback from students to the teacher that can be used to adjust the teaching focus or explanatory structure (e.g., Biddulph, Symington, & Osborne, 1986; Chinn & Osborne, 2008). There is evidence that student question asking and help-seeking is an embodiment of the outcome of their active self-assessment that there is a gap or discrepancy in their knowledge that they would like to address (Black et al., 2003; Cowie, 1998). Classroom studies have illustrated the value of classroom social norms whereby students are free to move around the room to access resources and ask for help from peers (e.g., Engle & Conant, 2002; Roth, 1995; Windschitl, 2001), highlighting the way the cultural, interpersonal, and material dimensions of a classroom combine, shape, and frame student opportunities to engage in self-initiated formative action.

Assessment task design is an important equity issue for student participation in assessment because of its links to students' opportunities to learn and to their opportunities to demonstrate and gain feedback on what they know and can do (Stobart, 2005). Tobin and Gallagher (1987) studied 200 science lessons and found that three to seven students monopolized whole-class interactions. These students asked and answered most questions and received higher quality feedback. The students Cowie (2005) interviewed were very aware of whom their teacher interacted with during a lesson, construing a lack of opportunity for interaction as a limitation on their ability to progress their learning. Although the consensus was that one-to-one interaction was most effective, some students preferred written feedback that they could reflect on at their leisure highlighting the importance of teachers knowing their students' interactional preferences.

Solono-Flores and Nelson-Barber (2001) introduced the notion of cultural validity to account for the need to take into consideration the influence of sociocultural context on how students make sense of and respond to science assessment items. They contended that current approaches to handling student diversity in assessment, such as adapting or translating tests and providing assessment accommodations, are limited and lack a sociocultural perspective. Solono-Flores and Nelson-Barber asserted that there are five aspects to cultural validity: (1) student epistemology, (2) student language proficiency, (3) cultural worldviews, (4) cultural communication and socialization styles, and (5) student life context and value (see also Friesen & Ezeife, 2009; Siegel, Wissehr, & Halverson, 2008). The increasing diversity of students in science classrooms suggests this will be an important area of focus in the future.

The knowledge assessed and equated with achievement in the classroom and beyond can be conceptualized as an equity and social justice issue. Science education researchers, working to foster the engagement and achievement of all students, are emphatic that the diverse "funds of knowledge" (González & Moll, 2002) that students and their communities have developed over time need to be invited into the classroom and into the science curriculum as resources that support student and teacher learning (Bang & Medin, 2010; Warren et al., 2001). Work on how this might be achieved is only just beginning (e.g., Calabrese Barton & Tan, 2009, 2010), but it is another important area for future development with implications for teacher relations with the wider school community and their involvement in curriculum and assessment.

Research on outside of school settings is also raising challenges to the focus and form of assessment. Fusco and Barton (2001) presented a case study from a youth-led community science project in inner-city New York to make the case that performance assessment needs to be reimagined to accommodate an inclusive critical vision of science education. The homeless youth involved in their science program chose to transform an empty lot across the street from their shelter into a usable/public space for the community. Over the course of the project, the youth prepared a book that recorded and displayed the collective history of their efforts. Fusco and Barton commented that the contents of the book raise questions about what the youths accomplished and learned through the project and also about how teachers might better understand the youths' growth and development within (and outside) the domain of science education. Carlone and colleagues (2011), in a study of two classrooms where the students developed similar understandings but with very different affiliations with science, provided a powerful argument that equitable assessment in science classroom needs to foster students' affiliation with science in the present and the longer term. They suggested this may involve changes in curriculum, assessment, and other aspects of pedagogy. Overall research that touches on matters of equity and inclusion in science education provides a very different perspective on assessment—one that places students rather than the goals of science education at the center.

Innovation in Summative Assessment

What follows are five short snapshots of innovative summative assessment (see Chapter 14 for more information on summative assessment). Orpwood and Barnett (1997) described a task in which Grade 1 students who have learned about the senses are asked to design a game for a student who is blind. The culminating assessments for an integrated unit focused on an *expo* of students' model houses (based on the English subject requirement for an expository description of work done) and a role play in which groups synthesized their learning to present an argument and plans for the development of the local lake to the *Minister for Planning* (a role played by an older student) at a town meeting (Rennie, Venville, & Wallace, 2011). Seven- to 8-year-old students in a small rural multicultural school in New Zealand presented a daily weather report over the school intercom as the culminating assessment of their unit on weather (Otrel-Cass, Cowie, & Glynn, 2009). Together with the teacher, individual students talked through a video of their presentation with their parents as part of a parent–teacher–student school report evening. Polman (2011) has demonstrated the value of science journalism whereby students prepare and post articles on a Web site and via a print version. Sadler and Zeidler (2009) have proposed "socioscientific reasoning" as a construct that subsumes practices significant for the negotiation of socioscientific issues. To assess scientific reasoning, they engage students in multiple cases that present contextualized socioscientific issues along with questions that provide opportunities for the students to demonstrate these practices.

Each of these tasks is distinguished by the opportunity they provided for collective and individual knowledge development and demonstration, by multimodal data generated over time, and by the authentic social purpose they offered for learning and the demonstration of learning. In this way, they go some way toward meeting the challenge of finding an assessment format and focus that is true to the transformative goals of science education to establish long-term and action oriented student engagement with science as recommended by Aikenhead, Orpwood, & Fensham (2011).

Implications for Teachers

Atkin and Black (2003) pointed out in the introduction to their book, *Inside Science Education Reform*, that "What really counts in education is what happens when teachers and students meet" (p. ix). Although CA is posited as a key means for accomplishing the vision that all students can and will learn science, evidence of change in teacher practice is mixed. A number of the studies described earlier, although they reported many positive student outcomes, also reported that change was challenging, took time, and did not include all teachers to the same extent. Indeed, there is substantial evidence that the potential of assessment to inform teaching and enhance learning is not being realized in practice (Abell & Volkmann, 2006; Shavelson et al., 2008; Yin et al., 2008). The dynamics and complexity of the process, as well as the knowledge demands involved in responding to the sense students make of and take from teaching and learning activities in science classrooms, have already been mentioned. Teachers *and* students can struggle with the shifts in roles and responsibilities required to place the student and the development of their learning autonomy at the heart of their CA practice. For some teachers, pedagogical and assessment change is likely to be just as substantial a change as learning science is for their students (Harrison, in press)—all the more so if science is perceived as a fixed body of knowledge that provides "right answers," with teachers responsible for delivering this to their students and students for passively absorbing it (Black & Wiliam, 2006).

Teacher orientation to students and their ideas influence the information that is of interest to them and the nature of the responses. Minstrell, Li, et al. (2009b), based on their research in K–12 science classrooms in the United States, identified two dominant instructional stances to formative assessment. Teachers whose conduct of formative assessment they judged as more effective focused on how as well as what students were actually learning. These teachers were more likely to identify instructional actions linked to learning needs, rather than simply topically related ones. The teachers they judged as less effective focused on content coverage or how much students had learned. Their instructional responses tended to involve spending more time on a topic, moving on, and making other longer-term adjustments. Mortimer and Scott (2003), working in science classrooms in England, distinguished between the authorative and dialogic functions of discourse in a way that resonates with Minstrell and colleagues' conception of the different forms of formative assessment. It offers a way forward for thinking about the teacher's role in science assessment. Within an authorative discourse, teachers hear what a student has to say from a school science point of view, and as a consequence, only one voice is heard. In contrast, within a dialogic discourse, teachers listen to the student's point of view, and multiple viewpoints are shared. Mortimer and Scott noted that movement between the two discourses is inevitable where the purpose is to support the meaningful learning of scientific knowledge. During a lesson, teacher talk might be dialogic as part of an interaction during a learning activity and their goal is to extend student thinking, whereas it might be authoritative when they draw a lesson to a conclusion. Russ, Coffey, Hammer, and Hutchison (2009) illustrated that it is the balance and timing of these two orientations that is important if the teacher wants their students to sustain a commitment to reasoning.

Based on their empirical work, Abell and Seigel (2011) developed a model of the dimensions of science teacher assessment literacy. The Abell and Seigel model combines the interaction of general principles and values with understanding of the habits of mind, processes, and knowledge important for proficiency in a particular domain and knowledge, along with knowledge and practices associated with designing and helping students learn in that domain. At the center is a view of learning that undergirds the values, principles, and knowledge of assessment needed to teach effectively. Abell and Seigel explained that if science learning is viewed as sense-making, then assessment needs be more than pencil-and-paper tests; it needs to include opportunities for students to apply knowledge. They listed the principles for assessment as assessment as a process through which teachers should learn, a process from which students should learn, a process that helps students be metacognitive, with assessment tasks that are equitable for all learners. These values and principles interact with four categories of science teacher knowledge of assessment: (1) assessment purposes (summative, formative, diagnostic, and metacognitive); (2) what to assess (curriculum goals and what is of value); (3) assessment strategies (formal, informal, and topic-specific); and (4) assessment interpretation and resulting actions. This model offers a tool to guide teacher professional learning through the way it encapsulates and adds detail to findings from other studies that change in teacher practices involves both *know-how* and *know-why* about the new assessment practice (Wiliam & Thompson, 2008), especially when the aim is to use assessment to develop student learning and learning autonomy.

Contemplating Prospects for Ways Forward for Science Classroom Assessment

Research has begun to explicate some of the opportunities and challenges for a synergy among curriculum, current views of learning/

learners, pedagogy, and assessment with the focus on offering considerable promise for moving forward both research and practice. A number of research teams are working to develop rubrics and other tools for understanding the development of student proficiency in argumentation, modeling, and sociocscientific reasoning. Teaching sequences congruent with inquiry, argumentation, and explanation-based pedagogies, and that afford the full range of science learning outcomes and embed opportunities for formative and summative assessment, have shown positive results. There is evidence that Web-based and other digital information and communications technologies (ICTs) have a role to play in innovation and the wider dissemination of material that is open to teacher customization, albeit the research indicates teachers need guidance in their use and flexible adaptation. Given the intrinsic appeal of these technologies and their increasing availability, this area is a promising prospect. One danger here is that investment in assessment tools and strategies will take time and funding from support for teacher learning. Research that indicates that the implementation of assessment strategies devoid of an understanding of the underlying principles and appreciation of how learning is accomplished should alert us to this danger and help avoid it. This would seem to be a challenge best met by students, teachers, researchers, curriculum developers, and assessment specialists/scholars working together, as has been the case with the work by Shavelson and his team.

The development of learning progressions holds promise as a contribution to teacher knowledge of the possible pathways for student learning—something that is vital to the development of effective teaching sequences and assessment practices that allow teachers to build on from student understanding (Black & Wiliam, 1998; see also Chapter 3 of this volume). Wilson and Bertenthal (2005) defined learning progressions as "descriptions of successively more sophisticated ways of thinking about an idea that follow one another as students learn: they lay out in words and examples what it means to move toward more expert understanding" (p. 3). Currently, learning progressions are being developed for the *big ideas* of science—that is, the ideas that will be useful across students' lives. These progressions also aim to address the why and how aspects of science knowledge. They span years or grades, providing teachers with a longer-term view of student learning—where it might have come from and might go to. They offer new possibilities for aligning curriculum, instruction, and assessment. The suggestion is that teachers can link formative and summative assessment opportunities to the learning goals in a progression and make plans in advance of and during instruction about when, what, how, and who to assess and to envision possibilities to guide feedback and formative action.

Duschl, Maeng, and Sezen (2011) provided a useful overview of over 10 science-related learning progressions, describing their development and the impact of their use, and distinguishing between validation and evolutionary learning progressions. Alonzo and Steedle (2009), for instance, have developed and validated a progression on force and motion, with delineation of the levels employing students' language. Songer et al. (2009), for their progression on biodiversity, developed two learning pathways—one in terms of content progression and the other in terms of inquiry reasoning. The Grades 3 to 5 learning progression on matter developed by Smith, Wiser, and Carraher (2010) was empirically established. This said, significant questions remain about the potential and appropriate "grain size" for a progression in terms of time span and level of detail (Duschl, 2008). Heritage (2011) reminds us of the centrality of teacher knowledge and skills in steering through an appropriate learning progression. Alonzo and Steedle (2009) found that a progression provides only a tentative description of the ways in which student thinking develops. Alonzo et al. (2006) noted that teachers need specific information about likely student alternative conceptions and that their clustering and connections need to be a focus for change at their year level for them to translate learning progressions into effective tasks and to provide individual feedback. Through their longer-term focus, learning progressions hold out the prospect and need for greater cross-year and school communication and collaboration around student learning. This will be important but is likely to pose a challenge for researchers and teachers.

At a time of increasing student diversity, assessment in support of pedagogy that draws on diversity as a resource in science teaching and learning is an area in need of urgent development—all the more so when there is a need to address the persistent participation and achievement gaps in science within some subgroups of the student population. From a student perspective, Calabrese Barton et al. (2011) summed up this issue/prospect in this way: "When a child's' worldview is left unvalued and expressionless in an educational setting, what should we expect in terms of engagement, investment and learning from that child?" (p. 4). There is still very little research that provides students with an opportunity to participate as equals in the critique and construction of their learning and assessment opportunities.

Teacher classroom practice is nested within a framework of expectations and obligations to individual students, to a class as a whole, to their peers and school, to parents, to the government, and to other audit and accountability agencies. Moss (2008) has pointed out that assessment practices afford different knowledgeable identities for teachers, administrators, and policy makers as well as for students, and so substantial and sustained change in teacher CA will likely require coordinated change across all these stakeholders. The current focus on more directly aligning the system of assessment (national to classroom), curriculum, and pedagogy comes with the prospect of this suggesting the need for research that tracks developments at all levels of the system and across all stakeholders.

Finally, this review has focused largely on studies from Western countries, but even across these countries, the context for science CA is very different. Studies in countries and cultures with different histories and different expectations around student effort and the role of examinations provide a very different context for CA (Carless, 2005; Kennedy, Chan, Fok, & Yu, 2008), as do differences in resourcing and class sizes. All in all there is much that can be built on and much to be done to improve what is already in place to ensure that students develop the scientific literacy they need to be active and informed citizens in today's society.

REFERENCES

Abell, S. K., & Siegel, M. A. (2011). Assessment literacy: What science teachers need to know and be able to do. In D. Corrigan, J. Dillon, & R. Gunstone (Eds.), *The professional knowledge base of science teaching* (pp. 205–221). New York: Springer.

Abell, S. K., & Volkmann, M. J. (2006). *Seamless assessment in science: A guide for elementary and middle school teachers.* Portsmouth, NH: Heinemann.

Aikenhead, G. (1996). Science education: Border crossing into the subculture of science. *Studies in Science Education, 27,* 1–52.

Aikenhead, G. (2006). *Science education for everyday life: Evidence-based practice.* New York: Teachers College Press.

Aikenhead, G., Orpwood, G., & Fensham, P. (2011). Scientific literacy for a Knowledge Society. In C. Linder, L. Ostman, D. Roberts, P. Wickman, G. Erickson, & A. MacKinnon (Eds), *Exploring the landscape of scientific literacy* (pp. 28–44). Routledge: New York.

Ainsworth, S. (2006). DeFT: A conceptual framework for considering learning with multiple Representations. *Learning and Instruction, 16,* 183–198.

Alonzo, A., Gearhart, M., Champagne, A., Coppola, B., Duschl, R., Herman, J., et al. (2006). Commentaries. *Measurement: Interdisciplinary Research & Perspective, 4*(1/2), 99–126.

Alonzo, A., & Steedle, J. (2009). Developing and assessing a force and motion learning progression. *Science Education, 93,* 389–421.

Anderson, C. (2007). Perspectives on learning science. In S. Abell & N. Lederman (Eds.), *Handbook of research on science education* (pp. 3–30). Mahwah, NJ: Lawrence Erlbaum.

Anderson, K., Zuiker, S., Taasoobshirazi, G., & Hickey, D. (2007). Classroom discourse as a tool to enhance formative assessment and practise in science. *International Journal of Science Education, 29*(14), 1721–1744.

Aschbacher, P., & Alonzo, A. (2006). Using science notebooks to assess students' conceptual understanding. *Educational assessment, 11,* 179–203.

Atkin, J., & Black, P. (2003). *Inside science education reform: A history of curricular and policy change.* New York: Teachers College Press.

Bang, M., & Medin, D. (2010). Cultural processes in science education: Supporting the navigation of multiple epistemologies. *Science Education, 94*(6), 1008–1026.

Barton, A., & Tan, E. (2010). We be burnin'! Agency, identity, and science learning. *Journal of the Learning Sciences, 19*(2), 187–229.

Basu, S. J., Barton, A. C., & Tan, E. (2011). *Democratic science teaching: Building the expertise to empower low-income minority youth in science.* Rotterdam: Sense.

Bell, B., & Cowie, B. (2001). *Formative assessment and science education.* Dordrecht, The Netherlands: Kluwer.

Biddulph, F., Symington, D., & Osborne, R. (1986). The place of children's questions in primary science education. *Research in Science & Technological Education, 4*(1), 77–88.

Black, P., & Harrison, C. (2004). *Science inside the black box.* London, UK: GL Assessment.

Black, P., Harrison, C., Lee, C., Marshall, B., & Wiliam, D. (2003). *Assessment for learning: Putting it into practice.* Buckingham, UK: Open University Press.

Black, P., Harrison, C., Hodgen, J., Marshall, B., & Serret, N. (2011). Can teachers' summative assessments produce dependable results and also enhance classroom learning?, *Assessment in Education, 18*(4), 451–469.

Black, P., & Wiliam, D. (1998). Assessment and classroom learning. *Assessment in Education,* 5(1) 7–71.

Black, P., & Wiliam, D. (2006). Developing a theory of formative assessment. In J. Gardner (Ed.), *Assessment and learning* (pp. 81–100). Thousand Oaks, CA: Sage.

Black, P., & Wiliam, D. (2009). Developing the theory of formative assessment *Educational Assessment, Evaluation and Accountability, 21*(1), 5–31.

Buck, G., & Trauth-Nare, A. (2009). Preparing teachers to make the formative assessment process integral to science teaching and learning. *Journal of Science Teacher Education, 20,* 475–494.

Calabrese Barton, A., Basu, J., Johnson, V., & Tan, E. (2011). Introduction. In J. Basu, A. Barton, & E. Tan (Eds.), *Democratic science teaching: Building the expertise to empower low-income minority youth in science.* Rotterdam: Sense.

Calabrese Barton, A., & Tan, E. (2009). Funds of knowledge, discourses & hybrid space. *Journal of Research in Science Education, 46*(1), 50–73.

Calabrese Barton, A., & Tan, E. (2010). We be burnin'! Agency, identity & science learning. *Journal of Learning Sciences, 19*(2), 187–229.

Calabrese Barton, A., Tan, E., & Rivet A. (2008). Creating hybrid spaces for engaging school science among urban middle school girls. *American Education Research Journal, 45,* 68–103.

Carless, D. (2005). Prospects for the implementation of assessment for learning. *Assessment in Education, 12*(1), 39–54

Carlone, H., Haun-Frank, J., & Webb, A. (2011). Assessing equity beyond knowledge- and skills-based outcomes: A comparative ethnography of two fourth-grade reform-based science classrooms. *Journal of Research in Science Teaching,* 48(5), 459–485.

Chinn, C., & Osborne, J. (2008). Students' questions: A potential resource for teaching and learning science. *Studies in Science Education, 44*(1), 1–39.

Cowie, B. (1998). The role of questions in classroom assessment. *SAMEpapers, 98,* 41–53.

Cowie, B. (2005). Pupil commentary on Assessment for Learning. *The Curriculum Journal, 16*(2), 137–151.

Cowie, B., & Bell, B. (1999). A model of formative assessment in science education. *Assessment in Education, 6*(1), 101–116.

Cowie, B., Moreland, J., Jones, A., & Otrel-Cass, K. (2008). *The Classroom InSiTE Project: Understanding classroom interactions and learning trajectories to enhance teaching and learning in science and technology* (Final report). Wellington, New Zealand: New Zealand Council for Educational Research.

Crawford, T., Chen, C., & Kelly, G. (1997). Creating authentic opportunities for presenting science: The influence of audience on student talk. *Journal of Classroom Interaction, 32*(2), 1–12.

Danish, J., & Phelps, D. (2010, December 14). Representational practices by the numbers: Howe kindergarten and first-grade students create, evaluate, and modify their science representations. *International Journal of Science Education.*

Driver, R. A., Newton, P., & Osborne, J. (2000). Establishing the norms of scientific argumentation in classrooms. *Science Education, 84*(3), 287–312.

Duschl, R. A. (2003a). Assessment of inquiry. In J. Atkin & J. Coffey (Eds.), *Everyday assessment in the science classroom* (pp. 41–59). Arlington, VA: National Science Teachers Association Press.

Duschl, R. A. (2003b). The assessment of argumentation and explanation: Creating and supporting teachers' feedback strategies. In D. Zeidler (Ed.), *The role of moral reasoning on socioscientific issues and discourse in science education* (pp. 139–159). Dorecht, The Netherlands: Kluwer Acdemic Publishers.

Duschl, R. A. (2008). Science education in three-part harmony: Balancing conceptual, epistemic, and social learning goals. *Review of Research in Education, 32,* 268–291.

Duschl, R. A., & Gitomer, D. H. (1997). Strategies and challenges to changing the focus of assessment and instruction in science classrooms. *Educational Assessment, 4,* 37–73.

Duschl, R. A., Maeng, S., & Sezen, A. (2011). Learning progressions and teaching sequences: A review and analysis. *Studies in Science Education, 47*(2), 123–182.

Engle, R. & Conant, F. (2002). Guiding principles for fostering productive disciplinary engagement: Explaining an emergent argument in a community of learners classroom. *Cognition and Instruction, 20*(4), 399–483.

European Commission. (2007). *Science education now: A renewed pedagogy for the future of Europe.*

Brussels, Belgium: European Commission, Directorate–General for Research.

Fensham, P. (2008). *Science education policy-making: Eleven emerging issues.* Report commissioned by UNESCO, Section for Science, Technical and Vocational Education. UNESCO.

Ford, M., & Forman, E. (2006). Disciplinary learning in classroom contexts. *Review of Research in Education, 30,* 1–32.

Frederiksen, J., & White, B. (1997). *Reflective assessment of students' research within an inquiry-based middle school science curriculum.* Paper presented at the annual meeting of the American Educational Research Association, Chicago.

Friesen, J., & Ezeife, A. (2009). Making science assessment culturally valid for Aboriginal students. *Canadian Journal of Native Education, 32*(2), 24–37.

Furtak, E., & Ruiz-Primo, M. A. (2008). Making students' thinking explicit in writing and discussion: An analysis of formative assessment prompts. *Science Education, 92*(5), 799–824.

Fusco, D., & Barton, A. C. (2001). Representing student achievements in science. *Journal of Research in Science Teaching, 38*(3), 337–354.

Gerard, L., Spitulnik, M., & Linn, M. (2010). Teacher use of evidence to customize inquiry science instruction. *Journal of Research in Science Teaching, 47*(9), 1037–1063.

Givry, D., & Roth, W. (2006). Toward a new conception of conceptions: Interplay of talk, gestures, and structures in the setting. *Journal of Research in Science Teaching, 43*(10), 1086–1109.

González, N., & Moll, L. (2002). Cruzando el puente: Building bridges to funds of knowledge. *Journal of Educational Policy, 16*(4), 623–641.

Harlen, W. (2003). *Enhancing inquiry through formative assessment.* Institute for Inquiry, San Francisco. Retrieved from www.exploratorium.edu/IFI/resources/harlen_monograph.pdf

Harlen, W. (2010). *Principles and big ideas of science education.* Gosport, Hants, UK: Great Britain Ashford Colour Press Ltd.

Harrison, C. (in press). Changing assessment practices in science classrooms. In D. Corrigan, R. Gunstone, & A. Jones (Eds.), *Valuing assessment in science education: Pedagogy, curriculum, policy.* Dordrecht: Springer.

Heritage, M. (2011). Commentary on road maps for learning: A guide to the navigation of learning progressions. *Measurement: Interdisciplinary Research & Perspective, 9*(2/3), 149–151.

Herrenkohl, L., & Guerra, M. (1998). Participant structures, scientific discourse, and student engagement in fourth grade. *Cognition and Instruction, 16,* 433–475.

Hickey, D., Ingram-Goble, A., & Jameson, E. (2009). Designing assessments and assessing designs in virtual educational environments. *Journal of Science Education and Technology, 18*(2), 187–208.

Hubber, P., Tytler, R., & Haslam, F. (2010). Teaching and learning about force with a representational focus: Pedagogy and teacher change. *Research in Science Education, 40*(1).

Kelly, G., & Brown, C. (2003). Communicative demands of learning science through technological design: Third grade students' construction of solar energy devices. *Linguistics and Education, 13*(4), 483–532.

Kennedy, K., Chan, J., Fok, P., & Yu, W. (2008). Forms of assessment and their potential for enhancing learning: Conceptual and cultural issues. *Education Research Policy Practice, 7,* 197–207.

Ketelhut, D., Nelson, B., Clarke, J., & Dede, C. (2010). A multi-user virtual environment for building and assessing higher order inquiry skills in science. *British Journal of Educational Technology, 41*(1), 56–68.

Kress, G., Jewitt, C., Ogborn, J., & Tsatsarelius, C. (2001). *Multimodal teaching and learning: The rhetorics of the science classroom.* London: Continuum.

Lee, O. (2001). Culture and language in science educating: What do we know and what do we need to know? *Journal of Research in Science Teaching, 38*(5), 499–501.

Lee, O., & Buxton, C. (2010). *Diversity and equity in science education: Research, policy and practice.* New York: Teachers College Press

Lemke, J. L. (1990). *Talking science: Language, learning, and values.* Norwood, NJ: Ablex.

Lemke, J. L. (2000). Multimedia literacy demands of the scientific curriculum. *Linguistics and Education, 10*(3), 247–271.

Liu, O., Lee, H., & Linn, M. (2011). An investigation of explanation multiple-choice items in science assessment. *Educational Assessment, 16*(3), 164–184.

McMillan, J. (2003). Understanding and improving teachers' classroom decision-making: Implications for theory and practice. *Educational Measurement: Issues and Practice, 22*(4), 34–43.

McNeill, K. L., & Krajcik, J. (2008). Teacher instructional practices to support students writing scientific explanations. In J. Luft, J. Gess-Newsome, & R. Bell (Eds.), *Science as inquiry in the secondary setting.* Washington, DC: National Science Foundation.

McNeill, K. L., Lizotte, D. J, Krajcik, J., & Marx, R. W. (2006). Supporting students' construction of scientific explanations by fading scaffolds in instructional materials. *The Journal of the Learning Sciences, 15*(2), 153–191.

Minstrell, J., Anderson, R., Kraus, P., & Minstrell, J. E. (2008). Bridging from practice to research and back: Perspectives and tools in assessing for learning. In J. Coffey, R. Douglas, & C. Stearns (Eds.), *Assessing science learning.* Arlington, VA: National Science Teachers Association.

Minstrell, J., Anderson, R., & Li., M. (2011, May 10/11). *Building on learner thinking: A framework for assessment in instruction.* Commissioned paper for the Committee on Highly Successful STEM Schools or Programs for K–12 STEM Education: Workshop.

Minstrell, J., & Kraus, P. (2007). *Applied Research on Implementing Diagnostic Instructional Tools* (Final report to National Science Foundation). Seattle, WA: FACET Innovations.

Minstrell, J., Li, M., & Anderson, R. (2009a). *Annual report for formative assessment project.* Seattle, WA: FACET Innovations.

Minstrell, J., Li, M., & Anderson, R. (2009b). *Evaluating science teachers' formative assessment competency* (Technical report submitted to NSF).

Minstrell, J., & van Zee, E. (2003). Using questioning to assess and foster student thinking. In J. Atkin & J. Coffey (Eds.), *Everyday assessment in the science classroom* (pp. 61–73). Arlington, VA: National Science Teachers Association Press.

Mortimer, E., & Scott, P. (2003). *Meaning making in secondary science classrooms.* Buckingham, UK: Open University Press.

Moss, P. (2008). Sociocultural implications for the practice of assessment I: Classroom assessment. In P. Moss, D. Pullin, J. Gee, E. Haertel, & L. Young (Eds.), *Assessment, equity, and opportunity to learn.* New York: Cambridge University Press.

Mutegi, J. (2011). The inadequacies of "science for all" and the necessity and nature of a socially transformative curriculum approach for African American science education. *Journal of Research in Science Teaching, 3,* 301–316.

National Research Council. (1996). *National science education standards.* Washington, DC: National Academy Press.

National Research Council. (2000). *Inquiry and the national standards in science education.* Washington, DC: National Academy Press.

O'Byrne, B. (2009). Knowing more than words can say: Using multimodal assessment tools to excavate and construct knowledge about wolves. *International Journal of Science Education, 31*(4), 523–539.

Organisation for Economic Cooperation and Development. (2005, November). *Policy Brief. Formative assessment: Improving learning in secondary classrooms.* Paris: Author.

Orpwood, G., & Barnett, J. (1997). Science in the National Curriculum: an international perspective. *Curriculum Journal, 8*(3), 331–249.

Otrel-Cass, K., Cowie, B., & Glynn, T. (2009). Connecting science teachers with their Māori students. *Set, 2,* 34–41.

Osborne. R., & Freyberg, P. (1985). *Learning in science: The implications of children's science.* Auckland, New Zealand: Heinemann.

Pluta, W., Chinn, C., & Duncan, R. (2011). Learners' epistemic criteria for good scientific models. *Journal of Research in Science Teaching, 48*(5), 486–511.

Polman, J. L. (2011, April). *Informal learning environments that build connections to local communities while engaging citizens.* Panel presentation, Informal Learning Environments SIG, at the annual meeting of the American Educational Research Association, New Orleans, LA.

Porter, C., & Parvin, J. (2009). *Learning to love science: Harnessing children's scientific imagination.* A report from the Chemical Industry Education Centre, University of York. Retrieved from www-static.shell.com/static/gbr/downloads/responsible_energy/ro1427_ses_report.pdf

Prain, V., & Hand, B. (2012). In B. Fraser, K. Tobin, & C. McRobbie (Eds), *Second international handbook of science education.* New York: Springer.

Rennie, L., Venville, G., & Wallace, J. (2011). Learning science in an integrated classroom: Finding balance through theoretical triangulation. *Journal of Curriculum Studies, 43*(2), 139–162.

Roberts, D. (2007). Scientific literacy/science literacy. In S. Abell & N. Lederman (Eds.), *Handbook of research on science education* (pp. 729–780). New York: Routledge.

Roth, W.-M. (1995). Inventors, copycats, and everyone else: The emergence of shared resources and practices as defining aspects of classroom communities. *Science Education, 79*(5), 475–502.

Roth, W.-M. (2005). *Talking science: Language and learning in science classrooms.* Lanham, MD: Rowman & Littlefield.

Ruiz-Primo, M. (2011). Informal formative assessment: The role of instructional dialogues in assessing students' learning. *Studies in Educational Evaluation, 37,* 15–24.

Ruiz-Primo, M., & Furtak, E. (2006). Informal formative assessment and scientific inquiry: Exploring teachers' practices and student learning. *Educational Assessment, 11*(3/4), 205–235.

Russ, R. S., Coffey, J. E., Hammer, D., & Hutchison, P. (2009). Making classroom assessment more accountable to scientific reasoning: A case for attending to mechanistic thinking. *Science Education, 93*(5), 875–891.

Sadler, P. (1998). Psychometric models of student conceptions in science: Reconciling qualitative studies and distractor-driven assessment instruments. *Journal of Research in Science Teaching, 35,* 265–296.

Sadler, T., & Zeidler, D. (2009). Scientific literacy, PISA, and socioscientific discourse: Assessment for progressive aims of science education. *Journal of Research in Science Teaching, 46*(8), 909–921.

Sandoval, W. (2003). Conceptual and epistemic aspects of students' scientific explanations. *Journal of the Learning Sciences, 12*(1), 5–51.

Sandoval, W., & Cam, A. (2010). Elementary children's judgments of the epistemic status of sources of justification. *Science Education, 95,* 383–408.

Shavelson, R., Young, D., Ayala, C., Brandon, P., Furtak, E. & Ruiz-Primo, M. (2008). On the impact of curriculum-embedded formative assessment on learning: A collaboration between curriculum and assessment developers. *Applied Measurement in Education, 21,* 295–314.

Shepard, L. (2007). Will commercialism enable or destroy formative assessment? In C. Dwyer (Ed.), *The future of assessment: Shaping teaching and learning.* Mahwah, NJ: Lawrence Erlbaum.

Siegel, M., Wissehr, C., & Halverson, K. L. (2008). Sounds like success: A framework for equitable assessment. *The Science Teacher, 75*(3), 43–46.

Simon, S., Erduran, S., & Osborne, J. (2006). Learning to teach argumentation: Research and development in the science classroom. *International Journal of Science Education, 28*(2/3), 235–260.

Smith, C., Wiser, M., & Carraher, D. (2010, March). *Using a comparative longitudinal study to test some assumptions about a learning progression for matter.* Paper presented at the National Association for Research in Science Teaching, Philadelphia.

Solono-Flores, G., & Nelson-Barber, S. (2001). On the cultural validity of science assessments. *Journal of research in science teaching, 38*(5), 553–573.

Songer, J. G., Trinh, H. T., Killgore, G. E., Thompson, A. D., McDonald, L. C., & Limbago, B. M. (2009). Clostridium difficile in retail meat products, USA, 2007. *Emerging Infectious Disease, 15,* 819–821.

Southerland, S., Smith, L., Sowell, S., & Kittleson, J. (2007). Resisting unlearning: Understanding science education's response to the United States' national accountability movement. *Review of Research in Education, 31,* 45–72.

Stobart, G. (2005). Fairness in multicultural assessment systems. *Assessment in Education, 12*(3), 275–287.

Tan, A. (2011). Home culture, science, school and science learning: Is reconciliation possible? *Cultural Studies of Science Education, 6,* 559–567.

Tobin, K., & Gallagher, J. (1987). The role of target students in the science classroom. *Journal of Research in Science Teaching, 24*(1), 61–75.

Tytler, R. (2007). *Re-imagining science education: Engaging students in science for Australia's future.* Camberwell, Victoria, Australia: ACER Press: Australian Council for Educational Research.

U.S. Department of Education. (2002). *No Child Left Behind Act of 2001* (Title I Paraprofessionals: Draft Non-Regulatory Guidance). Washington, DC: U.S. Department of Education, Office of Elementary and Secondary Education.

Varelas, M., Pappas, C., Tucker-Raymond, E., Kane, J., Hankes, J., Ortiz, I., et al. (2010). Drama activities as ideational resources for primary-grade children in urban science classrooms. *Journal of Research in Science Teaching, 47*(3), 302–325.

Waldrip, B., Prain, V., & Carolan, J. (2010). Using multi-modal representations to improve learning in junior secondary science. *Research in Science Education, 40*(1), 65–80.

Warren, B., Ballenger, C., Ogonowski, M., Rosebery, A. & Hudicourt-Barnes, J. (2001). Rethinking diversity in learning science: The logic of everyday sense making. *Journal of Research in Science Teaching, 38*(5), 529–552.

Wenger, E. (1998). *Communities of practice: Learning, meaning and identity.* New York: Cambridge University Press

White, D., & Gunstone, D. (1992). *Probing understanding.* London: Falmer Press.

Wiliam, D., & Thompson, M. (2008). Integrating assessment with instruction: What will it take to make it work? In C. A. Dwyer (Ed.), *The future of assessment: Shaping teaching and learning* (pp. 53–82). Mahwah, NJ: Lawrence Erlbaum.

Wilson, M., & Berthenthal, M. (2005). *Systems for state science assessment.* Washington, DC: National Academies Press.

Windschitl, M. (2001). The diffusion and appropriation of ideas: An investigation of events occurring between groups of learners in science classrooms. *Journal of Research in Science Teaching, 38*(1), 17–42.

Yin, Y., Shavelson, R., Ayala, C., Ruiz-Primo, M., Brandon, P., Furtak, E., et al. (2008). On the impact of formative assessment on student motivation, achievement, and conceptual change. *Applied Measurement in Education, 21*(4), 335–359.

28

Classroom Assessment in Writing

Judy M. Parr

Writing is not only a complex cognitive act but one that is socially, culturally, and contextually framed. Being a writer involves "navigating textually through our deeply layered semiotic, material and socio-cultural worlds" (Dressman, McCarthey, & Prior, 2011, p. 7). From this theoretical perspective, writing is a tool in students' negotiation of their many-faceted and changing worlds—cultural, social, and academic. In theorizing about writing, there has been movement from a view of writing primarily as a product and as a somewhat generic, transferable skill (or set of skills) to be taught and assessed to viewing it as an act that is social and is centrally influenced by purpose, content, and context.

However, the links between current theorizing about writing and pedagogy, including assessment, are not very well articulated. In general, assessment of writing is poorly aligned to current theory of writing (Behizadeh & Engelhard, 2011). For writing, the foremost component of any valid assessment is "a model (a theory) of student cognition in the domain . . . the theory or set of beliefs about how students represent knowledge and develop competence in a subject domain" (Pellegrino, Chudowsky, & Glaser, 2001, p. 44). Writing research has resulted in informative models of the cognitive processes involved in writing (e.g., Bereiter & Scardamalia, 1987; Berninger & Swanson, 1994; Flower & Hayes, 1981; Hayes, 1996; Hayes & Flower, 1980; Kellog, 1996), and these have, arguably, influenced pedagogy. But a model of learning that specifies the development of both product and processes in writing simply does not exist (Alamargot & Fayol, 2009); what develops in writing and what it develops toward (Marshall, 2004) are moot questions. Given these questions, assessment of writing is, arguably, qualitatively different from assessment of curriculum areas like history or math. In writing (as noted for reading by Phelps & Schilling, 2004), there is not a body of scholarship that defines the content of the subject of writing.

Further, current assessment theory and the majority of research on assessment in writing seem misaligned. Although assessment of writing was seen to be among the least studied aspects of writing research more generally (Juzwik et al., 2006), there is still a considerable body of research in writing assessment. This literature has tended to focus on issues that are predominantly technical (see Huot & Neal, 2006), relating to testing writing as a means of making summative judgments regarding performance against standards or for purposes of admission, placement, etc. Theorizing assessment, however, has changed. There has been a general reframing of the purpose of assessment (Black & Wiliam, 1998a, 1998b; Sadler, 1989; Wiliam & Black, 1996). It is now seen as a means to inform and improve teaching and learning. Assessment refers to "all those activities undertaken by teachers—and by students in assessing themselves—that provide information to be used as feedback to modify teaching and learning activities" (Black & Wiliam, 1998b, p. 140).

While many writing resource books for teachers continue to present a traditional view of classroom assessment (CA) as almost an afterthought phase in the planning cycle where what is taught is determined by curriculum objectives and writing process specifications (e.g., Tompkins, 2004), this reframing has markedly influenced others. Notably, Huot (2002) described how he deliberated long and hard to decide on the title for his book *(Re)-Articulating Writing Assessment for Teaching and Learning* to ensure that it would capture changing notions of assessment.

In this chapter, I consider the major ways in which teachers of writing may be supported to find out where their students are currently positioned in relation to desired outcomes for writing, and how teachers may best work with this evidence to enhance their instructional practices. An important part of enhancing writing involves helping students to become partners in their learning.

Classroom Practice and Theory and Research in Assessment

Although in the assessment literature, notions of assessment have moved toward formative purposes, testing to make a summative judgment about performance against standards or to admit or place students still figures in the context of the writing classroom teacher (see Chapter 14 and Section 3 of this volume). Such formative tests impact curricula and instruction through a complex phenomenon referred to as washback (Weigle, 2002). The form and function of these assessments influences what happens in writing classrooms in terms of rhetorical stance, instructional mode, and writing process; they privilege curricula content that appears related to the assessment, like particular forms of writing (Hillocks, 2002). Tests promote unintended learning, including a narrow definition of writing by students (Luce-Kapler & Klinger, 2005). To the extent that the design and implementation of such tests fail to furnish useful diagnostic information for the classroom participants, they consume valuable teaching time.

Assessment should provide information from which teachers learn about how successful their instruction has been and how they may need to adjust practice. It also provides information for students to inform their learning as, increasingly, assessment within a classroom context is seen as a social, collaborative activity (Black & Wiliam, 2009). However, there is a gap between the approaches promoted in the professional literature and those of the classroom. In their seminal article, Black and Wiliam (1998b), in noting a poverty of CA practice, are clear that teachers will not take up ideas, however attractive or no matter how extensive the supporting research, if the ideas are simply given in the form of general principles so that teachers shoulder the difficult task of translating them into practice. Writing suffers the additional barriers of a lack of specification of what content knowledge is needed (as previously noted) and likely (given research in reading: e.g., Wong-Fillmore & Snow, 2002) from a lack of knowledge on the part of teachers about the development of written language and how language works to achieve its social communicative meaning. Arguably, support is necessary for teachers to implement quality CA in writing that will impact teaching and learning and raise writing achievement.

Assessing Writing in the Service of Teaching and Learning

Historically, writing teachers responded to the conflicting needs of providing judgments about performance, of providing authentic assessment that would more likely represent student performance in a range of contexts, and to a lesser extent, of providing information useful for learning and instruction through the development of portfolios. Portfolios essentially comprise multiple instances of writing which could be gathered over time to represent richer, more complex information about a writer's efforts, progress, or performance (see Chapter 19 of this volume for a more extended discussion of portfolios). They were seen as an alternative, authentic, more equitable form of evaluating such performance that might have a positive effect on instruction and student performance (Darling-Hammond, Ancess, & Falk, 1995; Wiggins,

1993). The portfolio concept as applied to writing has been discussed in a number of collections (e.g., Black, Daiger, Sommers, & Stygall, 1994; Calfee & Perfumo, 1996; Hamp-Lyons & Condon, 2000; Yancey & Weisser, 1997). Whether portfolios are a form of evaluation has been questioned (Calfee, 2000; Elbow, 1994); rather, they could be viewed as "a pedagogically useful collection procedure that in some ways resembles an assessment procedure" (White, 1994, p. 29). The portfolio movement exemplified the need for multiple instances, and often collection over time, of evidence. Although portfolios seemed to link assessment to the classroom, in research concerning them, the link to teaching and learning was not directly addressed.

Engaging in ongoing CA means there are multiple opportunities to assess students' writing for a range of communicative purposes and under a range of conditions. A key characteristic of effective literacy teachers is that they know their learners. Observing and gathering information systematically about students' reading and writing behaviors and outcomes on an ongoing basis is an integral part of teaching (Parr & Limbrick, 2010; Pressley, Allington, Wharton-McDonald, Block, & Morrow, 2001; Pressley, Rankin, & Yokoi, 1996).

Viewed from the perspective of instruction, CA of students' writing can be thought of as providing the principal form of evidence for the inquiring or reflective teacher of writing. The notion of teaching as inquiry means that a teacher is constantly asking whether current practice is effective in that it is supporting all students in the class to learn. The hallmark of an effective teacher is that s/he is what has been termed an adaptive expert (Bransford, Derry, Berliner, & Hammerness, 2005). An adaptive expert is one who is able to change or tailor practice to meet the needs of each student in the class.

In order to accomplish this, a writing teacher should be clear about what the students in class should achieve at their particular level of the curriculum and seek evidence of where students are in relation to the desired outcomes. The teacher then has to use this evidence of writing performance, in tandem with research-based evidence of effective practice in the teaching of writing, to plan optimal instruction that moves to bridge the gap between what students currently know and can do and what they need to know and do. At the same time, reflective practitioners consider what they may need to learn in order to decide on and implement the instruction to help students progress to where they need to be. Clearly, this cycle of inquiry is iterative as there has to be ongoing assessment to monitor the efficacy of the new learning experiences for students and then of any subsequent changes to practice (Timperley, Wilson, & Barrar, 2007).

Identifying Patterns of Strengths and Gaps in Student Writing

Some indication to teachers regarding desired outcomes in writing comes from official sources. Most commonly, writing outcomes are indicated by curriculum goals and standards or benchmarks. These are variously arrived at mostly through professional judgment rather than empirical research or normative data. For example, in New Zealand, a standard for writing to be achieved by the end of Year 4 (Grade 3) states the following:

> By the end of year 4, students will create texts in order to meet the writing demands of the New Zealand Curriculum at level 2. Students will use their writing to think about, record and communicate experiences, ideas, and information to meet specific learning purposes across the curriculum. (Ministry of Education, 2009, p. 27)

This is followed by the key characteristics of students' writing at this level where it is stated that the knowledge, skills, and attitudes expected are described in the *Literacy Learning Progressions (LLP)* (Ministry of Education, 2010) and that students will independently write texts using language and a simple text structure that suit their audience and purpose. The standard goes on to read that the texts will include, when appropriate, the following:

- Content that is mostly relevant to the curriculum task; covers a range of ideas, experiences, or items of information; and often includes detail and/or comment supporting the main points
- Mainly simple and compound sentences that vary in their beginnings, structures, and lengths and that are mostly correct grammatically

- Attempts at complex sentences
- Words and phrases, in particular nouns, verbs, adjectives, and adverbs, that clearly convey ideas, experiences, and information. (Ministry of Education, 2009, p. 27)

The standard is then amplified with an example that contains aspects of the task and text relevant to the standard and commentary showing how a student engages with both task and text to meet the writing demands of the curriculum. There is a note that a number of such examples would need to be used to inform the overall teacher judgment for a student (where a student is in relation to any standard is based on professional opinion formed from evidence; this is the classroom teacher's overall teacher judgment).

While there are stated curriculum goals or standards at a district, state, or national level, at a classroom level there is the instantiation of these often more high level or generalized goals into the immediate, more specific focus and aims of teaching day to day. For a writing lesson or a group of lessons, a teacher of Grade 3 or 4 may have a main learning goal for students, such as that when writing to argue or persuade, they learn to present points both for and against and to provide an example that supports each point. Or a specific learning goal may be that students understand that writing to instruct often uses imperatives, and they are able to recognize, form, and employ such constructions appropriately.

The information that a teacher uses to find out how students are progressing, in relation to a specific goal or a more general goal, is influenced first by the purpose for gathering the evidence. Commonly, the purpose is to check learning in relation to the more specific aims for a lesson or series of lessons. The purpose may be to consider the patterns across the class for what they tell a teacher about instruction (past and planned) or to measure the extent of progress and gauge whether the pace of learning is on target for individuals to reach particular levels or standards. At other times, the purpose may be to gain a sense of performance against broader curriculum goals and standards. The effective writing teacher needs to integrate information from a number of different sources to come to an overall judgment about a student's performance relative to a goal or standard. Or the purpose may be to share a profile of the student's writing "strengths and gaps" (Sadler, 1989) with the student and parents.

The means is also influenced by the teacher's theory of what is important in writing and writing development for his/her students. Any tool for, or means of, gathering evidence reflects the designer's (or user's) theory of the task—what is involved in being a competent writer, producing a competent performance at a particular level. In selecting a means to gather evidence, a teacher has to ask, "To what extent is this means of gathering evidence a valid indicator of the competence or skills, including strategic metacognitive skills, or dispositions in writing that I want to find out about for my present purpose?" The nature of the construct assessed (and the means to assess the construct) needs to align with the purpose.

Evidence about ongoing student learning in writing in relation to desired outcomes is gathered by the classroom teacher in two major ways. Information about student writing, both process and product, is obtained through what has been termed interactive formative assessment, the moment by moment observations a teacher (or student) makes, and through planned formative assessment (Cowie & Bell, 1999). Interactive formative assessment in the writing classroom refers to information gleaned in the course of everyday interactions around writing. Planned formative assessment in writing usually involves a common task (or tasks) for students, most often the production of a sample (or samples) of writing to gain information on how well students have learned from the current teaching or how well they are progressing toward a learning outcome or standard.

In providing examples of how both interactive and planned formative assessment operate in the writing classroom, the type of support that helps classroom teachers assess writing effectively for their purposes is important. A significant support for any professional community involves the development of shared repertoires—a community's set of shared resources created to negotiate meaning in the joint pursuit of an enterprise (Wenger, 1998). The repertoire includes routines, tools, words, or concepts that the community has either produced or adopted in the course of its existence. Tools are considered to be externalized representations of ideas that people use in their practice (Norman, 1988;

Spillane, Reiser, & Reimer, 2002). When the ideas represented in the tool are valid—in the current case of classroom writing assessment if the ideas represent valid indicators of writing behavior at a particular developmental level—and if these ideas are represented in a quality way (a way that allows them to serve as indicators of the nature of such behavior), the tool is able to help achieve the purpose of the task. Mostly it is not simply the tool itself that enables the learning. Rather, it is how the tool is integrated into the routines of practice. In assessing writing, the routines of practice include collegial discussion of evidence of writing, particularly the moderation of writing samples.

Using the New Zealand context as an example, there are several key tools that could be regarded as resources that have become part of the repertoire of writing teachers. These include the *Assessment Tools for Teaching and Learning* or *asTTle* (Ministry of Education and the University of Auckland, 2004), a diagnostic tool for assessing writing and, more recently, the *LLP* (Ministry of Education, 2010) and the *New Zealand Curriculum Reading and Writing Standards* (Ministry of Education, 2009).

Interactive Formative Writing Assessment

In the course of daily writing time, the teacher has numerous opportunities to observe and note writing behaviors. The interactions in guided and shared writing, discussion of text in reading, sharing writing to elicit responses from others, and conferencing are all sites for gathering evidence to assess what students know in regard to writing and where they need support to strengthen or move their understanding. The evidence gained from interactions about students' writing development is often acted upon immediately, as the teacher takes the opportunity to teach at the point of need. At other times, the evidence or inference from what was observed is filed as a mental note, an entry in the teacher's log-in-the-head. On yet other occasions, more formal written logs or reports are developed to record ongoing observations or to annotate the features of the context (i.e., level of autonomy, persistence, resources used, and student affective response to own writing) in which a particular piece of writing was produced.

Conferencing

A key interactive site in the elementary or primary writing classroom that provides rich evidence of and for learning (including the opportunity to push learning forward) is conferencing. Practice oriented, classroom-based writers (e.g., Anderson, 2000; Calkins, 1994; Graves, 1983, 2003) clearly locate the role of the teacher as a follower of a developing writer's lead; young writers are to take responsibility for managing and reflecting on their own learning. In conferences, developing writers learn to interact with and craft meaning for a reader. Effective conferences provide writers with opportunities to develop the metacognitive awareness related to the writing process and the self-regulatory strategies needed for reflecting on their texts, together with the personal responsibility needed to become a writer (Graves, 2003). The role of the teacher is couched in terms of listening for clues about the kind of support writers need.

Although research studies are relatively limited, detailed analyses of conferences in action show the reality of practice to be quite different to the ideals of conferencing. Conferences have been shown to be predominantly teacher controlled, with the teacher adopting an overly authoritative role (Wong, 1998). Differences in the manner in which conferences have been conducted were found for low and high achieving writers (Freedman & Sperling, 1985; Glasswell, Parr, & McNaughton, 2003; Walker & Elias, 1987) and for students from different cultural backgrounds (Patthey-Chavez & Ferris, 1997). The focus of these studies has tended to be the properties of the interaction. However, the pedagogical effectiveness of any individual interaction is not in the formal properties but in the way in which these properties are used to achieve targeted instructional purposes in a particular context (Haneda, 2004).

Conferences contain opportunities for moment-by-moment assessment and subsequent decision making by teachers who have the potential to move learners' development forward in meaningful ways. Glasswell and Parr (2009) have shown, through a theorized example of the practice of an effective teacher, how a conference is used to assess a young writer and through skilled, deliberate teaching moves to ascertain the region of sensitivity where a student is primed to learn. The analysis of the teacher–student interactions around an evolving piece of writing illustrates several things. It shows how the teacher knows the student, having tracked his development over time, how the student initiates an interaction and provides evidence of ability to monitor and evaluate his progress, articulating what he perceives he has accomplished, and how the teacher uses the incoming information and her knowledge to recognize the teachable moment, "the space in which complex interactions among assessment, teaching, and learning become dynamically and productively linked to enhance student learning" (Glasswell & Parr, 2009, p. 354).

The literature suggests that, for even the most skilled teachers, conferencing around writing is complex and challenging (Anderson, 2000; Calkins, 1994; Glasswell et al., 2003). Arguably, knowing what to attend to in the on-the-fly stream of activity of a writing conference in order to assess and then guide the student's learning forward requires considerable expertise. It is important that a teacher knows what behaviors are likely to be significant indicators of developing ability to write.

The Literacy Learning Progressions

In New Zealand, a tool was developed to help in this endeavor. The *LLP* (Ministry of Education, 2010) describes and illustrates the literacy-related knowledge, skills, and attitudes that students need in order to meet the reading and writing demands of the New Zealand curriculum. The *LLP* descriptions are intended to be used as a reference point when teachers are gathering information about their students' literacy strengths and needs. They help direct teachers' attention to significant behaviors, attitudes, knowledge, and skills, cueing teachers as to what to notice particularly in interactions with students but also in considering products. Because of the role of writing as an interactive tool across the curriculum, there is a specific focus on purpose for writing in the *LLP* as students use writing to think about, record, and communicate ideas, experiences, and information. At each level in the progressions, a paragraph describes the writing demands of the texts and tasks of the curriculum at that level, then a paragraph describes the shift in writing expertise over 2 years (the *LLP* are largely at 2-year intervals because a curriculum level covers 2 years of schooling). A set of bullet points describes the expertise and attitudes that students demonstrate when they write texts in order to meet the demands of the curriculum at the level indicated. A few examples of these from the end of Year 4 include the following. As they write, students build on their expertise and demonstrate that they do the following:

- Understand their purposes for writing and how to meet those purposes.
- Write texts on a variety of topics and confidently express ideas and opinions.
- Encode words using their knowledge of consonant and vowel sounds, of common spelling patterns.
- Expand their writing vocabulary by using strategies such as the following:
    - Applying knowledge of the meaning of most common prefixes . . . and suffixes
    - Using reference sources to check meanings of words and to find words
- Reread as they are writing to check for meaning and fitness for purpose.

Finally, a paragraph describes the specific skills and items of knowledge that students draw on as they use their expertise in writing at the particular level. The kinds of texts students are expected to write are illustrated and cross-referenced with the National Standards document (Ministry of Education, 2009), where there are annotated exemplars.

The *LLP* have helped teachers understand their learners in numerous ways. In one study (Parr, 2011), 291 teachers responded using a 6-point Likert scale to questions developed from the principles articulated in the research literature as underpinning learning progressions. These included whether the descriptions represented actual observed performance by students; provided a big picture of what is to be learned, including making the writing demands of the curriculum clear; and how they aligned with assessment tools and allowed the mapping of formative assessment information (Hess, 2008). In relation to the latter, respondents were asked about the extent to which the *LLP* helped to locate current strengths and needs of students, helped teachers to see connections between what comes before and after a certain learning goal, helped teachers to decide on actions to take in teaching, and gave an indication of learning experiences most useful at a particular stage of development. Open-ended questions asked about what teachers learned and what they have done as a result to this learning.

The strongest agreement concerned items such as "providing a big picture of what is to be learned" and "providing a view of current learning within the bigger picture of development." Teachers also agreed strongly that the *LLP* helped them to learn about what was expected at different year levels in order that students would be able to access and cope with the writing (and reading) demands of the curriculum and with items concerning making connections between what had gone before and what came afterward, in terms of where the student is currently at and where s/he needs to be in moving forward.

The tool is integrated into the practice of assessment for learning (AFL) in the classroom through the use of the tool as a professional learning resource and, more significantly, through the routines of professional discussions that take place among teachers at grade level around specific examples drawn from their classrooms and students.

Planned Formative Writing Assessment

Planned formative assessment mostly includes examining samples and/or collections of writing, in draft or more final form. To produce writing samples for assessment requires developing a quality, rich task for writers and examining responses in a nuanced way so that the required evidence can be gained about the particular writing function or dimension under consideration. Many tasks that are used as indicators of writing ability do not provide information that is sufficiently detailed in terms of actual production of writing to serve diagnostic purposes. For example, a sentence-combining task will not give adequate information about students' ability to produce text, nor will an exercise to correct semantic or syntactic errors in a paragraph do this. While they may serve as rough proxies for performance, they are of little use as diagnostic measures.

Other tasks and their associated scoring schemes, while providing a judgment about writing quality, may not provide information about the particular function of writing that was the focus of instruction. For example, a generic writing test may not give a valid indication of how well a teacher has taught students to classify and organize information in order to report it. For the latter, a rich task would provide content information (as content knowledge is a major reason for variation even within a person in terms of writing performance) for the report in an unstructured way (including visuals perhaps), possibly including irrelevant material. Then the teacher would assess performance using criteria that pertain to such a purpose for writing.

The important consideration is whether the assessment chosen, especially if it is a standardized writing test, is aligned with the curriculum and with what has been taught. Otherwise, the evidence gained about performance is difficult to relate to classroom practice, to what has been taught, in order to utilize the information to reflect on the efficacy of such practice. Similarly, if the assessment is not aligned to the curriculum, it is of limited use in planning how to move learning forward. In this respect, the task the students respond to needs to be able to be analyzed in a way that gives maximum diagnostic information. Scoring writing holistically yields little information other than a generic level of performance. Analytic scoring rubrics, encapsulating desired qualities of writing, can be useful. However, given that writing varies according to social purpose, a one-size-fits-all rubric arguably has limited utility for classroom use.

These were issues that we were mindful of in designing a writing assessment, *asTTle* Writing (Ministry of Education & the University of Auckland, 2004), that could be used by the classroom teacher for diagnostic purposes. The view of writing underpinning the tool is aligned with theory that writing is a social and cultural practice that varies not only according to purpose but to cultural practice and situational context. We drew on the work of those who view writing broadly as serving social purposes (e.g., Chapman, 1999; Knapp & Watkins, 1994, 2005). Writing was conceptualized as serving six major purposes, a core set of generic processes that encapsulate what the text is doing (Knapp & Watkins, 2005). For each of the major purposes that inform, or processes that form, an analytic rubric was developed. The content of these rubrics drew on sociolinguistic research (e.g., Martin, Christie, & Rothery, 1987), regarding forms of text produced (i.e., genres) in and by specific social institutions (like within schooling) as having some stability, given the relative stability of social structures (Kress, 1993). Therefore, descriptions of features and text structures commonly associated with a generic social purpose were provided in the rubrics.

The rubrics assess student performance using criterion statements relating to seven dimensions of writing, from rhetorical considerations to surface features. While all dimensions of analysis of the text are seen as interdependent in terms of judging the effectiveness of the piece of writing, for purposes of assessment, the dimensions are considered and scored separately. Within the same framework and dimensions, the criteria at each of the curriculum levels (2 to 6) articulate a developmental progression. This helps teachers to work out what the next level of development, the way forward, would look like for any given writer. The scoring against criteria helps map a writer's development, allowing diagnosis of areas of difficulty and those of strength to be situated within the context of the communicative purpose of the task. The normative database underpinning the tool also allows teachers to compare their students with others (see Parr, 2010).

The tool was utilized by 300 schools that participated in a national professional development project in literacy that selected writing as their focus (there were three cohorts of schools, each lasting 2 years). The project was evidence-informed at all levels (see Parr & Timperley, 2010a), and the rubrics from the diagnostic instrument, *asTTle* Writing, were used both to score writing to provide evidence of level of performance and also to provide information for diagnostic purposes and for planning and assisting professional learning. Through skilled facilitation at the school level, the project aimed to enhance practice in teaching writing by establishing the learning needs of students and then what their teachers needed to know and do in order to best meet those needs. In writing, each cohort of students made significant gains beyond expectations (see Parr & Timperley, 2010a).

Part of the explanation for the considerable gains in writing achievement was likely to have been the support provided by the detailed scoring rubrics from the diagnostic tool (Parr, Glasswell, & Aikman, 2007) and, in later cohorts, from the *LLP*. Teachers are thought to gain a better understanding of writing and form concepts of a quality performance in the process of discussion with colleagues. Knowledge that is built in the processes of discussion and consensus decision making becomes part of the guild knowledge of the teacher (Sadler, 1989). In this process of constructing shared notions of a quality performance at different levels, teachers are aided by tools and routines, including annotated exemplars constructed by acknowledged experts. Detailed scoring rubrics also assist, as do tools like progressions and standards, as they help to make explicit what to notice and they operationalize and make concrete significant features (Parr, 2011).

Letting Developing Writers in on the Secret

For students to participate in their own learning, in our focus here on writing, they need to gain an understanding of the qualities of the desired performance, their current level of understanding, and what they have to do to achieve the desired performance (Hattie & Timperley, 2007). Research shows that when students are given clear and coherent messages about what they are meant to learn about writing (not about the task that they are meant to be doing) and what a quality performance looks like, they make accelerated progress in writing skills (Timperley & Parr, 2009). This empirical study examined the quality of writing instructional goals, how well they were conveyed to students through lesson activities, and how the students came to understand them. Two different but converging theoretical perspectives of self-regulated learning (SRL) and formative assessment were used as an analytical framework. Teachers' instructional practices during writing lessons were audiotaped in 17 different classrooms and a sample of students subsequently interviewed to assess their understanding of the dimensions of interest. The conditions monitored included the extent to which aims and mastery criteria were made explicit and how well feedback was aligned to those lesson aims. In most classes, students' interview responses reflected the extent to which teachers were explicit in these aspects of instructional practice. In general, when lesson aims and mastery criteria were unclear, students identified surface features of writing (e.g., spelling and length) as their learning aims. When these lesson attributes were clearly articulated by the teacher, students were able to identify deeper features of writing (e.g., rhetorical issues and structure or use of language) as the lesson aims. When the aims were clear but the mastery criteria and lesson activities were misaligned, however, students identified surface features of writing as the lesson aims, rather than those articulated by the teacher.

The provision of specific learning aims and performance criteria is contested territory and seen as problematic by some (Sadler, 2010). This is particularly so in writing where, arguably, the whole is more than the sum of the parts. This issue notwithstanding, teachers often use assessment rubrics and annotated examples that relate to different dimensions of writing, some specially written in *student-speak*, to make clear to students the elements of a quality performance and what they look like (Parr & Jesson, 2011).

Students also gain information about how they are progressing and what they need to do to improve from teacher feedback. The ability of teachers to provide quality written feedback was associated with students who made greater progress in writing (Parr & Timperley, 2010b). In this study, the quality of response was defined in terms of providing information about where students were positioned relative to the performance desired, key features of the desired performance, and what was needed to achieve the desired performance. Fifty-nine teachers in six schools provided data regarding their ability to give quality formative written feedback to a piece of writing. This quality score related significantly to gains in their students' achievement on a nationally standardized measure of writing ($r = 0.685$, $p < 0.01$). The ability to provide a written response that served AFL functions appeared to be a powerful component of teacher practice that developed student writing.

While such knowledge is fundamental to student engagement with their learning in writing, Sadler (2010) argued that the telling nature of quality feedback renders it less than adequate as students have to understand the concepts or criteria used in the feedback communication. And to convert feedback into action for improvement, there is a need for sufficient working knowledge of some fundamental concepts that teachers draw on when assessing and when giving feedback. There are three classes of concepts students need to acquire in developing appraisal expertise: (1) task compliance, (2) quality, and (3) criteria (Sadler, 2010). Task compliance refers to the congruence between the type of response stipulated in the task specifications and the type of response actually submitted.

The teacher, according to Sadler, draws on two types of knowledge in assessing. One concerns the notion of range of quality, which comes from exposure to a variety of work; this forms and maintains the teacher's abstract notion of quality itself (this carries across students and assessment events). Sadler treats quality as an integrated property, rather than something composed of or built up from judgments made on separate criteria. So students need exposure to a variety of works of varying quality, in a planned way, to develop a sense of quality. The second type of knowledge concerns comparability where any given level of performance also has many possible expressions. These two types of knowledge represent two dimensions, and each piece of student work can be located within this two dimensional space. The teacher as s/he marks progressively populates this space with judgments about real cases and from this constructs feedback. Teachers routinely invoke criteria that are salient to a particular judgment. Behind each criterion is a quality-related concept that students, too, can acquire.

To develop such tacit knowledge, students have to be immersed in learning environments where they acquire a sound working knowledge of needed concepts not in an abstract way but in a way where concepts are operationalized and applied to a concrete situation. Providing supported evaluative experience is a deliberate part of the design of teaching. In the writing classroom, environments to develop the ability to make complex judgments in evaluating writing could happen through engaging in peer or self-assessment or in moderation-type discussions around writing.

Self- and Peer Writing Assessment

Appraising your own work and that of your peers (peer evaluation is seen as easier than self-evaluation) is a way to develop evaluative and productive knowledge and expertise (Sadler, 1989; see also Chapters 21 and 22 of this volume). Such assessments help students' internal self-regulatory mechanisms and enhance their evaluative insights and writing. There is a large body of literature that shows that learners who are more self-regulated are more effective learners; they are more persistent, resourceful, and confident, and they are higher achievers (e.g., Pintrich, 1995; Zimmerman & Schunk, 2001; see also Chapters 3 and 4 of this volume). While the benefits of reflection and self assessment are readily claimed, and there is a developed rationale for linking self-assessment to achievement (see Ross, Rolheiser, & Hogaboam-Gray, 1999), there is limited empirical support of these claims (Rust, Price, & Donovan, 2003, is an exception).

Writing teachers seldom engage in activities designed to develop evaluative expertise. A study of methods teachers use in writing classrooms of 13- to 16-year-olds suggests that methods of evaluation and tasks that cede control to students are not a common occurrence (Hunter, Mayenga, & Gambell, 2006). However, teachers of writing (e.g., Bloom, 1997; Elbow, 1997; Glenn, 2009) do describe methods by which they incorporate student self-assessment into their classroom through reflective writing, through contracting criteria that describe the work required to reach a particular level or grade, and through written or oral dialogues in which student and teacher evaluate writing together or dialogue around the student writing. And there is some evidence to suggest that students are being accorded a more significant role as partners in learning about writing (Hawe, Dixon, & Watson, 2008).

There are a small number of empirical studies examining specific ways to support self- and peer assessment. In writing, approaches to understanding assessment criteria or standards have utilized the principle of annotated samples, commonly used as a basis for training raters, and have modified the procedure for learners. Exemplars help make criteria clear and form a focus for meaningful formative feedback about expected standards (Orsmond, Merry, & Reiling, 2002). In a small scale study involving the provision of scripts annotated according to criteria specific to a writing task, each participant assessed his or her own writing and that of a peer. The samples helped students gain a sense of perspective regarding the quality of their written work and to both self- and peer assess appropriately (Brown, 2005).

Conclusion

Writing is a complex act to teach and to assess. As students progress through schooling, writing increasingly becomes the principal means by which they are required to display what they have learned. The CA literature in writing is limited—there is work to be done—so the argument presented here has been partly developed from theorizing and from more general literature around what has been termed formative assessment and also from notions of teaching as inquiry. The broad argument, supported by some research, is that the use of assessment in the service of teaching and learning enhances writing achievement.

Ongoing CA provides multiple opportunities to assess students' writing for a range of communicative purposes under a range of conditions. Two major ways in which teachers accomplish this are through interactive and planned formative assessment. However, given the general lack of empirically verified models of the development of writing and the contested nature of what constitutes quality, teachers need considerable support in terms of what to notice in the stream of activity and also in the nature of written products at different levels of schooling. The use of tools like progressions and detailed scoring rubrics encapsulating a developmental aspect that provide scaffolding for CA has been described. The evidence obtained about the patterns of strengths and gaps in student writing achievement allows practice to be honed to better meet the learning needs of students, resulting in accelerated progress.

Furthermore, the argument for involving students in their development as writers has been made, and the potential ways to provide structured opportunities to develop the knowledge and skills required are noted. Moving beyond quality feedback to students, the pedagogical approach suggested here, drawing on the more recent work of Sadler (2010), involves helping students to see and understand the reasons for quality and to develop facility in making complex judgments through self- and peer assessment. Research on assessment in writing would benefit from study of how this can best be accomplished.

References

Alamargot, D., & Fayol, M. (2009). Modeling the development of written composition. In R. Beard, D. Myhill, M. Nystrand, & J. Riley (Eds.), *Handbook of writing development* (pp. 23–47). Thousand Oaks, CA: Sage.

Anderson, C. (2000). *How's it going? A practical guide to conferring with student writers.* Portsmouth, NH: Heinemann.

Behizadeh, N., & Engelhard, G. (2011). Historical view of the influence of measurement and writing theories on the practice of writing assessment in the United States. *Assessing Writing, 16,* 189–211.

Bereiter, C., & Scardamalia, M. (1987). *The psychology of written composition.* Hillsdale, NJ: Lawrence Erlbaum.

Berninger, V. W., & Swanson, H. L. (1994). Modifying Hayes and Flower model of skilled writing to explain beginning and developing writing. In E. C. Butterfield (Ed.), *Advances in cognition and educational practice (Vol. 2: Children's writing: Toward a process theory of development of skilled writing)* (pp. 57–82). Greenwich, CT: JAI Press.

Black, L., Daiger, D., Sommers, J. & Stygall, G. (Eds.). (1994). *New directions in portfolio assessment: Reflective practice, critical theory and large-scale scoring.* Portsmouth, NH: Boynton.

Black, P., & Wiliam, D. (1998a). Assessment and classroom learning. *Assessment in Education: Principles, Policy and Practice, 5*(1), 7–74.

Black, P., & Wiliam, D. (1998b). Inside the black box: Raising standards through classroom assessment. *Phi Delta Kappan, 80*(2), 139–144, 146–148.

Black, P., & Wiliam, D. (2009). Developing the theory of formative assessment. *Educational Assessment, Evaluation and Accountability, 21*(1), 5–31.

Bloom, L. Z. (1997). Why I (used to) hate to give grades. *College Composition and Communication, 48,* 360–371.

Bransford, J., Derry, S., Berliner, D., & Hammerness, K. (2005). Theories of learning and their roles in teaching. In L. Darling-Hammond & J. Bransford (Eds.), *Preparing teachers for a changing world* (pp. 40–87). New York: John Wiley.

Brown, A. (2005). Self-assessment of writing in independent language learning programs: The value of annotated samples. *Assessing Writing, 10,* 174–191.

Calfee, R. C. (2000). Writing portfolios: Activity, assessment, authenticity. In R. Indrisano & J. R. Squires (Eds.), *Perspectives on writing: Research, theory and practice* (pp. 278–304). Newark, NJ: International Reading Association.

Calfee, R. C., & Perfumo, P. (Eds.). (1996). *Writing portfolios: Policy and practice.* Hillsdale, NJ: Lawrence Erlbaum.

Calkins, L. (1994). *The art of teaching writing.* Portsmouth, NH: Heinemann.

Chapman, M. (1999). Situated, social, active: Rewriting genre in the elementary classroom. *Written Communication, 16,* 469–490.

Cowie, B., & Bell, B. (1999). A model of formative assessment in science education. *Assessment in Education: Principles, Policy and Practice, 6,* 101–116.

Darling-Hammond, L., Ancess, J., & Falk, B. (1995). *Authentic assessment in action.* New York: Teachers College Press.

Dressman, M., McCarthey, S., & Prior, P. (2011). On the complexities of writing and writing research. *Research in the Teaching of English, 46,* 5–7.

Elbow, P. (1994). Will the virtues of portfolio assessment blind us to their potential dangers? In L. Black, D. Daiker, J. Sommers, & G. Stygall (Eds.), *New directions in portfolio assessment* (pp. 40–55). Portsmouth, NH: Boynton/Cook.

Elbow, P. (1997). Taking time out from grading and evaluating while working in a conventional system. *Assessing Writing, 4,* 5–28.

Flower, L., & Hayes, J. R. (1981). A cognitive process theory of writing. *College Composition & Communication, 32,* 365–387.

Freedman, S., & Sperling, M. (1985). Written language acquisition: The role of response and the writing conference. In S. W. Freedman (Ed.), *The acquisition of written language* (pp. 106–130). Norwood, NJ: Ablex.

Glasswell, K., & Parr, J. M. (2009). Teachable moments: Linking assessment and teaching in talk around writing. *Language Arts, 86,* 352–361.

Glasswell, K., Parr, J. M., & McNaughton, S. (2003). Four ways to work against yourself when conferencing with struggling writers. *Language Arts, 80,* 291–298.

Glenn, J. (2009). *Using a feedback log to improve academic writing in secondary classrooms.* Unpublished doctoral thesis, University of Auckland, Auckland, New Zealand.

Graves, D. (1983). *Writing: Teachers and children at work.* Portsmouth, NH: Heinemann.

Graves, D. (2003). *Writing: Teachers and children at work* (2nd ed.). Portsmouth, NH: Heinemann.

Hamp-Lyons, L., & Condon, W. (2000). *Assessing the portfolio: Principles for practice, theory and research.* Cresskill, NJ: Hampton Press.

Haneda, M. (2004). The joint construction of meaning in writing conferences. *Applied Linguistics, 25,* 178–219.

Hattie, J., & Timperley, H. (2007). The power of feedback. *Review of Educational Research, 77*(1), 81–112.

Hawe, E., Dixon, H., & Watson, E. (2008). Oral feedback in the context of written language. *Australian Journal of Language and Literacy, 31,* 43–58.

Hayes, J. (1996). A new framework for understanding cognition and affect in writing. In M. Levy & S. Ransdell (Eds.), *The science of writing: Theories, methods, individual differences and applications* (pp. 1–27). Mahwah, NJ: Lawrence Erlbaum.

Hayes, J. R. & Flower, L. S. (1980). Identifying the organization of writing processes. In L. W. Gregg & E. R. Steinberg (Eds.), *Cognitive processes in writing* (pp. 3–30). Hillsdale, NJ: Lawrence Erlbaum.

Hess, K. (2008, February 18–19). *Developing and using learning progressions as a schema for measuring progress.* Paper presented at the U Penn CPRIE Symposium, Philadelphia.

Hillocks, G. (2002). *The testing trap: How state writing assessments control learning.* New York: Teachers College Press.

Hunter, D., Mayenga, C., & Gambell, T. (2006). Classroom assessment tools and uses: Canadian English teachers' practices for writing. *Assessing Writing, 11,* 42–65.

Huot, B. (2002). *(Re)-articulating writing assessment for teaching and learning.* Logan: Utah State University Press.

Huot, B., & Neal, M. (2006). Writing assessment: A techno-history. In C.A. MacArthur, S. Graham, & J. Fitzgerald (Eds.), *Handbook of writing research* (pp. 417–432). New York: Guilford Press.

Juzwik, M., Curcic, S., Wolbers, K., Moxley, K., Dimling, L., & Shankland, R. K. (2006). Writing into the 21st Century: An overview of research on writing 1999–2004. *Written Communication, 23*(4), 451–476.

Kellog, R. T. (1996). A model of working memory in writing. In C. M. Levy & S. Ransdell (Eds.), *The science of writing: Theories, methods, individual difference and applications* (pp. 57–72). Mahwah, NJ: Lawrence Erlbaum.

Knapp, P., & Watkins, M. (1994). *Context-text-grammar: Teaching the genres and grammar of school writing in infant and primary classrooms.* Broadway, New South Wales: Text Productions.

Knapp, P., & Watkins, M. (2005). *Genre, text, grammar: Technologies for teaching and assessing writing.* Sydney, Australia: University of New South Wales Press.

Kress, G. (1993). Genre as social process. In B. Cope & M. Kalantzis (Eds.), *The powers of literacy—A genre approach to teaching literacy* (pp. 22–37). London: The Falmer Press.

Luce-Kepler, R., & Klinger, D. (2005). Uneasy writing: The defining moments of high-stakes literacy testing. *Assessing Writing, 10,* 157–173.

Marshall, B. (2004). Goals or horizons— the conundrum of progression in English: Or a possible way of understanding formative assessment in English. *The Curriculum Journal, 15,* 101–113.

Martin, J. R., Christie, F., & Rothery, J. (1987). Social processes in education: A reply to Sawyer and Watson (and others). In I. Reid (Ed.), *The place of genre in learning: Current debates* (pp. 55–58). Geelong, Australia: Deakin University Press.

Ministry of Education. (2009). *The New Zealand curriculum reading and writing standards for Years 1–8.* Wellington, New Zealand: Learning Media.

Ministry of Education. (2010). *The Literacy Learning Progressions: Meeting the reading and writing demands of the curriculum.* Wellington, New Zealand: Learning Media.

Ministry of Education and the University of Auckland. (2004). *Assessment Tools for Teaching and Learning: asTTle.* Wellington, New Zealand: Ministry of Education.

Norman, D. (1988). *The psychology of everyday things.* New York: Basic Books.

Orsmond, P., Merry, S., & Reiling, K. (2002). The use of exemplars and formative feedback when using student derived marking criteria in peer and self assessment. *Assessment and Evaluation in Higher Education, 25,* 309–324.

Parr, J. M. (2010). A dual purpose database for research and diagnostic assessment of student writing. *Journal of Writing Research, 2*(2), 129–150.

Parr, J. M. (2011). Repertoires to scaffold teacher learning and practice in assessment of writing. *Assessing Writing, 16,* 32–48.

Parr, J. M., Glasswell, K., & Aikman, M. (2007). Supporting teacher learning and informed practice in writing through assessment tools for teaching and learning. *Asia-Pacific Journal of Teacher Education, 35,* 69–87.

Parr, J. M., & Jesson, R. (2011). If students are not succeeding as writers, teach them to self-assess using a rubric. In D. Lapp & B. Moss (Eds.), *Exemplary instruction in the middle grades* (pp. 174–188). New York: Guilford Press.

Parr, J. M., & Limbrick, E. (2010). Contextualising practice: Hallmarks of effective teachers of writing. *Teaching and Teacher Education, 26,* 583–590.

Parr, J. M., & Timperley, H. (2010a). Multiple black boxes: The role of formative assessment in learning within systems. *Improving Schools, 13(2),* 1–14.

Parr, J. M., & Timperley, H. (2010b). Feedback to writing, assessment for teaching and learning and student progress. *Assessing Writing, 15,* 68–85.

Patthey-Chavez, G., & Ferris, D. (1997). Writing conferences and the weaving of multi-voiced texts in college composition. *Research in the Teaching of English, 31,* 51–90.

Pellegrino, J., Chudowsky, N., & Glaser, R. (Eds). (2001). *Knowing what students know: The science and design of educational assessment.* Washington, DC: National Research Council/ National Academy Press.

Phelps, G., & Schilling, S. (2004). Developing measures of content knowledge for teaching reading. *Elementary School Journal, 105,* 31–49.

Pintrich, P. R. (1995). Understanding self-regulated learning. In P. Pintrich (Ed.), *Understanding self-regulated learning* (pp. 3–13). San Francisco, CA: Jossey-Bass.

Pressley, M., Allington, R., Wharton-McDonald, R., Block, C., & Morrow, L. M. (2001). *Learning to read: Lessons from exemplary first-grade classrooms.* New York: Guilford Press.

Pressley, M., Rankin, J., & Yokoi, L. (1996). A survey of instructional practices of primary teachers nominated as effective in promoting literacy. *Elementary School Journal, 96*(4), 363–384.

Ross, J. A., Rolheiser, C., & Hogaboam-Gray, A. (1999). Effects of self-evaluation training on narrative writing. *Assessing Writing, 6,* 107–132.

Rust, C., Price, M., & Donovan, B. (2003). Improving students' learning by developing their understanding of assessment criteria and processes. *Assessment and Evaluation, 28,* 147–164.

Sadler, R. (1989). Formative assessment and the design of instructional systems. *Instructional Science, 18,* 119–44.

Sadler, R. (2010). Beyond feedback: Developing student capability in complex appraisal. *Assessment and Evaluation in Higher Education, 35*(5), 535–550.

Spillane, J. P., Reiser, B. J., & Reimer, T. (2002). Policy implementation and cognition: Reframing and refocusing implementation research. *Review of Educational Research, 72,* 387–431.

Timperley, H. S., & Parr, J. M. (2009). What is this lesson about? Instructional processes and student understandings in the writing classroom. *The Curriculum Journal, 20*(1), 43–60.

Timperley, H., Wilson, A., & Barrar, H. (2007). *Best evidence synthesis iteration: Professional learning and development.* Wellington, New Zealand: Ministry of Education.

Tompkins, G. (2004). *Teaching writing: Balancing process and product* (4th ed.). Englewood Cliffs, NJ: Prentice Hall.

Walker, C. P., & Elias, D. (1987). Writing conference talk: Factors associated with high and low rated conferences. *Research in the Teaching of English, 21,* 266–285.

Weigle, S. C. (2002). *Assessing writing.* Cambridge: Cambridge University Press.

Wenger, E. (1998). *Communities of practice: Learning, meaning and identity.* New York: Cambridge University Press.

White, E. M. (1994). Portfolios as an assessment concept. In L. Black, D. Daiker, J. Sommers, & G. Stygall (Eds.), *New directions in portfolio assessment* (pp. 25–39). Portsmouth, NH: Boynton/Cook.

Wiggins, C. P. (1993). *Assessing student performance.* San Francisco, CA: Jossey-Bass.

Wiliam, D., & Black, P. (1996). Meanings and consequences: A basis for distinguishing formative and summative functions of assessment. *British Educational Research Journal, 22*(5), 537–548.

Wong, I. (1998). Teacher-student talk in technical writing conference. *Written Communication, 5,* 444–460.

Wong-Fillmore, L., & Snow, C. E. (2002). What teachers need to know about language. In C. T. Adger, C. E. Snow, & D. Christian (Eds.), *What teachers need to know about language* (pp. 7–54). McHenry, IL: Delta Systems Co.

Yancey, K. B., & Weisser, I. (Eds.) (1997). *Situating portfolios: Four perspectives.* Logan: Utah State University Press.

Zimmerman, B. J., & Schunk, D. H. (Eds.). (2001). *Self-regulated learning and academic achievement: Theoretical perspectives* (2nd ed.). Mahwah, NJ: Lawrence Erlbaum.

INDEX

Page references followed by (figure) indicate an illustrated figure; followed by (table) indicate a table.

ABOUT THE AUTHORS

Heidi L. Andrade is an associate professor of educational psychology and the associate dean for academic affairs at the School of Education, University at Albany—State University of New York. She received her EdD from Harvard University. Her research and teaching focus on the relationships between learning and assessment, with emphases on student self-assessment and self-regulated learning (SRL). She has written numerous articles, including an award-winning article on rubrics for *Educational Leadership* (1997). She edited a special issue on assessment for *Theory Into Practice* (2009), coedited *The Handbook of Formative Assessment* (2010) with Gregory Cizek, and is coediting a special issue of *Applied Measurement in Education* with Christina Schneider.

Susan F. Belgrad is a professor of education with California State University, Northridge, where she leads graduate courses and professional development for teachers in differentiated learning and assessment, creating student portfolios and supporting media-rich classrooms with brain-based and student-centered practices. She received her EdD from the George Peabody College of Education at Vanderbilt University and has authored books and articles on portfolio assessment, including the third edition of *The Portfolio Connection: Student Work Linked to Standards* (2007) with Kay Burke and Robin Fogarty. Her research is on the impact of teacher efficacy on student learning. She has taught at the elementary level and in early childhood special education and has served in leadership posts in higher education in early childhood and teacher leadership for pre-K–12.

Paul Black is professor emeritus of science education at King's College London. He has made many contributions in both curriculum development and in assessment research. He has served on advisory groups of the National Research Council (NRC) and as visiting professor at Stanford University. His work on formative assessment with Dylan Wiliam and colleagues at King's has had widespread impact.

Sarah M. Bonner is an associate professor in the Department of Educational Foundations and Counseling Programs at Hunter College, City University of New York. Prior to entering higher education, she worked in K–12 education for many years, as a teacher in programs for high-risk adolescents in Chicago and Southern Arizona, in dropout prevention and program development, and as an educational program evaluator. Her research focuses on the beliefs and skills of classroom teachers that relate to their formative and summative assessment practices and the cognitive and metacognitive processes used by test takers on tests of different types.

Marc A. Brackett is a research scientist in the Department of Psychology at Yale University, the deputy director of Yale's Health, Emotion, and Behavior Laboratory and head of the Emotional Intelligence Unit in the Edward Zigler Center in Child Development and Social Policy. He is an author on more than 80 scholarly publications and codeveloper of The RULER Approach to Social and Emotional Learning, an evidence-based program teaching K–12 students and educators the skills associated with recognizing, understanding, labeling, expressing, and regulating emotions to promote positive social, emotional, and academic development.

Susan M. Brookhart is an independent educational consultant. She is a former professor and chair of the Department of Educational Foundations and Leadership in the School of Education at Duquesne University, where she currently is senior research associate in the Center for Advancing the Study of Teaching and Learning (CASTL). She was the editor of *Educational Measurement: Issues and Practice,* a journal of the National Council on Measurement in Education (NCME) from 2007 to 2009. Her interests include the role of both formative and summative classroom assessment (CA) in student motivation and achievement, the connection between CA and large-scale assessment, and grading.

Gavin T. L. Brown is an associate professor in the Faculty of Education at The University of Auckland. After growing up in Europe and Canada thanks to a military upbringing, he worked as a high school and adult teacher of English and English for speakers of other languages (ESOL) in New Zealand. He spent 9 years in standardized test development before working as an academic at the University of Auckland and the Hong Kong Institute of Education. His research focuses on school-based assessment, informed by psychometric theory, with a special interest in the social psychology of teacher and student responses to educational assessment. He is the author of *Conceptions of Assessment* (Nova, 2008) and has authored studies conducted in Spain, Cyprus, Hong Kong, China, Queensland, Louisiana, and New Zealand about teacher and student beliefs.

William S. Bush is currently professor of mathematics education and director of the Center for Research in Mathematics Teacher Development at the University of Louisville. His research interests focus on the development and assessment of mathematics teacher knowledge and on mathematics assessments for students. He has led and participated in a number of large-scale teacher development projects funded by the National Science Foundation (NSF). He is a member of the National Council of Teachers of Mathematics (NCTM), the Association of Mathematics Teacher Educators, and the Kentucky Mathematics Coalition.

Cynthia Campbell is an associate professor of educational research and assessment at Northern Illinois University. Her research and teaching interests include classroom assessment (CA), test development, and linguistic analysis. Campbell has published extensively in these areas and has given numerous refereed presentations at the state, regional, national, and international levels. Currently, she is the president of the Mid-Western Educational Research Association and a member of the American Educational Research Association (AERA), the National Council on Measurement in Education (NCME), and the American Counseling Association.

Tedra Clark is a senior researcher at Mid-Continent Research for Education and Learning (McREL), where she leads applied research and evaluation projects aimed at improving educational outcomes through schoolwide interventions, classroom instruction, teacher professional development programs, and classroom assessment (CA). Dr. Clark was a coauthor and lead data analyst for a cluster randomized trial of the professional development program *Classroom Assessment for Student Learning (CASL),* funded by the U.S. Department of Education, Institute of Education Sciences. She was also the lead author of a large-scale research synthesis on CA funded by the Stupski Foundation. Prior to joining McREL, Dr. Clark was a graduate research assistant and adjunct professor of psychology at the University of Denver, where she facilitated both National Institutes of Health (NIH)- and National Science Foundation (NSF)-sponsored projects examining basic processes of learning and memory.

Elizabeth Ann Claunch-Lesback is the director of curriculum for National History Day (NHD) and is professor emeritus of history education at the University of New Mexico in Albuquerque. Dr. Claunch-Lesback's educational experience includes 14 years as a public school teacher and 12 years as a university professor. She has researched, presented, and written professionally on history education and adult education.

Bronwen Cowie is director of the Wilf Malcolm Institute of Educational Research, The University of Waikato. She has expertise in classroom-based focus group and survey research and has led a number of large externally funded projects focused on assessment for learning (AFL), curriculum implementation, and information and communication technology (ICT)/e-learning. Her particular research interests include student views of assessment and AFL interactions in primary science and technology classrooms.

Karla L. Egan is a research manager at CTB/McGraw-Hill where she manages a diverse group of research scientists and research associates and provides leadership on issues related to assessment development, assessment policy, and psychometrics. She provides guidance to state departments of education for their customized assessments, and she works with educators through standard setting and form selection workshops. She has led or supported over 60 standard settings for statewide test programs. Her research has been published in the *Peabody Journal of Education,* and as a noted expert in standard setting, she has been the lead author of several book chapters on this topic. She led the development of a framework for developing the achievement level descriptors that guide test development, standard setting, and score reporting. Her current research focuses on standard setting, test security, identification of aberrant anchor items, and language assessment for English language learners (ELLs).

Carolin Hagelskamp earned her PhD in community psychology at New York University and was a postdoctoral research associate at the Health, Emotion, and Behavior Laboratory at Yale University. Her academic research focuses on contextual factors in early adolescent development, including work–family, classroom climate, race/ethnicity, and immigration. She is currently director of research at Public Agenda, where she conducts public opinion research on social policy issues such as K–12 education reform.

Thomas M. Haladyna is professor emeritus of the Mary Lou Fulton Teachers College at Arizona State University. He specializes in item and test development and validation. He has authored or edited 14 books; more than 60 journal articles; and hundreds of conference papers, white papers, opinions, and technical reports. He has interviewed with and assisted media in many investigations of test fraud.

Lois Harris is an honorary research fellow at the University of Auckland and teaches in CQUniversity Australia's postgraduate program. Her research examines relationships between educational stakeholders' thinking and their practices, with recent studies investigating assessment and student engagement. She also has a strong interest in both qualitative and quantitative research methodologies. Previously, she was a secondary school teacher in the United States and Australia, working in both mainstream and distance education modes.

Margaret Heritage is assistant director for professional development at the National Center for Research on Evaluation, Standards, & Student Testing (CRESST) at the University of California, Los Angeles. For many years, her work has focused on research and practice in formative assessment. In addition to publishing extensively on formative assessment, she has made numerous presentations on the topic all over the United States, in Europe, Australia, and Asia.

Thomas P. Hogan is professor of psychology and distinguished university fellow at the University of Scranton, where he previously served as dean of the Graduate School, director of research, and interim provost/academic vice president. He is the author or coauthor of four books on measurement and research methods; several nationally used standardized tests; and over 150 published articles, chapters, and presentations related to psychological and educational measurement. He holds a bachelor's degree from John Carroll University and both master's and doctoral degrees from Fordham University, with a specialization in psychometrics.

Marc W. Julian is a research manager at CTB/McGraw-Hill. He manages a diverse group of research scientists and research associates, providing technical and managerial support to this team of researchers. Dr. Julian was the lead research scientist for *TerraNova, The Second Edition.* Dr. Julian has also served as the lead research scientist for many statewide assessment projects, including the groundbreaking Maryland School Performance Assessment Program (MSPAP). His research has been published in *Applied Measurement in Education, Educational Measurement: Issues and Practice, Journal of Educational Measurement,* and *Structural Equation Modeling,*

Suzanne Lane is a professor in the Research Methodology Program at the University of Pittsburgh. Her research and professional interests are in educational measurement and testing—in particular, design, validity, and technical issues related to large-scale assessment and accountability systems, including performance-based assessments. Her work is published in journals such as *Applied Measurement in Education, Educational Measurement: Issues and Practice,* and the *Journal of Educational Measurement.* She was the president of the National Council on Measurement in Education (NCME) (2003–2004), Vice President of Division

D of the American Educational Research Association (AERA) (2000–2002), and a member of the AERA, American Psychological Association (APA), and NCME Joint Committee for the Revision of the *Standards for Educational and Psychological Testing* (1993–1999).

Min Li, associate professor at College of Education, University of Washington, is an assessment expert deeply interested in understanding how student learning can be accurately and adequately assessed both in large-scale testing and classroom settings. Her research and publications reflect a combination of cognitive science and psychometric approaches in various projects, including examining the cognitive demands of state test science items, analyzing teachers' classroom assessment (CA) practices, developing instruments to evaluate teachers' assessment practices, and using science notebooks as assessment tools.

Maggie B. McGatha is an associate professor of mathematics education in the Department of Middle and Secondary Education in the College of Education and Human Development at the University of Louisville. Dr. McGatha teaches elementary and middle school mathematics methods courses as well as courses on coaching and mentoring. Her research interests are mathematics teacher professional development, mathematics coaching, and mathematics assessment.

James H. McMillan is professor and chair of the Department of Foundations of Education at Virginia Commonwealth University, where he has been teaching for 32 years. Dr. McMillan is also executive director of the Metropolitan Educational Research Consortium, a partnership between Virginia Commonwealth University and eight Richmond, Virginia, school districts that plans, executes, and disseminates results of applied research on issues of importance to the schools. He has published several books, including *Educational Research: Fundamentals for the Consumer* and *Classroom Assessment: Principles and Practice for Effective Standards-Based Instruction*, has published extensively in journals, and presented nationally and internationally on assessment in education and research methods.

Tonya R. Moon is a professor in the Curry School of Education at the University of Virginia. Her specializations are in the areas of educational measurement, research, and evaluation. She works with educational institutions both nationally and internationally on using better assessment techniques for improving instruction and student learning.

Connie M. Moss is an associate professor in the Department of Foundations and Leadership, School of Education at Duquesne University in Pittsburgh, where she also directs the Center for Advancing the Study of Teaching and Learning (CASTL). During her career, she has taught in urban public schools; directed regional and statewide initiatives focused on bringing excellence and equity to all students; and worked extensively in schools with teachers, principals, and central office administrators. Her current work includes the study of formative assessment with a particular focus on the relationships among effective teaching, self-regulated student learning, formative educational leadership, and social justice.

Jay Parkes is currently chair of the Department of Individual, Family & Community Education and an associate professor of Educational Psychology at the University of New Mexico where he teaches graduate courses in classroom assessment (CA), educational measurement, introductory and intermediate statistics, and research design. His areas of expertise include performance and alternative assessments, CA, and feedback, which he pursues both in dual language education and in medical education.

Judy M. Parr is a professor of education and head of the School of Curriculum and Pedagogy in the Faculty of Education at the University of Auckland. Her particular expertise is in writing, encompassing how writing develops, the cultural tools of literacy, and considerations of instructional issues like teacher knowledge and practice and, in particular, assessment of written language. A major research focus concerns school change and improvement in order to ensure effective practice and raise achievement. Judy has published widely in a range of international journals spanning literacy, technology, policy and administration, and school change. Two books cowritten or edited with Professor Helen Timperley bridge theory and practice: *Using Evidence in Teaching Practice: Implications for Professional Learning* (2004) and *Weaving Evidence, Inquiry and Standards to Build Better Schools* (2010).

Bruce Randel is an independent research consultant, based in Centennial, Colorado, providing services in education research, statistical analysis, educational measurement and psychometrics, and technical reporting. He is former principal researcher at Mid-Continent Research for Education and Learning (McREL) and senior research scientist at CTB/McGraw-Hill. His research interests include randomized controlled trials (RCTs), measurement of formative assessment practice, test and instrument development, and statistical analyses.

Susan E. Rivers is a research scientist in the Department of Psychology at Yale University. She is the associate director of the Health, Emotion, and Behavior Laboratory at Yale and a fellow at the Edward Zigler Center in Child Development and Social Policy. She is a codeveloper of The RULER Approach to Social and Emotional Learning and the achievement model of emotional literacy, as well as several curricula designed to help children, educators, and parents become emotionally literate. In her grant-funded research, she investigates how emotional literacy training affects positive youth development and creates supportive learning environments. Dr. Rivers is the coauthor of many scholarly articles and papers, and she trains educators and families on the RULER programs.

Michael C. Rodriguez is associate professor and coordinator of Quantitative Methods in Education in the Department of Educational Psychology at the University of Minnesota. He received his PhD in measurement and quantitative methods at Michigan State University. His research interests include item writing, test accessibility, reliability theory, meta-analysis, and item response models and multilevel modeling. He is a member of the Academy of Distinguished Teachers at the University of Minnesota; on the editorial boards of *Applied Measurement in Education*, *Educational Measurement: Issues & Practice*, and *Journal of Educational Measurement*; a member of the board of directors of the National Council on Measurement in Education (NCME); and a recipient of the Harris Research Award from the International Reading Association.

Maria Araceli Ruiz-Primo is an associate professor at the School of Education and Human Development, University of Colorado Denver. Her work focuses on two strands: (1) assessment of students learning at both large-scale and classroom level and (2) the study of teachers' assessment practices. Her publications reflect such strands: (1) developing and evaluating different strategies to assess students' learning such as concept maps and students' science notebooks and (2) studying teachers' informal and formal formative assessment practices such as the use of assessment conversations and embedded assessments. Her recent work focuses on the development and evaluation of assessments that are instructionally sensitive and instruments to measure teachers' formative assessment practices She also co-edited a special issue on assessment for the *Journal of Research in Science Teaching.*

M. Christina Schneider is a research scientist at CTB/McGraw-Hill. She has worked as the lead research scientist on numerous state assessment projects and is a member of the CTB Standard Setting Team, helping to establish cut scores for large-scale assessments across the United States. She was the principal investigator on a federally funded $1.7 million multisite cluster randomized trial investigating the effects of a professional development program in formative classroom assessment (CA) on teacher and student achievement. Her research has been published in *Applied Measurement in Education, Peabody Journal of Education, Journal of Multidisciplinary Evaluation,* and *Journal of Psychoeducational Assessment.* Her areas of expertise include formative CA, automated essay scoring, standard setting, identification of aberrant anchor items, and assessment in the arts.

Robin D. Tierney (University of Ottawa) is an independent researcher and writer in San Jose, California. Previously, she taught elementary English language arts and graduate level research methodology courses in Ontario, Canada. Her doctoral work focused on teachers' practical wisdom (phronesis) about fairness in classroom assessment (CA). She has presented at educational research conferences in Canada, Europe, and the United States and has published several articles about CA. Her current research interests include the quality and ethics of CA and the use of complementary methods in educational research.

Carol Ann Tomlinson is the William Clay Parrish Jr. Professor and chair of Educational Leadership, Foundations, and Policy at the University of Virginia's Curry School of Education where she also serves as codirector of Curry's Institutes on

Academic Diversity. Prior to joining the University of Virginia faculty, she was a public school teacher for 21 years.

Keith J. Topping is a professor and director of the Centre for Paired Learning at the University of Dundee in Scotland. His research interests are in the development and evaluation of methods for nonprofessionals (such as parents or peers) to tutor others one-to-one in fundamental skills and higher order learning across many different subjects, contexts, and ages. He also has interests in electronic literacy and computer-aided assessment and in behavior management and social competence in schools. His publications include over 20 books, 50 chapters, 150 peer reviewed journal papers, 30 distance learning packages, and other items. He presents, trains, consults, and engages in collaborative action and research around the world.

Cheryl A. Torrez is an assistant professor in the Department of Teacher Education at the University of New Mexico. Her research interests include curriculum and instruction in elementary classrooms, school–university partnerships, and teacher education across the professional life span. She is a former elementary school teacher and teaches undergraduate and graduate courses in curriculum and instruction and teacher inquiry. She is currently the vice president of the New Mexico Council for the Social Studies and cochair of the Teacher Education and Professional Development Community of the National Council for the Social Studies (NCSS).

Dylan Wiliam is emeritus professor of Educational Assessment at Institute of Education, University of London, where from 2006 to 2010 he was its deputy director. In a varied career, he has taught in urban public schools, directed a large-scale testing program, served a number of roles in university administration, including dean of a School of Education, and pursued a research program focused on supporting teachers to develop their use of assessment in support of learning. From 2003 to 2006, he was senior research director at the Educational Testing Service in Princeton, New Jersey, and now works as an independent consultant, dividing his time between the United States and the United Kingdom.

Yaoying Xu is an associate professor in the Department of Special Education and Disability Policy at Virginia Commonwealth University. She teaches graduate courses including assessment, instructional programming, and multicultural perspectives in education as well as a doctoral course that focuses on research design, funding, and conducting research in special education. Her research interests involve culturally and linguistically appropriate assessment and instruction for young children and students with diverse backgrounds, impact of social interactions on school performance, and empowering culturally diverse families of young children and students with disabilities in the process of assessment and intervention. She has published over 30 peer-reviewed journal articles and book chapters in the fields of general education, special education, and multicultural education.

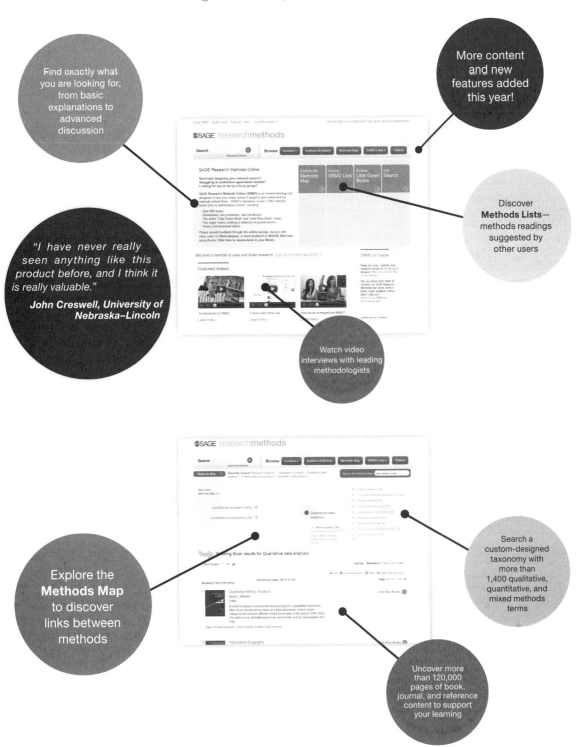